The Study of Shiʿi Islam

The Institute of Ismaili Studies
Shiʿi Heritage Series, 2

Previously published title:

1. Daftary, Farhad. *A History of Shiʿi Islam* (2013).

The Study of Shiʿi Islam

History, Theology and Law

Edited by

Farhad Daftary and Gurdofarid Miskinzoda

I.B.Tauris *Publishers*
LONDON • NEW YORK
in association with
The Institute of Ismaili Studies
LONDON, 2014

Published in 2014 by I.B.Tauris & Co. Ltd
6 Salem Road, London W2 4BU
175 Fifth Avenue, New York NY 10010
www.ibtauris.com

in association with The Institute of Ismaili Studies
210 Euston Road, London NW1 2DA
www.iis.ac.uk

Distributed in the United States and Canada exclusively by Palgrave Macmillan
175 Fifth Avenue, New York NY 10010

ISBN: 978 1 78076 506 8

A full CIP record for this book is available from the British Library
A full CIP record is available from the Library of Congress

Library of Congress Catalog Card Number: available

Typeset in Minion Tra for The Institute of Ismaili Studies

Printed and bound in Great Britain by T.J. International, Padstow, Cornwall

FSC www.fsc.org MIX Paper from responsible sources FSC® C013056

The Institute of Ismaili Studies

The Institute of Ismaili Studies was established in 1977 with the object of promoting scholarship and learning on Islam, in historical as well as contemporary contexts, and a better understanding of its relationship with other societies and faiths.

The Institute's programmes encourage a perspective which is not confined to the theological and religious heritage of Islam, but seeks to explore the relationship of religious ideas to broader dimensions of society and culture. The programmes thus encourage an interdisciplinary approach to the materials of Islamic history and thought. Particular attention is also given to issues of modernity that arise as Muslims seek to relate their heritage to the contemporary situation.

Within the Islamic tradition, the Institute's programmes promote research on those areas which have, to date, received relatively little attention from scholars. These include the intellectual and literary expressions of Shiʿism in general, and Ismailism in particular.

In the context of Islamic societies, the Institute's programmes are informed by the full range and diversity of cultures in which Islam is practised today, from the Middle East, South and Central Asia, and Africa to the industrialised societies of the West, thus taking into consideration the variety of contexts that shape the ideals, beliefs and practices of the faith.

These objectives are realised through concrete programmes and activities organised and implemented by various departments of the Institute. The Institute also collaborates periodically, on a programme-specific basis, with other institutions of learning in the United Kingdom and abroad.

The Institute's academic publications fall into a number of interrelated categories:

1. Occasional papers or essays addressing broad themes of the relationship between religion and society, with special reference to Islam.
2. Works exploring specific aspects of Islamic faith and culture, or the contributions of individual Muslim thinkers or writers.
3. Editions or translations of significant primary or secondary texts.
4. Translations of poetic or literary texts that illustrate the rich heritage of spiritual, devotional and symbolic expressions in Muslim history.

5. Works on Ismaili history and thought, and the relationship of the Ismailis to other traditions, communities and schools of thought in Islam.
6. Proceedings of conferences and seminars sponsored by the Institute.
7. Bibliographical works and catalogues that document manuscripts, printed texts and other source materials.

This book falls into category two listed above.

In facilitating these and other publications, the Institute's sole aim is to encourage original research and analysis of relevant issues. While every effort is made to ensure that the publications are of a high academic standard, there is naturally bound to be a diversity of views, ideas and interpretations. As such, the opinions expressed in these publications must be understood as belonging to their authors alone.

Shiʿi Heritage Series

Shiʿi Muslims, with their rich intellectual and cultural heritage, have contributed significantly to the fecundity and diversity of the Islamic traditions throughout the centuries, enabling Islam to evolve and flourish both as a major religion and also as a civilisation. In spite of this, Shiʿi Islam has received little scholarly attention in the West, in medieval as well as modern times. It is only in recent decades that academic interest has focused increasingly on Shiʿi Islam within the wider study of Islam.

The principal objective of the *Shiʿi Heritage Series*, launched by The Institute of Ismaili Studies, is to enhance general knowledge of Shiʿi Islam and promote a better understanding of its history, doctrines and practices in their historical and contemporary manifestations. Addressing all Shiʿi communities, the series also aims to engage in discussions on theoretical and methodological issues, while inspiring further research in the field.

Works published in this series will include monographs, collective volumes, editions and translations of primary texts, and bibliographical projects, bringing together some of the most significant themes in the study of Shiʿi Islam through an interdisciplinary approach, and making them accessible to a wide readership.

Table of Contents

Foreword*

Until forty years ago, the field of Shiʿi studies was the 'poor relative' of Islamic research and, for unjustifiable reasons, not included in the mainstream agenda. It is only since the 1970s that some specialists, albeit a small number, have started to focus their studies on Shiʿi Islam in its various components. After 1980, dramatic events such as the Lebanese civil war, the Iranian revolution and the war in Iraq, aroused the attention of the public at large and also of the scholarly community, and brought about a broadening of Shiʿi studies, especially those dealing with Twelver Shiʿism.

Alongside a plethora of studies devoted to political Shiʿism and its modern and contemporary developments, historical and philological publications on the history of classical Shiʿi thought have highlighted the great intellectual and spiritual wealth of the religion of this minority community of Islam, which, nonetheless, numbers almost 200 million believers. Beyond the shocking phenomena of the politicisation of the faith – with its autocratic religious authorities, strictly veiled women, indoctrinated mobs and bloody rituals of mourning – Shiʿi Islam, in its long and rich history, has been found to be one of the most abundant faiths in the world in terms of the number of its outstanding theologians, philosophers, mystics and men of letters, and others, the body of whose output comprises many thousands of works.

Unarguably one of the oldest religious currents in Islam, Shiʿism at first occupied a central position in the genesis and development of the religion. This phenomenon is not new: in a number of faiths, what has later come to be considered as 'orthodox' was often originally deemed to be 'heterodox', or even 'heretical', and has frequently become more entrenched as a reaction to these currents. We now know that this is the case with a certain number of Sunni theological doctrines which were shaped as a reaction to Shiʿi activities, such as establishing the written text of the Qurʾan, the shaping and character of the corpus of *ḥadīth* and *sīra*, prophetology, hagiography and the status of the Companions of the Prophet, theories of theological–political authority, Qurʾanic exegesis and the numerous themes of *kalām*, among others.

Moreover, studies into the mystical and esoteric dimensions of the various Shiʿi trends in the classical period have shown definitively the primordial role of Shiʿism in the adoption, transmission, adaptation and development in Islam of numerous intellectual and spiritual themes arising from the traditions of late antiquity, including Judaeo-Christian trends, Gnostic movements, Manichaeism and the Hellenistic doctrines of Neoplatonism, Pythagoreanism and Hermetism, as well as a dualist

* Translated from the French by Russell Harris.

Weltanschauung, emanationism, the hybrid nature of man, apophatic theology, the redemptive role of knowledge, the centrality of the Divine Guide, the double level of the scriptures, hermeneutics, the significance of the occult sciences, the cult of the secret, the initiatic structure and messianic cults.

At last there is enough data on Shiʿism to enable it to be presented in a new perspective and theoretical framework in which the early manifestation of Islam can be examined. It is true that Shiʿi sources can be just as slanted as Sunni sources (especially during the early Islamic centuries when intellectual activity was often taking place against the backdrop of civil wars), but a critical examination of the sources would appear to show that, beyond the ideological dimension, the contents of their major works are corroborated by a large number of modern studies into the difficulties inherent in editing the Qurʾanic text, the political nature of the development of a huge section of the corpus of *ḥadīth*, state disapproval of the various religious or historiographical bodies of work and the close relationship between literature and the genesis, or on the contrary, the suppression and impoverishment of Qurʾanic exegesis and its interaction with caliphal power.

These few examples will suffice to show the growing importance of Shiʿi studies for a better understanding of Shiʿism itself, and also of Islam in general, and on the larger scale they help to provide a clearer conception of how religious and philosophical traditions from late antiquity have remained at the core of this religion.

This significance has not escaped the acute perception of Dr Farhad Daftary, Co-Director and Head of the Department of Academic Research and Publications at The Institute of Ismaili Studies, who has devoted much time to Shiʿi studies at the Institute. *The Study of Shiʿi Islam: The State of the Field, Issues of Methodology and Recent Developments* colloquium, organised most efficiently by Dr Gurdofarid Miskinzoda, in September 2010, was the first public offering by this great intellectual initiative. The *Shiʿi Heritage Series* has been set up as an intrinsic part of the publications programme of The Institute of Ismaili Studies, and it is as part of this series that the present volume of papers from the colloquium is being published. The book mirrors the colloquium in setting out in a clear and discerning manner the great historical and doctrinal themes of Shiʿi Islam, such as history, theology, *ḥadīth*, Qurʾanic exegesis, philosophy and ritual. Several of the most renowned specialists in these fields have introduced and enriched each part with their edifying and innovative studies, thereby enlightening the reader with the latest intellectual developments on Shiʿism, providing a thorough background to a particular subject, and detailing the epistemological and methodological steps undertaken by the authors.

Mohammad Ali Amir-Moezzi
École Pratique des Hautes Études (Sorbonne) and
Senior Research Fellow, The Institute of Ismaili Studies

Preface

Islam is a major world religion as well as civilisation, with some 1.3 billion Muslims scattered in almost every region of the globe, especially in the Middle East, Asia and Africa. Currently, around 15 per cent of the Muslim population of the world belong to various communities of Shiʿi Islam, with the Ithnaʿasharis or Twelvers accounting for the largest numbers. The Ismailis, Zaydis and ʿAlawis represent other important Shiʿi communities.

In addition to their significant number, around 200 million, Shiʿi Muslims have played a crucial role, proportionally greater than their relative number, in furthering the intellectual and artistic achievements of the Islamic civilisation. Indeed, the Shiʿi scholars and literati of various Shiʿi branches and from various regions, including scientists, philosophers, theologians, jurists and poets, have made seminal contributions to Islamic thought and culture. There have also been numerous Shiʿi dynasties, families and artists as well as a variety of institutions of learning in Islam. Amongst such Shiʿi dynasties, particular mention may be made of the Būyids, the Fatimids, the Hamdanids and the Safawids as well as a host of lesser or local Shiʿi dynasties of North Africa, the Middle East and India. All in all, Shiʿi Muslims have contributed significantly over the entire course of Islamic history to the richness and diversity of the Islamic traditions, enabling Islam to evolve and flourish not merely as a religion, but also as a major world civilisation. In spite of its relative significance, however, Shiʿi Islam has received very little attention in the West, in both medieval and modern times. With a few exceptions, the state of Shiʿi studies has not fared much better in Muslim countries.

Sunni authors belonging to different literary and scholarly traditions were not in general interested in collecting accurate information on Shiʿi Islam and its internal divisions, as they treated all Shiʿi interpretations of Islam as deviations from the 'right path'. Medieval Europeans' knowledge and perceptions of Shiʿi Islam were even more deficient and fictitious since their overall knowledge of Islam was extremely limited. Such knowledge that medieval Europeans did have was rooted more in their 'imaginative ignorance' than in any accurate sources of information to which they could have obtained access if they had so desired. The earliest Western impressions of Islam, which were retained for several centuries, were almost exclusively rooted in religious polemics, since the medieval Europeans intended to uphold the theological claims of Christianity and to disclaim those of the Muslims. This basically negative perception of Islam was retained for almost a thousand years.

If the medieval Europeans remained incredibly ignorant about the most basic aspects of the Islamic message, they doubtless knew even less about its internal divisions, including especially the Sunni–Shiʿi division, and the intricacies of interpretation within the Islamic communities and their distinctive tenets. With the establishment of Twelver Shiʿism as the state religion of Safawid Persia in 907/1501, the ground was laid for better availability of information on Shiʿi Islam to Westerners who visited that country. However, European scholars, trained in theology and philological studies, had not yet found access to Islamic texts that would lead to a breakthrough in their study of Islam free from the assumptions of anti-Islamic polemics of the earlier generations. By the dawn of the 19th century, European orientalists were finally ready to investigate Islam as a religion in a scholarly and systematic manner with the goal of understanding rather than condemning it.

Scientific orientalism, based on the study of textual evidence, effectively began in Europe with the establishment in 1795 of the École des Langues Orientales Vivantes in Paris, with A. I. Silvestre de Sacy (1758–1838), the most distinguished orientalist of his time, appointed as the first Professor of Arabic at that academic institution. European scholars now started to produce their studies of Islam on the basis of the Arabic texts, then available mainly in manuscript form, and the Islamic tradition itself. However, the bulk of the original texts then available in France, Germany and other European countries had been written by Sunni authors and reflected their particular perspectives since few Shiʿi texts had found their way to European libraries during the 19th century. Consequently, the orientalists studied Islam according to the Sunni perspective of their manuscript sources and, borrowing classifications from their own Christian contexts, they too treated the Sunni interpretation of Islam as 'orthodoxy', in contrast with Shiʿism which was taken to represent a 'heterodoxy' or, at its extreme, a 'heresy'. The Sunni-centric approach to the study of Islam has continued to hold prominence to various degrees in Western scholarship in the field.

However, it is clear that terms such as 'heterodoxy' and 'orthodoxy' are not appropriate in the context of Islam and its study. Even the term 'schism' or 'split' does not fit closely the origins and development of the various branches of Islam and its early history. The split that led to the emergence of the two main divisions of Islam – Sunni and Shiʿi – does not, however, explain the development of the various understandings of political and religious authority that took quite a while to formulate, since the schism had originally taken place in the first century of Islam along with the events commonly associated with it. Even the features that the two major divisions and their sub-branches acquired following the split went beyond the original cause of the split and took a very long time to crystallise. Among these are: the distinctive interpretation of religious authority and the special place of the Imam, the distinctive legal tradition, distinctiveness in worship and rituals, and the places of pilgrimage.

It is therefore not surprising that until the middle of the 20th century, systematic progress in Islamic studies had not led to any significant improvement in the scholarly investigation of Shiʿi Islam and its various branches, as genuine Shiʿi textual materials of any genre remained relatively inaccessible to Western scholars. Subsequently, a selective group of scholars sought to devote more serious attention to the study of Shiʿi Islam. Led by Louis Massignon (1883–1962), these scholars investigated Shiʿism with particular reference to its spiritual, esoteric and mystic dimensions, and as manifested in its Twelver and Ismaili traditions. The contributions of Henry Corbin (1903–1978) were also invaluable in understanding Shiʿi thought in general and its theosophical and metaphysical aspects as developed particularly in Iran. By the 1960s, a number of Islamicists and religious scholars belonging to the Twelver community had also taken the initiative of elaborating the doctrines of their branch of Shiʿi Islam on a more systematic, though still traditional, basis. These religious scholars, such as ʿAllama Sayyid Muhammad Husayn Tabataba'i (1903–1981), also held teaching sessions at the religious seminaries of Iran, notably those in Qumm, Isfahan and Mashhad. These institutions have continued to train impressive numbers of Twelver Shiʿi scholars in Iran.

All in all, Shiʿi studies have remained extremely marginalised in the Muslim countries outside Iran and Iraq with their vibrant religious seminaries and Shiʿi theological traditions as well as extensive collections of Shiʿi manuscripts. In Iran itself, Islamic studies predominantly imply Shiʿi, and more specifically Twelver Shiʿi, studies, with full consideration of the fields of theology, philosophy and jurisprudence, as well as the Shiʿi contributions to Qur'anic and *ḥadīth* studies.

A new interest in the study of Shiʿi Islam in Iran, and to some extent globally, was kindled by the Islamic Revolution of 1979. The Islamic Revolution proved to be not only a turning point in the socio-political fabric of Iran but also in the popularity of the Iranian form of Twelver Shiʿism and its theological underpinnings, under the leadership of a politically powerful class of clerics. As a result, attention has been increasingly devoted to a series of new research topics such as relations between Shiʿi Islam and the authority–power structure of the state. At the same time, a great number of primary sources, including the classical texts of Twelver Imāmī Shiʿi tradition as well as Twelver works on history, theology and jurisprudence, are continuously edited and published under the auspices of Iran's religious seminaries. In sum, contemporary Iranian scholars and institutions have been making systematic contributions to the field of Shiʿi studies.

In the West, meanwhile, a select group of scholars belonging to a new generation, partially represented in this volume, have been producing some of the most influential works on various aspects of Shiʿi Islam. However, it should be noted that few scholars, in the West or in Muslim countries, have concerned themselves with all branches of Shiʿi Islam. In more recent decades, only Professor Wilferd Madelung has made original contributions to the study of the Twelver, Ismaili and Zaydi branches of Shiʿism, while Professor Josef van Ess has investigated theological aspects of the various Shiʿi traditions.

With these conceptual and historical points in mind, we have organised the chapters in this volume into eight main parts. These are: history and historiography, Qur'an and its Shiʿi interpretations, Shiʿi *ḥadīth*, Shiʿi law, authority, theology, rites and rituals, and philosophy and intellectual traditions. The introductions to each of the parts aim to provide an overview of that particular sub-field in the study of Shiʿi Islam within the more general context of Shiʿi and Islamic studies. They examine issues of methodology and recent developments in their respective sub-fields and represent a comprehensive overview of the topic, the state of research in that particular sub-field, how it has developed so far, primary aims at the current stage of its development and what needs to be done to further future research. Moreover, the author of each introduction has taken a unique approach to writing them for pragmatic reasons, in order to avoid repetitions and also to provide an extensive overview of the field in general.

The introductions are followed by what may be termed 'case studies' (studies on a particular topic), which are meant to explicate the type of issues and questions raised in the introductions and those that exist in the contemporary study of Shiʿi Islam, along with the methodologies and tools of research that are currently used to address these issues. Although the introductions refer to these case studies, they do in fact use the case studies to exemplify and highlight issues wherever appropriate without, however, limiting themselves to these alone. Of course, we acknowledge that these eight parts/topics do not cover all aspects of Shiʿi Islam, but going beyond this would have made the project unmanageable. It is hoped that the volume will inspire further research and discourse in the field leading to more exciting avenues for research in these and other areas. This collective volume is also the second volume in the Institute's *Shiʿi Heritage Series* of publications, which is a new venture that aims at promoting better understanding of and excellence in research in the field of Shiʿi studies.

In 2010 The Institute of Ismaili Studies organised a colloquium entitled *The Study of Shiʿi Islam: The State of the Field, Issues of Methodology and Recent Developments* to coincide with this volume. The colloquium aimed at providing a productive atmosphere for the exchange of ideas and scholarship by bringing together a large number of contributors to the volume and others. The panels reflected all sections represented in this volume. While focusing on the state of the field itself, the colloquium enabled serious discussions on current issues in the study of Shiʿi Islam. By providing leading as well as young scholars in the field with the opportunity to meet and discuss the state of the field and their current research, it sought to realise the aims of the Institute in promoting the understanding of Shiʿi Islam and enhancing further research.

We would like to thank all the contributors to this volume and all those who attended the colloquium for embarking on this journey with us and providing insights into the current state of the field. Some of the chapters have been translated from French or Arabic especially for the volume, for which we thank Nuha al-Shaar, Maria De Cillis, Russell Harris and Orkhan Mir-Kasimov. We would also like to express our gratitude to Kutub Kassam for his editorial skills, to Nadia Holmes who meticulously prepared the various drafts of this volume, and to Hamid Haji for having skilfully performed various editorial tasks.

FD and GM
May, 2013

Contributors

Farhad Daftary	Co-Director and Head of the Department of Academic Research and Publications, The Institute of Ismaili Studies
Gurdofarid Miskinzoda	Research Associate, Department of Academic Research and Publications, The Institute of Ismaili Studies
Mohammad Ali Amir-Moezzi	École Pratique des Hautes Études (Sorbonne) and Senior Research Fellow, The Institute of Ismaili Studies
Hassan Ansari	Senior Research Associate, Research Unit Intellectual History of the Islamicate World, Freie Universität Berlin
Meir M. Bar-Asher	Professor, Chair of the Department of Arabic Language and Literature, The Hebrew University of Jerusalem
Maria Massi Dakake	Associate Professor of Religious Studies, George Mason University in Fairfax, Virginia
Nader El-Bizri	Professor (civilisation sequence programme) and Director of the Anis Makdisi Program in literature and the humanistic disciplines, American University of Beirut
Hakim Elnazarov	Coordinator of the Central Asian Studies Unit, The Institute of Ismaili Studies
Gerald R. Hawting	Professor Emeritus, SOAS, University of London
David Hollenberg	Assistant Professor of Arabic Language and Religious Literature, The University of Oregon
Etan Kohlberg	Professor Emeritus of Arabic Language and Literature, The Hebrew University, Jerusalem
Wilferd Madelung	Professor Emeritus, University of Oxford and Senior Research Fellow, The Institute of Ismaili Studies

Toby Mayer	Research Associate, Department of Academic Research and Publications, The Institute of Ismaili Studies
Christopher Melchert	University Lecturer in Arabic and Islam, University of Oxford
Sabrina Mervin	Research Fellow at the Centre National de la Recherche Scientifique (CNRS), Paris
Azim Nanji	Professor, Aga Khan University, Karachi
Andrew J. Newman	Reader in Islamic Studies and Persian, Department of Islamic and Middle Eastern Studies, The University of Edinburgh
Ismail K. Poonawala	Professor of Arabic and Islamic Studies, University of California at Los Angeles
Nasser Rabbat	Aga Khan Professor of Islamic Architecture and Director, Aga Khan Program for Islamic Architecture, Department of Architecture, Massachusetts Institute of Technology
Andrew Rippin	Professor of Islamic History, University of Victoria, Canada
Sajjad Rizvi	Associate Professor of Islamic Intellectual History, University of Exeter
Sabine Schmidtke	Professor of Islamic Studies and Director of the Research Unit for Intellectual History of the Islamicate World, Freie Universität Berlin
Daniel De Smet	Director of Research at the Centre National de la Recherche Scientifique (CNRS), Paris
Roy Vilozny	The Hebrew University of Jerusalem and The Van Leer Jerusalem Institute
Paul E. Walker	Director for Academic Programs, Center for Middle Eastern Studies, University of Chicago
Sayyid Zayd al-Wazir	Yemen Heritage and Research Centre
Mohyddin Yahia	Professor, Dar al-Hadith University, Rabat, Morocco

Note on Transliteration and Dates

The system of transliteration used in this book for the Arabic and Persian scripts is essentially that adopted in the third edition of *The Encyclopaedia of Islam*. The lunar years of the Islamic calendar are generally followed throughout the text and endnotes by the corresponding Gregorian solar years (for example, 11/632). The years of the Islamic era, initiated by the emigration (*hijra*) of the Prophet Muḥammad from Mecca to Medina in September 622, commonly abbreviated in the Latin form AH (*Anno Hegirae*), have been converted to the corresponding dates of the Christian era, abbreviated as AD (*Anno Domini*), on the basis of the conversion tables given in Greville S.P. Freeman-Grenville, *The Muslim and Christian Calendars* (London, 1963). In Iran (called Persia in the West until 1936), a solar Islamic calendar was officially adopted in the 1920s. The Islamic dates of the sources published in modern Iran are, therefore, solar (Persian, Shamsi), coinciding with the corresponding Christian years starting on 21 March.

Abbreviations

The following abbreviations are used for certain periodicals, organisations and encyclopaedias cited frequently in the chapter notes:

AACMEC	*Association des amis du centre médiéval européen de Chartres*
BSOAS	*Bulletin of the School of Oriental and African Studies*
CEMOTI	*Cahiers d'études sur la Méditerranée orientale et le monde turco-iranien*
CERMOC	Centre de recherche sur le Moyen-Orient contemporain
DMBI	*Dāʾirat al-maʿārif-i buzurg-i Islāmī*
EI	*The Encyclopaedia of Islam*
EI2	*The Encyclopaedia of Islam*, new (second) edition
EI3	*The Encyclopaedia of Islam, Three*
EIR	*Encyclopaedia Iranica*
EIS	*Encyclopaedia Islamica*
EPHE	École Pratique des Hautes Études (Sorbonne)
IFEAD	Institut français d'études arabes de Damas
IJMES	*International Journal of Middle East Studies*
JAIS	*Journal of Arabic and Islamic Studies*
JAOS	*Journal of the American Oriental Society*
JNES	*Journal of Near Eastern Studies*
JRAS	*Journal of the Royal Asiatic Society*
JSAI	*Jerusalem Studies in Arabic and Islam*
NS	New Series
OM	*Oriente Moderno*
REMMM	*Revue des Mondes Musulmans et de la Méditerranée*
SI	*Studia Islamica*
ZDMG	*Zeitschrift der Deutschen Morgenländischen Gesellschaft*

PART I
HISTORY AND HISTORIOGRAPHY

Introduction

Wilferd Madelung

The study of the history of the Shiʿa within the wider history of Islam has been transformed in recent decades. When the history of the Muslim world first became a subject of modern academic research in the 19th century, historians naturally relied primarily on the major literary sources of mainstream Sunni Islam and adopted the Sunni historical perspective reflected in them. Sunni Islam and practice thus were viewed as the original and authentic Islam that developed out of the preaching of the Prophet Muḥammad and the Qurʾan. The Shiʿa, or *shīʿat ʿAlī*, were seen to be the radical followers of the fourth Rightly Guided successor of Muḥammad, who deviated from mainstream Islam only after the murder of ʿAlī (d. 40/661) when they began to claim that ʿAlī, as the cousin of the Prophet, had alone been entitled to succeed him and that after ʿAlī legitimate succession belonged to his descendants. The Shiʿa thus developed into a sectarian movement whose branches gradually moved further apart from mainstream Islam towards 'heterodoxy'. While the Sunni literary sources were in general recognised as reliably reflecting real history, deviant Shiʿi accounts were viewed with suspicion and considered unreliable.

In the early 20th century Western historiography turned more stridently anti-Shiʿi. The Umayyad caliphate (40–132/661–750) came to be viewed and admired as the golden age of Islam. Since the major historical sources for early Islam were written in the Abbasid age (132–656/750–1258), they were now seen as deeply biased against the Umayyad regime that was overthrown by the overtly Shiʿi Abbasid revolutionary movement. ʿAlī was perceived as an incompetent, yet inordinately ambitious rival of the early caliphs who plotted against them and was probably behind the murder of the second caliph ʿUmar and certainly responsible for the overthrow and murder of the third caliph ʿUthmān. The Umayyad claim of revenge for ʿUthmān provided legitimacy to the dynastic Umayyad reign which indeed had been envisaged and facilitated by the caliph ʿUmar. ʿAlī's cousin ʿAbd Allāh b. al-ʿAbbās, ancestor of the Abbasid caliphs, whose reports on the history of the early caliphate critical of ʿUmar are given prominence in the Sunni literary sources, was viewed as a brazen partisan liar.

By the middle of the 20th century, the growing distrust of Western historians in the reliability of mainstream Muslim literary sources for early Islam led to a revisionist crisis in historiography. Leading historians asserted that because of their late date, ideological bias and consistent back projection, all Muslim literary sources must be set aside entirely in critical research in favour of archaeological and non-Muslim literary sources. There could in particular be no hope of ever resolving the highly controversial issue of the origins and early history of the Shiʿa on the basis of the late Muslim sources.

In reaction to the extreme scepticism of the revisionist historians in respect to the literary sources dating from the Abbasid age, other scholars have sought to isolate and critically reinterpret documents and reports that can safely be dated back to pre-Abbasid Islam. For the origins of the Shiʿa, most significant have been the Qurʾan and the so-called Constitution of Medina negotiated by the Prophet Muḥammad. The latter document has been the subject of several thorough investigations and has generally been accepted as authentic, even by the revisionists, precisely because it stands in sharp contrast to the constitution of the caliphate of Quraysh that was implemented in Medina after the death of the Prophet. The Constitution of Medina does not give the Quraysh a privileged position in the Muslim community, which was composed of a group of Emigrants (*muhājirūn*) evidently including Qurayshīs, and various local Medinan Arab and Jewish tribal groups on a par. Muḥammad was the single head of the community, and no provisions for his succession were made in the Constitution.

The Qurʾan likewise did not grant Quraysh distinct leadership rights in Islam.[1] Nowhere does it express preference for the Emigrants over the Medinan Helpers (*anṣār*), although it exalts the merit of the earliest converts to Islam. The *Sūra* 57:10 placed those who joined Islam only after the conquest of Mecca in 9/630 lower in rank and merit than those who had done so before and made sacrifices in the cause of Islam. Yet these latecomers consisted mostly of the Quraysh and other non-Muslim tribes. The Qurʾan, however, provided clear, universally binding laws of inheritance and succession in Islam, which were promulgated in *Sūrat al-nisāʾ* (4:11–14) in the year 4/626. They gave unconditional precedence to direct descendants, awarding sons double the share of daughters. In the absence of a son, a daughter or daughters were sole primary heirs and could not be excluded by any rights of male kin. These Qurʾanic rules of succession were valid in either testate or intestate succession. A testament (*waṣiyya*) could merely name a legal executor (*waṣī*) for the division of shares of inheritance who would normally be rewarded for his service by a bequest. The executor could not become an heir and successor unless he was entitled to a primary Qurʾanic share.

A year later, *Sūrat al-aḥzāb* further restricted legitimate succession in lineal descent by outlawing adoption and recognising only blood relationships. Muḥammad himself had, years before his Prophetic mission, adopted his manumitted Syrian Arab slave Zayd b. Ḥāritha as his son. Zayd now lost his potential right of succession, although he remained as a client a highly trusted and favoured member of Muḥammad's household. *Sūra* 33:40 assured the community that 'Muḥammad is not the father of any of your men, he is God's Messenger and the seal of the prophets.' The lack of a

[1] For the following, see W. Madelung, 'Social Legislation in Sūrat al-Aḥzāb', forthcoming.

son seemed to rule out the succession of another prophet, but it also confirmed the legitimate succession of Muḥammad's surviving daughters.

In the Qur'an, the title to prophethood and religious authority (*imāma*) is inherited by continuous male descent. Ibrāhīm was the forefather of all later prophets. When God promised to make him the Imam of his people, Ibrāhīm asked Him to extend His compact to his offspring. God then excluded from the compact the wrongdoers, but evidently included the just among Ibrāhīm's progeny (Q.2:124). Exceptionally, however, God might elect a woman of the prophetic family for His unique favour, as He did with Maryam, the daughter of ʿImrān and mother of ʿĪsā. Might He not choose one of Muḥammad's daughters for His special favour in the absence of a son?

At that time, five years before his death, the Prophet certainly had not given up hope that a son might be born to him who would eventually become his successor. Three years on, his hopes seemed to be fulfilled when his Coptic concubine Maryam bore him a son. Muḥammad announced his son's birth to the Community at prayer time and declared that he had named him Ibrāhīm after his eminent forefather. A year later, however, the infant Ibrāhīm died. At the time of the Prophet's death, only his youngest daughter Fāṭima and her two sons and two daughters, all still minor, survived of his entitled descendants. A further surviving granddaughter of Muḥammad, Umāma, daughter of his eldest daughter Zaynab, was definitely excluded from succession under the rules of the Qur'an by the fact that her mother had predeceased the Prophet, who could have left her a bequest if he had written a testament.[2] Under the divine law of the Qur'an, Fāṭima was the Prophet's prime heiress and successor, entitled to seven-eighths of his inheritance, while His surviving nine wives were entitled to one eighth collectively.

A critical examination of the two early documents, the Qur'an and the Constitution of Medina, thus reveals that the establishment of the Sunni caliphate of the Quraysh decided in the famous assembly in the *Saqīfat Banī Sāʿida* (the hall of the Banū Sāʿida) was not simply a legitimate constitutional reform necessitated by the failure of the Prophet to name a successor and universally agreed by the Muslim community. The crisis after his death evidently was brought on by the exceptional circumstance that the legitimate successor to supreme leadership was a woman who, under the concepts of the time, could not personally perform some of the duties of her office such as leading the communal prayers or commanding the army. Sovereign queens, however, were well known to delegate such functions without detriment to their sovereign authority. Without an appointed executor of the Prophet's will, the community was obliged by the divine law first to pay homage to his daughter and follow her guidance and orders as they had followed her father. In modern world-historical terms, the establishment of the caliphate of the Quraysh must be judged to have been a *coup d'état* in which the ruling house was overthrown, the legitimate successor to the reign assaulted in her house and disinherited, the early constitution that gave equal

---

[2] See W. Madelung, *The Succession to Muḥammad: A Study of the Early Caliphate* (Cambridge, 1997), p. 41. n. 37, pp. 328–329.

autonomous rights to Emigrants and Medinan Muslims replaced by an institution that turned the Medinans, whose protection and support of the Prophet had secured the triumph of Islam, as well as all other Muslims into subjects of Quraysh.

The outcome of the assembly in the *Saqīfat Banī Sāʿida* was the great schism in Islam that has caused endless conflict and bloodshed over the centuries. The *shīʿat ʿAlī* grew out of the early minority group of legitimists who upheld the divine right of the family of the Prophet to succeed him. The Sunni majority were challenged to develop a new basis of religious legitimacy in the Sunna of the consensus of the Companions and especially the Sunna set by the acts of the Rightly Guided Caliphs.

The historical circumstances and events so far described must today be recognised as real by any critical historian and can no longer be dismissed as potentially fictitious back projection of later conflict in the Muslim community. This recognition also provides a firm basis for judging conflicting accounts and documents reported in the Sunni literary sources dating from the Abbasid age. The crisis of confidence in the reliability of these was indeed largely provoked by the fact that they contained so many reports apparently reflecting Shiʿi ideological views. These were commonly rejected by modern Western scholars as fiction produced in the early Abbasid age in order to please the new dynasty with its initially Shiʿi and anti-Umayyad ideology. Shiʿi literary sources were generally discarded out of hand. Anti-Shiʿi bias has certainly been deep and widespread, though not universal, in Western Islamic studies since the late 19th century. Historians of Shiʿism may face a long struggle to overcome this entrenched bias and to demonstrate that Shiʿis were not merely disgruntled dissident Muslims inclined to vilify the Companions of the Prophet and curse them in public.

The case of the Shiʿa has ever been obscured by the misunderstanding that the Shiʿi claim that ʿAlī was appointed by Muḥammad as his *waṣī* meant that he was entitled to succeed the Prophet in his office and that his position was illegally occupied by Abū Bakr and ʿUmar. As noted, a *waṣī* is merely a legatee and executor of the testament (*waṣiyya*) in which he is appointed, not normally the successor. Without title to any share of the Prophet's inheritance, ʿAlī could not become his legal successor. The Shiʿi claim itself is specious since in the absence of a testament there could be no *waṣī* in the legal sense. The claim was based on the famous proclamation of the Prophet, only months before his death, in favour of his cousin at Ghadīr Khumm which reasonably enough was widely understood as a confirmation that he intended to entrust his cousin with the execution of his will.

According to ʿAbd Allāh b. al-ʿAbbās, Muḥammad during his final illness wanted to write a testament, but was prevented by ʿUmar b. al-Khaṭṭāb, and the Shiʿis have ever since presumed that the Prophet merely intended to confirm ʿAlī as his *waṣī*.[3] Yet if he was so certain of his choice, why did he not write his last will earlier and

---

[3] For the following, see in general my *Succession to the Prophet Muḥammad*. It will be noted that my understanding of the history of the succession dispute has developed further after the publication of this book by my subsequent realisation that the Qur'anic rules of succession unambiguously made the Prophet's daughter Fāṭima his prime heiress and successor. This

why did he not ask ʿAlī to lead the communal prayers during his illness rather than Abū Bakr? According to other reports of Ibn al-ʿAbbās, ʿUmar explained to him that the Prophet had made ambiguous statements in favour of ʿAlī and in his mortal illness intended to appoint him successor. ʿUmar had, however, restrained him out of concern for Islam. He warned him that the Quraysh would not tolerate prophethood and succession to the rule to belong to one and the same of their clans and all the Arabs would rise in revolt against ʿAlī. The Prophet had been impressed by this advice and therefore kept silent. ʿUmar stressed to Ibn al-ʿAbbās that it was not Abū Bakr who wanted to prevent the succession of ʿAlī. Abū Bakr had, rather, done what was most prudent under the circumstances.[4]

ʿUmar must have declared his opposition to the appointment of ʿAlī as *waṣī* of Muḥammad right after the pronouncement of Ghadīr Khumm. The Prophet understood his warning correctly as ʿUmar's bid for the succession, a bid he probably had expected ever since ʿUmar's sudden conversion to Islam in Mecca after earlier violent hostility. He realised the seriousness of ʿUmar's warning, not so much because he believed that the Quraysh were united in opposition to his family. ʿUmar, he was certain, was much more feared and less admired by the Meccan Quraysh than he. ʿUmar had, however, built up a strong personal power base among the Arabs on the outskirts of Medina, and especially among the Banū Aslam, who were prepared to act on his signal. ʿAlī, in contrast, had so far not gained much popularity. Although personally a brave warrior and battle hero, he had as governor of Yemen just lost the loyal backing of his soldiers, forcing the Prophet to make his pronouncement. ʿUmar's warning clearly indicated that he was not opposed to ʿAlī personally, but to the privileged status of the Prophet's family which stood in the way of his own ambition to succeed to the rule of the Muslim community. Muḥammad was well aware of ʿUmar's strident male chauvinism and abhorrence of the rule of women over men. If ʿUmar were to gain power, the legitimate rights of the Prophet's only surviving daughter and his grandsons would hardly be secured.

The Prophet was now vitally concerned to keep his overambitious Companion and father-in-law at bay. There is evidence that ʿUmar, at the outbreak of Muḥammad's illness, attempted to take over the leadership of the communal prayers. The Prophet, hearing his voice, insisted that his old friend Abū Bakr must lead them in his stead. Abū Bakr, he recognised, had no personal power base, but was widely respected and better liked than ʿUmar in the Muslim community. If appointed executor of the Prophet's will, he could be trusted to protect the rights of his family.

All historical accounts agree that Muḥammad still wanted to leave a written will, and the majority report that it was ʿUmar's intervention that prevented him from doing so. As noted, ʿUmar himself claimed responsibility, justifying his action by the higher interest of Islam. The reports disagree on the identity of the intended

---

realisation has inevitably modified my views in particular about the roles of Abū Bakr and ʿUmar.

4 Madelung, *Succession*, pp. 66–67.

beneficiary and executor of the will. ʿĀʾisha reported that the Prophet, who was then ill, had asked her to call her father and her brother because he intended to write his testament in favour of Abū Bakr, but she did not mention what prevented him from writing it. Did ʿUmar intervene? ʿĀʾisha evidently would not have wished to blame him, and most later Sunni Muslims, who viewed ʿUmar as the Fārūq, the saviour of Islam, would rather not know. ʿAbd Allāh b. al-ʿAbbās reported that his father al-ʿAbbās, paternal uncle of Muḥammad, recognised approaching death in the Prophet's face and urged ʿAlī to ask him concerning the succession. He told ʿAlī that the Prophet would either give the reign to the Banū Hāshim or at least commend (*awṣā*) them to the good care of the Muslims. ʿAlī refused, expressing fear that if the Prophet denied them succession, the Muslims would never grant it to them.[5] Ibn al-ʿAbbās also told ʿUmar during his caliphate that the Banū Hāshim asserted that Muḥammad had actually named ʿAlī (*naṣṣa ʿalayh*) for the caliphate. He, Ibn al-ʿAbbās, had asked his father al-ʿAbbās about this, and his father had confirmed it.[6]

From these accounts it is evident that whereas ʿĀʾisha was convinced that the Prophet just before his death intended to make her father Abū Bakr executor of his will, ʿAlī was now in doubt about Muḥammad's intention, although he was certain that the Prophet had earlier intended to name his cousin. It is also plain that Muḥammad was most of all concerned to thwart the designs of ʿUmar in order to safeguard the Qurʾanic rights of his only surviving daughter and his descendants. The critical historian, however, will have to suspend judgement on the identity of his ultimate choice of his *waṣī*. The circumstantial evidence in favour of his old friend and father-in-law Abū Bakr and of his cousin and son-in-law ʿAlī is equal. ʿAbd Allāh b. al-ʿAbbās described the decisive occasion thus: shortly before the Prophet's death, when a number of his closest Companions were assembled to hear his last advice, he expressed the wish to write a letter for them after which they would not go astray. ʿUmar objected: 'The Apostle of God is overcome by pain. You have the Qurʾan, the Book of God is sufficient for us.' Those present started to quarrel, some of them demanding that the Prophet be allowed to write, others siding with ʿUmar. As their noise pained the Prophet, he asked them to leave him. Ibn al-ʿAbbās used to comment that utmost calamity was thus caused by their discord and noise which prevented the Prophet from writing his will.[7] He meant the great schism that has rent apart Islam until the present.

Further developments until the appearance of the *shīʿat ʿAlī* on the stage of history during the reign of the fourth caliph of Islam cannot be traced here in detail. Critical historians of early Islam, however, will have to understand that succession to the caliphate initially did not mean legitimate succession to the Prophet. The term *khalīfat rasūl Allāh,* caliph of the Apostle of God, had been used to designate Muḥammad's

5 Ibid., p. 22.
6 Ibid., p. 66.
7 Ibid., pp. 23–24.

temporary deputy in Medina during his absence on campaigns.[8] That Abū Bakr and ʿUmar could not have claimed the later common title *khalīfat Allāh*, which would under the circumstances have constituted a claim to succession to the rank of the Apostle of God, is plain. In the absence of a testament of the Prophet, ʿUmar at first hoped to realise his designs by denying the death of Muḥammad and asserting that the Prophet had gone to his Lord as Moses had done, leaving his people for forty days and returning after he had been pronounced dead.[9] In the meantime, ʿUmar must have expected that he would be able to rule without having to worry about any rights of inheritance. ʿUmar's bid for supreme power was quickly thwarted by Muḥammad's uncle al-ʿAbbās and Muḥammad's other father-in-law Abū Bakr who both testified that the Prophet was dead.

At the *Saqīfa* assembly, Abū Bakr was nominated by ʿUmar as *khalīfa* of the Prophet and most of those present pledged allegiance to him. His title to the new position, whose function could be defined as that of a *waṣī* chosen by the community, was based on the claim of a collective leadership privilege in Islam which had no basis in the Qur'an. Abū Bakr's title was disputed by some of the leading men of Quraysh in Mecca, most seriously by the old chieftain of the Umayya Abū Sufyān who, when informed of the election of the new caliph, remarked mockingly: 'Who, Abu'l-Faṣīl, the son of Abū Quḥāfa?' and offered ʿAlī his armed support against the new caliph of Quraysh. He most likely felt that if the rights of Muḥammad's cousin were disregarded by the Muslims they should at least have chosen ʿUthmān, the other close kinsman of the Prophet among the early Companions. Abū Sufyān's overture was rejected by ʿAlī, but his slighting remark was to cause lasting bitterness between the family of Abū Bakr and the house of Umayya.

Having confirmed the death of Muḥammad, Abū Bakr was faced with the problem of the Prophet's inheritance. His nomination by ʿUmar and continued need to rely on his power base threatened to turn him into a tool of his rival. When the daughter of the Prophet and his uncle al-ʿAbbās visited the caliph to ask for their share of the inheritance, Abū Bakr, according to the account of ʿĀ'isha, told them that he had heard the Apostle of God say: 'We the prophets do not leave anything to be inherited. Whatever we leave is alms.'[10] The account raises a question for critical historians familiar with the Qur'an, for the Qur'an does not confirm a residual right of agnates to inherit when a woman's share exceeds half of what a man in her position would have inherited. Under the Sunni law of succession, Muḥammad's daughter could not have inherited more than half of the estate, and al-ʿAbbās, as his paternal uncle, would have been entitled to a share of three-eighths. Was the pre-Islamic right of agnates, now necessarily residual, still generally recognised in Muslim legal practice or was it, rather, restored in the legal reforms introduced by ʿUmar? That the *ḥadīth*

---

[8] See K. Y. Blankinship, 'Imārah, Khilāfah, and Imāmah: The Origins of the Succession to the Prophet Muḥammad', in L. Clarke, ed., *Shīʿite Heritage: Essays on Classical and Modern Traditions* (Binghamton, NY, 2001), p. 28.

[9] Madelung, *Succession*, p. 38.

[10] Ibid., p. 50.

Abū Bakr claimed to have heard from the Prophet was nothing but a political lie, presumably invented by ʿUmar in the higher interest of Islam, was certainly understood by the two claimants. A statement so obviously contradicting the letter and the spirit of the Holy Book could not have been made by the Prophet, even if he were raving.

Fāṭima was hardly offended by the caliph's decision and perhaps relieved that the burden of distributing the alms fairly among the legal recipients now fell on his shoulders. She must at this point have been grateful to him that he, according to various sources, had restrained ʿUmar when he attacked her house, threatening to burn it, and had protected her husband ʿAlī from further persecution even though ʿAlī had still not pledged allegiance to the caliph. More hurtful must have been the caliph's rejection of her claim, made in a subsequent visit jointly with ʿAlī, that her father had gifted the produce of the oasis Fadak to her years before his death. Abū Bakr asked for legal evidence for the gift and then rejected the joint testimony of ʿAlī and Umm Ayman, the faithful old servant of the Prophet, as inadequate since Umm Ayman's testimony as a woman counted only a half and required that of a second woman. It clearly amounted to recourse to a legal formality with the intent of denying the course of justice. Abū Bakr and the public knew well that the Prophet had assigned the produce of Fadak to his daughter for her and her family's maintenance since ʿAlī, having inherited little from his parents, depended materially on his wife and that she used to give the surplus as alms to the needy. Muḥammad evidently had failed to notarise his gift since he expected his daughter to inherit on his death. Fāṭima and ʿAlī again must have felt the hands of ʿUmar behind Abū Bakr's verdict.

When Fāṭima died, six months after her father, ʿAlī buried her privately, as her father had been buried, and did not inform the caliph. Abū Bakr, according to ʿĀʾisha's account, decided to visit him on his request, against the advice of ʿUmar, who suggested that the Banū Hāshim might kill him if he went alone. Abū Bakr assured ʿAlī that his kinship ties to the Apostle of God were indeed dearer to him than his own kinship, but he repeated that he had heard the alleged *ḥadīth* from the Prophet. The family of Muḥammad could eat from the alms left by the Prophet. He solemnly promised that he would do nothing with this public money but what the Prophet had done. The following day ʿAlī pledged allegiance to Abū Bakr in public.[11]

Abū Bakr's assertion of his paramount commitment to the welfare of the Prophet's family must have partly reassured ʿAlī, but his repetition of the forged *ḥadīth* still worried him. The historical reports about Abū Bakr's caliphate indicate that ʿAlī still kept generally aloof from the caliph, although he supported him and sincerely advised him if invited to do so. He understood that with the death of Fāṭima the right of succession of the Prophet devolved upon her still minor sons and, if they should die prematurely, on her two daughters. He as a cousin of Muḥammad could not succeed him, though as a member of his family and father of Fāṭima's minor

[11] Ibid., pp. 52–53.

children he was obliged to safeguard their rights. This gave him a strong title to the caliphate which he hoped Abū Bakr would respect.

Before his death two years later, the first caliph appointed ʿUmar as his successor. As an appointee of Abū Bakr the second caliph had even less claim to legitimacy than his predecessor under the new constitution of the caliphate of Quraysh. Abū Bakr did consult a few of the early Qurayshī Companions after he had already made up his mind, but the reaction was predominantly negative. ʿAbd al-Raḥmān b. ʿAwf expressed reservations because of ʿUmar's well-known harshness, and Abū Bakr's kinsman Ṭalḥa protested on account of ʿUmar's ill treatment of people even during Abū Bakr's reign.[12] ʿUmar thus began his reign with the modest title of *khalīfat khalīfat rasūl Allāh*, deputy of the deputy of the Apostle of God. He soon, however, claimed another, military title: *amīr al-mu'minīn*, Commander of the Faithful, which suited his designs better. The title was to become hereditary for all subsequent caliphs, turning them primarily into supreme military commanders – a fateful development in Islam hardly in tune with succession to a prophet defined as a conveyor of a divine message. ʿAlī, too, was to adopt it as his favourite title, for he was – although aware of the threat of ʿUmar to the rights of the Prophet's family – in general an admirer of his conduct and religious reforms. He held on to his own claim, however, to know and understand the message and preaching of the Prophet better than any of his other Companions.

During the twelve years of his reign, ʿUmar undertook to implement his concept of the caliphate of Quraysh, which amounted to a new vision of Islam not entirely derived from the Qur'an. He had told the Prophet that Quraysh would not countenance a monopoly of his family on supreme religious and worldly authority. This meant excluding any superhuman implications in the privileged status the Qur'an accorded Muḥammad's *ahl al-bayt*. In his last Friday sermon, as reported by Ibn al-ʿAbbās, ʿUmar pointedly quoted the Prophet's order: 'Do not extol me as Jesus, son of Mary, has been extolled, but say: the servant of God and His messenger.'[13] The Family of the Prophet were one of the families of Quraysh, the Banū Hāshim a clan of Quraysh, who according to the Qur'an were privileged in the lifetime of the Prophet, but this did not imply permanent privilege. In his *dīwān* for the distribution of the revenue from conquered lands, ʿUmar granted the two grandsons of Muḥammad a stipend equal to that of the veterans of the Battle of Badr in recognition of the rights of their mother, and he granted the disinherited widows of the Prophet pensions more than double of them.[14] Fāṭima's daughters received no compensation. While still insisting that the Prophet had disinherited his daughter and wives, he turned over Muḥammad's estates in Medina that had been withheld from his daughter to al-ʿAbbās and ʿAlī as an endowment to be administered by them. Al-ʿAbbās thus was recompensed for his non-Qur'anic share of the Prophet's inheritance as an agnate,

---

12 Ibid., p. 55.
13 Ibid., p. 30.
14 Ibid., pp. 58–59.

while ʿAlī, who was not entitled to any share of Muḥammad's estate under Sunni law, was compensated for his share of the inheritance of his wife Fāṭima which, under Qurʾanic law, amounted to one fourth. ʿĀʾisha reported that ʿAlī soon usurped the rights of al-ʿAbbās in respect of these estates. In reality al-ʿAbbās had no rights under the Qurʾanic rules, and the inheritance of Fāṭima belonged primarily to her children who at the time of entitlement were still minor. The legal dispute between al-ʿAbbās and his nephew ʿAlī was provoked by ʿUmar's reform of Islamic law.

ʿUmar's idea of the right of Quraysh collectively to govern the Muslim community was not strictly egalitarian or meritocratic. Merit in Islam could in his view be inherited to some extent, and early merit in general trumped any later merit. The clans of Quraysh, he held, should be allowed to compete for leadership as they had done before Islam, but none should obtain a monopoly. It was legitimate for the caliph to appoint his successor, but ʿUmar was opposed to simple dynastic succession. Ultimately succession to the caliphate should be based on unanimous or near-unanimous election by Quraysh. ʿUmar was eager that the Banū Hāshim and ʿAlī should compete again for leadership and the caliphate, but they must not claim permanent privilege on the basis of their kinship with the Prophet. When he heard rumours of a plot to raise ʿAlī to power after his, ʿUmar's, death in a coup similar to the one at the *Saqīfa* assembly, he vigorously denounced such plans in his last Friday sermon. The coup (*falta*) in Abū Bakr's favour, he asserted, had been justified by the higher interest of Islam at the time and by the fact that the Muslims were longing for Abū Bakr as for no one else. For this reason God had warded off any evil consequences of the *falta*. The present plot was, rather, one of a mere clan (*rahṭ*) of Arabs who were conspiring to deprive the people (of Quraysh) of their right to decide. ʿUmar's description of ʿAlī and his family as a mere clan of Arabs became a standard slogan of the opponents of the Shiʿa.

The prophetic chain with its lineal descent, conspicuous in the Qurʾan and in Shiʿi thought, had little significance for ʿUmar. Prophets were chosen by God to convey a verbal message from Him, not because of some innate superior qualification. Muḥammad, as ʿUmar stressed in his last sermon, was merely a slave of God, and like other humans prone to misstep, as when he proposed to appoint his cousin to succeed him. The Prophet, however, had not been merely a passive conveyor of God's message. As the Qurʾan explained, he was privileged to put his, and his Companions', questions to God, who might or might not respond in a Qurʾanic message. ʿUmar personally took credit for having asked Muḥammad for the rule imposed in Q.33:53 that the Prophet's wives must only speak to men other than their close kin when veiled and behind a screen.[15] In his final sermon, ʿUmar warned the community not to neglect the religious duty of stoning as punishment for fornication and adultery which, he affirmed, had been part of the Qurʾan and was practised by the Prophet. Let no one go astray by neglecting it, saying: 'We do not find stoning in the Book of

[15] H. Lazarus-Yafeh, "Umar b. al-Khaṭṭāb – Paul of Islam?', in his *Some Religious Aspects of Islam: A Collection of Articles* (Leiden, 1981), pp. 8–9.

God.'[16] It is unlikely that the stoning verse to which 'Umar referred was ever part of the Qur'an. There are reports that in the time of the Prophet it was considered as taken from the Tora and that 'Umar vainly tried to persuade Muḥammad to include it in the Qur'an.[17] It is evident that 'Umar was deeply concerned that it should become a permanent part of the law of Islam. On account of Q.33:40 he certainly accepted that Muḥammad was the last prophet to receive a verbal message of God. In consonance, however, with the Qur'anic principle of abrogation (*naskh*) that had allowed the Prophet to adjust the divine law to arising circumstances, he saw himself entitled to adjust and interpret it as he had done while the Prophet had been alive. Firmly convinced that he had, with the support of the Banū Aslam, saved Islam at the *Saqīfa* assembly, he trusted that his reforms of ritual and law, too, were divinely sanctioned.

'Umar's reforms were largely to the detriment of women's rights. He was profoundly convinced of the innate inferiority of women to men and that this difference in rank was distinctly recognised in the divine law of the Qur'an. The idea that the double share of the inheritance for men stipulated by the Qur'an might be intended to obligate them to provide for women because of their general disadvantage in earning their livelihood and that it did not affect their immaterial value as human beings was foreign to his ideology. The value of a woman, he held, could be no more than half of a man in Islam. Men should not be obliged to support women they did not want, and unilateral repudiation of a wife by immediately effective triple pronouncement of divorce must be allowed and encouraged. Temporary marriage (*mut'a*) was banned by 'Umar certainly not because he held that marriage should be permanent, but rather because men should not be responsible for sustaining their unwanted children and their mothers. Women must be controlled by men, but not be a burden on them.

'Umar's reforms were almost universally appreciated at the time, even by women. The age of the idea of women's emancipation was still remote. There was some dissent from 'Abd Allāh b. al-'Abbās and early non-Qurayshī Companions like 'Abd Allāh b. Mas'ūd, who preferred holding on to the practices of the Prophet. The phenomenal achievements of the Muslim armies under 'Umar as Commander of the Faithful assured wide recognition of his title as the Fārūq, the Saviour of Islam, and the second in rank as head of the Muslim community after Muḥammad. Yet 'Umar must have been keenly aware that, contrary to his warning to the Prophet that Quraysh would never countenance a caliphate of his family, the majority of the Muslim community including Quraysh were longing for it, even if it meant dynastic succession. All dynastic caliphates down to the 10th/16th century, the Umayyad, Abbasid and Fatimid, have based their claim of legitimacy on belonging to the Prophet's Family. 'Umar perhaps might have delayed their succession by appointing his own successor as Abū Bakr had done. When it was suggested to him that he appoint his own son

[16] Madelung, *Succession*, p. 29.

[17] J. Burton, *The Sources of Islamic Law: Islamic Theories of Abrogation* (Edinburgh, 1990), pp. 129–135.

ʿAbd Allāh, who enjoyed considerable popularity and respect in the community, he declined, observing that ʿAbd Allāh was not even capable of divorcing his wife.[18]

In order to maintain the semblance of a genuine election, not just a confirmation of an obvious candidate, ʿUmar chose two members of the Prophet's Family for his electoral council of six early Companions of Quraysh: ʿAlī and ʿUthmān b. ʿAffān, grandson of Muḥammad's aunt Umm Ḥakīm, married consecutively to two of Muḥammad's daughters, and father of Muḥammad's grandson ʿAbd Allāh, who died at the age of six in the year 4/625.[19] ʿUthmān had long been recognised as a member of the Prophet's *ahl al-bayt*, and Muḥammad's widows had after his death first thought of asking him to intervene with Abū Bakr for their share of the inheritance, but were dissuaded by ʿĀʾisha.[20] The election for the succession of ʿUmar turned quickly into a competition between the two close kinsmen of Muḥammad. Both cast their first vote for the other, but then ʿAlī forcefully pleaded his own case, no doubt on account of his paternity of the two grandsons of the Prophet who, as his surviving male lineal descendants, were now fully entitled to his succession. However, ʿUthmān was elected in the year 23/644, with strong support from the majority of Quraysh.

ʿAlī was disappointed, but grudgingly pledged allegiance, hoping that the third caliph, as a kinsman of Muḥammad, would eventually respect the rights of the Prophet's grandsons. Such hope was disappointed in the following year (24/644–645), the 'year of the nose-bleed' (*sanat al-ruʿāf*), when ʿUthmān, fearing for his own life, made a testament in favour of his own son ʿAmr, still a minor , with al-Zubayr b. ʿAwwām, Muḥammad's maternal cousin, as his temporary successor until ʿAmr came of age.[21] Having been elected by Quraysh as a close kinsman of Muḥammad, ʿUthmān considered himself the first true successor of the Prophet and adopted the title *khalīfat Allāh,* vicegerent of God on earth, as Muḥammad had been the Messenger of God to humanity. His Umayyad nepotism and high-handed governing policy soon provoked criticism that he was putting himself in rank above his two predecessors and on a par with the Prophet. Later during his reign, when rebels demanded that he resign or they would kill him, he insisted that he would not take off a cloak with which God had dressed him. Muʿāwiya and the later Umayyad caliphs were to claim the title *khalīfat Allāh* in succession to him.

The revolt that eventually overthrew ʿUthmān's caliphate was not led, instigated or backed by ʿAlī, contrary to what Western historians have long contended. ʿAlī at first negotiated with the rebels on behalf of the caliph, but finally abandoned his mediation effort as ʿUthmān, under the influence of his cousin Marwān, would not keep his commitments to the rebels. During the siege of ʿUthmān's palace in Medina, the Prophet's grandson al-Ḥasan b. ʿAlī joined the defenders of the caliph and was slightly wounded. His brother al-Ḥusayn also volunteered to join, but was excused by the caliph and sent back to his father ʿAlī to urge him to join. ʿAlī declined, perhaps

[18] Madelung, *Succession*, p. 69.

[19] Ibid., p. 304.

[20] Ibid., p. 51.

[21] Ibid., pp. 88–89.

on the advice of his son Muḥammad b. al-Ḥanafiyya.[22] The prominent Companions who stirred up and actively promoted the revolt were first ʿAmr b. al-ʿĀṣ, who was deposed by ʿUthmān from the governorship of Egypt, and then Abū Bakr's daughter ʿĀʾisha and her kinsman Ṭalḥa. They were strongly opposed to ʿAlī and, after ʿAlī's succession to the caliphate, became leaders of the insurrection against him. Among the rebels against ʿUthmān, there were, however, also many supporters of ʿAlī, especially in Kūfa. Prominent among his supporters were ʿĀʾisha's younger half-brother Muḥammad b. Abī Bakr, who had been raised in ʿAlī's household and participated in the slaying of ʿUthmān, and the early Companion ʿAmmār b. Yāsir, who was manhandled by the retainers of the caliph.

These rebels against ʿUthmān formed a significant part of the armed *shīʿat ʿAlī* defending ʿAlī's caliphate. ʿAlī appreciated their support and did not accuse anyone of the violent death of ʿUthmān, holding that he had been killed in a popular uprising provoked by his own actions. As Muʿāwiya and the *shīʿat ʿUthmān* backing him demanded retribution for the wrongful killing of the caliph (*al-khalīfa al-maẓlūm*) and punishment of those involved in his death, these followers of ʿAlī were unconditionally opposed to any compromise with Muʿāwiya, and most of them joined the Khārijīs after ʿAlī's agreement to arbitration. The Khārijīs later even claimed ʿAmmār b. Yāsir, who was killed in the Battle of Ṣiffīn before the agreement, as one of their founders.

The electoral council (*shūrā*) constituted by ʿUmar was the first and last serious attempt to implement his concept of the caliphate of Quraysh. While the concept has been preserved as a fundamental dogma in the Sunni creed until the modern age, in historical practice it was immediately replaced by a competition among branches descended from Muḥammad's ancestor ʿAbd Manāf, the father of Hāshim and ʿAbd Shams, for recognition as legitimate successors of the Prophet on a dynastic basis. The great majority of the Muslim community never accepted the view that the line of prophetic descent had ended with Muḥammad since only male descent could count. Fāṭima's male descendants were commonly addressed, by Shiʿis and Sunnis alike, as sons of the Messenger of God, *yā Ibn rasūl Allāh*. As inter-Muslim war and oppression were seen to be spreading under the caliphate, hope for a Mahdī, a restorer of justice, found expression in popular prophecies about a descendant and namesake of Muḥammad who would fill the earth with justice before the end of time as it was filled with oppression and anarchy. While in early times not a few believed that the Mahdī might be a descendant of ʿUmar, ʿAbd Shams, al-ʿAbbās or even some non-Qurayshī, the later Sunni creed insisted, like the Shiʿi creed, on his descent from the Prophet. While the early Shiʿa adopted a substantial portion of Sunnism on account of ʿAlī's distinct admiration for some of ʿUmar's reforms of the *sharīʿa* of Islam, the Sunni world in later centuries has absorbed much of the Shiʿi veneration of the family of the Prophet.

---

[22] Ibid., pp. 133–134.

Critical historians of Islam and Shiʿism today can no longer reasonably adopt the perspective of the revisionist school and globally dismiss Muslim literary sources for the life of Muḥammad and early Islam as unreliable merely because they date from the Abbasid age. Like all historical sources, even contemporary newspaper reports, they have to be critically evaluated. If major Sunni sources like the annals of al-Ṭabarī and al-Balādhurī's *Ansāb al-ashrāf*, whose authors clearly professed their Sunni perspective of history, contain numerous documents and reports of an apparent Shiʿi flavour, it can only mean that they accepted them as the most reliable information available to them, not that Shiʿis were able to smuggle their fiction into them without the author's knowledge, as is so often assumed by Western historians. Such documents and reports in Sunni and Shiʿi sources alike must no longer merely be read as reflecting the Shiʿi 'eye of the beholder' with no relevance to a real history, which by definition of the sceptics can never be known. No other world religion has preserved so rich a literature about its origins and early and late medieval development as Islam, both Shiʿi and Sunni. Much of it is still awaiting critical, unbiased investigation.

1

Reflections on the Expression *dīn ʿAlī*: The Origins of the Shiʿi Faith*

Mohammad Ali Amir-Moezzi

In Shiʿi lands generally, and in Iran more particularly, there are a number of compound first names ending in ʿAlī. Many are very common: for instance, *Ḥusayn-ʿAlī, Muḥammad-ʿAlī, Jaʿfar-ʿAlī*; others have a more literary even poetic resonance: *Sayf-ʿAlī* ('Sword of ʿAlī'), *Nūr-ʿAlī* ('Light of ʿAlī'), *Maḥabbat-ʿAlī* or *Mihr-ʿAlī* ('Love of ʿAlī'), *Īmān-ʿAlī* ('Faith of ʿAlī'); still others are quite unusual if not very rare: *Shīr-ʿAlī* ('Lion-ʿAlī'), *Gurg-ʿAlī* ('Wolf ʿAlī'), *Chirāg-ʿAlī* ('Lamp of ʿAlī') and *Dīn-ʿAlī* ('Religion of ʿAlī').

This last appellation has always intrigued me: "ʿAlī's religion'. Is this not the same as Islam, as Muḥammad's religion? How might one explain this term, especially given that *Islām* and *dīn Muḥammad* are used as first names as well? Imagine my surprise when, a few years ago, I encountered the expression *dīn ʿAlī* in certain passages from early historiographical works. What does this term stand for? How can it be interpreted? Although the context is obviously not the same, this chapter is thus an attempt to answer a long-standing question. The chapter consists of five parts: (1) *Dīn ʿAlī* in the works of the historiographers; (2) The uniqueness of ʿAlī; (3) Themes concerning ʿAlī and the ʿAlids; (4) The basis for the religion of ʿAlī (the Qurʾanic bases; and the pre-Islamic bases); (5) Reactions and repercussions.

1. *Dīn ʿAlī* in the Works of the Historiographers

In certain passages of his monumental work *Taʾrīkh al-rusul waʾl-mulūk*, al-Ṭabarī (d. 310/923) reproduces some reports in which the expression *dīn ʿAlī* appears. The first is found in a long account reported by ʿAṭiyya b. Bilāl about the Battle of the

* I extend my gratitude to Professors Wilferd Madelung and Etan Kohlberg for their pertinent comments during the process of writing this chapter. Any imperfections that still remain are the responsibility solely of the author.

Camel in 36/656.[1] At one point during the battle, ʿAmr b. Yathribī al-Ḍabbī *al-rājiz*, a poet-warrior in the camp of the confederates allied against ʿAlī, kills three of his men, ʿIlbā' b. al-Haytham al-Sadūsī, Hind b. ʿAmr al-Jamalī and Zayd b. Ṣūḥān, before being laid low by ʿAmmār b. Yāsir, one of ʿAlī' s oldest supporters. After he had been brought down, he is said to have recited this *rajaz*:

> Let he who knows me not, learn that I am Ibn Yathribī, killer of 'Ilbā' and Hind al-Jamalī. As well as of the son of Ṣūḥān, all (adepts) of ʿAlī's religion.[2]

He is then led to ʿAlī, who does not accept his request for *amān*, and orders his execution. According to the author of this account, Ibn Yathribī was the only captive to whom ʿAlī denied a pardon. Al-Ṭabarī does not provide any clarification of his intransigence. The reader can reasonably conclude that the *rājiz* (poet-warrior) was executed for rather haughtily boasting about killing three of the most loyal of ʿAlī's companions. During the same period, another erudite scholar, Ibn Durayd Muḥammad b. al-Ḥasan al-Azdī (d. 321/933), reproduces the poem in his *Kitāb al-ishtiqāq*, adding that in order to justify this unique execution, ʿAlī is supposed to have said:

> He [i.e., Ibn Yathribī] claimed to have killed [my three companions] because they followed the religion of ʿAlī; well, the religion of ʿAlī is the religion of Muḥammad (*zaʿama annahu qatalahum ʿalā dīn ʿAlī wa dīn ʿAlī dīn Muḥammad*).[3]

According to Ibn Durayd's account, the reason for putting Ibn Yathribī to death was the distinction made by him between the religion of ʿAlī and that of Muḥammad,

---

[1] Al-Ṭabarī, *Ta'rīkh*, ed. M. J. de Goeje et al. (Leiden, 1879–1901), series 1, pp. 3196ff.; ed. M. A. F. Ibrāhīm (Cairo, 1960), vol. 4, pp. 514ff.

[2] *Anā li-man yunkirunī ibnu yathribī qātilu ʿilbā'i wa hindi'l-jamalī wa ibnin li-ṣūḥāna ʿalā dīni ʿAlī*; al-Ṭabarī, ed. de Goeje, series 1, p. 3199; ed. Ibrāhīm, vol. 4, p. 517, varies slightly: '*In taqtulūnī* [if you plan to kill me, know that etc.] *fa anā ibnu yathribī qātilu ʿilbā'i wa hindi'l-jamalī thumma bni ṣūḥāna ʿalā dīni ʿAlī*.' See also al-Mufīd, *Kitāb al-Jamal aw al-nuṣra fī ḥarb al-Baṣra* (Najaf, 1963), p. 146; Ibn Shahrāshūb, *Manāqib āl Abī Ṭālib*, ed. M. Burūjirdī (lithograph, Tehran, 1316–1317/1898–1899; Najaf, 1956), vol. 3, p. 156; al-Majlisī, *Biḥār al-anwār*, ed. based on the edition by Kumpānī, 90 vols, in 110 tomes (Tehran and Qumm, 1376–1392/1956–1972), vol. 32, p. 176, in which ʿAmmār b. Yāsir shouts at Ibn Yathribī: 'It is as a follower of ʿAlī's religion that I fight you (*uqātiluka ʿalā dīni ʿAlī*)'.

[3] Ibn Durayd, *Kitāb al-ishtiqāq*, ed. ʿA. M. Hārūn (Baghdad, 1399/1979), p. 413; the version of the poem by Ibn Durayd is slightly different: '*Qataltu ʿilbā'a wa hinda'l-jamalī wa ibnan li-ṣūḥāna ʿalā dīni ʿAlī*.' In the margins of the *unicum* dated the 7th/13th century, used by ʿAbd al-Salām Muḥammad Hārūn, are found earlier notes that often provide different understandings (see the editor's introduction, ibid., pp. 36–37). For the passage cited, the notes in the margin follow the version by al-Ṭabarī in the edition prepared under the guidance of de Goeje; ibid., p. 413, note 2, *in fine*.

thus implicitly accusing ʿAlī of professing a deviant religion compared with Islam.[4] Other passages in al-Ṭabarī call into question the explanation provided by *Kitāb al-ishtiqāq*, since in this case the expression is uttered by ʿAlī's supporters. One of these passages appears in a report by the famous Abū Mikhnaf (based on ʿUbayd Allāh b. al-Ḥurr al-Juʿfī) regarding Muʿāwiya's order to arrest and execute a large number of ʿAlid rebels led by Ḥujr b. ʿAdī. During an interrogation, one of ʿAlī's partisans, Karīm b. ʿAfīf al-Khathʿamī, is supposed to have had the following conversation with Muʿāwiya:

> Al-Khathʿamī: 'Fear God, Muʿāwiya [literally: God! God! O Muʿāwiya] for you will be led [inevitably] from this transitory place to the final and eternal resting place; there you will be questioned about the reasons for my execution and you will be asked to explain why you shed my blood.'
>
> Muʿāwiya: 'What say you regarding ʿAlī?'
>
> Al-Khathʿamī: '[I say] The same as you: I dissociate myself from the religion of ʿAlī, by which he submits to God (*atabarra'u min dīni ʿAlī alladhī kāna yadīnu llāha bihi*).' At this [declaration], having difficulty in devising a reply, Muʿāwiya remained silent.[5]

---

4 L. Caetani makes an error of interpretation by comparing this punishment of Ibn Yathribī to that of ʿAbd Allāh b. Saba', inflicted, according to tradition, by ʿAlī himself, *Annali dell'Islam* (Milan, 1905–1926), vol. 9, p. 142; re: ʿAbd Allāh b. Saba', see M. G. S. Hodgson, *EI2*). To accuse ʿAlī of professing a deviant religion is entirely different to claiming to defend ʿAlī's cause while professing an 'extremist' doctrine; this error is pointed out by W. Madelung in *The Succession to Muḥammad* (Cambridge, 1997), p. 178, n. 183. Another historiographical source, *Kitāb al-futūḥ* by Ibn Aʿtham al-Kūfī (d. 314/926) gives as the sole reason for the execution of Ibn Yathribī, his violent animosity towards ʿAlī; see Ibn Aʿtham, *al-Futūḥ*, Persian trans. Harawī (6th/12th century), ed. G. Ṭabāṭabā'ī Majd (Tehran, 1374 Sh./1995), pp. 432–433.

5 Al-Ṭabarī, ed. de Goeje, series 2, p. 143; ed. Ibrāhīm, vol. 5, p. 276. In speaking of these ʿAlids, Muʿāwiya calls them 'rebels among the Turābiyya Saba'iyya', a reference to the *kunya* Abū Turāb for ʿAlī (see E. Kohlberg, 'Abū Turāb', *BSOAS*, 41 [1978], pp. 347–352; repr. in *Belief and Law in Imāmī Shīʿism* [Aldershot, 1991] article VI) and to ʿAbd Allāh b. Saba'. See also the abridged version of this account in al-Balādhurī, *Ansāb al-ashrāf*, vol. 4/a, ed. M. Schloessinger and M. J. Kister (Jerusalem, 1972), p. 225. Admittedly, al-Khathʿamī's response is ambiguous, hence Muʿāwiya's embarrassment. His 'dissociation' from ʿAlī's religion is surely based on the obligation of *taqiyya*, but one wonders if the expression *dīn ʿAlī* does not in fact stem from Muʿāwiya or more generally from ʿAlī's adversaries. The expression does indeed seem to have posed a problem for at least some of ʿAlī's supporters, since it could establish a distinction between 'the religion of ʿAlī' and Islam. According to a report by al-Ṭabarī, during the Battle of the Camel, when in order to spare their lives the Azd of Baṣra declared themselves followers of ʿAlī's religion (*naḥnu ʿalā dīni ʿAlī*), a man from the Banī Layth of Kūfa (no doubt an ʿAlid) mocks them for what they have just said (al-Ṭabarī, ed. de Goeje, series 1, pp. 3,189–3,190; ed. Ibrāhīm, vol. 4, p. 512). However, as we shall see, the expression is sometimes unambiguously attributed to supporters of ʿAlī. Cf. also verses by ʿAlī's Companion al-Nuʿmān b. al-ʿAjlān al-Anṣārī, praising 'the religion of ʿAlī' after the Battle of Ṣiffīn, according to al-Minqarī,

Still according to al-Ṭabarī, during al-Mukhtār's revolt, Rufāʿa b. Shaddād al-Hamdānī, the former's supporter, recites the following verse while in the heat of battle:

> I am the son of Shaddād, adept of ʿAlī's religion / I am not an ally of ʿUthmān, offspring of a goat.[6]

Finally, according to a tradition reported by Ibn Abī Shayba (d. 235/849) in *al-Muṣannaf*, during the Battle of the Camel, Muḥammad b. al-Ḥanafiyya, the son of ʿAlī, spares the life of an adversary when the latter claims to have adopted ʿAlī's religion.[7]

Some elements of this account seem to indicate that the expression is authentic. First is the rarity of such occurrences and their somewhat fortuitous nature. In addition to the care taken in highlighting an expression, one of the features of the apocryphal is its repetitous and frequent usage.[8] I certainly do not claim to have thoroughly examined al-Ṭabarī's monumental *History* in its entirety, but I have read it attentively, and with these few passages, I believe we have a fairly accurate picture. What is more, the expression is alloted to the fiercest adversaries as well as to the loyal and devout supporters of ʿAlī, which tends to indicate that it was a current expression known by all and that its usage by reporters in historiographical traditions was not dictated by partisanship; this moreover would explain the somewhat fortuitous occurrences, with no particular motive for the context in which they appeared. During the course of the following study, we will consider other indications that the expression could have existed at the dawn of Islam.

2. The Uniqueness of ʿAlī

To my knowledge, ʿAlī is the only personality from early Islam – apart from the Prophet of course – with whom the term *dīn* is associated. Thanks to analyses by R. B. Serjeant and, especially, due to the pioneering study by M. M. Bravmann, we

---

Waqʿat Ṣiffīn, ed. A. M. Hārūn (Cairo, 1382/1962), p. 380 and Ibn Abiʾl-Ḥadīd, *Sharḥ Nahj al-balāgha*, ed. M. A. Ibrāhīm (Cairo, 1965), vol. 1, p. 149.

6 *Anā bnu shaddāda ʿalā dīni ʿAlī/lastu li-ʿUthmāna bni arwā bi-walī* (al-Ṭabarī, ed. Ibrāhīm, vol. 6, p. 50). Usage of *arwā* (lit. 'mountain goat') is a play on words with *ʿaffān* (the name of ʿUthmān's father, one meaning of which is 'animal with malodorous skin or hair'). Al-Majlisī reports this account based on al-Ṭabarī's *History*, but his version presents significant differences with the *Taʾrīkh*: for example, the individual is named al-Aḥraṣ b. Shaddād and his verse is a response to a verse by his adversary Ibn Dhabʿān al-Kalbī: 'I am Ibn Dhabʿān al-Karīm al-Mufaḍḍal / One of the leaders among those who dissociate themselves from the religion of ʿAlī (*anā bnu Dhabʿānaʾl-karīmiʾl-mufaḍḍali / min ʿaṣabatin yabraʾūna min dīni ʿAlī*)', *Biḥār al-anwār*, vol. 45, p. 381.

7 Ibn Abī Shayba, *al-Muṣannaf*, ed. S. M. al-Laḥḥām, 9 vols (Beirut, 1409/1989), vol. 8, p. 711.

8 See, e.g., J. Schacht, 'A Revaluation of Islamic Traditions', *JRAS* (1949), pp. 140–152; G. H. A. Juynboll, *The Authenticity of the Tradition Literature: Discussions in Modern Egypt* (Leiden, 1969), pp. 30ff.

know that just as in the earliest days of the new religion of the Arabs, *dīn* in pre-Islamic times designated a set of both secular and sacred laws.[9] By extension, *dīn* also referred to submission to a law or a leader, thus contrasting with the anarchy and wild behaviour associated with *jahl* or ignorance. Gradually becoming more exclusive in the Islamic period, the interpretation of 'religion' would have been derived from this original secular and/or religious sense of the term.[10] The use of the expression *dīn ʿAlī* is all the more remarkable since when speaking of his most notable contemporaries, namely the three other *rāshidūn* (rightly guided) caliphs, the sources employ the term *sunna*, almost never *dīn*. Here too, studies by M. M. Bravmann (correcting J. Schacht's analyses), followed by those of G. H. A. Juynboll, demonstrate that *sunna* was initially a clearly marked path on the ground from which one could only waver wilfully, and by extension the path of the elders or sages in a tribe that one ought to follow scrupulously. Although the Qur'an defines this term as 'path of God', at the dawn of the nascent religion, *sunna* designates a whole set of secular or religious forms of behaviour, attitudes and sayings of sages and role models par excellence, in this instance the Prophet himself and the first caliphs.[11] Both historiographical and purely religious sources allude to the *sunna*s of the first caliphs. Al-Balādhurī (d. ca. 302/892) refers to the *sunna* of Abū Bakr and ʿUmar, as well as that of the Khārijīs, during the arbitration at Ṣiffīn, as also does al-Ṭabarī.[12] The expression '*sunna* of the Two ʿUmars', that is, Abū Bakr and ʿUmar, is found again in poetry by Farazdaq (ca. 109/728)[13] and Ibn Abī Yaʿlā (d. 526/1133), who while citing the *Kitāb al-sunna* by al-Barbahārī (d. 329/941), refers to the *sunna* of Abū Bakr, ʿUmar and ʿUthmān.[14]

---

9 R. B. Serjeant, '*Ḥaram* and *ḥawṭah*, the Sacred Enclave in Arabia', in A. R. Badawi (ed.), *Mélanges Taha Husain* (Cairo, 1962), pp. 41–50, esp. p. 42 and p. 50, and 'The "Constitution" of Medina', *The Islamic Quarterly*, 8 (1964), pp. 3–16, esp. 13 (repr. in *Studies in Arabian History and Civilisation*, London, 1981, articles III and V); M. M. Bravmann, *The Spiritual Background of Early Islam* (Leiden, 1972), see index under '*dāna (dyn)*', '*dīn*', and pp. 4–7 '*Murūwah* and *dīn*'.

10 Bravmann, *The Spiritual Background*, p. 34 and note 1 in which the author argues that the theories advanced by Nöldeke and Horovitz on the Iranian origin of the term are superfluous; see also U. Rubin, *The Eye of the Beholder: The Life of Muḥammad as Viewed by the Early Muslims* (Princeton, 1995), see index under '*dīn*'.

11 Bravmann, *The Spiritual Background*, see index under '*sanna*', '*sunnah*'; G. H. A. Juynboll, 'Some New Ideas on the Development of *Sunna* as a Technical Term in Early Islam', *JSAI*, 10 (1987), pp. 97–118, esp. pp. 97f. (repr. in *Studies on the Origins and Uses of Islamic Ḥadīth* [London, 1996], article V); J. Chabbi, *Le Seigneur des tribus. L'Islam de Mahomet* (Paris, 1997), p. 652. For a very rare usage of the expression *dīn ʿUthmān* (forged probably in reaction to the expression *dīn ʿAlī*), see J. van Ess, *Theologie und Gesellschaft im 2. und 3. Jahrhundert Hidschra*, I–VI (Berlin, 1991–1997), see index under '*dīn*' and also vol. 4, pp. 565ff. (on the use of the term *dīn*).

12 Al-Balādhurī, *Ansāb al-ashrāf*, vol. 4/b, ed. M. Schloessinger (Jerusalem, 1961), p. 27; al-Ṭabarī, ed. de Goeje, series 1, pp. 3350–3351.

13 Cf. *Naqāʾiḍ Jarīr waʾl-Farazdaq*, ed. A. A. Bevan (Leiden, 1905–1909), p. 1013.

14 Ibn Abī Yaʿlā al-Farrāʾ, *Ṭabaqāt al-ḥanābila* (Damascus, 1923; repr. Beirut, ca. 1980), vol. 2, p. 32. Some reports make a distinction between *sunna* of the Prophet and *sīra* of the

In my research to date, I have encountered the expression *sunnat ʿAlī* only in the anonymous historiographical text from the 2nd–3rd/8th–9th centuries edited as *Akhbār al-dawla al-ʿAbbāsiyya.*[15] The remarkable analysis of this work by M. Sharon shows how this pro-ʿAbbasid source deals with ʿAlī and the ʿAlids,[16] whence the use of the term *sunna* with reference to ʿAlī in order to stress the latter's role as model in the same manner as the other *rāshidūn*. The rarity if not the nonexistence of the expression *sunnat ʿAlī* seems all the more surprising since as far as legal and ritual practice are concerned, ʿAlī seems to have taken the same decisions as the first two caliphs. This is no doubt why, much later, marked by their aversion to the Prophet's first three successors, in many cases the Shiʿis would follow the legal teachings of Ibn ʿAbbās rather than those of ʿAlī.[17] Imāmī literature would itself seek to justify this fact by invoking a form of *taqiyya* practised by ʿAlī, who feared being accused of deviation compared with the path followed by Abū Bakr and ʿUmar.[18] The striking ostracism of the *sunna* concerning ʿAlī is perhaps thus due to the fact that, in speaking of the latter, the term *dīn* was more frequently used, thus emphasising the radical difference of certain positions taken in the area of faith as compared to his predecessors. The traditionalist, Muḥammad b. ʿUbayd b. Abī Umayya (d. 204/819), a fierce opponent of the Kūfan Shiʿis, never ceased to vaunt the merits of the first three *rāshidūn*, exhorting his public to follow their *sunna*, no doubt by deliberately deleting ʿAlī from the list of role models to be followed.[19] It is surely as a reaction against using the expression *dīn ʿAlī*, that, writing at the turn of the 5th and 6th/11th and 12th centuries, Ibn Abī Yaʿlā reports that the *sunna* of the

---

caliphs (cf. al-Ṭabarī, ed. de Goeje, series 1, pp. 2786 and p. 2793; al-Yaʿqūbī, *Taʾrīkh*, ed. M. Th. Houtsma [Leiden, 1883], vol. 2, pp. 186–187). Bravmann believes that in this context these two terms are synonymous, *The Spiritual Background*, pp. 124f. For an excellent historical and doctrinal analysis of these passages, see T. Nagel, *Studien zum Minderheitenproblem im Islam*, vol. 1 (Bonn, 1973), pp. 7–44.

15 Ed. Dūrī-Muṭṭalibī (Beirut, 1971), p. 284.

16 Cf. M. Sharon, 'The ʿAbbasid Daʿwa Re-examined on the Basis of a New Source', *Arabic and Islamic Studies* (1973). In this regard, refer also to the important work by M. Q. Zaman, *Religion and Politics under the Early ʿAbbāsids* (Leiden, 1997), see index under '*akhbār*'.

17 Now consult W. Madelung, "Abdallāh b. ʿAbbās and Shiite Law', in U. Vermeulen and J. M. F. van Reeth, ed., *Law, Christianity and Modernism in Islamic Society* (Louvain, 1998), pp. 13–25.

18 According to a tradition going back to Imam Muḥammad al-Bāqir reported by Ibn Shabba, *Taʾrīkh al-madīna al-munawwara*, ed. M. F. Shaltūt (Qumm, 1410/1989–1990), p. 217; cited by Madelung, "Abdallāh b. ʿAbbās and Shiite Law', p. 24.

19 Ibn Ḥajar al-ʿAsqalānī, *Tahdhīb al-tahdhīb*, 12 vols (Hyderabad, 1907–1909; repr. Beirut, 1968), vol. 9, pp. 328ff. See also a similar opinion held by al-Shāfiʿī, analysed by J. Schacht, *Origins of Muhammadan Jurisprudence* (Oxford, 1950), p. 24. Including ʿAlī among the *rāshidūn* caliphs posed a problem until the ʿAbbasid period. Ibn Ḥanbal would have been the first great non-ʿAlid thinker to have sought to employ the image of ʿAlī to this end; see his *Kitāb al-sunna* (Mecca, 1349/1930), p. 214; Ṣāliḥ b. Aḥmad b. Ḥanbal, *Sīrat al-imām Aḥmad b. Ḥanbal*, ed. F. ʿAbd al-Munʿim Aḥmad (Alexandria, 1981), p. 82. Regarding the rehabilitation of ʿAlī, see also T. Nagel, *Rechtleitung und Kalifat* (Bonn, 1975), pp. 232f.

first three caliphs – ʿAlī is thus wilfully excluded – was called 'the original ancient religion', *al-dīn al-ʿatīq*.[20] *Dīn ʿAlī* would thus have been much more than a *sunna*, more than a collection of behaviour patterns or decisions relating to daily sacred or secular life. Rather, it seems to designate a whole set of beliefs, professions of faith one might say, touching upon both the sacred and profane, the spiritual as well as the temporal – hence justifying translation of the expression as 'religion of ʿAlī'. Let us attempt to discover the content of this 'religion', at least in its broadest terms.

In his outstanding work *The Succession to Muḥammad*, W. Madelung points out almost all the above-mentioned passages in which our expression appears.[21] An impressive work of erudition and subtle analyses, it treats with numerous fundamental problems in the history of early Islam; this might explain why its eminent author limits himself to a single allusion regarding *dīn ʿAlī*:

> *Dīn ʿAlī* could at this stage have only a limited meaning, most likely the claim that ʿAlī was the best of men after Muḥammad, his legatee (*waṣī*), and as such most entitled to lead the Community.[22]

As we shall see, the above would indeed encapsulate the very fabric of "ʿAlī's religion'; however, each of these facts holds a number of ideas and implicit conceptions – bearing upon both ancestral Arab beliefs as well as the new Islamic faith – that would enable the claim for exclusive legitimacy in the eyes of a number of believers. The meaning of the expression is perhaps limited in scope but nevertheless complex. The aim of this chapter is to attempt to discover the ramifications of this meaning and in modest terms to supplement the masterful study by this renowned Islamic scholar.

3. Themes Concerning ʿAlī and the ʿAlids

The sayings of ʿAlī himself offer a most rewarding field of investigation. As is known, authentic or not, they are numerous, filling pages and pages of sources in various literary genres.[23] ʿAlī's life seems to have been especially active: the period of his youth just at the birth of Islam; his relationship with Muḥammad first in Mecca and then Medina; his exploits in war, his spiritual dimension, his family; being overlooked

20 Ibn Abī Yaʿlā al-Farrāʾ, *Ṭabaqāt al-ḥanābila*, vol. 2, p. 32 (or *dīn al-ʿAtīq*, and in this instance it should be translated as 'the religion of ʿAtīq', ʿAtīq being one of the *laqab*s of Abū Bakr); equally the expression *dīn ʿUthmān* replaced at times *raʾy al-ʿUthmāniyya* (al-Ṭabarī, ed. de Goeje, series 2, p. 340) designating those who chose the Banū ʿUmayya over the Banū Hāshim, seems to have been a response to *dīn ʿAlī*.

21 In the course of the very long chapter on ʿAlī's reign, see pp. 178–179, and in the conclusion mainly devoted to Muʿāwiya's rule, p. 338.

22 Madelung, *The Succession*, pp. 178–179.

23 Cf. L. Veccia Vaglieri, 'Sul Nahj al-balāghah e sul suo compilatore ash-Sharīf ar-Raḍī', *Annali dell'Istituto Universitario Orientale di Napoli*, special issue (1958), pp. 7ff.

in the matter of the succession to the Prophet; his relationship with the first three caliphs; his short-lived reign – an uninterrupted period of civil war and so on – all constitute a myriad of backdrops reflected in the rich variety of sayings of the most highly placed and colourful character that the Islamic sources present to us.

However, among these many sayings on the most varied of subjects, two themes constitute veritable leitmotifs: the very fact of having been the first man to accept Muḥammad's prophetic message and of having vowed to have absolute faith in and loyalty to the new religion (the notion of *sābiqa*); and, especially, the fact of being the Prophet's closest male relative with the strongest blood ties to him (the notion of *qarāba*). As we shall see, the importance of this relationship is so fundamental that it encompasses and even explains the idea of *sābiqa*. In implicit or explicit terms, both from his own perspective and in the eyes of his supporters, these two claims made ʿAlī the only legitimate successor to the Prophet. One need only glance through the historiographical works, for example the sayings of ʿAlī, more specifically those regarding the direction of the community – in which his legitimist claims feature – to pick out the two themes which are omnipresent in the context of the Battle of Ṣiffīn,[24] his letters to Muʿāwiya and a letter to his elder brother ʿAqīl b. Abī Ṭālib,[25] or again, his sayings arising from the famous speech by Muḥammad at Ghadīr Khumm.[26]

These are the very themes that enable supporters of ʿAlī to recognise him as the sole legitimate *waṣī* (legatee) to Muḥammad. In the poem reported by al-Balādhurī of the warrior of the Banū ʿAdī who was on the side of ʿĀʾisha, Ṭalḥa and al-Zubayr, and fought against ʿAlī at the Battle of the Camel, this title for ʿAlī is an object of ridicule (a point which goes to prove the fact of its existence), since for the Banū ʿAdī, the only true 'legatee' of the Prophet is Abū Bakr, whose daughter is now in battle against the ʿAlids:

> We are ʿAdī and we are looking for ʿAlī (to kill him) … we will kill all those who oppose the *waṣī* [i.e., Abū Bakr].[27]

Al-Ṭabarī reports that after the assassination of the third caliph, ʿUthmān, poets competed to commemorate the event. Among them, al-Faḍl b. al-ʿAbbās b. ʿUtba b. Abī Lahab took this opportunity to sing the praises of ʿAlī:

---

[24] Al-Minqarī, *Waqʿat Ṣiffīn*, ed. ʿA. M. Hārūn (Cairo 1382/1962), pp. 470f; al-Thaqafī, *Kitāb al-ghārāt*, ed. J. al-Muḥaddith al-Urmawī (Tehran, 1395/1975), pp. 303ff; al-Masʿūdī, *Murūj al-dhahab*, ed. Barbier de Meynard, rev. C. Pellat (Beirut, 1968–1979), vol. 3, p. 201ff; (Pseudo-) Ibn Qutayba, *al-Imāma wa'l-siyāsa*, ed. M. M. al-Rāfiʿī (Cairo, 1322/1904), vol. 1, pp. 191f. Also, Madelung, *The Succession*, pp. 240–241 and pp. 270–271.

[25] Al-Thaqafī, *K. al-Ghārāt*, pp. 434–435; al-Balādhurī, *Ansāb al-ashrāf*, vol. 2, ed. M. B. al-Maḥmūdī (Beirut, 1974), pp. 74–75. Also, H. Lammens, *Etudes sur le règne du Calife Omaiyade Muʿāwia 1er* (Paris, 1908), p. 175; Madelung, *The Succession*, pp. 263–264.

[26] E.g., al-Ṭabarī, de Goeje, series 1, pp. 3350ff; on *ḥadīth*s concerning Ghadīr Khumm, see e.g., A. J. Wensinck, *Concordance et indices de la tradition musulmane* (Leiden, 1936), see under *wālī*. Also, L. Veccia Vaglieri, *EI2*, under *Ghadīr Khumm*.

[27] Al-Balādhurī, *Ansāb al-ashrāf*, vol. 2, pp. 245–246.

> Truly, among those who recall (*ʿinda dhī al-dhikri*), the best among men after Muḥammad is indeed the legatee of the Chosen Prophet / He who, as the first, the closest (*ṣinw* or *ṣunw*) to the Prophet recited the Prayer and who, as the first, defeated the misguided of Badr.[28]

In a letter probably written just before Ṣiffīn and which was reported by some of the historiographers and censored by others, Muḥammad, son of the first caliph, Abū Bakr, violently opposed Muʿāwiya. Referring to ʿAlī, he describes him as the first man to have responded positively to Muḥammad's Message, to whom he was related as brother and cousin, of whom he was the legatee, who was the leader of the faithful and the father of his (Muḥammad's) descendants.[29]

In one of his *ṭawīls*, the ʿAlid poet of Baṣra, Abu'l-Aswad al-Du'alī (d. 69/688), citing his favourite personalities among the immediate blood relations of the Prophet, limits himself to naming ʿAlī by the single term *waṣī*.[30] The same leitmotifs are found in sermons by al-Ḥasan, ʿAlī's eldest son, made at the mosque in Kūfa after ʿAlī's assassination; a sermon also reported by the Sunni al-Balādhurī and the pro-Shiʿi Abu'l-Faraj al-Iṣfahānī (d. 356/966).[31] Shiʿi sources, and more specifically works of *ḥadīth*, later took up the same themes to the full and embellished themes regarding the *sābiqa* and, even more so, the *qarāba* of ʿAlī.

4. The Basis of the Religion of ʿAlī

In what way do these ideas justify being given the appellation 'religion of ʿAlī'? How and why might they constitute articles of faith? If ʿAlī and his followers laid claim to them in such an obsessive manner and if among both those for and those against the

---

28 Al-Ṭabarī, ed. Ibrāhīm, vol. 4, p. 426; the term *ṣinw/ṣunw*, that I have translated as 'the closest', literally means 'similar, same' and designates the brother, cousin or son. W. Madelung cites the poem using the edition by de Goeje, series 1, p. 3065, and attributes it instead to the father of al-Faḍl, al-ʿAbbās b. ʿUtba who seems to have been the poet and spokesperson for the Banū Hāshim; *The Succession*, p. 186. Ibn Ḥanbal uses the term to define al-ʿAbbās's relationship to ʿAbd Allāh, Muḥammad's father; see his *Musnad*, ed. Muḥammad al-Zuhrī al-Ghamrāwī (Cairo, 1313/1896), vol. 1, p. 207 and vol. 2, p. 322.

29 Al-Balādhurī, *Ansāb al-ashrāf*, vol. 2, pp. 393ff; al-Minqarī, *Waqʿat Ṣiffīn*, pp. 118ff; al-Masʿūdī, *Murūj*, vol. 3, pp. 197ff. Al-Ṭabarī expressly admits to having censored the letter because the masses (*ʿāmma*) would not have tolerated it; ed. de Goeje, series 1, p. 3248. By this he surely means the Ḥanbalī activists of Baghdad whose hostility towards the great scholar was known to all; cf. al-Iṣfahānī, *Annalium Libri*, ed. Gottwald (Petropoli, 1884), vol. 2, p. 155; Ibn al-Jawzī, *al-Muntaẓam* (Hyderabad, 1357/1938), vol. 6, p. 172.

30 *Dīwān Abu'l-Aswad al-Du'alī*, ed. M. Ḥ. Āl Yāsīn (Beirut, 1974), pp. 119–120; Abu'l-Faraj al-Iṣfahānī, *Kitāb al-Aghānī*, 20 vols (Būlāq, 1285/1868), vol. 12, p. 321 (a shorter version of the poem).

31 *Ansāb al-ashrāf*, vol. 3, ed. M. B. al-Maḥmudī (Beirut, 1974), p. 28; Abu'l-Faraj al-Iṣfahānī, *Maqātil al-Ṭālibiyyīn*, ed. S. A. Ṣaqr (Cairo 1949; repr. Qumm, 1416/1995), p. 62.

ʿAlids the habit had been formed of designating them by the expression *dīn ʿAlī*, it is because they were based upon doctrinal and ideological justifications that seemed legitimate from a religious point of view and credible to those who professed them. It appears to me that two categories of 'legitimising proofs' supported these ideas and justified them by giving them the term *dīn ʿAlī*: proofs of an Islamic nature based on the text of the Qurʾan and even more so, proofs based on ancestral beliefs.

The Qurʾanic bases

Famous for his legendary knowledge of and scrupulous faithfulness to the text of the Qurʾan,[32] ʿAlī could not have failed to present elements of the revealed text in order to legitimise his claims. Here too, Madelung's scholarship will guide us. In a subsection of his dense and pertinent introduction to *The Succession to Muḥammad*, he assiduously examines all the Qurʾanic instances that might serve to justify the ʿAlid claim to lead the Community after the Prophet's death. To my knowledge, this is the first time the evidence has been brought forward with such erudition and precision; it even serves as a focus and fundamental argument for the discourse underlying the entire work.[33] In summarising this work we will thus limit ourselves to concentrating in the main on the Qurʾanic proofs.

Genealogical Table of the Prophet Muḥammad and Imam ʿAlī

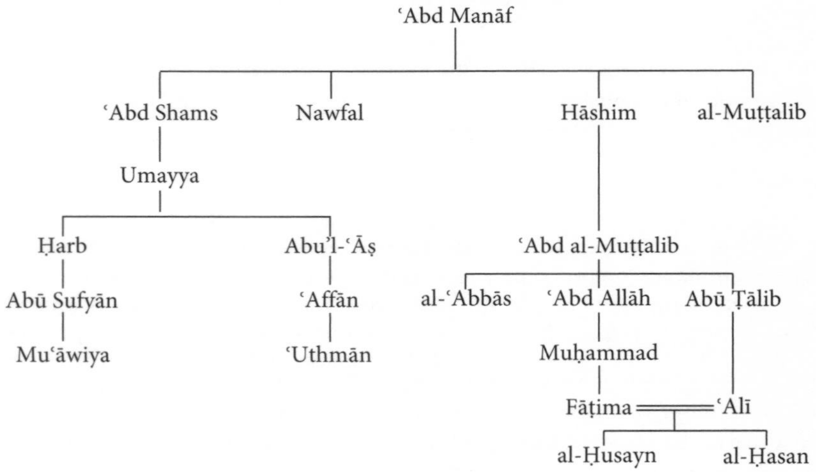

[32] See e.g., Ibn Saʿd, *al-Ṭabaqāt al-kubrā*, ed. Iḥsān ʿAbbās, 9 vols (Beirut, 1380/1960), vol. 2, p. 338; Ibn Ḥajar, *Tahdhīb*, vol. 7, p. 338; Ibn al-Athīr, *al-Nihāya fī gharīb al-ḥadīth wa'l-athar*, ed. al-Zāwī and al-Tināḥī, 4 vols (Cairo, 1963–1966; repr. Beirut, n.d.), vol. 3, p. 102.

[33] Madelung, *The Succession*, 'The obligation of the kinship and the families of the prophets in the Qurʾān', pp. 6–18; whence the reaction of certain critics of the book who perceive it as a kind of pro-Shiʿi apologia. This is certainly a flagrant misunderstanding; but further analysis is beyond the scope of the present chapter.

The Qur'an places great emphasis on respect for family and blood ties:[34]

> Surely God bids to justice and good-doing and giving to kinsmen (*dhi'l-qurbā*); and He forbids indecency, dishonour, and insolence, admonishing you, so that haply you will remember (Q.16:90)
>
> And give the kinsman his right (Q.17:26)
>
> They will question thee concerning what they should expend. Say: 'Whatsover good you expend is for parents (*wālidayn*) and kinsmen (*aqrabīn*), orphans, the needy, and the traveller.' (Q.2:215)

Generosity to close relatives and providing them with material support is a religious duty but on condition that the latter are converts to Islam; though even if they are not, the Muslim is called upon to be just and impartial to those of his relatives who may have maintained their pagan beliefs (Q.4:135; 6:152; 9:23–24 and 113–114).[35] However, in spite of these limitations, the Qur'an clearly establishes the superiority and pre-eminence of blood ties over all other kinds of bonds or alliances.

> Those who are bound by blood (*ūlu'l-arḥām*) are nearer to one another in the Book of God than the believers and the emigrants. (Q.33:6)

Singing the praises of past converts, the Emigrants and the Helpers, verses 72 to 74 of Sura 8 are followed by the following verse (probably added later on):

> And those who have believed afterwards and emigrated, and struggled with you – they belong to you; but those related by blood are nearer to one another in the Book of God.[36]

There is yet another important contributing factor for our subject: in the Qur'anic 'History of Prophets', close relatives of the prophets play a vital role: they are the protectors of the Messengers of God against their adversaries and after the Messengers die, they become their inheritors in both temporal and spiritual matters. The prophets of the Banū Isrā'īl are in fact descendants of one and the same family going back to Noah and Adam; the line of this same family continues up to Jesus (Q.3:33–34 and 19:58). The chain of prophets and the importance of their inheritors in the

---

34 The translation of the Qur'an used in this work is A. J. Arberry, *The Koran* (Oxford, 1964).

35 Madelung, *The Succession*, pp. 6–7.

36 Ibid., pp. 7–8.

economy of the sacred, as chosen from among their immediate family, are stressed by verses 84 to 89 of Sura 6:

> And we gave to him [i.e., Abraham] Isaac and Jacob – each one We guided, And Noah We guided before; and of his seed David and Solomon, Job and Joseph, Moses and Aaron – even so We recompense the good-doers – Zachariah and John, Jesus and Elias; each was of the righteous; Ishmael and Elisha, Jonah and Lot – each one We preferred above all beings; and of their fathers, and of their seed, and of their brethren; and We elected them, and We guided them to a straight path.
>
> That is God's guidance; He guides by it whom He will of His servants; had they been idolaters, it would have failed them, the things they did. Those are they to whom We gave the Book, the Judgement, the Prophethood.

All Noah's people are annihilated by the Flood, except for his family (*ahl*), apart from one son and the wife who had betrayed him (Q.11:40 and 45–46; 21:76–77; 23:27; 37:76–77). Similarly, Lot's relatives, except for his traitor-wife, were the only ones spared the catastrophe visited upon the people (Q.54:33–35; 56:10) since his family was composed of those who had ' purified themselves' (*yataṭahharūn*) (Q.27:56). Abraham, a central figure in the Qur'an, is the patriarch of the prophets of the Banū Isrā'īl. All the prophets and transmitters of Scriptures after him are in fact his direct descendants via Isaac and his grandson Jacob, thus forming an uninterrupted chain of Messengers and Guides (*imāms*) (Q.2:124; 19:49–50; 29:27; 57:26). Addressing Sarah and speaking about Abraham's family, the angels say:

> What, dost thou marvel at God's command? The mercy of God and His blessings be upon you, O *Ahl al-Bayt*. (Q.11:76)[37]

Moreover:

---

[37] Regarding this phrase, 'Family of the Home' seems to me to be a more precise translation than the more conventional 'People of the House'. *Ahl* in Arabic, both in South Arabian as well as in Ugaritic, corresponds to the Accadian origin *ālu* (W. von Soden, *Akkadisches Handwörterbuch*, Wiesbaden, 1965) and to the Hebrew *ohêl*. The latter designates the nomad's tent (e.g., Genesis 13:5; 18:1; Isaiah 38:12) or the tent as sanctuary (Exodus 33:7; Numbers 11:24) and as Residence/Home (*mishkan*) of God (Psalms 15:1; 27:5) (cf. Gesenius-Buhl, *Hebräisches und aramäisches Handwörterbuch* [17th edn, Leiden, 1951], p. 95, col. 2). *Ahl*, place of residence, home, eventually came to designate those who live in this place, thus the family; it is the same term that according to the *Tāj al-ʿarūs*, gave us the term *āl* (family, descendants), with the letter *h* eliminated: *āl wa aṣluhu ahl ubdilat al-hā' hamza fa ṣārat a-a-l-tawālat hamzatān fa ubdilat al-thāniya alifan fa ṣāra āl* (al-Zabīdī, *Tāj al-ʿarūs*, under *āl*). As for the term *bayt*, whether it means a constructed building, a tent or a natural site, it designates a place of residence; 'home' evokes the latter meaning. I shall return to other semantic levels related to *bayt*.

> Yet We gave the people of Abraham the Book and the Wisdom, and We gave them a mighty kingdom (*mulkan ʿaẓīman*). (Q.4:54)

Moses is assisted in his prophetic mission by his brother Aaron who partakes with him in an intimate relationship with God (Q.20:29–32 and 36; 21:48–49; 25:35). The enigmatic *baqiyya*, a relic containing the divine *sakīna* and signs of divine investiture and royalty of the Banū Isrāʾīl, belongs to the family of the chosen brothers (Q.2:248). Similarly, David has Solomon, his son, inheritor and successor, as his assistant (Q.1:78; 27:16; 38:30). Zachariah, John's father, asks God for a divine son who would inherit the status of prophethood possessed by Jacob's family (Q.19:5–6). As for non-Israelite prophets, in this instance Shuʿayb from the people of Midian and Ṣāliḥ from the Thamūd, their families also play a vital role as protectors and disciples (Q.11:91 and 27:49).[38]

This eminent place accorded close relatives of preceding prophets could not have been left without any parallel with Muḥammad's immediate family. Some Qur'anic passages are vague and indirect (Q.26:214, *"ashīrataka al-aqrabīn'*; Q.42:23, *'al-mawadda fi'l-qurbā'*). Others certainly do refer to the family and blood relatives of the Prophet. These are verses relating to the distribution of a fifth of the spoils (*khums*) and a part of *fay'* – property of the infidels acquired without battle – to close relatives (*dhu'l-qurbā*) of the Prophet (Q.8:41 and 59:7). In the matter of the 'close relatives', practically all the exegetical and historiographical sources are in agreement in recognising the descendants of the brothers Hāshim and al-Muṭṭalib, the sons of Muḥammad's great grandfather, ʿAbd Manāf, to the exclusion of another two of his sons, namely ʿAbd Shams and Nawfal. According to many reports, these allocations compensated somewhat for the fact that Muḥammad's immediate relatives could not benefit from alms or charity (*ṣadaqa, zakāt*). The reason given for this interdiction is that the charity came from the people's 'impurities', whence the purifying function of giving charity. The status of purity associated with the Prophet's family was thus considered incompatible with receiving charity. As in the case of the purity of Lot's family, examined above, the Qur'an also refers to the purity of Muḥammad's family:

> *O Ahl al-Bayt*, God only desires to put away from you abomination and to cleanse you. (Q.33:33)

The spiritual and religious importance of Muḥammad's family is equally noted in the famous verse of the Ordeal, *āyat al-mubāhala* (Q.3:61). Just as the Qur'an constantly establishes parallels between Muḥammad and previous prophets, in terms

[38] Madelung, *The Succession*, pp. 8–12. For discussions regarding the term *baqiyya*, cf. R. Paret, 'Die Bedeutung des Wortes *baqīya* im Koran', in *Alttestamentliche Studien Friedrich Nötscher zum 60. Geburtstag* (Bonn, 1950), pp. 168–171; A. Spitaler, 'Was bedeutet *baqīja* im Koran?', in *Westöstliche Abhandlungen Rudolf Tschudi zum 70. Geburtstag* (Wiesbaden, 1954), pp. 137–146.

of his prophetic mission, the fierce resistance of his people and, finally, his victory thanks to God's support, so the similar status of Muḥammad's family and families of past prophets regarding spiritual and temporal heritage seems obvious. Admittedly, according to the dogma of the 'seal of prophecy' Muḥammad's inheritor could not lay claim to prophethood; however, it is just as true that among elements of the prophetic heritage bequeathed by the Envoys of God to their close relatives, the Qur'an includes sovereignty (*mulk*), authority (*ḥukm*), wisdom (*ḥikma*), Scriptures (*kitāb*) and the imamate. Given this Qur'anic evidence, it seems to me that W. Madelung is right to conclude that the Qur'an advises consultation (*shūrā*) in certain cases but never for what bears upon the succession of prophets.[39]

I will be returning to many of these points. Here I would like to note that, given his privileged relationship with the Prophet, ʿAlī would surely not have missed the opportunity to point to this Qur'anic evidence in order to legitimise his declarations. In his *Ṭabaqāt*, Ibn Saʿd (d. 230/845) – an author who could hardly be suspected of pro-ʿAlid sympathies – recounts a report that seems especially telling in this regard. In a chapter devoted to 'the heritage of the Messenger of God and what he leaves behind' (*dhikr mīrāth rasūli'llāh wa mā taraka*), as derived from ʿAbbās b. ʿAbd Allāh b. Maʿbad, grandson of al-ʿAbbās b. ʿAbd al-Muṭṭalib, Ibn Saʿd reports that Fāṭima and al-ʿAbbās in the company of ʿAlī approached the elected caliph, Abū Bakr, to ask him for their rightful share of Muḥammad's heritage. Abū Bakr is said to have replied:

> 'The Messenger of God said: "We [the prophets] do not leave behind an inheritance; all that we leave behind is charity." And I am now in charge of all that the Messenger of God left behind.'

Citing the Qur'an, ʿAlī is said to have replied:

> '"Solomon inherited from David" (Q.27:16) and [invoking God when asking Him for a son] Zachariah says: "So give me, from Thee, a kinsman who shall be my inheritor of the House of Jacob" (Q.19:6).'
>
> Abū Bakr: 'By God, surely you know what I know.'
>
> ʿAlī: 'It is the Book of God that speaks here.' After this there was silence and then they parted.[40]

---

[39] Madelung, *The Succession*, pp. 12–18.

[40] Ibn Saʿd, *Ṭabaqāt*, vol. 2, p. 315. I. Hrbek, stressing among other things the incompatibility of the *ḥadīth* cited by Abū Bakr with the spirit and letter of the Qur'an, considers it apocryphal, 'Muḥammads Nachlass und die Aliden', *Archiv Orientální*, 18 (1950), pp. 143–149; Madelung, *The Succession*, pp. 360–361.

This legitimation by the Qurʾan was certainly a factor in the support that (according to the historiographers) the majority of the Qurʾan reciters (*qurrāʾ*) gave to ʿAlī at the time of his conflict with Muʿāwiya, especially before the start of the Battle of Ṣiffīn and the ensuing arbitration.[41] However, in this early period of Islam, legitimation by the Qurʾan could definitely not guarantee unanimous agreement. The new religion would require several generations of assimilation to profoundly affect people's outlook and to establish itself in their hearts before it could become the kind of social phenomenon capable of shaping minds. To be credible during this early period, a speech or event had to be rooted in ancient, ancestral beliefs and to be supported by the tribal culture of Arab paganism if it were to resonate among recently converted Muslims.

The pre-Islamic basis

For more than a century, a number of eminent Orientalists and specialists in Arabic and Islamic studies have brought to light and examined the remarkable continuity between the pre-Islamic period and the earliest days of Islam with regard to institutions, beliefs and rituals. These scholars include J. Wellhausen and I. Goldziher and the circle responsible for 'From Jāhiliyya to Islam' gathered around M. J. Kister and his colleagues and students, M. Lecker, U. Rubin, H. Busse and others, not to mention J. Henninger, R. B. Serjeant, T. Fahd, A. F. L. Beeston and J. Chelhod, and more recently E. Conte and J. Chabbi. Many of these have been led to study the system of family relations be it in its secular and sacred dimensions or its natural and supernatural aspects.

The outdated thesis presented by H. Lammens in *Le berceau de l'Islam*, according to which hereditary power and dynastic rulers were completely unknown if not utterly detested by the Arabs does not seem tenable any more.[42] Ever since the monumental study by E. Tyan, *Institutions du droit public Musulman*, it has been established that though tribal secular leadership was not actually always hereditary religious leadership and theocratic functions depended directly on the importance of a noble lineage, *nasab*, and that this concept was particularly upheld in the tribe of Quraysh.[43] Even W. M. Watt, who in his biography of Muḥammad at times seem to concur closely with the opinion held by Lammens,[44] concedes in his *Islamic Political Thought*, that the Arabs regularly elected their leaders from specific families.[45] In this regard, the studies by R. B. Serjeant seem decisive. Over the course of a number of publications, the author establishes most convincingly that Muḥammad's rapid success and the ultimate ease he experienced in rallying a large number of tribes to

[41] Cf. Minqarī, *Waqʿat Ṣiffīn*, pp. 88ff; al-Ṭabarī, ed. de Goeje, series 1, pp. 3385–3386.

[42] H. Lammens, *Le berceau de l'Islam: l'Arabie occidentale à la veille de l'Hégire* (Rome, 1914), p. 314 et passim.

[43] E. Tyan, *Institutions du droit public Musulman* (Paris, 1954–1956), vol. 1, pp. 97ff, 114ff.

[44] W. M. Watt, *Muhammad: Prophet and Statesman* (Oxford, 1961), esp. pp. 35–36.

[45] W. M. Watt, *Islamic Political Thought* (Edinburgh, 1968), p. 31.

his cause, were essentially due to the fact that he belonged to a Meccan and Qurashī family; an aristocratic and theocratic family in which religious functions, as was the case throughout Arabia, were hereditary. Were he not part of this lineage, which the English scholar terms 'The Holy Family', Muḥammad would have had no credibility with other tribes.[46]

Well before Muḥammad's time, the Quraysh were held to be a tribe that benefited from divine protection due to its sacred status as *ahl al-ḥaram*, the People of the Meccan Sanctuary and the area surrounding it. According to U. Rubin, early Muslim exegesis even maintained traces of this ancient belief.[47] Muḥammad's ancestor Quṣayy seems to have been the guardian and leader of the sanctuary; from then on, the different clans of his direct descendants inherited various responsibilities for the ritual functions relating to the pilgrimage: guarding the Kaʿba (*ḥijāba*), providing potable water (*siqāya*), food (*rifāda*) and banners (*liwāʾ*) as well as the privilege of *nadwa*, a term vaguely designating either the council of tribal leadership or the meeting place for the resolution of inter-tribal differences.[48] One finds traces of the hereditary sacred functions of Muḥammad's ancestors in poems by the Prophet's bard, Ḥassān b. Thābit (d. 54/674).[49] Muḥammad himself is said to have designated the 'Holy Family' of the Quraysh as consisting of the descendants of al-Muṭṭalib and those of his brother, Hāshim, the great-grandfather of the Prophet (see the genealogical tree above). The canonical works of *ḥadīth* leave no doubt about this by identifying the 'near kin' (*dhu'l-qurbā*) mentioned by the Qur'an as those that receive the *khums* and *fayʾ*; the receipt of alms is forbidden to them as descendants of al-Muṭṭalib and even more often of Hāshim.[50] Moreover, we know that ever since pre-Islamic times the Banū'l-Muṭṭalib and the Banū Hāshim were strongly bound to each other by the *ḥilf al-fuḍūl*.[51]

---

[46] R. B. Serjeant, 'The Saiyids of Ḥaḍramawt', *An Inaugural Lecture at the School of Oriental and African Studies*, 1956 (London, 1957), pp. 3–29; R. B. Serjeant, '*Ḥaram* and *ḥawṭah*, the Sacred Enclave in Arabia', pp. 41–58; R. B. Serjeant, 'The "Constitution" of Medina', pp. 3–16; R. B. Sergeant, 'The *Sunnah Jāmiʿah*, Pacts with the Yathrib Jews, and the *taḥrīm* of Yathrib: Analysis and Translation of the Documents Comprised in the So-called "Constitution of Medina"', *BSOAS*, 41 (1978), pp. 1–42 (repr. in *Studies in Arabian History and Civilisation*, articles VIII, III, V and VI).

[47] U. Rubin, 'The *īlāf* of Quraysh. A Study of Sūra CVI', *Arabica*, 31–32 (1984), pp. 165–188.

[48] R. B. Serjeant, '*Ḥaram* and *ḥawṭah*', pp. 53ff. U. Rubin, 'The Kaʿba: Aspects of Its Ritual Functions and Position in Pre-Islamic and Early Islamic times', *JSAI*, 8 (1986), pp. 97–131.

[49] Ḥassān ibn Thābit, *Diwan*, ed. W. N. ʿArafat (London, 1971), vol. 1, p. 109.

[50] Cf. A. J. Wensinck, *Handbook of Early Muhammadan Tradition* (Leiden, 1927), p. 266. On the part reserved for the Banū Hāshim in the *dīwān* by ʿUmar see Ibn Saʿd, *Ṭabaqāt*, vol. 3, pp. 294ff, completed in al-Balādhurī, *Futūḥ al-buldān*, ed. M. J. de Goeje (Leiden, 1866), series 1, pp. 448ff. On *ʿaṭāʾ* reserved for the Banū Hāshim see al-Zubayr b. Bakkār, *Jamharat nasab Quraysh*, ed. M. M. Shākir (Cairo, 1381/1961), p. 111. For an exclusively ʿAbbasid appropriation of these facts, refer to Abū Yūsuf, *Kitāb al-kharāj*, ed. I. ʿAbbās (Beirut and London, 1985), pp. 102–104, 142ff.

[51] W. M. Watt, *Muḥammad at Mecca* (Oxford, 1953), pp. 6–7; C. Pellat, 'Ḥilf al-fuḍūl', *EI2*.

In this connection, the tradition reported by Abū Dāwūd and al-Maqrīzī, on the authority of al-Zuhrī, Sa'īd b. al-Musayyib and Jubayr b. Muṭ'im, is the most significant: after the victory at Khaybar, the Prophet divided the share of the close relatives (*sahm dhi'l-qurbā*) between the Banū Hāshim and the Banū'l-Muṭṭalib, thus excluding the Banū Nawfal and the Banū 'Abd Shams (Nawfal and 'Abd Shams are two other brothers of Muṭṭalib and Hāshim). So, the reporter Jubayr b. Muṭ'im (a descendant of Nawfal), and 'Uthmān b. 'Affān (the future third caliph, descendant of 'Abd Shams) protest to Muḥammad saying:

> Messenger of God, because of the place God has accorded you amongst them, we do not deny the excellence of the Banū Hāshim. But what of our brothers, the Banū'l-Muṭṭalib? You have given them a share and you have excluded us while our relationship to you is the same as theirs.

Muḥammad replies:

> We [the Banū Hāshim] and the Banū'l-Muṭṭalib have never been separated, neither during the *Jāhiliyya* nor in Islam. We and they are one and the same.[52]

The saintliness of the Banū Hāshim becomes evident from the subtle analyses of the *Hāshimiyyāt*, a collection of poems by al-Kumayt b. Zayd al-Asadī al-Kūfī (d. 126/743),[53] undertaken by T. Nagel, M. Sharon and especially by W. Madelung in his monograph dedicated to this work.[54] It seems that among the descendants of Hāshim, Muḥammad recognised his own family as *the* 'Holy Family' par excellence.[55] Muḥammad would have designated this 'Holy Family' by the expression *ahl baytī*,

---

[52] Abū Dāwūd, *Sunan*, ed. M. M. 'Abd al-Ḥamīd, 4 vols (Cairo, n.d.), ch. 19, no. 51; al-Maqrīzī, *al-Nizā' wa'l-takhāṣum fī mā bayna banī Umayya wa banī Hāshim*, ed. Ḥ. Mu'nis (Cairo, 1984), p. 60 (slightly different and shorter version).

[53] Ed. J. Horovitz, *Die Hāšimijjāt des Kumait* (Leiden, 1904; Arabic text repr. in Qumm, n.d. [ca. 1970]).

[54] T. Nagel, *Untersuchungen zur Entstehung des Abbasidischen Kalifats* (Bonn, 1972), pp. 70ff and pp. 79ff; M. Sharon, *Black Banners from the East* (Leiden and Jerusalem, 1983), pp. 76ff; W. Madelung, 'The Hāshimiyyāt of al-Kumayt and Hāshimi Shi'ism', *SI*, 70 (1990), pp. 5–26.

[55] In this context, in terms of methodology, traditions concerning 'monotheism', signs of election and the saintliness of the ancestors and close relatives of the Prophet, specifically his grandfather 'Abd al-Muṭṭalib, his father 'Abd Allāh and his paternal uncle Abū Ṭālib ('Alī's father who adopted and raised Muḥammad after the death of 'Abd Allāh) cannot be exploited here due to their strong Islamic connotations that in turn prove their later date. Regarding these traditions and the historical problems they pose, see e.g., T. Fahd, *La divination arabe* (Strasbourg, 1971; 2nd edn, Paris, 1987), pp. 82ff and pp. 260ff; U. Rubin, 'Prophets and Progenitors in Early Shī'a Tradition', *JSAI*, 1 (1979); C. Gilliot, 'Muqātil, grand exégète, traditionniste et théologien maudit', *Journal Asiatique*, 279/1–2 (1991), pp. 68–70; M. A. Amir-Moezzi, *Le Guide divin*, pp. 103–104 and note 204 (*Divine Guide*, p. 40); Chabbi, *Le Seigneur des tribus*, pp. 166ff.

surely having in mind the Qurʾanic occurrences of the expression *ahl al-bayt* that we have examined above. Apart from the purity that the Qurʾan ascribes to Muḥammad's *ahl al-bayt* (Q.33:33), the sacred dimension linked to the term *bayt* must certainly have played a role as well. Indeed, the religious nature of the vocable, originating from the antique heritage of Semitic languages in which it means temple, sanctuary or a supernatural being's place of residence, is again clearly evident in the ways that the Qurʾan employs the term; for example, in the manner that it designates the Kaʿba or in *al-bayt al-maʿmūr* and in the expression *rabb al-bayt* in the early suras, 105, *al-Fīl* and 106, *Quraysh*.[56]

It is not a matter of determining here the full meaning that Muḥammad attributed to the expression *ahl al-bayt*, at one and the same time of religious, sacred and political import.[57] A great many studies have been dedicated to this, analysing both the diverse classical exegeses of the expression and the material which is of a historical and philological nature: from H. Lammens and R. Strothmann who see in it only an allusion to the Prophet's wives[58] and R. Paret, for whom the *ahl al-bayt* designates adherents of the cult of the Kaʿba,[59] to the meticulously prepared monographs by M. Sharon on the various connotations depending on changing times as well as religious and political trends;[60] studies which seem to me to be decisive regarding certain points and to which I will have the opportunity to return, and also considering W. Madelung, according to whom the expression essentially designates the descendants

---

[56] In Accadian, the term *bīt* designates the temple as a whole, or rooms of which it is made up (W. von Soden, *AHW*); the same evolution is encountered in Hebrew, as well as in Syriac and Arabic. In parallel with its profane, or secular, meaning of 'residence', the religious nature of the term is more specifically emphasised when it is preceded by an article such as *ha-b-baït* in Hebrew (Micah 3:12; Haggai 1:8) (Gesenius-Buhl, *Hebräisches*, pp. 95–98) or *al-bayt* in Arabic (e.g., Q.2:125, 127 etc.). Apparently, during the stage of nomadism, among the Arabs as well as the Hebrews, *bayt* was often followed by the word *il/el* (divinity, supernatural entity or protector), which gives us *batīl/Bêt-El* (whence 'Betyl'). This composite form originally designated the mobile sanctuary in which the symbols and objects required for worship were held, eventually itself becoming the symbol and/or object of worship. Cf. T. Fahd, *Le Panthéon de l'Arabie Centrale à la veille de l'Hégire* (Paris, 1968), ch. 1; J. Chabbi, *Le Seigneur des tribus*, see index under '*bayt*', '*beth*', '*bétyle*'. Regarding the meaning of the word in South Arabia see A. F. L. Beeston, 'The So-called Harlots of Ḥaḍramawt', *Oriens*, 5 (1952), pp. 21ff, 'Kingship in Ancient South-Arabia', *Journal of the Economic and Social History of the Orient*, 15 (1972), pp. 251ff.

[57] M. Sharon interprets the expression, in a pre-Islamic context, as 'the leading noble families' among tribes, and more exclusively the tribe of the Quraysh; see his '*Ahl al-Bayt* – People of the House', *JSAI*, 8 (1986), pp. 169–184, respectively pp. 183 and 179.

[58] Especially in Q.33:33; H. Lammens, *Fāṭima et les filles de Mahomet* (Rome, 1912), p. 97 et passim; R. Strothmann, *Das Staatsrecht der Zaiditen* (Strasbourg, 1912), pp. 19ff.

[59] Especially in Q.11:73 and 33:33; cf. his article 'Der Plan einer neuen, leicht kommentierten Koranübersetzung', in Paret, ed., *Orientalistische Studien Enno Littmann zu seinem 60. Geburtstag* (Leiden, 1935), pp. 121–130, esp. pp. 127f.

[60] '*Ahl al-Bayt* – People of the House'; 'The Umayyads as *ahl al-bayt*', *JSAI*, 14 (1991), pp. 115–152; see also his article 'The Development of the Debate around the Legitimacy of Authority in Early Islam', *JSAI*, 5 (1984), pp. 121–142.

of Hāshim in general.[61] Still, it is useful to recall, as I. Goldziher so aptly demonstrated, that, in spite of the benefit that the ʿAlids were to gain from it, the majority opinion had very early on identified Muḥammad's *ahl al-bayt* with the *ahl al-kisāʾ*, namely Fāṭima, ʿAlī, al-Ḥasan and al-Ḥusayn.[62] As an especially telling example, almost all of the numerous early exegeses of verse 33:33, regarding the purity of Muḥammad's *ahl al-bayt*, as reported by al-Ṭabarī in his monumental Qurʾanic commentary, lean in this direction.[63] Whatever the case may be, in the context of the problem which now preoccupies us, frankly it seems unthinkable that ʿAlī would not have claimed to belong to the Prophet's *ahl al-bayt*. He would have also laid claim exclusively for himself and his progeny to those things in the prophetic heritage concerned with spiritual and temporal matters, thus making of them a veritable collection of articles of faith called *dīn ʿAlī*.[64]

ʿAlī is actually related to Muḥammad by the two principal aspects of Arab familial ties (*qarāba*), namely *nasab* and *muṣāhara*. Terms difficult to render in translation, the first conveys the sense of genealogy, provenance or paternal lineage, ties by blood or by alliance, noble birth and affinity. The second, as rich in meaning as the first, evokes in its original sense the idea of fusing and thus affinity, relationship through women, an alliance by marriage. Thus, in general, *nasab* refers to a relationship by blood and *muṣāhara* to a link or alliance by marriage.[65] ʿAlī was Muḥammad's cousin, the son of his paternal uncle, one of the noblest relationships characterising *nasab* according to the tribal conception.[66] Once he became the Prophet's son-in-law, he was also related by *muṣāhara*, thus fulfilling with regard to the latter, the condition

---

61 'The *Hāshimiyyāt* of al-Kumayt', esp. pp. 15, 21, 24–25.

62 I. Goldziher, *Muslim Studies*, ed. S. M. Stern (London, 1971), vol. 2, pp. 103ff; see also sources noted by M. Sharon, '*Ahl al-Bayt* – People of the House', pp. 172–173.

63 Al-Ṭabarī, *Jāmiʿ al-bayān*, ed. M. M. Shākir and A. M. Shākir (Cairo, 1373–1388/1955–1969), vol. 22, pp. 5–7.

64 In his long letter to Muʿāwiya, reported by several historiographers (Minqarī, al-Balādhurī, al-Ṭabarī) and analysed by Madelung (*The Succession*, pp. 212ff), ʿAlī seems to have identified the *ahl al-bayt* with the Banū Hāshim and Banū'l-Muṭṭalib; however, concerning succession to the Prophet, he would most certainly have thought of himself and his sons, al-Ḥasan and al-Ḥusayn.

65 See P. Bonte, E. Conte, C. Hames and A. W. Ould Cheikh, *Al-Ansāb. La quête des origines* (Paris, 1991), pp. 65ff. The third aspect of the *qarāba* is the *riḍāʿa* (adoption by milk); see ibid., pp. 73ff. For a more detailed analysis, see J. Cuisenier and A. Miquel, 'La terminologie arabe de la parenté. Analyse sémantique et analyse componentielle', *L'Homme*, 5/3–4 (1965), pp. 15–79. In the Qur'an, these two terms are inseparably linked in verse 25:54: 'And it is He who created of water a mortal, and made him kindred of *blood* and *marriage* (*fa jaʿalahu nasaban wa ṣihran*)'. E. Conte proposes 'relatives (by blood ties) and allies (by virtue of marriage or women)', see *Al-Ansāb. La quête des origines*, p. 66.

66 At the moment when the tribe is defined as an organic group of relatives descended from the same lineage – *awlād al-ʿamm*; on this important notion, studies by the earliest major Arabic and Islamic scholars are still the most reliable reference works; see for example I. Goldziher, 'Polyandry and Exogamy among the Arabs', *The Academy*, 13/26 (1880); J. Wellhausen, 'Die Ehe bei den Arabern', *Nachrichten von der Königlichen Gesellschaft und der*

of *wālī*, that is, relative by blood and/or by alliance;[67] the significance this term was to acquire later in Shiʿism is well known.

Other facts pertaining to ancestral beliefs about the supranatural aspects of relationships also seem to have played a role in the establishment of 'the religion of ʿAlī'. In the context of our subject, these beliefs seem inextricably linked to certain aspects of Muḥammad's personality as perceived by certain of his contemporaries.[68] Muḥammad could have truly possessed a supranatural aura in their eyes. T. Fahd has shown the continuity of ancient magic-related personas such as the 'soothsayer' (*kāhin*), the 'poet' (*shāʿir*), the clairvoyant (*ʿarrāf*) and so forth alongside the prophetic figure of Muḥammad: one finds here and there, obviously with different combinations and justifications, communication with supernatural beings, different kinds of divination, inspirations and oracles, healing powers, use of a particular language, knowledge of hidden things, power over objects and so forth. By means of in-depth analyses, this great scholar has, in my view, demonstrated to what extent ancient Arab beliefs and prophethood encountered one another and influenced each other.[69] According to numerous passages in the Qur'an, Muḥammad was compared by his adversaries to *kāhin*s, *sāḥir*s and *shāʿir*s (Q.37:36; 52:29; 59:42). He was often accused of being possessed or inspired by *jinn*s (expressions *majnūn* or *mā bihi … min jinna*). J. Chabbi argues that this was a means by which the Prophet's adversaries sought to trivialise his actions, that is to say to portray him as a kind of magical character, not in a relationship with God but with different kinds of 'genies', characters familiar to Arabia from time immemorial.[70]

Linked to the famous question of Muḥammad's human 'informants', relentlessly upheld by his adversaries, Hūd b. Muḥkim/Muḥakkam (second half of 3rd/9th century) reports a saying by al-Ḥasan al-Baṣrī (d. 110/728), according to which one of these presumed informants was a servant of Ibn al-Ḥaḍramī, the famous soothsayer of the age of the *jāhiliyya*.[71] In another report, reproduced by al-Baghawī (d. 516/1122), the same al-Ḥasan speaks of ʿUbayd b. al-Khaḍir, an Ethiopian

Georg-Augustus-Universität zu Göttingen, 11 (1893); O. Proksch, *Über die Blutrache bei den vorislamischen Arabern und Mohammeds Stellung zu ihr* (Leipzig, 1899), esp. pp. 33ff.

67 Cf. Chabbi, *Le Seigneur des tribus*, p. 654.

68 On this point of view, now consult U. Rubin, *The Eye of the Beholder. The Life of Muḥammad as Viewed by the Early Muslims* (Princeton, 1995).

69 Fahd, *La divination arabe*, pp. 63ff ('Divination et prophétie'), pp. 88ff ('Prophète et divin') and p. 263, passim; see also T. Fahd, 'Le monde du sorcier en Islam', in *Le monde du sorcier* (Paris, 1966), pp. 155–204. On the difficulty in translating the term *kāhin* (priest – soothsayer – oracle – doctor), see *La divination arabe*, pp. 94f. Regarding *shāʿir* ('poet'), etymologically 'he who knows' and has theurgic knowledge, see also F. Rosenthal, *Knowledge Triumphant: The Concept of Knowledge in Medieval Islam* (Leiden, 1971), pp. 12–13.

70 *Le Seigneur des tribus*, pp. 182–183 and pp. 527–529.

71 Hūd b. Muḥkim/Muḥakkam al-Ḥawwārī, *Tafsīr*, ed. B. Sharīfī (Beirut, 1990), vol. 2, p. 389.

soothsayer.[72] According to Ibn al-Athīr, before his conversion to Islam, ʿUmar b. al-Khaṭṭāb regarded the Prophet as a *kāhin* and a *shāʿir*.[73] Finally, according to a report by Ibn Saʿd, not a supporter of the ʿAlid cause, at the beginning, Muḥammad himself was concerned about being a soothsayer.[74]

We know that in a number of ancient belief systems, body fluids such as blood, sperm, saliva, milk and sweat are considered to be agents for thaumaturgic transmission; they can bear and transmit beneficial or harmful elements, faculties, virtues or spiritual influences from the bearer to another, more specifically, by heredity, to their descendants.[75] The Arabs, too, held these kinds of beliefs. The *kāhin* was believed to have the power to master and direct consciously and wilfully what he transmitted by his bodily fluids.[76] Muḥammad appears to have been associated with this conception in a number of reports regarding him, both directly and allusively, in which the subject of different organic fluids is discussed.

The exchange of blood made two men brothers or allied relatives.[77] J. Wellhausen is right to compare the result of Arab blood pacts with *Verbrüderung* and *adoptio in fratres*.[78] In spite of the great discretion of the Islamic sources, it seems certain that rituals of 'the pact of chosen brotherhood' (*mu'ākhāt*), practised twice by the Prophet upon his arrival in Medina, were accompanied by the exchange of blood. A practice originating according to L. Caetani, from the ancient Arabic *ḥilf*[79] and already a subject of the pre-Islamic poetry of al-Aʿshā Maymūn,[80] it carried infinitely more weight than Qurʾanic and/or Islamic arguments in winning over the Anṣār in Medina. According to a report given by Ibn Hishām, on the occasion of the second meeting in ʿAqaba, faced with the reluctance of the Medinans to conclude a pact with him, Muḥammad declares:

---

72 Abū Muḥammad al-Baghawī, *Tafsīr al-Baghawī al-musammā bi-Maʿālim al-tanzīl*, Ḥ. ʿA. al-ʿAkk and M. Sawār (Beirut, 1992), vol. 3, p. 361. Regarding the Prophet's 'informants', now consult C. Gilliot, 'Les "informateurs" juifs et chrétiens de Muḥammad', *JSAI*, 22 (1998), pp. 84–126, a study which revisits and very usefully supplements the preceding works by A. Sprenger and T. Nöldeke (respectively: *Das Leben und die Lehre des Moḥammad*, 2 vols, [Berlin, 1861–1862], and 'Hatte Muḥammad christliche Lehrer?', *ZDMG*, 12, [1858], pp. 699–708).

73 *Usd al-ghāba*, ed. M. Fāyiḍ et al. (Cairo, 1963–1972), vol. 4, p. 74.

74 Ibn Saʿd, *Ṭabaqāt*, 1/1, p. 129.

75 Cf., e.g., A. van Gennep, *Les rites de passage* (Paris, 1909), pp. 41ff.

76 T. Witton Davies, *Magic, Divination and Demonology* (London, 1933; repr. Baghdad, n.d. [ca. 1960]), pp. 70ff; E. O. James, *The Nature and Function of Priesthood* (London, 1955), pp. 87ff; J. Henninger, *La société bédouine ancienne* (Rome, 1959), index; J. Chelhod, *Les structures du sacré chez les arabes* (Paris, 1986), pp. 189f.

77 W. Robertson Smith, *Kinship and Marriage in Early Arabia* (2nd edn, Cambridge, 1903), pp. 50f and his *Lectures on the Religion of the Semites* (2nd edn, Edinburgh, 1914), pp. 314ff, 479ff.

78 *Reste arabischen Heidentums* (Berlin and Leipzig, 1884), pp. 124, 127–128.

79 *Annali dell'Islam*, vol. 1, p. 408.

80 'They swear by darkly intense black blood: we never wish to separate,' cited by J. Wellhausen, *Reste arabischen Heidentums* p. 128, and reported by E. Conte, 'Entrer dans le sang. Perceptions arabes des origines', in *Al-Ansāb. La quête des origines*, p. 92.

> Your blood is mine. I am one of you and you are mine. Your enemies are my enemies; your friends, my friends. Choose twelve leaders among you in order to represent you in the ritual of the oath (*ḥilf*).[81]

During the Battle of Ḥunayn in the year 8/630, in the midst of the general disarray of Muslim victims when ambushed by the Hawāzin, the Prophet asks his uncle ʿAbbās b. ʿAbd al-Muṭṭalib to use his booming voice to remind the troops of bonds sealed by blood.[82] The different episodes narrated in Ibn Hishām's account demonstrate that this kind of speech, rooted in ancient culture, was more favourably received by the Arabs than the prophetic statements made by Muḥammad.[83] The second pact of brotherhood is of even more interest to us. This, of course, is the ritual of the *muʾākhāt*, promoted by Muḥammad (according to Ibn Ḥabīb)[84] among the Muslims of Mecca, from the Meccan period onwards; or (according to Ibn Hishām)[85] upon his arrival in Medina among both the Meccans and Medinans.

During the 'twinning' ritual, Muḥammad chose ʿAlī as his brother. What is remarkable is that according to Ibn Ḥabīb the *muʾākhāt*, made on 'the basis of law (?) and sharing' (*ʿalāʾl-ḥaqq waʾl-muʾāsāt*) implied that upon the death of either individual, the other, his 'brother', had priority as inheritor,[86] which seems authentic, since in verses 4:33, 8:75 and especially 33:6, the Qurʾan seems to call this institution into question vigorously by stressing the priority of a relationship over the pact of brotherhood.[87] On the basis of, among others, Roman legal sources concerning the governing of the Bedouin population in Syria during the 5th century AD and studied by Bruns and Sachau (once more proving this to be an age-old practice), E. Conte concludes that the *muʾākhāt*, sealed by blood, made 'twin brothers' of close relatives (*qarāʾib*), who were classified as first cousins (*ibnāʾl-ʿamm*) and as a consequence inheritors of the male lineage (*ʿaṣaba*); by establishing a relationship, the 'twinning' pact created a common filiation between 'brothers';[88] which is to say that the *muʾākhāt* itself enabled ʿAlī to claim the prophetic heritage; this may explain the almost complete silence of non-Shiʿi sources on this episode in the life of Muḥammad, a rather curious silence about one of the founding acts of the Muslim community in Medina.[89]

---

81 Ibn Hishām, *al-Sīra al-nabawiyya*, ed. M. Saqqā, I. Abyārī and ʿA. Shalabī (2nd edn, Cairo, 1955), vol. 1, pp. 446 and 454; al-Ṭabarī, de Goeje, series 1, pp. 1220–1221.

82 Ibn Hishām, *Sīra*, vol. 2, pp. 442–443.

83 Cf. on this subject, W. Atallah, 'Les survivances préislamiques chez le Prophète et ses Compagnons', *Arabica*, 24/3 (1977), pp. 299–310.

84 *Kitāb al-muḥabbar*, ed. I. Lichtenstaedter (Hyderabad, 1942), pp. 70ff.

85 Ibn Hishām, *Sīra*, vol. 1, pp. 344–346; also, Serjeant, 'The "Constitution" of Medina', p. 6.

86 Ibn Ḥabīb, *Kitāb al-muḥabbar*, p. 71.

87 See also W. M. Watt, 'Muʾākhāt', *EI2*; Conte, 'Entrer dans le sang. Perceptions arabes des origines', pp. 93–99.

88 Conte, 'Entrer dans le sang. Perceptions arabes des origines', p. 94.

89 Regarding the total silence of the sources, see D. Santillana, *Istituzioni di diritto musulmano malichita con riguardo anche al sistema sciafiita* (Rome, 1938), vol. 1, p. 196, note 8; consult also the 'skeletal' bibliography of the article 'Muʾākhāt' by W. M. Watt.

There is more. For the Arabs, just like nobility, *kahāna* is hereditary. The qualities of the *kāhin* or nobles are transmitted by various means, including the sperm of the father.[90] In pre-Islamic Arabia, in order to bear children of distinguished pedigree, the Bedouins went so far as to 'lend' their wives to nobles whose sperm was highly praised.[91] In terms of the qualities of saintliness, Islamic sources speak repeatedly about the power of transmission of the seminal substance from Muḥammad's ancestors, manifested by the 'Light' and symbolised by the *ṣulb* (kidney, loins), an organ regarded as the repository of the semen.[92] Passing via the uterus (*raḥim*) of the woman, the repository for her 'seed', the man's semen forms the milk in the mother's breast, which in turn enables the transmission of the father's qualities to his child; whence the inseparable link between sperm and milk that one finds in expressions such as 'milk is from man' (*al-laban min al-mar'*), 'the reproductive milk' (*laban al-faḥl*) or 'the unique sperm' (*liqāḥ wāḥid*) that designate both the man's seminal fluid as well as the woman's milk.[93] The father's sperm provides the child's flesh and blood (*dam wa laḥm*); the mother gives form to this matter and completes the formation of the child by her milk, which is compared to the father's sperm.[94] Issuing from the same Hāshimid seed as the Prophet and married to Fāṭima, ʿAlī also became the father of the male descendants of Muḥammad. And Fāṭima, whose most common title among the Shiʿis is 'the Confluence of two Lights' (*majmaʿ al-nūrayn*),[95] being born from Muḥammad's seed and the recipient of ʿAlī's, becomes the other factor in the transmission of prophetic virtues. ʿAlī seems to have been fully convinced of these laws.

According to a report by al-Ṭabarī, during his conflict with Muʿāwiya, just before the arbitration of Ṣiffīn, at the moment in Kūfa when part of his army had dispersed, ʿAlī at one point decided to engage in battle and to fight to the death if necessary. However, upon seeing al-Ḥasan and al-Ḥusayn he realised that if they were to perish, the Muslims would be entirely deprived of descendants of the Prophet. The conclusion one draws from al-Ṭabarī's account is that this was the main reason that led ʿAlī put a halt to the campaign.[96] As reported by al-Maqrīzī, some Muslims held the opinion that if ʿAlī had directly succeeded the Prophet,

---

90 For example Fahd, *La divination arabe*, pp. 23ff.

91 On this practice called *iktisāb*, i.e., 'obtaining' (of the seminal substance and thus noble race), see al-Alūsī, *Bulūgh al-arab fī maʿrifat aḥwāl al-ʿarab* (Cairo, 1928), vol. 2, p. 4. The custom still designated by the terms *iktisāb* or *kasb*, is to this day practised among some Yemeni tribes, cf. J. Chelhod, 'Du nouveau à propos du "matriarcat" arabe', *Arabica*, 28/1 (1981), p. 82.

92 For sources and studies on this subject see Amir-Moezzi, *Guide divin*, see index under '*ṣulb*', '*aṣlāb*' and '*nūr*'.

93 J. Schacht, *The Origins of Muhammadan Jurisprudence* (Oxford, 1950), p. 194 and n. 4; S. Altorki, 'Milk-Kinship in Arab Society: An Unexplored Problem in the Ethnography of Marriage', *Ethnology*, 19 (1980), pp. 233–244, esp. 234ff.

94 P. Bonte, 'Egalité et hiérarchie dans une tribu maure', in *Al-Ansāb. La quête des origines*, p. 158 et passim.

95 See al-Ṭurayḥī, Fakhr al-Dīn, *Majmaʿ al-baḥrayn wa maṭlaʿ al-nayyirayn* (Tehran, 1321/1903), index under '*majmaʿ al-nūrayn*'.

96 Al-Ṭabarī, ed. de Goeje, series 1, pp. 3346–3347.

as the father of al-Ḥasan and al-Ḥusayn, people would have concluded that the caliphate was a hereditary sovereignty (*mulk mutawārath*). This seems historically plausible.[97]

Saliva is also considered a factor in thaumaturgic transmission. The giving of saliva is the famous practice known as *taḥnīk*, termed 'sputation' by C. Gilliot.[98] However, according to Arab lexicographers, Ibn Manẓūr or al-Zabīdī for example, the verbal form means 'to rub the roof of the mouth' when accompanied with a complementary noun (*ḥannaka bi-* e.g., *ḥannakahu bi- tamratin*, rub the roof of another's mouth with a [crushed] date, *ḥannakahu bi'l-iṣbiʿ*, with a finger). Employed without a complement, it means to put one's saliva in someone's mouth (*ḥannaka Zaydun ʿAmran*, lit.: with his saliva, Zayd rubs the roof of ʿAmr's mouth); in the latter instance, the meaning may be clarified by the addition of the word, 'saliva' (*ḥannakahu bi-rīqihi*).[99] Saliva can protect, heal, transmit virtues or skills, but also destroy or humiliate. Depending on the intention of one who uses it, it may be an initiation, a blessing, a medicament or a malign act.[100] Both *ḥadīth* and *sīra* literature as well as historiographical works report many examples of *taḥnīk* by the Prophet. The aim is either therapeutic: Muḥammad in this manner cured the ailing hand of Umm Jalīl bint al-Mujallal's son[101] and epilepsy in a seven-year-old child;[102] or initiatory: Muḥammad transmitted knowledge to Ibn ʿAbbās;[103] or especially the transmission of blessings and moral virtues: there are many accounts of parents taking their children to the Prophet in order that he may practise *taḥnīk*;[104] other accounts speak of new converts who ask the Prophet to perform *taḥnīk*.[105]

---

97 *Al-Nizāʿ wa'l-takhāṣum*, p. 92.

98 In his fundamental article 'Portrait "mythique" d'Ibn ʿAbbās', *Arabica*, 32 (1985), pp. 127–184; pp. 143–144.

99 *Lisān al-ʿarab, Tāj al-ʿarūs.*

100 Van Gennep, *Les rites de passage*, pp. 138–139 (*taḥnīk* as initiatory ritual); J. Desparmet, *Le mal magique* (Algiers and Paris, 1932), pp. 98ff.

101 Ibn Ḥanbal, *Musnad*, ed. Muḥammad al-Zuhrī al-Ghamrāwī (Cairo, 1313/1896), vol. 3, p. 107.

102 Ibn Isḥāq, *Sīra Ibn Isḥāq al-musammāt bi-kitāb al-mubtada' wa'l-mabʿath wa'l-maghāzī*, ed. M. Ḥamidullāh (Rabat, 1976), p. 103; al-Bukhārī, *Ṣaḥīḥ*, 3 vols (Cairo, 1378/1958), 'ṭibb', 21.

103 Ibn Kathīr, *al-Bidāya wa'l-nihāya* (Beirut, 1977), vol. 8, p. 295. See Gilliot, 'Portrait "mythique" d'Ibn ʿAbbās', p. 143; cf. also Van Gennep, *Les rites de passage*, p. 138. In 1973, I witnessed ritual of *taḥnīk* among the Qādirī dervishes of Iranian Baluchistan; according to them, the master transmits *ʿilm* and *ʿamal* to the disciple, which to the dervishes mean initiatory knowledge and supernatural powers.

104 Al-Bukhārī, *Ṣaḥīḥ*, '*ʿaqīqa*', 1; '*adab*', 109; Muslim, *al-Jāmiʿ al-ṣaḥīḥ*, 2 vols (repr. Istanbul, 1383/1963), '*adab*', vol. 1, pp. 23–28, '*ṭahāra*', 101; Ibn Ḥanbal, *Musnad*, vol. 3, pp. 105–106, 171, 175, 181, 188, 254 and 288; vol. 4, p. 399; vol. 6, pp. 93, 212, 347. Abū Dāwūd, *Sunan*, '*adab*', 107. On this aspect of the practice, now consult A. Giladi, 'Some Notes on *taḥnīk* in Medieval Islam', *JNES*, 3 (1988), pp. 175–179.

105 Al-Bukhārī, *Ṣaḥīḥ*, '*manāqib al-Anṣār*', 45; '*zakāt*', 69, '*dhabā'iḥ*', 35; al-Tirmidhī, *al-Jāmiʿ al-ṣaḥīḥ/Sunan*, ed. A. M. Shākir, 5 vols (Cairo, 1356/1937), '*manāqib*', 44; Abū Dāwūd,

It is useful here to note the direct link between *taḥnīk* and *baraka/tabarruk*. In a number of *ḥadīth*s, both roots are used (*fa-yubarriku ʿalayhim wa yuḥannikuhum*; *ḥannakahu fa-barraka ʿalayhi*, etc.).[106]

Baraka, a word in Muslim hagiography which eventually comes to mean a kind of mysterious and beneficial flow, an energy or spiritual influx transmitted by contact, affecting living things and objects, originally meant abundant rain or the camping of a camel near a source of water; or yet again what the camel does during this stay, that is, chewing on its food and (once mixed in saliva) feeding its little ones with it. In his excellent article on this point, J. Chelhod demonstrates how this latter meaning led to the interpretation of *baraka* as the spiritual energy that the father transmits to his newly born child by placing him upon his knees and putting saliva in his mouth, blessing him and in this way according him his protection.[107] The common element between *taḥnīk* and *baraka* is the idea of a nourishing and invigorating liquid (rain, saliva and even a source of water) for both the body and the soul, which constitutes a true blessing.

Here too, as in the case of *mu'ākhāt* examined above, ʿAlī and his sons al-Ḥasan and al-Ḥusayn seem to have been ostracised by non-Shiʿi authors. There is no mention of them in the numerous *ḥadīth*s or accounts concerning *taḥnīk*s by the Prophet. Ibn Kathīr (d. 774/1373), a pro-ʿAbbasid author, goes so far as to say that as far as he knew, except for Ibn ʿAbbās, no one had received saliva from the Prophet;[108] it is unthinkable that he would not have been aware of at least some of the numerous traditions reported in the canonical works of *ḥadīth* noted above. How can one imagine that Muḥammad had thus 'blessed' a large number of his companions and followers, overlooking his own 'brother', cousin, future son-in-law who was also undoubtedly one of his closest companions? Yet still, is it conceivable that the Prophet would have 'blessed' a large number of children only to neglect, forget or deliberately deprive his very own grandchildren, his own male descendants, of this blessing? To my knowledge, only Shiʿi literature reports *taḥnīk*s that the Prophet practised upon

---

Sunan, 'jihād', 52. In their translation of the *Ṣaḥīḥ* by al-Bukhārī, O. Houdas and W. Marçais seem to wish to ignore the meaning of *taḥnīk* employed without a complementary noun; indeed the term is regularly translated with the complement (in this instance, 'a date'), even when the original text does not mention it; see El-Bokhâri, *Les traditions islamiques*, 4 vols (Paris, 1903–1914, repr. 1977), see vol. 2, pp. 681ff and n. 2. In the 5th volume (intro. and amends by M. Hamidullah, Paris, 1981), the error has not been corrected.

106 Refer to the preceding two footnotes.

107 J. Chelhod, 'La *baraka* chez les Arabes', *Revue de l'Histoire des Religions*, 148/1 (1955), pp. 68–88; see also by him, *Les structures du sacré chez les arabes*, index and esp. pp. 58–62.

108 Ibn Kathīr, *al-Bidāya wa'l-nihāya*, vol. 8, p. 295; elsewhere, he recognises that 'prophetic heritage' returns to the immediate family of the prophets, Ibn Kathīr, *al-Bidāya*, vol. 5, p. 290; also his *Tafsīr*, ed. Beirut, 1966, vol. 5, pp. 452f., but seems to maintain that this family consists of ʿAbbās and his descendants (*Tafsīr*, vol. 5, pp. 456–457, a pro-ʿAbbasid version of the *ḥadīth ahl al-kisā'*, in which these are identified as ʿAbbās and his sons).

ʿAlī and the sons born to Fāṭima – a practice that, according to the same sources, the Imams were to continue.[109]

Adopted at a very young age by his paternal uncle Abū Ṭālib, before the advent of Islam Muḥammad was 'the adopted brother' of his cousin ʿAlī. This *qarāba*, as well as the spiritual links between them were such that ʿAlī did not hesitate to embrace the religion proclaimed by Muḥammad. Friend and no doubt blessed confidant of the latter, his constant companion, 'twinned' with him by virtue of the *muʾākhāt* ritual, during which there may have been an exchange of blood, an intrepid warrior fighting for his Cause, ʿAlī married Fāṭima, Muḥammad's daughter and became the father of the only male descendants of the Prophet, al-Ḥasan and al-Ḥusayn. Some Companions had the privilege of one or many of these kinds of relations with Muḥammad, but none of them apart from ʿAlī had all these kinds of relationship with him. What is more, he had the exclusive privilege of two fundamental *qarābas*: 'twinning' and fathering male descendants. Thus, ʿAlī had cogent reasons, confirmed in his opinion by the Qurʾan and even more so by ancient beliefs, for believing in his own divine election and that of his progeny by Fāṭima later on. Surely it is this 'election' that constituted the essential core of what his contemporaries would have called *dīn ʿAlī*.

Reactions and Consequences

Whatever the expression *ahl bayt al-nabī*, which rapidly became synonymous with *āl Muḥammad, āl al-nabī, āl al-rasūl* and so on, was originally meant to communicate, ʿAlī would surely not have failed to claim it for himself and his household. Certain Hāshimids, especially the ʿAlids, seem to have made this claim from the 1st/7th century; this seems to be apparent, for example, in a few verses of ancient poets such as Abu'l-Aswad al-Duʾalī (d. 69/688), Kuthayyir ʿAzza (d. 105/723) and al-Kumayt b. Zayd (d. 126/743).[110] From the extensive and pertinent analyses of the expression and its religious and political implications conducted by M. Sharon in many of his publications, it transpires that popular opinion during this period identified the *ahl bayt al-nabī* with the Hāshimids in general and more specifically with the household of ʿAlī (this is also what emerges from a large number of *ḥadīth*s on the *ahl al-kisāʾ*, analysed by I. Goldziher; see above) – without, however, this popular respect actually translating into a recognition of the right to govern the

---

[109] For examples and sources see Amir-Moezzi, *Guide divin*, pp. 193–195 (*Divine Guide*, pp. 76–77). Here the Prophet not only introduces his saliva into the mouth but also into the eyes of the recipient. Moreover, he does the same with his sweat. See also Sulaym b. Qays (Ps.), *Kitāb Sulaym b. Qays al-Hilālī*, ed. M. B. al-Anṣārī, 3 vols (Qumm, 1416/1995), vol. 2, p. 779, no. 26. Yūsuf al-Baḥrānī, *al-Durar al-najafiyya* (Qumm, n.d.), pp. 281 and 287.

[110] For the first and third, see above. For the second, see al-Iṣfahānī, *Kitāb al-aghānī*, vol. 9, p. 14; al-Nāshiʾ al-Akbar, *Masāʾil al-imāma*, ed. J. van Ess (Beirut, 1971), p. 26.

community.[111] Of those who partook of this respect, some ʿAlids seem to have been the first to claim political legitimacy, in other words, that the caliphate was exclusively reserved for ʿAlī. One can reasonably assume that they were followers of '*dīn ʿAlī*'. M. Sharon examines the probable influence of the Jewish conception of the House of David, as strongly felt in Iraq, on the population in Kūfa, homeland and bastion of the ʿAlids. According to this conception, leadership of the community remains exclusively reserved for the descendants of the House of David.[112] Elsewhere, the same scholar seems to include the influence of the Christian concept of the 'Holy Family' (equally highly present in Iraq during the early centuries of Islam), by underscoring the constant comparisons that Shiʿi literature establishes between the figures of Mary and Fāṭima.[113]

He considers entirely plausible the historical existence of a recension of the Qurʾan from Kūfa in which ʿAlī and members of his family would have been mentioned numerous times,[114] just as Imami *ḥadīth*s, repeatedly and openly declared until the mid-4th/10th century.[115]

Quite apart from certain violent reactions against the importance accorded to a relationship with the Prophet or against the legitimacy of the Prophet's family, for example by the Khārijīs,[116] the anti-caliph ʿAbd Allāh b. al-Zubayr,[117] and some *ahl al-ḥadīth*,[118] non-ʿAlid members of the Prophet's family and their descendants,

---

[111] M. Sharon, 'The Umayyads as *ahl al-bayt*', addendum in response to the article '*Hāshimiyyāt*' by W. Madelung, pp. 151–152.

[112] Ibid., p. 126; Jewish Exilarchate (in Arabic *ra's al-jālūt*, from the Aramaic *rêsh galūtha*, lit. 'Leader of the Diaspora') resided in Iraq and represented, in himself, the divine election of descendants of the House of David. Also, M. Gil, 'The Exilarchate', in D. Frank, ed. *The Jews of Medieval Islam* (Leiden, 1995), pp. 33–65.

[113] Sharon, '*Ahl al-Bayt* – People of the House', p. 173. For sources and studies regarding these comparisons, now consult M. A. Amir-Moezzi, 'Fāṭema', section 1, *EIR*, vol. 9, pp. 400–402.

[114] 'The Umayyads as *ahl al-bayt*', p. 127.

[115] On this version of the Qur'an, see e.g., E. Kohlberg, 'Some Notes on the Imāmite Attitude to the Qur'an', in S. M. Stern, A. Hourani and V. Brown (ed.), *Islamic Philosophy and the Classical Tradition* (Oxford, 1972), pp. 209–224; Amir-Moezzi, *Guide divin*, pp. 200–227 (*Divine Guide*, pp. 79–91); M. M. Bar- Asher, 'Variant Readings and Additions of the Imāmī-Shīʿa to the Quran', *Israel Oriental Studies*, 13 (1993), pp. 39–74. And now consult M. A. Amir-Moezzi and E. Kohlberg, 'Révélation et falsification: introduction à l'édition du *Kitāb al-Qirāʾāt* d'al-Sayyārī', *Journal Asiatique*, 293 (2005), pp. 663–722.

[116] Cf., e.g., al-Ṭabarī, ed. de Goeje, series 1, p. 3350.

[117] According to an account by al-Zuhrī, reported by al-Balādhurī, Ibn Zubayr considered the Prophet's family to be 'petty and bad' (*uhayla sūʾ/saw*', *Ansāb al-ashrāf*) vol. 5, ed. S. Goetein (Jerusalem, 1936), p. 372.

[118] Those, for example, that transmitted traditions regarding the *kufr* of Muḥammad's father and ancestors; cf. Muslim, vol. 1, pp. 132–133; al-Ḥalabī, *al-Sīrat al-ḥalabiyya* (Beirut, n.d.), vol. 1, p. 29; al-Ṭabarī, *Jāmiʿ al-bayān*, vol. 11, pp. 30–31. For the anti-ʿAlid twist given to these traditions, see al-Zurqānī, *Sharḥ ʿalāʾl-Mawāhib al-laduniyya liʾl-Qasṭallānī* (Cairo, 1329/1911), vol. 1, p. 179, according to which 'the infidel father' of the *ḥadīth* in fact designates Abū Ṭālib, since in Arabic 'one who raises a child is also called father'.

in this instance the Umayyads and subsequently the Abbasids, would also have responded by trying to appropriate the title of *ahl al-bayt*. Although his prudent approach prevents M. Sharon from explicitly declaring his stance on the matter, on many occasions he seems to suggest that Umayyad and Abbasid attempts to identify with the *ahl bayt al-nabī* would have been in reaction to ʿAlid claims that were much older.[119] At one point, their common position against the Umayyads drew the ʿAlids and Abbasids[120] closer together. However, once in power, the Abbasids distanced themselves from the ʿAlids by describing themselves as the only 'Holy Family', as witnessed by, among other things, the attempt to undermine the status of Fāṭima and the presentation of ʿAbbās b. ʿAbd al-Muṭṭalib and his sons as the *ahl al-kisāʾ*.[121]

Moreover, the study of *dīn ʿAlī* seems to corroborate allusions made by G. H. Sadighi and E. Kohlberg that the process of ʿAlī's glorification, transforming his historical character into a semi-legendary figure of heroic and even sacred dimensions, can be traced back to very early times, namely the period of his caliphate or even that immediately after the death of the Prophet.[122] A certain reaction against the violent and repressive policies of the first Umayyads, especially Muʿāwiya and his son Yazīd, equally seems to have been a catalyst for this process.[123] 'ʿAlī's religion' seems thus to have been the early nucleus of what was later to become Shiʿism. Imami sources have retained some reports, admittedly rare, in which one finds the expressions *dīn ʿAlī*, *dīn Ḥasan* and *dīn Ḥusayn,* the latter two apparently variants of ʿAlī's religion under the imamates of these two sons.[124]

---

119 '*Ahl al-Bayt* – People of the House', p. 183; 'The Umayyads as *ahl al-bayt*', pp. 127, 151.

120 Gilliot, 'Portrait "mythique" d'Ibn ʿAbbās', pp. 159ff, esp. p. 161; Madelung, 'ʿAbd Allāh b. ʿAbbās and Shiʿite Law'.

121 Sharon, '*Ahl al-Bayt*', pp. 174, 176–179, esp. p. 177. Although not having especially examined the issue, it seems to me that many of the accounts regarding Ibn ʿAbbās's privileged relationship with the Prophet including the transmission of prophetic knowledge (reports presented and analysed in detail by Gilliot in 'Portrait "mythique"', esp. pp. 134, 140, 142–143, 151–152, 156) are modelled on the abundant reports about ʿAlī in early Shiʿi works. This issue merits further attention, see Sharon, *Black Banners from the East*, pp. 126–140 and more especially pp. 93–99 and J. van Ess, 'Les Qadarites et les Ghailānīya de Yazīd III', *SI*, 31 (1970), p. 285.

122 Gh. Ḥ. Ṣadīqī, *Jonbesh hā-ye dīnī-ye Īrānī dar qarn hā-ye dovvom va sevvom-e hejrī* (Tehran, 1372 Sh./1993), pp. 225–226 (this publication is a completed and updated version of the author's thesis, *Les mouvements religieux iraniens aux II et IIIe siècles de l'hégire* [Paris, 1938]); E. Kohlberg, 'Some Imāmī Shīʿī Views on the *ṣaḥāba*', *JSAI*, 5 (1984) (repr. in *Belief and Law*, article IX), pp. 145–146. See also F. Daftary, 'ʿAlī in Classical Ismaili Theology', in A. Y. Ocak, ed., *From History to Theology: Ali in Islamic Beliefs* (Ankara, 2005), pp. 59–82.

123 Madelung, *The Succession*, pp. 309–310.

124 We have already examined two reports by al-Majlisī (d. 1111/1699–1700) in his *Biḥār al-anwār* (notes 2 and 6 above). See also *Biḥār*, vol. 44, p. 125 (a letter from Ziyād b. Abīhi to Muʿāwiya in which he writes that the Ḥaḍramīs are followers of ʿAlī's religion – based on *Kitāb Sulaym b. Qays*, a work of uncertain attribution but cited by authors of the 4th/10th century); vol. 4, p. 213 (a letter from al-Ḥusayn to Muʿāwiya in which he refers to the same letter from Ziyād – based on the *Rijāl* by al-Kashshī, d. 4th/10th century);

With the doctrinal implications that ensued, Shiʿism – in its different forms and in relative terms, of course – seems to have been the development of components found in the religion of ʿAlī:[125] the cult of *qarāba*, the notion of prophetic

---

vol. 45, p. 136 (Yazīd b. Muʿāwiya says to Zaynab bint ʿAlī: 'Your father [ʿAlī] and your brother [al-Ḥusayn] excluded themselves from the religion.' Zaynab: 'If your grandfather [Abū Sufyān], your father [Muʿāwiya] and you had been Muslims, you would have returned to the grace and religion of God, the religion of my father and brother.' Based on the *Manāqib* by Ibn Shahrāshūb, d. 588/1192); also al-Mufīd (d. 413/1022): *al-Irshād*, ed. H. Rasūlī Maḥallātī (Tehran, 1346 Sh./1968), vol. 2, pp. 106–107 (during the Battle of Karbalā', Nāfiʿ b. Hilāl al-Bajalī, a supporter of al-Ḥusayn, recites the following verse: 'I am Ibn Hilāl al-Bajalī / I am a follower of the religion of ʿAlī / And the religion of the latter is the religion of the Prophet.' His adversary replies: 'I am the follower of the religion of Uthmān'; it remains for Nāfiʿ to retort: 'You are [in fact] a follower of the religion of Satan'; also *Biḥār al-anwār*, vol. 45, p. 19 and n.1 by the editor on the faulty metre of the poem; in the version reported by Ibn Shahrāshūb in *Manāqib āl Abī Ṭālib*, 3 vols [Najaf, 1956], vol. 3, p. 252, other verses are attributed to Nāfiʿ: 'I am the young Yemeni man of the Bajalīs / My religion is that of Ḥusayn and ʿAlī'; *Biḥār*, vol. 45, p. 27); Ibn Shahrāshūb, *Manāqib*, vol. 3, p. 251 (also during the Battle of Karbalā', verses by ʿAbd al-Raḥmān b. ʿAbd Allāh al-Yazanī: 'I am the son of ʿAbd Allāh of the Āl Yazan / My religion is that of Ḥusayn and Ḥasan'; *Biḥār*, vol. 45, p. 22). In addition, apart from written sources, Shiʿism has also retained *'Dīn ʿAlī'* as a personal name, as seen at the beginning of this chapter.

125 It is useful to note here a remarkable and probably ancient evolution in which the aspects which are specifically Arab and ancestral and which underlie a large part of *dīn ʿAlī*, progressively experienced a transmutation of an initiatory and esoteric nature in Shiʿism. This evolution seems to date especially from the period of the imamates of Muḥammad al-Bāqir (d. 115 or 119/732 or 737) and Jaʿfar al-Ṣādiq (d. 148/765) (cf. J. Ruska, *Arabische Alchemisten. II. Jaʿfar al-Ṣādiq, der sechste Imām* [Heidelberg, 1924]; M. E. G. Hodgson, 'How Did the Early Shīʿa Become Sectarian?', *JAOS*, 75, 1955). To illustrate this evolution, allow me to limit myself to examples drawn from early Imami *ḥadīths*: the replacement of the tribal concept of *ḥilm* by *ʿaql* (which I have, in this particular context, translated as 'intelligence of the sacred' or 'hiero-intelligence') which, in terms of wisdom, is equivalent to *ʿilm* (in the sense of 'initiatory knowledge') (cf. *Guide divin*, esp. pp. 15–28 and 174–199 [*Divine Guide*, pp. 6–11 and 69–79]). The content of the Prophet's saliva (or sweat) is said to be 'initiatory knowledge' (ʿAlī often begins his sermons with these words: 'O people! Question me before you lose me! I am the Bearer of initiatory knowledge; I carry in me the Prophet's saliva that he made me drink drop by drop. Question me for I hold the knowledge of Beginnings and Ends', for example, Ibn Bābūya al-Ṣadūq, *Amālī/Majālis*, ed. M. B. Kamareʾī [Tehran, 1404/1984], p. 341). After receiving Muḥammad's saliva in his eyes, ʿAlī acquired the power 'to see' and to know the true nature of people; see, for example, al-Ṣaffār al-Qummī, *Baṣāʾir al-darajāt*, ed. M. Kuchibāghī (2nd edn, Tabriz, n.d. [ca. 1960]), p. 390. When Muḥammad taught ʿAlī the 'thousand chapters' of knowledge, both men perspired and the sweat of each ran upon the body of the other (*Baṣāʾir*, p. 313; see also *Guide divin*, pp. 193–194 [*Divine Guide*, pp. 176–177]). In the series of traditions regarding the 'tripatriate division of humanity', some, surely the earliest, employ tribal terminology ('We [i.e., the Imams] are the descendants of Hāshim, our Shiʿis are Arabs of noble stock [*al-ʿarab*] and the others, Bedouins of inferior descent [*al-aʿrāb*]'; 'We are noble Arabs [*ʿarabī*], our believers are protected allies [*mawālī*] and those that do not possess the same doctrine as us are vile [*ʿilj*]'). Others, clearly later, take up the same division by introducing the initiatory dimension ('Men are divided into three categories: the wise initiator [*ʿālim*, i.e.,

heritage, the divine election of ʿAlī and his descendants, the ancestral and natural, but also supra-natural, aspects, thaumaturgic and initiatory elements linked to the prophetic 'Holy Family'.

the Imam], the initiated disciple [*mutaʿallim* 'the Imam's faithful'] and the foam carried by the wave [*ghuththāʾ* i.e., the non-believers]'; 'The [true] men are only of two kinds: the wise initiator and the initiated disciple. The others are but vile beings [*hamaj*]'). Regarding these traditions and their analysis, see M. A. Amir-Moezzi, 'Seul l'homme de Dieu est humain. Théologie et anthropologie mystique à travers l'exégèse imamite ancienne (Aspects de l'imamologie duodécimaine IV)', *Arabica*, 45 (1998), pp. 193–214.

2

The Study of the Ismailis: Phases and Issues

Farhad Daftary

The Ismailis represent an important Shiʿi Muslim community. In the past, in spite of their minority status within the broader Muslim society, the Ismailis succeeded in founding their Shiʿi Fatimid caliphate in rivalry with the Sunni Abbasid caliphate. The Fatimid caliphate, ruled by the Ismaili Imams, grew into a major empire, stretching from North Africa to Syria, making significant contributions to Islamic thought and culture. It was also in the Fatimid period that Ismaili thought and literature attained their summit. The Ismaili *dāʿī*s or missionaries, who were also the scholars and authors of their community, produced what became known as the classical texts of Ismaili literature on a variety of exoteric (*ẓāhirī*) and esoteric (*bāṭinī*) subjects, including *taʾwīl* or esoteric exegesis of Qurʾanic passages, the hallmark of Ismaili thought.

In 487/1094, the Ismailis were split into Nizārī and Mustaʿlian branches, with further subsequent subdivisions. This major schism occurred in the aftermath of the Fatimid Imam-caliph al-Mustanṣir's death and his succession dispute. The Mustaʿlian Ismailis who recognised al-Mustanṣir's son al-Mustaʿlī and the later Fatimid caliphs as their Imams eventually found their permanent stronghold in Yemen, and later in South Asia. On the other hand, the Nizārī Ismailis, who recognised the imamate of al-Mustanṣir's original heir Nizār and his successors, were initially concentrated in Persia and Syria, but later came to represent significant communities in Central Asia and South Asia. The Nizārī Ismailis also established a state of their own in Persia with a subsidiary in Syria under the initial leadership of Ḥasan-i Ṣabbāḥ (d. 518/1124). This state, founded in the midst of the ardently Sunni Saljūq sultanate, was eventually uprooted by the Mongol hordes in 654/1256. Subsequently, the Nizārī Ismailis, devoid of any political prominence, survived as minority religious communities.

Today the Ismailis are scattered in more than 25 countries of Asia, the Middle East, Africa, Europe and North America. The bulk of the Ismailis of the world, belonging to the Nizārī branch, now recognise His Highness Prince Karim Aga Khan IV as their 49th and present Imam. The Mustaʿlian Ismailis, who belong exclusively to the Ṭayyibī branch, have not had a manifest Imam since 524/1130; and in the absence of an Imam, the Ṭayyibīs (now subdivided into Dāʾūdī, Sulaymānī and ʿAlawī factions known as Bohras in South Asia) have been led by lines of *dāʿīs* with full authority.[1]

In medieval times, the Ismailis posed serious challenges to the religio-political Sunni order established under the Abbasids. The Ismailis were, indeed, perceived by the Abbasids as their chief adversary. This explains why the Abbasids launched a prolonged literary campaign against the Ismailis, who were maliciously misrepresented in Sunni polemical writings as the arch-enemies of Islam. The Crusaders, who remained ignorant of the religious identity of the Ismailis, added their own contributions to the misrepresentations and legends surrounding the Ismailis. As a result, the Ismailis were generally perceived by Sunni Muslims as deviators from the rightful religious path, while the medieval Crusader circles depicted them fancifully as a band of religious fanatics bent on senseless murder.

The medieval misrepresentations of the Ismailis did not undergo significant revisions at the hands of the orientalists of the 19th century, even as they became much better informed about Islam and its internal divisions, on the basis of the Islamic manuscripts available to them. The breakthrough in the study of the Ismailis had to await the recovery of a large number of authentic Ismaili texts in modern times, making it possible for scholars to embark on the process of deconstructing and dispelling the medieval and orientalistic misrepresentations of the Ismailis. In this chapter, we shall review the key developments in each of the three main phases in the perception and study of the Ismailis, namely the medieval Muslim and European perceptions, and the orientalistic studies, as well as the major steps in modern progress in Ismaili studies.

Medieval Muslim Perceptions

As the most revolutionary wing of Shiʿism with a religio-political agenda that aimed to uproot the Abbasids and restore the caliphate to a line of ʿAlid Imams acknowledged by them, the Ismailis from early on aroused the hostility of the Sunni establishment of the Muslim majority. With the foundation of the Fatimid caliphate in North Africa in 297/907, the Ismaili challenge to the established order had become actualised, and thereupon the Abbasid caliphs and the Sunni *ʿulamāʾ* launched what amounted to a widespread and official anti-Ismaili campaign. The overall aim of this systematic and prolonged literary campaign was to discredit and defame the entire Ismaili movement from its origins in the middle of the 2nd/8th century, so that the Ismailis could be readily classified and condemned as *malāḥida*, that is, heretics or deviators from the true religious path.

Sunni polemicists, starting with Abū ʿAbd Allāh Muḥammad b. ʿAlī b. Rizām al-Kūfī, better known as Ibn Rizām, who lived in Baghdad during the first half of

[1] For brief overviews of Nizārī and Mustaʿlian Ismaili history, see F. Daftary, *A Short History of the Ismailis* (Edinburgh, 1998), pp. 120–193.

the 4th/10th century, now began to fabricate the necessary evidence that would lend support to the condemnation of the Ismailis on specific doctrinal grounds. Ibn Rizām's anti-Ismaili treatise does not seem to have survived, but it was used extensively a few decades later by another polemicist, Sharīf Abu'l-Ḥusayn Muḥammad b. ʿAlī, better known as Akhū Muḥsin, whose own anti-Ismaili work written around 372/982 has not survived either. However, these early anti-Ismaili accounts have been preserved fragmentarily by several later authors, notably al-Nuwayrī (d. 733/1333), Ibn al-Dawādārī (d. after 736/1335) and al-Maqrīzī (d. 845/1442).[2] At any rate, the polemicists cleverly concocted detailed accounts of the sinister teachings and practices of the Ismailis, while also refuting the ʿAlid genealogy of their Imams as descendants of Imam Jaʿfar al-Ṣādiq (d. 148/765). Anti-Ismaili polemical writings provided a main source of information for Sunni heresiographers, such as al-Baghdādī (d. 429/1037),[3] who produced another important category of writings against the Ismailis.

A number of polemicists also fabricated travesties in which they attributed a variety of shocking doctrines and practices to the Ismailis. And, oddly enough, these forgeries circulated as genuine Ismaili treatises and were used as source materials by subsequent generations of polemicists and heresiographers. One of these forgeries in particular, the anonymous *Kitāb al-siyāsa* (*Book of Methodology*), acquired wide popularity as it contained all the ideas needed to refute the Ismailis as 'heretics' on account of their libertinism and atheism. This book, or perhaps another forgery entitled *Kitāb al-balāgh* (*Book of Initiation*), was seen shortly afterwards by Ibn al-Nadīm who cites it in his famous catalogue of Arabic books completed in 377/987.[4] The *Kitāb al-siyāsa*, which has been preserved only fragmentarily in later Sunni sources and was partially reconstructed by S. M. Stern,[5] reportedly expounded the intricate procedure used by Ismaili *dāʿī*s for winning new converts and instructing them through some seven stages of initiation or *balāgh* leading ultimately to unbelief and atheism. Needless to add, the Ismaili tradition knows of these fictitious accounts only through the polemics of its adversaries. Be that as it may, the polemical and heresiographical works, in turn, influenced the Muslim historians, theologians and jurists who had something to say about the Ismailis.

---

2 Shihāb al-Dīn Aḥmad b. ʿAbd al-Wahhāb al-Nuwayrī, *Nihāyat al-arab fī funūn al-adab*, vol. 25, ed. M. J. ʿA. al-Ḥīnī et al. (Cairo, 1984), pp. 187–317; Abū Bakr b. ʿAbd Allāh b. al-Dawādārī, *Kanz al-durar wa-jāmiʿ al-ghurar*, vol. 6, ed. Ṣ. al-Munajjid (Cairo, 1961), pp. 6–21, 44–156, and Taqī al-Dīn Aḥmad b. ʿAlī al-Maqrīzī, *Ittiʿāẓ al-ḥunafāʾ bi-akhbār al-aʾimma al-Fāṭimiyyīn al-khulafāʾ*, vol. 1, ed. J. al-Shayyāl (Cairo, 1967), pp. 22–29, 151–207; ed. Ayman F. Sayyid (Damascus, 2010), vol. 1, pp. 173–237; partial English trans., *Towards a Shiʿi Mediterranean Empire: Fatimid Egypt and the Founding of Cairo*, tr. Sh. Jiwa (London, 2009), pp. 122–187.

3 Abū Manṣūr ʿAbd al-Qāhir b. Ṭāhir al-Baghdādī, *al-Farq bayn al-firaq*, ed. M. Badr (Cairo, 1328/1910), pp. 265–299; English trans., *Moslem Schisms and Sects*, part II, tr. A. S. Halkin (Tel Aviv, 1935), pp. 107–157.

4 Ibn al-Nadīm, *Kitāb al-fihrist*, ed. M. R. Tajaddud (2nd ed., Tehran, 1973), pp. 238, 240.

5 S. M. Stern, 'The Book of the Highest Initiation and Other Anti-Ismāʿīlī Travesties', in his *Studies in Early Ismāʿīlism* (Jerusalem and Leiden, 1983), pp. 56–83.

The Sunni authors, who were generally uninterested in collecting accurate information on the internal divisions of Shiʿi Islam and treated all Shiʿi interpretations of Islam as deviations from the truth or 'heresies', also readily availed themselves of the opportunity of blaming the Fatimids and the entire Ismaili community for the atrocities perpetrated by the Qarmaṭīs of Bahrayn.[6] The Qarmaṭīs, as it is now known, seceded from the rest of the Ismaili community in 286/899 and never recognised continuity in the imamate which was the central doctrine of the Fatimid Ismailis. The Qarmaṭīs continued to await the return of their seventh and final Imam, Muḥammad b. Ismāʿīl, who would then initiate the final era of human history. At any rate, in 317/930, the Qarmaṭīs of Bahrayn attacked Mecca, massacred the pilgrims there and then carried away the Black Stone (*al-ḥajar al-aswad*) to their own capital, al-Aḥsāʾ, in eastern Arabia, presumably to symbolise the end of the era of Islam. The sacrilege of the Qarmaṭīs at Mecca shocked the entire Muslim world. The dissemination of hostile accounts and misrepresentations contributed significantly to turning the Sunni Muslims at large against the Ismailis.

By spreading defamations and forged accounts, the anti-Ismaili authors, indeed, produced a 'black legend' in the course of the 4th/10th century. Ismailism was now depicted as the arch-heresy of Islam, cleverly designed by a certain ʿAbd Allāh b. Maymūn al-Qaddāḥ or some other non-ʿAlid impostor, or possibly even a Jewish magician disguised as a Muslim, with the aim of destroying Islam from within.[7] By the 5th/11th century, this anti-Ismaili fiction, with its elaborate details and stages of initiation, had been accepted as an accurate and reliable description of Ismaili motives, beliefs and practices, leading to further anti-Ismaili polemics and heresiographical accusations as well as intensifying the animosity of other Muslims towards the Ismailis. It is interesting to note that the same 'black legend' served as the basis of the famous 'Baghdad manifesto' issued in 402/1111 against the Fatimids.[8] This declaration, sponsored by the Abbasid caliph al-Qādir (381–422/991–1031), was essentially a public refutation of the ʿAlid ancestry of the Fatimid Imam-caliphs. The manifesto was read in mosques throughout the Abbasid realm, to the deep annoyance of the then reigning Fatimid Imam-caliph, al-Ḥākim (386–411/996–1021). In addition, al-Qādir commissioned several theologians, including the Muʿtazilī ʿAlī b. Saʿīd al-Iṣṭakhrī (d. 404/1013), to write treatises condemning the Fatimids and their doctrines.

---

[6] See especially W. Madelung, 'The Fatimids and the Qarmaṭīs of Baḥrayn', in F. Daftary, ed., *Mediaeval Ismaʿili History and Thought* (Cambridge, 1996), pp. 21–34, 37–39, 41–42, 46–56, 54. See also F. Daftary, 'A Major Schism in the Early Ismāʿīlī Movement', *Studia Islamica*, 77 (1993), pp. 123–139; repr. in an abridged version in his *Ismailis in Medieval Muslim Societies* (London, 2005), pp. 45–61.

[7] W. Ivanow produced a number of studies on this 'black legend'; see especially his *The Alleged Founder of Ismailism* (Bombay, 1946).

[8] The text of the manifesto, with slight variations, may be found in Ibn al-Jawzī, *al-Muntaẓam*, ed. F. Krenkow (Hyderabad, 1357–1362/1938–1943), vol. 7, p. 255; Ibn Taghrībirdī, *al-Nujūm al-zāhira fī mulūk Miṣr wa'l-Qāhira* (Cairo, 1348–1392/1929–1972), vol. 4, pp. 229–231, and al-Maqrīzī, *Ittiʿāẓ*, ed. al-Shayyāl, vol. 1, pp. 43–44; ed. Sayyid, vol. 1, pp. 42–43.

The revolt of the Persian Ismailis led by Ḥasan-i Ṣabbāḥ (d. 518/1124) against the Saljūq Turks, the new overlords of the Abbasids, called forth another vigorous Sunni reaction against the Ismailis in general and the Nizārī Ismailis in particular. The new literary campaign, accompanied by military expeditions against Alamūt and other Nizārī fortresses in Persia, was initiated by Niẓām al-Mulk (d. 485/1092), the Saljūq *wazīr* and virtual master of their realm for more than two decades. Niẓām al-Mulk devoted a long chapter in his *Siyāsat-nāma* (*The Book of Government*) to the condemnation of the Ismailis who, according to him, aimed to 'abolish Islam, to mislead mankind and cast them into perdition'.[9] But the earliest polemical treatise against the Persian Ismailis and their central doctrine of *taʿlīm*, propounding the necessity of authoritative teaching by the Ismaili Imam of the time, was written by no less a figure than Abū Ḥāmid Muḥammad al-Ghazālī (d. 505/1111), the most eminent contemporary Sunni theologian and jurist. He was, in fact, commissioned by the Abbasid caliph al-Mustaẓhir (487–512/1094–1118) to write a major treatise in refutation of the Bāṭinīs, another designation meaning 'esotericists' coined for the Ismailis by their adversaries who accused them of dispensing with the *ẓāhir*, or the commandments and prohibitions of the *sharīʿa*, because they claimed to have found access to the *bāṭin*, or the inner meaning of the Islamic message as interpreted by the Ismaili Imam. In this widely circulating book, completed around 488/1095 and generally known as *al-Mustaẓhirī*, al-Ghazālī fabricated his own elaborate 'Ismaili system' of graded initiation leading to the ultimate stage of atheism.[10] Subsequently, al-Ghazālī wrote several shorter works in refutation of the Ismailis,[11] and his defamations were adopted by other Sunni writers who, like Niẓām al-Mulk, were familiar with the earlier anti-Ismaili 'black legend' as well. The Nizārīs themselves never responded to al-Ghazālī's polemics, but a detailed refutation of *al-Mustaẓhirī* was written much later in Yemen by the fifth Ṭayyibī Mustaʿlian *dāʿī muṭlaq*, ʿAlī b. Muḥammad Ibn al-Walīd (d. 612/1215).[12] The Sunni authors, including especially Saljūq chroniclers, participated actively in the renewed propaganda campaign against the Ismailis, while Saljūq armies failed to dislodge the Nizārīs from their mountain fortresses despite their superior military power.

---

9 Niẓām al-Mulk, *Siyar al-mulūk (Siyāsat-nāma)*, ed. H. Darke (2nd ed., Tehran, 1347/1968), p. 311; English trans., *The Book of Government, or, Rules for Kings*, tr. H. Darke (2nd ed., London, 1978), p. 231.

10 Abū Ḥāmid Muḥammad al-Ghazālī, *Faḍāʾiḥ al-Bāṭiniyya*, ed. ʿAbd al-Raḥmān Badawī (Cairo, 1964), especially pp. 21–36.

11 See F. Daftary, *Ismaili Literature: A Bibliography of Sources and Studies* (London, 2004), p. 177.

12 ʿAlī b. Muḥammad Ibn al-Walīd, *Dāmigh al-bāṭil wa-ḥatf al-munāḍil*, ed. M. Ghālib (Beirut, 1403/1982), 2 vols. See also H. Corbin, 'The Ismāʿīlī Response to the Polemic of Ghazālī', in S. H. Nasr, ed., *Ismāʿīlī Contributions to Islamic Culture* (Tehran, 1977), pp. 69–98, and F. Mitha, *Al-Ghazālī and the Ismailis: A Debate on Reason and Authority in Medieval Islam* (London, 2001).

Medieval European Perceptions

Soon the Ismailis found a new enemy in the Christian Crusaders who had supposedly arrived in the Holy Land to liberate their own co-religionists. The Crusaders seized Jerusalem, their primary target, in 492/1099 and subsequently engaged in extensive military and diplomatic encounters with the Fatimids in Egypt and the Nizārī Ismailis in Syria, with lasting consequences in terms of the distorted image of the Nizārīs in Europe. The Syrian Nizārī Ismailis attained the peak of their power under the leadership of Rāshid al-Dīn Sinān, who was their chief *dāʿī* for some three decades until his death in 589/1193. It was in the time of Sinān, the original 'Old Man of the Mountain' or 'Le Vieux de la Montagne' of the Crusader sources, that occidental chroniclers of the Crusades and a number of European travellers and diplomatic emissaries began to write about the Nizārī Ismailis, whom they designated as the 'Assassins'. The very term Assassin, based on the variants of the Arabic word *ḥashīshī* (plural, *ḥashīshiyya*) that was applied to the Nizārī Ismailis in a derogatory sense of 'irreligious social outcasts' by other Muslims, was picked up locally in the Levant by the Crusaders and their European observers. At the same time, the Frankish circles and their occidental chroniclers, who were not interested in collecting accurate information about Islam as a religion and its internal divisions despite their proximity to Muslims, remained completely ignorant of Muslims in general and the Ismailis in particular. In fact, the Syrian Nizārī Ismailis were the first Shiʿi Muslim community with whom the Crusaders had come into contact. However, the Crusader circles remained unaware of the religious identity of the Ismailis and had only vague and erroneous ideas regarding the Sunni–Shiʿi division in Islam.

Indeed, there is no evidence to suggest that even the most learned of the Crusader historians who spent long periods in the Latin Orient, where they had continuous contacts with the local Muslims, made any serious efforts to gather details on the Muslim communities of the region. Ironically, some of these occidental historians, such as William of Tyre (d. ca. 1184) and James of Vitry (d. 1240), were theologians who served as bishops and archbishops in the Crusader states and also aimed at converting local Muslims to Christianity. The Crusaders obviously also failed to realise that the Fatimids and the Syrian Nizārīs then belonged to rival wings of Ismailism, which itself represented a major branch of Shiʿi Islam. It may be noted here that Sinān had made attempts to establish peaceful relations with his Christian Crusader neighbours through exchanging emissaries with Amalric I (d. 1174), king of the Latin state of Jerusalem. On this occasion, too, the Crusaders did not obtain any information on Ismaili beliefs. Instead, William of Tyre curiously relates that it was at the time of this embassy that the Syrian Nizārīs proposed to collectively embrace Christianity.[13] Needless to say this story, reflecting a basic misunderstanding

[13] See William of Tyre, *Willelmi Tyrensis Archiepiscopi Chronicon*, ed. Robert B. C. Huygens (Turnhout, 1986), vol. 2, pp. 954–956; English trans., *A History of Deeds Done Beyond the Sea*, tr. E. A. Babcock and A. C. Krey (New York, 1943), vol. 2, pp. 392–394. See also

of Sinān's intentions, may be regarded as purely fictitious. It was under such circumstances that the Frankish circles themselves began to fabricate and put into circulation, both in the Latin Orient and in Europe, a number of sensational tales about the secret practices of the Nizārī Ismailis. It is significant to note that none of the variants of these tales are to be found in contemporary Muslim sources, including the most hostile ones written during the 6th–7th/12th–13th centuries.

The Crusaders were particularly impressed by the highly exaggerated reports and rumours of the assassinations attributed to the Nizārīs, and the daring behaviour of their *fidāʾīs*, self-sacrificing devotees who carried out such missions in public places and normally lost their own lives in the process. It should be recalled that in the 6th/12th century, almost any assassination of any significance committed in the central Islamic lands was readily attributed to the daggers of the Nizārī *fidāʾīs*. This explains why these imaginative tales came to revolve around the recruitment and training of the would-be *fidāʾīs* – because they were meant to provide satisfactory explanations for behaviour that would otherwise seem irrational or strange to the medieval European mind. These so-called Assassin legends consisted of a number of separate but interconnected tales, including the '*ḥashīsh* legend', the 'paradise legend' and the 'death-leap legend'. The tales developed in stages, receiving new embellishments at each successive stage, and finally culminated in a synthesis popularised by Marco Polo (d. 1324).[14] The Venetian traveller added his own original contribution in the form of a 'secret garden of paradise', where bodily pleasures were supposedly procured for the *fidāʾīs* with the aid of *ḥashīsh* by their mischievous leader, the Old Man, as part of their indoctrination and training.[15]

Marco Polo's version of the Assassin legends, offered as a report obtained from reliable contemporary sources in Persia, was reiterated to varying degrees by subsequent European writers, such as Odoric of Pordenone (d. 1331), as the standard description of the 'Old Man of the Mountain and his Assassins'. However, it did not occur to any European that Marco Polo may have actually heard the tales in Italy after returning to Venice in 1295 from his journeys to the East – tales that were by then quite widespread in Europe and could be traced to European antecedents on the subject, or that the Assassin legends found in Marco Polo's travelogue may have been entirely inserted, as a digressionary note, by Rustichello of Pisa, the Italian romance writer who was responsible for committing the account of Marco Polo's travels to writing. No more can be said on this subject at the present state of our knowledge, especially as the original version of Marco Polo's travelogue written by Rustichello

---

J. Hauziński, 'On Alleged Attempts at Converting the Assassins to Christianity in the Light of William of Tyre's Account', *Folia Orientalia*, 15 (1974), pp. 229–246, and M. Barber, *The New Knighthood: A History of the Order of the Temple* (Cambridge, 1994), pp. 100–104.

14 For a survey of these legends, see F. Daftary, *The Assassin Legends: Myths of the Ismaʿilis* (London, 1994), pp. 88–127.

15 Marco Polo, *The Book of Ser Marco Polo, the Venetian, Concerning the Kingdoms and Marvels of the East*, ed. and tr. H. Yule, 3rd revised ed. by H. Cordier (London, 1929), vol. 1, pp. 139–146.

in a peculiar form of old French mixed with Italian has not been recovered. In this connection, it may also be noted that Marco Polo himself evidently revised his travelogue during the last twenty years of his life, at which time he could readily have appropriated the popular Assassin legends regarding the Syrian Nizārī Ismailis then current in Europe. In fact, it was Marco Polo who transferred the scene of the legends from Syria to Persia. The contemporary Persian historian ʿAṭā-Malik Juwaynī (d. 681/1283), an avowed enemy of the Nizārīs who accompanied the Mongol conqueror Hūlāgū to Alamūt in 654/1256 and personally inspected that fortress and its famous library before their destruction by the Mongols, does not report discovering any 'secret garden of paradise' there, as claimed in Marco Polo's popular account.

Starting with Burchard of Strassburg, who visited Syria in 570/1175 as an envoy of Frederic of Barbarossa, the Hohenstaufen emperor of Germany, European travellers, chroniclers and envoys to the Latin Orient who had something to say about the 'Assassins' participated in the process of fabricating, transmitting and legitimising the legends. Subsequently, different Assassin legends or components of particular tales were 'imagined' independently and at times concurrently by different European authors, such as Arnold of Lübeck (d. 1212), the German abbot and historian, and James of Vitry (d. 1240), the French bishop of Acre and Crusader historian. The legends were embellished over time and followed an ascending tendency towards more elaborate versions. They culminated in the version attributed to Marco Polo, which combined a number of such legends with an additional component in the form of a 'secret garden of paradise'. By the 8th/14th century, the legends had acquired wide currency and were generally accepted as reliable and accurate descriptions of Nizārī Ismaili teachings and practices, in much the same way as the earlier anti-Ismaili 'black legend' of the Muslim writers. Henceforth, the Nizārī Ismailis were portrayed in late medieval European sources as a sinister order of drugged 'assassins' bent on indiscriminate murder and mayhem.

In the meantime, the word 'assassin', instead of signifying the name of a community in Syria, had acquired a new meaning in French, Italian and other European languages. It had become a common noun designating a professional murderer. With the advent of this usage, the origin of the term was soon forgotten in Europe, while the 'oriental group' designated earlier by that name in the Crusader sources continued to arouse interest among Europeans, mainly because of the enduring popularity of the Assassin legends which had acquired an independent life of their own. At the same time, a number of European philologists and lexicographers had begun to collect the variants of the term 'assassin', such as *assassini*, *assissini* and *heyssessini*, occurring in medieval occidental sources, also proposing many strange etymologies. By the 12th/18th century, a multitude of etymologies of this term had been proposed, while the Ismailis had received a few more notices from travellers and Christian missionaries sent to the Orient.[16] All in all, by the beginning of the 13th/19th century, Europeans still perceived the Ismailis in utterly confused and fanciful manners.

---

16 See, for instance, Camille Falconet (1671–1762), 'Dissertation sur les Assassins, peuple d'Asie', in *Mémoires de Littérature, tirés des registres de l'Académie Royale des Inscriptions et*

Orientalistic Studies of the Ismailis

A new phase in the study of Islam, and to some extent the Ismailis, occurred in the 19th century with the increasing access of the so-called orientalists to the textual sources of the Muslims – Arabic and Persian manuscripts that were variously acquired by the Bibliothèque Nationale, Paris, and other major European libraries. Scientific orientalism had been initiated in France with the establishment in 1795 of the École des Langues Orientales Vivantes in Paris. Baron Antoine Isaac Silvestre de Sacy (1758–1838), the most eminent orientalist of his time, became the first Professor of Arabic in that newly founded School of Oriental Languages; he was also appointed in 1806 to the new chair of Persian at the Collège de France. In due course, de Sacy acquired the distinction of being the teacher of the most prominent orientalists of the first half of the 19th century. At any rate, the orientalists, led by de Sacy, now began their more scholarly study of Islam on the basis of the manuscripts which were written mainly in Arabic and by Sunni authors. Consequently, they studied Islam according to Sunni perspectives and, borrowing classifications from Christian contexts, treated Shiʿism as the 'heterodox' interpretation of Islam, or even as a 'heresy', in contrast to Sunnism which was taken to represent Islamic 'orthodoxy'. Indeed, Western scholarship on Islam has continued variously to be shaped by its Arabo-Sunni perspectives. It was mainly on this basis, as well as the continued attraction of the seminal Assassin legends, that the orientalists launched their own studies of the Ismailis.

It was de Sacy, with his lifelong interest in the Druze religion,[17] who finally also solved the mystery of the name 'Assassin' in his famous *Memoir*.[18] He showed, once and for all, that the word Assassin was connected with the Arabic word *ḥashīsh*, referring to Indian hemp, a narcotic product of *cannabis sativa*. More specifically, he convincingly argued that the main variant forms of this term (such as *Assassini* and *Assissini*) occurring in base-Latin documents of the Crusaders and in different European languages were derived from the Arabic word *ḥashīshī* (plural, *ḥashīshiyya* or *ḥashīshiyyīn*); and he was able to cite Arabic texts, such as the history of the contemporary Syrian chronicler Abū Shāma (d. 665/1267), in which the Nizārī Ismailis were called *ḥashīshī* (plural, *ḥashīshiyya*).

A few contemporary Muslim historians occasionally used the term *ḥashīshī* (*ḥashīshiyya*) in reference to the Nizārī Ismailis of Syria and Persia without any

---

Belles Lettres, 17 (1751), pp. 127–170; English trans., 'A Dissertation on the Assassins, a People of Asia', in John of Joinville, *Memoirs of John Lord de Joinville*, tr. T. Johnes (Hafod, 1807), vol. 2, pp. 287–328, and Simone Assemani (1752–1821), *Ragguaglio storico-critico sopra la setta Assissana, detta volgarmente degli Assassini* (Padua, 1806).

17 Silvestre de Sacy, *Exposé de la religion des Druzes* (Paris, 1838), 2 vols.

18 Silvestre de Sacy, 'Mémoire sur la dynastie des Assassins, et sur l'étymologie de leur nom', *Mémoires de l'Institut Royal de France*, 4 (1818), pp. 1–84; repr. in Bryan S. Turner, ed., *Orientalism: Early Sources*, Vol. 1: *Readings in Orientalism* (London, 2000), pp. 118–169; English trans., 'Memoir on the Dynasty of the Assassins, and on the Etymology of their Name', in Daftary, *Assassin Legends*, pp. 129–188.

derivative explanation. This name seems to have been applied to the Nizārīs as a term of abuse and reproach. The Nizārīs were already a target for hostility by other Muslims and they would readily qualify for every sort of contemptuous judgement on their beliefs and behaviour. In other words, it seems that the pejorative term *ḥashīshiyya*, designating people of lax morality, reflected a criticism of the Nizārīs rather than an accurate description of their secret practices. And it was the name that gave rise to imaginative tales which supplied some explanation of the behaviour that would otherwise seem rather incomprehensible to ill-informed Europeans. Be that as it may, although de Sacy and other orientalists now correctly identified the Ismailis as a Shiʿi Muslim community, they were still obliged to study them on the basis of the hostile Sunni sources and the fictitious occidental accounts of the Crusader circles. Consequently, de Sacy and others endorsed, to varying degrees, the anti-Ismaili 'black legend' of the medieval Sunni polemicists and the Assassin legends of the Crusaders.

De Sacy's deficient evaluation of the Ismailis (albeit unintentional) set the frame within which other orientalists of the 19th century studied the medieval history of the Ismailis. It was under such circumstances that misrepresentation and plain fiction came to permeate the first European book devoted exclusively to the history of the Persian Nizārī Ismailis of the Alamūt period, which was written by Joseph von Hammer-Purgstall (1774–1856). This Austrian orientalist-diplomat endorsed Marco Polo's narrative in its entirety as well as all the medieval defamations levelled against the Ismailis by their Sunni detractors. Originally published in German in 1818, this book achieved great success in Europe and continued to be treated as the standard history of the Nizārī Ismailis until at least the 1930s.[19] With a few exceptions, European scholarship made little further progress in the study of the Ismailis during the second half of the 19th century, while Ismaili sources still remained generally inaccessible to orientalists. The outstanding exception was provided by the historical studies of the French orientalist Charles François Defrémery (1822–1883), who collected a large number of references from various Muslim chronicles on the Nizārīs of Persia and Syria.[20]

The Ismailis continued to be misrepresented to various degrees by orientalists such as Michael J. de Goeje (1836–1909), who made valuable contributions to the study of the Qarmaṭīs of Bahrayn but whose erroneous interpretation of Fatimid–Qarmaṭī

[19] J. von Hammer-Purgstall, *Die Geschichte der Assassinen aus Morgenländischen Quellen* (Stuttgart and Tübingen, 1818); English trans., *The History of the Assassins, derived from Oriental Sources*, tr. O. C. Wood (London, 1835; repr. New York, 1968); French trans., *Histoire de l'ordre des Assassins*, tr. J. J. Hellert and P. A. de la Nourais (Paris, 1833; repr. Paris, 1961). See also F. Daftary, 'The "Order of the Assassins": J. von Hammer and the Orientalist Misrepresentations of the Nizari Ismailis', *Iranian Studies*, 39 (2006), pp. 71–81.

[20] C. Defrémery, 'Nouvelles recherches sur les Ismaéliens ou Bathiniens de Syrie, plus connus sous le nom d'Assassins', *Journal Asiatique*, 5 série, 3 (1854), pp. 373–421, and 5 (1855), pp. 5–76, and his 'Essai sur l'histoire des Ismaéliens ou Batiniens de la Perse, plus connus sous le nom d'Assassins', *Journal Asiatique*, 5 série, 8 (1856), pp. 353–387, and 15 (1860), pp. 130–210.

relations was generally adopted.[21] There also appeared for the first time a history of the Fatimids by Ferdinand Wüstenfeld (1808–1899), a compilation from various Arabic chronicles with no extracts from any Ismaili source.[22] Lack of significant progress in the study of the Fatimids is clearly revealed by the fact that the next Western book on the subject, written some four decades later by De Lacy O'Leary (1872–1957) of Bristol University, still did not make any references to Ismaili sources.[23] Orientalism, thus, gave a new lease of life to the myths surrounding the Ismailis; and this deplorable state of Ismaili studies remained essentially unchanged until the 1930s. Even an eminent orientalist of the calibre of Edward G. Browne (1862–1926), who covered the Ismailis only tangentially in his magisterial survey of Persian literature, could not avoid reiterating the standard orientalistic tales of his predecessors on the Ismailis.[24] This should not cause any particular surprise, however, as very few Ismaili sources had been available to the orientalists of the 19th and early 20th centuries. Meanwhile, Westerners had continued to refer to the Nizārī Ismailis as the Assassins, a misnomer rooted in a medieval pejorative neologism.

The breakthrough in Ismaili studies had to await the recovery of genuine Ismaili texts on a large scale. A few Ismaili manuscripts of Syrian provenance had already surfaced in Paris during the 19th century, and some fragments of these texts were studied and published by Stanislas Guyard (1846–1884) and other orientalists.[25] Another small group of Ismaili texts, again of Syrian provenance, had been sent by a Protestant missionary to America.[26] At the same time, Paul Casanova (1861–1926), who would produce important studies on the Fatimids, was the first European orientalist to have recognised the Ismaili affiliation of the *Rasā'il Ikhwān al-Ṣafā'* (*Epistles of the Brethren of Purity*), a portion of which had found its way to Paris.[27] Earlier, the German orientalist Friedrich Dieterici (1821–1903) had published many parts of the *Rasā'il*, with German translation, without realising their Ismaili connection.[28] These

---

21 See M. J. de Goeje, *Mémoire sur les Carmathes du Bahraïn et les Fatimides* (Leiden, 1862; 2nd ed., Leiden, 1886), and his 'La fin de l'empire des Carmathes du Bahraïn', *Journal Asiatique*, 9 série, 5 (1895), pp. 5–30; repr. in Turner, *Orientalism*, vol. 1, pp. 263–278.

22 F. Wüstenfeld, *Geschichte der Faṭimiden Chalifen nach den arabischen Quellen*, in *Abhandlungen der Königlichen Gesellschaft der Wissenschaften zu Göttingen*, Historisch-Philologische Classe, 26, band 3 (1880), pp. 1–97, and 27, band 1 (1881), pp. 1–130, and 27, band 3 (1881), pp. 1–126; repr. together (Hildesheim and New York, 1976).

23 De Lacy Evans O'Leary, *A Short History of the Fatimid Khalifate* (London, 1923).

24 E. G. Browne, *A Literary History of Persia* (London and Cambridge, 1902–1924), vol. 1, pp. 391–415 and vol. 2, pp. 190–211, 453–460.

25 S. Guyard, ed. and tr., *Fragments rélatifs a la doctrine des Ismaélîs* (Paris, 1874), and his 'Un grand maître des Assassins au temps de Saladin', *Journal Asiatique*, 7 série, 9 (1877), pp. 324–489.

26 Edward E. Salisbury (1814–1901), 'Translation of Two Unpublished Arabic Documents Relating to the Doctrines of the Ismâ'ilis and other Bâṭinian Sects', *JAOS*, 2 (1851), pp. 259–324.

27 See P. Casanova, 'Notice sur un manuscrit de la secte des Assassins', *Journal Asiatique*, 9 série, 11 (1898), pp. 151–159.

28 See Daftary, *Ismaili Literature*, pp. 168, 170–171.

early discoveries of Ismaili sources were, however, few and far between, and it was largely the scholars working in Paris, the capital of orientalism in the 19th century, who had access to these codices.

Other types of information on the Ismailis had now started to appear. While travelling in Syria in 1895, the Swiss orientalist Max van Berchem (1863–1921) read almost all of the epigraphic evidence of the Syrian Nizārī fortresses.[29] Paul Casanova became the first orientalist to produce a study of the Nizārī coins minted during the Alamūt period.[30] Much information on the Nizārī Khojas of South Asia and the first of the modern Nizārī Imams to bear the title of the Āghā Khān (Aga Khan), originally bestowed by the Qājār monarch of Persia, became available in the course of a complicated legal case investigated by the High Court of Bombay, culminating in the famous judgement of 1866.[31]

More Ismaili manuscripts preserved in Yemen and Central Asia began to be recovered in the opening decades of the 20th century. In 1903, Giuseppe Caprotti (1869–1919), an Italian merchant who had spent some three decades in Yemen, brought a collection of Arabic manuscripts to Italy and sold it to the Ambrosiana Library in Milan. The Ambrosiana's Caprotti Collection of codices was later found to contain several Ismaili texts.[32] Of greater significance were the efforts of some Russian scholars and officials who, having become aware of the existence of Ismaili communities within the Central Asian domains of the Russian Empire, now attempted to establish direct contact with them. The Central Asian Ismailis, it may be recalled, all belong to the Nizārī branch and were concentrated mainly in the Badakhshān mountainous region, now divided by the Oxus River (Āmū Daryā) between Tajikistan and Afghanistan. Russians travelled freely in the Upper Oxus region on the right bank of the Panj River, a major upper headwater of the Oxus. Count Aleksey A. Bobrinskiy (1861–1938), a Russian scholar who studied the inhabitants of the Wakhān and Ishkāshim districts of Badakhshān in 1898, published the first account of the Nizārīs living there.[33] Subsequently, in 1914 Ivan I. Zarubin (1887–1964), the eminent

[29] M. van Berchem, 'Épigraphie des Assassins de Syrie', *Journal Asiatique*, 9 série, 9 (1897), pp. 453–501; repr. in his *Opera Minora* (Geneva, 1978), vol. 1, pp. 453–501; also repr. in Turner, *Orientalism*, vol. 1, pp. 279–309.

[30] P. Casanova, 'Monnaie des Assassins de Perse', *Revue Numismatiques*, 3 série, 11 (1893), pp. 343–352.

[31] 'Judgement of the Honourable Sir Joseph Arnould in the Khodjah Case, otherwise known as the Aga Khan Case …' (Bombay, 1867); see also *Bombay High Court Reports*, 12 (1866), pp. 323–363. This case has been summarised in Asaf A. A. Fyzee, *Cases in the Muhammadan Law of India and Pakistan* (Oxford, 1965), pp. 504–549. The Aga Khan Case has been analysed in Amrita Shodan, *A Question of Community: Religious Groups and Colonial Law* (Calcutta, 1999), pp. 82–116.

[32] See Eugenio Griffini (1878–1925), 'Die jüngste ambrosianische Sammlung arabischer Handschriften', *Zeitschrift der Deutschen Morgenländischen Gesellschaft*, 69 (1915), especially pp. 80–88.

[33] A. A. Bobrinskiy, 'Sekta Ismailiya v Russkikh i Bukharskikh predelakh Sredney Azii', *Étnograficheskoe Obozrenie*, 2 (1902), pp. 1–20. Now also see B. M. Zoeggeler et al., ed., *Graf*

Russian ethnologist and specialist in Tajik dialects, acquired a small collection of Ismaili manuscripts from the western Pamir districts of Shughnān and Rūshān in Badakhshān, which was presented to the Asiatic Museum of the Imperial Russian Academy of Sciences in St Petersburg.[34] In 1918, the Asiatic Museum received a second collection of Persian Nizārī texts.[35] These manuscripts had been acquired a few years earlier, from the Upper Oxus region, by Aleksandr A. Semenov (1873–1958), a Russian pioneer in Ismaili studies from Tashkent. These Ismaili manuscripts of Central Asian provenance are currently part of the collections of the Russian Institute of Oriental Manuscripts in St Petersburg.

The generally meagre number of Ismaili titles known to orientalists by the 1920s is well reflected in the first Western bibliography of Ismaili works prepared by Louis Massignon (1883–1962), the foremost French pioneer in Shiʿi and Ismaili studies.[36] Little further progress was made in the study of the Ismailis during the 1920s, aside from the publication of some of the works of the Persian *dāʿī*, poet and philosopher Nāṣir-i Khusraw (d. after 462/1070), while European orientalist studies on the subject essentially continued to display the misrepresentations of the Crusaders and the defamations of medieval Sunni polemicists. Nevertheless, the ground was rapidly being prepared for the initiation of a totally new phase in the study of the Ismailis – the modern phase based increasingly on Ismaili textual materials.

Modern Progress in Ismaili Studies

Modern scholarship in Ismaili studies, founded on the recovery and study of genuine Ismaili sources on a large scale, was actually initiated in the 1930s in India, where significant collections of Ismaili manuscripts have been preserved. This breakthrough resulted mainly from the efforts of Wladimir Ivanow (1886–1970) and a few Ismaili Bohra scholars, notably Asaf A. A. Fyzee (1899–1981), Ḥusayn F. al-Hamdānī (1901–1962) and Zāhid ʿAlī (1888–1958), who produced their pioneering studies using their family collections of Ismaili manuscripts. Subsequently, these collections

---

Bobrinskoj. Der lange weg vom Pamir in die Dolomiten/Il Conte Bobrinskoj: Il lungo Cammino dal Pamir alle Dolomite (Bozen, 2012).

34 See V. A. Ivanov, 'Ismailitskie rukopisi Aziatskago Muzeya. Sobranie I. Zarubina, 1916 g.', *Bulletin de l'Académie Impériale des Sciences de Russie*, 6 série, 11 (1917), pp. 359–386.

35 A. A. Semenov, 'Opisanie ismailitskikh rukopisey, sobrannïkh A. A. Semyonovïm', *Bulletin de l'Académie des Sciences de Russie*, 6 série, 12 (1918), pp. 2171–2202.

36 L. Massignon, 'Esquisse d'une bibliographie Qarmaṭe', in R. A. Nicholson and T. W. Arnold, ed., *A Volume of Oriental Studies Presented to Edward G. Browne on his 60th Birthday* (Cambridge, 1922), pp. 329–338; repr. in L. Massignon, *Opera Minora*, ed. Y. Moubarac (Paris, 1969), vol. 1, pp. 627–639. This bibliography does not include the Asiatic Museum's then recently acquired Ismaili texts.

were donated to various academic institutions, including especially The Institute of Ismaili Studies in London, and thus were made available to scholars at large.[37]

Asaf Fyzee, who studied law at Cambridge University and belonged to the most eminent Sulaymānī Ṭayyibī family of Ismaili Bohras in India, made modern scholars aware of the existence of an independent Ismaili *madhhab* or school of jurisprudence. Among his numerous studies on Ismaili law,[38] Fyzee produced a critical edition of the *Daʿāʾim al-Islām*, the major compendium of the foremost Ismaili jurist al-Qāḍī al-Nuʿmān (d. 363/974), which served as the legal code of the Fatimid state and is still used by the Ṭayyibī Ismailis of South Asia and Yemen.[39] Ḥusayn al-Hamdānī hailed from a distinguished Dāʾūdī Ṭayyibī family of scholars with Yemeni origins. He received his doctorate from London University's School of Oriental (and African) Studies, and was a pioneer in producing a number of Ismaili studies based on a collection of manuscripts which had been compiled by several generations of his ancestors in Yemen and Gujarāt;[40] he also called the attention of modern scholars to the existence of this literary heritage,[41] and made the manuscripts in his possession readily available to numerous scholars, such as Paul Kraus (1904–1944), who were then producing their own original studies. Zāhid ʿAlī, who was from another learned Dāʾūdī Bohra family, was for many years the principal of the Niẓām College at Hyderabad after receiving his doctorate from Oxford University, where he produced a critical edition of the *Dīwān* of Ibn Hāniʾ (d. 362/973), the foremost Ismaili poet of classical times, as his thesis.[42] Subsequently, Zāhid ʿAlī was to become the first author

---

[37] Asaf Fyzee donated some 200 manuscripts to the Bombay University Library; see M. Goriawala, *A Descriptive Catalogue of the Fyzee Collection of Ismaili Manuscripts* (Bombay, 1965), and A. A. A. Fyzee, 'A Collection of Fatimid Manuscripts', in N. N. Gidwani, ed., *Comparative Librarianship: Essays in Honour of Professor D.N. Marshall* (Delhi, 1973), pp. 209–220. Ḥusayn al-Hamdānī also donated part of his family's collection to the Bombay University, while another portion remained in the possession of his son, Professor Abbas Hamdani, who donated the bulk of these manuscripts in 2006 to The Institute of Ismaili Studies Library; see F. de Blois, *Arabic, Persian and Gujarati Manuscripts: The Hamdani Collection in the Library of The Institute of Ismaili Studies* (London, 2011). The Zāhid ʿAlī Collection of some 226 Arabic Ismaili manuscripts was also donated to The Institute of Ismaili Studies in 1997; see D. Cortese, *Arabic Ismaili Manuscripts: The Zāhid ʿAlī Collection in the Library of The Institute of Ismaili Studies* (London, 2003).

[38] See F. Daftary, 'The Bibliography of Asaf A. A. Fyzee', *Indo-Iranica*, 37 (1984), pp. 49–63.

[39] Al-Qāḍī Abū Ḥanīfa al-Nuʿmān b. Muḥammad, *Daʿāʾim al-Islām*, ed. Asaf A. A. Fyzee (Cairo, 1951–1961), 2 vols; English trans., *The Pillars of Islam*, tr. A. A. A. Fyzee, completely revised by I. K. Poonawala (New Delhi, 2002–2004).

[40] See Daftary, *Ismaili Literature*, pp. 287–288.

[41] See Ḥ. F. al-Hamdānī, 'Some Unknown Ismāʿīlī Authors and their Works', *Journal of the Royal Asiatic Society* (1933), pp. 359–378.

[42] Ibn Hāniʾ, *Tabyīn al-maʿānī fī sharḥ Dīwān Ibn Hāniʾ al-Andalusī al-Maghribī* (Cairo, 1352/1933).

in modern times to have written, in Urdu, a scholarly work on the Fatimid dynasty, based on a large variety of Ismaili sources.[43]

Wladimir Ivanow was a major force behind the modern progress in Ismaili studies.[44] Born in 1886 in St Petersburg, Ivanow joined the Asiatic Museum in 1915 as an assistant keeper of oriental manuscripts, and in that capacity travelled widely in Central Asia acquiring more than a thousand Arabic and Persian manuscripts for the Museum. It was at the Asiatic Museum that Ivanow had his first contacts with Ismaili literature, his main research interest in later years. Ivanow, who eventually settled in Bombay after leaving his native Russia in 1918 for good, collaborated closely with the above-mentioned Bohra scholars and a few emerging European scholars in the field. Meanwhile, he had established relations with some Nizārī Khojas of Bombay who, in turn, introduced him to Sultan Muhammad (Mahomed) Shah Aga Khan III (1877–1957), the 48th Imam of the Nizārī Ismailis. In 1931, the Ismaili Imam employed Ivanow on a permanent basis to conduct research into the literature, history and doctrines of the Ismailis. Henceforth, Ivanow also found ready access to the private collections of Ismaili manuscripts held by the Nizārī Ismailis of India, Badakhshān and elsewhere.

It was in Bombay during the early 1930s that this small group of pioneers, led by Ivanow, brought about the breakthrough in modern Ismaili studies. In 1933, Ivanow produced the first detailed catalogue of Ismaili works, citing some 700 separate titles written by a multitude of Ismaili authors such as Abū Ḥātim al-Rāzī (d. 322/934), Jaʿfar b. Manṣūr al-Yaman (d. ca. 346/957), al-Qāḍī al-Nuʿmān b. Muḥammad (d. 363/974), Abū Yaʿqūb al-Sijistānī (d. after 361/971), Ḥamīd al-Dīn al-Kirmānī (d. after 411/1020), al-Muʾayyad fiʾl-Dīn al-Shīrāzī (d. 470/1078), Nāṣir-i Khusraw (d. after 462/1070), and many later authors who lived in Yemen, Syria, Persia and other regions. This catalogue attested to the hitherto unknown richness and diversity of Ismaili literary and intellectual traditions.[45] The initiation of modern scholarship in Ismaili studies may indeed be traced to this very publication, which provided for the first time a scientific framework for research in this new field of Islamic studies. In the same year, Ivanow founded the Islamic Research Assocation in Bombay with the collaboration of Asaf Fyzee and other Ismaili friends. Several Ismaili works, including Ivanow's own editions of a number of Persian Nizārī texts and his major study of early Ismailism,[46] appeared in the series of publications sponsored by this institution. In 1937, Ivanow discovered the tombs of several Nizārī Imams in the villages of Anjudān and Kahak, in central Persia, enabling him to fill certain gaps in

[43] Zāhid ʿAlī, *Taʾrīkh-i Fāṭimiyyīn-i Miṣr* (Hyderabad, 1367/1948), 2 vols; see also his work on Ismaili doctrines entitled *Hamāre Ismāʿīlī madhhab kī ḥaqīqat awr uskā niẓām* (Hyderabad, 1373/1954).

[44] See F. Daftary, 'Bibliography of the Publications of the late W. Ivanow', *Islamic Culture*, 45 (1971), pp. 55–67, and 56 (1982), pp. 239–240, and his 'Ivanow, Vladimir', *EIR*, vol. 14, pp. 298–300.

[45] W. Ivanow, *A Guide to Ismaili Literature* (London, 1933).

[46] W. Ivanow, *Ismaili Tradition Concerning the Rise of the Fatimids* (London, etc., 1942).

the post-Alamūt history of the Nizārī Ismailis.[47] In fact, Ivanow himself succeeded in identifying what he termed the 'Anjudān revival', an important period stretching from around the middle of the 9th/15th century to the late 11th/17th century, representing a revival in the *daʿwa* and literary activities of the Nizārī Ismailis.

Ismaili scholarship received a major boost through the establishment in 1946 of the Ismaili Society in Bombay under the patronage of Aga Khan III. Ivanow also played a crucial role in the creation of the Ismaili Society, whose various series of publications were devoted mainly to his own monographs as well as editions and translations of Persian Nizārī texts. Ivanow acquired a large number of Arabic and Persian Ismaili manuscripts for the Ismaili Society's library, which were transferred in the early 1980s to The Institute of Ismaili Studies Library in London. These manuscript sources were initially also made available to a group of Western scholars, including Henry Corbin (1903–1978), who were then developing an interest in Ismaili studies.[48]

By 1963, when Ivanow published a revised edition of his Ismaili catalogue, many more textual sources had become known and progress in Ismaili studies had gained momentum.[49] In addition to many studies by Ivanow and the Bohra pioneers, as well as those of a dozen European scholars such as Rudolf Strothmann (1877–1960), Marius Canard (1888–1982), Paul Kraus (1904–1944) and Bernard Lewis, numerous Ismaili texts had now begun to be critically edited, preparing the ground for further progress in the field. In this connection, particular mention should be made of the Ismaili texts of Fatimid and later times edited together with French translations and analytical introductions by Henry Corbin, and published simultaneously in Tehran and Paris in his 'Bibliothèque Iranienne' series, and the Fatimid Ismaili texts published by the Egyptian scholar Muḥammad Kāmil Ḥusayn (1901–1961) in his 'Silsilat Makhṭūṭāt al-Fāṭimiyyīn' in Cairo. 'Ārif Tāmir (1921–1998), who belonged to the small Mu'minī Nizārī community in Syria, also made a number of Ismaili texts available to scholars, albeit often in defective editions.

The groundbreaking efforts of Ivanow in making the bulk of the Nizārī literature available to modern scholars had meanwhile enabled Marshall Hodgson (1922–1968) to produce the first comprehensive and scholarly study of the Nizārī Ismailis of the

---

47 W. Ivanow, 'Tombs of Some Persian Ismaili Imams', *Journal of the Bombay Branch of the Royal Asiatic Society*, New Series, 14 (1938), pp. 49–62. For Ivanow's archaeological studies, see his *Alamut and Lamasar: Two Medieval Ismaili Strongholds in Iran* (Tehran, 1960). For the most recent study of these and other Nizārī castles of Persia and Syria, see Peter Willey (1922–2009), *Eagle's Nest: Ismaili Castles in Iran and Syria* (London, 2005).

48 For some interesting details, see S. Schmidtke, ed., *Correspondence Corbin-Ivanow: Lettres échangées entre Henry Corbin et Vladimir Ivanow de 1947 à 1966* (Paris, 1999). See also Daniel de Smet, 'Henry Corbin et les études Ismaéliennes', in M. A. Amir-Moezzi et al., ed., *Henry Corbin: Philosophe et sagesses des religions du livre* (Turnhout, 2005), pp. 105–118.

49 W. Ivanow, *Ismaili Literature: A Bibliographical Survey* (Tehran, 1963). See also F. Daftary, 'Ismaili History and Literary Traditions', in H. Landolt, S. Sheikh and K. Kassam, ed., *An Anthology of Ismaili Literature* (London, 2008), pp. 1–29.

Alamūt period,[50] a work that finally replaced J. von Hammer-Purgstall's 19th-century orientalist monograph on the subject. Modern scholars now also acquired a much better understanding of the nature of the pre-Fatimid Ismaili *daʿwa* and community and the proper place of the Qarmaṭīs within early Ismailism, thanks to a number of studies by Samuel M. Stern (1920–1969) and Wilferd Madelung.[51] Later, Madelung summed up the contemporary state of scholarship on Ismaili history in his article 'Ismāʿīliyya', published in 1973 in the new edition of *The Encyclopaedia of Islam*.

Meanwhile, a number of Russian scholars had maintained the earlier interests of A. Semenov and their other compatriots in Ismaili studies, though often limited by their Marxist class-struggle analytical framework. Among such scholars particular mention should be made of Andrey E. Bertel's (1926–1995) and Lyudmila V. Stroeva (1910–1993).[52] Stroeva produced the only modern Russian account of the history of the Nizārī Ismaili state in Persia.[53] Driven by her Marxist ideology, however, Stroeva was obliged to draw significantly different conclusions compared with Hodgson's treatment of the same subject. At the same time, several Egyptian scholars with interests in the medieval history of their country, especially Ḥasan Ibrāhīm Ḥasan (1892–1968), Jamāl al-Dīn al-Shayyāl (1911–1967), Muḥammad Jamāl al-Dīn Surūr (1911–1992) and ʿAbd al-Munʿim Mājid (1920–1999), made further contributions to Fatimid studies. Indeed, the Fatimid period remains the best documented era of Ismaili history.

Progress was equally astonishing in broader areas of Ismaili studies, such as the enigmatic Ikhwān al-Ṣafāʾ and their enyclopaedic *Rasāʾil*, though controversies regarding the identity of these authors and the date of composition of their 52 epistles remain unresolved. Yves Marquet (1911–2008) produced a vast corpus of studies on the Ikhwān al-Ṣafāʾ, while Alessandro Bausani (1921–1988) and Carmela Baffioni, amongst others, have also contributed to this field. Abbas Hamdani has

---

50 Marshall G. S. Hodgson, *The Order of Assassins: The Struggle of the Early Nizārī Ismāʿīlīs against the Islamic World* (The Hague, 1955; repr. New York, 1980). This book was based on the author's doctoral thesis presented to the University of Chicago in 1951.

51 See particularly the following works of S. M. Stern: 'Heterodox Ismāʿīlism at the Time of al-Muʿizz', *BSOAS*, 17 (1955), pp. 10–33, and 'Ismāʿīlīs and Qarmaṭians', in *L'Élaboration de l'Islam* (Paris, 1961), pp. 99–108; both repr. in his *Studies in Early Ismāʿīlism*, pp. 257–288 and 289–298, respectively. Professor Madelung's contributions, based on his doctoral thesis presented to the University of Hamburg in 1957, are to be found in two substantial articles: 'Fatimiden und Baḥrainqarmaṭen', *Der Islam*, 34 (1959), pp. 34–88, slightly revised English trans., 'The Fatimids and the Qarmaṭīs of Baḥrayn', in Daftary, ed., *Mediaeval Ismaʿili History and Thought*, pp. 21–73; and 'Das Imamat in der frühen ismailitischen Lehre', *Der Islam*, 37 (1961), pp. 43–135. See further J. D. Latham and H. W. Mitchell, 'The Bibliography of S. M. Stern', *Journal of Semitic Studies*, 15 (1970), pp. 226–238, repr. with additions in S. M. Stern, *Hispano-Arabic Strophic Poetry: Studies by Samuel Miklos Stern*, ed. L. P. Harvey (Oxford, 1974), pp. 231–245; and F. Daftary, 'Bibliography of the Works of Wilferd Madelung', in F. Daftary and J. W. Meri, ed., *Culture and Memory in Medieval Islam: Essays in Honour of Wilferd Madelung* (London, 2003), pp. 5–40.

52 See Daftary, *Ismaili Literature*, pp. 223–224 and 398–401.

53 L. V. Stroeva, *Gosudarstvo ismailitov v Irane v XI–XIII vv* (Moscow, 1978).

expounded his own distinct hypothesis on the authorship and dating of the *Rasāʾil* in his numerous studies. Professor Hamdani essentially maintains that these epistles were composed by a group of Ismaili *dāʿīs* shortly before the foundation of the Fatimid state in 297/909.[54] There are still other scholars, like Ian R. Netton, who altogether dispute the Ismaili connection with the *Rasāʾil*.[55] Amongst the various regional Ismaili traditions that have received scholarly attention in recent decades, particular mention may be made of the contributions of Azim Nanji and Ali Asani to the study of the Satpanthi tradition of South Asian Nizārī Khojas, as reflected in their *ginān* devotional literature.

Progress in Ismaili studies has proceeded at a rapid pace during the last few decades through the cumulative efforts of yet another generation of scholars, such as Ismail K. Poonawala, Heinz Halm, Paul E. Walker, Hermann Landolt, Thierry Bianquis, Michael Brett, Pieter Smoor, Yaacov Lev, Farhat Dachraoui, Mohammed Yalaoui and Ayman F. Sayyid, some of whom have devoted their attention mainly to Fatimid studies. There are also those newcomers to the field, such as Christian Jambet, Daniel de Smet and Paula Sanders, who are making contributions to different aspects of Ismaili studies. Progress in the recovery of Ismaili literature is well reflected in Professor Poonawala's monumental catalogue, which identifies some 1,300 titles written by more than 200 authors.[56] Many Ismaili texts have already been published in critical editions, while an increasing number of secondary studies on various aspects of Ismaili history, thought and traditions have been produced by at least three generations of modern scholars, as documented in this author's *Ismaili Literature* published in 2004.

Modern progress in Ismaili studies has received steady impetus from the recovery, or better accessibility, of yet more Ismaili manuscripts, including various library holdings such as those of the American University of Beirut and Tübingen University, amongst others. The vast Arabic manuscript collections of the Dāʾūdī Bohra libraries at Sūrat, in Gujarāt, and Bombay (Mumbai), remain under the strict control of that community's leadership and are generally inaccessible to scholars. The bulk of the extensive Persian manuscript sources preserved by the Central Asian Nizārīs have now been identified, and they are largely accessible to scholars. Several hundred Ismaili manuscripts held by the Nizārī Ismailis of Tajik Badakhshān were recovered during 1959–1963,[57] and subsequently many more titles were identified in Shughnān and other districts in both Tajik and Afghan Badakhshān through the efforts of The Institute of Ismaili Studies. The Institute now holds the largest collection of Arabic

---

54 For a listing of A. Hamdani's relevant studies, see Daftary, *Ismaili Literature*, pp. 285–287.

55 I. R. Netton, *Muslim Neoplatonists: An Introduction to the Thought of the Brethren of Purity (Ikhwān al-Ṣafāʾ)* (London, 1982), especially pp. 95–108.

56 I. K. Poonawala, *Biobibliography of Ismāʿīlī Literature* (Malibu, CA, 1977). Professor Poonawala is currently working on a revised edition of this work with many additional titles.

57 See, for instance, Andrey E. Bertel's and M. Bakoev, *Alphabetic Catalogue of Manuscripts found by 1959–1963 Expedition in Gorno-Badakhshan Autonomous Region*, ed. B. G. Gafurov and A. M. Mirzoev (Moscow, 1967).

and Persian Ismaili manuscripts in the West, as well as some 650 manuscripts of *ginān*s, written mainly in the Khojkī script developed within the Nizārī Khoja community of South Asia.

Scholarship in Ismaili studies is set to continue unabated as the Ismailis themselves are becoming increasingly interested in studying their history and literary heritage, an emerging phenomenon attested by the growing number of Ismaili-related doctoral theses written in recent decades by the Ismailis. In this context, a major contribution is currently being made by The Institute of Ismaili Studies, established in London in 1977 by H. H. Prince Karim Aga Khan IV, the 49th and current Imam of the Nizārī Ismailis.[58] This academic institution is already serving as the central point of reference for Ismaili studies, while making its own contributions through various programmes of research and publications. Amongst these, particular mention should be made of the monographs appearing in the Institute's 'Ismaili Heritage Series', which aims to make available to wide audiences the results of modern scholarship on the Ismailis and their intellectual and literary traditions; and the 'Ismaili Texts and Translations Series', launched in 2000, in which critical editions of Arabic and Persian texts are published together with English translations and contextualising introductions. Numerous scholars worldwide participate in these programmes, as well as in the series devoted to a complete critical edition and annotated English translation of *Rasāʾil Ikhwān al-Ṣafāʾ* (*Epistles of the Brethren of Purity*), launched in 2008; and many more benefit from ready access to the Institute's collections of Ismaili manuscripts. With these modern developments, based on the accessibility of Ismaili textual materials, the sustained scholarly study of the Ismailis promises to deconstruct and dissipate the remaining misrepresentations of the Ismailis rooted in the 'hostility' or the 'imaginative ignorance' of earlier generations.

---

58 See Paul E. Walker, 'The Institute of Ismaili Studies', *EIR*, vol. 12, pp. 164–166.

3

Al-Maqrīzī's Connection to the Fatimids

Nasser Rabbat

Although many believed in their divine right to lead the Islamic *umma*, the descendants of the Prophet Muḥammad seldom ruled. Apart from the eventful caliphate of ʿAlī b. Abī Ṭālib (d. 40/661), and the even more tragic attempt to reclaim the caliphate by his son al-Ḥusayn (d. 61/680), the reigning families in the first few centuries of Islam, the Umayyads and the Abbasids, were members of Quraysh, the Prophet's tribe, but not his descendants. Thus, the rise of the Fatimids in 297/909 in Ifrīqiya and their conquest of Egypt in 358/969 to form a viable counter-caliphal project represented a potential turning point in Islamic history, which could have led to the Ismailification of the Islamic world and its unification under a dynasty of the descendants of the Prophet. But the plan failed and, instead, we now, ten centuries later, have a vast conglomeration of Sunni-controlled, yet somewhat secular nation-states punctured by religious Twelver Shiʿi states in Iran and Iraq, a couple of regimes asserting a Hashemite and ʿAlid pedigree in Jordan and Morocco respectively, and a few charismatic militant movements led by Sayyids (descendants of the Prophet), such as Hizbullah in Lebanon and the al-Mahdī Army in Iraq, in addition to the global communities of Ismailis criss-crossing the world with supreme leaders who trace their lineage back to the Fatimids but have no actual state to call their own.

There was a concerted effort to erase all traces of the Fatimids after their downfall and the restoration of the Abbasid caliphate in Egypt in 567/1171 at the hands of Ṣalāḥ al-Dīn al-Ayyūbī (d. 589/1193). Separated according to gender, members of the Fatimid family were sequestered in perpetuity to prevent their propagation, which resulted in most of the family dying off by the late 13th century. Ismailis in the army and the administration were purged on accusation of sedition and many were killed in battle, executed on the gallows or expelled from the country. Fatimid palaces were parcelled out among the Ayyubid *amīr*s and ultimately demolished so that they could be replaced by religious complexes in the 13th and 14th centuries.[1] Some

[1] On the actions against the Fatimids taken by Ṣalāḥ al-Dīn, see Abū Shāma, *Kitāb al-rawḍatayn fī akhbār al-dawlatayn al-Nūriyya wa'l-Ṣalāḥiyya*, ed. Muḥammad H. M. Aḥmad and M. M. Ziyāda (Cairo, 1956–1962), vol. 1, part 2, p. 506; al-Maqrīzī, *al-Mawāʿiẓ wa'l-iʿtibār bi-dhikr al-khiṭaṭ wa'l-āthār* (Būlāq, 1270/1853), vol. 1, pp. 396–398; al-Maqrīzī, *Ittiʿāẓ*

Fatimid mosques were closed off for almost a century, such as the al-Azhar Mosque, or neglected so that they fell into disuse, such as the Mosque of al-Qarāfa, and tombs of the Fatimid caliphs inside al-Qāhira were dug out and built over. Fatimid archives were deliberately destroyed and their libraries and artefacts sold off in auction and dispersed among many collectors and merchants, some of whom were so ignorant of their true value that they tore them apart to be sold as discrete objects or smelted them down to be disposed of as bullion. Finally, the Fatimid historical legacy was ignored or sabotaged, and their name in Ayyūbid and Mamlūk historiography changed to al-ʿUbaydiyyūn, after ʿUbayd Allāh al-Mahdī bi'llāh, the founder of the Fatimid state in 297/909, to drive home the rejection of the Fatimids' claim of descent from Fāṭima, the daughter of the Prophet and wife of ʿAlī b. Abī Ṭālib.

In that hostile Sunni environment towards anything Fatimid, it was exceedingly daring to cast them in a positive light or to accept their Prophetic and ʿAlid lineage in any form of writing, and only two prominent scholars did so. The first was the great Ibn Khaldūn (732–808/1332–1406), the most original socio-historical thinker in Islamic history, who accepted the Fatimids' lineage on the grounds of the veracity of their official genealogy, though he had little to say about their rule.[2] The second was his one-time companion and student, Taqī al-Dīn Aḥmad b. ʿAlī b. ʿAbd al-Qādir al-Maqrīzī (766–845/1364–1442), the historian with the most expansive repertoire of his generation, if not the entire 15th-century Mamlūk historiography, who went much further than his master in his defence of the Fatimids. In two of his major works, *al-Mawāʿiẓ wa'l-iʿtibār bi-dhikr al-khiṭaṭ wa'l-āthār* and *Ittiʿāẓ al-ḥunafāʾ bi-akhbār al-aʾimma al-Fāṭimiyyīn al-khulafāʾ* (which are in fact the most comprehensive historical sources we have on the Fatimids) al-Maqrīzī offers a flattering portrayal of the Fatimid caliphs and their achievements and accepts their genealogy, but stops short of espousing their religious doctrine, although he refuses to condemn it. In the *Khiṭaṭ*, he displays much more than 'an antiquarian interest in the Fatimids' as Paul Walker states.[3] He lauds their caliphate and describes the many spectacular structures and the order and decorum it established in Fatimid Egypt with utter admiration and respect that transcend the rhetorical need of setting the tone for his subsequent criticism of the Mamlūks, as asserted by Walker and others. In the *Ittiʿāẓ*, which is an expansive chronicle of the Fatimid period down to Ṣalāḥ al-Dīn's coup, al-Maqrīzī mounts a fervent defence of the authenticity of the Fatimids' lineage at a time when the learned consensus in Sunni Egypt was that the Fatimids were

---

al-ḥunafāʾ bi-akhbār al-aʾimma al-Fāṭimiyyīn al-khulafāʾ, ed. Jamāl al-Dīn al-Shayyāl and Muḥammad Ḥ. M. Aḥmad (Cairo, 1967–1973), vol. 3, p. 347.

[2] Yet this earned him the ire of his contemporaries; see Ibn Ḥajar al-ʿAsqalānī, *Inbāʾ al-ghumr bi-anbāʾ al-ʿumr* (Hyderabad, 1967), vol. 5, p. 331; similar report in Shams al-Dīn al-Sakhāwī, *al-Ḍawʾ al-lāmiʿ li-ahl al-qarn al-tāsiʿ* (Cairo, 1935), vol. 4, pp. 147–148.

[3] Paul Walker, 'al-Maqrīzī and the Fatimids', *Mamlūk Studies Review*, 7 (2003), pp. 83–97.

impostors who descended from a preacher with a suspect lineage, 'Ubayd Allāh, 'the fifth descendant of Maymūn al-Qaddāḥ b. Dayṣān, the Manichean'.[4]

In what follows, I will explain al-Maqrīzī's distinct stance on the Fatimids by examining it in the context of his lineage, his uncompromising ethics, and his criticism of his contemporary rulers, the Circassian Mamlūks.

Al-Maqrīzī grew up in the house of his maternal family in the venerable Ḥārat al-Burjuwān at the heart of Fatimid Cairo. In his own autobiographical writing, he tells us a fair amount about his father and grandfather, but beyond that his lineage is a bit obscure. He is said to have intentionally limited his genealogy to ten names, the last of which is Tamīm, who is ostensibly a direct descendant of the caliph al-Mu'izz li-Dīn Allāh (r. 341–365/953–975), the first Fatimid caliph in Egypt and the founder of Cairo.[5] Ibn Ḥajar al-'Asqalānī says that al-Maqrīzī once deleted all the names before his tenth ancestor in the copy of one of his books. On another occasion, al-Maqrīzī kept his answer to Ibn Ḥajar vague, when the latter asked him point-blank to verify a report about his grandfather's Anṣārī (a descendant of a Medinese Companion of the Prophet) origin. Al-Maqrīzī just questioned the authority of the biographer, but neither confirmed nor rejected his claim.[6]

Why he did so Ibn Ḥajar does not explain, although it is not difficult to guess. Al-Maqrīzī was probably divided between accepting the opportunity to attach himself to an extremely prestigious and safe though false ancestry, that is, the Anṣārī genealogy, or revealing that his real pedigree, at least in his belief, was even more glorious but doctrinally perilous. These cautious acts are justifiable in the context of the competitive and even cut-throat scholarly milieu in which al-Maqrīzī and his colleagues navigated. A public assertion of his Fatimid ancestry in Sunni Mamlūk Egypt could have ruined his carefully constructed career as an *'ālim,* and even as a private citizen. Even without any solid confirmation of his Fatimid pedigree,

---

[4] Al-Maqrīzī, *Itti'āẓ*, vol. 1, pp. 52–54. The Qaddāḥid genealogy is discussed in the same section.

[5] For al-Maqrīzī's own presentation of his genealogy in the preface of his books see his *Khiṭaṭ*, vol. 1, p. 4, where he stops at his great-grandfather; *al-Sulūk li-ma'rifat duwal al-mulūk*, ed. Muḥammad Muṣṭafā Ziyāda et al. (Cairo 1934–1972), vol. 1, p. 22, and *Durar al-'uqūd al-farīda fī tarājim al-a'yān al-mufīda* (Damascus, 1995), vol. 1, p. 47, with the ten names stopping at the name of Tamīm, the father of 'Abd al-Ṣamad, who is in fact the grandson of the caliph al-Mu'izz according to al-Sakhāwī's longer chain. The same line appears in al-Maqrīzī's obituary of his grandfather 'Abd al-Qādir in *Sulūk*, vol. 2, p. 365, and of his father 'Alī in ibid., vol. 1, p. 326.

[6] Ibn Ḥajar, *al-Durar al-kāmina fī a'yān al-mi'a al-thāmina,* ed. Muḥammad 'Abd al-Ḥamīd Khān (Hyderabad, 1972), vol. 2, p. 238; Ibn Ḥajar, *Inbā'*, vol. 9, p. 172; al-Jawharī al-Ṣayrafī, *Nuzhat al-nufūs wa'l-abdān fi-tawārīkh al-zamān,* ed. Ḥasan Ḥabashī (Cairo, 1970–1989), vol. 4, p. 242, distorts the report he is copying from Ibn Ḥajar to the point of making it impossible to understand.

al-Sakhāwī, in his maliciously disparaging biography, uses the derogatory patronymic al-ʿUbaydī to mock al-Maqrīzī.[7]

Yet al-Maqrīzī seems to have admitted his Fatimid ancestry to at least some of his close friends.[8] He even approvingly volunteers a number of panegyric stanzas written to him by his neighbour and colleague Shihāb al-Dīn al-Awḥadī (d. 811/1408) in which al-Awḥadī candidly and unapologetically calls him *ʿibn al-khalāʾif* (scion of the caliphs) and a descendant of al-Muʿizz and al-Ḥākim, the first and third Fatimid caliphs in Egypt.[9] In one stanza, al-Awḥadī bluntly proclaims, 'Be proud Taqīyy al-Dīn [al- Maqrīzī] among the people of your noble Fatimid lineage. And if you cited a report on their generosity and you encountered a contestant, then trace your ancestry back to the Ḥākimī (al-Ḥākim).' These laudatory lines appear nowhere else in either al-Awḥadī's or al-Maqrīzī's various biographies.[10] In fact, al-Maqrīzī is the only one who quotes examples from al-Awḥadī's *dīwān* of poetry in his intimate biographical dictionary *Durar al-ʿuqud al-fārida fī tarājim al-aʿyān al-mufīda,* including those laudatory verses. Their citing can only be explained as an implicit admission of al-Maqrīzī's purported Fatimid pedigree, even though it is couched in someone else's words. A similar indirect confirmation of his Fatimid ancestry occurred after al-Maqrīzī's death, when Ibn Taghrībirdī, who was his student and close collaborator, reported that al-Maqrīzī's nephew recited his uncle's genealogy and brought it up to al-Muʿizz, and from him to an even more illustrious forebear, ʿAlī b. Abī Ṭālib.[11]

It is thus very plausible that al-Maqrīzī's flattering portrayal of the Fatimids and their achievements in both his *Khiṭaṭ* and his *Ittiʿāẓ* was partly animated by his belief of being their scion.[12] He, however, does not heed al-Awḥadī's exhortation to outwardly 'trace his ancestry' to the Fatimids, but takes on something almost

---

[7] Shams al-Dīn al-Sakhāwī, *al-Ḍawʾ*, vol. 2, p. 21; Shams al-Dīn al-Sakhāwī, *al-Tibr al-masbūk fī dhayl al-sulūk* (Cairo, 1896), p. 21, where he lists the ancestors up to al-Muʿizz li-Dīn Allāh.

[8] Ibn Ḥajar, *Inbāʾ*, vol. 9, p. 172; Ibn Ḥajar, *al-Durar al-kāmina,* vol. 3, p. 5; copied with an indignant remark in al-Sakhāwī, *Ḍawʾ*, vol. 2, p. 23.

[9] Al-Maqrīzī, *Durar,* vol. 1, pp. 249–250; Muḥammad Kamāl al-Dīn ʿIzz al-Dīn, *al-Maqrīzī wa Kitābuhu Durar al-ʿuqūd al-farīda fī tarājim al-aʿyān al-mufīda* (Beirut, 1992), vol. 1, p. 234.

[10] See al-Awḥadī's biographies in Ibn Ḥajar, *Inbāʾ*, vol. 6, pp. 112–113; Ibn Ḥajar, *al-Majmaʿ al-muʾassis li-l-muʿjam al-mufahris,* ed. Yūsuf ʿAbd al-Raḥmān al-Marʿashlī (Beirut, 1994), vol. 3, pp. 38–39; al-Sakhāwī, *Ḍawʾ*, vol. 1, pp. 358–359; Ibn al-ʿImād al-Ḥanbalī, *Shadharāt al-dhahab fī akhbār man dhahab* (Cairo, 1931–1932), vol. 7, pp. 89–90.

[11] Ibn Taghrībirdī, *al-Nujūm al-zāhira fī mulūk Miṣr waʾl-Qāhira*, ed. Aḥmad Ramzī (Cairo, 1930–1956), vol. 15, p. 490 and Ibn Ḥajar, *al-Majmaʿ al-muʾassis*, vol. 3, p. 59, enumerate the forefathers of al-Maqrīzī back to the eighth ancestor, ʿAbd al-Ṣamad, and say that they have copied it from al-Maqrīzī himself. Ibn Taghrībirdī then adds that al-Maqrīzī's nephew, Nāṣir al-Dīn Muḥammad, dictated his uncle's genealogy after his death and brought it up to ʿAlī b. Abī Ṭālib through the Fatimid caliphs. The same report appears in al-Jawharī al-Sayrafī, *Nuzhat,* vol. 4, p. 244.

[12] Shākir Muṣṭafā, *al-Taʾrīkh al-ʿArabī waʾl-muʾarrikhūn: dirāsa fī taṭawwur ʿilm al-taʾrīkh wa-rijāluhu fī-l-Islām* (Beirut, 1978–1993), vol. 2, p. 148, raises this possibility as well, but

as daring. He mounts a fervent defence of the authenticity of their lineage back to Fāṭima in the introduction to his *Itti'āẓ*.[13] To that end, he presents all the reports on their genealogy in detail, both those accepting of and those denying its veracity. Furthermore, he takes the added precaution of stating at the beginning of every denial he cites that he 'disagrees with it' *(bara'a*, lit. claim innocence of), a way of emphasising both his objectivity and his personal opinion.[14] He then approvingly records Ibn Khaldūn's discussion defending the authenticity of the Fatimids' genealogy, an opinion that earned Ibn Khaldūn many curses from his contemporary biographers.[15] Finally, al-Maqrīzī asks his readers 'examine the facts fairly and not be deceived by the fabrications of the Fatimids' detractors', many of whom were his detractors as well.

Al-Maqrīzī's plea to his readers to accept the Fatimid genealogy did not go unnoticed. On the margin of the page in which al-Maqrīzī reports the Imāmī traditions on the rise of the Fatimids, a remark states that 'Maqrīzī – God forgiveness be upon him – is not to blame for mounting this defence of the Fatimids because his lineage goes back to them'.[16] This comment must have been added by either the copyist or the owner of the manuscript, both of whom were 15th-century scholars who might have known al-Maqrīzī personally.[17] This was not the only contemporary or near-contemporary reference to al-Maqrīzī's Fatimid ancestry. Ibn Ḥajar almost confirms it, but refrains from doing so probably out of fear for his friend al-Maqrīzī. Instead

---

Ayman Fu'ād Sayyid, *Musawwadat kitāb al-mawā'iẓ wa'l-i'tibār fī dhikr al-khiṭaṭ wa'l-āthār* (London, 1995), Introduction, p. 45, does not seem to think that it was the case.

13 Al-Maqrīzī, *Itti'āẓ*, vol. 1, pp. 15–54, where he logically argues the truth of their lineage and lists prominent scholars, such as Ibn Khaldūn, who accepted it. Al-Maqrīzī, *Khiṭaṭ*, vol. 1, pp. 348–349, is a summary of the *Itti'āẓ*'s discussion. Another Mamlūk historian who accepts their claim is Ibn 'Abd al-Ẓāhir, *al-Rawḍa al-bāhiyya fī Khiṭaṭ al-Qāhira al-Mu'izziyya*, ed. Ayman Fu'ād Sayyid (Cairo, 1996), pp. 6–7. Other Mamlūk historians who deny their lineage include Ibn Taghrībirdī, *al-Nujūm*, vol. 4, pp. 69–112; Abū Ḥamīd al-Qudsī, *Kitāb Duwal al-Islām al-sharīfa al-bāyiha: wa-dhikr mā zahara lī min ḥikam allāh al-khāfiyya fī jalb tā'fat al-atrāk ilā al-diyār al-Miṣriyya*, ed. Ulrich Haarmann and Subhi Labib (Beirut, 1997), pp. 12–15.

14 Al-Maqrīzī, *Itti'āẓ*, vol. 1, p. 15: although he otherwise revered Ibn Ḥazm, al-Maqrīzī disagrees with his denial of the Fatimids' genealogical claim and tries to explain it as a function of it having been generated in Umayyad al-Andalus; p. 23: al-Maqrīzī rejects Ibn al-Nadīm's denial in *al-Fihrist*; p. 38: al-Maqrīzī vehemently rejects the story of Ibn Bādīs in his *Ta'rīkh Ifrīqiya wa'l-gharb*, and affixes Ibn al-Athīr's discussion in support of the Fatimids' genealogy.

15 Al-Maqrīzī, *Itti'āẓ*, vol. 1, pp. 44–52. On the cursing of Ibn Khaldūn, see Ibn Ḥajar, *Inbā'*, vol. 5, p. 331, though not in his entry in *al-Majma' al-mu'assis*, vol. 3, pp. 157–160; similar reports in al-Sakhāwī, *Ḍaw'*, vol. 4, pp. 147–148.

16 Al-Maqrīzī, *Itti'āẓ*, vol. 1, p. 54, no. 2.

17 Ibid., vol. 1, p. 31. The copyist, who copied his text from an autographed version in 884/1479, is an Azharī as his *niṣba* indicates: Muḥammad b. Aḥmad al-Gīzī al-Shāfi'ī al-Azharī. The owner seems to have been Yūsuf b. 'Abd al-Hādī, a famous Damascene scholar of the 15th century (840–909/1437–1504). On his biography, see al-Sakhāwī, *Ḍaw'*, vol. 10, p. 308; Najm al-Dīn al-Ghazzī, *al-Kawākib al-sā'ira fī a'yān al-mi'ā 'āshira*, ed. Khalīl Manṣūr (Beirut, 1997), vol. 1, p. 317; Ibn 'Abd al-Hādī, *Rasā'il Dimashqiyya*, ed. Ṣalāḥ Muḥammad al-Khiyamī (Damascus, 1988), pp. 13–17.

he calls him al-Tamīmī (the descendant of Tamīm, either the son of al-Muʿizz, i.e., al-ʿAzīz, or his great-grandson), perhaps another way of ascribing him to the Fatimids without having to state it openly.[18]

Najm al-Dīn Muḥammad Ibn Fahd, a Meccan scholar who accompanied al-Maqrīzī during his several *mujāwarāt* (long stays) in Mecca, traces his teacher's ancestry in his *Muʿjam al-shuyūkh* to ʿAlī b. Abī Ṭālib via al-Ḥusayn, his second son and the great martyr of Shiʿism, and through the Fatimid line.[19] The confirmation of al-Maqrīzī's pedigree in this case is telling, for Ibn Fahd's own lineage goes back to ʿAlī as well, though in his case through his younger son, Muḥammad (Ibn al-Ḥanafiyya).[20] Moreover, Ibn Fahd was living in Mecca away from the religious politics of Cairo and under an ʿAlid Shiʿi ruling family, the Ḥasanid Sharīfs, who flaunted the same ancestry, albeit carefully when it came to dealing with the zealously Sunni Mamlūks.[21]

Al-Maqrīzī's choice of wording for the title of his *Ittiʿāẓ al-ḥunafāʾ bi-akhbār al-aʾimma al-Fāṭimiyyīn al-khulafāʾ* itself amounts to another bold public declaration of his belief in their genuineness. In the first clause, he is inviting his readers, whom he calls *ḥunafāʾ* (sing. *ḥanīf*), to draw moral lessons (*mawāʿiẓ*) from the history of the Fatimids. His use of the term *ḥunafāʾ*, however, is motivated by more than the necessity of rhyme. It is probably intentional and significant. A *ḥanīf* in the general sense accepted in the medieval period is the true Muslim, the believer in the original and true religion, that is, someone who transcends the sectarian division that prompted the Sunnis to vehemently denigrate both the Ismaili doctrine and the genealogical claim of the Fatimids.[22] But the most significant part of the title is the second clause, since it strongly emphasises the Fatimids' privilege as both *khulafāʾ* (caliphs) and *aʾimma* (Imams) of the Islamic community, that is, the supreme leaders of the community in both the theological/judicial and institutional senses; precisely how they saw themselves and how they were believed to be by their followers.[23]

This is not the same as saying that al-Maqrīzī harboured secret doctrinal leanings towards the Ismaili doctrine of the Fatimids – he was by all accounts a solid Sunni Shāfiʿī, even prejudiced against the Ḥanafīs for their perceived leniency. None

---

18 Ibn Ḥajar, *Rafʿ al-iṣr ʿan quḍāt Miṣr*, ed. Ḥamīd ʿAbd al-Majīd and Muḥammad Abū Sinna (Cairo, 1957), vol. 1, p. 2, in a complimentary remark on his friend al-Maqrīzī in his introduction.

19 Ibn Fahd, *Muʿjam al-shuyūkh*, ed. Muḥammad al-Zāhī and Hamad al-Jāsir (Riyadh, 1982), p. 63.

20 Ibn Fahd *père*'s genealogy to ʿAlī, which appeared in al-Maqrīzī's *Durar,* is copied in al-Sakhāwī, *Ḍawʾ*, vol. 9, p. 231.

21 On the Ḥasanid Sharīfs and their long hold on Mecca, see A. J. Wensinck (C. E. Bosworth), 'Makka', *EI2*, vol. 6, pp. 148–151, and G. Rentz, 'Hāshimids', *EI2*, vol. 3, pp. 262–263.

22 On the meaning and development of the term, see W. Montgomery Watt, 'Ḥanīf', *EI2*, vol. 3, pp. 165–166.

23 On the meaning and development of the Imamate, see W. Madelung, 'Imāma', *EI2*, vol. 3, pp. 1163–1169; on the caliphate, see D. Sourdel, 'Khilāfa, the History of the Institution', and A. K. S. Lambton, 'Khilāfa, in Political Theory', *EI2*, vol. 4, pp. 937–950.

of his biographers, including the most malicious among them, accuses him of that, although they heap all sorts of petty doctrinal failings on him. The remark that al-Maqrīzī himself tacks onto his exposé of the Fatimids' dogma in his *Musawadda* (draft) of the *Khiṭaṭ* is critical in understanding the difference between believing in the Fatimids glorious pedigree and accepting their dogma. In the remark, al-Maqrīzī distances himself *(yatabarra'*, takes *barā'a)* from the Ismaili doctrine he is about to explain, as he did in reporting the accounts denigrating the Fatimids' genealogy in the *Itti'āẓ*.[24] It is curious that the same remark does not appear in the old published copy of the *Khiṭaṭ*, although the *da'wa* section is copied in its entirety from the text of the *Musawadda*.[25] This is probably due to the transformation that al-Maqrīzī underwent in the period between the draft and the final redaction of the *Khiṭaṭ*. By the latter date, which was towards the end of his life, al-Maqrīzī did not feel the need to assert the solidity of his Shāfiʿī Sunni creed since he was no longer interested in competing for public positions or patronage. The defence of the Fatimid genealogy, however, appears in both the *Musawaddāt* and the *Khiṭaṭ*, as well as in the *Itti'āẓ*, underscoring al-Maqrīzī's strong conviction in its truthfulness throughout his life.

This belief, controversial as it might seem, is consistent with al-Maqrīzī's pronounced moral rectitude, which he displayed in so many junctures throughout his life, and which culminated in his retreat to his family home at the prime age of 48, where he was to spend the rest of his long life (thirty years) studying, writing and teaching in almost total seclusion. An early manifestation of this ethical stand is his changing his Ḥanbalī *madhhab* to embrace the Shāfiʿī *madhhab* at the young age of 20, which suggests that he was consciously considering a scholarly path. Another is his sympathy towards the by then uncommon Ẓāhirī *madhhab*.[26] Practically extinct today, the Ẓāhirī *madhhab*, which never took root in Egypt and Syria, upheld a strict literalist approach to interpretation and opposed all other *madhāhib* on basic interpretive issues. [27] Al-Maqrīzī, who says nothing about his adherence to Ẓāhirism,[28]

---

24 Ayman Fu'ād Sayyid, *Musawwadat Kitab al-Mawaiz*, 'Introduction', p. 45, and p. 94 of the text.

25 Al-Maqrīzī, *Khiṭaṭ*, vol. 1, pp. 348–349, 393–395, in which the same exposé is presented.

26 Ibn Taghrībirdī, *al-Manhal al-ṣāfī wa'l-mustawfī ba'da al-wāfī*, ed. Aḥmad Najātī, Muḥammad Muḥammad Amīn et al. (Cairo, 1956–1993), vol. 1, p. 396, where he says that there is nothing wrong in admiring the writing of Ibn Ḥazm; also ibid., vol. 2, p. 88, where he accuses his revered teacher al-Maqrīzī of favouring al-Burhān simply because he was a Ẓāhirī.

27 On the Ẓāhirī school, see R. Strothmann, 'al-Ẓāhiriyya', *EI*, vol. 8, pp. 1192–1193; P. Voorhoeve, 'Dāwūd b. 'Alī b. Khalaf', *EI2*, vol. 2, pp. 182–183; R. Aenaldez, 'Ibn Ḥazm', *EI2*, vol. 3, pp. 790–799.

28 Al-Sakhāwī, *Ḍaw'*, vol. 2, p. 22, copying his master Ibn Ḥajar, *Inbā'*, vol. 9, p. 170. In this regard, al-Maqrīzī was perhaps not so different from how he described the grammarian Abū Ḥayyān al-Andalusī (1256–1344) in his *al-Muqaffa' al-kabīr: tarājim Maghribiyya wa-Mashriqiyya min al-fatrah al-'Ubaydiyya*, ed. Muḥammad al-Ya'lāwī (Beirut, 1987–1991), vol. 7, p. 505: 'He was Ẓāhirī in *madhhab*, partial to Abī Muḥammad 'Alī b. Aḥmad b. Sa'īd b. Ḥazm, leaning towards the *madhhab* of Imam al-Shāfiʿī, and he revered Taqī al-Dīn Aḥmab b. Taymiyya [the Hanbalī controversial scholar of 14th-century Damascus] and concurred with his opinion.'

seems to have been close to many Ẓāhirīs, and is full of praise for them as righteous, just, self-restrained and chaste individuals.[29]

But what seems to have truly attracted al-Maqrīzī to Ẓāhirism was what can today be termed the 'militant' spirit that some of its last followers exhibited in the face of the religiously corrupt Mamlūk regime. This spirit exploded in the so-called 'Ẓāhirī Revolt' of 1386, an uprising that greatly impressed the young al-Maqrīzī, who painted a glowing image of its leader, the rather obscure Shaykh al-Burhān, in his *Durar*.[30] Al-Burhān, who was also a shaykh to al-Maqrīzī, foolishly and tenaciously led this revolt against the Mamlūks because they did not satisfy the strict Islamic prerequisites to rule. The uprising failed and many of its organisers were caught, tortured and imprisoned.

Al-Maqrīzī's impassioned and detailed description of the Ẓāhirī revolt substantially differs from other Mamlūk historians' reports.[31] His is the only one that goes deep into its theological roots in order to justify it. His reported leaning towards the Ẓāhirīs may thus have been motivated by his respect for their fortitude as committed individuals and their opposition to the Mamlūks on religious grounds rather than his adherence to their religious interpretations.

Another possible explanation for al-Maqrīzī's passionate support of the 'Ẓāhirī' revolt may be found in his complex set of religious beliefs, which, though not uncommon at the time, may appear a bit paradoxical to our modern eyes accustomed to a visible Sunni–Shiʿi sectarian division. Al-Maqrīzī, the pious and strict Sunni *ʿālim*, seems nonetheless to have harboured ʿAlid sympathies throughout his life. What his defence of the Fatimids hints at comes across more clearly in other writings focusing on the *ahl al-bayt* (the family of the Prophet), especially his *al-Nizaʿ wa'l-takhāṣum fī mā bayna banī Umayya wa banī Hāshim* (Book of Contention and Strife Concerning

[29] See al-Maqrīzī, *Durar*, vol. 1, pp. 191, 203; ʿIzz al-Dīn, *al-Maqrīzī wa kitābuhu*, vol. 1, pp. 204–205; for the biographies of his teacher al-ʿImād al-Ḥanbalī, and the Sharīf and *muḥaddith* Abū Bakr al-Hāshimī; al-Maqrīzī, *Sulūk*, 4, vol. 2, p. 761: in the biographical notice on Badr al-Dīn Muḥammad al-Bashtakī (d. 830/1427), who was a follower of Ibn Ḥazm's *madhhab*, al-Maqrīzī says, 'I have been chagrined by his loss, he has left no one like him'. Al-Maqrīzī admired moral rectitude wherever he encountered it; see for instance his report in *Khiṭaṭ*, vol. 2, pp. 279–280, where he praises the steadfastness of the Shāfiʿī judge al-Minawwī, who betrays Ẓāhirī leanings in his discourse, in upholding what he considers to be right.

[30] Al-Maqrīzī, *Durar*, vol. 2, pp. 44–55; ʿIzz al-Dīn, *al-Maqrīzī wa kitābuhu*, vol. 2, pp. 342–347. Al-Maqrīzī, *Sulūk*, vol. 2, p. 554, offers a compact report on the revolt and in *Sulūk*, 4, vol. 1, p. 23, produces a brief obituary of al-Burhān which carries the same positive assessment.

[31] For other historians' reports see Ibn Taghrībirdī, *Manhal*, vol. 2, pp. 87–89, who says that al-Maqrīzī exaggerated in his praise of al-Burhān because he was a Ẓāhirī; Ibn Ḥajar, *Inbā'*, vol. 2, pp. 232–234; idem, *al-Majmaʿ al-mu'assis*, vol. 3, pp. 73-75; al-Sakhāwī, *Ḍaw'*, vol. 2, pp. 96–98; a reconstruction of the revolt based mostly on Ibn Qāḍī Shuhbah, *Ta'rīkh Ibn Qāḍī Shuhbah*, ed. ʿAdnān Darwīsh (Damascus, 1977–1994), vol. 1, pp. 89–91, 186–189, 269, is Lutz Wiederhold, 'Legal-Religious Elite, Temporal Authority, and the Caliphate in Mamluk Society: Conclusions Drawn from the Examination of a Zahiri Revolt in Damascus', *IJMES* 31 (May 1999), pp. 203–235, esp. 209–216. It is revealing that al-Maqrīzī, unlike Ibn Qāḍī Shuhbah, never uses the word *fitna* (sedition) in his description.

the Relations between the Umayyads and the Hashemites).[32] In this undated short work, which seems to belong to his early career, al-Maqrīzī was trying to make metahistorical sense of the apparent failure of the ʿAlids, the Banū Hāshim of his title, to keep what was their divinely ordained birthright, namely the caliphate. After analysing the circumstances of the conflict between the Umayyads and the Hashemites (both Abbasids and ʿAlids), he comes down squarely on the side of the ʿAlids. He assumes the same stance in other similar treatises where the ʿAlids are unambiguously identified as the God-appointed rulers and guides of the Islamic community.[33] This opinion might have further animated his passionate support of the 'Ẓāhirī' revolt, for its main demand was the installation of a Qurayshī caliph, though not specifically an ʿAlid one, in fulfilment of a strict interpretation of Islamic tenets.

What sets al-Maqrīzī apart from his peers is his anxious sympathy for militant movements aimed at redressing the wrong they perceived at the top of the ruling system in the Islamic world. Never mind that both causes he championed, the ʿAlid and the Ẓāhirī, were ultimately doomed to failure. What matters is that al-Maqrīzī displayed an honest sense of justice and objection to deviation from the proper Islamic ways as he knew them. This is not to say that he was personally involved in any actual political movement. Instead he confined his contention strictly to his writing. This is another sign of that same personality trait that he had exhibited since he rejected his family's *madhhab* after the death of both his father and maternal grandfather: acquiescence on the surface accompanied by quiet resistance; that is, to protest by proxy at what he perceived as unjust but did not have the audacity to actively oppose. He was not to overcome this weakness until he decided after an intense and painful soul-searching to withdraw from public life around Rabīʿ al-Awwal 816/June 1413 and to report openly and unrestrainedly the failings of his contemporary Mamlūk rulers in the harshest possible terms and with no fear of retribution. This decision marked his transformation from a scholar-client to one or other of the Mamlūk grandees to an independent, even aloof, sharp critic of his time.

---

32 First edited and translated in 1888 as al-Maqrīzī, *Kitāb al-Nizaʿ wa'l-takhāṣum fī mā bayna Banī Umayya wa Banī Hāshim, Kampfe und Streitigkeiten zwischen den Banu Umajja und den Banu Hasim; eine Abhandlung von Takijj ad-Din al-Makrizijj*, ed. Geerhardus Vos (Vienna and Strasbourg, 1888). Several Arabic re-editions followed but they did not add much. For an English translation and commentary, see *al-Maqrīzī's Book of Contention and Strife Concerning the Relations between the Banu Umayya and the Banu Hashim*, ed. and tr. Clifford Edmund Bosworth (Manchester, 1983).

33 On al-Maqrīzī's pro-ʿAlid sympathy, see C. E. Bosworth, 'al-Maqrīzī's Epistle Concerning What Has Come Down to us about the Banu Umayya and the Banu'l-ʿAbbas', in Wadād Kādī, ed., *Studia Arabica and Islamica: Festschrift for Ihsan ʿAbbas* (Beirut, 1981), pp. 39–45; C. E. Bosworth, 'al-Maqrīzī's Exposition of the Formative Period in Islamic History and its Cosmic Significance: The *Kitāb al-Nizaʿ wa'l-Takhāṣsum*', in A. T. Welsh and P. Cachia, ed., *Islam: Past Influence and Present Challenge. In Honour of William Montgomery Watt* (Edinburgh, 1979), pp. 93–104, repr. in C. E. Bosworth, *Medieval Arabic Culture and Administration* (London, 1982) as nos IX and XI respectively.

PART II
THE QUR'AN AND ITS SHI'I INTERPRETATIONS

Introduction

Meir M. Bar-Asher

From early on, the Qur'an and its exegesis have constituted a central part of Shiʿi literature. Pioneering scholars of Islam, among them Nöldeke and Goldziher, in their groundbreaking works on the Qur'an, dealt with Shiʿi exegesis and offered erudite analyses of its features. The availability of manuscripts and printed editions of Qur'an commentaries, not known to previous generations, enables contemporary scholars to offer a more variegated picture of Shiʿi exegesis. We can now point to various schools of exegesis that may be characterised by such features as their exegetical methods, their attitudes toward Sunni Islam, their reliance on material borrowed from Sunni authors and so forth. Progress in research on the Qur'an and its exegesis today allows us to adopt a more nuanced comparative approach. Our increased acquaintance with theological schools of thought will enable future research to refine and develop the study of trends in Shiʿi exegesis.

All Shiʿi groups sought to discover reference points in the Qur'an to which they could anchor their beliefs. Various beliefs and doctrines that crystallised during the early phases of Shiʿism and later changed form and substance as a result of *inter alia* polemics with rival tendencies, are presented as though they were directly formulated in the Qur'an. In this, Shiʿi exegetes are no different from their Sunni counterparts. Both Sunnis and Shiʿis believe that the Qur'an is multilayered and that any concept or outlook can, with the help of various methods of interpretation, be discovered within the Qur'anic text. In a statement ascribed to the Imam Jaʿfar al-Ṣādiq (d. 148/765), he is said to have declared that: 'Every word in the Qur'an includes seven meanings (*awjuh*) and even seventy-seven, and it is the commentator's task to reveal them.'[1] Moreover, the Qur'an is believed to contain verses that convey an obvious or at least apparent (*ẓāhir*) message as opposed to others implying an esoteric, inner (*bāṭin*) sense. This principle is believed to be expressed in the Qur'an itself, for example: 'and He has lavished on you His blessings, outward and inward' (*wa-asbagha ʿalaykum niʿamahu ẓāhiratan wa-bāṭinatan* [Q.31:20]), and 'Forsake the outward sin, and the inward' (*wa-dharū ẓāhira l-ithmi wa-bāṭinahu* [Q.6:120]). The occurrence of the opposing pair of terms *ẓāhir* versus *bāṭin* in the very text of the Qur'an

[1] Al-Qāḍī al-Nuʿmān, *Kitāb asās al-ta'wīl*, ed. ʿĀrif Tāmir (Beirut, 1960), p. 27.

is used by the exegete as an anchoring point for a fundamental exegetical principle, namely the requirement to read the text thoroughly, making a continuous attempt to discover these two dimensions hidden in it.

The four case studies included in this part deal, on the one hand, with a number of significant methodological issues which are so fundamental that any study of Shiʿi exegesis cannot avoid touching upon them; on the other hand, they contain analytical descriptions of the features and content of this exegesis. Andrew Rippin's case study raises basic questions that are the cornerstone of the issue dealt with here: what is Shiʿi exegesis, and what characterises it and distinguishes it from its Sunni counterpart? The present author, in his case study, addresses another major issue of methodology – that of authority, that is, who is authorised to interpret the words of God in the Qurʾan? As the section on authority shows, there is an immense gap between the Sunni and the Shiʿi attitudes on this issue. The two other case studies – written respectively by Mohammad Ali Amir-Moezzi and David Hollenberg – illustrate, each in its own way, the particular features of Shiʿi exegesis and survey its content. Amir-Moezzi devotes his chapter to al-Ḥusayn b. al-Ḥakam al-Ḥibarī (d. 286/899), a distinguished commentator and *ḥadīth* scholar presumably representing the early phase of Zaydī exegesis, which is essentially very similar to Imāmī Shiʿi exegesis in the pre-Būyid period. Hollenberg, in turn, focuses on early Ismaili interpretation. His concern is with the extraordinary mix that characterises the genre and the attempt to explain how it relates to the doctrines and teachings that the Ismaili missionaries intended to convey. In addition, he examines the style and function of Ismaili *taʾwīl* with the aim of resolving a specific problem in the development of Ismaili doctrine – namely, the presence of Neoplatonic material in texts in which one would not expect to find it.

The present framework does not permit a broad survey of Shiʿi exegesis. Moreover, since the essential outlines of this exegesis have been delineated in earlier studies, beginning with Goldziher's *Die Richtungen der islamischen Koransauslegung*,[2] such a survey does not seem crucial. To avoid the unnecessary repetition of statements and insights dealt with in earlier scholarship as well as in the four case studies that follow, the overview I offer here of a number of key issues will necessarily be concise. The questions posed by Rippin – what is Shiʿi *tafsīr* and how is it best defined? – are, in my view, key questions and I shall therefore start my overview with them. This will be followed by a discussion of three other issues: the question of the integrity of the Qurʾan (or, what precisely is the text to be interpreted?); the principles and methods of Shiʿi exegesis; and the nature of *tafsīr* as a genre and as used in non-exegetical sources. These three issues will be followed by a general survey of the Shiʿi exegetical corpus.

---

[2] The book was published in Leiden in 1920 and has since been translated into Arabic by ʿAbd al-Ḥalīm al-Najjār as *Madhāhib al-tafsīr al-Islāmī* (Cairo, 1374/1955), and into English by Wolfgang H. Behn as *Schools of Koranic Commentaries* (Wiesbaden, 2006).

What is *Tafsīr* and How is Shiʿi *Tafsīr* Defined?

Andrew Rippin opens his case study with a series of questions: what qualifies a work to be called a Shiʿi *tafsīr* rather than something else? How 'Shiʿi' must it be to warrant being described as such? How do we know which works should be included in the category 'Shiʿi'? Is Shiʿi *tafsīr* a unified category? Do the works fit within a definition of the *tafsīr* genre or should they be marked off as a separate subcategory within the overall genre? How best can we incorporate Shiʿi *tafsīr* within the history of the genre? These are indeed essential questions, and they must be the basis of any discussion of the nature of Shiʿi exegesis. They can be further supplemented by a few other questions, for example: what distinguishes the exegesis of one Shiʿi faction from that of another? To what extent is the exegesis offered by a commentator of a certain Shiʿi faction of the same kind as that of another commentator belonging to the same faction? It seems that although one can offer answers to all these questions, the answers are by no means clear-cut or decisive. They vary according to the period or the commentator. By way of illustration, Goldziher considered the sectarian stance as the most distinctive feature of Shiʿi exegesis.[3] He is undoubtedly right in the case of early Imāmī Shiʿi exegesis, that is, pre-Būyid, and one can now add that his conclusion is also valid as regards early Ismaili exegesis of the same period – that is, up to the mid-4th/10th century. The Imāmī Shiʿi exegesis of later periods, that is, mainly that composed in the period that begins with the Būyids and which reaches its peak with the monumental *al-Tibyān fī tafsīr al-Qurʾān* by Abū Jaʿfar al-Ṭūsī (d. 460/1067), manifests, however, a new trend in exegesis in which the sectarian voice is toned down. Moreover, the resemblance of this exegesis to its Sunni counterpart is remarkable. Mahmoud Ayoub, whose article on Shiʿi *tafsīr* is cited by Rippin, attests to the diversity of the early Shiʿi exegesis and offers a periodisation of this exegesis.[4] The Shiʿi (mainly Imāmī Shiʿi) exegetical corpus, substantial parts of which have become available in the last few decades but which was inaccessible to the prominent scholars of the 19th and early 20th centuries, makes possible a more nuanced description and analysis than that offered by them.

Since I have expressed my views on this issue in detail in earlier studies, I will delineate them here only briefly. In attempting to characterise the major features of early Shiʿi exegesis – bearing in mind the kind of questions evoked by Rippin – I coined the term 'pre-Būyid school of exegesis' and suggested four criteria by which this school could be defined, as opposed both to later Shiʿi exegesis and to its Sunni counterpart. It seems to me that these features faithfully describe not only pre-Būyid exegesis but partially (i.e., features (b) and (d) below) also Ismaili exegesis of the

[3] This can be seen even from the title given to the chapter in which Shiʿi exegesis is discussed. It is entitled 'Sekterische Koranauslegung' (pp. 263–309 of the German edition), 'The Sectarian Interpretation of the Koran' (pp. 167–196 of the English translation).

[4] Mahmoud Ayoub, 'The Speaking Qurʾān and the Silent Qurʾān: A Study of the Principles and Development of Imāmī-Shiʿi *Tafsīr*', in Andrew Rippin, ed., *Approaches to the History of the Text of the Qurʾān* (Oxford, 1988), pp. 177–198.

corresponding period. These features are: (a) interpretation by means of *ḥadīth*; (b) selective concern with the text of the Qurʾan – that is, putting an emphasis mainly on verses with potential Shiʿi reference; (c) scant interest in theological issues (among Shiʿi doctrinal issues, mainly *walāya* and *barāʾa* draw significant attention); (d) an anti-Sunni stance and a hostile attitude to leading Companions of the Prophet.[5]

One may rightly claim that the first two characteristics are also present in early Sunni exegesis; such Qurʾan commentaries as those of Mujāhid (d. 104/723) or ʿAbd al-Razzāq (d. 211/826) are based almost entirely on *ḥadīth*. The second characteristic is also not exclusive to early Imāmī Shiʿi exegesis. However, the presence of all four characteristics in the same composition imparts a unique character that indisputably qualifies pre-Būyid Imāmī Shiʿi Qurʾan exegesis as a school in its own right. Later, beginning with Abū Jaʿfar al-Ṭūsī, a shift in the attitude of Imāmī Shiʿi exegesis becomes evident.[6] The exegesis of this period can be characterised as being more independent and more ambivalent about the use of *ḥadīth*. This can be clearly seen both in the marginal position of *ḥadīth*s in commentaries of this period and in the omission or abbreviation of the chains of transmitters (*isnād*s). The commentators who represent the new trend of Imāmī Shiʿi exegesis are ambivalent in their approach to Sunni Islam in general and to the generation of the Companions of the Prophet in particular. Theirs is a middle road. They have reservations about blatant criticism of the Companions of the Prophet and are careful not to detract from the images of the first three caliphs in the manner of their pre-Būyid predecessors.[7] All the characteristics used here as criteria for distinguishing between two major periods in the history of Shiʿism place the emphasis mainly, as Rippin has rightly noted, on points of content. Amir-Moezzi in his chapter on al-Ḥibarī, in line with his previous studies on early Shiʿism, stresses other dimensions that distinguish the pre-Būyid from the Būyid and post-Būyid periods. The earliest phase, that is the pre-Būyid phase, is marked, according to him, by its esoteric, mystical and magic dimensions. One might add that these features clearly also characterise the Ismaili interpretation of the equivalent period, such as *Kitāb al-kashf*, attributed to Jaʿfar b. Manṣūr al-Yaman (d. ca. 347/957), one of the leading disseminators of Ismaili-Fatimid *daʿwa*. These dimensions are abundantly present in both exegetical and non-exegetical works of this period, but they gradually disappear from writings post-dating the Būyid period. It is noteworthy that later in the history of Imāmī Shiʿism the ancient phase, with its markedly sectarian, isolationist and anti-Sunni elements that characterise the pre-Būyid period, re-emerges in the writings of leading authorities of the Ṣafawid period.[8]

---

[5] M. M. Bar-Asher, *Scripture and Exegesis in Early Imāmī Shiism* (Jerusalem and Leiden, 1999), pp. 71–86.

[6] Other explanations for this shift are offered by Amir-Moezzi, 'The *Tafsīr* of al-Ḥibarī (d. 286/899): Qurʾanic Exegesis and Early Shiʿi Esotericism' (English translation in Chapter 5 of this volume). References below are to the English version.

[7] For the details, see Bar-Asher, *Scripture and Exegesis*, pp. 84–86.

[8] For the names of the major exegetes of this period, see final section below.

The Question of the Integrity of the Qur'an (or, What is the Genuine Text to be Interpreted?)

A major bone of contention between Sunni and Shiʿi Islam concerns the integrity of the Qur'an. The Shiʿa disputed the canonical validity of the ʿUthmānic codex, the *textus receptus*, of the Qur'an and cast doubt on the quality of its editing, alleging political tendentiousness on the part of the editors – namely, the first three caliphs, particularly ʿUthmān b. ʿAffān (r. 23–35/644–656). Shiʿi (mainly Imāmī) criticism of the Qur'anic text was most severe in the first centuries of Islam. The editors were accused of falsification (*taḥrīf*) of the Qur'anic text both by the omission of some phrases and by the addition of others. Moreover, the claim that the Qur'an has been falsified is one of the principal arguments to which early Shiʿi – that is, mainly pre-Būyid – tradition resorted to explain the absence of any explicit reference to the Shiʿa in the Qur'an. In Shiʿi Qur'anic commentaries, many traditions are found accusing the Companions of the Prophet of violating the integrity of the Qur'anic text. In one of these traditions, cited in the commentary ascribed to the Imam Ḥasan al-ʿAskarī (d. 260/873–874), it is stated that 'those whose ambitions became their wisdom (i.e., the *ṣaḥāba*) falsified (*ḥarrafū*) the true meaning of God's Book and altered it (*wa-ghayyarūhu*)'.[9] A treasure trove of such traditions is *Kitāb al-qirāʾāt* (also known as *Kitāb al-tanzīl wa'l-taḥrīf*) by Aḥmad b. Muḥammad al-Sayyārī (fl. late 3rd/9th century), an annotated edition of which by E. Kohlberg and M. A. Amir-Moezzi is now available.[10]

It is noteworthy that the commentators do not attempt to validate their general claim with examples of texts that, in their opinion, have been altered. Just how unspecific these traditions are can be demonstrated by an account ascribed to Jaʿfar al-Ṣādiq, cited in relation to verse Q.2:279: 'On leaving the house of the [caliph] ʿUthmān, ʿAbdallāh b. ʿAmr b. al-ʿĀṣ met the Commander of the Faithful [ʿAlī] and said to him "O ʿAlī, we have spent the night on a matter with which we hope God will strengthen this community", ʿAlī answered: "I know how you spent the night: you falsified, altered and changed (*ḥarraftum wa-ghayyartum wa-baddaltum*) nine hundred words … falsified three hundred words, changed three hundred words and altered three hundred words."' ʿAlī then added this verse, Q.2:279: 'Woe to those who write the Book with their hands and then say, "this is from God" (*fa-waylun li-lladhīna yaktubūna al-kitāba bi-aydīhim thumma yaqūlūna hādhā min ʿindi*

[9] *Tafsīr al-ʿAskarī*, attributed to the Imam al-Ḥasan al-ʿAskarī (Qumm, 1409/1988), p. 95; E. Kohlberg, 'Some Notes on the Imāmite Attitude to the Qur'ān', in S. M. Stern et al., *Islamic Philosophy and the Classical Tradition: Essays Presented to Richard Walzer* (Oxford, 1972), pp. 209–224, at p. 212 and note 37.

[10] E. Kohlberg and M. A. Amir-Moezzi, *Revelation and Falsification: The Kitāb al-qirāʾāt of Aḥmad b. Muḥammad al-Sayyārī. Critical Edition with an Introduction and Notes* (Leiden, 2009).

llāhi).'[11] It is obvious that the numbers are not to be taken at face value, just as the three different verbs used to describe the editorial activity (*ḥarrafa*, *ghayyara* and *baddala*) in no way indicate discrete falsification techniques.

Numerous Shiʿi utterances refer to the nature of the original text of the Qur'an prior to its alleged corruption by the Sunnis. In a well-known tradition, which appears in the writings of most early Shiʿi commentators, Imam Muḥammad al-Bāqir declares: 'The Qur'an was revealed [consisting of] four parts: One part concerning us [the Shiʿa], one part concerning our enemies, one part commandments and regulations (*farā'iḍ wa-aḥkām*), and one part customs and parables (*sunan wa-amthāl*). And the exalted parts of the Qur'an refer to us (*wa-lanā karā'im al-Qur'ān*).'[12]

Other accounts refer to the length of the original Qur'an. It is believed to have contained 17,000 verses.[13] *Sūra* 33 (*al-Aḥzāb*) is often given as an example of a text that in the original Qur'an was two and two-thirds longer than *Sūra* 2 (*al-Baqara*),[14] which in turn was longer than the version in the 'Uthmānic codex.[15] A major concern of Shiʿi hermeneutical tradition was the identification of those parts of the Qur'an which were allegedly revealed concerning the family of the Prophet. Of extraordinary significance is the decipherment of names of persons referring to Shiʿi Islam or to its enemies who are believed to be alluded to in the Qur'an, for 'knowing the names of [these] persons is the religion of God (*maʿrifat al-rijāl dīn allāh*)', as we are told in a number of utterances attributed to the Imams.[16] The discrepancy between the Qur'anic text and the Shiʿi viewpoint is not necessarily one that a 'correct' interpretation can remedy. This discrepancy results from a textual gap between the incomplete Qur'anic text found in the possession of the Sunnis and the ideal text that, according to the Shiʿi belief, is no longer in anyone's possession but will be revealed by the Mahdī in the eschatological era.

Beginning in the Būyid period, here again in the wake of the political and social changes that Imāmī Shiʿism underwent, a tendency to moderation became apparent, and some of the criticism became muted. Leading Imāmī Shiʿi scholars, such as Muḥammad b. Muḥammad b. al-Nuʿmān, better known as al-Shaykh al-Mufīd (d. 413/1022), al-Sharīf al-Murtaḍā (d. 436/1044), Abū Jaʿfar al-Ṭūsī and – a century later – Abū ʿAlī al-Ṭabrisī (d. 548/1153), held the view that although the text of the

---

[11] Abu'l-Naḍr Muḥammad b. Masʿūd al-ʿAyyāshī (d. beginning of the 4th/10th century), *Tafsīr al-ʿAyyāshī*, ed. Hāshim al-Rasūlī al-Maḥallātī (Qumm, 1380/1960), vol. 1, pp. 47–48, tradition 62.

[12] *Tafsīr al-ʿAyyāshī*, vol. 1, p. 9, tradition 3, where a tripartite division is suggested. See also Kohlberg and Amir-Moezzi, *Revelation and Falsification*, p. 8, tradition 11 (the Arabic text) and p. 59, note 11 (of the English section).

[13] Ibid., p. 9, tradition 16 (the Arabic text) and pp. 61–62, note 16 (the English section).

[14] Ibid., p. 109, tradition 418 (the Arabic text) and pp. 198–199, note 418 (the English section).

[15] Ibid., p. 110, tradition 421 (the Arabic text) and p. 200, note 421 (the English section).

[16] See al-Ṣaffār al-Qummī, *Baṣā'ir al-darajāt* (Tabriz, 1380/1960), p. 526; Amir-Moezzi, 'The *Tafsīr* of al-Ḥibarī', Chapter 5.

Qur'an as we have it is incomplete, it does not contain any falsification. In other words, what is found in the 'Uthmānic codex is the truth, but not the whole truth, since it does not include all that was revealed to Muḥammad. As demonstrated by Etan Kohlberg, recurring changes took place throughout the history of Imāmī Shi'ism in its attitude regarding the question of the integrity of the Qur'an.[17] This process of change can be likened to the swing of a pendulum: in early Shi'ism, up to the mid-4th/10th century, Imāmī Shi'is maintained a very radical view; later – that is, in the Būyid period – a much more moderate view became prevalent; then, 'with the re-emergence during the Ṣafawid period of the Akhbāriyyūn, who set great store by individual traditions, the question of the attitude to the 'Uthmānic codex was revived'.[18] The dominant view in this period was a rejection of the *taḥrīf* theory. Yet some leading scholars of the late Ṣafawid period – such as Muḥammad Ṣāliḥ al-Māzandarānī in his commentary on al-Kulaynī's (d. 328/939–940 or 329/940–941) *Uṣūl min al-Kāfī*, Hāshim al-Baḥrānī in his *al-Burhān fī tafsīr al-Qur'ān* and Ni'mat Allāh al-Jazā'irī (d. 1112/1700) in his *al-Anwār al-nu'māniyya* – reverted to the views of pre-Būyid Imāmī scholars, accusing the Companions of the Prophet of falsifying the Qur'anic text.[19] The most radical representative of the falsification theory in modern times is al-Ḥusayn b. Muḥammad Taqī al-Nūrī al-Ṭabrisī (d. 1320/1905). A recurrent tradition, on which Nūrī bases his argument in favour of *taḥrīf*, draws an analogy between the Shi'is and the Jews. 'Just as the Jews and the Christians altered and falsified the Book of their prophet [*sic*!] after him, this community [i.e., the Muslims] shall alter and falsify the Qur'an after our Prophet – may God bless him and his family – for everything that happened to the Children of Israel is bound to happen to this community.'[20] It should be stressed, however, that Nūrī's extreme anti-Sunni tone was criticised even by the Shi'i scholars of his day. Nonetheless, the question of *taḥrīf* never ceased to be a burning issue in Shi'i-Sunni discourse, to the point that 'there is hardly a new book on the general subject of the Qur'anic sciences whose author can afford not to include a chapter dealing with *taḥrīf*.[21]

---

17 On the various positions taken by Imāmī Shi'is on this question, see Kohlberg, 'Some Notes on the Imāmite Attitude to the Qur'ān'.

18 Ibid., p. 217. See also Amir-Moezzi, 'The *Tafsīr* of al-Ḥibarī', Chapter 5.

19 Kohlberg and Amir-Moezzi, *Revelation and Falsification*, p. 28.

20 Al-Ḥusayn b. Muḥammad Taqī al-Nūrī al-Ṭabrisī, *al-Faṣl al-khiṭāb fī taḥrīf kitāb rabb al-arbāb* ([Tehran], 1298/1881 (litho.)), p. 35; see also R. Brunner, 'The Dispute about the Falsification of the Qur'ān between Sunnis and Shi'is in the Twentieth Century', in Stefan Leder et al., ed., *Studies in Arabic and Islam: Proceedings of the 19th Congress, Union Europeénne des Arabisants et Islamisants [Halle 1998]* (Leuven and Paris, 2002), pp. 437–446, at p. 439.

21 See Brunner, 'The Dispute', p. 445. The *taḥrīf* problem in modern times, with special emphasis on al-Nūrī al-Ṭabrisī's views, is extensively analysed by R. Brunner in his *Die Schia und die Koranfälschung* (Würzburg, 2001), especially pp. 39–69.

Principles and Methods of Shiʿi Exegesis

The methods of interpretation used by Shiʿi exegetes are much like those used by the Sunnis. These methods range widely and include, on the one hand, such textual interpretation as variant readings, lexical interpretation and grammatical commentary; and, on the other hand, contextual interpretation. The latter includes widespread use of traditions about the circumstances of the revelation of particular verses (*asbāb al-nuzūl*) and application of the *naskh* (abrogation) principle, as well as allegorical and typological interpretations.

Shiʿi exegetes, perhaps even more than their Sunni counterparts, support their distinctive views by referring to Qur'anic proof-texts. A major distinction is that the Shiʿi exegetes attempt to find in the Qur'an explicit references to such themes as the Imams' supernatural and mystical qualities, their authority to interpret the Qur'an and other religious scriptures, or such major Shiʿi doctrines as the immunity of the Imams from sins and errors (*ʿiṣma*) and the privilege of intercession (*shafāʿa*) on behalf of their community with which they were endowed.

More than any other branch of Islam, the Shiʿa in general and the Ismailis in particular allot a central role to esoteric writing. This style of writing is characterised by reliance on allegorical-typological interpretation, as well as by the use of cryptography and other encoding techniques. In the words of Henry Corbin, one of the leading scholars of Shiʿism in the 20th century, Shiʿism is 'the shrine of esotericism in Islam' (le sanctuaire de l'ésoterisme de l'Islam).[22] Another accurate and eloquent definition of the nature of Shiʿi exegesis is Amir-Moezzi's assertion that since its earliest days Shiʿism has defined itself as a 'hermeneutical doctrine'.[23]

In Shiʿism (as well as in various religious groups outside Islam), the penchant for esoteric writing stems from two major factors. The first is the notion of the group's supremacy and religious exclusivity. The group believes itself to be the holder of supreme religious truths – truths that should not be shared with everyone; even members of the group should learn these truths gradually and only after having made progress in the hierarchy of religious knowledge. This inner circle of secrecy is central to the Ismaili distinction between the chosen ones (*khāṣṣa*) and the common people (*ʿāmma*). A similar distinction exists in other groups with connections to Ismailism – for example, the Druze, with whom such connections are direct, and the Nuṣayrīs, with whom they are indirect.

The use of such techniques may provide spiritual meaning to the life of esoteric sectarian groups. As Hollenberg cogently puts it, following Samuel Thomas's monograph on the writings of the Qumran sects: 'esoteric literature … provides the community with the sense of a hidden, secret truth and reality reserved only to a

---

22 H. Corbin, *En Islam Iranien: Aspects spirituels et philosophiques* (Paris, 1971–1972), vol. 1, p. xiv, whence D. de Smet, '*Zahir* et *bāṭin*', in J. Servier, ed., *Dictionnaire de l'ésotérisme* (Paris, 1998), pp. 1387–1392.

23 Amir-Moezzi, 'The *Tafsīr* of al-Ḥibarī', Chapter 5.

select group of initiates. This creates a new and different reality, a "second world" in which the community members experience an alternative to the manifest world. Access to this alternative world is achieved through a radical transformation of the acolyte, a dramatic experience of receiving the hidden knowledge.'[24]

Sometimes the use of esoteric techniques derives from an existential necessity. Religious and ideological minorities may find themselves in danger as a consequence of the overt and careless expression of ideas unpalatable to the ruling majority. And indeed, many Shiʿi factions throughout history which flourished under Sunni rule required the use of survival techniques both in everyday life and when committing their religious doctrines to writing. Shiʿi scholars of all factions had to walk a fine line: on the one hand, they wished whenever possible to give expression to their views; on the other hand, they had to ascertain that the expression of such ideas did not arouse the wrath of their Sunni opponents. These two factors combined constitute the essence of the doctrine of *taqiyya* (caution) and *kitmān* (secrecy).

An illustration of the allegorical approach (*taʾwīl*) of Shiʿi Qurʾan exegesis may be seen in the interpretation of the Night Journey of Muḥammad, which, according to Muslim exegetical tradition, is referred to in the first verse of *sūra* 17 (*sūrat al-isrāʾ*). Although aware of the conventional understanding of this verse as referring to the actual journey during which the Prophet was borne from Mecca to Jerusalem, Ismaili as well as Nuṣayrī authors interpreted this passage as a symbol of the spiritual progress of the Imams or other persons within the divine realm.[25]

The Ismailis tend to employ allegory, *inter alia*, to interpret Muslim law. Thus, for example, 'the pillars of Islam' are given symbolic meanings in Ismaili writings: the five obligatory prayers correspond to the five divine ranks (*ḥudūd*) in the Ismaili hierarchical system; almsgiving (*zakāt*) means that those with knowledge should provide reliable mentors to guide the people; fasting (*ṣawm*) entails observing silence and not betraying religious secrets to the uninitiated; pilgrimage to Mecca (*ḥajj*) means paying a visit to the Imam – the manifestation of the house of God – since divine knowledge resides with him.[26] It is worth mentioning that this tendency, prevalent in Ismailism, is shared by certain other groups such as the Nuṣayrīs and the Druze. However, a significant difference should be noted. Moderate allegorists – for example Imāmī Shiʿis and most Ismailis – maintained that the allegorical interpretation that

24 See D. Hollenberg's chapter in this volume, 'The Empire Writes Back: Fatimid Ismaili *Taʾwīl* (Allegoresis) and the Mysteries of the Ancient Greeks', referring to S. I. Thomas, *The 'Mysteries' of Qumran: Mystery, Secrecy, and Esotericism in the Dead Sea Scrolls* (Atlanta, 2009).

25 For the Ismaili approach, see al-Qāḍī al-Nuʿmān, *Asās al-taʾwīl*, p. 337; for the Nuṣayrī interpretation, see the epistle of the Nuṣayrī author Abū ʿAbd Allāh al-Ḥusayn b. Hārūn al-Ṣāʾigh (fl. 4th/10th century) in M. M. Bar-Asher and A. Kofsky, *The Nuṣayrī-ʿAlawī Religion: An Enquiry into its Theology and Liturgy* (Leiden, 2002), pp. 89–97.

26 See I. K. Poonawala, 'Ismāʿīlī *Taʾwīl* of the Qurʾān', in A. Rippin, ed., *Approaches to the History of the Interpretation of the Qurʾān* (Oxford, 1988), pp, 199–222, at p. 218, referring to the *Kitāb al-iftikhār* by Abū Yaʿqūb al-Sijistānī (d. after 361/971), ed. I. K. Poonawala (Beirut, 2000), pp. 240–263.

extracts the true meaning of the Qurʾan does not aim to invalidate the plain meaning of the text.[27] But 'heterodox' groups, in contrast, often held that allegory was the only correct interpretation and thus belittled and even ignored the apparent sense of the texts. This distinction was especially striking with regard to legal matters. Consistent allegorical interpretation led its practitioners, more often than not, to adopt antinomian attitudes towards the religious precepts of the Qurʾan, and once a law assumed a symbolic meaning its literal meaning, according to these circles, was no longer binding. An explicitly antinomian interpretation of the pillars of Islam is included in the sixth epistle of the Druze canon entitled *al-Kitāb al-maʿrūf bi-l-naqḍ al-khafī* (the book known as 'the hidden destruction [of religion]').[28]

Esoteric language in Shiʿi exegesis is evident on two levels. The first level, the exegetes believe, is found in the Qurʾan itself; it underlines such obscure or general Qurʾanic expressions as *al-jibt waʾl-ṭāghūt* (demon and idols), *al-faḥshāʾ waʾl-munkar* (indecency and dishonour), *al-maghḍūb ʿalayhim* (those who earn [God's] anger) and *al-ẓālimūna* (evildoers), which refer to various enemies of the Shiʿa. The second level is that of the exegetical tradition itself. The commentator never claims explicitly that pair-expressions, such as those in the first two examples just mentioned, refer to Abū Bakr and ʿUmar, as well as to other enemies of the Shiʿa; rather he resorts to such code words as 'the first' (*al-awwal*) and 'the second' (*al-thānī*); *ḥabtar* (fox) is usually applied to Abū Bakr, while *zurayq* ('the blue-eyed' or 'shiny-eyed') refers to ʿUmar.[29] In other words, the transition from the covert stratum in the Qurʾan to the overt stratum of the interpretation is not direct but undergoes a further process of encoding. The underlying assumption is that Shiʿis are familiar with these code words which are an integral part of their religious-cultural upbringing.

Another central feature of early Shiʿi exegesis is the use of variant readings (*qirāʾāt*) of the Qurʾanic text or, in certain cases, the addition of words believed to have been omitted from it. Examples of these alterations are the common textual substitution of *aʾimma* (Imams) for *umma* (nation or community), or slight changes to the word 'Imam' itself. The implication of these variants is that the institution of the imamate

---

27 See, e.g., Bar-Asher, *Scripture and Exegesis*, pp. 122–124; M. Bar-Asher, 'Outlines of Early Ismāʿīlī-Faṭimid Qurʾān Exegesis', *Journal Asiatique*, 296 (2008), pp. 257–296, at pp. 268–272.

28 For an annotated edition of the text, see *Les Epîtres sacrées des Druzes (Rasaʾil al-ḥikma)*, ed. D. de Smet (Leuven, 2007), pp. 483–498 (the Arabic text), pp. 158–179 (the French annotated translation). See also S. de Sacy, *Exposé des la religion des Druzes* (Paris, 1838), vol. 2; D. R. W. Bryer, 'The Origins of the Druze Religion: An Edition of Hamza's Writings and Analysis of his Doctrine' (D.Phil. dissertation, University of Oxford, 1971), vol. 2, pp. 31–50.

29 For these and a plethora of derogatory appellations, see I. Goldziher, 'Spottnamen der ersten Chalifen bei den Schiʿiten', in I. Goldziher, *Gesammelte Schriften*, ed. J. Desomogyi (Hildesheim, 1967–1976), vol. 4, pp. 295–308; E. Kohlberg, 'Some Imāmī Shiʿi Views on the *ṣaḥāba*', *JSAI*, 5 (1984), pp. 143–175, repr. in Etan Kohlberg, *Belief and Law in Imāmī Shīʿism* (Aldershot, 1991), pp. 143–175, at pp. 160–167; Bar-Asher, *Scripture and Exegesis*, pp. 113–120. See also the numerous examples in the texts cited by Amir-Moezzi, 'The *Tafsīr* of al-Ḥibarī', Chapter 5.

and other principles associated with it originate in the Qur'an.[30] Such textual alterations are based not only on the assumption that the Qur'anic text is flawed and incomplete but also on the belief that the Qur'an itself, in its original version, is an encoded text. The Imams are thus needed to serve as hermeneutical guides introducing their initiated disciples into its secrets.[31] Scholars who held the view that the Qur'an is corrupt believed that in the eschatological era the true text will be revealed and the original intention of the Holy Scripture will then be uncovered.

It should be noted, however, that variant readings play an important role mainly in early Imāmī Shi'i exegesis. In later periods in the development of this faction, as well as in other Shi'i factions, the emphasis is put on other aspects of the Qur'anic text. When dealing with Ismaili *ta'wīl*, Hollenberg rightly stresses that in their endeavour to interpret the Qur'an, Ismaili missionaries often understand the Qur'anic text based on the similarity of a sound or a keyword, and this does not require them to master variant readings or any other field of knowledge crucial for the exegetes of the Qur'an.[32]

Other methods of Shi'i exegesis are based on word and letter order, and on calculations of the numerical value of letters. In his interpretation of *sūra* 108 (*al-Kawthar*), Abū Ya'qūb al-Sijistānī presents a transposition of the words and letters of the *sūra*, thus reading into it the Shi'i tenet of *wiṣāya*, the rank of succession among the Imams.[33] The technique of numerical calculation of letters is primarily applied to the mysterious letters (*fawātiḥ al-suwar*) appearing at the head of 29 *sūras*. For example, the letters *alif*, *lām*, *mīm* and *ṣād* (the total numerical value of which is 161) at the head of *sūra* 7 (*al-a'rāf*) allude, according to an account attributed to the Imam al-Bāqir, to the year 161 of the *hijrī* calendar (AD 777) which, it had been predicted (incorrectly as it turned out), would be the year of the fall of the Umayyad dynasty.[34]

Finally, it should be noted that Shi'i, and particularly Ismaili, exegesis is characterised by the use of a secret script designed to encrypt information – mainly names of persons – that the author wishes to conceal for precautionary reasons. Numerous examples of this practice are found in the *Kitāb al-kashf* of Ja'far b. Manṣūr al-Yaman and in the *Mizāj al-tasnīm* of the Yemeni *dā'ī* Ismā'īl b. Hibat Allāh (d. 1184/1770).[35]

---

[30] For the place of variant readings in Shi'i exegesis, see Kohlberg and Amir-Moezzi, *Revelation and Falsification*; M. M. Bar-Asher, 'Variant Readings and Additions of the Imāmī-Šī'a to the Qurān', *Israel Oriental Studies*, 13 (1993), pp. 39–74; repr. in Ibn Warraq (=G. Giorgione), ed., *Which Koran? Variants, Manuscripts, Linguistics* (New York, 2011), pp. 575–612.

[31] Amir-Moezzi, 'The *Tafsīr* of al-Ḥibarī', Chapter 5.

[32] See Hollenberg, 'Fatimid Ismaili *Ta'wīl*', Chapter 6.

[33] For this hermeneutical technique, see Bar-Asher, 'Outlines of Early Ismā'īlī-Faṭimid Qur'ān Exegesis', pp. 289–291. See also Hollenberg, 'Fatimid Ismaili *Ta'wīl*', Chapter 6,.

[34] See *Tafsīr al-'Ayyāshī*, vol. 2, pp. 7–8, traditions 2 and 3.

[35] For further details, see Bar-Asher, 'Outlines of Early Ismā'īlī-Faṭimid Qur'ān Exegesis', pp. 287–289.

Tafsīr as a Genre and *Tafsīr* as Used in Non-exegetical Sources

Shiʿi Qurʾan exegesis, especially that of the Imāmī and Zaydī factions, is of three types: (a) exegetical compositions par excellence which are of two kinds: first, comprehensive commentaries, in which the entire text of the Qurʾan is interpreted verse-by-verse; second, commentaries that focus exclusively on Shiʿi topics and usually pass in silence over verses that are not of particular Shiʿi interest; (b) small treatises dedicated to commentary on a certain *sūra* or a number of *sūras*;[36] (c) non-exegetical compositions covering various genres of religious literature. In these works, be they doctrinal, legal, historical or other, Qurʾanic passages are employed either as mere illustrations for authors to employ in their argumentation or, at times, as the axis around which the whole discussion revolves. For example, early Imāmī *ḥadīth* compositions are replete with exegetical material. Examples are *Baṣāʾir al-darajāt* of Abū Jaʿfar Muḥammad al-Ṣaffār al-Qummī (d. 290/902–903), which is a doctrinal work in the form of traditions transmitted in the names of the Imams or *al-Kāfī*, the monumental Imāmī *ḥadīth* compilation by al-Kulaynī. Similar to these is *Asās al-taʾwīl* by al-Qāḍī al-Nuʿmān (d. 363/974). Though its title alludes to its being an exegetical composition, it is in fact a doctrinal work focusing on the role of prophets and Imams in Ismaili belief. Elaboration of the concepts revolves around hundreds of Qurʾanic verses, and the entire work can undoubtedly be employed as a basis for delineating the methods and content of Ismaili hermeneutics.

The feature that marks the distinction between Imāmī and Zaydī exegesis on the one hand and Ismaili exegesis on the other hand is the complete absence in Ismailism of comprehensive, verse-by-verse commentaries. The reasons for the discrepancy between the relatively abundant Qur'an-related materials in Ismaili writings and the absence of comprehensive commentaries become clearer when viewed in the light of some of the basic principles of the Ismailis. The possible explanations for this discrepancy are twofold: (1) Given the continuing active and ever-present existence of the Imam and the institution of the imamate (unlike Imāmī Shiʿism with its belief in a hidden Imam, some of whose authority was in due course delegated to the *ʿulamāʾ*), the Imam is an authority always accessible to interpret the words of God to the believers, thus reducing the need for systematic, written exegesis; (2) A distinction is drawn between interpretation of the esoteric and the exoteric – a distinction that is important as the principle upon which Ismaili literature in general and Ismaili Qur'an exegesis in particular are based. Ismaili Qur'an exegesis, entrusted to the Imams or to their preachers (*duʿāt*), deals mainly with revealing the inner, hidden meaning of the Qur'an. The exegete is not required to interpret those parts of the Qur'an that can be understood literally. In other words, since large parts of the Qurʾan do not require esoteric interpretation, no comprehensive and systematic commentaries are needed for them; believers can make use of existing commentaries, even if they were composed by non-Ismailis. Striving to reach *taʾwīl* (the achievement of

36 Ibid., pp. 263–264.

inner meaning by way of typological or allegoric–symbolic interpretation), however, is considered prestigious and valuable. This point of view is explicitly expressed in al-Qāḍī al-Nuʿmān's words: 'We have put aside the visible because its visibility suffices us and because most people know it (*wa-taraknā al-ẓāhir iktifāʾan minnā bi-ẓuhūrihi wa-maʿrifat akthar al-nās bihi*).'[37]

Finally, it is worthwhile considering the place of the Qur'an among 'heterodox' groups that emerged within Shiʿism or had some affinity to it. Good examples are the Nuṣayrī-ʿAlawīs and the Druze, followers of the two independent religions that were initially 'heterodox' groups. The Qur'an holds a major place in their writings: one can hardly come across a page in the holy writings of these religions that does not contain a Qur'anic citation. These passages are often given fascinating esoteric interpretations in line with the doctrinal concepts of the particular religion. The fact that the Qur'an does not play a major role in the ritual life of their believers seems to have contributed to its relative marginalisation and explains the lack of interest in composing systematic commentaries on it.

Major Shiʿi Exegetes and their Works

The earliest Shiʿi Qur'an commentaries known to us date from the end of the 3rd/9th century. These include the works of Furāt b. Ibrāhīm al-Kūfī (d. *ca.* 3rd/9th century), *Tafsīr Furāt al-Kūfī* (Najaf, 1354/1935; new edition M. Kāẓim, Tehran, 1410/1990), ʿAlī b. Ibrāhīm al-Qummī (d. *ca.* 307/919), *Tafsīr al-Qummī* (ed. al-Ṭayyib al-Jazāʾirī, Najaf, ah 1386–1387) and Abu'l-Naḍr Muḥammad b. Masʿūd al-ʿAyyāshī (d. early 4th/10th century), *Tafsīr al-ʿAyyāshī* (ed. H. al-Rasūlī al-Maḥallātī, Qumm, ah 1380), all of whom flourished in the last decades of the 3rd/9th century and the beginning of the 4th/10th century, that is, prior to the Great Occultation (*al-ghayba al-kubrā*) which occurred in the year 329/941. Somewhat later is Muḥammad b. Ibrāhīm b. Jaʿfar al-Nuʿmānī (d. *ca.* 360/971), to whom a treatise constituting a sort of introduction to the Qur'an is ascribed (Majlisī, *Biḥār al-anwār* [Beirut, 1403–1983], vol. 95, pp. 1–97). Other compositions are the two commentaries ascribed to the sixth and eleventh Imams: *Ḥaqāʾiq al-tafsīr al-Qurʾānī* (ed. A. Zayʿūr, Beirut, 1413/1993), a small exegetical treatise of a Sufi character attributed to the sixth Imam, Jaʿfar al-Ṣādiq, and *Tafsīr al-ʿAskarī*, a comprehensive *haggadic* commentary on the first two *sūra*s of the Qur'an, attributed to the eleventh Imam, Ḥasan al-ʿAskarī ([d. 260/874], Qumm, 1409/1988). The most outstanding *tafsīr*s of the post-*Ghayba* period are *al-Tibyān fī tafsīr al-Qurʾān* by Abū Jaʿfar al-Ṭūsī (Najaf, 1376–1385/1957–1965), the *Majmaʿ al-bayān fī tafsīr al-Qurʾān* by Abū ʿAlī al-Faḍl b. Ḥasan al-Ṭabrisī (Beirut, 1374–1377/1953–1957), which is clearly dependent on the *Tibyān*, and the *Rawḍ al-jinān*

[37] *Asās al-taʾwīl*, MS 1148, The Institute of Ismaili Studies, London, 766 fos, at fo. 414, lines 4–6; Tāmir's edition, p. 214, has the less plausible version: *wa-maʿrifatihi* (instead of *wa-maʿrifat*).

wa-rūḥ al-janān (Tehran, 1349 Sh.), a Qurʾan commentary in Persian, by Abu'l-Futūḥ Ḥusayn b. ʿAlī al-Rāzī (fl. the first half of the 6th/12th century). Some very comprehensive Imāmī-Shiʿi *tafsīr* works, which are mainly compilations of early sources, were composed in Ṣafawid Iran. Among these the most prominent are *Taʾwīl al-āyāt al-ẓāhira fī faḍāʾil al-ʿitra al-ṭāhira* (Qumm, 1407/1986) by Sharaf al-Dīn ʿAlī al-Ḥusaynī al-Astarābādī (fl. 10th/16th century); *Kitāb al-ṣāfī fī tafsīr al-Qurʾān* (Beirut, 1389/1979) by Muḥammad b. Murtaḍā al-Kāshānī (d. 1091/1680) and *Kitāb al-burhān fī tafsīr al-Qurʾān* (Tehran, n.d.) by Hāshim b. Sulaymān al-Baḥrānī (d. 1107/1693 or 1109/1697). Representatives of modern Imāmī Qurʾan exegesis include *al-Mīzān fī tafsīr al-Qurʾān* (Beirut, 1403–1405/1983–1985) by Muḥammad b. Ḥusayn Ṭabāṭabāʾī (d. 1981) and *Min waḥy al-Qurʾān* by Muḥammad Ḥusayn Faḍl Allāh (d. 2010). Needless to say, exegetical material other than Qurʾan commentaries per se proliferates in all genres of Imāmī literature.[38]

Ismaili doctrinal writings include a vast amount of exegetical material, but little is known of specifically Ismaili exegetical compositions. Among the few quasi-exegetical works that have come down to us are *Kitāb asās al-taʾwīl* (ed. ʿĀ. Tāmir, Beirut, 1960) by al-Qāḍī al-Nuʿmān (d. 363/974) and *Kitāb al-kashf* (ed. R. Strothmann, London, 1952) attributed to the *dāʿī* Jaʿfar b. Manṣūr al-Yaman (d. ca. 346/957).[39]

The Zaydī exegetical tradition remains largely unexplored, and most Zaydī works of *tafsīr* are still in manuscript form. The Zaydī Imams al-Qāsim b. Ibrāhīm Rassī (d. 246/860), al-Nāṣir li'l-Ḥaqq al-Uṭrūsh (d. 304/917) and Abu'l-Fatḥ Nāṣir b. Ḥusayn Daylamī (d. 444/1052) are among those credited with a *tafsīr*.[40]

A Qurʾan commentary is also ascribed to Ziyād b. Mundhir Abu'l-Jārūd, the eponym of the Zaydi-Jārūdī, al-Jārūdiyya.[41] The work is not preserved; however, excerpts are incorporated in the aforementioned *tafsīr* of ʿAlī b. Ibrāhīm al-Qummī.[42] Another outstanding Jārūdī scholar who is credited with a *tafsīr* is Aḥmad b. Muḥammad al-Hamadhānī, better known as Ibn ʿUqda (d. 333/944).[43] To these works one may add the *Tafsīr al-Ḥibarī* (ed. M. R. al-Ḥusaynī, Beirut 1408/1987) by al-Ḥusayn b. al-Ḥakam al-Ḥibarī (d. 286/899), presumably representing the early phase of Zaydī exegesis. Finally it is worth mentioning the *Fatḥ al-qadīr* of Muḥammad b. ʿAlī b.

---

[38] For a detailed survey of Shiʿi *tafsīr* works, see also Āghā Buzurg al-Ṭihrānī, *al-Dharīʿa ilā taṣānīf al-Shīʿa* (Najaf, 1936–1938), vol. 3, pp. 302–307 and vol. 4, pp. 231–346.

[39] For other Ismaili hermeneutical works, see the index of I. K. Poonawala, *Biobibliography of Ismāʿīlī Literature* (Malibu, CA, 1977) under the entries *tafsīr* and *taʾwīl*; Bar-Asher, 'Outlines of Early Ismāʿīlī-Faṭimid Qurʾān Exegesis', pp. 261–269.

[40] See al-Ṭihrānī, *al-Dharīʿa ilā taṣānīf al-Shīʿa*, vol. 4, pp. 255, 261. See also B. Abrahamov, *Anthropomorphism and Interpretation of the Qurʾān: Kitāb al-Mustarshid* (Leiden, New York and Cologne, 1996) pp. 17–43; H. Ansari and S. Schmidtke, 'Iranian Zaydism during the 7th/13th Century: Abu'l-Faḍl b. Shahrdawīr al-Daylamī al-Jīlānī and his Commentary on the Qurʾān', *Journal Asiatique*, 299 (2011), pp. 205–211.

[41] See al-Ṭihrānī, *al-Dharīʿa ilā taṣānīf al-Shīʿa*, vol. 4, p. 251.

[42] See Bar-Asher, *Scripture and Exegesis*, pp. 46–56, 244–247.

[43] See al-Ṭihrānī, *al-Dharīʿa ilā taṣānīf al-Shīʿa*, vol. 4, p. 304.

Muḥammad al-Shawkānī (d. 1250/1834), one of the best-known and most prolific authors of the later Zaydiyya.

As for the exegesis of the *ghulāt* (such as the Druze and the Nuṣayrīs), although the Qur'an is widely cited and often commented on in their sacred writings, there is no evidence of Qur'an commentaries as such penned by these groups.

Concluding Remarks

It seems that since Shiʿism was reluctant to take the far-reaching step of presenting an alternative version to the *textus receptus* of the Qur'an, it used its exegesis to the text as an alternative. Through exegesis, Shiʿism was able to bridge the gap between its self-perception of superiority over its enemies and its inferior status in reality. By means of allegorical exegesis Shiʿis were able to unveil truths allegedly alluded to in the Qur'an. Shiʿi commentators believe it is not surprising that matters referring to Shiʿi Islam and its enemies are not explicitly referred to in the Qur'an, because those who are privy to hidden knowledge as well as being familiar with that which is revealed, that is, the Imams, know how to deduce the truths from the holy book. Instructive in this context is a tradition attributed to ʿAlī and cited by Aḥmad b. Abī Ṭālib al-Ṭabrisī (d. beginning of 6th/12th century), which depicts a tripartite division of the Qur'an: 'God in the breadth of His mercy and His compassion towards His creatures (*bi-saʿat raḥmatihi wa-raʾfatihi bi-makhlūqātihi*) and knowing that the falsifiers of His words would alter the divine text, divided His words [in the Qur'an] into three parts: one part is intelligible to both the learned and the ignorant; another part is intelligible only to those of pure mind, delicate sensitivity and correct discernment among those whose heart God had opened to Islam (*mimman sharaḥa allāhu ṣadrahu lil-islām*); and another part is intelligible only to God and His prophets and to those firmly rooted in knowledge.'[44]

This tradition, like many of its kind, is unequivocal. It suggests an explanation for the absence in the Qur'an of explicit references to Shiʿi Islam and its doctrines. It teaches that the truth is found in the Qur'an, though it is not visible to all creatures. There exists a hierarchy in the amount of truth that is unveiled to various followers.

[44] Aḥmad b. Abī Ṭālib al-Ṭabrisī, *Kitāb iḥtijāj* (Beirut, 1989), p. 253.

4

What Defines a (Pre-modern) Shiʿi *Tafsīr*? Notes towards the History of the Genre of *Tafsīr* in Islam, in the Light of the Study of the Shiʿi Contribution

Andrew Rippin

Does Shiʿi *tafsīr* have any special characteristics when viewed within the context of the overall genre of *tafsīr*? What qualifies a work to be called a Shiʿi *tafsīr* rather than something else? How 'Shiʿi' must it be to be included? How do we know which works are to be included in the category 'Shiʿi'? Is Shiʿi *tafsīr* a unified category? Do the works fit within a definition of the genre of *tafsīr* or are they to be marked off as a separate (sub)category within the overall genre? How best can we incorporate Shiʿi *tafsīr* within the history of the genre? Such are the questions that arise when contemplating the research that has been done thus far on the place of Shiʿi works in the overall history of the genre of *tafsīr*. My own interest in how to understand and appreciate the component elements and the history of the genre also drives these questions, which arise originally out of non-Shiʿi-focused contexts within scholarship on *tafsīr*.

One context for these questions is the recent scholarly discussion concerning what it means to call *al-Kashshāf ʿan ḥaqāʾiq ghawāmiḍ al-tanzīl* by al-Zamakhsharī (d. 538/1144) a 'Muʿtazilī' *tafsīr*, as discussed by Andrew Lane.[1] Regardless of the merits of, or problems with, the arguments that have been put forward concerning Lane's work (the reviews have been overwhelmingly sceptical concerning Lane's misgivings at calling al-Zamakhsharī's work 'Muʿtazilī', although otherwise his work has been unanimously praised), the discussion does raise awareness of the need to employ careful definitions and to provide analyses that can lead to meaningful generalisations. As Lane says of his study, it 'demonstrates that it would even be difficult to

[1] Andrew Lane, *A Traditional Muʿtazilite Qurʾān Commentary: The* Kashshāf *of Jār Allāh al-Zamakhsharī (d. 538/1144)* (Leiden, 2006). Reviews include: Karen Bauer, *JAOS*, 126 (2006), pp. 435–437; Andrew Rippin, *Islam and Christian-Muslim Relations*, 17 (2006), pp. 486–487; Suleiman Mourad, *Journal of Semitic Studies*, 52 (2007), pp. 409–411.

define what a "Muʿtazilite commentary" actually is';[2] 'difficult', yes, but then that is the task of scholarship.

The second context arises from the dynamics of the modern world. The struggle over the definition and control of Muslim cultural heritage is a part of the character of the modern technological age. I have noted with interest contemporary Iranian (and other – altafsir.com, for example) efforts to incorporate books understood to be Shiʿi within the Muslim canon of *tafsīr* works through the issuance of CDs and websites that feature vast collections of *tafsīr* works covering a spectrum of interests.[3]

This chapter will review the (generally implicit) definition of Shiʿi *tafsīr* (limited here to specifically Imāmī/Twelver-Shiʿi works[4]) that has been used in a variety of scholarly discussions up to this point, with the goal of extracting what the authors consider to be the major characteristics of the works that make them suitable to be called Shiʿi. Those ideas will then be considered within the context of analytical–typological definitions of *tafsīr* as a whole (particularly as proposed by Norman Calder) and I will discuss how Shiʿi *tafsīr* can be placed within that context, with consideration given to whether doing so adds or particularises anything significant in the study of *tafsīr* as an overall genre. Special attention will be paid to what I term the 'transition points' in the genre, as the form and content of the works undergo

---

[2] Lane, *A Traditional Muʿtazilite Qurʾān Commentary*, p. 229.

[3] On this point see my forthcoming article, 'The Impact of the Internet on the Qurʾān', in Göran Larsson and Thomas Hoffman, ed., *Muslims and the New Information and Communication Technologies* (New York and Heidelberg, 2013):

> More critically, there is another, perhaps more internal Muslim dispute that we are potentially witnessing as well, and that is the ownership and promulgation of the Muslim cultural and intellectual heritage. Vested in this amassing of data is that core sense of the definition of the Islamic heritage and of Islam itself. In some ways, the competing sites which bring Qurʾānic exegetical material together – I would suggest a comparison of the King Fahd Centre and the Aal al-Bayt Foundation – are the places in which the future of Islam is being staked, at least symbolically (in terms of cultural heritage). This is even further apparent in the work that is also taking place in Iran where the collections of *tafsir* texts are not limited to the Shiʿi standard works but include masses of Sunni works as well, in an effort which can only be interpreted as a Shiʿi effort to have their own works included in the general Muslim canon. [This is a point made in Peter Mandaville, 'Digital Islam: Changing the Boundaries of Religious Knowledge', *ISIM Newsletter*, 2 (1999), p. 1, although he seems to present this mainly in economic terms ('capturing a larger share of the market for digital Islam').] The struggle for control of what Gary Bunt has called the Islamic knowledge economy [Gary R. Bunt, *Muslims: Rewiring the House of Islam* (Chapel Hill, NC, 2009), p. 276] may be viewed as being constructed through such sites.

[4] On Ismaili *tafsīr*, see Meir M. Bar-Asher, 'Outlines of Early Ismāʿīlī-Fāṭimid Qurʾān Exegesis', *Journal Asiatique*, 296 (2008), pp. 257–295. Zaydī *tafsīr* has not enjoyed an extensive scholarly survey yet; see Binyamin Abrahamov, *Anthropomorphism and Interpretation of the Qurʾān in the Theology of al-Qāsim ibn Ibrāhīm* Kitāb al-Mustarshid (Leiden, 1996) and, for a brief overview, Feras Hamza, Sajjad Rizvi and Farhana Mayer, ed., *An Anthology of Qurʾanic Commentaries*. Volume 1: *On the Nature of the Divine* (Oxford, 2008), pp. 42–45.

significant reorientation, as a way of illustrating why this approach to Shiʿi *tafsīr* might be helpful within the larger context of the study of Qurʾanic commentaries.

There has already emerged a sense of a canon of Shiʿi *tafsīr* works in the scholarly world by virtue of what has been published and become generally available (which is a part of the interesting phenomenon of scholarship, certainly – the extent to which topics of research are driven by publishers), although no full scholarly catalogue of them is available to me. Guy Monnot's listing of authors is certainly dated.[5] Implicit definitions arise in the modern electronic context where content on websites and on CDs suggests certain 'canons' might be emerging (and, as such, need detailing and analysis). From the Sunni side, altafsir.com includes works by the following under the heading of Ithnāʿashariyya: al-Qummī (d. ca. 307/920), al-Ṭūsī (d. 460/1067), al-Ṭabrisī (d. 548/1153), Ṣadr al-Mutaʾallihīn al-Shīrāzī [Mullā Ṣadrā] (d. 1059/1649 [*sic*: usually 1050/1640]), [Muḥsin] Fayḍ Kāshānī (d. 1090/1680), al-Junābadhī (d. 14th/19th century, written in 1311/1893; the author's name is more accurately al-Junābādī) and al-Ṭabaṭabāʾī (d. 1402/1981). One Iranian CD of Islamic books, *al-Mojam* (version 3, dated 1421/2001), includes 87 Shiʿi works on the Qurʾan (not all strictly *tafsīr* because the total includes *ʿulūm al-Qurʾān* works and a significant portion of the total number of works is modern) and 112 from Sunni writers; Noor Jāmiʿ al-tafāsīr from Iran assembles 184 titles (in version 3 from 2006), with a similar division (and character) among the works to that of al-Mojam. The CD *Maktaba ahl al-bayt* from almarkaz.net (2005) again has similar numbers, although notably including al-Zamakhsharī in the list of Shiʿi rather than Sunni works, where Sunni-oriented scholarship would place him, which illustrates some of the point of the questions with which this chapter started.

Given that a certain consensus may be said to have emerged about which books are to be considered Shiʿi, it may well be that the answers to my basic questions can be deemed 'obvious'. The characteristic that marks Shiʿi *tafsīr* as Shiʿi is some aspect of its Shiʿi content (that itself being subject to definition, of course). Another approach might be to say that a *tafsīr*'s author is identified in biographical and theological writings as Shiʿi and that creates the definition.[6] A third thought may be to invoke the word 'esoteric'. This, however, is a highly problematic concept because it is never clear

[5] 'Islam: Exégèse coranique. I. 1. Introduction à l'exégèse duodécimaine', *Annuaire. Résumé des conferences et de travaux, Paris, EPHE, Ve section sciences religieuses*, 91 (1982–1983), pp. 309–317.

[6] Kevin Reinhart has pointed out in his 'On Sunni Sectarianism', in Yasir Suleiman, ed., *Living Islamic History: Studies in Honour of Professor Carole Hillenbrand* (Edinburgh, 2010), pp. 209–225, that the term Sunni, when applied to people or texts, is of no particular advantage in clarifying matters. It is used 'to mean whatever is not Shiʿi (or worse, whatever is not ʿAlid)' (p. 209). Reinhart reviews the usage of the terminology of 'denomination' and 'sect' as it applies in the Islamic case and his essay focuses on the sense in which, within theology, the dominant stream of Sunnism is sectarian in the sense of it proclaiming its own 'rightness' in opposition to the 'other' who is viewed with hostility and suspicion. Denominations, he points out, are what characterise other aspects of the Islamic world, with the over-reaching definition of the community as an umbrella that can contain multiple *madhhab*s and tolerate

in whose view any given material is, in fact, esoteric: one person's esoteric is another person's exoteric. Fundamentally, those who share in esoteric knowledge are making social power claims through their possession of it ('knowledge is power'). Further, it may well be argued that the mere act of writing a *tafsīr* in and by itself means that any true sense of esoteric – that which is hidden, limited in circulation, known to a small group, is rare or unusual – has been lost, especially given the common form that authors employ within the genre.

Here, I would like to consider this matter from the overall context of the discipline of *tafsīr*. Taking the focus away from content and external biographical identifications and considering the material on the basis of the text of *tafsīr* itself and its structures and methods will be a step towards elaborating an overall vision of the genre of *tafsīr* while, at the same time, clarifying the Shiʿi component and contribution in the genre. In this way, the vision of the genre can incorporate Shiʿi works, while acknowledging their distinctiveness, on the basis of what all works of *tafsīr* share and where their emphases fall, rather than leaving the Shiʿi works aside as a manifestation of a particular orientation within the Islamic community. The tendency to classify Shiʿi *tafsīr* on the basis of its content creates significant problems (as it does for the definition of a Muʿtazilī *tafsīr* on the basis of whether *every* opportunity to argue a doctrinal point is pursued), precisely because of the variation in the form, method and orientation of the works over history.

Scholarly Views of Shiʿi *Tafsīr*

Ignaz Goldziher's *Die Richtungen der islamischen Koranauslegung* provides the grounding for the modern scholarly study of Shiʿi *tafsīr*.[7] In a chapter headed 'Sectarian Interpretation',[8] Goldziher covers Shiʿi *tafsīr* as a part of 'tendentious' exegesis and as a manifestation of 'sectarian interest' and 'distinctive principles'. For Goldziher, sectarianism is a parallel to rationalism and mysticism in their common move 'away' from the 'simple word' of the Qur'an.

Goldziher's access to works that are now spoken of as Shiʿi *tafsīr*s was strikingly limited. Many of his references to ʿAlid interpretations of the text are provided through Sunni reports which reject such ideas. In describing Shiʿi *tafsīr*, Goldziher first draws attention to Shiʿi attitudes towards the 'incomplete state' of the text of the Qur'an and ʿAlī's role in creating a definitive *muṣḥaf*. With Goldziher's emphasis falling there, one is certainly left with the impression that the inclusion of such material in the text is what, for him, would primarily mark Shiʿi *tafsīr*. Virtually all of Goldziher's initial discussion of this issue is derived from Sunni sources describing the Shiʿi

---

the *dhimmīs*. When considering the group we identify as the Shiʿa, the variation in attitude through history is much like the case in Sunnism.

[7] Ignaz Goldziher, *Die Richtungen der islamischen Koranauslegung* (Leiden, 1920); English trans., *Schools of Koranic Commentators*, tr. Wolfgang H. Behn (Wiesbaden, 2006).

[8] Ibid., pp. 263–309 (German text), pp. 167–196 (English text).

position, although the detailed examples that he cites later are all from al-Qummī,[9] the main Shiʿi source to which he had access.[10] Goldziher also draws attention to what he sees as the 'characteristic mark' of Shiʿi *tafsīr* in the issue of authority: that the *isnāds* must be traceable to the *ahl al-bayt.*[11] The other characteristic Goldziher indicates is the particular Shiʿi character of the 'identification of the unknown',[12] which would extend (beyond the Sunni tendency to do the same, as he illustrates with the work of al-Suhaylī [d. 581/1185]) to include references to ʿAlī and the Mahdī (as illustrated again through the work of al-Qummī). Overall, Goldziher isolates matters related to the illegitimacy of the caliphate, the glorification of ʿAlī and the Imams, and the return of the Mahdī as the principal issues for which Shiʿi *tafsīr* is arguing.

For Goldziher, then, Shiʿi *tafsīr* is primarily characterised by its content in terms of religious beliefs, grounded in the claims that separate the Shiʿa from the Sunnis. Goldziher's attitude to Shiʿi *tafsīr* (and the Shiʿa in general) reflects his view of religion and Islam as a whole: that the truth and value of religion resides in its scripture and its prophet, before the religion became politicised and orthodoxised; any move away from the purity of religion results from a wilful destructive approach that enhances the political power-claims of later generations.[13]

In contrast to the work of Goldziher, the essay of Mahmoud Ayoub, 'The Speaking Qur'an and the Silent Qur'an',[14] illustrates the explosion in the number of texts of Shiʿi *tafsīr* that had become available to researchers in the span of some seventy years. That relative abundance of texts allows Ayoub to draw attention to the periodisation of Shiʿi *tafsīr*, emphasising the changing notions of the authority of the Imam, especially contrasting the pre-*ghayba*/post-*ghayba* ethos. For Ayoub, the earliest stage is characterised by *tafsīr*s stemming from disciples of the Imams, while the classical,

---

[9] Ibid., pp. 280–288 (German text), pp. 178–183 (English text).

[10] Goldziher also mentions (*Richtungen*, p. 279 (German text), p. 177 (English text)) what he terms 'the oldest' Shiʿi Qur'an commentary as the work of al-Baydakhtī (d. 311/923), *Bayān al-saʿāda fī maqām al-ʿibāda* (Tehran, 1314/1896). This is a mistake. The work appears actually to be that of Mullā Sulṭān Muḥammad Sulṭān ʿAlīshāh al-Junābādī (d. 1327/1909), *Bayān al-saʿāda fī maqāmāt al-ʿibāda*, written in 1311/1893. See Carl Brockelmann, *Geschichte der arabischen Litteratur* (Leiden, 1937–1949), supplement, vol. 2, p. 834; the work is now found at altafsir.com under al-Junābadhī. See also N. Hanif, *Biographical Encyclopaedia of Sufis (Central Asia and Middle East)* (New Delhi, 2002), p. 6. On the work itself, see online: http://www.iis.ac.uk/view_article.asp?ContentID=111970 (accessed 13 August 2013). Al-Junābādī was born in Bidukht, in central Khurāsān, where the Gonabadi branch of Niʿmatullahi Sufism is centred (see Habib Borjian, 'Bidokt', *EIR*, online: http://www.iranicaonline.org/articles/bidokt-1 (accessed 13 August 2013)), and thus the name as found in Goldziher, 'al-Baydakhtī'.

[11] Goldziher, *Richtungen*, p. 279 (German text), pp. 177–178 (English text).

[12] Ibid., pp. 289–296 (German text), pp. 183–188 (English text).

[13] On the religious perspective of Goldziher, see Dietrich Jung, *Orientalists, Islamists and the Global Public Sphere: A Genealogy of the Modern Essentialist Image of Islam* (London, 2011).

[14] Mahmoud Ayoub, 'The Speaking Qurʾān and the Silent Qurʾān: A Study of the Principles and Development of Imāmī Shiʿi *tafsīr*', in Andrew Rippin, ed., *Approaches to the History of the Interpretation of the Qurʾān* (Oxford, 1988), pp. 177–198.

post-classical and modern periods are characterised and differentiated mainly by their attitude towards Sunni sources.

Beyond the focus on periodisation, Ayoub's description of Shiʿi *tafsīr* clearly highlights the central issue of authority. *Tafsīr* is, for Ayoub, 'the link between the faithful and their spiritual guides, the Imams'.[15] The importance of Q.3:7 when linked to the definition of those who are 'firmly grounded in knowledge' as the Imams provides the underpinning of Ayoub's approach, along with an emphasis on the esoteric meaning of the Qur'an that the Imams make plain. Ayoub argues that the most particular characteristic of Shiʿi *tafsīr* is 'its insistence upon the continued validity and relevance of the sacred text to human life at all times' through the mediation of the *ahl al-bayt*.[16]

Meir Bar-Asher's study *Scripture and Exegesis in Early Imāmī Shiism* makes the point clearly that the Shiʿi ability and methods to 'read into' the Qur'an,[17] features that arose subsequent to the emergence of the Qur'anic text itself, were no different from those of the Sunnis.[18] He highlights the role of the authority of the Imams in the pre-occultation period, through whom, it was claimed, the only true access to the meaning of the text can be obtained. Centrally, Bar-Asher points to the characteristics of pre-Būyid exegesis, aspects which I would consider critical factors in the context of the discussion in this chapter, namely: (a) commentary by means of *ḥadīth*; (b) selective concern with the text of the Qur'an, paying attention mainly to verses with potential Shiʿi reference; (c) among Shiʿi doctrinal issues, only *walāya* and *barā'a* draw significant attention; (d) extreme anti-Sunni stance (hostile to Muḥammad's Companions).[19] These characteristics are embedded within textual and allegorical–typological methods of interpretation.

A significant additional contribution is found in the brief and eloquent entry written by Todd Lawson for *Encyclopaedia Iranica* on 'Hermeneutics',[20] with an appropriate nod to Henry Corbin's overview of the topic in *En Islam Iranien*.[21] Lawson is acutely aware of the complexities involved in understanding the category of Shiʿi *tafsīr*, given its apparent significant shifts in orientation over time. He unifies the category itself but sees the hermeneutic of the 4th century (late 10th or early 11th century AD) as moving away from the radicalism and absolutism of the pre-Būyid period, which he terms a 'hermeneutic of authority' because of its focus on the Imam. The new stance is a 'hermeneutic of compromise', characterised as less isolationist and more conciliatory (towards Sunnism), accompanied by a rise in the authority of the scholars over the Imam (as pointed out also by Bar-Asher,[22] who makes the

---

15 Ibid., p. 177.

16 Ibid., p. 192.

17 Meir M. Bar-Asher, *Scripture and Exegesis in Early Imāmī Shiism* (Leiden, 1999).

18 Ibid., p. 17.

19 Ibid., p. 19.

20 Todd Lawson, 'Hermeneutics', *EIR*, vol. 12, pp. 235–239, and online: http://www.iranicaonline.org/articles/hermeneutics (accessed 13 August 2013).

21 Specifically, volume 1, parts IV and V.

22 *Scripture and Exegesis*, pp. 75 and 80.

perceptive comment that what we see in this period is the presence of the author who was absent in earlier works). That then becomes inverted in the Ṣafawid period with a return to the radicalism (or 'sectarianism') of earlier times, tempered by the influences of Sufism and philosophy, and 'individualistic aspects' focused on the reader.

What Makes a Work 'Shiʿi'?

As I suggested at the outset, when we think of a category 'Shiʿi *tafsīr*', the question that is provoked when reviewing these descriptions is how much of a given tendency must be found within a work to declare it 'Shiʿi'? This really is the crux of the issue, as may be seen in several ways. Notably, the charge of 'being Shiʿi' was frequently levelled against writers whom today we view as staunchly Sunni. Additionally, what we might wish to claim as 'Shiʿi markers' in *tafsīr* vary significantly over time. The answer to the question of what defines a work as Shiʿi, then, is perhaps not as clear as it might be (as the above example of al-Zamakhsharī again makes plain).

The medieval isolation of the existence of *tafsīr*s that were defined as Shiʿi is apparent. One might thus argue that modern scholars are simply working within the medieval tradition, to some extent as defined by Sunnis, in specifying which books stand within the Shiʿi tradition. However, even this is not so obvious. For example, the listing in the bibliography of Ibn al-Nadīm (d. ca. 380/990) in his section 'On the Qurʾan and Qurʾanic sciences' begins with the work of Imam al-Bāqir (d. 114/733). As has been argued by Dimitry Frolov,[23] Ibn al-Nadīm stresses the leading role of Shiʿi scholars in the very formative stages of the development of *tafsīr* in the school of Kufa (as compared with the Sunni school of the Hijaz and the Muʿtazilī school of Basra).[24] As Frolov points out,

> both *al-Itqān fī ʿulūm al-Qurʾān* of al-Suyūṭī (d. 911/1505) and the *Fihrist* of Ibn al-Nadīm have been the main sources for the history of the Qurʾanic sciences in the works of European scholars. Both sources are often seen as parts of the same line of thought and as complementary to each other. If I am correct in my analysis, these books give alternative, not complementary views of the subject and should be treated as such.[25]

Al-Suyūṭī worked to privilege the Sunni line of authoritative *tafsīr* by giving precedence to Ibn ʿAbbās (d. ca. 68/687) and his followers, leaving Shiʿi writers only a marginal status at best. The very way in which the genealogy of the genre of *tafsīr* was written has affected our perception of it today.

---

23 Dimitry Frolov, 'Ibn al-Nadīm on the History of Quranic Exegesis', *Wiener Zeitschrift für die Kunde des Morganlandes*, 87 (1997), pp. 65–81.

24 Ibid., p. 76.

25 Ibid., p. 81.

It may also be observed that the borders of Shiʿi *tafsīr* are very permeable in other ways. The charge of crypto-Shiʿism appears to have been a common one to undermine one's intellectual rivals, as, for example, in the case of al-Ṭabarī.[26] Also, some works may be consciously 'catholic' in their approach to the discipline and to their religion, and embrace symbols that some might consider Shiʿi. That observation has been made by Guy Monnot,[27] for example, about the work *Gharāʾib al-Qurʾān* of Niẓām al-Dīn al-Nīsābūrī (d. 728/1327). Al-Nīsābūrī wrote commentaries on works of al-Qummī and al-Ṭūsī (authors who are normally understood to be Shiʿi writers), and in his *tafsīr* some of his glosses are 'Shiʿi' in sentiment (while, at other times, he is explicitly anti-Shiʿi in his remarks). Also, note should be taken of the Persian work of Kāshifī (d. 910/1504–1505) whom Kristin Sands describes as being attractive to both Sunnis and Shiʿis because of his carefully enunciated stance.[28] Indeed, the world of medieval scholarship overall appears to have been (periodically at the very least) reasonably catholic, given the use and circulation of books witnessed in bibliographies and the like. This is evidenced in the bibliographic works of both Ibn al-Nadīm and Ibn Ṭāwūs (d. 664/1266), for example. Note must also be made of the sources employed in *Kashf al-bayān* of al-Thaʿlabī (d. 427/1035) within the Nishapur school of *tafsīr* which include works that are thought of as Shiʿi *tafsīr*s, regardless of the reason for which such material may have been included in his work and for which al-Thaʿlabī was also subject to the censure of Ibn Taymiyya (d. 728/1328).[29]

This does suggest to some extent that there were certain 'tags' for medieval Sunni Muslims at least that marked a work as Shiʿi (most emphatically the attitude towards ʿAlī). However, it is also possible to say that the circulation of works within the genre of *tafsīr*, both Sunni and Shiʿi, was certainly widespread and, it would seem, such books were read as part of a single genre, even if only in a polemical way; it was also done in a neutralising ('declawed' in Saleh's very apt expression[30]) way, as in the example that Saleh gives of loving the Prophet's family as a totally appropriate Sunni activity.[31] This also emphasises the point that always needs to be kept in mind: regardless of whether the authors were Sunnis or Shiʿis, their work of interpreting the Qurʾan was conducted within a commonly accepted framework of what we still recognise today as a genre of literature known as *tafsīr*. Differences in assumptions about authority and a different set of pre-understandings about the meaning of the Qurʾan did not result in the genre of *tafsīr* itself taking on significantly different forms

26 See Franz Rosenthal, 'General Introduction', in his *The History of al-Ṭabarī*. Volume 1: *General Introduction and From the Creation to the Flood* (Albany, NY, 1989), pp. 59–62.

27 Guy Monnot, 'Islam: Exégèse coranique. I. 2. Recherches sur le commentaire doctrinal de Nīsābūrī', *Annuaire. Résumé des conferences et de travaux, Paris, EPHE, Ve section sciences religieuses*, 91 (1982–1983), pp. 317–318.

28 Kristin Sands, 'On the Popularity of Husayn Vaʿiz Kashifi's *Mavāhib-i ʿaliyya*: A Persian Commentary on the Qurʾān', *Iranian Studies*, 36 (2003), p. 483.

29 Walid Saleh, *The Formation of the Classical Tafsīr Tradition* (Leiden, 2004), pp. 218–220.

30 Ibid., p. 187.

31 Ibid., p. 186.

(or the form being renounced by one group or another) as a means of conveying the appropriate meaning of the text, which it could well have: the works stay within the generally accepted genre boundaries such that the work can always be recognised as a *tafsīr*. This remarkable outcome emphasises the interaction among intellectuals in both the formative and classical periods. All participants shared a common goal and used a common form to demonstrate that the principles that stand at the basis of their conception of Muslim society and the Muslim ethos can find an underpinning in the Qur'an (for that, I would argue, is the real purpose of *tafsīr*, rather than the oft-assumed superficial one of 'determining the meaning' of the text, which, as observed polemically by Ibn Taymiyya and many 19th-century reformers, was subsumed in the scholastic explorations of *tafsīr*).

Analysing the Genre of *Tafsīr*

Norman Calder's seminal article '*Tafsīr* from Ṭabarī to Ibn Kathīr' proposes a framework for the analysis of classical *tafsīr* that does not focus on content but rather on form and technique,[32] building on the work of John Wansbrough in his *Quranic Studies*.[33] Calder provides a descriptive analysis of what features are present in the scholastic discipline of *tafsīr*:

> (a) Following the text of scripture: 'canon and segmentation, lemma and comment';[34]
>
> (b) Authority is cited by community (polyvalency), intellect, and (revealed) text (*ḥadīth*: citation of named authority); authority and its citation is always in the hands of the author who both hides reports (in order to limit variety) and expresses preferences (in order to control variety) – all 'a declaration of loyalty: it defines the tradition within which one works'.[35]

For Calder, *tafsīr* is a process, and a manifestation in a literary genre, of a 'measuring of the Qur'anic text against' the following two fundamental elements:

---

[32] Norman Calder, '*Tafsīr* from Ṭabarī to Ibn Kathīr: Problems in the Description of a Genre, Illustrated with Reference to the Story of Abraham', in G. R. Hawting and A. A. Shareef, ed., *Approaches to the Qur'ān* (London, 1993), pp. 101–140. Calder laid out plans for a second study to extend the discussion historically and thematically with a focus on law; see the introduction to his collected works volume, Jawid Mojaddedi and Andrew Rippin, 'Introduction', in Norman Calder, *Interpretation and Jurisprudence in Medieval Islam* (Aldershot, 2006), pp. ix–xiii.

[33] John Wansbrough, *Quranic Studies: Sources and Methods of Scriptural Interpretation* (Oxford, 1977); repr. with Foreword, Translations and Extended Notes by Andrew Rippin (Amherst, NY, 2004).

[34] Calder, '*Tafsīr*', p. 101.

[35] Ibid., p. 103.

1. Instrumental structures: orthography, lexis, syntax, rhetoric, symbol/allegory
2. Ideological structures: prophetic history, theology, eschatology, law, *taṣawwuf*[36]

For Calder, the balancing of all these elements is reflective of the artistry of the author. An approach to defining *tafsīr* by its methods, one that will recognise the different weightings that various authors give to each instrumental and ideological structure, allows us to recognise both the differences and the commonalities within the entire genre. Rather than separating out Shiʿi *tafsīr* on an 'intuitive', content, or traditional/biographical basis, the analysis of *tafsīr* as a genre can better represent the scholastic discipline itself by paying attention to its inherent constituent structures and methods (as indeed has been done by Bar-Asher for the formative period in his *Scripture and Exegesis*). Most of all, it may shed light on some of the transition points in Shiʿi *tafsīr* that lie behind the periodisation of the genre, especially in the significance, meaning and theoretical underpinnings when those points are viewed in parallel with the transition points in the Sunni world.

Walid Saleh has forcefully argued in a number of works for significant transition points in the genre of (Sunni) *tafsīr*.[37] Not only does this attention to transitions suggest that care is needed in proposing any overarching definition and description of the genre but it is also a reminder that Sunni *tafsīr*, too, could be said to go through at least three phases: pre-al-Ṭabarī (the 'formative period'), al-Ṭabarī to Ibn Kathīr (the 'classical period'), Ibn Kathīr to the early 20th century (the 'post-classical' or 'mature' phase).[38] To emphasise the apparent shifts in the character of Shiʿi *tafsīr* is, therefore, potentially to overshadow the significant transitions happening in the genre overall and to miss definite parallels in form, principles and approach across Sunni and Shiʿi works.

Transitions in the Genre of *Tafsīr*

While the division of Sunni *tafsīr* into periods is by no means absolute (and it may well be argued that they are tendencies not grounded in specific historical events so much as in doctrine, although at the current state of the study of *tafsīr*, a tie to history does seem somewhat apparent), it is clear that a formative, classical and mature (post-classical) division is potentially meaningful, with al-Ṭabarī and Ibn Taymiyya as the critical transition points, as Calder suggested. Certainly, neither transition point is

---

36 Ibid., pp. 105–106.

37 See Saleh, *Formation* and Walid Saleh, 'The Last of the Nishapuri School of Tafsīr: Al-Wāḥidī and his Significance in the History of Qur'anic Exegesis', *JAOS*, 126 (2006), pp. 223–243.

38 I leave aside the modern period in this discussion. There are significant transitions in terms of form and method in contemporary times although such transitions do not entirely eliminate the production of 'mature' phase formulations.

absolute. Walid Saleh has especially argued against seeing al-Ṭabarī as a solitary pivot point,[39] although perhaps the intention here is more to make sure that the significance of later exegetes such as al-Thaʿlabī and al-Wāḥidī (d. 468/1075) gets its due. The instrumental structures of the formative period become increasingly overwhelmed by ideological structures in the classical period (not that ideological structures were absent in the formative period), while the shift to the post-classical, mature period marks a reorientation of authority from community and intellect to an emphasis on the revealed text (to use Calder's categories). The process of contraction and expansion in the material cited by the exegetes is to be seen as particularly significant. The transition points are also marked historically: the emergence of the classical period is marked by the rise of the power of the *ʿulamāʾ* in the affairs of the state and religion (for both the Sunnis and the Shiʿa, although likely not at the same historical moment), and the transition to the post-classical, mature period is marked by the disturbance in social power structures with the Mongol invasion for the Sunnis, and with the rise of the Ṣafawids against the Ottomans for the Shiʿa as the likely parallel.[40]

An approach that emphasises the links between Shiʿi *tafsīr* and Sunni *tafsīr* as the genre progresses through history and that maps out those changes would be most helpful to gaining a full appreciation of the genre of *tafsīr*. For example, such an approach will help us recognise that the distinct Shiʿi elements that have been pointed out in descriptions of Shiʿi *tafsīr* are manifestations of counterparts to various arguments being made within Sunni *tafsīr*. Arguments are made in Sunni texts, for example, about which verses need to be interpreted and whether to correct and/or supplement the text or understand it (or 're-establish' it, literally) in a certain way by using the interpretive tools of *majāz* and *taqdīr*; both of these terms can refer to this process of 're-establishing' the fully explicit text of the Qur'an by drawing out meanings embedded in phenomena such as metaphor and ellipsis. This may be seen as a counterpart to the Shiʿi 'readings' of the text and notions of textual integrity. Both act to correct and supplement the text to match the perceived needs and expectations of the community. All this involves issues of what ideological points need to be made (e.g., arguments about grammar and arguments about the Imam are parallel

---

39 See Saleh, *Formation*, for example p. 8, where it is suggested that al-Thaʿlabī 'has redone the whole of al-Ṭabarī's work and in doing so reconsidered the entire tradition'.

40 This obviously summarises very superficially detailed theories as discussed in many scholarly studies. For the case of the transition to the classical period in Sunnism, see, for example, Ira M. Lapidus, 'The Separation of State and Religion in the Development of Early Islamic Society', *IJMES*, 6 (1975), pp. 363–375. Much of the work on Ibn Taymiyya is relevant to the case of the transition to the post-classical, mature period; see, for example, the essays in Yossef Rapoport and Shahab Ahmed, ed., *Ibn Taymiyya and His Times* (Oxford, 2010). For the Shiʿi situation, Mohammad Ali Amir-Moezzi, 'Appendix: Some Implications of the Occultation: Individual Religion and Collective Religion', in his *The Divine Guide in Early Shiʿism: The Sources of Esotericism in Islam* (Albany, NY, 1994), pp. 133–139, provides an excellent summary; also see Wilferd Madelung, 'Authority in Twelver Shiism in the Absence of the Imam', in *La notion d'autorité au moyen age: Islam, Byzance, Occident*, ed. George Makdisi, Dominique Sourdel and Janine Sourdel-Thomine (Paris, 1982), pp. 163–173.

methodologically), and what range and conception of authority need to be used for interpretation (whether preferring the Imams or a certain range of early Companions of Muḥammad). Whether the Qurʾan is subjugated to the authority of the Imams or the authority of grammar, the process, goals and outcomes remain the same. From this point of view, Shiʿi *tafsīr* can be incorporated within the overall study of the discipline and genre of *tafsīr*, with its own distinctiveness recognised (something which, I am implicitly arguing, tends not to happen when Shiʿi *tafsīr* is treated as a topic in itself). This should also assist us in coming to an understanding of transition points in the genre overall. The historical and ideological factors leading to the transitions may not be identical between the Sunnis and the Shiʿa, and the historical moments at which they happen may not be simultaneous, but the methodological parallels and the similarities in the nature of the causes are striking. Insight into those transitions can come from both Sunni and Shiʿi works.

The Formative Period

To what extent, then, can the pre-occultation period (pre-329/941) of Shiʿi *tafsīr* be seen as parallel to the formative period of Sunni *tafsīr*? The character of the *tafsīr* works by al-ʿAyyāshī (d. ca. 320/932), Fūrat al-Kūfī (d. ca. 300/912), al-Qummī, al-Nuʿmānī (d. ca. 360/971), Jaʿfar al-Ṣādiq (d. 148/765) and al-Ḥasan al-ʿAskarī (d. 260/874) has been given some extensive attention, especially in Bar-Asher's work.[41] The characteristics that Bar-Asher cites about early Shiʿi *tafsīr*s – especially commentary by means of *ḥadīth,* selective concern with the text of the Qurʾan and limited attention to doctrinal issues – may well be argued to convey characteristics that have parallels or are held in common with Sunni *tafsīr* of the first three centuries as studied in Wansbrough's *Quranic Studies.*[42] This is especially so if one understands the 'selectiveness' of the commentary in its treatment of isolated verses to be the common form of early *tafsīr*, rather than focusing on the doctrinal goals of such citations. One can compare the early Shiʿi works to that of *Maʿānī 'l-Qurʾān* of al-Farrāʾ (d. 207/822), for example; the latter's focus is on verses in need of, or worthy of, comment about grammatical features and other problems in the Qurʾanic text. This precisely parallels the Shiʿi need to explicate verses that contain within them allusions to the sources of social authority, the Imams. Overall, the formative period is marked by a clear subjugation of the text of the Qurʾan to these emerging notions of authority, the Imam for the Shiʿa and the grammarians for the Sunnis.

---

[41] Bar-Asher, *Scripture and Exegesis*, Meir M. Bar-Asher, 'The Qurʾānic Commentary Ascribed to Imām Ḥasan al-ʿAskarī', *JSAI*, 24 (2000), pp. 358–379, and *idem*, 'Exegesis ii. In Shiʿism', *EIR*, vol. 9, Fasc. 2, pp. 116–119, online: http://www.iranicaonline.org/articles/exegesis-ii (accessed 13 August 2013).

[42] Specifically part IV of his book.

Wansbrough makes infrequent reference to Shiʿi *tafsīr* within his descriptions of formative Muslim *tafsīr*.[43] He does not treat it as a separate category but, rather, notes perceptively one particular characteristic that it shares with other *tafsīr*s of the era but which is employed in a different way – that is, Shiʿi *tafsīr*s' tendency to use symbolic and typological interpretation within a rhetorical and literary approach to the text. This is, in some senses, a facet that Goldziher had already drawn attention to,[44] but for Goldziher, the outcome as 'sectarian' marks it as separate, even though the process by which that outcome is achieved is the same as that of mystical or rational approaches.

The Transition to the Classical Period

The emergence of the classical period in Shiʿi *tafsīr* has frequently been seen to be paralleled in the Sunni world when comparing the works of writers such as al-Ṭabarī and al-Thaʿlabī with those of al-Ṭūsī (*al-Tibyān fī tafsīr al-Qurʾān*) and al-Ṭabrisī (*Majmaʿ al-bayān fī tafsīr al-Qurʾān*). The transition is significant in scope, as has often been pointed out. Bruce Fudge has summarised this assessment particularly well:

> al-Ṭabrisī was taught by both a former student and a son of Abū Jaʿfar al-Ṭūsī, and al-Ṭūsī's *Tibyān* was the first comprehensive work of Imāmī exegesis. Previous works were much more eccentric in style and sectarian in orientation, and made no pretence to follow the grand example of al-Ṭabarī and others in including all the verses and all potentially relevant scholarly commentary, nor were they inclined to accept ambiguity or plurality of interpretation. The *Tibyān*, by contrast, included both Shiʿi and Sunni sources, employed the range of Islamic sciences from grammar to jurisprudence, and divided each verse's commentary accordingly just as al-Ṭabrisī would do a century later (with the different rubrics 'Reading', 'Declension', 'Language', 'Meaning' etc.).[45]

Even on issues of the integrity of the text of the Qur'an (the prime Shiʿi tag of the formative period), al-Ṭabrisī's tendency to find ways to use the glossing technique to produce the same meaning as others had earlier accomplished through textual emendation is, of course, critical as a hermeneutical point that is at the core of all *tafsīr* activity in this period, Sunni and Shiʿi.

Calder characterises the *tafsīr*s of this period as manifesting the rejection of meditations on the text that have no authority as well as the rejection of mystical/allegorical

---

[43] See the section on 'Rhetoric and Allegory' in Wansbrough, *Quranic Studies*, pp. 227–246, and especially p. 245.

[44] Goldziher, *Richtungen*, pp. 297–309 (German text), pp. 188–196 (English text).

[45] Bruce Fudge, *Qurʾānic Hermeneutics: al-Ṭabrisī and the Craft of Commentary* (London, 2011), pp. 38–39.

interpretations (pointedly an anti-sectarian position),[46] unless any of those aspects is accompanied by scholastic rigour (as illustrated in the Sunni world by someone such as Fakhr al-Dīn al-Rāzī [d. 606/1209]). This explanation is critical in conceptualising the emergence of the *tafsīr* works of al-Ṭūsī and al-Ṭabrisī within the Shiʿi tradition.

This period also sees significant figures such as al-Shaykh al-Mufīd (d. 413/1022), al-Sharīf al-Raḍī (d. 406/1015) and al-Sharīf al-Murtaḍā (d. 436/1044). Al-Sharīf al-Raḍī's available works, *Takhlīṣ al-bayān fī majāzāt al-Qur'ān* and *Ḥaqā'iq al-ta'wīl fī mutashābih al-tanzīl*, while not fitting within the formal definition of classical *tafsīr*, do illustrate the broadening of the discipline in the move away from the formative period. They are centrally concerned with anthropomorphism, reflecting the rise of Muʿtazilī-influenced theology,[47] linked to a sophisticated understanding of the function of language (what Kamal Abu Deeb has referred to as 'poetic alertness'[48]). Fitting the Persian work of Abu'l-Futūḥ Rāzī (d. after 525/1131), *Rawḍ al-jinān wa-rawḥ al-Janān*, into this context would be appropriate also.

Shiʿi works from the 7th/13th to the 10th/16th century appear to be little studied. Monnot suggests that the relative paucity of *tafsīr*s in the 8th/14th and 9th/15th centuries is the result of the Mongol invasions.[49] Works by Miqdād al-Suyūrī (*Kanz al-ʿirfān*, d. 826/1423), Sharaf al-Dīn al-Najafī (*Ta'wīl al-āyāt al-ẓāhira*, 10th/16th century) and others (likely including those influenced by Ibn ʿArabī [d. 638/1240] as cited by Lawson[50]) are known, but there is still much work to be done in coming to an overview of those *tafsīr*s that contain Shiʿi elements; but that may well be true of the many Sunni works that are available from this part of the classical period but which are similarly little studied. Overall, it is the comprehensive nature of the *tafsīr*s that can be pointed to in which it is not just a matter of authority but also of what is included in terms of content.

As suggested above in passing, the emergence of comprehensive works of *tafsīr* in the classical period is marked in both Sunni and Shiʿi circles by the rise of the *ʿulamā'* against the power of the caliph in the Sunni case (symbolised in the *miḥna*) and of the Imam for the Shiʿa (I leave the cause and effect relationship between these two for another discussion). This is marked in both instances by the emergence of the voice of the exegete in guiding his reader through the accumulated material, as Bar-Asher has pointed out.[51] The two events are not historically coincident but both

[46] Calder, 'Tafsīr', p. 134.

[47] See Mahmoud Ayoub, 'Literary Exegesis of the Qur'ān: The Case of al-Sharīf al-Raḍī', in Issa J. Boullata, ed., *Literary Structures of Religious Meaning in the Qur'ān* (Richmond, 2000), pp. 292–309.

[48] Kamal Abu Deeb, 'Studies in the *Majāz* and Metaphorical Language of the Qur'ān: Abū ʿUbayda and al-Sharīf al-Raḍī', in Issa J. Boullata, ed., *Literary Structures of Religious Meaning in the Qur'ān* (Richmond, 2000), p. 322.

[49] Guy Monnot, 'Islam: Exégèse coranique. I. 1. Introduction à l'exégèse duodécimaine', *Annuaire. Résumé des conferences et de travaux, Paris, EPHE, Ve section sciences religieuses*, 91 (1982–1983), pp. 309–317, at p. 315.

[50] Lawson, 'Hermeneutics', *EIR*.

[51] Bar-Asher, *Scripture and Exegesis*, pp. 75 and 80.

are certainly marked by the rise of the professional learned classes, the prominence of grammarians as arbiters of language,[52] and the impact of the decline in centralised power in the empire (as potentially a cause of the first factor). The genre of *tafsīr* thus goes through a similar transition for both the Sunnis and the Shiʿis, while emphasising differing ideological aspects within the grounding of its material. The unity of genre is upheld; the forces that make it what it is may be said to be common across any sense of an ideological divide.

The Transition to the Mature Phase

With the emergence of the Shiʿi post-classical, mature phase, Todd Lawson and Robert Gleave have already made the argument for this transition having elements in parallel with those emerging in the Sunni world.[53] The later exegetes such as ʿAbd ʿAlī al-Ḥuwayzī (d. before 1105/1693; *Nūr al-thaqalayn*), Muḥsin Fayḍ Kāshānī (d. 1090/1679; *al-Ṣāfī*), Hāshim al-Baḥrānī (d. 1107/1695 or 1109/1697; *al-Burhān*) and al-Sharīf al-ʿĀmilī al-Iṣfahānī (d. 1138/1726; *Mirʾāt al-anwār*), while certainly not representing the entire scope of post-classical Shiʿi *tafsīr* by any means, are certainly better studied than others and they illustrate a transition to a more methodologically constrained (while still voluminous) approach within the genre. Todd Lawson's essay on Akhbārī *tafsīr* is a helpful overview in this regard. Of these writers, Lawson states that they

> care almost nothing for stylistics, points of grammar and so on, except in so far as such concerns might impinge upon finding the true reading of the verse in question through metonomy or metaphor for the Imam or some related topic such as *walāya*. The Akhbārī approach is distinguished by the employment of vast numbers of oral reports … that bear directly, or sometimes indirectly … on the meaning of the Qurʾan. … virtually all of these reports are traced to one of the members of the holy family of Shiʿism.[54]

Lawson's suggestion of a parallel between Akhbārī works and the work of al-Ṭabarī (as representative of *tafsīr biʾl-maʾthūr*, the point on which Lawson sees the parallel) seems to me to miss the mark, however,[55] and his footnote reference to al-Suyūṭī (d. 911/1505) is a better comparison – as pointed out to him by Norman Calder

---

[52] It would be worth investigating the role of grammarians who were identified as Shiʿi in order to complete this picture.

[53] Todd Lawson, 'Akhbārī Shīʿī Approaches to *tafsīr*', in Hawting and Shareef, ed., *Approaches to the Qurʾān*, pp. 173–210. Robert Gleave, *Scripturalist Islam: The History and Doctrines of the Akhbārī Shīʿī School* (Leiden, 2007).

[54] Lawson, 'Akhbārī Shiʿi Approaches', p. 175.

[55] Ibid., p. 176.

– and that seems to suggest he had second thoughts also.[56] An even better parallel would be to Ibn Taymiyya and Ibn Kathīr (d. 774/1373) who initiate a tendency that then reaches its solidification in a work such as al-Suyūṭī's *al-Durr al-manthūr fī'l-tafsīr bi'l-ma'thūr*; the key methodological principle is seen in the strict adherence to the notion of transmitted authority. Says Lawson: 'Many of the traditions cited are explicitly anti-Sunni in nature, and all either explicitly or implicitly uphold and promulgate the absolute authority of the Imams.'[57] Ibn Taymiyya's ranking of the sources of authentic interpretation accomplishes precisely the same thing,[58] bringing *tafsīr* within the constraints of the discipline of *ḥadīth* and removing the 'extraneous' disciplines.

Robert Gleave's work on the Akhbārīs also adds significantly to the picture.[59] He points out that the label Akhbārī itself gives 'the impression that the Akhbārī identity of a scholar was an unproblematic description'.[60] Such is, of course, not the case, and much development both in response to outside groups and inside controversies took place. Gleave notes that the critical hermeneutical point underlying the exegetical approach is the claim that, in legal issues, the intended meaning (*murād*) of the Qur'an is unavailable to the inquiring mind.[61] The text of the Qur'an becomes supplanted by the guidance of the Imams as found in the *akhbār*. Even that position becomes modified, as seen in the lasting impact that the work of Muḥsin Fayḍ has had, where the exegete at least has some role to play, especially as far as the *muḥkam* verses were concerned.

The rise of the *akhbārī/uṣūlī* difference among the Shiʿa has been traced by Madelung back to the 6th/12th century, at least in its terminological heritage. That the controversy is a Muslim dispute with an even longer heritage is also evident, as illustrated by the debates between the traditionalists and the Muʿtazila over how to establish the law. The specific impact of this on the genre of *tafsīr* in the Sunni world, such that it would change the character and composition of these types of works, finds its most remarkable methodological development in Ibn Taymiyya, as recently analysed by Walid Saleh.[62] As well, the observations of Tariq al-Jamil on Ibn Taymiyya's situation as related to his interactions with Ibn al-Muṭahhar al-ʿAllāma al-Ḥillī (d. 726/1325) are important for documenting the 8th/14th century interactions between

---

[56] Ibid., p. 205, n. 11. Although see his essay 'Exegesis vi: In Akbārī and Post-Safavid Esoteric Shiʿism', *EIR*, vol. 9, pp. 123–125, online: http://www.iranicaonline.org/articles/exegesis-iv (accessed 13 August 2013), where the parallel remains.

[57] Lawson, 'Akhbārī Shiʿi Approaches', p. 176.

[58] As reflected by his *Muqaddima fī uṣūl al-tafsīr*; see Walid Saleh, 'Ibn Taymiyya and the Rise of Radical Hermeneutics: An Analysis of *An Introduction to the Foundations of Qur'ānic Exegesis*', in Rapoport and Ahmed, ed., *Ibn Taymiyya and His Times*, pp. 123–162.

[59] Gleave, *Scripturalist Islam*, especially ch. 7.

[60] Ibid., p. 216.

[61] Ibid., pp. 66–67, 218.

[62] Saleh, 'Ibn Taymiyya and the Rise of Radical Hermeneutics', pp. 123–162.

scholars of the two schools at the time.[63] This is not to suggest that later Akhbārī approaches are a response to such interactions and attacks – given the legacy of the general hermeneutical dispute there is no need to posit such influence – but the issues that are at stake become much clearer when viewed in this overall light, and the impact on the genre of *tafsīr* becomes that much more apparent.

The rise of *ḥadīth* criticism among Shiʿi scholars in this period is certainly to be remarked as significant. However, Saleh's point concerning Ibn Taymiyya's position is apt: it must not be thought that Ibn Taymiyya's ideas had a 'sweeping' impact on the medieval Sunni world;[64] but he did have an influence as seen in the works of scholars such as Ibn Kathīr and al-Suyūṭī. The same point needs to be made with Akhbārī *tafsīr* also, so as not to exaggerate its dominance. Note should be taken that Diana Steigerwald, in her essay 'Twelver Shīʿī *ta'wīl*', does not separate out the classical/post-classical periods at all and mentions the Akhbārīs as having no particular distinguishing marks, emphasising that it is possible to survey the genre without drawing particular attention to this manifestation.[65] However, the underlying importance cannot be denied:

> The moment a Hadith-centered approach to *tafsīr* was articulated theoretically it became impossible to reject it out of hand: one could only submit to the fundamental validity of this approach, in so far as it places the Hadith (loosely redefined by Ibn Taymiyya to include all *tafsīr* material from the *salaf* generations) at the centre of how one interprets the Qur'an.[66]

The hermeneutical point of the restriction of *tafsīr* to authenticated material (authenticated by the appropriate standards to achieve the desired goals) represents a significant contraction in the scope of the material invoked within the genre in an action that appears to move away from a celebration of polyvalence and incorporation of multiple disciplines to a desire to control meaning, and where the author's opinion, even if it be based on material deemed authentic, is pushed into the background.

However, as I just suggested, it is possible to exaggerate the impact of this shift. On the Sunni side the line between Ibn Kathīr and al-Suyūṭī, for example, is by no means a straight one. One only needs to consider the emergence of the subgenre of *ḥāshiya* and the significance that it takes on during this period to see that continued expansion and working within the tradition was possible.[67] There are also hundreds

---

[63] Tariq al-Jamil, 'Ibn Taymiyya and Ibn al-Muṭahhar al-Ḥillī: Shiʿi Polemics and the Struggle for Religious Authority in Medieval Islam', in Rapoport and Ahmed, ed., *Ibn Taymiyya and His Times*, pp. 229–246.

[64] Saleh, 'Ibn Taymiyya and the Rise of Radical Hermeneutics', p. 152.

[65] Diana Steigerwald, 'Twelver Shīʿī *ta'wīl*', in Andrew Rippin, ed., *The Blackwell Companion to the Qur'ān* (Oxford, 2006), pp. 373–385.

[66] Saleh, 'Ibn Taymiyya and the Rise of Radical Hermeneutics ', p. 153.

[67] Little studied but best illustrated by Lane, *Traditional Muʿtazilite Qur'ān Commentary*, Appendix Four, 'Authors of Works based on the *Kashshāf*'. Walid A. Saleh, 'The Gloss as Intellectual History: The *Ḥāshiyas* on al-Kashshāf', *Oriens*, 41 (2013), pp. 217–259.

of works of *tafsīr* that exist from this period which have yet to be examined with a scholarly eye and thus it is treacherous to generalise. The main point would be to say that other modes of exegesis do not disappear from the intellectual framework on either the Sunni or Shiʿi side.

Shiʿi *Tafsīr* Within the Genre of *Tafsīr*

Overall, it is clear that what we describe as Shiʿi *tafsīr* constitutes a part of the overall genre of *tafsīr* that reflects that genre's growing and maturation pains and joys. The critical element in terms of a descriptive approach to the genre does emerge in the area of authority as it shifts over time from community to intellect and to revealed text, in Calder's terminology. In this regard, it is important to remember that Sunni *tafsīr* is always marked by a limiting of authority to exclude those outside the generations of early Companions and followers who did not accept the authority of all the *rāshidūn*. ʿAlī b. Abī Ṭālib was, after all, an accepted source of authority for the Sunnis, but the other Imams were not. For the Shiʿa, on the other hand, this sense of authority and its conveyance varied in its constraints over time in cycles that were different from those experienced in Sunni *tafsīr*, but it, too, was purposefully limited within each of its conceptions.

5

The *Tafsīr* of al-Ḥibarī (d. 286/899): Qur'anic Exegesis and Early Shi'i Esotericism*

Mohammad Ali Amir-Moezzi

Some preliminary clarifications, mainly concerning methodological and epistemological issues, seem useful to me in order to ensure an appropriate approach and a better understanding of the present study.

The work that will be examined here, the Qur'anic commentary of al-Ḥibarī, belongs to the pre-Būyid Shi'ism. Judging by its earliest extant sources, expected to contain its fundamental doctrines, this Shi'ism is deeply marked by the initiatory, esoteric, mystical and even magical teachings.[1] This is what we can see indeed in the collections of traditions compiled by the great scholars of the 3rd/9th and of the first half of the 4th/10th centuries, such as the Imāmī scholars al-Barqī (d. 274/887–888 or 280/893–894), al-Ṣaffār al-Qummī (d. 290/902–903), al-Kulaynī (d. 329/941) or the Ismaili al-Qāḍī al-Nu'mān (d. 363/974).[2] Let us specify at this point that the collections of these authors are not constituted exclusively of the esoteric doctrines. For example, they also include many important chapters on legal matters. But the fact that they do include esoteric doctrines gives them a specific, almost unique status within the Islamic literature of this period, and more particularly within the *ḥadīth*

---

* Originally published as 'Le *Tafsīr* d'al-Ḥibarī (m. 286/899): Exégèse coranique et ésotérisme shi'ite ancien', *Journal des savants* (January–June, 2009), pp. 3–23. Translated from French into English for this volume by Orkhan Mir-Kasimov.

[1] See M. A. Amir-Moezzi and Christian Jambet, *Qu'est-ce que le Shî'isme?* (Paris, 2004), especially Part 1.

[2] Notwithstanding their different political orientation, there is little doctrinal divergence between principal Shi'i trends of the early period. The followers changing from one branch to another is a common practice. The *ḥadīth*s of al-Qāḍī Nu'mān's collection are mostly the same as those of al-Kulaynī's. As we will see later, the commentary of al-Ḥibarī, belonging to the Zaydī trend, is held in high esteem by the Twelver Imāmīs. This is why I do not think that it would be pertinent to establish any sharp distinction between the early Shi'i authors belonging to different trends, especially in what concerns *ḥadīth* literature.

literature.[3] In what concerns the pre-Būyid Qur'anic commentaries, they also have some remarkable specific features:[4] not one of the extant commentaries of this kind covers the whole Qur'an; the exegesis includes only a varying selection of *sūras* and/or verses. The commentaries are composed exclusively of the traditions attributed to the 'People of the prophetic House' (*ahl al-bayt*), namely the Prophet, Fāṭima and the Imams;[5] this is what is called *al-tafsīr bi-l-ma'thūr* (literally, 'the commentary by the means of traditions'). This selection is typological and concerns mostly the verses which can typically receive Shiʿi exegesis in the theological, legal or historical areas or, more specifically, in relation to the *ahl al-bayt*, their followers or their opponents. Grammatical, lexicological, philological and rhetorical kinds of exegesis are almost totally missing. In this regard, it will be enough to mention the *tafsīr*s of pseudo (?) al-Ḥasan al-ʿAskarī (the version transmitted by Abu'l-Ḥasan Muḥammad b. al-Qāsim al-Astarābādī),[6] al-Sayyārī (3rd/9th century),[7] ʿAlī b. Ibrāhīm al-Qummī (d. after 307/919),[8] Furāt al-Kūfī (d. ca. 300/912),[9] al-ʿAyyāshī (d. beginning of

[3] For the Shiʿi *ḥadīth* literature (i.e., the teachings going back to the Prophet and to the Imams), see G. Lecomte, 'Aspects de la littérature du *ḥadîth* chez les Imâmites', in T. Fahd, ed., *Le Shîʿisme Imâmite* (Paris, 1970), pp. 91–101; K. Modīr Shānīhchī, 'Kotob-e arbaʿe-ye ḥadīth-e shīʿe', *Nāme-ye Āstān-e Qods*, 1–2 (NS), 18 (Mashhad, n.d. [ca. 1975]), pp. 43–65; E. Kohlberg, 'Shīʿī *Ḥadīth*', in A. F. L. Beeston et al., ed., *The Cambridge History of Arabic Literature*, vol. 1: *Arabic Literature to the End of the Umayyad Period* (Cambridge, 1983), pp. 299–307; M. A. Amir-Moezzi, *Le Guide divin dans le Shiʿisme originel: Aux sources de l'ésotérisme en Islam* (Paris-Lagrasse, 1992; 2nd ed., 2007), pp. 48–58; M. ʿA. Mahdavī Rād, A. ʿĀbidī and ʿA. Rafīʿī, 'Ḥadīth', in *Tashayyuʿ: sayrī dar farhang va tārīkhi tashayyuʿ* (it is the article 'tashayyo' of *Dā'irat al-maʿārif-ī tashayyuʿ*) (Tehran, 1373 Sh./1994), pp. 109–127; A. J. Newman, *The Formative Period of Twelver Shīʿism: Hadith as Discourse Between Qumm and Baghdad* (Richmond, 2000); R. Gleave, 'Between *Ḥadīth* and *Fiqh*: The "Canonical" Imāmī Collections of *Akhbār*', *Islamic Law and Society*, 8 (2001), pp. 350–382.

[4] For general information about these commentaries, see M. M. Bar-Asher, *Scripture and Exegesis in Early Imāmī Shiism* (Leiden and Jerusalem, 1999).

[5] For the reasons behind this translation of *ahl al-bayt*, see M. A. Amir-Moezzi, 'Considérations sur l'expression *dīn ʿAlī*: Aux origines de la foi Shiʿite', *ZDMG*, 150 (2000), pp. 29–68; repr. in M. A. Amir-Moezzi, *La religion discrète: croyances et pratiques spirituelles dans l'Islam Shiʿite* (Paris, 2006), chapter 1.

[6] Al-Imām al-Ḥasan al-ʿAskarī (attributed to), *Tafsīr* (Qumm, 1409/1988) (there exist several other editions of all works quoted here); on this work see M. M. Bar-Asher, 'The Qur'ān Commentary Ascribed to Imam Ḥasan al-ʿAskarī', *JSAI*, 24 (2000), pp. 358–379.

[7] On him and his works see now M. A. Amir-Moezzi and E. Kohlberg, 'Révélation et falsification: introduction à l'édition du *Kitāb al-qirā'āt* d'al-Sayyārī', *Journal Asiatique*, 293 (2005), pp. 663–722. On the commentary of al-Sayyārī , better known under the title 'The Book of Quranic Variant Readings', see M. A. Amir-Moezzi and E. Kohlberg, *Revelation and Falsification: The* Kitāb al-Qirā'āt *of Aḥmad b. Muḥammad al-Sayyārī*, critical edition, introduction and notes by E. Kohlberg and M. A. Amir-Moezzi (Leiden, 2009).

[8] ʿAlī b. Ibrāhīm al-Qummī, *Tafsīr*, ed. Ṭ. Al-Mūsawī al-Jazā'irī (Najaf, 1386–1387/1966–1967).

[9] Furāt b. Ibrāhīm al-Kūfī, *Tafsīr*, ed. M. al-Kāẓim (Tehran, 1410/1990).

4th/10th century) and, of course, al-Ḥibarī (see below).[10] I call this pre-Būyid Shiʿism or, more specifically, its foundational doctrines, the 'original esoteric and non-rational' tradition.[11]

The situation changed when the Būyids acquired access to the leadership shortly before the end of the first half of the 4th/10th century. The reasons for this are complicated and intertwined: the political supremacy of Shiʿism with the Fatimids, the Qarmaṭīs and the Ḥamdānids in the most important parts of the Islamic Empire, in addition to the Būyids being in the centre of the caliphate; the Occultation of the last Imam of the Twelvers in 329/941 as attested to by the tradition itself; and the orientation of Islamic thought towards rationalistic patterns. The combination of these historical, political and religious reasons led, in particular, to the emergence of a new class of Twelver jurist-theologians in the circles close to the Būyid princes, who aimed at justifying their rule. As the Abbasid caliph had still not been dismissed and the Sunnis still had a comfortable majority, these scholars felt an urgent need to legitimise their position and ensure that it was respected. They begin, therefore, to distance themselves from their predecessors belonging to the 'original non-rational tradition' and to criticise them. This is the beginning of the development, within Twelver Shiʿism, of the new 'theologico-legal rationalistic' tradition which will from now on constitute the dominant majority, pushing the primitive esoteric tradition into isolation.[12] In regard to the exegetical literature, the monumental commentary of al-Shaykh al-Ṭūsī (385–460/995–1067), the brilliant representative of this new tradition, *al-Tibyān fī tafsīr al-Qur'ān*, is a hallmark of this turning point. It is, indeed, most probably the first commentary that covers all Qur'anic verses where the features specific to the Shiʿi approach are almost entirely erased, toned down or simply drowned in the grammatical, lexicological, theological and legal forms of exegesis. Indeed, besides the authorities belonging to the *ahl al-bayt*, other personalities, even those belonging to Sunnism, are quoted, as well as the personal opinions of the author (which are called *al-tafsīr bi-l-ra'y*).[13] After this period, the commentaries related to the original tradition, to which the work of al-Ḥibarī belongs, become rare until the Ṣafawid times, after the 10th/16th century, and the partial reconstruction of the traditionalism of Imāmī Shiʿism.[14]

---

[10] Abu'l-Naḍr Muḥammad b. Masʿūd al-ʿAyyāshī, *Tafsīr*, ed. H. Rasūlī Maḥallātī (Qumm, 1380/1960). On these three last works see M. M. Bar-Asher, *Scripture and Exegesis*, chapter 1; also M. M. Bar-Asher, 'Exégèse sunnite et chiite', in M. A. Amir-Moezzi, ed., *Dictionnaire du Coran* (Paris, 2007), pp. 312–320.

[11] M. A. Amir-Moezzi, *Le Guide divin*, chapter 1.

[12] Ibid., and also Amir-Moezzi and Jambet, *Qu'est-ce que le shiʿisme?*, part 3, chapters 1 and 2.

[13] Al-Shaykh Abū Jaʿfar al-Ṭūsī, *al-Tibyān fī tafsīr al-Qur'ān*, ed. A. Ḥ. Qaṣīr al-ʿĀmilī (Beirut, ca. 1995). This commentary, as well as its close paraphrase written by al-Faḍl b. al-Ḥasan al-Ṭabrisī (d. 548/1154), *Majmaʿ al-bayān fi tafsīr al-Qur'ān* (Beirut, 1374–1377/1954–1957), are the two most influential Qur'anic exegeses of the rationalist trend.

[14] Let us limit ourselves to the names of some of the best-known works belonging to this traditionalist genre: al-Sayyid Ḥaydar al-Āmulī (8th/14th century), *Tafsīr al-Muḥīṭ al-aʿẓam*

I

Already in its earliest texts, Shiʿism defines itself as a hermeneutical doctrine. The teaching of the Imam/*walī* comes essentially to reveal the hidden meaning (or meanings) of the Revelation. Without the commentaries and the explanations of the *walī*, the Scripture revealed by the Prophet (*nabī*) remains obscure and its deepest levels cannot be understood. For instance, already in the fragments which seem to belong to the most archaic layers of the *Kitāb Sulaym b. Qays*, considered the oldest Shiʿi text (first half of the 2nd/8th century),[15] we can read:

> ʿAlī proclaimed: Question me before you lose me! By God, at the moment of revelation (*tanzīl*) of every verse, the Messenger of God recited it to me, so that, in my turn, I could recite it to him, and I had the knowledge of the interpretation of its hidden meaning (*taʾwīl*).[16]

In another place, the same work gives an explanation, remarkable for this early time, of the necessity of the *taʾwīl* as hermeneutics of the Qurʾan, explanation of the hidden meaning of the Book which brings forth its spirit hidden by the letter. It is the dialogue between ʿAbd Allāh Ibn ʿAbbās, cousin and Companion of the Prophet Muḥammad and follower of ʿAlī, and the ʿUmayyad Muʿāwiya b. Abī Sufyān, a bitter enemy, as is well known, of the latter:

---

waʾl-baḥr al-khiḍam, ed. M. al-Mūsawī al-Tabrīzī (Tehran, 1414/1993); al-Fayḍ al-Kāshānī (d. 1091/1680), *Tafsīr al-Ṣāfī*, 2 vols (Tehran, n.d.); Hāshim b. Sulaymān al-Baḥrānī (d. 1107/1695–1696 or 1109/1697–1698), *al-Burhān fī tafsīr al-Qurʾān*, 5 vols (Tehran, n.d.); ʿAbd al-ʿAlī b. Jumʿa al-Ḥuwayzī (d. ca. 1112/1700–1701), *Tafsīr nūr al-thaqalayn*, ed. H. al-Rasūlī al-Maḥallātī (Qumm, 1412/1991–1992); Abuʾl-Ḥasan al-Sharīf al-ʿĀmilī al-Iṣfahānī (d. after 1140/1727–1728), *Tafsīr mirʾāt al-anwār*, litho. ed. (Tehran, 1303/1885–1886) (the introduction of this commentary has been published in Qumm in 1393/1973); Sulṭān ʿAlī Gunābādī (d. 1327/1909), *Tafsīr bayān al-saʿāda* (Tehran, n.d). See also below the examples of the 'personalised commentaries' related to the same tradition.

[15] *Kitāb Sulaym b. Qays al-Hilālī*, ed. M. B. al-Anṣārī al-Zanjānī al-Khuʾīnī (Qumm, 1414/1994); on this major work see now H. Modarressi, *Tradition and Survival: A Bibliographical Survey of Early Shīʿite Literature* (Oxford, 2003), pp. 83–86, and M. A. Amir-Moezzi, 'Note bibliographique sur le *Kitāb Sulaym b. Qays*, le plus ancien ouvrage Shiʿite, in M. M. Bar-Asher and S. Hopkins, ed., *Le Shīʿisme Imāmite quarante ans après. Hommages à Etan Kohlberg* (Paris and Turnhout, 2009), pp. 33–48.

[16] *Kitāb Sulaym b. Qays al-Hilālī*, tradition no. 31, vol. 2, p. 802 (= 2:802), ed. M. B. al-Anṣārī, 3 vols (Qumm, 1426/1995); see also Abū Jaʿfar al-Ṭūsī, *al-Amālī*, ed. M. Ṣ. Baḥr al-ʿUlūm, vol. 2 Najaf, 1384/1964), p.136; al-Majlisī (d. 1110/1699), *Biḥār al-anwār* (Tehran and Qumm, 1376–1392/1956–1972), vol. 40, p. 186. Concerning the pair of terms *tanzīl/taʾwīl*, the revelation of the Scripture and the search for its hidden meaning, Daniel Gimaret translates them as the 'letter' and the 'spirit' of the Qurʾan, using this famous Paulinian pair; see Shahrastānī, *Livre des religions et des sectes*, tr. D. Gimaret and G. Monnot (Paris and Louvain, 1986), vol. 1, p. 543. In the rest of this chapter, I will resort to this translation which seems the most pertinent to me.

Ibn ʿAbbās: Do you forbid us [i.e., the *ahl al-bayt*] to read the Qur'an?
Muʿāwiya: No.
- Do you forbid us to seek the knowledge of its spirit?
- Yes.
- Then, [according to you] we must read the Qur'an without questioning ourselves what was the intention of God [when He revealed such and such a verse]?
- Yes.
- But which duty is most important: to read the Qur'an or to act up to it?
- To act up to it.
- And how can we act upon it if we are not aware of the divine intention which is within what God has revealed to us?[17]

This dialogue alone explains and justifies the old and recurring Shiʿi conception according to which the Qur'an remains 'mute' until the Imam operates its hermeneutics. The Imam is thus identified with the actual tongue, the true word of the Qur'an, which contains and reveals the 'Intention of God'. Hence, the pair of concepts includes the Qur'an as 'the mute Book or Guide' (*kitāb/imām ṣāmit*), and the Imam as the 'speaking Qur'an' (*qur'ān nāṭiq*).[18]

In one of the sermons attributed to ʿAlī, he declares:

> This light by the means of which we are guided, this Qur'an which you asked to speak and which will not speak. It is me who will inform you concerning it, what it contains of the knowledge of the future, of the teaching on the past, of the healing of your sufferings and of the setting in order of your relationships.[19]

The same doctrine is contained in the Shiʿi axiom *al-walāya bāṭin al-nubuwwa*, 'the *walāya* is the hidden aspect of the prophetic mission'. The *walāya*, the real substance of the Shiʿi religion,[20] is principally constituted by the nature and the function of the *walī*/Imam, and the fundamental initiatory role of the latter is the disclosing of the secrets hidden behind the letter of the Scriptures. To this extent, it seems safe to say that the axiom, expressed in a thousand different ways in Shiʿi works of all periods, defines Shiʿism as the hermeneutical doctrine par excellence of Islam and,

---

17 *Kitāb Sulaym b. Qays al-Hilālī*, tradition no. 26, vol. 2, pp. 782–783 ; see also al-Majlisī, *Biḥār al-anwār*, vol. 33, p. 173 and vol. 44, p. 128.

18 Mahmoud Ayoub, 'The Speaking Qur'ān and the Silent Qur'ān: A Study of the Principles and Development of Imāmī Tafsīr', in A. Rippin, ed., *Approaches to the History of the Interpretation of the Qur'ān* (Oxford, 1988), pp. 177–198.

19 Al-Imām ʿAlī b. Abī Ṭālib (attributed to), *Nahj al-balāgha* (compiled by al-Sharīf al-Raḍī), ed. ʿA. N. Fayḍ al-Islām (Tehran, 1351 Sh./1972), sermon no. 157, p. 499.

20 M. A. Amir-Moezzi, 'Notes à propose de la *walāya* imamite (aspects de l'imamologie duodécimaine X)', *JAOS*, 122 (2002), pp. 722–741 (repr. in *La religion discrète*, chapter 7); M. Massi Dakake, *The Charismatic Community: Shiʿite Identity in Early Islam* (New York, 2007) (a monograph on the concept of *walāya*). I will come back to this question below.

therefore, as its esoteric dimension: 'Everything has a secret. The secret of Islam is the Shiʿism', according to a lapidary tradition going back to the Imam Jaʿfar al-Ṣādiq.[21] The hermeneutic nature of Shiʿism, conveyed through the teachings of the Imams, is also strongly highlighted by the famous *ḥadīth* of the 'Fighter for the *ta'wīl*'. It is a prophetic tradition where it is said that Muḥammad proclaimed:

> There is among you [i.e., my followers] someone who fights for the spiritual interpretation of the Qur'an like I fought for the letter of the Revelation, and this person is ʿAlī b. Abī Ṭālib.[22]

A similar saying is attributed to ʿAmmār b. Yāsir, faithful Companion of the Prophet and of ʿAlī. He uttered it during the Battle of Ṣiffīn, where the armies of the latter opposed those of Muʿāwiya: 'By the One who holds my life in His Hand, we fight today against our enemies for the spirit of the Revelation, just as we fought them before for its letter.'[23]

According to the idea conveyed by these traditions, ʿAlī, the Imam par excellence, 'father' of all other Imams and the supreme symbol of Shiʿism, comes in order to achieve the mission of Muḥammad by revealing, through his hermeneutical teachings, the spirit hidden under the letter of the Revelation. The same idea is expressed in another prophetic tradition quoted by the Ismaili thinker Ḥamīd al-Dīn al-Kirmānī (d. after 427/1036): 'I am the master of the revealed letter [of the Qur'an] and ʿAlī is the master of the spiritual hermeneutics.'[24]

> Every revealed verse without exception, ʿAlī used to say, the Prophet recited to me, dictated it to me so that I write it down with my own hand. He taught me the esoteric (*ta'wīl*) and exoteric (*tafsīr*) interpretation [of every verse], abrogating and abrogated, firm and ambiguous. Simultaneously, the Messenger of God implored God that He would implant in me the understanding and the learning by heart. And indeed, I did not forget a single word of it.[25]

---

[21] Al-Kulaynī, *al-Rawḍa min al-Kāfī*, ed. H. Rasūlī Maḥallātī (Tehran, 1386/1969), vol. 2, p. 14; Ibn ʿAyyāsh al-Jawharī (d. 401/1011), *Muqtaḍab al-athar* (Tehran, 1346/1927), p. 23.

[22] Al-ʿAyyāshī, *Tafsīr*, vol. 1, p. 15; al-Khazzāz al-Rāzī (4th/10th century), *Kifāyat al-athar* (Qumm, 1401/1980), pp. 76, 88, 117, 135 (on p. 66 of this work, in a tradition attributed to the Prophet, it is the *qā'im*, the eschatological Saviour, who is presented as the 'fighter for the spiritual hermeneutics'); al-Majlisī, *Biḥār al-anwār*, vol. 19, pp. 25–26; al-Baḥrānī, *al-Burhān*, vol. 1, p. 17. See also M. M. Bar-Asher, *Scripture and Exegesis*, p. 88, note 1.

[23] See al-Masʿūdī (d. 345/956), *Murūj al-dhahab*, ed. C. Pellat (Beirut, 1965–1979), § 1676; French trans. C. Pellat, *Les Prairies d'or* (Paris, 1962–1997), vol. 3, p. 655: 'Par Celui qui tient ma vie dans sa main, tout comme nous les avons combattus (naguère) au nom de la révélation (du Coran), nous les combattons certes aujourd'hui pour son interprétation.'

[24] Al-Kirmānī, *Majmūʿat al-rasā'il*, ed. M. Ghālib (Beirut, 1983), p. 156.

[25] Al-Ḥākim al-Ḥaskānī (d. after 470/1077–1078), *Shawāhid al-tanzīl*, ed. M. B. al-Maḥmūdī (Beirut, 1393/1974), vol. 1, p. 35.

Other traditions, also transmitted by non-Shiʿi sources, underline the role of ʿAlī as someone initiated into the mysteries of the Qurʾan. These traditions are repeatedly quoted in Shiʿi works:

> The Qurʾan has been revealed according to seven letters (*sabʿat aḥruf*),[26] and every letter includes an apparent (*ẓāhir*) and a hidden (*bāṭin*) levels. ʿAlī b. Abī Ṭālib is the one who has the knowledge of the exoteric (*ẓāhir*) as well as of esoteric (*bāṭin*) [levels of the Qurʾan].[27]

Also, 'With the exception of the Prophet, nobody is more knowledgeable than ʿAlī in regard to what is contained between the two covers of the Book of God.'[28]

To conclude, let us cite the famous prophetic *ḥadīth*: "ʿAlī is with the Qurʾan and the Qurʾan is with ʿAlī.'[29] The prophets are thus the messengers of the letter of the divine Word intended for the majority of believers, and the Imams are the messengers of the spirit of the same Word taught to a minority of initiated. This minority is made up of the 'Shiʿis' of every religion. The historical Shiʿis, those of Islam, consider themselves therefore as the last link in this long initiatory chain which goes back to the beginning of humankind.[30] This dialectic, based on the complementary pairs of the Prophet and the Imam, of the *nubuwwa* and the *walāya,* of the letter of the Revelation and its spiritual hermeneutics (*tanzīl/taʾwīl*), is essential to one of the most

---

[26] On the complexity of the term *ḥarf*, pl. *ḥurūf, aḥruf*, in the context of Qurʾanic studies, see K. Versteegh, *Arabic Grammar and Quranic Exegesis in Early Islam* (Leiden, 1993), index *s.v.*

[27] Abū Nuʿaym al-Iṣfahānī (d. 430/1038), *Ḥilyat al-awliyāʾ* (Cairo, 1351/1932–1933), vol. 1, p. 65 (tradition attributed to Ibn Masʿūd); Sulaymān b. Ibrāhīm al-Qundūzī (d. 1294/1877), *Yanābīʿ al-mawadda* (Najaf, n.d.), p. 448 (tradition attributed to Ibn ʿAbbās).

[28] Al-Ḥākim al-Ḥaskānī, *Shawāhid al-tanzīl*, vol. 1, p. 36 (tradition attributed to ʿĀmir al-Shaʿbī). The doctrinal affiliation of al-Ḥaskānī is not clear. It seems that he was a Ḥanafī Sunni with strong Shiʿi sympathies, or even more probably a crypto-Shiʿi practising *taqiyya* (the duty of secrecy); see E. Kohlberg, *A Medieval Muslim Scholar at Work: Ibn Ṭāwūs and his Library* (Leiden, 1992), pp. 150–151.

[29] Sulaymān b. Aḥmad al-Ṭabarānī (d. 360/970–971), *al-Muʿjam al-ṣaghīr*, ed. ʿA. Muḥammad (Medina, 1388/1968), vol. 1, p. 255; al-Ḥakīm al-Nīsābūrī (d. 405/1014), *al-Mustadrak ʿalā al-Ṣaḥīḥayn* (Hyderabad, n.d.; repr., Riyad), vol. 3, p. 124. Finally, the well-known *ḥadīth* of 'two Precious Objects (*ḥadīth al-thaqalayn*)' should also be included among these traditions. In this *ḥadīth*, transmitted in different versions, the Prophet would have basically declared that he leaves behind him two precious objects to his community, the Qurʾan and his Family; see Amir-Moezzi, *Le Guide divin*, p. 215, and especially Bar-Asher, *Scripture and Exegesis*, pp. 93–98.

[30] This conception is the central topic of the work attributed to al-Masʿūdī, *Ithbāt al-waṣiyya* (Qumm, 1417/1996); see also M. Molé, 'Entre le Mazdéisme et l'islam: la bonne et la mauvaise religion', in *Mélanges Henri Massé* (Tehran, 1963), pp. 303–316; E. Kohlberg, 'Some Shīʿī Views on the Antediluvian World', *SI*, 52 (1980), pp. 41–66; repr. in Kohlberg, *Belief and Law in Imāmī Shīʿism* (Aldershot, 1991), article 16; Amir-Moezzi, *Le Guide divin*, parts II–1 and II–2.

specific features of Shiʿism, namely its 'dual world view', according to which every part of reality, from the highest to the most trivial, has at least two levels: one manifest, exoteric (*ẓāhir*) which conceals another, secret and esoteric one (*bāṭin*), and the concealed gives the meaning to the apparent.[31] I return later to this organic relationship between the figure of the Imam and the *walāya* which is its characteristic, both of which are most often represented by the figure of ʿAlī.

The antiquity and centrality of these doctrines undoubtedly explain the early appearance and abundance of the exegetical works in the Shiʿi milieu. The bibliographical and prosopographical works contain the lists of more than 100 works of this genre compiled roughly during the time of the historical Imams, that is, from the 1st/7th to the second half of the 3rd/9th century. There is no extant work from the period preceding the 3rd/9th century, with the exception of the fragments included in the later writings. In addition to the well-known names of the exegetical Shiʿi literature of the 3rd/9th century that we have already mentioned,[32] a significant part of these writings goes back to the direct disciples of the Imams like Abu'l-Jārūd (belonging to the Zaydī trend; born ca. 80/699), Jābir b. Yazīd al-Juʿfī (d. 127/744–745), Abān b. Taghlib (d. 141/758–759), Thābit b. Dīnār, better known by the name of Abū Ḥamza al-Thumālī (d. 150/767), or Muqātil b. Sulaymān (belonging to the Zaydī trend; d. 150/767) and Aḥmad b. Muḥammad b. Khālid al-Barqī (d. 274/887–888 or 280/893–894).[33] As we have mentioned, all these texts would have been the collections of exegetical *ḥadīth*s attributed to the Imams, probably without any addition on the part of the compiler who gave his name to the work.

II

Al-Ḥusayn b. al-Ḥakam b. Muslim Abū ʿAbd Allāh al-Kūfī al-Washshāʾ al-Ḥibarī (d. 286/899), the traditionist and exegete of the Qur'an, would have been, according to the last three elements of his name, the most often reported by his biographers, a native of Kūfa in Iraq, and traded or produced materials and clothes, because *al-washy* as well as *al-ḥibar* are the names of clothes probably made of silk or made from this precious material.[34] Notwithstanding the doubts expressed by some of his

---

[31] Amir-Moezzi and Jambet, *Qu'est-ce que le Shiʿisme?*, part I, chapter 1.

[32] See notes 6 to 10 above and related texts.

[33] On the writings of this period see Modarressi, *Tradition and Survival.*

[34] On him, see, for example, Abu'l-Faraj al-Iṣfahānī (d. 356/967), *Maqātil al-Ṭālibiyyīn*, ed. A. Ṣaqr (Cairo, 1368/1948), p. 435; al-Dāraquṭnī (d. 385/995), *al-Sunan*, ed. ʿA. H. al-Madanī (Cairo, 1386/1966–1967), vol. 1, p. 355; al-Najāshī (d. 450/1058), *Rijāl*, ed. M. J. al-Nāʾīnī (Beirut, 1408/1988), p. 5; al-Khaṭīb al-Baghdādī (d. 463/1071), *Taʾrīkh Baghdād* (Cairo, 1349/1930), vol. 8, p. 449; Ibn Mākūlā (d. 475/1082–1083), *al-Ikmāl* (Hyderabad, 1383/1963), vol. 3, p. 40; al-Samʿānī (d. 562/1166), *al-Ansāb* (Hyderabad, 1382–1402/1962–1982), vol. 4, p. 45; al-Dhahabī (d. 748/1348), *al-Mushtabah* (Cairo, 1962), vol. 1, p. 184; Ibn Ḥajar al-ʿAsqalānī (d. 852/1449), *Lisān al-mīzān* (Hyderabad, 1330/1911), vol. 2, p. 201, no. 911. Almost every onomastic element of our author is recorded in different versions following different sources: al-Ḥasan instead of

biographers, it seems clear that he was a Shiʿi of Zaydī trend. However, the Twelvers always made a claim on him, a fact that shows once more the permeability of the doctrinal borders between different Shiʿi groups, especially in the early times.[35] The information concerning the teachers and direct transmitters of al-Ḥibarī can be found in the works of his biographers, and the chains of transmission (*isnād*) are quoted in his own or in related works.[36] Some of his teachers are not Shiʿi, such as ʿAffān b. Muslim al-Ṣaffār al-Baṣrī, Ibārhīm b. Isḥāq al-Kūfī al-Ṣīnī or Jandal b. Wāliq al-Taghlabī al-Kūfī; but mostly they are Shiʿis and belong to the Zaydī branch. First of all, Imam Muḥammad b. ʿAlī al-Jawād (the ninth Imam of the Twelvers), al-Ḥusayn b. al-Ḥasan al-Fazārī al-Kūfī (considered as extremist Shiʿi, *ghālin*), al-Ḥusayn b. Naṣr b. Muzāḥim al-Minqarī (son of the well-known author of the *Waqaʿat Ṣiffīn*), al-Ḥasan b. al-Ḥusayn al-ʿUranī al-Anṣārī (one of the Zaydī leaders of his time), al-Faḍl b. Dukayn al-Kūfī (known as moderate Shiʿi), Mukhawwil b. Ibrāhīm al-Nahdī al-Kūfī (a Zaydī who took part in the armed revolt of Yaḥyā b. ʿAbd Allāh) and Yaḥyā b. Hāshim al-Ghassānī (an important Zaydī figure). The situation is the same with his disciples and transmitters. Among the non-Shiʿis we can mention Aḥmad b. Muḥammad Ibn al-Aʿrābī, Khaythama b. Sulaymān al-Qurashī and ʿAlī b. Muḥammad al-Nakhaʿī al-Qāḍī; among the Shiʿis: Furāt b. Ibrāhīm al-Kūfī (author of the well-known *Tafsīr*), Ibn ʿUqda Abu'l-ʿAbbās al-Kūfī (a Jārūdī Zaydī), Aḥmad b. Isḥāq b. al-Buhlūl al-Anbārī (a Zaydī judge), al-Ḥusayn b. ʿAlī b. al-Ḥasan al-ʿAlawī al-Miṣrī, as well as ʿAlī b. Ibrāhīm al-ʿAlawī al-Madanī and ʿAlī b. ʿAbd al-Raḥmān al-Sabīʿī al-Kūfī (all three of them are learned Zaydī notables).

Two works of al-Ḥibarī are extant. The first is *al-Musnad*, a collection of 63 traditions on different topics and going back to the Prophet's contemporaries (Ḥudhayfa, Khālid b. al-Walīd, Ibn ʿAbbās, Abū Ayyūb al-Anṣārī, ʿĀ'isha, ʿAlī, etc.). The great majority of traditions are devoted to the innumerable virtues of ʿAlī and his praise,

---

al-Ḥusayn; al-Ḥākim instead of al-Ḥakam; al-Ḥīrī, al-Jubayrī or al-Jabrī instead of al-Ḥibarī, etc.

35 Notwithstanding the reluctance of some rare Imāmī prosopographers to count him among the Shiʿi authors (for example, al-Baḥrānī (1107/1695–1696 or 1109/1697–1698), *Ghāyat al-marām*, litho. ed. (Iran, 1272/1855–1856), p. 364), the Shiʿism of al-Ḥibarī seems evident from the contents of his writings. His adherence to the Zaydī trend also seems to be confirmed by the religious identity of a great number of his teachers and transmitters (see below). Among the early Imāmīs, he is listed as Zaydī by al-Najāshī and in the *Fihrist* of Shaykh al-Ṭūsī (ed. M. Ṣ. Baḥr al-ʿUlūm [Najaf, 1380/1960], p. 137), and by modern authors such as Muḥsin al-Amīn (d.1371/1952), *Aʿyān al-Shīʿa* (Damascus, 1948), vol. 25, p. 342, and al-Khū'ī (d. 1413/1992), *Muʿjam rijāl al-ḥadīth* (Najaf, 1390/1970), vol. 4, p. 321 and vol. 5, pp. 224–225. Useful references concerning his Zaydism are, for example, Abu'l-Faraj al-Iṣfahānī, *Maqātil al-Ṭālibiyyīn*, pp. 215, 251, 435–437, as well as the Zaydī work of al-Sayyid Yaḥyā b. al-Ḥusayn al-Hārūnī, *Taysīr al-maṭālib* (Beirut, 1395/1975), pp. 55 and 61. It seems, however, that al-Ḥibarī more or less managed to hide his creed because many Sunni prosopographers, even if they give little credence to his reliability as a transmitter of *ḥadīth*, do not tell anything about his Shiʿism.

36 See the introduction of al-Sayyid Muḥammad Riḍā al-Ḥusaynī to his edition of the *Tafsīr* of al-Ḥibarī (Beirut, 1408/1987), pp. 47–71 (on the editions of this work, see below).

especially by the Prophet himself.[37] The second work is, of course, his Qurʾanic commentary, which has been published at least twice.[38] It is known under several titles: *Tanzīl al-āyāt al-munzala fī manāqib ahl al-bayt*, *Mā nazala min al-Qurʾān fī amīr al-muʾminīn*, *Mā nazala min al-Qurʾān fī ahl al-bayt*, *al-Āyāt al-muntazaʿa*, and more commonly, *Tafsīr al-Ḥibarī*.[39] The principal transmitter of the book is the learned Shiʿi Abū ʿUbaydallāh Muḥammad b. ʿImrān al-Marzubānī al-Baghdādī (born 296/908–909; d. 384/994).[40] The commentary itself and its supplement contain 100 traditions. Nearly all of them go back to the Companion Ibn ʿAbbās and concern the presumed allusions or the hidden meanings of the Qurʾan related to ʿAlī, the members of his family, his followers and his opponents. From this point of view, the work can be considered as a kind of *asbāb al-nuzūl* ('Occasions of Revelation') genre,[41] in a Shiʿi version which hides its identity behind the authority of Ibn ʿAbbās.

In order to get a better idea about al-Ḥibarī's Qurʾanic commentary, let us translate some extracts from it (we will not concern ourselves with the chains of transmission of the traditions – the *isnād* – which are not pertinent to our subject):

- Commentary of the *sūra* 2 (*al-Baqara*), verse 25: 'But give glad tidings to those who believe and work righteousness.' Ibn ʿAbbās: 'This verse was revealed concerning ʿAlī, Ḥamza [b. ʿAbd al-Muṭṭalib], Jaʿfar [b. Abū Ṭālib] and ʿUbayda b. al-Ḥārith b. ʿAbd al-Muṭṭalib.'[42]

---

[37] al-Ḥibarī , *al-Musnad*, ed. al-Sayyid Muḥammad Riḍā al-Ḥusaynī, in *Turāthunā*, 32–33 (1413/1992), pp. 275–385.

[38] First by al-Sayyid Aḥmad al-Ḥusaynī: al-Ḥusayn b. al-Ḥakam al-Ḥīrī [*sic*], *Mā nazala min al-Qurʾān fī ahl al-bayt ʿalayhim al-salām* (Qumm, 1395/1975); then by al-Sayyid Muḥammad Riḍā al-Ḥusaynī: al-Ḥusayn b. al-Ḥakam al-Ḥibarī, *Tafsīr* (Beirut, 1408/1987). I use this second edition, which is definitely the best of the two. It includes: a substantial introduction – however in traditionalist spirit – on the author and his works (pp. 9–229); the text of the Qurʾanic commentary containing 71 traditions, on the basis of two manuscripts (pp. 231–330); the supplement (*mustadrak*) of the commentary containing 29 traditions reported by our author and picked up by the editor in other sources (pp. 333–374); commentary on the traditions and their parallels in other works (pp. 377–542); the index (pp. 545–658); and bibliography (pp. 659–689).

[39] The introduction of al-Sayyid Muḥammad Riḍā al-Ḥusaynī to his edition of the *Tafsīr* of al-Ḥibarī, pp. 77f.

[40] On him see al-Khaṭīb al-Baghdādī, *Taʾrīkh Baghdād*, vol. 3, p. 135; Ibn Shahrāshūb (d. 588/1192), *Maʿālim al-ʿulamāʾ*, ed. M. Ṣ. Baḥr al-ʿUlūm (Najaf, 1380/1960), p. 118; *idem*, *Manāqib Āl Abī Ṭālib*, 3 vols (Najaf, 1956), vol. 3, p. 83; R. Sellheim, *EI2*, vol. 6, pp. 634–635.

[41] See A. Rippin, 'Occasions of Revelation', in *The Encyclopaedia of the Qurʾān* (Leiden, 2002), vol. 3, pp. 569–573; M. Yahia, 'Circonstances de la révélation', in Amir-Moezzi, ed., *Dictionnaire du Coran*, pp. 168–171. See also the interesting developments in A. Radtke, *Offenbarung zwischen Gesetz und Geschichte* (Wiesbaden, 2003), pp. 39–58.

[42] Tradition no. 4, p. 235: see al-Ḥibarī, *Tafsīr*, ed. M.R. al-Ḥusaynī (Beirut, 1408/1987). The personages mentioned here were, according to the traditional sources, among the first Muslims and protectors of the Prophet. In what concerns the occurrences of the traditions in other sources, in order not to overload the footnotes, we refer the reader to the excellent compilation by the editor M. R. al-Ḥusaynī , p. 377f. (see note 36 above).

- Qur'an 2 (*al-Baqara*), verse 45: 'Seek (God's) help with patient perseverance and prayer: It is indeed hard, except to those who bring a lowly spirit.' Ibn 'Abbās: Those who bring a lowly spirit are those who lower themselves in the prayer [before God] and who go to the prayer with enthusiasm. This concerns the Messenger of God and 'Alī.[43]
- Qur'an 2 (*al-Baqara*), verses 81–82: 'Nay, those who seek to gain in evil, and are girt round by their sins …' Ibn 'Abbās: 'This was revealed concerning Abū Jahl.' 'But those who have faith and work righteousness, they are companions of the Garden: therein shall they abide (for ever).' Ibn 'Abbās: 'This was revealed specially about 'Alī because he was the first convert [in Islam] and the first, after the Prophet, who performed the ritual prayer.'[44]
- Qur'an 3 (*Āl 'Imrān*), verse 61: 'Come! Let us gather together, our sons and your sons, our women and your women, ourselves and yourselves: Then let us earnestly pray, and invoke the curse of God on those who lie.' Ibn 'Abbās: '[This verse] was revealed concerning the "selves" of the Messenger of God and of 'Alī; [the expression] "our women and your women" refers to Fāṭima; "our sons and your sons" refers to "Ḥasan and Ḥusayn" [*sic*: both names are written without article].'[45]
- Qur'an 5 (*al-Mā'ida*), verse 55: 'Your (real) friends are (no less than) Allah, His Messenger and the (fellowship of) believers, those who establish regular prayers and regular charity, and they bow down humbly (in worship).' Ibn 'Abbās: 'This was revealed especially concerning 'Alī.'[46]
- Qur'an 5 (*al-Mā'ida*), verse 67: 'O Messenger. Proclaim the (message) which hath been sent to thee from thy Lord. If thou didst not, thou wouldst not have fulfilled and proclaimed His mission.' Ibn 'Abbās: 'This was revealed concerning 'Alī. Indeed, the Prophet received the order to declare 'Alī [his successor]. Therefore, he took his hand and said: "Of whosoever I am the master (*mawlā*), 'Alī is his master. O Lord! Love whoever loves 'Alī (*wāli man wālāhu*) and be an enemy of whoever opposes him."'[47] This tradition is completed by another which interprets Qur'an 13 (*al-Ra'd*), verse 43, reported by the traditionist 'Abd Allāh b. 'Aṭā who quotes the Imam Abū Ja'far Muḥammad al-Bāqir: 'God revealed

---

43 Tradition no. 6, p. 238.

44 Tradition no. 8, pp. 240–241. Abū Jahl was one of the well-known opponents of Islam.

45 Tradition no. 12, pp. 247. On this verse see P. Ballanfat and M. Yahia, 'Ordalie', in Amir-Moezzi, ed., *Dictionnaire du Coran*, pp. 618–620; on the conception see W. Schmucker, 'Mubāhala', *EI2*, vol. 7, pp. 276–277.

46 Tradition no. 22, p. 260. The occurrences are innumerable, as can be expected in Shi'i works (see Schmucker, 'Mubāhala', pp. 438–446).

47 Tradition no. 24, pp. 262–263. On the semantic complexity of the root WLY in Shi'ism and the related terms, see M. A. Amir-Moezzi, 'Notes à propose de la *walāya* imamite (aspects de l'imamologie duodécimaine X)' (n. 20 above). The maxim would have been uttered by the Prophet in Ghadīr Khumm (on this place, highly symbolic for the Shi'is, see L. Veccia Vaglieri, 'Ghadir Khumm', in *EI2*, vol. 2, pp. 993–994 ; M. Dakake and A. Kazemi Moussavi in *EIR*, vol. 10, pp. 246–249.

to His Messenger: "Say to the people: 'Of whosoever I am the master, 'Alī is his master.'" But the Prophet, afraid of the people, did not say this. Therefore, God revealed to him: "O Messenger, proclaim the (message) which hath been sent to thee from thy Lord. If thou didst not, thou wouldst not have fulfilled and proclaimed His mission." It was then that the Messenger of God took the hand of 'Alī, the day of Ghadīr Khumm, and said: "Of whosoever I am the master 'Alī is his master".'[48]

- Qur'an 9 (*al-Tawba*), verses 20–21: 'Those who believe, and suffer exile and strive with might and main, in God's cause, with their goods and their persons, have the highest rank in the sight of God. They are the people who will achieve (salvation). Their Lord doth give them glad tidings of a Mercy from Himself, of His good pleasure, and of gardens for them, wherein are delights that endure.' Ibn 'Abbās: 'This was revealed especially concerning 'Alī.'[49]
- Qur'an 13 (*al-Raʿd*), verse 7: 'But thou art truly a warner, and to every people a guide.' Abū Barza: 'I heard the Messenger of God say: "Thou art truly a warner" and he put his hand on his own chest [meaning that this verse refers to the Prophet], while reciting "to every people a guide" he pointed out 'Alī with his hand.'[50]
- Qur'an 14 (*Ibrāhīm*), verse 27: 'God will establish in strength those who believe, with the word that stands firm.' Ibn 'Abbās: 'This concerns the *walāya* of 'Alī b. Abī Ṭālib.'[51]
- Qur'an 32 (*al-Sajda*), verse 18: 'Is then the man who believes no better than the man who is rebellious and wicked?' Ibn 'Abbās: '"The man who believes" refers here to 'Alī b. Abī Ṭālib and the "rebellious and wicked" to al-Walīd b. 'Uqba b. Abī Muʿayṭ.'[52]
- Qur'an 33 (*al-Aḥzāb*), verse 33: 'God only wishes to remove all abomination from you, ye members of the Family, and to make you pure and spotless.' Around 10 traditions reported from several Companions of the Prophet (Ibn 'Abbās, Abu'l-Ḥamrā', Anas b. Mālik, etc.) and particularly from Umm Salama, the wife of the Prophet, identify the 'members of the Family' mentioned in the Qur'anic verse with the Five of the Cloak, that is, Muḥammad, 'Alī, Fāṭima, al-Ḥasan and al-Ḥusayn.[53]

[48] Tradition no. 41, pp. 285–287. The text seems to suggest that the phrase 'Of whosoever I am the master, 'Alī is his master' was originally included in the Qur'anic Revelation. On the Qur'an and the question of its falsification, see Amir-Moezzi and Kohlberg, 'Révélation et falsification' (n. 7 above); on studies concerning this topic, see the same article, notes 123 to 126 and related texts, pp. 695–697.

[49] Tradition no. 34, p. 274.

[50] Tradition no. 39, pp. 282–283. Abū Barza al-Aslamī is a Companion of the Prophet.

[51] Tradition no. 42, p. 288.

[52] Tradition no. 48, p. 295. Al-Walīd is an opponent of Muḥammad and 'Alī.

[53] Traditions nos 50–59, pp. 297–311. This interpretation, particularly appreciated by the Shiʿis, is also cited very frequently, including the Sunni sources; see ibid., pp. 502–533.

- Qur'an 66 (*Lam tuḥarrim = al-Taḥrīm*), verse 4: 'But if ye back up each other against him [i.e., the Prophet], truly God is his Protector, and Gabriel, and (every) righteous one among those who believe.' Asmā' bint 'Umays: '"The righteous one among those who believe" is 'Alī b. Abī Ṭālib.' The same verse is interpreted by Ibn 'Abbās as: 'the expression "each other" refers to 'Ā'isha and Ḥafṣa. "God is his Protector" refers to the Messenger of God. "The righteous one among those who believe" was revealed exceptionally concerning 'Alī.'[54]

It seems to me that this selection of sample quotations, conveying in general the same message, is enough to illustrate clearly the nature and contents of the *Tafsīr* of al-Ḥibarī. The different Qur'anic verses are thus considered as the codes referring to the persons or historical groups clearly identified by the personages respected for their knowledge of religious matters and of the Qur'an (wives and Companions of the Prophet, epigones of Shi'i Imams, etc.). In this identification of the figures 'hidden' behind the letter of the Qur'an, 'Alī has, by far, the lion's share. The pro-'Alid character of our *Tafsīr* is thus beyond doubt. But it is as if al-Ḥibarī, resorting to the persons who could be accused of Shi'i sectarianism, wanted to demonstrate, on the one hand, his impartiality and his moderation and, on the other hand, the objective reality of the sacredness of 'Alī and to a lesser degree of the other members of the *ahl al-bayt*. This kind of exegesis, where different figures from the Prophet's circle are perceived under the veil of a particular Qur'anic verse, can also be found in the works of the non-Shi'i authors, but is less evident and mostly, as has already been emphasised, in the context of the 'Occasions of Revelation'. Within Shi'ism it becomes a genuine literary genre. Two specific features of this genre are particularly amplified in the course of time. First, the elimination of the non-Shi'i figures from the chains of transmission in favour of the Shi'is and especially of the Imams considered as the principal transmitters of the tradition or the principal exegetes of the Qur'anic text. Secondly, the persons identified from behind the letter of the Qur'an will be, in the order of their frequency, 'Alī, other members of the 'Five of the Cloak' (Muḥammad, Fāṭima, al-Ḥasan and al-Ḥusayn), their historical opponents in accordance with the Shi'i views, other Imams, their followers and their opponents.

Let us call this genre 'individualised interpretations'. Though not very elegant, this expression has the advantage of being clear. Interpretations of this kind are numerous in Shi'ism. Let us quote some examples:

- In the 3rd/9th century: *Mā nazala min al-Qur'ān fī amīr al-mu'minīn* ('That which was revealed in the Qur'an concerning the Prince of believers', i.e., 'Alī)

[54] Traditions nos 67 and 68, pp. 323–325. Asmā' bint 'Umays was the wife of Ja'far b. Abī Ṭālib, cousin of the Prophet, and afterwards of Abū Bakr. 'Ā'isha, daughter of the latter, and Ḥafṣa, daughter of 'Umar, were the wives of the Prophet. Both of them are loathed by the Shi'is because of their hostility to 'Alī. They are considered spies of their 'hypocrite' fathers in the house of Muḥammad.

of Ibrāhīm b. Muḥammad al-Thaqafī (d. 283/896), the author of the well-known *Kitāb al-ghārāt*.[55]

- In the 4th/10th century: the *Tafsīr* of Furāt al-Kūfī (d. ca. 300/912), a disciple of al-Ḥibarī;[56] *Kitāb al-tanzīl fī l-naṣṣ ʿalā amīr al-muʾminīn* ('The Book of Revelation, in the text of the Qurʾan, on the Prince of believers'; also known by other titles) of Ibn Abī al-Thalj (d. 322/934 or 325/936–937);[57] *Asmāʾ amīr al-muʾminīn min al-Qurʾān* ('The Denominations of the Prince of the believers in the Qurʾan') of Ibn Shammūn Abū ʿAbd Allāh al-Kātib (d. ca. 330/941–942);[58] *Mā nazala fiʾl-khamsa* ('That which was revealed concerning the Five', i.e., the Five of the Cloak) and *Mā nazala fī ʿAlī min al-Qurʾān* ('That which was revealed concerning ʿAlī extracted from the Qurʾan') of ʿAbd al-ʿAzīz al-Jalūdī al-Baṣrī (d. 332/944);[59] *Taʾwīl mā nazala min al-Qurʾān fī ahl al-bayt* ('Esoteric interpretation of that which was revealed in the Qurʾan concerning the People of the House of the Prophet'; this title has several variants) of Muḥammad b. al-ʿAbbās al-Bazzāz known as Ibn al-Juḥām (was alive in 328/939–940);[60] *Mā nazala min al-Qurʾān fī ṣāḥib al-zamān* ('That which was revealed in the Qurʾan concerning the Master of the Time', that is, the Mahdī; title has several variants) of Ibn ʿAyyāsh al-Jawharī (d. 401/1010), author of *Muqtaḍab al-athar*.[61]
- In the 5th/11th century: *Āy al-Qurʾān al-munazzala fī amīr al-muʾminīn ʿAlī b. Abī Ṭālib* ('The Qurʾanic verses revealed on the Prince of the believers ʿAlī b. Abī Ṭālib') of al-Shaykh al-Mufīd (d. 413/1022);[62] two books of al-Ḥākim al-Ḥaskānī (d. after 470/1077–1078), namely *Khaṣāʾiṣ amīr al-muʾminīn fiʾl-Qurʾān* ('Specific characteristics of the Prince of believers in the Qurʾan')[63] and *Shawāhid al-tanzīl* ('Testimonies to the Revelation').[64]
- In the 6th/12th century: *Nuzūl al-Qurʾān fī shaʾn amīr al-muʾminīn* ('The Revelation of the Qurʾan concerning the rank of the Prince of believers') of Muḥammad b. Muʾmin al-Shīrāzī (exact dates unknown);[65] *Khaṣāʾiṣ al-waḥy al-mubīn fī manāqib amīr al-muʾminīn* ('Particular features of the clear Revelation

---

55 Al-Najāshī, *Rijāl*, p. 12; Āghā Buzurg al-Ṭihrānī (d. 1389/1970), *al-Dharīʿa ilā taṣānīf al-Shīʿa* (Tehran-Najaf, 1353–1398/1934–1978), vol. 19, p. 28. The work seems to be lost; generally, this would be the case when there is no reference to an edition of the text under discussion.

56 Furāt al-Kūfī, *Tafsīr* (n. 9 above).

57 Kohlberg, *A Medieval Muslim Scholar*, p. 355, no. 594.

58 Al-Najāshī, *Rijāl*, p. 52; al-Ṭihrānī, *al-Dharīʿa*, vol. 2, p. 65.

59 Al-Najāshī, *Rijāl*, p. 180; al-Ṭihrānī, *al-Dharīʿa*, vol. 19, pp. 28 and 30.

60 Kohlberg, *A Medieval Muslim Scholar*, pp. 369–371, no. 623.

61 Al-Najāshī, *Rijāl*, p. 67; Ibn Shahrāshūb, *Maʿālim al-ʿulamāʾ*, p. 20; al-Ṭihrānī, *al-Dharīʿa*, vol. 19, p. 30.

62 Kohlberg, *A Medieval Muslim Scholar*, p. 132, no. 83.

63 Ibn Shahrāshūb, *Maʿālim al-ʿulamāʾ*, p. 78.

64 Kohlberg, *A Medieval Muslim Scholar*, pp. 330–331, no. 542; al-Ḥākim al-Ḥaskānī, *Shawāhid al-tanzīl*, ed. M. B. al-Maḥmūdī (Beirut, 1393/1974). On the possible Shiʿi affiliation of al-Ḥaskānī, see note 28 above.

65 Kohlberg, *A Medieval Muslim Scholar*, p. 307, no. 488.

concerning the virtues of the Prince of believers') of Ibn al-Biṭrīq al-Ḥillī (d. 600/1203–1204).[66]

- In the 8th/14th century: *al-Durr al-thamīn fī khams mi'a āya nazalat fī amīr al-mu'minīn* ('The precious Pearl of the 500 verses revealed about the Prince of believers'; other variants of the title also exist) of al-Ḥāfiẓ Rajab al-Bursī.[67]
- In the 10th/16th century: *Ta'wīl al-āyāt al-ẓāhira fī faḍā'il al-ʿitrat al-ṭāhira* ('Esoteric interpretation of the letter of the Qur'anic verses concerning the virtues of the Pure Family', i.e., of the Family of the Prophet) of Sharaf al-Dīn al-Astarābādī.[68]
- At the turn of the 11th/17th and 12th/18th centuries: two works of Hāshim b. Sulaymān al-Baḥrānī, *al-Lawāmiʿ al-nūrāniyya fī asmā' amīr al-mu'minīn al-qur'āniyya* ('The flows of light on the Qur'anic names of the Prince of believers')[69] and *al-Maḥajja fī mā nazala fi'l-qā'im al-ḥujja* ('The broad way to what was revealed concerning the Qā'im the Proof', i.e., Mahdī).[70]
- In the 13th/19th century: *al-Āyāt al-nāzila fī dhamm al-jā'irīn ʿalā ahl al-bayt* ('The verses revealed in order to denounce those who were unfair to the Family of the Prophet') of Ḥaydar ʿAlī al-Shīrwānī,[71] and *al-Naṣṣ al-jalī fī arbaʿīn āya fī sha'n ʿAlī* ('The radiant text of forty verses on the rank of ʿAlī') of al-Ḥusayn b. Bāqir al-Burūjirdī.[72] It should be noted that works of this kind are still being written in Shiʿi circles.

III

What is particularly esoteric in this kind of Qur'anic exegesis? In the first instance, one might think that the perception of the Qur'anic text as an encrypted message which needs an exegesis in order to reveal its secrets can be considered in itself as an esoteric process of an initiatory kind. The 'individualised interpretation', revealing the historical personages behind the veil of the letter of the Qur'an, exemplifies a

---

66 Ed. M. B. al-Maḥmūdī (Tehran, 1406/1986).

67 Ed. al-Sayyid ʿAlī ʿĀshūr (Beirut, 1424/2003).

68 Ed. Ḥ. al-Ustād Walī (Qumm, 1417/1996).

69 Published in Qumm, 1394/1974–1975.

70 Ed. M. M. al-Mīlānī (Beirut, 1413/1992).

71 Al-Ṭihrānī, *al-Dharīʿa*, vol. 1, p. 48.

72 Ibid., vol. 24, p. 172. The work was published in Tehran, 1320/1902–1903 (I have not seen it). It must be noted that the Sunni authors with Shiʿi sympathies also wrote these kinds of works, but of course less commonly. Some examples are the pro-mystic Abū Nuʿaym al-Iṣfahānī (d. 430/1038) in his *Mā nazala min al-Qur'ān fī amīr al-mu'minīn* (al-Ṭihrānī, *al-Dharīʿa*, vol. 19, p. 28); the fragments of this work reported by other sources were edited by M. B. al-Maḥmūdī in *al-Nūr al-mushtaʿal al-muqtabas min kitāb Mā nazal min al-Qur'ān fī amīr al-mu'minīn* (Tehran, 1406/1985); Ibn al-Faḥḥām al-Nīsābūrī (d. 458/1066), author of *al-Āyāt al-nāzila fī ahl al-bayt* (Ibn Ḥajar, *Lisān al-mīzān*, vol. 2, p. 251), and al-Ḥākim al-Jushamī al-Bayhaqī (d. 494/1100–1101), belonging to the Muʿtazilī and Zaydī trend, in his *Tanbīh al-ghāfilīn* (Cairo, n.d.).

form of esotericism which seems older than more sophisticated esotericism incorporating complicated cosmogonical, Imamological, theological, eschatological and other doctrines. It is even not impossible that the first type of esotericism could have been at the root of the second one.[73]

But there is probably more than that. What is the message that this kind of Shiʿi Qurʾanic exegesis strives to convey, beyond the persons thus identified in the divine Revelation?[74] Do the 'individualised interpretations' in general, and the *Tafsīr* of al-Ḥibarī in particular, contain any secret Shiʿi teaching? Does there exist any 'subliminal message' that the authors of this literary genre would try to insinuate to the followers?

We have already mentioned the 'dual' world view, exemplified by the pairs of complementary terms such as prophet/Imam, *nubuwwa/walāya*, letter of the Revelation/its spiritual hermeneutics (*tanzīl/taʾwīl*), etc.[75] However, in Shiʿism, a second, 'dualist' world view completes and interprets the first one. According to this 'dualist' perspective, the universe is a broad battlefield where, from the time of the creation, the forces of knowledge fight with the forces of ignorance. In other words, the different Allies of God (*awliyāʾ*, i.e., prophets, Imams, saints of all times) and their insiders confront their opponents and the followers of the latter.[76] This cosmic battle begins even before the creation of the empirical world by the conflict between the soldiers (*junūd*) of the cosmic Intelligence (*al-ʿaql*), the cosmogonical Imam of the forces of Good and the archetype of the terrestrial Imam, and the soldiers of the cosmic Ignorance (*al-jahl*), the captain of the forces of evil and the archetype of the foe of the Allies of God.[77] The war continues as a struggle which, at any time, places the Imams of the different legislator prophets and their followers against their opponents led by the chieftains who deny the mission of the prophets and/or that of the Imams.[78] This dualism develops in relationship with a 'theory of opposites' (*ḍidd*, pl. *aḍdād*), exemplified by the fundamental 'pairs' such as Intelligence/Ignorance, Imam/enemy of the Imam (*ʿaduww al-imām*), people of the right/people of the left (*aṣḥāb al-yamīn/aṣḥāb al-shimāl*), guides of the light/guides of the darkness (*aʾimmat al-nūr/aʾimmat al-ẓalām*), or *walāya/barāʾa* , that is to say, the sacred love towards the Allies of God

[73] On the first kind of esotericism see Amir-Moezzi, 'Note bibliographique sur le *Kitāb Sulaym b. Qays*'. On the second kind, see idem, *Le Guide divin* as well as the series of articles entitled 'Aspects de l'imamologie duodécimaine', now published together in idem, *La religion discrète*.

[74] I insist on the adjective 'Shiʿi' because the Sunni literature also has a genre of 'individualised interpretations' intended to meet a totally different doctrinal need concerning the 'Occasions of Revelation'. The details in these two cases are altogether different.

[75] See note 31 above and the related text.

[76] On these two world views symbolised by the 'vertical axis' of the initiation and the 'horizontal axis' of the fight, see Amir-Moezzi, *Le Guide divin*, 'Quelques conclusions', pp. 308–310.

[77] See M. A. Amir-Moezzi, 'Cosmogony and Cosmology in Twelver Shiʿism', *EIR*, vol. 4, pp. 317–322.

[78] See al-Masʿūdī (attributed to), *Ithbāt al-waṣiyya* (Qumm, 1417/1996) and other references, see note 30 above.

and the disassociation from their opponents (I will come back to that last kind of opposition later on).[79] The opponents of the *walāya*, the people of the *barāʾa*, are not necessarily the pagans and the unbelievers. The Israelites who betrayed Moses by devoting themselves to the cult of the Golden Calf, or the Companions of the Prophet who betrayed him by putting aside ʿAlī, his only true initiate, are not the non-Jews or non-Muslims, but those who deny the esoteric part of the religion, depriving the latter of its deepest meaning. Indeed, during the era of Islam, the opponents, the foes, are those who deny the *walāya* of ʿAlī and, after that, the *walāya* of the Imams belonging to his line of descent. This includes, in this case, almost all the Companions, and in particular the first three caliphs, the Umayyads, the Abbasids, and, more generally, all those to whom the Shiʿis refer as 'the majority' (*al-akthar*) or the 'mass' (*al-ʿāmma*), that is to say, those who will later be referred to as 'the Sunnites'.[80]

This dualist vision, which emerged very early in the ʿAlid circles, gradually referred to as the Shiʿis, is evidently conveyed by the 'individualised commentaries' including that of al-Ḥibarī. As we saw, the maxims and negative concepts of the Qurʾanic text are mostly related to the opponents, real ones or ideologically supposed, of Muḥammad and of ʿAlī. At the same time, the positive discourse and notions are related, in the majority of cases, to ʿAlī, the members of his family or his followers. This hermeneutical conception is clearly announced in many traditions permanently used in the Shiʿi works:

> The Qurʾan is revealed in four parts: a quarter is about us (i.e., us, the members of the Prophet's Family), another quarter is about our opponent, the third quarter is about the lawful and the unlawful, and the last quarter is about the duties and the precepts. The noblest parts of the Qurʾan belong to us.[81]
>
> Seventy verses were revealed about ʿAlī, nobody else can be related to them.[82]
>
> Considering what was revealed concerning him, ʿAlī has no match in the Book of God.[83]

---

79 M. A. Amir-Moezzi, 'Seul l'homme de Dieu est humain. Théologie et anthropologie mystique à travers l'exégèse imamite ancienne (Aspects de l'imamologie duodécimaine IV)', *Arabica*, 45 (1998), pp. 193–214 (repr. in *La religion discrète*, chapter 8).

80 This attitude of the Shiʿis in regard to their opponents is expressed in a particularly concise manner by the term *ṣabb al-ṣaḥāba* ('swearing at the Companions'); on this topic, see I. Goldziher, 'Spottnamen der ersten Chalifen bei den Schiʿiten', repr. in J. De Somogyi, ed., *Gesammelte Schriften* (Hildesheim, 1967–1973), vol. 4, pp. 291–305; A. S.Tritton, *Muslim Theology* (London, 1947), pp. 27f., and particularly E. Kohlberg, 'Some Imāmī Shīʿī Views on the *ṣaḥāba*', *JSAI*, 5 (1984), pp. 143–175 (repr. in Kohlberg, *Belief and Law*, part IX).

81 Tradition often attributed to ʿAlī, but also to the Prophet, and reported with different variants. See, for instance, al-Ḥibarī, *Tafsīr*, tradition no. 2, p. 233; Furāt al-Kūfī, *Tafsīr*, pp. 45f; al-Ḥākim al-Ḥaskānī, *Shawāhid al-tanzīl*, nos 57f.

82 Tradition going back to Mujāhid: al-Ḥakīm al-Ḥaskānī, *Shawāhid al-tanzīl*, vol. 1, p. 43.

83 Tradition going back to Ibn ʿAbbās: al-Ḥakīm al-Ḥaskānī, *Shawāhid al-tanzīl*, vol. 1, pp. 39f.

A very early work that always circulated under the name of Sulaym b. Qays – the book that we have already mentioned – provides another textual basis of the dualist vision because it is wholly devoted to the exposure of the corruption of the majority Islam immediately after the death of the Prophet. This corruption would be the result of the betrayal of the greater number of the Companions, the first two caliphs at their head, and of their greed for power. These people misappropriated the leadership of the young Islamic community after they pushed aside ʿAlī, the only true initiate of Muḥammad, and deprived him of the power intended for him by the order of God and of his Messenger.[84] At the same time, the *Kitāb Sulaym b. Qays* reports a great number of traditions related to the 'individualised Qurʾanic commentaries':

> The verses *Sūra* 89 (*al-Fajr*), 25–26 are associated with Abū Bakr and ʿUmar: 'For, that Day, His chastisement will be such as none (else) can inflict. And His bonds will be such as none (other) can bind.'[85]
>
> The verses *Sūra* 9 (*al-Tawba*), 100 and *Sūra* 56 (*al-Wāqiʿa*), 10 are said to be linked to the person of ʿAlī: 'The vanguard (of Islam) – the first of those who forsook (their homes) and of those who gave them aid', and 'those foremost (in faith) will be foremost (in the Hereafter). These will be those nearest to God.'[86]
>
> The verses *Sūra* 98 (*al-Bayyina*), 7 and 6 are associated with the friends and the enemies of ʿAlī respectively: 'Those who have faith and do righteous deeds, they are the best of creatures.' And 'those who reject (Truth), among the People of the Book and among the Polytheists, will be in Hellfire, to dwell therein (for aye). They are the worst of creatures.'[87]
>
> The verses *Sūra* 14 (*Ibrāhīm*), 37, 22 (*al-Ḥajj*), 77 and 2 (*al-Baqara*), 143 are associated with ʿAlī: '[O our Lord] fill the hearts of some among men with love towards them'; 'O ye who believe! Bow down, prostrate yourselves, and adore your Lord, and do good, that ye may prosper'; 'Thus, have We made of you an intermediate community, that ye might be witnesses over the people.'[88] Same for the verses 11(*Hūd*), 17 and 13 (*al-Raʿd*), 43: 'those who accept a clear (sign) from their Lord, and whom a witness from Himself doth teach'; 'such as have knowledge of the Book'.[89]

---

[84] See note 15 above and the related text.

[85] *Kitāb Sulaym b. Qays al-Hilālī*, ed. M. B. al-Anṣārī al-Zanjānī al-Khuʾīnī (Qumm, 1414/1994), vol. 2, pp. 595–596 (tradition no. 4). However, it should be noted that the *Tafsīr* of al-Ḥibarī seems to be much more 'moderate' than the *Kitāb Sulaym b. Qays* or other pre-Būyid Qurʾanic commentaries, such as the works of al-Sayyārī, al-ʿAyyāshī or al-Qummī, to the extent that he never cites the figures respected by the non-Shiʿis, as for example the first three caliphs, among the opponents of the Prophet and/or of ʿAlī.

[86] Ibid., vol. 2, pp. 643–644 (tradition no. 11).

[87] Ibid., vol. 2, pp. 832–833 (tradition no. 41).

[88] Ibid., vol. 2, pp. 885–886 (tradition no. 54).

[89] Ibid., vol. 2, p. 903 (tradition no. 60).

> And of course, the well-known verse 33 (*al-Aḥzāb*), is associated with the Five of the Cloak:[90] 'And Allah only wishes to remove all abomination from you, ye members of the Family, and to make you pure and spotless.'[91]

One of the esoteric levels of this kind of Qur'anic commentary aims thus at justifying and maintaining the 'dualist world view' in the mind of followers, weaving it into the very framework of the holy Book. However, another level seems to play exactly the same role with regard to the 'dual world view'. On this level, the figure of 'Alī, brought forward in the commentaries on an impressive number of verses, transcends the historical personage. It comes to symbolise the figure of Imam par excellence, perfectly representing all the initiator guides of all times, as well as their nature and function, that is, the divine Alliance (*walāya*), with all its doctrinal complexity.

We have already noted the organic relationship that links the Revelation to the figure of Imam, who is the messenger of its spirit, the tongue of the Book which otherwise would remain 'mute', a sealed letter, because it would be incomprehensible and thus inapplicable. 'Alī is the symbol of this 'Master of hermeneutics' (*ṣāḥib al-ta'wīl*) who is *walī*/Imam, a conception exemplified by uncountable traditions. In addition, the first Imam of the Shi'is is also the supreme symbol and the personification of the *walāya*. This gives additional dimensions to such maxims, going back to the Prophet, as "Alī is with the Qur'an and the Qur'an is with 'Alī', the maxim that we mentioned above.

What is the meaning of *walāya* in Shi'ism? In its technical sense, *walāya* has three main semantic levels, complementary and interdependent:[92] the imamate, the love of the Imam/*walī* and the theology of the metaphysical Imam, that is, the Imam as the locus of the full manifestation of God. These three semantic levels, or significations, cannot be separated from each other, because they are all referred to by the one and unique term of *walāya* which makes it impossible to translate the latter by a single word. Indeed, in the Shi'i religious consciousness, these three levels are bound together by an organic link: the historical imamate, the intrinsic nature and the initiatory role of the terrestrial Imam leads to the religion of love of the revealed Face of God which is the cosmic Imam.[93] This is why the *walāya* constitutes the substance of the faith. Without the *walāya*, there is no religion. Without the spirit, the letter is dead; it is just a lifeless body, because the *walāya* forms the core, the depth, the secret heart of any prophetic mission and of any Revelation. This idea is exemplified by the recurrent expression *al-walāya bāṭin al-nubuwwa*. Al-Ṣaffār al-Qummī (d. 290/902–903) devoted many chapters of the second section of his work *Baṣā'r*

[90] See note 54 above and the related text.

[91] Ibid., vol. 2, pp. 909–910 (tradition no. 62)

[92] See the references in note 20 above.

[93] On this central conception of the Shi'i esotericism, see M. A. Amir-Moezzi, 'Aspects de l'imamologie duodécimaine. I. Remarques sur la divinité de l'imam', *Studia Iranica*, 25 (1996), pp. 193–216 (repr. in *La religion discrète*, chapter 3).

al-darajāt to this question.[94] According to several traditions going back to the Imams Muḥammad al-Bāqir and Jaʿfar al-Ṣādiq, the Primordial Covenant (*mīthāq*), to which the Qur'anic verse 7 (*al-Aʿrāf*)/172 is supposed to refer, relates to the *walāya*. At the moment of this Covenant, the best creatures took an oath of fidelity to the *walāya* of ʿAlī (who symbolises in this episode the cosmic Imam and the universal imamate). These best creatures were: the angels brought nigh (*al-muqarrabūn*), the messengers (*al-mursalūn*) among the prophets and the well-tried (*al-mumtaḥanūn*) among the believers.[95] This is why this *walāya* constitutes the essential reason for any prophetic mission:

> No prophet and no messenger was ever sent with a mission otherwise than by [or 'for'] our *walāya* (*bi-walāyatinā*, i.e., ours, us the Imams).[96]
>
> Our *walāya* is the *walāya* of God. No Prophet was sent for anything but for/by it.[97]
>
> The *walāya* of ʿAlī is written in the books of all the Prophets. The only mission of every prophet was to proclaim the prophecy of Muḥammad and the *walāya* of ʿAlī.[98]
>
> Even the Qur'an, in its complete and not falsified version should have clearly mentioned this fact.[99]
>
> Qur'an 42 (*al-Shūrā*), 13: 'The same religion has He established for you *O the Family of Muḥammad* as that which He enjoined on Noah – and that which We have sent by inspiration to thee *O Muḥammad* – and that which We enjoined on Abraham, Moses, and Jesus: Namely, that ye should remain steadfast in *the* religion *of the Family of Muḥammad* [here, 'the Family of Muḥammad' symbolises the holy theophanic Family par excellence], and make no divisions therein *and remain united*: to those who worship anything but God, *those who associate* [other *walāya-s*] *with the walāya of ʿAlī* [i.e., the sacrality of the divine Man], hard is

[94] Ed. M. Kūchihbāghī (2nd ed., Tabriz, n.d. [ca. 1960]), section 2, chapters 6–16, pp. 67–90; on the author and his works, see M. A. Amir-Moezzi, 'al-Ṣaffār al-Qummī (d. 290/902–903) et son *Kitāb baṣā'ir al-darajāt*', *Journal Asiatique*, 280 (1992), pp. 221–250 ; Newman, *The Formative Period of Twelver Shiʿism*, chapter 5.

[95] Al-Ṣaffār al-Qummī, *Baṣā'ir al-darajāt*, ed. Kūchihbāghī, section 2, chapter 6, pp. 67–68 and chapters 7–12. On the commentaries of this verse see also al-ʿAyyāshī, *Tafsīr*, vol. 2, p. 41; al-Baḥrānī, *al-Burhān*, vol. 2, p. 50; for the general information on this verse, see R. Gramlich, 'Der Urvertrag in der Koranauslegung (zu Sura 7, 172–173)', *Der Islam*, 60 (1963), pp. 205–230.

[96] Al-Ṣaffār al-Qummī, *Baṣā'ir al-darajāt*, section 2, chapter 9, pp. 74–75.

[97] Ibid., p. 75.

[98] Ibid., p. 72. See also al-Qundūzī, *Yanābīʿ al-mawadda*, p. 82.

[99] On the question of the falsification of the Qur'an, see note 48 above. In the following Qur'anic citation, the phrases in italics do not appear in the existing version of the Qur'an but, according to our text, they were included in the Revelation made to the Prophet before it was censored by the official authorities.

the (way) to which thou callest them *concerning the walāya of ʿAlī. Certainly* God guides, *O Muḥammad*, to Himself those who turn (to Him), *who accept your call to the walāya of ʿAlī* [instead of 'God chooses to Himself those whom He pleases, and guides to Himself those who turn (to Him)'].'[100]

In such a context, it appears quite natural that Islam, the ultimate religion of the most perfect among the prophets, should be more focused on the *walāya* than the other religions. In addition, if Muḥammad is the most accomplished of God's messengers, it is because he was initiated, even more than the others, in particular during his heavenly ascensions, to the mysteries of the *walāya* of Imam, that of the Man-God symbolised by cosmic ʿAlī:

> ʿAlī is a Sign of God [*āya*, just as a verse of the Qur'an] for Muḥammad. The latter did nothing else than call [people] to the *walāya* of ʿAlī.[101]
>
> The Prophet was taken up to the heaven twenty times. Not a single time he came back without God entrusting him the *walāya* of ʿAlī and that of the Imams [who will come] after him, much more than His recommendations concerning the canonical religious duties.[102]

The *walāya* is thus the secret message, the esoteric (*bāṭin*) dimension of Islam and of all the preceding religions: 'God made of our *walāya,* us the Family of the prophetic House, the axis (*quṭb*) around which the Qur'an turns, as well as the axis of all the Holy Scriptures. It is around this axis that the clear verses of the Qur'an (*muḥkam al-qur'ān*) turn, it fills all the sacred Books, by it the faith can be clearly recognised.'[103]

To deny the *walāya* of the Man-God, locus of the manifestation of God, means thus to deny all the heavenly Revelations because, in one word, this *walāya* is the supreme reason of the creation: 'The *walāya* of Muḥammad and that of his descendants is the ultimate goal and the highest purpose (*al-gharaḍ al-aqṣā wa'l-murād*

---

[100] Furāt al-Kūfī, *Tafsīr*, p. 387; al-Kulaynī, *al-Rawḍa min al-Kāfī* (note 21 above), vol. 2, p. 163, no. 502; *idem*, *al-Uṣūl min al-Kāfī*, ed. J. Muṣṭafawī, with Persian translation in four volumes (the date is not mentioned but the fourth volume, tr. H. Rasūlī Maḥallātī, is dated 1386/1966), vol. 2, p. 285, no. 32 (a shorter version).

[101] Al-Qummī, *Baṣā'ir al-darajāt*, chapter 7, pp. 71–72; section 2, chapter 9, p. 77.

[102] Ibid., chapter 10, p. 79. On the early Shiʿi conceptions of the heavenly ascension, see M. A. Amir-Moezzi, 'L'imam dans le ciel: Ascension et initiation (Aspects de l'imamologie duodécimaine III)', in M. A. Amir-Moezzi, ed., *Le voyage initiatique en terre d'islam: Ascensions célestes et itinéraires spirituels* (Louvain and Paris, 1997), pp. 99–116 (repr. in Amir-Moezzi, *La religion discrète*, chapter 5).

[103] Al-ʿAyyāshī, *Tafsīr*, vol. 1, p. 5; al-Majlisī, *Biḥār al-anwār*, vol. 19, p. 78; al-Baḥrānī, *al-Burhān*, vol. 1, p. 10.

al-afḍal). God created the creatures only to call them to the *walāya* of Muḥammad, of ʿAlī and that of the successors of the latter.'[104]

The goal of the coded allusions to ʿAlī and his *walāya* contained in the Qurʾan as well as in other Holy Scriptures is the transmission of the knowledge of the Man-God and the love of his person through the historical figure of the Imam. The believer is, therefore, directed, by the intermediary of this supreme spiritual example, to the knowledge of the mysteries of the Face of God.

The 'individualised commentaries' in general and the Qurʾanic commentary of al-Ḥibarī in particular seem to be, among other things, one of the most powerful vehicles for the two world views specific to Shiʿism and, more particularly, for the substance of the Shiʿi faith, the concept of *walāya*. The latter is indeed the only common element between these two world views. It is complementary to the *nubuwwa*, to which it gives sense in the perspective of the dual vision; and it is opposite to the *barāʾa* in the perspective of the dualist vision. This orientation, often implicit and allusive, constitutes, in my opinion, the secret dimension of this kind of Qurʾanic commentary and makes them a major factor in the preservation and transmission of the faith within a religion which defines itself as the hermeneutical and esoteric doctrine par excellence of Islam.

---

[104] Al-Imām al-Ḥasan al-ʿAskarī (attributed to), *Tafsīr*, p. 379, no. 264 (see note 6 above); Bar-Asher, 'The Qurʾān Commentary Ascribed to Imam Ḥasan al-ʿAskarī', p. 375 (see note 6).

6

The Empire Writes Back: Fatimid Ismaili *Ta'wīl* (Allegoresis) and the Mysteries of the Ancient Greeks

David Hollenberg

As is well known, the exegesis composed by the Ismaili missionaries (*dāʿīs*) is different from most other schools and branches within Islam. Rather than the massive, encyclopaedic, line-by-line Qur'an commentaries that characterise the bulk of exegetical literature in Islam, Ismaili exegesis is anthological: only choice lines and phrases of scripture, those which are believed to carry a secret, inner sense, receive comment. Perhaps what is most unusual is that while the Qur'an is always a crucial object of interpretation for Ismaili missionaries, their *ta'wīl* (allegorical interpretation) is not tethered to it: *realia*, historical events, the Hebrew Bible and Syriac Gospels, and any number of other objects are taken as fertile ground for allegoresis.

Consideration of Ismaili exegesis, then, might take one of two tacks. One could focus on just the bits of Ismaili *ta'wīl* devoted to the interpretation of the Qur'an. This approach has the advantage of comparing and thus situating Ismaili hermeneutics with those of other proximate traditions or schools. Or, one could consider the unusual mix that characterises the genre, and how it relates to the doctrines and teachings the Ismaili missionaries intended to convey. Since Meir Bar-Asher has taken the former approach in his recent article, in what follows, I will explore the latter.[1] More specifically, the following pages consider the style and function of Ismaili *ta'wīl* in order to resolve a specific problem regarding the development of Ismaili doctrine: the presence of Neoplatonic material in texts in which we would not expect them to be.

The Problem: Pre-Kirmānian Fatimid Neoplatonica

Largely thanks to the work of Wilferd Madelung, one of the things that we think we know about Ismaili doctrine concerns the role of Neoplatonic philosophy in its

[1] Meir Bar-Asher, 'Outlines of Early Ismāʿīlī-Faṭimid Qur'ān Exegesis', *Journal Asiatique*, 296 (2008), pp. 257–295.

development.[2] After the advent of the Fatimids in 297/909, the Ismaili community was split. Ismaili missionaries in north-west Iran, Khurāsān, Sijistān and Transoxania who did not recognise the Fatimid caliphs as their Imams synthesised Ismaili doctrine with Neoplatonic philosophy in order to win over wazirs and educated elites to the Ismaili cause.[3] The missionaries who accepted the Fatimid caliphs as Imams composed cabbalistic, allegorising *taʾwīl* on their behalf, and rejected mixing philosophy with Ismaili doctrine. Thus the sources ascribed to spokesmen for the fourth Fatimid Caliph, al-Muʿizz li-Dīn Allāh (d. 365/975), Jaʿfar b. Manṣūr al-Yaman (fl. mid-4th/10th century) and al-Qāḍī al-Nuʿmān (d. 363/974) are free of the philosophising one finds in the eastern dioceses. This distinction between Fatimid allegorising *taʾwīl*, on the one hand, and (non-Fatimid) philosophical Ismailism, on the other, persisted until Ḥamīd al-Dīn al-Kirmānī's (d. after 411/1020–1021) synthesis of *falsafa* and doctrine became the official doctrine of the Fatimid state.

The problem with this account is that there are at least two pre-Kirmānian Fatimid texts that *do* contain philosophical elements. The opening sections of *Kitāb al-fatarāt wa'l-qirānāt* (The Book of Periods and Conjunctions), attributed to Jaʿfar b. Manṣūr al-Yaman, and *al-Risāla al-mudhhiba* (The Epistle that drives off [Satan's Whispers]) discuss such topics as the First Cause, the First Emanation (*al-ibdāʿ al-awwal*),[4] the relationship between the Universal Intellect and the Universal Soul, and their relationship to the celestial and sublunar worlds – in short, metaphysical topics applying terminology similar to that of Islamic philosophers in the Greek philosophical tradition, and of non-Fatimid Ismailis in the east. While the authenticity and date of composition of *al-Risāla al-mudhhiba* remains an open question, Heinz Halm has authenticated the opening section of the *Kitāb al-fatarāt* to the period of al-Muʿizz.[5] If the Fatimid Caliph al-Muʿizz were indeed hostile to the blend of philosophy and doctrine, then why do philosophical elements appear in several of the writings of two of his leading spokesmen?

The work of several scholars supplies one possible explanation. Madelung established that as part of the Fatimid Caliph al-Muʿizz's effort to expand the empire, he attempted a rapprochement with the missionaries operating in the eastern lands. Towards that end, al-Muʿizz reformed Fatimid doctrine by reinstating the status of Muḥammad b. Ismāʿīl as the awaited redeemer, a central pillar of pre-Fatimid and non-Fatimid Ismailis. Michael Brett has suggested that just as al-Muʿizz reached out

---

2 Wilferd Madelung, 'Das Imamat in der frühen ismailitischen Lehre', *Der Islam*, 37 (1961), pp. 43–135; see especially pp. 102–114 on 'The Persian School'.

3 Paul E. Walker, *Early Philosophical Shiism: The Ismaili Neoplatonism of Abū Yaʿqūb al-Sijistānī* (Cambridge, 1993), pp. 9, 13–15.

4 David Hollenberg, *Neoplatonism in Pre-Kirmānīan Fatimid Doctrine: A Critical Edition and Translation of the Prologue of the* Kitāb al-fatarāt wa'l-qirānāt (Le Museon, 2009), p. 167 (Arabic text).

5 Heinz Halm, 'Zur Datierung des ismāʿīlitischen "Buches der Zwischenzeiten und der zehn Konjunktionen" (*Kitāb al-fatarāt wa'l-qirānāt al-ʿaṣara*) HS Tübingen Ma VI 297', *Die Welt des Orients*, 8 (1975), pp. 91–107.

to the Ismailis of the Iranian lands by elevating the status of Muḥammad b. Ismāʿīl, so too did he accept the Iranian missionary Abū Yaʿqūb al-Sijistānī's (active mid-10th century) Neoplatonism as a basis for the Fatimid doctrine. For Brett, al-Sijistānī's universalistic Neoplatonic theology served 'as a prescription for universal empire' and 'became the formula of the caliphate in Egypt'.[6] In their recent publications, Paul E. Walker and Farhad Daftary are more cautious in characterising the relationship between al-Sijistānī and al-Muʿizz, but seem to agree with the premise that al-Muʿizz employed Neoplatonica in order to convince the Iranian dissident Ismailis to join ranks with the Fatimid *daʿwa*.[7] Such a thesis would make sense of the two early Neoplatonic Fatimid sources: as a concession to the eastern Ismaili dioceses, al-Muʿizz instructed his spokesmen to sate the Easterners' appetite for philosophy by incorporating *falsafa* into Fatimid doctrine. Thus the Neoplatonica in the *Kitāb al-fatarāt* and the *Risāla al-mudhhiba* were a half-step on the way to its full adoption a generation later by al-Kirmānī.

While plausible, investigation of the content and form of the Neoplatonic and scientific material in the *Kitāb al-fatarāt* does not easily support this explanation.[8]

Greek Wisdom in the *Kitāb al-fatarāt*

After a description of the first two emanations of the pleroma, the Universal Intellect and Soul, the prologue to the *Kitāb al-fatarāt* describes the creation of the celestial world, the elements, and the mineral, vegetable and animal worlds including humanity.[9] An anonymous sage teaches this through a series of dicta, some of which are attributed to the ancient Greek sages: the throne of the All-Merciful created vapours and smoke which formed the luminous spheres and compound bodies, and these warm vapours produced a 'sperm-like' rain which gave birth to all the animals;[10] like other animals, humanity is dominated by the temperaments of heat and moisture, but is distinguished by a human soul's receptivity to intellect;[11] humanity is a microcosm

---

[6] Michael Brett, *The Rise of the Fatimids: The World of the Mediterranean and the Middle East in the Fourth Century of the Hijra* (Leiden, 2001), p. 218.

[7] Paul E. Walker, *Exploring an Islamic Empire: Fatimid History and Its Sources* (London, 2002), p. 34. Daftary writes that 'al-Muʿizz also attempted a limited doctrinal rapprochement with the Qarmaṭīs, including a partial endorsement of the Neoplatonic cosmological doctrine propounded by the Iranian *dāʿīs*.' Farhad Daftary, 'The Medieval Ismāʿīlīs of the Iranian Lands', in Carole Hillenbrand, ed., *Studies in Honour of Clifford Edmund Bosworth*, vol. 2: *The Sultan's Turret: Studies in Persian and Turkish Culture* (Leiden, 2000), p. 55.

[8] The material in the *Kitāb al-fatarāt* displays similarities with many near contemporary sources, but is identical to none of them. See David Hollenberg, 'Interpretation after the End of Days: The Fatimid-Ismaili *ta'wīl* of Jaʿfar ibn Manṣūr al-Yaman (d. ca. 960)' (Ph.D. thesis, University of Pennsylvania, 2006), pp. 43–207.

[9] Hollenberg, *Neoplatonism*, p. 190.

[10] Ibid., p. 192.

[11] Ibid., pp. 189–190.

of the universe, being formed by both Universal Intellect and Soul. The anonymous sage counsels that after the death of their bodies, those humans who directed their souls to employ reason while alive escape to the world of Intellect (or, in another paragraph, to the celestial spheres of Jupiter and Venus), while those who fall slaves to their whims suffer the torment of residing in the world of ether (or, in another section, the fire of Saturn and Mars). Guidance for believers comes in the form of specially endowed figures – 'prophets, legatees, Imams, and caliphs' – who receive the light of the Universal Intellect. Through the supernal resources (*al-mawādd*) that descend to them, these figures teach what is necessary for correct worship, purify the pollution of sin and disobedience, and direct believers to the First Cause.

Many of the concepts and terms used in this discussion – the mixing of the four primary 'natures' and 'secondary elements' (*ummahāt/ustuqussāt*);[12] humanity as a microcosm of the universe;[13] the dispersal of human souls to the celestial spheres[14] – draw from technical terms employed by 4th/10th-century *falāsifa* (Islamic philosophers in the Greek tradition) and the Arabic tradition of Greek science. Indeed, several statements, including one explicitly attributed to Aristotle, are so similar to their views and language that it is highly likely it was copied directly from a philosophical text.[15] Generally, the link of this material with salvation of an earthly hierarchy of the mission of God – the speaker-prophets, legatees, believers, dioceses – is similar to claims made by Iranian missionaries such as Abū Ḥātim al-Rāzī (d. 322/934) and al-Sijistānī. The problem is in the details.

---

[12] D. E. Pingree and Nomanul Haq, 'Ṭabīʿa', *EI2*, vol. 10, pp. 25–28. Walker, *Early Philosophical Shiʿism*, pp. 102–106. Daniel De Smet, *La Quiétude de l'intellect: néoplatonisme et gnose ismaélienne dans l'oeuvre de Ḥamîd ad-Dîn al-Kirmânî (Xe-XIe s.)* (Leuven, 1995), pp. 316–318. Al-Māturīdī describes the *aṣḥāb al-ṭawābiʿ* as holding the view that there are four natures (hot, cold, moist and dry) and that the mixtures of these natures comprise the rest of the material world. Abu'l-Manṣūr al-Māturīdī, *Kitāb al-tawḥīd* (Beirut, 1970), p. 141. I thank Patricia Crone for this reference.

[13] *Rasāʾil Ikhwān al-Ṣafāʾ* (Beirut, 2006), vol. 2, pp. 456–479. Miskawayh, *al-Fawz al-aṣghar*, ed. Ṣāliḥ ʿAḍīma and Roger Arnaldez (Paris, 1987), pp. 118–123.

[14] Ibn Sīnā claimed that the highest levels of human souls went to the celestial spheres after the death of the body, the second level were in contact with the souls of the celestial spheres, and the third level went to the seats of natural shadows and elemental bodies. Ibn Sīnā, *Aḥwāl al-nafs: Risāla fi'l-nafs wa-baqāʾihā wa-maʿādihā*, ed. Aḥmad Fuʾād al-Ahwānī (Cairo, 1952), pp. 187–188. As is well known, Ibn Sīnā was raised in an Ismaili home, but abandoned Ismailism early in his life.

[15] Hollenberg, *Neoplatonism*, p. 22 (Arabic text). The wise one Aristotle said: 'This soul came to love matter through which she appears and did not choose to go from it to her world from which she had appeared only because she is not certain that she only exists [in this world] via matter (*hayūla*). If she learned that when she leaves [matter] she would be joined to her cause and be purified from [matter's] crudities in the world of abiding and repose where there is no worry, sadness, loss, deficiency, imperfection and wear, she would rush to go over, desiring to acquire [that] station; [she would] not be satisfied with this world as a whereabouts (*muqām*).'

The metaphysics in the *Kitāb al-fatarāt*'s prologue possesses concepts that would be problematic for the Ismaili missionaries to the east. The most straightforward problem is that in the text God is referred to several times as *al-ʿilla al-ūlā* (the First Cause). While this way of conceiving of and referring to God was quite common for contemporary Islamic philosophers in the Greek tradition, Ismaili metaphysicians in Iran vigorously argued against this view. For them, God was beyond causality; it is only His emanations that can be conceived as in the realm of causation. Al-Sijistānī explicitly claimed that God cannot be called a cause;[16] the issue of causality is appropriate for discussing the creation of this world – well below the level of the pleroma. Rather than God, it was the *ibdāʿ*, the first emanation, which Abū Ḥātim al-Rāzī referred to as *al-ʿilla al-ūlā* (the first cause).[17]

If his intent was to appeal to Iranian Ismailis, it seems odd that the Fatimid author incorporated material that was objectionable to them on an issue so fundamental as the nature of God. Now, it is of course possible that this was an attempt to appeal to the Iranians but, due to his unfamiliarity with the metaphysics of his eastern counterparts, the Fatimid author made poor choices. However, there is evidence that the Fatimids had access to the doctrines of the Iranians through visitors from the eastern dioceses;[18] if the Fatimids' goal were to appeal to the Iranians, it seems likely that they would have copied excerpts from the Iranian Ismailis themselves rather than from *falsafa* proper. And there are also other problems.

It is not merely that the metaphysics is at odds with the views of those to whom it is supposedly trying to appeal; it is also internally inconsistent. For example, in one paragraph the sage states that the Soul is among the entities created *fī dafʿatan wāḥidatan* (in one stroke) – that is, beyond the rubric of time; in another paragraph, we read that the Soul is created 'with time' (as opposed to Intellect, which is created 'with eternity'). The sage refers once to God as 'beyond attributes and description'; elsewhere he describes Him, calling him the Originator and First Cause. There is also inconsistent usage of the terms for the primary and secondary elements. The author-compiler of these dicta seems disengaged from the intellectual content of the philosophical dicta he deployed. Why then, did he transmit them? Progress into understanding what he meant to signal begins with consideration of the genre and hermeneutical presuppositions of *ta'wīl*.

---

16 De Smet, *La Quiétude de l'intellect*, p. 136, citing Abū Yaʿqūb al-Sijistānī, *Kitāb al-iftikhār*, ed. Ismail K. Poonawala (Beirut, 2000), p. 32.

17 Abū Ḥātim al-Rāzī, *Kitāb al-iṣlāḥ*, ed. Ḥasan Mīnūchihr and Mahdī Muḥaqqiq (Tehran, 1988), p. 39.

18 An account of al-Muʿizz's meeting with an Ismaili from one of the eastern dioceses is recounted by al-Qāḍī al-Nuʿmān in *Kitāb al-majālis wa'l-musāyarāt*, ed. al-Ḥabīb al-Faqī et al. (2nd ed., Beirut, 1997), p. 374.

Ta'wīl and the Disclosure of the Universe's Secrets

Let us begin by considering the most basic unit of *ta'wīl*, the *mathal* (similitude). The term *mathal* is used 88 times in the Qur'an, often in the sense of metaphor but also as parable or aphorism, and in Ismaili *ta'wīl* it can connote each of these senses. As Alfred Ivry has put it, the *mathal* 'represents other than what it literally depicts … It is like it but it is not the thing itself'.[19] The most frequent *taʾwīl* formulation is 'X is a *mathal* for Y' where X, the *mathal* or *ishāra* (indication or sign), represents the exterior (*ẓāhir*) sign, and Y, the *mamthūl* (that which is signified), represents the hidden true reality (*ḥaqīqa*).

The missionaries' most common source of material for their *mathals* was the Qur'an, but they by no means limited themselves to it. Rituals (the five daily prayers; alms), *realia* such as natural phenomena (the sky, ground, light, water, birds), social institutions (marriage, circumcision),[20] the two sexes[21] and parts of the human anatomy[22] were all frequently adopted as objects of interpretation. *Mamthūls* were far more limited. They were usually aspects of the pleroma (*al-aṣlān*, or the two 'original sources' or supernal hypostases that emanate from God; the angelic triad *jadd*, *fatḥ* and *khayāl*) or the earthly hierarchy of the mission and its institutions (the speaker-prophets, legatees, Imams, missionaries, believers and the twelve dioceses into which the world is divided). There were a number of standard *mathal-mamthūl* themes: water as a *mathal* for knowledge, land (*al-arḍ*) as a *mathal* for the believers of the *daʿwa*, and birds as a *mathal* for the Imam's missionaries were topoi, and made the basis for more elaborate interpretations.[23]

In Western rhetoric, the common term for this method of interpretation is allegoresis, the decipherment of an object of interpretation (the 'vehicle') that was not

---

[19] Alfred L. Ivry, 'The Utilization of Allegory in Islamic Philosophy', in Jon Whitman, ed., *Interpretation and Allegory: Antiquity to the Modern Period* (Leiden, 2003), pp. 155–157.

[20] The pact of marriage is similar to the believers' pact with the Imam of the period. Thus to follow Moses in the period of Jesus is 'to commit adultery' and leaving the *daʿwa* is like divorce. Jaʿfar b. Manṣūr al-Yaman, *Ta'wīl sūrat al-nisā'*, MS 1103, The Library of the Institute of Ismaili Studies, London, fos 34, 36. I thank Mr Alnoor Merchant for his kind help with granting me access to this manuscript.

[21] Ibid., pp. 44–45.

[22] For example, the disclosure of the teeth in the smile is like the disclosure of the interior sense. Jaʿfar b. Manṣūr al-Yaman, *Sarā'ir wa-asrār al-nuṭaqā'*, ed. Muṣṭafā Ghālib (Beirut, 1404/1984), p. 197; the disclosure of the shaft of the penis [of Ismāʿīl] from the foreskin is like the disclosure of the law of Abraham from the law of Noah. Ibid., pp. 99–100.

[23] Bar-Asher points to prophetology, Imamology, enemies of the mission and religious commandments as among the most common themes in *ta'wīl*. Bar-Asher, 'Outlines of Early Ismāʿīlī-Faṭimid Qur'ān Exegesis', pp. 278–287. Poonawala points to physical objects found in the Qur'an as commonly interpreted *amthāl*: earth, the heavens, mountains and trees. Ismail K. Poonawala, 'Ismāʿīlī *ta'wīl* of the Qur'ān', in Andrew Rippin, ed., *Approaches to the History of the Interpretation of the Qur'an* (Oxford, 1988), pp. 212–222.

intended to be decoded, and the determination of a second meaning ('the tenor').[24] The missionaries would not have liked this as a description for *ta'wīl*. For them, the *mamthūl* was not an interpretation produced by human imagination, erudition or insight. Rather, God placed the *mathal*s and *mamthūl*s in this world as indicators, pointers to the higher world. *Ta'wīl* entails the disclosure of the authentic, original sense of God's similitudes through the interpreter's divine grace or support (*ta'yīd*).

Mathal and *mamthūl* are commonly linked by one of these three devices:

- Wordplay. This includes paronomasia, etymology, the interpretation of the letters of a word and manipulating word order or the order of letters in a word (*istinbāṭ*).[25] Often the basis of the wordplay is the similar sounds of two words (homophony). Also frequent is the use of a 'key letter' which occurs in both the *mathal* and *mamthūl* (metagraphy).
- Hiero-historical parallelism. Sets of different historical figures are taken as analogues. Thus an incident that occurred during the time of the ancient Israelites or the Prophet and early Muslims is said to parallel Ismaili sacred historical figures or contemporary events in the mission.
- Numeric equivalents. This entails interpretation based on the correspondence between two or more numbers or sets of numbers.

Each of these techniques is independent of the epistemological presuppositions of the intellectual fields with which the objects of interpretation are associated. They can be applied to anything. For a missionary to apply *ta'wīl* to two Qur'anic phrases based on the similarity of a sound of a keyword does not require him to master variant readings, syntax, lexicography or any other field of knowledge crucial for the *mufassirūn* (the exegetes of the Qur'an), neither does he need to follow the *akhbārī*s (historical chroniclers) in assembling a multitude of *akhbār* (historical reports) in order to posit the parallel of Moses and Aaron, with Jesus and Simon-Peter and with, in turn, Muḥammad and 'Alī. Ismaili *ta'wīl* resituates these intellectual fields and technical vocabularies, applying its own special hermeneutics to them. Objects of interpretation are a cipher, a secret code which the Imam and his retinue alone have the capacity to unlock.

In the *Kitāb al-fatarāt*, it is the third technique, numeric equivalents of *mathal* and *mamthūl*, that is most important. Like the Pythagoreans, and a great many other similar literatures across a broad variety of cultures, the authors of Ismaili *ta'wīl* assume that there is a hidden, geometric architecture reflected in the numeric symmetries that can be recovered by the Imam.[26]

---

[24] 'Allegory', in James. W. Halporn et al., *The New Princeton Encyclopedia of Poetry and Poetics* (Princeton, 1993), pp. 31–36.

[25] Bar-Asher, 'Outlines of Early Ismā'īlī-Faṭimid Qur'ān Exegesis', pp. 289–291.

[26] Walter Burkert, *Lore and Science in Ancient Pythagoreanism*, tr. Ewin Minar (Cambridge, 1972), pp. 465–479.

In the following *ta'wīl* from the *Kitāb al-fatarāt*, metaphysics and the earthly missionary are paired using the number equivalent, six.

> The Sage (peace be upon him) said that the first beginning of the primaries in the world are four, and four oppose them: Intellect with eternity (*dahr*), Soul with time, prime matter with place, and nature with bodies. Two supernal, emanated sources oppose [these four]; they are the Word and Command.
>
> Thus there came to be six primaries (*awā'il*) in the world of divinity. Likewise, there are [six primaries] from humankind parallel to them: deputies appearing with divine power speaking in every age and time, removing people from the oppression of animality and the waves of the sea of regret so that the similitude (*mathal*) by the All-Knowing, All-Powerful's governance may be completed. Knowing, pious, favoured, chosen, formed messengers, the best of the spiritual ones, kings, *honoured servants* [Q.21:26]. *They speak not until He hath spoken and they act by His command* [Q.21:27]. For these are the six ranks.

The sage teaches that the two original sources, here called 'Word' and 'Command', are opposed to (i.e., parallel with) 'four primaries' (Intellect, Soul, prime matter and nature). The two and four added together equal six, and these six are parallel to God's six messenger-deputies. While the sage draws from Greek scientific terminology, the point of the *ta'wīl* is to draw the symmetrical relationship between the six supernal *mathal*s and the six earthly *mamthūl*s. As in many *ta'wīl*s based on numeric equivalents, the basis of this *ta'wīl* is simply the discovery of the harmony between the six primaries and the speaker-prophets; the content of the Neoplatonic substrata is purely incidental.

In the following section the sage explains that both the human body and the universe were created by what is known in Ismaili doctrine as *al-aṣlān*, 'the two original sources' of the pleroma beyond the celestial spheres:

> Furthermore, the existence of the body (*al-juththa*) of the human was by the influence of the rising of the power from the two supernal sources which were the cause of the existence of the macrocosm. Therefore, one of the ancient wise ones said that the beginning of existence is two lines, one on the other in the middle, in this shape: —+—. Because of this, the Messiah was mounted on the cross to exemplify it, indicating the two sources. Then they became two circles, one on the other. One of the two was named 'the [outermost] sphere' (*al-falak al-mustaqīm*) and the other 'the sphere divided by the signs.' The [outermost] sphere turns the divided sphere every day and night on its rotation, disposed [to go] from east to west. From its rotations, all of the heavenly and earthly worlds, the spiritual subtleties and natural crudities, are generated.[27]

[27] Hollenberg, *Neoplatonism*, p. 191.

This *ta'wīl* is based on the geometric equivalent of the number 'two'. One of the 'ancient wise ones' (*ḥukamā' mutaqaddimūn*) describes the beginning of existence as two lines (*khaṭṭān*), one on the other; these are parallel to the two original sources in the pleroma, and the two posts of the cross upon which Jesus was crucified. The conception of two lines forming the ecliptic and equator of the universe ultimately derives from Plato's *Timaeus*,[28] a source well-known to the 10th-century philosophers in Baghdad. The pairing of the two lines with the cross and crucifixion suggests that the basis for the *ta'wīl* came from a Christian source.[29]

Most medieval Muslims, of course, were quite clear that Jesus was *not* crucified on the cross as God declared this explicitly (Q.4:157). Moreover, the cross is associated with both the doctrine of the Trinity and the Christian empire and is thus generally taken as an offensive symbol in Islam not to be tolerated in public display. All this raises the question as to why such an image was seen as an appropriate object for *ta'wīl*. The same question could be asked regarding the philosophical dicta: in the 4th/10th century, 'foreign' Greek sciences such as Greek philosophy and astrology were objectionable to most medieval Muslim scholars.[30] It is noteworthy that the narrator of the *Kitāb al-fatarāt* not only transmitted philosophical dicta, but did so explicitly on the authority of 'the ancient Greeks, and mentioned Plato, Aristotle and Euclid specifically. Why did an Ismaili missionary interpret such material as the cross and crucifixion and dicta attributed to ancient Greeks?[31]

As I have pointed out elsewhere, one aspect of Ismaili *ta'wīl* is that in its objects of interpretation, it often allegorises material that is not only unusual, but considered

---

[28] Plato, *Timaeus*, tr. Benjamin Jowett (Indianapolis, 1949), p. 526 (para. 36).

[29] Perhaps the source was from a commentary on the Arabic translation of *Timaeus* by the well-known Christian philosopher Yaḥyā b. 'Adī al-Takrītī (d. 363/974). It is possible that Yaḥyā b. 'Adī commented on the translation by Ibn al-Biṭrīq. Ibn al-Nadīm, *al-Fihrist* (Beirut, 1966), p. 256. Ḥunayn b. Iṣḥāq's translation of part of the 'Synopsis of the Platonic Dialogues' by Galen that recounts parts of the *Timaeus* has been edited by P. Kraus and R. Walzer, *Galeni Compendium Timaei Platonis* (London, 1951). I thank Sasha Treiger for these references. Also, fragments of Galen's medical commentary on the *Timaeus* have survived. See Carlos J. Larrain, *Galens Kommentar zu Platons Timaios* (Stuttgart, 1992); Cristina d'Ancona, 'The *Timaeus*' Model for Creation and Providence: An Example of Continuity and Adaptation in Early Arabic Philosophical Literature', in Gretchen J. Yeydams-Schils, ed., *Plato's Timaeus as Cultural Icon* (Notre Dame, 2003), pp. 206–235. The apologist Justin Martyr (fl. 2nd century) referred to the 'two bands' as a reference to the cross in his *First Apology*. Justin Martyr, *The First and Second Apologies*, ed. and tr. Leslie W. Barnard (New York, 1997), para. 60, p. 65.

[30] Ignaz Goldziher, 'The Attitude of Orthodox Islam Toward the Ancient Sciences', in M. L. Swartz, ed., *Studies on Islam* (New York, 1981), pp. 185–215. In the 5th/11th and 6th/12th centuries, among certain Sunni and Twelver scholars, *falsafa* and Greek science was admissible in Qur'anic exegesis. For example, see Robert G. Morrison, 'The Portrayal of Nature in a Medieval Qur'an Commentary', *Studia Islamica*, 93 (2002), pp. 115–137. However, in the 4th/10th century, this impulse seems to have been restricted to Ismaili missionaries. In this sense, Ismaili *ta'wīl* could be seen as the avant-garde of Islamic exegesis.

[31] D. Thomas, 'Ṣalīb', *EI2*, vol. 8, pp. 980–981.

dubious or loathsome to non-Ismaili Muslim contemporaries.[32] Thus missionaries composed *taʾwīl*s that interpreted the church hierarchy, the clothes of the priests and monks, the Eucharist and passages from the Bible in Hebrew or the Gospels in Syriac,[33] including biblical tales known to be problematic for Muslims. They took such materials as *mathal*s with hidden meaning that could only be decoded by the Imam and his missionaries to whom his aid (*taʾyīd*) filters down. The function of this strategy is clarified by consideration of similar esoteric literatures.

Esotericism and the Sectarian Ethos

In his recently published monograph, Samuel Thomas has drawn from sociological theories of sect formation and esotericism to analyse sources produced by the community at Qumran.[34] One such theory adapted by Thomas from the work of Stark and Bainbridge defines a sect as a community which exists in tension with its immediate social environment.[35] Sects perpetuate this dynamic through producing myths, doctrines and practices which create a sense of difference and antagonism with the surrounding world.[36] Esoteric literature such as 'prophetic exegesis' provides the community with a sense of a hidden, secret truth and reality reserved only to a select group of initiates. This creates a new and different reality, a 'second world' in which community members experience an alternative to the manifest world. Access to this alternative world is achieved through a radical transformation of the acolyte, a dramatic experience of receiving the hidden knowledge.[37]

As Thomas describes, sectarians employ esoterica by transforming mysteries – such ultimately unknowable topics as the origins of the universe or what happens to humans after death – into 'secrets' which are only accessible through special individuals.[38] In religious sects that employ this discourse, these secrets are not merely information; learning them entails an experience of transformation, a regulated and institutionalised anagnorisis which binds the saved community to one another, creates a

[32] David Hollenberg, 'Disrobing Judges with Veiled Truths: An Early Ismaili Torah Interpretation (*taʾwīl*) in Service of the Fatimid Mission', *Religion* (April, 2004), pp. 127–145.

[33] Daniel De Smet and J. M. F. Van Reeth, 'Les citations bibliques dan l'oeuvre du dāʿī Ismalién Ḥamīd ad-Dīn al-Kirmānī', in Urbain Vermeulen, ed., *Law, Christianity and Modernism in Islamic Society* (Louvain, 1998), pp. 147–160.

[34] Samuel I. Thomas, *The 'Mysteries' of Qumran: Mystery, Secrecy, and Esotericism in the Dead Sea Scrolls* (Atlanta, 2009).

[35] Rodney Stark and W. S. Bainbridge, *The Future of Religion: Secularization, Revival, and Cult Formation* (Berkeley, 1985), pp. 134–137.

[36] Thomas, *The 'Mysteries' of Qumran*, p. 66.

[37] Georg Simmel, *The Sociology of Georg Simmel*, tr. K. H. Wolff (Glencoe, IL, 1950); Kocku von Struckhard, *Western Esotericism: A Brief History of Secret Knowledge*, tr. N. Goodrick-Clarke (London, 2005).

[38] Thomas, *The 'Mysteries' of Qumran*, pp. 81–126.

sense of difference from outsiders, and provides a source of authority and legitimacy for the sect. Thus esoteric literature can serve a sectarian ethos.

This theory of esoteric literature is consonant with themes in Ismaili sources which depict the radical transformation of the acolyte. The anonymous sage in *Kitāb al-ʿālim waʾl-ghulām* (The Book of the Master and the Disciple) moves his audience to tears by pointing out deficiencies in their understanding of the Qurʾan, a speech which eventually yields the conversion of a youth, and also the youth's Sunni father and companions.[39] In his autobiography, Jaʿfar b. Manṣūr al-Yaman's father, Ibn Ḥawshab, vividly describes this moment of his own epiphany. While still a young man in a state of spiritual confusion and despair, an anonymous sage asks Ibn Ḥawshab about the meaning of a verse he had been reciting. 'What shall I say? By God, it is as if I had never read the verse!', the young Ibn Ḥawshab exclaims. This was the first step towards his eventual conversion.[40] Many similar 'conversion to the mission' stories occur in and outside Ismaili literature.[41] The acolytes experienced a sense that the gulf between ignorance and knowledge is vast; the knowledge of the Imam is far from that of the commonality, and the acolyte is in desperate need of it for his salvation.

One technique the Ismailis used to occasion this response was the interpretation of extremely familiar objects. Missionaries interpreted verses of the Qurʾan, the Islamic testimony of faith, well-known traditions of the Prophet and his family, and prayers and legal rulings to apply to the elements of the earthly missionary hierarchy. This type of *taʾwīl* transforms what is familiar into a mystery that requires explication.

If reconfiguring familiar themes is one *taʾwīl* strategy, the *Kitāb al-fatarāt* is an example of the obverse: showing that material considered anathema to Islam contains God's hidden signs. To interpret the Christian cross, biblical and Gospel verses in Hebrew and Syriac, and obscure statements of Aristotle, Plato and Euclid is to make accessible material that is beyond the reach of non-Ismaili Muslims. By disclosing the true meaning behind these foreign sources, missionaries demonstrate the universality of the Imam as they reinforce a sense of difference from and superiority to the broader Islamic milieu.

I began this chapter by asking what *taʾwīl* of 'wisdom of the Greeks' in two early Fatimid sources was meant to signal. While reflection on the nature of *taʾwīl* partly explains the potential utility of 'foreign' material to an Ismaili missionary, it does not explain precisely what the incorporation of this material was meant to signal during the reign of the Fatimid Caliph al-Muʿizz li-Dīn Allāh. Al-Muʿizz was reported to

---

39 James W. Morris, *The Master and the Disciple: An Early Islamic Spiritual Dialogue* (London, 2001), p. 5 (Arabic text).

40 Al-Qāḍī al-Nuʿmān, *Iftitāḥ al-daʿwa*, ed. W. al-Qāḍī (Beirut, 1970), pp. 33–39.

41 For example, the conversion of ʿAlī b. al-Faḍl in Muḥammad b. Mālik al-Yamānī, *Kashf asrār al-bāṭiniyya*, ed. M. Z. al-Kawtharī (Cairo, 1939), pp. 21–23; the conversion of Nāṣir-i Khusraw, in W. Ivanow, *Nasiri-Khusraw and Ismailism* (Leiden and Bombay, 1948), pp. 22–24. A non-Ismaili description of conversion is the conversion of Ḥamdān Qarmaṭ, in Thābit b. Sinān, *Taʾrīkh akhbār al-qarāmiṭa*, ed. S. Zakkār (Beirut, 1971), p. 96ff. I thank Patricia Crone for first introducing me to these references.

have explicitly repudiated 'the mix' (*ikhtilāṭ*) of *falsafa* and doctrine early in his career;[42] why did he change his mind?

The Iranian missionaries had been composing 'philosophical *taʾwīl*' for a generation and so it stands to reason that this shift had something to do with them. But, as we discussed above, the nature of the material makes it unlikely that it was meant as a doctrinal concession to the eastern Ismaili dioceses. As the next section demonstrates, a *taʾwīl* of the story of the speaker-prophet Adam in a source composed in the same period as the prologue to the *Kitāb al-fatarāt* provides an alternative explanation.

Adam's Escape from the Island of the Philosophers

As is well known, the status of the first of the speaker-prophets, Adam, and whether he instituted a law, was the locus of debate among Ismaili missionaries.[43] It is then instructive that in a lengthy *taʾwīl* of the story of Adam in another source ascribed to Jaʿfar b. Manṣūr al-Yaman, the *Sarāʾir al-nuṭaqāʾ* (Secrets of the Speaker-Prophets), a source composed near the same period as the prologue to the *Kitāb al-fatarāt*, there seem to be oblique references to the intellect and *falsafa*, and their proper role and status.

At the story's opening, we are told that Adam was born on an island in which the ruling king patronised 'philosophers and astronomers'. Upon his birth, the king's astrologers recognised that Adam would become a future ruler, and reported that if he did not take action Adam would grow up to rule the earth using 'intellectual governances' and 'divine *nomoi*' (*nawāmīs*). His parents, fearing for Adam's life, took him to a remote island, where Adam was befriended by animals and raised by a lioness, who taught him knowledge of their Imam. The Imam of the animals eventually appointed Adam to be his successor.[44]

In a *taʾwīl* of the story, it is revealed that the Imam of the period who is the Intellect. It is he who declared '*Verily I put on this earth a successor/deputy*' (Q.2:30).[45] Upon being chosen by the Intellect as its deputy and receiving the supernal resources, Adam chose four birds through the marriage of four women, who represent four of his representatives in the mission. He then 'directed them to a land within which they sought to erect an abode of refuge (*dār hijra*) in order to establish the statutes of

[42] Al-Qāḍī al-Nuʿmān, *Kitāb al-majālis*, p. 374.

[43] This is largely because the status of Adam was tied to the awaited redeemer, the *Qāʾim*, whom it was expected would return the world to the aboriginal religion of Adam in which worship did not require laws or works. As we might expect, the Fatimids, who began their reign by declaring the advent of the End of Days had arrived, rejected the view that Adam did not possess a law, and thus that the law had been abrogated with their rule.

[44] Jaʿfar b. Manṣūr al-Yaman, *Sarāʾir*, pp. 27–30.

[45] Ibid., p. 29. 'This is the speech of the Imam of the time who is the *Qāʾim* to the people of his period … for God would erect him and put him in place, so he was named "God" as he came by the deed of God.'

religion, and fight against his adversary, and his enemy Iblīs and his forces'.[46] Adam's mission is to spread the Intellect's message through erecting polities to sow revolution. In successive *ta'wīls* of the story's plot, it is explained that the evil king pursuing Adam is the chief missionary of an island who was originally close to the forces of the Intellect, but whose hubris led him to disobey the Intellect's election of Adam. The moral of the story is that it is not through the independent use of intellect through philosophy that one receives the benefits of the Intellect, but through joining and propagating the mission of the rightful Imam.

This *ta'wīl* depicts a struggle between two Ismaili dioceses: one in which renegades rule by using philosophy and astrology without recourse to a proper Imam, and another ruled by the Intellect who governs the animal-believers, and who bequeaths the imamate to the rightful Imam, Adam. The *ta'wīl* was a Fatimid polemic against the dissident Ismaili missionaries in Iran, who, according to the Fatimids, strayed from the path of the rightful (Fatimid) Imam and 'philosophised' without the Imam's guidance. This conception of intellect clarifies a statement by the anonymous sage in the *Kitāb al-fatarāt* when he condemned a group who vacillated on the importance of the law whom he refers to as 'specialists in philosophy and logic'. They 'do not understand the true sense (*ḥaqīqat al-amr*) of the Law-bringers (*aṣḥāb al-sharā'i'*). *They scoff at those* [Q.9:79] whose intellects are weak, but they only make themselves look foolish.'[47] Although this might refer to the *falāsifa* proper, when read in light of the Adam story in the *Sarā'ir*, it seems likely to have been intended to apply to the Iranian missionaries as well.

To return to our original question, it is clear that despite the many passages ascribed to the ancient Greeks adduced by the *Kitāb al-fatarāt*'s anonymous sage, the prologue is not a work of speculative metaphysics similar to that of the Iranian Ismailis. It is better viewed as a *ta'wīl* in the traditional Fatimid-Ismaili mode: the author of the *Kitāb al-fatarāt* reads the ancient Greeks' statements as a cosmic mystery that requires *ta'wīl* to be decoded. I would suggest that rather than an attempt to appeal to the dioceses to the east, this material is better viewed as a response: only the Fatimid Imam and his missionaries know the true meaning of the wisdom of the Greeks. It was, then, not a concession, but a riposte, a case of 'The Empire Writes Back'.

46 Ibid., p. 38.

47 Hollenberg, *Neoplatonism*, p. 200.

7

The Authority to Interpret the Qur'an

Meir M. Bar-Asher

A major issue regarding Qur'an exegesis, in both Sunni and Shi'i tradition, is the question of authority: who is authorised to interpret the sacred text? Are Muslim believers entitled to do so and, if so, does this extend to all of them? Overall one can point to two distinct approaches to this question. The first, which may be defined as scripturalist, holds that the Qur'an is the ultimate authority in all areas. The second consists of recognising the priority rather than the exclusivity of the Qur'an, and the need for exegesis. According to the first, namely the scripturalist approach, the Qur'an is, as many of its verses reiterate, a revealed text, and no additional source or exegetical endeavour is required to make its meaning clear. This view of the Qur'an as a self-explanatory text is attested in a number of prophetic traditions, one of which recounts that the Companion of the Prophet, Abū Wā'il Shaqīq b. Salama al-Asadī (d. 82/701), when asked about something in the Qur'an (*idhā su'ila 'an shay' min al-Qur'ān*), would reply: 'God expresses [literally: achieves] in it what he wills (*aṣāba allāhu bihi alladhī arāda*)';[1] which is to say that the words of God in the Qur'an are explicit and any interpretation is superfluous.

According to another tradition in the same spirit, the theologian Aḥmad b. Ḥanbal (d. 241/855) declared: 'Three things have no foundation: Qur'an exegesis, apocalyptic tales concerning the end of days and tales of the military campaigns of the Prophet (*thalāthat ashyā' lā aṣla lahā: al-tafsīr wa'l-malāḥim wa'l-maghāzī*).'[2] A further example of this attitude was to be found, as noted by Ignaz Goldziher, in one of the sub-sects of the Khawārij, which 'acknowledged only the Qur'an as having legislative authority, and rejected everything else as without competence for the regulation of religious affairs'.[3] Inevitably this resistance to the role of exegesis – which,

[1] Ibn Sa'd, *Kitāb al-ṭabaqāt al-kubrā* (Beirut, 1957–1958), vol. 6, p. 67; I. Goldziher, *Die Richtungen der islamischen Koransauslegung* (Leiden, 1920), p. 56 (=*Schools of Koranic Commentators*, tr. Wolfgang H. Behn [Wiesbaden, 2006], p. 37).

[2] Goldziher, *Die Richtungen der islamischen Koransauslegung*, p. 57 (German text), p. 37 (English text).

[3] I. Goldziher, *Introduction to Islamic Theology and Law* (English translation of *Vorlesungen über den Islam*, by A. and R. Hamori, Princeton, 1981), p. 173 with note 12.

according to Goldziher, was prevalent up to the beginning of the 2nd/8th century[4] – could not be sustained indefinitely. For while the scripturalist attitude within Islam can be seen as exemplifying the tendency – found also in other religions – to maximise the stature of the Holy Scripture, the need to make Scripture relevant for a living, dynamic community, and to find in the Qurʾan answers to questions which it does not explicitly address, became irresistible. As with other religions based on a holy text, this would lead to the emergence of an exegetical tradition and methods of interpretation, thereby allowing for the actualisation of the words of God. Later, however, this scripturalist approach was to disappear, and the Khawārij developed their own exegetical tradition.

Those who approached the Qurʾan as a primary rather than an absolute text maintained that it should be accompanied by exegesis that could help interpret its meanings. However, even when the value of exegesis was acknowledged, there were differing views on the degree of freedom to be given to commentators interpreting the Qurʾan. A glance at early exegetical writings, such as the monumental work of al-Ṭabarī (d. 310/923), clearly demonstrates this. At issue was a fundamental question, known as the debate between *ahl al-raʾy* (people of reason) and *ahl al-ḥadīth* (people of tradition): the first maintained that commentators were free to use their own reasoning in their endeavour to understand the Qurʾan; their adversaries argued that commentators were obliged to convey only those meanings of words and concepts in the Qurʾan that had been transmitted in the *ḥadīth*, and were not permitted to employ their own reasoning.

The latter view had both ideological and literary aspects. From the ideological point of view, the exegete was not free to pass judgement or express his own opinions unless these were based on traditions handed down to him, and which supported the view he aimed to express. The literary form (dependent, to a certain extent, on the ideological one) demanded that each idea, rule or article of faith be transmitted in the form of *ḥadīth*. Here again al-Ṭabarī's exegetical work serves as a corpus to illustrate the issue. In his introduction he voices reservations on the use of rational thinking in exegesis. The traditions that al-Ṭabarī cites on this question (most of which are ascribed to Ibn ʿAbbās) are of three kinds: (1) traditions that forbid the interpretation of the Qurʾan either on the basis of one's own judgement (*bi-raʾyihi*), or without (previous) knowledge (*bi-ghayr ʿilm*); it is further stated that he who transgresses 'should find his place in the fire [of hell] (*faʾl-yatabawwaʾ maqʿadahu min al-nār*)'; (2) traditions that warn of a similar punishment to whoever interprets the Qurʾan according to his own judgement; (3) traditions that warn of punishment for those who interpret the Qurʾan without previous knowledge.[5] Al-Ṭabarī himself treads the middle ground: on the one hand, he upholds exegesis by means of prophetical traditions (*al-tafsīr bi-l-maʾthūr*), along which lines he wrote the commentary that has had

---

[4] Goldziher, *Die Richtungen der islamischen Koransauslegung*, p. 55 (=*Schools of Koranic Commentaries*, p. 36).

[5] Abū Jaʿfar Muḥammad b. Jarīr al-Ṭabarī, *Jāmiʿ al-bayān ʿan taʾwīl āy al-Qurʾān* (Cairo, 1388/1968), vol. 1, pp. 34–35.

an incomparable influence on generations of Sunni and Shiʿi exegesis; on the other hand, he allows himself considerable scope for independent decisions.

The dilemma of the authority of reason versus that of tradition has preoccupied Sunni and Shiʿi commentators alike. There is, however, an essential difference between the two. The prevalent view in Shiʿi exegetical tradition, unlike that of Sunnism, is that the authority to interpret the Qur'an does not lie with ordinary believers but is rather a privilege exclusive to ʿAlī and his descendants, the Imams. This privilege accompanies their status as recipients of divine knowledge – one of several superhuman features with which they are believed to be endowed. It should be noted, however, that Shiʿi views on this issue are by no means uniform. As will be seen below, there are differences not only between various currents of Shiʿism – such as the Twelver Shiʿis and the Ismailis – but also within each specific current. From the earliest phase in the history of the Shiʿa, Shiʿi scholars endeavoured to anchor the concept of the Imams' exclusive authority as Qur'an interpreters within the Qur'an itself or, alternatively, within prophetical traditions.

I will now offer a brief survey of the principal verses and *ḥadīth*s employed as proof texts for this claim. Perhaps the most widely known of the verses invoked to endorse this concept is Q.3:7:

> It is He who revealed the Book to you, in which appear clear signs [or verses], which are the Essence of the Book, and other ambiguous [signs/verses] … and none knows its interpretation, save only God. And those firmly rooted in knowledge say, 'We believe in it'. All is from our Lord; yet none remember, but men possessed of minds (*huwa alladhī anzala ʿalayka al-kitāb minhu āyāt muḥkamāt hunna ummu al-kitāb wa-ukharun mutashābihāt … wa-mā yaʿlamu ta'wīlahu illā llāhu* ***wa'l-rāsikhūna fi'l-ʿilm*** *yaqūlūna āmannā bihi*'. *Kullun min ʿindi rabbinā wa-mā yadhdhakkaru illā ulū al-albāb*).[6]

The commentary on this verse raises the syntactic question of how to read the phrase '*al-rāsikhūn fi'l-ʿilm* (those firmly rooted in knowledge)': is it the second subject, next to Allah in the previous sentence (i.e., only God and those firmly rooted in knowledge know its meaning), or is it the subject of the next sentence (those firmly rooted in knowledge say)? The Sunni exegetical tradition leans towards the second interpretation. The prevalent attitude in Shiʿi exegesis, both Imāmī-Shiʿi and Ismaili – in which the verse was employed as a proof text for the Imams' authority in Qur'anic exegesis,

---

[6] See, for example, Abū Zakariyā' Yaḥyā b. Muḥammad al-Farrā', *Maʿānī al-Qur'ān* (Cairo, 1980), vol. 1, p. 191; al-Ṭabarī, *Jāmiʿ al-bayān*, vol. 3, pp. 182–184, who surveys many traditions supporting both interpretations but clearly prefers the second possibility (p. 184), as do al-Farrā' and other Sunni commentators. See also John Wansbrough, *Quranic Studies: Sources and Methods of Scriptural Interpretation* (Oxford, 1977), p. 152. The translations of Qur'anic verses throughout this chapter are those of A. J. Arberry, *The Koran Interpreted* (London, 1955), with occasional slight alterations.

preferred the first interpretation.[7] The words '*al-rāsikhūn fi'l-ʿilm*' became one of the most common phrases to denote the Imams in their role as exclusive interpreters of the Qurʾan.

Another verse employed in this manner is Q.4:83: 'When there comes to them a matter, be it of security or fear, they broadcast it; if they had referred it to the Messenger and to those in authority among them, those of them whose task is to investigate would have known the matter (*wa-idhā jāʾahum amr min al-amn wa'l-khawf adhāʿū bihi wa-law raddūhu ilā al-rasūl wa-ilā ulī al-amr minhum laʿalimahu alladhīna yastanbiṭūnahu minhum*).' There is an instructive tradition regarding this verse related in the name of the Imam ʿAlī al-Riḍā and reported by Abu'l-Naḍr Muḥammad b. Masʿūd al-ʿAyyāshī, one of the greatest Imāmī-Shiʿi scholars and Qurʾan commentators (flourished end of the 3rd/9th until the beginning of the 4th/10th century). The historical context of the tradition is a written exchange between al-Riḍā and his disciple ʿAbd Allāh b. Jundab.[8] Ibn Jundab mentioned a group of Shiʿi believers who had become enemies of the Shiʿa, to which the Imam responded: 'The Devil presented himself to them and led them astray with words of doubt and corrupted their faith.' Al-Riḍā went on to refer to the Shiʿi view on the authority of the Imams as interpreters of the Qurʾan. He stated that the believers in question had erred because they wished 'to seek the truth independently, inquiring why, who and how (*arādū al-hudā min tilqāʾi nafsihim wa-saʾalū li-mā wa-man wa-kayfa*)'. These issues were not within their authority and contradicted their obligation to obey the Imams, since 'it is the duty [of the believers] in their perplexity and ignorance to approach those of wisdom and authority', namely the Imams, the exclusive legitimate descendants of the Prophet.[9]

As stated earlier, the authority of the Imams as interpreters of the Qurʾan is reiterated in a number of traditions, some of which will be mentioned here. Among these, perhaps the most recurrent in both exegetical and non-exegetical works in all

---

[7] Abu'l-Naḍr al-ʿAyyāshī, *Tafsīr*, ed. H. al-Rasūlī al-Maḥallātī (Qumm, 1380/1960), vol. 1, p. 162; al-Nuʿmān b. Ḥayyūn al-Tamīmī al-Maghribī (=al-Qāḍī al-Nuʿmān), *Asās al-taʾwīl*, ed. ʿA. Tāmir (Beirut, 1960), p. 29.

[8] Ibn Jundab was also a disciple of al-Riḍā's grandfather and father, i.e., the Imams Jaʿfar al-Ṣādiq and Mūsā al-Kāẓim. On Ibn Jundab see Abū Jaʿfar al-Ṭūsī, *Rijāl* (Najaf, 1381/1961), pp. 229, 355, 379; ʿAbd Allāh al-Māmaqānī, *Tanqīḥ al-maqāl* (Najaf, 1349–1352), biography 6791, who adds in al-Ṭūsī's name that Ibn Jundab was a *wakīl* (i.e., spokesman and appointee) of the Imam Abū Ibrāhīm (i.e., al-Kāẓim) and al-Riḍā and was highly regarded by them (*rafīʿ al-manzila ladayhim*); Abū ʿAmr Muḥammad b. ʿUmar al-Kashshī, *Kitāb al-rijāl* (Najaf, n.d,), pp. 489–490. See also E. Kohlberg and M. A. Amir-Moezzi, *Revelation and Falsification: The Kitāb al-qirāʾāt of Aḥmad b. Muḥammad al-Sayyārī* (Leiden and Boston, 2009), English section, pp. 220–221 (§§ 492, 493).

[9] *Tafsīr al-ʿAyyāshī*, vol. 1, p. 260. The tradition is cited in a number of works of the Safawid period. See the editor's comment, ibid., note 4. A similar version is cited by al-Shaykh al-Mufīd (d. 413/1022) in his *al-Ikhtiṣāṣ*, ed. ʿAlī Akbar al-Ghaffārī (Tehran, 1379/1959), p. 258. See also Muḥammad b. al-Ḥusayn Ṭabāṭabāʾī's observation in his *al-Mīzān fī tafsīr al-Qurʾān* (Beirut, 1403–1405/1983–1985), vol. 5, p. 24.

the Shi'i currents is *ḥadīth al-thaqalayn* (the tradition of the two weighty things). According to both Shi'i and Sunni sources, Muḥammad related this *ḥadīth* to the believers during the sermon he delivered on the last pilgrimage to Mecca after its conquest (in the ninth year of the *hijra*), an event referred to in Muslim historiography as *khuṭbat ḥajjat al-wadāʿ*. There are, however, significant differences between the Sunni and Shi'i interpretations of this tradition. Furthermore, both Sunni and Shi'i texts comprise more than one version of this tradition.

According to one version, cited in the Sunni text *Sīrat rasūl Allāh* by Muḥammad Ibn Isḥāq (d. 151/768) as transmitted and edited by ʿAbd al-Malik b. Hishām (d. 218/834), Muḥammad said to his disciples:

> I have left with you something clear; if you hold fast to it, you will never fall into error – the Book of God and the practice of His Prophet (*qad taraktu fīkum mā in iʿtaṣamtum bihi lan taḍillū abadan amran bayyinan – kitāb Allāh wa-sunnat nabiyyihi*).[10]

The two things Muḥammad left in the hands of his community (which, in parallel traditions, are referred to as *thaqalān*) later became the first two principles of Muslim jurisprudence (*uṣūl al-fiqh*) – namely, the Qur'an and the Sunna (the prophetic practice).

Two other versions of this tradition are also recorded in Sunni texts: a widely known version, in which the *thaqalān* are the Qur'an (designated in many traditions *al-thaqal al-akbar*, 'the more weighty object') and the Family of the Prophet (*ahl al-bayt*), designated *al-thaqal al-aṣghar* ('the less weighty object'). The second version is a tradition in which only the first of the pair of *thaqalān* is mentioned – the Qur'an.

An example of the first of these two types of tradition is the following, cited in Muslim's *Ṣaḥīḥ*:

> I leave among you the two weighty things (*thaqalān*): the first is the book of God (*kitāb Allāh*), which contains correct guidance and light (*al-hudā wa'l-nūr*). Cling therefore to the book of God and hold fast to it. And he [Muḥammad] encouraged his disciples [to follow] the book of God (*fa-ḥaththa ʿalā kitāb Allāh wa-raghghaba fīhi*); then he said: 'and my family' (*ahl baytī*).[11]

The existence of a version mentioning *ahl al-bayt* (the Family of the Prophet) instead of *sunnat nabiyyihi* (the practice of His Prophet) provided the Shi'i exegetical

---

[10] Muḥammad Ibn Isḥāq, *Kitāb sīrat rasūl Allāh*, ed. F. Wüstenfeld (Leipzig, 1858–1859), vol. 2, p. 969. The English translation cited here is that of A. Guillaume, *The Life of the Prophet Muhammad* (Oxford, 1955), p. 651, with slight modifications.

[11] See, for example, Abu'l-Ḥusayn Muslim b. al-Ḥajjāj al-Qushayrī al-Naysabūrī, *Ṣaḥīḥ Muslim* (Cairo, 1374–1375/1981), vol. 4, p. 1873 (tradition 36); p. 1384 (tradition 37). See also A. J. Wensinck, *Concordance et indices de la tradition musulmane* (Leiden, 1936–1969), s.v. *thaqal*.

tradition with room for sectarian interpretation. An investigation of how Shiʿi tradition made use of *ḥadīth al-thaqalayn* brings to light two main features: first, a restrictive interpretation of *ahl al-bayt*, so that the term denotes only ʿAlī and the Imams, descendants of Fāṭima, and thus excludes others such as the wives of the Prophet or other branches of the Hāshimī House;[12] and second, an application of the *ḥadīth* as proof text for the authority of the Imams as the exclusive interpreters of the Qurʾan. The analogy between one tradition, according to which the second *thaqal* refers to the practice of the Prophet (*sunnat nabiyyihi*), and the other tradition, according to which it is his family (*ahl baytī* or *ʿitratī ahl baytī*), indicates the position of Shiʿi scholars on the exclusive exegetical role of the Family of the Prophet in the interpretation of the Qurʾan.[13] In other words, while in the Sunni exegetical tradition, the *practice* of the Prophet (*sunnat nabiyyihi*) is invoked for the interpretation of the Qurʾan (and is therefore mentioned in conjunction with the Book itself), in Shiʿi tradition, the Family of the Prophet plays the equivalent role – that is, only through the mediation of the Imams, the descendants of the Prophet, is the true meaning of the Qurʾanic text revealed to believers. An example of the Shiʿi version of this tradition is cited by al-ʿAyyāshī:

> I [Muḥammad] am your vanguard and you are destined to appear before me at the pool (of paradise). When you appear before me, I shall ask you about the *thaqalān*. Therefore consider how to replace me [in your concern for them], until you meet me. Then they asked: what are the *thaqalān*, O Messenger of God? He answered: The great *thaqal* is the Book of God. This is a rope whose one end is in the hands of the Lord while the other end is in yours; so hold on to it and you shall not err nor be degraded (*lā taḍillū wa-lā tadhillū*). The small *thaqal* is my family, the people of my household, and I have already been informed by the Merciful and Knowing One that the two will never be divided until they meet me … Do not compete with them and you shall not err, and do not neglect [your duties] for then you will be lost; and do not instruct them for they are more learned than you.[14]

The *thaqalān* are thus intertwined with each other forever. The first one, the Qurʾan, remains meaningless without the other, namely the Imams, who invest it with life;

---

12 For an indication that this tradition was indeed interpreted inclusively, see Muslim, *Ṣaḥīḥ Muslim*, vol. 4, p. 1873 (tradition 36) where the question is explicitly raised: 'And who are his family? … are not the Prophet's wives [included] in his family' (*wa-man ahl baytihi? a-laysa nisāʾuhu min ahl baytihi*)? The answer given there is that the Prophet's wives are indeed included in the term *ahl baytihi*, although in general it signifies the various households of Hāshim's family (p. 1384, tradition 37).

13 For more on the term *ahl al-bayt* and its political and factional connotations (from the pre-Islamic period to the Qurʾan and its commentators), see M. Sharon, 'Ahl al-Bayt – People of the House', *JSAI*, 8 (1986), pp. 169–184. See also W. Madelung, 'The Hāshimiyyāt of al-Kumayt and Hāshimī Shiʿism', *SI*, 70 (1989), pp. 5–26.

14 *Tafsīr al-ʿAyyāshī*, vol. 1, p. 4.

or in the words of Abū Jaʿfar al-Ṭūsī (d. 460/1067), the great Imāmī-Shiʿi theologian and Qur'an commentator of the Būyid period: 'This tradition [of the *thaqalān*] proves that it [i.e., the Qur'an] exists in every generation, since it is unlikely that he [Muḥammad] would decree that we keep something which we cannot keep, just as the family of the Prophet, and those we ordered to follow, are present at all times.'[15] From here to the creation of a well-known metaphor describing the Imams as 'the speaking Qur'an [*kitāb Allāh al-nāṭiq*]', the path is short indeed. This recurrent expression is employed inter alia by the Imāmī-Shiʿi scholar Abū Rajab al-Bursī (d. 813/1411) with regard to Q.23:62: 'With us is a Book speaking the truth (*wa-ladaynā kitāb yanṭiqu bi-l-ḥaqq*).' Al-Bursī comments: 'The Speaking Book is the friend [of God, i.e., the Imam] (*al-kitāb al-nāṭiq huwa al-walī*).'[16] In Ismaili Shiʿism, or more precisely in one of its two major branches, the Nizārīs, where the imamate has remained a permanently living institution, the role of the Imam as a 'speaking Qur'an' is to be taken in a more literal sense, for he is an authority always accessible to interpret the words of God to the believers, thus reducing the need for systematic, written exegesis. As I have learned from discussions with Ismailis upholding the 'living tradition' of their faith, this explanation is regarded as almost self-explanatory.[17] The version of this tradition as it appears in *Tafsīr al-ʿAyyāshī*, as well as in other Twelver Imāmī-Shiʿi and Ismaili sources,[18] differs in various details from the one cited above in Muslim's *Ṣaḥīḥ*. However, it is unique particularly in its ending, which underscores the duty to subject oneself to and obey the *thaqalān*: it is forbidden to compete with them or to presume a greater knowledge or authority than theirs.

---

[15] Abū Jaʿfar al-Ṭūsī, *al-Tibyān fī tafsīr al-Qur'ān* (Najaf, 1376–1385/1957–1965), vol. 1, pp. 3–4.

[16] Abū Rajab al-Bursī, *Mashāriq anwār al-yaqīn fī asrār amīr al-mu'minīn* (Beirut, n.d.), p. 135. On al-Bursī and on another tradition he cites in a similar spirit, see P. Lory, 'Souffrir pour la verité selon l'ésotérisme chiite de Rajab al-Borsī', in M. A. Amir-Moezzi, M. M. Bar-Asher and S. Hopkins, ed., *Le Shīʿisme Imāmite quarante ans après: Hommage à Etan Kohlberg* (Paris, 2009), pp. 315–323, at p. 319. See also M. Ayoub, 'The Speaking Qur'ān and the Silent Qur'ān: A Study of the Principles and Development of Imāmī Tafsīr', in A. Rippin, ed., *Approaches to the History of the Interpretation of the Qur'ān* (Oxford, 1988), pp. 177–198, at p. 183, note 17; and see now M. A. Amir-Moezzi, *Le Coran silencieux et le Coran parlant: Sources scripturaires de l'islam entre histoire et ferveur* (Paris, 2011).

[17] The split took place after the death of the Imam-caliph al-Mustanṣir (d. 428/1094). In the Indian subcontinent, as well as in other areas to which Ismaili believers migrated from India, these two branches are known as Bohra and Khoja. The Bohra are the Mustaʿlī-Ṭayyibīs living in West India. The Khoja (Persian, *kh[w]āja* 'sir', pl. *kh[w]ājān*) are the Nizarīs living in north-west India. The latter consider the Aga Khan to be their spiritual leader. Their main centres are in Punjab and Sind, along the lower Indus River. Khoja communities are also to be found in the Middle East, Pakistan, China, Burma, eastern and southern Africa, as well as North America and Europe.

[18] For Ismaili works in which the *ḥadīth al-thaqalayn* is cited, see for example the Ṭayyibī *dāʿī* ʿAlī Ibn al-Walīd, *Tāj al-ʿaqā'id wa-maʿdin al-fawā'id*, ed. ʿĀrif Tāmir (Beirut, 1967), p. 90. See also al-Qāḍī al-Nuʿmān, *Asās al-ta'wīl*.

Another well-known tradition relates that the Prophet defined ʿAlī's role as a fighter for the interpretation of the Qur'an, just as the Prophet himself fought for its revelation (*inna fīkum man yuqātilu ʿalā ta'wīl al-Qur'ān kamā qātaltu ʿalā tanzīlihi*). This tradition, which a few years ago was subjected to a meticulous analysis by Mohammad Ali Amir-Moezzi,[19] is recurrent in Sunni,[20] Imāmī-Shiʿi[21] and Ismaili works.[22] Moreover, in the Ismaili tradition, Muḥammad's role is likened to that of the other prophets; it is reduced to the mere revelation of the text, whereas ʿAlī's role – and hence also that of his descendants – is to concentrate on the concealed layer, which should be kept secret and be revealed only to the initiated. In Ismaili doctrine this division between the role of the Prophet and that of his descendants, the Imams, is epitomised in the clear-cut distinction between the 'speaking Imam' (*imām nāṭiq*) who is in charge of the revealed-exoteric layer of Scripture and the 'silent Imam' (*imām ṣāmit*) who, in turn, is responsible for its hidden-esoteric layer. Finally, noteworthy is an Ismaili tradition related in connection with Q.38 (*Ṣād*):39, which supports the distinction between Muḥammad and his descendants, the Imams. The tradition focuses on the Imams' affinity with the Qur'anic text, and the different levels of miraculous ability with which they were endowed:

> [God] the exalted the most high has determined the exoteric layer [of the Qur'an] as his Messenger's miracle, and the esoteric layer as a miracle of the Imams, from among his family. [The knowledge of the esoteric] exists only with them, and no one but they can produce anything similar; just as none but their forefather, Muḥammad the Messenger of God, could produce the visible text [of the Qur'an]. It is inherited knowledge and is deposited with them; it exists with no one but them; they discuss it with each group according to their understanding

---

[19] M. A. Amir-Moezzi, '"Le combattant du ta'wīl": un poème de Mollā Ṣadrā sur ʿAlī: Aspects de l'imamologie duodécimaine IX.', *Journal Asiatique*, 292 (2004), pp. 331–359; repr. in M. A. Amir-Moezzi, *La Religion discrète: croyances et pratiques spirituelles dans l'islam shiʿite* (Paris, 2006), pp. 231–251, where the expression taken from the *ḥadīth* – *le combattant du ta'wīl* – forms part of the title. For an English version of this article see now 'The Warrior of *Ta'wīl* …', in M. A. Amir-Moezzi, *The Spirituality of Shiʿi Islam* (London, 2011), pp. 307–337.

[20] See, for example, al-Muḥibb al-Ṭabarī, *al-Riyāḍ al-naḍira* (Tanta, 1372/1953), vol. 2, pp. 52–53.

[21] See, *Tafsīr al-ʿAyyāshī*, vol. 1, p. 115 and ibid., p. 17. See also Abu'l-Fatḥ ʿAlī b. ʿAbd al-Karīm al-Shahrastānī, *Kitāb al-milal wa'l-niḥal* (Beirut, n.d.), p. 189; al-Shahrastānī, *Livre des religions et des sectes*, tr. and ed. D. Gimaret, J. Jolivet and G. Monnot (Paris and Louvain, 1986), vol. 1, p. 543 and note 231, where other sources are cited.

[22] See 'Fragments of *the Kitāb al-rushd wa'l-hidāya*, the Arabic text edited by M. Kamil Hussein', in W. Ivanow, ed., *Collectanea*, 1 (Leiden, 1948), pp. 185–213, at p. 211. It is noteworthy that the text in question reflects Ismaili doctrine at the beginning of the 4th/10th century. See M. M. Bar-Asher, 'Outlines of Early Ismāʿīlī-Faṭimid Qur'ān Exegesis', *Journal Asiatique*, 296 (2008), pp. 257–296, at p. 267; *Tāj al-ʿaqā'id wa-maʿdin al-fawā'id* by the Yemenī Ismaili *dāʿī* ʿAlī b. Muḥammad Ibn al-Walīd (d. 612/1215), p. 90.

> and bestow upon the people of each rank[23] that which they deserve thereof; they deny [this knowledge] to those to whom it needs to be denied, and remove from it those who deserve to have it removed, according to the words of the Almighty Bestower [God]: 'This is our gift. Bestow it or cease without reckoning' (*fa-jaʿala ʿazza wa-jalla ẓāhirahu muʿjizata rasūlihi wa-bāṭinahu muʿjizata al-aʾimma min ahl baytihi, lā yūjadu illā ʿindahum wa-lā yastaṭīʿu aḥad an yaʾtiya bi-mithlihi ghayruhum kamā lā yastaṭīʿu an yaʾtiya bi-ẓāhir al-kitāb ghayru Muḥammad rasūl Allāh jaddihim fa-dhālika ʿilm manqūl fīhim mutawārith baynahum mustawdaʿ ladayhim, lā yūjadu ʿinda aḥad siwāhum, yukhāṭibūna kulla qawm minhu bi-miqdār mā yafhamūna wa-yuʿṭūna ahla kulli ḥadd minhu mā yastaḥiqqūna wa-yamnaʿūna minhu man yajibu manʿuhu wa-yadfaʿūna ʿanhu man istaḥaqqa dafʿahu li-qawl al-ʿazīz al-wahhāb: 'hādhā ʿaṭāʾunā fa-mnun aw amsik bi-ghayri ḥisābin'* [Q.38:39]).[24]

Muḥammad is described here as merely the deliverer of the Qur'an: the Prophet's greatest virtue is in delivering the Qur'anic text as it is. In contrast, the Imams are the guardians of knowledge, including, of course, knowledge of the esoteric meaning of the Qur'an. They have the authority to share this knowledge with the believers, each according to his capacity, whereas the exoteric knowledge is available to all those who undertake a careful study of the text. A nuance not familiar from Imāmī texts seems to emerge from this Ismaili text – namely, the believer can read the exoteric aspect of the text on his own, but he is dependent on the Imam for an understanding of its esoteric aspect.

Needless to say, the above texts represent only a few among many examples. Shiʿi exegesis, in all the currents, is rich in interpretations of Qur'anic verses and in traditions that aim to reinforce the status and exclusive authority of the Imams as the exclusively authoritative Qur'an interpreters.[25]

As we have seen, an examination of the question of authority reveals a great similarity between the exegetical texts of the Imāmī-Shiʿis and the Ismailis; the similarity also appears to extend, for the most part, to Zaydī Shiʿism. There exists, however, a substantial difference in the history of these three factions, and this would seem to have implications for the issue discussed here. In Zaydī and Ismaili Shiʿism the imamate remained a permanent institution throughout their history and the Imams (or the preachers – *duʿāt* – acting on their behalf) continue to exert authority over their communities, including the authority to interpret the Qur'an. In Imāmī Shiʿism, however, with the Occultation of the Twelfth Imam (260/874), the institution of the

---

23 Arabic *ḥadd*: stage, degree, a key term in Ismaili doctrine, in which the notion of hierarchy is fundamentally implied.

24 Al-Qāḍī al-Nuʿmān, *Asās al-taʾwīl*, pp. 31–32.

25 For further details regarding Imāmī-Shiʿi exegesis, see Bar-Asher, *Scripture and Exegesis*, pp. 93–101.

imamate ceased to exist. This raised the question: how was the authority of the Imams to be exerted in their absence?

Reviewing the exegetical literature of early Imāmī Shiʿism with regard to the question of authority, one discovers two distinct tendencies that can be defined in both chronological and doctrinal terms. Chronology and doctrine, it should be stressed, are in this case intertwined. By chronology, I mean the distinction between literature written up to the Greater Occultation (329/941), or according to another time-definition, before the rise to power of the Būyid dynasty (334–447/945–1055), and the literature written after the Occultation (or after the Būyid period had begun). Doctrinally, I mean the distinction between the traditional and the rational attitude; to put it differently, if I may use an anachronistic terminology, the distinction between the *akhbārī* and *uṣūlī* attitude in dealing with the authority issue. The pre-Occultation period is characterised by a traditional (*akhbārī* or more precisely proto-*akhbārī*) attitude, while the post-Occultation is characterised by a more rationalist (proto-*uṣūlī*) attitude.

In the pre-Occultation period, there clearly emerges from Imāmī-Shiʿi writings a rejection of rational interpretation of the Qurʾan and an emphasis on the exclusivity of the Imams as possessors of divine knowledge, including the ability to interpret the Qurʾan. At this stage the exegetical views of the authors are given indirectly. Loyal to the *ḥadīth* statement that 'whosoever interprets [rationally] a verse from the Qurʾan is an infidel (*man fassara bi-raʾyihi āya min kitāb Allāh fa-qad kafara*)',[26] early (pre-Occultation) Imāmī-Shiʿi commentators drastically reduced their participation in the process of interpretation, limiting themselves to citing traditions in the name of the Imams and only very rarely stating their own opinions on the material they present. This should not, however, lead us to the simplistic conclusion that the Imāmī-Shiʿi commentators at this period did not have an overall exegetical viewpoint, since their opinion – although not explicitly pronounced – may be implicitly discerned from their choice and selection of material cited and omitted. Moreover, as Etan Kohlberg demonstrated in a number of his studies, among which is his article 'Imam and Community in the pre-Ghayba Period', already in the early stages of Shiʿism there were leading disciples of the Imams who dared to challenge the authority of the Imam by expressing their independent views on matters of doctrine and law. 'A common mechanism for dealing with such dissidents was dissociation, by which they were effectively removed from the community.'[27] If we take as an example the attitude to the Companions of the Prophet – and more particularly, to the first three caliphs – we can see that the pre-Occultation commentators (mainly Abu'l-Naḍr al-ʿAyyāshī, ʿAlī Ibn Ibrāhīm al-Qummī and Furāt b. Ibrāhīm b. Furāt al-Kūfī) consistently incorporated all the traditions that denigrated them, anchoring these in specific Qurʾan verses. However, these commentators put forward their views in a *ḥadīth* format,

[26] *Tafsīr al-ʿAyyāshī*, vol. 1, p. 17, traditions 2, 4 and 5.

[27] E. Kohlberg, 'Imam and Community in the Pre-Ghayba Period', in Said A. Arjomand, ed., *Authority and Political Culture in Shiʿism* (Albany, NY, 1988), p. 39.

thus emphasising the minimal intervention on their part in the message they sought to convey.

Beginning with Abū Ja'far al-Ṭūsī, the leading Imāmī-Shi'i theologian and commentator of the Būyid period, there is evidence of a remarkable shift in the attitude of the Imāmī-Shi'i exegetes. Al-Ṭūsī – representing a new tendency which may be designated 'independent exegesis' – is ambivalent about the use of *ḥadīth* in his commentary. On the one hand, he does not deny his indebtedness to tradition and explicitly states that 'the Qur'an should only be interpreted according to correct traditions (*illā bi-l-athar al-ṣaḥīḥ*) transmitted by the Prophet, [the people] of his household and the Imams, peace be upon them, whose words are as exemplary (*ḥujja*) as those of the Prophet [himself]; it should not be interpreted rationally (*wa-inna al-qawla fīhi bi-l-ra'y lā yajūzu*)'.[28] Yet even a cursory review of his work – and that of his great follower, who lived nearly a century after him, Abū 'Alī al-Faḍl b. al-Ḥasan al-Ṭabrisī (d. 548/1153) – reveals that (as with al-Ṭabarī, perhaps even under his inspiration) a new path had been paved. While their comprehensive Qur'an commentaries are replete with early Imāmī-Shi'i traditions, these are presented in a radically different manner from the way similar traditions are cited in the pre-Būyid exegetical (and non-exegetical) works. This can be seen both in the marginal positioning of these traditions in the works of al-Ṭūsī and al-Ṭabrisī and in the omission or abbreviation of the chains of transmitters (*isnād*s). These commentaries primarily take the form of a continuous discourse in which the authors often voice their own opinions and preferences.

A striking evaluation of the pre-Būyid Imāmī-Shi'i exegesis is offered by al-Ṭabrisī in an instructive introduction to his Qur'an commentary. Insightful remarks attest to his subtle understanding of the substantial change that occurred in Imāmī-Shi'i literature after the Occultation of the Twelfth Imam. Al-Ṭabrisī explains why he and al-Ṭūsī based their commentaries upon similar texts that pre-date their work – namely, the exegetical writings of the pre-Būyid period. He begins by praising the work of the ancients, 'who attempted to reveal the secrets [of the Qur'an] ... and composed in this [field] impressive books, in many of which they ventured into the depth [of the sea of exegesis]'.[29] Out of such praise there emerges, however, an indication of what he considers to be the limitations of the early exegesis as well as a veiled criticism of it:

> Our colleagues [*aṣḥābunā*], may God be pleased with them, composed only abridgments [*mukhtaṣarāt*] in which they cited traditions in this [area] handed down to them; they did not pay attention to the interpretation of meanings or the disclosure

---

[28] Abū Ja'far al-Ṭūsī, *al-Tibyān fī tafsīr al-Qur'ān*, vol. 1, p. 4. In the lines following this quotation al-Ṭūsī mentions several Companions and sages of Medina who were renowned for their strong opposition to rational interpretation.

[29] Abū 'Alī al-Faḍl b. al-Ḥasan al-Ṭabrisī, *Majma' al-bayān fī tafsīr al-Qur'ān* (Beirut, 1374–1377/1955–1957), vol. 1, p. 20.

> of secrets. The only exception was the great scholar Abū Jaʿfar Muḥammad b. al-Ḥasan al-Ṭūsī, who in his book *al-Tibyān* … did more than just collect [traditions] without interpreting them and [he did not just] write them down [in an elegant fashion] without analyzing them (*lam yaqnaʿ bi-tadwīnihā dūna tabyīnihā wa-lā bi-tanmīqihā dūna taḥqīqihā*).[30]

Unlike the pre-Būyid works of exegesis, therefore, later Imāmī-Shiʿi exegesis, as exemplified by the writings of al-Ṭūsī – and by those of al-Ṭabrisī, which are no less impressive – is characterised by an in-depth study of content. It is not eclectic, as were earlier works, and – which is more relevant to our discussion – the commentators are more authoritative, not restricting themselves to the transmission of exegetical traditions in the name of the Imams but often expressing their own views in an explicit manner.

How should one understand the huge gap between the two exegetical approaches within Imāmī Shiʿism? Perhaps the answer lies in the internal developments that took place in this branch of Shiʿism in the post-Occultation period or, put differently, under Būyid rule. During this period, Imāmī Shiʿism had no authoritative religious leadership, and only the representatives (*sufarāʾ*, *wukalāʾ*) of the Imam were active.[31] Since not much time had elapsed since the imamate of the 11th Imam Ḥasan al-ʿAskarī (d. 260/873), the last active Imam, traces of his authority were still evident, as convincingly demonstrated in the remarkable work of Hossein Modarressi, *Crisis and Consolidation in the Formative Period of Shiʿite Islam*.[32] It is only natural that in the absence of a living leader imposing his authority on the community, the Shiʿi religious scholars would assume some of the responsibilities that until then had been exclusively in the hands of the Imams. Without taking into account the changes that Imāmī-Shiʿism underwent in the absence of the Imam, it is impossible to understand the independent voice of scholars that is reflected in the literature produced during this period. As we have noted, the important development within Imāmī Shiʿism coincided with the rise to power of the Būyids in the middle of the Abbasid period; this ushered in a golden age in the history of Shiʿism. Hitherto oppressed and persecuted, under the Būyids the Shiʿis were accorded a legitimacy that brought in its wake a rich crop of Shiʿi literature in all fields, characterised by a general shift in attitude. In the period just prior to the Great Occultation, the Imāmī-Shiʿi doctrine had embraced divergent and even opposing views; a tendency towards rationalism existed side by side with traditionalism, whose legitimacy was based upon *ḥadīth*s authorised by the Imams. However, after the Great Occultation, Imāmī-Shiʿism adopted the Muʿtazilī doctrine, which maintained that rational judgement should be applied to theology; the same approach held true for exegesis and the authority accorded to commentators

30 Ibid.

31 See E. Kohlberg, '*Safīr*', *EI2*, vol. 8, pp. 811–812.

32 H. Modarressi, *Crisis and Consolidation in the Formative Period of Shiʿite Islam* (Princeton, 1993), pp. 65–84.

in interpreting the Qurʾan. Post-Occultation Imāmī-Shiʿi scholars, basing themselves on *ḥadīth al-thaqalayn* and other core traditions, adhered *de jure* to the view that the Imams were the exclusive authority for the interpretation of the Qurʾan; at the same time, however, there was a tendency among the new exegetes to express their own opinions, delegating to themselves de facto some of the authority of the Imams. The delegation of authority from the Imams to their disciples, both during the lifetime of the Imams and after the disappearance of the last Imam, is well described and analysed by Liyakat N. Takim in his recently published book, *The Heirs of the Prophet: Charisma and Religious Authority in Shiʿite Islam*. I fully share Takim's view that the delegation of authority to Imāmī-Shiʿi scholars should not be viewed as an event that occurred immediately after the death of a certain Imam or the disappearance of the last Imam: 'Rather, it was a process that gradually diffused the charismatic authority of an Imam to the nascent charismatic office of those close disciples while he was still alive.' [33]

Concluding Remarks

Since the earliest phases in the history of Muslim exegesis, the question of the authority to interpret the Qurʾan has held centre stage. Initially the issue at stake was whether it is permissible or even possible for a human being to interpret the divine words of God as revealed in the Qurʾan. As in other religions, the prevalent approach during the first century of Islam was scripturalist, in the sense that the sacred book is a clear text requiring no additional source or exegetical endeavour to make its meaning clearer. Moreover, it is believed to be, as is stated in the text itself, a Book 'making clear everything (*tibyānan li-kulli shayʾin*)'. Inevitably this resistance to the role of exegesis could not be sustained indefinitely. For while the scripturalist attitude within Islam can be seen as exemplifying the tendency – found also in other religions – to maximise the stature of the Holy Scripture, the need to make Scripture relevant for a living, dynamic community, and to find in the Qurʾan answers to questions which it does not explicitly address, became irresistible.

New questions appeared: who is authorised to interpret the sacred text? Are Muslim believers entitled to do so and, if so, does this extend to all of them? To what extent is the commentator free in his endeavour to interpret the Qurʾan? Muslim scholars were far from unanimous in their approach to these questions. Sunnis and Shiʿis sharply disagreed as regards the question of authority. The dominant Sunni view was that the authority to interpret the holy text was delegated by the Prophet to his Companions and their followers and, later on, to the scholars who are viewed as holders of the Muslim heritage and consequently as those authorised to interpret it. In contrast, Shiʿis of all persuasions shared the view that the authority to interpret the

---

[33] L. N. Takim, *The Heirs of the Prophet: Charisma and Religious Authority in Shiʿite Islam* (New York, 2006), p. 86.

Qurʾan does not lie with ordinary believers but is rather a privilege exclusive to ʿAlī and his descendants, the Imams. This privilege accompanies their status as recipients of divine knowledge – one of several superhuman features with which they are believed to be endowed. The Shiʿi approach was anchored in a number of Qurʾanic verses and core prophetic traditions which became 'proof texts' for the question of authority. Among these the *ḥadīth al-thaqalayn* occupies a special place.

PART III
SHI'I *ḤADĪTH*

Introduction

Etan Kohlberg

For the Shiʿis, the term '*ḥadīth*' (literally 'narrative', 'report', often rendered as 'tradition') designates a pronouncement of the Prophet Muḥammad or one of the Imams, as well as a report describing their words, actions or habits. '*Ḥadīth*' also refers to the entire corpus of these traditions.[1] As such, *Ḥadīth* – no less than the Qurʾan – is of paramount importance for Shiʿi doctrine, history and law. *Ḥadīth* is arguably the earliest form of Shiʿi literature although a second category, that of scholastic writing (*kalām*), was also produced in the early period (2nd–4th/8th–10th century).[2]

One of the first scholars in the West to appreciate the significance of Shiʿi *Ḥadīth* was Ignaz Goldziher (1850–1921). Although Shiʿism was not his main field of research, he showed a lifelong interest in the subject, and his studies on Shiʿism are at least partially based on the literature of *Ḥadīth*. At the same time, the paucity of Shiʿi texts at his disposal placed a limit on what he could achieve in this area.[3] Since

---

1 In what follows, '*ḥadīth*' ('ḥ' in lower case) denotes an individual tradition, while '*Ḥadīth*' ('Ḥ' in upper case) refers to the corpus of traditions. Other terms occasionally used in the same meaning as *ḥadīth* are *khabar* (pl. *akhbār*), *athar* (pl. *āthār*) and *riwāya* (pl. *riwāyāt*). At times, a distinction is drawn between Prophetic *Ḥadīth* and *akhbār* of the Imams. See Robert Gleave, *Inevitable Doubt: Two Theories of Shīʿī Jurisprudence* (Leiden, 2000), p. 29; Robert Gleave, 'Between *Ḥadīth* and *Fiqh*: The "Canonical" Imāmī Collections of *Akhbār*', *Islamic Law and Society*, 8 (2001), p. 352; Gérard Lecomte, 'Aspects de la littérature du *ḥadīṯ* chez les imāmites', in T. Fahd, ed., *Le Shīʿisme Imāmite* (Paris, 1970), p. 96.

2 On this literature, see Josef van Ess, *Theologie und Gesellschaft im 2. und 3. Jahrhundert Hidschra* (Berlin and New York, 1991–1997), vol. 1, pp. 233–403. For the issue of disciples of the Imams who formulated their own opinions on doctrinal matters, see Hossein Modarressi, *An Introduction to Shīʿī Law: A Bibliographical Study* (London, 1984), pp. 25–27; Hossein Modarressi, *Crisis and Consolidation in the Formative Period of Shiʿite Islam* (Princeton, 1993), pp. 110–117; Etan Kohlberg, 'Imam and Community in the Pre-Ghayba Period', in Said A. Arjomand, ed., *Authority and Political Culture in Shiʿism* (Albany, NY, 1988) pp. 33–37, reproduced in his *Belief and Law in Imāmī Shīʿism* (Aldershot, 1991), article XIII. Unless otherwise indicated, the term 'Shiʿis' will be used to refer to Imāmī (or Twelver) Shiʿis.

3 For further details see Kohlberg, 'Western Studies of Shiʿa Islam', in Martin Kramer, ed., *Shiʿism, Resistance, and Revolution* (Boulder, CO, 1987), pp. 38–40, reproduced in his *Belief and Law in Imāmī Shīʿism*, article II. For Goldziher's methodology in his studies on *Ḥadīth* in general see Harald Motzki, 'Introduction', in Harald Motzki, ed., *Ḥadīth: Origins and Developments* (Aldershot, 2004), pp. xviii–xxi.

his days, and particularly in the decades following the Iranian revolution of 1979, there have been significant advances in the research on Shiʿism in general and Shiʿi *Ḥadīth* in particular, though the number of studies on Shiʿi *Ḥadīth* remains modest in comparison with work on *Ḥadīth* in Sunni Islam.[4]

The Corpus of Shiʿi *Ḥadīth*

Of the various fields of research on Shiʿi *Ḥadīth*, the study and analysis of early *Ḥadīth* texts have occupied a prominent place. The oldest of these texts are known collectively as *al-Uṣūl al-arbaʿumiʾa* (literally, *The Four Hundred [Original] Sources*).[5] In most cases, an *aṣl* is a personal notebook of material received from the Imam through oral transmission;[6] it is called after the disciple who first wrote down the Imam's words. Most *uṣūl* authors were disciples of the sixth Imam, Jaʿfar al-Ṣādiq (d. 148/765), though the compilation of *uṣūl* continued for several generations after his death. The number 400 is mentioned for example by al-Shaykh al-Mufīd (d. 413/1022),[7] but it is doubtful whether this should be taken literally. Today, only about 20 *uṣūl* are known to have survived in their original form. By their very nature, the *uṣūl* were not as a rule composed according to subject matter. At a later stage, they were incorporated into larger works known as *jawāmiʿ*, which in turn served (together with other material) as the basis for the definitive collections of *Ḥadīth* of the Buwayhid period.

Among the compilations of Shiʿi traditions that have come down to us, those concerned with the virtues and prerogatives of the Imam occupy a special position. An early work of this kind is the *Baṣāʾir al-darajāt* by Muḥammad b. al-Ḥasan al-Ṣaffār al-Qummī (d. 290/903). The first Western scholar to examine this text was Levi Billig, but his work remained unfinished at the time of his assassination in Jerusalem in 1936, and was never published. More recently, the *Baṣāʾir* was studied

---

[4] Some of these studies are mentioned in Andrew J. Newman, *The Formative Period of Twelver Shīʿism* (Richmond, 2000), pp. xiv–xviii; Motzki, 'Introduction', pp. lvii–lviii; Jonathan A. C. Brown, *Hadith: Muhammad's Legacy in the Medieval and Modern World* (Oxford, 2009), pp. 147–148. See also Mohammad Ali Amir-Moezzi, 'Remarques sur les critères d'authenticité du hadīth et l'autorité du juriste dans le shiʿisme imāmite', *SI*, 85 (1997), pp. 5–39 and the studies referred to at p. 5, note 1. Newman notes that 'there has yet to develop a field of Twelver *ḥadīth* as well-populated as that which has sprung up for Sunnī Islam' (*Formative Period*, p. xviii).

[5] See Kohlberg, '*Al-uṣūl al-arbaʿumiʾa*', *JSAI*, 10 (1987), pp. 128–166, reproduced in his *Belief and Law in Imāmī Shīʿism*, article VII, and in Motzki, ed., *Ḥadīth*, chapter 6.

[6] Hossein Modarressi, *Tradition and Survival: A Bibliographical Survey of Early Shīʿi Literature* (Oxford, 2003), vol. 1, p. xiv.

[7] As cited in Ibn Shahrāshūb, *Maʿālim al-ʿulamāʾ* (Najaf, 1380/1961), p. 3.

by Mohammad Ali Amir-Moezzi[8] and Andrew Newman.[9] Another work of major importance on this topic is the *Uṣūl min al-kāfī*, comprising the first two volumes of the *Kāfī* by al-Kulīnī (Kulaynī) (d. 329/941).[10] The merits and the right to rule of ʿAlī are the subject of a great number of traditions, which are often grouped together under the title *Khaṣāʾiṣ*, *Manāqib* or *Faḍāʾil ʿAlī*.

A special category of traditions concerning the imamate deals with the occultation of the Imam. In the pre-*ghayba* era (i.e., the period preceding the occultation in 260/874 of the twelfth Imam), traditions of this kind were circulated by the Wāqifa, who saw them as referring to the seventh Imam Mūsā al-Kāẓim (d. 183/799). In their view, al-Kāẓim had not died in prison but had gone into hiding and would return as the Qāʾim. Following the occultation of the Twelfth Imam, the Imāmī Shiʿis reshaped these traditions and interpreted them as referring to him.[11] Compilations of such *ḥadīth*s were directed not only against the Sunnis, but also against non-Imāmī Shiʿis. A typical work of this nature is the *Kifāyat al-athar fiʾl-nuṣūṣ ʿalāʾl-aʾimma al-ithnay ʿashar* by al-Khazzāz al-Rāzī (fl. second half of the 4th/10th century), which was probably written in refutation of Zaydī criticisms of the doctrine of 12 Imams.[12] The best-known compilations of traditions on the subject of the occultation of the Hidden Imam are the *Ikmāl (kamāl) al-dīn wa-itmām (tamām) al-niʿma* by al-Khazzāz al-Rāzī's teacher Muḥammad b. ʿAlī Ibn Bābawayh known as al-Ṣadūq (d. 381/991), the *Kitāb al-ghayba* by Muḥammad b. Ibrāhīm Ibn Zaynab al-Nuʿmānī (d. ca. 360/971) and the *Kitāb al-ghayba* by Abū Jaʿfar al-Ṭūsī (d. 460/1067). Traditions stating that the number of Imams is twelve are occasionally found in works predating the *ghayba*, though it remains to be established whether or not these are later interpolations.[13]

---

[8] Amir-Moezzi, 'al-Ṣaffār al-Qummī (m. 290/902–3) et son *Kitāb baṣāʾir al-darajāt*', *Journal Asiatique*, 280 (1992), pp. 221–250; an expanded version is included in his *Le Coran silencieux et le Coran parlant* (Paris, 2011), pp. 127–158.

[9] Newman, *Formative Period*, pp. 67–93 and index, s.v. *Baṣāʾir al-Darajāt*.

[10] See Mohammad Ali Amir-Moezzi and Hassan Ansari, 'Muḥammad b. Yaʿqūb al-Kulaynī (m. 328 ou 329/939–40 ou 940–41) et son *Kitāb al-kāfī*: Une introduction', *Studia Iranica*, 38 (2009), pp. 191–247, reproduced in Amir-Moezzi, *Le Coran silencieux*, pp. 159–206. See also Newman, *Formative Period*, pp. 94–112 and index, s.v. *al-Kāfī*. The first two volumes of the *Kāfī* were apparently all that Goldziher possessed of the 'Four Books' (on which see further below) (Kohlberg, 'Western Studies', p. 39).

[11] Jassim M. Hussain, *The Occultation of the Twelfth Imam* (London, 1982), p. 3; Heinz Halm, *Shiʿism*, tr. Janet Watson and Marian Hill (2nd ed., Edinburgh, 2004), p. 32; Modarressi, *Crisis*, pp. 60–61, 87; Hassan Ansari, 'L'Imamat et l'occultation selon l'Imamisme: Étude bibliographique et histoire des textes' (Ph.D. thesis, École Pratique des Hautes Études, Sorbonne, Paris, 2009), pp. 175–185, 256.

[12] Ansari, *L'Imamat*, pp. 110–115. For Zaydī criticism of the occultation, see the *Kitāb al-ishhād* by the late 3rd/9th century Zaydī author Abū Zayd al-ʿAlawī, cited in Modarressi, *Crisis*, p. 186 (Arabic), p. 223 (English).

[13] Kohlberg, 'From Imāmiyya to Ithnā-ʿAshariyya', *BSOAS*, 39 (1976), pp. 521–523, reproduced in his *Belief and Law in Imāmī Shīʿism*, article XIV; Amir-Moezzi, 'al-Ṣaffār al-Qummī',

Two other categories of *Ḥadīth* works should be mentioned. The first are those known as *Amālī*. These were dictated, usually by an eminent scholar, on successive sessions (*majālis*); hence the same work may sometimes be referred to both as *Amālī* and *Majālis*. Works of this genre derive from some of the most prominent Shiʿi scholars of the Buwayhid period, including Ibn Bābawayh, al-Shaykh al-Mufīd, al-Sharīf al-Murtaḍā (d. 436/1044) and Abū Jaʿfar al-Ṭūsī. The traditions found in the *Amālī* are not as a rule grouped thematically; instead they relate to a variety of historical, doctrinal and legal issues.

The second category are collections of *ḥadīth*s in which the reasons (*ʿilal*) behind various laws and tenets are explained. One of the eleven 'books' (*kutub*) making up the extant portion of *Kitāb al-maḥāsin* by Aḥmad b. Muḥammad al-Barqī (d. 274/887–888 or 280/893–894) is devoted to traditions of this kind.[14] Ibn Bābawayh's *ʿIlal al-sharāʾiʿ* is composed entirely of such *ḥadīth*s. Ibn Bābawayh is also the author of the *Maʿānī al-akhbār*, in which the meanings of difficult *ḥadīth*s and of obscure expressions and words are elucidated.

As in Sunni traditions, Shiʿi *ḥadīth*s consist of a chain of transmission (*isnād*) followed by the content (*matn*). Whereas a typical Sunni *isnād* will have a Companion (*ṣaḥābī*) transmitting from the Prophet, a Shiʿi chain of transmission normally goes back to an Imam, or to an Imam who transmits from his forefathers (*ʿan ābāʾihi*), or to an Imam who transmits from the Prophet, either directly or via the Imam's forefathers.[15] For Shiʿis, the reasons for excluding the Companions from the chains of transmission are twofold: first, most Companions either acquiesced in, or actively supported the usurpation of power from ʿAlī; second, the Companions lack probity (*ʿadāla*) and cannot therefore be considered reliable transmitters.[16]

In some Shiʿi compilations of *Ḥadīth* the chain of transmission is wholly or partially dropped. Thus Ibn Bābawayh states at the beginning of his *Man lā yaḥḍuruhuʾl-faqīh* that he wrote this book with truncated *isnād*s (*bi-ḥadhf al-asānīd*) so that its routes of transmission (*ṭuruquhu*) might not multiply.[17] Abū Jaʿfar al-Ṭūsī notes in his *Istibṣār* that in the first two volumes of the book he cited the complete *isnād*s of each tradition, but in the third volume he abbreviated them (*ikhtaṣartu*) by omitting the names

p. 241; Modarressi, *Crisis*, pp. 99–105; Roy Vilozny, 'Pre-Būyid Hadith Literature' (in this volume).

[14] Roy Vilozny, 'Réflexions sur le *Kitāb al-ʿilal* d'Aḥmad b. Muḥammad al-Barqī (m. 274/888 ou 280/894)', in Mohammad Ali Amir-Moezzi, Meir M. Bar-Asher and Simon Hopkins, ed., *Le Shīʿisme Imāmite quarante ans après. Hommage à Etan Kohlberg* (Turnhout, 2009), pp. 417–435.

[15] Kohlberg, 'An Unusual Shīʿī *isnād*', *Israel Oriental Studies*, 5 (1975), p. 142, reproduced in his *Belief and Law in Imāmī Shīʿism*, article VIII.

[16] Kohlberg, 'Some Imāmī Shīʿī Views on the *Ṣaḥāba*', *JSAI*, 5 (1984), pp. 143–175, reproduced in his *Belief and Law in Imāmī Shīʿism*, article IX; Brown, *Hadith*, pp. 124–126.

[17] Ibn Bābawayh, *Man lā yaḥḍuruhuʾl-faqīh* (Tehran, 1390/1970), vol. 1, p. 3, tr. Gleave, 'Between *Ḥadīth* and *Fiqh*', p. 374; see also Brown, *Hadith*, p. 130 (Ibn Bābawayh refrains from providing complete *isnād*s for each *ḥadīth* since 'he does not want the reader to concern himself with such specialised details'). See Modarressi, *An Introduction to Shīʿī Law*, p. 33.

of his immediate authorities. Instead, he gave the complete chains of transmission at the end of the work.[18] The practice of abbreviating the *isnād*s was followed by the anonymous redactor of the *Tafsīr* of Muḥammad b. Masʿūd al-ʿAyyāshī (d. early 4th/10th century),[19] while al-Ḥasan b. ʿAlī Ibn Shuʿba explains in the introduction to his *Tuḥaf al-ʿuqūl* that he omitted the *isnād*s for the sake of brevity (*wa-asqaṭtu l-asānīd takhfīfan wa-ījāzan*).[20]

Reconstruction of Early Sources

While many early works of Shiʿi *Ḥadīth* are lost, some can be (wholly or partially) reconstructed by tracing quotations found in later sources. Recent decades have seen considerable scholarly efforts in this direction, resulting in a series of publications of early works based entirely on such quotations. The following two examples, taken from the field of Qur'anic exegesis, are of relevance since early works of *tafsīr* are comprised wholly of *ḥadīths*.[21] There are, first, quotations from the Qur'an commentary of the Kūfan Abū Ḥamza al-Thumālī (d. between 148/765 and 150/767), which have been collected by ʿAbd al-Razzāq Muḥammad Ḥusayn Ḥirz al-Dīn.[22] The second example concerns Muḥammad b. al-ʿAbbās Ibn al-Juḥām (d. after 328/939–940), who is the author of a large commentary on the Qur'an entitled *Ta'wīl mā nazala min al-qur'ān al-karīm fī'l-nabī wa-ālihi*, and now lost. The second of its two volumes, consisting of exegetical traditions on *Sūrat al-isrā'* to the end of the Qur'an, was still available to the 10th/16th-century scholar Sharaf al-Dīn ʿAlī al-Ḥusaynī al-Astarābādī al-Najafī, who cites extensively from it in his *Ta'wīl al-āyāt al-ẓāhira fī faḍā'il al-ʿitra al-ṭāhira*.[23] These fragments have been published as an independent volume.[24]

---

[18] Abū Jaʿfar al-Ṭūsī, *al-Istibṣār*, ed. Ḥasan al-Mūsawī al-Kharsān (Tehran, 1390/1970), vol. 4, pp. 304–305. The method of citing abbreviated chains of transmission and providing complete *isnāds* at the end of the work is also followed by al-Ṭūsī in his *Tahdhīb al-aḥkām*.

[19] Al-ʿAyyāshī, *Tafsīr*, ed. Hāshim al-Rasūlī al-Maḥallātī (Qumm, 1380/1960–61), vol. 1, p. 2 (*ḥadhaftu minhu'l-isnād*). On this work see Meir M. Bar-Asher, *Scripture and Exegesis in Early Imāmī Shiism* (Leiden, 1999), pp. 60–63.

[20] Ibn Shuʿba, *Tuḥaf al-ʿuqūl ʿan āl al-rasūl* (Beirut, 1394/1974), p. 11. For the dating of this work see Ansari, *L'Imamat*, p. 250, note 1349.

[21] See Bar-Asher, *Scripture and Exegesis*, pp. 73–79; Amir-Moezzi, *Le Coran silencieux*, p. 103.

[22] The volume is entitled *Tafsīr al-Qur'ān al-karīm li-Abī Ḥamza Thābit b. Dīnār al-Thumālī* (Qumm, 1420/1999–2000) (referred to in Modarressi, *Tradition and Survival*, p. 377).

[23] Etan Kohlberg, *A Medieval Muslim Scholar at Work: Ibn Ṭāwūs and His Library* (Leiden, 1992), pp. 369–371, no. 623; Etan Kohlberg and Mohammad Ali Amir-Moezzi, *Revelation and Falsification: The* Kitāb al-qirā'āt *of Aḥmad b. Muḥammad al-Sayyārī* (Leiden, 2009), p. 35.

[24] Ibn al-Juḥām, *Ta'wīl mā nazala min al-Qur'ān al-karīm fī'l-nabī wa-ālihi*, ed. Fāris Tabrīziyān al-Ḥassūn (Qumm, 1420/1999–2000).

Numerous references to quotations of early works in later Shiʿi texts have been collected by Hossein Modarressi in his *Tradition and Survival* and by Hassan Ansari in his doctoral dissertation.[25] In these quotations, the titles of the early works are often omitted; yet the underlying assumption is that it is possible to identify these works by taking *isnād*s that end with a specific author and correlating them with references to written works in the classical bibliographical literature.[26] The importance of such reconstructions is underlined by Ansari, who takes it as a methodological axiom that a study of the doctrinal history of Imāmī Shiʿism which does not take account of 'sources of the sources' may result in misunderstandings and errors of perspective, since doctrinal history is inseparable from the history of texts.[27]

Approaches to the Study of Shiʿi *Ḥadīth*

The rich and variegated nature of Shiʿi *Ḥadīth* is mirrored in the different approaches to this material in the scholarly literature. The esoteric aspects of early Shiʿism as preserved in *Ḥadīth* have been investigated by Mohammad Ali Amir-Moezzi in many of his studies, notably in *The Divine Guide*.[28] He has drawn attention to the central position of a superhuman, omniscient Imam, and has underscored the esoteric and mystical nature of Shiʿi spirituality as an essential phenomenon for understanding Shiʿi Islam. The esoteric elements in Shiʿi *Ḥadīth* have also been noted by Hassan Ansari, Ehud Krinis[29] and Maria Dakake (in Chapter 8 of this volume) and Maria Dakake (in the chapter published in this volume). Other scholars have reiterated the role of the Imam as the bearer of knowledge superior to and more authoritative than the knowledge of other Muslims, while maintaining that esotericism was not an integral part of early Shiʿism and was introduced into Shiʿi *Ḥadīth* by extremist (*ghulāt*) elements.[30] Thus Hossein Modarressi notes that the scholars and *Ḥadīth* transmitters in Qumm, which by the 3rd/9th century had become the main Imāmī centre of

[25] The substantial Appendix ('L'annexe') of this dissertation (Ansari, *L'Imamat*, pp. 285–529) comprises in addition fragments of early works of *Ḥadīth* reconstructed from later sources ('Anciens ouvrages de hadiths perdus et reconstitués à partir de leurs fragments rapportés dans des sources postérieurs').

[26] Modarressi, *Tradition and Survival*, p. xv, referred to in Najam Haider, *The Origins of the Shīʿa: Identity, Ritual, and Sacred Space in Eighth-Century Kūfa* (Cambridge, 2011), p. 32. See Ansari, *L'Imamat*, p. 220.

[27] Ansari, *L'Imamat*, pp. 256–257.

[28] M. A. Amir-Moezzi, *The Divine Guide in Early Shiʿism: The Sources of Esotericism in Islam*, tr. David Streight (Albany, NY, 1994).

[29] In his forthcoming *God's Chosen People: Judah Halevi's 'Kuzari' and the Shīʿī Imām Doctrine* (Turnhout, 2013). This book is of interest *inter alia* since it demonstrates the relevance of early Shiʿi *Ḥadīth* for other disciplines.

[30] Modarressi, *Crisis*, pp. 19–51. See Tamima Bayhom-Daou, *Shaykh Mufid* (Oxford, 2005), p. 32.

learning, tried to contain extremist views by banishing proponents of these views from this city.[31]

A historical approach to early *Ḥadīth* is adopted by Andrew Newman in his *Formative Period.* He undertakes a comparative analysis of al-Barqī's *Kitāb al-maḥāsin*, al-Ṣaffār's *Baṣā'ir al-darajāt* (both composed in Qumm) and the *Kāfī* of al-Kulaynī (composed in Baghdad), examines the specific historical and social background of each of these works, analyses the methods of selection and organisation of the traditions (paying attention to both their *isnād* and *matn*), and points to the aims of the authors in compiling these works.

The development of Shi'i identity is examined by Najam Haider in his *Origins of the Shī'a.* He utilises the Kūfan tradition to evaluate the veracity of early sectarian narratives, and compares 'the structural characteristics of Kūfan texts drawn from the Sunnī, Imāmī and Zaydī collections to determine the point at which sectarian groups appear to have developed a sense of being "different"'.[32] According to Haider, quoting unique authorities through distinct *isnād*s in particular narrative forms indicates the presence of an independent sectarian identity, while shared authorities, transmitters and styles 'suggest a degree of overlap between groups'.[33] For his analysis, Haider chose traditions dealing with ritual practice, focusing on three case studies: *basmala* – its relation to the Qur'anic text, and the question of whether it should be uttered audibly or silently; *qunūt* (a curse or invocation) – whether it should be recited in the mandatory or supererogatory (*witr*) ritual prayers; and alcoholic beverages – the arguments cited in defence of a general prohibition on their consumption or the conditions under which this prohibition may be narrowed. His findings support the view – prevalent in Western scholarship – that an Imāmī sectarian identity originated in the early 2nd/8th century. In contrast, his conclusions on the origins of Zaydism suggest that the narrative drawn from the heresiographical literature (and largely adopted by Western scholars) – namely, that Zaydism was a product of the merging of two strains of Kūfan Shi'ism (Batriyya and Jārūdiyya) – does not stand up to scrutiny. Haider argues that an overwhelming majority of Zaydīs were initially Batrīs, and that it was only in the aftermath of the Battle of Fakhkh (169/786) that Zaydism was reoriented in a Jārūdī direction.[34]

The position of the authors (more precisely: the compilers) of the early *Ḥadīth* collections has been discussed in several studies. Andrew Newman has noted that although these authors do not express themselves in the first person, they nonetheless play a significant role in shaping the material through the choice and arrangement of

---

31 Modarressi, *Crisis*, pp. 34–35.

32 Haider, *Origins*, p. 250.

33 Ibid.

34 Haider, *Origins*, pp. 189–192, 213–214, 251–252. For a discussion of the Batriyya and the Jārūdiyya see W. Madelung, *Der Imam al-Qāsim ibn Ibrāhīm und die Glaubenslehre der Zaiditen* (Berlin, 1965), pp. 44–52; van Ess, *Theologie und Gesellschaft*, vol. 1, pp. 239–268. On the Battle of Fakhkh, see L. Veccia Vaglieri, 'Fakhkh', *EI2*, vol. 2, pp. 744–745.

the *ḥadīths* and the titles given to the various chapters.[35] This point also comes across in Roy Vilozny's analysis of al-Barqī's *Kitāb al-maḥāsin* (in the chapter published in this volume). Other scholars have noted the gradual change in the authors' role (roughly from the late 3rd/9th century), when authors begin to express their personal opinion, either in the introductory passages[36] or in comments within the text.[37]

From *ḥadīth* to *fiqh*

Some of the oldest Shiʿi works comprise traditions of a legal nature. Most of these works have not survived and are only known by their titles, for example *Kitāb al-ḥalāl wa'l-ḥarām*. Legal traditions are also much in evidence in the *uṣūl* works. In the 4th/10th and 5th/11th centuries, such traditions were incorporated into large-scale works, of which the most famous came to be known as the 'Four Books' (*al-kutub al-arbaʿa*).[38] These are al-Kulaynī's *al-Furūʿ min al-kāfī* (which is a continuation of his *al-Uṣūl min al-kāfī*), as well as the above-mentioned *Man lā yaḥḍuruhu'l-faqīh* by Ibn Bābawayh, *Tahdhīb al-aḥkām* by Abū Jaʿfar al-Ṭūsī and *al-Istibṣār*, also by al-Ṭūsī. Each of these works has its distinctive characteristics;[39] yet in their overall structure, they resemble the Sunni *muṣannaf* works in that all traditions relating to a particular subject are grouped under one heading. Authors of later generations collected the traditions found in the 'Four Books' and commented on them. Of these collections, the best-known are the *Wāfī* by Muḥsin al-Fayḍ al-Kāshānī (d. 1091/1680), the *(Tafṣīl) wasā'il al-shīʿa ilā taḥṣīl masā'il al-sharīʿa* by Muḥammad b. al-Ḥasan al-Ḥurr al-ʿĀmilī (d. 1104/1693)[40] and the *Mustadrak al-wasā'il* by Mīrzā Ḥusayn b. Muḥammad Taqī al-Nūrī al-Ṭabarsī/Ṭabrisī (d. 1320/1902).[41]

---

35 Newman, *Formative Period,* pp. 50–51, 54 and passim. See also Bar-Asher, *Scripture and Exegesis*, p. 62 (noting that al-ʿAyyāshī's opinions in his *Tafsīr* may be discerned from the choice and selection of material cited and omitted).

36 As, for example, al-Kulaynī in the introduction to his *al-Kāfī* or ʿAlī b. Ibrāhīm al-Qummī and al-ʿAyyāshī in the introduction to their respective *Tafsīr*s (see Bar-Asher, *Scripture and Exegesis*, pp. 35–36, 61–62).

37 As, for example, al-Nuʿmānī in his *Kitāb al-ghayba* (see E. Krinis, '*Galut* and *Ghayba*: The Exile of Israel and the Occultation of the Shīʿī Imam-Messiah – A Comparative Study of Judah Halevi and Early Imāmī-Shīʿī Writers', forthcoming) or Ibn Bābawayh in many of his works.

38 These are 'the nearest Shīʿī scholars have come to delimiting a "canon" of the *akhbār*' (Gleave, *Inevitable Doubt*, p. 34, note 15). Their canonicity derives from the fact that subsequent Imāmī thought 'gave reports from these collections a stronger "probative force" (*ḥujjiyya*) than those found in other collections' (Gleave, 'Between *Ḥadīth* and *Fiqh*', p. 350); Haider, *Origins*, p. 36.

39 See the discussion in Gleave, 'Between *Ḥadīth* and *Fiqh*', pp. 352–353, 355–356, 357.

40 On the significance of the *Wasā'il* see Haider, *Origins*, p. 37. See also Kohlberg, '*Al-uṣūl al-arbaʿumi'a*', p. 138.

41 On whom see Rainer Brunner, *Die Schia und die Koranfälschung* (Würzburg, 2001), pp. 39–69.

Other material, including both legal and extra-legal *Ḥadīth*, is preserved in the *Biḥār al-anwār* by Muḥammad Bāqir al-Majlisī (d. 1110/1699).[42]

Legal *Ḥadīth* in Shiʿism is of particular significance, since it predates the juristic literature (in contrast to the situation in Sunni Islam) and constitutes the single most important source of information on early Shiʿi legal practice. It was thus essential for Shiʿi jurists to determine the reliability of legal traditions. One way of achieving this was to check the piety, honesty and reliability of the transmitters.[43] Another was to examine whether a given tradition has multiple chains of transmission and is thus well-attested (*khabar mutawātir*) and not the result of collusion among the transmitters, or whether it has only one or a few chains of transmission and is thus a 'single' or 'isolated tradition' (*khabar al-wāḥid*, pl. *akhbār al-āḥād*). As Robert Gleave explains, a *khabar mutawātir* is said to bring 'certain' knowledge, while a *khabar al-wāḥid* brings only 'opinion' (*ẓann*) as to the law's content. Since the majority of traditions transmitted from the Imams belonged to the category of *khabar al-wāḥid*, much exegetical effort was expended to demonstrate that there was divine sanction for the use of *khabar al-wāḥid* in legal argumentation.[44] Among the leading scholars of the Buwayhid period, those who endorsed the use of *khabar al-wāḥid* as a valid basis for the law included Ibn Bābawayh[45] and (under certain conditions) Abū Jaʿfar al-Ṭūsī,[46] while al-Sharīf al-Murtaḍā regarded it as inadmissible, in line with his negative attitude to *Ḥadīth* as a whole and his adoption of the Muʿtazili thesis that the fundamental truths of religion must be established by reason alone.[47] Al-Murtaḍā's teacher, al-Shaykh al-Mufīd, accepted isolated traditions only if they could be supported by another proof such as a rational argument or a Qur'anic text.[48]

Following the onset of the 'Greater Occultation' (in 329/941) and the problems arising from the absence of the Imam, jurisprudence began to emerge as an independent Imāmī discipline, as it was felt that *Ḥadīth* was no longer a sufficient expression

---

42 E. Kohlberg, 'Beḥār al-anwār', *EIR*, vol. 4, pp. 90–93.

43 See B. Scarcia Amoretti, ''Ilm al-ridjāl', *EI2*, vol. 3, pp. 1150–1152. For further criteria, see Amir-Moezzi, 'Remarques sur les critères d'authenticité', pp. 8–12.

44 Robert Gleave, 'Modern Šīʿī Discussions of *Ḫabar al-wāḥid*: Ṣadr, Ḫumaynī and Ḫū'ī', *OM*, NS, 21 (2002), pp. 181–182. For the use of these terms in the Sunni methodology of *Ḥadīth* see G. H. A. Juynboll, 'Khabar al-wāḥid', *EI2*, vol. 4, p. 896; A. J. Wensinck [W. F. Heinrichs], 'Mutawātir', *EI2*, vol. 7, pp. 781–782; Wael B. Hallaq, *Sharīʿa: Theory, Practice, Transformations* (Cambridge, 2009), pp. 92–97; Brown, *Hadith*, pp. 104, 173, 178–180.

45 Ansari, *L'Imamat*, p. 85.

46 Modarressi, *An Introduction to Shīʿī Law*, p. 44; Norman Calder, 'Doubt and Prerogative: The Emergence of an Imāmī Shīʿī Theory of *Ijtihād*', *SI*, 70 (1989), pp. 62–64; Mohammad Ali Amir-Moezzi, 'al-Ṭūsī', *EI2*, vol. 10, pp. 745–746.

47 W. Madelung, 'Imāmism and Muʿtazilite Theology', in Fahd, ed. *Le Shīʿisme Imāmite*, pp. 25–26; idem, ''Alam-al-Hodā', *EIR*, vol. 1, p. 793; Calder, 'Doubt and Prerogative', pp. 59, 61.

48 Martin J. McDermott, *The Theology of al-Shaikh al-Mufīd (d. 413/1022)* (Beirut, 1978), pp. 298–299; W. Madelung, 'al-Mufīd', *EI2*, vol. 7, pp. 312–313; Modarressi, *An Introduction to Shīʿī Law*, pp. 42–43; Bayhom-Daou, *Shaykh Mufid*, pp. 96–97.

of the law,[49] and its condensed style was not suitable for judicial discussions. As noted by Gleave and Bayhom-Daou, the transition from *Ḥadīth* to *fiqh* was a gradual process. Thus Ibn Bābawayh, while relying almost exclusively on *Ḥadīth*, included in his *Man lā yaḥḍuruhu'l-faqīh* and in other works not only traditions but also editorial comment and judicial *fatwās* by himself and his father.[50] Al-Mufīd went further by basing his main legal book, *al-Muqniʿa*, on his personal opinion, while supporting it by citing *Ḥadīth*.[51] In the later legal literature, *Ḥadīth* is used mainly as proof-text rather than being regarded as the law itself. [52]

The status of *Ḥadīth* as a source of law was one of the major points of contention between Akhbārīs and Uṣūlīs.[53] Muḥammad Amīn al-Astarābādī (d. 1033/1624 or 1036/1627), regarded by some as the founder of the Akhbārī school, argued that the traditions of the Imams are the single most important source of law. They provide the community with an infallible guide to all aspects of life; they are also indispensable for a correct understanding of the Qur'an and the Prophet's utterances. Every Imāmī tradition recorded in the 'Four Books' is sound (*ṣaḥīḥ*), in the sense that it derives with certainty from an Imam (i.e., it is *qaṭʿī al-wurūd* or *al-ṣudūr*). Such traditions are to be accepted, even when they are isolated (*khabar wāḥid*). It is not essential to ascertain in each case whether or not a given *ḥadīth* constitutes a genuine expression of the Imam's thought; once its soundness has been established, the believer is allowed to follow its ruling even if it is based on precautionary dissimulation (*taqiyya*).[54] Later scholars who adhered to the Akhbārī school modified some of al-Astarābādī's views. Muḥsin al-Fayḍ al-Kāshānī, for example, maintained that isolated traditions cannot be regarded as deriving with certainty from an Imam. Against al-Astarābādī, he insisted on the major significance of the Qur'an as an independent source of law, which is not to be viewed merely through the prism of *Ḥadīth*.[55]

---

49 Bayhom-Daou, *Shaykh Mufid*, pp. 14–15.

50 Gleave, 'Between *Ḥadīth* and *Fiqh*', pp. 352, 355, 360, 364; Bayhom-Daou, *Shaykh Mufid*, pp. 94, 116; Ansari, *L'Imamat*, p. 84, note 364.

51 A. Kazemi-Moussavi, 'Hadith in Shiʿism', *EIR*, vol. 11, p. 448.

52 See Gleave, 'Between *Ḥadīth* and *Fiqh*', p. 351.

53 The conflict between these two schools has been the subject of several studies. See Etan Kohlberg, 'Aḵbārīya', *EIR*, vol. 1, pp. 716–718; Etan Kohlberg, 'Aspects of Akhbari Thought in the Seventeenth and Eighteenth Centuries', in N. Levtzion and J. O. Voll, ed., *Eighteenth-Century Renewal and Reform in Islam* (New York, 1987), pp. 133–160, reproduced in his *Belief and Law in Imāmī Shīʿism*, article XVII; Devin J. Stewart, *Islamic Legal Orthodoxy: Twelver Shiite Responses to the Sunni Legal System* (Salt Lake City, 1998), index, s.vv. 'Akhbārīs', 'Uṣūlīs'; Andrew J. Newman, 'The Nature of the Akhbārī/Uṣūlī Dispute in Late Ṣafawid Iran, Part 1: ʿAbdallāh al-Samāhījī's "*Munyat al-Mumārisīn*"', *BSOAS*, 55 (1992), pp. 22–51; Andrew J. Newman, 'The Nature of the Akhbārī/Uṣūlī Dispute in Late Ṣafawid Iran, Part 2: The Conflict Reassessed', *BSOAS*, 55 (1992), pp. 250–261; Gleave, *Inevitable Doubt*, pp. 5–9, 247–253.

54 Kohlberg, 'Aspects of Akhbari Thought', pp. 134–135. On al-Astarābādī see also Newman, 'The Nature of the Akhbārī/Uṣūlī Dispute', pp. 250–253.

55 Kohlberg, 'Aspects of Akhbari Thought', p. 137. For more on Akhbārī and Uṣūlī views of the relationship between Qur'an and *Ḥadīth* as sources of law, see Newman, 'The Nature of the Akhbārī/Uṣūlī Dispute', p. 260; Gleave, *Inevitable Doubt*, pp. 47–55, 60–66, 249.

From a literary perspective, the main contribution of the Akhbārīs consisted in bringing about a renaissance of the corpus of Shiʿi *Ḥadīth* dating back to Buwayhid and pre-Buwayhid times.[56]

The Writing of Shiʿi *Ḥadīth*

The question of the oral versus written transmission of *Ḥadīth* has been a subject of considerable scholarly debate. Initially, the studies devoted to this topic dealt almost exclusively with Sunni material;[57] in recent years, these have expanded to include discussions of the writing down of Shiʿi *Ḥadīth*. On this, there appears to be a large measure of scholarly agreement to the effect that traditions were being accurately recorded and transmitted in the early 2nd/8th century.[58] Most recently, this view has been upheld by Najam Haider,[59] building on the methodology developed by Harald Motzki and others.[60] Looking at the issue from a different perspective, Maria Dakake (in Chapter 8, this volume, p. 181) shows how the Shiʿi attitude towards writing was 'profoundly connected to uniquely Shiʿi conceptions of religious authority and community, as well as to certain esoteric conceptions of knowledge'. She notes further that the fact of adhering to a written text was itself a subtle mode of Shiʿi resistance to the dominant culture of early Islam.

Polemics and Dialogue

Shiʿi *Ḥadīth* did not grow in a vacuum, and Shiʿis were well aware of developments in the Sunni camp. There are numerous examples of Shiʿis who studied with Sunni masters (and – admittedly fewer – cases of Sunnis studying with Shiʿi scholars).[61] The knowledge which each side acquired about the literature of the other helped to further the dialogue between them but was also used in a polemical context. Ibn Bābawayh, for example, cites a great number of Sunni *ḥadīth*s in order to buttress Shiʿi doctrines about the imamate,[62] while the Baghdadi scholar Aḥmad b. ʿUbaydallāh b. ʿAyyāsh al-Jawharī (d. 401/1011) in his *Muqtaḍab al-athar* similarly relies on Sunni *ḥadīth*s

---

56 Kohlberg, 'Aspects of Akhbari Thought', p. 147.

57 Motzki, 'Introduction', pp. xxix–xxxi.

58 See Kohlberg, '*Al-uṣūl al-arbaʿumiʾa*'; Modarressi, *Tradition and Survival*; Ansari, *L'Imamat*. Contrast Calder's view that the juristic literature in general went through a prolonged phase of oral transmission; *Early Muslim Jurisprudence* (Oxford, 1993), pp. 161–171.

59 Haider, *Origins*, p. 250.

60 Particularly in his *Origins of Islamic Jurisprudence: Meccan Fiqh Before the Classical Schools*, tr. Marion Katz (Leiden, 2002); referred to in Haider, *Origins*, p. 29. See also Motzki, 'Introduction', pp. xxvii–xxix and the studies referred to at p. xxviii, note 69.

61 Stewart, *Islamic Legal Orthodoxy*, pp. 63–95.

62 Ansari, *L'Imamat*, pp. 79, 84.

to prove the validity of the doctrine of Twelve Imams.[63] *Ḥadīth*s in which ʿAlī's rights are upheld appear frequently in polemical works, such as *al-Ikhtiṣāṣ* of al-Mufid.[64] The Iraqi Shiʿi scholar and bibliophile ʿAlī b. Mūsā ibn Ṭāwūs (d. 664/1266) bought a large number of Sunni texts for his library, was at home with Sunni literature and repeatedly cites from Sunni works, including most of the six canonical books of Sunni *Ḥadīth*. His *Yaqīn*, for example, consists of quotations taken mostly from Sunni sources which show that the Prophet called ʿAlī by various honorific titles, including especially *amīr al-muʾminīn* (Commander of the Faithful); as Ibn Ṭāwūs explains, a Sunni authority provides more impressive proof (*huwa ablagh fiʾl-ḥujja*) for the correctness of a Shiʿi view than does a Shiʿi one.[65]

Some of the ways in which *Ḥadīth* was used in the dialogue between Sunnis and Shiʿis are examined in Gurdofarid Miskinzoda's study published in this volume. The study shows how a particular account – the story of 'pen and paper' – was employed, edited and embellished by both sides (and within each camp) in a prolonged process of adaptation and transformation. Miskinzoda's aim is to analyse and interpret the changes and developments which this account underwent, and not necessarily to seek to establish the historical kernel or to pass judgement on the historical value of the sources. As has been shown by Uri Rubin,[66] this methodology can be particularly fruitful in studies relating to the biography of the Prophet. In Chapter 8 of this

---

63 *Wa-qad dhakartu fī kitābī hādha min muqtaḍab al-āthār mā addathu ilaynā ruwāt al-ḥadīth min mukhālifīnā min al-naṣṣ ʿalā aʾimmatinā ʿalayhim al-salām min al-riwāyāt al-ṣaḥīḥa … muwāfiqan li-riwāyātinā* (Ibn ʿAyyāsh, *Muqtaḍab al-athar fiʾl-naṣṣ alāʾl-aʾimma al-ithnay ʿashar* [Qumm, n.d.], p. 1). On Ibn ʿAyyāsh al-Jawharī see Fuat Sezgin, *Geschichte des Arabischen Schrifttums* (Leiden, 1967), vol. 1, p. 549; Ansari, *L'Imamat*, pp. 97–99.

64 On the *Ikhtiṣāṣ*, see McDermott, *The Theology of al-Shaikh al-Mufīd*, pp. 27, 34. Those who doubt al-Mufīd's authorship of this work include Abu'l-Qāsim al-Khuʾī (d. 1413/1992) (see his *Muʿjam rijāl al-ḥadīth* (n. p., 1992), vol. 8, p. 197), Hossein Modarressi, who refers to the author as 'pseudo-Mufīd' ('Early Debates on the Integrity of the Qurʾan: A Brief Survey', *SI*, 77 (1993), p. 18, note 75), and Hassan Ansari (*L'Imamat*, p. 109, note 521 and the studies cited there). Another text with polemical overtones, the *Kitāb Sulaym b. Qays*, has been shown to have been written at a later date than the lifetime of its purported author, Sulaym b. Qays (allegedly a Kūfan disciple of ʿAlī) and to include additions and interpolations. See Modarressi, *Crisis*, pp. 100–101; Modarressi, *Tradition and Survival*, pp. 82–86; Patricia Crone, '*Mawālī* and the Prophet's Family: An Early Shiʿi View', in Monique Bernards and John Nawas, ed., *Patronate and Patronage in Early and Classical Islam* (Leiden, 2005), pp. 167–194; Amir-Moezzi, 'Note bibliographique sur le *Kitāb Sulaym b. Qays*, le plus ancien ouvrage shiʿite existant', in Amir-Moezzi, Bar-Asher and Hopkins, ed., *Le Shīʿisme Imāmite quarante ans après*, pp. 33–48 (expanded version in Amir-Moezzi, *Le Coran silencieux*, pp. 27–61); Ansari, *L'Imamat*, pp. 138, 140; Dakake (in Chapter 8 of this volume). There is room for further work on the authenticity of early texts of Shiʿi *Ḥadīth*.

65 Ibn Ṭāwūs, *al-Yaqīn fī imrat amīr al-muʾminīn*, ed. Muḥammad Bāqir al-Anṣārī and Muḥammad Ṣādiq al-Anṣārī (Beirut, 1410/1989), pp. 125, 271, 279. On this work, see Kohlberg, *A Medieval Muslim Scholar*, pp. 63–64.

66 Particularly in his *The Eye of the Beholder: The Life of Muḥammad as Viewed by the Early Muslims* (Princeton, 1995).

volume, Maria Dakake similarly demonstrates how early Shiʿi literature grew in the context of a constant dialogue with its proto-Sunni counterpart.

Zaydī and Ismaili *Ḥadīth*

The study of Zaydī *Ḥadīth* and Zaydī intellectual history in general has lagged behind the study of Imāmī Shiʿism, mainly as a result of the geographical isolation of Yemen.[67] One of the first Zaydī texts to become known in the West was the *Majmūʿ al-fiqh*, published in 1919 as a work of Zayd b. ʿAlī (d. 122/740).[68] As has since been shown, the *Majmūʿ* reflects Kūfan legal tradition of the second half of the 2nd/8th century and is unlikely to be the work of Zayd himself. The same holds true for other texts ascribed to Zayd, including the *Musnad*.[69] The first Zaydī collection of *Ḥadīth* – the *Amālī* of Aḥmad b. ʿĪsā (d. 247/861–862) – was only compiled in the mid-3rd/9th century.[70] However, the traditions contained in it are at least in part drawn from previous Zaydī written works: thus the bulk of the legal traditions of Muḥammad al-Bāqir (d. 117/735) are quoted from the *Aṣl* of Abu'l-Jārūd Ziyād b. Mundhir, the eponymous founder of the Jārūdiyya.[71] Zaydī *isnāds* exhibit a greater variety than Imāmī chains of transmission: while the Imams recognised by the Zaydīyya are regarded as the most reliable and trustworthy authorities, all other descendants of ʿAlī and Fāṭima through either al-Ḥasan or al-Ḥusayn are also commonly accepted as authorities, as are occasionally some non-ʿAlids.[72] Various issues relating to Zaydī

---

67 Some aspects of Zaydī *Ḥadīth* literature are surveyed in ʿAbdallāh al-ʿIzzī, *ʿUlūm al-ḥadīth ʿinda'l-Zaydīyya wa'l-muḥaddithīn* (Amman, 1421/2001). For modern research on the Zaydiyya, see Sabine Schmidtke and Jan Thiele, *Preserving Yemen's Cultural Heritage: The Yemen Manuscript Digitization Project* (Sanaa, 2011), pp. 19–25. A special issue of *Arabica*, 59 (2012) is entirely devoted to Zaydīsm.

68 *Corpus Juris di Zaid b. ʿAli*, ed. Eugenio Griffini (Milan, 1919). For the debate following the publication of this work see Sezgin, *Geschichte des Arabischen Schrifttums*, vol. 1, pp. 552–556 and the references in Motzki, 'Introduction', p. xxxii. Cf. Michael Cook, *Commanding Right and Forbidding Wrong in Islamic Thought* (Cambridge, 2000), p. 228.

69 W. Madelung, 'Zayd b. ʿAlī b. al-Ḥusayn', *EI2*, vol. 11, pp. 473–474.

70 Sezgin, *Geschichte des arabischen Schrifttums*, vol. 1, pp. 560–561. On Aḥmad b. ʿĪsā see Madelung, *al-Qāsim*, pp. 80–83 and index. His *Amālī* was transmitted by Muḥammad b. Manṣūr al-Murādī (d. 290/903), who was the most significant collector of Zaydī legal traditions in the 3rd/9th century (Madelung, *al-Qāsim*, pp. 82–84; Halm, *Shiʿism*, p. 202). The text of the *Amālī* in its entirety is available in a modern commentary entitled *Kitāb ra'b al-ṣadʿ* by ʿAlī b. Ismāʿīl b. ʿAbdallāh al-Mu'ayyad al-Ṣanʿānī (d. 1970) (Beirut, 1410/1990). See Haider, *Origins*, pp. 37–38.

71 W. Madelung, 'Abu'l-Jārūd', *EIR*, vol. 1, p. 327; Kohlberg, '*Al-uṣūl al-arbaʿumiʾa*', p. 147. Cf. Haider, *Origins*, pp. 33–34.

72 Madelung, *al-Qāsim*, p. 83; Etan Kohlberg, 'Some Zaydī Views on the Companions of the Prophet', *BSOAS*, 39 (1976), p. 98; Haider, *Origins*, pp. 42–43. On Zaydī *Ḥadīth*, see further Brown, *Hadith*, pp. 143–147. For the process of 'Sunnification' among the later Zaydīs (and the attendant change of attitude to the *ṣaḥāba*) see Cook, *Commanding Right*, pp. 247–251; Bernard

Ḥadīth remain to be explored. This task is likely to be facilitated by the increasing availability of Zaydī texts.

Unlike Imāmism and Zaydism, *Ḥadīth* never held centre place in Ismaili Shiʿism. As suggested by Poonawala, the reason may well have to do with the great emphasis which Ismailis placed on the internal/esoteric *(bāṭinī)* sciences.[73] It is, however, noteworthy that according to the Ismaili author Aḥmad b. Ibrāhīm al-Naysābūrī (5th/11th century), the *dāʿī* (summoner, religious agent) must be acquainted with the science of *Ḥadīth* – considered as one of the five divisions into which external knowledge (*ʿilm al-ẓāhir*) falls – so that he may draw on it 'to determine the accuracy of what he says to novices, in order to have them accept it from him'.[74] Al-Naysābūrī's frequent references to traditions of the Prophet, ʿAlī and Jaʿfar al-Ṣādiq bear witness to his deep knowledge of *Ḥadīth*.[75]

The only major author of Ismaʿili *Ḥadīth* is the renowned scholar and jurist al-Qāḍī al-Nuʿmān (d. 363/974). When he was commissioned by the fourth Fatimid caliph al-Muʿizz (r. 341–365/952–975) to collect legal traditions which would form the basis of Ismaili law, that law had not yet developed. Al-Nuʿmān thus used Imāmī and Zaydī sources, notably for his voluminous *Kitāb al-īḍāḥ*, of which only a small fragment has survived.[76] In this work, the *isnād* is fully quoted for each tradition. However, in all his other legal works the chains of transmission are abbreviated. This, for example, is the case in his legal compendium *Daʿāʾim al-islām*, which became the official code of the Fatimid state.[77] Al-Nuʿmān also followed this practice in some of his non-legal works, including the *Sharḥ al-akhbār* (in which he collected and commented on traditions on the merits of ʿAlī and other members of the *ahl al-bayt*)[78] and *al-Manāqib wa'l-mathālib*, a work on the virtues of the Prophet and the Banū Hāshim and the impiety

Haykel, *Revival and Reform in Islam: The Legacy of Muhammad al-Shawkānī* (Cambridge, 2003) (referred to in Haider, *Origins*, p. 43, note 81).

73 Ismail K. Poonawala, 'Hadith in Ismaʿilism', *EIR*, vol. 11, p. 450.

74 Aḥmad b. Ibrāhīm al-Naysābūrī, *al-Risāla al-mūjaza al-kāfiya fī ādāb al-duʿāt*, ed. and tr. Verena Klemm and Paul E. Walker as *A Code of Conduct: A Treatise on the Etiquette of the Fatimid Ismaili Mission* (London, 2011), pp. 14–15 (Arabic), p. 42 (English).

75 *A Code of Conduct*, pp. 7–8. See also Aḥmad b. Ibrāhīm al-Naysābūrī, *Kitāb ithbāt al-imāma*, ed. and tr. Arzina R. Lalani as *Degrees of Excellence: A Fatimid Treatise on Leadership in Islam* (London, 2010), p. 6 (English) and the studies cited in note 16.

76 W. Madelung, 'The Sources of Ismāʿīlī Law', *JNES*, 35 (1976), pp. 29–40; Poonawala, 'Al-Qāḍī al-Nuʿmān and Ismaʿili Jurisprudence', in Farhad Daftary, ed., *Mediaeval Ismaʿili History and Thought* (Cambridge, 1996), pp. 121–122.

77 On the *Daʿāʾim*, see Ismail K. Poonawala, *Biobibliography of Ismāʿīlī Literature* (Malibu, CA, 1977), pp. 56–57; Poonawala, 'Al-Qāḍī al-Nuʿmān and Ismaʿili Jurisprudence', pp. 126–129; Farhad Daftary, *Ismaili Literature: A Bibliography of Sources and Studies* (London, 2004), pp. 142–143; Farhad Daftary, *The Ismāʿīlīs: Their History and Doctrines* (2nd ed., Cambridge, 2007), p. 169.

78 In the introduction to this work al-Nuʿmān states that he abbreviated the chains of transmission (*ḥadhaftu asānīdahā*). See his *Sharḥ al-akhbār fī faḍāʾil al-aʾimma al-aṭhār*, ed. Muḥammad al-Ḥusaynī al-Jalālī (Beirut, 1414/1994), vol. 1, p. 88. On this work see Poonawala, *Biobibliography*, pp. 60–61; Daftary, *Ismaili Literature*, p. 145.

of the Umayyads.[79] In the introduction to the *Manāqib* al-Nuʿmān explains that he abbreviated the *isnād*s in the interest of brevity.[80] This explanation is similar to the one used by Imāmī Shiʿi scholars in justifying the abbreviation of *isnād*s (see above). Yet in the case of al-Nuʿmān there may have been an additional reason: since in his view the Imam is always present and his authority is all-embracing, when a *ḥadīth* is related from him there is no need for further validation in the form of a chain of transmission.[81] In conformity with Ismaili doctrine, al-Nuʿmān ignores traditions of the Twelver Shiʿi Imams after Jaʿfar al-Ṣādiq.[82] At the same time, he preserves a great many traditions which, judging by their content, may have been included in Imāmī compilations that are no longer available to us. A detailed study of al-Nuʿmān's works of *Ḥadīth* may thus shed further light on Shiʿi tradition as a whole.

79 As is attested by its full title: *Kitāb al-manāqib li-ahl bayt rasūl allāh al-nujabāʾ waʾl-mathālib li-banī Umayya al-luʿanāʾ*. On this work see Poonawala, *Biobibliography*, p. 60; Daftary, *Ismaili Literature*, pp. 144–145.

80 *Wa-natrukuʾl-asānīd waʾl-ikthār li-īthār al-takhfīf fī dhālika waʾl-ikhtiṣār* (al-Qāḍī al-Nuʿmān, *al-Manāqib waʾl-mathālib*, ed. Mājid b. Aḥmad al-ʿAṭiyya (Beirut, 1423/2002), p. 23).

81 Daftary, *The Ismāʿīlīs*, p. 170.

82 Ibid.

8

Writing and Resistance: The Transmission of Religious Knowledge in Early Shiʿism

Maria Massi Dakake

One of the subtler issues that distinguished Shiʿis from most non-Shiʿis in early Islam was their view on the written transmission of religious knowledge. The dominant intellectual culture in early Islam valued the oral transmission of religious teachings. While Gregor Schoeler and others have shown that there is strong evidence of fairly widespread use of private written notes among early scholars, oral transmission remained the ideal, and reliance on written notes was disparaged and rarely admitted. Yet a number of scholars have shown that this attitude towards written transmission was far less prevalent among those outside the dominant Islamic intellectual tradition, and carried little resonance with Shiʿis and Khārijīs among others. In fact, far from exhibiting any ambivalence about transmitting religious knowledge in writing, the Imāmī *ḥadīth* tradition seemed to encourage the practice. Yet the existing scholarship on writing in the early Islamic tradition does not sufficiently address the significance of Shiʿi divergence on this point, and most scholars researching oral and written transmission in early Islam mention Shiʿi differences on this issue merely as an aside. The early, written heritage of Shiʿism has been well documented by Shiʿi and Western scholars alike, but in this chapter I hope to bring out the deeper significance of the early Shiʿi use of writing and written texts. I argue that the Imāmī Shiʿi attitude towards writing is not a minor technical detail, but is, rather, profoundly connected to uniquely Shiʿi conceptions of religious authority and community, as well as to certain esoteric conceptions of knowledge. It was, on one level, driven by the imperatives of secrecy and survival among pre-*ghayba* Shiʿis, but on another, it constituted a subtle mode of Shiʿi resistance to the dominant intellectual culture of early Islam that both facilitated and demonstrated Shiʿism's divergence from the mainstream Muslim religious perspective.

Oral and Written Transmission of Knowledge in Early Islam

While studies have long confirmed that the Middle East of the early Islamic period was hardly as illiterate as is sometimes thought – there is substantial evidence of written contracts, letters and political documents,[1] for example – it nonetheless seems to be true that the transmission of specifically religious knowledge, or historical knowledge related to the religio-political situation of the early Islamic community, is widely thought to have been of a predominantly oral nature, with written compilations of religious or historical material emerging in substantial number only some time in the 3rd/9th century.

Nabia Abbott issued an important initial challenge to the notion that the transmission of such knowledge was either as primitive or as exclusively oral as may have been thought through her early, voluminous and detailed work on the early Arabic papyri. She further argued, on the basis of an admittedly credulous reading of early sources, that historical writing, as such, was fairly well developed by the end of the first Islamic century.[2] She further argued that the apparent antipathy towards the written transmission of religious knowledge was derived, not from an instinctive distrust of the written word or excessive pride in memory and oral recitation on the part of the Arabs, as is sometimes conjectured, but rather from a direct prohibition on the written preservation of this kind of knowledge established by the second caliph, ʿUmar b. al-Khaṭṭāb. According to a report found in an important early Islamic source, ʿUmar collected and burned all written Prophetic traditions and records of this sort during his caliphate, fearing that they would confuse Muslims and detract from the absolute authority and sacred character of the Qurʾan.[3] Juynboll later sought to temper Abbott's enthusiastic argument for the early prevalence of written history and tradition, taking her to task for an excessive and largely uncritical reliance on *isnād* evidence, and for what Juynboll argued was an over-emphasis on ʿUmar's role in inhibiting the written transmission of religious knowledge, citing her heavy reliance on the Islamic sources' own explanation of this role.[4] Yet, in a more recent study, Michael Cook similarly cited the tradition regarding ʿUmar's role in the discouragement or outright prohibition of the writing of religious knowledge, in conjunction with ʿUmar's reportedly unflattering comparison of the development of such a body of written, non-scriptural religious material to the written Mishna in Judaism.[5]

---

1 See, for instance, R. B. Serjeant, 'Early Arabic Prose Literature', in *Cambridge History of Arabic Literature: Arabic Literature to the End of the Umayyad Period* (Cambridge, 1983), pp. 114–153.

2 N. Abbott, *Studies in Arabic Literary Papyri* (Chicago, 1957), vol. 2, p. 39.

3 Ibn Saʿd, *al-Ṭabaqāt al-kubrā* (*Biographien Muhammeds*, 9 vols. (Leiden, 1905–1940), vol. 5, p. 140.

4 G. H. A. Juynboll, *Muslim Tradition* (Cambridge, 1983), p. 5.

5 See M. Cook, 'The Opponents of the Writing of Tradition in Early Islam', *Arabica*, 44 (1997), pp. 437–523, especially pp. 502–503, 509.

Whether or not the imposition of a strictly oral transmission of religious and historical tradition can be correctly or justly laid at the feet of the second caliph, the attribution of a prohibition on written transmission to such a figure as ʿUmar b. al-Khaṭṭāb (d. 23/644) is hardly insignificant for the association between the oral transmission of religious knowledge and religious 'orthodoxy'. In her study, Abbott observed that it was those who represented 'pious scholarship' who 'struggled to hold onto the idea of the absolute primacy of oral transmission';[6] that the restriction on written *ḥadīth* collections 'did have the effect of discouraging the writing-down of *ḥadīth* among the more orthodox and pious, but it had little effect on the heterodox Kharijites and the less submissive of ʿUmar's own generation and later generations among the faithful';[7] and that during the time of ʿUmar b. ʿAbd al-ʿAzīz (ʿUmar II), it was the 'pious scholars' who began, reluctantly, to write down their materials and traditions in order to 'forestall encroaching heresy',[8] perhaps in order to compete with less 'orthodox' groups who had no qualms about committing their material to writing. Abbott's statements seem to beg the question of just who constituted this unspecified group of 'pious scholars'; but her statements nonetheless suggest that some kind of general or at least symbolic connection between writing and heterodoxy or writing and resistance to the established Islamic intellectual tradition was fairly widespread in the earliest period of Islamic sectarian history.

Abbott mentions only the Khārijīs specifically as a group who rejected, or at least seemed to ignore, the second caliph's alleged prohibition on the writing of religious knowledge. But if the Khārijīs, who accepted the caliphate and personal piety of ʿUmar, would take his prohibition so lightly, then what could such a prohibition have meant to Shiʿis, who conceived of ʿUmar as the primary perpetrator of the historic injustice to the family of the Prophet? Indeed, Michael Cook observes an almost complete absence of any trace of the oral versus written controversy in either Khārijī or Shiʿi sources.[9] But beyond a mere absence of any notable controversy about written tradition in Shiʿi sources, one might expect to find ʿUmar's alleged prohibition on the writing of Prophetic tradition roundly condemned in Shiʿi sources, and presented in Shiʿi polemic as nothing short of an attempt to hide from the judgement of history evidence of the injustice and illegitimacy of his and his predecessor, Abū Bakr's, caliphates, and of the religious innovations which Shiʿis accuse them of sanctioning under their rule.

---

6 Abbott, *Studies*, vol. 1, p. 24.

7 Ibid., vol. 1, p. 7.

8 Ibid., *Studies*, vol. 2, p. 52.

9 See Cook, 'The Opponents', p. 444, where he notes: 'I have encountered almost nothing of relevance in non-Sunni sources. The oralism of the old Kūfan traditionists appears to have left no trace among the Imāmīs or the Zaydīs, just as that of the Basran traditionists seems scarcely to be reflected in Ibāḍī [Khārijī] literature.' See also p. 483, where he observes: 'It is in general the role of the ʿAlids to appear on the side of writing (a fact that is doubtless linked to the absence of evidence for the controversy [over writing] in Shiʿi sources).'

Yet Shiʿi tradition does not seem to have directly addressed ʿUmar's alleged ban on writing *ḥadīth*, at least not directly in relation to its own views on the written transmission of religious knowledge. The fact that they do not, against all expectation, would seem to call into question the authenticity, or at least the early circulation, of ʿUmar's reported ban on writing religious knowledge, for this seems to be something that would have hardly gone without early Shiʿi comment and criticism. There is little doubt, however, that to the extent that any kind of official taboo on the written transmission of religious or historical knowledge actually existed, Shiʿis largely ignored it. Such a conclusion can be derived not only from the lack of controversy over the issue in Shiʿi sources, but also from the fact that there is a significant representation of extant Shiʿi works among the earliest that we have in a variety of literary genres, including history,[10] *ḥadīth*,[11] heresiography[12] and poetry,[13] and their disproportionate survival likely has much to do with their having been recorded in writing somewhat earlier than many of their Sunni counterparts.

While the written text is easily susceptible to later tampering, in Shiʿi texts, such corruptions often meant either that new material was superadded to the core of the early text,[14] or else that controversial material was omitted.[15] In many cases, what is likely to have been the core text can still be discerned. Written texts could also be easily destroyed, of course, but to the extent that they physically survived, they may have been harder to ignore, and so to allow to be forgotten, or to substantially alter, than was the case for purely orally transmitted material.[16] For example, a significant number of Shiʿi works written in the 2nd–3rd/8th–9th centuries are still extant as independent texts, despite their being incorporated into later compilations. Perhaps

---

[10] For example, Naṣr b. Muzāḥim's *Waqʿat Ṣiffīn*, which dates to the second half of the 2nd century, Ibn Muzāḥim having died in 183, to say nothing of the partially extant historical compilations of early Shiʿi scholars, most notably, Abū Mikhnaf, whose work was substantially incorporated in the works of Ṭabarī and other later compilers.

[11] In this category, we have a number of extant *uṣūl*, or informal Shiʿi notebooks of *ḥadīth* traditions from the Imams al-Bāqir and al-Ṣādiq, which date from the early and mid-2nd/8th century.

[12] In this *genre*, there are the two 3rd/9th-century extant Shiʿi heresiographical works: al-Ḥasan b. Mūsā al-Nawbakhtī's *Firaq al-shīʿa* and Saʿd b. ʿAbd Allāh al-Ashʿarī al-Qummī's *Kitāb maqālāt wa'l-firaq*, which predate the earliest known non-Shiʿi heresiography, that of Abu'l-Ḥasan al-Ashʿarī, by a generation.

[13] The *Hāshimiyyat* of Kumayt b. Zayd, for example, almost certainly dates to the late Umayyad period.

[14] With regard to this phenomenon in the early work, *Kitāb Sulaym b. Qays*, discussed below, see Hossein Modarressi, *Tradition and Survival* (Oxford, 2003), p. 86.

[15] This has been shown to be the case with the extant recension of the *Tafsīr al-Qummī*; see Meir Bar-Asher, *Scripture and Exegesis in Early Imāmī Shīʿism* (Leiden, 1999), pp. 46–50.

[16] Note Gregor Schoeler's discussion in *The Genesis of Literature in Islam: From the Aural to the Read*, tr. S. Toorawa (Edinburgh, 2009), ch. 2, where he observes that in early traditions of Arabic poetry, wherein oral transmission was both traditional and inherent to the *genre*, transmitters seem to have been expected not simply to transmit the poems verbatim, but to improve them where appropriate.

because some of these early source materials were committed to writing while Shiʿi theology and Imamology was still under construction, we find in Shiʿi *ḥadīth* collections sections where traditions containing older formulations and terminologies have been placed side by side with newer ones, in some cases suggesting a clear line of development.[17] Similarly, the Shiʿi heresiographical work, *Firaq al-shīʿa*, which was composed during the *al-ghayba al-ṣughrā* (the lesser occultation), contains statements regarding the Twelfth Imam that effectively contradict later Shiʿi theology regarding his return.[18] As yet another example of the stubbornness of written material, we might note that despite the attempts of Imāmī Shiʿi scholarly authorities in the 4th/10th century to encourage the acceptance of the ʿUthmānī codex of the Qurʾanic text, they did not manage to erase from the record the substantial material that already existed in Imāmī Shiʿi *ḥadīth* literature detailing Shiʿi differences with the ʿUthmānic text.[19] In what follows, I examine the significance of writing and written documents for the early Shiʿi attempt to construct an historical counter-narrative of defining events in the early Islamic community, as well as for Shiʿis' slightly later project of preserving and disseminating the teachings of the Imams within their community.

Writing and the Shiʿi Counter-narrative of the Early Caliphate

By the time scholars generally agree that Islamic historical tradition had developed into a primarily written one (between the 3rd/9th and 4th/10th century), a more or less unanimous understanding of the events surrounding the rise of Islam and the early caliphate had emerged. The essential justness and legitimacy of the early caliphate was widely accepted, and dissenting opinions had largely been pushed to the margins.[20] But the well-known Shiʿi view of the events which took place from the death of the Prophet to the establishment of the Umayyad caliphate differs significantly from the version of these same events as found in the standard, extant historical compilations, all of which were composed in the Abbasid period. The era of the Madinan or Rightly Guided caliphate, as it is termed in the official Sunni tradition established in the early Abbasid period, represents for the Shiʿis, by contrast, the source and root of much injustice and religious error in the Islamic community.

---

[17] See, for example, my discussion of this phenomenon in relation to Shiʿi traditions regarding the 'pillars' of religion in *The Charismatic Community: Shīʿite Identity in Early Islam* (Albany, NY, 2007).

[18] See Ḥasan b. Mūsā al-Nawbakhtī, *Firaq al-shīʿa* (Cairo, 1992), p. 100.

[19] See al-Kulaynī, *Uṣūl al-kāfī*, ed. Muhḥammad Jaʿfar Shams al-Dīn (Beirut, 1990), vol. 1, pp. 479–506. For the most recent treatment of Imāmī views on the Qurʾan, see Etan Kohlberg and M. A. Amir-Moezzi, *Revelation and Falsification: The* Kitāb al-qirāʾāt *of Aḥmad b. Muḥammad al-Sayyārī* (Leiden, 2009), pp. 24–30.

[20] See W. Madelung, *The Succession to Muḥammad: A Study of the Early Caliphate* (Cambridge, 1997), for an exhumation of early dissenting opinions.

The work of Etan Kohlberg has made it clear, and it is now widely accepted, that the definitive establishment of this radically negative Shiʿi view of the early caliphate and of the Prophetic Companions who supported it can be traced to some time in the early (pre-Abbasid) 2nd/8th Islamic century.[21] This is precisely the period in which a standard version of history and tradition was beginning to be written down – most famously by the historian allegedly in the service of the Umayyad court, Ibn Shihāb al-Zuhrī (d. 124/741) – with official sanction, if not direct encouragement.[22] Although little remains to us of this 'Umayyad version of history', it is to be expected that in this version, the first three caliphs would have been presented as impeccable examples of Muslim leadership and Umayyad legitimacy would have been set on firm ground. If such a project can in fact be traced to the late Umayyad period (or early 2nd/8th century), then it seems reasonable to think that the more radical strain of Rāfiḍī Shiʿism emerging at this same time would have felt the need to present an internally consistent and morally compelling counter-version of the history of the early caliphate. From another point of view, the emergence of the more radical Rāfiḍī Shiʿi perspective in the late Umayyad period may itself have been part of a strenuous Shiʿi reaction to the development and recording of an 'official' version of history and tradition in this same period. It is worth noting that al-Zuhrī was a Madinan scholar who was a contemporary and associate of fellow Madinans, ʿAlī Zayn al-ʿĀbidīn and Muḥammad al-Bāqir, and that ʿAlī Zayn al-ʿĀbidīn reportedly knew and disapproved of al-Zuhrī's collaboration with the Umayyads. It may not be a coincidence, therefore, that the earliest attempts at combining the Shiʿi perspective on early Islamic history with the beginnings of an internally consistent sectarian theological doctrine, and earliest extant works attesting to this, can be traced to the time of Muḥammad al-Bāqir, around the turn of the first Islamic century.

Writing, Secrecy and Counter-history in *Kitāb Sulaym b. Qays*

If we look at the contested history of the events surrounding the establishment of the caliphate after the death of the Prophet, we see that writing and written documents play some role in both Shiʿi and Sunni accounts of these events, and have particular relevance for some of the traditional Shiʿi grievances against the two caliphs. One of the most commonly known examples of this is the reported request of the Prophet on his deathbed for a pen and tablet in order to write his last will and testament, which

---

21 See Etan Kohlberg, 'Some Imāmī Shīʿī Views on the Ṣaḥāba', *JAOS*, 5 (1984), pp. 146–147, where he notes the presence of these ideas among the earlier Saba'iyyah or Kaysaniyya Shiʿis, but states that the first Imāmī Shiʿi Imam to whom these ideas are attributed is Muḥammad al-Bāqir.

22 Abbott, *Studies*, vol. 2, pp. 33–34; Schoeler, *The Genesis of Literature in Islam*, pp. 50–56. See also allusions to al-Zuhrī's association both with the Umayyads and with the change from a predominantly oral to a predominantly written transmission methodology in Ibn Saʿd, *Ṭabaqāt*, vol. 2 pp. 135–136.

Shiʿis believe included, or would have included, a clear and explicit designation of ʿAlī b. Abī Ṭālib as the Prophet's successor. It is none other than ʿUmar who reportedly prevented compliance with the Prophet's request, arguing that the Prophet was delirious and not mentally fit to give such a final testament.[23] A second, equally well-known instance which relates more directly to the transmission of religious knowledge, is the reported rejection by Abū Bakr of ʿAlī's written codex of the Qurʾan, with accompanying Prophetic commentary, compiled in the months after the Prophet's death.[24] This, of course, constitutes an important basis of the Shiʿi claim that their Imams alone know the complete Qurʾan, and that they alone are in possession of its true interpretation.

One of the most important early works suggesting a link between the conscious effort to establish or preserve a Shiʿi counter-narrative of the early events of the Islamic community and the role of writing in both the events themselves and their transmission, is the late Umayyad Shiʿi polemical work, *Kitāb Sulaym b. Qays al-Hilālī*. This work presents itself as a collection of traditions, or *aḥādīth*, that the purported author, Sulaym b. Qays al-Hilālī, heard directly from ʿAlī b. Abī Ṭālib or from his well-known contemporary supporters, and then recorded in a single written text. Other than this work, there is no historical record of Sulaym b. Qays, and the name is either a completely fictitious ascription, or else a pseudonym.[25] According to the transmission history that the text provides for itself, Sulaym b. Qays, on his deathbed, gave the book to the known, but reportedly unreliable Shiʿi transmitter, Abān b. Abī ʿAyyāsh,[26] without having orally reviewed with him all of the contents of the book. Abān later conveyed the book to the generally reliable transmitter, ʿUmar b. Udhaynah, who is also the primary source through which far more well-accepted collections of traditions from Muḥammad al-Bāqir enter Shiʿi *ḥadīth* literature.[27] Given the nature of its reported transmission history, *Kitāb Sulaym* is sometimes classified by

---

[23] See al-Ṭabarī, *Taʾrīkh al-rusul waʾl-mulūk*, ed. M. J. de Goeje et al. (Leiden, 1879–1901), vol. 2, pp. 1806–1807, in which ʿUmar is not named specifically as the one who refuses the Prophet's request; and Ibn Saʿd, *Ṭabaqāt*, vol. 2, pp. 36–38, where ʿUmar is specifically identified as the one who refuses the Prophet's request in certain accounts cited by Ibn Saʿd, but not in others.

[24] Al-Ṭabrisī, *al-Iḥtijāj*, ed. Jaʿfar Subḥānī (Qumm, 1992), p. 207. See also, Ibn Saʿd *Ṭabaqāt*, vol. 2, p. 101, where ʿAlī's collection of the Qurʾan after the death of the Prophet is noted, without reference to Abū Bakr's rejection of it.

[25] See Modarressi, *Tradition and Survival*, p. 83; and Ardabīlī, *Jāmiʿ al-ruwāh wa izāhat al-ishtibāhāt ʿan al-ṭuruq waʾl-isnād* (Beirut, 1983), vol. 1, p. 374.

[26] Abān's reputation as an unreliable transmitter stems directly from accusations that he forged the *Kitāb Sulaym b. Qays*, which is the only major transmission he is credited with in Shiʿi bio-bibliographical sources, see Ardabīlī, *Jāmiʿ al-ruwāh*, vol. 1, p. 9; and Muḥammad b. Ḥasan al-Ṭūsī, *Ikhtiyār maʿrifat al-rijāl* (= *Rijāl al-Kashshī*), ed. Ḥasan al-Muṣṭafawī (Mashhad, 1348 Sh./1969), pp. 104–105, where all that is known about Sulaym comes from the text of this work itself.

[27] See Ardabīlī, *Jāmiʿ al-ruwā*, vol. 1, pp. 631–632.

Imāmī Shiʿi scholars as one of the '*uṣūl*' or 'notebooks',[28] although it differs significantly in style from the other extant *uṣūl* or from other Shiʿi collections of traditions. Firstly, the traditions included in the text are not generally limited to a single issue of theology or *fiqh*; rather, they tend to be lengthy traditions that include full, narrative accounts of some of the most important events in early Islamic history, as told from a distinctly Shiʿi point of view. While the book's contents are clearly polemical, its concern with historical events and the long, narrative style of its reports distinguish it from other Shiʿi works of *ḥadīth*. This text has often been dismissed as an unreliable source by Shiʿi and Western scholars alike because it bears the clear marks of later tampering and corruption.[29] But compelling internal evidence indicates that the core of the text is distinctly late Umayyad in origin, and can almost certainly be dated between AH 122 and 132.[30]

The book is primarily concerned with presenting an historical case for the superiority of ʿAlī and for the injustice that he suffered in being denied his right to the caliphate, while explaining the religious error and underhanded political manipulations of the first two caliphs, as well as of the third caliph, ʿUthmān b. ʿAffān, and a host of anti-Shiʿi figures: Zubayr b. al-ʿAwāmm, Ṭalḥa b. ʿUbayd, ʿĀʾisha bt. Abī Bakr, ʿAmr b. al-ʿĀṣ and Muʿāwiya b. Abī Sufyān – that is to say, precisely those prominent opponents of the ʿAlid cause whom the emerging Rāfiḍī Shiʿi doctrine of the early 2nd/8th century encouraged Shiʿis to dissociate from and to curse.[31] Given its early dating and its historical, if polemical, content, *Kitāb Sulaym* likely represents an early attempt at compiling a pro-ʿAlid version of the events of the early Islamic community – a version that may have been engendered, or at least radicalised, by the reported Umayyad attempt to record a written, official history in roughly this same time period in the early 2nd/8th century.

Turning to the content of *Kitāb Sulaym*, we see that one of the earliest historical events given broad coverage in the text is the Prophetic statement at Ghadīr Khumm. There are three complete accounts of this event included in the text, along with numerous references to it in other passages.[32] I have argued elsewhere that evidence in both Sunni and Shiʿi sources suggests that the Ghadīr Khumm tradition was in

---

[28] Etan Kohlberg, '*al-Uṣūl al-arbaʿumiʾa*', in Harald Motzki, *Ḥadīth: Origins and Development* (Ashgate, 2004), p. 128.

[29] For some of the range of opinion on the book, see Tustarī, *Qāmūs al-rijāl*, vol. 4, pp. 445–455; Ardabīlī, vol. 1, p. 374. The leading Shiʿi criticism of the text is undoubtedly found in Ibn al-Ghadāʾirī, *Kitāb al-ḍuʿafāʾ*. See Tustarī's summary of Ibn al-Ghadāʾirī's multiple reasons for discrediting the text in *Qāmūs*, vol. 4, pp. 450–453. For a more recent discussion of the various historical opinions among Shiʿi scholars regarding *Kitāb Sulaym*, see Muḥammad Taqī Subḥānī, '*Dar shināsāʾī va iḥyāʾī-yi Kitāb Sulaym b. Qays al-Hilālī*', *Āyina-i pazhūhish*, 37, pp. 19–28, esp. 21–24.

[30] See Maria Dakake, 'Loyalty, Love, and Faith: Shiʿi Identity in Early Islam' (Ph.D. thesis, Princeton University, 2000), Appendix I; and Hossein Modaressi, *Tradition and Survival*, p. 83.

[31] See Etan Kohlberg, '*Barāʾa* in Shiʿi Doctrine', *JSAI*, 7 (1986), pp. 139–175.

[32] *Kitāb Sulaym*, vol. 2, pp. 644–646, 758–759, 828–829.

fairly wide circulation in the late Umayyad period.[33] It seems reasonable, therefore, that this event would constitute an essential pillar of any purported Shiʿi counter-historical narrative originating at this time. The other major incident that is given detailed coverage in the text is the night of the *Saqīfa Banī Sāʿida* and its aftermath. *Kitāb Sulaym* presents essentially two complete accounts of this event, one of which (constituted by combining *ḥadīth*s 3 and 48 in the text) presents a strongly pro-Abbasid version of the events of that night, with both Ibn ʿAbbās and his father being important protagonists in the narrative,[34] and a second in which the Abbasid figures are absent.[35] It is the second version of the nomination of Abū Bakr which sounds most like the version found in other, later Shiʿi sources, and it is this account that is partially quoted by al-Kulaynī[36] and later Shiʿi *ḥadīth* compilers[37] on the authority of *Kitāb Sulaym*; whereas the first account, with its favourable representation of the Abbasid Hāshemites, is not cited by any later Shiʿi author that we have seen. It may well be that the first account represents the original version of these events, belonging to the earliest recension of *Kitāb Sulaym*, while the second represents a later account inserted into the text in the Abbasid era, when the Shiʿis were embroiled in a legitimist debate with the collateral Abbasid Hāshemite line. The text also includes narrative accounts of other incidents which have become well-known elements of the Shiʿi argument against the Sunni view of the early caliphs and Prophetic Companions, including a discussion of the issue of Fadak as part of Fāṭima's inheritance appropriated by the state under Abū Bakr, as well as a list of 'harmful innovations' enacted or sanctioned under the leadership of the first two caliphs.[38] The text also includes several narrative accounts in which ʿAlī defends his own legitimist claims and explains certain puzzling aspects of his historical behaviour.

Perhaps more important than the historical narratives *Kitāb Sulaym* claims to transmit, at least for our purposes here, is the role that writing plays in many of the book's accounts, including the exclusively written transmission history it provides for itself. Throughout the text, writing is connected with secret or hidden knowledge that is, above all, subversive in nature, and this is certainly the case with its transmission narrative as well. In this lengthy narrative, the secondary transmitter, Abān b. Abī ʿAyyāsh, admits that he was disturbed by the allegations made in the book he received from Sulaym, and so set out to confirm its contents, discreetly, with several key pro-ʿAlid figures, from the fourth Imam, ʿAlī Zayn al-ʿĀbidīn, to al-Ḥasan al-Baṣrī (d. 110/728) and Abū Ṭufayl ʿĀmir b. Wāthila (d. 100/718). All three corroborate the truth of its contents, indicating that they maintained a quiet awareness of the true nature of these disturbing events, as recounted in *Kitāb Sulaym*, despite their acquiescence to the existing state of affairs. Abū Ṭufayl reportedly initiates Abān into

33 See Dakake, *The Charismatic Community*, ch. 2.
34 *Kitāb Sulaym*, vol. 2, pp. 571–576 and 862–873.
35 Ibid., vol. 2, pp. 578–599.
36 Al-Kulaynī, *al-Kāfī*, ed. ʿAlī Akbar al-Ghaffārī (Tehran, 1983), vol. 8, pp. 343–344.
37 Al-Ṭabrisī, *al-Ihtijāj*, vol. 1, pp. 203–222.
38 *Kitāb Sulaym*, vol. 2, pp. 675–695.

the esoteric Shiʿi belief in *rajʿa*, while also warning him that such esoteric knowledge can be dangerous, and that it must be concealed, even from most Shiʿis.[39] The clear implication is that this book that Abān has shown him must remain secret as well, and the text's secret nature and its written transmission are clearly linked. Writing would likely have been strongly connected with esoteric and highly secretive knowledge at this time. The practical difficulty of reproducing a written text meant that few could have access to knowledge transmitted in this way. In fact, the indication in early Islamic sources seems to be that such written materials were used almost exclusively for the private purposes of an individual scholar, not as a medium for transmitting religious knowledge, or that if they were transmitted, they were transmitted as part of a family legacy.[40] As Schoeler makes clear in his work, while written texts were used for private purposes, all publication was oral/aural.[41] However, Sulaym commits these particular traditions to writing – the transmission narrative implicitly argues – not only because this was the most effective means of preserving the knowledge, but also for the purpose of safely transmitting it, intact, from one generation of elite Shiʿis to another.

The importance of the written word in the transmission of secretive knowledge is also well attested in the content, as well as the alleged transmission methodology, of *Kitāb Sulaym*. The text, for example, includes a narration of the Prophet's attempt to compose a final written testament and ʿUmar's prevention of it.[42] In another passage, Ibn ʿAbbās claims that ʿAlī showed him a book in his possession that contained a list of all those who would be saved and all those who would be damned in the Hereafter.[43] Another interesting example of the usefulness of written records is suggested in the passage in which Sulaym claims to give a first-hand account of the secret, treacherous dealings between the Umayyad caliph, Muʿāwiya, and his repressive governor in Iraq, Ziyād b. Abīhi. Sulaym informs us that he has been able to give the account – which takes the form of a letter written by Muʿāwiya to Ziyād – because he has a friend (who is secretly a fellow Shiʿi) in the service of Ziyād. This friend, he tells us, surreptitiously took the letter and read it to Sulaym, who immediately committed its contents to writing. Sulaym then reports that Ziyād later asked the servant to retrieve the letter, whereupon Ziyād erased the letter and ordered the servant to refrain from

---

39 Ibid., pp. 557–564.

40 See Cook, 'The Opponents of the Writing of Tradition in Early Islam', pp. 476–479.

41 Schoeler, *The Genesis of Literature in Islam*, pp. 40–45.

42 *Kitāb Sulaym*, vol. 2, pp. 794–795. This account is related by Ibn ʿAbbās, as is the version found in al-Ṭabarī (see note 26). In al-Ṭabarī's account, ʿUmar is not mentioned by name as the one who refuses the Prophet's request. Rather this is attributed to some unnamed persons present in the room with the Prophet, and the account further alludes to the fact that Ibn ʿAbbās did not generally relate the matter openly. In the *Kitāb Sulaym* version, Ibn ʿAbbās likewise initially refuses to give the name of ʿUmar as the culprit, only telling this later in confidence to Sulaym.

43 *Kitāb Sulaym*, vol. 2, p. 804. For similar traditions, see al-Ṣaffār al-Qummī, *Baṣāʾir al-darajāt* (Beirut, 2007), vol. 1, pp. 379–383.

revealing its contents to anyone. Sulaym then adds, with some palpable satisfaction: 'But [Ziyād] did not know that I had already copied it.'[44]

In contrast to the 'true' narrative of the early Islamic community, which was concealed and maintained in writing, the text indicates the falsity of anti-ʿAlid material transmitted orally and promoted publicly, mentioning specifically Muʿāwiya's pervasive attempts at spreading false praise traditions regarding ʿUthmān.[45] However, the text also accuses ʿAlid enemies of using written documents to keep secret records of their own subversive plans. The clearest and most interesting examples of this in the text are the numerous references to the '*aṣḥāb al-ṣaḥīfa*' – a group of anti-ʿAlid figures, including Abū Bakr and ʿUmar, who according to several accounts in *Kitāb Sulaym*, secretly recorded a pact amongst themselves to seek to usurp ʿAlī's legitimate authority upon the death of the Prophet.[46] The secret anti-ʿAlid document is allegedly written towards the end of the Prophet's lifetime, and in one account, the document is drawn up subsequent to the Prophet's announcement at Ghadīr Khumm (just weeks before the Prophet's death).[47] The text thus alleges that this group planned during the Prophet's own lifetime to directly subvert the latter's command regarding the authority of ʿAlī, and that they recorded their commitment to this intended subversion in a written document that was then concealed in the Kaʿba until after the Prophet's death.[48] Here, then, we have a connection established between writing and subversion from both sides of the coin: the *aṣḥāb al-ṣaḥīfa* write a document with the intent of subverting the legitimate transfer of authority from the Prophet to ʿAlī; while it is implied that Sulaym in turn compiles his 'counter-history' in order to subvert the consolidation of this initial subversion, with the hope of some day re-establishing just and legitimate authority over the community in the manner he and his fellow Shiʿis believe was ordained by the Prophet.

Shiʿi Accounts of the First Civil War

While the narratives in *Kitāb Sulaym* focus primarily on events surrounding, and immediately after, the Prophet's death, the text does provide some details regarding the various events of the First Civil War, such as the Battle of the Camel[49] and the

[44] Ibid., pp. 739–746.

[45] Ibid., pp. 785–786.

[46] Ibid., p. 727, where the list of those party to this secret pact also includes, besides Abū Bakr and ʿUmar, Abū ʿUbayda b. al-Jarrāḥ, Sālim (the client of Abū Ḥudhayfa) and Muʿādh b. Jabal.

[47] Ibid., pp. 730–731. In this account, those party to the pact include, in addition to the five cited in the previous reference, five members of the *shūrā* (ʿUthmān, Ṭalḥa, Zubayr, ʿAbd al-Raḥmān b. ʿAwf, Saʿd b. Abī Waqqāṣ, as well as ʿAmr b. al-ʿĀṣ and Muʿāwiya b. Abī Sufyān).

[48] Ibid., p. 727; a similar tradition is included in Abū Saʿīd ʿAbbād, *Aṣl*, in *Uṣūl sittat ʿashar* (Tehran, 1951–1952), p. 18.

[49] See *Kitāb Sulaym*, vol. 2, pp. 796–800.

Battle of Ṣiffīn,[50] and the text is also concerned with the immediate aftermath of the Umayyad takeover after ʿAlī's death.[51] It is remarkable, however, that the text does not deal in any detail with the massacre of Ḥusayn and his supporters at Karbalāʾ, even though the purported author of the text, Sulaym b. Qays, reportedly lived through the time of Ḥasan and Ḥusayn b. ʿAlī, dying well after the Karbalāʾ event. As central as the Karbalāʾ event would become in later Shiʿi consciousness, the event plays almost no role in the sectarian polemic of the text. It is mentioned in passing only a few times, and in each of these instances it is merely included in long lists of other Umayyad injustices.[52] There are several reasons we might hypothesise for this striking lacuna, one of which may be that the Karbalāʾ event was not a serious point of contention among early Islamic historians. In fact, the historiographical tradition regarding the Karbalāʾ incident is almost entirely unanimous as regards the justice and goodness of Ḥusayn, his supporters and his cause, and the evil and maliciousness of the perpetrators of the massacre. There was, perhaps, no need to present a polemically magnified counter-version of this historical event, since Shiʿis and non-Shiʿis, radicals and moderates alike, seem to have viewed the event with the same categorical judgement. The text of *Kitāb Sulaym* is primarily interested in addressing the more controversial aspects of the events surrounding the establishment of the caliphate, presenting its Rāfiḍī Shiʿi view as a challenge, perhaps, to the emerging historiography which was reportedly being sanctioned or even commissioned by Umayyad rulers such as Hishām b. ʿAbd al-Mālik (d. 125/743), on the one hand, and to the moderate Shiʿi perspective against which it was historically defining itself in this same period, on the other.

The events of the First Civil War, however, remained more contested, and in fact seem to have been a matter of particular concern to Shiʿi authors in this early period. Gregor Schoeler notes that the earliest written monographs about the events of the First Civil War were composed exclusively by Shiʿi authors.[53] It was Shiʿis who initially took it upon themselves to record this history, and in so doing, likely preserved much of it from official obfuscation, while also effectively framing the historical narrative of the First Civil War in a way that would influence all later historiography of this period. The importance of the early Shiʿi narratives of this event are clear, for example, in the extent to which the Shiʿi Abū Mikhnaf's (d. 157/774) account is wholly imported into Ṭabarī's narrative of both the First Civil War and the Karbalāʾ massacre, with

---

50 Ibid., pp. 805–813.

51 Ibid., pp. 782–785.

52 Ibid., p. 632, where the broken *bayʿa* of the Kūfans toward Ḥusayn is likened to the broken *bayʿa* of Zubayr and Ṭalḥa toward ʿAlī and the broken *bayʿa* of the Kūfans toward Ḥasan b. ʿAlī upon his father's death; and pp. 633 and 838, where it is mentioned but greatly overshadowed by the issue of the general Umayyad oppression of the Shiʿis. On pp. 774–775, Ḥusayn's martyrdom is mentioned along with that of ʿAlī, Ḥasan b. ʿAlī and Zayd b. ʿAlī, although, again, no details are given of the event and the notion of his martyrdom is not even connected with the site of Karbalāʾ.

53 Schoeler, *The Genesis of Literature in Islam*, p. 74.

approximately 85–90 per cent of al-Ṭabarī's account of these two events having been taken directly from Abū Mikhnaf's works. There are also written accounts of the individual battles of the First Civil War ascribed to late Umayyad Shiʿi authors who were disciples of Muḥammad al-Bāqir, including the prominent Jābir b. Yazīd al-Juʿfī and Abān b. Taghlib;[54] and the earliest, fully extant account of the Battle of Ṣiffīn (*Waqʿat Ṣiffīn*) was written by the late 2nd/8th century Shiʿi, Naṣr b. Muzāḥim. The factual accuracy of those accounts that are extant may be questioned in the typical ways, and the authenticity of the highly literary poems and speeches that ornament the narratives of Abū Mikhnaf and Ibn Muzāḥim, purportedly composed and recited in the midst of desperate battles and somehow preserved in memory for decades, seems improbable. But at the same time, some of these accounts preserve material that seems to be quite early in origin. For example, Naṣr b. Muzāḥim's *Waqʿat Ṣiffīn* contains passages that are clearly pre-Rāfiḍī in origin,[55] although Ibn Muzāḥim dies in 183, long after the Rāfiḍī and early Imāmī views of the *ṣaḥāba* had been established. His account makes no effort, as it well could have, to include narrative details and rhetoric that would support the Imāmī perspective as developed in the mid- to late 2nd/8th century. All of this suggests that Shiʿi accounts of the events of the First Civil War began to be collected at a very early date, and that they were preserved in writing, which made it convenient for the material to be incorporated in large chunks by later, even rather pro-Sunni authors, such as al-Ṭabarī, and which also allowed their more primitive content to survive the Imāmī theological refinements of mid- to late 2nd/8th century Shiʿism.

Writing, Secret Knowledge and Communal Survival in the Shiʿi *Ḥadīth* Tradition

If some early 2nd/8th-century Shiʿis struggled to preserve and promote a Shiʿi counter-narrative of the events after the Prophet's death and of the contested early history of the Muslim community, Shiʿi scholars from the mid-2nd/8th century seem more concerned with developing a systematic theological and legal basis for Shiʿi differences with the non-Shiʿi Muslim majority, although this clearly had already begun in a more rudimentary way among the followers of Muḥammad al-Bāqir (d. 115 or 119/733 or 737). A key element of this emerging theology, from the time of Jaʿfar al-Ṣādiq (d. 148/765) onwards, was the superior knowledge of the Imāmī Imams as the

---

54 Aḥmad b. ʿAlī al-Najāshī, *Rijāl al-Najāshī*, ed. M. J. al-Nāʾīnī (Beirut, 1988), vol. 1, pp. 76, 315; Modarressi, *Tradition and Survival*, pp. 99–101 and 115–116.

55 The Rāfiḍī Shiʿi perspective seems almost entirely absent from this text, as are the more elaborate arguments for ʿAlī's authority as they developed in later Shiʿi thought. For example, ʿAlī's legitimacy is premised simply on his precedence (*sābiqa*) in Islam; there is no real antipathy toward Abū Bakr or ʿUmar (who are in one account described as '*ṭayyib*', or 'good', see p. 293), and no accusations that they had usurped ʿAlī's authority. And in one passage ʿAlī prohibits his followers from cursing his, or their, enemies; see p. 103.

essential basis of their spiritual authority, and the importance of knowledge in general within the Imāmī community. Large sections of al-Kulaynī's *Uṣūl al-kāfī*, as well as earlier pre-canonical compilations, most notably Aḥmad al-Barqī's (d. 274/887–888 or 280/893–894), *Maḥāsin* and al-Ṣaffār al-Qummī's (d. 290/902–903) *Baṣā'ir al-darajāt* are devoted to this subject. The sheer amount of material on knowledge and its role in religious life distinguishes early Shiʿi *ḥadīth* compilations from the earliest Sunni canonical collections, where the sections on knowledge are much shorter and less systematic in organisation. But the discussions of knowledge in Shiʿi *ḥadīth* collections are also distinguished by the extent to which they represent true knowledge as hidden and inaccessible to some, or even to all but a few,[56] and by the role that writing and written texts – real or symbolic – play in the Shiʿi conception of spiritual knowledge.

While the Imams' knowledge came from a variety of unique sources, the Imāmī *ḥadīth* literature attributes some of their knowledge to a series of mysterious texts said to exist in the sole possession of the Imams, and passed from one Imam to the next. In many cases, traditions about these extraordinary written documents in the possession of the Imams appear to be extrapolations from simpler, earlier accounts. The widely reported account of the Prophet being denied his request to have his final will and testament recorded in writing is directly connected to traditions about a private testimony given to Fāṭima, either by the Prophet, or the Angel Gabriel, which she then dictated to ʿAlī. In Shiʿi *ḥadīth* tradition, this text, which is referred to as the codex of Fāṭima (*muṣḥaf Fāṭima*),[57] or sometimes the tablet of Fāṭima (*lawḥ Fāṭima*),[58] is said to contain knowledge of all future Imams and the history of the *ahl al-bayt*.[59] The tradition that ʿAlī kept a sheet of paper in the sheath of his sword that contained some written guidelines regarding the bloodwit (*diyya*)[60] may be the basis for the many references in Shiʿi *ḥadīth* to the 'Book of ʿAlī' (*Kitāb ʿAlī*), that is said to contain far more elaborate information concerning a variety of legal issues, as well as lists of future rulers and kings.[61] And the account of ʿAlī compiling the Qur'anic

---

[56] A famous early tradition repeatedly cited in Shiʿi *ḥadīth* sources from earliest times states the teachings of the Imams are difficult to grasp (*ṣaʿb*), and that they can only be understood by the angels, prophets and the rarest believers. See Jaʿfar al-Ḥaḍramī, *Aṣl*, in *al-Uṣūl al-sittatʿashar*, p. 65; al-Kulaynī, *Kāfī*, vol. 1, pp. 466–467; for fairly comprehensive collection of the tradition in earlier works, see Muḥammad Bāqir al-Majlisī, *Biḥār al-anwār* (Tehran, 1956–1972), vol. 2, pp. 183–197, 208–213.

[57] Al-Ṣaffār al-Qummī, *Baṣā'ir al-darajāt*, vol. 1, pp. 294–298, 304–325; M. A. Amir-Moezzi, *The Divine Guide in Early Shīʿism: The Sources of Esoterism in Islam*, tr. D. Streight (Albany, NY, 1994), p. 74.

[58] Al-Kulaynī, *Kāfī*, vol. 1, pp. 605–606, 610–611; al-Ṭabrisī, *Iḥtijāj*, pp. 162–166.

[59] In *Aṣl ʿĀṣim b. Ḥumayd al-Ḥannāṭ* in *al-Uṣūl al-sittat ʿashar* (Tehran, 1951–1952), p. 23, similar knowledge is said to be contained in the *waṣiyya* of Fāṭima.

[60] Bukhārī, Muḥammad b. Ismāʿīl, *Ṣaḥīḥ*, *K. al-ʿilm*, *ḥadīth* 111; Modarressi, *Tradition and Survival*, pp. 6, 12–13.

[61] For a full discussion of the *Kitāb ʿAlī*, see Modarressi, pp. 4–12 and Andrew Newman, *The Formative Period of Twelver Shīʿism: Ḥadīth as Discourse between Qumm and Baghdad* (Richmond, Surrey, 2000), p. 124.

revelations after the death of the Prophet and offering the collection to Abū Bakr – who did not accept it – becomes the basis for the idea that the Imams alone possess the true Qur'anic text and its Prophetic commentary.[62] This belief further led to traditions that asserted small, but significant omissions from the 'Uthmānī compilation of the Qur'anic text, which are detailed in one of the largest individual chapters in al-Kulaynī's *Uṣūl al-kāfī* containing over 90 traditions, related on the authority of several different Imams.[63] Later Imāmī tradition rejected all suggestions and assertions that compromised the essential integrity of the 'Uthmānī codex, insisting that it was only the inclusion of Prophetic commentary that distinguished 'Alī's collection from the 'Uthmānī codex.[64] But the assertion that the Imams possessed the only copy of a full Prophetic commentary on the Qur'anic text is powerful enough a claim on its own, especially given the relative paucity of direct Prophetic commentary on the Qur'an that is found in non-Shi'i tradition.

The Shi'i *ḥadīth* tradition also goes on to describe a series of books in the Imams' possession, all of which afford the Imams extraordinary, unparalleled, miraculous, even revelatory knowledge, including books containing the names of all Shi'is until the end of time,[65] as well as the original copies of earlier scriptures, including the Torah and the Gospel.[66] Perhaps as a corollary to these latter traditions, the Imams were said to possess knowledge of all languages[67] (presumably allowing them to read these earlier scriptures), as well as the esoteric 'language of the birds'.[68] It is not hard to see how extraordinary traditions developed from more ordinary ones, or how one extraordinary claim regarding the Imams' knowledge led to, or even logically necessitated, another. Questions of origin and authenticity aside, however, these traditions play a substantial role in Shi'i *ḥadīth* traditions that describe the nature of the Imams' knowledge. More importantly, such traditions unmistakably imply that true knowledge is the preserve of a few, and that it is kept that way, in part, through the use of written texts which could be easily hidden and secreted away, and transmitted quietly and in clandestine fashion, if need be, from one generation to the next.

If the soundest religious knowledge in the Sunni tradition was that which was most well-known, most widely circulated and transmitted, and made public in open teaching sessions via oral transmission and recitation, the most sacred knowledge in Shi'ism was that possessed exclusively by the Imams, and kept, in part, in secret written texts whose contents were never fully divulged, even to their followers. Whatever the references to such books and hidden knowledge possessed by the Imams might

---

62 See, for example, al-Kulaynī, *Kāfī*, vol. 1, pp. 284–286; al-Ṣaffār al-Qummī, *Baṣā'ir al-darajāt*, vol. 1, pp. 384–392.

63 Al-Kulaynī, *Kāfī*, vol. 1, pp. 479–506.

64 Bar-Asher, *Scripture and Exegesis*, p. 16.

65 Al-Ṣaffār al-Qummī, *Baṣā'ir al-darajāt*, vol. 1, pp. 341–346.

66 Al-Kulaynī, *Kāfī*, vol. 1, pp. 281–284, al-Ṣaffār al-Qummī, *Baṣā'ir al-darajāt*, vol. 1. pp. 276–288.

67 Al-Kulaynī, *Kāfī*, vol. 1, p. 284.

68 Amir-Moezzi, *Divine Guide*, p. 16.

mean, and regardless of their alleged content, to posit their very existence as the source of truest knowledge is already to assume a position of resistance – symbolic or otherwise – to the dominant Islamic intellectual culture. To establish that knowledge does not belong to the majority, but to the minority, and that this knowledge was such that it needed to remain hidden from the majority, is to create an intellectual and spiritual space in which the Shiʿi perspective could flourish and survive among its adherents without openly challenging the dominant tradition. At the same time, this conception of the nature of true religious knowledge as the hidden preserve of the spiritual elite (that is, the Shiʿis, by their own formulation), made the Shiʿi perspective, as it was understood by Shiʿis themselves, somewhat resistant to external intellectual challenges by undermining the very principles of knowledge creation and transmission upon which that prevailing intellectual tradition was based.

Writing and Shiʿi Transmission of the Imams' Teaching

Given the symbolic importance of the Imams as keepers of secret texts, it seems rather natural that their disciples would have used private written texts themselves to record and preserve the purported teachings of the Imams, and it is clear from both direct and indirect textual evidence that they did so regularly. These written records of the Imams' teaching sometimes took the form of thematically unified compilations – such as collections of *tafsīr* traditions from Muḥammad al-Bāqir, of accounts pertaining to early historical events, such as battles of the First Civil War, or of the Imams' teachings on a particular issue of law or ritual – but were more often simply informal collections of traditions an individual disciple had heard and recorded from the Imam or one of his associates. Although only a relative handful of these are currently extant, Shiʿi bibliographical works attest to hundreds of these collections with diverse content and unsystematic presentation, which are referred to as '*uṣūl*,' ('sources' or 'notebooks') because they contain the raw source material from which the later systematic and thematic collections of Shiʿi *ḥadīth* were compiled. While this process whereby private, informal written collections were later incorporated into systematic, published works has long been recognised as formative for the Imāmī Shiʿi *ḥadīth* tradition, more recent scholarship has argued for the existence of a somewhat similar process in the Sunni tradition as well, although the strong predilection for the ideal of oral transmission meant that this process was not fully acknowledged. Schoeler maintains that there was a period during which *ḥadīth* began to be written down in private, unsystematic collections, and that this period preceded the compilation of the early, pre-canonical Sunni *muṣannaf* works in the early 3rd/9th century, and to some degree, facilitated it.[69] Harald Motzki has also argued convincingly that these early *muṣannaf* works seem to have relied on both written and oral sources, some of which likely preserve material that authentically originates as early as the

[69] Schoeler, *The Genesis of Literature in Islam*, ch. 5.

first Islamic century.[70] Even if the processes whereby the Sunni and Shiʿi canonical *ḥadīth* traditions were formed are analogous in some ways, and went through similar stages, the use of written texts in the formation of the early Shiʿi tradition was based on a profoundly different set of historical circumstances and intellectual and religious premises, and as such, carried unique significance.

Sunnis, who viewed all authentic religious knowledge as originating ideally with the Prophet and his Companions, were separated from this ultimate source of knowledge by historical time, and the oral tradition of transmission enshrined in the *isnād* was a chain that allowed them to traverse that distance in a virtual sense, the personal, face-to-face transmission substituting for the direct teaching of the Prophet. For 2nd/8th-century Shiʿis, however, the living Imam, and not the *isnād*, was their link to the religious authority of the Prophet, and most Shiʿis in this period were separated from their Imam by geographical, rather than temporal distance. Muḥammad al-Bāqir and Jaʿfar al-Ṣādiq, the two Imams who collectively represent the origin of approximately 80–90 per cent of the Imāmī Shiʿi *ḥadīth* tradition, lived all their lives in Medina, while the majority of their disciples – including many who were transmitters of their teachings – were resident in Kūfa. Most Kūfan Shiʿis at this time would have had the opportunity of seeing their Imam only once or twice in their lifetimes – probably often in conjunction with performing the *ḥajj*[71] – while others would have been completely dependent on the reports they received of the Imams' teachings from their fellow Shiʿis who had the opportunity to visit them. Because even many of those who were able to visit the Imam would not have had the luxury of staying with him long enough to memorise and review whatever they had learned, it hardly seems unlikely that many would have availed themselves of written notes to better preserve what they had heard in order to share it with their fellow Shiʿis in Kūfa.

In contrast to the Sunni tradition, in which the practical use of written notes co-existed with the ideal that all religious knowledge be learned and transmitted orally, the Shiʿi Imams reveal no discomfort with their disciples' recording their teachings in written form. In fact, far from manifesting ambivalence about the use of written texts for this purpose, the sixth Imam is reported to have directly encouraged it, telling his followers, 'Write, for you will not remember (*yaḥfaẓūn*) unless you write,'[72] and 'The heart trusts in writing'.[73] These two traditions are found in a single chapter in al-Kulaynī's Book on the Superiority of Knowledge (*Kitāb faḍl al-ʿilm*)

---

[70] Harald Motzki, 'The *Muṣannaf* of ʿAbd al-Razzāq al-Sanʿānī as a Source of Authentic *Aḥādīth* of the First Century A.H.', *JNES*, 50 (1991), pp. 1–21.

[71] There are many traditions that indicate that Shiʿis would frequently visit the Imam in conjunction with their pilgrimage to Makka, or else during the *ḥajj* rituals themselves, which paradoxically would afford the Imam and his disciple some anonymity, and hence privacy, among the crowds of pilgrims. For example, see Zayd al-Narsī, *Aṣl*, in *Uṣūl sittat ʿashar*, p. 48 and al-Kulaynī, *Kāfī*, vol. 1, p. 449.

[72] Al-Kulaynī, *Kāfī*, vol. 1, pp. 104–105; for a slightly longer version of this, see *Aṣl Āṣim b. Ḥumayd al-Ḥannāṭ*, pp. 25 and 34.

[73] Al-Kulaynī, *Kāfī*, vol. 1, p. 104.

containing 15 *aḥādīth* that are almost entirely dedicated to encouraging the use of written texts in not only the preservation, but also the transmission of the Imams' teachings. One of these traditions is attributed to al-Ṣādiq by Mufaḍḍal b. ʿUmar, a figure accused of extremism and generally considered unreliable:[74]

> Write and spread your knowledge among your brothers. And if you die, then bequeath your books to your sons. For a time of tribulation will come upon people, in which there will be none to keep them company save their books.[75]

Another tradition suggests the manner in which these texts may have been used as tools for instructing the Shiʿi disciples in Kūfa. In this *ḥadīth*, ʿAbd Allāh b. Sinān, a reliable transmitter and disciple of al-Ṣādiq complains to the Imam, saying:[76]

> A group came to me to listen to your *ḥadīth*, but it was difficult for me, for I am not strong. [Al-Ṣādiq] said: 'So read them a *ḥadīth* from the beginning of it, and a *ḥadīth* from the middle of it, and a *ḥadīth* from the end of it.'[77]

This *ḥadīth* clearly suggests that ʿAbd Allāh b. Sinān possessed a written collection of the Imams' teachings from which he might instruct his fellow Shiʿis and that it was long enough to tire him if he attempted to read it all.

In addition to allowing the use of written texts for both preserving and transmitting the Imams' teachings, the *aḥādīth* in this chapter also allow the transmission of, and reliance upon, written texts without the author's explicit permission, that is, transmitting their contents on the basis of *wijāda*, or 'finding'. A disciple puts the following question to ʿAlī al-Riḍā:

> A man from among our companions gave me a book but did not say, 'Transmit this from me'. Is it permissible for me to transmit it from him?' [Al-Riḍā'] said: 'If you know that the book was his, then transmit it from him.'[78]

A similar issue is brought to the attention of the ninth Imam, Muḥammad al-Jawād:

> May I be your ransom! Our elders used to relate traditions from Muḥammad al-Bāqir and Jaʿfar al-Ṣādiq, while [the need for] *taqiyya* was intense, so they hid their books and did not transmit from them. And when they died, the books came to us. [The Imam] said: 'Relate *ḥadīth* from them, for they are truthful.'[79]

---

[74] See Modarressi, *Tradition and Survival*, pp. 333–334.
[75] Al-Kulaynī, *Kāfī*, vol. 1, p. 105.
[76] Modarressi, *Tradition and Survival*, pp. 157–161.
[77] Al-Kulaynī, *Kāfī*, vol. 1, p. 104.
[78] Ibid., p. 104.
[79] Ibid., p. 106.

These practices would hardly be acceptable in Sunni *ḥadīth* methodology, at least as it was ideally construed, and the chapter contains other pieces of advice from the Imam that could only be considered as endorsing rather bad *ḥadīth* methodology by these standards. There is, for example, a tradition indicating that one need not be too concerned with transmitting the Imams' words precisely, so long as one was able to convey the intended meaning accurately;[80] another in which al-Ṣādiq indicates that one may relate a tradition from either himself or Muḥammad al-Bāqir, since all his knowledge derives from his father;[81] and yet another that recommends citing one's sources for any *ḥadīth* one transmits, so that if the *ḥadīth* is untrue, blame will fall upon one's source rather than oneself.[82]

The *aḥādīth* in this chapter seem to provide the Imams' sanction for what can be described, at best, as a less than cautious methodology for transmitting their traditions, and at worst, as an endorsement, or belated justification, for practices that ultimately allowed a good deal of spurious and extremist material to enter into mainstream Imāmī Shiʿi *ḥadīth*. But it should be noted that, as is often the case in Imāmī *ḥadīth* collections, these traditions are attributed to both very sound and more questionable transmitters, and cannot necessarily be dismissed as merely serving an extremist agenda. Moreover, the less than airtight *ḥadīth* methodology promoted in these traditions is clearly displayed in many canonical, and reliable, Shiʿi *ahādīth*: some, for example, are not clear as to whether the tradition should be traced back to al-Bāqir or al-Ṣādiq, with the attribution left open by narrating the tradition on the authority of 'one of these two' (*aḥadahumā*), and many others contain imperfect or incomplete *isnād*s. In theory, however, none of this would have meant very much as long as the Imams were present to correct any errors or resolve any discrepancies,[83] as they would have been in the 2nd/8th, and, to a lesser extent, 3rd/9th centuries. In fact, *isnād* criticism as the basis of authenticating *ḥadīth* seems to emerge rather belatedly in Shiʿi tradition for this reason, and even then, seems to have carried less weight and significance than it did in the Sunni tradition. In his study of the formative Imāmī *ḥadīth* tradition, Andrew Newman observed that while the 4th/10th-century canonical compiler al-Kulaynī attempted to pare down some of the more extremist content of the expansive Imāmī *ḥadīth* literature in circulation, he clearly did so, not by excising traditions related from unreliable transmitters, but rather by eliminating traditions based on their extremist content (*matn*).[84] And indeed we sometimes see in the Shiʿi *rijāl* literature transmitters – even prominent ones – being criticised on the basis of the content of the *aḥādīth* ascribed to them, even as their sometimes prolific transmission or closeness to a particular Imam is simultaneously noted. More importantly, this differential approach to *isnād* and *matn* criticism, in conjunction with the prevalence, and apparently greater authority, of written texts in the early

80 Ibid., pp. 103–104.
81 Ibid., p. 104.
82 Ibid., p. 104.
83 Kohlberg, '*al-Uṣūl al-arbaʿumiʾa*', p. 139.
84 Newman, *The Formative Period of Twelver Shīʿism*, pp. 136–137.

Shiʿi tradition relative to its Sunni counterpart, meant that Shiʿi traditions were rarely excised on the exclusive basis of either the *isnād* or the *matn*. They were, for the most part, allowed to continue to circulate within the tradition, since the systematic Shiʿi *rijāl* literature emerged only after canonical and pre-canonical collections of Shiʿi *ḥadīth* had already been set in writing and so were, in essence, 'facts on the ground'.

In encouraging their followers to use written texts, and sanctioning a relatively lax approach to the use of *isnād*s in the process of transmitting their *aḥādīth*, the Imams' primary concern was probably to ensure the survival of their religious teachings, and to allow for their quiet and private circulation among their followers in Kūfa. The Imams may also have had far fewer scruples about the written transmission of religious knowledge by virtue of their residence in Madina, whose scholarly culture after the time of al-Zuhrī became more open to the use of writing than that of Kūfa.[85] And if the ideal of oral transmission still dominated the intellectual atmosphere of Kūfa, then the Kūfan Shiʿis' reliance on written texts, with the sanction of their Imams, would have allowed them to circulate their Imams' teachings without engaging or confronting the larger intellectual circles around them, while also reinforcing their sense of community, in part by emphasising their differences with the non-Shiʿi majority on the very source of religious knowledge, not merely its content.

Conclusion

The use of writing among the early Imāmī Shiʿis was a successful strategy for preserving their early teachings in a form that both concealed them from wider public view and allowed them to survive their compilers. Concealing such texts in writing during dangerous times allowed not only for their survival but, as we have seen, also for their incorporation within, and influence upon, the subsequent tradition by virtue of their early compilation which would have given them an air of credibility. Moreover, the fixed and stable form of written texts made incorporating them wholesale into later works easy and appealing, even for those who at least outwardly maintained their scruples regarding oral transmission. Indeed the practical result of the use of written texts to transmit Shiʿi ideas prevalent in the pre-*ghayba* period was that much of this early material was preserved, and continued to be circulated, even after the official compilation of Imāmī *ḥadīth* collections in the 4th–5th/10th–11th centuries. Although there were important Shiʿi scholars who sought to discredit some of the more extremist content of this earlier material, it was never excised from the tradition. The continued presence and influence of this early material is evident, for example, in the library of the 7th/13th-century Shiʿi scholar Ibn Ṭāwūs (as reconstructed by Kohlberg) and, much later, in the massive *ḥadīth* compilation of the Safawid author

[85] Schoeler, *The Genesis of Literature in Islam*, p. 50.

al-Majlisī, in his 110-volume *Biḥār al-anwār*.[86] In addition to its practical contribution to the preservation of some elements of early Shiʿi thought, the use of written texts was, on a deeper level, philosophically consistent with, and an extension of, the notion of the Imams' true knowledge as esoteric and hidden – exclusively possessed and cautiously and privately disseminated. As such, it presents a direct contrast to some of the prevailing conceptions of knowledge and its transmission in the contemporaneous Sunni tradition, and thus points to a unique and coherent Shiʿi view of the nature of religious knowledge which was consistent with its larger theological premises, and which existed as a subtext of Shiʿi sectarian differences with the non-Shiʿi community.

[86] Etan Kohlberg, *A Medieval Muslim Scholar at Work: Ibn Ṭāwūs and His Library* (Leiden, 1992).

9

Pre-Būyid *Ḥadīth* Literature: The Case of al-Barqī from Qumm (d. 274/888 or 280/894) in Twelve Sections*

Roy Vilozny

Introduction

It is doubtful whether one may speak about self-awareness of the concept of Twelve Imams amongst the Imāmī Shiʿis during the lifetime of Aḥmad b. Muḥammad al-Barqī, that is, the second half of the 3rd/9th century, and perhaps partly due to this, this chapter will comprise twelve sections. Building the present study in twelve parts has several aims, the first of which has already been achieved in the opening statement, which is to place al-Barqī, whose works are regarded retrospectively as important Twelver sources, in an era of pre-Twelver self-consciousness – a dissonance that naturally requires further clarification.[1] Second, of the main work by al-Barqī, *Kitāb al-maḥāsin*,[2] to which the bulk of this chapter will be devoted, only eleven parts have come down to us and hence, a biographical-bibliographical section followed by additional eleven sections, devoted to each of the eleven surviving parts of *al-Maḥāsin*, will add up to twelve. Third, constructing this chapter according to a certain numeral logic could be regarded as a modern Western demonstration for the use of the unique literary genre of which al-Barqī makes use in the first part of the printed editions of his *al-Maḥāsin*, *Kitāb al-ashkāl wa'l-qarā'in* ('The book of parallels and comparisons').[3]

* To Yoram Hazan *in Memoriam*.

1 See below under the section on al-Barqī – Life and Work.

2 Aḥmad b. Muḥammad al-Barqī, *Kitāb al-maḥāsin* (Tehran, 1951–1952; repr. Beirut, n.d.), 2 vols. References will be to this edition, followed by references to the Najaf 1964 edition (2 vols; repr. Beirut, 2008). For information regarding manuscripts of the text, see F. Sezgin, *Geschichte des Arabischen Schrifttums* (Leiden, 1967), vol. 1, p. 538.

3 It is worth mentioning that while *Kitāb al-ashkāl wa'l-qarā'in* is located first in the printed editions of the text, it may not have constituted the first part of the original version; see below under section II.

Al-Barqī's *al-Maḥāsin* is an outstanding example of inter-religious and inter-cultural influences during the initial stage of development of both Imāmī religion and literature. The fact that al-Barqī's work, although not sufficiently acknowledged by Western scholars,[4] has been consulted and cited by subsequent generations of Imāmī scholars[5] seems to be a good enough proof for its centrality and importance. And finally, since the canonisation of Imāmī literature took place after al-Barqī's lifetime, and mainly during the Būyid period (945–1055 AD), this chapter may also be regarded as a tribute to the early generation of Imāmī scholars, who played an essential role in paving the way towards the final crystallisation of the Shiʿi classical corpus.

I. Life and Work

Very little can be said about al-Barqī's character or personal world view, as the only two extant works of his, *Kitāb al-rijāl* and *Kitāb al-maḥāsin*, contain no personal utterances, neither in the form of a preface or an introduction, nor by an expression of his own opinions in the text itself.[6] In his work, so it seems, al-Barqī restricted himself to the role of the classical traditionist or biographer, whose sole task was to collect information, at times rearrange it, and write it. By adhering to this method, al-Barqī may be counted among the traditionists of the proto-Akhbārī school of Qumm. A few remarks about the man, which derive from an examination of both the dimensions of his work and its contents, seem appropriate and will be made further below. But prior to that, an attempt will be made to reconstruct al-Barqī's life, according to the information available to us in biographical and bibliographical sources.

---

[4] Apart from A. J. Newman, in the fourth chapter of his *The Formative Period of Early Shīʿism* (Richmond, 2000), 'Ḥadīth as Discourse between Qum and Baghdad', pp. 50–66, P. Sander, in his *Zwischen Charisma und Ratio: Entwicklung in der frühen imāmitischen Theologie* (Berlin, 1994), pp. 123–164, and the author of the present chapter in his 'A Shīʿī Life Cycle According to al-Barqī's *Kitāb al-maḥāsin*', *Arabica*, 54 (2007), and 'Réflexions sur le *Kitāb al-ʿIlal* d'Aḥmad b. Muḥammad al-Barqī (d. 274/888 or 280/894), in M. A. Amir-Moezzi, M. M. Bar-Asher and S. Hopkins, ed., *Le Shīʿisme Imāmite quarante ans après. Hommage à Etan Kohlberg* (Turnhout, 2009), pp. 417–435, no Western scholar has focused his research directly on al-Barqī.

[5] An outstanding evidence for the centrality of al-Barqī's *Kitāb al-maḥāsin* is its inclusion among the principal sources from which Muḥammad Bāqir al-Majlisī (d. 1110/1699) quotes in his voluminous *Biḥār al-anwār*.

[6] Aḥmad b. Muḥammad al-Barqī, *Kitāb al-rijāl* (Tehran, 1342 Sh./1963); H. Modarressi, *Tradition and Survival: A Bibliographical Survey of Early Shiʿi Literature* (Oxford, 2003), vol. 1, p. xvii, where Modarressi remarks that this text may have been written in a later period and is wrongly ascribed to al-Barqī.

Neither of the two main biographical sources on which the following is based, al-Najāshī[7] and al-Ṭūsī,[8] provides any information regarding al-Barqī's date of birth. What we do find are some details about his ancestors and origins. Al-Barqī's family hailed from Kūfa, where his great-grandfather was arrested and later executed by Yūsuf b. ʿUmar al-Thaqafī (the governor of Iraq during the years 120–126/738–744), supposedly for taking part in the failed rebellion of Zayd b. ʿAlī (Muḥammad al-Bāqir's half-brother) against the Umayyads in 122/740. Following this event the family migrated to a small village near Qumm called Barq Rūd or Barqat Qumm, which is the putative reason for the *nisba* al-Barqī.[9]

Aḥmad's father, Muḥammad, was a disciple of both the eighth Imam, ʿAlī al-Riḍā (d. 203/818), and the ninth Imam, Muḥammad b. ʿAlī (d. 220/835), and seems to have been the first family member to transmit Shiʿi traditions.[10] According to the *Fihrist* of Ibn al-Nadīm, which on this point differs from other biographical sources, it is Muḥammad, Aḥmad's father, who was behind the compilation of *Kitāb al-maḥāsin.*[11] Even if the information provided by Ibn al-Nadīm is not entirely correct, the fact that almost one-third of the traditions included in *al-Maḥāsin* are ascribed to Aḥmad's father[12] may indicate that it was not the work of a single author, but rather of both father and son.

Aḥmad followed in his father's footsteps both as an Imāmī devotee – he was the disciple of the ninth and tenth Imams, Muḥammad b. ʿAlī (d. 220/835) and ʿAlī b. Muḥammad (d. 254/868) – and as a compiler and transmitter of traditions.[13] In spite of his reliance on weak transmitters (*ḍuʿafāʾ*),[14] both al-Najāshī and al-Ṭūsī

---

[7] Aḥmad b. ʿAlī al-Najāshī who died in 455/1063, the author of *Kitāb al-rijāl*, one of most often quoted Shiʿi biographical sources. See B. S. Amoretti, "Ilm al-Ridjāl', *EI2*, vol. 3, pp. 1150–1152.

[8] Abū Jaʿfar al-Ṭūsī Muḥammad b. al-Ḥasan, a prominent Imāmī scholar, born in 385/995 in Ṭūs, was a disciple of al-Shaykh al-Mufīd in Baghdad and of his successor, al-Sharīf al-Murtaḍā, whom he himself, as the latter's prominent disciple, succeeded in 436/1044. Al-Ṭūsī is the author of two of the 'four books' of the Imāmiyya. He died in Najaf in 459–60/1066–1067. See M. A. Amir-Moezzi, 'al-Ṭūsī', *EI2*, vol. 10, pp. 745–746.

[9] See al-Najāshī, *Rijāl* (Beirut, 1988), vol. 1, pp. 204–207; al-Ṭūsī, *al-Fihrist* (Najaf, 1960), pp. 44–46; Newman, *The Formative Period of Early Shīʿism*, pp. 51–52; Ch. Pellat, 'al-Barḳī', *EI2*, vol. 12 (supplement), pp. 127–128.

[10] Pellat, 'al-Barḳī', pp. 127–128; Newman, *The Formative Period of Early Shīʿism*, p. 51.

[11] Ibn al-Nadīm, *Fihrist* (Cairo, 1348), pp. 309–310; Pellat, 'al-Barḳī', pp. 127–128.

[12] Newman, *The Formative Period of Early Shīʿism*, p. 53, notes that 739 traditions (28 per cent) in *Kitāb al-maḥasin* are ascribed to Aḥmad's father.

[13] See al-Ṭūsī, *Rijāl* (Najaf, 1961), p. 398, where Aḥmad is included among the companions of the ninth Imam, and p. 410, where he is included among the companions of the tenth Imam; Sezgin, *Geschichte des Arabischen Schrifttums*, vol. 1, p. 538; Newman, *The Formative Period of Early Shīʿism*, p. 51.

[14] See J. Robson, 'al-Djarḥ wa-l-Taʿdīl', *EI2*, vol. 2, p. 462, where it is explained that although a *ḍaʿīf* is a person 'weak in tradition', he is not rejected if his traditions are supported elsewhere.

considered Aḥmad to be trustworthy (*thiqa*)[15] and agree that he was the author of numerous books, including *Kitāb al-maḥāsin*.[16]

The death date of al-Barqī is given as either 274/888 or 280/894. It is noteworthy that both dates are later than that of the beginning of the Twelfth Imam's lesser occultation in 260/874.[17] It seems quite unlikely that in the fifteen or twenty years that passed from the occultation of the Twelfth Imam until the death of al-Barqī, the doctrine of Twelfth Imams could have taken root and it is therefore difficult, if not impossible, to consider al-Barqī as a 'Twelver'. This conclusion goes hand in hand with the lack of any direct or indirect references to the number 12 or to the concept of *ghayba* (occultation) in his *Kitāb al-maḥāsin*.[18]

Al-Barqī's death-date should also be considered from another perspective – it preceded one of the most important historical turning points in the early development of the Shiʿi religion and *ḥadīth* literature: the coming to power of the Būyid dynasty in the year 334/945. In fact, most of the classical Shiʿi *ḥadīth* compilations are the result of the work of scholars from the Būyid period, during which Shiʿi intellectual activity was encouraged by the ruling dynasty that enabled Shiʿi scholars to work freely.[19] Viewed in this light, al-Barqī's work is unique, as it is a rare example of a *ḥadīth* collection that survived from the pre-Būyid era.[20] One should also bear in mind that these political circumstances coincided with the growing need for a reliable corpus of *ḥadīth* in the absence of an Imam, especially after contact with the hidden Imam came to an end in 329/941 – the year which marks the end of the lesser and the beginning of the greater occultation.

---

15 See G. H. N. Juynboll, 'Thiqa', *EI2*, vol. 10, p. 446, where this term is defined as 'qualification used in the science of *ḥadīth* to describe a transmitter as trustworthy, reliable'.

16 See note 10.

17 Al-Najāshī, *Rijāl*, pp. 206–207; al-Ṭūsī, *Rijāl*, p. 398.

18 About the development of the term *ithnā-ʿashariyya* see: E. Kohlberg, 'From Imāmiyya to Ithnā-ʿashariyya', *BSOAS*, 39 (1976), pp. 521–534, repr. in E. Kohlberg, *Belief and Law in Imāmī Shīʿism* (Aldershot, 1991), article xiv. Of special relevance to our discussion is Kohlberg's observation on p. 523 that neither al-Barqī nor his contemporary, al-Ṣaffar al-Qummī (d. 290/903), provide any information regarding the concept of twelve Imams and the idea of occultation; see also E. Kohlberg, 'Early Attestations of the Term '*ithnā-ʿashariyya*', *JSAI*, 24 (2000), pp. 343–357, and A. Arjomand, 'Imam *absconditus* and the Beginning of a Theology of Occultation: Imāmī Shiʿism *circa* 280–90/900 A.D.', *JAOS*, 117 (1997), pp. 1–12; see also M. A. Amir-Moezzi, *The Divine Guide in Early Shiʿism: The Sources of Esotericism in Islam*, tr. D. Streight (Albany, NY, 1994), pp. 101–102, where references in early sources to the number of Imams and the occultation are discussed.

19 Etan Kohlberg, 'Shīʿī ḥadīth', in *Arabic Literature to the End of the Umayyad Period* (Cambridge, 1983), pp. 302–303.

20 Another important source of a proximate time is the *Baṣāʾir al-darajāt* of al-Ṣaffar al-Qummī (d. 290/903); see M. A. Amir-Moezzi, 'al-Ṣaffar al-Qummī (d. 290/902–903) et son *Kitāb baṣāʾir al-darajāt*', *Journal Asiatique*, 280 (1992), pp. 221–250; of particular relevance is Amir-Moezzi's observation on pp. 240–241 that, unlike the *Kitāb al-maḥāsin*, this text does include five traditions which refer specifically to the notion of twelve Imams.

Al-Barqī's biographical dictionary, *Kitāb al-rijāl*, mainly comprises lists of names of the companions of each Imam. It starts by listing the companions of the Messenger of God (*aṣḥāb rasūl allāh*), goes on to those of the commander of the faithful (i.e., ʿAlī, the first Imam), his two sons, al-Ḥasan and al-Ḥusayn, and so on until the Eleventh Imam.[21] Given that al-Barqī composed his *Rijāl* towards the end of his life, or at least was able to update it as long as he was alive, the fact that he stopped at the Eleventh Imam who died in 260/874 may indicate that the identity of the latter's successor was not known to him. If true, this would explain why his *Kitāb al-maḥāsin* contains no references to the Twelfth Imam or to his occultation. At the same time though, one could expect to find some clues as to the reality in which al-Barqī lived and worked – either when the Imam's identity was unknown or when there was simply no Imam. A separate section of his *Rijāl*, significantly shorter than the previous one which was devoted to men, is consecrated to women who transmitted traditions that they heard directly from the Prophet or the Imams.[22]

A special place is given at the end of the *Rijāl* to those who rejected Abū Bakr. That their number is said to have been twelve seems not to be connected to the special significance of this number in Twelver Shiʿism, especially in light of the above-mentioned lack of references to this number in al-Barqī's *al-Maḥāsin*. The fact that in their case al-Barqī not only provides a list of names, but also elaborates on the circumstances in which each of them rejected Abū Bakr, is remarkable.[23] According to al-Barqī, the first person who objected to Abū Bakr's appointment was the *muhājir*, Khālid b. Saʿīd al-ʿĀṣ, who did so by reminding Abū Bakr of the Prophet's words at the Battle of Qurayẓa: 'Oh, the people of Quraysh, keep my will that ʿAlī will be your Imam after me. Gabriel informed me so in the name of God.'[24]

The title of al-Barqī's main work, *Kitāb al-maḥāsin*, which may be translated as 'The book of good qualities', already reveals something about its contents. As any other cultural oeuvre, this text did not spring out of nowhere and the reflection of both external influences and internal Shiʿi tendencies can be seen already in its title. By the time of al-Barqī, such a title may well have rung a bell with the literate audience, who were familiar with other works of similar titles – a possible indication that they belong to the same literary genre – such as *al-Maḥāsin wa'l-aḍdād* of al-Jāḥiẓ, a contemporary of al-Barqī.[25]

Furthermore, for the Shiʿi believer whose notions of good and evil are deeply rooted in his dualistic world view,[26] the term 'good qualities' is necessarily associ-

---

[21] Al-Barqī, *Kitāb al-rijāl*, pp. 1–61; not surprisingly, the sixth Imam, Jaʿfar al-Ṣādiq, who is the most important Imam for the development of the Imāmī doctrine – also called Jaʿfariyya – had the largest number of companions (pp. 16–47), whereas the third Imam, al-Ḥasan, had the fewest (a very short list of ten names on p. 7).

[22] Ibid., pp. 61–62.

[23] Ibid., pp. 63–66.

[24] Ibid., p. 63.

[25] See I. Geries, *Un genre littéraire arabe: al-maḥāsin wa-l-masāwī* (Paris, 1977).

[26] See below under section VI.

ated with 'bad qualities'. Indeed, *Kitāb al-maḥāsin* of al-Barqī deals not only with 'good qualities' but also with their contrary 'bad ones'. The fact that in the title only the positive side is mentioned is in a way comparable with the fact that in many traditions the negative element is missing or, at times, only alluded to. As will be seen further below, the negative mirror reflection of praising the Shiʿi community by ascribing to them 'good qualities', that is, the condemnation of its opponents, may be inferred quite easily, even when apparently a tradition is not at all concerned with it.

Kitāb al-maḥāsin is a large collection of traditions ascribed to the Imams or to the Prophet. In its published editions the text includes 11 sub-books (*kitāb*, pl. *kutub*), which are all that survived of the original 90-odd sub-books.[27] Each sub-book within *al-Maḥāsin* has a title indicating its content and in most cases, excluding the sixth sub-book, is divided into chapters (*bāb*, pl. *abwāb*) that normally also have a subtitle of their own. Each chapter contains numerous traditions ascribed to one of the Imams or to the Prophet and mostly, but not always, dealing with a certain aspect of this sub-book's main subject. In view of the rich variety characterising *Kitāb al-maḥāsin*, especially when one also examines the titles of its missing parts that dealt with subjects such as medicine, astrology, grammar and many more, Pellat's suggestion that this book was intended as a sort of encyclopaedia for the believer seems plausible.[28] The combination of this with the remarks made above about its title and literary genre, may lead to the conclusion that *Kitāb al-maḥāsin* was conceived as a moral guide for all aspects of the believer's life – from daily legal details to the fundamentals of the creed, a conclusion that tallies with the eclectic character of the text.

Judging by the scope of his work and its presumed goal, al-Barqī must have been an exceptionally diligent scholar with great ambitions. Accomplishing a project such as this seems to be impossible without complete and hermit-like dedication. That he may have dedicated most of his life to this purpose could indirectly teach us something about his personality, since a project at this scale can only be undertaken by someone entirely devoted, not only to his work but apparently also to his faith. The possibility that *Kitāb al-maḥāsin* was written by more than one person was already mentioned above when referring to al-Barqī's father. Given the gigantic dimensions of the original text, the possibility that al-Barqī, like al-Majlisī in the case of his *Biḥār*, had a team working for him cannot be excluded. Finally, in attempting to form some general impression of the kind of person that al-Barqī was, his uncompromising avoidance of any personal opinions or utterances, although an accepted practice at the time, should be borne in mind as well.

The 11 sub-books that survived from the original *Kitāb al-maḥāsin* and comprise a total of 2,609 traditions are:[29]

---

[27] Al-Najāshī, *Rijāl*, pp. 205–206, gives a list of 93 sub-books that were included in *al-Maḥāsin*; al-Ṭūsī in his *Fihrist*, pp. 44–45, lists 97 sub-books.

[28] Pellat, 'al-Barḳī', pp. 127–128.

[29] For a concise account of the contents of *Kitāb al-maḥāsin* see also Newman, *The Formative Period of Early Shīʿism*, pp. 52–59.

1. *Kitāb al-ashkāl wa'l-qarā'in* ('The book of parallels and comparisons'). This sub-book includes 51 traditions in 11 chapters dealing mostly with instructions for good religious behaviour. The first 8 chapters (43 traditions) are numerological in character and are entitled according to the number with which they deal, from 'the chapter three' until 'the chapter ten'.[30] That the three last chapters do not share this numeric pattern and are entitled: 'the chapter of the benefit of saying good', 'the chapter of the Prophet's instructions' and 'the chapter of the instructions by the descendants of the Prophet', may indicate that originally they belonged to another sub-book. Worth mentioning is the fact that in this particular sub-book Aḥmad's father, Muḥammad, appears in only one chain of transmission.[31]
2. *Kitāb thawāb al-aʿmāl* ('The book of the reward for [good] deeds').[32] This sub-book includes 152 traditions in 123 chapters, mostly concerned with the reward for virtuous deeds, mainly religious duties as obedience to God, prayer, pilgrimage, ablution and repetition of various religious formulae. Of doctrinal importance are chapters 78–87 which describe the reward for different forms of loyalty to the family of the Prophet (*Āl Muḥammad*). Three recurring terms which are used in those chapters to describe the doctrinal principle of loyalty to the family of the Prophet (i.e., the Imams) are worth mentioning: *walāya*, *ḥubb* and *mawadda*.[33]
3. *Kitāb ʿiqāb al-aʿmāl* ('The book of the punishment for [evil] deeds').[34] It includes 143 traditions in 70 chapters, dealing mostly with the punishment for failing to fulfil religious duties (such as prayer, pilgrimage, alms and more) or for vice (killing, adultery, homosexuality, lying and more). Chapters 14–20, which have titles such as 'the punishment of the one who has doubts regarding the Messenger of God, ʿAlī and his descendants' or 'the punishment of the one who denies the right of the descendants of the Prophet and ignores their right to rule (*jahila amrahum*)', describe the punishment for disloyalty or rejection of the descendants of the Prophet, that is, the Imams. The general attitude towards sinners of this kind is to declare them as non-believers since loyalty to ʿAlī and his descendants is considered a fundamental pillar of the faith. To what degree this

---

[30] The resemblance to Ibn Bābawayh's *Kitāb al-khiṣāl*, which is built according to a similar numerological pattern, from 'the chapter one' until 'the chapter over one thousand', is worth mentioning; see in addition Kohlberg's remark about 'the chapter twelve' in Ibn Bābawayh's work and the absence of such a chapter in *Kitāb al-ashkāl wa'l-qarā'in*, in his 'From Imāmiyya to ithnā-ʿashariyya', p. 523.

[31] Al-Barqī, *Kitāb al-maḥāsin*, p. 10, no. 31 (ed. Beirut, p. 11, no. 4); See also note 12 above where it is stated that Aḥmad ascribes almost a third of the traditions in *al-Maḥāsin* to his father.

[32] Note that Ibn Bābawayh has a work with the same title: *Kitāb thawāb al-aʿmāl*.

[33] See Amir-Moezzi, *Divine Guide*, s.v. '*walāya*', and M. A. Amir-Moezzi, 'Notes à propos de la *walāya* Imāmite (aspects de l'imamologie duodécimaine, x)', *JAOS*, 122 (2002), pp. 722–741.

[34] Note that Ibn Bābawayh has also a work entitled *Kitāb ʿiqāb al-aʿmāl*.

principle is important can be seen in the following statement which is ascribed to Jaʿfar al-Ṣādiq: 'Had everyone on earth rejected the commander of the faithful [i.e., ʿAlī], God would have tortured them all and put them in hell.'[35]

4. *Kitāb al-ṣafwa wa'l-nūr wa'l-raḥma* ('The book of the chosen ones, the light and the mercy'). This sub-book includes 201 traditions in 47 chapters. Together with the fifth sub-book it represents the most interesting part of *Kitāb al-maḥāsin* as it includes a rich variety of traditions of both mythical and doctrinal character. As the title of this sub-book indicates, three central motives are significantly important in the attempt to portray the Shiʿi community as an elite chosen minority. Indeed, many traditions in this sub-book depict the creation of the Shiʿi believer as related to these three motives: being chosen on the one hand and the outcome of a unique relationship between the divine light and God's mercy on the other. That the believer's relationships with God, the Prophet, the Imams, his fellow believers and non-believers, are influenced by the character of his creation is only natural and has its far-reaching consequences both in this life and in the afterlife.[36]
5. *Kitāb maṣābīḥ al-ẓulam* ('The book of the lights of darkness'). This sub-book, which is the second largest of *Kitāb al-maḥāsin*, includes 467 traditions in 49 chapters (see the above remark about the fourth sub-book). While the previous sub-book dealt mainly with mythical elements of the Shiʿi belief and doctrine, in this sub-book one witnesses some preliminary attempts at creating a systematic theology. This is not to say that al-Barqī himself is expressing his personal views on different theological issues, but rather that traditions are gathered under chapters which can already be defined as theological; 'the chapter of reason (*al-ʿaql*)', 'the chapter of acknowledging the Imam', 'the chapter of God's guidance to the right path', 'the chapter about the necessity of an Imam (*ʿālim*) on earth at all times' and 'the chapter of *taqiyya* (the obligation to conceal one's beliefs)', to name only a few of the themes that are dealt with in this sub-book. The fact that in most cases the various doctrinal concepts which are expressed in this sub-book do not yet take their final shape is extremely important, since it enables us to examine the Imāmī theology at its very initial stages of development. In addition to theological questions of which the author of *Kitāb al-maḥāsin* was probably aware, one can find valuable information and come to conclusions regarding less obvious theological issues, such as dualism and pre-destination (see below under section VI).
6. *Kitāb al-ʿilal* ('The book of causes').[37] This sub-book includes 130 traditions with no division into chapters. It describes the causes or reasons for a large variety

---

[35] Al-Barqī, *Kitāb al-maḥāsin*, p. 89, no. 36 (ed. Beirut, pp. 61–62, no. 3).

[36] This sub-book was analysed and discussed at length in R. Vilozny, 'A Shīʿī Life Cycle' (see above, note 4).

[37] Ibn Bābawayh also has a work entitled *ʿIlal al-sharāʾiʿ* (The Reasons behind Religious Laws).

of phenomena, mostly from the field of religious law but also in general.[38] A justification (or a 'reason') to compile a book of this sort may be found in the following words which are ascribed to Jaʿfar al-Ṣādiq in one of the traditions of this sub-book: 'God has not done anything without a reason.'[39]

7. *Kitāb al-safar* ('The book of travel'). This sub-book includes 160 traditions in 39/40 chapters (after the 39th chapter there is a titleless chapter that is not included in this sub-book's list of contents). It is concerned with different aspects of travel, both religious and practical: times on which travelling is desired or not desired, various formulae that the traveller should recite before departing, on the benefits of offering alms to the poor on the day of departure, the importance of companions for a journey, where on the way one should not pray, and more.
8. *Kitāb al-ma'ākil* ('The book of foodstuffs'). This is by far the largest sub-book in *Kitāb al-maḥāsin*. It includes 981 traditions in 127 chapters. This sub-book deals with different kinds of food and with phenomena related to eating from different perspectives: legal, nutritional, medical, social and more. Some chapters in this sub-book are devoted to the way one should behave in circumstances that involve foodstuffs or eating. Chapters of this kind may describe the duty to feed others, to invite and accept invitation for dining, the ablution prior to eating, formulae that should be recited prior to a meal or after eating, and more. Many chapters are entitled according to the specific kind of food with which they deal: 'the chapter of meat', 'the chapter of kebab', 'the chapter of rice', 'the chapter of olives', and so forth. In this kind of chapter one may learn about the nutritional values of various foodstuffs as well as of legal restrictions regarding other kinds of foods (for example: 'the chapter of forbidden meats').
9. *Kitāb al-mā'* ('The book of water'). This sub-book includes 114 traditions in 20 chapters. It deals with the value of water in general – 'Water is the lord of beverages in this world and in the afterlife'[40] – and water from certain sources (Zamzam, Euphrates) in particular, as well as with some legal aspects of water and its consumption. Chapter 9 is devoted to sorts of water that should not be consumed: salty water and water of hot springs in the mountains that smell of sulphur. (Chapters 13–20 seem to belong to 'the book of foodstuffs' and not to 'the book of water'.)
10. *Kitāb al-manāfiʿ* ('The book of benefits'). This is the shortest sub-book: it includes 33 traditions in 6 chapters and is concerned mostly with different ways of reaching a decision in times of confusion or perplexity. According to this sub-book, there are three different ways to reach a firm resolution in times of confusion: *istikhāra* (turning to God in order to reach the better decision), *istishāra* (asking advice from other human beings) and *qurʿa* (lot-casting, performed by an Imam). To each of these methods a chapter in this sub-book is

[38] This sub-book was analysed and discussed at length in R. Vilozny, 'Réflexions sur le *Kitāb al-ʿIlal*' (see above, note 4).

[39] Al-Barqī, *Kitāb al-maḥāsin*, p. 333, no. 100 (ed. Beirut, p. 233. no. 100).

[40] Ibid., p. 570, no. 2 (ed. Beirut, p. 397, no. 2).

devoted. On the difficulty that these methods raise in a community guided by an Imam see below (section XI).

11. *Kitāb al-marāfiq* ('The book of the household'). This sub-book, the last in the printed editions, includes 174 traditions in 16 chapters. It deals with legal and practical aspects of house maintenance (building, cleaning, servants, animals and more). Alongside traditions that define the minimum size of a room on a roof in which one can sleep overnight,[41] we can find an instruction ascribed to the Prophet to sweep the courtyards in order not to become similar to the Jews.[42]

It seems to the author of the present lines that discussing in detail a small number of traditions would be the best way of acquainting the reader with the contents and characteristics of *Kitāb al-maḥāsin*. In the eleven sections that follow (II–XII) only a single tradition from each sub-book will be presented and analysed. Naturally, these eleven traditions, which serve as specific case studies of this chapter's main case study, al-Barqī, cannot cover every aspect and theme in a text of more than 2,600 traditions. However, as will be seen below, these traditions are representative for two main reasons: first, each of them gives the reader a taste of the essence and characteristics of the relevant sub-book, and second, in most cases the chosen tradition is only one example from within a group of traditions with a similar message. Furthermore, we will see that these eleven traditions that belong to a variety of fields deal, either directly or indirectly, with some of the most important aspects of the Shiʿi doctrine.

At any rate, the following selection should not be regarded as an attempt to cover the whole, but rather as 11 short in-depth probes into the heart of each of the surviving parts of the text. It seems that combined with the present biographical-bibliographical section, a fair overview of the text could be gained. Although the different selected traditions may at times seem to have no common denominator, since they merely reflect the eclectic character of *Kitāb al-maḥāsin*, we will see that a few general remarks can be made and prove relevant for them all (see below under conclusion).

II. *Kitāb al-ashkāl wa'l-qarā'in* ('The Book of Parallels and Comparisons')

'Al-Barqī – [missing chain of transmission] – Salmān [al-Fārisī, or 'Alī b. Abū Ṭālib],[43] may God be pleased with him, said: "Three things make me laugh and three things make me cry. The three that make me cry are: the departure [i.e., death] of those

---

[41] Ibid., p. 621, no. 62 (ed. Beirut, p. 430, no. 1).

[42] Ibid., p. 624, no. 76 (ed. Beirut, p. 432, no. 2).

[43] In al-Barqī's version, after 'Salmān' the verb 'said' appears twice and therefore it is not entirely clear whether this tradition is ascribed to Salmān or to 'Alī, to whom he was very close; in two places in al-Majlisī's *Biḥār al-anwār* (Tehran, 1956–1972), vol. 68, p. 266, no. 9 (from Fattāl's *Rawḍat al-wāʿiẓīn*) and vol. 70, p. 94, no. 73 (from Ibn Bābawayh's *Khiṣāl*) a somewhat different version of this tradition on the authority of Salmān is cited. At any rate, this is not a typical *isnād* and may well be related to Salmān's special status and relationship with 'Alī. For

beloved [by God]: Muḥammad and his party; the horror during the mortal throes; facing the Lord of the Universes on the Day upon which all secrets will become public, not knowing whether I am headed for heaven or for hell. As for the three that make me laugh: a person who is neglectful [of his duties] but whose deeds do not [lit., 'but who does not'] go unnoticed [by God];[44] a person who is chasing this world while death is chasing him; a person who is laughing his head off while not knowing whether his Lord is satisfied or angry at him".'[45]

It is more than likely that this tradition is expected to be read by people to whom it is clear beyond any doubt that an Imam does not share his feelings with an audience unless he has a very good reason to do so. This observation seems to be relevant in our case, whether the speaker in the present tradition is the first Imam or Salmān, whose status is here elevated almost to that of an Imam.[46] Information given by an Imam, who is regarded as a model for imitation, must be of an instructive or a guiding character. In the present case this would naturally mean that one's feelings with regard to the six facts mentioned in the tradition should be similar to those of the Imam. Furthermore, as crying and laughing represent deep emotions, having similar feelings towards these six facts cannot be the outcome of simple imitation and must be the result of a certain way of life. A summary of the main principles of this way would be:

1. To mourn the death of the Prophet and members of his party.
2. Awareness of death and of the horrible tortures which are part of it.
3. Fearing the Day of Judgement.
4. Belief in God's omniscience (particularly noticeable on the Day of Judgement).
5. Belief in the existence of heaven and hell.
6. Accepting the fact that throughout life one does not know what his fate in the afterlife will be.
7. Negligence in fulfilling one's duties does not meet equal attitude on the part of God.

more, see G. Levi Della Vida, 'Salmān al-Fārisī', *EI2*, vol. 12 (supplement), pp. 701–702; see also note 46 below.

44 This statement may well be alluding to the Qur'anic expression *wa-mā llāhu/rabbuka bighāfilin ʿammā taʿmalūn/yaʿmalūn* 'what you do does not go unnoticed by God' which appears nine times in different verses and another time in a slightly different rephrasing *wa-lā taḥsabanna llāha ghāfilan ʿammā yaʿmalu al-ẓālimūn* (Q.14:42).

45 Al-Barqī, *Kitāb al-ashkāl wal-qarā'in*, p. 4, no. 6 (ed. Beirut, p. 8, no. 6); quoted in al-Majlisī, *Biḥār al-anwār* (Tehran, 1956–1972), vol. 67, p. 386, no. 50; for another version of this tradition see also al-Barqī, p. 4, no. 7 (ed. Beirut, p. 8. no. 7) where the three things that made Salmān laugh in tradition no. 6 are presented as making [another Imam or Salmān] wonder.

46 See E. Kohlberg, 'The Term "Muḥaddath" in Twelver Shīʿism', in *Studia Orientalia memoiriae D. H. Baneth dedicata* (Jerusalem, 1979), pp. 39–47, repr. in his *Belief and Law*, article V. Of special relevance to the present case is Kohlberg's description (pp. 42–43) of the tension and doctrinal problems created by Salmān's special status as a *muḥaddath* (i.e., 'to whom an angel speaks').

8. Earthly desires are meaningless if the ephemerality of life is taken into consideration.
9. Laughter in light of one's ignorance regarding God's opinion about him is legitimate only to a certain extent.

That the inclusion of this tradition in the sub-book of 'comparisons and parallels' is justified seems to be obvious: Salmān (or the first Imam) is comparing the things that make him cry with those that make him laugh by presenting them as two parallel, even opposite, groups. A closer examination of the two different groups reveals that, excluding the first thing that makes him cry, Salmān cries or laughs at the very same things; the only thing varying between the two is the perspective. The other side of fearing death is ignoring it and chasing worldly pleasures. Not knowing whether you are headed for heaven or for hell is equivalent to ignorance regarding the degree of God's satisfaction or dissatisfaction. To these two pairs one may add the first thing that makes Salmān laugh, that is, the negligence of duties which does not go unnoticed by God, as this too points to peoples' lack of the desired balance or awareness of their own state vis-à-vis greater things, as God, heaven and hell, and death. The unique thing about the first thing, that is, the departure of the ones beloved by God, is that it refers to something external rather than to some inner fear or misbalance.

Despite the impression that there is nothing specifically Shiʿi about this tradition, one can assume that what makes Salmān (or ʿAlī, the first Imam) cry must also characterise true believers and that the things that make him laugh may apply to non-Shiʿis. In other words, listing various things under two opposing categories – crying and laughter – seems to fit very well the dualistic world view which is so typical of the Shiʿi religion.[47]

If this (as well as other traditions of this sort) is an authentic one, Salmān's (or the Imam's) choice to rephrase some principles using numerological structure, three against three in the 'chapter of three', may raise some questions; mainly: why would an Imam choose to use numerical elements to express his opinion? That the Imam uses this literary, or rhetorical, technique as a mnemonic device is only one possible answer. However, in this context, the striking similarity to the pre-Islamic Persian *andarz* literature is worth mentioning.

In his encyclopaedic entry, Shaked defines the *andarz*, or the 'instruction/guidance/advice literature' as a genre meant to provide various behaviour instructions, both religious and non-religious, usually from an authoritative figure to commoners.[48] Remarkably relevant for our present discussion is the fact that one of the stylistic means of this literature is the use of numbers. Various types of people, qualities and different matters are discussed under numerological titles. At times, good and bad qualities are listed against each other according to their quantity. This Persian

[47] For more about dualism, see below under section VI.

[48] See S. Shaked, 'Andarz', *EIR*, vol. 2, pp. 11–116; S. Shaked, *Wisdom of the Sasanian Sages* (Boulder, CO, 1979), Introduction, pp. xv–xviii.

genre is dated as early as the Avesta period and considerable parts of it were translated into Arabic during the first three centuries of Islam. Many *adab* writers quoted directly or indirectly from this literature and Shaked does not exclude the possibility that it also filtered into the literature of *ḥadīth*, although it is not easily traceable.[49]

Should traditions of this sort not be authentic, what they may represent is a later adaptation of the Shiʿi doctrine to this unique literary genre by arranging it according to a numerological pattern and ascribing it retrospectively to the Imams.

III. *Kitāb thawāb al-aʿmāl* ('The Book of the Reward for [Good] Deeds')

'Al-Barqī,Yaʿqūb b. Yazīd, Muḥammad b. Abī ʿUmayr, Bakr b. Muḥammad, Fuḍayl b. Yasār, Abū ʿAbdallāh [Jaʿfar al-Ṣādiq], peace be upon him, said: "Whenever we are mentioned [reading *dhukirnā*] in the presence of someone and as a result his eyes flow [with tears], be it only to the amount of a fly wing, God will forgive his sins even if they are as [many as] the foam of the sea".'[50]

That this tradition is intended to emphasise the importance of remembering the Imams – an elementary part of the believer's duty to love the Imams[51] – is self-evident. The emotional dimension which is presented in this tradition as critical for a reward, and which is expressed by shedding tears, seems to be worth closer examination. Why should the secreting of some tears, which may be as small as the wing of a fly, while remembering the family of the Prophet or the Imams, justify the erasure of one's sins, no matter how many they may be? It must mean that for Jaʿfar al-Ṣādiq, shedding tears, perhaps generally, but clearly when remembering the Imams, symbolises something extremely important.[52]

Although it is not explicitly stated in the tradition, one may conclude that the reward for remembering the Imams without shedding a tear must be smaller, but probably still existent.[53] Worth noting is the fact that 'The book of punishment for

---

[49] Ibid.

[50] Al-Barqī, *Kitāb thawāb al-aʿmāl*, p. 63, no. 110 (ed. Beirut, p. 44, no. 1); quoted in *Biḥār al-anwār*, vol. 71, p. 351, no. 18 (from al-Ḥimyarī, *Qurb al-isnād*, p. 18 and Ibn Bābawayh, *Thawāb al-aʿmāl*, p. 170) with two optional readings of the verb 'mentioned': active (*dhakaranā*) and passive (*dhukirnā*) which appears to be the better reading; and vol. 44, p. 282, no. 14 (from *Qurb al-isnād*, p.26) with the addition that 'God will be merciful towards whoever lends life to our cause (*aḥyā amranā*, i.e., the Shiʿi belief)'.

[51] On the duty to love the Imams, see Amir-Moezzi, *Divine Guide*, s.v. '*walāya*' and M. A. Amir-Moezzi, 'Notes à propos de la *walāya* Imāmite (aspects de l'imamologie duodécimaine, x), *JAOS*, 122 (2002), pp. 722–741.

[52] Another situation in which weeping plays an essential role are the *taʿziya* celebrations; see M. Ayoub, *Redemptive Suffering in Islām: A Study of the Devotional Aspects of ʿĀshūrāʾ in Twelver Shīʿism* (The Hague, 1978).

[53] See al-Barqī, *Kitāb thawāb al-aʿmāl*, p. 62, no. 107 (ed. Beirut, p. 43, no. 1) where the reward for remembering the family of the Prophet [without shedding tears] is cure of illnesses and protection against evil thoughts.

[evil] deeds' does not include punishment for remembering the Imams *without* shedding tears. To use legal terminology, 'shedding a tear' when remembering the Imams could be regarded as a desired deed rather than an obligatory one. It is as if the tear is seen as a proof or an indicator for the level of faith, and shedding it is necessarily the result of deep emotional involvement on the part of the believer.

Normally, in traditions of this sort, the believer is confronted with a certain model of behaviour for which a person may be rewarded or punished. The believer is naturally expected either to imitate the positive example or avoid the negative one. The implication of this rule in the case of the 'tear tradition' would be that a believer should aspire to reach the emotional state in which remembering the Imams brings him to tears.

The idea that the way to reach this level is not specified by the Imam may lead us to the conclusion that such matters are not in the hands of the believer: either you have it in you or you do not. On the other hand, one cannot ignore the strong mystical echo resulting from the combination of a principle of faith and an external expression of emotion. If so, the way to reach the desired emotional level, of shedding a tear while remembering the Imams, is clear: mysticism.

Finally, a few words about the remarkable contrast in the Imam's words between the smallest human tear and the foam of the sea seem to be worthwhile. One drop of salty water created by the eye of the believer while remembering the Imams is weighed against the foam created by all the salty water of the sea. The contrast between the salty water of a tear, as representing deep emotions and supreme values, and the foam created by other salty water, as representing the quantity of sins, is not likely to be coincidental and may well be related to the concept of purity versus impurity.[54]

IV. *Kitāb ʿIqāb al-aʿmāl* ('The Book of the Punishment for [Evil] Deeds')

'Al-Barqī, Muḥammad b. 'Alī, al-Faḍl b. Ṣāliḥ al-Asadī, Muḥammad b. Marwān, Abū 'Abdallāh [Ja'far al-Ṣādiq], peace be upon him, said: "The Messenger of God said: 'Whoever hates us, the family of the Prophet (*ahl al-bayt*), God will resurrect him as a Jew.' Someone said: 'Oh, the Messenger of God, even if he acknowledged the two *shahādas*?' [The Prophet] said: 'Yes, by those two pronouncements he is only protected from having his blood split or [paying] the poll-tax (*jizya*), which involves humiliation.' Then he repeated: 'Whoever hates us, the family of the Prophet (*ahl al-bayt*), God will resurrect him as a Jew.' Someone then asked: 'And how is that, oh,

[54] It is worth noting that the use of the expression 'as [many as] the foam of the sea (*zabad al-baḥr*)' to describe a very large amount of sins is common in Shiʿi sources. See for example al-Ṭūsī, *Miṣbāḥ al-mutahajjid*, p. 261, where recitation of the verse 'He is one God' [Q.112:1] 200 times in four *rakʿas* erases one's sins 'even if they were as many as the foam of the sea'.

Messenger of God?' [The Prophet] said: 'Had this person lived long enough until the false messiah (*dajjāl*)[55] appeared, he would have believed in him'."[56]

If the previous tradition dealt mainly with the principle of love towards the Imams, this one, which deals with hatred towards them, may be seen as its mirror image. In fact, by stating what the destiny of those who hate the Imams will be, the contrary, or at least the negation of this destiny may be ascribed to the ones who love the Imams – they will be resurrected as true believers, or at least not as Jews.

Two communities are presented in a pejorative way in this tradition: Muslims who acknowledge God's unity and the message of His Prophet (the two *shahādas*), but express hatred towards the Imams, and Jews who are only used as an example for bad destiny. The main tension in the tradition is that between the Shiʿi community and the Muslim non-Shiʿi one. Although there is no discussion of Muslims who acknowledge both *shahādas*, do not hate the Imams and neither love them nor are loyal to them, the existence of such a category could not be excluded. Restricting the discussion solely to Muslims who hate the Imams goes hand in hand with the Shiʿi dualistic perception of the world – one can be on the right side and love the Imams or on the wrong side and hate them.

Arguing that the two *shahādas* – the first pillar of Islam – are worthless if one hates the Imams is a private case of one of the common Shiʿi means of showing superiority over other forms of Islam, that is, depriving fundamental principles of Islam of any value, given that a person fails to fulfil his duties as a Shiʿi.[57] What is unique about the present tradition is that the Imam also supplies us with some further information on the worthlessness of the two *shahādas* when pronounced by an anti-Shiʿi Muslim – such a Muslim must have acknowledged them for the wrong reasons: protection from bloodshed or avoiding the poll tax.

It would be quite reasonable to assume that hating the Imams is a horrible sin for which the punishment has to be a dreadful one – being resurrected as a Jew must therefore be seen as just such a punishment.[58] That the Imam does not feel the need to explain why it is so bad to be resurrected as a Jew may indicate that this was at his time common knowledge. In other words, the state of the Jew – at least as the Imam

---

55 See A. Abel, 'Al-Dadjdjāl', *EI2*, vol. 2, pp. 76–77.

56 Al-Barqī, *Kitāb ʿiqāb al-aʿmāl*, p. 90, no. 39 (ed. Beirut, p. 62, no.1); quoted in *Biḥār al-anwār*, vol. 52, p. 192, no. 25 and vol. 69, p. 134, no. 13; and with some minor variations also in Ibn Bābawayh, *Kitāb ʿiqāb al-aʿmāl*, pp. 203–204.

57 See the discussion of the worthlessness of the performance of religious duties when one fails to acknowledge the basic Shiʿi principles in R. Vilozny, 'A Shīʿī Life Cycle', pp. 394–395.

58 Compare with al-Barqī, *Kitāb ʿiqāb al-aʿmāl*, p. 91, no. 42 (ed. Beirut, p. 63, no. 4) where the punishment for hating the Imams is being resurrected as leprous, or with al-Barqī, *Kitāb ʿiqāb al-aʿmāl*, p. 153, no. 76 (ed. Beirut, p. 100, no. 1) where the punishment is hell, and what determines in which category of hell one will be is the level of his hatred (the worst is hating by heart, tongue and hand).

saw it – including the consequence of being resurrected as one, must have been familiar to the common Shiʿi listener.[59]

The reason why a Muslim who hates the Imams will be resurrected as a Jew is related directly to the assumption that such a Muslim would probably believe in the false messiah, the *dajjāl*, if only he lived long enough to witness his appearance.[60] A subsequent conclusion may therefore be that believing in the *dajjāl* was a main accusation of Shiʿis against the Jews. This issue may have been so central in inter-religious debate that the Imam thought of it as a good enough argument to explain to his audience why an anti-Shiʿi will be resurrected as a Jew.

V. *Kitāb al-ṣafwa wa'l-nūr wa'l-raḥma* ('The Book of the Chosen Ones, the Light and the Mercy')

'Al-Barqī, Ibn Maḥbūb, ʿAmr b. Abī al-Miqdām, Mālik b. Aʿyan al-Juhanī: Abū ʿAbdallāh [Jaʿfar al-Ṣādiq], peace be upon him, came to me and said: "Oh Mālik, by God, you are truly/rightfully our party (*shīʿatunā*). Oh Mālik, indeed you may think that you have gone too far in describing our superiority [but this is not the case]. No one can describe God nor fully grasp the essence of His omnipotence and greatness. Just as no one can fully grasp God's attribute nor the essence of His omnipotence and greatness – since 'to God applies the highest attribute' [Q.16:60] – no one is able to describe the Messenger of God, may God pray upon him and his family, nor our superiority and what God bestowed upon us, nor the duties that He obliged [others to fulfil] with regard to us. Just as no one is able to describe our superiority, nor what God bestowed upon us, nor do justice to the duties that He obliged his fellow believers to fulfil with regard to Him. By God, Oh Mālik, when two believers meet and shake hands God looks at them with love and compassion, the sins then fall off of their faces and organs until they separate. Who then can describe God or those whose state with God is such?"'[61]

This tradition was chosen mainly due to the fact that it clearly underlines several central and recurring themes in the Imāmī self-perception: hierarchy, exclusivity, superiority and solidarity.

1. Hierarchy: even though the Imams' status in practice may often seem higher than that of the Prophet (compare, for example, the number of traditions ascribed to

---

[59] For more on the status of Jews in early Shiʿi literature, see M. M. Bar-Asher, 'On the Place of Judaism and Jews in the Religious Literature of the Early Shīʿa', *Peamim*, 61 (1994), pp. 16–36 (in Hebrew).

[60] On the concept of *dajjāl* in Shiʿi thought, see D. Cook, *Studies in Muslim Apocalyptic* (Princeton, 2000), pp. 221–225.

[61] Al-Barqī, *Kitāb al-ṣafwa wa'l-nūr wa'l-raḥma*, p. 143, no. 41 (ed. Beirut, p. 94. no. 1); quoted in *Biḥār al-anwār*, vol. 71, p. 226, no. 18 and in vol. 64, p. 65, no. 13 (from *Kitāb al-mu'min* of al-Ḥusayn b. Saʿīd, p. 31, no. 59) .

the Prophet with those ascribed to the fifth and sixth Imams in the Shiʿi *ḥadīth*), the commonly accepted doctrine is that reflected in the above-quoted tradition: God – the Prophet – the Imams – the believers. Although not explicitly stated, it is quite obvious that whoever is not included in this description, that is, non-Shiʿis, must be inferior. Remarkably, this hierarchical scheme is meant not only to establish the relative position of its constituent members, but also to present them as belonging to one group elevated above all others (see below). Several aspects of the tradition bear witness to the special affinity between representatives of the various levels that comprise this group; thus, a believer has a discussion with an Imam; the Imam describes this believer as being a member of his party; God is compassionate and loving towards the believers.[62]

2. Superiority: the notion of God's transcendent superiority as well as the notion of the Prophet's superiority over other human beings seem to be of less interest for the present discussion and are common also to other currents within Islam, as well as to other religions. However, presenting the superiority of the Imams and especially that of the Shiʿi community by comparing it to God's divine attributes or to His omnipotence is not self-evident. Claiming that the difficulty to grasp the status of the Imams or that of the believers is equal to the difficulty to grasp the nature of God may be a step in the direction of deification, even if the Imam had different intentions in mind.[63] On the other hand, presenting the status of the Imams and their community as something beyond human grasp may be regarded as an attempt to explain why the Shiʿis, despite their superiority, remained a persecuted minority. Had this status been graspable, it must have had its evident consequences in practice and not only in theory. Needless to say, this superiority has its unseen benefits: God's love and compassion and the erasure of sins which strongly allude to the eschatological era.
3. Solidarity: emphasis is placed on the act of two fellow believers shaking hands. The impression gained is that this specific action is so crucial for attaining God's love and compassion that questions regarding the fate of the believer who does not shake hands with his fellow believer may seem appropriate. Will such a believer be deprived of God's love and compassion? A possible answer may be that expressing solidarity in the form of shaking hands is a characteristic

[62] On the tension between the attempt to create hierarchy in the community and at the same time to elevate the status of its ordinary members, see E. Kohlberg, 'Imam and Community in the Pre-Ghayba Period', in Said Amir Arjomand, ed., *Authority and Political Culture in Shiʿism* (Albany, NY, 1988), pp. 25–53, repr. in *Belief and Law*, article XIII. On p. 31 this tension is demonstrated through the analysis of traditions that depict Imams and believers as being created from similar substances.

[63] For more on the close relationship between representatives of the different levels, God – Imams – believers, see M. A. Amir-Moezzi, 'Seul l'homme de Dieu est humain: Théologie et anthropologie mystique à travers l'exégèse Imāmite ancienne (Aspects de l'Imamologie Duodécimaine IV)', *Arabica*, 45 (1998), pp. 193–214, and M. A. Amir-Moezzi, *The Spirituality of Shiʿi Islam* (London, 2011), ch. 3, 'Some Remarks on the Divinity of the Imam', pp. 103–131.

common to all believers and it is therefore clear that all of them enjoy God's love and compassion. It is not the only case in which the believer's sins are forgiven, but depicting the erasure of sins as a result of this physical expression of solidarity seems noteworthy and may well be related to the above-mentioned aspect: creating a clear hierarchy but simultaneously maintaining firm relations between members of each level and between members of various levels. One could picture some sort of unique mechanism, comprising four layers that are both vertically and horizontally linked and separated at the same time.

4. Exclusivity: that all the above is limited only to members of the Shiʿi community is implied in the text and needs no further clarification. However, one thing seems to be embedded in members of the Shiʿi community and in others alike: people of both groups are unable to grasp the status of the believer with God. The difference is that while a true believer fulfils his duties towards his fellow believer as part of his obedience to God, the non-Shiʿi ignores them.

VI. *Kitāb maṣābīḥ al-ẓulam* ('The Book of the Lights of Darkness')

'Al-Barqī, ʿAlī b. Ḥadīd, Samāʿa b. Mihrān: I was at Abū ʿAbdallāh's [Jaʿfar al-Ṣādiq], peace be upon him, while he was hosting several of his companions.[64] When the issue of reason and ignorance was brought up,[65] he, peace be upon him, said: "If you know reason and its armies and ignorance and its armies, you will be guided to the right path." I [i.e., Samāʿa] said: "Oh, may I be your ransom, we know only what you teach us!" Abū ʿAbdallāh said: "God created from His light[66] reason, which was the first among the spiritual creatures, to the right of His throne and told it to turn around and it did. Then He told it to come close and it did. God, may he be exalted, said: 'I created you as a great creation and I honoured you above the rest of my creatures.' Then God created ignorance from the salty dark sea and told it to turn around and it did, and then He told it to come close and it did not. God asked it: "Are you being arrogant?' And He cursed it. Then God created for reason 75 armies. When ignorance saw the honour which God bestowed on reason and what he gave it, it [ignorance] developed hatred towards it [reason] and said: 'Oh, my Lord, this is a creature just like me; you created it and honoured it and strengthened it and I, who am his opponent have no strength against it. Give me armies equal to those you gave it.' God said: 'Yes, but if you disobey afterwards, I shall remove you and your armies from my mercy.' Ignorance said: 'I agree,' so God gave it 75 armies. Among the 75 armies

[64] Note that the word *mawālīhi*, which was translated as 'companions' may also be translated as 'followers' when vocalised as *muwālīhi*.

[65] Amir-Moezzi discusses at length the terms reason and ignorance in his *Divine Guide*; see '*ʿaql*' and '*jahl*'.

[66] On the concept of 'light', see U. Rubin, 'Pre-Existence and Light: Aspects of the Concept of Nūr Muḥammad', *Israel Oriental Studies*, 5 (1975), pp. 62–112; Amir-Moezzi, *Divine Guide*, '*nūr*'.

that God gave reason was goodness, who is the minister [or, assistant] of reason, He established as its opponent evil, who is the minister [or, assistant] of ignorance".'[67]

Following 'good and evil' there is a long list of 74 pairs, which may best be described as representing positive and negative human qualities. Finally, the Imam claims that all the armies of reason are to be found in a prophet, an Imam or in a believer whose heart was tested by God. In ordinary believers there must be a minimum of reason which enables them to complete the rest, avoid ignorance and thus to be on the same level with prophets and Imams.

Dualism and determinism, probably two of the most important aspects of the early Shiʿi doctrine, seem to be the main themes of the present tradition. The coming to being of the spiritual entities in this world was followed immediately by a primordial struggle between reason and ignorance. Although it is not explicitly stated in the tradition, it is reasonable to assume that this struggle will last as long as the world exists. Why God decided to create ignorance and ignite this eternal struggle is not explained in the tradition. For an observer from the outside this story could seem as a possible mythical solution for the existence of evil in a world created by an omnipotent God.[68] In Shiʿi eyes what we see is the background for the main axis around which everything in this world turns – reason versus ignorance, good versus evil.

Everything in this world must be affiliated with either of the two poles – reason/good and ignorance/evil – and there appears to be no room for flexibility. It is quite clear that this polar depiction of the spiritual entities is an allegory of the state of man, or of the inner struggle that exists in every human being (excluding prophets, Imams and 'believers whose hearts were tested by God') between good and evil.[69] Seeing man's inner complexity merely as a polar struggle between two possible extremities has far-reaching deterministic and dualistic implications. Furthermore, the 75 pairs of good and bad qualities seem to represent the entire spectrum of the human character or personality, as if man could develop only according to the qualities in this list. That these spiritual entities were created prior to the creation of man must mean that man was created into an existing dualistic pattern and, therefore, must adapt to it.

---

[67] Al-Barqī, *Kitāb maṣābīḥ al-ẓulam*, pp. 196–198, no. 22 (ed. Beirut, pp. 130–131, no. 22); quoted in *Biḥār al-anwār*, vol. 1, pp. 109–111, no. 7; see also al-Kulaynī, *Uṣūl al-kāfī*, vol. 1, pp. 20–23, no. 14; Ibn Bābawayh, *ʿIlal al-sharāʾiʿ*, vol. 1, pp. 113–115, no. 10; for other versions [for] of the creation of 'good' and 'evil' see *Kitāb maṣābīḥ al-ẓulam*, pp. 281–282, nos. 412–413 (ed. Beirut, pp. 191–92, nos. 2–3), where another interesting dimension comes to the fore: that in reality there is no perfect dualism; it is noteworthy that similar ideas are expressed in al-Mufaḍḍal b. ʿUmar al-Juʿfī's *Kitāb al-haft waʾl-aẓilla* which is one of the important texts adumbrating the early Nuṣayrī religion; see H. Halm, *Die islamische Gnosis* (Zurich and Munich, 1982), pp. 240–274.

[68] On the problematics that this question raises in general, see R. Schulze, 'Das Böse in der Islamischen Tradition', in J. Laube, ed., *Das Böse in den Welt-Religionen* (Darmstadt, 2003), pp. 131–200.

[69] According to the chapter of 'The creation of good and evil' in *Kitāb maṣābīḥ al-ẓulam*, pp. 283–284 (ed. Beirut, pp. 192–193), a person is good or evil solely as a result of God's determination, not as the outcome of an inner struggle.

Fortunately, all Shiʿi believers are created with the minimum number of armies of reason required in order to complete the rest and avoid ignorance. One can conclude that non-Shiʿis are likely to be created without this required minimum and, therefore, will inevitably be affiliated with ignorance and its armies. Naturally, this deterministic state of things is meant to present the Shiʿi community in a positive light as the chosen ones. However, the lack of independent judgement on the part of the believer could somewhat tarnish this ideal image (unless we choose to understand that having the required minimum of reason only provides the believer with the ability to complete the rest on his own, but he is not forced to do so).

Another expression for the cost of the effort to present the 'right side' in an idealistic manner can be seen in the way the tradition portrays reason and ignorance: Obedience on the part of reason and disobedience on the part of ignorance lead to an equal outcome, as each received from God the same quantity of armies. The difference between the two is that whereas reason obtained it as a reward for its blind obedience, ignorance earned it through intelligent arguments in its negotiations with God. Reading the story from this perspective may easily reverse its intended purpose and present ignorance as having the upper hand, especially since it is only due to its behaviour that reason and ignorance have become equal rivals.

VII. *Kitāb al-ʿilal* ('The Book of Causes')

'Al-Barqī, his father, al-Ḥasan b. Maḥbūb, Muḥammad b. Qazʿa: I told Abū ʿAbdallāh [Jaʿfar al-Ṣādiq], peace be upon him, that people among us say that Abraham circumcised himself using an adz over a wine jug(?). He [Jaʿfar al-Ṣādiq] said: "by God, it is not like they say, they lied about Abraham." He [b. Qazʿa] said: "How is that?" [Jaʿfar al-Ṣādiq] said: "In the case of the prophets, the foreskin used to fall off together with the navel [cord?] on the seventh day. When Ishmael was born to Abraham from Hagar his foreskin fell off with his navel and following this Sarah berated Hagar, as she would do to the slave girls. Hagar cried as it was hard for her and when Ishmael saw her he cried since she was crying. Abraham came in and asked: 'Ishmael, why are you crying?' And he told him that Sarah had berated his mother for such and such reasons and that he cried since his mother cried. Abraham went to his praying place and addressed his God asking him to relieve Hagar from that thing and God did it. Afterwards Sarah gave birth to Isaac and on the seventh day his navel fell off but not his foreskin and this saddened Sarah. When Abraham came in she asked him: "What is the thing that happened to Abraham's family and to the sons of the prophets? The navel of your son, Isaac, fell off whereas his foreskin did not.' Abraham went again to his praying place and addressed his Lord asking Him what is the thing that happened to Abraham's family and to the sons of the prophets – the navel of his son, Isaac, fell off, whereas his foreskin did not. God revealed to him: 'Oh, Abraham, this is the result of Sarah's condemnation of Hagar – I promised to myself that I would not make it [the foreskin] fall off to any of the prophets' sons after Sarah's rebuke of Hagar. Circumcise Isaac with a knife and let him taste the heat of the metal.'

And Abraham circumcised him using a knife and circumcision became the practice (*sunna*) among the people".'[70]

The attempt to provide answers to some of the fundamental mysteries of life in the form of a religious doctrine, normally accompanied by a codex of religious laws, does not necessarily make it easier for man to understand them. It is true that in God, who is seen in religions such as Islam as an omniscient and omnipotent entity, one should seek all the answers, but as the present tradition demonstrates, this is not enough. It is only natural that living according to a detailed legal system will raise endless questions to which the answer 'because God decided so' is not sufficient. Even when God's omniscience and omnipotence are taken for granted, the human mind requires a logical or a reasonable explanation for various phenomena – a thing that in itself must derive from a divine reason or cause (if one is to apply some religious thinking to the present discussion).

As we witness in the text, men came up with a variety of reasons for the custom of circumcision. The one given by the disciple in the text is based upon the version that he heard regarding the circumcision of Abraham. According to this version, Abraham had performed the procedure on himself and, being the founder forefather, by doing so he instituted the norm. If we consider this tradition to be authentic, what we have is a perplexed disciple who wants to verify whether a possible explanation for a religious custom is true or false. If not, the disciple's version may be nothing more than a literary stratagem to present the Imāmī point of view regarding the custom of circumcision. At any case, the question must have preoccupied the community.

In addition to the 'real' reason for the institution of the circumcision, an examination of the Imāmī version reveals several other meaningful aspects. The fact that the foreskin used to fall off by itself in the case of prophets and sons of prophets must have been the outcome of God's will and thus necessarily represents the desired physical condition.

A natural, not to say a miraculous, biological phenomenon that characterised prophets and their sons was stopped by God following the birth of Ishmael. In other words, Ishmael was the last son of a prophet whose 'circumcision' occurred naturally, without human interference. Sarah is to be blamed for God's decision to stop this phenomenon from happening any more, as it was a result of her reproach of Hagar after Ishmael's birth. In a way, her behaviour, following which the prophets and their children were deprived of a unique privilege, could be compared with that of Adam, in which too a woman was involved, and that resulted in his expulsion from paradise. Something in the ideal form of creation was damaged and it is man's duty to try to

[70] Al-Barqī, *Kitāb al-ʿilal*, pp. 300–301 (ed. Beirut, p. 208, no. 6); a short version of this tradition is in *Biḥār al-anwār*, vol. 12, p. 8, no. 22 and a full one in vol. 101, pp. 113–114, no. 27; both quotations in the *Biḥār* are from *ʿIlal al-sharāʾiʿ* of Ibn Bābawayh (vol. 2, pp. 505–506, no. 1), and there is no reference to *Kitāb al-maḥāsin*; the last three words 'among the people' are based on the version of *ʿIlal al-sharāʾiʿ* which is cited in *Biḥār* (vol. 101, pp. 113–114, no. 27) and ends with the words: *fiʾl-nās*. The reading '*fī Isḥāq*' which appears in *al-Maḥāsin* could – with difficulty – be understood as 'according to the precedent established in the case of Isaac'.

regain it, but as we learn both from the present tradition and the story of Adam, pain will be for ever part of this effort.

However, the fact that it is Sarah who is responsible for this divine decision does not mean that her part in the story is wholly negative. After all, it is she who is behind the custom of circumcision as we know it until today, and her son, Isaac, was the first to undergo it. As for Abraham and Ishmael, they represent the last examples of the 'pre-Sarah–Hagar incident', in which bodies of prophets and sons of prophets used to get their divinely desired shape – the model for generations to come – in a natural way.

An interesting paradox may arise when one tries to settle this tradition with the Imāmī belief that the Prophet and all Imams were born circumcised. An attempt to resolve this contradiction from an internal perspective, or from a Shiʿi point of view, could rely on the well-known affinity between Abraham and Muḥammad, who are regarded as the forefathers and representatives of the true monotheistic belief – Islam as a late representation of *dīn Ibrāhīm*. From an external perspective, this contradiction requires no particular resolution, as it is quite common in this sort of literature that an attempt to supply explanation to one phenomenon – in our case the reason for a legal practice – may contradict another principle – that the Prophet and the Imams are different from ordinary people.

VIII. *Kitāb al-safar* ('The Book of Travel')

'Al-Barqī, al-Qāsim b. Yaḥyā, his grandfather, al-Ḥasan b. Rāshid, Mufaḍḍal b. ʿUmar: I was travelling to Mecca in the company of Abū ʿAbdallāh [Jaʿfar al-Ṣādiq] When we arrived at a certain wadi he said: "Put up your camp here and do not enter the wadi." We put our camp and shortly afterwards we found ourselves in the shadow of a cloud. It rained over us until the wadi was flooded and washed away whoever was in it.'[71]

In this deceptively simple story several important goals are achieved; let us discuss them from the obvious to the obscure. As mentioned in the general description of *Kitāb al-maḥāsin*, this book was probably meant as a guide to all aspects of the believer's life. In the present tradition we get clear instructions as to where one should not put up a night camp while travelling.[72] The warning against camping in a wadi in the desert is the obvious message and could also be found in modern tour guides. Ascribing this warning to an Imam shortly before water washes away anyone who did not follow his advice is something slightly different. The practical warning is given to the

[71] Al-Barqī, *Kitāb al-safar*, p. 364, no. 106 (ed. Beirut, p. 257, no. 4); quoted in *Biḥār al-anwār*, vol. 73, p. 279, no. 18.

[72] This tradition is included in a chapter which is devoted for this purpose and therefore entitled 'the chapter of places where one should not camp'. Other traditions in this chapter warn against camping in a wadi since it is normally inhabited by lions and snakes. See al-Barqī, p. 364, no. 103–105 (ed. Beirut, p. 257, nos 1–3).

believer in a literary way, through a story with a moral. Alongside the main message of this tradition, which justifies its inclusion in 'the book of travel', some fundamental virtues of the hero, that is, the Imam, can be inferred quite easily: (1) The Imam's knowledge also covers practical aspects of journeying, which may be regarded as further evidence of its being all-encompassing. (2) The Imam foresees the future. (3) Being saved from the flood or dying in it may symbolise the general rule according to which following the Imam means salvation whereas failing to do so implies perdition.

IX. *Kitāb al-maʾākil* ('The Book of Foods')

'Al-Barqī, Muḥammad b. ʿAlī b. Asbāṭ, Sayyāba b. Ḍurays, Ḥamza b. Ḥamrān, Abū ʿAbdallāh [Jaʿfar al-Ṣādiq], peace be upon him: ʿAlī b. al-Ḥusayn [the fourth Imam] used to order a lamb on days on which he had been fasting. The lamb would be slaughtered and its organs cut and cooked. In the evening, while he was still fasting, he used to take care of the pots until he could smell the meat soup. Then he used to say: "Bring the bowls and pour to this family and to that family" until the last pot. Afterwards bread and some dates would be brought and this used to be his dinner.'[73]

The present tradition, like the previous one, could be approached from two different angles: first, what practical information related to 'foodstuffs' does it convey? And second, what Imāmī aspects are integrated in the story? Let us start this time with a few remarks about the fourth Imam, ʿAlī b. al-Ḥusayn, and finish with a short remark about the practical dimension of this tradition.

It is well known that generosity and satisfaction with little were important qualities in pre-Islamic times and an indispensable characteristic of proper manhood or *muruwwa*, at times translated as 'gentlemanly behaviour'.[74] Add to these two an ascetic dimension and you get a perfect model for how a man should behave in post-Jāhilī times. That the fourth Imam is presented in this light is, therefore, not surprising, especially due to the fact that the other crucial manly qualities, namely courage and bravery on the battlefield, could not be ascribed to him. Based on the assumption that this tradition aims at presenting the Imam on the one hand as a model for imitation and on the other as a superhuman being who could hardly be imitated, one could determine that it represents an extreme form of asceticism and generosity that could hardly be reached by ordinary human beings. The believer is therefore not expected to reach the level of asceticism represented by the Imam, but rather to consider the latter's behaviour as a point of reference. Finally, the situation described in the tradition would not have been so extreme, unless the Imam, like others at his

---

[73] Al-Barqī, *Kitāb al-maʾākil*, p. 396, no. 67 (ed. Beirut, p. 281, no. 4); quoted in *Biḥār al-anwār*, vol. 46, pp. 71–72, no. 53 (also from *Manāqib āl Abī Ṭālib* of Ibn Shahrāshūb, vol. 3, p. 294, which indicates that the purpose of this tradition goes beyond practical or legal aspects of food); compare with the famous Jāhilī story about Ḥātim's generosity.

[74] See I. Goldziher, *A Short History of Classical Arabic Literature*, tr. J. Desomogyi (Hildesheim, 1966), pp. 1–2.

time, probably really liked lamb soup, and in the light of this assumption the scene is painted with some even more dramatic colours.

The practical or legal message of this tradition is not different from that of other traditions in 'the chapter of feeding in Ramaḍān' whose main aim is to underline the importance of inviting fellow believers to the meal of fast-breaking during the month of Ramaḍān – an act even 'more valuable than fasting itself'.[75]

X. *Kitāb al-māʾ* ('The Book of Water')

'Al-Barqī, Yaʿqūb b. Yazīd, Yaḥya b. al-Mubārak, ʿAbdallāh b. Jabala, Ṣārim: One of our fellow believers in Mecca suffered from [an illness] until he was at the point of death. I met Abū ʿAbdallāh [Jaʿfar al-Ṣādiq], peace be upon him, on the road and he asked me: "Ṣārim, how is so-and-so?" I said: "I left him at the point of death." [Abu ʿAbdallāh] told me: "If I were in your place, I would give him to drink some drainpipe water [i.e., fresh rainwater]. We looked for it everywhere but could not find it. While we were searching, a cloud appeared, there was thunder and lightning and it started to rain. I came to someone at the mosque, gave him a dirham, took a cup and filled it with drainpipe water. I brought it to him [to the sick person] and gave him to drink. I stayed by him until he drank a wheat mush and recovered".'[76]

Through a tradition in the 'book of water' we are exposed to several further aspects of the Imāmī community and its leader, the Imam. The principle of solidarity between members of the community, which was discussed above on the theoretical level (see section V above), takes a concrete form in the present story – nursing a dying fellow believer. The vertical dimension of the solidarity that characterises the community, that is, between the leader and the believers, can also be clearly deduced. By chance, a believer meets the Imam somewhere on the way and a conversation takes place. That the leader of a community is accessible in such circumstances could be regarded as one side of the vertical solidarity. That the Imam is aware of the severe state of an ill member of the community and shows real concern and empathy is another remarkable aspect.

The fact that in addition the Imam points to an efficient cure for the disease reveals something important not only about his relationship with the community but also about himself. By advising Ṣārim to make the ill person drink water from

[75] Al-Barqī, p. 396, no. 66 (ed. Beirut, p. 281, no. 3); see also traditions nos. 64–65 (ed. Beirut, no. 1–2) where inviting a believer to the meal of breaking the fast (*ifṭār*) is compared to freeing a slave.

[76] Al-Barqī, *Kitāb al-māʾ*, p. 574, no. 24 (ed. Beirut, p. 399, no. 1); quoted in *Biḥār al-anwār*, vol. 63, pp. 357–358, no. 44 and vol. 96, p. 245, no. 17. It is worth noting that following this tradition which forms 'the chapter of the value of drainpipe water' appears a tradition that focuses on the purifying and healing values of 'water from the sky'. It seems that drainpipe water is no different from 'water from the sky' and that the reason for including these two traditions in different chapters is merely the different terminology used in each of them.

a drainpipe the Imam fulfils a role similar to that of a shaman – a specialist in folk medicine or home remedy – but, as the story unfolds, we realise that the Imam's superhuman powers go far beyond that. Advising someone to fetch rainwater to a dying person when such water is unavailable can be very frustrating. When, following the Imam's advice, clouds appear in the sky, there is lightning and it starts to rain, the Imam is presented as no less than a miracle-worker,[77] and in this light the recovery of the dying person could only be expected.

To conclude, the image of the Imam that arises from this tradition could be summarised as that of a leader elevated from among ordinary people, both by his vast knowledge and by his ability to perform miracles, yet who at the same time is very much involved in the life of the community, concerned about the well-being of specific individuals in it and accessible in informal ways.

XI. *Kitāb al-manāfiʿ* ('The Book of Benefits')

'Al-Barqī, Muḥammad b. ʿĪsā, Khalaf b. Ḥammād, Isḥāq b. ʿAmmār: I told Abū ʿAbdallāh [Jaʿfar al-Ṣādiq], peace be upon him: "Sometimes I am torn between two opposing courses of action, with one part of me ordering me to act and another forbidding me." [Jaʿfar] said: "If you are in such a situation, pray two *rakʿa*s and seek God's advice by *istikhāra*[78] a hundred times, then consider which of the two options is more difficult [to follow] and act accordingly since this is the right choice. If God wills, may your *istikhāra* be for a state of well-being, since sometimes a man is given a choice [between a positive result] and having his hand cut off, his offspring killed or his property destroyed".'[79]

Surprisingly, an Imam, who is normally considered as the ultimate address in times of perplexity, advises a believer in such a state[80] to make up his mind by other means – *istikhāra* – a contradiction to which several possible solutions may be suggested.[81]

---

77 On the Imams as performers of miracles, see J. Loebenstein, 'Miracles in Shīʿī Thought: A Case-Study of the Miracles Attributed to Imām Jaʿfar al-Ṣādiq', *Arabica*, 50 (2003), pp. 199–244; L. N. Takim, *The Heirs of the Prophet: Charisma and Religious Authority in Shiʿite Islam* (Albany, NY, 2006), pp. 62–64.

78 See T. Fahd, 'Istikhāra', *EI2*, vol. 4, pp. 259–260.

79 Al-Barqī, *Kitāb al-manāfiʿ*, p. 599, no. 7 (ed. Beirut, p. 415, no. 7); Cf. the version in Kulaynī's *al-Kāfī*, vol. 3, p. 472, where instead of the word *aʿzam* 'more difficult' in al-Barqī's version appears the word *aḥzam* (i.e., sounder, based on a better judgement).

80 In two other traditions from 'the chapter of *istikhāra*' the Imam, Jaʿfar al-Ṣādiq, is quoted as encouraging the believer to perform *istikhāra* prior to any [meaningful] action and not necessarily in times of perplexity. See al-Barqī, p. 598, nos 3–4 (ed. Beirut, p. 415, nos 3–4).

81 Noteworthy in this context is *Kitāb fatḥ al-abwāb bayna dhawī al-albāb wa-bayna rabbi al-arbāb fī al-istikhārāt* (Beirut, 1989) by the Shiʿi scholar Ibn Ṭāwūs (d. 664/1266), which is devoted mainly to different aspects of *istikhāra*, as well as for other forms of consulting God (for example: *qurʿa*, lot casting); see also E. Kohlberg, *A Medieval Muslim Scholar at Work: Ibn Ṭāwūs and his Library* (Leiden, 1992), s.v. *istikhāra*.

First, that the Imam exists and is not yet hidden (prior to the occultation) does not necessarily mean that he is available at all times and can be consulted on all matters by every member of the community. Second, whether or not the tradition is authentic, or the sixth Imam who is really behind the recommendation to perform *istikhāra*, it may be seen as an attempt to provide Imāmī legitimacy to a pre-Islamic custom. Third, if the tradition is not authentic, it may in fact be an example of an anachronism in which post-occultation thinking is being expressed through the words of an Imam, as it supplies the believer with instructions to find his way out of a problematic situation without having to consult an Imam.

A closer look at the details provided in the tradition regarding the process of the *istikhāra*, as well as an attempt to evaluate its efficiency, may lead to some further observations. The *istikhāra* does not end by a definite result given by God to the person who performs it, and the latter still has to figure out for himself which of the two options is more difficult to follow. Furthermore, the 'right' decision is normally not the easy one to take and may involve catastrophic consequences. Indeed, sometimes a minor catastrophe could be unavoidable on the way to prevent a major one from happening, but yet, a combination between the fact that at the end of the process the believer is still the one responsible for the decision and the fact that this decision may lead to a catastrophe, makes one question the efficiency of the process. That Jaʿfar al-Ṣādiq claims that a person who is not satisfied by the results of his *istikhāra*, and therefore becomes upset, is 'the most hated by God' since his behaviour is equal to 'blaming God',[82] may be regarded as further evidence for the problematic consequences that may follow the performance of *istikhāra*. It is as if the Imam is trying very hard to protect this custom against people who, following an unsuccessful attempt, may doubt it. As in similar cases in other contexts, it seems that Jaʿfar's statement would not have been necessary, had the performance of *istikhāra* not been a problematic one.

XII. *Kitāb al-marāfiq* ('The Book of the Household')

'Al-Barqī, his father, Aḥmad b. al-Nadr, ʿAmr b. Shimr, Jābir, ʿAbdallāh b. Yaḥya al-Kindī, his father (who was in charge of bringing water to ʿAlī for the purpose of ritual ablution[83]), ʿAlī [b. Abī Ṭālib], peace be upon him, said: "The Messenger of God, may God pray upon him and his family, said: 'Oh, ʿAlī, Gabriel came to me last night and greeted me from the door. I said: "Come in!" But he replied: "We do not enter a house that contains what this house contains." I believed him, but I did not know about anything [untoward] in the house. I clapped my hand and suddenly there appeared a puppy with whom al-Ḥusayn b. ʿAlī had played the day before and

[82] Al-Barqī, p. 598, no. 5 (ed. Beirut, p. 415, no. 5).

[83] This is my translation of the Arabic term *ṣāḥib maṭharat ʿAlī*; see al-Kulaynī, *al-Kāfī*, vol. 6, p. 528, note 2.

who had slipped under the bed at nightfall. I drove him out of the house and then he [Gabriel] came in. I asked him: "Oh, Gabriel, don't you enter a house in which there is a dog?" He said: "No and neither do we set foot in a house in which there is a *junub* [i.e., someone in a state of major ritual impurity] or a statue/an idol".'[84]

The legal dimension of this tradition, that is, that one should not keep a dog at home, place a statue or be at home in a state of major ritual impurity, may well be implied from the angels' refraining from setting foot in a house that contains any of these things and is of little relevance to the present discussion.[85] Of much greater interest is the way the relationships between the different characters of the story are depicted.

The angel's visit to the Prophet's house seems to be a casual thing – he drops by and the Prophet invites him in. That on this specific visit he refused to come in is presented as an exception to the norm. ʿAlī is of course the first person with whom the Prophet would share his experiences and it is therefore far from surprising that he told him about the visit. It seems that the whole purpose of the angel's visit was to instruct the Prophet on a legal ruling, or in other words to increase his legal knowledge. The Prophet immediately passes this new information onto his cousin and son-in-law, who also happens to be the first Imam, whose knowledge – as well as that of his successors – has to be equal to that of the Prophet according to the Shiʿi doctrine.

Juxtaposed with the principle of *ʿiṣma*, that is, the immunity from sin and error which is ascribed to all prophets and Imams, this story raises some important questions. Could it be that Muḥammad, who was certainly a prophet when this episode occurred, was about to spend the night with a dog in his house?[86] Or that the future Imam, Ḥusayn, although still a young boy, would play with a dog which is an impure animal? A positive answer on these questions would contradict the Imāmī view of *ʿiṣma*, according to which the Prophet and the Imams were immune from error and sin already prior to their mission, and certainly afterwards, while they were already functioning as Prophet or Imams. However, theoretical discussions of this kind about the nature of *ʿiṣma* and the attempt to apply this principle to stories about prophets and Imams were not yet common in the time of al-Barqī and are typical of the rationalisation of the post-Būyid era.[87]

---

84 Al-Barqī, *Kitāb al-marāfiq*, p. 615, no. 41 (ed. Beirut, p. 427, no. 10); quoted in *Biḥār al-anwār*, vol. 2, p. 615, no. 41.

85 In several other traditions in the same chapter the angel Gabriel is quoted saying that angels do not enter a house that contains a dog, a human image, a statue [of a man], or a receptacle of urine. See al-Barqī, pp. 614–615, nos. 38–40 (ed. Beirut, p. 427, nos. 7–9).

86 Compare with tradition no. 34 on al-Barqī, pp. 612–613 (ed. Beirut, pp. 426–427, no. 3) where ʿAlī is telling that when the Prophet sent him to Medina he instructed him to erase all images, to flatten all graves and to kill all dogs; see also F. Viré, 'Kalb', *EI2*, vol. 4, pp. 489–492.

87 See, for example, the discussion about *ʿiṣma* in al-Shaykh al-Mufīd, *Kitāb awāʾil al-maqālāt* (Tabriz, 1371/1951), pp. 8–9, or in al-Sharīf al-Murtaḍā's *Kitāb tanzīh al-anbiyāʾ* (Najaf, 1960).

Conclusion

The purpose of this chapter is twofold. First, to shed some light on the life and works of the Qummī traditionist Aḥmad b. Muḥammad al-Barqī, one of the less familiar Shiʿi scholars from the pre-Būyid era, who lived and worked during the second half of the 3rd/9th century. Second, to examine through the case study of al-Barqī some of the characteristics of the Shiʿi *ḥadīth* literature before its final crystallisation and canonisation during the Būyid period (945–1055 AD). This literature deals with some of the fundamental notions of the Shiʿi religion at its early stage of development, so it is only natural that some of these notions should have come to the fore in the course of this chapter.

Despite the great variety of themes that seems to have preoccupied al-Barqī, and notwithstanding the various literary genres and stylistic means of which he made use, there is a common denominator which transcends the thematic and stylistic borders throughout the *Kitāb al-maḥāsin*. Regardless of whether a tradition deals with a mythical story about the creation of 'reason and ignorance' or with the medical value of 'drainpipe water', the superiority and exclusivity of the Shiʿi community, represented in many cases through the special status of the Imam, will somehow find its expression in it.

10

The Story of 'Pen and Paper' and its Interpretation in Muslim Literary and Historical Tradition*

Gurdofarid Miskinzoda

Introduction

Muslim literary and historical tradition contains numerous reports about the last days of Prophet Muḥammad (d. 11/632) and his death. They cover several events which acquired increasing significance as the history of Islam unfolded. Here, I focus on a small episode of the Prophet's deathbed wish to write, which is reported to have happened during one of the last days of his life. The main report associated with this episode is known in Muslim tradition as the '*ḥadīth* of pen and paper'. The main sentence ascribed to the Prophet in this *ḥadīth* in most cases reads as: '*aktubu lakum kitāban lā taḍillū baʿdahu abadan* (I will write something for you after which you will never go astray)'. Close examination of the various versions of this *ḥadīth* and reports associated with it indicate considerable differences between the variants and sources that include those.

My aim is to show that the variants of this report pose a number of problems. In fact, the text (sentences, sequence of events and quotations ascribed to various personages) is confusing to the extent that, eventually, it is not clear what the incident was really about. In analysing the various versions of this report in the Sunni as well as Shiʿi sources, I am not concerned with the reliability of the reports, but rather with the processes of change, adaptation, redaction and transformation that take place within the text of the *ḥadīth* and the story associated with it. The aim of this chapter, therefore, is to show that the main value of such a story is not whether what it tells us is true or false, but rather what is its purpose. To ask how and why various authors

* This chapter is a considerably modified version of a section of Chapter 5 of my doctoral thesis 'On the Margins of *sīra:* Mughulṭāʾī (689–762/1290–1361) and his Place in the Development of *sīra* Literature' (Ph.D. thesis, University of London, 2007), pp. 206–231. It has benefited greatly from the comments of Professor Gerald R. Hawting on my thesis. Further comments have been kindly provided by Professor Etan Kohlberg. I am indebted to both of them for their useful feedback and insight on the earlier versions of the chapter.

included and interpreted the story considering the nature of our sources is, probably, more important than to investigate its validity as a historically authentic report.

Background and Context of the Story

In many *sīras* (biographies of the Prophet), *ḥadīth* collections and other representatives of Muslim literary and historical tradition, this *ḥadīth* and the story associated with it is connected with reports about the Prophet's night visit to the cemetery, his announcement that he had been offered the choice between meeting his God and going to paradise (i.e., death) and the key to worldly treasures (i.e., life), and his command to Abū Bakr (d. 13/634) to lead the prayer when he himself was unable to attend public prayers. The theme of the Prophet's choice between paradise and meeting God and possessing the keys of worldly treasures is associated with two main recurring ideas that prepare the reader for the eventual death of the Prophet. One is that all prophets have the choice of when to die.[1] As one of the prophets, in fact the last one, Muḥammad therefore also had that choice, thus placing him within the wider idea of prophethood. The other is his desire to prepare the community for his departure. Although not expressly stated, it can be inferred from our reports.[2] Reports that tell us what happened also mention several important figures, but the names depend on the preference of the narrator and his emphasis on their role and significance. Several names (e.g., ʿUmar, ʿAlī, Zaynab, ʿAbd al-Raḥmān b. Abī Bakr, Umm Salama) are added or removed from the episode as dictated by the preference of our narrators.

However, some *sīras* do not include this episode as a separate incident, but either merge it with other events commonly associated with the last days of the Prophet, or avoid it altogether. In those sources where we find the episode, it is also part of a wider context of several important events of the Prophet's life. The principal among these are the last pilgrimage (*ḥijjat al-wadāʿ*), ʿAlī's mission to Yemen, ʿUsāma b. Ḥāritha's

---

[1] See Ibn Hishām, *al-Sīra al-nabawiyya* (Cairo, 1999), vol. 4, p. 212, tr. A. Guillaume, *The Life of Muḥammad: A Translation of Ibn Ishaq's Sirat Rasul Allāh* (Karachi, 2001), p. 680. Ibn Sayyid al-Nās also quotes a report on the authority of ʿĀʾisha who heard the Prophet saying that: '*mā min nabiyyin yamūt ḥattā yukhayyar* (none of the prophets died until they are given a choice).' See Ibn Sayyid al-Nās, *ʿUyūn al-athar fī funūn al-maghāzī waʾl-shamāʾil waʾl-siyar* (Beirut, 1993), vol. 2, p. 407. Also see Raven, '*Sīra* and the Qurʾān', in J. D. McAuliffe, ed., *Encyclopaedia of the Qurʾān* (Leiden and Boston, 2006), vol. 5, p. 41.

[2] For an example of such reports, see al-Diyārbakrī who includes the speech of Muḥammad in which he warns that he is to depart from the Muslims and that they must remain true to God even after he has gone. This speech is placed among the reports about the last public prayer attended by the Prophet. Al-Diyārbakrī, *Taʾrīkh al-khamīs fī aḥwāl anfas nafīs* (Cairo, 1885), vol. 2, p. 181. Also, see Ibn Kathīr's section on the verses of the Qurʾan and *ḥadīth*s which forewarn of the death of the Prophet. Ibn Kathīr, *al-Sīra al-nabawiyya* (Cairo, 1964), vol. 4, pp. 442–445; tr. Trevor Le Gassick, *The Life of Muḥammad: al-Sīra al-nabawiyya* (Reading, 2000), vol. 4, pp. 320–322.

expedition to Palestine, the beginning of the Prophet's illness, the actual death of the Prophet, the meeting in the Hall of the Banū Sā'ida and the burial of the Prophet. The connection between these events and those following the death of the Prophet, as well as the reign of the first four caliphs, *al-khulafā' al-rāshidūn* (the Rightly Guided Caliphs), is undoubtedly crucial.[3] A significant role as far as the emphasis, choice of versions and interpretations of details are concerned is played by the narrator's preference and sectarian affiliation. It is noticeable that the overall context, language and arguments within which the *ḥadīth* of 'pen and paper' and the story associated with it is placed in the Shi'i sources in comparison with more famous *sīras* mainly representing the Sunni tradition is markedly distinct. However, the underlining themes and issues remain the same.

Summary of the Narrative

The account of the Prophet's wish to write something may be summarised as follows. It occurred during his last days, when his situation deteriorated and he abstained from attending public prayers. At some point during his illness the Prophet fell unconscious. When he regained consciousness, he requested a medium to write in order to put in writing something that he thought might serve his community in the long term. People present in the room began disputing whether they should bring him what he had asked for. The quarrel and noise increased, and the Prophet ordered them to leave and did not write anything. Some reports relate that the Prophet, following his failure to write, gave them three recommendations. Most agree that the incident took place on a Thursday, but, some place it on the same day as the Prophet's death, which is said to be Monday. The main sources for majority of the reports about the episode are 'Ā'isha and 'Abd Allāh b. 'Abbās.[4]

It seems the purpose of the incident is to depict the end of the Prophet and the beginning of new community politics. The story suggests that the Prophet accepted and permitted the way in which the community was to choose to deal with its own affairs in his absence, which is perhaps connected with the emergence of *ḥadīth*s, such as 'My *umma* will never agree on an error.'[5]

This idea is developed by various authors, but is expressly stated by Ibn Ḥazm (d. 456/1064) and Ibn Sayyid al-Nās (d. 734/1334) whose versions of the account will also be discussed below. In this respect, it can be argued that the episode was probably important as part of a group of reports that form a smooth transition from the life of the community under the leadership of the Prophet to the affairs of the community following his death. Despite the many contradictory details, it seems that the main

---

3 See, for example, Wilferd Madelung, *The Succession to Muḥammad* (Cambridge, 1997), pp. 20–23.

4 On Ibn 'Abbās, see L. Veccia Vaglieri, ''Abd Allāh b. 'Abbās', *EI2*, vol. 1, pp. 40–41.

5 See Ignaz Goldziher, *Introduction to Islamic Theology and Law*, tr. Andras and Ruth Hamori (Princeton, 1981), p. 50.

task of the episode is to provide legitimacy for the developments and changes in the life of a newly emerged community following the Prophet's death and the rule of the first four caliphs. Although most of our authors present a balanced narrative, the stress varies among the narrators. In the Shiʿi sources, the emphasis is placed on the idea that this event represents a 'calamity' and a missed opportunity for the designation of the rightful successor, namely ʿAlī b. Abī Ṭālib (d. 35/656), to the leadership of the community.

The analysis below suggests that the episode might also reveal an important aspect of a theological discourse. Thus, I argue that reading the story as a problem of succession of Abū Bakr or ʿAlī to the Prophet is not the only development in the tradition. This 'reading' of the story perhaps emerged in the light of subsequent discussions of pro- and anti-ʿAlid propaganda and debates around the rightful succession to the Prophet. The focal point of the story, in my opinion, is about the permissibility of writing down something besides the Book of Allah, that is, the Qurʾan, and the question of religious authority: the human spoken word on the one hand, and the authority of the word of God expressed in the Qurʾan on the other.

The Presentation of the Story in Different Works

Dealing with this episode, Ibn Saʿd (d. 230/845) cited a total of nine reports, producing thereby the first and longest version of it in a section on the Prophet's wish to write in his *al-Ṭabaqāt*, while scarcely hinting at his preferred version. His first cited report is quite neutral and contains only general information about the event:

> The Prophet's (peace be upon him) condition worsened and he said: 'Bring me the inkholder and paper (*dawāt wa-ṣaḥīfa*). I will write something for you after which you will never go astray (*aktubu lakum kitāban lā taḍillū baʿdahu abadan*).' Somebody from among those present with him (*ʿindahu*) said: 'Surely, the Messenger of Allah is delirious (*la-yahjuru*).' It was said to him (*wa-qīla lahu*): 'Shall we give you what you have asked for?'[6]

This and other versions of the report are organised under the theme of *Dhikr al-kitāb alladhī arāda rasūl allāh (ṣ) an yaktubahu li-ummatihi fī maraḍihi alladhī māta fī-hi* (On the writing that the Messenger of Allah (peace be upon him) wished to leave for his *umma* during his illness of which he died).[7] Taken together, Ibn Saʿd's versions highlight several central messages: that the incident took place; that the writing was meant for the entire *umma*, not for a particular person; that the Prophet had asked to write it during the illness of which he eventually died; and that once failing to write down what he had wished, he gave verbal guidance to his followers. It is important

---

[6] Ibn Saʿd, *Kitāb al-ṭabaqāt al-kubrā* (Beirut, 1957–1968), vol. 2, p. 242.

[7] Ibid., p. 242.

to draw attention to the central message of Ibn Saʿd's reports, because as we move to other sources, a change of emphasis is noticeable.

The major source for Ibn Saʿd's reports, al-Wāqidī (d. 207/822), does not go into any detail about the illness, death or last days of the Prophet in his own book. His *Kitāb al-maghāzī* finishes with the account of Usāma b. Zayd's expedition to Muʾta, whither he was sent to avenge the death of his father Zayd b. Ḥāritha in 8/629.[8] The last passages of al-Wāqidī's work are reports about Usāma, his father Zayd and their close relationship with the Prophet. The only detail al-Wāqidī provides about the death of the Prophet is the date as the afternoon of Monday, 12th of Rabīʿ al-awwal of the year 11 of the *hijra*.[9] However, as Wim Raven also mentions, al-Wāqidī probably had a separate book on the death of Muḥammad, of which we have only quotations in the work of Ibn Saʿd and other authors.[10] One can only guess whether this book of al-Wāqidī would have contained anything on the episode, but the fact that the episode first appears in Ibn Saʿd's *al-Ṭabaqāt* at least suggests that al-Wāqidī, his teacher, was familiar with it. Moreover, the *isnād*s of, at least, two other versions cited by Ibn Saʿd also feature al-Wāqidī. Unlike al-Wāqidī, Ibn Hishām (d. 218/833) includes several details on the last days of the Prophet, but does not mention the story of 'pen and paper'. In fact, it is a well-known characteristic of Ibn Hishām's work to leave out some sensitive material.[11] Ibn Saʿd's version of the story will, therefore, serve as the main background against which the story in other sources is compared.

Already Ibn Saʿd's second version (cited on the authority of Sufyān b. ʿUyayna – Sulaymān b. Abī Muslim (uncle of Ibn Abī Najīḥ – Saʿīd b. Jubayr) differs considerably from his first. It is in this second version that many issues emerge. First, the day when the incident supposedly happened is mentioned: '*yawm al-khamīs wa-mā yawmu al-khamīs* (Thursday, what a Thursday that was)', an expression that becomes one of the main literary motifs of the episode. The report also emphasises the quarrel and confusion among the people about the Prophet's intention and well-being: '*fa-tanāzaʿū wa-lā yanbaghī ʿinda nabī tanāzuʿ fa-qālū mā shaʾnuhu a-hajara, istafhimūhu* (They quarrelled, [but] it is not acceptable to quarrel in the presence of the Prophet. What does he want? Is he delirious? Ask him.)'

Upon hearing their confused remarks the Prophet orders them to leave him telling them that his condition was better than what they were saying *daʿūnī fa-lladhī anā fī-hi khayrun mimmā tadʿūnanī ilayhi*. He then mentions the three 'recommendations' (*wa-ūṣī bi-thalāthin*): the first is to drive away the associaters from the Arabian Peninsula (*akhrijū al-mushrikīn min jazīrat al-ʿArab*); the second is to accept the delegations in the same manner that he had done (*wa-ajīzū al-wafd bi-naḥwin*

[8] For al-Wāqidī's version of the last days of Muḥammad, see his *Kitāb al-maghāzī* (London, 1966), vol. 3, p. 1118ff.

[9] Al-Wāqidī, *Kitāb al-maghāzī*, vol. 3, p. 1120.

[10] See, Raven, '*Sīra* and the Qurʾān', p. 34.

[11] Among other examples left out are stories about the intended suicide of Muḥammad and the 'satanic verses', both of which can be found in many other recensions of Ibn Isḥāq's work, including that used by al-Ṭabarī. Ibid.

mimmā kuntu ujīzahum); and the third he either did not mention or the reporter forgot it (*fa-lā adrī qālahā fa-nasītuhā aw sakata ʿanhā ʿamdan*).[12]

Al-Ṭabarī (d. 310/923) includes exactly the same tradition with several grammatical changes of minor importance transmitted with the same *isnād* as Ibn Saʿd in his only two reports on the incident.[13] Ibn Kathīr (d. 774/1373) cites the same report on the authority of al-Bukhārī (d. 256/870) and going back to Ibn ʿAbbās through Sufyān, Sulaymān al-Aḥwal and Saʿīd. Apart from three minor differences between the versions of Ibn Saʿd and Ibn Kathīr, the latter excludes the last sentence (i.e., *fa-lā adrī qālahā fa-nasītuhā aw sakata ʿanhā ʿamdan*), probably to lessen the impact of the admission that the third recommendation had been forgotten.[14]

Ibn Saʿd's third version is on the authority of Muḥammad b. ʿAbd Allāh al-Anṣārī – Qurrat b. Khālid – Abu'l-Zubayr – Jābir b. ʿAbd Allāh al-Anṣārī. It introduces the name of ʿUmar (*wa-takallama ʿUmar b. al-Khaṭṭāb*). The medium of writing is mentioned as a *ṣaḥīfa* (*daʿā bi-ṣaḥīfa*). As in the previous version, the theme of not being led astray emerges. Again, due to the lack of united approval for his request, the Prophet is said to have abandoned the idea altogether.[15]

Version four is transmitted on the authority of ʿAlī, which introduces his name to the incident. It also differs considerably from the previous ones in terms of its contents. For example, according to this report it is ʿAlī who is asked by Muḥammad to bring the medium of writing for him: *ʿyā ʿAlī iʾtinī bi-ṭabaqin aktubu fī-hi mā lā taḍillu ummatī baʿdī*'. Of minor importance is the change in what the Prophet asks for, namely a *ṭabaq*, not *katif* or *saḥīfa*, and *dawāt* and *qalam*.[16]

There are other major differences between this particular version and those quoted earlier. The first is that having heard the request, ʿAlī offers to remember what the Prophet had to say (*fa-qultu innī aḥfaẓu dhirāʿan min al-ṣaḥīfa*), while the Prophet's

---

[12] Ibn Saʿd, *al-Ṭabaqāt*, vol. 2, p. 242.

[13] See al-Ṭabarī, *Taʾrīkh al-rusul wa'l-mulūk* (Beirut, 1998), vol. 3, p. 249.

[14] Ibn Kathīr, *al-Sīra al-nabawiyya*, vol. 4, p. 451 (=*The Life*, vol. 4, p. 326).

[15] Ibn Saʿd, *al-Ṭabaqāt*, vol. 2, p. 243.

[16] Ibn Saʿd, *al-Ṭabaqāt*, vol. 2, p. 243. In al-Ṭabarī: *ʿbi'l-lawḥ wa'l-dawāt aw al-katif wa'l-dawāt*'. See al-Ṭabarī, *Taʾrīkh*, vol. 3, p. 249. The use of words such as *ṣaḥīfa, dawāt, ṭabaq* and *katif* seems quite problematic in this context. They all refer to various writing materials, but one thing can be certain that paper (*qāghaḍ*) itself was introduced to Arabia not earlier than 134/751. See Cl. Huart and A. Groham, 'Kāghad', *EI2*, vol. 4, p. 419. *Katif* most probably refers to a shoulder bone of an animal used for writing and therefore, seems the most probable medium of writing at the time of the story. See, T. Fahd, 'Katif', *EI2*, vol. 4, p. 763. *Ṣaḥīfa* refers to any surface or material suitable for writing and in the earlier periods referred to the text of the Qurʾan written down, but when used to refer to paper here is again questionable. See A. Ghédira, 'Ṣaḥīfa', *EI2*, vol. 8, p. 834. *Dawāt*, an ink holder, later became a symbol of knowledge, tradition and scholarship, and was also frequently used for ornamentation. Its use in conjunction with *qāghaḍ* and *ṣaḥīfa* here appears anachronistic. See E. Baer, 'Dawāt', *EI2*, vol. 12, p. 203. For a more detailed discussion on paper in the Islamic societies, see Johannes Pedersen, *The Arabic Book*, tr. Geoffrey French (Princeton, 1984), and Jonathan Bloom, *Paper Before Print: The History and Impact of Paper in the Islamic World* (New Haven, 2001). The fact that this episode has been known as that of 'pen and paper' is therefore also part of the problem.

head was on his lap (*fa-kāna ra'suhu bayna dhirāʿī*). Second, the three recommendations are also different from the ones mentioned in version two. In this version they are: prayer, alms and *mā malakat aymānukum*[17] (*fa-jaʿala yūṣī bi'l-ṣalāt wa'l-zakāt wa-mā malakat aymānukum*).[18]

The theme of the three recommendations is developed mainly through their association with the Prophet's wish to write. However, the problem with the three recommendations is as follows: they are different in both versions and while Ibn ʿAbbās says that he either did not remember the third one, or that the Prophet did not mention it, ʿAlī mentions *mā malakat aymānukum* as the third recommendation. It is then not surprising that in the later works considerable attention is given to the identification of the third recommendation, precisely because it was not stated clearly or at all. Therefore, there was plenty of room for interpretation, guessing and polemic. Third, the report mentions the actual death of the Prophet; that he took his last breath there and then on ʿAlī's lap. The last thing that Muḥammad ordered was the *shahāda* (*wa-amara bi-shahāda … ḥatta fāḍat nafsuhu*).[19]

Version six,[20] on the authority of al-Wāqidī going back to ʿUmar, returns us to the theme of the latter's involvement in the episode. It mentions the demand of the women present at the Prophet's house to bring him what he needs (*fa-qāla al-niswatu i'tū rasūl Allāh (ṣ) bi-ḥājatihi*).[21] According to this report, it was ʿUmar who did not allow for this to happen. Although the women wanted to go ahead with it, ʿUmar thought it was unnecessary: '*qāla ʿUmar fa-qultu [u]skutna fa-innakunna ṣawāḥibuhu*[22] *idhā mariḍa ʿaṣartunna aʿyunakunna wa-idhā ṣaḥḥa akhadhtunna bi-ʿunqihi* ('Umar said: Be quiet. You are indeed his [?] Companions; if he is ill you cry your eyes out, and if he recovers you grab him by his neck)'. The report also includes the last sentence in

---

[17] Broadly speaking, '*mā malakat aymānukum*' means something or someone for or over which a person has the right; or a possession of some sort. The phrase is usually connected with Q.16:71.

[18] Ibn Saʿd, *al-Ṭabaqāt*, vol. 2, p. 243. Something close to the words identified with ʿAlī regarding the three recommendations is later ascribed to the two wives of the Prophet, ʿĀ'isha and Umm Salama.

[19] Ibn Saʿd, *al-Ṭabaqāt*, vol. 2, p. 243.

[20] Ibn Saʿd's fifth version does not add anything new, but excludes many details, which reduces it to conveying that one of the events preceding the Prophet's death was his wish to write something down to remain as a guide for his people.

[21] In Ibn Saʿd's last version similar words are ascribed only to Zaynab: '*fa-qālat Zaynab zawjat al-nabī (ṣ) a lā tasmaʿūn al-nabī (ṣ) yaʿhudu ilaykum*'. See Ibn Saʿd, *al-Ṭabaqāt*, vol. 2, p. 245.

[22] The phrase '*uskutna fa-innakunna ṣawāḥibuhu*' in other instances is attributed to the Prophet, who compares his wives to the companions of Yūsuf (*ṣawāḥib Yusūf*), because they each argued for their own candidate to lead the prayer instead of the Prophet. In another instance, it refers only to ʿĀ'isha, who refused to summon her father Abū Bakr. See Ibn Saʿd, *al-Ṭabaqāt*, vol. 2, p. 219; Ibn Hishām, *al-Sīra*, vol. 4, p. 212; al-Diyārbakrī, *Ta'rīkh al-khamīs*, vol. 2, p. 181.

which the Prophet is so annoyed with the men around him that he reprimands them by saying that the women were better than they were (*hunna khayrun minkum*).[23]

Ibn Saʿd's longest version (eighth)[24] is also transmitted on the authority of al-Wāqidī. The last two reports deserve a closer look, because they contain most of the interesting details on the incident. The first important new element in this version is ʿUmar's reference to the Qurʾan, arguing that there is no need for a new 'writing', because they already have the book of God: '*wa-ʿindakum al-Qurʾān ḥasbunā kitāb Allāh* (You have the Qurʾan, the Book of Allah is sufficient for us)'.[25] This remark led to a quarrel between those who agreed with ʿUmar and those who wanted to fulfil the Prophet's wish (*fa-khtalafa ahl al-bayt*[26] *wa-khtaṣamū fa-minhum man yaqūl qarribū yaktub lakum rasūl Allāh (ṣ) wa-minhum man yaqūl mā qāla ʿUmar*). The Prophet, saddened by their quarrel, abandoned the idea and ordered everyone to leave (*fa-lammā kathura al-laghaṭ waʾl-ikhtilāf wa-ghammū rasūl Allāh (ṣ) fa-qāla qūmū ʿannī*).

Another new sentence is then added to the description of the incident. It is a saying in most cases attributed either to ʿUbayd Allāh b. ʿAbd Allāh or to Ibn ʿAbbās: '*al-raziyya kullu al-raziyya mā ḥāla bayna rasūl Allāh (ṣ) wa-bayna an yaktuba lahum dhālika al-kitāb min ikhtilāfihim wa-laghaṭihim*' (What a loss it was that due to their disagreement and noise the Messenger of God (peace be upon him) was prevented from writing that down)'.[27]

---

[23] Ibn Saʿd, *al-Ṭabaqāt*, vol. 2, pp. 243–244.

[24] Ibn Saʿd' seventh report is also on the authority of al-Wāqidī going back to Jābir. It is the shortest among his reports, and is also quoted by al-Balādhurī. The report not only confirms that due to the clamour and dispute Muḥammad abandoned the idea to write down his message, but argues that the writing was meant for the community so that they do not go astray and are not led astray (*lā yaḍillū wa-lā yuḍallū*). See, Ibn Saʿd, *al-Ṭabaqāt*, vol. 2, p. 244 and al-Balādhurī, *Ansāb al-ashrāf* (Cairo, 1959), vol. 1, p. 562.

[25] The idea of 'a book besides the Book of God' most commonly appears in connection with the permission or prohibition of writing down the prophetic traditions. There is a considerable literature on the permissibility of writing down of tradition in early history of Islam. Opinions on this topic vary considerably, but for major arguments, see Ignaz Goldziher, 'Disputes over the Status of *Ḥadīth* in Islam', in H. Motzki, ed., *Ḥadīth: Origins and Developments* (Aldershot, 2004), pp. 55–66; originally published as 'Kämpfe um die Stellung des Ḥadīṯ im Islam', in I. Goldziher, *Gesammelte Schriften*, ed. J. de Somogyi (Hildesheim, 1967–1973), vol. 5, pp. 86–98; Gregor Schoeler, 'Oral Torah and *Ḥadīth*: Transmission, Prohibition of Writing, Redaction', tr. Gwendolyn Goldbloom, in Motzki, ed., *Ḥadīth*, pp. 67–108; originally published as 'Mündliche Thora und Ḥadīt im Islam. Überlieferung, Schreibverbot, Redaktion', *Der Islam*, 66 (1989), pp. 213–251, and Michael Cook, 'The Opponents of the Writing of Tradition in Early Islam', *Arabica*, 44 (1997), pp. 437–530. I am more inclined to agree with Cook in that hostility to the writing down of tradition existed in all major centres of learning in early Islam and was a prevailing attitude at one point. Cook also argues that this hostility has Jewish origins. I also find his explanations concerning the demise of the emphasis on the oral tradition in Islam more convincing.

[26] Note the use of '*ahl al-bayt*' here.

[27] Ibn Saʿd, *al-Ṭabaqāt*, vol. 2, p. 244. Cf. Momen's translation: 'The greatest of all calamities is what intervened between the messenger of God and this writing' in Moojan Momen,

The report is even more interesting when compared with Ibn Kathīr's version and his arguments on the matter of the Prophet's wish to write. Ibn Kathīr, who reports it on the authority of al-Bukhārī, excludes 'Umar's name from the text perhaps to avoid mentioning that it was 'Umar who rejected Muḥammad's request:

> *wa-fī al-bayt rijāl [*leaves out: *fī-him 'Umar b. al-Khaṭṭāb] fa-qāla al-nabī (ṣ) hallumū aktub lakum kitāban lā taḍillū ba'dahu abadan fa-qāla ba'ḍuhum [*instead of: *fa-qāla 'Umar] inna rasūl Allāh (ṣ) ghalabahu al-waja'u wa-'indakum al-Qur'ān ḥasbunā kitāb Allāh.*

and also:

> *fa-minhum man yaqūl qarribū yaktub lakum [*leaves out: *rasūl Allāh (ṣ)] kitāban lā naḍillū ba'dahu wa-minhum man yaqūl ghayr dhālika [*instead of: *mā qāla 'Umar].*[28]

Ibn Kathīr downplays the effect of this rejection and quarrel on the Prophet's mood and decision and instead says: '*fa-lamma aktharū al-laghw wa'l-ikhtilāf [*leaves out: *wa-ghammū rasūl Allāh (ṣ)] qāla rasūl Allāh (ṣ) qūmū [*leaves out: *'annī]*'.[29]

Al-Bukhārī, on whose authority Ibn Kathīr reports, includes several versions of this report in his *Ṣaḥīḥ* and, at least one of them does mention the name of 'Umar. There is little doubt that Ibn Kathīr was familiar with it, yet he chooses the one that serves his purpose best, namely the version that does not mention 'Umar.[30] Al-Diyārbakrī (d. ca. 960s/1550s), who also cites al-Bukhārī as his source for this report, lessens the emphasis on the Prophet's discontent by omitting '*wa-ghammū rasūl Allāh*', but retains all references to 'Umar.[31]

Concerns over 'Umar's action dominate Ibn Ḥazm's version of the story, who similar to al-Diyārbakrī includes 'Umar's name. Ibn Ḥazm defends 'Umar's action and argues that although his action had caused the Prophet to abandon the writing he only meant good (*fa-qāla 'Umar b. al-Khaṭṭāb (r) kalimatan arāda bi-hā al-khayr fa-kānat sababan li-imtinā'ihi min dhālika al-kitāb*).[32] Moreover, he maintains,

---

An Introduction to Shi'i Islam (New Haven, 1985), pp. 15–16.

[28] Ibn Kathīr, *al-Sīra al-nabawiyya*, vol. 4, p. 451 (=*The Life*, vol. 4, p. 327).

[29] Ibid.

[30] For the *ḥadīth* containing the name of 'Umar, see *Ṣaḥīḥ al-Bukhārī: The Translation of the Meaning of Ṣaḥīḥ al-Bukhārī* (Beirut, 1973), vol. 1, p. 86, and al-'Asqalānī, *Fatḥ al-Bārī: sharḥ Ṣaḥīḥ al-Bukhārī* (Riyadh, 1421/2000), vol. 1, p. 275. For the *ḥadīth* not containing 'Umar's name, see *Ṣaḥīḥ al-Bukhārī*, vol. 5, p. 512, and al-'Asqalānī, *Fatḥ al-Bārī*, vol. 8, p. 166 and vol. 6, p. 204.

[31] Al-Diyārbakrī, *Tā'rīkh al-khamīs*, vol. 2, p. 182.

[32] Ibn Ḥazm, *Jawāmi' al-siyar wa-khamsa rasā'il ukhrā* (Cairo, 1956), p. 263.

ʿUmar's responsibility is alleviated because other participants had also agreed with his decision (*wa-sāʿadahu qawmun*).[33]

Ibn Ḥazm goes on further to argue that if the writing had any significance for the religion and the *sharīʿa*, neither the words of ʿUmar nor those of somebody else would have prevented the Prophet from writing it down (*illā annahu lā shakka law kāna min wājibāt al-dīn wa-lawāzim al-sharīʿa lam yathnihi ʿanhu kalām ʿUmar wa-lā ghayrihi*).[34] Moreover, Ibn Ḥazm not only defends ʿUmar's action, but emphasises that the community would not have gone astray without the leadership of the Prophet after his death. Thus he interprets the episode and expresses his own preference not merely through which report he includes or excludes, but also through direct explanation and interpretation. Similar effort is seen in al-Ḥalabī's (d. 1044/1635) work, who explains ʿUmar's reaction to the Prophet's request by saying that the former wanted to ease the Prophet's task (*ay wa-innamā qāla dhālika (r) takhfīfan ʿalā rasūl Allāh (ṣ)*).[35]

However, issues with the report do not stop here. The last report (version nine) in Ibn Saʿd's *al-Ṭabaqāt* leaves the reader completely confused by introducing four new details and excluding most of the previously mentioned ones. The first additions are words ascribed to ʿUmar in which he refers to Rūm (that is, the Byzantine Empire) and certain towns in it (*fulāna wa-fulāna madāʾin al-Rūm*), perhaps expressing his disbelief that the Prophet could die before these towns were conquered:

> The Messenger of God (peace be upon him) is not going to die until we become victorious over them [i.e., the *madāʾin* in *al-Rūm*] (*laysa bi-mayyitin ḥattā naftatiḥahā*). Even if he dies (*wa-law māta*), we will wait for him as the children of Israel waited for Moses (*[i]ntaẓarnāhu kamā intaẓarat banū Isrāʾīl Mūsā*).[36]

ʿUmar promises that they (the Muslims) would wait for his comeback as did the children of Israel who waited for Moses to return. A similar remark is made in two instances involving a council of war held by Muḥammad before the Battles of Badr (2/623–624) and al-Ḥudaybiyya (6/627–628). Uri Rubin discusses these instances in detail and argues that they allude to Qurʾan 5:24: 'They said: "Moses, we will never enter it so long as they are in it. Go forth, you and your Lord, and do battle; we will be sitting here".'[37] Alluding to this verse, al-Miqdād b. al-Aswad replies to Muḥammad's request: 'By God, we shall not tell you what the children of Israel told their prophet: "Go forth, you and your Lord, and do battle; we will be sitting here". Nay, we say: "Go

---

33 Ibid., pp. 263–264.

34 Ibid., p. 264.

35 Al-Ḥalabī, *al-Sīra al-ḥalabiyya: Insān al-ʿuyūn fī sīrat al-Amīn al-Maʾmūn* (Beirut, 1980), vol. 3, p. 456.

36 Ibn Saʿd, *al-Ṭabaqāt*, vol. 2, p. 244.

37 Uri Rubin, 'The Life of Muḥammad and the Islamic Self-Image', in H. Motzki, ed., *The Biography of Muḥammad: The Issue of the Sources* (Leiden, 2000), pp. 3–17.

forth, you and your Lord, and do battle; we will be fighting with you".'[38] The contrast is made between the faithful Muslims and the disobeying Israelites. Rubin also shows that there are several versions in which the honour of expressing readiness to fight on the side of the Prophet by referring to this Qur'anic verse moves from a particular person, namely al-Miqdād, to the Ansār as a group and later to the Arabian *umma* as a whole.[39]

Also, in the same report of Ibn Saʿd, it is Zaynab, the wife of the Prophet, who is identified as the person demanding the fulfilment of his request. In other words, the anonymous reference to a group of women is changed to an identified Zaynab. The last sentence of the report conveys the impression that the Prophet died at that very moment following the departure of the people. In sum, Ibn Saʿd in his last version leaves many newly introduced and unanswered problems for his readers and for later scholars. One of the authors, who could have shed light on these and other problems concerning the episode, was al-Balādhurī (d. ca. 890s), a student of Ibn Saʿd. Al-Balādhurī is chronologically the second scholar to include the episode in his work, but he does not address these issues either because he did not want to or because they were not problematic for him.

Al-Balādhurī, who begins with a report through Ibn Saʿd going back to ʿĀ'isha,[40] puts Abū Bakr in the centre of the episode. In fact, the section where al-Balādhurī gathers all the reports on the incident is entirely devoted to Abū Bakr and what the Prophet said about him. It is a first major change of the emphasis in the interpretation of the episode. As mentioned earlier, reports in Ibn Saʿd's *al-Ṭabaqāt* emphasise the very fact that an episode where the Prophet wanted to write something for his community had taken place. Al-Balādhurī moves the emphasis to the purpose of the writing, suggesting that it was to confirm Abū Bakr's succession to the Prophet so that there was no disagreement on the matter (*ḥattā aktuba li-Abī Bakr kitāban lā yukhtalafu ʿalayhi maʿahu*).[41]

Beginning with and following the work of al-Balādhurī, most of the reports preserved in the Sunni-oriented sources emphasise (to various degrees) that Abū Bakr was the chosen one, and the incident of writing becomes part of the Prophet's confirmation of this very point. The desire is to show that it was Abū Bakr who was chosen to be the leader and that the Prophet's writing, as well as his last attendance at a public prayer, were meant to confirm Abū Bakr's ability to lead the Muslims. This is partly shown in a move from the writing being intended for the community

---

[38] Ibid., p. 7.

[39] For more details, see ibid., pp. 7–16.

[40] The report's chain includes Ibn Saʿd's name despite the fact that the latter does not quote it in his *al-Ṭabaqāt*.

[41] Al-Balādhurī, *Ansāb*, vol. 1, p. 541. Also, see al-Diyārbakrī, *Ta'rīkh al-khamīs*, vol. 2, p. 182; al-Ḥalabī, *al-Sīra al-ḥalabiyya*, vol. 3, p. 456; Ibn Ḥazm, *Jawāmiʿ*, p. 264. And it is ʿAbd al-Raḥmān b. Abī Bakr or ʿĀ'isha who were asked to bring the medium to write (*daʿā ʿAbd al-Raḥmān b. Abī Bakr fa-qāla i'tinī bi-katif*) or to summon Abū Bakr for the purpose (*udʿī lī abāki wa-akhāki*).

in general towards an argument that it was meant for an unidentified person (Ibn Saʿd, where we find the episode for the first time), through to the name of Abū Bakr (al-Balādhurī). Some of the later authors attempt to use the report as a clear proof that the writing was meant to confirm the succession of Abū Bakr (Ibn Kathīr and al-Ḥalabī quoting Ibn Kathīr). It is, of course, quite natural that an opposite to this tendency would be noticeable in the Shiʿi sources, which would argue that the reason behind the Prophet's wish to write was to confirm ʿAlī as his rightful successor.

In another version al-Balādhurī has a new sentence along the same line: '*thumma qāla: daʿīhi maʿādh Allāh an yakhtalif al-muʾminūn fī Abī Bakr*',[42] while also introducing the theme of those people who would oppose Abū Bakr's appointment. It is also noteworthy that none of the six versions adduced by al-Balādhurī contain the name of ʿUmar or ʿAlī, and all concentrate on ʿĀʾisha and her father Abū Bakr.

Thus, a new concern emerges. The indication of Abū Bakr as successor and the Prophet's confidence that God and the believers would not go against this decision, is ironically intertwined with the suspicion that some people may reject it and wish for something else (e.g., al-Balādhurī: *fa-innī akhāfu an yatamannā*; Ibn Ḥazm: *yatamannā mutamannin aw yaqūla qāʾil, wa-yaʾbā Allāh waʾl-muʾminūn illā Abā Bakr;* al-Diyārbakrī: *abā Allāh waʾl-muʾminūn an yukhtalafa ʿalayka yā Abā Bakr*; al-Ḥalabī: *abā Allāh waʾl-muʾminūn an yukhtalaf*).[43] In other words, the emergence of Abū Bakr as the successor creates the corresponding theme of those who secretly wish something that they do not have the right for. It is variously expressed as *yatamannā mutamannin* (one may wish), *yaẓunnu ẓānn* (one might assume) and *yaqūlu al-qāʾil* (one might say).

Slightly different but conveying the same message is al-Ḥalabī's version, which he quotes directly on the authority of ʿĀʾisha without further *isnād*. An important change here is the addition of '*anā awlā*', most probably alluding to the claim of ʿAlī's supporters for his precedence in initiation to Islam (*fa-innī akhāfu an yatamannā mutamannin aw yaqūl qāʾil anā awlā wa-yaʾba Allāh waʾl-muʾminūn illā Abā Bakr*).[44]

Ibn Ḥazm's second version also follows along similar lines to those of al-Balādhurī, al-Diyārbakrī and al-Ḥalabī. However, Ibn Ḥazm again tends to add his personal interpretation of events as well. For example, he laments the fact that the Prophet did not have an opportunity to record his message. Had he done so, Ibn Ḥazm says, this would have prevented much of the bloodshed which followed his death (*faʾl-kitāb kāna rāfiʿan li-hādha al-nizāʿ*).[45]

This kind of openly expressed personal view, in my opinion, is one of the striking characteristics of Ibn Ḥazm's short *sīra*. None of our authors, apart from Ibn Kathīr,

42 Al-Balādhurī, *Ansāb*, vol. 1, p. 542.

43 Al-Balādhurī, *Ansāb*, vol. 1, p. 542; Ibn Ḥazm, *Jawāmiʿ*, p. 264; al-Diyārbakrī, *Taʾrīkh al-khamīs*, vol. 2, p. 182; al-Ḥalabī, *al-Sīra al-ḥalabiyya*, vol. 3, p. 456. Ibn Hishām also includes similar expression, but he connects them with the Prophet's request for Abū Bakr to lead the prayer. See his *al-Sīra*, vol. 4, pp. 212–213.

44 Al-Ḥalabī, *al-Sīra al-ḥalabiyya*, vol. 3, p. 456.

45 Ibn Ḥazm, *Jawāmiʿ*, p. 264.

whom I will discuss later, talk directly about the repercussions of this incident for the later history of Islam. Ibn Ḥazm goes beyond the usual 'silently expressing' method of *sīra* authors and shares his own position with the reader, often ignoring *isnād* altogether. He seems to be the only one among his generation of authors who does this. Moreover, he is also comparatively free with the use of the chain of transmitters and reports, and tries to mix and match different parts of various reports with each other in order to produce a short and comprehensive narrative of the main events of the Prophet's life. Yet he does not seem to shy away from sensitive details. Although this sort of attitude does not make him a strict observer of *isnād* and some other niceties of *sīra* and *ḥadīth* tradition, it serves the main purpose of *sīra* literature, that is, to compose a chronologically arranged narrative of the Prophet's life, yet retaining the multitude of variants and the chronological order of events.

Another author who not only attempts to produce a smooth narrative, but also shows his own interpretation of the purpose behind the episode and the various reports associated with it, is Ibn Sayyid al-Nās. The technique of condensing various reports can be demonstrated by the way in which he combines the Prophet's request to Abū Bakr to lead the prayer, his last attendance of public prayer, and the story of 'pen and paper'. Yet, Ibn Sayyid al-Nās' approach causes difficulty in making sense of the reports existing in other sources, because he merges fragments and details from various reports in one continuous narrative. However, when read against the reports of the episodes in other sources, his version seems rather confusing.

For example, Ibn Sayyid al-Nās' version does not make it clear whether this incident happened in the mosque or in the house of 'Ā'isha, because the scene of Muḥammad's last attendance at the mosque comes in-between. While other authors suggest that the incident took place in the house (e.g., Ibn Sa'd: *kunnā 'inda al-nabī*; al-Balādhurī: *fa-kāna fī al-bayt laghaṭ*; Ibn Ḥazm: *ijtama'a 'indahu* [that is, at the Prophet's place]). Then suddenly the three recommendations appear which are not only different, but are also attributed to 'Ā'isha and Umm Salama, not 'Alī or Ibn 'Abbās as in other sources. The three recommendations are: *lā yutraka bi-jazīrat al-'arab dīnān, ṣalāt* and *mā malakat aymānukum*. Then Ibn Sayyid al-Nās quotes a report from 'Ā'isha on the choice of a prophet on whether to die and finishes with her saying that these were the last words of the Prophet: '*fa-kānat tilka ākhir kalima takallama bi-hā rasūl Allāh (ṣ)*'.[46]

Another variant approach to the story is seen in Ibn Kathīr's *sīra*. The climax of the dispute associated with this small but significant episode in the life of Prophet Muḥammad is evident in the way Ibn Kathīr deals with it. He turns it into an open battlefield of theological and sectarian dispute. Having cited several versions of the report from his chosen authorities, albeit in his own redaction, Ibn Kathīr writes:

> This *ḥadīth* has served to feed the imaginations of certain foolish persons (*ba'ḍ al-aghbiyā'*), the advocators of improper innovative practices (*ahl al-bid'a*), such

[46] Ibn Sayyid al-Nās, *'Uyūn*, vol. 2, p. 407.

> as the *Shīʿa* and others, all claiming that the Messenger of God (peace be upon him) wished to write in the text referred to above what they purport in their own statement. This claim of theirs constitutes adherence to obscurity and disregard for what is fully established. The Sunnis (*ahl al-sunna*) accept what is fully established and reject what might be viewed as allegorical. This is the methodology of those firmly rooted in knowledge (*al-rāsikhūn fiʾl-ʿilm*), as God, the Almighty and Glorious characterised them in His Book.[47] This area is one of those where the feet of the lost ones (*ahl al-ḍalālāt*) slip. The Sunnis, however, follow no path (*madhhab*) but pursue the truth alone, moving with it along whatever path it leads. Whatever he (peace be upon him) wished to write down has come previously in those clear and reliable *ḥadīth*s (*al-aḥādīth al-ṣaḥīḥa*) that lend themselves to interpretation.[48]

The evidence presented so far shows that although choosing which version to include to some extent hints at the preference and the position of an author (unless they quote it and then refute its contents either directly or by bringing in other versions), several voice their preferences more openly: Ibn Ḥazm, Ibn Sayyid al-Nās and Ibn Kathīr. Among those Ibn Kathīr goes much further than, at least, the *sīra* tradition commonly purports to do, by strongly advocating and defending his own position in open polemic. His statement is interesting not only in what it contains, but also in how he actually uses that contents to argue for his case. Here, for the first time among our compared *sīra*s, we actually see direct legal and theological polemics as related to this *ḥadīth* and the story associated with it.

Ibn Kathīr adds theological disputes to the common concerns of *sīra* (such as those pertaining to authenticity of the reports, reliability of the chain of transmitters, lexical and grammatical commentaries, authenticity of poetry), and in doing so uses specific terminology, such as *al-rāsikhūn fiʾl-ʿilm, madhhab, al-tamassuk biʾl-mutashābih, muḥkam, ṭarīqa* and *ahl al-ḍalālāt.*

Four other reports following this polemic, which are in line with al-Balādhurī's versions, lead Ibn Kathīr to his final argument on the matter:

> He [the Prophet] (peace be upon him) had delivered a great *khuṭba* on a Thursday, five days before he died, where he stated the good qualities of the trustworthy one from among the other Companions (*faḍl al-Ṣiddīq min bayni sāʾir al-ṣaḥāba*). Part of that was his command to him [i.e., Abū Bakr] (*maʿa mā kāna qad naṣṣa*[49] *ʿalayhi*) to lead the rest of the Companions in prayer, the explanation for which would come in the presence of them [i.e., the *ṣahāba*] all. Perhaps, this *khuṭba* of his was in place of what he wanted to put in writing (*wa-laʿalla khuṭbatahu hādhihi kānat ʿiwaḍan ʿammā arāda an yaktubahu fī al-kitāb*). He (peace be upon him) had washed himself prior to this important *khuṭba* and was poured upon from seven

---

47 Q.3:7.

48 Ibn Kathīr, *al-Sīra al-nabawiyya*, vol. 4, pp. 451–452 (=*The Life*, vol. 4, p. 327).

49 Note Ibn Kattīr's use of the term *naṣṣ* (specific designation) in this context.

unopened water-skins ... In sum, he [the Prophet] (peace be upon him) washed, then went out and prayed together with the people and addressed them. As was earlier reported in a *ḥadīth* from 'Ā'isha.[50]

Ibn Kathīr's main message is that all the efforts of the Prophet concerning this writing were directed towards the announcement of Abū Bakr as his successor. The announcement was so important that even the Prophet had to purify himself by washing before embarking on it. Moreover, Ibn Kathīr states not only which versions of the reports are the accepted ones (this he does through selecting and carefully editing them), but also *what they really convey* and *how they should be* understood.

Ibn Kathīr also diverges from the *sīra* tradition in one other aspect, namely the choice of his authorities. Among the six reports that Ibn Kathīr cites, four are transmitted on the authority of al-Bukhārī and two on the authority of Ibn Hanbal.[51] None of his authorities are that of *sīra* tradition, but of *ḥadīth* and *fiqh*.[52] For Ibn Kathīr the final authority lies with the *ḥadīth*; his *tafsīr* is therefore often termed as '*tafsīr bi'l-ḥadīth*'. His *sīra* could also be termed as '*sīra bi'l-ḥadīth*'.

In sum, although Ibn Kathīr chooses to include the episode, he is very much aware of the sensitivities associated with it. Although he does not reject the story, he forcefully rejects what the outside tradition and actualities might do with it. The very point in including the story in his *sīra* is to argue against that possibility. This, in my opinion, shows his awareness of the potential dangers of the information and/or lack of it in this episode in particular, and the tradition in general.

It is quite understandable that the Shi'i sources would have a different account of this story. Shaykh al-Mufīd (d. 413/1022), for example, puts much emphasis on the events following the Farewell Pilgrimage: the incident at Ghadīr Khumm and the last days of the Prophet's life. His description of these events differs considerably from the sources discussed so far.[53]

In his version of the story of 'pen and paper', 'Alī plays a central role in all the events preceding the death of the Prophet: there is a clear designation for him to succeed the Prophet, he is accompanying the Prophet to the cemetery of al-Baqī', he is asked to fight for the interpretation of the Qur'an after the death of the Prophet, and the Prophet gives him his ring, his sword and his armour. Unlike most of the sources discussed above, Shaykh al-Mufīd, includes only one version of the *ḥadīth* without mentioning the *isnād*:

---

50 Ibn Kathīr, *al-Sīra al-nabawiyya*, vol. 4, p. 453. (=*The Life*, vol. 4, p. 328)

51 Al-Bukhārī, *Ṣaḥīḥ*, vol. 9, *ḥadīth* number 468, vol. 7, *ḥadīth* number 573; vol. 4, *ḥadīth* number 393.

52 Al-Ḥalabī also refers quite often to legal authorities, as he does in the case of the story of 'Abd al-Muṭṭalib's vow, and in fact, attempts to prove precepts of the *jāhiliyya* by applying to them the regulations of Islamic law. In this case, however, he abstains from engaging in further theological and legal polemic.

53 Shaykh al-Mufīd, *Kitāb al-Irshād: The Book of Guidance into the Lives of the Twelve Imams*, tr. Ian K. A. Howard (London, 1981), p. 127.

> ... When he, peace be on him, recovered consciousness, one of them said: 'We will not bring you ink and parchment, Apostle of God'.
>
> 'May God remove him who made you say "no",' he said. 'However, I will appoint a trustee over you in a better way through my family'. Then he turned his head away from the people. They rose to leave but al-ʿAbbās, al-Faḍl b. al-ʿAbbās and ʿAlī b. Abī Ṭālib and his family, in particular, remained with him.[54]

Shaykh al-Mufīd's aim was to prove that ʿAlī was the most excellent of the Prophet's Companions and was clearly designated as his successor. In the Shiʿi sources ʿAlī, as expected, plays a much bigger role. Therefore, al-Mufīd's recension of the event has significant variations and additional details, which are specifically Shiʿi in their approach and the purpose they play in the overall scheme of things. The message that Shaykh al-Mufīd gives is quite obvious: it was ʿUmar who disobeyed the Prophet and forbade the people to bring him ink and parchment, people regretted their disobedience, the Prophet was displeased with ʿUmar and made it clear that ʿAlī is to be the trustee over the Muslims. Apart from the latter argument, all the others, as seen above, are present in non-Shiʿi sources as well.

It is important to note that Shaykh al-Mufīd includes a different version of the same report in his *Amālī*.[55] This version resembles Ibn Saʿd's version eight, especially because it mentions the sentence ascribed to ʿUmar: 'Do not give him anything, for he is overwhelmed with pain; you have the Qur'an, the Book of Allah is sufficient for you (*lā tuʾtūhu bi-shayʾin fa-innahu qad ghalabahu al-wajʿ wa-ʿindakum al-Qurʾān ḥasbunā kitāb Allāh*).'[56]

Al-Shahrastānī refers to this incident as 'the first dispute that took place during the Prophet's sickness'. It is interesting to note that he also reports it on the authority of al-Bukhārī, but unlike Ibn Kathīr, retains the reference to ʿUmar:

> When the last sickness of the Prophet became acute, he said, 'Bring me an inkpot and writing materials; I shall write something for you so that you will not be led astray after my departure.' ʿUmar said, 'The Prophet has been overcome by pain, God's Book is sufficient for us'. A noisy argument arose among those gathered; whereupon the Prophet said, 'Go away; there should be no quarrelling in my presence'. Ibn ʿAbbās says, 'What a tragedy which prevented us from having some writing of the Prophet!'[57]

---

[54] Shaykh al-Mufīd, *Kitāb al-irshād*, pp. 130–131.

[55] Shaykh al-Mufīd, *Amālī al-Shaykh al-Mufīd* (Najaf, n.d.), pp. 22–23, tr. Mulla Asgharali M. M. Jaffer as *Al-Amaali: The Dictations of Sheikh al-Mufid* (Stanmore, Middlesex, 1998), pp. 58–59.

[56] Shaykh al-Mufīd, *Amālī al-Shaykh al-Mufīd*, p. 22 (trans., p. 59).

[57] Muḥammad b. ʿAbd al-Karīm al-Shahrastānī, *Muslim Sects and Divisions: The Section on Muslim Sects in Kitāb al-Milal waʾl-Niḥal*, tr. A. K. Kazi and J. G. Flynn (London, 1984), p. 18.

However, it is surprising that other major Shiʿi authors, such as al-Kulaynī (d. 329/940–941) in his *al-Kāfī*, al-Nasāʾī (d. 303/915) in his *Kitāb khaṣāʾiṣ amīr al-muʾminīn*, and Muḥammad Bāqir al-Majlisī in his *Mirʾāt al-ʿuqūl*, do not include this *ḥadīth*. Although, both al-Kulaynī and al-Majlisī include a *ḥadīth* about the last days of the Prophet, they only have the version in which the Prophet is said to have taught ʿAlī a thousand words (*ḥarf*).[58]

There is little doubt, therefore, that our authors were quite conscious of the various interpretations of this story. What is apparent, as far as the variations are concerned, is that among the first generation of authors (2nd–3rd/8th–9th centuries), al-Wāqidī and Ibn Hishām do not mention the episode at all. However, already al-Wāqidī's student Ibn Saʿd includes nine versions of the report in his work. Although most of Ibn Saʿd's versions are cited on the authority of al-Wāqidī, the latter himself had not included them in his *Kitāb al-maghāzī*, possibly because they were not relevant to *maghāzī,* the main concern of his work, and possibly because he had a separate work on the death of the Prophet, wherein he might have included them.

Why Ibn Saʿd should have included so many reports which contradict each other is not obvious. At least, al-Balādhurī's main concern can be discerned from the central issue that his adduced versions deal with, namely Abū Bakr's fitness for succeeding the Prophet. The reports quoted by al-Balādhurī are also united in that they claim that the purpose of the writing was to confirm Abū Bakr's succession in writing. They are all transmitted on the authority of ʿĀʾisha.

Al-Ṭabarī quotes only two short reports on the incident. In the 5th/11th-century work of Ibn Ḥazm, we see a changing attitude towards the episode. He is the first to express his opinion and interpret what the early reports might have meant by providing some sort of explanation, rather than hinting at it through the selection of variants of the reports that more or less corresponded to his own view; a technique that might have been used more often and consciously by our authors than we are ready to admit. Ibn Sayyid al-Nās (8th/14th century), as mentioned earlier, ignores all issues and chooses to deal with them by carefully editing his chosen material. His student Mughulṭāʾī, for example, does not mention this episode at all in his *al-Ishāra*.[59]

In sum, the treatment of this incident in different sources varies considerably. There are, however, several phrases or sentences (such as '*yawm al-khamīs wa-mā yawmu al-khamīs*' and '*al-raziyya kull al-raziyya*') that unite them and indicate that they all refer to one and the same episode of Muḥammad's life.

---

58 Al-Kulaynī, *al-Uṣūl min al-kāfī* (Najaf, 1958), pp. 296–297; al-Majlisī, *Mirʾāt al-ʿuqūl fī sharḥ akhbār āl rasūl* (Tehran, 1394/1974), vol. 3, pp. 286–287.

59 Mughulṭāʾī b. Qilīj, *al-Ishāra ilā sīrat al-Muṣṭafā wa-taʾrīkh man baʿdahu min al-khulafāʾ*, ed. Muḥammad Niẓām al-Dīn al-Futayyiḥ (Damascus, 1416/1996), pp. 349–350.

Conclusion

So, the question is: what can be inferred from this variety of reports and their interpretation? I would like to suggest that the underlying message of the story might have been different in its earlier stages before it was transformed to express exclusively the vital problem of the succession to the Prophet.

First, let us consider the main concerns of the reports, central among which is the approaching death of the Prophet, that is, the end of prophecy and revelation. This raises the question of future guidance of the Muslims and at the same time triggers two major concerns. One is that the future guidance should be something other than or in addition to the received revelation (because the Prophet wanted to write down something else as a guide for the Muslims that would help them not go astray), and second in that the Prophet appoints somebody to lead the Muslims after his death. This also indicates that with the death of the Prophet, the revelation also comes to an end. His wish to write something down is rejected because the Muslims already have the Qurʾan as a clear guide and, therefore, do not need anything else to be written down besides it. In fact, people are even surprised that the Prophet is considering doing such a thing and openly express their opposition to it. Similarly, the Prophet expresses concerns about a possible opposition to his appointment.

The rejection of putting something else besides the Book of Allah down in writing also suggests that the book already existed in some written form and was accepted as the only guide by the believers. This rejection also suggests that the decision not to put down something else in writing besides the scripture was taken according to the 'consensus' of those present, and that even the Prophet had to accept it and give in. Thus, the major message of these traditions is that the scripture is the most important guide for the Muslims and that there was no need for something else besides it to be written down.

This line of argument, therefore, also suggests that the issues of factionalism and the succession to Muḥammad are not the only underlying concerns of the story. Factionalism between the pro- and anti-ʿAlid and pro- and anti-Abū Bakr camps, in my opinion, overshadows a more important concern in the story. That is, the story seems to emphasise that only the scripture can be written down and there was no need to add anything else to it. This is also explained by the surprise of all those present at hearing the Prophet's wish to put in writing something else besides it; that nothing but the Book of Allah can be written down and serve as guidance; not even the words of the Prophet. Moreover, even the Prophet acknowledges this.

The case of the story of 'pen and paper', if the suggested interpretation is accepted, tells us that the issue of who is going to succeed the Prophet is not the only development connected with the episode. The more important question here is the nature of authority, namely the word of God as opposed to the word of man. In other words, whether something other than the Book of Allah could be written down and considered authoritative alongside it.

In the story of 'pen and paper', the early sources disclose a twofold tendency. The first one develops according to an assumption that the Prophet's writing was meant for the Muslim community in general (e.g., Ibn Saʿd and al-Ṭabarī). The other one, because of external developments, attempts to emphasise a new interpretation of the purpose of the writing, which is to confirm Abū Bakr's succession. Among such external developments are the general Sunni consensus that Abū Bakr was to succeed the Prophet and the consolidation of the special position of the 'Rightly Guided' Caliphs. Al-Balādhurī's version can be considered the beginning of this tendency. The opposite position is represented by the Shiʿi-oriented sources, which argue that the writing was to confirm the designation of ʿAlī as the rightful successor of the Prophet.

A significant change is then seen in the work of the 8th/14th-century Ibn Kathīr. His text is a polemic on theological, sectarian and legal points. His main concern is not what is done with the story in the *sīra* text (which he shows through the careful selection and editing of the quoted versions anyway), but what can be done with the story outside the *sīra* tradition. Ibn Kathīr ignores the very details in the reports that lead him to arguments against other interpretations of the incident, thereby showing his dislike of its contents and problems.[60] Yet he might have had them in mind when he argues for his own position towards the story, which he considers the only correct one.

This is new to the *sīra* tradition in particular, because *sīra* authors usually employ a 'silently expressing' method. Probably shaken by Ibn Kathīr's harsh response to some interpretations of this story, several later authors do not include it. For example, al-Suyūṭī (d. 911/1505) does not mention the incident in his *Khaṣāʾiṣ al-kubrā*, although he pays particular attention to various details about the death of the Prophet. The episode emerges again in the *sīra*s of the 10th/16th-century al-Diyārbakrī and the 11th/17th-century al-Ḥalabī, where we find important changes in approach and style.

Finally, this particular example also demonstrates that once a given story and *ḥadīth*s associated with it were committed to writing, it did not mean that they remained fixed in that final form. Quite the opposite, for even in the written tradition the various elements of a story continued to be transformed. In some cases the transformation left little or nothing of the original version of the story. Therefore, there is little clarity concerning why, how and what happened in this particular case, which naturally leaves the door open for a variety of interpretations of the story of 'pen and paper'.

---

[60] See Calder, '*Tafsīr* from Ṭabarī to Ibn Kathīr', where he argues that Ibn Kathīr's *tafsīr* is in fact 'a significant deviation from the norms of the genre; perhaps as a major turning-point in its development' (p. 101). Calder argues that Ibn Kathīr has objections to the story which the authorities, such as al-Ṭabarī, before him considered part of the tradition (pp. 116–127). In some cases he is even ready to use the Bible against the accepted *tafsīr* tradition to prove his point. He shows a very rigid attitude and accepts, similar to his teacher Ibn Taymiyya, only what has value for the practical implication of the law. He, for example, rejects the story, whereas the earlier authorities of *tafsīr* accepted it. For a study of the influence of *ḥadīth* on Ibn Kathīr as a historian, see Laoust, 'Ibn Kathīr historien', *Arabica*, 2 (1955), pp. 42–88.

PART IV
SHI'I LAW

*Introduction**

Mohyddin Yahia

The chapters comprising the fourth part of this volume regard the major components of Shiʿi law – with the exception of the first one which focuses on the common religious atmosphere of the early centuries before a 'schism' irremediably separated Sunni and Shiʿi Muslims. There is no doubt that these chapters will be of interest to all scholars of Islam, whether experts of Islamic law or not. These contributions are particularly welcome given that, as it is known, studies on the history of *fiqh* are rare in the currently prolific production in the field of studies on Islam. Apropos the scientific curiosity about the *fiqh* of minorities or 'sects', it is no exaggeration to say that it has remained fractional over the past decades; by browsing through the *Index Islamicus*, it is evident that articles on the subject can be counted on the fingers of one hand. One of the main reasons for such an unfortunate disaffection is that our knowledge in this field depends on the availability of original sources and first-hand editions of texts. It is only natural that, in the case of minorities, the interest of the researchers has given priority to the historical works rather than the technicalities of *fiqh*.

The situation is even less favourable because the experts still often tend to be over-dependent on the discourse of the heresiographers whose indirect information remains questionable. They have long called for a more direct access to primary sources; yet referring to these works has often proved to be a sensitive issue, in relation to schismatic communities. Amongst the interesting aspects of the following chapters is that they have specifically examined the *fiqh* of the minorities on the basis of what is said by their members. Even before considering the perspective of social history or historical anthropology, one should have at one's disposal a sufficient number of studies capable of conveying to specialists of other disciplines the precise meaning of the texts on *fiqh*. Only such studies are able to provide the key to understanding the more general works, not to mention the historical unpublished information which they might also contain.

The reader might ask whether it is appropriate to juxtapose studies that focus on the *fiqh* of different communities. Would it not be an artificial device and the sign of an incongruent eclecticism controlled by a purely editorial logic? It will be seen that

* Translated from the French by Maria De Cillis.

this is not the case. Any expert on *fiqh* knows that the differences between schools of law specific to these different communities do not bear the significance to which they are usually ascribed.[1] In fact, despite the absence of a unifying theme, some threads run throughout the chapters included in this part under the banner of Shiʿi law and bring them together into a coherent whole notwithstanding their apparent divergence. First, these studies have in common the fact that they have mainly focused on the period before the legal *madhāhib* took their final shapes, and therefore, at a time when *fiqh* was not the decisive criterion for the identity of the religious groups. In addition, these different issues are not limited to the *fiqh* of one of these groups but can be found or reformulated in that of another rite, throughout several schools of thought. In particular, one can cite the question of the authority of the Imam in legal matters, the value of *ijmāʿ* as a source of *fiqh*, the legitimacy of *ijtihād* independent from the established legal schools, and the question of the fundamental relationship between *usūl* and *furūʿ*. Finally, some studies address broader issues; so, for example, the chapter by Melchert sheds light on the thorny issue of the starting point of the separation between Shiʿi and Sunni Islam.

It is clear that research in the field of Islamic studies would be severely damaged should it be deprived of the input from the studies on dissident communities deemed as 'peripheral'. The field of Islamic studies must maintain its unity. Just as sometimes 'the exception proves the rule' better than the rule itself, likewise, the answer to the most fundamental and common issues can sometimes be found outside the majority or so-called 'orthodox' version of Islam. This point is still valid even though the days when Ignaz Goldziher – repudiating any specialisation – managed to encompass within his expertise the entire Islamic knowledge available in his time, are long gone.

I

The first chapter in this section, Christopher Melchert's 'Renunciation (*Zuhd*) in the Early Shiʿi Tradition', is a continuation of previous research on the origin of Islamic mysticism, where the author had sought to question the affiliation historically drawn between Sufism and the early *zuhd* (renunciation).[2] Contrary to the representation

---

1 See, for example, what distinguishes the Ismaili *fiqh* from the Twelver Imāmī *fiqh* (see note 31 below). On the major differences between Imāmī *fiqh* and Sunni *fiqh*, see Y. Linant de Bellefonds, 'Le droit imâmite', in Toufic Fahd, ed., *Le Shîʿisme Imâmite,* Colloque de Strasbourg (6–9 May 1968) (Paris, 1970), pp. 183–200.

2 C. Melchert, 'The Transition from Asceticism to Mysticism at the Middle of the Ninth Century C.E.', *SI*, 83 (1996), pp. 51–70.

conveyed by Sufism itself,[3] which is reflected in the majority of orientalist works,[4] the idea of such an affiliation would be an expression of pious anachronism.

In this chapter, the author compares the statements attributed to the *Ahl al-bayt* and contemporary *zuhhād*, touching upon aspects of the moral recommendations and spiritual practice. The sources employed are the great collections of traditions and *akhbār*, both Sunni and Shiʿi, related to the pious ancients (*salaf*). The author notices that, in the first centuries of Islam, a large number of attitudes and views on the subjects in question were common for the Sunnis and Shiʿis alike, to the extent that they were formulated identically both by the Sunni and the Shiʿi authors. No essential difference separates the two groups. Beyond the theological antagonisms, 'Sunni Muslims' and 'Shiʿi Muslims' – if these groups can be referred to by these names in this early age – shared a great deal of religious and spiritual references. However, with the advent of Sufism, the religious orientation of the two groups began to differ significantly.

This conclusion reinforces the idea, often expressed, according to which the distinction between the two major components of Islam fades away as one goes back to the period of the origins. The author conveys the view that the 'schism' between the two groups – at least as far as the creed is concerned – did not occur before the middle of the 3rd/9th century. He suggests this hypothesis without stating it explicitly; aware of the fact that it is in need of more solid historical data, this hypothesis contradicts the vision Shiʿi orthodoxy has of its own identity. Such a portrayal rests on a dogma, according to which the words of the Imams have never ceased to be a bridge, a vital mediation between the Prophet and the believers.[5] One must conclude that the first circles devoted to the cause of ʿAlī b. Abī Ṭālib (d. 40/661) had, vis-à-vis the traditions of the Imams, a reverence far more nuanced than the one which dominated thereafter.

It might be opportune to include at this point in the debate a trend which, although minor within Shiʿi Islam, adopts an original approach to Sufism. Applied to this trend, the conclusion provided by Melchert would not be at this time an implausible one, should one address Shiʿi Islam in a broader sense which refers not so much to the belonging to a politico-religious party, but rather to fidelity to the esoteric teachings

---

[3] On this 'endogenous' perspective, see Abū Bakr Sirāj al-Dīn, 'The Origins of Sufism', *Islamic Quarterly*, 3 (1956), pp. 53–64.

[4] The most argued defence of this thesis is given by Louis Massignon in his classic *Essai sur les origines du lexique technique de la mystique Musulmane* (Paris, 1954), which offers an overview of Muslim mysticism and asceticism of the early centuries of Islam. This view has hardly changed in more recent works on the history of Sufism such as A. M. Schimmel, *Mystical Dimensions of Islam* (Chapel Hill, NC, 1975), due to the state of the sources relative to that period. R. Gramlich retrieves the same perspective, although he presents it in a more nuanced way in *Weltverzicht, Grundlagen und Weisen islamischer Askese, Harrassowitz* (Wiesbaden, 1997), p. 11ff.

[5] M. A. Amir-Moezzi and C. Jambet, *Qu'est-ce que le Shīʿisme?* (Paris, 2004); H. Laoust, 'Comment définir Le sunnisme le chiisme', *Revue des Études Islamiques*, 47 (1979) pp. 8–43; also published as an offprint (Paris, 1985); M. A. Amir-Moezzi, *Le Coran silencieux et le Coran Parlant: sources scripturaires de l'islam entre histoire et ferveur* (Paris, 2011).

of the Prophet transmitted to the *ahl al-bayt*. According to this current of thought, Sufism basically owes its existence to Shiʿi Islam and to the vivifying force that the latter infused within Sunnism through doctrines or by other means.[6] This picture, taking into consideration Melchert's current research, could even hold true for the earlier period, that of the *zuhhād* of the first two centuries. Since their religious orientation was very close to that of the Shiʿis, it might have easily received such influence. In this light, the statement that 'in fact, it is difficult to say whether a particular author was Sunni or Shiʿi before the 4th century',[7] sounds less audacious than it could seem at first sight. With reference to the contacts and mutual influences between Shiʿis and Proto-Sunnis, one may typically mention the relationship between the first eight Imams and the great figures of spirituality of that time. Attestations on this relationship can be found in the biographies of ascetics and mystics such as Ḥasan al-Baṣrī Uways al-Qaranī – believed to be disciples of ʿAlī – and Ibrāhīm. b. Adham, Bishr al-Ḥāfī, Bayāzid who belonged, according to tradition, to the circle of Jaʿfar al-Ṣādiq (d. 148/765), not to mention Ḥallāj, who was still assiduously attending the gatherings of Shiʿi groups in the middle of the 3rd century. It is only from the eighth Imam (ʿAlī al-Riḍā, d. 203/818), that they (the Imams) did no more openly associate themselves with the Sufis. Subsequently, Shiʿi Islam and Sufism followed two distinct paths without this causing the relations between the two to be severed.[8]

The present study by Melchert is not inconsistent with the refusal to consider the Sufis of the 3rd/9th century as being responsible for the continuation of ancient asceticism. It is less certain, however, whether this study may represent a decisive conclusion. Indeed Shiʿi Islam, whilst admitting the legitimacy of asceticism, did not allow itself to be absorbed within the nascent Sufism. The author suggests that, on the contrary, it did not find in it its original source. This argument, however, remains fragile and, in the current state of the research, the classical explanation for the origins of Sufism retains its value. The author of these lines should be allowed an explanatory digression on this point. If, to use Melchert's conceptual framework,[9] the ascetic and the mystic are, in the Weberian sense, two opposing ideal types, then why at that early time were there only ascetics and not mystics? It is not clear, moreover, whether the meaning ascribed by the author to the word *zuhd* is that of the Muslim tradition. Melchert cannot escape from the rebuke of having projected upon it a foreign concept. According to the Qur'an,

[6] 'Le chiisme est à l'origine de ce qu'on appellera plus tard le soufisme'. S. H. Nasr, 'Le Shîʿisme et le Soufisme, relations principielles et historiques', in Fahd, ed., *Le Shîʿisme Imâmite*, p. 216. Such a thesis cannot be defined as being purely 'endogenous', as it is similarly supported by T. Andrae, in his work *Die Person Muhammeds im Leben und Glauben seiner Gemeinde* (Stockholm, 1918), pp. 297–298.

[7] Nasr, 'Le Shîʿisme et le Soufisme', p. 225.

[8] Ibid., p. 226.

[9] The author refers at the beginning of his previously mentioned article on *zuhd* to a sociologic theory, and more precisely, to the theory of Gert H. Mueller. It consists in defining asceticism and mysticism by contrasting them with each other, to make them the two extreme poles of the religious attitude. Melchert, 'The Transition from Asceticism to Mysticism', p. 52.

zuhd involves neither the excessive mortifications of Christian-type asceticism, without however excluding them, nor solitary withdrawal from society: '*Zuhd* is not a demonstration of ascetic behaviour; it is a deeper feeling expressed as either contentment, trust in God or both.'[10] This is essentially a means to purify the faith and, as such, it is the very condition of mysticism. The question of the means is a secondary one; it does not imply the denial of the legitimate needs of the body. Rather than opposing asceticism and mysticism, the evidence found in the earliest documents invites us to postulate, conversely, their mutual relationships. Such early evidence is quite plentiful. According to al-Ashʿarī, the Murjiʾī ascetic of the 2nd century, Abū Shamīr, considered faith as something which – by definition – has to include love for God and humility. So, some amongst the Muʿtazilīs clothed themselves with wool, taking on the name of *sūfiyāt al-muʿtazila*; for al-Ashʿarī, these were true Sufis and the famous ʿAmr b. ʿUbayd (d. 143/760) was one of them.[11]

The present survey by Melchert only confirms that the Shiʿa did not derogate from what had become the general rule amongst the *zuhhād*. In addition, the concept of *tawakkul* (trust in God) already present in the middle of the 2nd century with Ibrāhīm b. Adham (d. 165/781) led to a kind of purely interior *zuhd* and to a sensitivity which was indifferent to mortification.[12] Finally, there is no need to invoke any hypothetical historico-social factor to explain the transition from asceticism to mysticism. It will suffice to remember that the Qurʾan contains mystical 'germs',[13] and that during the first two centuries, the condition of Islamic science did not allow *zuhhād* to express their spiritual states other than through a vocabulary borrowed from the contemporary Islamic sciences themselves and the Qurʾan – as demonstrated by L. Massignon in his famous *Essai*. The vocabulary of Muqātil, another ascetic (d. 150/767), anticipates that of the later mystical thought,[14] and it is worth noting that it was precisely the *zuhhād* that transmitted those *qudsī ḥadīth*s (divine sayings) whose content is undeniably mystical (such as *ʿashiqanī wa ʿashiqtuhu*).[15]

---

[10] L. Kinberg, 'What is Meant by Zuhd', *SI*, 61 (1985), p. 34.

[11] J. van Ess, *Theologie und Gesellschaft im 2. und 3. Jahrhundert Hidschra* (Berlin, 1991–1997), vol. 3, pp. 130–134, 142; ibid., vol. 2, p. 289.

[12] Ibid., vol. 2, p. 237: concerning the Muʿtazilī ascetic, Wāṣil b. ʿAṭāʾ (d. 131/748), it was said: 'Er verschnürte nicht seine Börse über einem Dînâr noch berührte er seinen Dirham. Er kannte nicht das Gewand, das er zuschnitt.' From this, it should be therefore concluded: 'Da wird also zwar seine Askese, seine Unempfendlichkeit gegenüber weltlichen Besitz hervorgehoben; aber es war innerweltliche Askese.' See B. Reinert, *Die Lehre vom* Tawakkul *in der klassischen Sufik* (Berlin, 1968), chapters 1 and 2.

[13] L. Massignon, 'Taṣawwuf', *Shorter Encyclopaedia of Islam* (Leiden, 1953), p. 582; L. Massignon, *Essai sur les origines du lexique technique*, p. 104ff.

[14] P. Nwyia, *Exégèse coranique et langage mystique* (Beirut, 1991), p. 35ff.

[15] 'He loved me and I loved him'; see L. Massignon, *al-Hallaj, martyre mystique de l'Islam* (Paris, 1922), vol. 2, p. 511; Massignon, *Essai sur les origines*, p. 120.

II

The chapter by Ismail K. Poonawala examines the origins of Ismaili *fiqh*, and more specifically, the work of al-Qāḍī al-Nuʿmān (d. 363/974).[16] This study complements other studies undertaken by the same author on this key figure,[17] these being publications that in themselves constitute major references on the doctrinal history of Ismailism.

Given the crucial role of the Fatimid caliphate in the establishing of Ismaili *fiqh*, both in terms of its doctrine and in terms of its codification, any reference to al-Qāḍī al-Nuʿmān, who was the principal architect of this work, presupposes knowledge of an earlier *fiqh*. But on this point the historical sources, which are relatively discrete, merely state that the Ismailis adopted the *fiqh* of the countries where they lived.[18] Anyway, it is to al-Qāḍī al-Nuʿmān specifically that Ismaili *fiqh* owes its existence; he was indeed its founder and not simply the eponym, as in the classical schools of *fiqh*. If the expression *madhhab nuʿmānī* did not emerge, this is undoubtedly due to the fact that the Ismaili law arose under unique conditions. The Qāḍī built his system on the basis of a quite relative *ijtihād*, since it largely borrowed from existing schools as well as written sources, instead of relying on an oral tradition.[19] But this eclecticism does not represent the real difference that separates it from other systems of *fiqh* since each of them, inheriting from an earlier tradition and adopting from it in a free and original way, did not invent any entirely new doctrine. So, for instance, Mālik b. Anas (d. 179/795) respected the *ʿamal* of the Medinese school, Shāfiʿī owes his formation to the Meccan school of *fiqh* dominated by the figure of Muslim b. Khālid al-Zanjī (d. 179/795), and the same discourse is true, *mutatis mutandis*, for other *mujtahid*s of the 2nd century of the *hijra*. With regard, however, to the historical process generally

---

[16] The most recent synthesis on this scholar is that of F. Daftary, 'Al-Qāḍī al-Nuʿmān, Ismāʿīlī Law and Imāmī Shiʿism', in M. A. Amir-Moezzi, M. M. al-Bar-Asher, S. Hopkins, ed., *Le Shîʿisme Imâmite, quarante ans après, hommage à Etan Kohlberg* (Turnhout, 2009). On titles published, see the critical apparatus of the article, quoted below, by I. K. Poonawala, in *Mediaeval Ismaʿili History and Thought.*

[17] These include: 'al-Qadi al-Nuʿman's Works and the Sources', *BSOAS*, 36 (1973), pp. 109–115, 'A Reconsideration of al-Qadi al-Nuʿman's *madhhab*', *BSOAS*, 37 (1974), pp. 572–579, where Poonawala refutes the assumption that al-Qāḍī al-Nuʿmān was in his youth the follower of a creed different from Imamism (some sources claim that he passed from Malikism to Ismailism); 'Al-Qadi al-Nuʿman and Ismaʿili Jurisprudence', in F. Daftary, ed., *Mediaeval Ismaʿili History and Thought* (Cambridge, 1996), pp. 117–143; the article is mainly devoted to the specific doctrinal Ismaili law and its historical evolution.

[18] On the state of *fiqh* prior to the doctrine of al-Qāḍī al-Nuʿmān, see Poonawala, 'al-Qadi al-Nuʿman', p. 133, n. 2, information from the unpublished thesis of S. T. Lokhandwalla, 'The Origins of Ismaʿili Law' (Ph.D. thesis, University of Oxford, 1951).

[19] See Madelung, 'The Sources of Ismāʿīlī Law', repr. in *Religious Schools and Sects in Medieval Islam* (London, 1985), pp. 33–40 of the original pagination included in volume. The article quotes about 20 books from which comes the material of the fragment published as *Kitāb al-īdāḥ*. See also Daftary, 'Al-Qāḍī al-Nuʿmān', p. 184.

followed by the Sunni schools, with the exception of their specific doctrinal lines, the contrast with the Ismaili *fiqh* is obvious. The Schools, gradually constituted, are the result of a collective effort; to the basic doctrine, which was the result of the works by the Schools' eponym, later generations have added other materials, completing or modifying it in some respects, and this process may have lasted up to two centuries after the death of the same eponym. Schools no longer hesitated, during this phase, to borrow the solutions found by their rivals. A period of openness preceded the clear delimitation which will characterise the schools in the classical period.[20]

But let us now turn to a more fundamental question inspired by these remarks: what need did the Ismaili community have for endowing itself with a distinctive expression – today we would say an identifying expression – of Islamic law when such a decision would unavoidably bear important consequences on its destiny, designating it to its milieu and accentuating its visible difference? On this question the author remains silent, but it is possible to advance the hypothesis that the reason for this is of contingent, even accidental nature. It does not appear that this measure is in contradiction with the fundamentally esoteric nature of Ismaili thought. Ismailism which, with the advent of the Fatimid caliphate becoming for the first time the official ideology of a state, did not deny the points which provided the essential aspects of its doctrine: its cosmology, its prophetology, its doctrine of the imamate (*walāya*) and its initiatory doctrine.[21] Al-Qāḍī al-Nuʿmān simply added what was lacking, it could be said, a law that would make it a complete *Weltanschauung*. But if this law was, on the one hand, relatively independent from theology then, on the other hand, it was also intrinsically linked to the socio-political institutions; detach it from the latter, and it would have turned into a merely private ethic with no impact on the social order.[22] The sources are unanimous in saying that the *Daʿāʾim al-Islām*[23] was the result of a political request. The work was composed by al-Qāḍī al-Nuʿmān, probably

---

20 On the current views of how Sunni schools were formed, see W. Hallaq, *The Origins and Evolution of Islamic Law* (Cambridge, 2004), pp. 150–177; C. Melchert, *The Formation of the Sunni Schools of Law, 9th – 10th Centuries CE* (Leiden, 1997). These books are changing the classical representation of older works such as the contribution by J. Schacht in M. Khadduri and H. J. Liebesny, ed., *Law in the Middle East*, vol. 1: *Origin and Development of Islamic Law* (Washington, 1955), pp. 57–84.

21 Poonawala, 'Al-Qāḍī al-Nuʿmān', p. 127; Madelung, *Religious Trends*, pp. 94–95; H. Halm, *Kosmologie und Heilslehre der frühen Ismāʿīlīya: Eine Studie zur islamischen Gnosis* (Wiesbaden, 1978).

22 B. Fillion, 'La spécificité du droit musulman', in M. Flory and J. Henry, ed., *L'enseignement du droit musulman* (Paris, 1989), pp. 93–104.

23 On the general content of *Daʿāʾim al-Islām*, see R. Brunschvig, '*Fiqh* Fatimide et histoire de l'Ifriqiya', in *Hommage à Georges Marçais* (Algiers, 1957), pp. 13–20, repr. in R. Brunschvig, *Études d'Islamologie* (Paris, 1976), vol. 1, pp. 63–70. The book was published in Cairo by A. A. A. Fyzee, in two volumes in 1951–1961. See R. Strothmann, 'Recht der Ismailiten', *Der Islam*, 31 (1954), pp. 131–146; this article, devoted to *Daʿāʾim al-Islām*, had already set out the main features of the Ismaili law relative to Imāmī Shiʿi *fiqh*.

around 349/960[24] on the order of the Fatimid Imam-caliph al-Muʿizz li-Dīn Allāh (r. 341–365/953–975). As a code promulgated officially in the empire, the *Daʿāʾim al-Islām* preserved its character of authority in the Ismaili community, long after the fall of the Fatimids. Ismaili *fiqh* cannot therefore trace its origins, as other schools do, to the first generations of followers of the Prophet, not even, according to the views of modern historians, to the pious figures of the 1st and 2nd centuries who were debating legal issues against the background of traditions inherited from the disciples more or less close to the Prophet.[25] His endeavour reminds rather of the short-lived attempt initiated by the Abbasid Caliph Abū Jaʿfar al-Manṣūr, when he asked Mālik, as it is reported, to use his *Muwaṭṭaʾ* as a reference throughout the empire.[26] The caliph had to abandon his plan at the refusal of the Medinese jurist.

In an earlier article, I. K. Poonawala had raised the question of the authenticity of works attributed by researchers to al-Qāḍī al-Nuʿmān.[27] He then analysed how al-Nuʿmān, in his major works of *fiqh* (*Kitāb al-iqtiṣār, Kitāb al-ikhtiṣār, Kitāb al-īḍāḥ*) used different sources.[28] In the first part of the present chapter, it is possible to find information that supplements this research. The author mentions the various books of *fiqh* which preceded the composition of the *Daʿāʾim al-Islām* and points out, citing al-Nuʿmān himself, the circumstances, characteristics and objectives of their composition. This adds details to those attained through previous studies.

Regarding the law itself, addressed from a comparative perspective, the main feature of the *Kitāb al-īḍāḥ* is that it appears as a compromise between Zaydī *fiqh* and Imāmī *fiqh*, this result holding validity for Ismaili *fiqh* in general.[29] Moreover, the *Daʿāʾim al-Islām* reveals a strong influence of the Mālikī doctrine as it is applied in North Africa, particularly with regards to the *fiqh* on marriage and on commercial transactions,[30] to the extent that the differences between the two schools are, on some points, sometimes minimal and sometimes substantial.[31] These issues raise not only the question concerning the real sources of Ismaili *fiqh* and the loans made to other rituals, but above all the actual relationship between *furūʿ* and *uṣūl*. The problem, far

[24] F. Dachraoui, 'al-Nuʿmān', *EI2*, vol. 8, pp. 117–118.

[25] Hallaq, *The Origins and Evolution of Islamic Law*, pp. 57–78 and 102–121.

[26] Mālik b. Anas would have objected that the Companions were dispersed throughout the empire, each of their judgements made in accordance with his *ʿilm* and his *ijtihād*. See Y. Dutton, *The Origins of Islamic Law: The Qurʾan, the Muwattaʾ and Madinan Amal* (Richmond, 1999), pp. 29 and 192, n. 86, for references to sources that mention this event.

[27] 'Al-Qāḍī al-Nuʿmān's Works and the Sources', pp. 109–115.

[28] It is possible to find the current editions of such works within the critical apparatus of Poonawala, 'al-Qāḍī al-Nuʿmān'.

[29] Madelung, 'The Sources', p. 32, note 22.

[30] Daftary, 'Al-Qāḍī al-Nuʿmān', p. 185; Madelung, *Religious Trends*, p. 40, *addendum*.

[31] On the points that distinguish the Twelver Imāmī *fiqh* from the Ismaili *fiqh*, see A. A. A. Fyzee, 'Shiʿi Legal Theories', in Khadduri and Liebesny, ed., *Law in the Middle East*, vol. 1, pp. 113–131; Fyzee, 'Aspects of Fāṭimid Law', *SI*, 31 (1970), pp. 81–91; Strothmann, 'Recht'; R. Brunschvig, '*Fiqh* Fatimide', p. 15.

from being clarified as any question of comparative *fiqh* requires a long and painstaking investigation, deserves a deeper examination.

At this stage of the research, a preliminary observation should suffice. To make *ijtihād* depend on one of the three sources exclusively reflects a desire to remain loyal to the earliest Shiʿi tradition. But is this not wishful thinking, given the abundant evidence of eclecticism found in *Daʿāʾim al-Islām*? In addition, W. Madelung has shown that there is little change in the solutions proposed in the *Kitāb al-īḍāḥ* and those of the *Daʿāʾim al-Islām*, although the *Ikhtilāf uṣūl al-madhāhib* shows the above-mentioned theoretical change. Madelung suggests that al-Qāḍī al-Nuʿmān, in so doing, would have yielded to the requests of the Imam al-Muʿizz. Anyway, it is reasonable to assume that the positive law of *Daʿāʾim al-Islām* probably has a less direct link with the *uṣūl* than it appears, and that its '*uṣūl*ist' theory is therefore superimposed, or even external to it. From this perspective, it is also reasonable to argue that legal solutions are better justified afterwards through the *uṣūl* rather than being logically deduced from them. One might also think that with reference to those issues which are not resolved by the traditions of the Imams, a form of 'loan' is allowed, provided that it has the approval by the Imam in office. In stating this, al-Nuʿmān would have adopted an approach that is not far from the historical process followed by other schools of *fiqh*.[32] The concurrences with other systems, and the probable reality of borrowing from them, strongly support this supposition.

It is therefore legitimate to wonder about the quality of *mujtahid muṭlaq* (a full *mujtahid*, able to establish a legal system of his own like the classical founders of legal schools) attributed to al-Qāḍī al-Nuʿmān, as well as in the case of other rites which conferred this title to their eponyms. To this it must be added the fact that al-Nuʿmān had apparently received no training either in *fiqh* or in *ḥadīth*.[33] According to classical theory, matured late, for Sunni as well as Shiʿi *uṣūl*, the ultimate degree of *ijtihād* requires from the jurist who has reached this stage a total independence of thought and it also forbids *taqlīd*.[34] From this point of view, certainly a little anachronistic, both the *Kitāb al-īḍāḥ* and the *Daʿāʾim al-Islām* might appear to be the works of a compiler rather than of a fully independent *mujtahid*. For us, this is an additional argument against the emergence of *madhhab Nuʿmānī*. However, one needs to keep in mind that the strict criteria imposed by the science of *uṣūl* date from the period of maturation of this science. They required that a *mujtahid*, prior to having been granted this title, belonged to a well-defined *madhhab*; and that he might show

---

32 Hallaq, *The Origins and Evolution*, p. 122ff.

33 Madelung, 'The Sources', p. 30.

34 For a quick and convenient overview of the issue of *ijtihād*, see. É. Chaumont, 'Ijtihad in Islam and History According to Some Classical Sunni Jurists and Theologians', in R. Gleave and E. Kermeli, ed., *Islamic Law, Theory and Practice* (London, 1997), pp. 7–23, and for a more complete analysis: 'Tout chercheur qualifié dit-il juste?', in A. Bolluec, ed., *The Controversy in Religious Forms* (Paris, 1995). Regarding the notion of *ijtihād* in Shiʿism, see A. Zysow, 'Ejtehād', *EIR*, online: http://www.iranicaonline.org/articles/ejtehad (accessed 13 August 2013).

his intellectual aptitude to overcome the limitations of this *madhhab*. But al-Qāḍī al-Nuʿmān who, so to speak, created his knowledge *ex nihilo*, falls out of this established framework.

All in all, the jurist of the Imam did not compose a major original work in the field of *uṣūl al-fiqh*. It is precisely this gap which fills another of his works entitled the *Ikhtilāf uṣūl al-madhāhib wa'l-radd ʿalā man khālafa l-ḥaqq fīha*, written before the *Daʿāʾim al-Islām*. This is, in truth, a treatise which delivers the *uṣūlī* doctrine of its author, thus allowing us to comprehend the methodological turn represented by the *Daʿāʾim*. In this light, it is possible to affirm, as I. K. Poonawala does, that the *Ikhtilāf*, written around 343/954, 'fills a major void in the chain of Nuʿmān's works that clearly reflects the development of his legal thought'. One will therefore recognise that one of Poonawala's greatest merits is that of having dedicated a significant portion of his article to this subject. In it one can find a substantial analysis of the work and translation of some excerpts.[35] On this occasion, al-Qāḍī al-Nuʿmān uses the subtle argumentation of a theoretician: he follows, step by step, his polemic against the *uṣūl* of the other schools which, according to al-Nuʿmān, must be reduced to the materials obtained by the way of inspiration – the Qurʾan, the Prophetic Sunna, the traditions of the Imams without any exclusivity, namely, without these being limited to the traditions of the Imams of his community. This is precisely, as previously observed, the thread followed by al-Nuʿmān in the development of his positive law.

The *Ikhtilāf* is duly dedicated to the discussion of the value of *ijmāʿ* which we can find analysed towards the end of the chapter. Such a development proves that the concept of *ijmāʿ* had never ceased to raise interest after Shāfiʿī. There is little doubt that the discussion mainly targeted the Sunnis, given that for the latter only this criterion could be found in orthodoxy. As it is known, this supra-individual authority has no reason to exist in the case of Shiʿism which replaces it with the *magisterium* of the infallible Imam. Al-Qāḍī al-Nuʿmān attempts, as other theologians – notably the Muʿtazilīs – did before him, to destroy the doctrinal value of the concept of *ijmāʿ*. With reference to this, Poonawala notices that the interest of the *Ikhtilāf* is wider than the scope of Ismaili studies alone. The book sheds light on the little-known prehistory of Sunni or Shiʿi *uṣūl al-fiqh*, and helps towards bridging the gap between Shāfiʿī and the first treatises which emerged about a century after his death.[36]

It is, therefore, this defence of Shiʿi *uṣūl* that engages al-Qāḍī al-Nuʿmān, not only in the doctrinal principles of his own school. He is also implicitly claiming for himself the status of *mujtahid muṭlaq*, logically announcing, in the second step, the

---

[35] A summary of this work is also present in Fyzee, *Law in the Middle East*, pp. 125–127.

[36] W. Hallaq, *A History of Islamic Legal Theories* (Cambridge, 1997), pp. 33–34. With reference to Shiʿism, the first works on *uṣūl* appeared later with the *Tadhkira* of Shaykh al-Mufīd (d. 413/1022); see H. Modarressi Ṭabātabāʾī, *An Introduction to Shīʿī Law* (London, 1984), p. 7. Nevertheless, the tradition dates back to the first attempts in this direction for about a century since a contemporary of al-Kulaynī, Ibn Abī ʿAqīl al-ʿAmmānī, is deemed to have been the first to write on the subject; see H. Löschner, *Die Grundlagen dogmatischen of šīʿitischen Rechts* (Cologne, 1971), p. 32.

development of a legal monument where the sayings of the early Shiʿi Imams are giving way to those of the Ismaili Imams. The enterprise is not dissimilar to that of Ibn Ḥazm, before his *Muḥallā*. The author further notes that *Daʿāʾim al-Islām* asserts much more clearly than the previous work of al-Qāḍī al-Nuʿmān the duty of obedience to the Fatimid caliph who was at the same time the Ismaili Imam. According to the author of these lines, this point might also well represent a discreet invitation to the reader to look there for the reason of the previously reported characteristics of Ismaili *fiqh*.

III

The chapter by S. Zayd al-Wazir has a different quality in comparison to the previous ones. Written by an official member of the Zaydī community, its point of view may seem ideological and even apologetic. The author does not spare raising his voice, using a vehement vocabulary, against the abuses performed by the Sunni caliphate in history. The Umayyad rulers were despots, 'caesars'[37] – as the author calls them – who illegitimately arrogated for themselves the regency of the divine right.[38] To this transgression of the principle of the law of God, they added a serious breach to the duty of justice. They shamelessly deprived the community of what rightfully belonged to it: the *zakāt*. They monopolised the public treasury of the Muslims, instead of redistributing it to the community to increase material solidarity amongst its members, without preventing money from becoming a source of conflict amongst believers. Under their caliphate of usurpation, the common good becomes private property. The premises to such a disastrous policy emerged in the practice of previous rulers, with the exception of ʿAlī, as they allowed themselves to interfere unduly with the process of distribution of *zakāt* which, governed by the rule of consultation, is 'democratic' in principle. Therefore, the information contained in the Sunni books is deceptive and the historical realities have been falsified. It is the task of the (currently) disinterested scholarly research to restore this reality, returning to the commandments of the Qur'an. The sacred text, informed by the teachings of Imam ʿAlī, defines the recipient of *zakāt* and establishes the right of the community to scrutinise the institution of *zakāt*. In contrast with the Sunni caliphs, the Zaydī rulers have actually implemented the provisions of *fiqh* on public money. The scholar shows this by recounting the policy on taxation and agriculture of the Imam al-Hādī and his successors, which

[37] This term is, however, unsuitable. The Sunni caliphs said they were Imams by divine right; the temporal monarchs of Europe did not make such claim to the extent that their political legitimacy rested on the consecration conferred by the head of the Church, therefore on the intervention of an authority independent, in its origins, from the temporal power.

[38] Indeed, all of them give themselves the title of 'Deputy of God' (*khalīfat Allāh*) and not 'Deputy of the Messenger of God' (*khalīfat rasūl Allāh*), like their predecessors; a change which mainly regarded the *ʿulamāʾ*. See P. Crone and M. Hinds, *God's Caliph: Religious Authority in the First Centuries of Islam* (Cambridge, 1986), pp. 11–23.

marks a striking contrast with the policy in these fields employed by the Abbasid caliphate. This part of the article, well documented, provides historians with first-hand information.

To this polemical reading of history, which repeats the traditional grievances of the Zaydī community against the Sunni caliphate, the article adds new information on the Zaydī *fiqh*. It is important to note, as does the author, that any Zaydī jurist is entitled to exercise *ijtihād muṭlaq*. It is well known that this power is reduced to the minimum in Sunnism, if not totally absent. In Twelver Imāmism, the *mujtahid* is considered to be the spokesman of the hidden Imam, and a greater freedom is left to any scholar on this point, although this freedom is exercised only in the *uṣūlī* branch. According to the author, the principle was fully implemented only in Zaydism. As a result, a specific feature of the Zaydī legal tradition is that the concept of *madhhab* cannot be applied to it; if one must speak of a 'Zaydī school of law,' then one must at least state that this is certainly less unified than the other schools of law.

It appears from the chapter that the Zaydī *fiqh* is particularly original when it comes to financial issues. *Zakāt* appears to have a different nature, when compared to its interpretation by the Sunni schools, which results from a dissenting interpretation of the Qur'an. The public good does not consist solely of incomes from obligatory taxation, but also of voluntary donations made by individuals, and Zaydī scholars of law invite the donation of surplus money for charitable purposes. Some goods are automatically taken from the property of rulers who cannot own them. The Zaydī *fiqh* makes it more difficult to accumulate wealth in the hands of a minority, as illustrated by the principle of co-partnership in the management of agricultural resources.[39]

Such information suggests that Zaydī *fiqh* has a spirit of its own and bears the mark of exegetical debates which are probably very old. It is guided, perhaps more than other schools, by ethical principles and the principle of common good. There is no doubt that this last contribution will encourage scholars specialised in comparative law to become interested, more than they have been so far, in one of the least-known schools of law in the Muslim world.

IV

Finally, mention should be made of the familiar issue of temporary marriage (*zawāj al-mutʿa*) which is permitted in Twelver Imāmī Shiʿi *fiqh*. It is known that such an institution is vigorously opposed by the Sunnis to the point of becoming one of the main arguments of divergence between the two communities. As often occurs in matters of *fiqh*, the legal controversy obscures the historical origins. These origins

[39] The author refers here to the provision of *kharāj al-muqāsama*, from the Ḥanafī school under which, according to classical Ḥanafī *fiqh*, the peasant was compelled to pay *kharāj*. However, with the changing socio-political conditions, many Ḥanafī *fuqahā'* protested against these dispositions present in the Ḥanafī doctrine. See B. Johansen, *The Islamic Law on Land Tax and Rent* (London, 1988), pp. 15–17 and 101–102.

could, however, reveal to us the true socio-cultural reasons of this controversy, reasons of which we have otherwise no knowledge.[40]

One of the ways in which this issue is addressed by contemporary scholars is through an analysis of the sayings of the Imams as they are reported in the classical treatises on Shiʿi *fiqh*. The purpose is to produce, on the basis of these materials, hypotheses on the period of the origins. Supposedly dating back to the first two centuries of Islam and particularly to the beginning of the Abbasid caliphate, this corpus of material constitutes a priori a preferred means to access the prehistory of Shiʿi *fiqh*, 'before any codification process took place and before any work of *fiqh* was composed'. In contrast to Sunni Islam, this phase of coding logically followed the compilation and harmonisation of the sayings of the Imams.[41] The works on Shiʿi *fiqh* were necessarily composed later than their Sunni counterparts, a fact which doubtlessly explains why, on the question of the origin of the *fiqh*, the attention of researchers from the time of J. Schacht onwards, has turned enthusiastically towards the Sunni, or more exactly, the proto-Sunni milieux.[42] Shiʿi tradition has issued a simple answer to this issue: Shiʿi *fiqh* is neither a late nor an *ex nihilo* creation but goes back to the era of the Imams who answered directly to the legal questions raised by the faithful. The authoritative character of their opinions was the result of the spiritual election naturally attached to the lineage of the *ahl al-bayt*.[43] This explains why the first Shiʿi jurist-theologian authors such as al-Kulaynī (d. 329/939) only exceptionally authorised the use of logical reasoning, which subsequently appeared amongst his successors.[44] This also explains that a proper Imāmī *madhhab* of *fiqh* could only be formed after the compilation of the great bodies of traditions of the Imams: at that time, it would have adopted the same tools that were utilised by the Sunni schools (sources, materials, processes of reasoning and deontic logic), whilst the sayings of the Imams in legal matters will not appear, in retrospect, in disagreement with the

---

40 This has been attempted by A. Gribetz in one of the most comprehensive studies on this issue, *Strange Bedfellows: Mutʿat al-nisāʾ and Mutʿat al-ḥajj: A Case Study on Sunnī and Shīʿī Sources of tafsīr, ḥadīth and fiqh* (Berlin, 1994), which aims to explain the origin of the Imāmī institution in connection with the modification of the rules of the pre-Islamic pilgrimage in the time of the Prophet (see pp. 43–46 and pp. 182–183).

41 See note 52.

42 Following the work by J. Schacht, two other works have addressed the question: H. Motzki, *Die Anfänge der islamischen Jurisprudenz* (Stuttgart, 1991), chapter 1, and B. Krawietz, *Hierarchie der Rechtsquellen im tradierten sunnistischen Islam* (Berlin, 2002), pp. 12–86. See also our study on al-Shāfiʿī, *Shâfiʿî et les deux sources de la loi islamique* (Turnhout, 2007), ch. 1 ('Review of the work on primitive *fiqh*').

43 The same character is acknowledged for the Prophet in Sunni circles, although majority opinion recognises his right to practise the *ijtihād*, and even admits a certain margin of error (to the Prophetic *ijtihād*) which, however, does not affect the transmission of the legal message. See É. Chaumont, 'La problématique classique de l'*Ijtihâd* et la question de l'*Ijtihâd* du Prophète: *Ijtihâd, Waḥy* et *ʿIṣma*', *SI*, 75 (1992), pp. 105–140.

44 R. Brunschvig, 'Les *uṣûl al-fiqh* imâmites à leur stade ancien', in Fahd, ed., *Le Shîʿisme Imâmite*, pp. 201–212. This explains why, for a long time, the only authorised foundations for *fiqh* were the Qurʾan, the Prophetic Sunna and the sayings of the Imams.

solutions proposed by the *fuqahā*ʾ. Attested in the sources, the opposite current – which recurs more openly to different forms of legal reasoning[45] – seems to have been in the minority.[46] The hostile attitude towards *raʾy* (legal opinion) of many non-Shiʿi traditionists of that period (*ahl al-ḥadīth*) could be compared to this conception of the law typical of original Shiʿism.[47]

These facts can also be explained in a different way which seems to be more justified given the current state of research. For the Imāmī sensitivity in general, which dates back to the origins of Islam, the legal domain had to pertain par excellence to *ẓāhir*, the exoteric facet – the bark which hides the marrow, that is to say, the *bāṭin*, the essential truth contained in Revelation.[48] Such truth is not accessible to reason, and this explains why the Imams were wary on opinion, analogy and *kalām*. On the questions that defied human understanding, the Imams recommended their followers to remain silent.[49] The result was to be a certain indifference towards the field of law and thereby, an attitude towards it that would have been profoundly different from that of the later Shiʿi communities when definitely consolidated. Original Shiʿi Islam would have tolerated compliance to any ritual, and to any theological sensitivity that emanated from it. Such a standpoint would have strengthened the regular use of the discipline of *taqiyya* within those circles.[50] It should be noted that such a hypothesis is consistent with the conclusion of Melchert's chapter if one considers how a relative indifference to the scholastic divergences promotes a kind of common milieu, a sort of continuum without precise contours between the various theological sensitivities of the time.

---

[45] H. Modarressi Ṭabātabāʾī, *An Introduction to Shīʿī Law*, pp. 22–25. The Imams are ascribed the opinion according to which, in relation to certain questions, they indicate only the principles of the law rather than providing the details of a particular solution. Preaching by example, they would have practised *ijtihād* and also let their listeners to find for themselves the answers to legal questions. In other words, the Imams are not believed to have served as legal consultants like the *muftī*s.

[46] M. A. Amir-Moezzi, *Le Guide divin dans le Shîʿisme originel* (2nd ed., Paris, 2007), pp. 39–40.

[47] See A. Amīn, *Ḍuḥā l-Islām* (Cairo, 1947), vol. 2, p. 160, and the traditions contained in the *Sunan* by al-Dārimī (d. 255/869) which condemn the employment of *raʾy* and the recourse to *fatwā* (in all editions, these traditions appear in the early sections, chapter 18 and following chapters). Indeed, many are those amongst the *ahl al-ḥadīth* who, refusing to go beyond the text, preferred not to comment on matters of *fiqh*; the grand master of Shāfiʿī in prophetic traditions, Sufyān b. ʿUyayna (d. 198/813), was one of them.

[48] Jaʿfar al-Ṣādiq (d. 148/765) said about someone obsessed with ablutions and prayers (that is to say, a believer attached to the letter of the law to such a point that he ignored its meaning), that he was the toy of Satan and that he had no spiritual discernment (*ʿaql*); account reported by al-Kulaynī and quoted by Amir-Moezzi, *Le Guide divin*, p. 25. In the same light can be understood the explication given by the Imams on the *ẓāhir* (ibid. p. 31, n. 43): this term covers the field of *fiqh*. The Qurʾan affirms that faith (*īmān*) is greater than its corporeal prescriptions, and faith is on the level of the *bāṭin*; it follows that it is the essential part of Islam.

[49] Ibid., pp. 36–37.

[50] M. G. Hodgson , 'Bāṭiniyya', *EI2*, vol. 1, pp. 1098–1100.

The issue of temporary marriage allows us to take a look at the whole picture in a more nuanced way, in effect, exclusively in relation to the attitude attributed to the Imams and without any reference to the classical position of the Jaʿfarī *madhhab*. It seems that neither the Imams nor their entourage might have developed a dominant doctrine on the subject given the great diversity of opinions on the matter at that time. This result is rich in implications; it confirms that original Shiʿi Islam was far from being indifferent to the legal aspect of religion and that the Imams would not have let these matters be subjected to the free interpretation of the believers. Moreover, it suggests that Shiʿi *fiqh* must have experienced, besides the politico-religious separations, a uniform evolution. The proliferation of original views must have been followed by a phase of 'canalisation' of such perspectives in ways just discovered by the Sunni *madhāhib*, then by the consolidation of established schools. This was to be followed by an effort of selecting and harmonising the legal opinion of the predecessors, in order to develop a coherent system, the latter phase being more or less parallel with the search for unifying *usūl*. If this approach is extended to other legal controversies, it would make it difficult to envisage – *mutatis mutandis* – the history of Shiʿi *fiqh* as being anything different from that of Sunni *fiqh*. However, an important difference separates the two. The former did not arrange all of its doctrine, in a more or less arbitrary way, on the account of a supposed founder. This is also an indication that it does not go back to the times of the first Imams, but probably to a later date – a few generations after the Sunni legal traditions emerged in the course of the 2nd century. However, we have little information on the crucial period of the 3rd century which preceded the establishment of the Jaʿfarī *madhhab*.[51]

It must be noticed that such analyses do not rely on the authenticity of the sayings attributed to the Imams, or more precisely, their paternity. This question is often not addressed because the assumptions made are taken to allow divergence from it.[52] Such approaches assume that, whether authentic or not, such sayings necessarily reflect the views generally admitted in the first Shiʿi community.[53] Without this

51 Stewart believes that the Jaʿfarī *madhhab* was formed to ensure a place for Shiʿi Islam within the plural consensus which characterised Sunni Islam towards the end of the 4th/10th century. See D. J. Stewart, *Islamic Legal Orthodoxy* (Salt Lake City, 1998), pp. 111–114. For more detailed views on how the Sunni schools were formed from local traditions of the 2nd century, see W. B. Hallaq, *Authority, Continuity and Change in Islamic Law* (Cambridge, 2005), pp. 57–85. This author has shown in particular that the *madhāhib* were not founded by figures such as Abū Ḥanīfa, Mālik b. Anas, al-Shāfiʿī, which are only eponyms who only played a decisive role in scholarly circles that began before them and continued to evolve after them.

52 In Islamic studies, two important trends collide on the question of value to be given to the early sources. A hypercritical current criticises a school that assumes that a correct analysis allows, within certain limits, to draw from these sources a reliable historical reconstruction. See H. Berg, ed., *Method and Theory in the Study of Islamic Origins* (Leiden, 2003).

53 This is the position held by an expert on *ḥadīth*, Juynboll, who recently passed away, even if the author strongly suspects that most of these sayings to not go back to the characters mentioned at the beginning of the *isnād*. See G. H. A. Juynboll, *Studies on the Origins and Uses of Islamic Ḥadīth* (Aldershot, 1996). One can simply suppose that those *akhbār* go back to the

preliminary assumption, which can be described as being minimalist, it is impossible to infer anything from the primitive material contained in the much later works. With the much less radical attitude of a researcher such as Motzki, who does not exclude altogether the information provided by the chain of the *isnād*, it would be possible to make a further step in the analysis. The method he proposes, called '*isnād cum matn* analysis',[54] would certainly allow him to narrow the search and to go back a little further, reaching the level of the first links in the chains of the transmitters. It is believed, however, that this method of analysis is adequate, since the existence of two attitudes amongst the Imams is discovered, one being more liberal than the other. According to this approach, Shiʿi Islam's initial tolerance has been undermined and obscured by later Imāmism which, under the pressure of Sunni Islam, did retain a rigorous position on this issue. Surely an anthropologist would draw a supplementary explanation from the fact that the ethical and spiritual dimension of a religion are not necessarily correlated, and that the natural law, varying in ages and climates, is only a concept, therefore making it legitimate for someone to question its meaning. But it is also permissible to wonder whether the dual attitude found amongst the Imams on this particular issue did not contain – in an embryonic stage – the subsequent opposition that would later be evident between the Uṣūlī and Akhbārī schools,[55] since this great division 'does not date from the 11th/17th century, but its traces can be found as early as the 2nd–3rd/8th–9th centuries'.[56] This observation seems to be confirmed by the fact that the Akhbārīs, overall, seem to be closer to the original, purely esoteric current of thought than the Uṣūlī school, which is closer to a more exoteric and legalist trend.[57]

On this point, R. Gleave, for example, brings in a contradictory debate; we indeed know about the existence of traditions going back to the time of the Imams which show that they were sometimes contradicted by some of their followers.[58] The sources themselves do not hide that the thesis on the infallibility of the Imam, although domi-

---

days when they were released and that falsification concerns the chain of transmission rather than its content. This means that these sayings can provide real information; therefore, the hypercritical attitude (mentioned above) would be excessively sceptic.

[54] This is illustrated in H. Motzki's article, 'The Prophet and the Cat, On Dating Mālik's *Muwatta*' and Legal Traditions', *JSAI*, 22 (1998), pp. 1–22.

[55] See, on this issue, the reference given by Amir-Moezzi, *Le Guide divin*, pp. 33–34, notes 47–49. See also R. Gleave, *Inevitable Doubt: Two Theories of Shīʿī Jurisprudence* (Leiden, 2000), pp. 5–6. The traditionalist (*akhbārī*) movement is, as such, actually late, representing a reaction against the incorporation of *ijtihād* into *fiqh*. For the latter author, however, the traditionalists imprudently made their views to date back to the period of the origins (*Inevitable Doubt*, p. 8 and *Scripturalist Islam*).

[56] Amir-Moezzi, *Le Guide divin*, p. 34.

[57] It is the traditionalists from the School of Qumm that transmit the primitive tradition of Imamism and not the rationalist School of Baghdad that dates back to a later period and is influenced by Muʿtazilism (ibid., p. 48).

[58] See W. Madelung, 'Authority in Twelver Shiism in the Absence of the Imam', in G. Makdisi, D. Sourdel and J. Sourdel-Thomine, ed., *La notion d'autorité au Moyen Âge: Islam, Byzance, Occident, Colloques internationaux de La Napoule, session de 1978* (Paris, 1982), p. 164.

nant, was not strictly unanimous. Even if their authority was not denied, it was not synonymous of infallible perfection: the Imams remained ordinary men who were physically indistinguishable from their peers, if not for their piety, coupled with excellent knowledge. Some believers had doubted that the Imams could know the invisible and have access to the *ʿilm al-ghayb*.[59] This controversy was naturally fraught with legal implications as noted above; it implied a radical change in the architectural structure of the *sharīʿa*.[60] Some in the circles of the Imams went as far as to contradict the Imams, questioning them on the *ratio legis* of this or that article of law.[61] Gleave thus reinforces the thesis that challenges the timeless character of this doctrine within Shiʿism and postulates the existence of early debates about the nature of the Imams. He goes even further by implicitly adding that the dogma of infallibility enjoyed a slow maturation before it imposed itself as evidence within the theological thought. The fact that the extent of issues included in the area covered by this infallibility increased over time in the great theological authorities of the 4th and 5th centuries, Ibn Bābūya (d. 381/991) and al-Murtaḍā (d. 436/1044), would point in this sense.[62] It is therefore legitimate to extrapolate and to suppose that such a statement was more modest and pragmatic in its infancy. This extrapolation is even more plausible since it has a parallel in Sunnism. The *taʿdīl al-ṣaḥāba*, namely, the Companions' impeccable integrity in terms of testimony, does not seem to have been unconditionally recognised among ancient traditionalists. As for previous cases, this dogma also has a history and was subject to disagreements.[63] It shows, once again, that 'as a religious phenomenon ... Shiʿism went through a long evolution which changed its character several times'.[64]

It remains to assess the magnitude of this contesting trend within the nascent religion. It may well have been very limited.[65] It is argued that the dogma in question was attributed to authorities as old as the theologian Hishām b. al-Ḥakam (d. 179/795–96). The doctrine of total submission to the Imams, which implies a belief in a certain perfection of the guide, appears in early writings such as those of al-Ṣaffār (d. 290/903) as well as later writers. In addition, the Imams would never encourage the development of a purely speculative thought, as they considered the rational faculty to be inferior to spiritual discernment.[66]

---

59 Modarressi Ṭabāṭabāʾī, *An Introduction*, p. 27. See also E. Kohlberg, 'Imam and Community in the Pre-Ghayba Period', in *Belief and Law in Imāmī Shīʿism* (Aldershot, 1991), article XIII.

60 See notes 44 and 45 above.

61 Modarressi Ṭabāṭabāʾī, *An Introduction*; Amir-Moezzi, *Le Guide divin*, p. 36, n. 55, cites figures such as Abū Jaʿfar al-Sakkāk, a disciple of Jaʿfar al-Ṣādiq (2nd/8th century) or Abū Jaʿfar b. Qibā (4th/10th century).

62 W. Madelung, "Iṣma', *EI2*, vol. 4, pp. 182–184.

63 G. H. A. Juynboll, *Muslim Tradition* (Cambridge, 1983), pp. 190–206.

64 H. Halm, *Le Chiisme* (Paris, 1995), p. 3.

65 The rationalist trend was a minor one in the early period. See Amir-Moezzi, *Le Guide divin*, pp. 34–40.

66 Ibid., p. 38, n. 64.

It would not be improbable to think that the early challenge of the law-making authority of the Sunna might have hidden similar debates about the status of the Prophetic *ḥadīths*.[67] Thus, the thesis of scholars such as R. Gleave enriches the debate without exhausting it. It is always difficult to extrapolate a conclusion from a specific issue pertinent to Shiʿi Islam in general. Finally, it rests on the authenticity of statements contrary to the general opinion, and this principle of selection may appear arbitrary to some. Nevertheless, views on this widely debated issue illustrate once again, if needed, the richness contained in classical sources and the need to examine them from a new angle.

[67] In fact, they never completely ceased as attested by the concept of *sunna ghayr tashrīʿiyya* (non-legislating Sunna); see M. H. Kamali, *Principles of Islamic Jurisprudence* (Cambridge, 1991), pp. 52–53, or on the theory of the Mālikī al-Qarāfī (d. 684/1285), see S. Jackson, 'From Prophetic Actions to Constitutional Theory', *IJMES*, 25 (1993), pp. 71–90.

11

Renunciation (*Zuhd*) in the Early Shiʿi Tradition

Christopher Melchert

Both the Sunni and Shiʿi parties will tend to see themselves as coherent bodies from the time of the First Civil War (35–40/656–661). Actually, the people who called themselves *ahl al-sunna wa'l-jamāʿa* were one party among many until the later 9th century. Indeed, as Marshall Hodgson has observed, the term *sunnī* continued to have multiple applications (opposition to Shiʿism, *kalām* and Sufism) long after it became the majority party in the later 9th century, each of these multiple applications a vestige of its time as a minority party before then.[1] Shiʿism, on the other hand, had a natural principle of self-identification according to which Imam any group supported. Here as well, though, lines were much blurred compared with later; for example, consider the Abbasids' various tacks, first supporting ʿAbd Allāh b. Muʿāwiya on the Zaydī principle that the proper ruler was whichever member of the House of the Prophet was militarily successful, then themselves on the same principle, later still invoking rather the Rāfiḍī principle of *naṣṣ* designation.[2]

From the 11th century AD, Sunni-Shiʿi interaction takes the familiar form of the Sunni majority ignoring the Shiʿi minority while the minority pays wary attention to the majority.[3] Again, however, there was much blurring of lines before then. The depth of support for the House forced mature Sunnism to recognise ʿAlī as the fourth caliph and fourth best Companion, an impressive list of Sunni heroes were

---

[1] Marshall G. S. Hodgson, *The Venture of Islam* (Chicago, 1973), vol. 1, pp. 278ff. The formation of Sunnism across the 9th century still awaits a specialist monograph, but see, provisionally, John B. Henderson, *The Construction of Orthodoxy and Heresy: Neo-Confucian, Islamic, Jewish, and Early Christian Patterns* (Albany, NY, 1998), esp. p. 53 on the chronology of Sunnism.

[2] See Patricia Crone, 'On the Meaning of the ʿAbbāsid Call to *al-Riḍā*', in C. E. Bosworth, et al., ed., *The Islamic World: From Classical to Modern Times. Essays in Honor of Bernard Lewis* (Princeton, 1989), pp. 95–111, and Claude Cahen, 'Points de vue sur la révolution ʿAbbāside', *Revue Historique*, 230 (1963), pp. 295–338.

[3] For example, Sunni views are included in al-Ṭūsī Shaykh al-Ṭā'ifa (d. 460/1067?), *al-Khilāf*, ed. ʿAlī al-Khurāsānī, et al. (Qumm, 1416–1421/1995–2000), but Shiʿi views are not in, among others, al-Qaffāl al-Shāshī (d. 507/1114), *Ḥilyat al-ʿulamā' fī maʿrifat madhāhib al-fuqahā'*, ed. Yāsīn Aḥmad Ibrāhīm Darādaka (Amman, 1988).

remembered as preferring ʿAlī to ʿUthmān, and Sunni *rijāl* criticism did not rely on a single category of 'Shiʿi' but distinguished between *tashayyuʿ*, which had to be overlooked, and *rafḍ*, which usually rendered someone's testimony unacceptable.[4] Not only is the 9th-century split between traditionalists and semi-rationalists observable within both Sunni and Shiʿi camps, it appears to be continuous with 10th-century Ḥanbalī–Shiʿi strife, at least in Baghdad.[5]

This chapter is concerned with the early development of Islamic piety, particularly renunciation (*zuhd*).[6] In the later 9th century, this issued into classical Sufism, which the Shiʿis were slow to take up.[7] The traditional explanation has been that Shiʿis were reluctant to recognise the Sufi master as a charismatic figure for fear that he would rival the Imam. That is why the present volume has sections for Law, Qur'an and *Ḥadīth* but not Sufism, as a survey of Sunni Islam surely would. My chapter mainly addresses not Shiʿi attitudes toward classical Sufism, but, rather, attitudes towards the renunciation that went before. My principal finding is that this also is an area where lines were blurred. There is little to distinguish professed Shiʿi ideas of renunciation from early Sunni ideas. It is only with the Sufi era in Sunnism, from the late 9th century, that Sunni and Shiʿi ideas about piety appear to significantly diverge.

Sources

My main source on the Shiʿi side is al-Kulaynī (d. 329/941), *al-Kāfī*, the first large Twelver collection of *ḥadīth*, secondarily al-Qāḍī al-Nuʿmān (d. 363/974), *Daʿā'im*

---

4 On ʿAlī as fourth best, see Christopher Melchert, *Ahmad ibn Hanbal* (Oxford, 2006), pp. 94–98. Ibn Qutayba provides a long list of Sunni heroes remembered as Shiʿa (i.e., preferring ʿAlī to ʿUthmān); *al-Maʿārif*, ed. Tharwat ʿUkāsha (6th ed., Cairo, 1992), p. 624. On *rijāl* criticism, see among other studies Liyakatali Takim, 'Evolution in the Biographical Profiles of Two ḥadīth Transmitters', in L. Clarke, ed., *Shīʿite Heritage* (Binghamton, NY, 2001), pp. 285–299. Aḥmad ibn Ḥanbal said that all Kūfans had preferred ʿAlī to ʿUthmān except two: Ṭalḥa ibn Muṣarrif (d. 112/730–731?) and ʿAbd Allāh ibn Idrīs (d. 192/807–808); Aḥmad, *Kitāb al-ʿilal wa-maʿrifat al-rijāl*, ed. Waṣī Allāh ibn Muḥammad ʿAbbās (Beirut, 1988), vol. 2, p. 535; *Kitāb al-jāmiʿ fi'l-ʿilal wa-maʿrifat al-rijāl*, ed. Muḥammad Ḥusām Bayḍūn (Beirut, 1410/1990), vol. 2, p. 47 (references to the latter ed. henceforth in *italic*). Kūfans comprise a little more than two-thirds of the names on Ibn Qutayba's list.

5 Christopher Melchert, 'The Imāmīs between Rationalism and Traditionalism', in Clarke, ed., *Shīʿite Heritage*, pp. 273–283.

6 I prefer 'renunciation', proposed by Michael Cooperson, to the more conventional 'asceticism' because I consider it useful to maintain a consistent distinction between *asceticism* and *mysticism*, as sketched in Christopher Melchert, 'The Transition from Asceticism to Mysticism at the Middle of the Ninth Century C.E.', *SI*, 83 (1996), pp. 51–70. Actually, it is Arabic *ijtihād* that corresponds most closely to Greek *askēsis*, while Arabic *zuhd* corresponds most closely to Greek *apatheia*.

7 For an up-to-date historical survey, see Ahmet T. Karamustafa, *Sufism* (Edinburgh, 2007).

al-Islām, the principal handbook of Ismaili law.[8] My main sources on the Sunni side are Ibn al-Mubārak (d. 181/797), *al-Zuhd*, in the recension of al-Ḥasan b. al-Ḥusayn (d. 246/860–861); Ibn Abī Shayba (d. 235/849), *al-Muṣannaf*, in the recension of Baqī b. Makhlad (d. 276/889) but without additions from him; Aḥmad b. Ḥanbal (d. 241/855), *al-Zuhd*, in the recension of his son ʿAbd Allāh; and Abū Nuʿaym al-Iṣbahānī (d. 430/1038), *Ḥilyat al-awliyāʾ*. The first three obviously predate my main Shiʿi sources by one to three generations. The last is from a century later. However, Abū Nuʿaym always names his sources and frequently quotes these earlier collectors, along with a few others such as Wakīʿ b. al-Jarrāḥ, which quotations can be checked and continually prove accurate. Therefore, I am inclined to consider Abū Nuʿaym a faithful transmitter of earlier knowledge, as reliable a guide to renunciation as it was remembered in the 9th century as the 9th-century collectors themselves whose works are extant. How reliably he and our 9th-century sources represent renunciation as it was thought of and practised in the early 8th century and before is of course a separate question.

It is regrettable that we have so little Shiʿi material from the 9th century. I have consulted two collections specifically of renunciant sayings, al-Ḥusayn b. Saʿīd al-Ahwāzī (fl. earlier 3rd/9th century), *al-Muʾmin*, and Muḥammad b. Hammām al-Iskāfī (d. 336/947–948), *al-Tamḥīṣ*.[9] Both are short and specialised (Ahwāzī offers encouragements of fraternal love, Ibn Hammām disparagements of this world) and will not be further cited. They do both confirm that the Twelver tradition attributed renunciant sayings especially to Jaʿfar al-Ṣādiq. From Kāmil Muṣṭafā al-Shaybī we have two modern studies with very interesting titles: *al-Fikr al-shīʿī waʾl-nazaʿāt al-ṣūfiyya* (ʻShiʿi thought and Sufi tendenciesʼ) and *al-Ṣila bayna al-taṣawwuf waʾl-tashayyuʿ* (ʻThe relation between Sufism and Shiʿismʼ).[10] For the most part, I have found him to offer interesting although often doubtful characterisations of Sufism and its antecedents (for example, valiant attempts to identify styles of renunciation peculiar to Syria, Kūfa and Baṣra) but little on early Shiʿism.

The Community Defined by Piety

The early Shiʿa certainly professed themselves to be interested in piety. They were defined, of course, by their recognising the correct Imam. ʻHe who dies without knowing the Imam of his time dies a Jāhilī deathʼ was a leading principle of theirs, although

---

[8] Citation of this source may justify inclusion of this chapter in the part on Law. Furthermore, juridical handbooks such as the *Daʿāʾim* are concerned mainly with identifying actions as required, recommended, indifferent, discouraged or forbidden. Inasmuch as renunciant literature is about identifying the recommended and discouraged, it also is juridical.

[9] Al-Ahwāzī, *al-Muʾmin* (Qumm, 1404/1984) and Ibn Hammām, *al-Tamḥīṣ* (Qumm, n.d.).

[10] Kāmil Muṣṭafā al-Shaybī, *al-Fikr al-Shīʿī waʾl-nazaʿāt al-ṣūfiyya* (Baghdad, 1386/1966); *al-Ṣila bayna al-taṣawwuf waʾl-tashayyuʿ* (Baghdad, 1382–1383/1963–1964).

one that Sunni Muslims might also accept.[11] But we are also told that Muḥammad al-Bāqir declared, 'Our party (*shīʿa*) is nothing but whoever obeys God (mighty and glorious is He).'[12] More elaborately, he is given as explaining:[13]

> Does it suffice for one who adheres to *tashayyuʿ* that he speak of his love for the people of the House? By God, our party is nothing but whoever fears God and obeys him. They are known by humility, submissiveness, honesty, much recollecting God, fasting, prayer, filial piety, keeping faith with poor neighbours and the indigent, debt-ridden and orphans, truthful speech, reciting the Qurʾan and speaking only good of people ... Whoever is obedient to God is our friend and whoever is rebellious toward God is our enemy.

This is actually going a little further than definitions of Sunnism. Before Sunni and Shiʿi were distinct, 'the Muslims' and 'the pious' might be identified, as in a saying ascribed to al-Ḥasan al-Baṣrī (d. 110/728): 'The good has gone and the bad remains. Whoever is left of the Muslims is dejected.'[14] Even more often, 'believer' is equated with 'pious'; for example, when the Companion Ibn Masʿūd (d. 32/652–653?) is quoted as saying, 'The believer (*muʾmin*) sees his sins as if he were sitting at the foot of a mountain, fearing that it should fall over onto him, whereas the reprobate (*fājir*) thinks his sins are like a fly that passes by his nose.'[15] But note also express reluctance to identify Sunnism with a renunciant lifestyle, also anxiety over heretical renunciants; for example, in another saying attributed to Ibn Masʿūd: 'Moderate exertion (*iqtiṣād*) in the Sunna is better than strenuous exertion (*ijtihād*) in innovation.'[16]

---

[11] Hodgson, *Venture,* vol. 2, p. 348. See al-Kulaynī, *al-Kāfī, kitāb al-rawḍa*; ed. ʿAlī Akbar al-Ghaffārī, corr. Muḥammad al-Ākhūndī (Tehran, 1389–1391/1969–1971), vol. 8, p. 146, and Aḥmad ibn Ḥanbal, *Musnad imām al-muḥaddithīn* (Cairo, 1313/1895), vol. 4, p. 96; *Musnad al-imām*, ed. Shuʿayb al-Arnaʾūṭ et al. (Beirut, 1413-1421/1993-2001), vol. 28, pp. 88–89 (references to the latter ed. henceforth in *italic*). Admittedly, Sunni collections usually stress versions that warn 'whoever dies apart from the *jamāʿa* dies a Jāhilī death'; e.g., Aḥmad, *Musnad,* vol. 1, pp. 275, 297, vol. 2, p. 70, vol. 3, pp. 445–446, vol. 5, p. 387, *vol. 4, pp. 290–291, vol. 9, pp. 284–286, vol. 24, pp. 452, 459–463, vol. 38, pp. 319–320, 324–325*. Aḥmad himself glossed 'the Imam of his time' as 'he of whom all the Muslims say "This is an Imam"': Ibn Hāniʾ, *Masāʾil al-imām Aḥmad b. Ḥanbal*, ed. Zuhayr al-Shāwīsh (Beirut, 1400/1979), vol. 2, p. 185.

[12] Al-Kulaynī, *Kāfī, kitāb al-īmān waʾl-kufr, bāb al-ṭāʿa waʾl-taqwā*, vol. 2, p. 73.

[13] Ibid., vol. 2, pp. 74–75.

[14] Aḥmad, *al-Zuhd*, ed. ʿAbd al-Raḥmān ibn Qāsim (Mecca, 1357/1939), p. 258 (= repr. Beirut, 1403/1983), p. 316 (references to the latter ed. henceforth in *italic*).

[15] Ibn al-Mubārak, *al-Zuhd waʾl-raqāʾiq*, ed. Ḥabīb al-Raḥmān al-Aʿẓamī (Malegaon, 1386; repr. with different pagination Beirut, 1419/1998), no 69; also in Bukhārī, *al-Jāmiʿ al-ṣaḥīḥ, Kitāb al-daʿawāt* 4, *bāb al-tawba,* no 6308; Ibn Masʿūd < Prophet in Aḥmad, *Musnad,* vol. 1, p. 383, *vol. 6, pp. 131–132*.

[16] Aḥmad, *Zuhd*, p. 159 *198*. *Iqtiṣād* means literally sticking to the middle of the road. A similar statement is attributed to another Companion, Ubayy ibn Kaʿb (d. 32/652–653?), in Ibn al-Mubārak, *Zuhd*, no. 8 among additions from Nuʿaym ibn Ḥammād, also Abū Nuʿaym, *Ḥilyat al-awliyāʾ* (Cairo, 1352–1357/1932–1938), vol. 1, p. 252. An Ismaili source admittedly

Sunnism crystallised in the late 8th century and across the 9th, by which time the Muslims were no longer a tiny minority at the top of society living off tribute, hence by which time no majoritarian party could demand a style of life that would interfere with making a living or, indeed, that would disqualify ordinary persons. On this point, Al-Kulaynī apparently preserves the outlook of an earlier generation of Muslims better than his Sunni contemporaries. He could afford to when Shiʿism remained safely minoritarian.

Fear of God

Muḥammad al-Bāqir begins his definition of the righteous Shiʿa by describing them as those who fear God. According to Jaʿfar al-Ṣādiq, 'God spoke to Moses saying, "'My servants have not approached me by anything that I like better than three characters".' Moses said, 'O my lord, what are they?' He said, 'Moses, renunciation of the world, precaution regarding sins and weeping from fear (*khashya*) of Me.'[17] The literary form is certainly familiar. As for dialogue between God and an early prophet, I might mention a typical report from Abū Fazāra Rāshid b. Kaysān, a late Kūfan Follower: 'I have heard that Dāwūd asked his Lord, "My Lord, indicate to me a work that will bring me into Paradise." He said, "Prefer my fancy (*hawā*) to yours."'[18] As for the number three, Muḥammad b. Kaʿb al-Quraẓī (Medinese, also Kūfa, d. 120/737–738 or before) said, 'If God wishes well for a servant, he puts three characters in him: discernment in the faith, renunciation of the world and sightedness concerning his faults.'[19] There are many Sunni descriptions of weeping from fear of God. Sometimes the Prophet, sometimes Abū Hurayra (d. 58/677–678), is quoted as saying, 'He will not enter the Fire who weeps from fear (*khashya*) of God, until the milk returns into the teat.'[20] ʿAbd Allāh b. ʿAmr (d. Mecca 63/683), seen weeping, said, 'Do you wonder that I should weep from fear of God? If you are not weeping, pretend to weep, until

attributes a similar statement to Jaʿfar al-Ṣādiq: 'A little work in the *sunna* is better than much work in innovation'. See al-Qāḍī al-Nuʿmān, *Daʿāʾim al-Islām, kitāb al-ṣalāt* 24, *dhikr ṣalāt al-sunna waʾl-nāfila,* ed. Asaf A. A. Fyzee (Cairo, 1379–1383/1960–1963; repr. Damascus, n.d.), vol. 1, p. 216.

17 Al-Kulaynī, *Kāfī, kitāb al-duʿāʾ, bāb al-bukāʾ*, vol. 2, pp. 482–483.

18 Al-Khuttalī, *Kitāb al-maḥabba lillāh,* in Bernd Radtke, ed., *Materialien zur alten islamischen Frömmigkeit* (Leiden, 2009), pp. 108–109; Ibn Qutayba, *ʿUyūn al-akhbār* (Cairo, 1343–1349/1925–1930), vol. 2, p. 263.

19 Ibn al-Mubārak, *Zuhd*, no. 282.

20 From the Prophet: Aḥmad, *Musnad,* vol. 2, p. 505, *vol. 16, pp. 330–331*; Hannād, *Kitāb al-zuhd*, ed. ʿAbd al-Raḥmān b. ʿAbd al-Jabbār al-Faryawāʾī (Kuwait, 1406/1985), vol. 1, p. 268, Tirmidhī, *al-Jāmiʿ al-ṣaḥīḥ, kitāb al-zuhd* 8, *bāb mā jāʾa fī faḍl al-bukāʾ min khashyat Allāh*, no 2311. From Abū Hurayrah: Wakīʿ, *Kitāb al-zuhd*, ed. ʿAbd al-Raḥmān ʿAbd al-Jabbār al-Faryawāʾī (Riyadh, 1415/1994), vol. 1, pp. 249–250; Aḥmad, *Zuhd*, p. 178, *222–223*; al-Nasāʾī, *al-Mujtabā, bāb faḍl man ʿamila fī sabīl Allāh ʿalā qadamih.*

one of you says *ayh, ayh*. This moon weeps from fear of God (be he exalted).'[21] Many more such quotations could be cited in addition to these.

Both Shiʿi and Sunni literatures are concerned with balancing hope and fear. Al-Kulaynī quotes Jaʿfar al-Ṣādiq as saying the believer has both hope and fear in his heart. 'If this were weighed, it would not outweigh that, and if that were weighed, it would not outweigh this.'[22] Compare Muṭarrif b. ʿAbd Allāh b. al-Shikhkhīr (Basran, d. 95/713–714): 'If the believer's fear and hope were weighed, neither would outweigh the other.'[23] Similarly, Maṭar b. Ṭahmān (Basran, d. 125/742–743) is quoted as saying, 'If the believer's fear and hope were weighed in the balance, neither would be found to exceed the other at all.'[24] The Sunni literature provides some sayings in favour of letting fear outweigh hope, more in favour of letting hope outweigh fear, but the predominant sentiment seems to be that hope and fear should be evenly balanced. The wise man Luqmān is quoted as saying to his son, 'Hope in God without feeling safe from His trickery (*makr*). Fear God without despairing of His mercy.' His son said, 'How can I do that, father, when I have only one heart?' Luqmān replied, 'My son, the believer is like one with two hearts, one heart with which to wish and one heart with which to fear.'[25] The Prophet is quoted as saying, 'If the unbeliever knew all that God has of mercy, he would not despair of Paradise, while if the Muslim knew all that God has of torment, he would not feel safe from Hell-fire.'[26]

Weeping, No Laughing

To this day, weeping is a prominent feature of Shiʿi devotions. Jaʿfar al-Ṣādiq is quoted as saying, 'If you are not weeping, pretend to weep.'[27] He is also quoted as approving a specific technique to stimulate weeping. One Isḥāq b. ʿAmmār told him, 'It happens that I pray and wish to weep but it does not come. Often, I have recollected some of my family who have died. Then I soften and weep. Is that permissible?' Jaʿfar answered, 'Yes, remember them, and if you have softening, then weep and pray to your Lord (blessed and exalted is He).'[28] In Sunni literature, the Prophet is quoted as saying, 'Weep. And if you do not weep, pretend to weep (*fa-in lam tabkū*

[21] Ibn Abī Shayba, *al-Muṣannaf, kitāb al-zuhd* 92, *mā qālū fi'l-bukā' min khashyat Allāh*; ed. Muḥammad ʿAbd Allāh al-Jumʿa and Muḥammad Ibrāhīm al-Luḥaydān (Riyadh, 1425/2004), vol. 12, p. 425.

[22] Al-Kulaynī, *Kāfī, kitāb al-īmān wa'l-kufr, bāb al-khawf wa'l-rajā'*, vol. 2, p. 67.

[23] Aḥmad, *Zuhd*, pp. 238–239, 293; Ibn Abī Shayba, *Muṣannaf, kitāb al-zuhd* 66, *Muṭarrif ibn al-Shikhkhīr*, vol. 12, p. 344.

[24] Abū Nuʿaym, *Ḥilya*, vol. 3, p. 76.

[25] Ibn al-Mubārak, *Zuhd*, no 912; Aḥmad, *Zuhd*, pp. 106–107, 132.

[26] Bukhārī, *Ṣaḥīḥ, kitāb al-riqāq* 19, *bāb al-rajā' wa'l-khawf*, no 6469.

[27] Al-Kulaynī, *Kāfī, kitāb al-duʿā', bāb al-raghba wa'l-rahba*, vol. 2, p. 483.

[28] Ibid., vol. 2, p. 483.

fa-tabākaw).'[29] So is Abū Bakr (d. 13/34): 'Weep! And if you are not weeping, pretend to weep.'[30] Another Companion, Abū Mūsā al-Ashʿarī (d. 50/670–671), is quoted as saying the same with an explanation: 'O people, weep. If you do not weep, pretend to weep. The people of the Fire are weeping tears till they are cut off, then they weep blood such that if boats were sent among them, they would float.'[31]

To the contrary, the Sunni tradition also records doubts about demonstrative weeping. In a book devoted to weeping, Ibn Abī al-Dunyā cites nine examples of disapproval of weeping in public.[32] The Companion Abū Umāma (d. 100/718–719) reproached someone for weeping and praying in prostration (i.e., in the course of the ritual prayer in the mosque): 'If only this were in your house.'[33] Al-Ḥasan al-Baṣrī was notable for looking always sad, but when a man began to weep loudly in his session, he said, 'Satan is now making this one weep.'[34] He warned a man who sobbed at a sermon of his, 'God will surely ask you what you meant by this.'[35] A number of other sayings are directed against deliberately induced weeping. Ibrāhīm b. ʿAbd Allāh al-Kattānī (fl. early 2nd/8th century) said, 'I have heard that weeping is nine-tenths hypocrisy, one-tenth for God, so if it comes to someone for God once a year, that is a lot.'[36] Shuʿayb al-Jubbāʾī (Yemeni, fl. 1st/8th century) said, 'When a man's reprobation is complete, he gains control of his eyes so that whenever he wishes to weep, he weeps.'[37] Muḥammad b. Sīrīn (Baṣran, d. 110/729), on being asked about those who sobbed on hearing the Qur'an, proposed a test: 'If they were to sit on a wall and the Qur'an was recited to them from beginning to end, if they fell off, then they would be as they say.'[38] ʿĪsā b. Zādhān (fl. earlier 2nd/8th century) predicted, 'There will befall the people a time when Satan lives in people's eyes and whoever wishes to weep will weep.'[39] Mālik b. Dīnār (Baṣran, d. 130/747–748) said, 'When a slave has reached perfection in debauchery, he gains control of his eyes.'[40] This is explained in an extension attributed to Sufyān al-Thawrī (Kūfan, d. 161/777): 'When a slave has perfected debauchery, he gains control of his eyes so that he weeps with

29 Ibn Māja, *al-Sunan, kitāb al-zuhd* 19, *bāb al-ḥuzn wa'l-bukā'*, no 4196; Abū ʿUbayd, *Faḍā'il al-Qur'ān*, ed. Marwān al-ʿAṭiyya, Muḥsin Kharāba and Wafāʾ Taqī al-Dīn (Damascus, 1415/1995), p. 135; Hannād, *Zuhd*, vol. 1, p. 270; Aḥmad, *Zuhd*, pp. 27, *36*.

30 Ibn al-Mubārak, *Zuhd*, no. 131; Wakīʿ, *Zuhd* 1:254; Aḥmad, *Zuhd*, pp. 108, *135*; Ibn Abī Shayba, *Muṣannaf, kitāb al-zuhd* 92, *mā qālū fi'l-bukā'*, vol. 12, p. 424.

31 Aḥmad, *Zuhd*, pp. 199, *247*; Abū Nuʿaym, *Ḥilya*, vol. 1, p. 261.

32 Ibn Abī al-Dunyā, *al-Riqqa wa'l-bukā'*, ed. Muḥammad Khayr Ramaḍān Yūsuf (Beirut, 1416/1996), pp. 53–54.

33 Ibn al-Mubārak, *Zuhd*, no. 156.

34 Aḥmad, *Zuhd*, pp. 274, *334*.

35 Abū Nuʿaym, *Ḥilya*, vol. 6, p. 305, quoting a lost section of Aḥmad, *Zuhd* (< ʿAl.; = abbreviation for ʿAbd Allāh).

36 Aḥmad, *Zuhd*, p. 229, *279* (< ʿAl.).

37 Ibn al-Mubārak, *Zuhd*, no 129; Wakīʿ, *Zuhd*, vol. 2, p. 788.

38 Abū Nuʿaym, *Ḥilya*, vol. 2, p. 265.

39 Aḥmad, *Zuhd*, pp. 275, *335*.

40 Ibid., pp. 322–323, *390*.

them whenever he wills.'[41] Weeping at the recitation of the Qur'an is still considered appropriate in Sunni circles today, but weeping is of course much more conspicuous in the course of Shiʿi ceremonies such as visiting tombs.

Unsurprisingly, the early Shiʿi and Sunni traditions are both sceptical of laughter. In the former, Jaʿfar al-Ṣādiq is quoted as saying, 'The believer's laughter is smiling.'[42] There are many Sunni parallels. Abū Sulaymān al-Dārānī (Syrian, d. 215/830–831) said, 'The laughter of the knower (*ʿārif*) is smiling.'[43] Jābir b. Samura is remembered as saying of the Prophet after the dawn prayer, 'They would converse, taking up the matter of the Jāhiliyya. They would laugh while he would smile.'[44] In the Shiʿi tradition, again, Jaʿfar al-Ṣādiq is quoted as saying, 'Much laughter kills the heart', also, 'Much laughter dissolves faith as water dissolves salt.'[45] Compare, in the Sunni tradition, the saying of the Prophet: 'Do not laugh much, for much laughter kills the heart.'[46] There are many other discouragements of laughing in the Sunni tradition similar to Jaʿfar's discouragement in the Shiʿi. Al-Ḥasan al-Baṣrī said, 'Much laughter kills the heart.'[47] Sufyān al-Thawrī said, 'Do not overeat, for it hardens the heart; suppress laughter and do not laugh much, for it kills hearts.'[48]

Al-Kulaynī balances sayings against laughter with encouragements of moderate laughing. Jaʿfar al-Ṣādiq asked Yūnus al-Shaybānī how their jesting (*mudāʿabah*) was. He said, 'Little.' Jaʿfar said, 'Do not do it. Jesting is part of goodnaturedness (*ḥusn al-khuluq*). It conveys pleasure to your brother. The Messenger of God … would jest with a man he wished to please.'[49] Muḥammad al-Jawād said, 'God (mighty and glori-

---

41 Abū Nuʿaym, *Ḥilya*, vol. 7, p. 72.

42 Al-Kulaynī, *Kāfī, kitāb al-ʿishra, bāb al-duʿāba wa'l-ḍaḥik*, vol. 2, p. 664.

43 Abū Nuʿaym, *Ḥilya*, vol. 9, p. 267.

44 Muslim, *Ṣaḥīḥ, kitāb al-masājid* 52, *bāb faḍl al-julūs fī muṣallāh*, no 1525, Kūfan *isnād*; ibid., *kitāb al-faḍā'il* 17, *bāb tabassumuh*, no. 2322; Aḥmad, *Musnad*, vol. 5, p. 91, *vol. 34, p. 431*. G. H. A. Juynboll ascribes this to Simāk ibn Ḥarb (Kūfan, d. 123/740–41): Juynboll, *Encyclopedia of Canonical Ḥadīth* (Leiden, 2007), p. 566. Jābir b. Samura is also quoted as describing the Prophet so: 'He would be long silent and laugh little. His companions would mention before him things of poetry and their affairs. They would laugh, while he would often smile'; Tirmidhī, *Jāmiʿ, al-adab* 70, *bāb mā jā'a fī inshā' al-shiʿr*, no 2850; Abū Dāwūd al-Ṭayālisī, *Musnad Abī Dāwūd al-Ṭayālisī* (Hyderabad, 1321; repr. Beirut, n.d.), no 771; Aḥmad, *Musnad*, vol. 5, p. 86, *vol. 34, pp. 405–406*. And again from Jābir b. Samura: 'The Messenger of God's thighs were slender. He did not laugh, only smile'; Tirmidhī, *Jāmiʿ, al-zuhd* 12, *bāb qawl Ibn Samura*, no 3645; Aḥmad, *Musnad*, vol. 5, pp. 97, 105, *vol. 34, pp. 466–467, 511*. See also Wakīʿ, *Zuhd*, vol. 1, pp. 266–267.

45 Al-Kulaynī, *Kāfī, kitāb al-ʿishra, bāb al-duʿāba wa'l-ḍaḥik*, vol. 2, p. 664.

46 Hannād, *Zuhd*, vol. 2, pp. 501, 553 (shortened version of same), Basran *isnād*; Tirmidhī, *Jāmiʿ, kitāb al-zuhd* 2, *man ittaqā al-maḥārim*, no. 2305, Basran *isnād*, different from Hannād's; Ibn Māja, *Sunan, kitāb al-zuhd* 19, *bāb al-ḥuzn wa'l-bukā'*, no 4193, Medinese *isnād*, also *Kitāb al-zuhd* 24, *bāb al-waraʿ wa'l-taqwā*, no 4217; Aḥmad, *Musnad*, vol. 2, p. 310, *vol. 13, pp. 458–459* with *isnād* like Tirmidhī's; Abū Nuʿaym, *Ḥilya*, vol. 1, p. 167.

47 Abū Nuʿaym, *Ḥilya*, vol. 2, p. 152.

48 Ibid., vol. 7, p. 36.

49 Al-Kulaynī, *Kāfī, kitāb al-ʿishra, bāb al-duʿāba wa'l-ḍaḥik*, vol. 2, p. 663.

ous is He) likes jesting in a group without indecency (*rafath*).'[50] According to Mūsā al-Kāẓim, 'Yaḥyā b. Zakarīyā' would weep but not laugh, while 'Īsā b. Maryam would laugh and weep.' The narrator's comment is preserved: 'It was as if what 'Īsā did was better than what Yaḥyā did.'[51] Similarly in the Sunni tradition is to be found praise of laughter over some things. Al-Ḥasan quoted the Prophet as saying:[52]

> There are two kinds of laughter, laughter that God loves and laughter that God despises. As for the laughter that God loves, it is that a man bare his teeth in the face of his brother on first recognising him, from longing to see him. As for the laughter that God despises, it is that a man speak harshly or meaninglessly, to laugh or to provoke laughter.

Likewise, there is Sunni praise for alternate laughing and weeping. Muḥammad b. Sīrīn was heard weeping by night, laughing by day.[53] He would laugh over poetry he recited, then blanch on hearing *ḥadīth* about the Sunna.[54] He often laughed until tears ran.[55] Ibn al-Mubārak reports a Companion's observation, 'I never saw anyone who smiled more than the Messenger of God', although also observations that the Prophet never laughed, only smiled.[56] Sometimes, to be sure, the emphasis is on secret weeping, presumptively sincere. Muʿāwiya b. Qurra (Basran, d. 113/731–732) said, 'Who will lead me to one who weeps by night but smiles by day?'[57] Muḥammad b. Wāsiʿ (Basran, d. 123/740–741) would weep by night, then grin in his friends' faces in the morning.[58]

Recollection

The devotional exercises that Muḥammad al-Bāqir describes begin with 'much recollecting God, fasting, prayer'. 'Recollection' (*dhikr*) so regularly appears in early renunciant literature as something audible that it seems this ought to be taken as its primary meaning. Al-Kulaynī quotes Jaʿfar al-Ṣādiq as saying, 'Lightning will not strike one who recollects (*al-dhākir*).' On being asked, 'What is a *dhākir*?', he said, 'One who recites 100 verses.'[59] More often, *dhikr* refers to reciting not the Qur'an but short phrases. For example, Jaʿfar al-Ṣādiq reports that the Prophet would say

50 Ibid.
51 Ibid., vol. 2, p. 665.
52 Hannād, *Zuhd*, vol. 2, p. 552.
53 Abū Nuʿaym, *Ḥilya*, vol. 2, p. 272.
54 Ibid., vol. 2, p. 274, quoting a lost § of Aḥmad, *Zuhd* (< 'Al.).
55 Abū Nuʿaym, *Ḥilya*, vol. 2, p. 274.
56 Ibn al-Mubārak, *Zuhd*, nos 145, 146, 148.
57 Abū Nuʿaym, *Ḥilya*, vol. 2, p. 299.
58 Ibn Abī al-Dunyā, *Riqqa*, p. 70.
59 Al-Kulaynī, *Kāfī*, *kitāb al-duʿā'*, *bāb anna al-ṣāʿiqa lā tuṣību dhākiran*, vol. 2, p. 500.

astaghfiru 'Llāh seventy times a day and *atūbu ilā 'Llāh* seventy times a day.[60] ʿAlī al-Riḍā said 100 times after the morning prayer and again 100 times after the sunset, 'In the name of God, the Merciful, the Compassionate, there is no power or strength save by God, the High, the Great.' He urged that no one quit sunset prayer till he had said this 100 times.[61] According to Jaʿfar al-Ṣādiq, Fāṭima would say on going to bed *Allāhu akbar* thirty-four times, *al-ḥamdu lillāh* thirty-three times, *subḥāna 'Llāh* thirty-three times, then recite the throne verse, the last two chapters of the Qurʾan, and the first and last 10 verses of Q.37 (*al-Ṣāffāt*).[62] Jaʿfar quoted the Prophet as saying that 'The one who recollects God among the neglectful (*al-dhākir lillāh, al-ghāfilīn*) is like the one who fights to protect the ones fleeing (*al-muqātil ʿan al-fārrīn*).'[63] It is easy to find Sunni parallels. The Prophet is quoted as saying, 'I ask God's forgiveness and repent to him 100 times a day.'[64] A Kūfan Follower, ʿAwn b. ʿAbd Allāh (d. before 120/738), is credited with saying, 'The one who recollects God among the neglectful (*al-dhākir Allāh, al-ghāfilīn*) is like the fighter behind the fleers (*al-fārrīn*).'[65] Almost the same statement, 'The one who recollects God among the indifferent is like the fighter behind those who have turned to flee (*al-mudbirīn*)', is also attributed to the Basran Ḥassān b. Abī Sinān (fl. first half 2nd/8th century).[66]

The Shiʿi tradition expects believers to pray in groups, probably repeating verbal formulae. Jaʿfar al-Ṣādiq is quoted as saying,[67]

> There is no group of forty men who meet and pray to God (mighty and glorious is He) concerning a matter save that God will answer them. If they are not forty, then four will not pray to God ten times (mighty and glorious is He) save that God will answer them. If they are not four, then one will not pray to God forty times save that God the mighty and all-powerful will answer him.

He foresees prayer by a designated leader, with his followers to respond by 'Amen' at the end: 'The one who prays and the one who says *āmīn* share in the reward.'[68]

We have abundant evidence from the Sunni tradition of a similar expectation of group prayer. The Prophet is supposed to have said, 'There is no group who have met to recollect God, desiring by that nothing but his face, save that a crier from Heaven cries "Arise forgiven: your bad characters have been replaced by good (*sayyiʾāt*,

---

[60] Ibid., *bāb al-istighfār*, vol. 2, p. 505.

[61] Ibid., *kitāb al-duʿāʾ*, *bāb al-qawl ʿinda al-iṣbāḥ wa'l- imsāʾ*, vol. 2, pp. 531–532.

[62] Ibid., *Kāfī*, *bāb al-duʿāʾ ʿinda al-nawm*, vol. 2, p. 536.

[63] Ibid., *Kāfī*, *kitāb al-duʿāʾ*, *bāb dhikr Allāh … fi'l-ghāfilīn*, vol. 2, p. 502. A slightly different version on the same page is attributed to Jaʿfar.

[64] Ibn Abī Shayba, *Muṣannaf*, *Kitāb al-duʿāʾ* 49, *mā dhukira fi'l-istighfār*, vol. 10, p. 87.

[65] Ibn al-Mubārak, *Zuhd*, no 357; Abū Nuʿaym, *Ḥilya*, vol. 4, p. 241, quoting a lost section of Aḥmad, *Zuhd*; Ibn Abī Shayba, *Muṣannaf*, *kitāb al-zuhd* 54, *kalām ʿAwn b. ʿAl.*, 12:307.

[66] Aḥmad, *Zuhd*, p. 328, *396*.

[67] Al-Kulaynī, *Kāfī*, *kitāb al-duʿāʾ*, *bāb al-ijtimāʿ*, vol. 2, p. 487.

[68] Ibid., vol. 2, p. 487.

ḥasanāt)".'[69] Al-Ḥasan al-Baṣrī related from the Messenger of God, 'When a group gather to recollect God (mighty and glorious is He), God tells his angels, "I have forgiven them, so wrap them with mercy." The angels say, "Our Lord, among them is so-and-so." God says, "They are a group who will not be lost by one sitting with them."'[70] Khulayd al-ʿAṣarī (Basran, fl. early 2nd/8th century) said that the adornment of mosques is men who help one another at recollecting God (*dhikr Allāh*).[71]

At the same time, the Sunni tradition also reports considerable suspicion and disparagement of group chanting. ʿAbd Allāh b. Masʿūd (d. Medina, 32/652–653) reproached someone for sitting in the mosque, having his circle repeat *Allāhu akbar*, *subḥān Allāh*, and so on, for set numbers of times.[72] People came to al-Rabīʿ b. Khuthaym (Kūfan, d. 63/682–683) 'for you to praise God and for us to praise Him with you, and for you to recollect God and for us to recollect Him with you.' He told them, 'God be praised — why don't you come to us saying, "We have come for you to drink and for us to drink with you and for you to commit adultery and for us to commit adultery with you?"'[73] Aḥmad (d. 241/855) was himself asked whether it was discouraged for a group to meet to pray to God and raise their hands: 'I do not dislike it for brothers so long as they have not met deliberately, unless they are many.' Isḥāq b. Rāhawayh's gloss shows the reason: 'Unless they are many' means that they should not make a habit of it such that they become known for it.[74] Devotions should be directed toward pleasing God, not the people.

The Shiʿi tradition certainly shows concern that devotions be practised for the sake of God alone. Jaʿfar al-Ṣādiq is quoted as saying, 'Our *shīʿa* are those who, when they are alone, recollect God often.'[75] ʿAlī al-Riḍā is quoted as saying, 'The servant's prayer in secret is worth seventy in public.'[76] Compare some sayings in the Sunni tradition. The Prophet himself is quoted as saying, 'The best recollection is the hidden, the best provision that which suffices.'[77] ʿĀʾisha (d. 57/676–677) is quoted as saying, 'The hidden recollection that the guardian angels do not record is multiplied over other prayers seventy times.'[78] 'The hidden recollection (*al-dhikr al-khafī*)' is evidently the one spoken is such a subdued voice that the guardian angels do not notice. ʿUqba b.

---

[69] Aḥmad, *Musnad*, vol. 3, p. 142, *vol. 19, p. 437*; Abū Nuʿaym, *Ḥilya*, vol. 3, p. 108. Similar is attributed to Sahl b. Ḥanẓala, Companion, by Ibn Abī Shayba, *Muṣannaf, kitāb al-duʿāʾ* 50, *fī thawāb dhikr Allāh*, vol. 10, p. 95; Aḥmad, *Zuhd*, pp. 205, *254*.

[70] Aḥmad, *Zuhd*, pp. 395, *472*.

[71] Ibid., pp. 237, *291* (< ʿAl.); Abū Nuʿaym, *Ḥilya*, vol. 2, p. 233 (quoting a lost section of Aḥmad, *Zuhd*, < Aḥmad).

[72] Aḥmad, *Zuhd*, pp. 358, *428–429* (< ʿAl.).

[73] Ibid., pp. 331, *399* (< ʿAl.).

[74] Al-Kawsaj, *Masāʾil al-imām Aḥmad b. Ḥanbal wa-Isḥāq b. Rāhawayh*, ed. Abu'l-Ḥusayn Khālid b. Maḥmūd al-Rabāṭ, Wiʾām al-Ḥawshī, and Jumʿa Fatḥī (Riyadh, 1425/2004), vol. 2, p. 598, no. 3499.

[75] Al-Kulaynī, *Kāfī, kitāb al-duʿāʾ, bāb dhikr Allāh kathīran*, vol. 2, p. 499.

[76] Ibid., *kitāb al-duʿāʾ, bāb ikhfāʾ al-duʿā*, vol. 2, p. 476.

[77] Aḥmad, *Musnad*, vol. 1, pp. 72, 180, 187, *vol. 3, pp. 76, 131–132, 168–169*.

[78] Ibn Abī Shayba, *Muṣannaf, kitāb al-duʿāʾ* 94, *fī rafʿ al-ṣawt bi'l-duʿāʾ* 2, vol. 10, p. 143.

ʿAbd al-Ghāfir (Basran, d. 83/702–703) said, 'One prayer (*daʿwa*) in secret is preferable to seventy in public.'[79] Ḥassān b. ʿAṭiyya (Damascene, d. 120s/738–747) said, 'A secret prayer (*duʿā'*) is seventy times preferred over a public.'[80] Al-Ḥasan al-Baṣrī is quoted as saying, 'There is no Muslim who resorts to his bed to recollect God save that his bed becomes a mosque for God and he is written in God's view among those who recollect (*al-dhākirīn*).'[81]

In a leading early Ismaili work, I have found a number of recommendations of recollecting not exactly God but death. Here, it seems that 'recollection' must refer to something like 'contemplation' rather than the repetition of phrases. The Prophet is said to have told one of the *anṣār*, 'I commend to you the recollection of death, for it will make you forget the matter of the world.'[82] Likewise, the Prophet commented that 'the one who most recollects death is the readiest for it.'[83] Muḥammad al-Bāqir is quoted as saying, 'Recollect death often, for no man recollects death often without renouncing the world.'[84] There is much talk of contemplating death in Sunni renunciant sources, as well. Al-ʿAlā' b. Ziyād (Basran, d. 94/712–713) recommended imagining oneself on the point of death, hence acting in obedience to God.[85] Shumayṭ b. ʿAjlān (Basran, fl. early 2nd/8th century) said, 'Whoever sets up death before his eyes will not care about the narrowness or wideness of the world.'[86] Al-Rabīʿ b. Abī Rāshid (Kufan, fl. early 2nd/8th century) said, 'If the recollection of death departs from me for an hour, it corrupts my heart.'[87]

'Recollection' in this sense more often goes by the name of *tafakkur*. Jaʿfar al-Ṣādiq says, 'The best worship is prolonged contemplation (*tafakkur*) of God and his power.'[88] Jaʿfar is told, and evidently approves, contemplation for an hour is better than staying up all night (in ritual prayer and Qur'anic recitation).[89] This is exactly what Abu'l-Dardā' and al-Ḥasan al-Baṣrī are quoted as saying: 'Contemplation for an hour is better than staying up all night.'[90] The Companion Ibn ʿAbbās is quoted as saying, 'Two moderate sets of bowings (*rakʿatān muqtaṣidatān*) with

79 Aḥmad, *Zuhd*, pp. 311, *377*.

80 Abū Nuʿaym, *Ḥilya*, vol. 6, p. 73.

81 Ibid., p. 271.

82 Al-Qāḍī al-Nuʿmān, *Daʿā'im*, ed. Fyzee, vol. 1, p. 224 = ed. ʿĀrif Tāmir (Beirut, 1416/1995), vol. 1, p. 264.

83 Ibid., 1:224; ed. Tāmir, vol. 1, p. 264.

84 Ibid., 1:224; ed. Tāmir, vol.1, p. 264.

85 Aḥmad, *Zuhd*, pp. 255, *p. 312*.

86 Abū Nuʿaym, *Ḥilya*, vol. 3, p. 129.

87 Ibn al-Mubārak, *Zuhd*, no 266; Ibn Abī Shayba, *Muṣannaf*, *kitāb al-zuhd* 84, *bāb al-Shaʿbī*, vol. 12, p. 405; Abū Nuʿaym, *Ḥilya*, vol. 5, pp. 75–76. Also attributed to Ṣāliḥ al-Murrī (Basran, d. 172/788–789?): Ibn al-Mubārak, *Zuhd*, no 260.

88 Al-Kulaynī, *Kāfī*, *kitāb al-īmān wa'l-kufr*, *bāb al-tafakkur*, vol. 2, p. 55.

89 Ibid., vol. 2, p. 54.

90 Ibn Abī Shayba, *Muṣannaf*, *kitāb al-zuhd* 13, *kalām Abi'l-Dardā'*, and *kitāb al-zuhd* 72, *kalām al-Ḥasan al-Baṣrī*, vol. 12, pp. 219, 365; also Aḥmad, *Zuhd*, pp. 272, *332* (al-Ḥasan).

contemplation are better than staying up all night with a straying mind (*wa'l-qalb sāhin*).'[91] Umm al-Dardā' (Syrian, d. after 81/700) is often quoted as saying *tafakkur* and *iʿtibār* (observing things and taking warning) had been the best work of her husband, Abu'l-Dardā' (d. early 30s/650s).[92]

Restricted Eating and Drinking

Second among the devotional exercises that Muḥammad al-Bāqir describes is fasting. Fasting during Ramaḍān is a duty for all Muslims, likewise as atonement for various offences. Apart from encouragements of formal fasting, al-Kulaynī also reports many injunctions to eat little. He quotes Jaʿfar al-Ṣādiq as saying, 'Much eating is hateful', 'The servant is closest to God when his stomach is light, while the servant is most despised by God when his stomach has been filled', 'God despises much eating' and 'There is nothing God despises more than a full stomach.'[93] Adding to a tradition going back to Christian renunciants centuries earlier, Jaʿfar is quoted as observing, 'The son of Adam has no alternative to eating in order to maintain his body. When one of you eats food, let him make a third of his stomach for food, a third of his stomach for drink, and a third of his stomach for his soul. Do not fatten yourselves as swine are fattened for slaughtering.'[94]

Many recommendations and examples of eating little are to be found in the Sunni tradition. Al-Qāsim b. Mukhaymira, who lived in Syria (d. 100/718–719), quoted the advice of Luqmān to his son: 'My son, beware of satiety, for it betrays you by night and humiliates by day.'[95] ʿUmar (d. 23/644) is said to have reproached ʿĀṣim b. ʿAmr, a Hijazi Follower, for gnawing on a piece of meat. 'It is excess enough that a man should eat everything he desires.'[96] Samura b. Jundub, a Companion who settled in Basra (d. 58/677–678), was told that his son had not slept the previous night. He asked, 'Is it overeating (*basham*)?' Told that it was, he said, 'If he died, I would not pray over him', suggesting that overeating was virtual apostasy.[97] The Kūfan al-Aswad b. Yazīd al-Nakhaʿī (d. 75/694–695) fasted until he had turned green and yellow and

---

91 Ibn al-Mubārak, *Zuhd*, no. 288, with 'moderate' presumably referring to their length.

92 Ibid., no 286; Aḥmad, *Zuhd*, pp. 135, *168*; Abū Nuʿaym, *Ḥilya*, vol. 1, p. 208, vol. 4, p. 253, vol. 7, p. 300; *tafakkur* alone *apud* Ibn Abī Shayba, *Muṣannaf*, *kitāb al-zuhd* 13, *kalām Abi'l-Dardā'*, vol. 12, p. 219.

93 Al-Kulaynī, *Kāfī*, *kitāb al-aṭʿima*, *bāb karāhiyat kathrat al-akl*, vol. 6, p. 269 except the last, vol. 6, p. 270.

94 Ibid., vol. 6, pp. 269–270.

95 Abū Nuʿaym, *Ḥilya* 6:82.

96 Ibn al-Mubārak, *Zuhd*, no 769.

97 Wakīʿ, *Zuhd* 1:302; Aḥmad, *Zuhd*, p. 199 *248*; Aḥmad b. Ḥanbal (attrib.), *Kitāb al-waraʿ*, ed. Zaynab Ibrāhīm al-Qārūṭ (Beirut, 1403/1983), p. 102; ed. Muḥammad Sayyid Basyūnī Zaghlūl (Beirut, 1409/1988), p. 84.

lost an eye.[98] Al-ʿAlāʾ b. Ziyād (d. 94/712–713) was a Baṣran who lived on one loaf a day and fasted until he had turned green.[99] Al-Ḥasan al-Baṣrī said that a Muslim did not eat with all his belly.[100]

More generally, we have the theme of licit eating. Early Muslims seem to have been deeply concerned not to take into their bodies what had not been rightly purchased. A man told Abū Jaʿfar (Muḥammad al-Bāqir) that he was weak of work (worship) but hoped to eat only what was licit. The Imam commented, 'What devotion (*ijtihād*) is better than chastity of the belly and genitals?'[101] Sunni sources often report concern for eating only what is licit. For example, ʿĀmir b. ʿAbd Qays (fl. 1st/7th century) would eat fat (*samn*) only from *arḍ al-ʿarab*, the pre-conquest territory of the Arabs, since it was unknown what other fat had been mixed with anything from elsewhere.[102] Yūsuf b. Asbāṭ, a Kufan who lived in Antioch (d. 195/810–811), would eat only what was licit and make do with dust if he found none.[103] But this concern for eating only the licit seems to have died out in the early 9th century. Wakīʿ (Kūfan, d. 197/812) declared, 'If a man swore to eat nothing but the licit, wear nothing but the licit, and not walk except in the licit, we would tell him, "Take off your clothes and throw yourself in the Euphrates." ... The purely licit we do not know today. ... The world has the status of carrion: take from it what will sustain you.'[104]

Al-Kulaynī encourages eating cold food rather than hot. Jaʿfar al-Ṣādiq quotes ʿAlī as saying, 'Lay by what is hot in order for it to cool off, for the Messenger of God ... had some hot food brought near him but said, "Lay it by for it to cool off. God has not fed us what is hot. Blessing is in the cold."'[105] Then we are told:[106]

> Supper was brought for Abū ʿAbd Allāh (Jaʿfar al-Ṣādiq) in the summertime. A table was brought with bread on it. He was also brought some soup and meat. He said, 'Let me have this food' and approached, then put his hand on it but raised it again, saying, 'I take refuge with God from the Fire; I appeal to God to preserve me

---

[98] Ibn Abī Shayba, *Muṣannaf, kitāb al-zuhd* 43, *kalam al-aswad*, vol. 12, p. 294; multiple reports, Abū Nuʿaym, *Ḥilya* vol. 2, pp. 103–104.

[99] Ibn al-Mubārak, *Zuhd*, no 965; Abū Nuʿaym, *Ḥilya* vol. 2, p. 243.

[100] Ibn al-Mubārak, *Zuhd*, no 271.

[101] Al-Kulaynī, *Kāfī, kitāb al-īmān wa'l-kufr, bāb al-ʿiffa*, vol. 2, p. 79. Comment repeated twice, ibid., vol. 2, p. 80.

[102] Aḥmad, *Zuhd*, pp. 220, *270*. See Ibn al-Mubārak, *Zuhd*, no. 866, where he says he eats fat from some places but not others, and Ibn Saʿd, *Biographien*, ed. Eduard Sachau et al. (Leiden, 1904–1940), vol. 7, pp. 74–75; *al-Ṭabaqāt al-kubrā* (Beirut, 1957–1968), vol. 7, pp. 104–105, where he says that he eats fat from the desert.

[103] Ibn Ḥibbān, *Kitāb al-thiqāt*, ed. Muḥammad ʿAbd al-Muʿīd Khān (Hyderabad, 1393–1403/1973–1983), vol. 7, p. 638; Ibn Ḥajar, *Tahdhīb al-tahdhīb* (Hyderabad, 1325–1327; repr. Beirut, n.d), vol. 11, p. 408.

[104] Abū Nuʿaym, *Ḥilya*, vol. 8, p. 370.

[105] Al-Kulaynī, *Kāfī, kitāb al-aṭʿima, bāb al-ṭaʿām al-ḥārr*, vol. 6, pp. 321–322, followed by three more prophetic *ḥadīth* reports with almost the same words, vol. 6, p. 322.

[106] Ibid., vol. 6, p. 322.

from the Fire; I appeal to God to preserve me from the Fire. We have no patience for this, so how the Fire? We are not strong enough for this, so how the Fire? We cannot bear this, so how the Fire?' He kept on saying that until the food had cooled. Then he ate and we with him.

The idea is evidently that hot food makes it akin to Hell-fire – better, then, to avoid it. There is no Sunni parallel that I have remarked, except for the archaic discussion of calling for ritual ablutions after touching anything touched by fire.[107]

Supererogatory Ritual Prayer

Third among the devotional exercises that Muḥammad al-Bāqir describes is the ritual prayer. This refers, of course, not to the required five daily prayers but to additional, supererogatory prayer. *Ijtihād* in renunciant literature refers especially to ritual worship (corresponding more closely than other terms to Greek *askēsis*). This is what Jaʿfar al-Ṣādiq refers to when he warns that ritual performance must be accompanied by right action: 'I enjoin on you fear of God, *waraʿ*, and *ijtihād*. Know that there is no benefit to *ijtihād* without scrupulosity.'[108] Scrupulosity (*waraʿ*) means avoiding not only what is plainly forbidden but anything remotely likely to be forbidden. In the Sunni tradition, it is said of ʿAbd al-Raḥmān b. al-Aswad (Kūfan, d. 99/717–718) that he would pray with 700 bowings a day. 'They used to say he was the least of the people of his house in *ijtihād*. I have heard that he became bone and skin. They used to say the Aswad family were among the people of Paradise.'[109] Recalling the heightened piety of an earlier generation, al-Ḥasan al-Baṣrī is quoted as saying, 'They used to exert themselves (*yajtahidūna*) in prayer (*duʿāʾ*), and you would hear nothing but whispering.'[110]

Unsurprisingly, the Shiʿi tradition recommends supererogatory ritual prayer. According to an Ismaili source, ʿAlī b. al-Ḥusayn Zayn al-ʿĀbidīn (d. Medina, 95/714) would pray 1,000 sets of supererogatory prayer per day.[111] There are very many reports in the Sunni literature of prodigious routines of supererogatory prayer. For example, the Kūfan *mukhaḍram* Murra b. Sharāḥīl (d. 76/695) is said to have prayed 500 bowings a day in his youth, 250 in old age.[112] ʿAlī b. ʿAbd Allāh b. al-ʿAbbās

[107] For which see Marion Holmes Katz, *Body of Text: The Emergence of the Sunnī Law of Ritual Purity* (Albany, 2002), pp. 102–123.

[108] Al-Kulaynī, *Kāfī*, *kitāb al-īmān wa'l-kufr*, *bāb al-waraʿ*, vol. 2, p. 76.

[109] Aḥmad, *Zuhd*, pp. 360, 430.

[110] Ibn Abī Shayba, *Muṣannaf*, *kitāb al-duʿāʾ* 94, *fī rafʿ al-ṣawt bi'l-duʿāʾ*, vol. 10, p. 144; Wakīʿ, *Zuhd* vol. 2, p. 616.

[111] Al-Qāḍī al-Nuʿmān, *Daʿāʾim*, ed. Fyzee, vol. 1, p. 211; ed. Tāmir, vol. 1, p. 261.

[112] Al-ʿIjlī, *Taʾrīkh al-thiqāt*, arr. Ibn Ḥajar al-Haythamī, ed. ʿAbd al-Muʿṭī Qalʿajī (Beirut, 1405/1984), p. 424; al-Jāḥiẓ, *al-Bayān wa'l-tabyīn*, ed. ʿAbd al-Salām Muḥammad Hārūn (Cairo, 1367–1369/1948–1950), vol. 3, p. 129.

(Medinese, d. 118/736–737) prayed over 500 bowings a day.[113] The Palestinian Rajāʾ b. Abī Salama (d. 161/777–778) prayed 1,000 prostrations a day.[114]

Al-Kulaynī also reports advice on how to pray apart from the ritual prayer. Jaʿfar al-Ṣādiq demonstrated gestures: 'Mention of a desire [at this he showed the insides of his palms to heaven]; thus is fear (*rahba*) [at this he put the backs of his hands to heaven]; thus is self-abasement (*taḍarruʿ*) [at this he moved his fingers right and left]; thus is chastity (*tabattul*) [at this he raised his fingers once and put them down once]; thus is supplication (*ibtihāl*) [at this he extended his hand before his face to the *qibla*]. One does not supplicate until a tear flows.'[115] Someone once presumed to correct the Imam:[116]

> A man passed by me as I was praying in the course of my ritual prayer with my left. He said, 'Abū ʿAbd Allāh, with your right.' I said, 'O servant of God, God (be He blessed and exalted) has a claim on this as He has on this.' Desire is that you extend your hands and show their insides. Fear is that you extend your hands and show their backs. Self-abasement is that you move the right pointing finger to right and left. Chastity is that you move the left pointing finger and raise it to heaven slowly (*rislan*), then put it down. Supplication is that you extend your hands and arms to heaven, supplication coming when you see the occasions of weeping.

Compare the Prophet from the Sunni tradition: 'If you ask God (for something), ask him with the palms of your hands; do not ask Him with their backs.'[117] Shahr b. Ḥawshab (Syrian, d. 112/730–731) gave this recommendation: spread the hands toward the face for *masʾala* (asking for a good), palms reversed for *taʿawwudh* (taking refuge with God from some danger).[118]

Concern for the Poor

Muḥammad al-Bāqir's recommendation of filial piety seems completely unremarkable, so that there can be no need to demonstrate Sunni parallels. As for the next on his list, 'keeping faith with poor neighbours and the indigent, debt-ridden and orphans', it is not particularly prominent in the rest of al-Kulaynī's collection of pious

113 Abū Nuʿaym, *Ḥilya*, vol. 3, p. 207; cf. Abū Dāwūd, *Kitāb al-zuhd*, ed. Muṣṭafā Maḥmūd Ḥusayn (Tanta, 1424/2003), p. 231, nos 451–452.

114 Abū Nuʿaym, *Ḥilya*, vol. 6, p. 91.

115 Al-Kulaynī, *Kāfī*, *kitāb al-duʿāʾ*, *bāb al-raghba waʾl-rahba*, vol. 2, p. 480.

116 Ibid., vol. 2, p. 480. Also, '*Masʾala* is extending the palms; *istiʿādha* is raising (*ifḍāʾ*) the palms (toward the *qibla*); chastity is indicating with the finger; self-abasement is moving the finger; supplication is extending both of one's hands' (ibid., vol. 2, p. 481).

117 Ibn Abī Shayba, *Muṣannaf*, *kitāb al-duʿāʾ* 45, *al-rajul idhā daʿā bi-baṭn kaffih*, vol. 10, p. 78; *isnād* Kufan in lower part, Basran upper.

118 Ibid., vol. 10, p. 79.

recommendations and it has some but not very numerous parallels in the Sunni literature. The Kūfan Khaythama b. ʿAbd al-Raḥmān (d. after 80/699–700) willed that he be buried in the cemetery of the poor of his tribe.[119] The Basran Muṭarrif b. ʿAbd Allāh (d. 95/713–714) wore wool and sat with the poor for the sake of humility.[120] People attended the session of the Kūfan Sufyān al-Thawrī in rags, and the rich there were said to be humbled, the poor exalted.[121]

Qurʾanic Recitation

Next on Muḥammad al-Bāqir's list is truthful speech, again unremarkable. 'Reciting the Qur'an' overlaps with recollection, as observed above. This devotional form is apparently more prominent in Sunni renunciant literature than Shiʿi. It is sometimes described as being superior to participation in the Holy War or other pious activities. ʿAbd Allāh b. Masʿūd said that one who recollects God, glossed as 'a man who recites the Book of God' (*rajul yatlū kitāb Allāh*), is better than a man who rides on the Holy War.[122] Salmān (d. Medina, 34/654–655) said, 'If one man stayed up all night giving eggs to slave girls (*qaynāt*) while another stayed up reciting the Qur'an and recollecting God, I think the one recollecting God would be the better.'[123] Sufyān al-Thawrī said it was better to recite the Qurʾan than to go frontier raiding.[124] There are as many reports in the Sunni literature of prodigious routines of Qurʾanic recitation as there are of supererogatory prayer. ʿUthmān would recite the Qurʾan in a single *rakʿa* by night.[125] ʿAlqama (Kufan, d. after 70/689–690?), recited the whole Qurʾan in a night around the Kaʿba.[126] Murra b. Sharāḥīl (Kūfan, d. 76/695–696) recited the Qurʾan daily and so was safe from the *fitna* of Ibn al-Zubayr.[127] Saʿīd b. Jubayr (Kūfan, d. 95/714) entered the Kaʿba and recited the entire Qurʾan in a single *rakʿa*, also daily during Ramadan and every three days during the rest of the year.[128] Al-Zuhrī (d. 125/742–743) recited the Qurʾan before breakfasting on the 21st, 23rd, 25th, 27th and

119 Ibn Abī Shayba, *Muṣannaf, kitāb al-zuhd* 60, *Khaythama ibn ʿAr.*, vol. 12, p. 321; Aḥmad, *Zuhd*, pp. 359, 429 (< ʿAl.).

120 Abū Nuʿaym, *Ḥilya*, vol. 2, p. 200.

121 Ibid., vol. 6, pp. 364–365.

122 Ibn Abī Shayba, *Muṣannaf, kitāb faḍāʾil al-Qurʾān* 29, *man qāla qirāʾat al-Qurʾān afḍal min siwāh*, vol. 10, p. 241.

123 Ibid., vol. 10, pp. 241–242.

124 Abū Nuʿaym, *Ḥilya*, vol. 7, p. 65.

125 Ibn Saʿd, *Biographien*, vol. 3, p. 153; *Ṭabaqāt*, vol. 3, pp. 75–76; Aḥmad, *Zuhd*, pp. 127, 158; Abū Nuʿaym, *Ḥilya*, vol. 1, p. 57.

126 Ibn Abī Shayba, *Muṣannaf, kitāb ṣalāh* 851, *man kāna yuḥibbu idhā qadima an yaqraʾa al-Qurʾān*, vol. 3, pp. 618–619. Also, 'He recited the Qurʾan in a night': ibid., *kitāb al-zuhd* 44, *kalām ʿAlqama*, vol. 12, p. 295.

127 Abū Nuʿaym, *Ḥilya*, vol. 4, pp. 162–163.

128 Ibid., vol. 4, p. 273.

29th of Ramadan.[129] Thābit al-Bunānī (Basran, d. 127/744–745) recited the Qurʾan daily as well as fasting perpetually.[130] And so on and so on.

Other Austerities

Night-time devotions are recommended in a saying from Jaʿfar al-Ṣādiq in the Ismaili tradition: 'I despise that a servant should recite the Qurʾan, then awaken in the night and not get up until morning is near, only then getting up and beginning to pray.'[131] The idea is that he should rather recite the Qurʾan after the evening prayer, go to bed, then get up for further devotions as soon as he wakes up, whenever that is. Compare the example of Abū Isḥāq al-Sabīʿī (Kūfan, d. 129/746–747), who would not go back to sleep if he awoke at night.[132] Sufyān al-Thawrī told his disciples it was all right to sleep at any length but not to go back to sleep after one had once woken up.[133]

Hostility to music is a common theme of pious literature, Sunni and Shiʿi. Jaʿfar al-Ṣādiq is said to have glossed Q.22:30, 'Avoid the abomination of idols, and avoid the speaking of falsehood', as 'singing'; likewise Q.6:31, 'Among the people are those who buy diverting tales to lead [people] away from the path of God without any knowledge'; and likewise Q.25:72, 'And those who will not bear false witness.'[134] He said, 'Playing lutes (*ḍarb al-ʿīdān*) makes hypocrisy spring up in the heart as water makes verdure spring up'; alternatively, 'Listening to singing and idle talk (*lahw*) makes hypocrisy spring up in the heart as water makes plants spring up.'[135] And he said, 'Whoever strikes strings (*rubṭ*) in his house for forty days, God gives a devil power over him. … When he is in that state, the life drops from him and he does not care what he says or what is said of him.'[136] On the other side, Sunni denunciations of music are plentiful. The Prophet is quoted as saying, 'Singing plants hypocrisy in the heart.'[137] Pouring out wine and smashing musical instruments are often paired as prime examples of *al-amr bi'l-maʿrūf wa'l-nahy ʿan al-munkar* ('commanding right and forbidding wrong').[138] Zubayd al-Yāmī, a Kūfan worshipper (d. 122/739–740 or after), seized and broke the reed flute he saw one slave girl carrying, the tambourine

---

129 Ibid., vol. 3, p. 170.

130 ʿAbd Allāh b. Aḥmad, *ʿIlal*, vol. 1, p. 486, *vol. 1, p. 181.*

131 Al-Qāḍī al-Nuʿmān, *Daʿāʾim*, ed. Fyzee, vol. 1, p. 213; ed. Tāmir, vol. 1, p. 264.

132 Abū Nuʿaym, *Ḥilya*, vol. 4, p. 340, quoting a lost section of Aḥmad, *Zuhd*.

133 Ibid., vol. 7, p. 60.

134 Al-Kulaynī, *Kāfī, kitāb al-ashriba, bāb al-ghināʾ*, vol. 6, pp. 431–433.

135 Ibid., vol. 6, p. 434.

136 Ibid., vol. 6, p. 434.

137 Abū Dāwūd, *Sunan, kitāb al-adab* 60, *bāb karāhiyat al-ghināʾ wa'l-zamr*, no. 4927. Further examples *apud* al-Ājurrī, *Taḥrīm al-nard wa'l-shaṭranj wa'l-malāhī*, ed. Muṣṭafā ʿAbd al-Qādir ʿAṭā (Beirut, 1408/1988), pp. 93–102.

138 As in Ghazālī's exemplary discussion of the duty, *Iḥyāʾ ʿulūm al-dīn*, book 19. Many examples are cited by Michael Cook, *Commanding Right and Forbidding Wrong in Islamic Thought* (Cambridge, 2000).

of another.[139] Aḥmad b. Ḥanbal (d. Baghdad, 241/855) said of singing, 'It establishes hypocrisy in the heart. I dislike it.'[140] He approved of breaking a lute or mandolin and denied that the breaker owed anything to the owner in compensation.[141]

Al-Kulaynī quotes Jaʿfar al-Ṣādiq as relating of the Messenger of God, 'Leaning in the mosque is the monasticism (*rahbāniyya*) of the Arabs. The believer's session is his mosque and his cell is his house.'[142] The Sunni tradition more often recommends the Holy War as the new monasticism; for example, the Companion Abū Saʿīd al-Khudrī (d. Medina, 64/683–684) is quoted as saying, 'I enjoin you to fear God, for it is the chief of everything. Incumbent on you is *jihād*, for it is the *rahbāniyya* of Islam.'[143] But sitting in the mosque is certainly encouraged in the Sunni tradition and sometimes identified with monasticism. 'Uthmān b. Maẓʿūn came to the Prophet and asked, among other things, 'O Messenger of God, permit us monasticism (*tarahhub*).' He said, 'The *tarahhub* of my community is sitting in the mosque waiting for the ritual prayer.'[144] Abū Idrīs al-Khawlānī (Syrian, d. 80/699–700) is quoted as saying, 'The mosques are the nobles' places of sitting (*majālis al-kirām*).'[145] Note how, similarly to Jaʿfar with Arabism, he conflates concepts of right religion and social status. The Muslim's house is identified with a monk's cell in a number of sayings in the Sunni tradition. Abu'l-Dardā' is supposed to have said, 'What a good cell for a man is his house. In it, he restrains his sight and tongue. Beware of the market, for it negates and distracts (*tulghī, tulhī*).'[146] Al-Ḥasan al-Baṣrī said, 'The believers' cells are their houses.'[147]

Some Shiʿi advice on clothing is very similar to Sunni. Al-Kulaynī quotes the Prophet as saying, 'Wear white, for it is better and purer. Shroud your dead in it.'[148] Sunni *ḥadīth* collections report exactly the same words.[149] But al-Kulaynī's repeated

---

139 Abū Nuʿaym, *Ḥilya*, vol. 5, p. 32.

140 ʿAbd Allāh b. Aḥmad, *Masāʾil al-imām Aḥmad b. Ḥanbal*, ed. Zuhayr al-Shāwīsh (Beirut, 1401/1981), p. 316.

141 Abū Dāwūd, *Kitāb masāʾil al-imām Aḥmad*, ed. Muḥammad Bahja al-Bayṭār (Cairo, 1353/1934; repr. Beirut, n.d.), p. 279.

142 Al-Kulaynī, *Kāfī, kitāb al-ʿishra, bāb al-ittikāʾ wa'l-iḥtibāʾ*, vol. 2, p. 662.

143 Ibn al-Mubārak, *Zuhd*, no. 840.

144 Ibid., no. 845.

145 Ibid., no. 840.

Aḥmad, *Zuhd*, pp. 380, *455*.

146 Wakīʿ, *Zuhd*, vol. 2, p. 516; Aḥmad, *Zuhd*, pp. 135, *168*; Ibn al-Mubārak, *Zuhd*, no. 14 among additions < N.; Jāḥiẓ, *Bayān*, vol. 3, p. 132.

147 Ibn al-Mubārak, *Zuhd*, no. 15 among additions < N.; Ibn Abī Shayba, *Muṣannaf, kitāb al-zuhd* 72, *kalām al-Ḥasan al-Baṣrī*, vol. 12, p. 380; Abū Nuʿaym, *Ḥilya*, vol. 3, p. 19, quoting a lost section of Aḥmad, *Zuhd*.

148 Two versions: al-Kulaynī, *Kāfī, kitāb al-zī wa'l-tajammul, bāb al-libās*, vol. 6, p. 445.

149 Tirmidhī, *Jāmiʿ*, *kitāb al-adab* 46, *bāb mā jāʾa fī lubs al-bayāḍ*, no 2810; Aḥmad, *Musnad*, vol. 5, pp. 10, 12, 13, 17, 18, 19, 20–21, *vol. 33, pp. 297, 318–319, 327–328, 354–355, 364, 372–373, 381–382*; ʿAbd al-Razzāq, *Muṣannaf*, ed. Ḥabīb al-Raḥmān al-Aʿẓamī (Johannesburg, 1390–1392/1970–1972), vol. 3, pp. 428–429 (3 versions). Similar advice is to be found *apud* Abū Dāwūd, *Sunan*, *kitāb al-ṭibb* 14, *bāb fi'l-amr bi'l-kuḥl*, no. 3878, repeated *kitāb al-libās* 13, *bāb*

discouragement of wool seems unlike the Sunni tradition. He reports that Jaʿfar said, 'Linen (*kattān*) is the dress of the prophets and makes the flesh grow.'[150] He reports that Jaʿfar said, 'Do not wear wool or hair save in illness (*min ʿilla*).'[151] He reports that ʿAlī said, 'Wear clothes of cotton (*quṭn*), for it is the dress of the Messenger of God and our dress. He did not wear wool or hair save from illness (*min ʿilla*).'[152] A section of *ḥadīth* relating to clothing comprises only encouragement to wear the best clothing one can.[153]

The contrary tendency can also be found. Al-Kulaynī quotes someone as saying,[154]

> I saw Abū ʿAbd Allāh (Jaʿfar al-Ṣādiq) wearing a rough shirt under his clothes, on top of it a woollen *jubba*, on top of it a rough shirt. I felt it and said, 'God make me your ransom: the people dislike to wear wool.' He said, 'On the contrary: Abū Muḥammad b. ʿAlī (al-Ḥasan) wore it and ʿAlī b. al-Ḥusayn (Zayn al-ʿĀbidīn) wore it. They would wear their roughest clothing when they got up to perform the ritual prayer. That is what we do.'

A Sunni source reports in rough conformity with this last report that Sufyān al-Thawrī discovered Jaʿfar al-Ṣādiq to be wearing wool underneath a silken *jubba*.[155] More generally, the Sunni tradition seems overwhelmingly friendly to the wearing of wool. Mūsā never wore anything but wool, likewise ʿĪsā.[156] Ibn Masʿūd (d. 32/652–653?) said, 'The prophets milked sheep, rode asses and wore wool.'[157] According to al-Ḥasan al-Baṣrī, the Prophet Muḥammad rode an ass (not a horse), wore wool, licked his fingers and ate on the floor.'[158] It was a mark of humility.[159] Strictures against wearing wool are also to be found, but they belong to the category of sayings against outward humility and inward pride; for express example, al-Ḥasan al-Baṣrī, quoted as saying of those who wear wool, 'They have hidden pride in their hearts

---

fi'l-bayāḍ, no. 4061; Tirmidhī, *Jāmiʿ*, *kitāb al-janāʾiz* 18, *bāb mā yustaḥabbu min al-akfān*, no. 994; Ibn Māja, *Sunan*, *kitāb al-libās* 5, *bāb al-bayāḍ min al-thiyāb*, no. 3567; Aḥmad, *Musnad*, vol. 1, pp. 247, 274, 328, 355, 363, *vol. 4, pp. 94, 282, vol. 5, pp. 161–162, 352–353, 398.*

150 Al-Kulaynī, *Kāfī*, *kitāb al-zī wa'l-tajammul*, *bāb al-kattān*, vol. 6, p. 449.

151 Ibid., *bāb lubs al-ṣūf wa'l- shaʿr*, vol. 6, p. 445.

152 Ibid., vol. 6, p. 450.

153 Al-Kulaynī, *Kāfī*, *kitāb al-zī wa'l-tajammul*, *bāb al-libās*, vol. 6, pp. 441–444.

154 Ibid., *bāb lubs al-ṣūf wa'l-shaʿr*, vol. 6, p. 450.

155 Abū Nuʿaym, *Ḥilya*, vol. 3, p. 193.

156 Al-Ḥasan al-Baṣrī on Moses, Abū Nuʿaym, *Ḥilya*, vol. 2, p. 137; Zuhrī on ʿĪsā, Abū ʿUbayd, *al-Khuṭab wa'l-mawāʿiẓ*, ed. Ramaḍān ʿAbd al-Tawwāb (Cairo, 1406/1986), p. 163; also Khaythama b. ʿAbd al-Raḥmān (d. after 80/699), Abū Nuʿaym, *Ḥilya*, vol. 4, p. 117.

157 Kufan *isnād*; Aḥmad, *Zuhd*, pp. 60, *78*.

158 Ibn al-Mubārak, *Zuhd*, no 995 (not < Ibn al-Mubārak).

159 For further discussion and examples, see Christopher Melchert, 'Baṣran origins', pp. 223–225. Shaybī believes that wool-wearing originated with Kūfan renunciants who took it up as a sign of their opposition to al-Ḥajjāj (*Ṣila*, vol. 1, pp. 280–286), but I believe there is equal evidence of it in other centres, most notably (in the generation of the Followers) Basra.

while outwardly showing humility in their clothing. By God, one of them is more proud of his dress than the wearer of a silken robe in his.'[160] Jaʿfar al-Ṣādiq is not alone in being reported to have worn wool underneath more comfortable clothing, hence to avoid making any show of humility; likewise, among others, the Basran Hārūn b. Rabāb (fl. early 2nd/8th century), the Kūfan ʿAbd al-Wāḥid b. Zayd (fl. early 2nd/8th century), and the Mesopotamian Maymūn b. Mihrān (d. 117/735–736) wore wool under other clothes to hide their renunciation.[161]

Al-Kulaynī also reports various encouragements of notably modest austerity. One is a long story of Jaʿfar al-Ṣādiq's being approached by Sufis who bid others to join them. He tells them that it is best to give away some of one's wealth but not all of it. It would be impossible for everyone to join them, lest women, the elderly and the sickly perish. And if everyone joined them, no one would be left to receive charity as atonement or *zakāt*.[162] Jaʿfar is also quoted as identifying proper renunciation not with outward austerity but entirely an inward attitude: 'Renunciation of the world is not wasting money or forbidding what is licit. Rather, renunciation of the world is that you be no more sure of what is in your hand than of what God has.'[163] Al-Kulaynī quotes ʿAlī to similar effect: 'Renunciation of the world is shortness of hope, thankfulness for every blessing and scruple before everything God (mighty and glorious is He) has forbidden.'[164]

Sunni parallels can be found. ʿAbd Allāh b. Masʿūd went to some Kūfans who had withdrawn and established themselves somewhere in the vicinity to worship: 'What induced you to do what you have done?' They said, 'We wished to go away from the crowd (*ghumār al-nās*).' Ibn Masʿūd told them, 'If the people did what you have done, who would fight the enemy? I will not go away till you return.'[165] ʿAlī is quoted as saying that he was most fearful of length of hope and following fancies (referring especially to heresy), since length of hope makes one forget the Afterworld, while following fancy turns one away from the truth.[166] Sufyān b. ʿUyayna (d. Mecca, 198/814) said, 'Renunciation of the world is shortness of hope, not eating what is

160 Ibn Saʿd, *Biographien*, vol. 7/1, p. 123 = *Ṭabaqāt*, vol. 7, p. 169; Jāḥiẓ, *Bayān*, vol. 3, p. 153; Ibn Qutayba, *ʿUyūn*, vol. 2, p. 372.

161 Hārūn b. Rabāb, Abū Nuʿaym, *Ḥilya*, vol. 3, p. 55; ʿAbd al-Wāḥid b. Zayd, ibid., vol. 6, p. 232; Maymūn b. Mihrān, ibid., vol. 4, pp. 91–92.

162 Al-Kulaynī, *Kāfī, kitāb al-maʿīsha, bāb dakhala al-ṣūfiyya ʿalā Abī ʿAbd Allāh*, vol. 5, pp. 65–70. The express reference to Sufis is probably anachronistic, inasmuch as the first to be called a Sufi was an Iraqi contemporary of Jaʿfar's – perhaps, though, not by much, for the term was used to designate disreputably extreme renunciants before about the mid-9th century. See further Melchert, 'Baṣran Origins', pp. 229–230.

163 Al-Kulaynī, *Kāfī, kitāb al-maʿīsha, bāb maʿnā al-zuhd*, vol. 5, pp. 70–71.

164 Ibid., vol. 5, p. 71.

165 Ibn al-Mubārak, *Zuhd*, no. 1104 (not < Ibn al-Mubārak).

166 Wakīʿ, *Zuhd*, vol. 2, pp. 439–441; Ibn al-Mubārak, *Zuhd*, no. 255; Aḥmad, *Zuhd*, pp. 130, *162–163*; Hannād, *Zuhd*, vol. 1, p. 291; Ibn Abī Shayba. *Muṣannaf, kitāb al-zuhd* 11, *kalām ʿAlī b. Abī Ṭālib*, vol. 12, p. 200.

rough or wearing a hood (*ʿabāya*).'[167] I have provisionally located this inward redefinition of renunciation (emphatically not the same thing as calling for inward attitudes to match outward appearances) in the last third of the 8th century AD (just the time of Sufyān b. ʿUyayna). The Imāmiyya seem to have embraced exactly this tendency, presumably for similar reasons: that they now included Muslims of all social classes, so that the rich among them needed to be shielded from complaints from the middling while the middling had to be offered a style of piety that would not prevent them from earning a living.[168]

Comments in Twelver literature on Sufis are uncommon. I have mentioned the Sufis whose call for withdrawal from society is rejected by Jaʿfar al-Ṣādiq. In the biographical literature, I have remarked Aḥmad b. Hilāl al-ʿAbartānī (fl. early 3rd/9th century), an Imāmī, who made fifty-four pilgrimages, twenty on foot, but whom the Imam nonetheless denounced as a deceiving Sufi (*ṣūfī mutaṣanniʿ*).[169] Wool-wearing occasionally turns up also in the record of early non-Imāmī Shiʿism. I have earlier mentioned the Sufis who, in alliance with the local Zaydiyya, took over Kufa for a few weeks on behalf of two Ḥasanids in 255/869.[170] Although he was not called a Sufi, the ʿAlid ʿAbd Allāh b. Muʿāwiya clothed himself in wool when he commenced his open rebellion against the Umayyads (127/744).[171] Ḥallāj, executed in 309/922, sometimes identified himself with the Shiʿa and is included among them by, among others, Ibn al-Nadīm.[172] Provisionally, I propose that al-Kulaynī is markedly more hostile to wool-wearing than Sunni *ḥadīth* collectors in part because it was the badge of non-Imāmī Shiʿa.

Conclusion

There is evidently considerable overlap between reported Shiʿi and Sunni sayings about renunciation. The Sunni sayings are attested earlier. Moreover, reattributions seem more likely to cluster around a few very prominent figures (such as the Imams on the Shiʿi side, the Prophet on both Shiʿi and Sunni) than be dispersed among many individuals. On both counts, *it seems probable that the Sunni literary tradition is the*

---

[167] Wakīʿ, *Zuhd*, vol. 1, p. 222; also Abū Nuʿaym, *Ḥilya* 6:386, citing Ibn Abī Shayba, with 'wearing wool' instead of 'wearing a hood'.

[168] Melchert, 'Baṣran Origins', pp. 230, 234.

[169] Al-Kashshī, *Rijāl al-Kashshī*, ed. Aḥmad al-Ḥusaynī (Karbala, n.d.), pp. 449–450.

[170] Al-Ṣūlī, *Kniga listov* (i.e., *Kitāb al-awrāq*), ed. Anas Khalidov (St Petersburg, 1998), p. 366; Melchert, 'Baṣran Origins', p. 232.

[171] Noticed by Josef van Ess, *Theologie und Gesellschaft* (Berlin, 1991–1995), vol. 2, p. 88. This and three other examples from the next century noticed by Shaybī, *Fikr*, p. 68 and *Ṣila*, vol. 2, pp. 12–13.

[172] Ibn al-Nadīm, *Fihrist*, *fann* 5, *maqāla* 5; *Kitāb al-Fihrist*, ed. Gustav Flügel, with Johannes Roedigger and August Mueller (Leipzig, 1872), pp. 190–192. For Ḥallāj interpreted principally as a Shiʿi rather than Sufi, see Said Amir Arjomand, 'The Crisis of the Imamate and the Institution of Occultation in Twelver Shiʿism', *IJMES*, 28 (1996), pp. 506–508.

earlier, and that influence ran primarily from the Sunni side to the Shiʿi rather than the other way around. At the same time, sayings seem to float from person to person in the Sunni literature, so that it seems more certain that these sayings were current among proto-Sunnis of the 8th century than that they must be attributed to exactly the individuals to which our sources of the 9th century attribute them. Whichever way influence flowed, overlap between Sunni and Shiʿi sayings about renunciation seem to indicate a common piety. I have looked for evidence of geographical specialisation in the Sunni record without success – this is in contrast to the record of opinions about law, where evidence of geographical specialisation is abundant. This suggests to me that the renunciant tradition has its origin at an earlier point than the legal tradition. It must have continued in the Shiʿi tradition as much as the Sunni, so that although Shiʿi tradition attributes all sayings to Imams, Shiʿi opinions and practices concerning renunciation must have been similar to Sunni throughout the 8th and 9th centuries.

Of special interest, then, are the parts of the Sunni renunciant tradition that do not appear in the Shiʿi record, such as preference for wearing wool. Divergence between Sunni and Shiʿi attitudes toward renunciation constitute further evidence of Sunni-Shiʿi differentiation, presumably in the course of the 9th century. It may be that sayings about wool were not taken into the Shiʿi tradition as documented by al-Kulaynī just because of Shiʿi resistance in the late 9th and early 10th centuries to taking up the Junaydi Sufi synthesis. This is the usual argument for the long-delayed development of Sufism in the Shiʿi tradition, namely that loyalty to the Imams, the defining character of Shiʿism, conflicted with loyalty to the *awliyāʾ*, a defining character of Sufism.[173] However, it appears also that *the Imāmī rejection of wool-wearing reflects earlier disquiet with non-Imāmī Shiʿi wool-wearers.*

Two questions concerning the development of Sufism seem most salient. First is the degree to which the emergence of Sunni Sufism reflects Shiʿi influence. This has often been alleged, as by Annemarie Schimmel: 'The thoughts of Jaʿfar and other early mystical thinkers must have been at work beneath the surface, permeating the mystical life until they appeared in the sayings of a number of Sufis.'[174] But this depends on taking attributions to Jaʿfar al-Ṣādiq at face value, a rash move for any scholar today. More modestly, with better documentation, Sara Sviri has characterised quotations of Shiʿi Imams in Sufi sources of the 10th century as 'Shīʿī material that became included in Ṣūfī literature'.[175] I am inclined to doubt whether much of the material to which Sviri refers, none of which is distinctly Shiʿi, actually has Shiʿi origins. More likely, similar to sayings about renunciation that al-Kulaynī attributes to various Imams, earlier Sunni collectors attributed to various renunciants of the early 8th century and before, it had circulated from the start among proto-Sunnis. The thesis that Shiʿi

173 See Karamustafa, *Sufism*, pp. 18, 20.

174 Annemarie Schimmel, *Mystical Dimensions of Islam* (Chapel Hill, NC, 1975), p. 42.

175 Sara Sviri, 'The Early Mystical Schools of Baghdad and Nīshāpūr', *JSAI*, 30 (2005), pp. 457–462 (quotation from p. 457). See Christopher Melchert, 'Khargūshī, *Tahdhīb al-asrār*', *BSOAS*, 73 (2010), pp. 33–34.

esoterism, looking for Qurʾanic allusions to the house of the Prophet, gave rise to Sufi esoterism depends also on supposing that the esoterism of 10th-century Shiʿi texts such as (above all) *Rasāʾil Ikhwān al-Ṣafāʾ* was not a development of the 10th century but already a character of 8th-century Shiʿism. I doubt this can ever be more than a supposition in the absence of 8th-century Shiʿi texts, or at least 9th-century. Inasmuch as it is a matter of 10th-century attributions to famous Imams, not a multitude of lesser names, it doubtfully deserves the presumption of greater reliability than Sunni attributions. *The present study of renunciant sayings weakly supports the larger argument that Sufism did not flow from an earlier Shiʿi tradition.*

The second great question is why Sufism was for so long exclusively Sunni. Although I offer here no answer, the absence of sayings about wool in al-Kulaynī's collection of renunciant sayings seems likely to document active resistance in his generation and the one before to the Junaydi synthesis. Among the Sunnis, 'Sufi' moved from a term for disreputable marginal figures to one for respectable orthodox ones at about the middle of the 9th century.[176] Shiʿa of some sort had worked closely with primitive Sufis, just before Sufism became respectable, but the Twelvers seem to have been opposed to them from the start. As, then, there seems to be a measure of continuity between Ḥanbali opposition to would-be Sunni *mutakallimīn* in the 9th century and to Shiʿa in the 10th, *there seems to be a measure of continuity between Imāmī opposition to would-be Shiʿi Sufis in the 9th century and a refusal to develop a form of Sufism in the 10th.* It was a part of Twelver consolidation and an important aspect of conscious Sunni–Shiʿi differentiation in the 10th century.

[176] B. Radtke, 'Taṣawwuf', *EI2*, vol. 9, pp. 313–314; Melchert, 'Baṣran Origins', esp. pp. 222–223, 234–240.

12

The Evolution of al-Qāḍī al-Nuʿmān's Theory of Ismaili Jurisprudence as Reflected in the Chronology of his Works on Jurisprudence

Ismail K. Poonawala[*]

Shiʿi Ismaili law, codified by al-Qāḍī al-Nuʿmān (hereafter referred to as Nuʿmān) in his enduring work *Daʿāʾim al-Islām* (The Pillars of Islam) with the approval of the fourth Fatimid Imam-caliph al-Muʿizz li-Dīn Allāh, is almost a millennium old.[1] Ever since its promulgation, most probably in 349/960,[2] as the official code of the Fatimid empire, the *Daʿāʾim* has reigned supreme, particularly with the Mustaʿlī-Ṭayyibī Ismailis of Yemen and the Indian subcontinent after the fall of the Fatimids in Egypt in 567/1171. However, this centuries-old law has not met the necessities of modern life for the Ismaili communities of the Dāudīs, Sulaymānīs and ʿAlawīs who follow this school of Islamic jurisprudence. Those advocating the *status quo* (maintaining the traditional system), notably the conservative religious establishments of all the three above-mentioned communities, have had little to offer in terms of a constructive legal reform which might adapt Ismaili law as formulated by its founder, al-Qāḍī al-Nuʿmān, to the modern conditions of life. For example, the religious authorities have buried their heads in the sand regarding family law, once considered the most sacred aspect of Islamic law, and which has undergone modifi-

---

* I would like to thank Hamid Haji for resetting the entire chapter with elegant Arabic font. He very kindly and carefully read the first set of proofs.

1 For Nuʿmān's life and works, see Ismail K. Poonawala, *Biobibliography of Ismāʿīlī Literature* (Malibu, CA, 1977), pp. 48–62; al-Qāḍī al-Nuʿmān, *Daʿāʾim al-Islām*, ed. Asaf A. A. Fyzee (Cairo, 1951–1961); tr. Asaf A. A. Fyzee, completely revised and annotated by Ismail K. Poonawala, *The Pillars of Islam*, vol. 1: *Acts of Devotion and Religious Observances*; vol. 2: *Laws Pertaining to Human Intercourse* (New Delhi, 2002–2004). All references to the *Daʿāʾim* are hereafter given to its translation because it is fully annotated. All English translations from Nuʿmān's works, unless stated otherwise, are by me.

2 There is no textual evidence to determine the exact date of its composition; however, I have argued my case on the basis of chronology of Nuʿmān's works and other corroborative evidences. See Ismail K. Poonawala, 'al-Qāḍī al-Nuʿmān and Ismaʿili Jurisprudence', in Farhad Daftary, ed., *Mediaeval Ismaʿili History and Thought* (Cambridge, 1996), p. 126.

cations in all Muslim countries except India.[3] In a previous work of mine, I have suggested that the entire structure of family law, including the law of Personal Status, needs to be reconsidered leaving aside the whole theory of law in itself.[4]

The structure of the *Daʿāʾim* and Nuʿmān's discussion of the fundamental principles of Ismaili law evolved for an extensive period of time, particularly after his profound scrutiny of a vast collection of legal traditions. Before he undertook the compilation of the *Daʿāʾim*, Nuʿmān already had several legal works to his credit. Moreover, he had acquired first-hand experience of interpreting textual evidence and its application, initially in the capacity of a provincial judge and then as the supreme *qāḍī* of the Fatimid empire.[5] He had also written a number of refutations, including the three founding figures of the major Sunni schools of law, Abū Ḥanīfa, Mālik and Shāfiʿī. The *Daʿāʾim*, compiled at the height of his career and with the blessing and supervision of the Imam al-Muʿizz li-Dīn Allāh, demonstrates the mature legal reasoning of Nuʿmān.[6]

Therefore, the following pages are first devoted to the elucidation of Nuʿmān's theory of Ismaili jurisprudence as reflected in the chronology of his legal works and then to the examination of his major polemical work entitled *Kitāb ikhtilāf uṣūl al-madhāhib* (The Book of Disagreement about the Positive Laws in Various Schools of Jurisprudence; henceforth referred to as *Ikhtilāf*),[7] which was compiled before the *Daʿāʾim*. It is the opinion of this author that the *Ikhtilāf* has not received sufficient

---

3 For example, see Norman Anderson, *Law Reform in the Muslim World* (London, 1976), pp. 34–85.

4 See Ismail K. Poonawala, 'The Reform Movement in the Context of Islam Globally'; keynote address delivered at the United Reformist Dawoodi Bohra Conference held in Daventry, England, 31 July–1 August 2004, *Conference Report*, pp. 17–19.

5 Nuʿmān was first appointed as a *qāḍī* of Tripoli by the third Fatimid Imam-caliph al-Manṣūr (r. 334–341/946–953) soon after his accession to the caliphate in 334/946. In 337/948 when the caliph moved his capital to the new city of al-Manṣūriyya, he promoted Nuʿmān as the supreme *qāḍī* of the Fatimid domain. Al-Qāḍī al-Nuʿmān, *Kitāb al-majālis wa'l-musāyarāt*, ed. al-Ḥabīb al-Fiqī, et al. (Tunis, 1978), pp. 51, 57, 69, 80–81; Poonawala, 'al-Qāḍī al-Nuʿmān and Ismaʿili Jurisprudence', p. 120.

6 For the description of the circumstances under which the caliph al-Muʿizz li-Dīn Allāh asked Nuʿmān to compile the *Daʿāʾim*, see Poonawala, 'al-Qāḍī al-Nuʿmān and Ismaʿili Jurisprudence', p. 126.

7 It is referred to hereafter as the *Ikhtilāf*. The term *uṣūl* in the title does not imply *uṣūl al-fiqh* as it came to indicate later on. In his article 'Was al-Shāfiʿī the Master Architect of Islamic Jurisprudence?', *IJMES*, 25 (1993), pp. 588 ff., Wael Hallaq has convincingly argued that the term *uṣūl* had a wide range of application during the early centuries of Islam until the middle of the 4th/10th century. Referring to the above-mentioned work of Nuʿmān, Hallaq states: 'And in his refutation of the *uṣūl* principles of Sunni juristic thought, al-Qāḍī al-Nuʿmān, writing around the middle of the 10th century, confirms the data provided by the biobibliographical sources.' See also Wael Hallaq, *The Origins and Evolution of Islamic Law* (Cambridge, 2005), pp. 127–128; he states that by the middle of the 4th/10th century, an elaborate and comprehensive theory of *uṣūl* had emerged. For the meaning of *madhhab*/s and the formation of legal schools see, Hallaq, *Origins*, pp. 150 ff., and his *A History of Islamic Legal Theories: An Introduction to Sunnī Uṣūl al-Fiqh* (Cambridge, 1997), chap. 2.

attention from contemporary students of Ismaili law.[8] An analysis of the evolution of Nuʿmān's legal thought and the encouragement he received from his patron al-Muʿizz is essential for an understanding of Ismaili law. At the same time, its scrutiny will reveal the challenging task faced by the later generations of Ismaili thinkers and jurists, especially after the disappearance of the 21st Imam al-Ṭayyib b. al-Āmir around 524/1130, of modifying any aspect of the law, either minor or major, in the absence of the Imam.[9] It should be noted that the Ismaili case is slightly different than the Twelver Imāmī. For the Mustaʿlī-Ṭayyibīs, their law fully developed before the disappearance of their Imam, while the situation was the opposite for the Imāmīs whose law developed and blossomed after the disappearance of the twelfth Imam in 260/874.

Before proceeding further, it is necessary to indicate that I have dealt with the question of the authenticity of Nuʿmān's works and their sources elsewhere.[10] I have also addressed the related issue of the chronology of his more than 40 works in a separate but yet to be published study.[11] Therefore, I will only briefly review the chronology of Nuʿmān's surviving legal works, published and unpublished.[12] This will help us in not only understanding the evolution of Nuʿmān's legal thinking but will also assist us in situating the *Ikhtilāf* within the chronology of his juridical works.

Let us begin with his first major work *Kitāb al-īḍāḥ*. It was a very large collection of legal traditions that Nuʿmān undertook with the blessings of the first Fatimid Imam-caliph al-Mahdī and completed it during his reign. Although the whole book, or a major part of it, was still available during the 16th century in India, it was considered lost by the following century according to al-Majdūʿ (d. ca. 1183/1769).[13] In his *Fihrist*, a bibliography of Ismaili works, al-Majdūʿ states that except for a small portion from the beginning of the chapter on ritual prayer, the book in its entirety could not to be found in the *daʿwa* collection.[14] *Kitāb al-īḍāḥ* constituted a compre-

[8] It is edited by [Shamʿūn] Ṭayyib ʿAlī Lokhandwalla (Simla, 1972) with a long introduction in English, which is a revised version of his dissertation written under the supervision of Joseph Schacht. Unfortunately, most Western scholars are unaware of this edition and still use the one edited by Muṣṭafā Ghālib (Beirut, 1973), which is unreliable.

[9] For the split within the Ismaili community after the assassination of the Fatimid Imam-caliph al-Āmir, see Farhad Daftary, *The Ismāʿīlīs: Their History and Doctrines* (2nd ed., Cambridge, 2007), pp. 238 ff.

[10] Ismail K. Poonawala, 'Sources for al-Qāḍī al-Nuʿmān's Works and their Authenticity', in Bruce Craig, ed., *Ismaili and Fatimid Studies in Honor of Paul E. Walker* (Chicago, 2010), pp. 87–99.

[11] Poonawala, 'The Chronology of al-Qāḍī al-Nuʿmān's Works', unpublished study.

[12] I have dealt with the chronology of Nuʿmān's legal works in my work 'al-Qāḍī al-Nuʿmān and Ismaʿili Jurisprudence', pp. 120–130.

[13] For his life and works, see Poonawala, *Biobibliography of Ismāʿīlī Literature*, pp. 204–206.

[14] Ismāʿīl b. ʿAbd al-Rasūl al-Majdūʿ, *Fahrasat al-kutub waʾl-rasāʾil*, ed. ʿAlī Naqī Munzavī (Tehran, 1966), p. 33. He states:

وهذا الكتاب الذي ذكره القاضي النعمان (رض) غير موجود في خزانة الدعوة إلّا اليسير منه من أوّل كتاب الصلاة إلى

hensive collection of legal traditions that was classified and arranged into legal topics like other collections of *ḥadīth* books. Referring to it in the introduction of his *Kitāb al-iqtiṣār* Nuʿmān states:

> I scrutinised various books [of traditions] transmitted on the authority of *Ahl al-bayt* with regard to what is lawful and unlawful in the established practices, juridical decisions and formal legal opinions. These books included those works that were accessible to me by way of *samāʿ*,[15] or *munāwala*,[16] or what I was able to obtain either through the *ijāza*[17] or the *ṣaḥīfa*.[18] The traditions ascribed to *Ahl al-bayt* varied from [being described as] *mashhūr*,[19] to *maʿrūf*[20] to *maʾthūr*.[21] I further observed that the transmitters either agreed or disagreed about most of the traditions. Again [I found that] most of those traditions were [not arranged in a more manageable form of] either *mulakhkhaṣ* or *muṣannaf* [according to the

---

أكثره، أعني كتاب الصلاة.

The extant part is edited by Muḥammad Kāẓim Raḥmatī in *Mīrāth-i Ḥadīth-i Shīʿa*, ed. Mahdī Mihrīzī and ʿAlī Ṣadrāyī Khūyi (Qumm, 1382 Sh.), vol. 10, pp. 35–218. W. Madelung's article, 'The Sources of Ismāʿīlī Law', *JNES*, 35 (1976), is based on this extant section. However, Madelung's contention that Nuʿmān probably was a Sunni and never received formal training in Shiʿi *ḥadīth* and *fiqh* is incorrect. See Poonawala, 'al-Qāḍī al-Nuʿmān and Ismaʿili Jurisprudence'; and Poonawala, 'al-Qāḍī al-Nuʿmān and His Refutation of Ibn Qutayba', in Omar Alí-de-Unzaga, ed., *Fortresses of the Intellect: Ismaili and other Islamic Studies in Honour of Farhad Daftary* (London, 2011), p. 278.

15 *Samāʿ* constitutes 'hearing', and 'that which is heard' directly from a teacher. As a term in Islamic eduction it means a 'certificate of hearing, authorisation or licence' to transmit from a teacher. Rudolph Sellheim, 'Samāʿ', *EI2*, vol. 8, p. 1018.

16 *Munāwala* means that a transmitter of Prophetic traditions who has collected those traditions hands over his collection/book to his student with permission to transmit. The *munāwala* (i.e., handing over the book) is considered a superior method of transmission to that of *ijāza*. Zamakhsharī, *Asās al-balāgha: Muʿjam fi'l-lugha wa'l-balāgha* (Beirut, 1996), s.v. n-w-l.

17 *Ijāza* constitutes authorisation or licence. It means that an authorised guarantor of a text or of a whole book (whether it is his own work, or a work received through a chain of transmitters going back to the author) gives a person the authorisation to transmit it. George Vajda, 'Idjāza', *EI2*, vol. 3, p. 1020.

18 *Ṣaḥīfa* literally means a plaque or a leaf on which either fragments of the Qur'an or the *ḥadīth* are written. Ameur Ghédira, 'Ṣaḥīfa', *EI2*, vol. 8, p. 834; Muḥammad Zubayr Ṣiddīqī, *Ḥadīth Literature: Its Origins, Development, Special Features and Criticism* (Calcutta, 1961), p. 15; Mohammad Mustafa Azmi, *Studies in Early Ḥadīth Literature: With a Critical Edition of Some Early Texts* (Beirut, 1968), pp. 189–199.

19 *Mashhūr* (widespread, widely accepted, well known) is a tradition with more than two transmitters, some such being *ṣaḥīḥ* and others not. A large number of traditions belong to this category, and they are the foundations of jurisprudence. Ṣiddīqī, *Ḥadīth Literature*, pp. 193–194; James Robson, 'Ḥadīth', *EI2*, vol. 3, p. 25; Hallaq, *History*, p. 65.

20 *Maʿrūf* (acknowledged) is applied to a weak tradition confirmed by another weak one, or it is a tradition superior in *matn* or *isnād* to one called *munkar* (ignored). James Robson, 'Ḥadīth', *EI2*, vol. 3, p. 26.

21 *Maʾthūr* means transmitted tradition.

> topic], hence uncertainty [about their authenticity] multiplied among a great majority of people and many of them, who were not well versed in [religious] learning, considered those traditions unsound.
>
> Hence, I thought it proper to collect those traditions, arrange them according to the topics [of law], and compile them into a book as handed down by the transmitters. I have entitled it *Kitāb al-īḍāḥ* (Book of Elucidation), because in it I have elucidated the issues [dealt with in those traditions] and have expanded the chapters [on various topics]. In it I have also indicated [the subjects] on which the transmitters agreed and [other matters about] which they disagreed, without transgressing the bounds of their statements. And I have expounded what has been the firmly established [practices that I have discerned] in those traditions with decisive proofs and clear demonstrations. Thus, [the size of] the book reached roughly around 3,000 folios.[22]

Subsequently, Nuʿmān made a number of abridgements but only two have survived. The first is *Kitāb al-akhbār* (or *al-ikhbār*),[23] which was completed during the reign of al-Mahdī, and the second is *Kitāb al-iqtiṣār*, completed during the reign of the second Fatimid Imam-caliph al-Qā'im. The former has yet to be edited while the second has already been published as stated above (see n. 22). Referring to both abridgements, Nuʿmān states in the introduction of *Kitāb al-iqtiṣār*:

> Then I abridged from it [i.e., *Kitāb al-īḍāḥ*] a book, which I entitled *Kitāb al-akhbār/ikhbār* [The Book of Traditions] wherein I related the traditions about which the transmitters agreed and disagreed with regard to the principles for [issuing] legal opinions. I approximated the meanings [of those traditions] by discarding, in general, the *furūʿ* (positive rules derived from the *uṣūl*), *asānīd* (the

---

[22] Nuʿmān, *Kitāb al-iqtiṣār*, ed. Muḥammad Waḥīd Mīrzā (Damascus, 1957), pp. 9–10. Nuʿmān states:

أمّا بعد، فإنّي تصفّحتُ في الكتب المرويّة عن أهل البيت صلوات الله عليهم ممّا كان لي من سماع، أو مناولة، أو أخذتُه بإجازة، أو صحيفة مع ما يُنسب منها إليهم من المشهور والمعروف والمأثور في السنن والأحكام ومسائل الفتيا في الحلال والحرام. فرأيتُ كثيراً منها قد اختلف الرواةُ فيه ومنه ما أجمعوا عليه، وأكثره غير ملخّص ولا مصنّف. فكثرتْ فيها على أكثر الناس الشبهة، وأنزلهُ كثير منهم ممّن لم يتّسع في العلم في منازل التهمة.

فرأيتُ جمعهُ وتصنيفه وبسطه وتأليفه على ما أدّتهُ الرواةُ في كتاب سمّيتُه **كتاب الإيضاح**، أوضحتُ فيه مسائله وبسطتُ أبوابه وذكرتُ ما أجمعوا عليه وما اختلفوا فيه على ما أدّاه الرواةُ إلينا، لم أعدُ قولهم. وبيّنتُ الثابت من ذلك بالدلائل والبراهين. فبلغ زهاء ثلاثة آلاف ورقة.

وأنا إن مدّ الله في عمري أؤمّل تفريع أصوله ليكون مشتملاً على جميع ما يحتاج إليه ممّا نزل، فيوجد إن شاء الله تعالى.

[23] Only the first volume of this work is extant. Poonawala, *Biobibliography of Ismāʿīlī Literature*, p. 53.

> chains of authority), and *al-ḥujaj* (arguments in favour or against). Consequently, [the size of the book] came close to 300 folios.[24]

Traditions collected by Nuʿmān in this book contain conflicting doctrines on certain issues of law. However, in such cases Nuʿmān puts forth his own preference for what he considered to be the correct and reliable tradition.[25] The *Akhbār/Ikhbār* was followed by *al-Iqtiṣār.* Nuʿmān states:

> Then I deemed appropriate, may God grant success [to my efforts], that I should confine myself to [collecting only those traditions] about which there is a firm agreement among the transmitters or about which they have strongly disagreed. [This book should be] precise to facilitate its understanding and to make it easier [to handle and remember]. Thus, I have collected [those traditions] in this book and entitled it *Kitāb al-iqtiṣār* (*The Digest*). It is to be hoped, God willing, that those who would confine themselves to it [only] will find it sufficient [for their needs], when God, the High and Exalted, would guide them to its [proper] understanding.[26]

Kitāb al-iqtiṣār was followed by *al-Muntakhaba*, also called *al-Urjūza al-muntakhaba*, a versified version of jurisprudence and easy to memorise. It was composed during the reign of the second Fatimid Imam-caliph al-Qāʾim.[27] It appears that during the reign of the third Fatimid Imam-caliph al-Manṣūr (r. 334/946–341/953), Nuʿmān was occupied with the administration of justice and wrote on other subjects, such as history and biographies. Thus, after a period of several years came *Kitāb al-ikhtiṣār* which was completed around 348/959–960. Its full title is *Kitāb al-ikhtiṣār li-ṣaḥīḥ al-āthār ʿan al-aʾimma al-aṭhār*, or *Mukhtaṣar* (or *Ikhtiṣār*) *al-āthār fīmā ruwiyā ʿan al-aʾimma al-aṭhār* (The Compendium of Sound Tradition Trans-

---

24 Nuʿmān, *Kitāb al-iqtiṣār*, p. 10; he states:

ثم جرّدتُ منه كتاباً سمّيتُه **كتاب الإخبار**، أخبرتُ فيه عمّا أجمع الرواةُ عليه واختلفوا فيه من أصول الفتيا، وقرّبتُ معانيه بطرح عامّة الفروع والأسانيد والحجج. فاجتمع في نحو ثلاث مائة ورقة.

25 The first volume contains the following seven chapters: Purity, ablution, prayer, poor-tax, fasting, pilgrimage and *jihād*. The manuscripts I was able to examine are without the author's introduction. It is difficult to state whether the introduction was deliberately removed or that the manuscript copy, from which the later copies were transcribed, was defective.

26 Nuʿmān, *Kitāb al-iqtiṣār*, p. 10; he states:

ثم رأيتُ، وبالله توفيقي، أن أقتصر على الثابت ممّا أجمعوا عليه واختلفوا فيه بمجمل من القول لتقريبه وتخفيفه وتسهيله. فجمعتُ ذلك في هذا الكتاب وسمّيتُه **كتاب الاقتصار**، وفيه إن شاء الله لمن اقتصر عليه كفاية إذا وفّقه الله عزّ وجلّ لفهمه.

27 Referring to it Nuʿmān states in *Kitāb al-iqtiṣār*, p. 10:

وقد نظمتُه أيضاً موزوناً رجزاً مزدوجاً في قصيدة سمّيتُها **المنتخبة**، انتخبتُها لمن أراد حفظها. والله يعين على العلم مَن هداهُ لطلبه ويوفّقه للعمل به إن شاء الله تعالى.

See Appendix I for its reference in *al-Muntakhaba*.

mitted from the Pure Imams).[28] Explaining the reason for its compilation in his *al-Majālis wa'l-musāyarāt*, Nuʿmān states:

> Some judges, governors and students asked me to compile a concise book, which contains the statements of the family of the Prophet [on the points of legal issues] approximating their teachings and is easy to handle and memorise. So, I began to work on it and anticipated that when it was completed [its size would be such that] it would be transcribed for a *dīnār* or less for those who wanted to have a copy. Hence, I entitled it *Kitāb al-dīnār* (Book for One *Dīnār*) and explained the [reason for its title] in the introduction. Whatever portion [of it] I had completed I presented it to al-Muʿizz and requested from him that I should read it to him so that it would be [identical to its direct] transmission from him.[29]

Therefore, Nuʿmān wrote a note to al-Muʿizz and sent it with the portion of the book that he had already completed. Al-Muʿizz, in turn, replied to Nuʿmān's request with a note in his own hand, written on the back of Nuʿmān's note, with the following message:

> In the name of God, the Merciful and Compassionate. May God preserve you, O Nuʿmān! I became interested in the book and leafed through it. What filled me with [pleasure and] admiration are the soundness of the traditions [you have related] and the brevity of its style. However, there are some [technical] terms in it which many of our friends would have difficulty in understanding, so explain those terms in a way that they can [easily] understand them … and entitle it *Kitāb al-ikhtiṣār li-ṣaḥīḥ al-āthār ʿan al-aʾimmat al-aṭhār*. The reason for [suggesting this title] is that it corresponds more [with its contents] than the [title] *Kitāb al-dīnār* [you had given]. Moreover, it contains the learning of God's Friends [i.e., the Imams], which all human beings ought to seek in earnest.[30]

---

[28] The extant copies of *al-Ikhtiṣār* are in the recension of Nuʿmān's grandson Ḥusayn b. ʿAlī b. al-Nuʿmān. In the first *ijāza* given by al-Nuʿmān to his son ʿAlī for transmission of the text, the latter states that he had read the book with his father in 348/959–960. Hence it implies that *al-Ikhtiṣār* was completed either in that year or a little earlier. The second *ijāza* written by Ḥusayn b. ʿAlī states that the permission for its transmission was given to him by the Imam-caliph al-Ḥākim. For the texts of both *ijāza*s, see Appendix II.

[29] Nuʿmān, *Kitāb al-majālis*, pp. 359–360; he states:

وسألني بعضُ القضاة والحكّام والطلبة بسط كتاب مختصر من قول أهل البيت (صلع) لهم، يقرّب معناه ويسهل حفظه، وتخفّ مؤنته. فابتدأتُ شيئاً منه، وقدّرتُ أنّ الكتاب إذا كمل قام على من يريد انتساخه بدينار فما دونه. وسمّيتُه كتاب الدينار، وذكرتُ ذلك في بسط افتتاحه، ورفعتُ ما ابتدأتُه منه إلى المعزّ (صلع)، وطالعتُه فيه وسألتُه قراءته عليه، وسماعه منه ليكون مأثوراً عنه. وكتبتُ مع ما رفعتُه منه إليه رقعةً ذكرتُ فيها ذلك له.

[30] Ibid., pp. 359–360; it reads:

فوقّع إليّ صلوات الله عليه بخطّه في ظهرها:

باسم الله الرحمٰن الرحيم. صانك الله يا نعمان، وقفتُ على الكتاب وتصفّحتُه، فرأيتُ ما أعجبني فيه من صحّة الرواية وجودة الاختصار، ولكنّ فيه كلمات تعتاص على كثير من أوليائنا معرفتُها، فاشرحْها بما يقرب من أفهامهم، فيستوي في

Al-Muʿizz permitted Nuʿmān to relate the entire book on his authority and that of his forefathers.[31] Hence, compared with his earlier works, such as *al-Īḍāḥ* and some of its abridgements, in this work Nuʿmān gives the *isnād* of every tradition at the highest point of its transmission authority. For example, *qāla rasūl Allāh* (the Prophet said), *ʿan ʿAlī* (from ʿAlī), or *qāla Abū Jaʿfar Muḥammad* (i.e., al-Bāqir said), or *ruwīnā ʿan ahl al-bayt* (it has been narrated to us from the family of the Prophet). Therefore, the *Ikhtiṣār* enjoys the same prestige as the *Daʿāʾim* as an authoritative source for Ismaili law.

I have elaborated elsewhere that the *Ikhtiṣār* was a major step forward in the direction of codification of Ismaili law by Nuʿmān.[32] A major change in the latter work relates to the fact that all the previous legal works commence with a chapter on ritual purity, but the *Ikhtiṣār* begins with a chapter on knowledge (*ʿilm*) and a discussion about the most authoritative and sound fountainhead from which to derive knowledge. Nuʿmān, in this way, made it clear that knowledge of law and theology should be obtained from the rightful Imam who is from the progeny of the Messenger of God. The Shiʿi-Ismaili theory of the imamate is the key to unlocking all the Ismaili religious and legal formulations. Not surprisingly, we observe that the *Daʿāʾim*, composed after the *Ikhtiṣār*, commences with a chapter on the *walāya* (devotion to the Imams). It is identified not only as the first pillar of Islam but also as the most excellent of all the pillars. Nuʿmān further adds that it is through the *walāya* and through the *walīy* (Imam) that true knowledge of the rest of the pillars can be obtained. It is the longest chapter in the *Daʿāʾim*. It also contains the most comprehensive discussion concerning the question of the imamate with its various

---

معرفته والإحاطة بعلم ألفاظه الشريفُ والمشروفُ. فإنه يجيء طريفاً قريب المأخذ. وسمّه كتاب الاختصار لصحيح الآثار عن الأئمّة الأطهار. فإنّ ذلك أشبهُ به من كتاب الدينار، لأنّ فيه من علم أولياء اللّه ما يحقّ على كافّة الخلق طلبُه بأرواحهم فضلاً عن أموالهم.

Although Idrīs ʿImād al-Dīn has reproduced the above account from Nuʿmān's *Kitāb al-majālis waʾl-musāyarāt*, without mentioning its title, he erroneously states that it was an abridgement of the *Daʿāʾim*. In his 'Some Unknown Ismāʿīlī Authors and their Works', *JRAS* (1933), p. 369, Ḥusayn al-Hamdānī was also misled by Idrīs' statement when he stated: 'Chronologically speaking, the *Daʿāʾim* and *Mukhtaṣar* were among the last works of the Qāḍī.' Based on its contents, Shamʿūn Lokhandwalla (see introduction to his edition of the *Ikhtilāf*, p. 22) has argued that it preceded the composition of the *Daʿāʾim*, and the present writer fully concurs with that conclusion. It seems to me that Idrīs was probably misled by close resemblance between the two: the *Daʿāʾim* and the *Ikhtiṣār*. However, on closer examination one finds doctrinal differences between them, though of minor nature. If it was an abridgement of the *Daʿāʾim*, Nuʿmān would have stated it in its introduction.

31 Referring to the comments and some changes suggested by al-Muʿizz, see Nuʿmān, *Kitāb al-majālis*, p. 360; he states:

ثم وقّع بعد ذلك بإثبات أشياء تصلح فيما رفعتُه منه، وحذف أشياء ممّا كتبتُه وأثبتُّه فيه، وذكرها وعلّم عليها. قرأتُه بعد ذلك قراءةً عليه، وأثبتُّ فيه كلَّ ما صحّحه وارتضاه، وأسقطتُ ممّا كنت كتبتُ فيه ما أمر بإسقاطه منه وحذفتُه لفظاً منه. وأذن لي أنْ أرويَهُ – لمن أخذ عنّي - عنه، عمّن ذكره فيه من آبائه الطاهرين (صلع) بعد أن أثبتَ ذلك عنهم. فعظُمتْ فائدتي فيه، وجلّت نعمتُه عليّ به. ولم أكن تعرّضتُ برفعي ذلك إليه [إلى] غير ذلك ليصحّ لي ما كنت آثرتُه عن آبائه وجمعتُه من كتب الرواة عنهم، وسمعتُه قبل ذلك منهم ... .

32 Poonawala, 'al-Qāḍī al-Nuʿmān and Ismaʿili Jurisprudence', pp. 123–124.

aspects and implications. In fact, with succinct style, the chapter on the *walāya* summarises all the topics discussed in the *Ikhtilāf*.

Nuʿmān compiled the *Ikhtilāf* prior to his composition of the *Ikhtiṣār*. In the opinion of the present writer, the *Ikhtilāf* fills a major void in the chain of Nuʿmān's works that clearly reflects the development of his legal thought and therefore worthy of analysis. The full title given by Nuʿmān is *Kitāb ikhtilāf uṣūl al-madhāhib wa'l-radd ʿalā man khālafa 'l-ḥaqq fīhā* ('The Book of Disagreement about the Positive Laws in Various Schools of Jurisprudence and the Refutation of those who Opposed the Truth Concerning those Laws'). It is believed to have been composed around 343/954, because at the beginning of the book Nuʿmān has copied the decree issued by al-Muʿizz on the occasion of his confirmation to the highest judiciary office in the Fatimid realm.[33] The royal edict gave Nuʿmān wide authority and his jurisdiction extended to every case when either the *maẓālim*[34] matters were brought directly to him, or as an appeal from any corner of the Fatimid domain. He was granted sole jurisdiction over matters related to the royal entourage, the various classes of the caliph's bondsmen and the soldiery stationed in the capital. In all the above matters, Nuʿmān was conferred with absolute judicial powers.

Besides Idrīs ʿImād al-Dīn (d. 872/1468), the *Ikhtilāf* is mentioned by Ibn Shahrāshūb (d. 588/1192) and Ibn Khallikān (681/1282). I have indicated elsewhere that the sources for the information concerning the books of Nuʿmān, both by Ibn Khallikān and Idrīs date back to contemporaneous historians.[35] It is also worth noting that all the extant copies of the *Ikhtilāf* are the recension of Nuʿmān's grandson, ʿAbd al-ʿAzīz b. Muḥammad b. al-Nuʿmān.[36] The front page, following the title, contains a brief foreword written by the grandson. It states as follows:

> The *qāḍī al-quḍāt* ʿAbd al-ʿAzīz b. Muḥammad b. al-Nuʿmān said: 'I have related this book, *Ikhtilāf uṣūl al-madhāhib wa'l-radd ʿalā man khālafa 'l-ḥaqq fīhā*, from my father al-Qāḍī Muḥammad b. al-Nuʿmān, may God be pleased with him and may He please him, and my father related it from his father al-Qāḍī al-Nuʿmān b. Muḥammad b. Manṣūr b. Aḥmad b. Ḥayyūn al-Tamīmī, may God be pleased with him and may He please him and honour his return and abode in the hereafter, who composed this book after having presented it [for approval] to our lord, the Imam al-Muʿizz li-Dīn Allāh, the Commander of the Faithful, may the salutations of God be upon him and his pure forefathers and the noble Imams from his progeny. It was his [Nuʿmān's] compilation and he related it. [Nuʿmān has stipulated that] the rights of its transmission after him belong to his sons and each one of

[33] The edict is dated 28 Rabīʿ I, 343/30 Sept. 954. For the full text of the edict see Appendix III. For its English translation see Lokhandwalla, op. cit., pp. 52–58.

[34] *Maẓālim* (lit., unjust actions), at an early stage in its development as an institution of government, came to denote the structure through which the ruling authorities assumed the responsibility for dispensing justice. For details, see J. Nielsen, 'Maẓālim', *EI2*, vol. 6, pp. 933–935; Hallaq, *Origins*, pp. 99–101.

[35] Poonawala, 'Sources for al-Qāḍī al-Nuʿmān's Works and their Authenticity.'

[36] He was appointed the chief *qāḍī* in 394/1004 by al-Ḥākim. For information on his life, see *The Governors and Judges of Egypt* (*Kitāb al-umarā' wa-kitāb al-quḍāt*) of al-Kindī, ed. Rhuvon Guest (Leiden, 1912), pp. 599–603.

> them will present the book and obtain the permission from the reigning Imam of his time. Hence, my father Muḥammad b. al-Nuʿmān was granted a second permission to relate it by our lord al-ʿAzīz bi'llāh, the Commander of the Faithful, may God bless him. Later on I presented it to our lord, the Imam al-Ḥākim bi-Amr Allāh, the Imam of the time, who granted me the permission to relate it on his behalf and gave me the exclusive permission to dictate it to his slaves and recorded the signature in his own exalted hand at the back of the book, which states, 'We have permitted our *qāḍī* ʿAbd al-ʿAzīz b. Muḥammad b. al-Nuʿmān to disseminate and dictate this book.'[37]

The importance of this work is demonstrated by the fact that permission was granted for its transmission by three successive Imam-caliphs, viz., al-Muʿizz, al-ʿAzīz and al-Ḥākim. At the beginning, Nuʿmān explains the reason for its compilation and states the following:

> [After the *basmala* and the *ḥamdala*] … Now, [I have to state] that I found the people of the *qibla* [Muslims], despite their agreement on the apparent text of the Qur'an and confirmation of [the prophethood of] the Messenger of God, they disagreed not only with regard to legal opinions [on a point of law] in most of the *furūʿ* [positive rules for the behaviour of men derived from the *uṣūl*], but also with regard to certain fundamental principles [the *uṣūl*] and various modes of [their] interpretations (*ta'wīl*). Thus, they pursued different paths and became divided into sectarian groups and parties even after they had heard and recited the words of God, the Mighty and the Exalted, saying: *Establish the true religion and do not be divided about it* (Q.42:13);[38] and *Those who were given the scripture diverged only after clear proof came to them* (Q.98:4); and *Religion with God is Submission. Those to whom the Scripture has been given differed only after knowledge came to them, through outrage amongst themselves* (Q.3:19); and *Will they not ponder on the Recitation, or are there locks on their hearts?* (Q.47:24); and *Do they not ponder on the Recitation? Had it been from any other than God, they would have found much contradiction in it* (Q.4:82). Thus, God, may His praise be high, found dissension and disagreement blameworthy and summoned them to unity and harmony. He has commanded that and urged them to [unite]. He made them desirous of performing the religious rites [correctly] and prohibited dissent from it.
>
> Therefore, I will begin this book with the [discussion of the] reason of their disagreement, which they themselves invited and prompted, and in consequence of it put themselves into [predicament]. I will follow it up with the reports of all what they said and how they established the fundamental [principles of jurispru-

---

[37] Nuʿmān, *Ikhtilāf*, pp. *alif-bā'*. See also Appendix IV for its text in Arabic.

[38] The full text of the verse reads: *He has instituted for you that religion which He ordained on Noah and what We have revealed to you and what We enjoined on Abraham and Moses and Jesus, saying, 'Establish the true religion and do not be divided about it.'* All English translations of the Qur'an cited in this chapter, unless stated otherwise, are by Alan Jones, *The Qur'ān: Translated into English* (London, 2007).

> dence] for themselves. I will expose the incorrectness of those principles and then interject the creed of the People of Truth (*ahl al-ḥaqq*)[39] concerning [the principles] about which they disagreed. I will elucidate and make those principles transparent with proofs. Subsequently, I will mention the doctrine of every sectarian group and their supporting arguments for what they alleged. Then, I will refute their stance for abandoning the truth in what they unduly assumed for themselves.[40]

Nuʿmān states that the reason for discord among the Muslim community following the Prophet's death was that they did not entrust their affairs to the care of the person who was rightfully authorised by the Qurʾan and the Prophet to assume the helm of the nascent Islamic state.[41] Nuʿmān then cites various traditions generally related by Shiʿi sources to prove that ʿAlī b. Abī Ṭālib was the most learned of the Companions of the Prophet regarding the Qurʾan and the occasions of its revelation (*asbāb al-nuzūl*). Therefore, he was well versed in Qurʾanic law and it is claimed that he said, 'Ask me before you lose me.'[42] It is also claimed that he said, 'Had a pillow been folded for me to sit [on] to dispense justice, I would have judged the People of the Qurʾan with the Qurʾan, the People of the Torah with the Torah, and the People of the Gospel with the Gospel, so no two people would have disagreed with regard to the edicts of [their respective] religion.'[43] Having made his most important points with regards to ʿAlī b. Abī Ṭālib that he was the rightful successor of the Messenger

---

39 Ismaʿili *dāʿīs* use this term for self reference. Abū Yaʿqūb Isḥāq al-Sijistānī, *Kitāb al-iftikhār*, ed. Ismail K. Poonawala (Beirut, 2000), *passim*.

40 Nuʿmān, *Ikhtilāf*, pp. 1–2. See also Appendix V for the Arabic text.

41 Recent studies on the issue of succession to the Prophet are by Wilferd Madelung, *The Succession to Muḥammad: A Study of the Early Caliphate* (Cambridge, 1997); and his 'Shīʿism in the Age of the Rightly-Guided Caliphs', in L. Clarke, ed., *Shīʿite Heritage* (Binghamton, NY, 2001), pp. 9–18; Khalid Blankinship, 'Imārah, Khilāfah, and Imāmah: The Origin of the Succession to the Prophet Muḥammad', in Clarke, ed., *Shīʿite Heritage*, pp. 19–43; Shaykh Muhammad Mahdi Shams al-Din, 'The Authenticity of Shīʿism', in Clarke, ed., *Shīʿite Heritage*, pp. 45–54; Khalil Athamina, 'The Pre-Islamic Roots of the Early Muslim Caliphate: The Emergence of Abū Bakr', *Der Islam*, 76 (1999), pp. 1–32; Tarek Fatah, *Chasing a Mirage: The Tragic Illusion of an Islamic State* (Mississauga, Ontario, 2008).

42 The Arabic reads:

ومن ذلك الحديث المأثور عنه أنه كان كثيراً ما يقول: سلوني قبل أن تُفقدوني.

Nuʿmān, *Ikhtilāf*, p. 4. In *Ghurar al-ḥikam* of al-Āmidī (as cited by Muḥammad Bāqir al-Majlisī, *Biḥār al-anwār*, annotated by al-Sayyid Jawād al-ʿAlawī and al-Shaykh Muḥammad Ākhundī, Tehran, 1374 Sh./1995, vol. 40, p. 153), the full text of the tradition is reported as follows:

سلوني قبل أن تفقدوني، فأنّي بطرق السماوات أخبر منكم بطرق الأرض.

43 Nuʿmān, *Ikhtilāf*, p. 3; it states:

الحديث المأثور عن علي صلوات الله عليه أنه قال، وقد رأى اختلاف الناس بعد رسول الله صلى الله عليه وآله: أما لو ثُنّيت لي وسادةٌ وجلستُ للناس لقضيتُ بين أهل القرآن بالقرآن، وبين أهل التوراة بالتوراة، وبين أهل الإنجيل بالإنجيل. ولما اختلف اثنان في حكمٍ من أحكام الدين.

See also al-Majlisī, *Biḥār al-anwār*, vol. 40, pp. 136–137.

of God for the leadership of the Muslim community and that he was the most knowledgeable about the interpretation and injunctions of the Qurʾan, Nuʿmān continues with a discussion about the fundamental principles of the law that had developed before him. He summarises them as follows:

> Most of the jurists state that whatever legal ordinances and related matters concerning lawful and unlawful matters that are clearly mentioned in the text of the Qurʾan, should be followed and acted upon. Whereas the matters that are not stated explicitly in the Qurʾan should be sought in the *sunna* of the Messenger of God. If those matters are treated or referred to in the *sunna* of the Messenger of God, they should be adhered to and acted upon without overstepping them.
>
> Now, whatever is not accounted for in either the Qurʾan or the *sunna* of the Messenger of God, should be sought in the reports of the Companions. If those matters are dealt with in their assertions and have been agreed upon by the Companions, we should adopt them. However, if we discover certain things in their statements, but at the same time also find that they had disagreed among themselves on those very issues, in such cases we have a choice; either we choose the report of one Companion or the other with which we are satisfied.
>
> Some jurists, on the other hand, have maintained that if they could track down a particular thing/issue that they were looking for in the statements of the Companions, they should accept it and not depart from it. However, if what they were looking for cannot be found in either the Qurʾan, the *sunna* of the Messenger of God, or in the accounts of the Companions, they should consider another option, whether the legal scholars had agreed on that matter. If they had agreed upon it, they should adopt it and not depart from their consensus.
>
> Yet, another group of jurists disagreed with the rest and declared certain things to be lawful or unlawful merely by justifying their own opinions and conclusions.[44]

Nuʿmān states that by such an action the latter faction of the jurists simply turned away from their opponents and followed other leaders. Nuʿmān adds that this group did not stop there and accused their rivals of unbelief. Yet, other jurists asserted their belief in the doctrine of *qiyās* (judicial reasoning by analogy),[45] while others advocated the doctrine of *raʾy* (personal, or considered opinion)[46] and *ijtihād* (jurisprudential interpretation),[47] while others upheld the principles of *istiḥsān*

[44] For the Arabic text, see Appendix VI.

[45] Monique Bernard, 'Ḳiyās', *EI2*, vol. 3, p. 1023. It is a collective name for a variety of legal arguments including, *inter alia*, analogy, *argumentum a fortiori*, *reductio ad absurdum*, or deductive arguments; see Hallaq, *Origins*, pp. 113–116, 140–144, and his *History*, pp. 83–107.

[46] It is a discretionary opinion or reasoning based on precedent or on subjective considerations, see Hallaq, *Origins*, pp. 113–114; Hallaq, *History*, pp. 15, 19.

[47] Joseph Schacht, 'Idjtihād', *EI2*, vol. 3, pp. 1026–1027. It is a process of legal reasoning through which the jurist derives or rationalises law on the basis of the Qurʾan and the *sunna*; during the early centuries of Islam it meant the exercise of one's discretionary opinion based on *ʿilm*. See Hallaq, *Origins*, pp. 114–115, 146; Hallaq, *History*, pp. 117–121.

(juristic preference),[48] *naẓar* (speculation, arbitrary reasoning), or *istidlāl* (inductive reasoning).[49]

According to Nuʿmān, all the aforementioned groups originated from a common intent, their belief that the Qur'an and the *sunna* of the Messenger of God do not provide them with all the information needed to decide all cases they encountered during their lives. Nuʿmān, therefore, asserts that all these groups are united on an unsound principle, which constitutes nothing more than following their own fancies and whims.

To support his contention that God, the Mighty and High, has perfected his religion and warned the people against speculations in religious matters, Nuʿmān cites numerous verses from the Qur'an. These include, God said: *And who is further astray than him who follows his whim without guidance from God?* (Q.28:50); *They only follow guesswork, and guesswork is of no avail against the truth* (Q.53:28). Additionally He said: *O David, We have made you a viceroy in the land. Judge between the people in truth. Do not follow caprice, lest it lead you away from the way of God* (Q.38:26). Addressing His Messenger, God said: *So [O Muḥammad] judge between them by what God has sent down; and do not follow their whims* (Q.5:48). After citing the above verses Nuʿmān quotes a well-known tradition of the Messenger of God: 'Follow, and do not innovate, for every innovation is an error, and every error leads to hellfire.'[50]

Following the above introductory remarks, Nuʿmān first takes issue with his adversaries' claims that there are several things, lawful or unlawful, not mentioned in either the Qur'an or the *sunna* of the Messenger of God. The main objective of Nuʿmān's argument in this case is to demonstrate that this claim is preposterous. In support of his argument he draws heavily on Qur'anic verses. It should be remarked here that Nuʿmān was simply following in the footsteps of the Shiʿi *ʿulamā'* who, by the time of Nuʿmān's writing, had fully elaborated the Shiʿi doctrine of the imamate. One of the fundamental elements of that doctrine is that the Imam is presumed to be the most learned person in the Muslim community.[51] Nuʿmān was a fierce proponent of the doctrine of the imamate. Of course, he was selective in his selec-

---

[48] Rudi Paret, 'Istiḥsān', *EI2*, vol. 4, pp. 255–256. It is a juristic preference based, in the early period, upon practical considerations, and later, on a particularised textual *ratio legis*; see Hallaq, *Origins*, pp. 116–117, 144–145; Hallaq, *History*, pp. 107–113.

[49] R. Arnaldez, 'Manṭiḳ (esp. Logic in the judicial science)', *EI2*, vol. 6, pp. 4514–4552. *Istidlāl* means arguments based on the *dalīl*, and it covers various inferences that do not belong to the category of *qiyās*. See Hallaq, *History*, pp. 112, 130, 131, 141; he states that arbitrary reasoning was often characterised as *ra'y* and *naẓar*. He further adds that in certain cases, reasoning, appearing under the labels of *ra'y* and *naẓar*, was nothing short of systematic *qiyās*.

[50] Nuʿmān, *Ikhtilāf*, pp. 10–11, 16; it reads:

قال رسول الله صلى الله عليه وآله: إتّبعوا ولا تبتدعوا، فكلّ بدعةٍ ضلالةٌ، وكلّ ضلالةٍ في النار.

It is transmitted by Muslim, Abū Dāwūd, Nasā'ī, Ibn Māja, Dārimī and Ibn Ḥanbal. A. J. Wensinck, *Concordance et indices de la tradition musulmane* (Leiden, 1992), s.v. ḍ-l-l. See also Nuʿmān, *The Pillars of Islam*, vol. 1, p. 110.

[51] For more details see Ismail Poonawala, 'The Imām's Authority during the Pre-Ghaybah Period: Theoretical and Practical Considerations', in Clarke, ed., *Shīʿite Heritage*, pp. 103–122.

tion of Qur'anic verses and took them out of context. However, to be fair, this was the norm of his day since there were a considerable number of sectarian groups and all of them tried to justify their claim by Qur'anic verses and traditions of the Prophet.

Let us return to Nu'mān and analyse how he developed his arguments that the Qur'an contains everything that the faithful might need to guide him during his life. It is a recurring argument. First, he quotes from the Qur'an to stress the point that it is a comprehensive Book. He uses the passage, God says: *We have neglected nothing in the Book* (Q.6:38).[52] Addressing His Messenger, God says: *We have sent down to you the Scripture as an explanation (tibyān^{an}) of everything and guidance and mercy and good news to those who submit* (Q.16:89). Nu'mān argues that the above verses clearly demonstrate that God explained everything in His Book and He did not neglect any aspect pertaining to Islam. The term '*bayān*,' Nu'mān explains is applied to what is obvious, clear, manifest and known.[53] Hence, one does not need to resort to *qiyās*, *ra'y*, *ijtihād*, *istiḥsān*, *naẓar* or *istidlāl* for explanations. If those people who advocate the above theories would ask us: 'Where is this explanation (*bayān*) [what you have stated] in the Qur'an?' In his defence Nu'mān states: 'We will respond with the following verses wherein God quite clearly says: *And We have sent down to you [O Muḥammad] the reminder for you to make clear to men what has been sent down to them* (Q.16:44). He says: *Whatever the Messenger gives you, take it. Whatever he forbids you to have, leave it alone* (Q.59:7). God also says: *If they were to refer it to the Messenger and to those who have authority among them (uli'l-amr minhum), those among them able to investigate the matter would know [how to handle it]* (Q.4:83). Moreover, God states: *Obey God and obey the Messenger and those of you who have authority (uli'l-amr minkum)* (Q.4:59). God also says: *Today I have perfected your*

---

[52] Alan Jones has translated *al-kitāb* as 'record', while most of the translators, such as Bell, Yusuf 'Alī, Pickthall, Arberry and Abdel Haleem have rendered *al-kitāb* as 'Book'. I have preferred the latter.

[53] Nu'mān, *Ikhtilāf*, p. 17. He states:

وكذلك سمّاه الله تعالى حكماً وتبياناً وهدًى وشفاءً. وأخبر رسول الله صلى الله عليه وآله أنه من اتّبع الهدى في غيره أضلّه الله. فكيف يزعم هؤلاء الجاهلون أن شيئاً تعبّد الله به خلقه لم يُنزله في كتابه؟

The terms *bayān* and *tibyān* occur four times in the Qur'an: 3:138, 55:4, 75:19 and 16:89. It is worth noting that in his *Risāla*, ed. Aḥmad M. Shākir (2nd ed., Cairo, 1979), p. 20; tr. Majid Khadduri, *al-Shāfi'ī's Risāla*: *Treatise on the Foundations of Islamic Jurisprudence* (2nd ed., Cambridge, 1987), p. 66, Shāfi'ī states: 'No misfortune will ever descend upon any of the followers of God's religion for which there is no guidance in the Book of God to indicate the right way.' Soon thereafter he cites the following verses of the Qur'an: 14:1, 16:46, 16:91 and 42:52. It is followed by several sections elucidating the term '*al-bayān*.' Shāfi'ī discusses certain characteristics of the Qur'an as an introduction to a fuller treatment of the Qur'an from a juridical viewpoint. In his *History*, pp. 21–29, Hallaq has succinctly summarised the contents of the *Risāla*.

religion for you and completed My blessing for you and have approved Submission (al-islām) as a religion for you (Q.5:3)'.[54]

Nu'mān adds that the *bayān* of the Messenger of God and the *uli'l-amr* are included in the ordinance of the Qur'an. This, therefore, is clear evidence that the *uli'l-amr* comprehends the lawful and unlawful, and all related matters that a person would need to know during the course of his life. He adds that the *uli'l-amr* need neither *qiyās*, *ra'y*, *istidlāl*, *ijtihād*, *istiḥsān*, nor *naẓar*. Addressing His Prophet, God said: *We have sent down to you the Scripture with the truth, for you to judge between the people by that which God has shown you* (Q.4:105). Ridiculing the above-stated theories, Nu'mān adds rhetorically, 'God said to the Messenger of God '*that which God has shown you*,' He did not say to His Messenger, 'that which [O Muḥammad] you considered as your personal opinion,' or 'that which is reached through your juristic preference,' or 'that which you arrived at by analogical reasoning,' or 'that which you reached by speculation,' or 'that which you reached by inductive reasoning,' or 'that which you concluded from your personal reasoning.'[55]

Nu'mān continues and states that people queried the Messenger of God with many issues in different situations, but he did not respond by exercising his personal opinion or analogical deduction. Rather he waited until the revelation came. There are several verses of the Qur'an that point in that direction: for example, *They ask you about menstruation. Say, 'It is a vexation. Withdraw from women during menstruation'* (Q.2:222); and *They will ask you about the Spirit. Say, 'The Spirit is part of the affair of my Lord, and you have been given only little knowledge'* (Q.17:85); and *They ask you about what they should spend. Say, 'The surplus'* (Q.2:219); and *They ask you about orphans. Say, 'Setting their affairs right is good'* (Q.2:220); and *They ask you about the sacred month and fighting in it. Say, 'Fighting in it is grievous, but turning [people] from God's way and unbelief in Him … is more grievous with God'* (Q.2:217).

Nu'mān sarcastically adds: 'How preposterous it is then to allege that God did not perfect His religion and left it to the people to perfect it! Even the Jinn, when they heard the Qur'an recited to them exclaimed: *We have heard a marvellous recitation, which guides to righteousness. We believed in it* (Q.72:1–2). God has called the Qur'an *ḥukm*^{an} [*'Arabiyy*^{an}] (a criterion in Arabic) (Q.13:37), and *tibyān*^{an} [*li-kulli shay'*^{in}] (an explanation of everything) (Q.16:89), and *hud*^{an} (a guidance) (Q.16:89; 10:57; 41:44), and *shifā'*^{an} (a remedy) (Q.10:57). How dare they say that the Qur'an is lacking in guidance! The Messenger of God said, "One who follows

54 In his *Uṣūl al-sharī'a* (Beirut, 1983), p. 70, Muḥammad Sa'īd 'Ashmāwī states that the verse was revealed when the Prophet was making a pilgrimage and the thrust of the meaning refers to the ritual practices required for the perfection of Islam as a religion. See also Hallaq, *History*, p. 233.

55 Nu'mān, *Ikhtilāf*, p. 13; it reads:

وكان بيانُ الرسول وبيانُ أولي الأمر داخلان في حكم الكتاب إذ كان الكتاب أوجب ذلك، ونطق به ودلّ عليه. فصار جميعُ الحلال والحرام والقضايا والأحكام والفرائض، وجميعُ ما تعبّد اللّٰه العباد به، بهذا القول مثبتاً في الكتاب بهذا المعنى واضحاً بيّناً، غير مشكلٍ ولا مقفلٍ. ولا يحتاج إلى القياس عليه، ولا استدلال فيه، ولا الرأي، ولا الاجتهاد، ولا الاستحسان، ولا النظر، كما زعم هؤلاء المختلفون.

guidance from a source other than the Qurʾan, God will make him lose his way."[56] Thus, how dare those ignorant people claim that the very matters with which mankind worship God, He did not reveal in His Book? Who taught them such knowledge? Did it not come through the Messenger of God? God says: *Say [O Muḥammad], 'I follow what is revealed to me from my Lord.'* (Q.7:203). God also says: *And He has taught you [O Muḥammad] what you did not know. God's bounty to you is great* (Q.4:113). Even the angels, addressing God, proclaimed: *Glory be to You. The only knowledge we have is what You have taught us. You truly are the Knowing and the Wise* (Q.2:32). How then those uninformed people allege that they derive legal rulings pertaining to what is lawful and unlawful that are not mentioned in the Qurʾan and the *sunna*? Did they not contradict the Qurʾan and claim for themselves a position higher than that of the prophets and the angels?'[57]

Let me add another reason Nuʿmān has given at the end of the book for the compilation of the *Ikhtilāf*. It is not altogether different from what he had given at the beginning of the book, but it recalls his personal encounter with someone who held a different view on this matter. He states:

> The reason for my compilation of this book in such a way is that I was a neighbour of someone who held the doctrine of *ijtihād*. I explained to him that it was an unsound assertion and I protested against it with the same arguments that I have presented in this book until he ceased from [asserting] it. I thought that he had confessed the truth and returned [to the right path]. But, subsequently he wound up with the composition of a booklet in which he elaborated the views of those who uphold the doctrine of *ijtihād* and persisted in his arguments that he had held before.
>
> I have related in this book all that he had compiled in his booklet of the arguments of the proponents of that theory. I have added additional affirmations and arguments that have reached me, but were not mentioned by him. And I have demonstrated unsoundness [of such belief] and refuted their arguments. I did not intend to invalidate only the theory of *ijtihād*, so that the one to whom this book reaches might think that I was satisfied with other principles advocated by the schools that are antagonistic to the truth which I have discussed in this book. Hence, I saw it fit to mention all their statements and refute them [one by one] seeking success and recompense from the Almighty.[58]

It is at this stage in the book that Nuʿmān introduces the *madhhab* of the People of Truth, the Ismaili legal doctrine and outlines the principles of its legal thought.[59] First, he copies the royal decree of the Fatimid Imam-caliph al-Muʿizz, which was

[56] This tradition of the Prophet is transmitted by Tirmidhī and Dārimī. Wensinck, *Concordance*, s.v. ḍ-l-l.

[57] I have summarised the Arabic text in translation. Nuʿmān, *Ikhtilāf*, pp. 16–18.

[58] For the Arabic text see Appendix VII.

[59] For the development of the concept of *madhhab* as a group of jurists and legists who are strictly loyal to a distinct, collective legal doctrine attributed to an eponym, after whom the school is known to acquire distinctive characteristics, see Hallaq, *Origins*, pp. 150 ff.

issued on the occasion of his investiture with the highest judicial office in the Fatimid realm and was read publicly. It was transcribed on Monday 28 Rabīʿ I, 343/ [30 September 954].[60] What interests us the most are the instructions given by al-Muʿizz to Nuʿmān. They basically cover the fundamental principles of Ismaili law as elaborated by Nuʿmān. What follows is the summary of the directives issued by al-Muʿizz.

Firstly, in all his legal decisions and judgements, Nuʿmān should follow the Book of God, which is described in His words as: *Falsehood cannot come to it from before it or from behind it, a Revelation sent down from One* [*who is*] *Wise and Praiseworthy* (Q.41:42). Al-Muʿizz states: 'Verily, God has clarified in His Book all matters that are either lawful or unlawful in His eyes. He has also expounded His commands and illuminated His signposts.'

Secondly, if Nuʿmān cannot find any reference [concerning a particular issue] either in the Qurʾanic text or in the *sunna* of the Messenger of God or his precepts, he seeks it in the acts and decisions (*madhāhib*) of the virtuous, pious and Rightly Guided Imams who are from the progeny of the Messenger of God, the forefathers of the Commander of the Faithful. They are the treasures of God's knowledge and the hidden secrets of His revelation. They are designated by God as guides for mankind and the luminaries in the darkness who are supposed to rescue them from the bewilderment of blindness and the gloom of destruction. They are the exemplary models who should be followed in religious and mundane matters.

Thirdly, if something appears to him as ambiguous and difficult [to resolve], or dubious and problematic, he should refer it to the Commander of the Faithful, so that he might be able to guide him in the appropriate direction. Indeed, the Commander of the Faithful is the best (*baqiyya*)[61] of the Rightly Guided deputies of God and from the progeny of the Rightly Guiding Imams. The Almighty has commanded people to turn to the Imams for guidance, to direct their questions to them and to acquire knowledge from them. God has also enjoined His servants to refer to the Imams, as God has said: *If they were to refer it* [*any matter*] *to the Messenger and to those who have authority* (*uli'l-amr*) *among them, those among them able to investigate the matter would know* [*how to handle*] *it* (Q.4:83). The Almighty has also said: *Ask the people* [*who have*] *the reminder* (*ahl al-dhikr*) *if you do not know* (Q.16:43). Moreover, the Messenger of God has declared, 'I am leaving among you two things of great weight (*al-thaqalayn*), the Book of God and my kindred (*ʿitratī*), the People

---

[60] For its Arabic text, see Appendix III.

[61] The word *baqiyya*, lit. means remainder, remnant, relic; however, when used in a genitive construction (*iḍāfa*) annexed to a word referring to a tribe, family, or a community, it means *the most excellent of them*. For example, فلانٌ من بقيّة القوم means *such a one is the most excellent*, or *the best of the people*. Edward Lane, *Arabic-English Lexicon*, Reprint (Cambridge: The Islamic Society, 1984), s.v. b-q-y; older sources are indicated therein. The word was used by al-Muʿizz in his sermon announcing the death of his father al-Manṣūr, see *Inside the Immaculate Portal: A History from Early Fatimid Archives*. A new edition and English translation of Manṣūr al-ʿAzīzī al-Jawdharī's biography of al-Ustādh Jawdhar, edited & translated by Hamid Haji (London: I.B.Tauris, 2012), p. 70 (Arabic text). Lokhandwalla's translation "remnant" is incorrect. I am thankful to Hamid Haji for drawing my attention to the above reference.

of My House (*ahl baytī*). As long as you will adhere to them, you will never be led astray, because these two shall never be separated until they return to me at the Pool.'[62]

As previously mentioned, Nuʿmān had already elaborated these principles at the beginning of the book. Now, they are reinforced by al-Muʿizz's royal decree. Another significant point Nuʿmān makes with regard to the edict and the instructions contained in it, is that it was the norm for all previous Imams beginning with the first Imam-caliph al-Mahdī to issue similar edicts whenever they appointed a *qāḍī*. Nuʿmān states that al-Manṣūr had also issued similar directives to him on the occasion of his appointment to that office. Nuʿmān asserts that the Imams did not enjoin their *qāḍī*s with the ability to exercise *qiyās*, *naẓar*, *istiḥsān*, *ra'y* or *ijtihād* as was the case with the rest of the Sunni caliphs. Nuʿmān adds that the overall Muslim community is united in their view that if a person does not know something related to religion and someone else has that knowledge, he ought to seek the latter's advice. Hence, Nuʿmān poses a rhetorical question and states:

> How is it then permissible for anyone to exercise his own individual opinion, or employ a different means of deduction? God has said: [*They*] *will reckon that they have something to stand on. Truly, they are the ones who lie* (Q.58:18). If that would have been the case, everyone would have exercised his opinion and all people would be equal in knowledge. As a result there would not have been any distinction between the learned and the ignorant. But, the Almighty has stated: *But only those with knowledge will understand them* (Q.29:43). He also stated: *Ask the people* [*who have*] *the reminder if you do not know* (Q.16:43). But people differed as to the identity of *ahl al-dhikr*. Some people said that they were the *fuqahā'* (jurists). Had that been the case, it would have been said to them, 'But, those jurists disagree among themselves. Some of them consider certain things lawful, while the others regard those very things unlawful. How would it be permissible for God to command people to ask them such matters of great significance? Similarly, some people asserted that the *uli'l-amr*, whose obedience is commanded by God, were the commanders of the *sarāyā* (military detachment sent by the Prophet).[63] Such an interpretation is incorrect, because the command to obey God, His Messenger, and *uli'l-amr* is addressed to all Muslims alike and is not limited to only those who only participated in some military expeditions sent by the Prophet.'[64]

---

[62] This tradition, known as *ḥadīth al-thaqalayn* (two weighty things) is transmitted by Ibn Ḥanbal, Muslim, Tirmidhī and Dārimī; Wensinck, *Concordance*, s.v. th-q-l. See also Nuʿmān, *The Pillars of Islam*, vol. 1, p. 37. Muslim's version contains 'God's Book' and 'My Family'.

[63] For the meaning of the *sariyya*, pl. *sarāyā*, see *The History of al-Ṭabarī*, vol. 9: *The Last Years of the Prophet, The Formation of the State, A. D. 630–632/A. H. 8–11*; tr. and annotated by Ismail K. Poonawala (Albany, NY, 1990), p. 62. See Nuʿmān' refutation in *The Pillars of Islam*, vol. 1, p. 32.

[64] I have summarised the Arabic text of the *Ikhtilāf*, pp. 25–28.

Thus far I have merely discussed and analysed the introduction of the book, consisting of about 28 printed pages of the text. The rest of the book contains over 200 pages which is devoted to the presentation of the views of the rival schools of jurisprudence and their refutations. Nuʿmān organises the book into several sections. First, he addresses the *aṣḥāb al-taqlīd* and at the end of the debate asserts that the same charge cannot be levelled against the Shīʿa.[65] This is followed by a section covering the *aṣḥāb al-ijmāʿ*. This is divided into three sections/chapters: the people who uphold *ijmāʿ* and their refutation; disagreement with regard to its *ḥujjiyya* (authoritativeness of methodological principles);[66] and an account of *ijmāʿ* with regards to place and time.[67] It is preceded by those who maintain the doctrine of *naẓar*. *Aṣḥāb al-qiyās*[68] comes next and is followed by those who assert the doctrines of *istiḥsān* and *istidlāl*. The last topic pertains to those who uphold the doctrine of *raʾy* and *ijtihād*.[69] Ultimately, it concludes with a recapitulation of Nuʿmān's representations of those groups and the main arguments.

An Account of *Aṣḥāb al-Taqlīd* and their Refutation[70]

Nuʿmān commences this chapter and states that God did not command the faithful to follow anyone after His Messenger except the *uliʾl-amr* whom the Prophet had designated as the vanguards of the community. However, the community disregarded this particular instruction of the Messenger of God and followed inappropriate individuals. After alluding to the historical events that followed the death of the Prophet, Nuʿmān narrates the story of ʿAdī b. Ḥātim al-Ṭāʾī who came to the Messenger of God to accept Islam while he was still wearing a cross made of gold around his neck. The Messenger of God, therefore, asked him to remove it and he recited to him the *sūrat barāʾa* (also known as *sūrat al-tawba*, chapter nine of the Qurʾan) until the end of the verse where God states: *They have taken their rabbis and monks as lords apart from God* (Q.9:31). Thus, Nuʿmān criticises that the Muslim community has become almost identical with the former communities of the Jews and the Christians whose story God has told us in the aforecited verse.

Nuʿmān narrates a tradition on the authority of the Imam Jaʿfar al-Ṣādiq stating that the Imam had rightly interpreted this verse as referring to the Muslim community of his days and said that they (i.e., the misguided of the community) did not, indeed, fast for, nor pray to their leaders; but these leaders permitted the community to do things that were ultimately unlawful, and so the people considered those things to be lawful; and [similarly] when their leaders forbade things that were lawful, the people considered those things to be forbidden.[71] The Prophet had

65 It consists of 26 pages and is the fourth longest chapter.
66 For *ḥujjiyya* see Hallaq, *History*, pp. 75–77, 126, 133, 166.
67 It is the longest chapter and comprises 59 pages.
68 It comprises 49 pages and is the second longest chapter.
69 It comprises 33 pages and is the third longest chapter.
70 For the meaning of *taqlīd*, see Hallaq, *Origins*, p. 147; Hallaq, *History*, pp. 121–123.
71 See also Nuʿmān, *The Pillars of Islam*, vol. 1, p. 2.

foreseen the situation that would prevail in his community. This was the reason that he said: 'You will surely follow the paths of the communities before you as a horseshoe upon a horseshoe and an arrow feather on an arrow feather, to the extent that if they had entered a lizard's hole, then you too would surely have done the same.'[72] The correct version of another popular tradition, known as the *ḥadīth al-thaqalayn*, identifies the two weighty things as 'the Book of God' and 'my kindred' (i.e., the People of the Messenger of God's House). It is not what the majority of the Muslims claim: 'the Book of God' and 'my *sunna*.' Nuʿmān states that the latter version is nothing more than tampering with the original text of the tradition.

Nuʿmān states that the main argument they present for their justification of *taqlīd* (blind following, submission) is a tradition ascribed to the Prophet which states, 'My Companions are like the stars; whichever one of them you choose to follow, you will be rightly guided.'[73] Nuʿmān then points out the fact which is well known to students of Islamic history: the Companions not only disagreed among themselves, they also fought among themselves and killed each other. The first thing a great majority of the *Muhājirīn* and *Anṣār* disagreed on was the injunction of the Messenger of God concerning the leadership of the community after him. Without going into the detail Nuʿmān alludes to the gathering at the *Saqīfat Banī Sāʿida* where a heated debate ensued between the *Anṣār* and the *Muhājirīn* that supposedly led to Abū Bakr being selected as the successor of the Prophet.[74]

Having made this significant point, Nuʿmān moves on to demonstrate that the Companions hardly agreed on anything. Nuʿmān reports that when Abū Bakr intended to fight the people of the Yamāma on the pretext of their not paying the *zakāt*, ʿUmar advised the caliph against such a move.[75] Nuʿmān then calls the reader's attention to ʿUmar's ignorance of the Qurʾan, especially with regard to its injunctions.[76] In many cases the second caliph ʿUmar b. al-Khaṭṭāb had given wrong

---

72 Ibid., vol. 1, p. 1; older sources are indicated there.

73 Ibid., vol. 1, p. 107. Walīy al-Dīn Muḥammad al-Tabrīzī, *Mishkāt al-maṣābīḥ*, ed. Muḥammad Nāsir al-Dīn al-Albānī (Damascus, 1961), vol. 3, p. 219; tr. James Robson, *Mishkat al-masabih* (Lahore, 1975), vol. 2, p. 1320; various versions are cited.

74 For details as to what happened in the *Saqīfat Banī Sāʿida*, see Poonawala, *The History of al-Ṭabarī*, vol. 9, p. 189 ff., where other parallel sources are cited; Fred Donner, *The History of al-Ṭabarī*, vol. 10: *The Conquest of Arabia* (Albany, NY, 1993), pp. 1 ff.

75 This report cannot be verified from historical sources. It probably refers to the incident of Buṭāḥ wherein Khālid b. Walīd killed Mālik b. Nuwayra and married his wife. ʿUmar was angry at what Khālid did and pressed Abū Bakr to dismiss him, saying: 'In his sword there really is forbidden behaviour.' Whereupon Abū Bakr replied: 'O ʿUmar I will not sheathe a sword that God has drawn against the unbelievers.' Donner, *The History of al-Ṭabarī*, vol. 10, pp. 98–104; al-Yaʿqūbī, *Taʾrīkh al-Yaʿqūbī*, ed. Muḥammad Ṣādiq Baḥr al-ʿUlūm (Najaf, 1964), vol. 2, p. 122; Ibn al-Athīr, *al-Kāmil fiʾl-taʾrīkh*, ed. C. J. Tornberg (repr., Beirut, 1979), vol. 2, pp. 357–360.

76 In his *al-Iḥkām fī uṣūl al-aḥkām* (Cairo, 1345/1926–1927), vol. 2, p. 125, Ibn Ḥazm gives specific examples where ʿUmar lacked adequate knowledge of the Qurʾan. Moreover, in the section entitled '*Fīhi bayān sabab al-ikhtilāf al-wāqiʿ bayn al-aʾimma fī ṣadr hādhihi al-umma*' (vol. 2, pp. 124 ff.), Ibn Ḥazm gives a vivid picture of differences among the nascent Muslim community concerning their knowledge of the Qurʾan and *ḥadīth*.

legal decisions, but thanks to ʿAlī's timely intervention and advice, ʿUmar revoked his judgements. Hence, the origin of the famous saying, 'Had it not been for ʿAlī, ʿUmar would have perished.'[77]

It is worth noting here that Nuʿmān then goes on to expound the linguistic meaning and usage of the verb *ṣaḥiba* and its noun formation *aṣḥāb* in the Qur'anic usage and in the Prophet's utterance during his final illness. When the Messenger of God got irritated with some of his wives for not carrying out his recommendations he said to them, 'You are like Joseph's little female companions (*innakunna ṣuwayḥibātu Yūsuf*).'[78] Of course, the term '*ṣuwayḥibāt Yūsuf*' was not a compliment, rather it had a negative connotation. Nuʿmān then states that the word *nujūm* was used metaphorically in the tradition they alleged that the Messenger of God had said: 'My Companions are like the stars; whichever of them you choose to follow, you will be rightly guided.' If it is authentic, Nuʿmān appropriates it and states that it refers to the Imams from his progeny and not to the Companions as the literal meaning of the tradition suggests.[79]

Clarifying his position that he is not bent on belittling the Companions, Nuʿmān states that his intention was not to disparage the Companions but to refute their argument supporting blind following. Nuʿmān adds that the same argument against *taqlīd* applies to those who blindly follow the *tābiʿūn* (the Followers), and those who follow the generation who came after them, that is, the *lāḥiqūn*. However, Nuʿmān adds, the most famous people to whom the word *taqlīd* is associated with are those who uphold the doctrine of the *ra'y*, *istiḥsān*, *qiyās*, *naẓar* and *ijtihād*, like Abū Ḥanīfa al-Nuʿmān al-Kūfī, Mālik b. Anas al-Madanī and Muḥammad b. Idrīs al-Shāfiʿī. A great majority of the people are the followers of those three figures. Nuʿmān's statement implies that the three major Sunni schools of jurisprudence had already crystallised by the middle of the 4th/10th century. It should be noted that Ibn Ḥanbal does not come into the picture at all, which clearly implies that he was not considered a major jurist or the founder of the Ḥanbalī *madhhab* at that time.[80] Nuʿmān then proceeds to criticise the founders of the three schools of jurisprudence.

Nuʿmān points out that Abū Ḥanīfa frequently changed his opinions and he is the one who is credited with saying: 'This knowledge of ours rests on opinion (*ra'y*) only, and in our opinion it is the best that can be attained. However, if someone comes to us with a better opinion, we shall reverse our opinion and adopt his view.'[81]

---

[77] For details and sources see Nuʿmān, *The Pillars of Islam*, vol. 1, p. 106.

[78] For details see Poonawala, *The History of al-Ṭabarī*, vol. 9, p. 180.

[79] For details and older sources, see Nuʿmān, *The Pillars of Islam*, vol. 1, p. 107.

[80] Hallaq, *Origins*, pp. 159 ff. He states that the beginning of legal Ḥanbalism, which had already established itself as a theological school, is to be located in the juristic activities of the generations that followed him.

[81] The Arabic reads:

قال أبو حنيفة: علمنا هذا رأي، وهو أحسن ما رأيناه، فمَنْ أتانا بخيرٍ منه رجعنا إليه فيه وقبلنا منه.

This saying of Abū Ḥanīfa is reported on the authority of his student al-Ḥasan b. Ziyād al-Lu'lu'ī (d. 204/819–820). Abū Ḥanīfa himself did not write any book, but his juridical opinions were recorded by his disciples. See also Joseph Schacht, 'Abū Ḥanīfa', *EI2*, vol. 1, pp.

Abū Ḥanīfa believed in the doctrine of *qiyās* and claimed that it is the most useful one. Nuʿmān then relates a story of a man from Khurāsān who performed the pilgrimage whereupon he met Abū Ḥanīfa and wrote down on his authority his legal opinions concerning certain issues. The following year the man returned to Mecca for pilgrimage, met Abū Ḥanīfa and asked him about the same issues. But Abū Ḥanīfa contradicted what he had previously said *in toto*. At this the Khurāsānī beat his face in confusion and let out a cry. The people gathered around him and asked him the reason. He said, 'O people! This man [Abū Ḥanīfa] gave me his legal opinion on certain issues last year. I then returned home and on the basis of his opinions I made certain things lawful and unlawful for my people. When I came to him this year he revoked his earlier opinions altogether.' Whereupon Abū Ḥanīfa exclaimed, 'But that was only the considered opinion I held at that time; and now I believe otherwise, so I revoked it.' The Khurāsānī rejoined, 'Woe to you! Perhaps if I were to depend on what you say this year, contrary to what you said last year, then you would certainly again reverse your opinion the next year!' Abū Ḥanīfa responded, 'I do not know; perhaps I might.' The Khurāsānī thereupon exclaimed, 'But, I know that upon you lies the curse of God!'[82]

Likewise, Nuʿmān criticises Mālik. Ashhab b. ʿAbd al-ʿAzīz, the foremost of Mālik's followers who reported that one day he was in the company of his master when he was asked about the irrevocable divorce (*ṭalāq al-batta*). Mālik said, 'It is pronounced thrice [at one time and considered thrice valid.]' Thereupon Ashhab seized his tablet to write it down on his authority. Mālik asked, 'What are you doing?' Ashhab replied that he was inscribing what he had just said. Mālik said, 'How do you know that by the evening I might change my opinion and say that it is only one valid pronouncement?'[83] Nuʿmān asks rhetorically, 'How, then, can these fickle minded people be followed?'

As for Shāfiʿī, Nuʿmān states that he first followed Mālik and others from the people of Mecca and Medina and gave his legal opinions accordingly. He then went to Iraq and met with Muḥammad b. al-Ḥasan al-Shaybānī and revoked many of his previous opinions. Later on, he went to Egypt and settled there whereupon he reversed many of his earlier opinions that he had given while he was in the Ḥijāz and Iraq.[84] Nuʿmān notes that Shāfiʿī strictly forbade his followers from the unequivocal adoption (*taqlīd*) of either his opinion or his fellow jurisconsults. He rebuked the jurists who adopted the opinions of their predecessors (*aṣḥāb al-taqlīd*) without inquiring into the reasons behind their decisions.[85] Despite his warning, some of his disciples followed him and adopted his authority. Nuʿmān then adds

---

123–124; Nuʿmān, *The Pillars of Islam*, vol. 1, p. 108.

82 This story is also reported by Nuʿmān in *The Pillars of Islam*, vol. 1, p. 110.

83 Nuʿmān reports the same story in *The Pillars of Islam*, vol. 1, p. 108.

84 For the life and doctrine of Shāfiʿī, see E. Chaumont, 'al-Shāfiʿī', *EI2*, vol. 9, pp. 181–185.

85 Nuʿmān, *Ikhtilāf*, p. 43; the Arabic reads:

وكان ينهى عن التقليد أشدَّ النهي، ويُعيب أهله، ويردّ على من قال به. واتّبعه على ذلك بعض أصحابه، وقال بعضهم: نتّبعه في كلّ شيءٍ، ونقول بقوله فيه إلا في نهيه عن التقليد. فإنا نخالفه فيه ونقلّده.

that even Shāfiʿī used to give legal opinions by exercising his *ra'y* and *istiḥsān*.[86] What should be noted is that Nuʿmān does not give any credit to these major figures for their efforts in developing certain principles for resolving new issues and only ridicules them.[87]

Having criticised his opponents, Nuʿmān expected that the same accusation of *taqlīd* could be levelled against him and the Shiʿa. Hence, he sets out to distinguish between the forms of *taqlīd*. He states that the followers of the various schools of Sunni jurisprudence adhered to the legal decisions of their leaders even though they were deduced through personal opinion without any textual evidence from the Qur'an or the *sunna* of the Messenger of God. Some of these legal opinions concern serious matters related to religion, namely whether they are lawful or unlawful. The Qur'an strictly forbids speculation in regards to religious matters and what is lawful and unlawful. God says: *And do not say, because of what your tongues falsely describe, 'this is lawful, and this is forbidden,' so that you may invent falsehood against God. Those who invent falsehood against God will not prosper. A brief enjoyment – and then they will have a painful punishment* (Q.16:116–117). Nuʿmān states that issuing legal opinions based on analogy or logical deduction amounts to introducing innovation (*bidʿa*) in religion and it contravenes what the Qur'an has just stated in the above verse. God also says: *Follow what has been sent down to you from your Lord and do not follow friends to His exclusion. Little you are reminded* (Q.7:3). Addressing his adversaries Nuʿmān asks, 'What will you say to God on the Day of Judgement when your own leaders will disown you for following them?' Nuʿmān reminds them that they will face a similar scenario, referred to in the Qur'an when the Almighty says: *When those who were followed disown those who follow them, and they see the doom and their cords are severed with them, and those who followed say, 'If only we might have another turn so that we might disown them, and they have disowned us!'* (Q.2:166–167)

Nuʿmān then asserts that the Shiʿa follow their Imams as models to be emulated and to seek their guidance with regards to matters they do not possess knowledge of. In doing so, they simply obey the commands of God when He says: *Ask the people* [*who have*] *the reminder* (*ahl al-dhikr*) *if you do not know* (Q.16:43), and *Obey God and obey the Messenger and those of you who have authority* (*uli'l-amr*) (Q.4:59). The Messenger of God also said, 'I am leaving among you two things; the Book of God and my kindred (*ʿitratī*), the People of my House (*ahl baytī*). As long as you will adhere to them, you will never be led astray, because these two shall never be separated until they return to me at the Pool.'[88] Nuʿmān reiterates, 'The Imams are the custodians of the secret knowledge of revelation. This knowledge they pass on from one generation to the next and they do not resort to *ra'y*, *ijtihād*, *qiyās* or *istiḥsān*.'

---

[86] It should be noted that Shāfiʿī argued against *istiḥsān*, see *al-Risāla*, pp. 25, 503 ff.; tr. *Al-Shāfiʿī's Risāla*, pp. 70, 304 ff.

[87] Nuʿmān repeated these reports in *The Pillars of Islam*, vol. 1, pp. 107–122, wherein he states: 'Subsequently, the question of giving formal legal opinions was restricted among the commonalty to Abū Ḥanīfa, Mālik, and Shāfiʿī.'

[88] See n. 62 above.

Nuʿmān further clarifies the Ismaili belief about the Imams by distancing himself from the extreme Shiʿa. He identifies a tradition from Jaʿfar al-Ṣādiq who was asked about what the Shiʿa say with regards to the Imams. The Imam asked him about it and the inquisitor said, 'Some of them say, "The Imam receives revelation"; others say, "[Divine words] resonate in the Imam's ear"; others say, "The Imam sees [the angels] in dreams"; and others say, "The Imam is inspired when he gives his legal decision"; yet others say, "The Imam is visited by Gabriel." Which, therefore, of their assertions should I then take to be the truth, may I be thy ransomed?' Jaʿfar al-Ṣādiq said, 'Praise the Lord, the Exalted, from such statements of the liars and the ignorant! Do not take anything of what they say as the truth. Rather the things permitted by us are taken from the Book of God, and likewise are the things prohibited by us.'[89]

Nuʿmān reiterates that the *uli'l-amr* and *ahl al-dhikr* are not the *fuqahā'* as they allege. Nuʿmān then calls the reader's attention to the Sunni caliphs and remarks, 'Look at their caliphs, how ignorant they were! Abū Bakr, the first caliph, in his first public address said, "I have been given authority over you, although I am not the best among you. If I err, then correct me."'[90] Nuʿmān asks rhetorically, 'Is it considered an admirable trait of one who assumes the leadership of the community?' This quote infers that Nuʿmān certainly did not believe so. Nuʿmān reports that addressing a crowd of people ʿUmar b. al-Khaṭṭāb, the second caliph, once said from the pulpit, 'O people, do not overdo what is given to your wives as dowries, for if this were something to be desired in society or a pious act in the eyes of God, the Messenger of God would have been the first to act in this way. But he never gave a dowry in excess of 500 dirhams.' Thereupon a woman standing among the last rows of the assembly rose and said, 'O Commander of the Believers, why do you deny the rights God granted us? He says: *And [if] you have given one of them [your wives] a large sum, take nothing from it.*' (Q.4:20) Whereupon ʿUmar lapsed into silence and could not reply. Then he turned to those present and said, 'You heard me making an error and you did not contest it, while a woman has refuted me.'[91] Nuʿmān states that he does not want to elaborate further on ʿUmar's ignorance about the Qur'an and its injunctions. He simply refers to the quote that he himself acknowledged and said, 'But for ʿAlī, ʿUmar would surely have perished.'[92] This demonstrates the situation with their caliphs.

Nuʿmān then cites numerous verses of the Qur'an that are generally interpreted by the Shiʿa as referring to the Imams. Let me present some examples. In *sūrat al-nisā'* He says: *Or do they envy the people for what God has given them of His bounty?* (Q.4:54). Nuʿmān states that 'the people envied' are the Imams because God has bestowed the imamate on them.[93] In the same *sūra* He says: *God commands you to pay back to their owners things entrusted to you and to judge fairly if you judge*

---

[89] See also *The Pillars of Islam*, vol. 1, pp. 66–67; the inquisitor is identified as Sadīr al-Ṣayrafī.

[90] Ibid., vol. 1, p. 105; older sources are indicated there.

[91] Ibid., vol. 1, pp. 104–105.

[92] Ibid., vol. 1, p. 106.

[93] Ibid., vol. 1, p. 28. Additional sources are indicated there.

between the people (Q.4:58).[94] The fragment 'to pay back the things entrusted,' is in reference to the Imams who return the knowledge, the books and the weapons entrusted to them and their successors.[95] Again in the same *sūra* He says: *O you who believe, obey God and obey the Messenger and those of you who have authority* (Q.4:59). The phrase, 'those of you in authority' refers to the Imams.[96] In *sūrat al-māʾida* He says: *Your protector is God and His Messenger, and those who believe: those who perform prayer and pay the zakāt and bow down* (Q.5:55). This verse was revealed with regard to ʿAlī who was the foremost among the Imams.[97] In *sūrat al-ʿankabūt* the Almighty says: *No. It is clear signs in the breasts of those who have been given knowledge* (Q.29:49). The phrase, 'those who have been given knowledge' is also in reference to the Imams.[98] In *sūrat al-raʿd* God says: *You are simply a warner; and for every people there is a guide* (Q.13:7). The phrase, 'You are simply a warner' refers to the Messenger of God; and in every age there is an Imam from the progeny of the Prophet to guide the community towards the message brought by him.[99] In *sūrat āl ʿImrān* He says: *Only God knows its interpretation and those who are well grounded in knowledge* (Q.3:5). Once again, 'those who are well grounded in knowledge' is in reference to the Imams.[100] In *sūrat al-naḥl* He says: *Ask the people [who have] the reminder* (Q.16:43). The expression, 'the people of the reminder' is in reference to the Imams.[101] Nuʿmān concludes this chapter and reiterates that what he has illustrated above is a clear distinction between *taqlīd* and *taṣdīq*. The former consists of blindly following their 'leaders' and 'jurists' who were not supposed to [mis]lead them, while the latter consists of giving credence to what is stated in the Qurʾan and submitting to the appropriate designated authorities for guidance.

At this juncture, I would like add a few comments. The word *taqlīd* generally carries the negative connotation of blind following. It plays an important role in the religious sciences of Islam during the classical period and is a part of any debate concerning authority and epistemology from the earliest of times to modern Islamic discourse.[102] As noted above by Nuʿmān, al-Muzanī (d. 264/878, Shāfiʿī's chief disciple and an outstanding jurist and dialectician) confirms that his master had prohibited *taqlīd* of either himself or other jurisconsults (*muftīs*).[103] This statement of Shāfiʿī implies that a learned *faqīh* should not simply follow his opinions but should understand his arguments and the basis for expressing such a view. However, Nuʿmān glosses over the implications of Shāfiʿī's statement and for the sake of his

---

94 Nuʿmān clarifies this further in *The Pillars of Islam*, vol. 1, p. 28. He states that the verse refers to the imamate/caliphate; hence it means when the Imams gain political power, they should rule the domain equitably.

95 For details, see ibid.

96 Ibid., p. 29.

97 Ibid.

98 Ibid, p. 30. Older sources are indicated there.

99 Ibid.

100 Ibid., p. 31.

101 Ibid., pp. 30, 37, 98.

102 N. Calder, *EI2*, 'Taḳlīd', vol. 10, pp. 137–138.

103 Ibid; see also Hallaq, 'Was al-Shāfiʿī the Master Architect of Islamic Jurisprudence?' pp. 590–591, 594, 598; Hallaq, *History*, p. 33.

argument only presents it as a warning against *taqlīd*. It should be noted that Shāfiʿī's distrust of *taqlīd* in juristic matters is reflected in the works of the Ẓāhirī school's jurist, Ibn Ḥazm. In *al-Iḥkām*, Ibn Ḥazm states that one should return to the evident meaning of the tradition and should not follow the traditional authorities, which he refers to as *taqlīd*.[104] Ibn Qutayba, a staunch traditionist, is very cautious in his selection of words when he compares and contrasts the views of the *aṣḥāb al-kalām wa-aṣḥāb al-raʾy* (i.e., the rationalists, the Muʿtazila) and the *aṣḥāb al-ḥadīth* (traditionists). In describing how the latter group achieved consensus on the basic principles of faith through revelation and submission to the acknowledged authorities of the *ʿulamāʾ* and the *fuqahāʾ*, Ibn Qutayba avoids use of the word *taqlīd*. On the other hand, he accuses the Muʿtazila of labelling others as the followers of traditional authorities (*yattahimūna ghayrahum fiʾl-naql*), since it was against their rational principle of *ʿaql*.[105] Also one should differentiate between *taqlīd* in juristic matters and *taqlīd* in credal matters, but this matter is beyond the scope of this chapter.

An Account of *Aṣḥāb al-ijmāʿ* and their Refutation[106]

The Sunni schools of jurisprudence maintain that the doctrine of *ijmāʿ* is one of the fundamental principles of Islamic law and therefore must be followed and obeyed. They consider it unlawful to oppose *ijmāʿ*. Thus, some jurists who assert this position, Nuʿmān states, consider those who dissent from their view as infidels. Their argument for the justification of the doctrine of *ijmāʿ* is chiefly based on their interpretation of the term *umma*, which occurs in the Qurʾan on several occasions. The verses generally cited to legitimise *ijmāʿ* are as follows. God says: *Thus We have made you a moderate community (ummat^an wasaṭ^an) for you to be witnesses (shuhadāʾ) to the people and for the Messenger to be a witness to you* (Q.2:143). In another passage He says: *He has chosen you and has not laid upon you any difficulty in your religion, the faith of your forefather Abraham. He has named you 'those who surrender' (al-muslimīn) both previously and in this* [*Recitation*], *that the Messenger*

[104] Ibn Ḥazm, *al-Iḥkām fī uṣūl al-aḥkām*, vol. 6, *al-Bāb al-sādis waʾl-thalālūn fī ibṭāl al-taqlīd*. In this long chapter entitled 'On invalidating blind imitation' (p. 123), Ibn Ḥazm states:
ويكفي من هذا أنّ كلّ ما ذكرنا من الفقهاء الذين قلّدوا مبطلون للتقليد، ناهون عنه، مانعون منه، مخبرون أنّ فاعله على باطل. وقد حدّثنا حمام عن الباجي عن أسلم القاضي عن المازني عن الشافعي أنّه نهى الناس عن تقليده وتقليد غيره. وحدّثنا عبد الرحمن بن سلمة ... قال: سمعتُ مالكاً وقال له ابن القاسم: ليس أحد بعد أهل المدينة أعلم بالبيوع من أهل مصر. قال له مالك: من أين علموا ذلك؟ قال: منك، يا أبا عبد الله. قال مالك: ما أعلمها أنا، فكيف يعلمونها هم؟ قال أبو محمد: كيف، وقد أغنانا الله تعالى عن قولهم في ذلك بما نصّ في كتابه من إبطال التقليد؟ فمن ذلك قول الله عزّ وجلّ: ﴿مَثَلُ ٱلَّذِينَ ٱتَّخَذُواْ مِن دُونِ ٱللَّهِ أَوْلِيَآءَ كَمَثَلِ ٱلْعَنكَبُوتِ ٱتَّخَذَتْ بَيْتًا وَإِنَّ أَوْهَنَ ٱلْبُيُوتِ لَبَيْتُ ٱلْعَنكَبُوتِ﴾ [سورة العنكبوت ٢٩:٤١]. ثم قال الله تعالى على أثر هذه الآية: ﴿وَتِلْكَ ٱلْأَمْثَٰلُ نَضْرِبُهَا لِلنَّاسِ وَمَا يَعْقِلُهَآ إِلَّا ٱلْعَٰلِمُونَ﴾ [سورة العنكبوت ٢٩:٤٣].

[105] Ibn Qutayba, *Taʾwīl mukhtalaf al-ḥadīth* (Beirut, 2004), pp. 12–14.

[106] For the concept of *ijmāʿ* see M. Bernard, 'Idjmāʿ', *EI2*, vol. 3, pp. 1023–1026; Hallaq, *History*, *passim*; Hallaq, *Origins*, *passim*.

may be a witness (shahīd^an) against you and that you may be witnesses (shuhadāʾ) against the rest of mankind (Q.22:78).[107] He also states: *Those who believe in God and His messengers – they are the loyal ones (ṣiddīqūn) and the witnesses (shuhadāʾ) with their Lord* (Q.57:19). He further says: *You are the best community (khayra ummat^in) brought forth for the people. You enjoin what is reputable and you forbid what is disreputable and you believe in God* (Q.3:110).

Consequently, the Sunnis allege that the word *umma,* mentioned by God in His Book refers to the community of Muḥammad and made to bear witness (*shuhadāʾ*) to the entire Muslim community. They further allege that the word *muʾminīn* (i.e., the active participle of those who believe in God and His messengers), mentioned in the above verse and further characterised by two additional traits of being *ṣiddīqīn* and *shuhadāʾ*, also applies to the entire Muslim community. Nuʿmān unequivocally disagrees with these sweeping generalisations and argues that it is ridiculous, irrational and unbelievable that the whole Muslim community can be characterised as *muʾminīn, ṣiddīqīn* and *shuhadāʾ*, for the simple reason that any community is comprised of a variety of people, good and evil, learned and ignorant, guided and misguided, gracious and barbaric, and obedient and rebellious. According to Nuʿmān, all those categories of people cannot be identified as honest and righteous, or with the traits mentioned in the Qurʾan.

Nuʿmān adds that when God characterised the community of Muḥammad as 'a moderate community,' certainly He meant that it possesses the characteristics of justice, fairness and honesty. If that is the case, Nuʿmān asks, 'How can certain jurists assert that all Muslims are qualified to be included in the community of Muḥammad?' Nuʿmān continues that the aforementioned verse further characterises the community of Muḥammad as one, which invites people to goodness – enjoins what is approved and forbids the opposite (*taʾmurūna biʾl-maʿrūf wa-tanhawna ʿan al-munkar*). Thus, how can one who is deficient in those characteristics be counted as representing the community, which the Almighty has described, when in fact he represents quite the contrary of what God has stipulated for that community? Nuʿmān states that if the jurists believe that the above verse pertained to all the Muslims then it carries serious implications for God's justice. For example, when the testimony of some Muslims is unacceptable even in the matter of a small measure of dates, how could they act as a witness for mankind on the Day of Judgement? Nuʿmān asserts that it will be a mockery of God's justice and certainly it cannot happen.

Elsewhere in the Qurʾan concerning the issue of the community, there is the verse about which Abraham had prayed, God says: *You are the best community (khayra ummat^in) brought forth for the people* (Q.3:110). If God had meant by this verse that all Muslims were 'the best community', then it would not have been clear about which people the Muslims had been brought forth. God never intended for

[107] I have preferred George Sale's translation, *The Koran: Translated into English from the Original Arabic*, with an introduction by Sir Edward Denison Ross (London, n.d.), p. 335. Alan Jones translation of this verse is incorrect. Richard Bell, Yusuf Ali and A. J. Arberry have also rendered it correctly.

those who are considered to be riff-raff and rabble to be counted among the community of Muḥammad.

Nuʿmān then proceeds by explaining the linguistic meaning and the Qur'anic usage of the term *umma*. He argues that in addition to being a collective noun, the word *umma* is also applied to a single person. A good example of such a usage in the Qur'an is when God states: *Abraham was a nation obedient (ummatan qānitan) to God* (Q.16:120).[108] Nuʿmān further demonstrates from its Qur'anic usage that the word *umma* has multiple nuances and is used with different meanings and in different contexts. In addition to denoting a community of humans, it also represents a community of beasts and birds. For example God states: *There is no beast in the earth nor bird that flies with its wings but they are communities (umam) like you* (Q.6:38). In another *sūra* He says: *The people were one community (ummatan wāḥidatan)* (Q.2:213). In the chapter on Joseph, it is used to indicate a period of unspecified time. God states: *The one of the two who had been saved [now] remembered after a time (baʿda ummatin)* (Q.12:45). Nuʿmān also points out that some people without naming them, on the other hand, argue that the word *umma* means a group of the *ʿulamāʾ* and not the whole community. To support their contention, they cite the Qur'anic verse, which states: *Let there be a community from you, summoning [people] to good (wa'l-takun minkum ummatun yadʿūna ila'l-khayr)* (Q.3:104).

Marshalling his evidence from the Qur'an, Nuʿmān argues further that the above positive description of the *umma* cannot be extended to include a great majority of the Muslim community. The plurality of the people is generally negatively characterised in the Qur'an. For example, God says: *Except those who believe [in God] and do good works, and they are few (qalīlun mā hum)* (Q.38:24); *But most of them are ignorant (aktharahum yajhalūn)* (Q.6:11); and *But most of them do not know (aktharahum lā yaʿlamūn)* (Q.6:37, 7:131, 8:34, 10:55, 28:13, 39:49, 44:39, 52:47); and *Most of them do not understand (aktharahum lā yaʿqilūn)* (Q.5:103, 29:63); and *But they are not aware (wa-mā yashʿurūn)* (Q.2:9, 3:69, 6:26, 123); and *But most of the people are not believers (wa-mā akthar al-nās bi-mu'minīn), even if you are eager for that* (Q.12:103); and *And most of them do not believe in God (aktharuhum mushrikūn) unless they associate others with Him* (Q.12:106).

Finally, Nuʿmān argues that the word *umma*, used to indicate the community of Muḥammad in the above verses with positive traits, is the community that solely constitutes the members of the Prophet's family and the Imams from their progeny. Nuʿmān adds that the word of God is the most veracious of those that speak in this matter. He then connects the emergence of the Muslim community (that is, submissive to God's commands), in its strict and narrow sense, to the prayer of Abraham and Ishmael. Nuʿmān knows very well how Abraham is portrayed in the Qur'an. It says: *Abraham was neither a Jew nor a Christian. He was a man of pure faith, one who surrendered. He was not one of those who associate others with God* (Q.3:67). Nuʿmān thereafter elaborates on the prayers of Abraham and God's response in the

[108] I have preferred Marmaduke Pickthall's translation in *The Meaning of The Glorious Koran: An Explanatory Translation* (London, 1969) to retain the word *umma*. Jones has translated the *umma* as 'an example'. See also Nuʿmān, *The Pillars of Islam*, vol. 1. pp. 43 ff.

following verses when God says: *When Abraham was tested by his Lord with certain words, and he fulfilled them. God said, 'I am making you a leader for the people.' Abraham said, 'And of my seed?' God replied, 'My covenant does not extend to those who do wrong' … And when Abraham and Ishmael were raising the foundations of the house,* [*Abraham said*], *'Our Lord, accept* [*this*] *from us … and make from our seed a community that will surrender to You'* (Q.2:124–128).

Nuʿmān adds that God responded to the supplication of Abraham and Ishmael by establishing from their seed a community submissive to God, and to send them a messenger from among them, that is, from that submissive community, a messenger who would recite His signs to them, and purify them and instruct them in the Book and wisdom.[109] This, according to Nuʿmān, constitutes irrefutable evidence, which demonstrates that the Imams and the Muslim community to which Muḥammad was sent can only be from the progeny of Abraham and Ishmael. To further support his contention, Nuʿmān cites additional verses from *sūrat al-Baqara* to demonstrate that the *Ahl al-bayt* are the intended people of the joint prayer of Abraham and Ishmael (Q.2:128–143), because in addition to the Messenger of God, his *Ahl al-bayt*, that is ʿAlī, Fāṭima, Ḥasan and Ḥusayn, did not serve idols.

Nuʿmān concludes this chapter by drawing the reader's attention to another dimension of the Qur'anic studies, namely that certain words such as *umma,* are often used in a 'general sense' (*maʿnā ʿāmma*), but a 'specific meaning' (*maʿnā khāṣṣa*) is sometimes intended.[110] Space and time do not permit me to go into more of the details elaborated by Nuʿmān in the two additional chapters on *ijmāʿ*. Briefly, a wide variety of opinions regarding the modes of its justification (*ḥujjiyya*) which existed at that time are enumerated and refuted by Nuʿmān. Unfortunately, most of the early sources on this subject did not survive. Between Shāfiʿī's *Risāla* and Nuʿmān's work there is a gap of more than a century. In the opinion of this writer, the importance of Nuʿmān's work, therefore, lies in the fact that it fills a major lacuna in our knowledge about that period. The *Ikhtilāf* presents a variegated picture that had not yet clearly emerged. Therefore it is worthwhile to give a summary of what the *Ikhtilāf* depicts in those two chapters. Let me first state that the overwhelming view one gets from reading the *Ikhtilāf* is that the facts on the ground were quite different from what one is made to believe by the later sources. In

---

[109] See also Nuʿmān, *The Pillars of Islam*, vol. 1, pp. 43 ff.

[110] Nuʿmān, *Ikhtilāf*, p. 79; he states:

إذا كان اسم الجماعة يقع عليهم كلّهم، ويقع على بعضهم كما بيّنّا ذلك في الأمّة والمؤمنين والناس في غير ذلك من العامّ الذي يراد به الخاصّ.

According to Shāfiʿī it is: the explicit general declaration of the Book intended to be all particular.

بيان ما نزل من الكتاب عامّ الظاهرِ يُراد به كلّهِ الخاصُّ.

See Shāfiʿī, *al-Risāla*, pp. 58–62; tr. *Al-Shāfiʿī's Risāla*, pp. 99–101. See also al-Suyūṭī, *al-Itqān fī ʿulūm al-Qurʾān*, ed. Muḥammad Abu'l-Faḍl (Beirut, 1988), vol. 3, pp. 44–49; he states:

العامّ على ثلاثة أقسام: الأول: الباقي على عمومه، لم يرد شموله لجميع الأفراد، لا من جهة تناول اللفظ، ولا من جهة الحكم، بل هو ذو أفراد استعمل في فرد منها. والثاني: العامّ المراد به الخصوص، أُريد عمومه وشموله لجميع الأفراد من جهة تناول اللفظ لها، لا من جهة الحكم. والثالث: العامّ المخصوص.

several ways the situation was fluid and a wide variety of opinions circulated as depicted by Hallaq first in his *History* and later in his *Origins*. The importance traditionally given to Shāfiʿī's *Risāla* in the development of the science of *uṣūl al-fiqh* seems to be overstated. The *Risāla*, in the words of Chaumont, remained a dead letter for more than a century.[111]

There was a lot of discord among the jurists concerning the evidence, generally known in Arabic sources as the *ḥujjiyya*, on which the *ijmāʿ* should be established. Some jurists asserted that it should only be predicated on the textual evidence of the Qur'an and the *sunna*, while others maintained that it should be based on the *ijmāʿ* of the Companions only because of their precedence in accepting Islam and their pre-eminence over the later generations of Muslims. Jurists further argued that it was this group that the Qur'anic references with the traits of *al-shuhadā'*, *al-ṣiddīqīn* and *ummat*^an^ *wasaṭ*^an^ refer to.

Other jurists debated the definition of *ijmāʿ* – should it be defined as a consensus of all the Muslims, or only of one group rather than another? Yet others argued that it should be restricted to the agreement/consensus of a few, rather than extending it to include the majority, because the majority of the people are ignorant. Those who argued that *ijmāʿ* was inclusive cited a tradition of the Prophet that states, 'God's hand is with the majority.'[112] They also report another tradition which states, 'Indeed, Satan is in the [company of] one [person], but he is far removed from [the company of] two or more people.'[113] Nuʿmān adds that this is precisely the belief of the Ḥashwiyya[114] and the Nawāṣib.[115] Then, Nuʿmān indicates that there are those who limit the application of the term *umma* to a smaller group within the commu-

---

[111] Chaumont, 'al-Shāfiʿī;' Hallaq, 'Was al-Shāfiʿī the Master Architect?'

[112] يد اللّٰه على الجماعة. It is transmitted by Tirmidhī and Nasā'ī. Wensinck, *Concordance*, s.v. j-m-ʿ. Ibn Qutayba, *Ta'wīl mukhtalaf al-ḥadīth*, p. 5.

[113] Nuʿmān, *Ikhtilāf*, p. 84; he states:

وعليكم بالجماعة فإن الشيطان مع الواحد، وهو من الاثنين أبعد.

In the *aḥādīth* sources it reads:

الشيطان مع من فارق الجماعة، أو إن الشيطان مع الواحد.

This tradition is transmitted by Ibn Ḥanbal, Tirmidhī and Nasā'ī. Wensinck, *Concordance*, s.v. j-m-ʿ; sh-ṭ-n. See also Shāfiʿī, *al-Risāla*, p. 474; tr. *al-Shāfiʿī's Risāla*, p. 286; Shāfiʿī, *Kitāb al-umm* (Beirut, 2005), vol. 1, p. 109; he states:

... فليلزم الجماعة، فإن الشيطان مع الفذّ، وهو من الاثنين أبعد.

[114] Ḥashwiyya is a contemptuous term with the meaning of 'scholars' of little worth, particularly ultra-traditionists (*aṣḥāb al-ḥadīth/ahl al-ḥadīth*) who interpret the Qur'an and *ḥadīth* literally in anthropomorphic language. Editor/s, 'Ḥashwiyya', *EI2*, vol. 3, p. 269; A. S. Halkin, 'The Ḥashwiyya', *JAOS*, 54 (1934), pp. 1–28.

[115] In his *Kitāb al-zīna* (MS collection of Asghar Ali Engineer's father, Bombay, fols. 176–177), Abū Ḥātim al-Rāzī states that the Prophet appointed (*naṣaba*) ʿAlī as his successor at Ghadīr al-Khumm, but the Muslims displayed enmity towards him (*nāṣaba*) after the death of the Prophet and appointed someone other than ʿAlī to succeed the Prophet. The term is therefore applied to those who bear hatred towards the family of the Prophet. However, according to Sunni sources the above appellation applies to the Khawārij who made it a matter of religious obligation to bear hatred towards ʿAlī. See also Nuʿmān, *Daʿā'im*, *The Pillars of Islam*, vol. 1, pp. 190–191.

nity. To vindicate their contention they cite verses from the Qur'an that equate the majority of the people with negative attributes.

Without giving specific names, Nuʿmān states that some people from Baghdad argue that *ijmāʿ* should be established by *naql*, that is, based on sound reports transmitted by uninterrupted authorities dating back to the Prophet. This group asserts that *ijmāʿ* cannot be based on *ra'y*, *ijtihād* or *qiyās*. Yet, others from Baghdad assert that *ijmāʿ* can be established only when all the Muslims (*ahl al-qibla*) agree on a particular matter/issue. If just one person dissents from their view, that *ijmāʿ* is nullified. Some others argue against such a rigid position and maintained that a consensus arrived at by a majority is valid despite disagreement from one person or a small group of people.

Another disagreement among Muslims that Nuʿmān identifies concerned the time when *ijmāʿ* had been achieved. Was it at the end of each century, or by each generation? Does a living jurist's agreement or disagreement count, or does the jurist's opinion only count after his death? The rationale behind such reasoning, Nuʿmān adds, is the probability that a living jurist might change his mind and revoke his agreement at any time as we have previously noted in the cases of both Abū Ḥanīfa and Shāfiʿī. Others claimed that *ijmāʿ* was successfully achieved by every generation or during each era even if it diverged from that of the previous generation or era.

Another disagreement ensued concerning *ijmāʿ* and its relation to a location or region. Mālik b. Anas and his followers alleged that the Muslims should follow the people of Medina because it was the Messenger of God's abode (*dār al-hijra*) following his emigration to Medina. Consequently, the people of Medina were more knowledgeable than any other group about the *sunna* of the Messenger of God.[116] Nuʿmān flatly rejects this justification and cites several Qur'anic verses to illustrate that Medina was inhabited and surrounded by all sorts of people (i.e., Bedouins, hypocrites and the Jews). It is reported that Mālik once visited Iraq, and in some of his remarks he belittled the inhabitants of Iraq for their lack of religious knowledge (*ʿilm*, i.e., knowledge of the textual sources of Islam). Some of those who heard Mālik's criticism retorted by saying that a number of the Companions, such as ʿAlī b. Abī Ṭālib, ʿAbd Allāh b. ʿAbbās[117] and ʿAbd Allāh b. Masʿūd[118] lived among them. So they did not lack the knowledge (*ʿilm*) that Mālik claimed. In his rejoinder Mālik reported a concocted tradition which states: 'Indeed, Medina exiles/ejects her wicked people as a blacksmith's bellows blow away the impurities of iron ore.'[119]

---

116 See Shāfiʿī, *Kitāb al-umm*, chapter on *ikhtilāf Mālik wa'l-Shāfiʿī*, vol. 2, pp. 2775 ff.

117 He is considered one of the greatest scholars of the first generation of Muslims. L. Veccia Vaglieri, "Abd Allāh b. al-ʿAbbās', *EI2*, vol. 1, pp. 40–41.

118 He was a Companion of the Prophet and reader of the Qur'an. J. Vadet, 'Ibn Masʿūd', *EI2*, vol. 3, pp. 873–875.

119 Nuʿmān, *Ikhtilāf*, pp. 99–100; it states:

فقال مالك، إن رسول الله صلى الله عليه وعلى آله قال: إن المدينة تنفي خبثها كما تنفي الكيرُ خَبَثَ الحديد.

It is transmitted by Bukhārī, Abū Dāwūd, Nasā'ī, Ibn Māja, Mālik and Ibn Ḥanbal, see Wensinck, Concordance, s.v. kh-b-th. It states:

المدينة تنفي الناسَ كما ينفي الكيرُ خبثَ الحديد.

Nuʿmān adds that Mālik not only lied but also fabricated the above tradition and ascribed it to the Messenger of God. Similarly, others made the same claims asserting that their definition of *ijmāʿ* was the only valid one. Such was the case with the people of the Ḥijāz that comprised the inhabitants of the two *ḥarams*, Mecca and Medina. The people of Iraq, namely the people of Kūfa and Baṣra, made similar claims. All those people based their claims on the fact that many of the Companions lived in those cities. Some people, on the other hand, maintained that the valid *ijmāʿ* is the one that was agreed upon by Mālik, Abū Ḥanīfa, Shāfiʿī, Awzāʿī[120] and their followers.

Nuʿmān concludes his discussion concerning *ijmāʿ* with a popular tradition of the Messenger of God, which is cited by almost all the heresiographers.[121] It states: 'The Israelites were divided into 72 sects and my community will be divided into 73 sects, only one group will be redeemed while the rest will perish.' People asked the Prophet, 'Which is the group that will be saved?' And he replied, '*Ahl al-sunna wa'l-jamāʿa*.' Thereupon people further asked him, 'What is the *sunna* and what is the *jamāʿa*?' He responded, 'That is what I myself and my Companions follow and practise today.'[122] Nuʿmān asserts that not a single Companion exercised either *ra'y*, *qiyās*, *naẓar*, *istiḥsān*, *ijtihād* or *istidlāl* with respect to *dīn Allāh*, that is, Islam, as long as the Messenger of God was alive. Nuʿmān further affirms that he and his group, namely, the Shiʿa-Ismailis, are the true representatives of *Ahl al-sunna wa'l-jamāʿa* because they have adhered both to the *sunna* of the Messenger of God and his *jamāʿa*, that is, the *Ahl al-bayt* and the rightful Imams.[123]

Let me add a few comments on the concept of *ijmāʿ*, ranked as the third principle, but in practice is the most important underpinning in Islamic law according to the classical theory of *uṣūl al-fiqh*. In fact the two scriptural sources – the text of Qur'an and *sunna* – in the final analysis were authenticated through *ijmāʿ*.[124] Thus, *ijmāʿ* takes precedence over both the Qur'an and the *sunna*. In theory *ijmāʿ* is defined as the unanimous agreement/consensus of the Muslim community on a particular *ḥukm* (legal ruling) imposed by God. Technically, however, it is the consensus of the recognised jurists at a given time in history. Historically, the concept of *ijmāʿ* as a source of law and a tool validating a *ḥukm* in light of the truth given by the Qur'an and the *sunna* of the Prophet arose out of the growing need of the community, especially after the conquests and the increasing pressures brought on the community by the sectarian dissensions within Islam. The need for such a

[120] He was the main representative of the ancient Syrian school of Islamic law. Joseph Schacht, 'Awzāʿī', *EI2*, vol. 1, p. 772–773; Hallaq, *Origins*, pp. 107, 154, 156, 166, 171.

[121] See, for example, ʿAbd al-Qāhir al-Baghdādī, *al-Farq bayn al-firaq*, ed. Muḥammad Muḥy al-Dīn (Cairo, n.d.), pp. 5–7; Muḥammad ʿAbd al-Karīm al-Shahrastānī, *Kitāb al-milal wa'l-niḥal*, ed. ʿAbd al-ʿAzīz Muḥammad al-Wakīl (Cairo, 1968), p. 11.

[122] This tradition is transmitted with a slight variation of words by Abū Dāwūd, Tirmidhī, Ibn Māja, Ibn Ḥanbal, Wensinck, *Concordance*, s.v. j-m-ʿ; f-r-q.

[123] In his *Kitāb al-zīna* (see ʿAbd Allāh al-Sāmarrā'ī, *al-Ghuluww wa'l-firaq al-ghāliya fi'l-ḥaḍāra al-Islāmiyya*, Baghdad, 1972, pp. 252–256), Abū Ḥātim al-Rāzī also makes the claim that he and his group belong to the *ahl al-sunna wa'l-jamāʿa*.

[124] Fazlur Rahman, *Islam* (London, 1966), p. 74; Hallaq, *Origins*, pp. 128 ff.; Hallaq, *History*, pp. 75 ff.

principle was necessary following the Prophet's death because the point of reference in legislative matters, that is, the Messenger of God, the source of revelation, was no longer alive for the community to resort to for a resolution of their problems.

The idea was most probably given its theoretical formulations during the 2nd/8th century. The definition of *ijmāʿ* as a source of law, therefore, raised the question of the probative validity (*ḥujjiyya*) of its very existence. In his *Kitāb uṣūl al-dīn*, ʿAbd al-Qāhir al-Baghdādī acknowledges that *ijmāʿ* for the purposes of *al-ḥukm al-sharʿī* (a legal ruling based on the *sharīʿa*) is limited to the *ijmāʿ* of the community during a specified period of time. The basis of it, he adds is the tradition of the Prophet that states, 'My community will never agree on error.'[125] Al-Baghdādī further states that the Khawārij and the Muʿtazilī theologian al-Naẓẓām rejected the very concept of *ijmāʿ*.[126]

Credit for the development of the concept of *ijmāʿ* is generally attributed to Shāfiʿī when he questioned the idea of the Medinan consensus by indicating the imprecise nature of their concept of 'the usage of Medina'. Thenceforth, Shāfiʿī replaced the Mālikī *ijmāʿ*, which was merely an affirmation of an existing practice and reality that prevailed in Medina, with his assertion of a basic truth of the infallibility of the unanimous pronouncements of the Muslim community.[127] Unfortunately, we do not have the sources at our disposal to trace the history of the development of *ijmāʿ* as a juridical source and other technical issues related to it, such as the *ḥujjiyya* and the method by which an agreement is reached, especially during the intervening period of roughly a century and a half after the death of Shāfiʿī and al-Qāḍī al-Nuʿmān's *Ikhtilāf uṣūl al-madhāhib*, composed around the middle of the 4th/10th century. Another issue of debate was related to the question, 'Can an agreement be reached by word, or deed, or can it be explicitly stated, or simply indicated by one's silence.' Herein lies the importance of Nuʿmān's work, which provides us with a vivid picture of the prevailing currents and counter currents at the time of its composition in the Islamic world.

For the Muʿtazila, who uphold the primacy of reason and with their predisposition towards ethics rather than logic, the principle of *ijmāʿ* was no more than an ethical theory left to the individual believer and his personal convictions. In his *al-Mughnī fī abwāb al-tawḥīd*, al-Qāḍī ʿAbd al-Jabbār takes over the objection raised by al-Naẓẓām, without mentioning his name, and states:

---

[125] ʿAbd al-Qāhir al-Baghdādī, *Kitāb uṣūl al-dīn* (Istanbul, 1928), p. 18; he states:

وأمّا الإجماع المعتبر في الحكم الشرعي فمقصورٌ على إجماع أهل عصرٍ من أعصار هذه الأمّة على حكم شرعي، فإنها لا تجتمع على ضلالةٍ.

The tradition transmitted by Ibn Māja (Wensinck, *Concordance*, s.v. j-m-ʿ) states:

إنّ أمّتي لا تجتمع على ضلالةٍ.

[126] Al-Baghdādī, *Kitāb uṣūl al-dīn*, p. 19. According to Abu'l-Ḥusayn ʿAlī al-Ashʿarī, *Maqālāt al-Islāmiyyīn*, ed. H. Ritter (2nd ed., Wiesbaden, 1963), p. 478, the majority of people agreed that *ijmāʿ* is possible while ʿAbbād (b. Sulaymān) maintained that the community can never come to terms on a matter over which they disagreed. W. Montgomery Watt, "Abbād b. Sulaymān', *EI2*, vol. 1, pp. 4–5; Josef van Ess, 'al-Naẓẓām', *EI2*, vol. 7, pp. 1057–1058.

[127] Shāfiʿī, *Kitāb al-umm*, vol. 2, pp. 275 ff.; the chapter is entitled *Kitāb ikhtilāf Mālik wa'l-Shāfiʿī*.

> As for the demonstration of the legal validity of *ijmāʿ* by reason, it is impossible. Because no evidence can demonstrate that a certain group of people is immune to error in their words or deeds, just as nothing can prove it for each matter of religious obligation. Moreover, there is a distinction between the person who imposes the validity of *ijmāʿ* by means of reason and the person who decides the probative value of disagreement, or ascribes the probative value to the statement of each individual. And this [validity of *ijmāʿ*] is greater in corruption [of public and private life] than the unquestioning acceptance of a doctrine whose validity we have demonstrated before.[128]

For Ibn Ḥazm, a representative of the Ẓāhirī school, *ijmāʿ* was only limited to the Companions.[129] His system of jurisprudence rejects the use of *qiyās* and insists on proof texts, that is, the Qurʾan and the *sunna*. He, therefore, can permit *ijmāʿ* that is derived either from a revealed text or the *sunna* of the Prophet. One can state that the technical issues do not carry much weight in his system because *ijmāʿ* is more or less reabsorbed by the Qurʾan and the *sunna*. The expression *uluʾl-amr* that is often used by Ibn Ḥazm, indicates that the commanders and scholars, at any given time, ought to guide the community by imposing those things which God and His Messenger have commanded. Therefore the problem of the successive generations is resolved and the need to verify the opinions of the whole community in every generation also does not arise with the approach of Ibn Ḥazm.

The Ḥanafīs denounced the Ẓāhirī position. Both Bazdawī[130] and al-Sarakhsī[131] criticise the weakness of the arguments presented by the Ẓāhirīs. Al-Bazdawī, clarifying the import of *umma*, states that the *umma* is understood as only those who have not adopted *ahwāʾ* (pernicious doctrines) and *bidaʿ* (innovations).[132] Once the question of what constitutes *ijmāʿ* is resolved, the issue of the method by which it has arrived at may be tackled. There also is a difference in opinion among the jurists of this school. The differing views state that an agreement on a particular issue can be arrived at by either word (or pronouncement) or deed (or act), and it can be either explicit or indicated by simply observing silence. Since *ijmāʿ* is a

---

[128] Al-Qāḍī ʿAbd al-Jabbār, *al-Mughnī fī abwāb al-tawḥīd*: *al-sharʿiyyāt*, vol. 17 (being a pirated ed., the name of the editor, publisher and year of publication are unavailable), p. 199. The Arabic reads as follows:

فأمّا الاستدلال على صحّة الإجماع من جهة العقل، فبعيدٌ، لأنه لا دليل يدلّ في جماعة مخصوصة على أنهم لا يخطئون فيما يعملون ويقولون، كما لا دليل يدلّ على ذلك في كلّ واحد من المكلّفين. فلا فرق بين من أوجب كون الإجماع حجّة عقلاً وبين من أوجب كون الخلاف حجّة، أو جعل قول كلّ مكلّف حجّة. وهذا أعظم فساداً من التقليد الذي دللنا من قبل على بطلانه.

[129] Ibn Ḥazm, *al-Iḥkām fī uṣūl al-aḥkām*, vol. 4, pp. 128 ff. It is the 22nd chapter with over 100 pages and is entitled: في الإجماع، وعن أيّ شيء يكون الإجماع، وكيف ينقل الإجماع

[130] He is ʿAlī b. Muḥammad b. al-Ḥusayn al-Pazdawī. His *Uṣūl* is printed with ʿAlāʾ al-Dīn al-Bukhārī's *Kashf al-asrār* (reprint, Beirut, 1394/1974).

[131] Muḥammad b. Aḥmad al-Sarakhsī was a Ḥanafī jurist of the 5th/11th century. N. Calder, 'al-Sarakhsī', *EI2*, vol. 9, pp. 35–36.

[132] Al-Ashʿarī, *Maqālāt al-Islāmiyyīn*, p. 478, states that people differed as to whether the discord of *ahl al-ahwāʾ* concerning the *aḥkām* counts or not.

judicial source that allows for the formulation of solutions to new problems that might arise, it is conditioned by the passing of time during which a fresh *ijmāʿ* is formed.

This conditioning process raises another important and vexing question as to whether the formulation of a new *ijmāʿ* requires the disappearance of the past generation or not. Opinions of the major schools are at odds with each other on this issue. For the Mālikīs and the Ẓāhirīs it is not a problem, but the situation varies with other schools. According to Āmidī and his master Shāfiʿī, Abū Ḥanīfa, the Ashāʿira and the Muʿtazila, extinction of a generation was not a necessary condition for the formulation of a new *ijmāʿ*.[133] But, for Ibn Ḥanbal, the formulation of a new *ijmāʿ* is subject to the total disappearance of the past generation.[134] For al-Sarakhsī the disappearance of the generation is not critical because he states that generations overlap and it is not possible to distinguish the end of one from the beginning of the next.[135] Ghazālī, on the other hand, suggests that the existence of *ijmāʿ* occurs when an agreement has taken place, even if only for an instant.[136] In short, *ijmāʿ* was a powerful and useful source to introduce change into the prevailing *status quo.*

An Account of those who Maintain the Doctrine of *Naẓar* and their Refutation[137]

Those who maintain this doctrine state that they resort to *naẓar* and rational argument only for those things that have not been explicitly specified either in the Qur'an or the *sunna* of the Messenger of God. On the other hand, they affirm that whatever is specified in the Book they accept it as commanded by Allāh: *Whatever the Messenger gives you, take it. Whatever he forbids you to have, leave it alone* (Q.59:7). Moreover, they state that if a particular issue could not be validated through the use of *naẓar* they would not accept it. Nuʿmān refutes their claim by asserting that rational arguments are not permitted in religious matters. The Qur'an addresses all things and neglects nothing that is an essential part of religion and human life.[138] The Messenger of God also said: 'Follow [me] and do not innovate.'[139]

---

[133] Al-Āmidī (d. 631/1233), a theologian, was a Ḥanbalī and later became a Shāfiʿī. D. Sourdel, 'al-Āmidī', *EI2*, vol. 1, p. 434.

[134] Al-Āmidī, *al-Iḥkām fī uṣūl al-aḥkām* (Beirut, 1983), vol. 1, p. 367 ff.

[135] Al-Sarakhsī, *Uṣūl al-Sarakhsī*, ed. Abu'l-Wafā' al-Afghānī (Hyderabad, 1953–1954), vol. 1, p. 315.

[136] Al-Ghazālī, *al-Mustaṣfā min ʿilm al-uṣūl* (Beirut, 1994), vol. 1, p. 121.

[137] For the meaning of *naẓar* see n. 49 above.

[138] He restates the Qur'anic verses 6:38, 16:89, 5:3, 16:43 and 4:83. In his *al-Uṣūl min al-kāfī*, ed. ʿAlī Akbar al-Ghaffārī (3rd ed., Tehran, 1388/1968–1969), vol. 1, pp. 59–62, 69–71, Kulaynī maintains the same position and states:

جميع ما يحتاج الناس إليه إلّا وقد جاء فيه كتاب أو سنّة، أو ما من شيءٍ إلّا وفيه كتاب وسنّة.

[139] A tradition transmitted by Dārimī states: اتَّبِعْ ولا تَبَدَّعْ [وقُرِئ تَبْتَدِعْ] . Wensinck, *Concordance*, s.v. t-b-ʿ.

Their main argument for the justification of the use of *naẓar* is based on two Qurʾanic verses that state: *And in yourselves, do you not see*? (Q.51:23)[140] and *Reflect, those of you who have eyes* (Q.59:2).[141] Thus, they argue that God has commanded His servants to reflect and exercise their *naẓar*. Nuʿmān flatly rejects their argument by asserting that those verses do not imply what they allege. If they really reflect back upon themselves they will realise their shortcoming. God did not leave any imperfection in his religion, as they imply, for them to perfect it with their perceptions and rational arguments. God unequivocally states: *Today I have perfected your religion for you and completed My blessing for you and have approved al-islām as a religion for you* (Q.5:3). Messengers of God did not use their *naẓar* in what they preached and what they commanded and forbade. Nuʿmān affirms that the Book and the *sunna* of the Messenger of God categorically rebut their claim, hence he does not see any reason to present additional rational arguments to refute their contention. Since human reasoning based on one's own *naẓar* or *raʾy* has no place in religion, Nuʿmān accuses them of going beyond the pale of Islam. Nuʿmān then cites the story of Moses and Khiḍr narrated in the *sūrat al-kahf* (Q.18:60–82) to support his contention. Moses's impatience in matters beyond his comprehension proved to be incorrect and he had to part with the company of Khiḍr. Furthermore, without going into details, Nuʿmān states that al-Walīd b. al-Mughīra and Abū Ṭālib, who were known for their prudence during the pre-Islamic days, failed to comprehend the Qurʾanic message at the beginning of the Prophet's mission.[142]

If debate was allowed in religious matters, Nuʿmān argues, people would have declared themselves what is *ḥalāl* (lawful) and what is *ḥarām* (unlawful). But God rejected such a position and states: *And do not say, because of what your tongues falsely describe, 'This is lawful, and this is forbidden', so that you may invent falsehood against God* (Q.16:116). He further states: *O people, … do not follow the footsteps of Satan … He [i.e., Satan] commands you … to say about God what you do not know* (Q.2:169). Nuʿmān then refutes their claim that God revealed only the *uṣūl* (basic principles, fundamentals) in the Qurʾan, but entrusted them with the *furūʿ* (secondary, derived matters) to exercise their *ijtihād*.

Another justification they present is that what is validated through *qiyās* is validated through *naẓar*. Nuʿmān states that he has already demonstrated the incorrectness of *qiyās*, hence there is no need to elaborate it here. Finally, he concludes this section by citing the following verses from the Qurʾan. Addressing his Messenger God states: *Do not move your tongue about it to hasten it. Upon Us is its [the Qurʾan] putting together and its recitation. When We recite it, follow its recitation. Upon Us is its explanation* (Q.75:16–19); *and We have sent down to you the reminder (dhikr) for you to make clear to men what has been sent down to them* (Q.16:44); and *Say [O Muḥammad], … I only follow what is revealed to me* (Q.46:9);

---

140 The Arabic reads: أَفَلَا تُبْصِرُونَ.

141 The Arabic reads: فَٱعْتَبِرُوا۟ يَٰٓأُو۟لِى ٱلْأَبْصَٰرِ. This verse is considered to have the greatest bearing upon the authoritativeness of *qiyās*; see Hallaq, *History*, pp. 106, 130. He states that *qiyās* was considered as nothing more than the various forms of arbitrary reasoning characterised as *raʾy* or *naẓar*.

142 Nuʿmān, *Ikhtilāf uṣūl al-madhāhib*, pp. 126–127.

and *Nor does he [the Prophet] speak out of caprice. This is simply a revelation that is being revealed* (Q.53:3–4).

An Account of *Aṣḥāb al-qiyās* and their Refutation[143]

The main argument of this group, like others, for the promotion of *qiyās* as a new judicial source is that the first two material sources, viz., the Qur'an and the *sunna* of the Messenger of God, do not respond to the need for resolving issues not foreseen in those texts and do not define rules applicable to new situations. The task of *qiyās* is therefore to determine rules of procedure which respect the spirit of rules dealt with by the material sources. Consequently, they claim that *qiyās* appeals to the principles of analogical deduction. The use of *qiyās* is therefore only valid in so far as it leads to the discovery of legal ruling for a new case on the basis of the revealed text/s and *ijmāʿ*.[144] Nuʿmān reiterates that he has already refuted such a claim by other groups that the Qur'an does not provide guidelines relevant to new situations; however, in this section he will elaborate specific arguments raised by this group to justify the exercise of *qiyās* and will refute their claims.

At the outset he points out that the *aṣḥāb al-qiyās* are divided into three distinct groups concerning the use of *qiyās* and the range of its application. The first group maintains that it is obligatory to exercise *qiyās* in matters related to the concept of divine unicity (*tawḥīd*) and formulating judicial decisions (*aḥkām*) applicable to new situations. The second group upholds its use only for formulating judicial decisions, while forbidding its use in matters related to the divine unicity. The third group, on the other hand, maintains a position contrary to the second group. Nuʿmān refutes their claim by asserting that the majority of the commonalty (i.e., the Sunni schools of jurisprudence) rejects *qiyās* in matters pertaining either to *tawḥīd* or *aḥkām*. Moreover, he had already refuted a similar claim by other groups that the Qur'an had not foreseen new situations to outline rules of procedure; hence there is no need to replicate.[145]

Next, Nuʿmān grapples with the theory of *qiyās shabah* (analogy of resemblance or similitude) as defined by this group. According to this proposition a case is compared to another case in its similarity, comparing an ordinance to another ordinance, and a judicial decision to another judicial decision. The purpose of the comparison is that an issue should resemble another issue in all aspects, including its meaning (*maʿānī*) and motives (or reasons, *asbāb*). Nuʿmān then poses a question: What happens if a case resembles another case in only some aspects? Do you still exercise analogy or abandon it? If the answer is 'no,' it implies that *qiyās* is invalid, because no two cases in this world resemble each other in every respect.[146]

143 For the meaning of *qiyās* see n. 45 above. Shāfiʿī (*al-Risāla*, p. 477) states that *qiyās* and *ijtihād* are two terms with the same meaning.

144 M. Bernard, 'Ḳiyās,' *EI2*, vol. 5, pp. 238–242; Hallaq, *History*, pp. 82 ff.

145 He refers to the Qur'an and *ḥadīth al-thaqalayn*. See n. 62 above.

146 Nuʿmān, *Ikhtilāf*, p. 138; it reads:

Consequently, he asserts that the same dictum is true of all judicial decisions and God's commands concerning what is lawful and unlawful. Nuʿmān states that after being cornered they might change their position and restate their case that two issues do not have to resemble in each other in all aspects, only in certain aspects. Nuʿmān's response to this shift in their position is that it cannot be permitted. Therefore, he concludes that the theory of *qiyās* is invalid and absurd.

Nuʿmān then moves on to demonstrate that human reason, or speculation regulated to the form of *qiyās shabah,* is also of no avail concerning the rules of *sharīʿa*. The first category of examples he cites consists of similar situations but the rules applicable to them are quite different.[147] For the expiation of oaths, different types of penance are prescribed and one is given several options: one can either feed ten poor people, give them clothing or emancipate a slave.[148] Whereas the punishment for a bandit is that he could be either killed, crucified or have his hands and feet cut off on alternate sides.[149] The fine for a *muḥrim* (a pilgrim assuming the state of ritual consecration) who hunts game is that he shall forfeit the equivalent of that which he had hunted/killed, in terms of domestic animals, or charity or fasting.[150] The second category of examples, on the other hand, deals with dissimilar situations yet the judicial rulings stipulated in all such cases are identical. *Tayammum* (rubbing the face, hands and forearms with clean sand or dust) is obligatory for those who cannot find water after breaking the state of purity by either relieving oneself, dozing off, having a wet dream or polluting oneself after sex.[151]

Next, Nuʿmān criticises Imam Abū Ḥanīfa, the main proponent of the theory of *qiyās*. The conversation between the latter and Imam Jaʿfar al-Ṣādiq ridiculing Abū Ḥanīfa's use of *qiyās* is quite striking. It is reported that once Abū Ḥanīfa al-Nuʿmān b. Thābit al-Kūfī visited Imam Jaʿfar al-Ṣādiq who said to him, 'O Nuʿmān, on what basis do you give a legal ruling?' He responded, 'Based on the Book of Allāh, and what I do not find in it I seek it in the *sunna* of the Messenger of God. Whatever I find neither in the Book of Allāh nor in the *sunna* of the Messenger of God I use deductive reasoning (*qistuhu*) to relate it to what I have found in these sources.' Imam Abū ʿAbd Allāh Jaʿfar al-Ṣādiq said, 'Woe unto you! Surely, the first to rely on

---

ثم سألنا أهل القياس عن معنى القياس عندهم، ما هو؟ فوجدناهم يذهبون فيه إلى تشبيه الشيء بالشيء، وتمثيل الأمر بالأمر، والحكم بالحكم. فيقال لهم: هذا التشبيه الذي شبّهتموه والتمثيل الذي مثّلتموه في الأشياء من بعضها لبعض، هو أن يشبه الشيءُ غيرَهُ من كلّ جهاته وجميع معانيه وأسبابه. فلا تحكمون له بحكمه تقيسونه عليه حتّى يكون كذلك، أم بأن يكون يشبه من بعض الجهات، وإن خالفها في غيرها؟ فإن قالوا: لا نقيس شيئاً على شيءٍ حتّى يكون موافقاً له في التشبيه به، والتمثيل من جميع جهاته، فقد أبطلوا القياس، وتركوا القول به، لأنّ شيئاً لا يكون يشبه شيئاً من كلّ جهاته موجوداً في العالم أبداً من مثل ما مثّلوه، وقاسوا عليه من الأحكام والحلال والحرام.

147 Nuʿmān, *Ikhtilāf*, p. 154; he states:

لمّا رأيتَ الله عزّ وجلّ قد حكم في أشياء متّفقات بأحكام متّفقات، وفي أشياء متّفقات بأحكام مفترقات، وفي أشياء مفترقات بأحكام متّفقات، علمتَ أنّ الأحكام لم تقع من الله تعالى لعللٍ تُدرك بخواطر الآدميين، ولا توقف على حقائقها بالنظير والتخيير.

148 See Nuʿmān, *The Pillars of Islam*, vol. 2, pp. 82–83.

149 Ibid., vol. 2, p. 479.

150 Ibid., vol. 1, pp. 383–388.

151 Ibid., vol. 1, pp. 148–151.

deductive reasoning was Satan and fell into error, for when God commanded him to prostrate himself before Adam, he declared, *I am better than him. You created me from fire and him from mud* (Q.7:12). He used deductive reasoning and assumed that fire (as an element) was nobler than earth. He further presumed that who is created from a nobler element is better than the one who is created from an inferior element'. Then the Imam asked him, 'O Nuʿmān, which of the two is nearer to cleanliness, semen or urine?' Abū Ḥanīfa replied, 'Semen, but I don't say that they are alike.' The Imam said, 'Why then did God decreed ablution after [the flow of] urine, and a ritual bath after [the extrusion of] semen? Don't you think that according to your reasoning the ruling should have been quite contrary, or the same ruling?' Abū Ḥanīfa remained silent. The Imam said, 'Which of the two is the greater offence, murder or unlawful sexual intercourse?' Abū Ḥanīfa said, 'Murder'. The Imam said, 'Why then did God decree that two witnesses are necessary in the case of murder so that the murderer could be executed with their testimonies and four witnesses were necessary in that of unlawful intercourse and that the adulterer cannot be punished without the testimonies of less than four?' Abū Ḥanīfa could not reply. The Imam said, 'Fear God, O Nuʿmān, and don't say: *What your tongues falsely describe, 'This is lawful, and this is forbidden'* (Q.16:116)'. Thereupon Abū Ḥanīfa was dumbfounded and could not utter a word.[152]

Nuʿmān takes up another form of *qiyās*, viz., *qiyās al-ʿilla* (causative inference), which bases analogy on an explanatory principle. This mode of *qiyās* considers a new thing according to its original meaning (*aṣl*) as expressed in the text/s. Consequently, the ruling of the *aṣl* is applied to that of the derived case (*farʿ*).[153] In this type of cases the ruling of the latter is deduced from the former, given either by the text of the Qur'an or *ḥadīth* which is infallible. Hence, the derived ruling is equated with certainty. It is reported that the Messenger of God prohibited the sale of one *kurr* (a measure of weight)[154] of wheat (*burr*) for two *kurr*s. Subsequently, based on *qiyās al-ʿilla* the *aṣḥāb al-qiyās* prohibited the sale of one *kurr* of rice for two *kurr*s of rice.[155] Nuʿmān states that those who advocate the use of *qiyās* give various reasons for the justification of their deduction why such a sale was forbidden by the Messenger of God. Without going into the details, Nuʿmān rejects their speculation for the justification by asserting that one does not know the rationale behind such a prohibition in the original case. God simply commands his servants to do certain things or forbids them to avoid other things. He does not state the rationale as to why such a thing is lawful or unlawful. What this group does is simply to opine that such and such was the rationale. Hence, Nuʿmān asserts that one cannot discover the exact rationale behind such a ruling. Nuʿmān then raises various hypothetical

152 Nuʿmān, *Ikhtilāf*, pp. 141–142. See also Nuʿmān, *The Pillars of Islam*, vol. 1, pp. 112–113; it is restated here with slight variation in wording.

153 Nuʿmān, *Ikhtilāf*, p. 143; it reads:

القياس في نفسه هو تشبيه الشيء بغيره والحكم به، هو الحكم للفرع بحكم أصله إذا استوت علّتهما فيما وقع الحكم من أجله.

154 Walther Hinz, *Islamische Masse und Gewichte: Umgerechnet ins Metrische System* (Leiden, 1970), pp. 42–43.

155 This example also appears in the later sources; see Hallaq, *History*, pp. 91–92.

questions even when one presumes that the *ʿilla* was specified in each and every case. What would happen if the circumstances change? Does the *ʿilla* remain constant? What would happen if the *ʿilla* ceases to operate in some cases, or the situation changes in other cases? Does that *ḥukm* (rule) remain valid, or does it become invalid? Nuʿmān then adds that the precise version of the above tradition reads: 'Verily, the Messenger of God forbade the sale of wheat by wheat, barley by barley, dates by dates and salt by salt except in equal quantity. Whoever increases or demands more than the equal amount is indeed practicing usury.'[156] In all those cases the Messenger of God prohibited disparity in transactions. Similarly the Messenger of God said: '[To exchange] silver for silver, or gold for gold, in equal amounts, on the spot [is lawful]; and he who increases or asks for more engages in usury.'[157] Nuʿmān reiterates that the *aḥkām* are not based on any particular *ʿilla* that could either be specified or comprehended by human reason. Referring to all those groups who advocate the use of *qiyās*, he cites the Qur'anic verse which categorically rejects human speculation in religious matters and states: *These are nothing but names you have invented yourselves, you and your forefathers. God has sent no authority for them. Even though their Lord has already brought them guidance, such people merely follow guesswork and the whims of their souls.* (Q.53:23)[158]

Nuʿmān gives another example by which *ahl al-qiyās* try to justify their use of *qiyās*. It is reported that a woman named al-Khathʿamiyya asked the Messenger of God whether or not she could perform pilgrimage on behalf of her father who was too old to undertake such a journey. The Messenger of God said yes and asked her: 'Do you think that if your father had incurred a monetary debt would you have paid it back?' Upon hearing the woman's response in the affirmative, the Messenger of God said: 'The debt owed to God is therefore more deserving [to be discharged.]' Hence, they claimed that the Prophet compared the obligation to fulfil the pilgrimage, which is man's obligation towards God, to a monetary debt, which is man's obligation towards another human being. Thus, they claim that the above *ḥadīth* quite eloquently expresses the permission to exercise *qiyās*.[159] Nuʿmān refutes their claim by stating they have fabricated a lie and ascribed it to the Messenger of God. Their attribution of falsehood to the Prophet, he adds, is rebutted by God when He addresses the Messenger of God: *Say, I only follow what is revealed to me* (Q.6:50); and *By the star when it sets, your comrade [Muḥammad] has not gone astray, nor has he erred, nor does he speak out of caprice. This [recitation] is simply a revelation that is being revealed* (Q.53:1–4). Nuʿmān reiterates that they ought to take the Messenger of God's words as expressed by God: *Whatever the Messenger gives you, take it*

[156] Nuʿmān, *Ikhtilāf*, p. 145; Arabic reads:

فأقول إن الحديث عن الرسول عند العامّة في الطعام أنه نهى عن البرّ بالبرّ، والشعير بالشعير، والتمر بالتمر، والملح بالملح إلا سواء بسواء، فمن زاد واستزاد فقد أربى.

It is transmitted by Muslim and others. Wensinck, *Concordance*, s.v. b-r-r.

[157] See also Nuʿmān, *The Pillars of Islam*, vol. 2, p. 24.

[158] This translation is by M. A. S. Abdel Haleem, *The Qur'an: A New Translation* (Oxford, 2004), pp. 347–348.

[159] The same case is discussed in later sources also to justify *qiyās*; see Hallaq, *History*, p. 93.

(Q.59:7). God did not tell that it was a *qiyās* on the Prophet's part. Turning the tables around, Nuʿmān states, 'If they allege that it was a *qiyās* on the part of the Messenger of God then why do they not approve of performing the pilgrimage on behalf of an able bodied person as a financial debt could be discharged on behalf of another person? However, they agree that the obligation to perform the pilgrimage could only be discharged in the case of a dead or for an aged person who is physically unable to undertake such a journey. If they still maintain that the Messenger of God's ruling was based on *qiyās*, they should make it lawful for someone else to fast or pray on behalf of others. But the fact is that they do not allow such an undertaking.' Hence, Nuʿmān asks, 'How is it permissible for them to argue that it was based on *qiyās*?' Finally, Nuʿmān points out contradiction in their argument and states that both the pilgrimage and a monetary debt belong to the category of *aṣl* and, according to their own theory of analogy, the ruling of the *aṣl* cannot be deduced from another ruling of the *aṣl*. This is an obvious violation of the rule.

Nuʿmān then states that Dāwūd b. ʿAlī (d. 270/883), the Imam of the school of the Ẓāhiriyya, and his son Muḥammad criticised the use of *qiyās* and rejected it categorically.[160] He also harshly criticises Shāfiʿī for admitting to the use of *qiyās* and his attempts to regulate its operation.[161] Moreover, Nuʿmān cites two examples, namely the punishment for adultery and atonement for forgetfulness during prayer, given by the proponents of *qiyās* to justify their use of *qiyās* in identical cases. Their inverted argument, a case of perverted logic, runs as follows. If the exercise of *qiyās* is invalidated then it is possible for someone to argue that the punishment for adultery by stoning and penance of offering a prostration for forgetfulness during prayer can also be invalidated because both cases are based on specific incidents. It is reported that the Messenger of God stoned a certain person called Māʿiz.[162] However, the advocates of deduction by analogy contend that if the use of *qiyās* is rejected then someone can refuse to stone another person called Saʿd, contending that he does not want to transgress his limits by stoning the latter (another person) whom the Prophet did not stone. Similarly another person could challenge that he is not bound to offer a prostration as expiation for his forgetfulness during any prayer except the noon (*ẓuhr*) prayer because the Messenger of God did it during the *ẓuhr* prayer only. They further contend that their validation of stoning punishment for adultery is based on whether the guilty person is married and free while the colour of his skin, ethnicity or name do not matter. Nuʿmān wholeheartedly agrees with their argument. His only disagreement is about the route they have taken to reach such a judgement. Nuʿmān states that he does not establish the validity of the stoning punishment and the prostration for forgetfulness during the prayer through the mechanism of *qiyās*, rather on the authority of the Imams who have uninterruptedly transmitted the traditions from the Messenger of God. Space does not permit me to go into further details. Finally, Nuʿmān concludes the chapter by

[160] Joseph Schacht, 'Dāwūd b. ʿAlī b. Khalaf', *EI2*, vol. 2, pp. 182–183; Hallaq, *History*, p. 32.

[161] Hallaq, *History*, p. 32.

[162] The name of Māʿiz occurs in the later sources but in a different context of abrogation. Ibid., p. 70.

stating that *aḥkām al-dīn,* especially concerning the rulings as to what is lawful and unlawful, cannot be established by analogical deduction, or on the rationale of probability, or by recourse to human fancy. *Aḥkām al-dīn* are based on the Qurʾan and the *sunna* as transmitted by the Imams.

An Account of those who Uphold the Theory of *Istiḥsān* and their Refutation[163]

Nuʿmān opens this chapter by stating that all groups that advocate various theories under the guise of *raʾy*, *qiyās*, *ijtihād*, *naẓar*, *istiḥsān* or *istidlāl* ultimately resort to human reason in religious matters. Hence, whatever he has stated so far about other groups equally applies to this group as well. To drive home his point that the Qurʾan contains everything and that it warns people against following their own fancies and assumptions in religious matters, Nuʿmān restates various verses from the Qurʾan.[164]

This group justifies the theory of *istiḥsān* (juristic preference) by citing the Qurʾanic verse which states: *So give good tidings to My servants, who listen to the declaration and follow the best of it (aḥsanahu). Those are the ones whom God has guided. Those are the [ones] possessed of understanding (uluʾl-albāb)* (Q.39:17–18). Thus, Nuʿmān states, they assumed that those who give legal ruling based on juristic preference are commended by God. Nuʿmān debunks their incorrect interpretation through linguistic and contextual analysis of the above verse. He states that the antecedent to which the pronoun (in *aḥsanahu*) refers are the people *who avoid serving idols and turn penitent*. Good tidings are given to *those who listen to the declaration (qawl) and follow the best of it*. Declaration refers to the Qurʾan as God states in the same *sūra*: *God has sent down the fairest discourse (aḥsan al-ḥadīth), a consistent Scripture, mathānī … That is God's guidance, by which He guides those whom He wishes; and those whom God leads astray have no guide* (Q.39:23). *The fairest discourse* refers to His Book and not to what they allege. Equating juristic preference to what is commendable according to their fancies, Nuʿmān states that it is forbidden by God when He states: *And do not say, because of what your tongues falsely describe, 'This is lawful, and this is forbidden,' so that you may invent a falsehood against God* (Q.16:116).

Another argument against this group is: what would they say if their opponents reject what they consider commendable/preferable and proclaim a different ruling that is commendable to them? Would it not lead to chaos concerning what is lawful and unlawful?[165] It could also be argued that when *istiḥsān* is permissible with regard to *furūʿ* (positive rules derived from the sources, *uṣūl*) it should also be

---

[163] For *istiḥsān,* see n. 48 above.

[164] Such as Qurʾan 7:3, 6:155, 16:116. 38:26 and 53:28.

[165] Nuʿmān, *Ikhtilāf*, p. 180; he states:

فيقال لهم: ما حجّتكم على من خالفكم إذا استحسن ضدّ ما استحسنتموه، فقال بخلاف ما قلتموه؟ وهل تدعون لأنفسكم في ذلك حالةً إلا جاز لخصمكم دعوى مثلها لنفسه؟ فإن دفعتموه فيما نازعكم فيه بلا حجّة ولا برهان لكم عليه كابرتموه. وإن سلّمتم له ما أوجبتموه لأنفسكم أوجبتم في الشيء الواحد أنه حلال حرام …

permissible for the *uṣūl*. Once it becomes permissible to exercise *istiḥsān* in matters dealing with the *uṣūl* it becomes obligatory to accept that the Jews, Christians, Zoroastrians and idol-worshippers are right in what they consider commendable about their religion.[166]

An Account of those who Uphold the Theory of *Istidlāl* and their Refutation[167]

This group maintains that the Book of God in itself is a legal indicant (*dalīl*), hence every argument or all evidence (*ḥujja*) is derived from it. Indeed, the *sunna* has become evidence because the Qur'an commanded followers to obey the Messenger of God (who established the *sunna*). They further assert that whatever is specified and explained in the Qur'an removes doubt from the listener as God states: *Obey God and obey the Messenger* (Q.4:59); and *Forbidden to you are: carrion, blood, the flesh of the pig* (Q.7:3); and *Forbidden to you are: your mothers, your daughters, your sisters…* (Q.4:23) However, what is unspecified or alluded to or expressed by parables, their true import could be discovered through *istidlāl* (arguments based on the *dalīl*, or legal inference). Similarly in the *sunna* of the Messenger of God, certain things are obvious and have no need for *dalīl* (argument or inference), while others are stated in general terms in need of interpretation (*ta'wīl*). Hence, what is not explicitly stated we infer (*istadlalnā*) from what is obvious. For example God says: *Perform prayer* (Q.2:43). And the Messenger of God explained the details, timing, and so forth. Nuʿmān rebuts their claim and states that their assertion that the Book of God itself is a *dalīl* which needs explanation. The Book by itself does not speak and was in need of the Messenger of God to explain its rules, regulations and uphold its teachings. Yes, the Qur'an is the proof for the veracity of the Messenger of God and he was the *dalīl* during his lifetime while his successors, the Imams, are the guides for the succeeding generations. This is the very reason why the Qur'an states: *O you who believe, obey God and obey the Messenger and those of you who have authority* (Q.4:59).[168] Had the Qur'an been the guide (*dalīl*) by itself to truth as they claim, Nuʿmān states that there would not have been a need for the Messenger of God or those who have authority. It only demonstrates their arrogance.

---

166 Ibid., p. 181; he states:

فإن جوّزتم الاستحسان في فروع الدين لزمكم أن تجيزوا ذلك في أصله، وإلا فمن أين يجوز لكم أن تحكموا في الفروع بغير حكم الأصول؟ وإن أنتم حكمتم بذلك فقد أوجبتم لليهود والنصارى والمجوس وعبدة الأوثان أنهم مصيبون فيما استحسنوه من دياناتهم.

167 For the meaning of *istidlāl* see n. 49 above.

168 Nuʿmān has argued above that *who have authority* refers to the Imams.

An Account of those who Uphold the Theories of *Ijtihād* and *Raʾy* and their Refutation for Abandoning the Truth[169]

They assert that the exercise of *ijtihād* is obligatory (*al-farḍ ʿalayhim*) in order to resolve cases not explicitly stated either in the Book of God or the *sunna* of the Messenger of God. After exercising his *ijtihād* if the jurist finds the matter discernible he can issue a ruling whether it is lawful or unlawful. Justification for the use of *ijtihād* is based on an alleged tradition reported on the authority of the Prophet. It is related that the Prophet sent Muʿādh b. Jabal to Yemen on a mission. The Prophet asked him, 'How will you decide on matters that come up?' He replied, 'I will decide according to the Book of God.' The Prophet asked, 'What if you do not find it there?' He replied, 'Then according to the *sunna* of the Messenger of God.' The Prophet asked, 'What if you do not find in the *sunna* of the Messenger of God?' He answered, 'Then I will exert effort to form my own judgement (*ajtahid raʾyī*).' Thereupon the Messenger of God struck his chest and said, 'Thank God for guiding the Messenger of God's messenger.'[170]

Nuʿmān tries to show that the above tradition is not authentic and presents his supporting evidence from the Qur'an and the *sunna*. He states that those from the commonalty who reject the principle of *ijtihād* indicate that the tradition is *maqṭūʿ* – the *isnād* is said to be broken.[171] Although the tradition is transmitted by several transmitters, the chain of authority stops with the nephew of al-Mughīra b. Shuʿba[172] who stated that he related it on the authority of men from Banī Ḥimṣ[173] who stated that it was on the authority of Muʿādh b. Jabal. Therefore, Nuʿmān says it is a weak tradition and its transmitters are unknown individuals. Even if it is presumed that the tradition is established, Nuʿmān argues, most probably the words

---

[169] For the meanings of *ijtihād* and *raʾy*, see n. 47 and 49 above.

[170] It is a widely related tradition to imply that reasoning by inference is approved by the Prophet. Hallaq, *History*, pp. 86, 106.

[171] *Maqṭūʿ* is a tradition that goes back to a Successor regarding words or deeds of his. Shāfiʿī used it in the sense of *Munqaṭiʿ*, which has been used of an *isnād* including unspecified people, or one later than a Successor who claims to have heard someone he did not hear. It is also used of one later than a Successor quoting directly from a Companion. However, it is commonly applied when there is a break in the *isnād* at any stage later than the Successor. James Robson, 'Ḥadīth', *EI2*, vol. 3, pp. 25–26. See also John Burton, *An Introduction to the Hadīth* (Edinburgh, 1994), p. 112; he states that this type of *ḥadīth* was the source of a great quantity of badly needed material. The degree to which it was relied on was dictated by necessity and governed by due regard to the transmitter's reputation. Jonathan Brown, *Hadith: Muḥammad's Legacy in the Medieval and Modern World* (Oxford, 2009), p. 279.

[172] He was a Companion and considered as one of the chief *dāhiya*s of his time. *Dāhiya* literally means 'smart fellow' or 'old fox', also holding negative connotations such as a man of dubious morals, or one who could get himself out of even the most hopeless situation. It was said about al-Mughīra that if he were shut behind seven doors, his cunning would find a way to burst open all the locks. See Henry Lammens, 'al-Mughīra b. Shuʿba', *EI2*, vol. 7, p. 347.

[173] Banū Ḥimṣ cannot be identified but Muḥammad Murtaḍā al-Zabīdī in his *Tāj al-ʿarūs* (Kuwait, 1977), vol. 17, p. 533, states that the city of Ḥimṣ in Syria was named after Ḥimṣ b. Ṣahr from Banī ʿImlīq.

of Muʿādh 'I will exert effort to form my own judgement' meant that he would seek the evidence from the Book and the *sunna*. Nuʿmān adds that when ʿUmar b. al-Khaṭṭāb persisted in his question to the Prophet about the meaning of *al-kalāla*,[174] he told him to refer to the verses that were revealed to him rather than telling him to exert his effort and form his own opinion. He further adds: What would happen if *ijtihād* was permitted and two persons exercising their rights of *ijtihād* reach contradictory conclusions about the same legal case? According to their argument both are correct in their judgements, but the fact is that the truth resides with only one party. This was the position taken by Muḥammad b. Dāwūd and his father, the founder of the Ẓāhirī school, for their opposition to the principle of *ijtihād*. Nuʿmān also objects to this group's assumption that the exercise of *ijtihād* is obligatory without providing any evidence. Moreover, their assumption that they are not obliged to find the correct solution is quite strange. If this is the case one surmises what the obligation is, because God categorically states: [*It is improper*] *to say about God what you do not know* (Q.2:169). In another verse He states: *After the truth what is there except error?* [*So*] *how are you turned about?* (Q.10:32), and *Do not follow the whims of a people who strayed previously and led many astray and strayed from the level path* (Q.5:77). God did not say, '*ijtahidū*,' He commanded: *Ask the people* [*who have*] *the reminder if you do not know* (Q.16:43).

Nuʿmān rejects Shāfiʿī's argument in defence of *ijtihād* concerning the command to face the Sacred Mosque in prayer very weak because it is known to every Muslim. If a person is ignorant about it, he should seek it from knowledgeable people and it is not permitted for him to use his *ijtihād*. Another tradition states, 'When a governor/judge formulates an independent judgement in a legal case and gets it right he gets a double reward, while the one who formulates his judgement but errs, gets one reward [for fulfilling the obligation of *ijtihād*].'[175] Nuʿmān rejects this tradition because it contradicts other traditions. He states that the correctly transmitted tradition reads, 'Judges are of three types: two are [condemned to] fire and one is [destined for] paradise. One who decides unjustly while knowing full well that he is not just [in his ruling] is destined for fire. One who rules unjustly but is not aware [that his ruling is unjust] is destined for fire because he has stripped the people of their rights. One who rules with justice is destined for paradise.'[176] Nuʿmān also criticises Abū Ḥanīfa, Shāfiʿī and Abū ʿUbayd al-Qāsim b. Sallām (d. 224/838),[177] but space does not permit me to elaborate.

As stated above it is the third longest chapter and Nuʿmān expands on an additional four justifications presented by this group and refutes them meticulously. In what follows I will summarise those justifications and Nuʿmān's main arguments

---

[174] See Qur'an 4:12, 176. For its meaning and more details see Nuʿmān, *The Pillars of Islam*, vol. 2, pp. 367, 369; Cilardo Agostino, *The Qur'ānic Term Kalāla: Studies in Arabic Language and Poetry, Ḥadīth, Tafsīr and Fiqh, Notes on the Origins of Islamic Law* (Edinburgh, 2005).

[175] It is transmitted by Bukhārī, Muslim, Abū Dāwūd, Tirmidhī, Nasā'ī, Ibn Māja and Ibn Ḥanbal. Wensinck, *Concordance*, s.v., a-j-r.

[176] It is transmitted by Abū Dāwūd and Ibn Māja, Wensinck, *Concordance*, s.v., q-ḍ-y.

[177] He was a grammarian, Qur'an scholar and a jurist. H. L. Gottschalk, 'Abū ʿUbayd al-Ḳāsim b. Sallām', *EI2*, vol. 1, p. 157.

against them. The second justification is based on a long verse which states: *Or like the one who passed by a settlement collapsed on its supports: he said, 'How will God give life to this [settlement] now that it is dead?' God caused him to die for a hundred years, and then brought him back to life. He said, 'How long have you tarried?' He said, 'A day or part of a day.' He said, 'No, you have lingered a hundred years …'* [to the end of the verse] (Q.2:259). They allege that *ijtihād* is permitted because God did not reject the speculation of the man who said, *'A day or part of a day.'* Nuʿmān states that their argument does not hold much water because the thrust of the verse is to show that man's speculation is wrong. Nuʿmān reinforces his argument with linguistic and contextual analysis of the verse.

The third justification is based on the verse that states: *God will not take you to task for making inadvertent errors in your oaths, but He will take you to task for agreements you have made through oaths. Expiation [for broken oaths] is the feeding of ten destitute people with the average of the food with which you feed your families or clothing of them or freeing of a slave. Whoever does not find* [the means for that] *should fast for three days* (Q.5:89). They argue that since God permitted selection/choice, why should a similar choice not be permitted with regard to *ijtihād*? Different rulings reached by different *mujtahid*s are thus similar to the choices given by God. Nuʿmān argues that choices are given by God and not left with the *mujtahid*s to deduce. What would happen if the choices are not provided by God? One *mujtahid* might rule that the one who breaks an oath should be killed and the second might rule that [his hand] should be cut off, and the third might rule that he should be flogged while the fourth might rule that he should be imprisoned. Don't they think that they are transgressing the punishments prescribed by God?

The fourth justification is also based on the above verse and they argue as follows. There is no difference between the three choices specified and leaving the selection or entrusting the exercise of *ijtihād* to them concerning an incident that might happen or a mishap should descend upon them. Nuʿmān refutes their argument by stating that their reasoning is far-fetched and God did not permit it. The last justification is derived from the verse about the maintenance of divorced women which states: *The well-to-do according to his means and the needy according to his* (Q.2:236). Nuʿmān rebuffs their reasoning by pointing out the verse which states: *Let a man of ample means spend some of those means; and those whose provision is measured, let them spend some of what God has given them* (Q.65:7). Nuʿmān asserts that the latter verse clearly indicates that the maintenance of divorced women is not left to their inference (*ijtihād*) as they falsely claim, but was left to the Messenger of God and the Imams to further clarify the matter as God states: *And We have sent down to you [O Prophet] the reminder for you to make clear to men what has been sent down to them* (Q.16:44).

Finally, let me return to Nuʿmān for some concluding remarks. In sharp contrast to other schools of jurisprudence, it should be noted that Ismaili law developed and flourished under the patronage of the Fatimid dynasty. Nuʿmān, therefore, put the theory of the imamate, fully articulated by him, to its appropriate use in *The Pillars of Islam*, which was his crowning achievement and blessed by the Imam-caliph al-Muʿizz. As soon as the *The Pillars of Islam* was completed it was proclaimed by al-

Muʿizz to be the official code of the Fatimid state. The law, thus promulgated through the *Daʿāʾim* was for the simultaneous use of the state and the Ismaili community. The *Daʿāʾim*, which I have elaborated elsewhere, was thus the first juristic text to give a legalistic place to the doctrine of the imamate/*walāya*.[178] Nuʿmān has correctly stated that of the seven pillars of Islam, it is the first pillar of *walāya* which is the most excellent and through it and through the *walīy* (the Imam), around whom the *walāya* revolves, the true knowledge of the rest of the pillars of Islam can be obtained. For the Fatimids, *walāya* was not merely a religious belief, it was the very foundation of their claim to political leadership of the Muslim world. The chapter on *walāya* along with that on the *jihād*, containing the *ʿahd* ascribed to ʿAlī b. Abī Ṭālib dealing with the ruler's conduct towards his subjects and the excellent qualities and practices that he should observe, represents the Ismaili theory of the state as well as its civil constitution.

In the absence of the Imam and the subsequent precarious existence of the Mustaʿlī-Ṭayyibī communities, first in the Yemen and then in the Indian subcontinent, it was not easy to consider any modification of this law, especially anything concerned with family law. However, the situation dramatically changed during the second half of the last century throughout Muslim countries. Hence, it is time that the religious authorities take into consideration the present situation and growing complaints by various segments of the community to render justice to the weaker segments of the society.[179]

[178] Poonawala, 'al-Qāḍī al-Nuʿmān and Ismaʿili Jurisprudence', p. 127.

[179] Ibid., p. 132.

Appendix I

Relevant verses from Nuʿmān's *al-Urjūza al-muntakhaba* (الأرجوزة المنتخبة، قصيدة مزدوجة نظمها في أبواب الفقه).[180]

الحمد لله العليّ الداني … ذي المنّ والآلاء والإحسانِ
وخُصّ ذو الطول وذو الأنعامِ … بأفضل الصلاة والإكرامِ
قائمُهم مِن بينهم بوَعْدِهِ … وخير من خلقهِ من بعدهِ
ذاك **أبو القاسم عبد الله** … **محمّد القائم** بالإلهِ
مهديُّنا خيرُ هداةِ الأمّةِ … وأفضلُ الملوكِ والأئمّةِ
وكنتُ قد جمعتُ عن آبائهِ … **في الفقه ما أوعبت في استقصائهِ**
ثمّ تدبّرتُ الذي جمعتُهُ … فكان فيه كُلّما أردتُهُ
لو كان مبسوطًا على التأليفِ … منتظم التلخيص والتصنيفِ
لكنّه جاء على الروايةِ … مختلط الوجوهِ في الحكايةِ
فمنه ما ألّف في أبواب … لم تأت بالإشباع والإيعابِ
وجاء في خلالها اختلافٌ … بين الرواةِ إذ هم أخيافٌ
وكلٌّ هذا فلهُ سبيلٌ … عليه من شاهده دليلٌ
وكنتُ قد **بسطتُهُ بنظمهِ** … **وشرح ما علمتُهُ من علمهِ**
في كتبٍ جامعةٍ شريفةٍ … مشبعةٍ موعوبةٍ طريفةٍ
كلّ كتابٍ جمعتُ أبوابهُ … وكلّ بابٍ ألّفتُ أسبابهُ
حكيتُ فيها علل اختلافهم … حكاية المحتجّ لائتلافهم
وجئتُ بالشاهد والبرهانِ … لثابتِ القولِ مع التبيانِ
من بعد ذكري عند كلِّ مسألةٍ … ما جاء فيها باختلاف النقلةِ
بذكر نقلها من الكتابِ … نصًّا وبالإسناد والأنسابِ
بغير ما رأيٍ ولا قياسٍ … إلّا على المثبت في الأساسِ
فكملت في مائتي كتابٍ … **تزيد عشرين على الحسابِ**
ثم اختصرتُ لفظها في مختصر … أجملتُ فيه جملاً من الخبر

ثمّ اختصرتُ بعد منها كتبًا … **جامعةً جمعتُ فيها عجبًا**
أزحتُ عنها طرق الإسنادِ … وكلّ منحولٍ من الأضدادِ
وجئتُ بالثابت فيها محضًا … من بعد أن مخضتُ عنها مخضًا

[180] MS in the collection of my father Mullā Qurbān Ḥusayn Poonawala. The word *risāla* added to the title given in the edited versions of Idrīs, *ʿUyūn al-akhbār*, p. 565: رسالة الأرجوزة المنتخبة and *ʿUyūn al-akhbār* (ed. Ghālib), vol. 6, p. 46: الرسالة الأرجوزة المختارة المنتخبة are incorrect.

It was composed after *Mukhtaṣar al-īḍāḥ* as Nuʿmān states:[181]

ثمّ اختصرتُ لفظها في مختصر أجملتُ فيه جملاً من الخبرِ
ثمّ رأيتُ جمعهُ مزدوجًا **قصيدةً** قوّمتُ فيها العوجا
مشبّعة الأبواب في اختصار يقرّب معناها من النظّارِ
ويسهل الحفظُ بها للعلم إذا رأوها ذو الحِجىَ والنَّهَمِ[182]
حصرتُ فيها الأوجه المفترقة تجمع ما في الجزء منها ورقة
من قول أهل البيت إذ جمعتُهُ عن الثقاة بعد أن صنّفتُهُ
سمّيتُها إذ تمّت المنتخبة لأنّني انتخبتُها للطلبة

This *Urjūza* by Nuʿmān was probably the first versified version of jurisprudence and it may have been regarded as a model for the later Sunni compositions. It is in two parts/volumes: the first deals with the *ʿibādāt* and the second with the *muʿāmalāt* and covers all topics of law covered in the *Daʿāʾim*. It was composed, as the author states in the introduction to facilitate its memorisation by the students. It is not edited and is mentioned by Ibn Khallikān.[183] Al-Majdūʿ gives its title as *al-Qaṣīda al-muntakhaba*.[184]

Appendix II

إجازات لمختصر الآثار

[إجازة القاضي الحسين بن علي بن القاضي النعمان من الحاكم]

بسم اللّٰه الرحمٰن الرحيم وبه نستعين

الحمد للّٰه على ما أولى به من آلائه حمدًا يقتضي المزيد من فضله ونعمائه، وصلّى اللّٰه على محمدٍ خاتم أنبيائه وعلى الأئمّة من ذرّيته، أوليائه. قال القاضي الحسين بن عليّ بن القاضي النعمان: رويتُ هذا الكتاب وغيره من الكتب المرويّة عن موالينا الأئمّة الصادقين من أهل بيت رسول اللّٰه، صلّى اللّٰه عليه

[181] Al-Qāḍī al-Nuʿmān, *al-Urjūza al-muntakhaba*, MS 2v–3r.

[182] Variant reading in another MS (in the collection of Mullā Qurbān Ḥusayn): والفهم

[183] Ibn Khallikān, p. 416; he states: وله القصيدة الفقهية لقّبها بالمنتخبة قصيدة مزدوجة نظمها في أبواب الفقه.

[184] Al-Majdūʿ, *Fahrasa*, pp. 34–35.

وسلّم أجمعين، التي صنّفها جدّي القاضي النعمانُ بن محمد رضوان اللّٰه عليه، عن أبي القاضي عليّ بن النعمان، رضي اللّٰه عنه وأرضاه، سماعاً وإجازةً بإسناده الذي أذكره قبل صدر هذا الكتاب. ثمّ ذكرتُ ذلك لمولانا الإمام الحاكم بأمر اللّٰه أمير المؤمنين صلوات اللّٰه عليه واستأذنتُه في رواية ما في هذه الكتب عنه صلوات اللّٰه عليه، و[عن] (في نسختين: أن) إملاء هذا الكتاب على مَن يرغب في روايته بعد أن أحضرتُه إيّاه وقرأتُ عليه بعضه. فأَذِنَ لي في ذلك. فامتثلتُ أمْرَهُ العالي وبدأتُ بالصدر الذي أرويه عن أبي رضي اللّٰه عنه. وهو:

[إجازة القاضي علي بن القاضي النعمان من العزيز]

بسم اللّٰه الرحمٰن الرحيم

الحمد للّٰه حقّ حمده والشكر له كنه شكره، وصلّى اللّٰه على محمدٍ نبيّه، وعلى الأئمّة أولي أمرهِ وأهل ذكرهِ. قال القاضي علي بن النعمان: قرأتُ هذا الكتاب على أبي القاضي النعمان بن محمد بن منصور بن أحمد بن حيّون، رضي اللّٰه عنه وأرضاه سنةَ ثمانٍ وأربعين وثلاثمائة، وأذِنَ لي في روايته عنه بإسناده. فلمّا توفّي، رضي اللّٰه عنه، ونَدَبَني مولانا الإمام المعزُّ لدين اللّٰه أمير المؤمنين، قدّس اللّٰه روحه وصلّى عليه وعلى الأئمّة من آبائه والصفوة من أبنائه، إلى ما كان نَدَبَ أبي إليه، واقتصر به عليه من الاستفادة منه والرواية عنه، أحضرتُه صلوات اللّٰه عليه هذا الكتاب مع غيره من الكتب المروية عنه عليه السلام، وذكرتُ له قراءتي إيّاها على أبي، وإذنهِ لي في روايتها عنه. فأذِنَ لي في رواية صدر هذا الكتاب، وصدور غيره من الكتب التي قرأتُها على أبي رضي اللّٰه عنه، وأجازَلي في رواية ما فيها عنه صلوات اللّٰه عليه. فامتثلتُ أمْرَهُ العالي إلى حين وفاتهِ قدّس اللّٰه روحه. ولمّا أُفضيت خلافةُ اللّٰه إلى مولانا، وليّ اللّٰه، الإمام العزيز باللّٰه أمير المؤمنين، صاحب العصر والزمان، ووليّ أهل الإسلام والإيمان، ذكرتُ ذلك له ورفعتُه إليه، فاستأذنتُه فيه صلوات اللّٰه عليه. فأجازَ لي

وأذن لي في روايته عنه حسب ما تقدّم لي من ذلك من المعزّ لدين اللّٰه قدّس اللّٰه روحه وصلّى عليه. فامتثلتُ أمْرَهُ العالي وبدأتُ بالصدر الذي أرويه من هذا الكتاب عن أبي رضي اللّٰه عنه، وهو:

[إجازة القاضي النعمان من المعزّ]

بسم اللّٰه الرحمٰن الرحيم

الحمد للّٰه شكراً على آلائهِ وإحسانهِ ونعمتهِ وامتراء للمزيد من فضلهِ وامتنانهِ وابتغاءِ رضوانهِ ورحمتهِ، وصلّى اللّٰه على محمدٍ خاتم أنبيائه المصطفين ورسله، وعلى عليّ بن أبي طالبٍ خليفتهِ في أمّتهِ، ووصيّهِ في أهلهِ، وعلى الأئمّة من ذرّيته الطيّبين الطاهرين الخلفاء المهديين الذين أقامَ بهم أركانَ الدينِ وأنهجَ بهم سُبُلَ الهُدى للمهتدين، وأنارَ بهم شُهُبَ الإسلام للمسلمين، وأورثَهم الإمامةَ إلى يوم الدين. فهُمُ القدوةُ والعمادُ، وهم أمَنَةُ الأنام، وأئمّة العبادِ لكلّ قومٍ في كلّ عصرٍ منهم إمامٌ هادٍ صلوات اللّٰه عليهم أجمعين، ورحم اللّٰه أوليائهم وأتباعهم من المؤمنين الأوّلين منهم والآخرين.

قال القاضي النعمان بن محمد: كنتُ قد جمعتُ من قول موالينا الأئمّة الطاهرين من أهل بيت رسول اللّٰه صلّى اللّٰه عليه وعليهم أجمعين كتبًا في علم الفُتْيا، وصنّفتُها وبوّبتُها وجزّأتُها وألّفتُها. وحكيتُ الروايات على اختلاف الرواةِ عنهم فيها، وأثبتُّ الثابت عنهم منها، وجئتُ بالدلائل على ذلك والبيان والشواهد والبرهان. فكَثُرَ عددُ أجزائها وعَظُمَتِ المؤنةُ فيها على ذوي ابتغائها. واختصرتُ منها موزونًا ومنثورًا في مختصراتٍ لم تؤدّ كثيرًا من الطالبين إلى الغايات. فأعجزتْهم تلك لتكثارِها، واستقلّوا الفائدةَ في هذه لاختصارها. وسألَني غيرُ واحدٍ من القضاة والحكّام والأولياء الطالبين علم الحلالِ والحرامِ أنْ أجمع لهم كتابًا متوسّطًا في ذلك يقرّب معناه، ويكتفي به من كتبه وقراءته [كما

صححناه، وفي كلتي النسختين: وقرائه، وقرءه] ويحفظه الحدثُ الصغيرُ، ويفيد منه الشيخُ الكبيُر، ويتّسع له المشغولُ والخليُّ، ويناله الفقيرُ والغنيُّ. فألّفتُ لهم هذا الكتاب متوسّطًا بين التطويل والاختصار، وسمّيتُه مختصر الآثار. ولمّا اعتبرتُ مقدار هذا الكتاب، فرأيتُه يقصر عن إدخال الأسانيد فيه، ورأيتُه أنّ ذلك ما لا غناءَ به عنه، رأيتُ أن أخُصَّهُ بأقرب الأسانيد وأعلاها وأصحّحها وأثبتها وأسناها. فرفعتُ ما أردتُ إثباته فيه شيئًا بعد شيءٍ إلى وليّ الأمر وإمام الزمان وصاحب العصر مولاي أمير المؤمنين الإمام المعزّ لدين اللّٰه صلوات اللّٰه عليه وعلى أبائه الأئمّة الطاهرين. فأسقطتُ من ذلك ما أمَرَ، أدام اللّٰه علوّ أمره، بإسقاطه، وأثبتُّ في هذا الكتاب ما ارتضاه وأمَرَ بإثباته، وقرأتُه عليه قراءةً. فكلٌّ مثبتٍ فيه فمنه. وأنا أرويه لمن أخذه عنّي [و]عنه وعن آبائه الطاهرين فقد استضاءَ نورًا، [و]مَن اقتبسَ من نورِ أمير المؤمنين وقد استعذب ماءَ مَن يشرب من رأسِ العين.

Appendix III

مختارات من كتاب عهد القضاء للقاضي النعمان من المعزّ [185]

بسم اللّٰه الرحمٰن الرحيم

هذا كتابٌ من عبد اللّٰه ووليّه معد أبي تميم المعزّ لدين اللّٰه أمير المؤمنين لنعمان بن محمد القاضي، أنّ أمير المؤمنين للمحلّ الذي اصطفاه اللّٰه به من الخلافة السنيّ قدرُها والإمامة العليّ خطرُها، وأن جعله سراجاً منيراً في أرضه، يُهتدى به ويُستضأ بنوره، ونصبه علماً لخلقه، وقائماً بحقّه، ومُوطّداً دعائم الإيمان، ومُؤكّداً وثائق الإسلام، ومُنهجاً شرائع جدّه محمدٍ رسول اللّٰه صلى اللّٰه عليه وآله، رأى أن يرفع من قدر القضاء حسب ما رفعه اللّٰه عزّ وجلّ ... **وقد كان أمير المؤمنين الذي وقف عليه من ورعِك، وديانتِك، وأمانتِك، ونزاهتِك،**

[185] Nuʿmān, *Ikhtilāf*, pp. 19–24.

وحميدِ طريقتِك استكفاك القضاء بالمنصورية وأعمالها، وأطلق لك النظر فيمن تظلّم إليك من أهل المدن التي فيها القُضاة والحكّام وغيرها بجميع الكور، وإنفاذ الحقّ على من وجب عليه، وإعطائه مستحقّه. ثم رأى عندما وقف عليه من صدقِ مُوالاتك، وتوخّيك الحقَّ في أحكامك، وما كشفه عنك الامتحان، ومخضك به الاختبار، وحسنت منك فيه الآثار، توكيد ذلك لك، وادّعامه وتشديده ... وليكنْ أمرُك جارياً، وحكمك نافذاً في كلّ من تظلّم إليك أو تظلـ[ـمـ]ـه من عندك من كافّة أهل مدائن أمير المؤمنين، وعامّة كورة الدانية منه والشاسعة منه، وأن يتطاول أحدٌ من قُضاة المهدية والقيروان إلى رفع أحدٍ من أهل البوادي التي حولهما، إلى أنفسهم، إذ كان أمير المؤمنين إنما أطلق لكلّ قاضٍ فيهما النظر في المدينة التي هو فيها، وما أحاط به قطرها، وليس له أن يتعدّى إلى النظر فيما خرج عنها، وأطلق لغيرهم من القضاة النظر في بوادي مدنهم، وأن لا يقيم أحدٌ منهم حاكماً ولا أميناً بجميع الكور التي لا قضاةَ فيها، **ولا ينظر بين أحدٍ من أولياء أمير المؤمنين، وطبقات عبيده، وسائر جُنده المقيمين بحضرته، وأن يكون النظرُ في جميع ذلك كلّه لك، مطلقة فيه يدُك، لا يُنازعك فيه أحدٌ من القضاة والحكّام** ... **مقتدياً في أحكامك وأقضيتك بكتاب الله** ... **وما لم تجد فيه نصّه ولا في سنّة جدّ أمير المؤمنين محمدٍ رسول الله** صلى الله عليه وآله ربّ العالمين حُكْمَهُ **التمسهُ في مذاهب الأئمّة** من ذرّيته الطاهرين ... الذين استحفظهم اللّهُ أمرَ دينهِ، وأودعهم خزائن علمه، ومكنون وحيه، وجعلهم هداةَ العبادِ ... الطريقة المثلى والمُقتدى بهم في أمر الدين والدنيا. **وما التبس عليك فأشكل، واشتبه فأعضل، انهيتهُ إلى أمير المؤمنين ليُوقّفك على وجه الحكم فيه** ... وقال جلّ ذكره وتبارك اسمه: ﴿وَلَوْ رَدُّوهُ إِلَى ٱلرَّسُولِ وَإِلَىٰٓ أُوْلِى ٱلْأَمْرِ مِنْهُمْ لَعَلِمَهُ ٱلَّذِينَ يَسْتَنۢبِطُونَهُۥ مِنْهُمْ﴾[سورة النساء ٤:٨٣]. وقال عزّ اسمه: ﴿فَسْـَٔلُوٓا۟ أَهْلَ ٱلذِّكْرِ إِن كُنتُمْ لَا تَعْلَمُونَ﴾ [سورة النحل ١٦:٤٣].

وقال النبيّ الناطق الصادق محمد صلى اللّٰه عليه وآله: إني تاركٌ فيكم الثقلين، كتاب اللّٰه وعترتي أهل بيتي، فلن تضلّوا ما إن تمسّكتم بهما، فإنهما لن يفترقا حتّى يردا على الحوض ... كُتب يوم الاثنين لليلتين بقيتا من شهر ربيع الأول سنةَ ثلاث وأربعين وثلاثمائة ... .

Appendix IV

إجازة لكتاب اختلاف أصول المذاهب

بسم اللّٰه الرحمٰن الرحيم

الحمد للّٰه على ما أسبغ من عطائه حمدَ عبدٍ شاكرٍ لآلائه، مستدع للمزيد من نعمائه، وصلى اللّٰه على محمد خاتم أنبيائه، المشفّع لأمّته يوم لقائه، وعلى وصيّه والأئمّة من آله أصفيائه. **قال قاضي القضاة عبد العزيز بن محمد بن النعمان: رويتُ هذا الكتاب وهو اختلاف أصول المذاهب والردّ على من خالف الحقّ فيها عن أبي القاضي محمد بن النعمان** رضي اللّٰه عنه وأرضاه، **ورواه أبي عن أبيه القاضي النعمان بن محمد** بن منصور بن أحمد بن حيّون التميمي، رضي اللّٰه عنه وأرضاه وأكرم منقلبه ومثواه، **مصنّف هذا الكتاب بعد عرضه إيّاه على مولانا وسيّدنا الإمام المعزّ لدين اللّٰه** أمير المؤمنين صلوات اللّٰه عليه وعلى آبائه الطاهرين والأئمّة من ولده الأكرمين، **وإجازته له وكان تصنيفه وروايته له ولولده من بعده بعد عرض كلّ راوٍ منهم له على إمام زمانه واستيذانه إيّاه في روايته عنه، وإجازة مولانا العزيز باللّٰه أمير المؤمنين** صلوات اللّٰه عليه **لوالدي محمد بن النعمان** رضي اللّٰه عنه قاضيه **إجازةً ثانيةً. فعرضتُ ذلك على مولانا الإمام الحاكم بأمر اللّٰه** إمام العصر. **فأجاز لي روايته عنه وأطلق لي إملاءه على عبيده، ووقّع على ظهره توقيعاً معظّماً بخطّ يده العالية**: ’أجزنا سماع هذا

الكتاب وإملاءه لقاضينا عبد العزيز بن محمد بن النعمان'. والحمد للّٰه ربّ العالمين.[186]

Appendix V

بداية من كتاب اختلاف اصول المذاهب[187]

بسم اللّٰه الرحمٰن الرحيم

الحمد للّٰه الذي أنزل الكتابَ على عبدهِ محمدٍ البشير النذير ...

أمّا بعد، فإني رأيتُ أهلَ القبلة بعد اتّفاقِهم على ظاهر نصِّ القرآن، وتصديق الرسول، قد اختلفوا في الفُتيا، في كثيرٍ من الفروع وفي بعض الأصول، وفي وجوهٍ كثيرةٍ من التأويل، وذهبوا في ذلك مذاهب، وتفرّقوا فرقاً، وتحزّبوا أحزاباً، بعد أن سمعوا قولَ اللّٰه عزّ وجلّ وتلوهُ: ﴿أَنْ أَقِيمُوا ٱلدِّينَ وَلَا تَتَفَرَّقُوا۟ فِيهِ﴾ [سورة الشورى ١٣:٤٢]؛ ﴿وَمَا تَفَرَّقَ ٱلَّذِينَ أُوتُوا۟ ٱلْكِتَـٰبَ إِلَّا مِن بَعْدِ مَا جَآءَتْهُمُ ٱلْبَيِّنَةُ﴾ [سورة البيّنة ٤:٩٨]. وقوله عزّ وجلّ: ﴿إِنَّ ٱلدِّينَ عِندَ ٱللَّهِ ٱلْإِسْلَـٰمُ وَمَا ٱخْتَلَفَ ٱلَّذِينَ أُوتُوا۟ ٱلْكِتَـٰبَ إِلَّا مِن بَعْدِ مَا جَآءَهُمُ ٱلْعِلْمُ بَغْياً بَيْنَهُمْ﴾ [سورة آل عمران ١٩:٣]. وقوله: ﴿أَفَلَا يَتَدَبَّرُونَ ٱلْقُرْءَانَ أَمْ عَلَىٰ قُلُوبٍ أَقْفَالُهَآ﴾ [سورة محمد ٢٤:٤٧]، ﴿وَلَوْ كَانَ مِنْ عِندِ غَيْرِ ٱللَّهِ لَوَجَدُوا۟ فِيهِ ٱخْتِلَـٰفاً كَثِيراً﴾ [سورة النساء ٨٢:٤]. فذمَّ جلّ ثناؤهُ التفريق والاختلاف، ودعا إلى الاجتماع والائتلاف، وأمر بذلك، وحضَّ عليه، ورغَّب في إقامة الدين، ونهى عن التفريق فيه. وقد رأيتُ، وباللّٰه أستعين وعليه أتوكّل، وعلى تائيد وليّهِ وإرشادهِ وموادّهِ أعولُ، وإيّاهُ لفاقتي أسترشدُ وأستعدُّ، ومن زواخرِ بحرهِ أغترفُ وأستمدُّ، بأن أبسط هذا الكتاب وابتدئ فيه بعلّةِ اختلافهم والذي دعاهم إليه، وحملهم عليه، وسبّبهم فيه، وأتلوا ذلك بذكرِ جملةِ قولهم، وما أصَّلُوهُ لأنفسهم، وبيانِ فسادهِ عليهم، وأشفّعهُ بذكرِ مذهب أهل الحقِّ فيما

[186] Nuʿmān, *Ikhtilāf*, pp. a–b.
[187] Nuʿmān, *Ikhtilāf*, pp. 1–2.

اختلفوا فيه، وإيضاحهِ وبيانهِ، والشواهد له والدلائل عليه. ثم أذكرُ بعد ذلك قولَ كلِّ فرقةٍ واحتجاجها بما قالتهُ، والردّ عليها فيما فارقتْ فيه الحقَّ بما انتحلتهُ، وقولَ أهلِ الحقِّ في ذلك بحسب ما أخذناه عن أئمّتنا عليهم السلام، رجاءَ ثوابَ الخدمة في ذلك، والعناية بأسبابه. فأمّا البرهان فلأولياء اللّٰه المفيدين له والفاتحين لأبوابه.

Appendix VI

ذكر جملة قول المختلفين في أحكام الدين:[188]

أجمع المنسوبون إلى الفقه من العامّة أنّ ما كان من الأحكام وعلم الحلال والحرام ظاهراً في نصّ القرآن وجب الحكم والعمل به، وأنّ ما لم يوجد بزعمهم من ذلك في القرآن أُلتمس في سنّة الرسول صلّى اللّٰه عليه وعلى آله. فإنّ وُجد في السنّة أُخذ به ولم يتعدّ إلى غيره. وقال كثيرٌ منهم: 'وما لم يكن من ذلك في كتاب اللّٰه جلّ ذكره ولا في سنّة رسول اللّٰه صلّى اللّٰه عليه وعلى آله نظرناه في قول الصحابة. فإن أصبناهم قد قالوه وأجمعوا عليه أخذنا به، وإنْ أصبناهم اختلفوا فيه تخيَّرنا قول من شئنا منهم، فقلنا به'.

وقال بعضهم: 'ومن أصبناه قال به منهم لم نخرج عن قوله، وما لم نجده في كتاب اللّٰه ولا في سنّة رسول اللّٰه صلّى اللّٰه عليه وعلى آله ولا في قول أحدٍ من الصحابة نظرنا، فإنْ كان مما اجتمع العلماء عليه قلنا به، ولم نخرج عن إجماعهم فيه.'

... واختلفوا فيمن قلّدوه، فذهب كلُّ فريقٍ منهم إلى قول قائلٍ ممن تقدّمهم. فقالوا بقوله، وأحلّوا ما أحلّه لهم، وحرّموا ما حرّمه عليهم، وأقاموا قوله حجّةً عندهم، وأعرضوا عن قول من خالفه ... وخطّأ بعضهم بعضاً، وكفّر قومٌ

[188] Nuʿmān, *Ikhtilāf*, pp. 8–10.

منهم قوماً ممّن خالفهم، وفارقهم آخرون ... وقالوا: 'لنا أن نستنبط كما استنبطوه ولا نقلّدهم.' فقال بعضهم بالقياس، وقال آخرون بالرأي والاجتهاد. وقال آخرون بالاستحسان، وقال الآخرون بالنظر، وقال آخرون بالاستدلال. وهذه ألقاب لقّبوا بها مذاهبهم لينسبوها إلى الحقّ بزعمهم. وكلُّها يرجع إلى أصلٍ واحدٍ، ويجمعها معنى فاسدٍ وهو اتّباع الهوى والظنّ ... .

Appendix VII

وكان سبب جمعي هذا الكتاب في مثل هذا وذلك إني جاريتُ بعض من يذهب إلى القول بالاجتهاد. فأبنتُ له فساد القول به، واحتججتُ عليه بمثل ما ذكرتُ من الحجّة في هذا الكتاب حتّى انقطع. وقد رأيتُ أنه اعترف بالحقّ ورجع. ثمّ انتهى إلى بعد ذلك أنه جمع كرّاسةً ذكر فيها قول القائلين بالاجتهاد، وحجّتهم فيه إصراراً منه بعد الحجّة على ما كان عليه. وقد حكيتُ في هذا الكتاب جميع ما صنّفه في كرّاسته من قول أصحابه، وغير ذلك ممّا انتهى إليّ من قولهم وحججهم ممّا لم يذكره، وأبنتُ فساده والحجّة عليهم فيه. ولم أر أن أقصد إلى إبطال الاجتهاد خاصّة. فيرى من انتهى ذلك عنّي إليه إنّي ارتضيتُ ما سواه ممّا صنّفه في هذا الكتاب من أصول مذاهب المخالفين للحقّ. فرأيتُ، وباللّه التوفيق، ذكر جميع أقاويلهم والحجّة فيما أصّلوه عليهم، رجاءَ ثواب اللّه تعالى في ذلك جلّ ذكره، وإيّاه أسألُ وأرجو أن يجعل ذلك خالصاً لوجهه وصلّى اللّه على محمدٍ عبده ورسوله وعلى الأئمّة الأبرار من أهل بيته وسلّم تسليماً.[189]

[189] Nuʿmān, *Ikhtilāf*, pp. 232–233.

13

The Theory of *Māl* among the Zaydīs*

Sayyid Zayd al-Wazir

I

When discussing the theory of *māl* (property, possession, money, it can also mean *zakāt*, or taxes) in Islam, special attention should be given to all historical narratives of the early period, especially those concerning claim to the absolute authority of the 'Rightly Guided Caliphs' (*al-khulafā' al-rāshidūn*), and how this claim came to be manipulated for political purposes. Our main attention should focus on the changes that occurred to the function of *māl*, and therefore we must investigate these changes which were skilfully concealed even by different transmitted reports.

It should be noted that scholars who were affiliated with the authority of the time gave the Abbasid and Umayyad rulers more authority, which was not even available to the Rightly Guided Caliphs. This gave them the leeway to manipulate decisions concerning the financial matters of the state and the natural function of money. As a result, they managed to transfer the authority over financial matters from a human regulation that was formulated by the Companions at the meeting of *al-Saqīfa* to a divine regulation, thus transforming the caliphate from a purely civil institution to a royal religious monopoly, where the caliph – as the vicegerent of God on earth – was given broad and absolute authority. As a result, the caliph was able to change the function of the Muslim treasury from a public property that belonged to the whole *umma* to a private one that belonged to the ruler, the *walī al-amr*. The new caliph became the successor 'caliph' of God – rather than the successor of the messenger of God – and the money was designated as the money of God, which the caliph as the deputy of God had a monopoly over, to be used for whatever purpose he decided and distributed to whomever he chose.

This tactic adopted by the scholars affiliated with the government was successful because the period of the Rightly Guided Caliphs was the closest to the time of the Prophet, and who adhered very closely to his teachings and implemented it vehemently. The manipulation of this practice and presenting it as a natural function of

* Translated from the Arabic by Nuha al-Shaar.

the caliphate was one of the ways to convince the *umma* and make it accept these changes in a period when literary culture among Muslims was in the process of formation and not yet established. It was a period when anecdotes and myths were mixed with historical facts, which allowed the rulers and the scholars affiliated to them to establish their own authority, while the people accepted these distorted versions of reality as historical facts.

In light of this, it should be first noted that the regulations concerning the treasury and other financial matters were religiously sanctioned as given facts. Therefore, there is also a need to distinguish that which is divine from that which is human, because looking at these human regulations as divinely sanctioned prevents a clear understanding of them. This can be seen in relation to the absolute financial authority given to a Rightly Guided Caliph, and also his unquestionable religious authority, while his authority in terms of the financial policy was not divinely legitimised. The Muslims agreed to establish these financial rights in accordance with the collaborative leadership on which the caliphate during the period of the Rightly Guided Caliphs was based. A closer look at the intentions behind the transformation of human regulations into divinely sanctioned ones shows that it was intended to demolish the authority of the the public treasury of Muslims, while maintaining the authority of the treasury of the ruler. We know from the undistorted facts reaching us that Muslims gave the trustee of the public treasury absolute authority that exceeded the authorities of the caliphs in this respect. In fact, the trustee of the public treasury of Muslims would oppose those decisions which were not obtained by the approval of the Companions, either by the consultation process, namely the *shūrā*, or by agreeing to them. The trustee of the public treasury of Muslims was the one who would publicly decide on the salary of the caliph, as in the case of Abū Bakr.[1]

However, as a result of corruption in the administration during the time of the Caliph 'Uthmān and because of the strong influence of the Umayyads, the trustee of the public treasury gave his resignation to the righteous people inside the mosque, meaning inside the council, the *majlis shūrā,* and in the presence of the caliph himself. He did not give it to the house of the caliphate or to the caliph.[2] Thus, to reinforce the individual authority of the caliph in the governing system that was based on the

[1] Ibn Sa'd reported on the authority of 'Atā' that after people pledged alligiance to Abū Bakr, he was heading to the market in the morning to work when he was seen by 'Umar. 'Umar asked him where he was going. Abū Bakr replied: 'To the market'. Then 'Umar asked: 'What would you do there when you have become the trustee of Muslim affairs?' Abū Bakr replied: 'How I would then feed my children?' Then 'Umar said: 'Let us go to Abu 'Ubayda and he will allocate you a salary.' They went to Abu 'Ubayda who allocated to Abū Bakr a salary that is equal to the provision of a man from the immigrants (*al-muhājirūn*), who is not from the higher class or the lower class, and clothing for the winter and the summer, which could be replaced when they are torn out. Ibn Sa'd on the authority of Ibn Maymūn also said that when Abū Bakr was made caliph, he was given 2,000 *dinārs* as a salary, but he said: 'Please give me more, because I have children and the new post will not allow me to take part in trade.' So he was given 500 *dirhams* more. See online: www.omelketab.net.

[2] Ṭāhā Ḥusayn, *al-Fitna al-kubrā': 'Uthmān* (9th ed., Cairo, 1947), p. 190.

rule of the 'caliph-caesar', and to conceal the authority of the trustee of the public treasury, the following claims were put forward: (a) the trustee of the public treasury of Muslims had certain authorities, and (b) the Caliph Abū Bakr had a special independent financial policy, while 'Umar, 'Uthmān and 'Alī each had their own policies which they implemented – but without linking these policies to a collaborative form of leadership, or an obligatory consultative process. In addition, the claim that it is the right of each caliph to have his own financial policy was a way to reject the consultative process (*al-khalīfa al-shūrī*) from the political memory in order to reinforce the legitimacy and acceptance of the rule of the 'caliph-caesar'.

Thus, one should be wary of the different reports that have been reinvented and attributed to the period of the time of the Rightly Guided Caliphs. A researcher should also critically investigate the different reports about the financial policies of the Rightly Guided Caliphs and the intentions behind them. To this effect, I took upon myself to critically reread this history in light of the teaching of the Qur'an, and in light of the existence of a collaborative leadership and an obligatory consultative process.[3]

II

I shall now discuss the function of *māl* among the Zaydīs, in general and the Zaydī Hadawī,[4] in particular. However, I will focus on the purposes and the ways in which this money is spent rather than its sources. This is because the Zaydī position on the sources of money does not differ from other branches. The Zaydīs seem to have a unique position when it comes to the function of this money and that is what sets them apart from other groups. In fact, it does not only exist in theory, but has also been implemented in practice in Yemen.

A discussion of this function is not an easy task because of the wider context of legal reasoning in the Zaydī tradition, which allows the absolute use of personal opinions and reasoning in all matters (*al-ijtihād al-muṭlaq*), and not only in matters of doctrine. The Zaydī school was established on the basis of this absolute use of opinion and reasoning. To put it differently, the Zaydī doctrine seems to be a more accurate expression here. This absolute use of opinion and reasoning facilitated the emergence of scholars who have different approaches, use their personal opinions and judgements, and who are not affiliated with any political establishment or are not restrained by any pressing pattern. This leads to flexibility and diversity in Zaydī thought due to the diversity in employing personal opinion, *ijtihād*. This also led to the development of various branches among the Zaydīs that have their own attitude

[3] For more details, see my book *al-Fardiyya: azmat al-fiqh al-siyāsī 'ind al-muslimīn* published by the Yemeni Heritage and Research Centre (Sanaa, 1420/2000).

[4] The Zaydī Hadawī are an offshoot from the Zaydīs. The Zaydīs allowed *ijtihād*, but Imam al-Hādī's thought differed from their principles as he was influenced by the Mu'tazila-Balakhī and also the Ḥanafī school of thinking; thus his followers are known as the Zaydī Hadawī.

regarding these issues. This is the reason behind the difficulties for the existence of a unifying pattern such as that present within the Mālikī, Ḥanafī, Shāfiʿī or Hanbalī schools of law. However, the Zaydīs followed a different path which is not limited by any strict jurisprudential model that limits its flexibility. This openness led them to establish certain rules that became essential in making judgements, taking into consideration all that which corresponds to this rule, even if it disagrees with the opinions of their Imams.[5] This also helped them to adopt *marjaʿiyyat kul mujtahid muṣīb* (the rule which states that personal opinions and judgements of all recognised scholars – *mujtahid*s – are considered correct and valid) as a solution to all the disagreements between the different juridical judgements that are based on personal opinions. It underlines the difficulty of finding one main line of thinking, and makes it equally hard to write about Zaydī doctrine with a specific legal framework as a result of the existence of the many judgements that are based on the exercise of personal opinions (*ijtihād*). However, the Zaydī perspective on the function of *māl* is more complex than this.

III

A close look at the various Zaydī positions shows the importance of the social function of *māl*, which is to be used for the welfare of the society. It has been proven that when this function was mismanaged, the *umma* suffered and people were exploited at the hands of the ruling elites.

During his reign, Muʿāwiya (d. 60/680) relied upon the saying that 'Money is the money of God';[6] however, Abū Dharr al-Ghaffarī (d. 32/652) recognised his true intention (that is, that Muʿāwiya wanted to exclude people from overseeing and benefiting from this money)[7] to ensure this money belonged to the caliph and not to the people, since he was the successor (caliph) of God. Since then, there was a division in the understanding of the concept of the ownership of money between the perspective of a Rightly Guided Caliph and the perspective of a greedy king. In fact, it seems that the latter perspective won in the end. This also means that the social function of the money ceased and the public treasury of the Muslim people was not used for social purposes.

Although the Zaydī approach was somewhat influenced by these changes, it indeed preserved the public right to *māl*, remaining loyal to its own understanding of the nature and the social function of money. The fulfilment of this function has also remained something that is demanded from a Zaydī Imam, so if he failed in

---

[5] See ʿAbd Allāh b. Miftāḥ, *Sharḥ al-azhār min al-ghayth al-midrār* (Cairo, 1377), pp. 46–48; Ḥusayn Aḥmad al-Siyāghī, *Uṣūl al-madhhab al-Zaydī al-Yamanī wa-qawāʿiduh* (Sanaa and Damascus, 1984).

[6] Ibn al-Athīr, *al-Kāmil fī al-taʾrīkh* (Beirut, 1385/1956), vol. 3, p. 114.

[7] Ibid., p. 115.

implementing social justice, he would lose his status as an Imam, and it was the right of people to rebel against him.

IV

The implementation of the social function of *māl* reached its peak at the time of ʿAlī b. Abī Ṭālib,[8] upon whose teachings the Zaydī school is based. This application of finance theory was supported by the Commander of the Faithful and the Companions of the Prophet. Among them an important place was held by Abū Dhir al-Ghafarī, who had struggled to achieve social justice since the appearance of the feudal system and ownership over large properties towards the end of ʿUthmān's reign.[9] When al-Ghafarī demanded that an end be put to the accumulation of wealth since he felt it was a form of monopoly enjoyed by the rich people and the rulers alike, he was attacked by these powerful landowners and rulers. As a punishment for raising objections, al-Ghafarī was exiled by Muʿāwiya to Medina under ʿUthmān's instructions. Later, he was exiled by ʿUthmān from Medina to the desert.[10] However, his legacy remained through history among the aggrieved.

It can be said that the economic monopoly of God's caliph started to appear when Muʿāwiya pronounced that 'Money belongs to God'. Acquisition of money came to be seen as the right of the caliph himself because of his position as the caliph of God. It was the first time that Muʿāwiya made a connection between wealth and power. Thus, Abū Dhir al-Ghafarī's teachings were overridden by Muʿāwiya's alternative form of governing, which was soon sanctified by the scholars who were affiliated to the Umayyad authority. From the beginning there were various oppositions to his policies, but without a majority consensus.

It has been narrated that ʿUthmān said: 'This money belongs to God. I will give it to those whom I wish to have it, and withhold it from those whom I do not wish to have it. So God will banish each one who disobeys me.' Then ʿAmar b. Yāsir said: 'I am the first who will do so', and he was assailed and beaten by the Umayyads.[11] It could be that ʿUthmān did not say this because the term 'God's caliph' had not yet come into use. It may have been attributed to him to support the claim that he held the title of 'God's caliph'.

According to Ṭāhā Ḥusayn:

> The finances of Muslims came to belong to the caliphs. They spent the money as they desired, and not as God desired it to be spent. Muʿāwiya bribed many people

[8] For examples of his rulings on social matters, see Jūrj Jurdāq, *al-Imām ʿAlī Ṣawt al-ʿadāla al-insāniyya* (Beirut, 1970), 5 vols.

[9] For information on the emergence of these ownerships, see Ḥusayn, *al-Fitna al-kubrā*, p. 105.

[10] Ibn al-Athīr, *al-Kāmil*, vol. 3, p. 115.

[11] Ibn al-ʿUbrī, *Taʾrīkh mukhtaṣar al-duwal* (Beirut, n.d.), p. 106.

> in Kufa and Basra and instigated them to rise up against ʿAlī, and continued to do so even after things were set right for him. He continued to win the support of people by misusing the people's money. The Umayyad caliphs who came later continued his policy, and thus wasted the money, ignoring the tradition of the Prophet, the two shaykhs [Abū Bakr and ʿUmār], and ʿAlī, God's mercy may be upon him.[12]

He also stated: 'Muʿāwiya's extravagance with Muslims' money, his preferential treatment of the strongest over the weakest, and the extravagance of the strongest in the people's money and blood, were all contrary to the pledge of allegiance that he made to his people.'[13]

Imam Zayd b. ʿAlī, the founder of the Zaydī doctrine (d. 122/740), struggled for the right of the *umma* to benefit from its money, rejecting that only the caliph had the right to manage this money. He promised in his speech, when pledging allegiance as Imam, to return the social function of the stolen money. In his speech in 122/739 when he revolted against the Umayyad caliph Hishām b. ʿAbd al-Malik, he clearly defined his public policy. What interests us in particular here is what has been mentioned about his financial policy. He said: 'We are inviting you to adhere to the Book of Allah and the *sunna* of his Prophet, to fight against the oppressors, to give the disadvantaged people their share of this booty equally, and to set right injustice, and to support the people to whom it rightly belongs. So do you give me your allegiance on this basis?'[14] This shows that money, for him, was a means and not an end in itself. It has a social function that leads to achieving social and economic justice. This function was suspended during the reign of the Umayyads and others, which led to an economic monopoly that was manifested in injustice in the distribution of wealth. This in turn resulted in social injustice leading to elitism in society. He demanded the termination of the ruler's monopoly over public money, to put an end to monopoly in society, and to return to the practice of using the money to create social solidarity and implement justice and equality by its fair distribution.

In looking carefully at the origin of this theory, we immediately recognise that it is based on the Qur'anic verse 15:7 that clearly denies that the money should only be in the possession of the rich. This is in order not to jeopardise social solidarity (both in terms of material and spiritual matters), which is based on righteousness and piety (Q.5:2). Moreover, even the consultations and negotiations around money should be based on righteousness and piety, in the same way that social relationships and manners are also based on piety (Q.2:189). A society that is based on righteousness and virtue rejects monopoly and exploitation and welcomes spending money on social welfare (Q.3:92).

---

12 Ṭāhā Ḥusayn, *Mirʾat al-Islām* (Cairo, 1959), p. 232.

13 Ḥusayn, *al-Fitna al-kubrā*, p. 196.

14 Muḥammad Abū Zahrā, *al-Imām Zayd ḥayātuh wa-ʿaṣruh, arāʾuh wa-fiqhuh* (Cairo, n.d.), pp. 56–57.

This theory had been misused before the time of Zayd and was replaced by monopoly over the money. After Zayd's time, the matter became worse because the monopoly reached its apex during the age of the Abbasid caliph, Abū Jaʿfar al-Manṣūr (d. 158/775). He claimed to be God's sultan on earth and the treasurer of His alms and the one responsible for the distribution of this money. He said that God had made him the lock on His deposit box ('If God wants, He would unlock me and allow me to give money to you, but if He does not wish to give money, he would keep me locked.')[15] It is at this point that the money stopped being used for social purposes and was openly mismanaged and spent in one direction to strengthen the authority of one person, the ruler. The *umma* was excluded completely from participating in overseeing this money or even supervising how it was spent. According to these events it becomes clear that the Umayyad caliphs – excluding ʿUmar b. ʿAbd al-ʿAzīz (d. 101/720) and Yazīd (d. 126/744) – were not the only ones who abused this public right since the Abbasid caliphs did the same thing, reinforcing further the absolute right of the ruler to control the money.

The attempts by Zayd to restore the use of money for social purposes undoubtedly failed; money was used only by and for the rich people, and the poor were excluded from control over it. Thus, money was used to further enrich the wealthy. It was not used for the common social good, the purpose for which it had been intended. In this context, it could be said that the Zaydī theory of money is very significant.

V

The teachings of Imam Zayd as reflected in his book *Majmūʿ al-fiqh al-kabīr*, and in his messages and speeches preserved by his students, show that he objected to the monopoly over money by the rich and powerful. Therefore, the concept of using money for the community's welfare and social justice was also a priority for his successors, and it became a valuable legacy.

The Imams continued to work to create a community in which material causes were in agreement with spiritual ones, as reflected in the Qur'anic verse 2:177. Hence, the Zaydīs legalised ownership, but at the same time restricted it by a number of conditions that have been applied to ownership contracts based on their understanding of the distinctive *ḥadīth*: 'there shall be no harming, injuring or hurting, of one man by another, in the first instance, nor in return, or requital in Islam'.[16] This Zaydī policy faced opposition from some governors, including some who belonged to the Zaydī Hadawī.

When talking about social justice we should mention that the Zaydī tradition considered the voluntary and obligatory contribution of each individual as part of

[15] See his speech in Jalāl al-Dīn al-Suyūṭī, *Ta'rīkh al-khulafā'*, ed. Muḥyi al-Dīn ʿAbd al-Ḥamīd (Cairo, 1371/1952), p. 263.

[16] Aḥmad, article online: http://www.islamweb.net.

the social function. Even though this theory was not fully implemented, it reduced individual exploitation. Thus, it can be said that the Zaydīs had classified the incomes from both voluntary and obligatory sources as a way to promote social solidarity. This stance is in line with the teaching of the holy Qur'an, which encourages alms giving. I would like to clarify that this teaching and the emphasis on giving was not a passive one, but that it was actively sought after. However, ultimately it is left up to each individual whether to give or not according to their circumstances.

In addition to giving alms to the public, there is the duty to give money to parents, relatives and travellers (Q.2:215, 51:19, and 70:24–25). So here there is a recognised right that is defined and no religious scholar can manipulate it. Some jurists tried to interpret it as a kind of *zakāt*, or alms. This opinion was held by Muḥammad b. ʿAbd Allāh al-Andalūsī, known as Ibn ʿArabī (d. 543/1148), who says that this prescribed due is the *zakāt* and the Islamic law has defined its measure, kind and time. Anything else apart from it is not known because it has not been properly prescribed in terms of measure, kind and time. This interpretation, however, was refuted by those two verses that specifically refer to the needy and the beggar. The verse on *zakāt*, however, is defined in eight ways, and the word *maʿlūm* means 'acknowledged' and 'made clear'. Imam al-Zamakhsharī (d. 538/1143) was between the two opinions: it can either be *zakāt*, because it is defined and measured, or it can be charity which a believer applies on himself and which he fulfils at certain times (*awqāṭ maʿlūma*).[17] This is the closest interpretation to the meaning of the verse.

In addition to *zakāt*, charity, and giving money to parents, relatives and travellers, and the prescribed due *al-ḥaqq al-maʿlūm*, there is the interest in public welfare. There are numerous verses that encourage good deeds for the welfare of society, both morally and materially. Included in these verses are Qur'an 2:215, 272 and 3:115.

In this context, one can mention what is called *zakāt al-fitr*. Imam Aḥmad b. Yaḥyā' al-Murtaḍā (d. 840/1436), extended the time of its distribution from the sunrise on the day of ʿĪd to the sunset of the same day.[18] In fact, ʿAbd Allāh b. Hamzā (d. 614/1217) extended the distribution of it over the period of three days in order to allow people to spend more during the days of the feast, and to give more time to those who missed the time of giving. All the ways of spending we encounter concerning voluntary charity can also be found in the context of obligatory spending, such as *zakāt* (money tax), *khums* (one-fifth, or 20 per cent), *ʿushr* (one-tenth, or 10 per cent), *ʿafw* (surplus money), etc. This shows that in both cases the money given has a social function that benefits all groups in the society.

Zakāt may seem to be the clearest evidence of how money is used to promote social solidarity. It is not considered as part of government revenue, but is a revenue that belongs to the *umma*. It is taken from the money of the rich and distributed to the poor. It represents a social productive episode; it is taken from the private income

---

17 Al-Zamakhsharī, *al-Kashshāf ʿan ḥaqāʾiq al-tanzīl wa ʿuyūn al-aqāwīl fī wujūh al-taʾwīl* (Beirut, n. d.), vol. 4, p. 156.

18 ʿAbd Allāh b. Miftāḥ, *Sharḥ al-azhār al-muntazaʿ min al-gayth al-midrār* (2nd ed., Cairo, 1357), p. 548.

of a person or properties, such as gold, silver, agricultural crops and animals (e.g., camels, cows and sheep).[19] *Zakāt* is considered as part of the social spending, whether it is collected by the government or not. It is a religious duty, like prayer, pilgrimage, etc., and should be performed by the individual in line with the eight ways in which it is defined in the Qur'an, even in the absence of a just government.

Due to the social welfare function of *zakāt*, the money is neither taken from the poor nor given to the rich. In the opinion of Imam Zayd b. ʿAlī: 'Alms are not taken from the one who only has 50 *dirhams*, and should not be given to the one who has 50 *dirhams*.[20] This is also by al-Hādī Yaḥyā b. al-Ḥusayn who said: 'It is not permitted for one to take charity if he has any form of money upon which charity is due.' The Prophet also said to Muʿādh: 'Let them know that there is a due charity on their money. It should be taken from their rich and given to their poor.' So he made the one from whom charity is taken the rich person, and the one to whom it is given the poor.[21] The poor man takes what he needs from the alms according to the number of family members he has to support.[22] So everything here primarily depends on need, and we should pay attention to the fact that charity is not given to shroud the dead and to build a mosque; this money is used for the benefit of those who are alive and are in need. The author of *al-Majmūʿ al-kabīr* explained this saying in the following way: 'It is decreed by God, the Almighty that alms are to be used to comfort the poor and to satisfy their hunger and fulfil the requirements set out in the rest of the eight categories. The money collected from *zakāt* should not be spent to cover the expenses of someone's shroud, or the building of a mosque.'[23]

This was also the opinion of the great Imams of the Zaydīs in Ṭabaristān – al-Nāṣir al-Uṭrūsh and al-Mu'ayyad bi'llāh (d. 421/1030). Zayd's opinion was supported by Imam Mālik, Abū Ḥanīfa and al-Shāfiʿī, while others said that it was permissible.[24] Because the money is a means to benefit Muslims, the need itself is the point of reference here. Therefore, even the rich have the right to benefit from it when in need.[25] The same thing can be said for the traveller or the passer-by. He can take from the alms what he needs to help him to get home, but if he did not travel, he should return what he had been given so that it could be used by someone else.[26] Thus, money corresponds to a social need and is a kind of sustenance that should be given to the one in need. It is for this reason that the Zaydī tradition bans charity from being given to unjust Imams because it strengthens them in their injustice: 'As for those who

[19] Ḥusayn b. Aḥmad al-Siyāghī, *al-Rawḍ al-naḍīr: sharḥ Majmūʿ al-fiqh al-kabīr* (2nd ed., Taif, 1968), vol. 2, pp. 620–621.

[20] Ibid., p. 601.

[21] Ibid., p. 602.

[22] Al-Hādī, *al-Aḥkām fī al-ḥalāl wa'l-ḥarām* (Sanaa, 1420/2000), vol. 1, p. 226.

[23] Al-Siyāghī, *al-Rawḍ al-naḍīr*, vol. 2, pp. 621–622.

[24] Ibid., pp. 621–622.

[25] ʿAbd Allāh b. Miftāḥ, *Sharḥ al-azhār*, vol. 1, p. 517.

[26] Ibid., p. 534.

persevere in helping unjust people to establish and build their business … without them, the oppressors would not exist.'[27]

Aḥmad b. ʿĪsā (d. 247/861), the grandson of Imam Zayd, decreed that charity should not be given to the unjust: 'The one who is able to give money to charity should never give it to an unjust Imam, but should spend it in the way that God would like it to be spent.'[28] Imam al-Qāsim b. Ibrāhīm also said: 'No one should pay a due sum on his money, land, or property apart from that which has been prescribed by God, and which he is obliged to pay in the form of *zakāt*. He should not pay this *zakāt* unless there is a just Imam to whom he should give it, or he should find out those deserving of his charity and pay it to them directly.'[29]

According to the opinion of the Commander of the Faithful, ʿAlī, the extorted money is not lost when it is distributed among men. Al-Hādī and his followers refused the idea of compulsory provisions on which the oppressor puts his hand as a provision given to him by God. So he and his followers established their doctrines. Muḥammad ʿAmāra said: 'In the matter of provisions, there is an important intellectual basis from which many points can be deduced. Some of them are related to social justice, when those who steal the money of the poor are charged, even if they refuse to admit the right of the poor to the money generation after generation.'[30]

Because of its social function and benefit to people, *zakāt* should be withheld from the one who does not spend it on himself or if it does not go towards the benefit of society; for example, giving it to an immoral poor person would facilitate him in his wrongdoing and immorality, and therefore the one who gives it to him would share in his corruption. If there were no just Imam, or if there were a just Imam but the owner of the money is not in his province and is not able to protect him, then the owner should better spend this money according to the societal needs.[31]

Now we come to the function of *māl al-ʿafw* (the money that exceeds one's need), something which was ignored and had not been implemented, despite the clear reference to it in the Qur'an (2:199). According to Ibn Manẓūr (d. 711/1311), *ʿafw* (*ʿafw al-māl*) is that which remains after expenditure, and he refers to Qur'an 2:199. Al-Jawharī (d. 393/1003) says in *al-Ṣiḥāḥ:* '*ʿafw* is the land that has not been inhabited yet and has no traces', and the *ʿafw* of the money is that which remains after expenditure. It is said, 'I gave him the *ʿafw* of the money, meaning without him asking for it.'[32] Al-Azharī (d. 370/981) said citing Ibn al-Sakīt: '*ʿafw al-bilād* is that which no one has ruled over or owned yet'; and he said: '*ʿafw al-māʾ* is that which remains

[27] Imām Yaḥyāʾ b. al-Ḥusayn, *Rasāʾil al-ʿadl waʾl-tawḥīd*, ed. Muḥammad ʿAmāra (Cairo, n.d.), vol. 2, p. 13.

[28] *Al-Jāmiʿ al-kāfī fī fiqh al-Zaydiyya* (manuscript), vol. 1, p. 405.

[29] *Majmūʿ kutub wa-rasāʾil al-imām al-Qāsim al-Rassī*, in ʿAbd al-Fattaḥ Shāʾif Nuʿmān, *al-Imām al-Hādī Yaḥyāʾ b. al-Ḥusayn b. al-Qāsim al-Rassī* (Sanaa, 1410/1989), vol. 2, p. 546.

[30] Imam Yaḥyāʾ b. al-Ḥusayn, *Rasāʾil al-ʿadl waʾl-tawḥīd*, vol. 2, p. 13.

[31] ʿAbd Allāh b. Miftāḥ, *Sharḥ al-azhār*, vol. 1, p. 517.

[32] Ismāʿīl b. Ḥimād al-Jawharī, *al-Ṣiḥāh tāj al-lugha wa-ṣiḥāḥ al-ʿArabiyya* (2nd ed., Beirut, 1979/1399), vol. 6, pp. 2431–2432.

after people have drunk';[33] he also said: 'The origin is that *ʿafw* in language is the remaining of something.'[34] Imam al-Hādī made reference to the Qur'an to this form of charity in his financial theory. He used to distribute the revenue for the benefit of people and for the protection of their affairs.[35] For al-Hādī, *ʿafw* is the surplus which if spent does not harm the one who did so, and it is not a form of charity, but it is obligatory, whether one likes it or not. Imam al-Zamakhsharī, whose opinions are approved by the Zaydī Hadawī, agreed with Imam al-Hādī's opinion regarding *ʿafw* (surplus money). He went on to say that *ʿafw* is the opposite of effort; it is to give more than effort can give.[36]

Some have abandoned completely this clear financial source and go as far as to to say that *māl al-ʿafw* had been abrogated by alms giving. This opinion corresponds to the need of a society which has been redefined and where everything has changed. It is no wonder that the Qur'anic verses which call for social justice would not remain intact within this changing society. However, the abrogating verse (Q.2:106), does not mean that the other verses have been abrogated completely, but shows that the latter replaces the former because it fits the purpose of the new circumstances better.

Voluntary action is also based on a compulsory moral commitment, since the collective conscience of the *umma* made it an obligatory thing. For example, when people were subject to the famine in the year of al-Ramāda (the year of the famous drought), the Caliph ʿUmar b. al-Khaṭṭāb (d. 23/644) ordered, after consulting the Companions, that rich people should dine and share their food with the poor. This then turned from a voluntary duty to an obligatory one. In addition, when the Companions noticed that landowners did not fulfil their voluntary duties, the Caliph, supported by the Companions, declared that if it were all up to him, he would take from the money of the rich people a sum and give it to the poor. He decided to implement this policy the following year, but he was martyred before that. It is clear that voluntary action is a moral commitment; if one does not fulfil it, he should be judged by the *umma*. On the basis of the use of personal opinions of the Companions, the religious scholars infer what they call *al-maṣāliḥ al-mursala*, which make the private money subject to public use in cases of necessity.

Thus, according to the Zaydī law, the property of metals (such as gold, silver, iron, copper), sheep and treasures should be also used for the benefit of society, and not for the benefit of the government.[37] This is in line with what has been emphasised by ʿUmar b. ʿAbd al-ʿAzīz in his financial reform policies. This system is based on that

---

33 Abū Manṣūr Muḥammad b. Aḥmad al-Azharī, *Muʿjam tahdhīb al-lugha* (Beirut, 1422/2001), vol. 3, p. 2489.

34 Ibid., p. 2491.

35 Yaḥyā' b. al-Ḥusayn al-Hādī, *Jawāb masā'il al-Ḥusayn b. ʿAbd Allāh al-Ṭabarī* (Sanaa, 1420/2000), p. 665.

36 Al-Zamakhsharī, *al-Kashshāf*, vol. 1, p. 360.

37 Al-Siyāghī, *al-Rawḍ al-naḍīr*, vol. 2, p. 610ff.

introduced by ʿUmar, even if the application has been altered because of differing circumstances.[38]

VI

Now we come to the last section of this study and ask whether the Zaydīs or Zaydī Hadawīs have implemented all these principles in practice. The answer will become clear by looking at the example of Imam al-Hādī Yaḥyā' b. al-Ḥusayn when he entered Yemen in 284/897 supported by several Yemeni tribes, and invited people to ascribe to his doctrine. When he took the pledge of allegiance as the Commander of the Faithful, he founded the Zaydī state in Yemen. This state became the centre for the implementation of the Zaydī principles. There was also a Zaydī state in Ṭabaristān under the leadership of al-Ḥasan b. Zayd, which preceded the emergence of this Zaydī state in Yemen. It is beyond the scope of this chapter to discuss the ideas of this state, although it should be mentioned that their ideas are in general agreement with the common Zaydī principles, except for some jurisprudential judgements that are based on personal opinions, especially those of Nāṣir al-Ḥasan b. ʿAlī b. Uṭrūsh (d. 304/917). It can be said that talking about the social function of finance among the Zaydīs of Yemen is indirectly addressing the same function among the Zaydīs of Ṭabaristān. It will suffice here to outline the main principles of the financial and agricultural policy applied by Imam al-Hādī, followed by his followers and even the oppressors among them. This will highlight the theory of the Zaydīs as it was expressed by Zayd b. ʿAlī in his famous speech included in his *al-Majmūʿ al-kabīr*, his teachings, his letters and his books, which were followed by the other Zaydī Imams after him.

In order to know the difference between the implementation of the financial principles by Imam al-Hādī, and its implementation at the time of the Abbasid caliphate, it suffices here to mention the statement of al-Ṭaqṭaqī that 'the governors bribed the wazirs in order to remain in charge of their provinces, while the accountants (*rijāl al-ḥisba*) accepted bribery, when they inspected traders'.[39]

Shā'if, quoting the *Dīwān* of Ibn-Muʿtaz, who was an Abbasid caliph for one day, draws a picture of the way in which the tax was collected. He said: 'As for the tax-collectors, they used to beat the money owners, pulling them by their faces, and hanging them by their hands and feet, in order to get from them whatever money they could, claiming that they were taking from them that which was the due right of the Muslims. However, in reality most of this money went to them and to those who appointed them.'[40]

On the contrary, the financial policy of Imam al-Hādī, according to Imam Abū Zahrā, was based on the just distribution of wealth throughout Yemen in order to

38 ʿAbd al-ʿAzīz al-Dawrī, *Muqaddima fī ta'rīkh ṣadr al-Islām* (Beirut, 1984), p. 87.

39 Shā'if, *al-Imām al-Hādī*, pp. 44–45; al-Masʿūdī, *Murūj al-dhahab* (Sanaa, n.d.), vol. 4, p. 259.

40 Shā'if, *al-Imām al-Hādī*, pp. 44–45, *Diwān ibn al-Muʿtaz*, p. 481.

achieve stability and security. This is because people would not be reassured unless fair judgement was deployed. He worked to spread justice in all its forms, especially social justice. Therefore, he organised the treasury and collected alms and tributes, which were then distributed among people. Also, he believed that a quarter of the alms collected should be spent on the people of the same village where the alms had been donated. He devoted all his energy to organising the treasury according to these principles.[41]

Al-Hādī chose the most reliable methods to estimate the value of fruit and involved those who knew most about it. He used to take oaths from them that they would be fair and would not transgress against anyone, as he would for example advise al-Ḥusayn b. ʿAbd Allāh al-Ṭabarī.[42] Because of his belief in the social function of money, he refused to manipulate the money of people in any way that could be considered unjust. When his friends said to him: 'If you were going to take only a portion of 33, a third of 10, and half of 10th, not much will be collected as a result.' He replied: 'I do not want to collect anything at all from this. By God, if this and this were to meet [referring to the heaven and earth] against my ribs, I would not take anything which is not right.'[43]

His words were combined with actions. According to al-Muqaddasī, he abolished all the taxes and royalties which were imposed on people by the unjust princes and shaykhs. He did not take anything from traders except the prescribed *zakāt*,[44] thus again underlining his point that the purpose of *māl* is to facilitate happiness, not misery. Then he turned to agricultural policy and organised the relationship between the owner and the partner on the basis of 'the land belongs to the one who works on it'. The Zaydī scholars, however, lessened the scale of the implementation of this policy, and instead chose to implement the system of co-partnership. Thus, they chose the most beneficial method causing the least hardship to all concerned also refusing the barter and rent system as it was implemented in the lower Yemen, which had been made acceptable by Shāfiʿī scholars. By implementing this co-partnership system, the influence of the concept of 'the land belongs to the one who works on it' was reduced. This was done on the basis of another saying: 'There shall be no harming, injuring or hurting, of one man by another, in the first instance, nor in return, or requital in Islam,' which reduces the freedom given to the owner of the land in the barter and rent system of the lower Yemen.

The barter system was based on the payment of a farm tax, whether the land produced crops or not. This meant that the hired peasant was required to pay the tax that was agreed upon, even at times of dryness and lack of crops. This represents an aspect of injustice to which a peasant was subjected. As for the co-partnership system, it was based on the efforts of the partner and the money of the owner. A

---

41 Abū Zahrā, *al-Imām Zayd* (Sanaa, n.d.), p. 512; Shā'if, *al-Imām al-Hādī*, p. 222.

42 Al-Hādī, *Jawāb masā'il al-Ḥusayn*, included in *al-Majmūʿa al-fākhira*, pp. 662–663.

43 ʿAlī b. Muḥammad al-ʿAlawī, *Sīrat al-Hādī ilā al-Ḥaqq Yaḥyā b. al-Ḥusayn*, ed. Suhayl Zakkār (Beirut, n.d.), p. 61; Shā'if, *al-Imām al-Hādī*, p. 224.

44 ʿAbd al-Fatāḥ, *al-Imām al-Hādī*, p. 224.

certain percentage of the payment was made in return for a certain percentage of effort. If the owner were to pay all the cost, he would share the crop equally with the partner. However, if the partner were to contribute some of the cost, then he would get two-thirds. If the partner were to pay all the expenses and indemnity, while the owner provided the land only, then the partner would get the entire product except for the sixth of it which was paid to the owner in return for the ownership of the land. In addition, the Zaydī partner was armed with his gun and supported by his tribe, a relationship that was regulated by alliances and tribal ties that secured his rights to the extent of violating the rights of the landowner if necessary.

Both the partner and the landowner accepted this policy to avoid being bound by the saying of the Prophet, also adopted by Imam Zayd who reported it on the authority of ʿAlī: 'The Prophet, peace be upon him, had forbidden the renting of the land in a contract for the third or the quarter, and he said: "If anyone of you owes a land, he should either sow it himself, or give to his brother".'[45] On the basis of this *ḥadīth,* the Zaydī Hadawīs adopted the co-partnership policy following the example of the Prophet, who had allowed the co-partnership in the event of Khaybar in return for half of the product itself. On this basis, Imam Zayd allowed the temporary sharecropping contract.[46] Therefore, the co-partnership system was adopted while *qibal* (land rent) was forbidden in the upper Yemen.[47] In lower Yemen, *qibal* was allowed without any prohibition. The adoption of the co-partnership by the upper Yemen should be seen in the context of the revolutionary nature of Zaydī thought. In the same way, the adoption of the *qibal* system by the Shāfiʿī religious scholars in lower Yemen was the result of the close relationship between this doctrine and politics.

While the co-partnership system in the north had resolved the problem between the peasant and the owner in a way that satisfied both of them, the *qibal* system had doubled the exploitation of peasants in the south. Therefore, landowners could not exploit peasants in the upper Yemen, while in the lower Yemen peasants were exploited. The peasants in the upper Yemen were facing the oppression of the state; the peasants in the lower Yemen were faced with injustice from both landowners and the state. The two systems resulted in a situation or a system that guaranteed a better position for the partner, while the peasant became subject to worse conditions. On the other hand, the Zaydī Hadawīs had refused the system of land-tax *jibāya*, and the insurance *ḍamān*, in other words, the very old engagements system. Mutawakkil ʿalallāh, Ismāʿīl b. al-Qāsim (d. 1087/1677) tried to impose it in 1077/1665–1666 on the people of al-Ḥīma.[48] However, under the pressure of the religious scholars, he gave up

---

45 Al-Siyāghī, *al-Rawḍ al-naḍīr*, p. 650.

46 Ibid., p. 664.

47 The *qibal* was a land rent for a fixed amount per annum, to be agreed by the landlord and the tenants. This fixed rent does not put into consideration the actual production value of the land. It guarantees the rent for the landlord at the expense of the farmers who work and cultivate the land.

48 Muḥsin b. al-Ḥasan Abū Ṭālib, *Taʾrīkh al-Yaman ʿaṣr al-istiqbāl ʿan al-ḥukm al-ʿthamānī al-awwal* (Sanaa, 1411/1990), p. 97.

this system at the next harvest. He removed the land-tax and *qibal* system and only kept what was taken before in the previous years.[49]

It seems that the systems of *iltizām*, *jibāya* or *ḍamān* – which are all different variations on the same unpopular system of *iltizām* – has been deeply rooted in the lower Yemen since the time of the Ottomans as a result of the political agreement between Ottoman leaders and the chieftains of the region. This agreement established a form of exchange of loyalty and benefits, where the chieftain was obliged to pay a specific amount to the Ottoman government in the name of alms or duties. In return, the Ottomans gave him the freedom to obtain whatever he wanted from the peasants' crops. In this way, the chieftain became very rich at the expense of the peasants. This situation did not occur in the Zaydī Yemen. In fact, the *qibal* system is a heavy burden upon those who are subjected to it. It must be treated in a religious manner by a new judgement that invalidates the previous one. The co-partnership *sharāka* system – an old religious system – however, does not need that, because it is not as bad.

The implementation of the decentralised administration by Imam al-Hādī in the province ruled by him facilitated the acceptance of the *sharāka* system. He explained to his governors how they should tax people and what they should leave for them. When the alms were collected, he ordered that each prince should distribute a quarter of the food collected to the needy in his province. He said: 'If God were to bestow upon us and upon Muslims, we would allocate half of it to the needy, and if the Muslims were to do without it, we would have given all of it to the needy.'[50] He ordered the governors to obtain what provisions they needed from the collected alms, while what remained should be divided according to the needs of his country, and the rest should be kept.[51]

It becomes clear that the *sharāka* system and the decentralised administration have aided each other at times. However, the system of the central government has taken over, and thus destroyed the decentralised system of administration, but it did not actually affect the *sharāka* system. It follows that *māl* should serve social solidarity and, therefore, it should be spent and not kept. Al-Hādī, therefore, refused to collect alms from those whom he could not protect. This shows that money is a means and not an end in itself. It should not be collected or spent for personal benefits, but for the benefit of all sections of society.

VII

In order to protect the continuity of the use of *māl* for promoting social solidarity, the Zaydīs adopted a series of measures to prevent turning *māl* into a private ownership. Among the most important measures taken is the forbidding of the accumulation of

---

49 Abū Ṭālib, *Ta'rīkh al-Yaman*, p. 100.

50 Al-ʿAlawī, *Sīrat al-Hādī*, p. 47; see, Shā'if, *al-Imām al-Hādī*, pp. 214–215.

51 See the section on the reign of al-Hādī, in al-ʿAlawī, *Sīrat al-Hādī*, pp. 46–48.

māl. The holy Qurʾan has conclusively forbidden it, not only because it is money that has been set aside, but also because it places the wealth in the hands of one person and deprives the community of it. This prevents the money from being used to promote social benefit, and is an obstacle to fair dealings among people. Abū Dhir al-Ghafarī had recognised the damage caused by the accumulation of wealth and its role in the emergence of large ownerships, so he said: 'O rich people, comfort the poor, tell those who accumulate gold and silver and do not spend it for the sake of God that they will be punished with painful burns on their foreheads and on their sides and backs.'[52] The wealthiest landowners and those who accumulated wealth were sceptical about Abū Dhir's position, accusing him of being under the influence of a mysterious man called Ibn al-Sawdāʾ. This Ibn al-Sawdāʾ was apparently influenced by the Mazdakīs in Iraq or Yemen, but Abū Dhir had embraced his position with good intent.[53]

The discussion of whether or not Ibn al-Sawdāʾ existed is beyond the scope of this chapter. In my opinion, however, Abū Dhir in taking this position was inspired by the teaching of the Qurʾan (9:35) and not by the Mazdakīs or Ibn al-Sawdāʾ. This reveals the level of distortion that has occurred to the facts about Abū Dhir. The Qurʾanic verse also shows that the accumulation of wealth is forbidden because it prevents the money being used for the benefit of all social sectors.

At the same time, the Zaydīs had adopted as part of their theory of *māl* a policy of not wasting money or spending it in unbeneficial ways, following the Prophetic *ḥadīth* reported by al-Zamakhsharī:

> It is reported from the Prophet, peace be upon him, that someone came to him with a golden egg that he acquired as a result of a raid and said: 'Take it from me as a charity'. However, the Messenger of God, peace be upon him, turned away from him. Then the man approached him again from the right side and said the same thing, but again the Prophet turned away from him. Then he approached him from the left side, and again the Prophet turned away from him and said in an angry tone: 'Give it to me', and then he threw it against him in a way that if it were to touch him, it would have injured him badly. Then he said: 'Some of you give away all your money to charity, and then beg people [for help]. Charity should however [derive] from competence.'[54]

The point here is perhaps that one should have a balanced attitude even in giving to charity, starting from one's own self, one's relatives and then wider society, and in this way poverty and neediness could be eradicated.

---

52 Ibn al-Athīr, *al-Kāmil*, vol. 3 , p. 114.
53 Aḥmad Amīn, *Fajr al-Islām* (11th ed., Beirut, 1975), pp. 110–111.
54 Al-Zamakhsharī, *al-Kashshāf*, vol. 1, p. 360.

VIII

In conclusion, it must be acknowledged that the principles mentioned above have not been fully implemented. However, the scale of the implementation has differed from one principle to another. The most important point is that the Zaydī tradition had one of the most strict doctrines in mentoring of financial affairs. These principles have not been interpreted in a way to conform to the policies of those who could have benefited from them unjustly.

It is true that the Zaydī Hadawī school has given the Imam absolute authority concerning the way in which money is to be spent, and also guaranteed the right of the scholars to observe and to make him account for the way in which he spends it. They are entitled even to rebel against him if they see fit. The preservation of the right to rebel against the unjust ruler has maintained a sharp tool against potential injustice, since the ruler knew very well that he was being observed by the *umma*, represented especially by its scholars who would not allow him to mismanage the money in the public treasury, monopolising it or spending it for the wrong reasons.

This is because claiming a monopoly over money means not taking the necessary counsel, which also means that it is permissible to rebel against an unjust ruler, fighting him or even killing him if necessary. It was thus this right to rebel against the unjust Imam which has made the Zaydī Hadawī Imam – even if he had obtained authority over the public money as a result of political machinations – aware of the consequences of his actions. This ultimately reduced the damage of his actions in comparison with other rulers, kings or sultans.

It would be wrong to say that the Zaydī Hadawī tradition has not been influenced by other doctrines in connection with this subject. In fact, it has been affected in certain aspects but despite that, justice in terms of the fair distribution and use of the public money has remained a requirement and a priority to determine the legitimacy of the just Imam in the Zaydī tradition. The scholars of the Zaydī Hadawī school did not violate any conditions, but in some cases, all that the weakest among them did was to deny that the Imam had violated any ruling or principles. Instead, they occupied themselves with finding justifications for his actions and did not criticise him. This led to the preservation of the principle, even if it has not been universally applied.

Finally, it is clear that the Zaydī position on money is that it should be spent to promote social solidarity. The social function of money facilitates all aspects of life (as stated in Q.18:46). Money is not beneficial unless it improves people's lives. A ruler is like a father: if a father is busy accumulating wealth, then happiness will disappear in his house. In the same way, if a ruler is busy accumulating his wealth, then happiness will vanish from the society over which he rules. This is because it confines the wealth in the hands of one family, while the rest of the society remains deprived of it, and righteousness and good deeds which are best in the eyes of God will be relegated to the background.

Alongside its emphasis on forbidding the accumulation of wealth, the Zaydī tradition does not encourage the donating of all of one's money to avoid a reverse situation where the person himself then becomes in need of help from other people. This position is supported by the Qur'an Q.3:280), which encourages mutual social collaboration among people. It acknowledges that repaying one's debts is necessary. But once the situation of such a person is improved, he may still be exempt from repaying the debt and this can be seen as a form of charity and good deeds. Thus, the call to exempt someone from repaying their debts implies a form of lifting difficulties from the shoulders of someone who might otherwise turn to others for financial help. It was in this context that Imam ʿAlī forbade, with the full consent of the right Companions and the trustworthy of the public treasury of Muslims, the accumulation of wealth. He used to spend the money that exceeds need on those deserving of charity. Abū Dhir was also a good example of one who refused to accumulate wealth and insisted that the *ʿafw* (the money that exceeded one's need) should be distributed.

It should also be noted that the Zaydīs allowed public ownership, but at the same time restricted it by a number of conditions that have been applied to ownership contracts to prevent any forms of injustice or monopoly. As has been noted, the accumulation of wealth violates the conditions that have been applied to ownership contracts because it holds back the surplus money that could otherwise have been spent for the benefit of society.

PART V
AUTHORITY

Introduction

Andrew J. Newman

The question of 'authority' in Shi'i Islam, and Twelver Shi'ism in particular, has been a matter of concern to scholars from the very earliest days of the emergence of the field. As a distinct Western discipline, Twelver studies has only recently appeared on the scene. The event that heralded the emergence of Twelver Shi'i studies as a distinct field – the Strasbourg colloquium 'Le Shî'isme Imâmite' – occurred only in May 1968, but a decade before the Iranian Revolution.[1] From that time through until that Revolution, study of the faith presupposed the division of Twelver history into two periods. The first was the period from the late 9th century – following the occultation of the Twelfth Imam in 874 – to the 16th century, when the faith was a minority one within a Sunni-dominated political structure and when Twelver scholars in the main composed their writings in Arabic. Scholars of this period of Shi'i history were interested in a variety of issues of Shi'i doctrine and practice including, for example, the compatibility of certain aspects of Shi'ism and Sufism. These could be researched via meticulous attention to the extant Arabic-language texts. The second period of the faith's history was understood to have commenced in 1501, when the newly arisen Safawid dynasty in Iran captured the ancient capital of Tabriz and declared Twelver Shi'ism to be the official faith of the territory under its control. The history of the faith from this date overlapped with the study of the formation of the modern Iranian nation-state.

Owing to the noticeable interaction between religion and politics in this period of Iranian history, especially since the mid-19th century – for example, the Tobacco Protest and the Constitutional Revolution – the scholars of this period of the faith's history raised questions concerning clerical authority and the nature of clerical involvement with and recognition of the established political institution during the Imam's absence. For these scholars the religious texts written by Twelver scholars over these past five centuries, more often than not continued to be composed in Arabic, were still the embodiment of developments in Twelver doctrine, if not always practice. However, these texts now competed for attention as 'source material' with an assortment of other, both Persian-language but also European-language sources,

[1] The papers were published as T. Fahd, ed., *Le Shî'isme Imâmite* (Paris, 1970). Apart from those few cited below as attending this gathering, the majority of academics at Strasbourg cannot be said to have been known at the time as especially interested in the faith.

including political and economic documents, court and personal histories, travelogues, works of literature and works of art/architecture, and even oral histories.

In 1968, Wilferd Madelung and Joseph Eliash represented the former tendency within the field. Together, these scholars explored an eclectic series of questions of Twelver doctrine and practice based on meticulous examination of the Arabic-language texts. In this tradition also Henry Corbin (d. 1978) and Sayyid Hossein Nasr were interested in aspects of medieval Islamic philosophy and in the compatibility of certain aspects of Shiʿism with Sufism. In these years the latter group of scholars included A. K. S. Lambton,[2] Leonard Binder,[3] Hamid Algar and Nikki Keddie.[4] The agenda of the former group may be said to have prevailed at Strasbourg; Corbin, Madelung, Nasr and Eliash were all present in Strasbourg while, although of the latter four both Lambton and Binder had published prior to 1968, only Lambton attended the May gathering.

But the 1968 colloquium took place in the years following the appearance of works in 'modernisation theory', such as those of Daniel Lerner in 1958 and Manfred Halpern in 1963.[5] As applied to the Middle East, 'modernisation' studies, of which these two were among the earliest offerings, presumed that Islam was in the process of 'withering away' and that the Middle East was fast becoming both secularised and 'western', processes spearheaded by a new, technocratic and distinctly secular middle class. Although the field as a whole grew after 1968, as their colleagues in other fields of Islamic and Middle Eastern studies, the still-small number of scholars of both periods of Shiʿi history, despite their differing interests and sets of sources, may be said to have accepted that Shiʿism and indeed, Islam and religion overall, seemed to be fast becoming phenomena of history, to be studied as such.

The Field and the Revolution

While 'Islamism' was already a force in the region, especially in the aftermath of the military defeats of 1956, 1967 and 1973, the 1979 Iranian Revolution and the very distinctly 'Islamic' character it rapidly assumed drove home the failure of 'modernisation theory' as useful in interpreting both past and future trends and events in the

---

[2] These scholars' interests in such issues are reflected in their publications to that time. See A. K. S. Lambton's 'Quis Custodiet Custodes: Some Reflections on the Persian Theory of Government', *SI*, 6 (1956), pp. 125–146; and 'A Reconsideration of the Position of the [*sic*] *Marjaʿ al-Taqlid* and the Religious Institution', *SI*, 20 (1964), pp. 115–135.

[3] See his 'The Proofs of Islam: Religion and Politics in Iran', in G. Makdisi, ed., *Arabic and Islamic Studies in Honor of Hamilton A. R. Gibb* (Leiden, 1965), pp. 118–140.

[4] See the famous 'Algar/Keddie debate' on the Shiʿi view of political authority in N. Keddie, ed., *Scholars, Saints and Sufis: Muslim Religious Institutions since 1500* (Berkeley and London, 1972), a collection based on a 1969 conference. See also Algar's *Religion and the State in Iran, 1785–1906* (Berkeley and London, 1969).

[5] D. Lerner, *The Passing of Traditional Society* (New York, 1958); M. Halpern, *The Politics of Social Change in the Middle East and North Africa* (Princeton, 1963).

region. Since then, scholars in the field of Shiʿi studies, as those in other branches of Middle Eastern Studies, have been trying to explain the faith's 'failure' to disappear.[6] To be sure, the number of Western scholars interested in Islam generally and the faith in particular has grown exponentially since the Revolution. Since 1979, the available body of Twelver primary source material in Arabic and Persian has also grown, particularly with the appearance in Iran especially of out-of-print lithographs and previously unpublished materials. Nevertheless, the field cannot be said to have investigated or experienced any 'paradigm shift'. First and foremost, the field remains split between those scholars interested in pre- and those focussing on post-16th-century Shiʿism. Secondly, the overviews of the faith since produced by many of those in both groups recall aspects of Nasr and Corbin's pre-1979 identification of affinities between Sufism and Shiʿism to discuss what constitutes 'genuine' Shiʿism.

These scholars agree that Twelver clerics have allocated to themselves more of the Hidden Imam's authority over the interpretation and implementation of matters of doctrine and practice. But, most maintain that 'genuine' Shiʿism is inherently apolitical and esoteric/otherworldly and that overt clerical authority and the concomitant clerical involvement in 'secular' political matters is recent, dating from the Safawid period and that since that period only a very few clerics have ever engaged in such activity. Thus, many argue, the Islamic Republic is not a legitimate expression of the true nature of the Shiʿi faith. Rather, it is the result of the action of a few, charismatic figures who latched on to broader Iranian discontent with the regime of the last Shah for their own, very 'political', purposes.

More often than not, beholden to the 'great man' theory of history, when referring both to the processes at work both in the Safawid period and in Iran's Islamic Revolution, these scholars have a single individual in mind. Thus, for example, in his enormously influential 1984 *The Shadow of God and the Hidden Imam*, Said Arjomand highlighted the faith's 'pious antipathy toward political power', an understanding derived from the earlier work of Corbin and Nasr. He identified Muḥammad Bāqir al-Majlisī (d. 1110/1699) as having been at the head of a 'triumphant hierocracy' which assumed control of Safawid society and the state in the late 17th century and sought to suppress all intellectual inquiry and minority religious tendencies; the activities of al-Majlisī and like-minded co-religionists were 'an important cause' of the Afghan invasion and the overthrow of the Safawid dynasty. And, when addressing the present, Arjomand argued that Ayatollah Khumaynī (d. 1989) utilised earlier 'Mahdī-istic' tendencies within the faith to promote a distinctly this-worldly political agenda.[7] The identification of al-Majlisī as such an intolerant but also powerful and influential figure long pre-dated the Iranian Revolution. Indeed until, perhaps,

---

[6] Results of the post-Mubarak elections in Egypt suggest that radical secularisation may not have been an inherent element of the 'Arab Spring'.

[7] S. A. Arjomand, *The Shadow of God and the Hidden Imam: Religion, Political Order, and Societal Change in Shiʿite Iran from the Beginning to 1890* (Chicago and London, 1984), pp. 21–23, 190f, 261–263, 269–270.

Khumaynī himself, no figure in Twelver Shiʿi history had been the object of such continued vilification in the Western sources as al-Majlisī.

The origin of many of the field's conventional wisdoms about various aspects of Safawid society and its preoccupation with al-Majlisī and his apparent influence can be traced to the work of Browne. In 1924 Browne declared al-Majlisī 'one of the greatest, most powerful and most fanatical *mujtahid*s of the Safawi period', and suggested that what 'left Persia exposed to perils' – a reference to 'the troubles which culminated in the supreme disaster of 1722', the Afghan invasion – was 'the narrow intolerance so largely fostered by him and his congeners'.[8] In 1958, Lockhart described al-Majlisī as 'an extremely bigoted *mujtahid*' and 'a rigid and fanatical formalist'. He also stated that al-Majlisī's influence over Shah Sultan Ḥusayn (r. 1105–1135/1694–1722) was substantial and was demonstrated by the latter's appointment of himself as *mullā-bāshī*' 'or head of the Mullas'.[9] Nasr referred to al-Majlisī's persecution of 'the intellectual methods of the *ḥakīm*s and philosophers' and, echoing both Browne and Lockhart, implied such persecution contributed to the fall of the dynasty to the Afghans.[10] In the aftermath of Arjomand's post-Revolution revival of the focus/blame on al-Majlisī, in 1985, in his introductory work on the faith, citing only Browne and Lockhart, Momen called al-Majlisī 'one of the most powerful and influential Shiʿi *ulama* of all time', and noted his 'suppression of Sufism and philosophy, the propagation of dogmatic legalistic form of Twelver Shiʿism and the suppression of Sunnism and other religious groups'.[11]

Seven years later, although his focus was on very early Shiʿi history, Amir-Moezzi also linked Safawid-period developments in rationalist Twelver jurisprudence more generally with the politicisation of the faith. Amir-Moezzi suggested that 'early Imāmīsm' was 'an esoteric doctrine' from which flowed Shiʿi 'theology, cosmogony, ethics, politics, the practical aspects of worship, mysticism, law, eschatology, and so forth'. The Safawid period, with the establishment of Twelver Shiʿism as the realm's official faith, witnessed the rise of 'independent Doctors of the Law'. As early as the reign of Ṭahmāsp I (r. 930–984/1524–1576), the second Safawid Shah, aided

[8] E. G. Browne, *A Literary History of Persia* (Cambridge, 1924; repr., 1953), vol. 4, pp. 403, 120; see also pp. 404, 194–195, 366.

[9] Laurence Lockhart, *The Fall of the Safavid Dynasty and the Afghan Occupation of Persia* (Cambridge, 1958), pp. 32–33, 70, 71 n. 1. Lockhart referred to Browne, vol. 4, p. 120, cited above. In fact, al-Majlisī was never the realm's chief *mulla*.

[10] S. H. Nasr, 'The School of Iṣpahān', in M. M. Sharif, ed., *A History of Muslim Philosophy* (Wiesbaden, 1968), vol. 2, p. 931. Some years later Nasr described al-Majlisī as 'the most formidable spokesman for the reaction which set in within Shiʿi religious circles during the later Safavid period' and noted his condemnation of the *ḥukam* (philosophers). See his 'Spiritual Movements, Philosophy and Theology in the Safavid Period', in P. Jackson and L. Lockhart, ed., *The Cambridge History of Iran*, vol. 6: *The Timurid and Safavid Periods* (Cambridge, 1986), p. 694.

[11] M. Momen, *An Introduction to Shiʿi Islam* (New Haven and London, 1985), pp. 115–116, 115, n. 7, citing only to Browne, vol. 4, p. 404, and Lockhart, *The Fall of the Safavid Dynasty*, p. 70.

by religio-political and economic crises, and 'the disappearance of the charisma of the sovereigns', the 'independent Doctors' began to accrue 'power'. The rationalist *Uṣūlī* school, heir to the methodology of al-Shaykh al-Mufīd (d. 413/1022) and al-ʿAllāma al-Ḥillī (d. 726/1325), crushed the *Akhbārī* opposition and '*ijtihād* ... officially and effectively became one of the methodological bases of Imāmite law'. Its use 'brought significant political and religious power to the jurist-theologian' as the mass of followers 'was relegated to relying on 'imitation (*taqlīd*), that is, to following the *mujtahid* and his instructions scrupulously'. The latter promoted themselves as the Imam's 'general representative (*nāʾib ʿāmm*) to the community' and jurisprudence (*fiqh*) became 'the dominant discipline' of study and 'political ambition and power, the latter two defined by the Imams as being destroyers of the "true Religion", were from then on presented as guarantees of its just application'. The 'jurist-theologian took the place of the Imam', with the intent 'to drag Imāmīsm into the political arena, apply it on the collective level and crystallise it as an ideology'.[12]

Two more recent contributions suggest that the field still remains loyal to paradigms of enquiry that ultimately pre-date the Iranian Revolution. Rahnema's 2011 volume attests to the continued preoccupation with al-Majlisī and his influence, even as a new 'great man' – Mahmoud Ahmadinejad – has replaced Khumaynī as the ultimate recipient/benefactor of al-Majlisī's 'legacy'.[13] In his 2011 overview of the faith, where he addresses Shiʿism in Safawid Iran, Dabashi highlights the manner in which the 17th century was marked by the intellectual interaction between Sufism and Shiʿism at the level of elite discourse, a framework still beholden to the interest of Corbin and Nasr in identifying affinities between the two.[14]

A Minority Discourse

To date, the study of the evolution of clerical authority in the absence of the Imam in Twelver Shiʿism has indeed produced a picture of that process that is linear and undynamic. This is largely because the process has been explored and understood mainly with reference to the legacy of but a handful of Twelver scholars already known in the West prior to 1979. By and large, for the pre-modern epoch the best-known Twelver scholars are those whose careers and contributions date them to the Būyid, Mongol/Timurid and Safawid periods, the three periods in which Twelver Shiʿism is generally known as having been tolerated by the political establishment and during the last of which it, finally, became the established faith.

---

[12] M. A. Amir-Moezzi, *The Divine Guide in Early Shiʿism: The Sources of Esotericism in Islam*, tr. David Streight (Albany, NY, 1994), pp. 125–126, 137–139. The original was published as *Le Guide Divin Dans le Shīʿisme Originel* (Paris, 1992).

[13] A. Rahnema, *Superstition as Ideology in Iranian Politics: From Majlesi to Ahmadinejad* (Cambridge, 2011).

[14] H. Dabashi, *Shiʿism: A Religion of Protest* (Cambridge, MA, 2011). See chapter 5.

The actual number of these scholars and those of their works that have been the subject of any sort of systematic, comparative study are limited. For the first two of these three periods alone, for example, the number of such scholars is small indeed. For the Būyid period (334–447/945–1055), these comprise Muḥammad b. ʿAlī, known as Ibn Bābawayh (d. 381/991), Muḥammad b. Muḥammad b. Nuʿmān, al-Shaykh al-Mufīd, ʿAlī b. al-Ḥusayn, al-Sharīf al-Murtaḍā (d. 436/1044) and Muḥammad b. Ḥasan al-Ṭūsī (d. 460/1067). For the Mongol and Timurid periods (798–807/1258–1405), these include Jaʿfar b. Ḥasan al-Ḥillī, al-Muḥaqqiq (d. 676/1277), Ḥasan b. Yūsuf, al-ʿAllāma al-Ḥillī and Muḥammad b. Makkī al-ʿĀmilī, al-Shahīd al-Awwal (d. 786/1384). Of these, all may be said to have been advocates of the accrual by the scholarly elite of the authority of the Hidden Imam over the interpretation of both doctrine and practice and in the implementation of matters of daily import to the life of the community.

While the Imams were the legitimate and only possessors of authority over matters of doctrine and practice whilst they were present in the community, from the onset of the occultation there was no agreement on who then came into possession of that authority. In the years following the onset of the occultation, in particular in the immediately following half-century or so, when some felt the Imam's return was imminent, authority in the interim was perhaps less of an issue. As that 'interim' was increasingly viewed as a rather longer-term affair, its nature was increasingly debated. In fact, within the larger community of self-identified believers, the views on authority offered by the above-named scholars across these two periods, and even as further promulgated by Safawid-period scholars in this tradition, were likely in the minority. There is much evidence for the contemporary questioning of and challenges to the scholarly tradition with which these figures were identified. The above scholars' claims for such authority over doctrine and practice and their interpretations thereof were in fact debated, argued and struggled for and won or, possibly, not won, partially or even totally. Sometimes these 'debates' took place in the streets, and many of the participants were not among the small number of formally trained, 'professional' clerical elites of the periods in question. There is even some question too as to the extent to which the mass of believers in these two earlier periods, scattered as they were across the region, were even aware of the views of these scholars. In sum, the doctrines and practices being set forth in the texts produced by the scholars in this tradition ought not to be confused with the reality of belief and practice 'on the ground' among those who identified themselves as believers during these periods.

Evidence of such questioning and such challenges is extant in *al-Dharīʿa ilā taṣānīf al-Shīʿa*, the great bibliographical dictionary of Āghā Buzurg al-Ṭihrānī (d. 1970). The author lists titles in the genre of literature known as *khilāf* (disputation) scattered across a number of volumes, most especially in works listed as *masāʾil* (issues), *jawābāt* (answers), *radd* (reply) and *naqḍ* (refutation).[15] A preliminary count of such

[15] Āghā Buzurg al-Ṭihrānī, *al-Dharīʿa ilā taṣānīf al-Shīʿa* (Tehran and Najaf, 1353-1398 Sh.), respectively, vol. 20, pp. 329f; vol. 5, pp. 170f; vol. 10, pp. 173f; vol. 24, pp. 283f. See also vol. 7,

titles, absent detailed attention to duplicates and cross-referencing, reveals both more than 1,000 titles and something of a bulge of entries across two of the three periods of pre-modern Twelver Shiʿi history: the Būyid period and the Safawid period. These questions and challenges are often referenced in the writings of the few well-known Twelver scholars listed above, as well as those of many lesser-known ones, wherein the author refers to opponents holding differing views on issues of doctrine and practice. As often, the authors of these texts also refer to unnamed opponents.

These references are often insufficient to allow these 'voices' – especially as these may be rooted among the non-scholarly, 'popular' classes, always the majority in any epoch – to be as fully identified and their arguments to be as fully recovered as might ultimately be desirable. Disagreement on both issues of authority over doctrine and practice and the actual interpretations thereof was probably more the norm than the exception. Reference to a fuller range of participating voices in past discourse can enable a more complete reconstruction of the processes and stages by which both the faith and authority within it evolved over time.

A Modern-day Case Study: ʿĀshūrāʾ and Authority

In privileging a more complex approach to understanding the evolution of authority within the faith, students of pre-modern Twelver Shiʿism might refer to studies of 'modern' Twelver beliefs and practices both in Iran but, especially also, outside Iran. Ten per cent of the world's one billion Muslims profess various forms of Shiʿi Islam – Twelver, Ismaili or Zaydī. While Twelvers in particular form the majority population in both Iraq and Iran, they also form sizeable minorities in Lebanon, Kuwait, Bahrain, Syria, Turkey, Saudi Arabia, Afghanistan, Azerbaijan, Tajikistan as well as India and Pakistan, areas in East Africa, South Asia, Europe and North America. It follows that if most Iranians today are Twelvers, most Twelvers are not Iranians.

Research undertaken both by historians and anthropologists on 'Āshūrā' commemorations across the Shiʿi world in particular has revealed vastly different understandings about these practices by elites and non-elites. In 1978, in one of the few pre-Iranian Revolution examples of the scholarly acknowledgement of the presence of Twelver communities outside Iran, Ende addressed disagreement among the Shiʿa of Syria/Lebanon and Iraq on 'the practice of chest-beating and the use of chains and swords for self-torture during the processions' – which he called 'flagellations' – in the annual commemorations of the killing of Imam Ḥusayn at Karbalāʾ in 680, on the tenth of the Muslim month of Muḥarram. Ende examined a 1920s work by the Lebanese scholar Sayyid Muḥsin al-Amīn al-ʿĀmilī (d. 1952) in which the latter defended the mourning of the Imam's killing but condemned the flagellations. This

pp. 235f, at *khilāf*; vol. 1, pp. 360–362, at *ikhtilāf*; and, vol. 10, pp. 239f, at *rasāʾil* (essays). On the genre generally, see D. Gimaret, '*Radd*', *EI2*, vol. 8, p. 362. On the *jawāb* literature, see also al-Tihrānī, vol. 5, p. 171, vol. 5, p.213.

text was the subject of a rebuttal written by a Shiʿi scholar from Nabatieh, in the Jabal ʿĀmil region, in 1926 or early 1927, to which Sayyid Muḥsin replied in 1927 in a work published in 1928.

The Sayyid condemned as 'innovation (*bidʿa*)' 'not only the flagellations but also, among other things, the use of musical instruments and the appearance in the processions of unveiled women impersonating Imam Ḥusayn's female relatives'. Ende noted that this text and the subsequent refutations were published in Iraq, to which Lebanese opponents of Sayyid Muḥsin had 'brought the news of what they considered a scandalous attack on the religious establishment'. Ende argued that Sayyid Muḥsin's purpose was to excise the 'innovation' and thereby utilise the commemorations as a form of 'Shiʿi missionary work'. Ende pointed to efforts by the 'Āmilī scholars in Iraq to incite what Ende called 'the uneducated masses' against Sayyid Muḥsin and his supporters. In the process, these scholars denounced their opponents as 'Umayyad' and called themselves "Alids'. Sayyid Muḥsin's opponents were, he noted, successful in convincing Iraqi Shiʿa of their claim, and 1929 processions involved more flagellants than ever before.

Ende also argued that 19th-century Iranian immigrants into Nabatieh had initiated the flagellations. These were opposed at the time by at least one senior cleric. The latter complained to the Ottoman authorities, who declined to intervene, and the practice was soon taken up by local non-Iranians and came to attract the attention of numbers of Shiʿa and non-Shiʿa from nearby and more distant locales. Ende also noted the association of the debate with issues of *taqlīd* and *ijtihād* in Najaf. The eminent *mujtahid* of the day, the *marjaʿ* Abu'l-Ḥasan al-Iṣfahānī (d. 1946), a supporter of Sayyid Muḥsin, enjoyed the support of his 'followers', one of whom, perhaps as or more importantly, was leader of a local armed brotherhood. Ende called attention to the importance of the 'debate' of both the recent takeover of the Hijaz by Wahhabi elements and the efforts of Reza Shah Pahlavi (r. 1925–1941) in Iran to move against public Muḥarram commemorations. The latter especially resonated among the many Iranian clerics then resident in Najaf in the later 1920s. Ende also highlighted the common interests of both certain clerics and local business elements in promoting the flagellations and providing catering services to the onlookers. And, in closing, Ende suggested that the practices constituted 'an expression of deep allegiance of the uneducated masses' to the sayyids and that as such, in the face of 'modern developments' some 'may consider it unwise' to forbid them.[16]

A 2005 article by Deeb effectively updated Ende's discussion. Deeb noted that when 'rural' elements came to Beirut, they brought the 'traditional form' of 'Āshūrā' commemorations with them. In the 1950s and 1960s, onlookers viewed them as 'backward', but opposition to them did not appear until the 1980s, in the wake of the 1978 disappearance of Mūsā al-Ṣadr, two Israeli invasions – 1978 and 1982 – and the Iranian Revolution. Deeb suggested that in both Iran and Lebanon the Revolution

[16] W. Ende, 'The Flagellations of Muḥarram and the Shiʿite 'Ulamā', *Der Islam*, 55 (1978), pp. 19–36.

especially encouraged a shift away from the dominant, politically quietist discourse on 'Āshūrā' to a discourse more appropriate to 'revolutionary Shi'ism'. In the process, however, she noted splits between elites and 'backward (*mutakhallif*)' elements. The former encouraged longer sermonising (*majālis*) and more restrained accounts of the events of Karbalā', avoiding 'unfounded exaggerations that they see as being "merely" to heighten emotions'. The more recent *majālis* also encouraged an alternative view of Imam Ḥusayn's sister Zaynab, who was taken captive by Yazīd after the event. Zaynab had been portrayed as extremely emotional – 'crying, screaming, wailing ... buried in grief'. She now became the 'courageous' defiant opponent of the 'oppressor' and leader of the post-Karbalā' community. The traditional processions whose self-flagellation (*latam*) extended to the shedding of blood were condemned by leading clerics and were even subject to a 1990s banning order by Hizbullah. Instead, calls were made for blood donations to local blood banks during 'Āshūrā', which were well taken up.

Women too came to occupy a relatively more prominent position in the Hizbullah-organised processions (*masirat*). Like the men, they were organised into groups in military-style ranks and engaged in organised chanting. In these the form of self-flagellation that causes the shedding of blood by the male participants was not performed. Even crying was discouraged by some elites, including Sayyid Muḥammad Ḥusayn Faḍlallāh (d. 2010), although Deeb noted Faḍlallāh's critics claimed he had over-intellectualised 'Āshūrā'. Finally, also, the new *majālis* attempted to shift the message of 'Āshūrā' to a more outward-looking, revolutionary one, and away from one of 'mourning, regret and salvation'. Nevertheless, the traditional forms of commemoration were still carried on at the time of Deeb's 2000 sojourn in Nabatieh, for example. Proponents of these 'commented that the display of self-injurious *latam* was a demonstration of the readiness of their youth to defend the community and fight against the Israeli occupation'.[17]

In a series of articles based on field research in north-west Pakistan in the early 1990s, Heglend focused on the role of women in commemorations of the martyrdom of the Imam. She suggested that in their 'communal mourning ceremonies' (*majāles*) Shi'i women who had come to the region from India and settled in Peshawar:

> nurtured resilience in the face of repeated reminders of their religious dependency and lack of agency. They appropriated rituals – including sermons (delivered by women), chanting and self-flagellation – for their own spiritual, religious, and social meanings. Their energising ritual performances allowed them to build up, within a protected framework, characteristics and abilities which they may later, depending on surrounding conditions, be able to apply more overtly for influence, self-advancement, and loosening strict gender controls.

---

[17] L. Deeb, 'Living Ashura in Lebanon: Mourning Transformed to Sacrifice', *Comparative Studies of South Asia, Africa and the Middle East*, 25 (2005), pp. 122–137, esp. pp. 124, 126f. For reference to 2010 commemorations in Nabatieh, see note 24 below.

These women were able to reach out to Shiʿa women of other ethnic groups and thereby 'helped meld Shiʿa [*sic*] into a more dedicated, vociferous, and cohesive interest group'.

Heglend noted also that this expansion took place in this period in reaction to a 'growing religious transnationalism', present in the forms of Shiʿism preached by Iran's Islamic Republic, as well as mounting sectarian – Sunni versus Shiʿi – violence and the concomitant rise, among both groupings, of 'fundamentalist ideology'. These, she argued, combined to limit the role of women and 'reinforced men as repositories of holy power and succour, and reminded women of their own unworthiness to shed blood on behalf of Imam Ḥusayn and Shiʿa Islam, as did men'. In turn, 'through their ritual practice women proclaimed their passionate devotion to Imam Ḥusayn and thereby their religious, spiritual, and social worthiness, subtly resisting negative gender definitions'.

Her 2003 article, also deriving from this material, directly addressed those 'ritual aspects of women's subtle resistance to the patriarchal demands and gender definitions promoted by male Shiʿa clerics and leaders', that is the default figures within the community who 'hold positions of authority and make decisions about what is religiously appropriate and what is not'. The *majāles* became the means for women to leave the home to develop 'social networks, abilities, and reputations'. These women 'roam the city, attending rituals in a number of different homes daily (sometimes as often as five or more gatherings), travelling to other towns or even to home communities in India for mourning rituals'. Their comportment at the single-sex gatherings as well as in mixed, but segregated, settings did not match expectations of male authority figures. The mourning rituals also offered opportunities for female performers, from very young girls to university students, to exhibit their talents, in chanting, preaching, as readers of the Qur'an and as hostesses, for example.

National/transnational issues were downplayed in favour of personal and family matters. In the process, also, the dominant male-inspired attitude toward women generally and the role of women in these commemorations in particular were challenged, thereby enhancing 'their own sense of self-worth and competence'. The ritual swinging of arms over their heads to thump their chests for hours over the day and even the night also allowed the women to challenge male authority figures' representations of women's 'delicate nature'. Terms such as 'agency' mark Heglend's analysis, even with regard to middle-class women, as do 'resilience' and 'resistance'. Not unexpectedly, Heglend noted, the male authorities developed an alternative narrative which stressed that because these women had so little to do at home that they had time to attend so many gatherings, and that their 'more emotional' nature explained the intensity of their mourning rituals.[18]

[18] M. Heglend, 'Shiʿa Women's Rituals in Northwest Pakistan: The Shortcomings and Significance of Resistance', *Anthropological Quarterly*, 76 (2003), esp. pp. 413–414, 421, 424, in which she also discussed her research and cited her earlier publications on these rituals.

Aghaie, in his 2004 study of Muḥarram commemorations in contemporary Iran, devoted a chapter to manner in which the alternative, 'gendered' visions of Karbalā' as offered by opposition elements in the late Pahlavi period and the further development of these under the Islamic Republic. For men, the Karbalā' model encouraged a revolutionary anti-Western vision. In post-1979 models, women emerged as more 'self-aware' than in the traditionalist visions of the 1950s and 1960s, but also as part of that larger confrontational, anti-Western vision. Thus, for example, in Iran – as in Lebanon – visions of Zaynab altered in these years. Aghaie examined a series of texts that appeared in the 1970s and also after the Revolution to underline his argument. Herein the ideal woman was presented as a willing supporter of the martyr, as maintaining her modesty throughout, and, as in the case of Zaynab, as 'victims of humiliation through captivity' and as mourners of the dead. Such women were also seen to be acting both as the conscience of the community as well as 'spokespersons, preservers and transmitters' of the message of the Imam. The latter encompassed the role of educator of both men and boys. Zaynab was seen to be caring for the Imam's son, her nephew, the future Imam Zayn al-ʿĀbidīn, and for the families of the martyrs, although she was herself suffering the loss of her sons and her brother. As a spokesperson, she was seen also to rebuke Yazīd after the battle. Men, Aghaie noted, could assume such roles as these, but women could not assume male roles.[19] The contributions in Aghaie's later, edited volume, *The Women of Karbala*, examined further the role of women in the Muḥarram commemorations in Shiʿi communities both in Iran, across the Arab world, South Asia and the US. Explicitly or implicitly, all these addressed not only women's role in these rituals but, also, the 'politics' of the authority by which this participation might be validated.[20]

For many years, Pinault has been researching the position of the Twelver Shiʿa in the subcontinent, focussing on Muḥarram commemorations throughout the region. A 1999 work on commemorations in India logged the complaints of contemporary 'educated [Indian] Shiʿas' as to the 'potential for abuses attendant on popular attitudes towards Muharram liturgies: they knew of Shiʿas who acted as if the zealous performance of *mātam* at Muharram compensated for the failure to observe religious obligations during the rest of the year'.[21] The Iranian vice-counsel in Hyderabad, India, in 1991, likewise offered criticisms of this zealousness: '[s]ome Shiʿas wrongly feel that during the other ten months of the year [i.e., apart from Muharram and Safar] they can do what they want, as long as they perform *mātam* during Muharram. We need to educate people concerning this.'

---

[19] K. Aghaie, *The Martyrs of Karbala: Shiʿi Symbols and Rituals in Modern Iran* (Seattle, 2004), pp. 113f.

[20] K. Aghaie, ed., *The Women of Karbala: Ritual Performance and Symbolic Discourses in Modern Shiʿi Islam* (Austin, TX, 2005).

[21] *Mātam* being defined as the 'gestures of mourning (ranging from weeping and breast beating to self-flagellation)'. See D. Pinault, 'Shia Lamentation Rituals and Reinterpretations of the Doctrine of Intercession: Two Cases from Modern India', *History of Religions*, 38 (1999), p. 286.

Part of this critique stemmed from a concern with the manner in which practices associated with the *mātam* – 'especially the more spectacular and bloody forms of *mātam* like *qameh-zanī* ("dagger-striking" in which the mourner gashes himself on the forehead or scalp with a knife or other bladed implement) and *zanjīr-zanī* (the *zanjīr* is a flail comprising several entwined chains each of which terminates in a long metal blade)' – would cause Shiʿism to be perceived by non-believers. Pinault noted the *mātam* enjoyed special popularity among 'hundreds of teenaged boys and young men' in both Hyderabad [India] and Leh (the district capital of Ladakh), but that *zanjīr-zanī* and even 'simple *hath ka mātam* (the more common form of ritual mourning, involving rhythmic repetitive breast-beating with the palm of one's hand)' were criticised by believers and non-believers.

As evidence of the latter, Pinault cited a 1997 interview with the Shiʿi prayer leader in Leh who noted the negative impression 'bloody *mātam*' would have on 'outsiders' and the latter's reference to a *fatwa* issued against *zanjīr-zanī* in 1994 by none other than Ayatollah Sayyid Ali Khamenei, who warned that the 'propagandists of the Satan of Imperialism' would use this against the faith. Echoing other portions of the ruling by Ayatollah Khamenei, the local prayer leader was careful not to question the sincerity of such behaviour. But he was just as careful to suggest that, according to Pinault, 'being an educated member of the Shiʿa community entailed socially responsible behaviour on the part of the individual; therefore one should not engage in actions (such as *zanjīri-mātam*) for one's private benefit if these actions risk harming the reputation of the Shiʿa faith in the eyes of the outside world'.

Pinault himself concluded that '[i]n Leh the Shiʿas who seemed most inclined to critique traditional lamentation practices were the more-educated and affluent members of the community; they also tended to be older than the individuals who engage in the bloodier forms of *mātam* (the *zanjīr* wielders by and large are teenaged boys and young men in their early twenties)'. For their part, the latter were critical of the opposition they experienced from 'local maulvis, municipal health officials, older Shiʿas in the community, and "outsiders"' – the latter were identified as those trained in Iran and elsewhere who passed through the area during Muḥarram. Quoting one participant as stating 'I'm the owner of my own body', Pinault suggested that the issue was one of 'control'. The continued popularity of such zealous expressions as these in Hyderabad and Ladakh attested that 'self-flagellation, then, in the face of disapproval, becomes an assertion of personal freedom'.

The issue was clearly also one of self-definition at what Pinault termed 'the popular level'. He noted that proponents argued that '*mātam* is a practice that is primarily and characteristically Shiʿa. *Mātam* is something Shiʿas do; and the bloodier forms of *mātam*, *qameh-zanī*, and *zanjīr-zanī*, comprise *mātam* par excellence. Thus as an outward-directed demonstration, bloody *mātam* serves to demarcate forcefully Shiʿa gatherings from non-Shiʿa, whether Muslim, Buddhist, or Hindu, a practice that can be especially useful in a setting such as India, where Shiʿas are a minority population within Islam, and where Islam in turn is the religion of a minority that sees itself as surrounded by Hindu and Buddhist majorities.' Pinault noted that the general critical view of these practices, while perhaps especially apparent in the years following the Iranian Revolution, could be dated to the 1930s.[22]

Pinault had also been a frequent visitor to Pakistan and, in a 2008 volume, focused on the decline of pluralist toleration and the rise of sectarianism in the country since its establishment, especially, in recent years. A chief focal point thereof involved *mātam*. Pinault sketched the socio-economic and political decline into sectarianism from the 1980s, with the rise of Shiʿi assertiveness in the face of the resulting aggressive promotion of Ḥanafī Sunnism resulting from the Islamisation agenda of Zia ul-Haqq (d. 1988). Deobandi resurgence and the rise of Taliban Sunni fundamentalism further encouraged widespread anti-Shiʿi discourse. In this atmosphere, Khamenei's 1994 ruling on the extreme practices associated with Muḥarram, the Musharraf government's 2002 bans on Sunni and Shiʿi organisations and even local elite condemnation of *mātam*-related practices as 'innovation' were ineffectual. *Mātam*, which had been an event witnessed by Hindus and non-Shiʿi Muslims alike, became associated with public practices which were the means of asserting of one's distinctive identity and were undertaken by those who were condemned by elites as 'uneducated' but who themselves proclaimed these 'extreme' practices to be 'a duty'. 'Without them', one informant noted to Pinault, 'we'd be left with only one *mazhab*.'

Chapter five, based on a 2005 visit to the country, recounted a visit to the Iranian Cultural Centre in Lahore whose director cited condemnations of various extreme practices associated with *mātam* – that is, any form of self-cutting which draws blood – issued by 'Iranian religious scholars and Iranian *mullas*'. The director also cited a 2002 Urdu translation of a book of Khamenei's *fatwa*s – the dust jacket thereof described the author as 'The Grand *Marja*ʿ of Shiʿism' – which included a lengthy section on mourning ceremonies in which many of the rulings addressed *mātam* and denounced public striking of oneself and any shedding of blood as these 'cause bodily harm or insult the sect in the eyes of onlookers'. These rulings, Pinault noted, went beyond Khamenei's 1994 statements, although common to both was the concern for how the faith might be seen by Sunni clerics, their followers and the larger world. There was even a condemnation as suicide the practices associated with *mātam* if the practitioner died as a result of undertaking these practices.

Pinault noted the change in the Iranian outlook from the years immediately following the Revolution: in 1987, for example, Ayatollah Khumaynī's urging of

---

[22] Pinault, 'Shia Lamentation Rituals', pp. 295–305. The portion of the ruling cited by Pinault is as follows:

> 'If the action of striking oneself with a weapon were actually carried out in private homes behind closed doors, then the harm coming from support for this practice would be solely a question of bodily injury. But when this action takes place before witnesses and in front of television cameras and the eyes of enemies and foreigners, and even before the eyes of our own young, at this point there is an additional harm that must be measured. It is not a question of individual or physical harm, but of great injuries linked to the reputation of Islam.'

Pinault's source was Sayyid Ali Khamenei, *ʿĀshūrāʾ* (Qumm, 1994), p. 22.

Iranians then in Mecca performing the *ḥajj* to be open in their condemnation of the Saudis as 'pagans' produced demonstrations and rioting. In response to efforts by Sunni governments to mobilise their populations against Iranian rhetoric by playing the 'Shiʿi card', Iran adopted a policy of 'internationalism' in its discourse. This involved Iran downplaying the sectarian divide, and this brief applied to Pakistan. Pinault noted that pro-Iran elements in the country thus, for example, blamed the 2006 murder of a prominent Shiʿi cleric on American agents, not on Pakistani Sunni elements.[23]

This single 'case study' of the modern expressions of this so very distinctive Twelver ritual – based on contributions from colleagues across several disciplines – certainly suggests not only that authority thereover has long been contested in the modern period but that the alternative visions thereof can be usefully understood with reference, at least, to discourses involving generation, class and gender, all against changing broader socio-economic and political backdrops. In this particular instance, the outcomes of these still ongoing contests between this wide range of participating voices across the Shiʿi world remain uncertain.[24]

This example can only encourage those for whom the more distant past is of primary research interest to parse past instances of doctrine and practice – and ritual – with special reference both to the disagreement thereon and to such varied axes, using the full range of available sources as imaginatively as possible to recover a broader range of 'voices' than have captured attention to date. In the process, a fuller picture of the evolution of Shiʿi doctrine and practice can be delineated which does not privilege the linear, static and largely teleological dynamic presently dominating many overviews of the faith.

Investigation of disputations on issues of practice would seem particularly fruitful in light of Haider's recent suggestion that in the very early years of the faith – especially the 8th century – in the self-identification process 'the "proper" performance of rituals effectively outweighed adherence to (or advocacy of) problematic theological tenets'. Indeed, he argued elsewhere, 'scholars in the late seventh and early eighth century equated "proper religion" with ritual practice' to the point where 'they affirmed the veracity of individual transmitters [of *ḥadīth*] primarily by observing them in the mosque rather than questioning them on theological matters such as God's justice or the imāmate'.[25]

---

23 D. Pinault, *Notes from a Fortune-Telling Parrot: Islam and the Struggle for Religious Pluralism in Pakistan* (London and Oakville, CT, 2008), pp. 59f, 66f, 95f. The forms of *mātam* referred to herein as practised in Gujarat, Pakistan, may be viewed in the 2007 short film 'Ten Days', made by Nadeem Kazmi, on whom see online: http://www.britslam.com/who-we-are/66-aliquam-curabitur-odio-arcu.html (accessed 6 January 2012).

24 Thus, injurious *latam* was practised in Nabatieh in December, 2010. See the videos at http://bloggingthecasbah.blogspot.com/2011/08/ashoura-in-nabatieh-south-lebanon.html (accessed 6 January 2012).

25 N. Haider, *The Origins of the Shīʿa: Identity, Ritual, and Sacred Space in Eighth-Century Kūfa* (Cambridge, 2011), p. 253; N. Haider, 'Prayer, Mosque, and Pilgrimage: The Emergence of

Authority, Mullā Ṣadrā, Fatimid Discourse and Early Twelver *Khilāf* Literature

The three chapters in this part all examine the issues relating to Shiʿism and authority and, concomitantly, aspects of the popularisation and legacy of that authority. Sajjad Rizvi's chapter addresses the concept of *walāya takwīniyya*. This he defines as 'the existential and absolute cosmic authority of the Imams'. Rizvi references both present and past discussions – the latter in the Safawid period in particular – of extremist notions of the Imams' status but also, and more importantly, Safawid-period thinkers' understanding of the concept as rooted in early tradition and the Shiʿi *ḥadīth*. Rizvi then examines, first, the understanding of *walāya* by Mullā Ṣadrā (d. 1044/1635) across several of his important contributions. But the author also tests the 'schema' as found in the writings of Ṣadrā's student and son-in-law Muḥsin Fayḍ Kāshānī (d. 1091/1680), as Fayḍ discussed *walāya* in relation to 'the perfect human (*al-insān al-kāmil*)', as a discourse separate to those discussions on the issue offered by his father-in-law. The works of the Safawid-period Twelver Neoplatonist Qāḍī Saʿīd Qummī (d. 1108/1696) are also examined and are found to be extending the discussion of such *wilāya* in relation to 'the perfect human'. The latter act 'as a mirror of the divine' whereas individuals 'exist in his shadow as pale reflections of his perfect humanity'. That 'universal *wilāya*' he 'equates … with its primary exponent Imām ʿAlī'.

These ideas needed to be 'translated', as it were, 'to vernacularise Shiʿi thought in order to disseminate and establish it as the faith of the [Safawid] empire and its peoples'. The author suggests that perhaps the first to do this, by writing in Persian, was Mīrzā Rafīʿā Nāʾīnī (d. 1073/1672). Nāʾīnī's work, although it did not address 'the perfect human' *per se*, did offer a picture of the Imams as at once perfecting knowledge, immune from error and possessors of a personality through all of which the Divine can be seen.

Rizvi then considers the discussions of *ḥikmat* by Nāʾinī's own son-in-law, and student of Ṣadrā, ʿAbd al-Razzāq Lāhījī (d. 1073/1662). For Lāhijī, following Ibn ʿArabī (d. 638/1240), the human is placed at the 'pinnacle of the manifestation of the Divine'. It is the person of the Imam who is the intermediary 'in the process of emanation' from that Divine, but who plays this role also in respect of the 'unfolding of the cosmos and of intellects emanating from the one'. A contemporary Sufi writing in India in 1644, Mullā Muḥammad Ṣādiq Iṣfahanī, endowed Imam ʿAlī with this role but, being a Sunnī, extended it to the caliphs as well.

The articulation did not disappear with the passing of the Safawid period. Āghā Muḥammad Bīdābādī (d. 1197–8/1783) studied with some of the last Safawid-period thinkers and carried on the discussion about 'the perfect human'. A student of his recentred the discussion on the figure of Imām ʿAlī, focusing on the Imam's own

Sectarian Identity in 2nd/8th Century Kufa', *Islamic Law and Society*, 16 (2009), p. 159.

words, and, citing both the *ḥadīth* and the works of Ibn ʿArabī, saw the niche in the light verse as, in fact, the perfect human – Imam ʿAlī himself.

Rizvi also cites Qājār-period scholars, noting, for example, the effort of the author of one text to integrate *walāya takwīniyya* and political theory, such that the ruler can better understand his role as the representative of the Imam.The author concludes that it was in the Safawid period that the *walāya* of Ibn ʿArabī was 'naturalised in a Shiʿi context', with its roots firmly based in the Twelver *ḥadīth* such that 'it became a Shiʿi doctrine'. Nevertheless, this was an argument being formulated. The blending of the two sets of discourses by these thinkers starting in the Safawid period was part and parcel of the conceptualisation of the faith, the Imams and the nature of their authority in this period that witnessed both the formal establishment of the faith and a resulting close working relationship between those in the ʿUṣūlī tradition and the political institution. Although both the political establishment and the scholarly elite benefited from this relationship, to be sure, the ideas formulated in this period, however arcane they may seem, had the greater longevity and very practical impact: Rizvi perceptively notes the importance given to *walāya takwīniyya* in the works of Ayatollah Khumaynī.

Paul E. Walker examines a wide range of primary sources composed in the Fatimid period to discuss the manner in which the Fatimids both understood the theory and practice of the imamate and conveyed it to the masses and those who constituted Fatimid officialdom themselves. Taken as a whole, the intended audiences for all these included both Ismailis, non-Ismaili Muslims and even non-Muslims. Walker notes that specifically four treatises on the imamate written in the Fatimid period are still extant. Of these, three were composed during the reign of al-Ḥākim (r. 386–411/996–1021).

One of these three was in fact composed for the Būyid wazir of Baghdad and as such was, Walker suggests, intended for a larger Shiʿi audience. Walker notes the presence of arguments about the necessity of the imamate and the infallibility of the Imam himself. The issue of lineage – the descent from the Prophet and ʿAlī – was also key, as was the specific designation by one Imam of his successor. A second chapter set out to prove the imamate to the Fatimid believers. In effect, claiming all these for the Imam-caliph al-Ḥākim himself, the author of the essay argued the Imam was the best of all men and that, therefore, their ruler was also Allah's shadow on earth. As such, in these official treatises, the Imam-caliph emerges as of a status superior to that of humans, holding the function of the Prophet himself and as such is above mortal comment.

Walker then examines a series of other works by important figures in the Fatimid *daʿwa* which also addressed the imamate. Two of these were composed by the famous Fatimid jurist and founder of Ismaili jurisprudence, al-Qāḍī al-Nuʿmān (d. 363/974). In one, the jurist author goes so far as to name and criticise other Muslim groups that opposed the Fatimids. Walker also calls attention to the relevance of both *majālis* literature, poetry and polemical/apologetic materials to the study.

Walker then surveys the 'festival sermon'/*khuṭba* given by the Imam-caliph on important occasions in the Islamic calendar. These especially, he notes, were specifically intended for the ruler's subjects and thus reveal something of what was felt necessary to be related to a potentially very diverse assembly – in attendance would have been Sunnis and Shiʿa, as well as those of various ranks and professions, including 'commoners' and non-Muslims. In one, delivered in North Africa in 945, Walker notes a direct appeal to the Kutāma Berber tribe. Walker points to the deliberate employment in others of terms and phrases that could be 'read' differently by Sunnis and Shiʿa where, in others, the distinctly Shiʿi, and Fatimid, and therefore anti-Umayyad and anti-Abbasid viewpoint was unequivocal. In two the death of the previous Imam was announced.

Finally, Walker calls attention to imperial letters, letters of appointment and decrees as sources for pronouncements on the imamate. Whilst still in North Africa, he notes, the Fatimids appointed no wazirs but by the early 11th century that had changed: Allah needed no such wazir, but mortals did, one document explained. If, Walker notes, the Fatimids claimed infallibility then those whom they appointed were beholden to them as individuals – and, as living Imams, as possessors of unshared authority – not to abstractions of doctrine derived by Sunni scholars. The author concludes that once the state had come into existence, the Fatimids were clear and consistent in their view of the imamate and its ultimate authority.

Andrew J. Newman's chapter suggests that claims to authority over doctrine and practice put forth by those Būyid-period Twelver scholars in the rationalist tradition already well known to scholars of the field likely did not enjoy approval of the majority of the faithful in their own time. Newman notes that work with a wide variety of source materials available on Qajar, and especially 20th and 21st centuries, Twelver discourse on myriad issues of doctrine and practice has revealed the participation therein of a range of non-elite 'voices'.

The chapter then focuses on a range of works authored by Muḥammad b. Muḥammad b. Nuʿmān, al-Shaykh al-Mufīd and ʿAlī b. al-Ḥusayn, al-Sharīf al-Murtaḍā, including, especially, their replies to questions sent to them in Baghdad from more distant communities of the faithful. Both sets of texts reveal the presence both of a range of views on Twelver authority over doctrine and practice, together with a range of practices being undertaken by those considering themselves members of the believing community that were at odds with the views of al-Mufīd and al-Murtaḍā. The range of replies each sent to these distant communities in particular reveal the efforts of each to assert both the authority of his own interpretations generally and the authoritativeness of their interpretations on particular issues. At the time, Newman suggests, the outcome of such doctrinal and practical disputations certainly cannot have been clear nor, indeed, could the future course of the faith, let alone its continued existence.

In fact, the same may be said of all three chapters. Each author has documented claims being advanced by the protagonists in question. The very making of the 'claims' highlighted by each author attests to the presence of alternative understandings and counter-claims. The chapters herein mark important steps in the direction of recovering a picture of the pre-modern evolution of each of the discourses in question.

14

'Seeking the Face of God': The Safawid *Ḥikmat* Tradition's Conceptualisation of *Walāya Takwīniyya*

Sajjad Rizvi

In the early 1990s, Hossein Modarressi wrote an important and influential account of the development of early classical Shiʿi thought that culminates and summarises a whole tradition of reformist Shiʿi thinking of the 20th century.[1] A more moderate face of Shiʿi Islam was presented, one in which the infallibility of the Imams was interrogated, and exaggerated notions of the cosmic roles of the Imams dismissed as *ghulūw* (exaggeration) or, at the very least, emerging from circles of individuals with liminal, mixed and confused allegiances, victims of and proponents of *takhlīṭ*, that admixture of correct and corrupt doctrine. This group of extremists rejected in the *ḥadīth* literature as *ghulāt* or *mufawwiḍa* (the latter because they supposedly held that the act of creation had been delegated by God to the Imams) were prominent in the classical period, attacking their opponents as *muqaṣṣira*, those whose beliefs about the Imams had shortcomings (such as the denial of their infallibility).[2]

Modarressi, it seems, agrees with the notion, common among Shiʿi reformists such as Mīrzā Riḍā-Qulī Sharīʿat-Sanglajī (d. 1944), Shaykh Muḥammad al-Khāliṣī (d. 1963), Ḥaydar ʿAlī Qalamdārān (d. 1989), and more recently ʿAbdolkarim Soroush (b. 1945) and Mohsen Kadivar (b. 1959) that the Imams were *ʿulamā'-yi abrār* (righteous but fallible scholars) and locates the popularisation of extreme views

[1] Hossein Modarressi, *Crisis and Consolidation in the Formative Period of Shiʿite Islam* (Princeton, 1993).

[2] Ibid., pp. 19–48. Among the early tradents, it was Ibn Bābawayh al-Qummī known as al-Shaykh al-Ṣadūq (d. 381/991) who was the most prominent opponent of the *mufawwiḍa* – see *ʿUyūn akhbār al-Riḍā'*, ed. Ḥusayn Aʿlamī (Beirut, 1984), vol. 1, pp. 216–220 (*bāb mā jā'a ʿan al-Riḍā' ʿalayhi al-salām fī wajh dalā'il al-a'imma ʿalayhim al-salām wa'l-radd ʿalā l-ghulāt wa'l-mufawwiḍa laʿnahumullāh*) – although the main attack upon the *mufawwiḍa* and tendencies of extreme veneration and consideration for the Imams known as *ghulūw* came from the classical specialists on the narrators of *ḥadīth* (*rijāl*); see Abū Jaʿfar al-Ṭūsī (d. 460/1067), *al-Rijāl*, ed. Jawād Qayyūmī Iṣfahānī (Qumm, 2000), where he mentions 33 narrators accused of *ghulūw* or *tafwīḍ*.

on the status of the Imams in the Safawid period, and, in particular, blames Safawid philosophers for expounding a view of the imamate as a cosmic necessity.[3] He argues that while early on the Imams had repudiated those who held exaggerated beliefs about their status, these very beliefs crept into the mainstream and were disseminated by theologians in later periods.[4] Safawid philosophers, such as Mullā Ṣadrā (d. 1635), who proposed a cosmic role for the Imams later termed *walāya takwīniyya* or the existential and absolute cosmic authority of the Imams, were thus a continuation of the early tendency of extremism, a revival of the *mufawwiḍa*.[5] In fact, in contemporary polemics, it seems that proponents of 'philosophy' defend *walāya takwīniyya* and those opposed to the Sadrian school and who favour reform tend to oppose it.[6]

[3] Ḥaydar ʿAlī Qalamdārān, *Rāh-i najāt az sharr-i ghulāt* (Qumm, 1974) and *Armaghān-i āsimān dar bayān-i ʿavāmil va ʿilal-i irtiqāʾ va inḥiṭāt-i Musalmānān* (Qumm, 1961); Yann Richard, 'Sharīʿat Sanglajī: A Reformist Theologian of the Riḍā Shāh Period', in Said Arjomand, ed., *Authority and Political Culture in Shiʿism* (Albany, NY, 1988), pp. 159–177; Rainer Brunner, 'A Shiite Cleric's Criticism of Sunnism: Mūsā Mūsawī', in Rainer Brunner and Werner Ende, ed., *The Twelver Shia in Modern Times* (Leiden, 2001), pp. 178–187; Aḥmad Kasravī, *Shīʿīgarī* (n.p., 1983); ʿAbd al-Karīm Surūsh, *Basṭ-i tajriba-yi nabavī* (3rd printing, Tehran, 1379 Sh./2000), pp. 269–281; Muḥsin Kadīvar, *'Qarāʾat-i farāmūsh-shuda, bāzkhwānī naẓarīya-yi ʿulamāʾ-yi abrār talaqqī-yi avvalī-yi Islām-i Shiʿi az aṣl-i imāmat'*, *Madrasa* I.3 (Tehran, 1385/2006), pp. 92–102. For the latter, see Ḥasan Anṣārī's critique on his blog online: http://ansari.kateban.com/entry1386.html (accessed 13 August 2013).

[4] It is worth emphasising that *ghulūw* is a highly contested concept and even early *ḥadīth* collections sometimes characterised as containing extremist material had chapters condemning *ghulūw*. For example, Abū Jaʿfar Muḥammad al-Ṣaffār al-Qummī (d. 290/902), the author of *Baṣāʾir al-darajāt*, one of the earliest collections of Imāmī *ḥadīth* which includes material sometimes characterised as extremist on the knowledge of the Imams and their cosmological *walāya*, is also credited with a work refuting the extremists (*Kitāb al-radd ʿalā l-ghulāt*); see M. A. Amir-Moezzi, *Le Coran silencieux et le Coran parlant* (Paris, 2011), p. 134. For a study sympathetic to Modarressi and which also argues that the cosmological notion of *walāya* is a later ahistorical approach to the classical perplexity following the death of the 11th Imam, see Said Arjomand, 'The Consolation of Theology: Absence of the Imam and Transition from Chiliasm to Law in Shiʿism', *Journal of Religion*, 76 (1996), pp. 548–571.

[5] A genealogy of the term *walāya takwīniyya* is a desideratum but not attempted in this chapter; one's impression is that it cannot be traced before the Qajar period. One might argue that this theological embrace of *tafwīḍ* in a different guise (as criticised by its opponents) mirrored developments in juristic and ritual practice such as the triple *shahāda* and the *tawliya* in the call to prayer discussed in Liyakat Takim, 'From *bidʿa* to Sunna: The *wilāya* of ʿAlī in the Shiʿi *adhān*,' *JAOS*, 120 (2000), pp. 166–177; cf. Joseph Eliash, 'On the Genesis and Development of the Twelver-Shiʿi Three-tenet Shahāda,' *Der Islam*, 47 (1971), pp. 265–272; Werner Ende, '*Bidʿa* or *sirr al-īmān*? Modern Shiʿi Controversies over the Third *shahāda* in the *adhān*', in M. A. Amir-Moezzi, Meir Bar-Asher and Simon Hopkins, ed., *Le Shīʿisme Imāmite Quarante ans après. Hommage à Etan Kohlberg* (Turnhout, 2009), pp. 203–217.

[6] For example, those in favour include the school of ʿAllāma al-Ṭabāṭabāʾī (d. 1981), prominent among whom writing in Arabic these days is Sayyid Kamāl al-Ḥaydarī whose lectures on the topic are published: *al-Walāya al-takwīniyya ḥaqīqatuhā wa-maẓāhiruhā*, bi-qalam Shaykh ʿAlī Ḥammūd al-ʿIbādī (Qumm, 2010). Prominent critics of the concept in recent times include the late reforming *marjaʿ* Sayyid Muḥammad Ḥusayn Faḍlallāh (d. 2010); for example,

Walāya takwīniyya as the absolute power and authority to act upon the cosmos and manipulate it (*walāyat al-taṣarruf*) becomes an expression of the notion that the Imam as the perfect human manifests the totality of the divine attributes and names.[7]

Modarressi writes:

> The introduction of Sufi ideas and interpretations into Islamic philosophy in the Safawid period brought about a new Shīʿite school of Islamic philosophy in the eleventh/seventeenth century and helped the Sufi cosmological theories of Ibn al-ʿArabī to be established in Shīʿite philosophical thought. Some of the adherents of this philosophical school put forward a theory of the Imām's 'existential authority' (*al-wilāya al-takwīniyya*) that was virtually the same as the Mufawwiḍa's cosmological theory on the authority of the 'first creature' or the 'perfect man' in the creation and supervision of the world. Although many of the followers of that Sufi philosophical school have not supported that concept of the Imām's existential authority to its full logical conclusion, others have done so. Those that have must be regarded as the true heirs to the Mufawwiḍa (even though they strongly deny it, at least verbally) because their doctrines are identical. Although always a very small minority, some of their ideas, which were in line with the pro-Mufawwiḍa reports in the collections of *ḥadīth*, as well as their terminology, have gained some degree of support in the community.[8]

So the concept of *walāya takwīniyya*, for Modarressi, is the result of the marriage of *tafwīḍ*, that particular doctrine that God had delegated His creative agency to the Imams who therefore are the true creators and sustainers of the cosmos, and the notion of the Perfect Human (*al-insān al-kāmil*) in the thought of the school of Ibn ʿArabī as the complete manifestation of the divine who deploys the totality of the divine names and attributes. The clear implication is that such notions about the status of the Imams are extrinsic to the Shiʿi tradition and traceable either to the influence of non-Muslim ideas coming through the *ghulāt* in southern Iraq in the classical period, or from Sunni thinkers such as Ibn ʿArabī and his Sufi followers. As such, the notion of *walāya takwīniyya* is, in a sense, inauthentically Shiʿi, a continuation of Modarressi's argument elsewhere with respect to the accusation of belief in a corrupted

see his *Naẓrat Islāmiyya ḥawl al-walāya al-takwīniyya* on his official website: http://arabic.bayynat.org.lb/books/welaya_100.htm (accessed 2 June 2011).

[7] This chapter is not concerned with political and nomological understandings of the *walāya* of the Imams. For a useful survey of those and their intersections with cosmological notions into the Safawid period, see Muḥammad Karīmī Zanjānī Aṣl, 'Jāyigāh-i valāyat dar fiqh-i siyāsī-yi imāmiyya (tā suqūṭ-i silsila-yi Ṣafavī)', in Bahāʾ al-Dīn Khurramshāhī and Jūyā Jahānbakhsh, ed., *Muḥaqqiq-nāma: maqālāt-i taqdīm shuda bih Ustād Duktūr Mahdī Muḥaqqiq* (Tehran, 2001), vol. 2, pp. 1112–1159.

[8] Modarressi, *Crisis and Consolidation*, p. 49.

Qurʾanic text (the notion of *taḥrīf*) or even the doctrine of messianic deliverance (belief in a *mahdī*).[9]

Leaving aside the polemical intent of this passage, what is quite clear is that the nexus of *ghulūw* and *taqṣīr* within which one tends to interpret Shiʿi sacred history remains one that affects communities to this day and indeed the academic field as well: *ghālī* and *muqaṣṣir* remain terms of abuse. At the same time other scholars have focused on precisely those *ghulāt* circles as defining early Shiʿi thought and adherence.[10] But I do not want to focus on the polemics but rather what the passage does suggest: that Safawid thinkers genuinely thought their reformulation of the *walāya* of the Imams had firm roots in the early tradition and in the *ḥadīth*. This chapter will therefore focus on their presentation of the theory of what we now term *walāya takwīniyya*.

For Safawid thinkers, the Shiʿi faith is at its heart centred upon the notion of *walāya* as a dual concept of the ontological status of the Imams and the devotion and initiatic adherence that disciples and followers owe to the Imams. Such a concept is not an invention of that period; Amir-Moezzi has, I think successfully, demonstrated its earlier precedents.[11] However, it becomes the cornerstone of the new dispensation and revival of Shiʿi heritage that was a central concern of the Safawid project intellectually and spiritually. It was the work of the late Henry Corbin that made the most significant contribution to our understanding of the centrality of *walāya* to Shiʿi Islam: as the central mode through which God was manifest in the pleroma of the *ahl al-bayt* through and beyond history, and the primary esoteric hermeneutic for understanding revelation.[12] The cosmos and indeed history is therefore defined through the *walāya* of the *ahl al-bayt* as the mediation between God and human, a 'hiéro-histoire' through which 'esoteric' Islam, in Corbin's words, defies the 'socialisation' of the spiritual, or the poverty of a historicisation of a religious dispensation.[13] The triumph of

---

9 Hossein Modarressi, 'Early Debates on the Integrity of the Qurʾān', *SI*, 77 (1993), pp. 5–39.

10 Mohammad Ali Amir-Moezzi, *Le guide divin dans le shiʿisme originel: aux sources de l'ésoterisme en Islam* (Paris, 1992), and *La religion discrète: croyances et pratiques dans l'islam Shiʿite* (Paris, 2006), and see also his review of Modarressi in *Bulletin Critique des Annales Islamologiques*, 14 (1998) pp. 53–57; cf. Ronald P. Buckley, 'Jaʿfar al-Ṣādiq and Early Proto-Shiʿism' (Ph.D. thesis, University of Exeter, 1993). For a study of the really marginal extremists, see William F. Tucker, *Mahdis and Millenarians: Shiʿite Extremists in Early Muslim Iraq* (Cambridge, 2008), and Tamima Bayhom-Daou, 'The Second-Century *ghulāt*: Were they Really Gnostic?' *JAIS*, 5 (2003–2004), pp. 13–61. More recently, Robert Gleave has perceptively noted that early debates on *ghulūw* and *taqṣīr* are replicated in academic approaches to the study of Shiʿi Islam; see 'Recent Research in the Early History of Shiʿism', *History Compass*, 7 (2009), pp. 1593–1605.

11 Mohammed Ali Amir-Moezzi, 'Notes à propos de la *walāya imāmite*', *JAOS*, 122 (2002), pp. 722–740, and idem, 'Seul l'homme de Dieu est humain: Théologie et anthropologie mystique à travers l'exégèse Imāmite ancienne', *Arabica*, 45 (1998), pp. 193–214.

12 Henry Corbin, *En Islam Iranien: aspects spirituels et philosophiques I: Le Shiʿisme duodécimain* (Paris, 1971), p. 4.

13 Ibid., pp. 35–36.

walāya therefore lies in its political incompletion. It is the Imams who define history, initiate it and accomplish and complete it at the end of times. It is their *walāya* that frames history and expresses their authority and power over time and space. While one may quibble with Corbin's esotericising project, his identification of Shiʿi Islam as more than 'Imāmism' understood in a limited manner is an important genuflection to the notion of *walāya takwīniyya* as a cosmological and ontological status that the *ahl al-bayt* possess. It is both a prophetic (and Gnostic) philosophy and an initiatic approach to religion. In a significant chapter entitled 'prophétologie et imāmologie', Corbin demonstrates the coupling of Shiʿi *ḥadīth* on the imamate with the concept of *walāya* in the Shiʿified school of Ibn ʿArabī from Sayyid Ḥaydar Āmulī (d. after 1385) to Mullā Ṣadrā: the Imams as inheritors of the prophets complete the function of prophecy as revelation and as the face of God, the *deus revelatus*.[14] The rational idea of the necessity of the Imam, or the proof of God (*ḥujja*) found in the *ḥadīth* and the *kalām* tradition, becomes an existential *sine qua non* of the cosmos as well as the epistemological condition for knowing God.[15] Corbin's main source in this chapter is Mullā Ṣadrā's famous commentary on the *Kitāb al-ḥujja* of al-Kulaynī's *al-Kāfī*. For those who support the notion of *walāya takwīniyya*, this conception arises out of the reading of the *ḥadīth* including those ecstatic sayings attributed to Imam ʿAlī (and considered by specialists of Shiʿi *ḥadīth* to be of dubious provenance) such as the *khuṭbat al-bayān* (The Expository Sermon).[16] These texts present the Imam as eternal principle, pre-existing, existing outside history and surviving history implicit in the famous saying of Imam ʿAlī (mirroring a similar saying of the Prophet): 'I was a *walī* even when Adam was still in the mixture of water and clay (*kuntu walīyan wa-Ādam bayn al-māʾ wa'l-ṭīn*).'

The concept of *walāya takwīniyya* expounded by Safawid philosophers and developed up to the present day by their heirs, including Sayyid Rūḥullāh Khumaynī (d. 1989), Sayyid Kāẓim ʿAṣṣār (d. 1975) and especially ʿAllāma Sayyid Muḥammad

[14] Ibid., pp. 220–221. On the Shiʿi school of Ibn ʿArabī, see Kāmil Muṣṭafā al-Shaybī, *al-Ṣila bayn al-taṣawwuf wa'l-tashayyuʿ* (Cairo, 1969).

[15] Corbin, *En Islam Iranien I*, pp. 229–234, 312.

[16] Ibid., pp. 253–258. On the genre of such sermons found in sources such as *Mashāriq anwār al-yaqīn fī asrār Amīr al-muʾminīn* of Ḥāfiẓ Rajab al-Bursī (d. ca 843/1411), see M. A. Amir-Moezzi, 'Remarques sur la divinité de l'Imam', *Studia Iranica*, 25 (1996), pp. 193–216, and Todd Lawson, 'The Dawning-places of the Lights of Certainty in the Divine Secrets Connected with the Commander of the Faithful by Rajab Bursī', in L. Lewisohn, ed., *The Heritage of Sufism II: The Legacy of Medieval Persian Sufism (1150–1500)* (Oxford, 1999), pp. 261–276. For the text of the famous sermon *khuṭbat al-bayān* (and its versions and excerpts), see Rajab al-Bursī, *Mashāriq anwār al-yaqīn fī asrār amīr al-muʾminīn* (Beirut, 1992), pp. 170–172; Sayyid Ḥaydar Āmulī, *Jāmiʿ al-asrār wa-manbaʿ al-anwār*, ed. Henry Corbin and O. Yahia (Tehran, 1969), pp. 383, 411; Qāḍī Saʿīd Qummī (d. 1696), *al-Arbaʿīnīyāt li-kashf anwār al-qudsīyāt*, ed. Najaf-Qulī Ḥabībī (Tehran, 2002), p. 38; Mīrzā Abu'l-Qāsim Rāz Shīrāzī (d. 1286/1869), *Sharḥ kitāb khuṭbat al-bayān* (Shiraz, n.d.); Sayyid Jaʿfar Kashfī (d. 1267/1851), *Tuḥfat al-mulūk*, ed. ʿAbd al-Wahhāb Furātī (Qumm, 2002), pp. 95–96; Shaykh ʿAlī al-Yazdī al-Ḥāʾirī (d. 1333/1915), *Ilzām al-nāṣib fī ithbāt al-ḥujjat al-ghāʾib* (Beirut, 1984), vol. 2, pp. 178–242 (these are most extensive).

Ḥusayn Ṭabāṭabāʾī (d. 1981), has increasingly become a dominant mode for understanding the onto-theological role of the Imams and, for Modarressi, is a continuation of classical, quasi-Gnostic, *ghulūw*.[17] A cursory survey of contemporary practice and belief suggests that it is now the dominant paradigm in Imāmī circles for understanding the nature and function of the Imams in the cosmos.[18] Here I examine this concept of *walāya takwīniyya* as expressed in Safawid texts as the natural result of a philosophising but also mysticising discourse of the Imam beyond a mere result of a theological syllogism or the teacher of rules of comportment.

Defining *Walāya*

Let's start with the most famous of the philosophers of the Safawid period, Mullā Ṣadrā (d. 1044/1635). Instead of looking at his commentary on *al-Kāfī*, there are important passages in his *al-Shawāhid al-rubūbiyya* (Divine Witnessings) that indicate for us the development of the theory of *walāya* in the direction of a 'Shiʿi philosophy'. His discussion of prophecy and *walāya* comes right at the end of the text and indicates its centrality to the God-cosmos and God-humanity relationship in his thought. The first step in understanding *walāya takwīniyya* is to examine its relationship with the function and status of prophecy (*nubūwa*).

Drawing upon the prophetic doctrine of the Ibn ʿArabī school, Mullā Ṣadrā regards *walāya* as the esoteric aspect and indeed the continuation of the prophetic dispensation. Prophecy as communication of revelation from an angel and as a

[17] On Khumaynī's deployment of *walāya takwīniyya*, see his important commentaries on the works of the school of Ibn ʿArabī (d. 638/1240) that focus on the notion of *walāya* as expressed in the *Faṣṣ shīthī* (Ring-setting on Seth) of the *Fuṣūṣ al-ḥikam* (Ring-settings of Wisdom) of Ibn ʿArabī: *Taʿlīqāt ʿalā Sharḥ Fuṣūṣ al-ḥikam wa-Miṣbāḥ al-uns* (Tehran, 1410/1990), *Sharḥ duʿāʾ al-saḥar*, ed. Sayyid Aḥmad Fihrī (Tehran, 1416/1995), *Miṣbāḥ al-hidāya ilā l-khilāfa wa'l-walāya* (Beirut, 1983), *Imāmat va insān-i kāmil az dīdgāh-i Imām Khumaynī* (Tehran, 1381 Sh./2002); see Christian Yahya Bonaud, *L'Imam Khomeyni, un gnostique méconnu du XXe siècle: métaphysique et théologie dans les oeuvres philosophiques et spirituelles de l'Imam Khomeyni* (Paris, 1997); Alexander Knysh, "Irfān Revisited: Khumaynī and the Legacy of Islamic Mystical Philosophy', *Middle East Journal*, 46 (1992), pp. 631–653. On ʿAṣṣār's work in this area, see his 'Tafsīr sūrat al-Fātiḥa', in *Majmūʿa-yi āthār-i ʿAṣṣār*, ed. Sayyid Jalāluddīn Āshtiyānī (Tehran, 1376 Sh./1998). As for Ṭabāṭabāʾī, the *locus classicus* is his *Risālat al-walāya* (Kuwait, 1987), now tr. Fazel Asadi Amjad and Mahdi Dasht Bozorgi as *The Return to Being* (London, 2009).

The key intermediaries between the Safawid period and the modern one were Mīrzā Muḥammad Riḍā Qummshihī (d. 1889) in his *Dhayl Faṣṣ al-shīth*, ed. Manūchihr Suhā (Qazvin, 1975), Mullā Hādī Sabzavārī (d. 1873) in his *Sharḥ al-asmāʾ*, ed. Najafqulī Ḥabībī (Tehran, 1376 Sh./1997) and Sulṭān-ʿAlī Shāh Gunābādī (d. 1909) in his *Vilāyatnāma* (Tehran, 1380 Sh./2001). For a discussion of the Qajar position on *walāya*, see Sajjad Rizvi, 'Being (*wujūd*) and Sanctity (*wilāya*): Two Poles of Intellectual and Mystical Inquiry in Qajar Iran', in Robert Gleave, ed., *Religion and Society in Qajar Iran* (London, 2005), pp. 113–126.

[18] There are few contemporary scholars who would openly deny it.

legislative function (*nubuwwa tashrīʿiyya*) culminated with the Prophet Muḥammad, after whom there is no prophet.[19] This prophetic cycle of ushering in the religious dispensation is then followed by the function of guidance, warning and giving good news that continues – through the infallible Imams, other givers of good news and through the proponents of the law or the *mujtahids*. Thus the role and the authority of the Prophet remain in force through these three categories of people. He then explains who the *awliyā'* are and how they relate to the Prophet:

> The *awliyā'* have a great share in prophecy not least because it has been reported that he – blessings and peace be with him – said: 'God has servants who are not prophets yet the prophets deem them fortunate.'[20] He [also] said: 'In my community are those who are inspired and spoken to [by angels – *muḥaddathūn*].' He said: 'Whosoever memorises the Qur'an, the function of prophecy develops within him.'[21] It [the function of *walāya*] has access to the unseen and is a witness to the prophet.
>
> So this is the difference between the prophet and the *walī* with respect to prophecy. It is said about him that he is a 'prophet' and the *walī* is an inheritor (*wārith*). Both *walī* and *wārith* are names of God as God is the *walī* of those who believe [Q.2:258 *inter alii*] and God is the best of inheritors [Q.21:89]. *Walāya* is a divine quality as is inheritance. The *walī* only takes prophecy from the prophet after he inherits the truth from him once it is passed onto the *walī*. That is the most perfect way for his truth. Some *awliyā'* take it [prophecy] as an inheritance from the Prophet as they have witnessed him such as his family – with whom be peace – and then the *ʿulamā'* of the disciplines take it from them generation after generation until the Day of Judgement as the chain extends. But the *awliyā'* also take it [prophecy] directly from God because they inherit it and practice it. They are the followers of the messengers similar to the lofty chain preserved such that 'falsehood does not come before them or behind them, but a revelation (*tanzīl*) from the Wise, the Praised' [Q.41:42].
>
> Abū Yazīd [Basṭāmī] said [to the *ʿulamā'*]: 'You take your knowledge from a dead person who took from one dead but we take our knowledge from the Living who

---

19 Mullā Ṣadrā Shīrāzī, *al-Shawāhid al-rubūbiyya fi'l-manāhij al-sulūkiyya*, ed. Sayyid Muṣṭafā Muḥaqqiq Dāmād (Tehran, 1382 Sh./2003), p. 438. There are plenty of precursors for this relationship between *walāya* and prophecy; for example, see Bursī, *Mashāriq anwār*, p. 44.

20 This *ḥadīth* is not found in major collections. However, similar wordings are present in the *Tamhīdāt* of ʿAyn al-Quḍāt Hamadānī (d. 525/1131), ed. ʿAfīf ʿUsayrān (Tehran, 1962), p. 44, and a similar *ḥadīth* praising the luminous *awliyā'* around the empyrean of God who are not prophets is found in Majlisī's *Biḥār al-anwār* (Beirut, 1982), vol. 22, p. 252.

21 Another *ḥadīth* that is not found in collections but is similar to a text quoted on the authority of ʿAbd Allāh in Abu'l-Ḥusayn Warrām b. Abi'l-Firās al-Mālik al-Ashtarī's *Tanbīh al-khawāṭir wa-tanzīh al-nawāẓir* (Beirut, n.d.), vol. 2, p. 11.

> does not die.'[22] Similar to this, He said to his prophet when He mentioned the prophets: 'They are the ones who God guides and through their guidance He directs' [Q.6:90]. And when they had died, God inherited from them as He is the best of inheritors. Then came to the Prophet that guidance by which He had guided them. The knowledge of the *awliyā'* today is exactly the same, through the guidance of the Prophet and the prophets who took from God who cast it in their chests from His very self as a mercy to them and as a providential grace that preceded them with their Lord as He said in favour of his servant Khiḍr: 'We gave it to him as a mercy from us and taught him knowledge from our very self (*min ladunnā*)' [Q.18:65].[23]

Walāya is therefore a Qur'anically embedded status that is divine and only by analogy applied to special chosen friends of God who continue the function of prophecy by linking humans with the divine and by indicating the divine through their interventions in the cosmos. The Safawid philosophers and theologians insisted upon the reality of secondary causality and considered the proximate cause of miracles to be the individual to whom they were ascribed and not God who is considered to be their ultimate agent. In his commentary on the Light Verse, Mullā Ṣadrā glosses the 'lamp' (*miṣbāḥ*) as the Muḥammadan reality, which has a central intermediary function as first creation and the most noble of the contingents (*al-ʿaql al-awwal wa'l-mumkin al-ashraf*) that exists within the world to enlighten and ennoble it, emanating the light of goodness and munificence.[24] There is thus a sense in which the *walī* provides the cosmos with its reason for existing and bestows value upon it. This cosmic role of the Imam/*walī* (taken up by his student Muḥsin Fayḍ as we shall shortly see) is placed within the theory of the perfect man as the manifestation of the totality of the divine names and their agency, even the divine name 'God' (*Allāh*) in the chapter later in the commentary that culminates in a pastiche of Ibn ʿArabī's chapter headings in *Fuṣūṣ al-ḥikam*: *ḥikma ilāhiyya fī kalimat ādamiyya* (divine wisdom in the Adamic name).[25] Mullā Ṣadrā sums up the *walī* as the perfect human manifestation of the divine in the following manner:

> He created the perfect human as a similitude for Him, the Most High, in essence, in quality and in act. True knowledge of this wonderful nature, this subtle order, and knowledge of this precious wisdom and hidden secrets bears within it a great secret of knowledge of God; in fact, knowledge of Him, the Most High, is not possible without knowledge of the perfect human who is the gate to God the Great, who is the firm bond, the taut rope by which one ascends to the higher realm, who is the

---

22 See Ibn ʿArabī, *al-Futūḥāt al-Makkiyya* (Beirut, n.d.), vol. 1, p. 31.

23 Mullā Ṣadrā, *al-Shawāhid al-rubūbiyya*, pp. 439–440.

24 Mullā Ṣadrā, *Tafsīr al-Qur'ān al-karīm*, ed. Muḥammad Khājavī (Qumm, 1993), vol. 4, p. 365.

25 Mullā Ṣadrā, *Tafsīr*, vol. 4, pp. 390ff.

straight path to God the Knowing, the Wise, and who is the gracious book issuing from the Merciful, the Compassionate. So it is incumbent on everyone to know what is in this hidden book and to understand this valuable secret.[26]

In the thought of the last century or so, a number of philosophers have related *walāya* to the cosmic role of the Imam, as the face of the divine through which existence descends and also the mode through which existence is folded up in the return to the One: *walāya* as procession and reversion of the Neoplatonic type is prevalent in works such as ʿAllāma Ṭabāṭabāʾī's *Risālat al-walāya*, the *Valāyatnāma* of the Gunābādī Sufi Sulṭān-ʿAlī Shāh and the *Miṣbāḥ al-hidāya* of Āyatollāh Khumaynī.[27] Within this schema, the divine function of *walāya* needed to be emulated by all humans who share the vicegerency of the divine in the quest for apotheosis (*taʾalluh*). In the particular terms of the *Valāyatnāma*, all humans possess two aspects of *walāya* that need to be actualised: *taklīfiyya*, relating to their general vicegerency of the divine that they adopt once they make the rational choice to be believers, and *takwīniyya*, pertaining to their acquisition of the authority and power over the cosmos in imitation of the divine. The special status of the Imams is therefore, in terms of intensity, a more perfect acquisition and performance of this function. The Sadrian principle of gradation and modulation within a singular reality pertains therefore to *walāya* just as it does to existence (*wujūd*). The *Valāyatnāma* closely follows Sadrian thought: *walāya* is a pure divine act identified with the divine existence which then issues through the divine act of creation through the word 'be', through the divine will (*mashiʾa*) and, as such, is synonymous with key terms from the lexicon of the school of Ibn ʿArabī, namely, the breath of the Merciful (*nafas al-raḥmān*), and the Muḥammadan reality (*ḥaqīqa Muḥammadiyya*).[28] As *walāya* descends from the precinct of the One, it is expressed in the primordial entities such as intellects, souls and, of course, the reality of the *ahl al-bayt*.[29] Once *walāya* is manifest in the cosmos, it acts as a force to propel entities towards their self-realisation and return to the One. The entities in the cosmos are hierarchically arranged and it is the human who has primary place within this structure because he possesses the twofold *walāya*. With respect to the moral obligation (*taklīf*) that the human acquires through an act of free will, human activity in faith is founded upon and expressive of *walāya*, as evinced in a famous narration from Imam Muḥammad al-Bāqir.[30] Since *walāya* propels humans towards

---

[26] Ibid., pp. 400–401.

[27] There are numerous printings of the former including a new translation: *The Return to Being: A Translation of Risalat al-walayah*, tr. Fazel Asadi Amjad and Mahdi Dasht Bozorgi (London, 2009) – a recent trend in writings on *ʿirfān* is for scholars to pen commentaries on this treatise; Sulṭān-ʿAlī Shāh, *Vilāyatnāma*; Rūḥullāh Khumaynī, *Miṣbāḥ al-hidāya*. For a discussion of the latter, see Yahya Bonaud, *L'Imam Khomeyni, un gnostique méconnu du XXe siècle* (Paris, 1997), pp. 268–277.

[28] Sulṭān-ʿAlī Shāh, *Valāyatnāma*, pp. 16–18.

[29] Ibid., pp. 24–27.

[30] Ibid., p. 33.

perfection, they require a *walī* to effect and inspire this process. It is the instruction and direction of the *walī* that awakes a natural disposition in humans that is *walāya*.[31] In particular, it is the *walāya* as love and devotion to the Imams that allows believers to actualise their moral obligation and their faith.

With respect to authority over the cosmos, all humans possess *walāya* because they are created in the image of the divine and *in potentia* can manifest the totality of the divine names. *Walāya takwīniyya* is merely the potential for humans to imitate the divine, and this propensity that they possess is actualised through contact and instruction from those who manifest such acts and attributes, namely the Imams, because the effusion of the absolute *walāya* of God to them is more perfect and more complete than it is to the rest of the cosmos.[32]

Muḥsin Fayḍ on the Perfect Human

Another influential schema of *walāya takwīniyya* is presented in *Kalimāt-i maknūna* ('Hidden Words') of Muḥsin Fayḍ Kāshānī (d. 1091/1680), the student and son-in-law of Mullā Ṣadrā. Fayḍ is primarily concerned with developing a theory of the perfect human within the context of the procession and reversion of being from and to the One.[33] His explicit discussion of *walāya* is restricted to a simple comparison to prophecy as possible expressions of the perfect human (*al-insān al-kāmil*) and as such the propaedeutic to his examination of the doctrine of the imamate, leaving *walāya* as the exclusive human property of the Imams.[34] Generally the school of Mullā Ṣadrā does not restrict *walāya* in this way, and, following Sayyid Ḥaydar Āmulī, considers *walāya* to be a hierarchy of sanctity whose seal is ʿAlī.[35] However, in his discussion of the perfect human, Fayḍ has an extensive discussion of the doctrine of *walāya takwīniyya* with certain key features.

First, since the One is manifest through His names, and those names are identical with the perfect human, the *insān kāmil* manifests the divine and is in fact the reason for the creation. He manifests the totality of the divine names.[36] The Sadrian tradition is careful to distinguish between reasons and causes (*asbāb*, *ʿilal*): *tafwīḍ* is based on the notion that the Imams are the immediate efficient cause of the cosmos and humanity. But this doctrine insists that they are the reasons for why there is

---

31 Ibid., p. 244.

32 Ibid., pp. 30–32.

33 For another useful study of Fayḍ on *walāya*, see Shigeru Kamada, 'Fayḍ al-Kāshānī's *Walāya*: The Confluence of Shiʿi Imamology and Mysticism', in Todd Lawson, ed., *Reason and Inspiration in Islam: Theology, Philosophy and Mysticism in Muslim Thought. Essays in Honour of Hermann Landolt* (London, 2005), pp. 455–468.

34 Muḥsin Fayḍ Kāshānī, *Kalimāt-i maknūna*, ed. Ṣādiq Ḥasanzāda (Qumm, 1386 Sh./2007), pp. 167–178.

35 Sayyid Ḥaydar Āmulī, *Jāmiʿ al-asrār wa-manbaʿ al-anwār*, pp. 101, 341–342, 398.

36 Fayḍ Kāshānī, *Kalimāt-i maknūna*, pp. 112–115.

something rather than nothing and not an actual Aristotelian cause for the existence of things.[37]

Second, since the perfect human has access to all forms of knowledge and the knowledge of the realities of all things (their 'names' as it says in the Qur'an), it is as if he possesses God's view of reality (*baṣar al-ḥaqq*). Because of this privileged immediate knowledge of the cosmos, he can control and deploy the cosmos as he wishes and, as such, becomes the controlling force of the cosmos with authority over it.[38] Fayḍ says:

> The perfect human is like the spirit of the cosmos, and the cosmos is his body. Just as it is the spirit indeed that controls the body and has authority over it through the bodily and spiritual faculties that it possesses, similarly the perfect human controls the cosmos and has authority over it through the divine names that have been placed in him and taught to him and rooted in his disposition.[39]

The manifestation and deployment of the names, for Fayḍ, is then connected to the famous words of the *khuṭbat al-bayān*.

Third, the perfect human is both the reason for the cosmos and the process of its reversion to the One (*maʿād*). In this context, he introduces another synonym for the *walī*, namely the vicegerent (*khalīfa*). Fayḍ says:

> The vicegerent is the uppermost goal of the existence of the cosmos and the highest reason for the creation of Adam. He is the loftiest fruit and purest kernel of creation from the most excellent of all the entities because it [the cosmos] needs him … Because of this, God made all the creatures high and low subject to him, obedient to him … The spheres, the animals, the plants and the rocks … are all created for the human and the human is created for the perfect among them and the perfect for the most perfect and the most perfect for God.[40]

---

[37] Other Shiʿi theologians, however, notably among them those classified as the Shaykhīya, have been happy to identify the Imams as the four Aristotelian causes (*al-ʿilal al-arbaʿa*) of the universe primarily to safeguard divine transcendence (*al-tanzīh*) and the elevated status of the family of the Prophet (and such a theme arguably continues a tendency within the apophatic Neoplatonism of classical Ismaili philosophy). See Shaykh Aḥmad al-Aḥsāʾī (d. 1826), *Sharḥ al-ziyāra al-jāmiʿa* (Beirut, 1999), 4 vols; idem, *Ḥayāt al-nafs*, ed. Mīrzā ʿAlī al-Ḥāʾirī (Kuwait, n.d.), pp. 23–24; Shaykh Muḥammad Bū-Khamsīn (d. 1893), *Najāt al-hālikīn fī ḥaṣr al-ʿilal al-arbaʿ fī Muḥammad wa-ālihi al-ṭāhirīn* (Kuwait, 2005); Mīrzā ʿAbd al-Rasūl al-Ḥāʾirī al-Iḥqāqī (d. 2005), *al-Wilāya: baḥth ḥawl al-wilāya min waḥī al-Qurʾān* (Kuwait, 1999), 2 vols.

[38] Fayḍ Kāshānī, *Kalimāt-i maknūna*, pp. 115–116.

[39] Ibid., p. 116.

[40] Ibid., p. 122.

Fayḍ therefore hints at the hierarchy within the human realm that aspires towards perfection. The folding up and reversion of the cosmos is similarly dependent upon the perfect man. Fayḍ says:

> The reversion of the cosmos is the essence of the human, and the reversion of the human is to the divine essence through the keys of His cosmos, and the keys of His kingdom open the gates of the heavens and the earth with mercy and forgiveness and wisdom and knowledge.[41]

Finally, the cosmic authority of the *walī* over creation is such that it is he that bestows upon it value, and his absence deprives the world of value, condemning it to perdition. He reiterates the eschatological role of the perfect human who is the final act of his *walāya takwīniyya*. Fayḍ continues the similitude of the spirit and the body:

> Just as the reason for the existentiation of the cosmos and its survival is the perfect human and the just Imam who is the vicegerent of God on earth, and just as the goal of creating the body is the rational soul, it is necessary that the abode of the cosmos is corrupted by the passing away of this human from it, just as the body corrupts and is annihilated with the separation of the rational soul from it. God only discloses him to the cosmos through mediation. With the cutting off of the extension that necessitates the survival of its existence and its perfections, the cosmos passes away with his passing away. Whatever spiritual realities and perfections were in it depart for the afterlife and with that the heavens are rent asunder, the sun is folded up, the stars wane and extinguish.[42]

Fayḍ's contemporary, the Shiʿi Neoplatonist thinker Qāḍī Saʿīd Qummī (d. 1108/1696) in a number of famous Arabic commentaries on *ḥadīth* demonstrates his ability to reconcile a Neoplatonic scheme of the procession from and reversion to the One and the role of the *walī* within the scheme with his close reading of narrative material. Qummī uses the concept of *walāya kubrā* or *walāya muṭlaqa* to express the concept that we are examining.[43] In his treatise *al-Ṭalāʾiʿ waʾl-bawāriq*, which is a study of the concept of the perfect human, he says:

> The absolute *walī* is the holder of universal *walāya* and the holder of the station of union and one who unites in himself the totality of the godly words and the source of realities from the east to the west.[44]

---

[41] Ibid., p. 124.

[42] Ibid., pp. 124–125. Note the Qurʾanic language of the end of time.

[43] Qāḍī Saʿīd Qummī, *al-Arbaʿīnīyāt li-kashf anwar al-qudsīyāt*, ed. Najafqulī Ḥabībī (Tehran, 2002), pp. 38, 266.

[44] Ibid., p. 270.

In this sense, Qummī draws a parallel between the *walī* and the Universal Intellect in which reside the forms of all things that exist and from which all things that exist issue. In this sense, the *walī* has a cosmic role as an ontological intermediary. The perfect human acts as a mirror of the divine and individual humans exist in his shadow as pale reflections of his perfect humanity.[45] In other works, consistent with Fayḍ, he equates the universal *walāya* with its primary exponent Imam ʿAlī, and that *walāya* also has a critical role to play in the acquisition of knowledge since all learning is derived from the niche of *walāya* and, as such, is a Prophetic and Imamic inheritance.[46]

Vernacularising *Walāya*

A key function of Safawid religious policy was to vernacularise Shiʿi thought in order to disseminate and establish it as the faith of the empire and its peoples.[47] We now turn to some of the Persian *ḥikmat* works that discuss the notions of *walāya takwīniyya* in the later Safawid and post-Safawid periods. The first text that merits a mention is *Shajara-yi ilāhiyya* of Sayyid Rafīʿ al-Dīn Muḥammad Ṭabāṭabāʾī better known as Mīrzā Rafīʿā Nāʾinī (d. 1083/1672), a contemporary of Mullā Ṣadrā and a leading theologian of Isfahan. He later wrote his own short commentary and summary of the text (*Thamara-yi Shajara-yi ilāhiyya*). On the whole, the work represents an early exposition of Shiʿi philosophical theology in Persian for the Safawid age. Much of the discussion is standard theological reasoning: the Imam is a necessity for the correct direction of society and his existence is an act of grace (*luṭf*) from God to facilitate the fulfilment of the moral obligation that believers owe God.[48] In the *Thamara*, he is more explicit on the role of the Imams as successors to the Prophet bearing the same attributes of perfection and fulfilling the role of manifesting the divine: it is in their perfections of knowledge, protection from error and personality that one understands God.[49] However, in the work of Mīrzā Rafīʿā, the lexicon of the school of Ibn ʿArabī on the perfect human is notably absent.

---

[45] Ibid., pp. 270–272. For an excellent study of Qāḍī Saʿīd Qummī on this theme, see Henry Corbin, *Face de Dieu, Face de l'homme* (Paris, 2008), pp. 245–313.

[46] Qāḍī Saʿīd Qummī, *Sharḥ al-arbaʿīn*, ed. Najafqulī Ḥabībī (Tehran, 2000), p. 353.

[47] For some discussions of processes of vernacularisation, see Rasūl Jaʿfarīyān, *Dīn va siyāsat dar dawra-yi Ṣafavī* (Qumm, 1991); Manṣūr Ṣifatgul, *Sākhtār-i nahād va andīsha-yi dīnī dar Īrān-i ʿaṣr-i Ṣafavī* (Tehran, 2002); Seyyed Hossein Nasr, *Islamic Philosophy from its Origin to the Present: Philosophy in the Land of Prophecy* (Albany, NY, 2006), pp. 235–256; Kathryn Babayan, *Mystics, Monarchs and Messiahs: Cultural Landscapes of Early Modern Iran* (Cambridge, MA, 2002), pp. 439–482; Jean Calmard, 'Shiʿi Rituals and Power II. The Consolidation of Safavid Shiʿism', in Charles Melville, ed., *Safavid Persia* (London, 1996), pp. 139–190.

[48] Mīrzā Rafīʿā Nāʾīnī, *Shajara-yi ilāhiyya* in *Ḥikmat-i ilāhī dar mutūn-i fārsī*, ed. ʿAbdullāh Nūrānī (Tehran, 2006), pp. 265–266.

[49] Mīrzā Rafīʿā Nāʾīnī, *Thamara-yi shajara-yi ilāhiyya*, in *Ḥikmat-i ilāhī*, pp. 325–327.

Nāʾinī's contemporary and the famous son-in-law and student of Mullā Ṣadrā, ʿAbd al-Razzāq ʿFayyāḍʾ Lāhījī (d. 1662), wrote a major work on *ḥikmat* for Shāh ʿAbbās II entitled *Gawhar-i murād*.[50] As had become standard in the Safawid period, Lāhījī deals with the question of cosmological *walāya* in two different parts of his text. First, in his discussion of how the cosmos unfolds and manifests the divine, as is consistent with the school of Ibn ʿArabī, he portrays the human at the pinnacle of the manifestation of the divine. The most intense and sublime level of being that is manifest is that of the Muḥammadan reality expressed in the person of the Imam who can therefore manifest the totality of the divine names and articulate their power.[51] In this sense, the Imam also plays a key role as an intermediary in the process of emanation, of the progression of being from the One. So the Imam finds a role in the ontology of Lāhījī. Elsewhere, in his exposition of the imamate, and following the theological arguments for its necessity and its conditions that are well known from the tradition, he alludes to the cosmological mediation that the Imam performs.[52] The Imam plays a mediating role not only in the unfolding of the cosmos and of intellects emanating from the One, since he is also identified with the primordial *nous*, he manifests and mediates in the two aspects of the intellect, the theoretical and the practical. The theoretical intellect provides us with the ideas and universals for all that we may seek to know, knowledge of the ontology that we inhabit, and the practical intellect confers value upon not only human moral psychology but also upon the moral agency that we possess. This point is further elaborated within his section on the miracles of the saints in which he links the ability to produce the extraordinary to a psychological account of the extraordinary faculty of imagination in the soul of the saint.[53]

Another contemporary of Lāhījī, a Sufi writing in Shāhjahānābād (Delhi) in 1055/1644, Mullā Muḥammad Ṣādiq b. Muḥammad Ṣāliḥ Iṣfahānī, wrote a massive compendium on doctrines entitled *Shāhid-i Ṣādiq*. Written from a broadly Sunni perspective influenced by the school of Ibn ʿArabī, the work discusses *walāya* in terms quite similar to our Safawid thinkers but does not restrict the cosmological power to the Imams, even if here once again it is Imam ʿAlī who exemplifies such a status.[54] The author also extends the role to the caliphs and this may well be an explicit attempt at

---

[50] For a study, see Sajjad Rizvi, ʿA Sufi Theology fit for a Shiʿi King: The *Gawhar-i murād* of ʿAbd al-Razzāq Lāhījīʾ, in A. Shihadeh, ed., *Sufism and Theology* (Edinburgh, 2007), pp. 83–98.

[51] ʿAbd al-Razzāq Lāhījī, *Gawhar-i murād* (lithograph, Tehran, 1860), pp. 208–215; idem, *Guzīda-yi Gawhar-i murād*, ed. Ṣamad Muvaḥḥid (Tehran, 1985), pp. 201–202. I did not have a chance to consult the modern semi-critical edition by Zayn al-ʿĀbidīn Qurbānī Lāhījī (Tehran, 1993).

[52] Lāhījī, *Guzīda-yi Gawhar-i murād*, pp. 292ff. Lāhījī's shorter work *Sarmāya-yi īmān* has a more straightforward approach to the imamate (lithograph, Tehran, 1893, pp. 70–99).

[53] Lāhījī, *Gawhar-i murād*, pp. 326–328.

[54] Muḥammad Ṣādiq Iṣfahānī, *Shāhid-i Ṣādiq*, MS India Office Islamic (British Library) 1537, fol. 10aff.

recovering a conception of Sufi *walāya* from the Safawid Shiʿification of it.[55] Ṣādiq's work is worth citing here because it shows that the concept of a cosmological *walāya* was not an exclusively Shiʿi phenomenon.

Āqā Muḥammad Bīdābādī (d. 1198/1783) had studied with the last generation of philosophers in Safawid Isfahan. In a short Persian treatise entitled *al-Mabdaʾ wa'l-maʿād*, he describes the nature of being and its emanations into the cosmos with the human at the pinnacle of the disclosure of the divine.[56] While he does not explicitly talk about *walāya*, he does present an exposition of the notion of the perfect human (*insān-i kāmil*). The human is the most perfect of the manifestations of being and the most perfect of revelations (*tanazzulāt*) because he unites in his self the totality of the divine names and discloses the reality of the divine essence. The human plays a pivotal role in the procession of being from the One and its reversion, because he is not only the perfect manifestation of the divine, but also possesses the perfections of the faculties that worldly things such as animals and plants have. In this sense, the human is both the face of God on earth mirroring the divine, as well as the face of the cosmos reflecting back to God.

A generation earlier, a Nūrbakhshī Shiʿi Sufi, Mullā ʿAbd al-Raḥīm Damāvandī Rāzī (d. 1160/1747), wrote a Persian treatise on the divine names entitled *Miftāḥ-i asrār al-Ḥusaynī* in which the concept of the cosmological role of the Imam is presented. The words of Imam ʿAlī are the miraculous expressions of the divine for him. In a section on the nature of divine unity, he quotes the famous (apocryphal) conversation between ʿAlī and his disciple Kumayl b. Ziyād al-Nakhaʿī (d. 82/701) on the nature of reality (*Mā al-ḥaqīqa?*) through the gloss of the Shiʿi commentator on Ibn ʿArabī, ʿAbd al-Razzāq Kāshānī (d. 735/1335).[57] In this, ʿAlī is an exemplar for the mystic seeking mystical union and the divine guide along that path whose intercession can affect the seeker's success. Elsewhere he argues that the perfect human, the Imam, manifests the divine names and hence has authority over the cosmos.[58] Later, he quotes (without acknowledging) Mullā Ṣadrā's words cited above from *al-Shawāhid* on the nature of *walāya* and its relationship to prophecy.[59] Damāvandī seems to be engaging in a polemic with Sufis; for him *walāya* and the secrets of its extent must be tied to the family of the Prophet and to the Imams and in this endeavour he copiously cites *ḥadīth*.[60] Spiritual perfections and the ability for another to

55 Ibid., fol. 19b–20a. There are probably many more such examples from Mughal India, Ottoman Turkey and Central Asia that are distinct attempts at preventing the school of Ibn ʿArabī from being captured wholly for a Shiʿi cause.

56 Āqā Muḥammad Bīdābādī, *al-Mabdaʾ wa'l-maʿād* in Sayyid Jalāl al-Dīn Āshtiyānī and Henry Corbin, ed., *Muntakhabātī az āthār-i ḥukamāʾ-yi ilāhī-yi Īrān* (Qumm, repr. 1999), vol. 4, pp. 382–383, 403–404.

57 Mullā ʿAbd al-Raḥīm Damāvandī, *Miftāḥ-i asrār al-Ḥusaynī* in Āshtiyānī and Corbin, ed., *Muntakhabātī az āthār*, vol. 3, pp. 737–752.

58 Ibid., p. 783.

59 Ibid., p. 796.

60 Ibid., pp. 796–803.

manifest *walāya takwīniyya* is thus constrained; the true Sufis and mystics are those who draw upon the niche of prophecy (that is, the *walāya* of the Shiʿi Imams) and subordinate their claims to authority.[61] The culmination of his argument lies in his interpretation of the Light Verse in which the niche symbolises the person of the perfect human and the efficacy and power that the Imams possess even in the dreams of believers. The niche, which symbolises the light of God in the heavens and the earth, is the perfect human who manifests the divine names and is exemplified in Imam ʿAlī; the names that he manifests are necessary concomitants of the very being of the divine.[62] For this point, Damāvandī weaves together exegesis of the *ḥadīth* of the Imams alongside quotations from Ibn ʿArabī and those from his Shiʿi followers such as Ibn Abī Jumhūr al-Aḥsāʾī (d. 907/1502). However, Damāvandī is careful to avoid accusations of extremism; all manifestations of being have a totemic quality, and they symbolise the divine – but one can easily fall into identifying the symbol with what is being symbolised and represented. The perfect human is therefore a symbol for the divine and not the divine itself.[63] He therefore has a real presence in wakeful states and in sleep – and his appearance in dreams is as real as a physical encounter and equally efficacious. For this, again, Damāvandī draws upon *ḥadīth* as well as the glosses of Ibn ʿArabī.[64] The complementarity of approaches between the 'rationalising mysticism' of Ibn ʿArabī and his school, and a deeper mystical and philosophical contemplation of the Shiʿi *ḥadīth* corpus was well established before the end of the Safawid period and retains a hegemonic status even today.

There are also works in Arabic that present the *ḥikmat* tradition's exposition of *walāya takwīniyya*. Mullā Naʿīmā Ṭāliqānī, a thinker of the late Safawid period wrote a treatise on the mystical understanding of being and its manifestations within the cosmos entitled *Aṣl al-uṣūl* around the time of the fall of Isfahan to the invading Afghan tribesmen in 1135/1722. He does not explicitly discuss the issue of *walāya,* but within his examination of theology and the emanation and manifestation of being *qua* God in the cosmos, he draws upon the scheme of the school of Ibn ʿArabī concerning the unfolding of the divine presences (*al-ḥaḍarāt al-ilāhiyya*) with the perfect human as the most perfect manifestation who discloses the totality of the divine names.[65] A key question in understanding cosmogony is to make sense of how God manifests and discloses Himself in the cosmos. One standard version of the presentation of the cosmic role of *walāya* is to use an exegesis of the famous saying of the hidden treasure (*kanzan makhfīyan*). God's self-disclosures obtain throughout the cosmos in a variegated and graded manner, but the true way to understanding Him is through that creation that discloses his nature as the hidden treasure, and that is the person of the perfect human or the *walī*. Ṭāliqānī says:

---

[61] Ibid., p. 800.

[62] Ibid., pp. 812–818.

[63] Ibid., p. 820.

[64] Ibid., pp. 822–830.

[65] Mullā Muḥammad Naʿīmā Ṭāliqānī, *Aṣl al-uṣūl*, ed. Sayyid Jalāl al-Dīn Āshtiyānī (Tehran, 1978), pp. 77–79.

> The (perfect) human is the microcosm that is a small mirror which manifests the names and attributes of the Most High ... The human is chosen from the cosmos to fulfil the role of exposing the divine presence of singularity and indeed the divine presence itself as well as the presences of the names and the attributes. He is the epitome of the book of existence and of the divine presences. God discloses himself through the perfect human to the world of humanity and he emanates a perfect being capable of taking on human characteristics. So he made the human an existent, living, knowing, hearing, seeing and being capable, willing, speaking just as he is all of these ... but with the simple difference that his essence is identical to these names and attributes while the human's manifestation of these names and attributes is not identical to his (divine) essence.[66]

Ṭāliqānī is, therefore, deliberately stepping back from possible criticism of his theory of *walāya* and the perfect human. The *walī* exhibits and manifests the divine names but not in a way in which God discloses them or in a way which suggests an identification of the human with the divine essence. That would entail a falling away into a Christian conception of incarnation or of the human participating in the divine essence (or substance) itself, and would violate both monotheism and the monistic intent of the theory.

Similarly, Mīrzā Ḥasan Lāhījī (d. 1121/1709), a grandson of Mullā Ṣadrā, in a work in Arabic entitled *Zawāhir al-ḥikam* which deals with the whole range of philosophy and theology, analyses the cosmic role of the Imam in two places. First, in the description of the cosmos and the descent of being, he identifies the human as the pinnacle of the creation.[67] Second, in the section on philosophical theology, he presents a discussion on the imamate. While the language is conventionally theological and engages in polemics, he asserts the importance of the Imam as the vicegerent of God on earth and his complete representation to the cosmos; it is through the Imam that God is known and in this sense the imamate continues the function of prophecy of revealing the divine.[68] Similarly, he takes the person of ʿAlī b. Abī Ṭālib as exemplar and describes him as the font of all philosophy in whose hands lie the secrets of the universe and all knowledge. The Imam mediates within the processes of being and of knowledge, and his ability to perform miracles is only an expression of that authority.[69] He is the complete book, the complete revelation that ought to be read to understand the nature of reality.

Finally, the concept of *walāya takwīniyya* is closely integrated into a theory of the polity and governance in a famous Qajar work of advice, *Tuḥfat al-mulūk*, written in Persian in 1233/1818 by Sayyid Jaʿfar Dārābī Kashfī (d. 1267/1851) and addressed

---

66 Ṭāliqānī, *Aṣl al-uṣūl*, p. 72.

67 Mīrzā Ḥasan Lāhījī, *Zawāhir al-ḥikam*, in Āshtiyānī and Corbin, ed., *Muntakhabātī az āthār*, vol. 3, pp. 369–375.

68 Ibid., pp. 406–410.

69 Ibid., pp. 416–417.

to the prince Muḥammad Taqī Mīrzā Ḥusām al-Salṭana (d. 1270/1853), governor of Luristān and son of Fatḥ ʿAlī Shāh Qājār (d. 1250/1834).[70] Kashfī's work is significant because it has often been said in the last two centuries that the notion of *walāya takwīniyya* is a form of extreme consideration for the status of the Imams whose propagation is associated with the Shaykhīya, and Kashfī was a prominent member of the *uṣūlī* establishment condemning them.[71] Yet his espousal of the *ḥikmat* conception of *walāya takwīniyya* is quite clear in his work. The work is divided into three sections: on moral psychology (on the nature of reason/intellect and its faculties); on the relationship between the intellect and the cosmos that it perceives (which concerns motivation, will and action); and on the properties and effects of practical reason on moral and political agency. The second section is therefore the key one for us because it concerns the relationship between inner states and the wider cosmos, and it is there that one finds the discussion of *walāya*. Kashfī's contention is that a proper understanding of the functioning of the human intellect and *walāya* as a principle central to the intellect are critical for successful deployment of governance in which the ruler acts as a representative of the Imam/*walī*. The political and ethical theory that underlies Kashfī's work contends that if we perfect our souls through spiritual exercises and especially develop our intellects, we become better moral agents in the pursuit of the good and ultimately of happiness. The study of philosophy is part of the process of perfecting the soul and in itself a spiritual exercise.[72] However, this philosophy, or rather wisdom, is not acquired but bestowed in the heart as it requires a context in which we know and function as cognitive beings.[73] A key part of the context is *walāya*: the person of the Imam who is identical to the first Intellect or the first being from which all individual intellects emanate. Thus as we have seen in the Neoplatonic scheme of Safawid thought, the *walī* is both the intermediary in the procession from the One and in the eschatological scheme of the reversion back to the One.[74] As such the *walī* manifests God and is the 'secret' of the divine.

---

[70] Kashfī, *Tuḥfat al-mulūk*, pp. 31–32. For discussions of this work, see Said Arjomand, 'Political Ethic and Public Law in the Early Qajar Period', in Robert Gleave, ed., *Religion and Society in Qajar Iran* (London, 2005), pp. 26–29; Jamīla Kadīvar, *Taḥavvul-i guftumān-i siyāsī-yi Shīʿa dar Īrān* (Tehran, 2000), pp. 194, 197, 200–201; Abdul-Hadi Hairi, 'The Legitimacy of the Early Qajar Rule as Viewed by the Shiʿi Religious Leaders', *Middle Eastern Studies*, 24 (1988), pp. 280–283.

[71] See Syed Hussain Arif Naqvi, 'The Controversy about the Shaykhiyya Tendency among Shia 'Ulama in Pakistan', in Brunner and Ende, ed., *The Twelver Shia*, pp. 135–149. Kashfī's own son became a Bābī and so the tension with Shaykhīs and Bābīs is quite palpable; see Abbas Amanat, *Resurrection and Renewal: The Making of the Babi Movement in Iran, 1844–1850* (Ithaca, NY, 1989), pp. 247–248.

[72] Kashfī, *Tuḥfat al-mulūk*, pp. 40–43.

[73] Ibid., p. 45.

[74] Ibid., pp. 76–79.

Conclusion

These are just some observations from the *ḥikmat* tradition. The notion of cosmological *walāya* therefore is deployed in two areas: in the ontology to explain the unfolding of the cosmos and the disclosure of being, and in the Imamology where the explicit links are made between belief in a necessary, infallible Imam and the cosmic mediation that he possesses and performs. As such, it draws upon the theme of the perfect human common to the school of Ibn ʿArabī especially in its Shiʿi form, as well as the copious *ḥadīth* and other textual materials on the status of the Imams in Shiʿi theological literature. There is far more evidence to demonstrate the development of what one might describe as a Shiʿi philosophy embedded in the theory of the Imam as expositor of *walāya takwīniyya*. This chapter has not been an archaeology of the term *walāya takwīniyya*, nor does it consider the evidence for or against Modarressi's interpretation of the classical period – ever since the publication of his work in Persian there has been quite a controversial literature on it.[75] What constitutes properly, even *authentically*, Shiʿi thought is a polemical problem of the present and certainly none of the thinkers that I have discussed would ever use the term. The simple fact that *walāya* was the manifestation of existence and the hermeneutic for understanding reality was sufficiently true not to need a label to explain and present it as a distinctive partisan phenomenon.

However, when we are considering what might qualify a particular discipline or learned tradition to be Shiʿi, it is worth thinking about what features define an intellectual tradition as Shiʿi. At the centre of any such analysis, based not least on the *ḥadīth* mentioned earlier that places *walāya* at the foundation of the faith, one ought to consider whether a philosophy of *walāya* makes this a tradition of philosophising 'Shiʿi'. One could object that much of the architecture of such a notion of *walāya* as a cosmological authority is derived from a non-Shiʿi source, the school of Ibn ʿArabī. But even there it is not inconclusive whether there were older Shiʿi influences on his thought. Once *walāya* from the Ibn ʿArabī school was naturalised in a Shiʿi context, it became a Shiʿi doctrine; and one that was identified and disseminated as the original intention of the teachings of the Imams as expressed in texts such as the book on the proof of God in *al-Kāfī* of al-Kulaynī. Thinkers such as Mullā Ṣadrā and Fayḍ Kāshānī, whilst being accomplished tradents, did not concern themselves with the careful authentication of texts, chains of authority and the possibilities of classical language – the prevalence of texts which they knew did not derive from partially canonised sources demonstrates their awareness of this – but rather recognised that

[75] Sayyid Ḥusayn Mudarrisī, *Maktab dar farāyand-i takāmul: naẓarī bar taṭavvur-i mabānī-yi fikrī-yi tashayyuʿ dar sih qarn-i nakhustīn*, tr. Hāshim Īzadpanāh (Tehran, 2007). For one website that gathers a number of critiques from a *ḥawza* background, see: http://toraath.com/index.php?name=Sections&req=listarticles&secid=4 (accessed 11 June 2011). In the summer of 2008, BBC Persian also ran a special on the book, see: http://www.bbc.co.uk/persian/arts/story/2008/08/080806_an-ash-shiite-modaressi.shtml (accessed 11 June 2011). Modarressi responded to some critiques in January 2009 on the Radio Zamaneh website.

texts are what one makes of them through processes of exegesis, deployment, internalisation and profession. The theological and philosophical structure in a sense took precedence over any corroborating scripture – it was the heart of the believer illuminated by the love and fidelity to *walāya* that guided one to truth. And for this reason, pivotal texts such as the *khuṭbat al-bayān* had to be the pronouncements of the Imam.

15

The Role of the Imam-caliph as Depicted in Official Treatises and Documents Issued by the Fatimids

Paul E. Walker

Background

Whereas, after the first four *Rāshidūn* caliphs, the Sunnis became less and less concerned with the personal qualifications of the Imam, who he was and how he was chosen, the Shiʿa never escaped having to decide such matters. Devotion to the Imam is a religious obligation; as a consequence, determining who he is constitutes a central tenet of faith. Commencing with ʿAlī b. Abī Ṭālib (d. 40/661) and then his sons, questions of succession were always critical, and the death of an Imam seemed almost inevitably to produce controversy and disagreement about the continuing line of the imamate. The term 'Ismaili' in fact denotes an answer to one such dispute; the problem of who was the Imam after Jaʿfar al-Ṣādiq (d. 148/765). But, if this difficulty was inherent to early Shiʿism, it was even more momentous for pre-Fatimid Ismailis and the first generations of Fatimid Imam-caliphs. And the problems connected to it, although they eventually abated, were not easily resolved either then or now. Modern scholarship may have even made the situation less clear. Fatimid pronouncements regarding pre-Fatimid Imams are not necessarily better; they are instead often obscure and hint at a baffling array of seemingly irresolvable doctrines.

There were three facets to the question. One concerns the issue of who was an Imam and what was his status. Here, for example, arises the dilemma of whether ʿAlī was an Imam, as some held, or of a higher rank and thus not counted as one of the Imams. Was Ḥasan an Imam? Was he perhaps a 'trustee' (*mustawdaʿ*) Imam until Ḥusayn took over as the 'permanent' (*mustaqarr*) Imam? A similar question applies to other, later cases, as, for example, that of Ismāʿīl b. Jaʿfar (d. after 138/755) and his son Muḥammad b. Ismāʿīl. Most significantly, who exactly were the Imams, if there were any, after this Muḥammad b. Ismāʿīl and how are they related to al-Mahdī, the first of the Fatimid caliphs? And problems of this type are numerous in the earliest literature.

A second subject involves determining the status and person of the *mahdī-qāʾim*, the messiah, who, according to many, will close out the era of Islam's prophet and usher in a form of paradise without law. The earliest Ismaili doctrine held that he was (is) Muḥammad b. Ismāʿīl b. Jaʿfar al-Ṣādiq. But, if so, how to admit that there are to be more Imams after him, as, for example, the Fatimid Imam-caliphs? How are the two related?

A third area, the theory of the imamate and the general conditions for it, is, by comparison, simpler. Over all the first two sets of questions, and others associated with the two, seem to dominate Ismaili doctrine in the pre-Fatimid period and the era of the first four caliphs, that is, through to the end of al-Muʿizz's reign. Subsequently, the issue of who had been an Imam and exactly what the line of descent was became much less urgent and the doctrine of the *mahdī-qāʾim* also receded into the background, his advent in any form having been delayed far into the future. Nevertheless, while the earlier issues remained uppermost, disputes among the various Ismaili factions were so serious as to lead to irreconcilable splintering. One major result had the Qarmatians in the east break with the Fatimids, leaving two Ismaili groups, one opposed to the other on these very issues.

The investigation of the split in this case and others and to the problem of the genealogy of the Fatimid Imams drew the attention of scholars long ago, some of whom then and later proposed solutions based on the pronouncements found in various sources, of both a hostile and a sympathetic kind. All in all, the Arabic materials are fairly voluminous. No one had managed to survey more than a limited portion of them until Madelung published in 1961 his definitive study of the subject.[1] For this article, he examined not only the range of modern scholarship from the writings of the early 19th-century orientalist A. I. Silvestre de Sacy to Zāhid ʿAlī's Urdu *Hamāre Ismāʿīlī madhhab*, which contained information about a number of unpublished early works not available elsewhere, but also a fairly complete list of Fatimid Ismaili sources, many in manuscript, a feat that at the time (there was no Institute of Ismaili Studies back then) was quite difficult to achieve. It was a tour de force when it was written and, in many ways, remains so to the present day.

Most fortunately, Farhad Daftary paid close attention to Madelung's work and, as a result, most of the information gathered by him – and there is a lot of it – reappears nicely summarised in *The Ismāʿīlīs: Their History and Doctrines*, which was published nearly thirty years later in 1990 (a second, revised edition was published in 2007). Heinz Halm likewise drew on it for several sections of his *Das Reich des Mahdī*.

Issues associated with the problem of connecting the Fatimid Imam-caliphs to a line of Imams running back to Jaʿfar al-Ṣādiq or determining who is, was or will be the *mahdī-qāʾim* never entirely disappeared as Madelung has shown. Odd versions might pop up or reappear in unlikely places. However, the basic scholarship on this aspect of the topic already exists. It is possible to revisit it, and even to add some additional notes, but it seems more productive to investigate the imamate in the Fatimid period from a slightly different angle, concentrating on the theory and doctrine as

[1] Wilferd Madelung, 'Das Imamat in der frühen ismailitischen Lehre', *Der Islam*, 37 (1961), pp. 43–135; repr. in W. Madelung, *Studies in Medieval Shiʿism* (Farnham, UK, 2012), article VII.

expressed formally in works composed at that time specifically on the imamate, in public pronouncements such as *khuṭbas*, letters and decrees, and in other official and semi-official pronouncements. To this we can add some additional material from poetry – specifically, panegyrics devoted to the Imams and the imamate. Another area to explore involves polemical and apologetic exchanges with political or religious opponents and detractors. Much, if not most, of all this material denotes the theory and practice of the Ismaili regime as it was expressed by and under the Fatimid caliphs. A major question to investigate involves the status, religious and political, of the Imam and how his authority informs the government over which he rules. How did the imamate operate both in theory and in practice? In what manner is the Imam's status conveyed to the empire he governs, to the citizens of that state and the ranks of officials between him at the top and the others below? A particularly interesting sub-question involves his relationship, as Imam, to those in his realm who were not Ismailis. For most of the period the majority of his subjects did not recognise his imamate in religious terms, although most acknowledged his right to rule. A substantial portion of them were Sunnis; others were not even Muslim. How did he deal with the latter group (Jews and Christians), and attract and hold their loyalty?

Fatimid Period Ismaili Works Devoted to the Imamate

There are four treatises specifically on the imamate now available. Others once existed – such as one by al-Qāḍī al-Nuʿmān (d. 363/974) – but apparently they have not survived. Still, the four extant treatises are a prime place to start. The oldest is al-Manṣūr's *Tathbīt al-imāma* ('Confirming the Imamate'). That it has been attributed to the Imam al-Manṣūr himself makes it unusually high in obvious authority.[2] Madelung offered a preliminary study of it in an article entitled 'A Treatise on the Imamate of the Fatimid Caliph al-Manṣūr bi'llāh'.[3] Here is how Madelung describes this work:

> The book is addressed to an unnamed questioner, evidently a follower, who asked the author about the establishment of proof for the imamate of the Commander of the Faithful ʿAlī b. Abī Ṭālib and his title to it. Al-Manṣūr promises to provide cogent proof and asks the questioner to rely on it in rational investigation before looking into the historical reports (*riwāyāt*) of the various parties who affirm the inevitable need of the people for an Imam. Throughout his discussion, it is evident that al-Manṣūr, in agreement with the general Shiite position, saw the imamate as a primary necessity of reason.

[2] Abū Ṭāhir Ismāʿīl al-Manṣūr bi'llāh, *The Shiʿi Imamate: A Fatimid Interpretation*, ed. and tr. Sami Makarem (London, 2013). This edition appeared after the present article was written.

[3] In Chase F. Robinson, ed., *Texts, Documents and Artefacts* (Leiden, 2003), pp. 69–77.

Three of the four treatises on the imamate belong to the era of al-Ḥākim. One of them does not actually claim the title but seems to be properly labelled, as its editor and translator has done, *al-Risāla fī'l-imāma* ('Letter on the Imamate').[4] It was composed by the *dāʿī* Abu'l-Fawāris Aḥmad b. Yaʿqūb in answer to questions put to him dealing with the following topics: the necessity for the institution of the imamate; refutation of the idea that the Qur'an, the Traditions and the *sharīʿa* can substitute for the Imam; reasons why the Imam must be installed by divine appointment, rather than be elected by the community; proofs for the validity of divine appointment; disparity among people necessitates divine appointment; reasons why the Imam after the Prophet could only be ʿAlī b. Abī Ṭālib; behind ʿAlī's refraining from claiming his right to the imamate; why it is not possible to have more than one Imam at the same time; why it is not permissible that the imamate be transferred from ʿAlī's descendants; the institution of the imamate is God's will; reasons for the impossibility of the rightful Imam not to have an heir; the possibility of the Imam's being a minor; the reason why Muḥammad b. Ismāʿīl was the rightful Imam rather than Mūsā b. Jaʿfar (d. 183/799); how allegiance to a concealed Imam is justified; why the names of the concealed Imams were kept secret; and how a rightful Imam can be distinguished from a pretender.

The remaining two are by the well-known *dāʿīs* al-Kirmānī (d. after 411/1020) and al-Naysābūrī (d. after 386/996), and both were written in the later years of al-Ḥākim. That by al-Kirmānī is slightly earlier. It was addressed obliquely to the Būyid wazir of Baghdad and is therefore a public work intended for a general Shiʿi audience.[5] The author called it *al-Maṣābīḥ fī ithbāt al-imāma* (*Lights to Illuminate the Proof of the Imamate*). In general the proofs in this work are often quite philosophical and thus fairly dense. The book is not easy reading. Nonetheless, two key sections have particular importance. Part two consists of a proof of the imamate and its necessity in its first chapters as follows: (1) proofs of the imamate, and (2) the necessity of the Imam's infallibility.

Al-Kirmānī's part one deals with the Prophet's role but the second focuses specifically on the imamate. From his stipulations in these chapters we can extract a few main points that help explain his concept of the Imam's role:

> An Imam is charged with warning the people of his time and admonishing them, announcing glad tidings, news of God's reward, and cautioning them against His punishment. (p. 78)
>
> God imposed on the believers three acts of obedience in one verse, each linked to the other. No one can accept the first without the second or the second without

[4] Sami Nasib Makarem, ed. and tr., *The Political Doctrine of the Ismāʿīlīs: The Imamate* (Delmar, NY, 1977), Arabic text pp. 1–41; English trans. pp. 21–51.

[5] Ḥamīd al-Dīn al-Kirmānī, *Master of the Age: An Islamic Treatise on the Necessity of the Imamate*, with a critical edition and translation of the Arabic text of Ḥamīd al-Dīn al-Kirmānī's *al-Maṣābīḥ fī ithbāt al-imāma* (*Lights to Illuminate the Proof of the Imamate*), by Paul E. Walker (London, 2007).

> the third. 'Oh, you who believe obey God and obey the Messenger and those in authority among you' [Q.4:59]. It is necessary therefore that there exist for the community someone who is rightly the subject of their obedience, and they are to follow his command in regard to God and the religion of God. (p. 77)
>
> It is essential that there be an Imam for every age in whose name God summons his people; 'The day we shall summon all peoples with their Imams' [Q.17:71]. (p. 77)
>
> It was necessary to put in the place of the Messenger someone to whom to refer those issues of religion about which there were differences. After the Prophet, someone must issue rulings in matters about which the people differ. That someone is the Imam. (p. 76)

Common sense requires that among people there be a ruler. The ruler is the Imam.

> What the Prophet brought can be added to or subtracted from, and it is likewise possible to alter his regulations and pronouncements and thus to introduce deviation in them. Therefore, there must be a person put in charge of these matters who guards them and prevents additions, subtractions, or alternations. (p. 71)
>
> Someone has to take up the Prophet's role in conveying the wisdom and protection he established, and to arrange the perpetual designation of another when the time of that person's passing approaches. (p. 71)
>
> *Characteristics of the Imam that make necessary his having infallibility*: If it were possible that he not be infallible, the community might proceed along a path contrary to that of the Prophet. That deviation would lead to injustice and would encourage people to break away and secede from the community. (p. 79)

The argument put forward by al-Kirmānī in the treatise uses the qualifications of an Imam – what he stands for and what he does – to establish who is and who is not qualified for the imamate. Chief among the required traits of the Imam is lineal descent from the Prophet and from ʿAlī and the explicit designation of the preceding Imam, but there are other characteristics at play. Here is one description of them from this work:

> The person who preserves the Book and the law with its regulations, who summons to Islam and to them both and who defends it both by exhortation and intimidation, who prays with the people, teaches them the waymarkers of their religion, extracts them from issues about which they differ and which are referred to him, who adjudicates according to what God revealed, who seeks from God forgiveness for he who seeks forgiveness from him, who purifies them, who applies to them the corporal punishments, who responds concerning questions put to him, who conveys what the Messenger has said in its true form, who takes from them what is due God and expends it as it should be, who occupies the place of the prophet

> among the community in accord with his command based on the designating of the person who assumes his place. That person is the Imam. (p. 117)

It should be noted that here al-Kirmānī intends this statement as a description of the imamate generally; it is not specifically Shiʿi. However, it is also not prescriptive except in that it suggests how failing to exemplify any of the traits on the list disqualifies a claimant who is deficient in that manner from the imamate. In the same treatise al-Kirmānī devotes considerable space to the demerits of pretenders, both in the past and in his own time.

Al-Naysābūrī's *Ithbāt al-imāma* (*Proof of the Imamate*) is less easy to summarise in part because, although he, like the others, intends a 'proof', his is more of a celebration of the imamate aimed at an audience of devoted adherents.[6] The author, who wrote within the safety and security of the Fatimid empire, proves the imamate to those who are already loyal Ismailis. His treatise has the air of celebration of existing fact; it is replete with comparisons that are rhetorically evocative rather than statements of an argument. According to his treatise, the Imam is the best of creatures and the ultimate end of the created world; he is the best of human beings, God's shadow on earth, the sun, gold, the brain and head of the world. His position is that of the Universal Intellect (*al-ʿaql al-kullī*) in its realm; the Imam is the Universal Intellect of this world. He is the speaking-prophet (*nāṭiq*) and the messiah of his time.

Nevertheless, it is essential to read what he has to say about the imamate in general. Here is an example:

> The imamate is the pivot of religion and its foundation. Around it revolve all religious and worldly affairs and the welfare of the next life and this. By means of it the dealings of the servants and the well-being of the land maintain their proper order. By means of it the reward in the abode to come arrives. Through it one attains knowledge of the absolute unity (of God) and of the revealed message based on proofs, demonstrations, and irrefutable evidence; and therein one reaches an understanding of the law and its foundation, and of the interpretation thereof and its explanation. (pp. 379–380)
>
> At no time or season can the world be without an Imam whereas the Prophet lives at one time and not another. (p. 380)

---

[6] Aḥmad b. Ibrāhīm al-Naysābūrī, *Ithbāt al-imāma* (*Proof of the Imamate*), Arabic text and English tr. by Arzina Lalani as *Degrees of Excellence: A Fatimid Treatise on Leadership in Islam* (London, 2010). For analysis of doctrines in these two works, see my article entitled '"In Praise of al-Ḥākim": Greek Elements in Ismaili Writings on the Imamate', in Emma Gannagé et al., ed., *The Greek Strand in Islamic Political Thought: Proceedings of the Conference at the Institute for Advanced Study, Princeton, 16–27 June 2003* (special issue of *Mélanges de l'Université Saint-Joseph*, 57 (2004), pp. 367–392; repr. in Paul E. Walker, *Fatimid History and Ismaili Doctrine* (Aldershot, 2008), article IX. The translations that follow are mine, citing pages of this article.

> The Imam occupies the place of the Messenger in his own time and era ... An Imam exists in the world at all times; at no time is it lacking one. The Imam upholds the law and maintains its veracity as we have said. What has now become clear and is thus firmly established is that religion revolves around the Imam and that, except by depending on the acts of the Imam with respect to the law of the prophet in his era, no one has a connection to that prophet or to his position and to his law in such a manner that its validity has undergone no change or alternation in any way. No one apprehends the true reality of the law and its interpretation or meaning except through him. (p. 380)

For most of his treatise al-Naysābūrī adheres to an argument based on the notion of 'disparity' (*tafāwut*) and differences of merit (*tafāḍul*). He expresses this principle as follows:

> At this point we will mention the disparity and differences of merit in each principle and kingdom of nature and show that for each genus and species its ultimate limit and highest degree points to the Imam in every time and period ... (p. 381)

But other examples that are equally relevant in this context follow:

> [T]he Imam is the ultimate of man, his highest degree, his consummation and perfection. The affairs of men are put in order by the Imam. Just as the usefulness of all that precedes men reverts to men, so the usefulness of all men reverts to the Imam. From them man learns the virtues and sciences. From them they acquire discernment and perspicacity. Through them is the betterment of their dealings in religious and worldly matters, and their salvation. By them are they led to acknowledge the Maker and admit to the necessity of thankfulness to the Benefactor and how to display that thanks. Through them they learn about the Messenger and the kind of obedience due him. (p. 383)
>
> [T]he Imam becomes the essence (*mukhkh*) of the whole universe. Thereupon the refinements of the spirit of reason and pure thought and the entirety of the intelligible spirit unite in him, along with the whole of the spirit of holiness (*rūḥ al-quds*) of which humans possess only a tiny portion, not great, except what they obtain from the Imam and his favour to those on whom he chooses to bestow it ... (p. 384)
>
> No human can remove himself from the rule of the Imam and his control in the same way that no animal can escape the control of humans. Those wild beasts having no benefit or merit that do evade the control of men are by the judgement of reason and the law to be killed, destroyed and annihilated precisely because they are not servile to men nor under his control and direction. Similarly whoever

> refuses to obey the Imam and thus behaves like a wild beast is the same as a harmful beast whose killing, destruction and annihilation has become permissible in accord with the determination in law, reason, nature and social order (*siyāsa*) of his having rebelled against the rule (*mulk*) of the Imam. (p. 384)
>
> He is the leader of the world and the governor (*sā'is*) of it. It has become clear that leadership (*ri'āsa*) and rulership (*siyāsa*) are required of necessity by nature, creation, natural character, innate disposition. A person who denies the law and religion, cannot deny, either in reason or in actuality, that the world has a governor (*sā'is*), a leader (*ra'īs*) and a ruler (*mudabbir*), since it is required by necessity. Based on the evidence from creation and the natures we have already cited, it follows necessarily also that he must be the most excellent of all, the noblest of them, most perfect, most knowledgeable and most pure, and that the foremost leader (*muqaddim*) is the Imam in all things and he is the ruler and the head. (p. 385)

In summary, al-Naysābūrī has just claimed for al-Ḥākim, the Imam of his day, the following: man is the best of creatures and end of the world; the Imam is the best of men and the best is naturally perforce the ruler and leader of them. As the holder of power the Imam is God's shadow on earth. He is the sun that illuminates the hearts of God's friends. The Imam occupies the place that corresponds to that of the Universal Intellect or Logos in its realm. He is the complete and ultimate sage; the brain of the world in its entirety, its head.

There are additional useful comments by the same authority in another of his works: the *Mūjaza*,[7] a treatise on the proper comportment of the *dāʿīs*. Since this latter work focuses more narrowly on the *daʿwa* and its activities, its aim is less theoretical. In many ways we may take what it says as a practical guide to the operations of the Ismaili religious establishment. Some examples of how it speaks about the Imam and his relationship to the agents who support him follow:

> The *dāʿī* must see to the affairs of the *daʿwa* and its proper administration, thereby relieving the Imam of that obligation, for the Imam has appointed him to manage the *daʿwa* and maintain the welfare of the various regions. When he manages these affairs properly, arranging them as they should be, he settles matters by the order of the Imam, for these matters belong solely to God and to His representative and it is not for anyone to speak ill of him. (p. 71)
>
> The *dāʿī* must constantly entreat the believers to obey the Imam and love him, appeal for him, dedicating their wealth and souls to his cause, and in pleasing him and obeying him, and undertaking holy war with him if he so orders them. The *dāʿī*

---

[7] See Aḥmad b. Ibrāhīm al-Naysābūrī, *A Code of Conduct: A Treatise on the Etiquette of the Fatimid Mission, A critical edition of the Arabic text and English translation of Aḥmad b. Ibrāhīm al-Naysābūrī's* al-Risāla al-Mūjaza al-kāfiya fī ādāb al-duʿāt, ed. and tr. Verena Klemm and Paul E. Walker (London, 2011).

> should make clear to them that God is pleased by his being pleased and obeying Him means obeying him; their salvation lies in obeying and in pleasing him. Also he will make clear that there is no obligation of any kind on the Imam. What is bestowed on the people by the Imam in the way of worldly goods and knowledge, he does as a favour and a kindness and what he holds back he does so justly. (p. 73)
>
> A *dāʿī* should know that the kingdom is the protector of the faith; the kingdom of the Imam is built on religion. If the affairs of both the religion and the *daʿwa* are in proper order and well maintained, the kingdom will run properly and without disorder. All of the populace will be servants of the Imam, whether in his presence or in other regions; they become like his army, supporters, and well-wishers, none able to betray or rebel against him, because all the people become his adversaries, his enemies, and opponents if there are defects in the religion and the *dāʿī* is unable or is remiss in dealing with the governing of the religion and managing it because he is himself ignorant, impious, or incompetent and unsound and untrustworthy, and he will ruin the beliefs of the believers. They will apostatize and chaos will reign. (pp. 74–75)

In terms of degree of authority, nothing can be higher than the words of an Imam. That would apply also to sermons (*khuṭbas*) composed by an Imam, and perhaps other documents directly approved by an Imam. Therefore, the treatise by al-Manṣūr cited above has obvious weight; those by *dāʿīs* less so. Still, the latter three works on the imamate, discussed here, likely expressed official doctrine even if we do not have explicit proof. For them to have been preserved by later Fatimid authorities may alone indicate approval.[8]

It is amply clear, however, that these authors are not advisors to the caliph. What they write is in no way a mirror for the prince. And neither would even remotely have hoped to play that role. For them, in describing what an Imam does, and what his subjects might expect that he would do, is almost precisely what the Muslims understand as the function of the Prophet in his capacity as the divinely appointed leader of its community. The current Fatimid Imam-caliph occupies the place of the Prophet (except in regard to receiving revelations). What the Imam does is what he should do and only he, among all humans, knows exactly what that is. Ordinary humans cannot comment critically on his actions any more than they can on those of God. Like the acts of the Divine, they are simply not subject to human scrutiny, and they may be thus occasionally quite as unintelligible and perplexing as are the mysteries of many of God's ways.

---

[8] Of the other such material attributed to Imams, there is the by now famous letter of al-Mahdī to his followers in the Yaman, recorded from memory by Jaʿfar b. Manṣūr al-Yaman and a letter to Shaybān a *dāʿī* in India by al-Muʿizz. There may be more. Al-Manṣūr wrote a testament (*waṣiyya*) to his successor that has not been explored, although The Institute of Ismaili Studies possibly holds a manuscript copy.

Such restrictions do not, however, prevent these authors from boasting about what the Imams do and have done. But, lauding the Commander of the Believer's commanding of the good and forbidding of the wrong, his charity and justice, is not prescriptive in any sense. There is no obligation involved. Such praise is simply a record from the perspective of the caliph's subjects of what good they have received from him and his actions, or what traits they happen to observe in him.

Works by Members of the *daʿwa* that Touch upon the Subject of the Imamate

From the growing list of works by the leading members of the Fatimid era *daʿwa* recovered in the last decades, many contain potentially important passages concerning the imamate. The following represent a few examples:

From al-Qāḍī al-Nuʿmān we have important comments on the imamate in his *Daʿāʾim al-Islām* (*Pillars of Islam*)[9] and the *Kitāb al-himma fī ādāb atbāʿ al-aʾimma* (*Book of Resolution with Respect to the Comportment of the Followers of the Imams*).[10] His *Kitāb al-majālis waʾl-musāyarāt*[11] is in essence an account of the Imam in action, governing and ruling on various matters and issues. Yet another work of his, the *Sharḥ al-akhbār fī faḍāʾil al-aʾimma al-āṭhār* (*Explanation of the Reports about the Excellences of the Past Imams*) is also relevant.[12] For al-Kirmānī, various titles other than his *Maṣābīḥ*, but particularly *Maʿāṣim al-hudā* (on the superiority of ʿAlī over the *Ṣaḥāba*), *al-Risāla al-wāʿiẓa* (against the proto-Druze), *al-Kāfiyya* (refutation of the Zaydī Imam) might be cited here.

Of those listed above,[13] two (at least) by al-Qāḍī al-Nuʿmān are essential to any discussion of the Imam's authority and status. His *Pillars of Islam* contains over a hundred pages (pp. 19–122 of the translation) on the duty of allegiance to the Imams (the 'Book of *Walāya*'). There the author assembles all the *ḥadīth*s related from earlier Imams about adherence to the imamate beginning with that of ʿAlī b. Abī Ṭālib. In it he also castigates and refutes by name many of the Islamic groups that opposed the Fatimids. Many Sunnis, for example, claim that there is no distinction between ordinary members of the community and the House of the Prophet with respect to religious authority.

---

[9] Ed. Asaf A. A. Fyzee. Cairo, 1951–1961; English trans. by Fyzee and completely revised by Ismail K. Poonawala as *The Pillars of Islam* (New Delhi, 2002 and 2004).

[10] Ed. M. Kāmil Ḥusayn (Cairo, 1948).

[11] Ed. al-Ḥabīb al-Faqhī, Ibrāhīm Shabbūḥ and Muḥammad al-Yaʿlāwī (Tunis, 1978).

[12] 3 vols (Beirut, 1994).

[13] This list might easily be expanded. I have not included the works of al-Sijistānī and Nāṣir b. Khusraw, and there are other treatises from the *daʿwa*, both by named authors and anonymous. To search it all for comments about the imamate would take time and effort, well beyond the current project. It is true that much was already done by Madelung, and more recently by Daftary, but there is more.

> [The Imam] Jaʿfar b. Muḥammad said: 'You must understand that none from among the earlier communities in times gone by, nor from among bygone generations, nor any community of which we have report is more iniquitous than this community [of ours]. This is because they assert that there is no distinction between them and the members of the Household of the Prophet and that the latter have no priority over them. He then who makes such an assertion has surely magnified falsehood against God and has perpetrated great slander and manifest sin. (pp. 41–42)
>
> If you maintain that the right of judgement and the authority as to that matter rest with some as distinguished from others, then tell us, with corroboration from the Book or the *sunna* or the consensus [of the community], who is thus distinguished in preference to others? They will never find the answer to that. If it is the people themselves who appoint the Imam, then the Imam derives his authority from their authority. Thus he does not possess any authority until they invest him with it. They, the people, then, are in effect the 'Imams' according to the plain meaning of this [assertion], while he (the Imam) is one among their officials. They, therefore, have the power to dismiss him. (p. 52)

Another treatise on the list, al-Qāḍī al-Nuʿmān's *Book of Resolution with Respect to the Comportment of the Followers of the Imams*, is often especially important for concepts of authority and the imamate.[14] Here below are some chapter titles, which help indicate what topics it covers.

> 1. It is essential for the followers of the Imams to acknowledge unwavering allegiance and loyalty to them and to accept and obey their leadership.
> 4. Respecting the Imams by confessing to their august and exalted authority.
> 7. Restrictions on those in the *daʿwa* of the Imam in regard to matters that are reported to them; they inform him without taking up the issue or speaking about something not permitted to them.
> 8. Having patience for the agents of the Imams and being thankful for what great benefit befalls them.
> 10. Every faithful believer must submit all matters to the Imams.
> 2. It is necessary to hold in high esteem those appointed by the Imams and to love them, and to express animosity to their enemies, break off relationships and detest such people.
> 14. The command to attend to all that the Imams approve and to prohibit doing what they oppose.
> 25. The protocol for seeking a need from the Imams.

[14] The existing translation by Jawad Muscati is incomplete and the Arabic is rendered there so loosely as often to distort the meaning considerably.

26. The prohibition of objecting to an action of the Imams and the command to follow their lead by accepting the charge of those charged [by them] with matters of protection thus behaving justly among those of the community under that person's supervision.

The *Majālis* Literature

From the preceding group three represent a special type of source that offers us a glimpse inside the *daʿwa* and its recurring sessions of teaching and exhortation. In addition, the earliest, the *Majālis* of al-Qāḍī al-Nuʿmān, in contrast to the later two, features the involvement of the Imam, as he sat for his followers in a kind of court. While we assume that the Imam approved the lectures, we do not necessarily have proof in all cases. Those of al-Nuʿmān are, therefore, particularly important since he records the direct involvement of his Imam and a fair amount of what he reports concerns in one way or another the general subject of the imamate. In fact it seems that he composed this work precisely to illustrate how and in what manner the Imam governs his community.

Poetry

No survey of this topic is complete without taking note of the poetry produced under the Fatimids, much of which consists of laudatory verse in praise of the Imams. Some of it, such as in the North African phase, was composed by non-Ismailis, or, as with the famous Ibn al-Hāniʾ (d. 362/973), of uncertain affiliation. A substantial amount, however, is by major figures including Tamīm b. al-Muʿizz (the caliph's oldest son (d. 374/985), al-Muʾayyad (d. 470/1078) and Nāṣir b. Khusraw (d. ca. 470/1077) where what they say ought to be accepted as quasi-official (with allowance for the role of poetic licence). As but one example Tahera Qutbuddin, in her expert study of al-Muʾayyad's work,[15] offers a substantial chapter (pp. 143–218) devoted to the appropriate theme: 'Praise of the Imam'. There she presents both the Arabic text and a full English translation of the material along with detailed analysis. In many ways it constitutes a fine model for what else might be attempted with other Fatimid era poets.[16]

The themes she develops in that section cover the Imam's descent from the Prophet and his legatee (ʿAlī) in uninterrupted succession (*tasalsul*) and designation (*naṣṣ*); the Imam's servitude to and representation of God; his attributes and

---

[15] *Al-Muʾayyad al-Shīrāzī and Fatimid Daʿwa Poetry: A Case of Commitment in Classical Arabic Literature* (Leiden, 2005).

[16] It is important to recognise here the many studies of Pieter Smoor, one of which is especially pertinent: 'Wine, Love and Praise for the Fāṭimid Imāms: The Enlightened of God', *ZDMG*, 142 (1992), pp. 90–104.

functions; his role in relation to the prophets and his similarity to Jesus; Qur'anic praise of the Imam; the Imam's titles; the regard and acts mandatory upon mankind vis-à-vis the Imam; the condition of the Imam's followers and enemies in this world and the Hereafter; yearning for homeland and the Imam as consolation; Imam as the true beloved; old age and youth with the Imam as refuge in the Hereafter; censure of Fate and the Imam as protection against its vicissitudes; blessings and prayers for the Imam. It is thus obvious that the poetry of al-Mu'ayyad is a rich mine of material concerning the imamate.

Polemics with Adversaries and Apologies

Once there existed a considerable literature of polemic and apology.[17] Fatimid authors composed refutations of a full range of their opponents, and the other side did likewise. Much of this material involves an argument about the imamate and the status of one caliphate over the other. As an example from a relatively short period during the reign of al-Ḥākim, we hear of anti-Ismaili works by the following: one by the famous Mālikī-Ashʿarī jurist and theologian, Abū Bakr al-Bāqillānī (d. 402/1013) called *Kashf al-asrār wa hatk al-astār*. Another theologian, the Muʿtazilī ʿAlī b. Saʿīd al-Iṣṭakhrī (d. 404/1013–14) wrote a refutation and condemnation of Fatimid doctrine.[18] The Zaydīs Abu'l-Qāsim al-Bustī (d. 420/1030) and his Imam Abu'l-Ḥasan al-Mu'ayyad bi'llāh Aḥmad b. Ḥusayn b. Hārūn (d. 411/1020), who resided in the Caspian region, did likewise. Neither al-Bāqillānī's work, nor that of al-Iṣṭakhrī appears to have survived, but major portions of al-Bustī's *Kashf al-asrār wa naqd al-afkār* are available.[19] The Zaydī Imam's treatise against the Fatimids was answered by al-Kirmānī in a work he called *al-Risāla al-kāfiya fi'l-radd ʿalā al-Hārūnī al-Ḥusaynī al-Zaydī* and that we have, though not what it responded to.[20]

Al-Kirmānī composed other refutations, among them one directed at the famous physician Abū Bakr al-Rāzī (d. 313/925) – his *al-Aqwāl al-dhahabiyya* – against the latter's *al-Ṭibb al-rūḥānī*. Similiarly, al-Qāḍī al-Nuʿmān, according to Poonawala's *Biobibliography*, composed refutations of the Khawārij, a Shāfiʿī scholar named Ibn Surayj, al-Shāfiʿī himself, Ibn Qutayba, Mālik, Abū Ḥanīfa and more. It is likely that these examples represent only the tip of an iceberg. Unfortunately, as yet we have recovered only a few of them. And of course the issues of contention are not all about the imamate in any case.

---

17 To be extra clear the latter term means 'something said or written in defence or justification of what appears to others to be wrong or of what may be liable to disapprobation'.

18 Al-Iṣṭakhrī died in 404/1013–1014 and therefore his anti-Fatimid work likely dates to the period 402–404.

19 Ed. ʿĀdil Sālim ʿAbd al-Jādir in his *al-Ismāʿīliyyūn* (no. 2) (Kuwait, 2002), pp. 187–369.

20 Ed. Muṣṭafā Ghālib as part of his *Majmūʿat rasāʾil al-Kirmānī* (Beirut, 1983), pp. 148–182.

The Imam's Sermons (*khuṭba*s)

Festival sermons, those given by the Imam-caliph on the annual *ʿīd*s, the feast of fast-breaking and the feast of sacrifice, and those for Fridays of Ramaḍān, are ideal for documenting the public attitude of the Imams who gave them. To a certain extent those given in their names by preachers (*khaṭīb*s) of lesser ranks ought to supply useful information as well. Unfortunately, we possess only a tiny few of either kind.[21] What remains is to extract from them a sense of what the Imams were saying specifically about the imamate. Here are some of the specific concerns voiced in these sermons and, in the following quotations from them, we find references to the imamate, its supporters and its enemies. This material begins to tell us first what the Imams actually said to their subjects and it, thus, reveals secondarily a little about what, in the context of a public forum, they felt the need to relate to those who followed them.

An element in the rhetorical strategy of these *khuṭba*s may have involved the use of phrases that a Sunni audience would understand differently from the Shiʿa among them. For example the commonly employed words *ʿAlī walī Allāh* ("ʿAlī is the *walī* of God'), which eventually appeared on all Fatimid coins and are quite standard in Shiʿa discourse of every type, are readily taken by Sunnis to mean "ʿAlī is the friend of God'. Ordinarily, because this sense of the word *walī*, which is perfectly valid for it, is not objectionable, it causes no resistance or hostility on their part. For the Shiʿa, however, it means more than 'friend'. ʿAlī was, in their view, the 'guardian' (*walī*, in a different sense) of God's community on earth. He was thus the agent of God with exclusive authority to act as regent for the Muslims; he was their guardian.

To bear witness or testify that Muḥammad was the prophet and messenger of God is a standard feature of the *khuṭba* in general. Most of the attributes ascribed to Muḥammad in Fatimid *khuṭba*s, moreover, agreed well with such statements in those not by them. What is different and uniquely Fatimid is the reference to him as the 'grandfather', for example, of the current caliph, or, as it most often appears, as 'our grandfather', as in the invocation of God's blessings on 'our grandfather' (*jaddinā*). The meaning, of course, is ancestor or forefather, but it carries a special connotation in conjunction with references to ʿAlī b. Abī Ṭālib, who is always called 'our father' (*abūnā*). See, for instance, the *khuṭba*s of al-Āmir where this type of reference appears prominently in both parts of the sermon. Additional examples occur in those of al-Manṣūr from 335/946 and 336/947.

References and characterisations of ʿAlī are particularly important as a sign of the ancestral lineage of the Fatimids and of the Shiʿi assertion of legitimacy for its imamate. ʿAlī bears the title Commander of the Believers, which, for the Shiʿa, applies to him alone among the Companions of the Prophet, since they do not recognise any of the others as valid successors to the imamate. In his position as heir to the Prophet,

---

[21] I have published the Arabic text and a translation of all those we have, plus a survey of the historical materials about them in a collection entitled *Orations of the Fatimid Caliphs: Festival Sermons of the Ismaili Imams* (London, 2008).

both physically and spiritually, he carries also the title of Legatee (in Arabic *waṣī*). Another appellation denotes his close family relationship to Muḥammad, which for the Shiʿa means, in reference to ʿAlī, brother. For them the Prophet had adopted him as his own brother. He was, moreover, in the same position as had been Aaron with respect to his brother Moses. The Prophet had stated, according to a *ḥadīth* of special importance to the Shiʿa, that "Alī is to me as Aaron was to Moses'.

Here follow some examples from the surviving *khuṭbas*:

> and bless the first to respond to him [i.e., the Prophet], ʿAlī, the Commander of the Believers and Lord of the Legatees, the establisher of excellence and mercy, the pillar of knowledge and wisdom, the root of the noble and righteous tree generated from the sacred and pure trunk. And [blessings be] on his successors, the lofty branches of that same tree, and on what comes from it: the fruit that grows there.[22]

> God bless our grandfather, Muḥammad, the guide to the shining path, and our father, the Commander of the Believers, ʿAlī b. Abī Ṭālib, his brother and son of his paternal uncle, whom he sanctioned for the position of executor, and the chaste Imams among the descendants of both, the clear evident proofs of God to His creatures.[23]

> And bless, O God, our father, the Commander of the Believers, ʿAlī b. Abī Ṭālib, who held the place with respect to him that had Aaron with Moses, the one who spoke to God.[24]

From a brief mention of a ritual of mutual cursing in Q.3:61, an entire tradition developed around the implied story of Muḥammad having brought under his cloak on that occasion his immediate family members. They were the *aṣḥāb al-kisāʾ* (the Companions of the Cloak). The question then became who exactly belonged to this set. For the Shiʿa this has never been much of a question since they include only the Prophet, ʿAlī, Fāṭima, al-Ḥasan and al-Ḥusayn. The non-Shiʿa dispute the matter and have alternate interpretations of the tradition.[25] However, in the Fatimid *khuṭbas*, as one would expect, the Shiʿi point of view prevails, as in the following passages from them:

> O God, bless Your servant and Your messenger with a perpetually perfect blessing, increase him with an honour to his honour and a nobility to his nobility. Bless also all of the Companions of the Cloak (*aṣḥāb al-kisāʾ*), the pure ones, the immaculates:

---

[22] Qirwāsh's *khuṭba* (no. 11).

[23] Ibid.

[24] *Khuṭba* of al-Āmir (no. 12).

[25] For additional information, see the articles in the *EI2* by W. Schmucker, 'Mubāhala', vol. 7, pp. 276–277; A. S. Tritton, 'Ahl al-kisā'', vol. 1, p. 264; and I. Goldziher, C. van Arendonk and A. S. Tritton, 'Ahl al-bayt', vol. 1, pp. 257–258.

> ʿAlī, the Commander of the Believers, Fāṭima the radiant, mistress of the women of the two worlds, and al-Ḥasan and al-Ḥusayn, the two most noble and most righteous, and [bless] the rightly guided Imams among the progeny of al-Ḥusayn, the luminaries of guidance, the full moons of the darkness, the masters of mankind, friends of the Most Merciful, the proofs of times, and pillars of the faith.[26]

In Fatimid era *khuṭba*s both Ḥasan and Ḥusayn are cited as Imams and members of the five Companions of the Cloak, although they make quite clear that the imamate continued after them solely among the descendants of Ḥusayn.

> … al-Ḥasan and al-Ḥusayn, the two most noble and most righteous, and [bless] the rightly guided Imams among the progeny of al-Ḥusayn, the luminaries of guidance, the full moons of the darkness, the masters of mankind, friends of the Most Merciful, the proofs of times, and pillars of the faith.[27]

> … al-Ḥasan and al-Ḥusayn, the two lords of the youth among the people of paradise; and the Imams from the progeny of al-Ḥusayn, the chaste ones, the remainder of the Messenger of God and his fruit, his two heirs, his proof to the servants, the mountains of religion, lords of the believers and saints of the worlds.[28]

One *khuṭba*, however, speaks more explicitly about the duties and rights of the imamate:

> God said: 'O you who believe, obey God and obey the Messenger and those with authority among you' [Q.4:59]. Thus He makes obedience a duty, attaching it to obedience to the regulators of His affairs. They are the ones who uphold, on behalf of God, His truth and those who summon to him whoever desires to obey Him. He singled them out by the imamate, which is the highest of the ranks below prophecy. He prescribed for the servants rights due them and ordered them to fulfil these. He stipulated that they are connected to obeying him, doubling their reward on the measure of how well they follow those whose authority is ordained. The Imam has not the option to reduce the rights of his flock, nor is the flock to decrease the rights of their Imam. Among the rights of the flock against their Imam is the maintaining of the Book of God and the Sunna of His Prophet, may God bless him and his family, and restitution from those who treat them unjustly for those so treated, and from the powerful among them for the weak, from the noble of them for the lowly, investigating their manner of life and the differing conditions of it, looking solicitously upon his dependants in his efforts, watching over them with his eye. For He, great and glorious is He, concerning what He praised of the character of

---

26 From the *khuṭba* by al-Manṣūr on the *ʿīd al-fiṭr* 335 (no. 5).

27 Ibid.

28 *Khuṭba* of al-Manṣūr on the *ʿīd al-aḍḥā'* in the year AD 335 (no. 6).

His Prophet and His Messenger said: 'There has come to you a messenger from among yourselves; a sorrow that befalls you grieves him; he is anxious concerning you; with the believers he is kind and compassionate' [Q.9:128]. When he does that, the flock should revere him, honor him and extend assistance to him, standing prepared and ready, on behalf of what is right according to the book of God and the Sunna of His Prophet, may God bless him and his family.[29]

Imperial Letters and Decrees

Of literally thousands upon thousands of official decrees and letters issued by the Imam in the Fatimid period, or those assigned by him to act in his name, we now have access to perhaps 300, nearly all copies of the original preserved in later histories and chancery collections. There are examples of many different types: edicts and legislations of new regulations, letters of appointment to office, letters of explanation, commemorations of ritual events and ceremonies, celebrations of one sort or another. All may be seen to contain phrases, or even a whole paragraph, about the Imam and his authority.[30] From one source or another, we have the complete text of at least five appointments to the office of wazir, and one each for that of chief *qāḍī*, head of the *maẓālim* (grievances) court, the *naqīb al-ashrāf* (head of the ʿAlid nobility), *amīr* (leader) of the *ḥajj*, *amīr* of the *jihād*, teacher in a *madrasa*, and a few others. There are two examples or more for the *ḥisba* (market supervision). Quite importantly, we have also two for the chief *dāʿī*. For the offices respectively of chief *qāḍī* and chief *dāʿī* there exists only one example each: al-Ḥusayn b. ʿAlī b. al-Nuʿmān as judge in 389/999 and al-Mu'ayyad as *dāʿī* in 450/1058. But for al-Mu'ayyad we have a second appointment or recall to the same position and the text of that decree is also preserved. The *maẓālim* is represented by one for al-Qāḍī al-Nuʿmān from 343/954–955 and another for Ruzzik b. Tala'iʿ during the wazirate of his father.

One valid test for those that are truly Fatimid is the presence in the text of a phrase asking for God's blessings (or the addressee's praise) to be on 'the Messenger of God, our grandfather (*jaddinā*) … and on [ʿAlī] our father (*abīnā*)'. The issuing person is, of course, the Fatimid caliph and normally a decree of appointment supposes that it is he who speaks and who creates the commission (the *ʿahd*) involved. Only a Fatimid could refer to Muḥammad as his 'grandfather' (forefather, progenitor) and ʿAlī b. Abī Ṭālib as his 'father', as is fairly standard in Fatimid decrees almost across the board.

The Fatimids in North Africa had appointed no wazirs and the notion of delegating that level of authority to a subordinate seemed not to have existed. But with al-Jarjarā'ī (d. 436/1045) the situation had changed radically. However, his decree

[29] *Khuṭba* of al-Qā'im 302 (no. 1).

[30] In an article entitled 'The Responsibilities of Political Office in a Shiʿi Caliphate and the Delineation of Public Duties under the Fatimids', in Asma Afsaruddin, ed., *Islam, the State, and Political Authority: Medieval Issues and Modern Concerns* (New York, 2011), pp. 93–110), I have investigated the topic of public duty as it was explained in the diploma of investiture.

(dated 418/1028) states quite clearly that wazirs do not diminish the status of the Imam-caliph. One decree that lacks a name of the appointee carefully explains that it is God and God alone who requires no wazir. But humans do. If any one, they say, could have not needed a wazir, it would have been Moses. Nonetheless, it was he who asked God to appoint him a wazir, Aaron, his brother (per Qur'anic report). Muḥammad's wazir was ʿAlī. Thus two of the greatest prophets, men of the highest capacities and each exempt from even the possibility of error, found it useful to have a wazir. Though Aaron and ʿAlī were ideal wazirs, the decree goes on to cite Joseph as the true model. His shepherding of the public welfare on behalf of pharaoh, especially of financial matters, is what the caliph expects of his new wazir.

From the decree appointing al-Qāḍī al-Nuʿmān over the *maẓālim* courts we have the following:

> The Commander of the Believers … being satisfied with the discharge of your judicial duties [in previous appointments], he now invests you with the absolute authority to look into the *maẓālim*.
>
> Having also taken note of your true loyalty to the Imams and your upholding of justice in your decisions, and having seen what tests and trials have revealed about you … the Commander of the Believers thinks it proper, in order to strengthen, buttress, reinforce and augment this appointment, to issue a public decree addressed to you so that the hopes of any who seek justice from you may be encouraged and those against whom your judgements might go will be filled with fear. The schemes of those who want to contravene justice by avoiding you and resorting to others may be frustrated.[31]

From the decree issued to al-Mu'ayyad fi'l-Dīn al-Shīrāzī recalling him to the position of chief *dāʿī* in 454/1062:

> You took charge of the rightly guiding *daʿwa*, healing souls with your healing discourse, the star of inner perception shining bright from the rising point of your tongue. You furnished proof of what is with us, the People of the House of Prophecy, of the honour of knowledge, and you expounded upon our being the interpreters of God's hidden secret. You 'proclaimed among the people the pilgrimage' to our *daʿwa*, 'they come walking and riding on every lean mount' (Q.22: 27). You snared each fleeing heart with the net of belief.[32]

Note in such state decrees of appointment how it remains important to cite the appointee's service to the Imam, to the *daʿwa* in his favour, and, in turn, his high

---

[31] Al-Qāḍī al-Nuʿmān, *Ikhtilāf uṣūl al-madhāhib*, pp. 47–48; adapted here from Poonawala's translation of this passage in his editor's introduction to *The Pillars of Islam*, vol. 1, p. xxviii.

[32] Tr. Tahera Qutbuddin, *al-Mu'ayyad*, pp. 384–385.

regard for the recipient, who, among other roles, teaches the people about the Imam's being the interpreter of 'God's hidden secret'.

From a decree of investiture for the chief justice (al-Ḥusayn b. ʿAlī b. al-Nuʿmān, in 389/999), we have evidence that offers a unique opportunity to read the exact language used by the Fatimids to express the Imam's policy in making this appointment (or any other appointment for that matter): what did the caliph expect of his chief justice and precisely what duties does the document specify for this office? Though drafted in the chancery, it states the policy of the ruler. Here are the main points of the text:[33]

> This is what the servant of God and His agent al-Manṣūr Abū ʿAlī al-Ḥākim bi-Amr Allāh, Commander of the Believers, entrusts to al-Qāḍī Ḥusayn b. ʿAlī b. al-Nuʿmān in appointing him to act as presiding judge over Cairo the Victorious, and Fustat, Alexandria and its dependencies, the Holy Cities [Mecca and Medina], may God the exalted protect them both, the military districts of Syria, and the governorates of the Maghrib, along with [the responsibility for] those mounting the pulpits, the leaders of the congregational mosques and those assigned to look after them, and those who call to prayer, the rest of those who operate in these and others of the mosques. He is to supervise all matters pertaining to their welfare and he is to oversee the mint and the weighing of gold and silver. This is in addition to what the Commander of the Believers may employ him to do or not do, have in mind for him or propose to him …
>
> [The caliph] orders him to arrange his sitting for judgement in places near the vicinities of the litigants, to remove barriers and open his doors to them, to make his court session agreeable to all, to divide between them his phrases proportionately, not to favour in that a powerful man because of his power nor to ruin in that a weak man because of his weakness, but rather lean to the truth and incline in its direction, upholding thus the truth always and maintain the balanced scale …
>
> [The caliph] commands him to take great care in supervising the notary witnesses who fall under him and who affect deeply the implementing of judgements and extracting of decisions. Try to see into their conditions with appropriate perception, apprehending their private affairs with sufficient realisation. He should ask about their religious schools, investigating their private and public lives, affairs that are open and those that are kept secret. Those of them he finds are just and of good faith, upright and self-respecting, intent on the truth, bearing witness to what is right, of good character, a manner near to perfection, he will retain …
>
> [The caliph] orders him to act in accord with the standard set for him by the Commander of the Believers in regard to those in charge of the funds of orphans and of

---

33 Taken from Shihāb al-Dīn Aḥmad al-Qalqashandī, *Ṣubḥ al-aʿshāʾ fi ṣināʿat al-inshāʾ* (Cairo, 1912–1938), vol. 10, pp. 384–388.

> bequests, those persons who are defective in the mind, those unable to handle their own funds. He is to proceed in a way that these matters will be in conformity with what pleases God and His agent, protecting them and preserving through those trustworthy persons assigned over them …
>
> [The caliph] commands him to watch over the mint and the weighing of gold and silver by means of trustworthy persons who guard both from every sort of adulteration. Those who work in either will not have the means to introduce into the operation any manner of debasement; because it is through cash and coin that tenements, estates and goods are obtained, slaves purchased, marriages contracted, claims paid. The introduction of deception and the entry of any thing like it is injurious to the religion and causes harm to the Muslims. The Commander of the Believers declares to God that he is innocent of both …
>
> This is what the Commander of the Believers has commissioned. Fulfil his commission, being led by his guidance, directed by his direction …

The responsibilities of all who occupy lesser ranks, in direct contrast with that of the Imam, are not exempt from human enquiry and from the expectations of the governing authority. But the interplay between the exalted concept of rule by a divinely sanctioned Imam, whose knowledge of right and wrong depends on God alone, who infallibly determines what can and cannot, should and should not, be done, and the actions proper to those he appoints to serve him as intermediaries between himself and his subjects, is not quite the same as it would have been under the Abbasids. The Fatimids claim infallible, divinely protected authority; no power is above them save that of God Himself. There is no consensus of Muslims to which they themselves adhere. Those the Fatimids appoint to office are beholden to them and not to an abstract notion of Islamic doctrine derived from the collective determinations of the scholars, as among Sunnis.

Nearly all Fatimid decrees of this type contain statements about duties in a general manner. They are thus common to the work of almost any office. It would be rare not to find some version of the command to 'order the good and prohibit the bad', to fear God and rely on Him, or to treat the rich the same as the poor, the powerful as if they were weak, the weak as if they were powerful, elites like the masses, masses like the elites. All *qāḍī*s – presumably all – were carefully admonished to deal with the funds of orphans in a proper manner (i.e., returning it to them in a timely fashion).[34] The clerks in the chancery merely had to invent slightly different ways of saying it for each subsequent occasion. But provisions of this kind are a generic component of such

[34] That this provision is a standard feature of appointment decrees for the judiciary surely indicates that violations of the judge's responsibilities in this area were not infrequent. In fact we have several cases of Fatimid judges who fell victim to their own venality with respect to the funds of orphans.

decrees and do not express a Fatimid trait or condition any more than the decrees issued by another dynasty. And for that reason this material is of much less interest.

In fact other portions of these decrees, not directly related to the statement of duties, have more interest. Normally they commence with a section praising God, followed by a paragraph invoking His blessings on the Prophet, on ʿAlī and the Imams, and then a statement about the Commander of the Believers, who is the Imam-caliph of the present, the one who issues the decree. The balance of the text covers the specifics of the position in question, the qualification of the person being appointed to it, and finally instructions on how to perform the job properly, that is, the duties which the job entailed. For a governor of Alexandria, for example, there will be fulsome praise of the city and its importance. Most decrees laud the appointee by stating that the Commander of the Believers considered all his men and found that only he – the new office holder – had all the qualifications required. One qualification, curiously, cited specifically and quite often, is having come from a noble lineage. High lineage seems to be especially important for holding public responsibility. (Lineage was after all the key to Fatimid legitimacy itself.) The section containing instructions might have both those specific to the position and others that are more generally true of public office.

Nevertheless, on the matter of the imamate and the overriding authority of that rank, there was little or no compromise. The one area of greatest contrast between Fatimid and non-Fatimid delineations of public duty is the appeal in the latter to observe and adhere to the prevailing consensus of the Islamic scholarly community, in other words, to follow the lead of illustrious predecessors.[35] That provision is absent from Fatimid documents, which focus exclusively on the guidance of the Imam. Thus the major difference and what distinguishes Fatimid doctrine from that of its rivals is its insistence on the pure and unshared authority of the living Imam – an authority that is comprehensive for all aspects of Islamic law and practice, in fact for government and governing in every respect.

But such a position is less explicit in the evidence than it might have been. Having no wish to aggravate the situation with highly charged rhetoric, the Fatimids preferred a quieter approach, one that befitted a diverse population where the point was made by omitting a doctrine favoured elsewhere, the net effect of which served, even so, to strengthen the authority and sole discretion of the Imam. By not admitting any other, none could be cited or appealed to. An official within such an administration had no choice but to acknowledge the caliph's authority. Public responsibility involved less a duty to the community, either as an abstraction or as an actual society of citizens, than to the Imam-caliph who was its supreme head and its highest embodiment. The actions of a public official should reflect those of its leader, his wishes, and his alone.

---

[35] A good example of the Abbasid (or other Sunni) type is the commission (*ʿahd*) composed by Ibn ʿAbbād in the name of Muʾayyad al-Dawla appointing ʿAbd al-Jabbār *qāḍī al-quḍāt* of Rayy in 367/977, which explicitly cites the *ijmāʿ* (consensus) and 'the statements of the famous predecessors and well regarded scholars of the community' as guides to the law as material on which the judge should rely (*Rasāʾil*, pp. 35–36).

It is therefore obvious that Fatimid era authorities expressed a fairly clear and consistent doctrine concerning the imamate and the ultimate authority it entailed. Although certain works by figures in the pre-Fatimid and early *daʿwa* indicate differences and elements of confusion, that is less and less common in official pronouncements once the Fatimid state had come into existence. Moreover, there is no lack of material from this later period (i.e., 297–567/910–1171) and nearly every document or writing from that period offers confirmation of that fact. Therefore, the information available is correspondingly large, even immense, only a portion of which has been discussed above. I doubt that collecting it all, assuming it were even possible, would add either extra clarity or much that might be new; better to concentrate on works of major importance and items that are not now readily accessible. Thus while there is more to be done, material to study and analyse, and aspects of the concept of authority still to investigate, we know at this point a great deal about the rule of the Imams in the Fatimid empire both in theory and, most especially, in practice.

16

'Minority Reports': Twelver Shiʿi Disputations and Authority in the Būyid Period

Andrew J. Newman

To date, scholars of Twelver Shiʿism have produced numerous studies of what might, in fact, be most usefully understood as clerical *claims* to authority during the absence of the Imam from the community rather than, as might be understood, the actual exercise of such authority.[1] The primary source texts cited in these studies were, therefore, part of a larger discourse: the authority of the clerical class as understood today was not either *in place* or *a given* from the outset of the occultation. Over the course of Twelver history, such authority was to be won but it could also be lost, either partially or even totally.

Indeed, over the history of the faith 'debates' over the nature and extent of authority have taken place in written form and even in the streets, between as well as within groups supporting and opposing the extension of such authority. For the Qajar (1779–1925), Pahlavi (1925–1979) and perhaps especially the Islamic Republic (1979–) periods in Iran, for example, there is a rich array of textual and non-textual material available through which it is possible to examine both arguments emanating from a variety of quarters about the exercise of the authority of the Imam over matters of doctrine and practice as well as the broader politico-spiritual context in which such claims were advanced and disputed.

For earlier periods in the faith's history clerical claims to authority, even if they have not been recognised as such, have been relatively less well covered by scholars in the field. Such as it has been, this coverage has also generally been limited to the nature and extent of such claims as they were advanced by the most senior elements of the clerical class, the literate few whose names and key works are already well known to the field. To date researchers have devoted less time to the recovery of the views of non-elites on such issues, let alone any others.

[1] On the rise of Twelver Shiʿi studies in the West, see A. Newman, *The Formative Period of Shiʿi Law: Hadith as Discourse between Qum and Baghdad* (Richmond, Surrey, 2000), pp. xiii–xviii. See also Etan Kohlberg, ed., *Shīʿism* (Aldershot, 2003), especially pp. xxiif.

The sum total of the faith's 'spiritual scene' in any period cannot be that reconstructed solely based on reference to a handful of such individuals. Indeed, privileging the views of these few scholars on issues related to authority, let alone any other matters, can only encourage a sense of the linear, inevitable nature of the trajectory of developments in Twelver doctrine and practice over the centuries. Because the 'voices' of these elements who, in any period, certainly constitute the majority, remain unheard, the processes by which the faith evolved remain, at best, imperfectly appreciated.

With reference to the Safawid period in Twelver Shiʿi history – the last of the three pre-modern periods in which the faith enjoyed a measure of 'official' tolerance – efforts made to 'recover' these voices have yielded some successes. Careful examination of primary source materials produced in a series of 'debates' over the period has revealed evidence of the participation of non-elite elements therein. Indeed, non-elites were sufficiently powerful to bring about the resignations of two prominent clerics of the period from their court-appointed posts: Bahāʾ al-Dīn Muḥammad, Shaykh Bahāʾī (d. 1030/1620–1621) was forced to step down from being Isfahan's *Shaykh al-Islām* and Fayḍ al-Kāshānī (d. 1091/1680) had to relinquish his post as the leader of the capital's Friday congregational prayer services.[2]

Although the authors of the texts examined, following standard practice, do not name their opponents, an inability to identify all the unnamed participants in these confrontations as fully as might be desirable does not negate the reality of their active participation in the life of the community at the time. The active involvement of such elements in these 'exchanges' also underlines the reality of their concerns over the very practical dimensions and implications of what has too often been otherwise supposed to be 'high', that is, esoteric, religious discourse carried on among a handful of clerical

[2] On the issue of Friday congregational prayer, for example, see our 'The Myth of the Clerical Migration to Safawid Iran: Arab Shiʿite Opposition to Ali al-Karaki and Safawid Shiʿism', *Die Welt des Islams*, 33 (1993), pp. 88f, 99f, 105–106; idem, 'Fayd al-Kashani and the Rejection of the Clergy/State Alliance: Friday Prayer as Politics in the Safavid Period', in L. Walbridge, ed., *The Most Learned of the Shiʿa* (New York, 2001), pp. 34–52; L. Walbridge, 'The *Vezir* and the *Mulla*: a late Safavid period debate on Friday prayer', in M. Bernardini, M. Haneda and M. Szuppe, ed., *Études sur l'Iran médiéval et moderne offertes* à *Jean Calmard*, *Eurasian Studies*, 1–2 (2006), pp. 237–269. On Bahāʾī, see our 'Towards a Reconsideration of the Isfahan School of Philosophy: Shaykh Bahāʾī and the Role of the Safawid Ulama', *Studia Iranica* (Paris), 15 (1986), pp. 165–199. On the anti-Sufi polemic, see our 'Clerical Perceptions of Sufi Practices in Late Seventeenth-Century Persia: Arguments Over the Permissibility of Singing (Ghina)', in L. Lewisohn and D. Morgan, ed., *The Heritage of Sufism*, vol. 3, *Late Classical Persianate Sufism: The Safavid and Mughal Period (1501–1750)* (Oxford, 1999), pp. 135–164; idem, 'Sufism and Anti-Sufism in Safavid Iran: The Authorship of the "Ḥadīqat al-Shīʿa" Revisited', *Iran*, 37 (1999), pp. 95–108. And, more recently, idem, 'Clerical Perceptions of Sufi Practices in Late 17th Century Persia, II: al-Ḥurr al-ʿĀmilī (d. 1693) and the Debate on the Permissibility of Ghinā', in Y. Suleiman, ed., *Living Islamic History: Studies in Honour of Professor Carole Hillenbrand* (Edinburgh, 2010), pp. 192–207.

elites. The result of these efforts to recover the voices of the 'non-elite' has been the emergence of a much more dynamic picture of the Safawid-period spiritual scene.

This chapter explores a range of works on theology and the practical points of the law (*furūʿ*) works produced in the Būyid period – the first of the three pre-modern periods in which the faith enjoyed a measure of tolerance, the second being the Mongol/Timurid period – for evidence of a similar range of voices, and concerns. The voices and views of those clerical elites of the time best known to the field of Shiʿi studies today are seen to have been more probably in the minority, and a range of elites and non-elites to have been actively engaged in discourse over matters of both doctrine and practice.

Theological and *Furūʿ* Disputations in the Works of al-Shaykh al-Mufīd

The Būyid period – perhaps best dated to the years between 945 and 1055, based on the Būyids' 'taking' and 'losing' of Baghdad – is well known as having been 'populated' by several key Twelver scholars famous for having elaborated a series of distinctive principles of doctrine and practice. Certainly among those who come to mind first and foremost are Muḥammad b. Muḥammad b. Nuʿmān, known as al-Shaykh al-Mufīd (d. 413/1022), and ʿAlī b. al-Ḥusayn, al-Sharīf al-Murtaḍā (d. 436/1044). By contrast with such of their well-known co-religionist predecessors as Muḥammad b. Yaʿqūb al-Kulaynī (d. 329/941) and Muḥammad b. ʿAlī al-Qummī, al-Shaykh al-Ṣadūq (d. 381/991–992) and others of the Qummī traditionists,[3] al-Mufīd and al-Murtaḍā are best known in the field for having promoted recourse to individual human reasoning (*ʿaql*) in the interpretation of doctrine and practice. Al-Mufīd and al-Murtaḍā were not the earliest Twelver scholars to have offered such arguments.[4] But, they are certainly among the best known both of the earliest of those who did and, perhaps as importantly, of those in this tradition a very large number of whose works are extant.

Al-Mufīd himself is certainly mainly thought of in the field as a rationalist scholar who defended the faith in debates with a number of Sunni scholars.[5] His discussions

---

[3] On al-Kulaynī and the Qumm 'school', see our *The Formative Period.*

[4] See the references to Ibn Abī ʿAqīl and Ibn al-Junayd al-Iskāfī, both of the early and middle 4th/10th century, in H. Modarressi Tabataba'i, *An Introduction to Shīʿī Law* (London, 1984), pp. 35–38, and to Ibn al-Junayd below.

[5] For a still-useful introduction to al-Mufīd and his thought, see M. J. McDermott, *The Theology of al-Shaikh al-Mufīd (d. 413/1022)* (Beirut, 1978). See also W. Akhtār's chapter on al-Mufīd in his *Early Imamiyyah Shiʿite Thinkers* (New Delhi, 1988), pp. 79–122. See also the two seminal works on al-Mufīd by Dominique Sourdel: 'Les Conceptions Imamites au débutdu XIe siècle d'après le Shaykh al-Mufīd', in D. S. Richards, ed., *Islamic Civilisation* (Oxford, 1973), pp. 187–200, mainly an investigation of the Shaykh's *Awāʾil al-maqālāt*, on which see further below; idem, 'L'Imāmisme vu par le Cheikh al-Mufīd', *Revue des Etudes Islamiques*, 60 (1972), pp. 217–296, which includes translations from *Awāʾil* (249f). See also Tabatabai, *An Introduction*, pp. 40–44; H. Halm, *Shiʿism*, tr. Janet Watson (Edinburgh, 1991), pp. 49–50; M. Momen,

with such Sunnis as the ʿAsharī Ibn al-Bāqillānī (d. 402/1013) and the Muʿtazilī Qāḍī ʿAbd al-Jabbār (d. 415/1025), for example, and his preference for Baghdādī over Baṣran Muʿtazilism are well attested in the secondary literature.[6] To date, however, less attention has been paid to al-Mufīd's participation in disputations within the Twelver community as on offer both in his theological works and his works on *furūʿ*.

Both Sourdel and McDermott privileged al-Mufīd's *Awāʾil al-maqālāt*, with the latter calling it al-Mufīd's 'most important' work of theology. In the process of addressing over 150 issues,[7] the text is, however, also replete with references to disagreements between Twelvers, to whom al-Mufīd refers as Imāmīs,[8] as well as with other Shiʿi and Sunni groups. From these discussions, moreover, it is clear both that the Twelver theologians conversing on these issues were themselves in disagreement on a range of issues and that al-Mufīd, even as he *asserted* the case for the validity of his own interpretations and his own authority to offer them, frequently agreed with non-Twelver interpretations and did not always hold the majority view within the faith. In his discussion of the acquisition of knowledge of the Divine, for example, al-Mufīd noted that he 'and many (*kathīr*) of the Imāmīs' and the Baghdādī Muʿtazila upheld the understanding that this was acquired by one's own reasoning or listening to the revelation. According to al-Mufīd, the Baṣran Muʿtazila, 'the determinists and *al-ḥashwiyya* among the traditionists (*aṣḥāb al-ḥadīth*)',[9] however, argued that this knowledge comes to the mind of the believer with no effort on the latter's behalf.

On the fact of the imamate itself as a prophetic mission, and its being imposed on the Imams, al-Mufīd noted that a number (*jumhūr*) of Imāmīs agreed with him, as did most of the Muʿtazila and most of *aṣḥāb al-ḥadīth*. On the question of the createdness of the Qurʾan, al-Mufīd noted that 'all the Imāmīs except for a few who deviate from them' – a phrase he also used with respect to minority Twelver opinion on the infallibility of the Imams – agreed the Qurʾan was 'produced in time'. In none of the above instances, or when he made similar references in elsewhere, did al-Mufīd offer any additional elaboration of the 'alternative' Twelver views to which he referred, nor identify their proponents.

Al-Mufīd did occasionally single out 'the Nawbakhtīs among the Imāmīs' for holding views at variance with others within the community. These and his frequent, but unparsed, references to the Imāmī *fuqahāʾ*, among whom there were disagreements,

---

An Introduction to Shiʿi Islam (New Haven and London, 1985), p. 79; M. A. Amir-Moezzi, *The Divine Guide in Early Shiʿism, The Sources of Esotericism in Islam*, tr. David Streight (Albany, NY, 1994), p. 134; T. Bayhom-Daou, *Shaykh Mufīd* (Oxford, 2005).

[6] For a list of al-Mufīd's writings, see McDermott, *Theology of al-Shaikh al-Mufīd*, pp. 27ff. See also Akhtār, *Early Imamiyyah Shiʿite Thinkers,* pp. 88f. The former's analyses of al-Mufīd's encounter with Muʿtazilism are still authoritative, although Akhtār does repay attention.

[7] Counting each section beginning with '*al-qawl fī*' as a single 'issue'.

[8] On the 'Imāmīs' as a reference to the Twelvers, see al-Mufīd, *Awāʾil al-maqālāt*, ed. A. S. Wajdī, incl. al-Mufīd's *Taṣḥīḥ al-iʿtiādāt* (2nd ed., Tabriz, 1370–1371), p. 49.

[9] The standard work on *al-ḥashwiyya*, who seem to be a separate group to the Imāmīs in *Awāʾil*, remains A. S. Halkin, 'The Ḥashwiyya', *JAOS*, 54 (1934), pp. 1–28. But, see also the brief article thereon in *EI2*, vol. 3, p. 269.

Imāmī relaters of traditions (variously labelled *aṣḥāb al-āthār* or *aṣḥāb al-naql*) and Imāmī practitioners of *kalām*, among whom there were also splits, bespeak – if only in his own mind – the presence of some formalised jurisprudential and theological 'tendencies' if not necessarily fully fledged 'schools'.[10] Thus, for example, al-Mufīd noted the agreement of himself, the Imāmī *fuqahā'* and the Imāmī *aṣḥāb al-athār* that the Imams could hear the speech of the angels without seeing them, but noted that the Nawbakhtīs and some Imāmīs (*jamāʿa min ahl al-Imāma*) rejected this as they held traditions on this were not sufficient.[11]

Al-Mufīd did occasionally invoke consensus (*ijmāʿ*). On the issue of free will, for example, he claimed that he was in agreement with the 'consensus of the Imāmīs (*ijmāʿ al-Imāmiyya*)', the Zaydīs and the Baghdādī Muʿtazila, most Murji'a and *aṣḥāb al-ḥadīth* that man does create his own acts. The Baṣran Muʿtazila disagreed, using the term 'creator (*khāliq*)' in respect of men and their actions. In this, he said, they are outside Muslim consensus.[12] Al-Mufīd did not, in this instance, substantiate his claim for consensus. But, further along, he explained that *ijmāʿ* is a 'proof (*ḥujja*)' among Imāmīs because it includes the statement of 'the Imam (*al-Ḥujja*)'. On this principle, he noted the Muʿtazila, the Murji'a, the Khawārij and *aṣḥāb al-ḥadīth* among both the Qadarīs and the Determinists were all in disagreement.[13]

As to the authenticity of the Qur'an, in a relatively lengthy discussion, al-Mufīd noted that some Imāmīs (*jamāʿa min ahl al-Imāma*) argued that nothing was missing from the extant text except for interpretations and explanations (*ta'wīl wa tafsīr*) offered in what he referred to as the text of Imam ʿAlī. He professed himself in agreement with this view. As for what may have been added to the text (*al-ziyāda*) of the Qur'an, he continued, an additional *sūra* could never have been added without its being detected. An additional 'word or two' or 'letter or two' might have been added without being noted but, he added, he doubted it. Al-Mufīd did note that the Nawbakhtīs held there had been additions and omissions and closed by worthies maintained this.[14]

The authenticity of the Qur'an was a 'real' issue for al-Mufīd and the community at the time. Later Sunni historians recorded clashes between Sunnis and Shiʿa in Baghdad in 392/1003 and 398/1007 on this issue. It may have been the spark that enflamed existing tensions; indeed Sunni-Shiʿi riots are again reported for 409/1018. In any case, gangs of youths and 'popular preachers' feature in these accounts. Despite his own position on the issue and his acknowledged lack of involvement in

---

10 Al-Mufīd, *Awā'il*, pp. 66, 57–58, 102, 100, 58, 72–74, 75, 79, 80, 81, 87, 95, 97, 98, 99, 110. Elsewhere (100), al-Mufīd did speak of Imāmī practitioners of *kalām*. On the Banū Nawbakht, see our *The Formative Period*.

11 Ibid., pp. 80–81.

12 Ibid., pp. 64–65.

13 Ibid., pp. 137–138.

14 Ibid., pp. 93–95. For a recent introduction to this issue, see E. Kohlberg and Mohammad Ali Amir-Moezzi, ed., *Revelation and Falsification: The Kitāb al-Qirā'āt of Aḥmad b. Muḥammad al-Sayyārī* (Leiden and Boston, 2009).

these disturbances, after both the 398/1007 and 409/1018 riots, al-Mufid was made a scapegoat for the Shiʿi involvement therein and banned from the city.[15]

Al-Mufid also composed a commentary on *al-Iʿtiqādāt*, a work of theology produced by Ibn Bābawayh (d. 381/991), his own teacher. To be sure, as with *Awāʾil*, *Taṣḥīḥ al-iʿtiqādāt*'s point-by-point criticisms of Ibn Bābawayh on some 39 issues merit attention for their own sake. But this text offers further evidence of disagreement within the community. Also on offer herein is al-Mufid's harsh critique of Qummī traditionism in particular and references to his own methodological alternative to that traditionism, and his views on the hierarchical structure within the community during the Imam's absence. Thus, for example, he criticised Ibn Bābawayh's discussion of 'decree and destiny' (*al-qadar wa'l-qaḍā*)', in which his teacher had argued that discussion of *qadar* was forbidden. Al-Mufid stated this interpretation was based on a text that was anomalous (*shādhdh*) and could be interpreted in different ways 'well known to learned men (*ʿulamāʾ*)'.[16]

Ibn Bābawayh had cited traditions ascribed to the Imams that condemned religious dialectics (*al-jadāl*) and said its practitioners – whom he named as *ahl al-kalām* – would perish, said al-Mufid. Al-Mufid himself then argued this prohibition applied only to those who were not conversant with its methods and easily confused, and that the practice of *kalām* was enjoined on those who were masters of the discipline.[17] Likewise, in his comments on Ibn Bābawayh's arguments for the necessity of dissimulation (*al-taqiyya*), al-Mufid noted that 'The Two Truthful Ones', a reference to the fifth and sixth Imams, had ordered one group to keep the truth hidden from 'the enemies of the faith'. The second group was commanded to challenge these enemies openly and to call them to the Truth, as they knew they would not face any harm for doing so.[18]

In a lengthy discussion of souls and spirits (*al-arwāḥ wa'l-nufūs*) al-Mufid identified *ḥashwiyya* elements among the Shiʿa as having propounded the view that particles (*dharr*) were created for which Allah later created bodies; this as an aspect of the idea that spirits (*arwāḥ*) were created before bodies (*ajsād*). Al-Mufid noted that Ibn Bābawayh had availed himself of a tradition that had but a single chain of transmission (*āḥād*). He noted also that some of Ibn Bābawayh's views mirrored the views of those – whom he did not identify – who accepted the principle of the transmigration of souls (*al-tanāsukhiyya*), even if his teacher did not realise this, and that Ibn Bābawayh's support for the idea of the perpetuity of souls was the basis on which

[15] See McDermott, *Theology of al-Shaikh al-Mufid*, pp. 17–22, citing accounts from the later Ḥanbalī historian Ibn al-Jawzī (d. 597/1201) and Ibn al-Athīr (d. 630/1233).

[16] Al-Mufid, *Awāʾil al-maqālāt*, ed. A. S. Wajdī, incl. al-Mufid's *Taṣḥīḥ al-iʿtiqādāt* (2nd ed., Tabriz, 1370–1371), pp. 194–195. See also pp. 231f, on 'inspiration (*al-waḥy*)', where Ibn Bābawayh was also criticised for citing a *shādhdh* text.

[17] Al-Mufid, *Taṣḥīḥ*, pp. 201f.

[18] Ibid., pp. 241f.

Sunnis had criticised the Shiʿa of atheism (*al-zandaqa*). This, al-Mufīd said, is what can happen if traditions are accepted without checking their authenticity.[19]

On the matter of 'exaggeration and delegation (*al-ghuluww wa'l-tafwīḍ*)' al-Mufīd criticised the reported view of a teacher of Ibn Bābawayh, Muḥammad b. al-Ḥasan b. al-Walīd (d. 343/954–955), on 'falling short (*taqṣīr*)', that is failing to accord the Prophet and the Imams their rightful place. Al-Mufīd held that when Ibn al-Walīd and other – unnamed – Qummī traditionists argued that in denying that the Prophet and the Imams could be distracted in their prayers they were, in fact, guilty of the fault of exaggeration (*ghuluww*).[20] In the text's final chapter, al-Mufīd noted that Ibn Bābawayh failed, beyond a brief notice, to outline a system for determining which traditions were to be followed and which not. Here al-Mufīd referred to his own *al-Tamhīd* and *Maṣābīḥ al-Nūr* for explication of these means and then offered a summary of the most key points to be kept in mind.[21]

Finally, al-Mufīd's *al-Fuṣūl al-Mukhtarā* comprises a selection of materials from different works of al-Mufīd assembled by al-Sharīf al-Murtaḍā, al-Mufīd's own student. Herein were discussions of Shiʿi history, critiques of non-Twelver Shiʿi groups, debates with Muʿtazilīs, and discussions on the occultation, the imamate, issues of theology and jurisprudence.

These also contain references to disputes over methodology. However, in the process, perhaps most interestingly, those whose methodology al-Mufīd adjudged to be problematic are identified, if only very partially. Thus, a Muʿtazilī critic is cited as asking about those Imāmīs who followed previous rulings uncritically (*muqallidūn*), whether they were unbelievers (*kuffār*) and deserving of an eternity in Hell. Al-Mufīd replied that although he did not condemn all such *muqallidūn* per se, among them were those who had 'no obligation to know and reason upon proofs' owing to their lack of wisdom (*ʿuqūl*)'. This applied, he said, to many of those 'of the Sawād and outlying districts, the Bedouin, both Arab and Persian, and the common people'. Those Imāmī *muqallidūn* who could use their reasoning but do not, he said, are those who 'deserve eternity in Hell'.[22]

Al-Mufīd's Disputations in *Furūʿ* Literature

The field's preoccupation with al-Mufīd's rationalist discourse perhaps explains the lack of attention to date paid to his writings on the practical points of jurisprudence (*furūʿ al-fiqh*). Indeed, with conventional discussions to date suggesting he was

---

19 Ibid., pp. 207f. On the *Ḥashwiyya*, see also pp. 227–228.

20 Ibid., pp. 33, 238–241.

21 Ibid., pp. 245–248. These are outlined, in brief, in the book on adjudication in al-Mufīd's *al-Muqniʿa*, on which see below.

22 Al-Mufīd, *al-Fuṣūl al-mukhtāra* (Qumm, 1396), pp. 76–80. See McDermott, *Theology of al-Shaikh al-Mufīd*, pp. 243–245. For a reference to 'Imāmī practitioners of *kalām* in Khurasan, Fars and Iraq', see *al-Fuṣūl*, p. 76.

mainly engaged with mounting theological defences to, largely, external opponents, and his documented scepticism of the reliability of and reliance on the texts, it might be well imagined that al-Mufīd had little time to produce any discussions thereof.

In this regard then, al-Mufīd's great work of *furūʿ* – *al-Muqniʿa fi'l-fiqh* – repays attention,[23] not only revealing splits within the community on matters of daily practice but also, as with some of his theological rulings, offering evidence of both his consistent claims for the authority of the *faqīh* during the Imam's absence and the manner in which he supported his arguments, and the minority status of his own interpretations. In the section on *al-zakāt*, for example, al-Mufīd offered an early argument for the authority of the senior clerics during the Imam's absence. Here he stated that it was a religious obligation (*farḍ*) that *al-zakāt* be delivered to the Prophet, or the Imam, as the former's successor (*khalīfa*). If the Imam were absent, *al-zakāt* should be delivered to whomever the Imam had appointed. If *al-sufarā'*[24] were absent, it was incumbent on the people to deliver *al-zakāt* to 'the trustworthy *fuqahā*'. This was because, he continued, 'the *faqīh* is more knowledgeable as to its disposition than someone who has no 'understanding of his faith (*fiqh diyānātihi*)'.[25] There were no supporting texts cited in the course of this discussion. By contrast, in sections addressing and defining various aspects of *al-zakāt*, al-Mufīd did quote the Imams. The sections on *zakāt al-fiṭra*[26] and on the categories of recipients of *al-zakāt*, for example, contained such references.[27]

As to *al-khums*, al-Mufīd noted disagreement within the community on what to do with these revenues during *al-ghayba*. One group felt that the obligation to pay these lapsed during the absence of the Imam. One group felt the *al-khums* should be buried in the ground, for the Imam (*al-qā'im*) to recover when he reappeared. Some, he said, saw a connection between the progeny of the family of the Prophet and the poor among the Shiʿa, based on the principle of recommendation/desirability (*istiḥbāb*). A fourth group maintained the revenue should be set aside for the Imam

---

[23] Where the field has yet to accord this work much attention, his student Muḥammad b. al-Ḥasan al-Ṭūsī (d. 460/1067) commenced a commentary on it during the lifetime of his teacher. The finished product, completed only after al-Mufīd's death, was al-Ṭūsī's *Tahdhīb al-aḥkām*, the first of his two great compilations of the Imams' statements, which in turn comprise the last two of the four great compilations thereof produced by the end of the Būyid period.

[24] Al-Mufīd did not here explain this reference. The understanding of the term as referring to the four named individuals understood to have been in direct contact with the Twelfth Imam from the onset of the latter's disappearance to the death of the fourth in 941 is generally thought to date to the later *Kitāb al-ghayba* of al-Mufīd's student al-Ṭūsī. Here, however, the reference may be less formal, perhaps referring to any individual designated by the Imam.

[25] Al-Mufīd, *al-Muqniʿa fi'l-fiqh* (Qumm, 1417/1996), p. 252.

[26] Ibid., pp. 247–252.

[27] Ibid., pp. 241–242, citing a text on the authority of Zarāra. A second, cited from Ismāʿīl al-Ashʿarī, had appeared in Muḥammad b. Yaʿqūb al-Kulaynī, *al-Kāfī*, ed. ʿAlī Akbar al-Ghaffārī (Tehran, 1377–1379/1957–1960), vol. 3, p. 547. The third and last text in this section, cited from Muḥammad b. ʿIsā, had also appeared in al-Kulaynī, *al-Kāfī*, vol. 3, p. 563.

(*Ṣāḥib al-amr*). But, if the believer was concerned that he himself might die before the Imam's reappearance, 'he commends[28] it to someone whom he trusts insofar as his wisdom (*'aql*) and his faith (*diyānātihi*) to give it to the Imam … or he commends it to someone who takes his place (*yaqūm maqāmihi*) in trustworthiness (*al-thiqa*) and faith (*al-diyāna*) until the Imam of the Age appears'. The latter, al-Mufīd declared, is more clear (*awḍaḥ*). He noted that the same question had been raised with respect to *al-zakāt*. That tax did not lapse with the occultation, he said, nor was it to be spent; it was obligatory to set it aside and commend it to someone who would convey it to those who deserve it.[29]

If he stopped just short of formally naming the *faqīh* in this discussion of *al-khums*, al-Mufīd's own reference here to his earlier discussion on *al-zakāt* made it clear enough to whom he was referring. As in his discussion of *al-zakāt* during the occultation, the discussion on this aspect of *al-khums* contained but a single supporting textual reference, in which it was said that the earth would disgorge its treasure at the reappearance of the Imam.[30] However, as in the case of his discussion on *al-zakāt*, as noted above, elsewhere in his book on *al-khums* al-Mufīd did cite texts. Two texts were cited in the discussion on the amount of the *jizya*, for example, the second of which was not available in earlier collections.[31]

In *al-Muqni'a*'s book on adjudication (*al-qaḍā*) al-Mufīd cautioned that no one should undertake judgement unless he was 'a complete [perhaps mature] and wise person (*'āqil kāmil*)', knowledgeable in the Qur'an and the *sunna*, in what is abrogating and abrogated, in the concepts of the 'universal' and the 'particular', in both Arabic and about Arabs, and was also someone who did only right actions and was pious. Al-Mufīd cited but a single supporting tradition here, from Imam 'Alī, on there being four sorts of judges of whom three were in Hell and only one was in Paradise. The latter was the one who judged on the basis of the Truth.[32]

In the very short section on commanding what was good and condemning what was evil *(al-amr bi'l-ma'rūf)* and the implementation of judicial punishments (*al-ḥudūd*), al-Mufīd declared that the responsibility for this was reserved for the Imams and those 'whom they designated of princes (*al-umarā'*) and rulers (*al-ḥukkām*). 'And they entrusted *(fawwaḍū)* looking after this to the *fuqahā'* of their Shi'a when possible (*ma'a al-imkān*)', if they were not afraid of a tyrannous ruler

---

28 Using the root '*w-ṣ-y*'.

29 Al-Mufīd, *al-Muqni'a*, pp. 285–286. Eliash erred in attributing to al-Ṭūsī these statements of al-Mufīd. See Joseph Eliash, 'Misconceptions Regarding the Juridical Status of the Iranian 'Ulama', *IJMES*, 10 (1979), p. 20.

30 Ibid., pp. 285–286.

31 Ibid., pp. 272–274. Both are cited from Muḥammad b. Muslim. The text of the first is nearly identifical to al-Faqīh, vol. 2, p. 5/1671, and with a different *sanad*, to *al-Kāfī*, vol. 3, p. 566/1. See also pp. 288–291.

32 Ibid., pp. 721–722. This text is cited with an addition from Imam Ja'far in *al-Kāfī*, vol. 7, p. 407, and the compilation of his teacher Muḥammad b. 'Alī al-Qummī, Ibn Bābawayh, *Man lā yaḥḍuruhu al-faqīh*, ed. Ḥ. M. al-Kharsān (Najaf, 1957), vol. 3, p. 4.

(*sulṭān al-jawr*). 'Whoever fears oppressors (*al-ẓālimūn*)' for himself or the faith,' he added, the obligation lapses.

Al-Mufīd then noted that the *fuqahāʾ* were to gather the community together for the five [daily] prayers, prayers on special occasions, and other prayers when they were able and to render judgements among them 'based on the Truth (*biʾl-ḥaqq*)'. 'This is because the Imams have "entrusted (*fawwaḍū*)" this to them, when they are able.' This, he said, was proven in the *akhbār* and judged correct by those who were knowledgeable. Neither the *fuqahāʾ* nor those among them who were appointed (*naṣab*) by *sulṭān al-jawr* to render judgements were permitted to render judgements contrary to the firm ruling (*ḥukm*) of the family of the Prophet 'except if they were compelled to do this, based on *taqiyya* and fear for the faith and oneself'. Only potential bloodshed of believers exempted one from this. Despite his reference to available textual evidence, al-Mufīd cited no such supporting traditions on any of these points.[33]

The *Khilāf* Tradition: *al-Masāʾil al-Sarawiyya*

A further promising source for references to differing understandings on matters of theory and practice within the community is literature in the *khilāf* (disputation) genre. Within this broad rubric are treatises whose titles variously include such words as *masāʾil* (issues), *jawābāt* (answers), *radd* (reply) and *naqḍ* (refutation).

Al-Mufīd's essays in this genre include responses to queries and criticisms originating from both outwith and within the Twelver community. The subjects of three of the latter – those addressed to Ibn Nubātā, a prominent Shiʿi preacher born in Diyārbakir, another either to Ibn Bābawayh, his own teacher, or the father of Ibn Qūlūya, Jaʿfar b. Muḥammad (d. 369/979), and another to Muḥammad b. ʿAlī al-Karājakī (d. 449/1057), his student – are not clear. Three others, to unnamed individuals, dealt with the occultation itself, the 'coming forth (*khurūj*)' of the Mahdī and the *furūʿ*, and so were perhaps addressed to believers. Another essay critiqued the argument for recourse to *al-raʾy* (personal opinion) put forward by the Twelver scholar Ibn al-Junayd al-Iskāfī (d. 381/991–992). Elsewhere, Ibn Bābawayh was criticised for maintaining that Ramaḍān is never shortened by a day, the Shiʿi anthropomorphist

33 Ibid., pp. 810–812. He did cite three texts – from the Prophet, Imam ʿAlī and Imam Jaʿfar respectively – on the importance of *al-amr biʾl-maʿrūf*. All three were apparently new to this volume. On the Friday congregational prayer in particular, see pp. 162–165, where there is no reference to the Imam or a deputy, per se, let alone the *faqīh*, but a requirement that the prayer be performed if a suitable 'Imam' was available. On the evolving meanings of *al-jawr*, from Ibn Bābawayh's definition of the term as a false claimant to the Imam to those offered in the Safawid period, see our 'The Myth', pp. 83–84. On al-Mufīd's view of working for 'the oppressors', in which he argued that, 'according to the Imāmīs', such service if served oppression should be avoided, as should receiving compensation from them, if possible, see also *Awāʾil*, p. 138.

and determinist Abu'l-Ḥusayn Muḥammad al-Asadī (d. 312/924) is critiqued on 'the created', and partisans of al-Ḥallāj were refuted.[34]

Within this genre, al-Mufīd's *al-Masāʾil al-Sarawiyya* comprised replies to 11 questions coming from one Sayyid Fāḍil in Sārī, completed sometime after 381/991–992. The questions posed illustrate the extent of debates and uncertainties over issues of doctrine and practice outside Baghdad. The topics addressed included such matters as *mutʿa* (temporary marriage), shapes and beings created before Adam, matters involving the grave and death, what *aṣḥāb al-akhbār* among the Imāmīs maintain concerning fate and unbelief, the path to *ʿilm*, the legitimacy of the ʿUthmānic Codex, the marriages of ʿAlī and the Prophet and, finally, the fate of those condemned to Hell on the Day of Judgement.[35] Al-Mufīd's replies to one of these in particular show him keen to rebut both the bases of traditionism's methodology, the practical results of recourse to traditionism and complement his discussions on the necessarily hierarchical structure of authority in the community during the occultation as offered in the theological and *furūʿ* works discussed above.

The Sayyid's eighth question concerned the different books of *fiqh* from the Imams, such as that of Ibn Bābawayh in his books of *akhbār*, in which the *asānīd* (chains of transmitters) included allowed these texts to be traced back to the Imams, where the books of ʿAlī b. al-Junayd (d. mid-4th/10th century) on matters of *fiqh* did not contain *asānīd*. Was the latter, based on opinion, permissible or should reliance be given to those texts traced back through unbroken links? It 'is not licit for any man', al-Mufīd replied, 'to decide for himself what is the true meaning when a difference occurs about the meaning of the Book [the Qurʾan] or the *sunna* or the conclusion of a rational demonstration'. The individual (*aḥad*), said al-Mufīd, was not permitted to undertake action on the basis of this revelation until he had acquired both 'knowledge of such matters and the skill in reasoning which will lead him to understand'. If the individual lacked the necessary knowledge, 'let him go to one who does know, and not make a statement based on his own opinion and speculation'. If the individual did so, acted on the basis of his own judgement and was right, he would not be rewarded (*maʾjūr*). If he did so and was wrong, he would not be excused.

Al-Mufīd noted that Ibn Bābawayh[36] and *aṣḥāb al-ḥadīth* related traditions narrated on the authority of a single transmitter (*akhbār al-āḥād*) or otherwise untrustworthy traditions without carefully checking these sources and failed to use their intellectual resources to distinguish what was reasonable in the revelation from what was not. They were not 'people of reason and investigation', nor were they 'in the habit of thinking out and discussing what they relate'. ʿAlī b. al-Junayd, said al-Mufīd, relied on the path of the faith's opponents and analogy (*al-qiyās*, accepted

---

34 McDermott, *Theology of al-Shaikh al-Mufīd*, pp. 27ff. On Ibn al-Junayd, see also below.

35 On this work, see al-Ṭihrānī, vol. 5, pp. 222–223. The essay can be found in the collection of al-Mufīd's essays entitled *ʿIddat rasāʾil* (2nd ed., Qumm, n.d.), pp. 207–231.

36 Al-Mufīd's reference to Ibn Bābawayh as deceased suggests the reply was composed after 381/991–992.

by Sunnis), such that what the Imams had said became mixed with his own opinion (*al-ra'y*). He also relied on *āḥād* traditions, not those with unbroken *asānīd*.[37]

In what was most likely a reference to the famous tradition reported by ʿUmar b. Ḥanẓala, al-Mufīd interpreted Imam Jaʿfar al-Ṣādiq's injunction concerning hesitation to mean that the layman should refer the matter in question to 'someone more learned than himself'.[38] This expert, in turn, should employ rational proofs and avoid recourse to such tools as *al-qiyās*. Al-Mufīd named himself as one such expert, noting 'I have given answers about many disputed traditions in questions that came to me from Nishapur, Mosul, Fars, and the district known as Mazanderan.'[39]

The Sayyid's ninth question turned on the legitimacy of the ʿUthmānic Codex of the Qur'an, in the process referring to a text thereof collated by Imam ʿAlī himself. As noted already, al-Mufīd addressed this matter in his *Awā'il al-maqālāt*. There he said that a *jamāʿa min ahl al-Imāma* (a group of the people of the imamate) argue that nothing is missing from the extant text but that what is missing are the interpretations and explanations (*ta'wīl wa tafsīr*) offered in the text of Imam ʿAlī, and that he agreed with this. In his reply herein, al-Mufīd rejected *āḥād* traditions on the matter, apparently cited by the Sayyid, and said that the extant recension should be accepted. But, he referred to the tradition about Imam ʿAlī's 'edition' and conceded that only the awaited Mahdī had the full and complete text.[40]

In sum, al-Mufīd's theological works document splits within the contemporary Twelver community on a broad range of issues. Al-Mufīd's *furūʿ* attest to a similarly broad range of views. In named pockets of the community outside Baghdad, there were clearly different understandings on issues of theological doctrine, analytical methodology and daily practice. Throughout both sets of materials al-Mufīd consistently advanced the authority of the senior *ʿulamā'* trained in the rationalist sciences over the interpretation of theological issues, jurisprudential methodology and the conduct of practices of daily import to the life of the community. Those of the latter that he addressed were, he argued, not to lapse but were to continue under the guidance of the *fuqahā'* as they were both the most skilled and knowledgeable and because they had been 'entrusted' so to do by the Imams. Non-experts, he suggested, would pay the penalty for failure to recognise the necessity of recourse to the *fuqahā'*. Al-Mufīd was not reticent to claim his status as one such *faqīh*.

But, clearly, on all these points not all, and, in some instances, very few of the faithful – both those whom al-Mufīd himself clearly considered as also members of the *ʿulamā'* class and those describable as 'non-elites' – were of the same understandings and, by his own admission, al-Mufīd's position was often both in the minority and in agreement with that of Sunni interlocutors. The discussion on *al-khums*

---

37 On Ibn al-Junayd, and al-Mufīd's criticism of him, see also Ṭabāṭabā'ī, *An Introduction to Shiʿi Law*, pp. 35–39; McDermott, *Theology of al-Shaikh al-Mufīd*, pp. 305f.

38 On this text, see our *The Formative Period*, pp. 107–108, 152, 181 and n. 28.

39 Al-Mufīd, *al-Masā'il al-Sarawiyya*, pp. 221–225. Al-Mufīd noted that he had critiqued Ibn al-Junayd's essay to those in Egypt whom he attempted to reconcile the *akhbār*.

40 Ibid., pp. 225–226.

stands out for the varied understandings on what was to be done with the revenues during the Imam's absence; of the four on offer only one – his own – included any role for the *'ulamā'*.

Disputation and Authority in the Works of al-Sharīf al-Murtaḍā

Like al-Mufīd, the field has tended to consider his own teacher, al-Sharīf al-Murtaḍā mainly in terms of his contributions to rationalist theological discourse. Indeed, where McDermott, for example, characterised al-Mufīd's recourse to reason as 'defensive' – to demonstrate that 'there is no conflict between Imāmite doctrine and reason' – he suggested that al-Murtaḍā availed himself of reason in the first instance to argue, for example, that the necessity of the imamate can be proved from reason alone.[41] As his teacher also, al-Murtaḍā was active in addressing matters of *uṣūl al-fiqh* and *furū'*, and was much more involved in disputes both with opponents of the faith and with fellow Twelvers than is usually accepted to date,[42] despite the suggestion to the contrary represented by Madelung's 1980 translation of al-Murtaḍā's essay on the legitimacy of working for the established political institution.[43] Attention to other essays of al-Murtaḍā in this genre reveals a further series of different understandings of doctrine and practice within yet other scattered, but named, pockets of the community.

Jawābāt al-Masā'il al-Mawsiliyya al-Thālitha

Al-Murtaḍā's *Jawābāt al-masā'il al-Mawsiliyya al-thālitha* ('Responses to the Third Issues of Mosul'), with answers to 110 questions, is especially interesting as it offers insights into his understanding of issues of both *uṣūl al-fiqh* and *furū'*. In fact, before his first reply, al-Murtaḍā opened with a discussion of *uṣūl al-fiqh*, denouncing reliance on both *al-qiyās* and *khabar al-wāḥid* (sing. of *akhbār al-āḥād*) in the attainment of 'firm knowledge (*'ilm*)' of 'the totality of rulings in the law (*jamī' aḥkām al-shar'iyya*)'. The former, he said, is used by our opponents. 'Some of our shaykhs', he said, approve use of both. But, 'all of our companions (*aṣḥāb*)' reject acting on the

---

[41] McDermott, *Theology of al-Shaikh al-Mufīd*, pp. 374–375, 385. Momen (p. 79) concurs with this evaluation and Halm (p. 51) suggests that 'In him reason (*'aql*) certainly gained the upper hand over tradition (*naql*).'

[42] For lists of these, see Āghā Buzurg al-Ṭihrānī, Muḥammad Muḥsin, *al-Dharī'a ilā taṣānīf al-Shī'a* (Tehran and Najaf, 1357–1398/1938–1978), vol. 20, pp. 329f; vol. 5, pp. 170f; vol. 10, pp. 173f. See also Akhtār, *Early Imamiyyah Shi'ite Thinkers*, pp. 186–190.

[43] W. Madelung, 'A Treatise of the Sharīf al-Murtaḍā on the Legality of Working for the Government *(Mas'ala fī'l-'amal ma'a'l-sulṭān)*', *BSOAS*, 43 (1980), pp. 18–31. This essay was, in fact, a response to critiques of his service to the Būyid 'state' launched from within the community.

basis of both. This, he says, he discussed in his previous reply to the people of Mosul, in 380/990.

Ijmāʿ among the people of 'the truthful sect (*al-firqa al-muḥaqqa*) among the Imāmīs (*min al-Imāmiyya*)', that is, the Twelvers, is a means of attaining *ʿilm* in relation to the *aḥkām* (rulings). 'We have learned', he said, 'that the statement of the Imam – even when he remains unidentified – enters into their words and is not absent from them.' It is a proof (*ḥujja*) because the statement of the Imam is a proof. 'The statement of the Imam … is part of the statements of the Imāmīs.' This was true even during the occultation: 'the truth in all of the *uṣūl* is with the Imāmīs, not their opponents.' The Imam 'is the most knowledgeable and the best in all of the *ijmāʿ*'. It cannot be said that the Imam is not part of *ijmāʿ*. This is because, al-Murtaḍā explained, during the occultation the Imam is present among the *ʿulamāʾ*. 'We do not know who each scholar (*ʿālim*) is among the *ʿulamāʾ*, or each *faqīh* among the *fuqahāʾ* in various countries, while we are sure of the *ijmāʿ* of each *ʿālim* whom we know or do not know. In this case, the Imam is as one whom we do not know of the Imāmī *ʿulamāʾ*.'

There might be issues (*masāʾil*), al-Murtaḍā admitted, which obviated this approach, and where the external aspect (*ẓāhir*) of the Qurʾan or the *sunna* of the Prophet and His family was definitive and its correctness clear. There might be *aḥkām* that are known from the earlier Imams. If so, this was sufficient. If it were asked, he continued, what does one do if the Imāmī community disagrees and there were no clear evidence (*dalīl*) from the Qurʾan or the *sunna*? 'Allah does not leave the believer, who is obligated to follow the law (*al-mukallif*), without a *ḥujja* and a path to *ʿilm* on the basis of which to act', he said. 'If there were a legal ruling (*ḥukm sharʿī*) on which Imāmīs disagreed in our time and it was not possible to rely on their *ijmāʿ* in which the Imam was present', then it would be clear that there had to be firm evidence (*dalīl qāṭiʿ*) on it in the Qurʾan or the *Sunna*. It might be argued, al-Murtaḍā said, that Imāmī shaykhs had relied on the *akhbār* narrated from reliable sources as the bases of their *aḥkām*. They had narrated traditions from the Imams even when the *akhbār* did not agree and when there were no stated preferences.

If this were suggested, al-Murtaḍā said, his answer would be that that all Imāmī Shiʿa, whether they agreed or disagreed, nevertheless rejected recourse to *al-qiyās* and *akhbār al-āḥād*. There were those who maintained that *al-qiyās* was acceptable. But, how could one agree on *aḥkām* based on *akhbār* whose correctness was not certain? *Aṣḥāb al-ḥadīth* narrate what they heard and relate it from their predecessors; it is not necessary or unnecessary that there be a *ḥujja* or *dalīl* in the *aḥkām*. If these *aṣḥāb* relied on a *ḥadīth* that was not definitely correct, this was a mistake. 'Do you not see that they themselves rely on *akhbār al-āḥād* in such issues of *uṣūl al-dīn* as *tawḥīd*, prophecy and the imamate. Any rational person (*ʿāqil*) knows this is not a *ḥujja*.' Some might even hold with the principle of compulsion (*al-jabr*) or of anthropomorphism (*al-tashbīh*) as a result of being led astray by such texts.

One should know, he said in the last few lines of this discussion, that for those issues on which we mention that the Imāmīs stand alone (*infirād al-Imāmiyya fīhī*) one would find explanations by means of evidence (*dalāla*) and paths [of transmitters] (*ṭuruq*) in works on disputation (*khilāf*).[44] The 110 replies that follow cover issues relating to ablutions, prayer, *al-zakāt*, *al-khums*, marriage, divorce, adultery, inheritance, theft and relations with *ahl al-kitāb* (people of the book).[45] Reply 30 was an extended discussion of *al-khums*. The original question seems to have turned on the tax being mandatory on all earnings, on all that is gained in war as well as on items of minerals, items from the sea and from treasure.

If, al-Murtaḍā said, Muslims take something by sword from *dār al-ḥarb* (abode of war), the shares belonging to the Imam are divided into five, four to be shared among those who participated in the war. The fifth is to be further divided, with three shares belonging to the Imam and the remaining three to the orphans of the Prophet's house, the poor and *ibn al-sabīl* (the wayfarer). 'The proof (*ḥujja*) for this', he said, 'is the *ijmāʿ* of the truthful sect.' Clearly addressing a point raised in the original question that itself had been raised by opponents, al-Murtaḍā noted it might be argued that this specification was based on the generality (*ʿumūm*) of Q.8: 41,[46] where the first part says 'a fifth of it is for Allah and for the Messenger and for the near of kin' and only then 'the orphans and the needy and the wayfarer' and that 'you' [i.e., the Shiʿa] have understood the latter also to refer to 'the near of kin'. Then the question is, 'how have you restricted this to the Banū Hāshim in particular?'

The reply, said al-Murtaḍā, would be as follows. The generality specifies the firm *dalīl*. 'The truthful sect' has reached a consensus on the ruling already cited, and this is not sustaining the external sense. 'Near of kin (*qurbā*)' by its generality can refer only to the kin of the Prophet. If by this is specified the kin of the Prophet and his family, then one is going beyond that externality. Similarly, he ended, the phrase 'and the orphans and the needy and the wayfarer' requires including all who fit that description: Muslims, Dhimmīs and the rich and the poor. That generality is not intended. It was meant to be specified.[47]

Reply 45 dealt with the issue of permission being in place for a woman to marry without the approval of her 'guardian (*walī*)'. Al-Murtaḍā opened his reply by stating that Abū Ḥanīfa (d. 148/767), the eponymous 'founder' of the Ḥanafī Sunni legal school, had agreed with this, if she had attained reason (*ʿaqālat*) and had come of age (*kamālat*). He then cited Abū Ḥanīfa's student Abū Yūsuf (d. 182/798) and Muḥammad[48] as having said that marriage required the guardian's approval but that

[44] Al-Murtaḍā, *Jawābāt al-masāʾil al-Mawsilīyyāt al-thālitha*, in *Rasāʾil al-Sharīf al-Murtaḍā*, ed. S. M. Rajāʿī (Qumm, 1405 Sh.), vol. 1, pp. 201–213. The essay is discussed in al-Tihrānī, vol. 5, p. 235. The text of any 'first' series of questions from Mosul is not extant. The text of the second is also found in volume 3 of *Rasāʾil al-Sharīf al-Murtaḍā*, pp. 169–198.

[45] The original question is itself only infrequently stated, and can only be inferred from the points made in the reply.

[46] 'And know that whatever thing you gain, a fifth of it is for Allah and for the Messenger and for the near of kin and the orphans and the needy and the wayfarer, if you believe in Allah and in that which We revealed to Our servant, on the day of distinction, the day on which the two parties met; and Allah has power over all things.'

[47] Al-Murtaḍā, *Jawābāt al-masāʾil*, pp. 226–228.

[48] This is probably a reference to al-Shāfiʿī (d. 204/ 820).

if the woman chose to marry herself it was incumbent on the guardian (*ʿala al-walī*) to give permission. He then cited Mālik b. Anas (d. 179/795) as having said that a woman who was ugly and objectionable did not need permission but someone who did not fit that description did need approval of a guardian. Dāʾūd[49] said that if she was a virgin she did need permission, but that if she were a widow or divorced she did not. 'The *dalīl* of the correctness of our school (*madhhab*) is the *ijmāʿ* of the truthful sect'. Again, clearly addressing a further point raised, al-Murtaḍā noted this might be challenged by citing the Prophet's statement that the marriage of any woman who married without permission of her guardian (*walī*) was invalid (*bāṭil*). The reply, he stated, would be that this statement was a *khabar al-wāḥid* and as such could not lead to *ʿilm*. In addition, al-Murtaḍā said, this text's transmission was contested (*maṭʿūn*), and considered weak by *aṣḥāb al-ḥadīth*. The 'critics (*nuqqād*) of the *ḥadīth*' had also objected to it, although he cited no names or examples of either.

It might be, he closed, that this was an issue particular (*khāṣṣ*) to the community (*al-umma*). This was because the text had been cited with different wording: 'The marriage of any woman who married without permission of her *mawlā* was invalid.' The *mawlā* of the community, he said, was called a *walī*.[50] In what was clearly a follow-up question, reply 46 dealt with whether a woman might marry without witnesses. Al-Murtaḍā stated that they were not a condition (*sharṭ*), though it was better. This, he said, was what Dāʾūd said. Al-Murtaḍā then cited Mālik as saying that if the marriage was not held in secret then witnesses were not needed. The proof of the correctness of 'our statement' was, he continued, 'the *ijmāʿ* of the truthful sect' and also that Allah had spoken of marriage many times without making witnesses a condition. The *ḥadīth* of the Prophet that 'there is no marriage without a just *walī* and witnesses' might be cited, he noted. Although al-Murtaḍā did not here characterise this text as *wāḥid* per se, he said that it did not lead to *ʿilm* and could not be acted upon although it was probable (*muḥtamal*). The statement 'there is no marriage' was made without any denial of correctness or favour/preference (*tafaḍḍul*). It was as if the Prophet had said 'there is no superior (*fāḍilan*) marriage except with a guardian and witnesses'.[51]

Reply 47 addressed the legality of temporary marriage (*mutʿa*). The Imāmī Shiʿa do not disagree about this form of marriage, stated al-Murtaḍā flatly. The distinction was that it is marriage for a 'fixed period of time (*muʿajjal*)' not a marriage which is 'eternal (*muʾabbad*)'. In this form of marriage there were no witnesses.

The evidence for the correctness of this position was, first, 'the *ijmāʿ* of the truthful sect', in which the *ḥujja* (the hidden Imam) was included, and Q.4:24, after the enumeration of those women with whom marriage was forbidden.[52] The marriage

---

[49] This is probably a reference to Dāwūd b. Khalaf al-Ẓāhirī (d. 270/883).

[50] Al-Murtaḍā, *Jawābāt al-masāʾil*, vol. 1, pp. 235–236.

[51] Ibid., vol. 1, pp. 236–237.

[52] The full verse reads: 'Also (prohibited are) women already married, except those whom your right hands possess; thus hath Allah ordained against you. Except for these, all others are lawful, provided ye seek them with gifts from your property, desiring chastity, not lust, seeing

was lawful based on the term used in the *sharīʿa*, the term *istimtāʿ* (deriving benefit). In law it can only refer to a special fixed-term agreement (*ʿiqd*) and was not a matter of 'pleasure'. Otherwise the discussion would revolve around a contract for pleasure and not a fixed-term agreement. He ended the reply by noting that there was no disagreement that such marriage was practised during the time of the Prophet. Without a prohibition against it, it must be permissible.[53] To be sure, most of the other replies are not as detailed as these. Replies 93 to 104, for example, dealt with issues relating to inheritance. These were quite brief, with al-Murtaḍā summarising the issue, offering a ruling and claiming the *ḥujja* for the ruling as the *ijmāʿ* of 'the truthful sect'.

On occasion al-Murtaḍā referred to 'the path of caution (*ṭarīqat al-iḥtiyāṭ*)' as an additional *ḥujja*. Thus, for example, reply 19 referred to a question on *ṣalāt al-ḍuḥā*, the voluntary supererogatory prayer organised in the morning, mid-morning, or late morning, and valued among the Sunnis. Al-Murtaḍā was terse and succinct: '*Ṣalāt al-ḍuḥā* is innovation (*bidʿa*) and is not permitted.' His reasons were 'the path of caution and *ijmāʿ* together'. In reply 27, al-Murtaḍā also refers to both principles when stating that a *dirham* is the least that can be given as *zakāt*.[54]

Jawābāt al-Masāʾil al-Miyyāfāriqīn

A second essay in this genre that repays attention is al-Murtaḍā's *Jawābāt al-masāʾil al-Miyyāfāriqīn* (Diyārbakir), birthplace of the Shiʿi scholar Muḥammad b. Ismāʿīl, Ibn Nubāta (d. 374/984–5).[55] In this series of replies, the questions posed and al-Murtaḍā's replies to two questions on prayer, the first two of the 66 issues raised, are especially interesting. The first reply addressed the question of whether or not the congregational prayer was permissible if led by someone of whose *dīn* (faith) there was uncertainty (*ʿadam al-mawthūq bi dīnihi*). Al-Murtaḍā's reply was brief but to the point. 'The congregational prayer entails much virtue and great reward (*faḍl kathīr wa thawāb kabīr*) if we are certain of the Imam and the correctness of his faith and his justness.' According to the People of the House (i.e., the Imams), someone who does not meet the legal requirements (*fāsiq*) cannot lead the prayer.

The second question was clearly a follow-up: 'Is it permitted to pray the congregational prayer behind [i.e., being led by] an Imāmī and an opponent together? And, are these two prostrations (*rakʿa*) with the sermon (*khuṭba*) to take the place of four [prostrations]?' He again gives a brief and direct reply. 'The congregational prayer entails two prostrations, no more. And, there is no congregating except with a just

---

that ye derive benefit from them, give them their dowers as prescribed; but if, after a dower is prescribed, agree mutually, there is no blame on you, and Allah is All-knowing, All-wise.'

53 Al-Murtaḍā, *Jawābāt al-masāʾil*, vol. 1, p. 237.

54 Ibid., vol. 1, pp. 221, 223. In reply 36 (vol. 1, p. 230) caution is held to mandate a stricter course of action than *ijmāʿ*.

55 McDermott, *Theology of al-Shaikh al-Mufīd*, p. 30, identifies this region as Diyārbakir. On al-Mufīd's essay apparently to the same individual, see al-Ṭihrānī, vol. 5, p. 196.

Imam, or with he whom the just Imam has designated (*naṣabahu*). If this situation does not obtain, pray the noontime prayer of four prostrations. He who is compelled to pray with someone whose leadership is not permitted owing to *taqiyya* must thereafter pray the noontime prayer of four [prostrations].'[56]

Reply 66 addressed matters relating to *al-khums*: 'Is *al-khums* to the family of the Prophet obligatory on booty (*al-ghanīma*) [taken] in the land of polytheism (*al-shirk*) or on all profits (*al-makāsib*), commerce (*al-tijāra*), property (*al-ʿaqār*) and agriculture (*al-zarʿ*), or in this period, is it not necessary [to render this] to them?' Al-Murtaḍā replied that *al-khums* is to be levied on all booty taken in raiding (*al-ghazw*) from the property of *ahl al-shirk*. He added that the levy is also necessary on minerals, treasure and what is taken from the sea, and also on all profits from commerce, agriculture and manufacturing on an annual basis.

After the time of the Prophet the shares of Allah and the Prophet belong to the Imam who takes the latter's place, in addition to the share of the Imam that belongs to 'the near of kin'. The remaining shares belonged to the orphans of the Prophet's family, the poor and the *abnā' al-sabīl*. 'It is as if', al-Murtaḍā said, 'it is divided into six shares, and three of these belong to the Imam, on him be peace, and three of them belong to the Prophet's family, on him and them be peace.' This is true, however, as a substitute for alms. If, he said, 'in some periods' this was forbidden 'then alms were permitted to them'.[57]

These questions clearly had their origins in challenges facing pockets of believers living cheek-by-jowl with, and perhaps as a minority among, non-Twelvers. Al-Murtaḍā's knowledge of and affinity for citing Sunni opinions on some issues might have been especially useful, and welcome, for those in such situations on selected issues such as marriage, for example. The appearance of questions on temporary (*mutʿa*) marriage in the *masā'il* addressed to al-Murtaḍā, as in the case of al-Mufīd in *al-Sarawiyya*, clearly suggests that even outside Baghdad the community was now well identified with this distinctive practice and being challenged on it.

Al-Murtaḍā's reply to those in Diyārbakir on *al-khums* lacks the reference to *ijmāʿ* in his reply to the Mosulīs on the same subject, but taken together they exemplify his perceived understanding, based on the questions submitted, of the need to stress 'first principles' among these outlying Twelver communities. The question on *ṣalāt al-ḍuhā* and, from those in Diyārbakir, on the congregational prayer suggests, however, that believers – adjudged aware, or not, of the finer points of doctrine and practice – were perhaps also under pressure locally to be less open in their display of some of these distinguishing practices or lacking in suitable 'personnel', or some combination of the two. What might be judged lacking in these are overt references to the authority of the community's senior *'ulamā'* in a manner as open as those

[56] Al-Murtaḍā, *Jawābāt al-masā'il al-Miyyāfāriqīn*, in *Rasā'il al-Sharīf al-Murtaḍā*, vol. 1, pp. 271–272. This is identical to the position offered by al-Mufīd in *al-Muqniʿa*, p. 163, where he stated the prayer 'lapsed'. In neither case was there any reference to the Imam-*faqīh*/*nā'ib* formulation with respect to this prayer. For an introduction to this, see our essays cited in n. 2.

[57] Al-Murtaḍā, *al-Miyyāfāriqīn*, vol. 1, p. 306.

offered by al-Mufīd, for example, in his several references to these as having been 'entrusted'.

In other works, however, al-Murtaḍā was less reticent to express his views on the responsibilities of the senior clerics during the occultation. In his more general *Jumal al-ʿilm wa'l-ʿamal*, al-Murtaḍā was perfectly clear about the handling of *al-zakāt* during the occultation: 'The best and preferable is delivering *al-zakāt* – especially with regard to properties that are visible ... to the Imam, and to his successors deputising on his behalf (*al-nā'ibīn ʿanhu*). If that is not possible', he then says 'its extraction is to the trustworthy *fuqahā'* for them to deliver it where it is due.'[58] If al-Murtaḍā did not formally refer to the status of the *faqīh* as *nā'ib* (deputy), or did he use the term 'entrust' as had al-Mufīd, his intent was certainly clear.

In these particular *masā'il*, if al-Murtaḍā may not have felt it opportune, for the reasons outlined above at least, to go further in these replies to obligate formally the lay classes to follow the rulings of the senior, rationalist clerics, his preferences were, also, not unclear. His critique of recourse to the traditions and his detailed delineation of *ijmāʿ* – in a manner that complemented the definition offered by al-Mufīd – and his repeated recourse to it in the Mosuli *masā'il* were clearly the product of his perception of the need to assert the claims of the senior clerics to authority over the use of *ijmāʿ* in particular and the interpretation of doctrine and practice generally. The Diyārbakir replies lacked a discussion of *uṣūl al-fiqh* similar to that given the Mosulīs. But, the implication in his reference herein to the absence of a proper prayer leader as resulting in the failure to gain the *faḍl kathīr wa thawāb kabīr* that accrued from performing the prayer with the proper Imam was clear enough. The two questions are indicative of practice – in the case of question 2, the suggestion clearly being that a Sunni was leading the prayer, if only jointly. Based on this reply, was not the next, at least implicit, step for the Diyārbakir community to request that an appropriate individual be sent out, implicitly also, as designated by such a clearly already-trusted authority as al-Murtaḍā himself, and thereupon to cease efforts to undertake, and to gain the reward from, this prayer by any means other than those he was setting down? In this manner, they would be firmer in their public declaration of their faith than these questions implied they had been to date. Al-Murtaḍā's subsequent condemnation of chess and backgammon suggests his view that a correspondingly 'lax' attitude to 'leisure' was also in circulation among the community in Diyārbakir.[59]

Summary and Conclusions

To date, discussions of the pre-modern evolution of key points in Twelver doctrine and practice have mainly addressed the formulations of a relative handful of Twelver

[58] Al-Murtaḍā, *Jumal al-ʿilm wa'l-ʿamal* in *Rasā'il al-Sharīf al-Murtaḍā*, vol. 3, p. 81. On this work, see also al-Tihrānī, vol. 5, p. 144.

[59] Al-Murtaḍā, *al-Miyyāfāriqīn*, p. 295.

scholars long known in Shiʿi studies. Such an approach necessarily encourages an understanding of the process of the ever-expanding authority of senior clerics, trained in the rationalist religious sciences over both as linear and inevitable. Research into exchanges over a variety of issues of doctrine and practice in the Safawid period has recovered evidence of the participation of 'non-elites' in the period's spiritual discourse such that a more dynamic picture thereof has emerged.

For the earlier Būyid period, works produced by the same very few scholars that the field has long considered representative of trends in Shiʿi discourse over its history also offer indications of a more vibrant spiritual discourse over matters of doctrine and practice and the authority to interpret both than has hitherto been suggested. Taken together, the works by al-Shaykh al-Mufīd and al-Sharīf al-Murtaḍā considered herein reveal efforts by both to encourage acceptance of and to cement further their own role and that of clerics trained in the rationalist tradition generally within the community as the legatees of the Hidden Imam. In these works the link between recourse to rationalist interpretation and the leading, if not exclusive, authority being claimed by clerical proponents thereof over both the articulation of doctrine and practice, and certain of the Imam's practical responsibilities during the latter's absence is clearly on offer. Although the two evidently disagreed on some particular matters, on this later point they were clearly in agreement.

At the same time, and more interestingly, these works also indicate that, in the process of advancing both their general claims to such authority and specific rulings on particular points of doctrine and practice, both men were engaged in a series of 'uphill struggles' on what today might seem to be some very basic, long-accepted points of doctrine and practice. On issues of both theology and *furūʿ* their interpretations frequently corresponded to Sunni interpretations and were otherwise more often in the minority than not.

Al-Mufīd and al-Murtaḍā did not identify their Twelver interlocutors to the degree that modern scholarship would certainly find desirable. Nevertheless, the information on these available in these particular works points to both 'centre/ periphery' and socio-economic dimensions to these differing understandings of doctrine and practice – both within Baghdad itself, namely the 'Qur'an riots', between Baghdad and outlying pockets of the faithful and even within those outlying centres – as possibly underlying features of such disagreements and axes along which to base further research. Taken together with the already well-documented external challenges faced by the community in this period of its history, the future course of Twelver Shiʿism, let alone its very survival, could not have appeared to the many different groups of faithful, let alone the faith's many and varied sets of opponents at the time, as the foregone conclusion it seems to many today.

PART VI
THEOLOGY

Introduction

Wilferd Madelung

Scholarly studies of Shiʿi theology have rapidly progressed in quantity and quality over the past century. Their progress has been greatly facilitated by the large-scale edition and publication of Shiʿi theological literature, even though research continues to rely primarily on manuscripts. During the 19th century Shiʿi theology was studied mostly on the basis of Sunni sources, heresiographies, refutations and polemics. The relatively few Shiʿi works published in lithographs in the East rarely reached Western university libraries and were largely ignored by Western scholars. Long seen through a Sunni perspective as Islamic heterodoxy, Shiʿi theology can now be viewed in its own right.

The schism dividing Shiʿism and Sunnism about the leadership of the Muslim community occurred after the death of the Prophet, long before the development of theology as a scholarly discipline in Islam. The Shiʿa thus appeared in history first as a politico-religious opposition movement to the caliphate. The movement soon divided further as sections recognised different members of the Family of the Prophet as their Imams and began to form separate communities within Islam with their own doctrinal tradition. Theology developed separately in these communities as it did in the various early Sunni schools of thought, and there was never a single dominant Sunni or Shiʿi theology. Traditionalist revelationist, rationalist and mystical esoteric tendencies were variously represented from the outset in Shiʿi and Sunni Islam. The evolution of the theological tradition of the major surviving branches of the Shiʿa, Zaydiyya, Imāmiyya and Ismāʿīliyya until modern times can largely be studied on the basis of their extant literary heritage, though much early literature has been lost.

Systematic study of Zaydī theology on the basis of Zaydī manuscripts from Yaman was initiated by Rudolf Strothmann (d. 1960). Strothmann first recognised the pivotal role of the early Zaydī Imam al-Qāsim b. Ibrāhīm al-Rassī (d. 246/860) in the development of Zaydī theological thought and described him as the 'inaugurator of deliberately Zaydī literature'. Imam al-Qāsim, according to Strothmann, broadly espoused Muʿtazilī theological doctrine in his writings. Before him the Zaydiyya had been divided in their allegiance to various partisan leaders, with widely differing theological tendencies and views. Other scholars in the first half of the 20th century argued that the original Zaydī theological doctrine was identical with that of the Muʿtazilī school of Baghdad.

Subsequent research has shown that early Zaydī theology was consistently and explicitly anti-Muʿtazilī. It rejected the basic Muʿtazilī thesis of the intermediate status of the unrepentant grave sinner (*ṣāḥib kabīra, fāsiq*) between the faithful believer and the unbeliever, and upheld strict predestination against the Muʿtazilī doctrine of human free will. Although it espoused an anti-anthropomorphic concept of God like the Muʿtazila, it disagreed substantially with Muʿtazilī teaching about the divine attributes. It is now evident that early Zaydī theology, as set forth by Sulaymān b. Jarīr and other Zaydī scholars in the *kalām* debates of the 2nd/8th century, was essentially identical with contemporary Ibāḍī Khārijī theological teaching except for the doctrine concerning the imamate. This essential agreement was noted at the time by the early Kūfan Ibāḍī scholar ʿAbd Allāh b. Yazīd al-Fazārī as well as the Sunni traditionalist scholar al-Qāsim b. Sallām (d. 224/839) in his *Kitāb al-īmān*.

Imam al-Qāsim b. Ibrāhīm also did not adopt Muʿtazilī theological principles and concepts, even though he sharply deviated from early Zaydī predestinarian doctrine to emphasise the justice of God in rewarding and punishing in accordance with freely chosen human acts of obedience or disobedience. His theological thought was distinctly more rationalist than the traditionalist early Zaydī theology and was partly formed in debates with Christians in Egypt. Concerning the unicity of God and His attributes, his teaching differed from Muʿtazilī doctrine by its insistence on the absolute otherness of the Creator to all creation and His essential goodness (*jūd*). In the formulation of his theology, however, Imam al-Qāsim avoided as far as possible distancing himself expressly from earlier Zaydī doctrine. Like the early Zaydiyya, he did not concede an intermediate status to the unrepentant Muslim grave sinner.

Imam al-Qāsim's rationalist and anti-predestinarian teaching did, however, open the door to Muʿtazilī theology among the Zaydiyya. His grandson Yaḥyā al-Hādī ila'l-Ḥaqq (d. 298/911), the founder of the Zaydī imamate in Yaman, mostly adopted the theological doctrine of Abu'l-Qāsim al-Balkhī (d. 319/931), the contemporary head of the Baghdādī school of the Muʿtazila. As noted by Strothmann, the Zaydiyya in Yaman, in championing the teaching of Imams al-Qāsim and al-Hādī, have ever remained predominantly Muʿtazilī. The followers of Imam al-Qāsim in the Caspian coastal regions of northern Iran, however, embraced Baṣran Muʿtazilī school doctrine. Several Caspian Zaydī Imams and prominent ʿAlids studied theology in Baghdad and Rayy under the Baṣran Muʿtazilī scholars Abū ʿAbd Allāh al-Baṣrī (d. 369/979) and Qāḍī ʿAbd al-Jabbār (d. 415/1022) and explicitly supported their teaching in their theological works. Recent research by H. Ansari and S. Schmidtke has highlighted the continued close cooperation between Zaydī and Muʿtazilī scholars in northern Iran during the 5th/11th and 6th/12th centuries.[1] Among the Zaydī Daylamites, in contrast, the theological teaching of Imam al-Ḥasan al-Nāṣir li'l-Ḥaqq (d. 304/917) prevailed. He agreed with Imam al-Qāsim's anti-predestinarian position,

[1] See Hassan Ansari and Sabine Schmidtke, 'Muʿtazilism in Rayy and Astarābād: Abū'l-Faḍl al-ʿAbbās b. Sharwīn', *Studia Iranica*, 41 (2012), pp. 57–100, and related articles.

but in general backed early Kūfan Zaydī and Imāmī Shi'i theological views, polemically criticising the Mu'tazilī doctrine.

Much of the literary heritage of the Caspian Qāsimiyya, including many Mu'tazilī works of the school of Qāḍī 'Abd al-Jabbār, was transferred to Yaman in the age of Imam Aḥmad al-Mutawakkil 'alā Allāh (d. 566/1170), who recognised the Baṣran Mu'tazilī teaching of the Caspian Imams as equally authoritative as the teaching of Imam al-Hādī current in Yaman. Baṣran Mu'tazilī doctrine was promoted in Yaman especially by the Qāḍī Shams al-Dīn Ja'far b. Abī Yaḥyā (d. 573/1777) and his school. There was, however, opposition to it, most vigorously from the Muṭarrifiyya, a Zaydī sectarian movement founded by Muṭarrif b. Shihāb in the 5th/11th century. Muṭarrif recognised the teaching of Imams al-Qāsim b. Ibrāhīm and the early Yamanī Imams as authoritative, but interpreted it, elaborating a theological system that deviated substantially from the Mu'tazilī doctrine. He taught that the course of the world after its original creation was governed entirely by the natural causality of four elements and that God would interfere in it only by occasional miracles. Widespread throughout northern Yaman during the 6th/12th century, the Muṭarrifiyya were severely persecuted and nearly wiped out by Imam 'Abd Allāh b. Ḥamza al-Manṣūr billāh (d. 614/1217), a strong supporter of Baṣran Mu'tazilī theology.

The theological doctrine of the last school of Mu'tazilī thought, founded by Abu'l-Ḥusayn al-Baṣrī (d. 436/1044), became known among the Zaydiyya in Yaman through the works of Rukn al-Dīn Ibn al-Malāḥimī (d. 536/1141) which reached Yaman in the later 6th/12th century. It was, however, to gain less favour among the Zaydiyya than among the Imāmī Shi'a in Iraq and Iran. In the 7th/13th century the Sayyid Ḥumaydān b. Yaḥyā composed several popular treatises denouncing the Mu'tazila and many of the subtleties of their theological thought. He praised the basic simplicity of the teaching of the early Zaydī Imams al-Qāsim b. Ibrāhīm and al-Nāṣir li'l-Ḥaqq. Mu'tazilī theology was also criticised in the neo-Sunni Zaydī school founded by the Sayyid Muḥammad b. Ibrāhīm al-Wazīr (d. 840/1436), which accepted the Sunni canonical *ḥadīth* collections as authoritative and inclined to traditionalist and Ash'arī theological views. It reached its peak in the teaching of Muḥammad b. 'Alī al-Shawkānī (d. 1250/1834), *muftī* and chief judge under several Imams.

With its strong rationalist and sober bent, Zaydī Islam has been generally averse to mystical and esoteric thought and mostly denounced Sufi practices except asceticism. It opposed all Sunni Sufi orders. In the 8th/14th century the Zaydī scholar 'Alī b. 'Abd Allāh b. Abī al-Khayr and his disciple Ibrāhīm al-Kayna'ī (d. 793/1391) founded a moderate Sufi order advocating ascetic practices and upholding Mu'tazilī theology. The order initially spread throughout northern Yaman but did not survive long.[2]

The theology of the moderate majority of the Imāmiyya or Twelver Shi'a was generally assumed by Western scholars in the early 20th century to have been Mu'tazilī originally and throughout history except for its cardinal doctrine of the permanent,

---

[2] See W. Madelung, 'Zaydī Attitudes to Sufism', in F. de Jong and B. Radtke, ed., *Islamic Mysticism Contested* (Leiden, 1990), pp. 124–144.

divinely installed imamate. This moderate, generally quietist Imāmiyya was seen as being in discord with a more militant, 'extremist' Shiʿa (*ghulāt*) that first emerged among the Kaysāniyya, asserting the imamate and Mahdīship of Muḥammad b. al-Ḥanafiyya and adopting Gnostic, dualist and antinomian beliefs from the various religions then established in Mesopotamia. As the Kaysāniyya disintegrated, many of the extremists joined the followers of the Ḥusaynid Imams, especially in the time of Imam Jaʿfar al-Ṣādiq (d. 148/765), bringing their heterodox theological thought with them. The *ghulāt* came to form a permanent wing in the Imāmiyya, but always remained ideologically separate from the moderate main body.

The hypothesis of an original identity or close affinity between Imāmī and Muʿtazilī theology became untenable after the publication of al-Ashʿarī's *Maqālāt al-Islāmiyyīn* and al-Khayyāṭ's *Kitāb al-intiṣār*. These and other heresiographical texts provided solid evidence of a sharp conflict between Imāmī and Muʿtazilī scholars in the early *kalām* debates of the 2nd/8th century. The Imāmī *kalām* theologians disagreed with fundamental Muʿtazilī principles in affirming that God wills and creates all evil as well as good in the world, that His foreknowledge of events is not eternal and immutable, and in ascribing motion to God in His action. If there was later agreement between Imāmiyya and Muʿtazila, it was secondary, not original.

Progressive study of Imāmī religious literature revealed the complexity of the development of later Imāmī theological thought. In the Būyid age, the prominent scholars of the school of Baghdad explicitly espoused Muʿtazilī theology on the unicity and justice of God, but upheld the Imāmī tenet of intercession of the Imams for the sinners of their community against the Muʿtazilī thesis of eternal punishment of the unrepentant grave sinner. While the Shaykh al-Mufīd (d. 413/1022) adopted the doctrine of the Muʿtazilī school of Baghdad, his pupils, the Sharīf al-Murtaḍā (d. 436/1044) and the Shaykh al-Ṭāʾifa Abū Jaʿfar al-Ṭūsī (d. 460/1067), backed Baṣran Bahshamī Muʿtazilī school doctrine. In their chapter in this volume on 'al-Shaykh al-Ṭūsī', H. Ansari and S. Schmidtke present evidence that in his later, mostly lost theological works, Shaykh al-Ṭūsī endorsed some of the views of the reformist Muʿtazilī theologian Abu'l-Ḥusayn al-Baṣrī (d. 436/1044) against Bahshamī doctrine. Abu'l-Ḥusayn al-Baṣrī's theological views, as further developed by Rukn al-Dīn Ibn al-Malāḥimī (d. 536/1141), were comprehensively backed by Sadīd al-Dīn Maḥmūd al-Ḥimmaṣī al-Rāzī in his large *Kitāb al-Munqidh min al-taqlīd* completed in 581/1185. They evidently had a wider impact among the Imāmiyya than among the Zaydiyya.

During the age of Mongol domination, philosophical and mystical Sufi theological thought gradually came to prevail over *kalām* theology among the Imāmiyya in Iran and Iraq. Naṣīr al-Dīn al-Ṭūsī (d. 672/1274) first introduced some of the theological teaching of Avicenna into his writings addressed to the Imāmī community. In the second half of the 9th/15th century, before the rise of the Safawid state in Iran, Ibn Abī Jumhūr al-Aḥsāʾī produced a synthesis of *kalām* theology, Avicennan philosophy, *ishrāqī* philosophy of Shihāb al-Dīn al-Suhrawardī, and Sufi thought of the school of Ibn al-ʿArabī. The same currents of thought were represented in the theological teaching of the so-called School of Isfahan during the Safawid age. The school reached its peak in the philosophical theology of Mullā Ṣadrā (d. 1050/1641) which transformed traditional Islamic philosophy by asserting the primacy of existence over essence and substantive motion. This transformation allowed Mullā Ṣadrā to revive and reinterpret some early Imāmī tenets, in particular that of *badā'* (change of decision in view of a change of circumstances), that had been largely explained away by the Muʿtazilī and philosophical theologians before him. While at the higher level of theological thought among the late medieval and modern Imāmiyya philosophy largely replaced *kalām*, at a lower credal level Muʿtazilī principles were mostly retained.

The doctrine of *imāma*, the imamate, was for the Imāmiyya a theological issue, not merely a legal question as it was for other Muslims including the Zaydiyya. The early Imams Muḥammad al-Bāqir and especially Jaʿfar al-Ṣādiq taught that God would never for a moment leave the earth without an Imam to guide mankind. *Imāma* was closely tied to *nubuwwa*, prophethood. Prophets were the Imams of their age; prophets and Imams were the *ḥujja*s, proofs or arguments, of God unto mankind.

It was about their doctrine of the imamate that the Imāmiyya were commonly divided into moderates and *ghulāt*. Those who in general adhered to Muʿtazilī theology and other rationalist theologians like the Imāmī participants in the early *kalām* debates mostly held that the Imams were protected by God from all error and sin, were granted knowledge of everything God granted His prophets, but were entirely human, created and ruled by God.[3] The Imams were tools of God through whom He guides, rules and judges mankind, but they have no autonomous share in His creation, rule and judgement. There were other followers of the Imams who viewed them as endowed with superhuman knowledge and powers. The early Imams had also stated that if God were ever to leave the earth without an Imam, it would dissolve in mud (*sākhat*). Such statements could be interpreted as attributing a cosmological role to the Imams in the creation and rule of the physical world.

Belief in the superhuman, semi-divine nature of the Imams was widespread in the later and modern Imāmiyya among scholars generally espousing philosophical and mystical theology, often with an *Akhbārī* traditionalist bent opposed to *Uṣūlī* rationalism. Some recent and contemporary scholars in the East and West have proposed that belief in the superhuman nature of the Imams and in their being endowed with spiritual knowledge transcending mere human reason prevailed in the original Imāmī Shiʿa and in Shiʿism in general. Most notably, H. Corbin (d. 1978) maintained that mystical thought in Islam originated among the early Shiʿa. M. A. Amir-Moezzi has argued in his *Le Guide divin dans le Shîʿisme originel* that original Shiʿism should not be viewed as a politico-religious opposition movement, but as an esoteric religion committed to secret teaching reserved for the trusted few followers of the Imams upon an oath of initiation. The Imams were recognised as pre-existent,

[3] See al-Kulaynī, *al-Uṣūl min al-kāfī*, ed. ʿAlī Akbar al-Ghaffārī (Tehran, 1388/1968), vol. 1, p. 144, where Imam Jaʿfar is quoted as stating that God does not sorrow (*ya'saf*), is pleased or resents, like human beings. Rather He creates supporters (*awliyā'*) for Himself who experience sorrow and pleasure on His behalf, yet are *makhlūqūn marbūbūn*.

angelic, semi-divine beings and were dispensers of a knowledge revealed to them by a cosmic Intellect (*ʿaql*) that transcended human reason. So-called *ghulāt* teaching was in fact the teaching of the Imams which prevailed among the Imāmiyya until the *ghayba* of the Twelfth Imam, when Muʿtazilī rationalism transformed the original Shiʿa into an ordinary, publicly proselytising sect and denounced the original Shiʿa as *ghulāt*. This view of the original Shiʿa is, however, difficult to maintain as all early sources, Shiʿi and anti-Shiʿi, consistently indicate that the distinction between moderate Shiʿa and *ghulāt* was well known throughout the age of the presence of the Imams. In the chapter in this volume on 'Early Imāmī Theology as reflected in the *Kitāb al-Kāfī* of al-Kulaynī' it is proposed that although the theology taught by the early Imams of the Imāmiyya, especially Imam Jaʿfar al-Ṣādiq, differed substantially from Muʿtazilī doctrine in various respects, its rationalism essentially agreed with that of the Muʿtazila in denying any claim to transcendent esoteric knowledge.

It is now evident, however, that *ghulāt* interpretation of the statements of the Imams as described by Amir-Moezzi was common in the age of the presence of the Imams, certainly from the time of Imam Jaʿfar. Out of the Imāmī *ghulāt* tradition arose various sectarian movements which developed their own doctrinal and literary tradition separate from the main body of the Imāmiyya, although they adhered to the Ḥusaynid line of Imams. Most notable is the Nuṣayriyya, in modern times also known as ʿAlawiyya, founded by Muḥammad b. Nuṣayr al-Namīrī in the time of the 11th Imam, al-Ḥasan al-ʿAskarī (d. 260/874). Nuṣayrī theological doctrine was partly founded on the writings of the prominent Imāmī *ghālī* al-Mufaḍḍal b. ʿUmar al-Juʿfī (d. before 179/795), author of the *Kitāb al-haft wa'l-aẓilla* (*Book of the Seven and the Shadows*), and espouses deification of the Imams, metempsychosis and antinomian repudiation of the *sharīʿa* of Islam. Early Nuṣayrī doctrine has been the subject of comprehensive study by H. Halm and,[4] most recently, by M. Bar-Asher and A. Kofsky.[5] Little is known, however, about any later developments in Nuṣayrī religious thought.

Ismaili Shiʿism has commonly been viewed and denounced in Sunni Islam as an arch-heresy, and anti-Ismaili polemical literature comprising systematic distortion and fictitious slander has a long tradition. In the early 20th century, Western scholars of Islam mostly gave credit to these strident polemics and on their basis described the Ismāʿīliyya as originating in a plot by Persian dualists to destroy Islam from the inside and the Fatimid Imams as being worshipped by them as God-kings. The story of Ismaili studies based on Ismaili literature in the past century has been briefly recounted by F. Daftary in his contribution to the present volume. Ismaili theology must now be viewed as an authentically Islamic development from early

---

[4] See in general his *Die islamische Gnosis: Die extreme Schia and die ʿAlawiten* (Zurich, 1982), and the article 'Nuṣayriyya' in *EI2*, vol. 8, pp. 145–148.

[5] See especially their *The Nuṣayrī-ʿAlawī Religion: An Enquiry into its Theology and Liturgy* (Leiden, 2002). A comprehensive study of the religion and history of the Nuṣayriyya has most recently been produced by Y. Friedman, *The Nuṣayrī-ʿAlawīs* (Leiden, 2010).

Imāmī religious thought of the age of Imam Jaʿfar al-Ṣādiq over whose succession the Ismāʿīliyya separated from the Twelver Shiʿa.

Ismaili theology has always upheld the concept of an entirely transcendent God who is above existence and non-existence, beyond recognition and all attributes that *kalām* theology ascribed to Him. He created the world by a single Command (*amr*) and is not further involved in its creation. Ismaili doctrine from its pre-Fatimid beginnings also elaborated a cyclical hiero-history of seven Speaker-Prophets, each followed by a Legatee (*waṣī*) and seven Imams. The cycle of the sixth Speaker-Prophet, Muḥammad, was closed with Imam Muḥammad b. Ismāʿīl b. Jaʿfar who went into concealment and was expected to reappear as the Mahdī, when he would proclaim the hidden inner meaning (*bāṭin*) of all previous religions.

The cosmology of the pre-Fatimid Ismaili *daʿwa* has been analysed and described by H. Halm as gnostic in a wide sense.[6] It was formulated in the epistles of ʿAbdān, the first author of the *daʿwa*. In the early Fatimid age, the Transoxanian *dāʿī* Muḥammad al-Nasafī (d. 332/943) introduced Pythagorean numerology and Neoplatonic philosophical thought and terminology into Ismaili cosmology and distanced himself expressly from the 'unscientific' cosmological doctrine of the Mufaḍḍal ideological tradition espoused by the Imāmī *ghulāt*.[7] It was a momentous turn away from the early Imāmī religious tradition towards the contemporary philosophical thought of Greek origin. As the pre-Fatimid *daʿwa* had split before the rise of the Fatimid caliphate, al-Nasafī's reformed doctrine was at first ignored by the *daʿwa* of the Fatimid Imams, but under the fourth Fatimid Imam-caliph, al-Muʿizz li-Dīn Allāh (d. 365/975), it was absorbed into the Fatimid *daʿwa*.

The pre-Fatimid Ismāʿīliyya had already developed a broad interest in all contemporary disciplines of science, whether scriptural, rational or occult. ʿAbdān is known to have arranged his extensive literary work as an encyclopaedia of the various contemporary sciences. After him the Ikhwān al-Ṣafāʾ, a group of philosophically minded scholars in Baṣra, composed their encyclopaedia of 51 epistles on all scientific disciplines. The Ikhwān al-Ṣafāʾ formulated Ismaili thought while outside the Fatimid *daʿwa*. The long-disputed date of their activity can now be definitely established as the first quarter of the 4th century of *hijra* (912–936) from the discovery by M. Fierro and P. Carusi that the author of the *Rutbat al-ḥakīm* and *Ghāyat al-ḥakīm* (Picatrix) was Maslama b. al-Qāsim al-Qurṭubī al-Zayyāt (d. 353/964), not Maslama al-Majrīṭī (d. ca. 398/1007) as was often assumed.[8] Maslama al-Qurṭubī visited Baṣra in 325/946–947 and joined the activity of the Ikhwān al-Ṣafāʾ there. He returned

---

6 H. Halm, *Kosmologie und Heilslehre der frühen Ismāʿīlīya* (Wiesbaden, 1978).

7 See W. Madelung, '*Kawn al-ʿĀlam:* The Cosmogony of the Ismaili *dāʿī* Muḥammad b. Aḥmad al-Nasafī', in B. D. Craig, ed., *Ismaili and Fatimid Studies in Honor of Paul E. Walker* (Chicago, 2010), pp. 23–31.

8 See M. Fierro, 'Bāṭinism in al-Andalus: Maslama b. Qāsim al-Qurṭubī (d. 353/964), Author of the *Rutbat'l-hakīm* and the *Ghāyat al-ḥakīm (Picatrix)*', *SI*, 84 (1996), pp. 87–112; P. Carusi, 'Alchimia Islamica e Religione: La legittimazione di una scienza della natura', *OM*, NS, 19 (2000), pp. 461–502.

to Cordova with the 51 epistles and there composed his abridged version *al-Risāla al-Jāmiʿa*. The *Epistles* of the Ikhwān al-Ṣafāʾ apparently never became part of the Fatimid *daʿwa* literature. They were, however, adopted by the post-Fatimid Ṭayyibī *daʿwa* in Yaman and were then attributed to one of the concealed Imams before the rise of the Fatimids.

The 4th/10th century has appropriately been called by L. Massignon the Ismaili century in Islam. Ismaili openness to all currents of contemporary intellectual life and broad involvement in scholarship reached a peak at that time, as reflected in the activity of the Ikhwān al-Ṣafāʾ. After the Fatimid conquest of Egypt in 358/969, Cairo became the main centre of scholarship and learning in the Islamic world under the patronage of the Fatimid Imam-caliphs. Ismaili theology, however, remained a secret subject confined to its initiates. The progressively extreme heretication of Ismailism and effort to exclude it from Islam by the majority of Muslims led to communal seclusion, socially as well as intellectually, and strict concealment, especially where the Fatimid government could not provide protection and security.

Before the fall of the Fatimid caliphate, the Ismāʿīliyya split into two major branches with separate ideological traditions which have survived to the present. The Nizārī branch broke away from the Fatimid *daʿwa*, proclaiming from its stronghold in Alamūt a new *daʿwa* which placed the Imam of the age at the centre of its theology, acknowledging his supreme teaching authority and viewing him as the visible aspect of the utterly transcendent God. The Mongol conquest of Alamūt in 654/1256 put an end to the public activity of the new *daʿwa* and forced the Nizārī community into strict concealment and secret underground teaching. The great expansion of Sufi orders espousing mystical thought during the age of Mongol domination permitted temporary alliances of the Nizārī Imams with some of them. Nizārī religious thought and practice also adapted to varying religious environments in India, Central Asia, Iran and Syria. Unlike the Imāmiyya in Safawid Iran, however, the Nizārī Ismāʿīliyya did not engage with the major philosophical currents of the age.

The *daʿwa* of the Ṭayyibī branch saw itself as a continuation of the Fatimid *daʿwa* in the absence of the Imam. The Ṭayyibī *daʿwa* in Yaman preserved a large portion of the literary heritage of the Fatimid *daʿwa*, but added the Epistles of the Ikhwān al-Ṣafāʾ to it, according high authority to their teaching. Ṭayyibī esoteric doctrine also adopted the reformed cosmological system of the Fatimid *dāʿī* Ḥamīd al-Dīn al-Kirmānī (d. 411/1020), which recognised ten superior Intellects in accordance with the philosophy of al-Fārābī. In the Fatimid *daʿwa*, al-Kirmānī's cosmology generally had not been preferred to the earlier cosmological doctrine of al-Nasafī recognising a single Universal Intellect and a single Universal Soul. On the basis of al-Kirmānī's system, Ṭayyibī esoteric *ḥaqāʾiq* doctrine elaborated a gnostic theory of the origins of the world with a mythical 'drama in heaven' according to which the Third Intellect, in seeking to occupy the rank of the Second Intellect, fell behind the Tenth Intellect and thus produced the lower material world. Ṭayyibī esoteric doctrine has been analysed perceptively and with empathy by H. Corbin. Much of its extensive literature, however, has not yet been the subject of scholarly study and remains unpublished in manuscript.

As Ismaili theology and religious thought have been studied on the basis of Ismaili sources, it has become evident that from its origins in the 3rd/9th century it radically turned away from Islamic traditionalism, strictly adhering to the literal meaning of the Qur'an and the *sunna* attributed to the Prophet Muḥammad and his Companions. Yet its motivation was entirely rooted in the preaching of the Prophet and in the Qur'an. Muḥammad had seen himself in a line of divinely guided prophets and Imams whose guidance he was called to renew for his own age and its circumstances. Divine guidance, the Ismāʿīliyya held, must inevitably change as human circumstances change, although there was also a hidden inner meaning in it that never changed and would become fully apparent towards the end of this world. The truth of their theology could not be derived from the exoteric literal meaning of the Qur'an, but by its consistency with the concealed inner meaning of the Holy Book revealed through *ta'wīl* interpretation. Despite all the attacks and accusations, the Ismaili Shiʿis have always viewed themselves as an authentic part of the Muslim world.

17

Early Imāmī Theology as Reflected in the *Kitāb al-kāfī* of al-Kulaynī

Wilferd Madelung

The development of early Imāmī Shiʿi theology has been studied in Western scholarship primarily on the basis of heresiographical and doxographical literature. This literature, especially the *Maqālāt al-Islāmiyyīn* of al-Ashʿarī, provides plentiful information on the theological views put forward and defended in the early *kalām* debates with other Muslim and non-Muslim scholars in which several Imāmī scholars, most prominent among them Hishām b. al-Ḥakam (d. 179/795–796), were engaged. The doctrine of the Imams, who did not participate in *kalām* debates but whose teaching was considered as authoritative and was elaborated by the Imāmī scholars, is never expressly quoted in these sources. The evolution of the teaching of the Imams must be examined primarily on the basis of Imāmī sources. Most informative and comprehensive in this respect is the first section of the *Kitāb al-uṣūl min al-kāfī* of Abū Jaʿfar Muḥammad b. Yaʿqūb al-Kulaynī (d. 329/941), which deals systematically with Imāmī theology.[1] A detailed study of this text evidently would require a substantial monograph. In the present chapter, only a few points may be raised which are apt to modify our understanding of the history of Imāmī theology significantly.

The teaching of the Imams, it must be kept in mind, was almost entirely reactive, rarely initiative. Unlike the Prophet Muḥammad, the Imams did not feel called upon to spread a message. They did not hold regular teaching sessions like other heads of doctrinal schools, even for their followers, and did not compose books. They merely answered questions from individuals, either orally or in writing. These answers might involve precautionary dissimulation (*taqiyya*), even if given to adherents. It was the task of the Imāmī scholars to sift their true answers from the false or misleading ones. This situation left considerable room for disagreement among the Imāmī scholars attempting to elaborate Imāmī theological doctrine in the *kalām* debates. Such disagreement among the followers of the Imams was then often referred to the Imams in questions for their resolution.

1 Al-Kulaynī, *al-Uṣūl min al-kāfī*, ed. ʿAlī Akbar al-Ghaffārī (Tehran, 1388/1968), vol. 1, pp. 9–167.

The first chapter of al-Kulaynī's *Uṣul* deals with *al-ʿaql wa'l-jahl*, reason, the intellect and ignorance. The first report in the chapter quotes Imam Muḥammad al-Bāqir describing God's creation of the intellect in terms similar to those of the famous *ḥadīth* of the Prophet.[2] After having tested the strict obedience of the intellect to His orders, God stated: 'My glory and my Majesty: I have not created any creature that is dearer to me than thee, I have perfected thee among whomever I love. My commandment is to thee and to thee is my prohibition. Thee I shall punish and thee I shall reward.'[3] The entire chapter renders highest praise to intelligence and rationality as the supreme virtue of mankind. Reason is the very foundation of religion (*dīn*). Imam Jaʿfar al-Ṣādiq stated:

> The first of matters, their origin, their power and their structure without which nothing is beneficial is the intellect which God has made an ornament of His creation and a light for them. By the intellect the servants recognise the Creator and that they are created, that He is their ruler (*mudabbir*) and they are the ruled, that He is the Everlasting and they are those perishing. With the intellect they inquire about what they see of His creation, His heavens and earth, His sun and His moon, His night and day, and about His being their Creator and Ruler from eternity to eternity, and through it they recognize good in contrast to evil, that darkness is in ignorance and that light is in knowledge. To this they are guided by reason.[4]

Reason is also the foundation of good character and ethics. Imam Jaʿfar said: 'The most perfect of people in intellect is the best of them in ethics (*akmalu'l-nāsi ʿaqlan aḥsanuhum khuluqan*).'[5] As God's command and prohibition are addressed to the intellect in humankind, God rewards and punishes individuals in accordance with their intellect. Good works performed in ignorance are of no avail. Imam Jaʿfar quoted the Messenger of God saying: 'If you are informed of a good state of a man, look for the goodness of his intellect, for he will be requited only for his intelligence.' The Prophet, according to Imam Jaʿfar, also said: 'If you see a man performing much prayer and much fasting, do not emulate him until you look at the quality of his intellect.'[6]

The unambiguous affirmation of the primacy of reason over prophetic revelation in religion places early Imāmī theology close to the rationalist theology of the Muʿtazila. This must seem surprising in view of the severe conflict between early Muʿtazilī and Imāmī scholars on many substantial points of theology recorded by the heresiographical sources, which do not note the rationalist basis of early Imāmī

---

[2] Discussed by I. Goldziher, 'Neuplatonische und gnostische Elemente im Ḥadīṯ', *Zeitschrift für Assyriologie*, 22 (1909), pp. 317–324.

[3] Al-Kulaynī, *Uṣūl*, vol. 1, p. 10

[4] Ibid., p. 29.

[5] Ibid., p. 23.

[6] Ibid., p. 26.

theological thought. Imāmī rationalism is, however, confirmed and denounced by the early Ibāḍī *kalām* theologian ʿAbd Allāh b. Yazīd al-Fazārī who, writing around the middle of the 2nd/8th century, regularly associates the Rāfiḍa, that is, the Imāmī Shiʿa, with the Muʿtazila in their assertion of the priority of reason in Islam over the prophetic message, the Qur'an and transmitted tradition.[7]

Modern historians of Imāmī thought have sometimes maintained that the intellect and reason extolled by the Imams are not the ordinary human intellect and reason, but a higher superhuman reason to which only prophets and the Imams are privy and which they reveal to their trusted adherents. While such belief in a superhuman intelligence of the Imams may have been common among the extremist Shiʿa (*ghulāt*), the teaching of the Imams as presented by al-Kulaynī did not envisage the existence of a higher reason above 'mere human reason'. Intelligence, the Imams explained, was the greatest and most precious gift of God to humans, not an inborn trait of human nature. God gives it to individuals to various extents and withholds it from some. To prophets and the Imams He gave perfect and comprehensive intelligence. Their intelligence, however, differed from that of others only quantitatively, not qualitatively. Imam Mūsā al-Kāẓim told Hishām b. al-Ḥakam: 'God sent His prophets and Messengers to His servants only in order that they recognise God's reality (*li-yaʿqilū ʿani llāh*).' On the same occasion he recited to him the numerous verses of the Qur'an that appeal to the hearers to observe and meditate about the wonders of creation in order to recognise the Creator.[8] Imam Jaʿfar stated: 'God never sent a prophet or a Messenger before his intellect was perfected and his intellect was more excellent than all the intellects of his community.'[9] The principal task of the prophets evidently was to summon their community to rational recognition of the Creator and of the fundamental truths of religion. Only secondarily were they to reveal matters that reason and perception could not reach. The Imams, equally endowed with perfect intellects but without a divine message, were also primarily obligated to guide their followers to rational recognition of the fundamental truths of religion and secondarily to preserve and reliably transmit the divine commands and prohibitions revealed by their ancestor, the Prophet. Imam Jaʿfar stated: 'The proof (*ḥujja*) of God unto the servants is the Prophet, but the proof between the servants and God is the intellect.'[10] Imam Mūsā explained to Hishām b. al-Ḥakam: 'God has two proofs unto the people, an apparent (*ẓāhir*) proof and a hidden (*bāṭin*) proof. The apparent proof consists of the Messengers, the prophets, and the Imams, and the hidden proof is the intellects.'[11]

In view of the emphatic rationalism of the theology espoused by the Imams, the explicit adoption of rationalist Muʿtazilī doctrine by the leading Imāmī scholars in

---

[7] See W. Madelung, 'ʿAbd Allāh b. Yazīd al-Fazārī and the Teaching of Ibn ʿUmayr', in L. Mühlethaler and G. Schwarb, ed., *Theological Rationalism in Medieval Islam: New Texts and Perspectives* (Leuven, 2013).

[8] *Uṣūl*, vol. 1, pp. 13–16.

[9] Ibid., p. 12.

[10] Ibid., p. 25.

[11] Ibid., p. 16.

the Būyid age, Shaykh al-Mufīd, Sharīf al-Murtaḍā and Shaykh al-Ṭūsī, can no longer be viewed as a sudden radical break with the early Imāmī theological tradition during the presence of the Imams. Rather, it appears that the Imams, in answering questions on disputed issues, progressively came to endorse Muʿtazilī perspectives, concepts and positions. This was certainly the case in regard to questions concerning *tawḥīd*, the reality and unicity of God and His attributes. It was less obvious in regard to the principle of God's *ʿadl*, justice, and *qadar*, divine determinism, where the Imams basically opposed the Muʿtazilī dogma that God does not create or will evil, while also maintaining that God gives humans freedom of choice between good and evil.

The first controversial *kalām* question authoritatively settled by Imam Muḥammad al-Bāqir was probably that concerning whether God may be described as a *shayʾ*, meaning a 'thing' or 'something'. The question arose when the early Murjiʾī theologian of Tirmidh, Jahm b. Ṣafwān (d. 128/745) asserted that God was not a thing. The Qurʾan indeed does not call God *shayʾ*, but affirms that 'no thing is like unto Him (*laysa ka-mithlihī shayʾ*)' (Q.2:11). Most Muslims, however, understood any denial of God being a *shayʾ* as implying His being nothing. They interpreted the Qurʾanic verse as meaning that God is a thing unlike all other (created) things. Jahm b. Ṣafwān, to be sure, did not mean to affirm that God was nothing. He recognised God as most real, the only reality; all created things were in his view entirely determined and controlled by Him and had no independent reality. Most Muslim scholars, including the Muʿtazila, however, adopted the popular formula that God, the Creator, is a thing entirely unlike all other things created by Him.

Imam al-Bāqir, according to al-Kulaynī, was asked by ʿAbd al-Raḥmān b. Abī Najrān: 'Do I conceive [of God as] a thing (*atawahhamu shayʾan*)?' The Imam answered: 'Yes, [something] neither cognisable nor delimited. Whatever your imagination falls upon is different than He, nothing resembles Him and imaginations cannot reach Him. How could imaginations reach Him when He is different from what can be cognised and different from what is represented in imagination? [He must] only be conceived of as a thing that is neither cognisable nor delimited.'[12]

The Imam's instruction left the early Imāmī scholars ample room for *kalām* speculation as to what it meant to be a thing different and incomparable to all other things. Even if *shayʾ* was interpreted to mean merely existent (*mawjūd*), as was widely held by *kalām* scholars, there remained the question of the quiddity of the existent. The Imams mostly did not prohibit all speculation beyond God's own description of Himself in the Qurʾan as did many strictly traditionalist Muslim scholars.

Hishām b. al-Ḥakam grew up in a Dayṣānī dualist milieu and seems to have been converted to Imāmī Shiʿism by Imam Jaʿfar al-Ṣādiq. He then engaged in *kalām* debates with dualist scholars, seeking to convert them. He reported that a *zindīq* from Egypt visited Imam Jaʿfar in Mecca and questioned him at length in Hishām's presence. The *zindīq* asked the Imam about his Lord, Allah, and Imam Jaʿfar explained that he would not assert God to be the letters *alif*, *lām*, *hāʾ*, *rāʾ* and *bāʾ*, but would

---

[12] Ibid., p. 82.

refer to a meaning and thing that is the Creator of all things and their Maker (*ṣāniʿ*). This meaning was named by God Allah, al-Raḥmān, al-Raḥīm, al-ʿAzīz and other names. The *zindīq* countered: 'We have never found any thing imaginable that is not created.' The Imam replied: 'If that were as you say, the testimony of God's unicity (*tawḥīd*) would be lifted, for we have not been obliged to anything unimaginable (*lam nukallaf ghayra mawhūm*). Rather we say that everything imaginable and perceived by the senses is created ... Thus it is necessary to affirm the Maker because of the existence of the made (creatures).' The *zindīq* then charged: 'But you have delimited Him as you affirmed His existence.' The Imam answered: 'I do not delimit Him, but affirm Him since there is no position between negation and affirmation.' Later in the conversation the *zindīq* questioned: 'Does He then have existence (*inniyya*) and a quiddity (*māhiyya*)?' Imam Jaʿfar replied: 'Yes, no thing can be confirmed except with existence and a quiddity.' Still further on the Imam states: 'It is indispensable to affirm a qualification (*kayfiyya*) that is not deserved or shared by anything else, is incomprehensible and unknowable by anyone but Him.'[13]

Hishām b. al-Ḥakam evidently understood these explanations of the Imam as a licence to engage in *kalām* speculation about the quiddity of God, even though ultimately no one could have certain knowledge about it. Imam Jaʿfar later, however, distanced himself sharply from the views put forward by Hishām and other Imāmī scholars in the debates. ʿAlī b. Abī Ḥamza al-Baṭāʾinī complained to Imam Jaʿfar that Hishām narrated on the authority of the Imams (*ʿankum*) that God is a body, solid and luminous (*ṣamadī nūrī*); recognition of Him was, by necessity (*maʿrifatuhū ḍarūra*), granted by God to whomever He wishes. The Imam denounced this view, affirming that no one knows how He is except He. He has neither a body nor a form (*ṣūra*).[14] Yūnus b. Ẓabyān reported to Imam Jaʿfar that Hishām b. al-Ḥakam asserted that God is a body, arguing that all things are either a body or an action (*fiʿl*) of the body. It was inadmissible for the Maker to be in the meaning of an act, but it was admissible for Him to be in the meaning of the agent (*fāʿil*). The Imam dismissed this argument, questioning whether Hishām did not know that a body as well as a shape is confined and finite, subject to increase and decrease. God rather must be described as the embodier (*mujassim*) of bodies and the shaper of shapes.[15] It is evident that Imam Jaʿfar, as the *kalām* debates progressed, supported a more Muʿtazilī concept of God as a transcendent immaterial and shapeless being.

The same happened in respect to the doctrine of divine attributes. Hishām b. al-Ḥakam did not adopt the Muʿtazilī concept of distinct attributes of essence that eternally and immutably applied to God and attributes of act that were subject to change and applied to God's ever-changing actions. Hishām considered all divine

---

[13] Ibid., pp. 84–85. According to note 1 on p. 85, the text of this tradition as quoted by Ibn Bābawayh in his *Kitāb al-tawḥīd* reads 'to affirm an essence without qualification (*dhāt bilā kayfiyya*)' instead of 'to affirm a qualification'. Ibn Bābawayh's version is most likely a later modification.

[14] Ibid., p. 104.

[15] Ibid., p. 106.

attributes as merely descriptive and held that they could not further be described as eternal or temporal. They all were subject to change as their objects changed, and Hishām described all acts of God, including creation, as motions. This view received no support from Imam Jaʿfar and the later Imams. Abū Baṣīr quoted Imam Jaʿfar as stating:

> God was from eternity our Lord, knowledge was His essence (*dhātuh*) when there was nothing to be known, sight was His essence when there was nothing visible, hearing was his essence when there was nothing to be heard, omnipotence was His essence when there was no object of His power. When he originated the things and something knowable existed, His knowledge fell on the knowable, His hearing on the hearable, His sight on the visible, and His omnipotence on the object of His power.

Abū Baṣīr asked: 'Was God from eternity moving?' The Imam replied: 'God is exalted above that. Motion is an attribute originated by the act.' Abū Baṣīr further inquired: 'Was God from eternity speaking (*mutakalliman*)?' The Imam answered: 'Speech is an originated attribute that is not eternal; God was without being a speaker.'[16] Imam Jaʿfar here unambiguously sets forth early Muʿtazilī doctrine about the divine attributes. The attributes he describes as eternal, knowledge, sight, hearing and power, are those primarily recognised by the Muʿtazila as attributes of essence.[17] Like the Muʿtazilī scholar Abu'l-Hudhayl, he describes them as identical with God's essence and immutable. Motion and speech are merely attributes of God's acts and thus originated in time.

Divine speech (*kalām*), the Qur'an, was viewed by the Muʿtazila and most Muslim scholars who distinguished between attributes of essence and attributes of act as an attribute of act and hence as created by God: 'it was not and then it was'.[18] Al-Kulaynī does not mention Imam Jaʿfar's famous statement concerning the nature of the Qur'an that was quoted by Aḥmad b. Ḥanbal during his trial in defence of his own position: 'The Qur'an is the speech of God, neither creator nor created.'[19] This statement was the basis of Hishām b. al-Ḥakam's *kalām* doctrine concerning the Holy Book. He and his companions professed that the Qur'an is neither creator nor created. According to some reports he added that it also ought not to be said that it is uncreated since it is a descriptive attribute that cannot be described further. The early heresiographer Zurqān narrated that Hishām also stated that the term Qur'an can be used in two senses. If what can be heard is meant, God created the sound and the letter structure

---

16 Ibid., p. 107.

17 It may be noted here that life (*ḥayāt*), which was another primary divine attribute of essence in Muʿtazilī theory, is not mentioned by Imam Jaʿfar and rarely by the later Imams. This obviously does not mean that they did not count it as an eternal attribute of essence.

18 See al-Ashʿarī, *Maqālāt al-Islāmiyyīn*, ed. H. Ritter (3rd ed., Wiesbaden, 1400/1980), p. 582.

19 Al-Dārimī, *K. al-Radd ʿalā l-Jahmiya*, ed. G. Vitstam (Leiden, 1960), p. 88.

(*rasm*) of the Qur'an. As for the Qur'an itself, it is an act of God like knowledge and motion. As such it is neither identical with God nor other than He.[20] Here the Qur'an evidently is viewed as a thought act of God.

Imam Jaʿfar's adoption of the Muʿtazilī concept of divine attributes and the distinction between attributes of essence and of acts rendered his statement about the Qur'an, presumably made earlier, problematic, as it could be understood as endorsing the co-eternity of the Qur'an with God. This had not been the intention of either the Imam or Hishām b. al-Ḥakam. Imam Jaʿfar had merely wished to raise the rank of the speech of God above all creation. Al-Ḥasan b. ʿAbd al-Raḥmān al-Ḥimmānī reported that he, al-Ḥimmānī, informed Imam Mūsā: 'Hishām b. al-Ḥakam claims that God is a body, no thing is like unto it, omniscient, hearing, seeing, omnipotent, speaking (*mutakallim*), articulating (*nāṭiq*). Speech, power and knowledge apply in the same way to Him, none of them is created.' The Imam answered: 'May God confound him, does he not know that the body is confined and that speech is other than the speaker? God forbid, I absolve myself from this opinion. There is no body, no shape, no delimitation, and every thing other than He is created …'[21]

In the controversial question of the possibility of human vision (*ru'ya*) of God, Imāmī doctrine shifted from early affirmation that God can and should be seen by the heart of the faithful, but not be seen by the eyes, to total denial of any vision of God as also espoused by the Muʿtazila. Imam Jaʿfar narrated that the Commander of the Faithful ʿAlī, while preaching in the mosque of Kūfa, was asked by a bold man called Dhaʿlab: 'Commander of the Faithful, have you seen your Lord?' ʿAlī replied: 'Woe to you, Dhaʿlab, I would not worship a Lord I have not seen.' Dhaʿlab inquired: 'Commander of the Faithful, how have you seen your Lord?' ʿAlī said: 'Woe to you, Dhaʿlab, eyes do not see Him by the witnessing of looks (*bi-mushāhadat al-abṣār*), but hearts can see Him by the realities of faith (*bi-ḥaqā'iq al-īmān*) …'[22] Imam Jaʿfar, however, interpreted Q.6:103: 'looks do not reach Him, but He reaches looks' as meaning comprehension by imagination (*iḥāṭat al-wahm*) rather than eyesight, referring to Q.6:104: 'Whoever looks out, it is for the benefit of himself, and whoever is blind, it is against it.'[23] Imagination and to look out for one's benefit was an activity of the heart, not of the eye. Any 'vision of the heart through the realities of faith' could not and should not lead to imagining God.

Imam Jaʿfar's interpretation was backed and further elaborated by Imams ʿAlī al-Riḍā and Muḥammad al-Jawād, both questioned by Abū Hāshim al-Jaʿfarī about the meaning of Q.6:103. Imam al-Jawād explained: 'Abū Hāshim, imaginations of the hearts are finer than looks of the eyes. With your imagination you may reach Sind,

---

20 Ibid., pp. 40, 582–583.

21 Ibid., p. 106.

22 Ibid., p. 138.

23 Ibid., p. 98.

Hind and countries you have not entered, but you cannot reach them with your look. Imaginings of hearts cannot reach Him, how much less so can the looks of eyes!'[24]

Hishām b. al-Ḥakam, despite his engagement on speculation about a material and spatially defined God, was constrained by the statement of Imam Jaʿfar to deny categorically the possibility of any vision of God by the human eye or heart. Unable to argue on the basis of God's transcendence above matter and space, he asserted that human eyesight penetrates only air and cannot reach anything not contained by the atmosphere. The heart, he maintained, likewise cannot imagine anything not contained in air and thus is unable to reach God.[25] The later Imams did not mention any more the heart's vision of God as envisaged by Imam ʿAlī b. Abī Ṭālib and denied any possibility of *ruʾya*. Imam al-Riḍā reported as a *ḥadīth* of the Prophet that when, during his nightly Ascension, he reached a station the angel Gabriel had never trodden, God revealed to him merely 'of the light of His majesty (*nūr ʿaẓamatih*) what He wished'.[26]

Early Imāmī theology was explicitly anti-Qadarī in its affirmation that God wills, creates and controls everything and every event, evil as well as good, in the world. God wills and creates the evil acts of humans and of the devil although he prohibits them and punishes the perpetrators. Imāmī theology, however, fully agreed with the Muʿtazilī thesis that God's justice requires that His reward and punishment must be based on responsibility, capability (*istiṭāʿa*) and free choice of the human agents. God does not reward or punish obedience or disobedience if He has not created the capability to obey or disobey in the human individual. Humans are free to choose, but their will to act or abstain from acting is not effective unless God gives them the capability to act.

This theory combining divine arbitrary creation with human responsibility and freedom of choice was envisaged in a widely reported response of the Commander of the Faithful ʿAlī to a Shaykh among his followers who questioned him about their campaign to Ṣiffīn against the Syrians, whether it had been in accordance with the ordainment and determination (*qaḍāʾ wa-qadar*) of God. Imam ʿAlī assured him that it was so and that they would be rewarded by God for all their voluntary efforts. The shaykh now asked him how their campaign could have been voluntary if it was ordained and determined by God. ʿAlī explained to him that it was not a compelling ordainment and binding determination. If it were so there could be no valid reward or punishment. God imposes obligation with a choice and prohibits with a warning; He does not compel.[27] The later Imams described this doctrine as an intermediate

[24] Ibid., p. 99. The Abū Jaʿfar addressed in tradition 11 is obviously Abū Jaʿfar al-Thānī, i.e., Muḥammad al-Jawād, not Imam al-Bāqir. Abū Hāshim Dāwūd b. al-Qāsim al-Jaʿfarī was a contemporary of Imams ʿAlī al-Riḍā and Muḥammad al-Jawād.

[25] Ibid., pp. 99–100.

[26] *Uṣūl*, p. 98.

[27] Ibid., p. 155.

position between *jabr*, compulsion, and *qadar*, autonomous power, or between *jabr* and *tafwīḍ*, empowerment.[28]

The obvious tension in the combination of a Creator of both good and evil and a just Judge who rewards and punishes human agents on the basis of their choice of good or evil inevitably posed problems for the Imāmī *kalām* theologians endeavouring to elaborate a rationally consistent theological system. Their task was, to some extent, lightened by another early Imāmī doctrine, that of *badā'*, a change of a decision of God in view of a change of circumstances. The tenet of *badā'* arose first among the Kaysānī Shiʿa and was adopted by the Imāmiyya in the age of Imam Muḥammad al-Bāqir. Ḥumrān b. Aʿyan reported that he asked Imam al-Bāqir about the meaning of Q.6:2: 'and He decided a term (*ajalan*) and a(nother) term named with Him'. The Imam answered: 'They are two terms, one is definitely decided (*maḥtūm*) and the other suspended (*mawqūf*).' Al-Fuḍayl b. Yasār reported that Imam al-Bāqir stated: 'God's knowledge is of two kinds: A knowledge that is stored (*makhzūn*) with Him of which He does not inform anyone of His creation and a knowledge about which He informs His angels and His Messengers. Whatever He informs His angels and His Messengers about will certainly occur. But of the knowledge that is stored with Him, He will advance whatever He wishes, delay whatever He wishes and confirm whatever He wishes.' Al-Fuḍayl also quoted Imam al-Bāqir as stating: 'some matters are suspended (*mawqūfa*) with God; He advances of them what He wishes and delays what He wishes'.[29]

It is evident that *badā'* here did not imply a radical or arbitrary decision. It meant the advancement or delay of an act of creation that did not change the overall design and intention of the Creator. The doctrine of *badā'* as explained by Imam al-Bāqir reflected recognition that the course of history after God's grant of freedom of choice to many of his creatures cannot be entirely predetermined by a just God even if every event in the world is ultimately determined and created by Him. God's decision on human acts and human history thus must remain 'suspended', subject to advancement and postponement, until the autonomous choice of His creatures has occurred, when His definite decision is made.

Imāmī theology rejected the concept of an eternal immutable will of God (*irāda, mashī'a*) unconditionally ruling the world that was embraced by the great majority of traditionalist Muslim scholars. God's will, rather, consisted of numerous ad hoc acts of will in time. Imam Jaʿfar evidently realised the crucial importance of the doctrine of *badā'* in Imāmī theology. He repeatedly described affirmation of *badā'* as an outstanding act of worship. Mālik al-Juhanī narrated that he heard Imam Jaʿfar say: 'If people knew what reward there is in upholding *badā'*, they would not let up speaking about it (*mā fatarū ʿani'l-kalāmi fīh*).'[30]

28 Ibid., pp. 159–160.
29 Ibid., p. 147.
30 Ibid., p. 148.

The doctrine of *badāʾ* was scornfully denounced by most Muslim scholars as implying arbitrary change of opinion in God. Even the Muʿtazila, who, like the Imāmiyya, held that God's will consists of a succession of temporal acts of will, were shocked by the implication that God does not have eternal foreknowledge of every event in the world. They generally asserted that God had foreknowledge from pre-eternity of all His future acts of will and changing decisions required by the free will and autonomous acts of His creatures. Yet how could there be a real choice of these creatures if God knew their choice from eternity? If God has foreknowledge of all future events, His foreknowledge must be determinative, and human free will and choice are an illusion, as determinist opponents of the Muʿtazila ever charged. If God grants His creatures real choice, His foreknowledge of their choice of acts must be 'suspended' just like His will and decision concerning them.

The early Imāmī *kalām* theologians speculated freely about the knowledge of God and accepted that God cannot know things either before they exist or before He wills them. They affirmed that the non-existent (*maʿdūm*) is not subject to knowledge. God's knowledge was tied to His will if not identical with it. Since God's will develops over time in multiple acts of will, His knowledge must also develop and change in time. Most Muslim theologians, including the Muʿtazila, maintained that God knows everything and all future events as He knows the past. If God's creation proceeded in acts of will, God knew these future acts of will from eternity. They accused the Imāmī scholars of describing God as ignorant (*jāhil*) in pre-eternity. It was no doubt partly in order to counter such accusations that Imam Jaʿfar adopted the Muʿtazilī concept of divine attributes with its distinction between attributes of essence and of act. According to ʿAmr b. ʿUthmān al-Juhanī he affirmed: 'No change of circumstance occurs to God from ignorance (*inna llāha lam yabdu lahū min jahl*).'[31]

The adoption of the Muʿtazilī tenet that knowledge is an eternal attribute of God by Imam Jaʿfar was, however, inevitably problematical. This appears obvious in another statement of his reported by ʿAbd Allāh b. Sinān: 'No change of view about anything occurs to God but that it was in His knowledge before it occurred.'[32] If the changed circumstances implied in *badāʾ*, not merely the possibility of *badāʾ*, were known to God from pre-eternity, His foreknowledge becomes necessarily determinative. Human autonomous choice and free will are then an illusion created by God in the human mind. 'Man is compelled under the guise of a freely choosing agent', as the Ashʿarī theologians and the philosopher Avicenna argued.[33] The tenet of *badāʾ*, originally implying a partial suspension of divine knowledge, lost its significance as Imāmī theology adopted Muʿtazilī concepts.

---

31 Ibid., p. 148.

32 Ibid., p.148.

33 See W. Madelung, 'The Late Muʿtazila and Determinism: The Philosophers' Trap', in B. Scarcia Amoretti and L. Rostagno, ed., *Yād-nāma in Memoria di Alessandro Bausani* (Rome, 1991), vol. 1, pp. 245–257.

18

Al-Shaykh al-Ṭūsī: His Writings on Theology and their Reception[*]

Hassan Ansari and Sabine Schmidtke

I

While the theological thought of Twelver Shiʿism during the 3rd/9th and 4th/10th centuries has been studied relatively well (as much as is possible on the basis of the few, mostly secondary sources that are preserved),[1] little is known about its doctrinal developments from the early 5th/11th century onwards. Whereas most of the theological works by al-Sharīf al-Murtaḍā (d. 436/1044) have been preserved and are now available in critical editions and have partly been studied,[2] only some of the

[*] This publication was prepared within the framework of the European Research Council's FP 7 project 'Rediscovering Theological Rationalism in the Medieval World of Islam'. We take the opportunity to thank Camilla Adang for helpful remarks on an earlier draft of this chapter.

[1] See the still authoritative overview by Wilferd Madelung, 'Imamism and Muʿtazilite Theology', in Toufic Fahd, ed., *Shīʿisme Imāmite* (Paris, 1970), pp. 13–29; repr. in W. Madelung, *Religious Schools and Sects in Medieval Islam* (London, 1985), article VII. For the early period, see also W. Madelung, 'The Shiite and Khārijite Contribution to Pre-Ashʿarite *Kalām*', in P. Morewedge, ed., *Islamic Philosophical Thought* (Albany, 1979); repr. in his *Religious Schools and Sects*, article VIII; Tamima Bayhom-Daou, 'The Imam's Knowledge and the Quran according to al-Faḍl b. Shādhān al-Nīsābūrī (d. 260 A.H./874 A.D.)', *BSOAS*, 64 (2001), pp. 188–207; Josef van Ess, *Theologie und Gesellschaft im 2. und 3. Jahrhundert Hidschra: Eine Geschichte des religiösen Denkens im frühen Islam* (Berlin, 1991–1997), vol. 1, pp. 233–403; Hossein Modarressi, *Crisis and Consolidation in the Formative Period of Shiʿite Islam: Abū Jaʿfar ibn Qiba al-Rāzī and His Contribution to Imāmite Shīʿite Thought* (Princeton, 1993); Hossein Modarressi, *An Introduction to Shīʿī law: A Bibliographical Study* (London, 1984), pp. 23–50; ʿAbbās Iqbāl, *Khāndān-i Nawbakhtī* (Tehran, 1345/1966); Ḥasan Anṣārī, 'Abū Sahl Nawbakhtī', *DMBI*, vol. 5, pp. 579–583; Martin J. McDermott, *The Theology of al-Shaikh al-Mufīd (d. 413/1022)* (Beirut, 1978); Paul Sander, *Zwischen Charisma und Ratio: Entwicklungen in der frühen imāmitischen Theologie* (Berlin, 1994).

[2] For his doctrinal thought, see Madelung, 'Imamism and Muʿtazilite Theology', pp. 25ff; McDermott, *Theology*, pp. 373ff; Muḥammad Riḍā al-Jaʿfarī, 'al-Kalām ʿindā'l-Imāmiyya, nash'atuhu, taṭawwuruhu wa-mawqiʿ al-Shaykh al-Mufīd minhu II', *Turāthunā*, 8 (1413/1992–1993), pp. 77–114. It was only in recent years that al-Murtaḍā's most comprehensive works on *kalām* were made available through publication, namely (i) *Rasā'il al-Sharīf al-Murtaḍā*,

kalām writings by his most prominent student, the *Shaykh al-ṭāʾifa* Muḥammad b. al-Ḥasan al-Ṭūsī (d. 460/1067), are extant.[3] Al-Murtaḍā had departed from the theological views of his teacher al-Shaykh al-Mufīd, who had maintained in many issues the doctrines of the Muʿtazilī School of Baghdad, in favour of those of the school of Abū Hāshim al-Jubbāʾī (d. 321/933), the Bahshamiyya, due to the influence of his teacher ʿAbd al-Jabbār al-Hamadhānī (d. 415/1025), head of the Bahshamiyya of his time. Quṭb al-Dīn Saʿīd b. Hibat Allāh al-Rāwandī (d. 573/1177–1178) enumerates more than 90 doctrinal differences between al-Mufīd and al-Murtaḍā in his lost work *al-Khilāf alladhī tajaddada bayna'l-Shaykh al-Mufīd wa'l-Murtaḍā*.[4]

As was the case with al-Shaykh al-Ṭūsī, virtually all leading Twelver Shiʿi scholars who flourished during the first half of the 5th/11th century had studied either with the Shaykh al-Mufīd, with al-Sharīf al-Murtaḍā or both. These include Abu'l-Ḥasan Muḥammad b. Muḥammad b. Aḥmad al-Buṣrawī (d. 443/1051), author of *al-Mufīd fi'l-taklīf*, a work that presumably dealt with theology and legal issues (lost);[5] Abu'l-Ṣalāḥ Taqī b. Najm b. ʿUbayd Allāh al-Ḥalabī (d. 447/1055), author

ed. Mahdī Rajāʾī, 4 vols (Qumm, 1405/1984–1985); (ii) *al-Dhakhīra ilā ʿilm al-kalām*, ed. Aḥmad al-Ḥusaynī (Qumm, 1411/1990–1991). On this work, see also S. Schmidtke, 'II Firk. Arab. 111: A Copy of al-Sharīf al-Murtaḍā's *Kitāb al-Dhakhīra* Completed in 472/1079–1080 in the Firkovitch-Collection, St. Petersburg', [Persian] *Maʿārif*, 20 (1382/2003), pp. 68–84; (iii) *al-Mulakhkhaṣ fī uṣūl al-dīn*, ed. Muḥammad Riḍā Anṣārī Qummī (Tehran, 1381/2002); (iv) his autocommentary *Sharḥ Jumal al-ʿilm*, ed. Yaʿqūb al-Jaʿfarī al-Marāghī (Qumm, 1414/1993–1994). In fact al-Murtaḍā's authorship is not entirely certain; see Ḥasan Anṣārī, 'Taʿlīq-i Sharḥ-i Jumal al-ʿilm-i Karājikī', online: http://ansari.kateban.com/entry1249.html (accessed 6 October 2011); (v) *Masāʾil al-Murtaḍā*, ed. Wafqān Khuḍayr Muḥsin al-Kaʿbī (Beirut, 1422/2001); (vi) *al-Mūḍiḥ ʿan jihat iʿjāz al-Qurʾān (al-Ṣarfa)*, ed. Muḥammad Riḍā Anṣārī Qummī (Mashhad, 1424/2003). A detailed investigation of al-Murtaḍā's theological thought on the basis of these works is still a desideratum. Generally on his life and work, see ʿAbd al-Razzāq Muḥyī al-Dīn, *Adab al-Murtaḍā min sīratihi wa-atharihi* (Baghdad, 1957); Aḥmad Muḥammad Maʿtūq, *al-Sharīf al-Murtaḍā, ḥayātuhu, thaqāfatuhu, adabuhu wa-naqduhu* (Beirut, 2008).

[3] See Section II below.

[4] See Āghā Buzurg al-Ṭihrānī, *al-Dharīʿa ilā taṣānīf al-Shīʿa* (Beirut, 1983), vol. 1, pp. 361–362, no. 1901; *Muʿjam al-turāth al-kalāmī*, taʾlīf al-Lajna al-ʿilmiyya fī Muʾassasat al-Imām al-Ṣādiq, taqdīm wa-ishrāf Jaʿfar al-Subḥānī (Qumm, 1424/2003–2004), vol. 1, p. 203, no. 645; Etan Kohlberg, *A Medieval Muslim Scholar at Work: Ibn Ṭāwūs and his Library* (Leiden, 1992), p. 217, no. 264. For al-Mufīd's theological views, see McDermott, *Theology*; Sander, *Zwischen Charisma und Ratio*; Muḥammad Riḍā al-Jaʿfarī, 'al-Kalām ʿindā'l-Imāmiyya: Nashʾatuhu, taṭawwuruhu wa-mawqiʿ al-Shaykh al-Mufīd minhu', *Turāthunā*, 8 (1413/1992–1993), pp. 144–299; Hassan Ansari, *L'imamat et l'occultation selon l'imamisme: Étude bibliographique et histoire des textes* (Ph.D. dissertation, École pratique des hautes études, Paris, 2008), pp. 105ff; Tamima Bayhom-Daou, *Shaykh Mufid* (Oxford, 2005). All his extant theological writings are included in *Muṣannafāt al-Shaykh al-Mufīd Abī ʿAbd Allāh Muḥammad b. Muḥammad b. al-Nuʿmān b. al-Muʿallim al-Ukbarī al-Baghdādī*, 13 vols (Beirut, 1413/1993).

[5] On him, see Ḥusayn Farhang Anṣārī, 'Buṣrawī', *DMBI*, vol. 12, pp. 193–194; Modarressi, *Introduction*, p. 43. Al-Buṣrawī had compiled a list of al-Murtaḍā's writings. The latter had issued an *ijāza* for al-Buṣrawī (dated Shaʿbān 417/September–October 1026) allowing him to transmit all works included in that list. The text of the *ijāza* including the list of al-Murtaḍā's

of *al-Kāfī fi'l-taklīf*, on theology and legal issues,[6] and *Taqrīb al-maʿārif*;[7] Abū Yaʿlā Sallār [Sālār] b. ʿAbd al-ʿAzīz al-Daylamī (d. 448/1057 [?]), who wrote *al-Tadhkira fī ḥaqīqat al-jawhar wa'l-ʿaraḍ* and apparently a work entitled *Tatmīm al-mulakhkhaṣ*, completing al-Murtaḍā's *al-Mulakhkhaṣ* (both are lost);[8] Abu'l-Fatḥ Muḥammad b. ʿAlī b. ʿUthmān al-Khaymī al-Karājikī (d. 449/1057), who wrote extensively on theology, including a commentary on al-Murtaḍā's *Jumal al-ʿilm* (apparently lost);[9]

---

writings is quoted by ʿAbd Allāh b. ʿĪsā Afandī al-Iṣfahānī, *Riyāḍ al-ʿulamāʾ wa-ḥiyāḍ al-fuḍalāʾ* (Qumm, 1403/1982–1983), vol. 4, pp. 38–39; vol. 5, p. 158. See also ʿAbd al-Razzāq Muḥyī al-Dīn, *Adab al-Murtaḍā min sīratihi wa-atharihi* (Baghdad, 1957), pp. 131ff. (where the list and the *ijāza* have also been edited) Al-Buṣrawī had apparently also assembled al-Murtaḍā's statements on definitions (*jamʿ al-Shaykh al-jalīl al-ʿālim Abi'l-Ḥasan al-Buṣrawī* [not: 'al-Ḥusayn al-Baṣrī'] *Ibn Qārūra* [not: 'Mārūra'] *raḥimahu llāh* ...); see Dānishpazhūh, 'Chahār farhangnāma-yi kalāmī', *Dhikrā al-alfiyya li-l-Shaykh al-Ṭūsī*, vol. 2, pp. 728ff ('Abu'l-Ḥusayn al-Baṣrī' as given here must certainly be read as 'Abu'l-Ḥasan al-Buṣrawī').

6 Abu'l-Ṣalāḥ al-Ḥalabī, *al-Kāfī fi'l-fiqh*, ed. Riḍā al-Ustādhī (Isfahan, 1400/1979–1980; repr. Qumm, 2009). See also Modarressi, *Introduction*, pp. 43, 63.

7 The work has been published twice: (i) *Taqrīb al-maʿārif fi'l-kalām*, ed. Riḍā al-Ustādhī (Qumm, 1404/1984) (partial edition); (ii) *Taqrīb al-maʿārif*, ed. Fārīs Tabrīziyyān al-Ḥassūn (Qumm, 1417/1996–1997). The second edition is available online: http://www.aqaed.com/book/131/ (accessed 14 July 2011). According to Ibn Shahrāshūb, Abu'l-Ṣalāḥ wrote a commentary on al-Murtaḍā's *Dhakhīra* (lost); see Ibn Shahrāshūb, *Maʿālim al-ʿulamāʾ fī fihrist kutub al-Shīʿa wa-asmāʾ al-muṣannifīn minhum, qadīman wa-ḥadīthan* (Najaf, 1961), p. 29, no. 155; cf. also Afandī, *Riyāḍ al-ʿulamāʾ*, vol. 1, p. 100; *Dharīʿa*, vol. 13, p. 277, no. 1011; *Muʿjam al-turāth al-kalāmī*, vol. 4, p. 68, no. 7856. For Abu'l-Ṣalāḥ and his writings, see also *Muʿjam ṭabaqāt al-mutakallimīn*, ta'līf al-Lajna al-ʿIlmiyya fī Mu'assasat al-Imām al-Ṣādiq, taqdīm wa-ishrāf Jaʿfar al-Subḥānī (Qumm, 1424/2003–2004), vol. 2, pp. 196–197, no. 170; Ahmad Pakatchi, 'Abu'l-Ṣalāḥ-i Ḥalabī', *DMBI*, vol. 5, pp. 601–611; Majmaʿ al-Fikr al-Islāmī, Qism al-Mawsūʿa, *Mawsūʿat mu'allifī al-Imāmiyya* (Qumm, 1420/2000), vol. 7, pp. 396–397; Sayyid Ḥusayn Ḥā'irī, 'Kitābshināsī-yi Abu'l-Ṣalāḥ-i Ḥalabī', *Jung-i Anjumān-i Fihristnagārān-i nuskhahā-yi khaṭṭī. Daftar-i duvvum: Majmūʿa-yi maqālāt-i yādmān ʿAllāma Shaykh Āqā Buzurg Tihrānī*, ed. Muḥsin Ṣādiqī (Qumm, 1389/2010), pp. 215–259.

8 See *Dharīʿa*, vol. 3, pp. 343–344, no. 1236; vol. 4, p. 24, no. 75; *Muʿjam al-turāth al-kalāmī*, vol. 2, p. 160, no. 3223. He is mostly known for his legal work *Kitāb al-marāsim* which has been published repeatedly, e.g., (i) *al-Marāsim fi'l-fiqh al-Imāmī*, ed. Muḥammad Bustānī (Beirut, 1980); (ii) *al-Marāsim al-ʿalawiyya fi'l-aḥkām al-nabawiyya*, ed. Muḥsin al-Ḥusaynī al-Amīnī (Qumm, 1414/1994). See also Ibn Shahrāshūb, *Maʿālim*, p. 135f; Muntajab al-Dīn, *Fihrist*, ed. ʿAbd al-ʿAzīz al-Ṭabāṭabāʾī, p. 84f, n.; Afandī, *Riyāḍ al-ʿulamāʾ*, vol. 2, pp. 438–440; Āghā Buzurg al-Ṭihrānī, *Ṭabaqāt aʿlām al-Shīʿa wa-huwa al-Nābis fi'l-qarn al-khāmis*, ed. ʿAlī Naqī Munzawī (Beirut, 1971), p. 86; *Muʿjam ṭabaqāt al-mutakallimīn*, vol. 2, pp. 210–211, no. 179; Modarressi, *Introduction*, pp. 14, 43, 63; Leonardo Capezzone, 'Maestri e testi nei centri imamiti dell'Iran Selgiuchide secondo il *Kitāb al-Naqḍ*', *Rivista degli Studi Orientali*, 79 (2006), p. 17f, no. 12.

9 The Abraham Firkovitch collection has at least three fragments of an unidentified Muslim commentary on al-Murtaḍā's *Jumal al-ʿilm* which may possibly belong to al-Karājikī's commentary; see Gregor Schwarb, 'Sahl b. al-Faḍl al-Tustarī's *Kitāb al-Īmāʾ*', *Ginzei Qedem: Genizah Research Annual*, 2 (2006), p. 79. Ḥasan Anṣārī has suggested that *Sharḥ Jumal al-ʿilm wa'l-ʿamal*, which has been published as a work by al-Murtaḍā (see n. 3 above), was in fact by al-Karājikī; see his 'Taʿlīq-i Sharḥ-i Jumal al-ʿilm-i Karājikī'. Some of al-Karājikī's writings

Abū Yaʿlā Muḥammad b. Ḥasan b. Ḥamza al-Jaʿfarī (d. 463/1070 [?]),[10] and *qāḍī* ʿAbd al-ʿAzīz b. Niḥrīr b. ʿAbd al-ʿAzīz b. al-Barrāj al-Ṭarābulusī (b. ca. 400/1009, d. 481/1088–1089).[11] Mention should also be made of Abū ʿAlī al-Ḥasan b. Aḥmad b. ʿAlī b. al-Muʿallim al-Ḥalabī (d. after 453/1061), who was a student of Abu'l-Ṣalāḥ al-Ḥalabī and wrote a commentary on al-Murtaḍā's *Mulakhkhaṣ*.[12] While al-Karājikī, Abū Yaʿlā al-Jaʿfarī and possibly Abu'l-Ḥasan al-Buṣrawī remained faithful to al-Mufīd, maintaining as a rule the Baghdādī positions,[13] all other theologians of this generation apparently followed al-Murtaḍā in their preference for the doctrines of the Bahshamiyya. Some of these theologians were also familiar with at least some aspects of Abu'l-Ḥusayn al-Baṣrī's (d. 436/1044) theological thought, albeit in a negative manner. It was mostly the latter's criticism of the Twelver Shiʿi notion of the imamate, expressed for example in his refutation (*naqḍ*) of al-Murtaḍā's *Kitāb al-shāfī*, that was known to and refuted by Sallār [Sālār] b. ʿAbd al-ʿAzīz[14] and by al-Karājikī.[15] None of these refutations is extant.

---

were published in his *Kanz al-fawā'id*, an anthology consisting mostly of some of his theological works that have been published repeatedly: (i) (Tabriz, 1322/1904–1905); (ii) ed. ʿAbd Allāh Niʿma, 2 vols (Beirut, 1985; repr., Qumm, n.d.). Most recently *al-Asbāb al-ṣādda ʿan idrāk al-ṣawāb* has been published in the edition of Maḥmūd Naẓarī in *Mīrāth-i Bahāristān (majmūʿa-yi 14 risāla), daftar-i duvvum* (Tehran, 1389/2010), pp. 577–594; the editor argues convincingly that this text is by al-Karājikī. On his life and work, see ʿAbd al-ʿAzīz Ṭabāṭabā'ī, 'Maktabat al-ʿAllāma al-Karājikī li-aḥad muʿāṣirīhi', *Turāthunā*, 43–44 (Rajab-Dhu'l-ḥijja 1416/1995–1996), pp. 365–404; Modarressi, *Introduction*, p. 44; Ansari, *L'imamat*, pp. 119ff.

10 See Ḥasan Anṣārī, 'Abū Yaʿlā Jaʿfarī', *DMBI*, vol. 6, pp. 434–435; Capezzone, 'Maestri e testi nei centri imamiti', p. 17, no. 10.

11 On him, see Sayyid Muḥammad Baḥr al-ʿulūm, 'Ibn Barrāj', *DMBI*, vol. 3, pp. 95–97; *Muʿjam ṭabaqāt al-mutakallimīn*, vol. 2, p. 217f; Modarressi, *Introduction*, pp. 43, 63, 121.

12 See Kamāl al-Dīn ʿUmar b. Aḥmad Ibn al-ʿAdīm, *Bughyat al-ṭalab fī tārīkh Ḥalab*, ed. Suhayl Zakkār (Damascus, 1988), vol. 5, pp. 2276–2284; *wa-lahu kitābun fi'l-uṣūl sharaḥa fīhi al-Mulakhkhaṣ* (ibid.), vol. 5, p. 2276).

13 That Abu'l-Ḥasan al-Buṣrawī adhered to the views of al-Mufīd is suggested by Najīb al-Dīn Abu'l-Qāsim ʿAbd al-Raḥmān b. ʿAlī b. Muḥammad al-Ḥusaynī's commentary on al-Ṭūsī's *Muqaddama* (MS 1338, ff. 18b, 39b, Atif Efendi Library, Istanbul). Whenever his views are mentioned they agree with those of al-Shaykh al-Mufīd. On this commentary, see Section III below.

14 *Al-Radd ʿalā Abi'l-Ḥusayn al-Baṣrī fī naqḍihi Kitāb al-Shāfī*; see *Dharīʿa*, vol. 3, p. 344; vol. 10, pp. 179–180, no. 378; *Muʿjam al-turāth al-kalāmī*, vol. 3, p. 366, no. 6477.

15 *Risālat al-Tanbīh ʿalā aghlāṭ Abi'l-Ḥusayn al-Baṣrī fī faṣlin fī dhikr al-imāma*, see Ṭabāṭabā'ī, 'Maktabat al-ʿAllāma al-Karājikī', p. 393; *Dharīʿa*, vol. 4, p. 437, no. 1943; *Muʿjam al-turāth al-kalāmī*, vol. 2, pp. 333–334, no. 4022. During the 6th/12th century, a *Naqḍ kitāb al-taṣaffuḥ li-Abi'l-Ḥusayn* is moreover known to have been composed by Rashīd al-Dīn Abū Saʿīd ʿAbd al-Jalīl b. Abi'l-Fatḥ Masʿūd b. ʿĪsā *al-mutakallim* al-Rāzī (fl. early 6th/12th century), a refutation of Abu'l-Ḥusayn's doctrinal views as laid down in his *Taṣaffuḥ al-adilla*. On the *Naqḍ al-taṣaffuḥ*, see *Dharīʿa*, vol. 24, p. 286, no. 1466; *Muʿjam al-turāth al-kalāmī*, vol. 5, p. 410, no. 12248. On its author, see Ibn Funqud, *Maʿārij nahj al-balāgha*, ed. Muḥammad Taqī Dānishpazhūh (Qumm, 1409/1988–1989), p. 36; Muntajab al-Dīn, *Fihrist*, ed. ʿAbd al-ʿAzīz Ṭabāṭabā'ī, p. 110; see also Ibn Shahrāshūb, *Maʿālim*, pp. 144–145. See also Ḥasan Anṣārī, "Ilm

During the early 6th/12th century Bilād al-Shām (Tripoli and Aleppo) had emerged as a significant centre of Twelver Shiʿi learning, alongside Rayy and Khurāsān in Iran.[16] Mention should be made of Abu'l-Faḍl Asʿad b. Aḥmad al-Ṭarābulusī (d. early 6th/12th century) who had composed a number of works on theology, among them *ʿUyūn al-adilla fī maʿrifat Allāh* and *al-Bayān fī ḥaqīqat al-insān*.[17] The Imāmī theologian Rashīd al-Dīn Abū Jaʿfar Muḥammad b. ʿAlī Ibn Shahrāshūb al-Māzandarānī who hailed from Sārī in Māzandarān (b. 489/1096) later on went to Aleppo where he died on 16 Shaʿbān 588/27 August 1192. Among his writings, his *Kitāb aʿlām al-ṭarāʾiq fiʾl-ḥudūd waʾl-ḥaqāʾiq* is partly concerned with theology.[18] Among Ibn Shahrāshūb's students was Muḥyī al-Dīn Muḥammad b. ʿAbd Allāh b. Zuhra al-Ḥalabī (d. 639/1241–1242), author of *al-Arbaʿīn ḥadīthan fī ḥuqūq al-ikhwān*.[19] The latter belonged to the leading family of the Imāmī community in Aleppo, the Banū Zuhra,[20] and one of its most prominent members was Abu'l-Makārim ʿIzz al-Dīn Ḥamza b. ʿAlī b. Zuhra al-Ḥusaynī al-Ḥalabī (b. Ramaḍān 511/1117, d. 585/1189–1190), author of *Ghunyat al-nuzūʿ ilā ʿilmay al-uṣūl waʾl-furūʿ*.[21] In the first

---

al-kalām al-imāmī wa-madrasat Abi'l-Ḥusayn al-Baṣrī al-kalāmiyya', online: http://ansari.kateban.com/entry779.html (accessed 6 October 2011); Capezzone, 'Maestri e testi nei centri imamiti', p. 22, no. 44–45.

16 The doctrinal and cultural situation of Twelver Shiʿism during this period in Iran is evident from ʿAbd al-Jalīl Qazwīnī's *Kitāb al-naqḍ*, written around 560/1164. On this work, see Capezzone, 'Maestri e testi nei centri imamiti'; Jean Calmard, 'Le Chiisme imamite en Iran à l'époche Seldjoukide d'après le *Kitāb al-Naqḍ*', *Le Monde Iranien et I'lslam*, 1 (1971), pp. 43ff.

17 See Ḥasan Anṣārī, 'Asʿad b. Aḥmad al-Ṭarābulusī', *DMBI*, vol. 8, p. 310f.

18 See Aḥmad Pakatchi, 'Ibn Shahrāshūb', *DMBI*, vol. 4, pp. 90–92. On the work, *Aʿlām al-ṭarāʾiq*, and extant manuscripts, see Ḥasan Anṣārī, 'Aʿlām al-ṭarāʾiq', *Nashr-i dānish*, 18 (1380/2001), pp. 29–30; *Fihrist al-kutub al-mawjūda biʾl-Maktaba al-Azhariyya*, 6 vols (Cairo, 1946–1952), vol. 6, pp. 182–183.

19 Muḥyī al-Dīn Muḥammad b. ʿAbd Allāh b. Zuhra al-Ḥalabī, *al-Arbaʿīn ḥadīthan fī ḥuqūq al-ikhwān*, ed. Nabīl Riḍā ʿAlwān (Qumm, 1405/1984; 2nd ed., Beirut, 1987).

20 For the Banū Zuhra, see Ṣādiq Sajjādī, 'Āl Zuhra', *DMBI*, vol. 2, pp. 15–19; Marco Salati, *Ascesa e Caduta di una Famiglia di Asraf Sciiti di Aleppo: I Zuhrawi o Zuhra-Zada (1600–1700)* (Rome, 1992); Arabic tr. by Muḥammad ʿAlī and published under the title *Kitāb Āl al-Zahrāwī* (Ḥimṣ, 2007), online: http://www.scribd.com/doc/17222448/Zahrawi-family-by-Mr-Marco-Selati- (accessed 17 January 2012); Marco Salati, 'Note in margine ai Banū Zuhrā / al-Zuhrāwī / Zuhrā zāda di Aleppo: Alcuni documenti dai tribunali sciaraitici della fine del xvii e l'inizio del xviii secolo (1684–1701)', *Annali di Ca' Foscari*, 49 (2010), pp. 23–42; Sayyid Muḥsin al-Amīn, *Aʿyān al-shīʿa*, ed. Ḥasan al-Amīn (Beirut, n.d.), vol. 6, pp. 249–250; Anne-Marie Eddé, *La principauté ayyoubide d'Alep (579/1183–658/1260)* (Stuttgart, 1999), pp. 438ff.

21 Among his other works (all lost) are *Naqḍ shubah al-falāsifa*, *Masʾala fiʾl-radd ʿalāʾl-munajjimīn*, *Masʾala fī anna naẓar al-kāmil al-ʿaql ʿalā infirādihi kāf fī taḥṣīl al-maʿārif al-ʿaqliyya*, *Masʾala fī nafy al-ruʾya wa-iʿtiqād al-imāmiyya wa-mukhālifīhim mimman yunsab ilāʾl-sunna waʾl-jamāʿa*, *Masʾala fī kawnihi taʿālā ḥayyan*, *al-Masʾala al-shāfiyya fiʾl-radd ʿalā man zaʿama annaʾl-naẓar ʿalā infirādihi ghayr kāf fī taḥṣīl al-maʿrifa bihi taʿālā*, *Masʾala fiʾl-radd ʿalā man dhahaba ilā annaʾl-wujūb waʾl-qubḥ lā yuʿlamān illā samʿan*; see Muḥammad Bāqir al-Majlisī, *Biḥār al-anwār*, ed. Muḥammad Bāqir al-Bihbūdī (Beirut, 1403/1983), vol. 106, p. 24ff.; al-Ḥurr al-ʿĀmilī, *Amal al-ʿāmil* (Baghdad, 1965–1966), vol. 2, p. 105f. His brother,

part of his *Ghunya*, which is devoted to theology, he adheres to the doctrinal views of al-Sharīf al-Murtaḍā.[22] Among Abu'l-Makārim's students, we know of Muʿīn al-Dīn Abu'l-Ḥasan Sālim b. Badrān al-Māzinī al-Miṣrī (alive in 619/1222), who later became a teacher of Naṣīr al-Dīn al-Ṭūsī (d. 672/1274) to whom he issued an *ijāza* for Abu'l-Makārim's *Ghunya* (dated 18 Jumādā II 619/30 July 1222).[23]

An important shift in the development of Imāmī doctrinal thought occurred with Sadīd al-Dīn Maḥmūd b. ʿAlī b. al-Ḥasan al-Ḥimmaṣī al-Rāzī (d. after 600/1204), who had completed his comprehensive theological *summa*, *al-Munqidh min al-taqlīd*, on 9 Jumādā I 581/8 August 1185 in al-Ḥilla.[24] Al-Ḥimmaṣī's work is apparently the earliest testimony for an Imāmī reception of the theological thought of Abu'l-Ḥusayn al-Baṣrī whose views al-Ḥimmaṣī adopted whenever these disagreed with those of the Bahshamiyya.[25]

Jamāl al-Dīn Abu'l-Qāsim ʿAbd Allāh b. ʿAlī b. Zuhra al-Ḥusaynī al-Ḥalabī (b. Dhu'l-ḥijja 531/ December 962–January 963, d. after 597/1200), is known to have composed *Jawāb su'āl warada min Miṣr fi'l-nubuwwa*, *Kitāb al-Tabyīn li-mas'alatay al-shifāʿa wa-ʿuṣāt al-muslimīn*, *Tabyīn al-maḥajja fī kawn ijmāʿ al-Imāmiyya ḥujja*, *Mas'ala fī nafy al-taḥābuṭ* (or: *Mas'ala fī nafy al-takhlīṭ*), *Jawāb su'āl warada ʿan al-Ismāʿīliyya* and *Jawāb sā'il sa'ala ʿan al-ʿaql*. See al-Ḥurr al-ʿĀmilī, *ʿAmal al-ʿāmil* (Baghdad, 1965–1966), vol. 2, p. 163f; Majlisī, *Biḥār al-anwār*, vol. 106, p. 25; Afandī, *Riyāḍ al-ʿulamā'*, vol. 3, p. 227f; *Mawsūʿat ṭabaqāt al-fuqahā'*, ta'līf al-Lajna al-ʿIlmiyya fī Mu'assasat al-Imām al-Ṣādiq, ishrāf Jaʿfar al-Subḥānī (Beirut, 1999–2001), vol. 6, p. 162f; Salati, *Ascesa*, p. 130, no. 4.

22 The *Ghunya* was published twice: (i) a partial edition, comprising the second and third part of the work on legal methodology and law, is included in *al-Jawāmiʿ al-fiqhiyya* (Tehran, [lithograph], 1276/1859–1860; repr., Qumm 1404/1984); see also Modarressi, *Introduction*, p. 65; (ii) *Ghunyat al-nuzūʿ ilā ʿilmay al-uṣūl wa'l-furūʿ*, ta'līf Ḥamza b. ʿAlī b. Zuhra al-Ḥalabī, ed. Ibrāhīm al-Bahādurī (Qumm, 1417/1996), comprising all three parts on *uṣūl al-dīn*, *uṣūl al-fiqh* and *fiqh*. A Persian paraphrase of the *Ghunya*, most likely by ʿImād al-Dīn Ḥasan b. ʿAlī al-Ṭabarī (alive in 701/1301), was published as *Muʿtaqad al-Imāmiyya: Matn-i Fārsī dar kalām u uṣūl u fiqh-i Shīʿī az sada-yi haftum*, ed. Muḥammad Taqī Dānishpazhūh (Tehran, 1961). See Ḥusayn Mudarrisī Ṭabāṭabā'ī, *Kitābiyyāt: Majmūʿa-yi maqālāt dar zamīna-yi kitābshināsī* (New Jersey, 2009), p. 32 n. 6. On ʿImād al-Dīn, see Rasūl Jaʿfariyān, 'Fawā'id-i tārīkhī u nukāt-i kitābshināsānī dar āthār-i ʿImād al-Dīn al-Ṭabarī', *Āyana-yi pazhūhish*, 50 (1377/1998), pp. 12–16.

23 For a facsimile reproduction of the autograph *ijāza*, see Muḥammad Taqī Mudarris Raḍawī, *Aḥwāl u āthār-i Khʷāja Naṣīr al-Dīn Ṭūsī* (Tehran, 1370/1991), pp. 161–167, esp. 164. On Sālim b. Badrān, see also *Muʿjam ṭabaqāt al-mutakallimīn*, vol. 2, p. 381f, no. 263.

24 Ed. Muḥammad Hādī al-Yūsufī al-Gharawī (Qumm, 1412/1991). A theological text entitled *al-Muʿtamad min madhhab al-shīʿa al-imāmiyya* has been edited by Muḥammad Riḍā Anṣārī Qummī (*Mīrāth-i Islāmī-yi Īrān*, vol. 6, pp. 16–34). See also *Muʿjam al-turāth al-kalāmī*, vol. 5, p. 180, no. 11094. The editor suggests that this text is also by al-Ḥimmaṣī al-Rāzī. On the life and work of al-Ḥimmaṣī (with further references), see the editors' introduction to Rukn al-Dīn Maḥmūd b. Muḥammad al-Malāḥimī al-Khwārazmī, *Kitāb al-muʿtamad fī uṣūl al-dīn*, ed. Martin McDermott and Wilferd Madelung (London, 1991), p. viii, and the introduction to our edition of *Khulāṣat al-naẓar: An Anonymous Imāmī-Muʿtazilī Treatise (Late 6th/12th or Early 7th/13th Century)* (Tehran and Berlin, 2006), p. xf; see also Capezzone, 'Maestri e testi nei centri imamiti', p. 25, no. 68.

25 Al-Ḥimmaṣī evidently had immediate access to Abu'l-Ḥusayn's theological writings, notably his *Kitāb al-ghurar* (see *al-Munqidh*, vol. 1, pp. 203, 504f ; see also *Dharīʿa*, vol. 23,

For the period following al-Ḥimmaṣī until the time of Naṣīr al-Dīn al-Ṭūsī, who had 'modernised' Twelver Shiʿi theology, very little is known about Imāmī theology – most theologians are again known by name only.[26] At the time of al-Ḥimmaṣī, al-Ḥilla had emerged as an important centre of Twelver Shiʿism and a number of renowned theologians were active there during the 7th/13th century. Mention should be made in particular of Sadīd al-Dīn Sālim b. Maḥfūẓ al-Ṣūrāwī al-Ḥillī (d. ca. 630/1232),[27] of al-Muḥaqqiq al-Ḥillī (d. 676/1277), author of *al-Maslak fī uṣūl al-dīn*,[28] of Muḥammad b. ʿAlī b. Muḥammad Ibn Juhaym (d. 680/1282), who was one of the teachers of the ʿAllāma al-Ḥillī (d. 726/1325),[29] of the latter's father, Sadīd al-Dīn Yūsuf b. ʿAlī (alive in 665/1267)[30] and of the ʿAllāma al-Ḥillī himself.[31] It was also during this period that the Banu'l-ʿAwdī emerged in al-Ḥilla, a family of several

---

pp. 151ff; Camilla Adang, 'A Rare Case of Biblical "Testimonies" to the Prophet Muḥammad in Muʿtazilite Literature: Quotations from Ibn Rabban al-Ṭabarī's *Kitāb al-dīn wa'l-dawla* in Abu'l-Ḥusayn al-Baṣrī's *Ghurar al-adilla*, as Preserved in a Work by al-Ḥimmaṣī al-Rāzī', in C. Adang, S. Schmidtke and D. Sklare, ed., *A Common Rationality: Muʿtazilism in Islam and Judaism* (Würzburg, 2007), pp. 297–330, and possibly his *Taṣaffuḥ al-adilla* (see, e.g., *al-Munqidh*, vol. 1, p. 63), and he regularly refers to the *Kitāb al-fā'iq* by Rukn al-Dīn Maḥmūd b. Muḥammad al-Malāḥimī al-Khwārazmī (d. 536/1141), the chief representative of Abu'l-Ḥusayn's doctrine a century after his death (see *al-Munqidh*, vol. 1, pp. 56–57, 208, 344).

26 For the doctrinal development of Twelver Shiʿism since the time of Naṣīr al-Dīn al-Ṭūsī, see the following works by Sabine Schmidtke: *The Theology of al-ʿAllāma al-Ḥillī (d. 726/1325)* (Berlin, 1991); *Theologie, Philosophie und Mystik im zwölferschiitischen Islam des 9./15. Jahrhunderts: Die Gedankenwelten des Ibn Abī Jumhūr al-Aḥsā'ī (um 838/1434–35–nach 906/1501)* (Leiden, 2000); and 'Ibn Abī Jumhūr al-Aḥsā'ī und sein Spätwerk *Sharḥ al-Bāb al-ḥādī ʿashar*', in A. Neuwirth and A. Chr. Islebe, ed., *Reflections on Reflections: Near Eastern Writers Reading Literature. Dedicated to Renate Jacobi* (Wiesbaden, 2006), pp. 119–145. For the theological views of Naṣīr al-Dīn al-Ṭūsī, see ʿAbd al-Amīr al-Aʿsam, *Naṣīr al-Dīn al-Ṭūsī: Mu'assis al-manhaj al-falsafī fī ʿilm al-kalām al-Islāmī* (Beirut, 1975; 2nd rev. ed., Beirut, 1980); ʿAbbās Sulaymān, *Taṭawwur ʿilm al-kalām ilā'l-falsafa wa-manhajuhā ʿinda Naṣīr al-Dīn al-Ṭūsī: Dirāsa taḥlīliyya muqārana li-Kitāb Tajrīd al-ʿaqā'id* (Alexandria, 1994), online: http://www.al-mostafa.info/data/arabic/depot2/gap.php?file=004180.pdf (accessed 17 January 2012).

27 He was also the teacher of al-Muḥaqqiq al-Ḥillī and ʿAlī b. Mūsā Ibn Ṭāwūs (d. 664/1266). On him, see al-Sayyid Ḥasan al-Ṣadr, *Takmilat amal al-ʿāmil*, ed. Ḥusayn ʿAlī Maḥfūẓ et al. (Beirut, 2008), vol. 3, pp. 106–107; *Muʿjam ṭabaqāt al-mutakallimīn*, vol. 2, p. 383f, no. 264.

28 Ed. Riḍā al-Ustādhī (Mashhad, 1373/1994). He also wrote a brief *ʿaqīda* that has been published repeatedly (see *Muʿjam al-turāth al-kalāmī*, vol. 5, pp. 7–8, no. 10225), and a *fatwā* concerning the status of one who upholds the doctrine that the non-existent (*maʿdūm*) is stable (*thābit*); see Sabine Schmidtke, 'The Doctrinal Views of the Banu'l-ʿAwd (early 8th/14th century): An Analysis of Ms Arab. f. 64 (Bodleian Library, Oxford)', in M. A. Amir-Moezzi, M. Bar-Asher and S. Hopkins, ed., *Le Shīʿisme Imāmite quarante ans après: Hommage à Etan Kohlberg* (Turnhout, 2009), p. 388f, nos 8 and 9 (with further references). On al-Muḥaqqiq al-Ḥillī, see also Riḍā al-Ustādhī, *Aḥwāl wa-āthār-i Muḥaqqiq-i Ḥillī, ṣāḥib sharā'iʿ* (Qumm, 1383/2004).

29 On him, see *Muʿjam ṭabaqāt al-mutakallimīn*, vol. 2, p. 408f, no. 278.

30 On him, see Schmidtke, *Theology*, p. 10 (with further references).

31 See Schmidtke, *Theology*; ʿAbd al-ʿAzīz Ṭabāṭabā'ī, *Maktabat al-ʿAllāma al-Ḥillī* (Qumm, 1416/1996).

generations of theologians.[32] Apart from al-Ḥilla, Baḥrayn developed into an important centre of Twelver Shiʿi learning and numerous theologians are known to have been active there during the 7th/13th century, notably Kamāl al-Dīn Aḥmad b. ʿAlī b. Saʿīd b. Saʿāda al-Baḥrānī,[33] his student ʿAlī b. Sulaymān al-Baḥrānī (fl. first half 7th/13th century)[34] and Kamāl al-Dīn Maytham b. ʿAlī b. Maytham al-Baḥrānī (d. 699/1299–1300), the author of *Qawāʿid al-marām fī ʿilm al-kalām*.[35] A number of additional texts of unclear authorship are also known to have been written at the beginning of this period, namely the *Kitāb al-Yāqūt* by a certain Abū Isḥāq Ibrāhīm b. Nawbakhtī,[36] *Khulāṣat al-naẓar* by an unknown author,[37] and a brief anonymous Twelver Shiʿi theological tract in which Abu'l-Ḥusayn al-Baṣrī is mentioned.[38]

---

[32] See Schmidtke, 'Doctrinal Views', pp. 357–382; Ḥusayn Mudarrisī Ṭabāṭabāʾī, 'Mufāwaḍa-i dar masʾala-yi shayʾiyyat-i maʿdūm', *Kitābiyyāt* (New Jersey, 2009), pp. 39–51.

[33] See ʿAlī Riḍā Sayyid Taqawī, 'Baḥrānī, Abū Jaʿfar Kamāl al-Dīn', *DMBI*, vol. 11, pp. 383–384.

[34] See Ḥasan Anṣārī, 'Miṣbāḥ al-ʿirfān wa-miftāḥ al-bayān-i ʿAlī b. Sulaymān al-Baḥrānī u dīgar-i āthār-i ū', online: http://ansari.kateban.com/entry1789.html (accessed 17 October 2011); Wilferd Madelung, 'Baḥrānī, Jamāl al-Dīn', *EIR*, vol. 3, p. 529; Robert Gleave, 'Shaykh ʿAlī b. Sulaymān al-Baḥrānī', *EI3*, vol. 3, p. 151f.

[35] Ed. Aḥmad al-Ḥusaynī (Qumm, 1406/1985–1986). See also Sayyid Jaʿfar Sajjādī, 'Ibn Maytham', *DMBI*, vol. 4, pp. 716–717; *Kitābshināsī-i āthār-i dastnivīs-i ʿAllāma Kamāl al-Dīn Abū ʿAlī Maytham b. ʿAlī Baḥrānī Māḥūzī: Darguzhashta-yi sāl-i 699 H. dar Kitābkhāna-yi Buzurg-i Ḥaḍrat-i Āyat Allāh al-ʿUẓmā Marʿashī Najafī: Ganjīna-yi Jahānī-i Makhṭūṭāt-i Islāmī* (Qumm, 2007). Most of the theological writings by Maytham al-Baḥrānī were commissioned by the *amīr* ʿAbd al-ʿAzīz b. Jaʿfar b. al-Ḥusayn al-Nīsābūrī (b. 626/1228–1229, d. 672/1274); see Ḥasan Anṣārī, 'Chand kitāb-i kalāmī taqdīmī bih yak amīr-i fāḍil-i Shīʿī', online: http://ansari.kateban.com/entry1792.html (accessed 17 October 2011). Generally on the scholars of Baḥrayn during this period, see Ali al-Oraibi, *The Shiʿi Renaissance: A Case Study of the Theosophical School of Bahrain in the 7th/13th Century* (Ph.D. dissertation, McGill University, Montreal, 1992); Ali al-Oraibi, 'Rationalism in the School of Bahrain', in Lynda Clarke, ed., *Shiite Heritage: Essays on Classical and Modern Tradition* (Binghamton, NY, 2001), pp. 331–343. The rich Twelver Shiʿi scholarship of Baḥrayn during the 8th/14th and 9th/15th centuries is documented in the chains of transmission of Ibn Abī Jumhūr al-Aḥsāʾī (d. after 906/1501); many scholars are known by name only. See Schmidtke, *Theologie, Philosophie und Mystik*, pp. 282ff (Appendix 3: Die Überliefererketten des Ibn Abī Ǧumhūr al-Aḥsāʾī).

[36] Following Muḥammad Khān Qazwīnī, Ḥasan Anṣārī has shown that the work was most probably written at the beginning of the 7th/13th century; see his "Allāma Qazwīnī u Kitāb al-Yāqūt-i Ibn Nawbakht', online: http://ansari.kateban.com/entry1794.html (accessed 17 October 2011). For earlier scholarship on the work and its author, see Schmidtke, *Theology*, p. 48f (with further references).

[37] See Ansari and Schmidtke, ed., *Khulāṣat al-naẓar: An Anonymous Imāmī-Muʿtazilī Treatise*.

[38] Preserved in a collective manuscript (ff. 5b–12a) that was copied during the second half of the 7th/13th century and is held by the library of the Faculty of Medicine at the University of Shiraz ('Allāma Ṭabāṭabāʾī Library). See our 'The Zaydī Reception of Ibn Khallād's *Kitāb al-Uṣūl*: The *taʿlīq* of Abū Ṭāhir b. ʿAlī al-Ṣaffār', *Journal Asiatique*, 298 (2010), pp. 275–302.

II

Abū Jaʿfar Muḥammad b. al-Ḥasan al-Ṭūsī ('Shaykh al-Ṭā'ifa', born in Ṭūs, Ramaḍān 385/September–October 995, died in Najaf, 22 Muḥarram 460/2 December 1067) began his scholarly career in his homeland Khurāsān and specifically in multicultural Nīshāpūr where he grew up and received his first education.[39] Apart from Shiʿi doctrine, he probably studied Shāfiʿī law here[40] and was exposed to the doctrinal thought of the Muʿtazilī School of Baghdad that was predominant in Khurāsān at the time. During this period he had specifically studied Abū Manṣūr al-Ṣarrām's *Bayān al-dīn* with his Imāmī teacher Abū Ḥāẓim al-Nīsābūrī, [41] and according to al-Ṭūsī's student al-Ḥasan b. Mahdī al-Saylaqī,[42] it was due to al-Ṣarrām's influence that al-Ṭūsī upheld the Muʿtazilī notion of the threat (*al-waʿīd*).[43] When he came to Baghdad in 408/1017–1018, al-Ṭūsī studied first with al-Mufīd, who died in 413/1022, and subsequently with al-Murtaḍā. It was undoubtedly the latter's influence that caused al-Ṭūsī to renounce the notion of *al-waʿīd* and to accept the demarcation lines between Muʿtazilism and Imāmism as they had been formulated particularly

[39] For his teachers during this period, see ʿAbd al-ʿAzīz Ṭabāṭabā'ī, 'Ḥayāt al-Shaykh al-Ṭūsī wa-mashā'ikhuhu', in the introduction to his edition of al-Ṭūsī's *Fihrist kutub al-Shīʿa wa-uṣūlihim wa-asmā' al-muṣannifīn wa-aṣḥāb al-uṣūl* (Qumm, 1420/1999–2000), pp. 32–36 [the original Persian version was published as 'Shakhṣiyyat-i ʿilmī wa-mashāyikh-i Shaykh-i Ṭūsī', *Mīrāth-i Islāmī-yi Īrān* 2 (1374/1995), pp. 361–412]; Ḥasan Anṣārī, 'Nokte-yī dar bāre-ye yekī az ostādān-e na shenākhte-ye Shaykh Ṭūsī dar Nīshābūr', online: http://ansari.kateban.com/entry1357.html (accessed 10 October 2011). A comprehensive study on the life and writings of al-Ṭūsī is the one by Āghā Buzurg al-Ṭihrānī in his introduction to the edition of al-Ṭūsī's Qur'an commentary, *al-Tibyān fī tafsīr al-Qur'ān*, ed. Aḥmad Qaṣīr al-ʿĀmilī, 10 vols (Najaf, 1957–1963), vol. 1, pp. 1–74. For a Persian translation of the introduction, see Āghā Buzurg al-Ṭihrānī, *Zindigīnāma-yi Shaykh Ṭūsī*, tr. ʿAlī Riḍā Mīrzā Muḥammad and Ḥamīd Ṭabībiyān (Tehran, 1360/1982) (republished repeatedly; we have used the edition of 1376/1997). See also Mohammad Ali Amir-Moezzi, 'Al-Ṭūsī, Muḥammad b. al-Ḥasan', *EI2*, vol. 10, pp. 745–746; Muḥammad Wā'iẓ-Zādeh Khurāsānī, 'Ḥayāt al-Shaykh al-Ṭūsī', in the introduction to *Rasā'il al-Shaykh al-Ṭūsī [al-Rasā'il al-ʿashr]* (Qumm, n.d.), pp. 5–62; *Dhikrā al-alfiyya li-l-Shaykh al-Ṭūsī. Yādnāma-yi Shaykh al-Ṭā'ifa Abū Jaʿfar Muḥammad b. Ḥasan Ṭūsī*, 3 vols (Mashhad, 1348–1354/1970–1976); Ansari, *L'imamat*, pp. 124ff.

[40] See al-Subkī, *Ṭabaqāt al-Shāfiʿiyya al-kubrā*, ed. Maḥmūd Muḥammad al-Ṭanāḥī and ʿAbd al-Fattāḥ Muḥammad al-Ḥilw, 10 vols (Cairo, 1964–1976), vol. 4, p. 126, where it is stated that he had Shāfiʿite tendencies (*kāna yantamī ilā madhhab al-Shāfiʿī*).

[41] See *Fihrist*, p. 225, no. 873. See also Āghā Buzurg al-Ṭihrānī, *Ṭabaqāt aʿlām al-shīʿa. al-Qarn al-rābiʿ: Nawābigh al-ruwāt fī rābiʿat al-mi'āt*, ed. ʿAlī Naqī Munzawī (Beirut, 1390/1970), p. 16. For Abū Manṣūr al-Ṣarrām, see *Fihrist*, ed. Ṭabaṭabā'ī, p. 537.

[42] On him, see Āghā Buzurg, *Ṭabaqāt aʿlām al-Shīʿa wa-huwa al-Nābis*, p. 56. See also Ḥasan Anṣārī, 'Guzār az ikhwān al-Ṣafā-yi ismāʿīlī bi-zaydiyya az maṣīr-i imāmiyya', *Kitāb-i māh-i dīn*, 120–122 (1386/2007), pp. 4–15.

[43] The first to report this was the ʿAllāma al-Ḥillī in his *Khulāṣat al-aqwāl fī maʿrifat al-rijāl* (n. p., 1417/1996–1997), p. 250.

by al-Murtaḍā.[44] Following the latter's death in 436/1044, al-Ṭūsī became the most authoritative Imāmī theologian in Baghdad.

During the Saljūq invasion of Baghdad in 447/1056, al-Ṭūsī's home and library were burnt down while al-Ṭūsī himself managed to flee to Najaf where he spent the rest of his life. As a result, many of his writings were destroyed, including some of his most important theological works. In his *Fihrist*, he lists the following writings of his on theology – the arrangement of titles in the autobibliography (which is retained in the following list) possibly reflects their relative chronology. Since all titles are mentioned after the *Fihrist* in the autobibliographical list, it is likely that they were all written after he had completed an initial version of the latter work (most likely around 415/1025), in most, if not all, cases perhaps even after the death of al-Murtaḍā in 436/1044:[45]

- *Kitāb mā yuʿallal wa-mā lā yuʿallal* (lost).[46] The title suggests that the work was concerned with the notion of *ʿilla* in theology and legal methodology.[47] This is noteworthy as there are no other works known to have been written by Imāmī theologians prior to al-Ṭūsī that were exclusively concerned with this topic. With the exception of al-Najāshī's *Rijāl*, the work is not cited by any later Twelver Shiʿi author and it is possible that it was destroyed during the Saljūq invasion of Baghdad.[48]
- *Muqaddama fi'l-madkhal ilā [ṣināʿat] ʿilm al-kalām*, an introductory work in which the author discusses the theological notions of existent (*mawjūd*), acci-

[44] See al-ʿAllāma al-Ḥillī, *Khulāṣat al-aqwāl*, p. 250; see also al-Shaykh al-Ṭūsī, *al-Iqtiṣād fīmā yajibu ʿalā'l-ʿibād* (Najaf, 1399/1979), pp. 193ff where the author denies the notion of mutual cancellation (*iḥbāṭ*) that is founded on the notion of the threat.

[45] See *Fihrist*, pp. 192–194. The process of compilation of the *Fihrist* still needs to be investigated in detail, but the date suggested is based on al-Ṭūsī's remark in his entry on Ibn Nūḥ al-Sīrāfī (*Fihrist*, p. 37) that the latter had died only a few years ago. See Ḥasan Anṣārī, 'Ibn Nūḥ Sīrāfī', *DMBI*, vol. 5, pp. 61–62; see also Mūsā Shubayrī Zanjānī, 'Abu'l-ʿAbbās-i Najāshī u ʿaṣr-i way', in Mu'assasa-yi kitābshināsī-yi Shīʿa, ed., *Jurʿa-ay az daryā* (Qumm, 1389/2010), vol. 1, p. 99. It should be noted, however, that the order of the titles given differs slightly in some of the manuscripts. This is reflected in the two published editions of the *Fihrist* by Ṭabāṭabā'ī and by Baḥr al-ʿUlūm. There is so far no study on the chronology of al-Ṭūsī's entire literary œuvre. A preliminary study addressing this issue is ʿEliyyeh Riḍā-Dād and Sayyid Kāẓim Ṭabāṭabā'ī, 'Gāhshumārī-yi āthār-i Shaykh-i Ṭūsī', *Faṣlnāma-yi muṭālaʿāt-i Islāmī*, 80 (1387/2008), pp. 49–73, online: http://www.sid.ir/fa/VEWSSID/J_pdf/55213878002.pdf (accessed 17 January 2012).

[46] In the edition of Baḥr al-ʿUlūm, the *Kitāb mā yuʿallal wa-mā lā yuʿallal* is mentioned as the first among the theological writings. In several manuscripts that have been consulted by Ṭabāṭabā'ī the *Kitāb mā yu'allal* follows upon *al-Mas'ala fi'l-aḥwāl.*

[47] For a contemporary Ashʿarī discussion of *ʿilal* in theology and *uṣūl al-fiqh*, see Imām al-Ḥaramayn al-Juwaynī, *al-Shāmil fī uṣūl al-dīn*, ed. ʿAlī Shāmī al-Nashshār et al. (Alexandria, 1969), pp. 629ff [*Kitāb al-ʿIlal*].

[48] See *Fihrist*, p. 193: 11; al-Najāshī, *Rijāl*, p. 403, no. 1068. See also *Dharīʿa*, vol. 19, p. 36, no. 185.

dents (*aʿrāḍ*) and substances (*jawāhir*), attributes (*ṣifāt*), reason (*ʿaql*) and the nature of reasoning (*naẓar*) and actions (*afʿāl*), taking into consideration the views of the Bahshamiyya and rivalling strands within the Muʿtazila. Despite its brevity, this was evidently considered by al-Ṭūsī to be an important work, as he characterised it as being without precedent (*lam yuʿmal mithluhu*).[49] This high esteem was shared by al-Najāshī who included the title in his list of al-Ṭūsī's writings, which otherwise contains only the more comprehensive works.[50] Its popularity is also indicated by the various commentaries that were written on it later on (see Section III below) and by the numerous extant manuscripts of the *Muqaddama*.[51] Moreover, al-Ṭūsī refers to the *Muqaddama* later on in his *Kitāb*

---

[49] See *Fihrist*, p. 193:11–12.

[50] See al-Najāshī, *Rijāl*, p. 403, no. 1068. The work is also listed by Ibn Shahrāshūb in his *Maʿālim*, p. 115: 4.

[51] (i) According to Āghā Buzurg, the earliest extant manuscript of the text, copied by Niẓām al-Dīn Maḥmūd b. ʿAlī al-Khwārazmī and dated 26 Rajab 444/21 November 1052 (together with an *ijāza* by al-Ṭūsī issued on 26 Muḥarram 445/18 May 1053) was held in the private library of Fakhr al-Dīn Naṣīrī in Tehran. The current whereabouts of the manuscript are unknown. See Āghā Buzurg al-Tihrānī's introduction to al-Ṭūsī's *Tibyān*, p. 31f, and his *Ṭabaqāt aʿlām al-shīʿa wa-huwa al-Nābis*, p. 191; Muḥammad Taqī Dānishpazhūh, 'Chahār farhangnāma-yi kalāmī', p. 145 n. 1 (Dānishpazhūh did not consult the manuscript himself; the authenticity of the manuscript is therefore not confirmed and it may have been forged; on the Fakhr al-Dīn Naṣīrī collection see the various articles included in *Nāma-yi Bahāristān* (1381/2003), vol. 5, pp. 165–198; ʿAlī Ṣafī Pūr, 'Raddi-bandī-yi andāzi-yi dastbord wa-bar sakhtigi dar dastnivishthā', *Majalla-yi Kitābdārī*, 43 (1388/2009), pp. 139–174; (ii) British Library MS Or. 10968/1, ff. 1a–17b, copied by ʿAlī b. Ḥasan b. al-Raḍī al-ʿAlawī al-Ḥusaynī and completed on 1 Dhu'l-Ḥijja 716/14 February 1317, with numerous collation notes and comments in the margin in the same hand. For a brief description of the codex, see Muḥammad Mahdī Najaf, 'Min al-makhṭūṭāt al-ʿArabiyya fi'l-maṭḥaf al-Brīṭānī Landan iv', *Turāthunā*, 23 (1428/2007), p. 277. The British Library purchased the manuscript on 12 January 1929 from Wladimir Ivanow (1886–1970) who had acquired the codex in October 1928 in Shiraz. On the title page of the manuscript there is an (illegible) library stamp dated 1307/1889–1890. A reproduction of this manuscript is preserved in the Markaz-i iḥyā'-i mīrāth-i islāmi in Qumm (shelfmark 403/1) and the Marʿashī library in Qumm (shelfmark 1257, *majmūʿa*); see Sayyid Jaʿfar Ḥusaynī Ashkavarī and Ṣādiq Ḥusaynī Ashkavarī, *Fihrist-i nuskha-hā-yi ʿaksī-i Markaz-i Iḥyā'-i Mīrāth-i Islāmī*, 2 vols (Qumm, 1377/1998–1999), vol. 2, pp. 7–9; Abu'l-Faḍl Ḥāfiẓiyān Bābulī, *Fihrist-i nuskha-hā-yi ʿaksī-yi Kitābkhāna-yi Buzurg-i Ḥaḍrat Āyat Allāh al-ʿUẓmā Marʿashī Najafī: Ganjīna-yi jahānī-yi makhṭūṭāt-i Islāmī* (Qumm, 2008), vol. 3, p. 575. See also online: http://www.aghabozorg.ir/showbookdetail.aspx?bookid=188789 (accessed 14 July 2011). We thank ʿAlī Ṭabāṭabā'ī Yazdī for having made a copy of the British Library manuscript available to us; (iii) Malik 458 (8th/14th century); see *Fihrist-i kitāb-hā-yi khaṭṭī-yi Kitābkhāna-yi Millī-i Malik*, ed. Īraj Afshār, Muḥammad Taqī Dānishpazhūh et al. (Tehran, 1352/1973), vol. 1, p. 532; al-Sayyid Aḥmad al-Ḥusaynī, *al-Turāth al-ʿArabī al-makhṭūṭ fī maktabāt Īrān al-ʿāmma* (Qumm, 1431/2010), vol. 12, p. 205. It seems that a reproduction of this manuscript is held by the Marʿashī library in Qumm; see Ḥāfiẓiyān Bābulī, *Fihrist-i nuskha-hā-yi ʿaksī-yi Kitābkhāna-yi Buzurg-i Ḥaḍrat Āyat Allāh al-ʿUẓmā Marʿashī*, vol. 4, p. 56f, no. 1334; (iv) Malik 5712/8 (copied between 990–995/1582–1587); see *Fihrist-i kitāb-hā-yi khaṭṭī-yi Kitābkhāna-yi Millī-i Malik*, vol. 8, p. 475; *Muʿjam al-turāth al-kalāmī*, vol. 5, p. 231, no. 11376. Muṣṭafā Dirāyatī (*Fihristvāra-yi*

al-iqtiṣād.[52] The *terminus post quem* for the compilation of the work is al-Sharīf al-Murtaḍā's year of death, 436/1044, as is indicated by the eulogy *raḥimahu llāh/raḍiya llāh ʿanhū* whenever he is mentioned in the text.

- An autocommentary on the said *Muqaddama* entitled, according to al-Najāshī, *Riyāḍat al-ʿuqūl* is lost.[53] It is possible that the commentary was completed soon after the *Muqaddama*, as the two works are mentioned next to each other in al-Ṭūsī's autobibliography.
- *Masʾala fi'l-aḥwāl* (lost), a work which al-Ṭūsī praises in his *Fihrist* as '*malīḥa*'.[54] Apart from al-Ṭūsī's autobibliography and al-Najāshī's and Ibn Shahrāshūb's references to the work,[55] no later author seems to cite it. The title suggests that it was concerned with the Bahshamī notion of the 'states' (*aḥwāl*).
- *Kitāb sharḥ mā yataʿallaq bi'l-uṣūl min Jumal al-ʿilm wa'l-ʿamal [Kitāb tamhīd al-uṣūl/al-Tamhīd fī ʿilm al-uṣūl]*, a commentary on the first part of al-Sharīf al-Murtaḍā's *Jumal al-ʿilm wa'l-ʿamal* which is concerned with theology.[56] The *terminus post quem* for this commentary was 436/1044, the year al-Murtaḍā died.[57] Throughout the work, al-Ṭūsī faithfully explains al-Murtaḍā's views and refrains

---

dastnivishthā-yi Īrān (Dinā), 12 vols (Tehran, 1389/2010), vol. 2, p. 11f) has mixed up several of al-Ṭūsī's epistles. The information he provides on the extant manuscripts is therefore of no use. M. T. Dānishpazhūh has published an edition of the *Muqaddama* on the basis of (iii) and (iv) in 'Chahār farhangnāma-yi kalāmī', pp. 183–217 [republished in *Rasāʾil al-Shaykh al-Ṭūsī (al-Rasāʾil al-ʿashr)* (Qumm, n.d.), pp. 63–90]. For a new edition of the *Muqaddama* based on (ii), including the numerous marginal commentaries on the text, and on the copy of the text as preserved in Atıf Efendi Library 1338 (see Section III below for a detailed description of this manuscript), see the Appendix to our Persian preface to *Twelver Shīʿite Theology in 6th/12th Century Syria: ʿAbd al-Raḥmān b. ʿAlī b. Muḥammad al-Ḥusaynī and his Commentary on al-Shaykh al-Ṭūsī's* Muqaddama. Facsimile Publication with Introduction and Indices by Hassan Ansari and Sabine Schmidtke (Tehran, 2013).

52 See al-Ṭūsī, *al-Iqtiṣād fīmā yajibu ʿalā'l-ʿibād*, ed. Ḥasan Saʿīd (Tehran, 1375/1955), p. 48.

53 See *Fihrist*, p. 193:12; al-Najāshī, *Rijāl*, p. 403, no. 1068; similarly Ibn Shahrāshūb, *Maʿālim*, p. 115:4–5. See also *Dharīʿa*, vol. 14, p. 85. The title *Riyāḍat al-ʿuqūl* is also in the margins of one of the extant manuscripts of al-Ṭūsī's *Fihrist*; see *Fihrist*, ed. Ṭabāṭabāʾī, p. 448 (*ḥāshiya*, no. 8).

54 See *Fihrist*, p. 193:13.

55 See al-Najāshī, *Rijāl*, p. 403, no. 1068; Ibn Shahrāshūb, *Maʿālim*, p. 115:5–6.

56 Al-Ṭūsī's student and colleague Abu'l-Qāsim ʿAbd al-ʿAzīz b. Niḥrīr b. ʿAbd al-ʿAzīz b. al-Barrāj al-Ṭarābulusī (b. ca. 400/1009–1010, d. 481/1088) has written a commentary on the *ʿamal* part of al-Sharīf al-Murtaḍā's *Jumal al-ʿilm wa'l-ʿamal* that is concerned with legal issues, *Sharḥ Jumal al-ʿilm wa'l-ʿamal li-Ibn al-Barrāj*, ed. Kāẓim-i Mudīr Shānahchī (Mashhad, 1394/1974). See also Modarressi, *Introduction*, p. 121; Muḥammad Baḥr al-ʿUlūm, 'Ibn Barrāj', *DMBI*, vol. 3, pp. 95–97.

57 See the eulogy for al-Murtaḍā mentioned in the introduction to *Tamhīd*, pp. 1:8–9.

from voicing his own opinions. The work is preserved in three manuscripts[58] and has been edited by ʿAbd al-Muḥsin Mishkāt Dīnī.[59]

All titles mentioned up to this point are included in al-Najāshī's list of al-Ṭūsī's writings in his *Rijāl*. Since al-Najāshī died in 450/1058 this is the *terminus ante quem* for all of them.

- *al-Masāʾil al-rāziyya fiʾl-waʿīd* (lost),[60] a collection of responsa concerned with the threat as the title seems to suggest.
- *Kitāb al-iqtiṣād fīmā yajibu ʿalāʾl-ʿibād* [*al-Iqtiṣād al-hādī ilā ṭarīq al-rashād / al-Iqtiṣād fīmā yataʿallaq biʾl-iʿtiqād*], a concise *summa* of theological and legal doctrines that is extant in several manuscripts and has been published repeatedly.[61] Throughout the work al-Ṭūsī shows himself to be a close follower of the views of al-Murtaḍā, and the numerous references to the author's *Tamhīd*[62] suggest that the *Iqtiṣād* was in fact based on this earlier work. Its *terminus post quem* is indicated by references to the author's *Miṣbāḥ al-mutahajjid*[63] which was known to have been composed towards the end of al-Ṭūsī's stay in Baghdad.[64] Thus the *Iqtiṣād* was either completed during the same period or when al-Ṭūsī was already in Najaf.
- Towards the end of his autobibliography, al-Ṭūsī lists a comprehensive work on theology that he describes as *Kitāb fiʾl-uṣūl kabīr kharaja minhuʾl-kalām fiʾl-tawḥīd wa-baʿḍaʾl-kalām fiʾl-ʿadl*.[65] The title suggests that this work, which is lost, was his most comprehensive book in this discipline and that he may not have completed it. The fact that it is placed at the end of his autobibliography indicates that al-Ṭūsī had composed it at an advanced stage of his life, certainly after 448 when he was in Najaf. The work may be identical with his *al-Kāfī fiʾl-kalām*

---

58 See *Muʿjam al-turāth al-kalāmī*, vol. 2, p. 328, no. 3999; Dirāyatī, *Fihristvāra-yi dastnivishthā-yi Īrān*, vol. 3, p. 321.

59 Tehran 1405/1363/1984. Mishkāt Dīnī has also prepared a Persian translation of the text: *Tamhīd al-uṣūl dar ʿilm-i kalām-i Islāmī*, tarjama u muqaddama u taʿlīqāt-i ʿAbd al-Muḥṣin Mishkāt al-Dīnī (Tehran, 1358/1980).

60 See *Fihrist*, ed. Ṭabāṭabāʾī, p. 450.

61 See *Fihrist*, p. 193:20. The work was first published by Ḥasan Saʿīd (Tehran 1375/1955), a second edition was published in Najaf (1399/1979). A Persian translation of the work was published as *Tarjuma-yi al-iqtiṣād ilā ṭarīq al-rashād*, tr. ʿAbd al-Muḥsin Mishkāt al-Dīnī (Mashhad, 1360/1981). For manuscripts of the text, see *Muʿjam al-turāth al-kalāmī*, vol. 1, p. 414f, no. 1738.

62 See *Iqtiṣād* (Najaf, 1399/1979), pp. 52, 68, 86, 99, 124, 127, 184, 197, 211, 215, 219, 231, 233, 237, 247, 257, 272, 278, 301, 303, 333, 343, 352, 358.

63 See, e.g., *Iqtiṣād* (Najaf, 1399/1979), p. 417.

64 See Shubayrī Zanjānī, 'Abuʾl-ʿAbbās-i Najāshī u ʿaṣr-way', p. 100.

65 See *Fihrist*, p. 194:3–4. In one of the manuscripts of the *Fihrist* this phrase reads as follows: *wa-lahu Kitāb al-Kāfī kabīr fiʾl-kalām mā tamma*. See *Fihrist*, ed. Ṭabāṭabāʾī, p. 451, n. 5.

which is listed by Ibn Shahrāshūb among al-Ṭūsī's writings – Ibn Shahrāshūb remarks that it had remained incomplete (*al-Kāfī fi'l-kalām ghayr tāmm*).[66] Since al-Ṭūsī's '*Kitāb fi'l-uṣūl kabīr*' is listed in the *Fihrist* after two other works of his that can be dated, namely his *Kitāb ikhtiyār maʿrifat al-rijāl* (completed in 456/1064) and his *Kitāb al-majālis (al-amālī) fi'l-akhbār* (completed between 455/1063 and 458/1066),[67] these dates suggest a *terminus post quem* for the compilation of his '*Kitāb fi'l-uṣūl kabīr*'.
- al-Ṭūsī's student al-Ḥasan b. Mahdī al-Saylaqī has added an additional title by al-Ṭūsī to his copy of the *Fihrist* at it seems, which had likewise remained incomplete according to the information provided: *wa-min muṣannafātihi allatī lam yadhkurhā fi'l-Fihrist Sharḥ al-sharḥ fi'l-uṣūl, kitāb mabsūṭ amlā ʿalaynā minhu shay'an ṣāliḥan wa-māta wa-lam yutimmhu wa-lam yuṣannaf mithluhu.*[68] It is likely that this was a commentary on his *Riyāḍat al-ʿuqūl* which he began to compose after he had started writing his above-mentioned 'extensive work on theology' (*kitāb fi'l-uṣūl kabīr*). Saylaqī's characterisation of the work as comprehensive (*mabsūṭ*), together with the fact that al-Ṭūsī dictated it at an advanced stage of his life, leave no doubt that this supercommentary, together with the above-mentioned *summa* that also remained incomplete, constituted important testimonies for the most advanced stage of development of al-Ṭūsī's doctrinal thought.

From this list it is evident that our knowledge of al-Ṭūsī's doctrinal views is based only on his commentary on al-Murtaḍā's *Jumal al-ʿilm* and on his briefer writings in this discipline, namely his *Muqaddama* and his *Kitab al-iqtiṣād*. In these, al-Ṭūsī shared al-Murtaḍā's preference for the doctrines of the Bahshamiyya. By contrast, all of al-Ṭūsī's more comprehensive works on theology are lost and it is unclear to what extent he maintained Bahshamī positions in them, particularly in those works that he composed at a more advanced stage of his life. Both al-Ṭūsī's '*Kitāb fi'l-uṣūl kabīr*' and his *Sharḥ al-sharḥ* seem to have been beyond the reach of later Imāmī theologians, although both works were evidently composed when al-Ṭūsī was already in Najaf. Al-Ḥimmaṣī al-Rāzī, for example, who had used al-Ṭūsī's *Tamhīd* and al-Murtaḍā's

---

66 See Ibn Shahrāshūb, *Maʿālim*, p. 115:16; see also note 66 above. It remains unclear to what extent this work was related to the commentary al-Ṭūsī had intended to write either on his *Tamhīd* or on al-Murtaḍā's *Dhakhīra*. Al-Ṭūsī had stated in his *Tamhīd* that he intended to write a commentary on either of the two works; cf. *Tamhīd*, p. 1:
فإني إن شاء الله في ما بعد أستأنف شرحًا مستوفى لهذا الشرح أو الذخيرة فإن الذخيرة أيضًا محتاجة إلى الشرح وخاصة النصف الأول منه وأذكر هناك الأدلة المعتمدة والمعترضة وقوي شبه المخالفين في كل فصل وأسأله تعالى أن يعين على عمل هذين الكتابين فإنهما إذا خرجا إلى الوجود لم يبق ورائهما شيء يُذكر إلا ما لا فائدة في ذكره لوهنه وضعفه أو في ما ذُكر يكون دليل عليه أو بينة عليه.

67 For these dates, see Shubayrī Zanjānī, 'Abū'l-ʿAbbās-i Najāshī u ʿaṣr-way', p. 100.

68 Quoted in 'Ḥāshiyat Khulāṣat al-aqwāl' by al-Shahīd al-thānī Zayn al-Dīn b. ʿAlī al-ʿĀmilī (d. 966/1558); see *Rasā'il al-Shahīd al-Thānī li-Zayn al-Dīn b. ʿAlī al-ʿĀmilī al-mashhūr bi'l-Shahīd al-Thānī*, 2 vols (Qumm, 1421/2000–2001), vol. 2, p. 1053.

Dhakhīra extensively throughout his *Munqidh*,[69] evidently had neither of these two works at his disposal. The later Imāmī literature contains only a few glimpses that seem to suggest that in some of his lost writings al-Ṭūsī departed from the doctrines of the Bahshamīs, presumably due to the influence of the doctrinal views of Abu'l-Ḥusayn al-Baṣrī. One indication that suggests that al-Ṭūsī did adopt at least some doctrinal aspects of Abu'l-Ḥusayn's thought is given in a *fatwā* by Sharaf al-Dīn Abū ʿAbd Allāh al-Ḥusayn b. Abi'l-Qāsim b. Ḥusayn b. Muḥammad al-ʿAwdī al-Asadī al-Ḥillī (fl. first half of the 8th/14th century) concerning the status of one who upholds the doctrine that the non-existent (*maʿdūm*) is stable (*thābit*). Following Abu'l-Ḥusayn al-Baṣrī, who denied the Bahshamī notion of the states (*aḥwāl*) and thus the claim founded on this notion that an essence (*dhāt*) is distinguished from all other essences and stable (*thābit*) by virtue of an attribute of essence (*ṣifat al-dhāt*) that is necessarily attached to every essence, independently of whether it is existent or not, Sharaf al-Dīn rejected the Bahshamī position that the non-existent (*maʿdūm*) is stable, is a thing (*shay'*), and concluded that the upholder of this position is an unbeliever. To support his argument, Sharaf al-Dīn refers, among other earlier theologians, to al-Ṭūsī who, Sharaf al-Dīn claims, had maintained the same view in his *Riyāḍat al-ʿuqūl*.[70] This would imply that in his autocommentary (or perhaps rather his supercommentary)[71] on the *Muqaddama* al-Ṭūsī had criticised or even rejected the Bahshamī notion of states in its entirety, doubtless due to the influence of Abu'l-Ḥusayn al-Baṣrī.

A second indication suggesting that al-Ṭūsī's doctrinal thought had undergone significant developments is included in his more concise epistles devoted to *kalām*,[72] particularly his *al-Masā'il al-kalāmiyya*. In this text, which cannot be dated,[73] he

[69] See *al-Munqidh*, vol. 2, pp. 213, 220, 222, 377.

[70] See Schmidtke, 'Doctrinal Views', pp. 383, 389, no. 9 (with further references).

[71] It is likely that Sharaf al-Dīn had al-Ṭūsī's *Sharḥ Riyāḍat al-ʿuqūl* in mind rather than his *Riyāḍat al-ʿuqūl*.

[72] Editions of these are included in *Rasā'il al-Shaykh al-Ṭūsī [al-Rasā'il al-ʿashr]* (Qumm, n.d.). An edition by Muḥammad Taqī Dānishpazhūh of another tract, *Sharḥ al-ʿIbārāt al-muṣṭalaḥa bayna'l-mutakallimīn*, which in the view of the editor is also by al-Ṭūsī, is included in *Dhikrā al-alfiyya li-l-Shaykh al-Ṭūsī: Yādnāma-yi Shaykh al-Ṭā'ifa Abū Jaʿfar Muḥammad b. Ḥasan Ṭūsī*, 3 vols (Mashhad, 1348–54/1970–1976), vol. 1, pp. 236–240; see ibid., p. 148 for a description of the single extant manuscript of the text (Sipahsālār); see also Dirāyatī, *Fihristvāra-yi dastnivishthā-yi Īrān*, vol. 1, p. 1051, no. 26349. This text is identical in Dānishpazhūh's view with *Iṣṭilāḥāt al-mutakallimīn* mentioned by Āghā Buzurg in his *Dharīʿa*; see n. 85 below.

[73] We do not have any reason to doubt the authenticity of *al-Masā'il al-kalāmiyya*, while that of the *Risāla fi'l-iʿtiqādāt* is less certain. The edition of *al-Masā'il al-kalāmiyya* is based on five manuscripts (the earliest being copied in the 10th/16th century), while the edition of *Risāla fi'l-iʿtiqādāt* is based on a single manuscript copied in 948/1541. For the extant manuscripts of *al-Masā'il al-kalāmiyya*, the commentaries on the text and the extant manuscripts of *Risāla fi'l-iʿtiqādāt*, among them one (preserved in Najaf) that apparently contains an indication that the text had been composed by al-Ṭūsī, see Muḥammad ʿAlī Rawḍātī, 'Dū risāla-yi kalāmī az Shaykh-i Ṭūsī', online: http://www.kateban.com/tusi_102.html (accessed 22 December 2011);

adduced the earlier definition of the *mutakallimūn* of God as being eternal (*qadīm azalī*), whose existence has no beginning (*anna wujūdahu lam yasbiqhu' l-ʿadam*) alongside the alternative notion of God being the necessary existent (*wājib al-wujūd)*, that is, whose non-existence is impossible *(la yajūzu ʿalayhi'l-ʿadam)* and who is not dependent in his existence on anything else (*annahu lā yaftaqiru fī wujūdihi ilā ghayrihi*).[74] Earlier Bahshamī authors, such as ʿAbd al-Jabbār,[75] the latter's Zaydī student Abu'l-Ḥusayn Aḥmad b. al-Ḥusayn b. Abī Hāshim al-Ḥusaynī al-Qazwīnī, known as Mānkdīm Shashdīw (d. ca. 425/1034),[76] and al-Sharīf al-Murtaḍā,[77] had already started replacing the traditional *kalām* notion of eternality (*qidam*) referring to 'beforeness' or to that whose existence has no beginning and is thus uncaused, with the notion of necessity (*wujūb al-wujūd*), but they still refrained from defining God as the necessary existent by virtue of himself (*wājib al-wujūd li-dhātihi*) and from using the matrix of necessary existent (*wājib al-wujūd*) versus contingent (*mumkin al-wujūd*), by virtue of itself (*li-dhātihi*) or by another (*li-ghayrihi*), as it had been fully formulated by Ibn Sīnā and was commonly used in *kalām* from the 6th/12th century onwards.[78] In his *al-Masā'il al-kalāmiyya*, al-Ṭūsī is thus one of the earliest *mutakallimūn* to have employed the more progressive matrix.[79] Again, he may have done so partly due to the influence of Abu'l-Ḥusayn al-Baṣrī. Although the latter had

---

idem, 'Fihrist-i nuskhahā-yi muṣannafāt-i Shaykh al-Ṭā'ifa-yi mawjūd dar kitābkhāna-yi Rawḍātī', online: http://www.kateban.com/tusi_120.html (accessed 22 December 2011); Dānishpazhūh, 'Chahār farhangnāma-yi kalāmī', pp. 142–144.

[74] Cf. his *al-Masā'il al-kalāmiyya*, p. 93:

«3» مسألة: الله تعالى واجب الوجود لذاته بمعنى أنه لا يفتقر في وجوده إلى غيره ولا يجوز عليه العدم بدليل أنه لو كان ممكن الوجود لافتقر إلى صانع كافتقار هذا العالم وذلك محال على المنعم المعبود. «4» مسألة: الله تعالى قديم أزلي بمعنى أن وجوده لم يسبقه العدم، باق أبدي بمعنى أن وجوده لم يلحقه العدم بدليل أنه واجب الوجود لذاته، فيستحيل سبق العدم عليه وتطرقه إليه.

See also ibid., p. 96 [*mas'ala* 21]. See also his *Risāla fi'l-iʿtiqādāt*, p. 104, where this notion is more advanced. However, the authenticity of this tract is uncertain (see n. 74 above):

(4) والدليل على أن الله تعالى واجب الوجود: لأنا نقسم الموجود إلى قسمين، واجب الوجود وممكن الوجود، فواجب الوجود هو الذي لا يفتقر في وجوده إلى غيره ولا يجوز عليه العدم، وهو الله تعالى. وممكن الوجود هو الذي يفتقر في وجوده إلى غيره ويجوز عليه العدم، وهو ما سوى الله تعالى وهو العالم. فلو كان البارئ تعالى ممكن الوجود لافتقر إلى مؤثر، والمفتقر ممكن فيكون البارئ تعالى واجب الوجود بهذا المعنى وهو المطلوب. (5) والدليل على أن الله تعالى قديم أزلي: لأن معنى القديم والأزلي هو الذي لا أول لوجوده فلو كان البارئ تعالى لوجوده أولًا لكان محدثًا وقد ثبت أنه تعالى واجب الوجود فيكون قديمًا أزليًا.

[75] See his *al-Mughnī fī abwāb al-tawḥīd wa'l-ʿadl*, ed. Ṭāhā Ḥusayn (Cairo, 1960–), vol. 4, p. 250; vol. 6, p. 54; vol. 11, p. 433.

[76] See his *[Taʿlīq] Sharḥ al-uṣūl al-khamsa*, p. 128.

[77] See his *Mulakhkhaṣ*, p. 217.

[78] The matrix and the Avicennan terminology are commonly used in Ibn al-Malāḥimī's *Kitāb al-fā'iq* and in his *Muʿtamad*. On the development of the notion of eternality (*qidam*) towards necessity (*wujūb*) among the *mutakallimūn*, see Robert Wisnovsky, *Avicenna's Metaphysics in Context* (New York, 2003), pp. 223ff; idem, 'One Aspect of the Avicennan Turn in Sunnī Theology', *Arabic Sciences and Philosophy*, 14 (2004), pp. 65–100. Wisnovsky was unaware of the important developments in Muʿtazilī *kalām* that were due to Abu'l-Ḥusayn al-Baṣrī.

[79] By contrast, this is certainly not the case in either his *Iqtiṣād* or in his *Tamhīd*.

apparently avoided the philosophical terminology,[80] his notion of *muḥdath* clearly departed from that of the earlier Muʿtazilī theologians and agreed in substance with Ibn Sīnā's notion of the contingent (*mumkin al-wujūd*).[81]

III

Apart from al-Ṭūsī's autocommentaries on his *Muqaddama*, several additional commentaries are known to have been written on the text, al-Quṭb al-Rāwandī's (d. 573/1177–1178) lost *Jawāhir al-kalām fī sharḥ Muqaddama al-kalām* being the earliest one.[82] The numerous marginal comments included in MS BL OR 10968/1 constitute another commentary on the text. These may have originated with the copyist of the manuscript, ʿAlī b. al-Ḥasan b. al-Raḍī al-ʿAlawī al-Ḥusaynī, who wrote in 716/1317, or perhaps with an earlier Imāmī scholar as is suggested by the clearly Bahshamī tendencies expressed throughout the *ḥawāshī*.[83] Moreover, it is likely that Qāḍī Saʿīd al-Qummī (d. 1107/1696) has also commented on the work.[84] Another

80 As was the case already with ʿAbd al-Jabbār, Abu'l-Ḥusayn uses, however, the notion of *wujūb al-wujūd*; see Abu'l-Ḥusayn al-Baṣrī, *Taṣaffuḥ al-adilla*. The extant parts introduced and edited by Wilferd Madelung and Sabine Schmidtke (Wiesbaden, 2006), pp. 5, 13.

81 See Wilferd Madelung, 'Abū'l-Ḥusayn al-Baṣrī's Proof for the Existence of God', in James E. Montgomery, ed., *Arabic Theology, Arabic Philosophy: From the Many to the One. Essays in Celebration of Richard M. Frank* (Leuven, 2006), p. 275. It was most likely due to the influence of Abu'l-Ḥusayn that the notions of necessary existent (*wājib al-wujūd*) versus contingent (*jā'iz al-wujūd*) were also employed by al-Juwaynī; see his *Kitāb al-shāmil*, pp. 111, 116.

82 See Muntajab al-Dīn ʿAlī b. Bābūya al-Rāzī, *al-Fihrist*, ed. ʿAbd al-ʿAzīz Ṭabāṭabā'ī (Beirut, 1406/1986), pp. 87–89; *al-Dharīʿa*, vol. 5, p. 277, no. 1298; vol. 14, p. 85; *Muʿjam al-turāth al-kalāmī*, vol. 2, p. 478, no. 4692. For Quṭb al-Dīn al-Rāwandī and his writings, see the editor's introduction to his *Lubb al-lubāb*, ed. al-Sayyid Ḥusayn al-Jaʿfarī al-Zanjānī, 2 vols (Qumm, 1431/2009–2010), vol. 1, pp. 5–57; ʿAbd al-ʿAzīz Ṭabāṭabā'ī, 'Nahj al-balāgha ʿabra'l-qurūn (7): Shurūḥuhu ḥasab al-tasalsul al-zamanī', *Turāthunā* 10 (1415/1994–1995), pp. 254ff; Capezzone, 'Maestri e testi nei centri imamiti', p. 24f, no. 67. According to Āghā Buzurg al-Ṭihrānī, another commentary on the *Muqaddama* was composed by Sayyid ʿAzīz Allāh al-Ḥusaynī al-Ardabīlī in 967/1559–1960. See *al-Dharīʿa*, vol. 14, p. 85f, no. 1839; *Muʿjam al-turāth al-kalāmī*, vol. 4, p. 91, no. 7960 (with reference to a manuscript in the Āstān-i quds library in Mashhad that was not available to us); for a description of this manuscript, see *Fihrist-i kutub-i khaṭṭī-yi Kitābkhāna-yi Āstān-i Quds-i Raḍavī* (Mashhad, 1315–/1936–), vol. 1, p. 58, no. 194. Muḥammad ʿAlī Rawḍātī, who has inspected the Mashhad manuscript, has established, however, that it is a commentary on al-Ṭūsī's *al-Masā'il al-kalāmiyya*; see his 'Dū risāla-yi kalāmī az Shaykh-i Ṭūsī'. Afandī mentions a commentary by ʿAzīz Allāh on an unspecified work of al-Ṭūsī, see *Riyāḍ al-ʿulamā'*, vol. 3, pp. 314–315; see also al-Ṣadr, *Takmilat amal al-ʿāmil*, vol. 3, p. 419.

83 For an *editio princeps* of these comments, see the annex to our Persian preface to *Twelver Shīʿite Theology in 6th/12th Century Syria*.

84 See *al-Dharīʿa*, vol. 2, p. 123, no. 495; vol. 13, p. 93, no. 298 according to which al-Shaykh al-Ṭūsī has composed a tract entitled *Iṣṭilāḥāt al-mutakallimīn*, information that is not confirmed elsewhere. It may well be that this title refers rather to his *Muqaddama ilā ʿilm*

so far unknown commentary (*taʿlīq*) on al-Ṭūsī's *Muqaddama* is preserved as Atıf Efendi Library MS 1338/1 (ff. 1a–110a).[85] The author is identified on the title page (written in a different hand to the text) as Najīb al-Dīn Abu'l-Qāsim ʿAbd al-Raḥmān b. ʿAlī b. Muḥammad al-Ḥusaynī and the wording of the title indicates that the commentary was noted down (*ʿulliqa*) by someone else, most likely a student of ʿAbd al-Raḥmān.[86] This is corroborated by a reference to ʿAbd al-Raḥmān on f. 64a:4ff that clearly originated with his otherwise unknown student (*wa-stadalla sayyidunā al-sharīf al-ajall Najīb al-Dīn Abu'l-Qāsim b. …* [word missing] *waffaqahu llāh*). The fact that the scribe of the title page was evidently unable to recognise Abū Jaʿfar al-Ṭūsī whose name he renders erroneously as Abū Jaʿfar *al-Ṭabarī* as the author of the *Muqaddama*[87] suggests that he was not well versed in Twelver Shiʿi literature. The copyist of the text itself, possibly an Imāmī, seems not to have been familiar with the author of the *taʿlīq*. This is suggested by the above-quoted reference to ʿAbd

---

al-kalām. The only extant manuscript is preserved in the private library of Rājah Muḥammad Mahdī al-Fayḍābādī in India, whose collection has not yet been catalogued. For Qāḍī Saʿīd, see also Muḥammad ʿAlī Rawḍātī, *Duvvumin dū guftār* (Isfahan, 1386/2007); Sajjad Rizvi, '(Neo) Platonism Revived in the Light of the Imams: Qāḍī Saʿīd Qummī (d. AH 1107/AD 1696) and his Reception of the Theologia Aristotelis', in Peter Adamson, ed., *Classical Arabic Philosophy: Sources and Reception* (London and Turin, 2007), pp. 176–207. Rawḍātī suggests that most works attributed to Saʿīd al-Qummī in fact originated with his contemporary Muḥammad Saʿīd al-Ḥakīm.

85 Published as *Twelver Shīʿite Theology in 6th/12th Century Syria* (see n. 51 above). Incomplete and mostly erroneous descriptions of the manuscript are included in Ramazan Şeşen (Ramaḍān Shishin), *Nawādir al-makhṭūṭāt al-ʿArabiyya fī maktabāt Turkiyā* (Beirut, 1975–1982), vol. 1, p. 224; Ramazan Şeşen, *Mukhtārāt min al-makhṭūṭāt al-ʿArabiyya al-nādira fī maktabāt Turkiyā* (Istanbul, 1997), p. 197; Ramazan Şeşen, 'Esquisse d'une histore du développement des colophons dans les manuscrits Musulmans', in François Deroche, ed., *Scribes et manuscrits du Moyen-Orient* (Paris, 1997), p. 200. See also the entry in the catalogue online: http://yazmalar.gov.tr/detay_goster.php?k=158630# (accessed 29 February 2012) and Ali Rıza Karabulut, *İstanbul ve Anadolu kütüphanelerinde mevcut el yazması eserler ansiklopedesi*, 3 vols (Istanbul 2005), p. 1175, no. 3833/9; here the text is described as 'Sharḥ muqaddamat Abī Jaʿfar al-ʿAbdalī al-Ṭabarī' and the work is listed among the works of al-Shaykh al-Ṭūsī and Naṣīr al-Dīn al-Ṭūsī (Karabulut clearly used Şeşen as his source for this manuscript and he fails to distinguish between the Shaykh al-Ṭāʾifa and Naṣīr al-Dīn). See also *Muʿjam al-turāth al-kalāmī*, vol. 4, p. 91, no. 7958 where the text is misattributed to Naṣīr al-Dīn al-Ṭūsī (d. 672/1274). In modern scholarship, Josef van Ess seems to have been the only one to consult the text; see his *Theologie und Gesellschaft*, vol. 6, pp. 25, 27. He incorrectly identifies its author as "Abd al-Raḥmān b. ʿAlī al-Ṭabarī [*sic*]'.

86 The title reads as follows:

عُلِّق من كلام السيد الأجل الشريف الطاهر نجيب الدين أبي القاسم عبد الرحمان بن علي بن محمد الحسيني أكرم الله مثواه | شرح لمقدمة أبي جعفر الطبري [كذا] مسكناً العدلي مذهباً رحمة الله عليه

The top of the title page also has the following note which suggests that the manuscript had circulated mostly, if not exclusively, in Sunnī circles: *hādhā'l-kitāb min kutub al-muʿtazila fi'l-kalām fa-lā taghfal*. In addition, there is an ownership note that is crossed out. The note reads as follows:

ملك العبد الفقير سالم بن محمد بن علي رزقه الله معرفته.

87 See note 86 above.

al-Raḥmān (f. 64a:4f) where the name of the latter's father was left out, certainly because the scribe ignored it. It should also be remarked that the scribe erroneously gives al-Ṭūsī's name as Muḥammad b. al-Ḥusayn (instead of al-Ḥasan) (f. 1b:1).[88] Throughout the text, numerous *balāgh* notes can be found,[89] as well as some marginal corrections and glosses,[90] possibly written by the same hand as the title page. On f. 23b there is a *ḥāshiya* signed by a certain Raḍī b. Muḥammad b. Qāsim. The text ends with a colophon (f. 110a) in which the copyist identifies himself as Salmān b. Masʿūd b. ʿAlī b. Saʿīd b. ʿAbd Allāh al-Hawbal. The date given, end of Ṣafar 590/February 1194, shows that the copy was completed only some eight years after the author of the commentary had died (in 582/1186, see below).[91] The colophon is followed by a collation note dated two months later, 11 Rabīʿ II 590/5 April 1194.[92] Apart from ʿAbd al-Raḥmān's *taʿlīq* on the *Muqaddama*, the codex contains a copy of *al-Mulakhkhaṣ fi'l-jadal* by the renowned Shāfiʿī scholar Abū Isḥāq al-Shīrāzī (d. 476/1084),[93] copied by a different scribe, al-Ḥasan b. ʿAlī b. Muḥammad b. Abi'l-Ḥusayn b. Manṣūr, and completed in Rabīʿ I 590/March 1194.[94] The second text begins still within the same

---

[88] The same mistake is attested in the manuscripts that have been used by Dānishpazhūh; see his edition of the *Muqaddama* in *Rasā'il al-Shaykh al-Ṭūsī*, p. 87.

[89] Ff. 17b, 24a, 32a, 33b, 35a, 41a, 43a, 46b, 58b, 60b, 66b, 67b, 70b, 71a, 72a, 72b, 88b, 92a, 93a, 101b, 102b, 103b,

[90] Ff. 3a, 6a, 8b, 9b, 10b, 11b, 13b, 14b, 15b, 16a, 16b, 22b, 25a, 27a, 27b, 28b, 29a, 30a, 31a, 32b ('Ibn Ḥazm al-Andalusī al-Manṭiqī'), 33b, 35b, 37b, 43a, 44a, 48b, 50a, 50b, 51a, 51b, 52a, 54a, 55a, 56a, 58b, 64a, 68b, 69b, 71b, 72b, 73a, 73b, 74a, 75a, 75b, 82a, 84a, 94a, 95b, 97a, 98a, 101a, 102a, 103b, 105b, 107a, 108a, 110a.

[91] The colophon reads as follows:
فرغ من نساخة هذا الكتاب الفقير إلى رحمة الله تعالى سلمان بن مسعود بن علي بن سعيد بن عبد الله الهوبل في العشر الآخر من شهر صفر من شهور سنة تسعين وخمسمائة غفر الله له ولوالديه ولصاحبه ولجميع المسلمين والمسلمات إنه هو الغفور الرحيم وحسبنا الله وكفى ونعم الوكيل وصلى الله على رسوله سيدنا محمد خاتم النبيين وعلى آله الطيبيين الطاهرين وسلم عليه وعليهم أجمعين.

[92] The note reads as follows:
كمل قصاصة ومعارضة على الأصل المنقول منه بمن الله وعونه يوم الاثنين لإحدى عشرة ليلة خلت من شهر ربيع الآخر من شهور سنة تسعين وخمسمائة سنة.

[93] For a brief description of the manuscript, see online: http://yazmalar.gov.tr/detay_goster.php?k=158631 (accessed 29 February 2012). The title page reads as follows (f. 111a:)
الملخص في الجدل صنفه الشيخ الإمام العالم أبو اسحاق ابراهيم بن علي الفيروزآبادي الشيرازي رحمة الله عليه
This book was apparently edited as part of a dissertation in two volumes submitted by Muḥammad Yūsuf Ākhand Jīyāzī (Mecca, 1407/1987). On the author, see Nūr Allāh Kasā'ī, 'Abū Isḥāq al-Shīrāzī', *DMBI*, vol. 5, pp. 167–171; Eric Chaumont, *La question de l'ijtihād selon abū Isḥāq al-Shīrāzī al-Fīrūzābādī al-Shāfiʿī, m. 476/1084* (Ph.D. dissertation, Université Catholique de Louvain, Louvain, 1989); Eric Chaumont, 'Encore au sujet de l'ashʿarisme d'Abū Isḥāq al-Shīrāzī', *SI*, 74 (1991), pp. 167–177. Among the extant manuscripts of *al-Mulakhkhaṣ*, there is a copy of it preserved in al-Maktaba al-Gharbiyya (Dār al-makhṭūṭāt), Sanaa, no. 886; see Aḥmad Muḥammad ʿĪsawī [et al.], *Fihris al-makhṭūṭāt al-Yamaniyya li-Dār al-makhṭūṭāt wa'l-Maktaba al-Gharbiyya bi'l-Jāmiʿ al-kabīr - Ṣanʿā'* (Qumm, 1426/2005), vol. 1, p. 63.

[94] See the colophon on f. 198b:
وفرغ من نسخته هذا الكتاب الحسن بن علي بن محمد بن أبي الحسين بن منصور (؟) في شهر ربيع الأول من سنة تسعين وخمسمائة وهو يسأل الله طالبًا في المغفرة له ولوالديه ولجميع المؤمنين والمؤمنات ... والحمد لله حمد الشاكرين وصلواته

quire in which the copy of the *taʿlīq* has ended.[95] This, as well as the fact that both texts were transcribed in 590/1194, suggests that the owner of the codex, without any doubt a Twelver Shiʿi, had first commissioned Ibn al-Hawbal to copy the *taʿlīq* on the *Muqaddama* and then Ibn Manṣūr to transcribe Abū Isḥāq's *Mulakhkhaṣ*.

While the Imāmī biographical sources ignore the author of the *taʿlīq*, the Shāfiʿī author ʿAbd al-ʿAẓīm al-Mundhirī (b. 581/1185, d. 656/1258) includes an entry on him in his *al-Takmila li-wafayāt al-naqala*, providing the following genealogy: *al-sharīf al-ajall al-fāḍil Abu'l-Qāsim ʿAbd al-Raḥmān b. al-sharīf al-ajall Abi'l-Ḥasan ʿAlī b. Muḥammad [b. Muḥammad] b. Qāsim al-ʿAlawī al-Ḥusaynī*.[96] The fact that both ʿAbd al-Raḥmān and his father ʿAlī are characterised as *al-sharīf al-ajall* suggests that both were scholars in their own right. Al-Mundhirī adds that ʿAbd al-Raḥmān was born around 520/1126 in Damascus, that he had lived in Aleppo and that he died in Cairo on 13 Shawwāl 582/27 December 1186. It is noteworthy that al-Mundhirī provides no details about ʿAbd al-Raḥmān's literary œuvre nor does he mention his affiliation with Twelver Shiʿism, although it is beyond doubt on the basis of the *taʿlīq*.

Al-Dhahabī (d. 748/1348) includes the same information among the events for the year 582/1186–1187 in his *Ta'rīkh al-Islām*,[97] adding that ʿAbd al-Raḥmān was the grandfather of the renowned al-Sharīf ʿIzz al-Dīn al-Ḥāfiẓ, whose biography is well known. The Shāfiʿī scholar al-Ḥāfiẓ ʿIzz al-Dīn Aḥmad b. Muḥammad b. ʿAbd al-Raḥmān al-Ḥusaynī (b. Cairo 636/1238, d. Cairo 695/1295) was a student of his compatriot al-Mundhirī whose *Takmila* he later on continued in his *Ṣilat al-takmila li-wafāyāt al-naqala*.[98] ʿIzz al-Dīn al-Ḥusaynī states that his genealogy goes back to

---

على رسوله الأمي وعلى أهل بيته الطيبين وسلامه

The colophon is followed by a *waqf* statement:

هذا الكتاب يوقف على ابراهيم بن قدمه (؟) من مالكه رحمة الله عليه وهو معي بالولاية لي وكتب موسى بن عطية بن محمد حامدًا لله تعالى رحم الله تعالى الكاتب والمصنف والناظر والمتأمل بإمعان النظر السديد ولا يسوء الظن بالمسلمين

[95] The codex consists of quinions, senions and septions: 1 V (10), 8 VI (106), 1 V (117), 2 VII (145), 2 VI (169), 1 V (189), 1 V–1 (198). We are using the method for the description of the composition of the quires as established by Jan Just Witkam; see his *Arabic Manuscripts in the Library of the University of Leiden and Other Collections in the Netherlands: A General Introduction to the Catalogue* (Leiden, 1982), p. 14; see also François Déroche et al., *Islamic Codicology: An Introduction to the Study of Manuscripts in Arabic Script* (London, 1426/2005), p. 71. Both scribes provide quire signatures in the outer corner of the upper margin of the recto of the first leaf of the quire. However, while Ibn Hawbal gives the numbers of ordinal form (*thānīya, thālitha, rābiʿa, khāmisa, sādisa, sābiʿa, thāmina, tāsiʿa, ʿāshira*), the copyist of the *Mulakhkhaṣ* employs numerals (11, 12, 13, 14, 15, 16, 17).

[96] ʿAbd al-ʿAẓīm b. ʿAbd al-Qawī al-Mundhirī, *al-Takmila li-wafayāt al-naqala*, ed. Bashshār ʿAwwād Maʿrūf, 4 vols (Beirut, 1981), vol. 1, p. 72, no. 5. The only Imāmī biographer who took notice of ʿAbd al-Raḥmān so far is ʿAbd al-ʿAziz Ṭabāṭabāʾī, *Muʿjam aʿlām al-Shīʿa*, p. 243, who mentions his biography as stated by al-Mundhirī.

[97] Muḥammad b. Aḥmad al-Dhahabī, *Ta'rīkh al-Islām*, ed. ʿUmar ʿAbd al-Salām Tadmurī (Beirut, 1988), vol. 12, p. 751.

[98] ʿIzz al-Dīn Aḥmad b. Muḥammad al-Ḥusaynī, *Ṣilat al-takmila li-wafayāt al-naqala*, ed. Bashshār ʿAwwād Maʿrūf (Beirut, 2007). On ʿIzz al-Dīn, see the editor's introduction to *Ṣilat al-takmila li-wafayāt al-naqala*, vol. 1, pp. 5–54 (with further references); Rudolf Sellheim,

ʿAlī b. Ḥusayn al-Sajjād (d. 95/713) and adds that his family was of Kūfan origin: *ʿIzz al-Dīn Abu'l-Qāsim Aḥmad b. Abī ʿAbd Allāh Muḥammad b. Abi'l-Qāsim ʿAbd al-Raḥmān b. Abi'l-Ḥasan ʿAlī b. Muḥammad b. Muḥammad b. Qāsim b. Muḥammad b. Ibrāhīm b. Muḥammad b. ʿAlī b. ʿUbayd Allāh b. ʿAlī b. ʿUbayd Allāh b. al-Ḥusayn b. ʿAlī b. al-Ḥusayn b. ʿAlī b. Abī Ṭālib …*[99]

About his father Muḥammad ʿIzz al-Din al-Ḥusaynī reports the following details:[100] Sharaf al-Dīn Abū ʿAbd Allāh Muḥammad was born in Cairo on 26 Ramaḍān 573/18 March 1178 where he also died on 6 Ṣafar 666/27 October 1267. ʿAbd al-Raḥmān, ʿIzz al-Dīn al-Ḥusaynī's grandfather, must therefore have left Aleppo prior to 573/1178 when his son was born, and he had died when his son was only nine years old. It is possible that ʿAbd al-Raḥmān was forced to flee from Aleppo as a result of the growing oppression of Shiʿis under the Zengids and the Ayyubids.[101] Sharaf al-Dīn apparently grew up as a Sunni, as his main education took place after his father's death, and

---

"Izzaddīn al-Ḥusainī's Autograph seiner *Ṣilat at-Takmila*: Traditionarier-Biographien des 7./13. Jahrhunderts', *Oriens*, 33 (1992), pp. 156–180. ʿIzz al-Dīn has also compiled a work entitled *al-Aḥādīth al-thamāniyya al-asānīd al-muntaqāt* that is preserved in an apparently unique manuscript (Istanbul, MS Koprülü (Fāḍil Aḥmad Pāshā) 371, ff. 105–202); for a brief description of the manuscript, see Karabulut, *İstanbul ve Anadolu kütüphanelerinde*, vol. 1, p. 229. Details on the transmission of the work and the material it contains are given on the title page as follows:

الأحاديث الثمانية الأسانيد المنتقاة من سماعات الشيخ الجليل مسند الوقت نجيب الدين أبي الفرج عبد المنعم بن علي بن نصر بن منصور الحراني خرجها له السيد الإمام عز الدين أبو القاسم أحمد بن محمد بن عبد الرحمن بن علي الحسيني رضي الله عنهما آمين رواية الشيخ الإمام صدر الدين أبي الفتح محمد بن محمد بن ابراهيم الميدومي عنه

99 *Ṣila*, vol. 2, p. 558; see also the editor's introduction to his *Ṣilat al-Takmila*, vol. 1, p. 7. ʿIzz al-Dīn al-Ḥusaynī apparently had two sons, *al-qāḍī* Sharaf al-Dīn Abu'l-Ḥasan Muḥammad, who had studied with his father the latter's work *Ṣilat al-Takmila* (the autograph manuscript of *Ṣilat al-Takmila* (Köprülü I 1101) has 17 *samāʿāt*, in most of them Muḥammad is mentioned as *sāmiʿ*; see Sellheim, 'Autograph', pp. 165ff; see also the editor's introduction to the *Ṣila*, vol. 1, pp. 25–26 and 50 for a facsimile reproduction of the *samāʿ* dated Rabīʿ I 685/April 1286) and Badr al-Dīn Abū Muḥammad al-Ḥasan (b. ca. 676/1277–1278, d. Jumādā I or Rabīʿ II 743/1342) who inherited from his father the office of *naqīb al-ashrāf*; see the editor's introduction to the *Ṣila*, vol. 1, p. 17.

100 *Ṣila*, vol. 2, p. 558f. See *Mashyakhat qāḍī'l-quḍāt Shaykh al-Islām Badr al-Dīn Abī ʿAbd Allāh Muḥammad b. Ibrāhīm b. Jamāʿa*, takhrīj ʿAlam al-Dīn al-Qāsim b. Muḥammad b. Yūsuf al-Birzālī, ed. Muwaffaq b. ʿAbd Allāh b. ʿAbd al-Qādir (Beirut, 1988), vol. 2, p. 496; al-Dhahabī, *Ta'rīkh al-Islām*, vol. 15, p. 137; Khalīl b. Aybak al-Ṣafadī, *al-Wāfī bi'l-wafayāt*, ed. Sven Dedering (Beirut, 1394/1974), vol. 3, p. 235; Aḥmad b. ʿAlī al-Maqrīzī, *Kitāb al-muqaffā al-kabīr*, ed. Muḥammad al-Yaʿlāwī (Beirut, 1991), vol. 6, p. 22; Mūsā b. Muḥammad al-Yūnīnī, *Dhayl mir'āt al-zamān* (Hyderabad, 1954–1955), vol. 2, p. 403.

101 On the situation of Twelver Shiʿis under the rule of Zangids and Ayyubids, see Ḥasan Anṣārī, 'Dīn u dawlat dar dawlathā-yi Āl Zangī wa-Ayyūbiyyān: Darāmadī bar adabiyyāt-i siyāsī-yi Islāmī', *Kitāb-i māh-i dīn*, 104–105 (1385/2006), pp. 6–33; Nikita Elisséeff, *Nūr ad-Dīn, un grand prince Musulman de Syrie au temps des Croisades (511–569 h./1118–1174)*, 3 vols (Damascus, 1967); Wilferd Madelung, 'The Spread of Māturīdism and the Turks', *Actas do IV Congresso de Estudos Árabes e Islâmicos, Coimbra-Lisboa 1968* (Leiden, 1971), pp. 109–168; Eddé, *La principauté ayyoubide*, pp. 436ff. See also Carole Hillenbrand, 'The Shīʿīs of Aleppo in the Zengid Period: Some Unexploited Textual and Epigraphic Evidence', in H. Biesterfeldt

the teachers Sharaf al-Dīn is known to have studied with were exclusively Sunnis.[102] It was possibly from his father that ʿIzz al-Dīn inherited the prestigious position as *naqīb al-ashrāf*,[103] and it is plausible that he in turn had inherited this office already from his father ʿAbd al-Raḥmān, although the biographical sources are silent about this. When talking about his grandfather ʿAbd al-Raḥmān it is noteworthy that, in contrast to al-Mundhirī and al-Dhahabī, ʿIzz al-Dīn al-Ḥusaynī explicitly refers to his grandfather's literary œuvre, albeit in a general manner, and that he states that the latter had for some time taught Arabic grammar and *uṣūl*, referring either to theology or legal methodology or both.[104] Like al-Mundhirī and al-Dhahabī, ʿIzz al-Dīn does not mention his grandfather's Imāmī affiliation.[105] Moreover, neither ʿIzz al-Dīn nor any other biographer provides any details as to the teachers of his grandfather ʿAbd al-Raḥmān.

Throughout the *taʿlīq* the author regularly refers, apart from some earlier Muʿtazilī thinkers and al-Shaykh al-Ṭūsī, to the Sharīf al-Murtaḍā, whose *Kitāb al-dhakhīra* he explicitly names on one occasion,[106] and to al-Murtaḍā's student Abu'l-Ḥasan al-Buṣrawī.[107] On one occasion he also explicitly mentions al-Ṭūsī's autocommentary on the *Muqaddama* which he must have had at his disposal.[108] It is possible that the present *taʿlīq* is primarily a paraphrastic commentary on al-Ṭūsī's *Sharḥ al-muqaddama*. Towards the end of the text the author refers to Abu'l-Ḥusayn al-Baṣrī (f. 95a)

---

and Verena Klemm, ed., *Differenz und Dynamik in Islam: Festschrift für Heinz Halm zum 70. Geburtstag/ Difference and Dynamics in Islam* (Würzburg, 2012), pp. 163–180.

102 See *Ṣila*, vol. 2, p. 559.

103 This office is mentioned in a *samāʿ* issued for *Ṣilat al-Takmila* where it is stated (quoted in the editor's introduction to the *Ṣila*, vol. 1, p. 25). Note also that ʿAbd al-Raḥmān is characterised in the following *samāʿ* as *al-muftī*:
سمع جميع هذه المجلدة والمجلدة قبلها على مصنفها سيدنا وشيخنا الفقيه الإمام العالم الحافظ ناصر السنة السيد عز الدين أبي القاسم أحمد بن الإمام العلامة شرف الدين أبي عبد الله محمد ابن الإمام المفتي نجيب الدين أبي القاسم عبد الرحمان الحسيني الشافعي نقيب النقباء فسح الله في مدته ونفع المسلمين ببركته ..

104 *Sila*, vol. 2, p. 559:
وأبوه أبو القاسم عبد الرحمن كان أحد الفضلاء المشهورين وله تصانيف حسنة وطريقة جميلة وأقرأ العربية والأصول وغيرهما مدة وانتفع به

105 The extant biographical works on the scholars of Aleppo also convey no information on ʿAbd al-Raḥmān. The only extant biographical work that is devoted to the history of Twelver Shiʿis in Aleppo, Ibn Abī Ṭayy al-Ḥalabī's (d. ca. 630/1232–1233) *al-Ḥāwī fī rijāl al-imāmiyya*, is preserved only incompletely and ʿAbd al-Raḥmān is not mentioned in the preserved parts of the work that have been collected by Rasūl Jaʿfariyān, in *Turāthunā*, 65 (Rabīʿ I 1422/2001), pp. 106–10; 66–67 (Rabīʿ II 1422/2001), pp. 122–131. He is also not mentioned in the various Sunni biographical dictionaries specifically devoted to Aleppo, namely *Zubdat al-ḥalab min taʾrīkh Ḥalab*, ed. Sāmī al-Dahhān (Damascus, 1370/1951) and the incompletely preserved *Bughyat al-ṭalab fī taʾrīkh Ḥalab*, ed. Suhayl Zakkār (Damascus, 1988), both by Kamāl al-Dīn ʿUmar b. al-ʿAdīm (d. 660/1262). On Ibn al-ʿAdīm's works, see also David Morray, *An Ayyubid Notable and his World: Ibn al-ʿAdīm and Aleppo as Portrayed in his Biographical Dictionary of People Associated with the City* (Leiden, 1994).

106 See f. 14a:16.

107 See ff. 18b, 39b.

108 See f. 14a:17 (discussing al-Ṭūsī's notion of annihilation).

'and his followers' (*wa-man qāla bi-qawlihi*) among those who negated the Bahshamī notion of the 'states' (*aḥwāl*). If indeed the present *taʿlīq* is based on al-Ṭūsī's *Sharḥ al-muqaddama,* this reference may have originated with al-Ṭūsī rather than with ʿAbd al-Raḥmān. This would be another indication that al-Ṭūsī had discussed some of the doctrinal views of Abu'l-Ḥusayn al-Baṣrī in his autocommentary. Be that as it may, the commentator clings to the doctrines of the Bahshamīs throughout the *taʿlīq* as seems to have been characteristic for Twelver Shiʿi theologians of Aleppo during his time. He may very well have been under the influence of, and perhaps even closely connected to, Abu'l-Makārim ʿIzz al-Dīn b. Zuhra (on him, see above). At various occasions ʿAbd al-Raḥmān explicitly remarks that his only intention is to explain the views of al-Ṭūsī in his *Muqaddama.*[109]

The text of the commentary begins without any introductory remarks that would provide information about the circumstances that led to the compilation of the *taʿlīq*. Moreover, neither has al-Ṭūsī's *khuṭba* been quoted in full nor has his final remark been included, and the commentary ends with only a brief concluding statement (f. 115a). Some information as to why the *taʿlīq* was compiled is given on f. 53b of the text. Here ʿAbd al-Raḥmān remarks, among other things, that the preceding discussion relates to a query, possibly by a student (*ijābatan li-suʾāl al-sāʾil wa-muwāfaqatan li-gharaḍ al-ṭālib*).[110]

---

109 See f. 96b:17–20:

واعلم بأنّ معظم هذا الفصل مبني على القول بإثبات الأحوال واثبات المعدوم وفيه بعد ذلك ما فيه خلاف بين أهل النظر ونحن نذكر مسئلة مسئلة منه فنبين ماهيتها بحول الله وقوته على حسب ما يليق بهذا الكتاب.

F. 97a:15:

وتحقيق هذه الأقوال وبيان الصحيح منها تقصر عنه رتبة هذا التعليق فلا وجه لذكره.

110 See f. 53b:3–9 (here the work is also explicitly qualified as a *taʿlīq*):

واعلم بأنا وإن أشبعنا في هذا الفصل ما لم نتشبع في باقي فصول هذا الكتاب فإنما كان ذلك إجابة لسؤال السائل وموافقة لغرض الطالب ومن أراد انتزاع هذا الفصل من جملة تعليق هذا الكتاب وجعله كتابًا مفردًا بذاته كان مصيبًا في إرادته مسددًا في قصده فإنه يطلع به على جلّ العلوم التي لها تعلق بالكلام والألفاظ بحول الله وقوته

PART VII
RITES AND RITUALS

Introduction

Gerald R. Hawting

The ritual life of Shiʿi Islam has much in common with that of the Sunnis and other Muslims. Daily prayer (*ṣalāt*), fasting (*ṣawm*, *ṣiyām*) during Ramaḍān, the giving of a certain percentage of one's wealth as alms (*zakāt*) and participation in the annual rituals in and around Mecca (*ḥajj*), all are required of Shiʿis as they are of other Muslims. Certain details in the performance of these rituals may differ between Shiʿis and Sunnis, but then there are differences in the details between the followers of different Sunni schools as well, in addition to the variations that inevitably arise in different social and geographical settings.

There are other areas of ritual, however, which are more specific to Shiʿism and rarely shared by Sunnis. The most obvious are the practices associated with the 10th of Muḥarram (the day of ʿĀshūrā'), when the death of the third Imam, al-Ḥusayn b. ʿAlī b. Abī Ṭālib, in battle against the forces of the Umayyad caliphate on 10 Muḥarram 61/10 October 680, is commemorated and mourned. The other distinctive practice that distinguishes Shiʿi from other forms of Islam is that of 'visitation' (*ziyāra*) to various shrines, mausoleums and other places that have come to be regarded as holy because of their association with individuals revered and important for the religion. 'Visitation', while its legitimacy is disputed by some Sunnis, is known in the Sunni tradition, but what makes the Shiʿi form of the practice distinctive is its prominence as part of religious life, as well as its orientation towards places connected with their Imams and other descendants of the Prophet.

Furthermore, there are festivals and holidays that commemorate events understood by the Shiʿa as decisive in the history of their tradition, such as the ʿĪd Ghadīr Khumm (when, according to Shiʿi interpretation, the Prophet designated ʿAlī as his successor) on the 18th of Dhu'l-Ḥijja, and the ʿĪd al-Mubāhala (when it is believed that the Prophet marked out ʿAlī, Fāṭima, al-Ḥasan and al-Ḥusayn as those closest to him) on the 24th of the same month. Branches of the Shiʿa also have festivals and rituals that are particular to them, such as the celebration by the Ismailis of their own Imam's birthday.

Academic analysis of the ritual aspects of Islam has most often been made through the disciplines of history and anthropology. Typically, anthropologists have been concerned with the functions and meanings of rituals performed in contemporary Islamic societies, while historians have been more interested in their origins and development. Anthropological analysis usually deals with rituals observed in specific societies at specific times, whereas historical analysis often focuses on textual evidence, referring to normative and idealised accounts, questionably related to the realities of everyday life.

Of course, the two approaches often complement one another and overlap as methods for the understanding of Islamic ritual. Anthropologists and historians together ascribe considerable importance to ritual life in the formation, reinforcement and assertion of identities; both acknowledge that the form and meaning of rituals change over time and between communities; and both accept that political, social and economic circumstances are relevant for understanding the developments, often contested, in the performance and understanding of ritual.

Early scholarly investigations focused on the origins and historical development of Muslim rituals. Naturally the institutions that mainly attracted attention were those associated with the 'five pillars of Islam', and it was the Sunni forms of them, as known through law books and collections of *ḥadīth*s, that occupied centre stage. Scholars such as Ignaz Goldziher, Christian Snouck Hurgronje, Carl-Heinrich Becker and Arendt Jan Wensinck produced studies of institutions connected with Muslim prayer rituals, fasting practices, the pilgrimage to Mecca and the *zakāt*, which are still important today even though they worked with evidence that, by today's standards, was relatively limited.[1] Snouck Hurgronje was somewhat unusual in that his work on Mecca and the *ḥajj* combined textual evidence with his own observations of life in Mecca.

Various assumptions and methods were shared by such scholars, although they might sometimes differ radically in their conclusions.[2] They generally accepted that the Prophet Muḥammad was instrumental in establishing the fundamental forms of Muslim rituals, although developments after his death and in lands outside Arabia may have been extremely important for the forms that the rituals took on subsequently. They regarded the Qur'an, the different parts of which they related to the stages of Muḥammad's prophetic career, as offering a way into the Prophet's mind and as evidence for his elaboration of the rituals. They assumed that the rituals of Islam must be related, genetically, to those of previous religions. Following Muslim tradition, they considered that in Arabia during the Prophet's lifetime the two most obvious sources of influence would have been the religious practices of the pre-Islamic

---

[1] See, for example, I. Goldziher, 'Die Sabbathinstitution im Islam', in *David Kaufman Gedenkbuch* (Breslau, 1900), pp. 86–102; C. Snouck Hurgonje, *Het Mekkaansche Feest* (Leiden, 1880), repr. in his *Verspreide Geschriften* (Bonn and Leipzig, 1923), vol. 1, pp. 1–124; C. Snouck Hurgonje, 'Nieuwe bijdragen tot de kennis van den Islam', in *Bijdragen tot de Taal-, Land-, en Volkenkunde van Nederlandsche Indie*, 4th series (The Hague, 1882), vol. 6, pp. 357–421, repr. in his *Verspreide Geschriften*, vol. 2, pp. 1–58; C. H. Becker, 'Zur Geschichte der islamischen Kultus', *Der Islam*, 3 (1912), pp. 74–99; A. J. Wensinck, 'Die Entstehung der muslimischen Reinheitgesetzgebung', *Der Islam*, 5 (1914), pp. 62–80. For translations into English, in whole or in part, see G. R. Hawting, ed., *The Development of Islamic Ritual* (Aldershot, 2006).

[2] Compare, for example, the study of Becker cited above with that of Eugen Mittwoch, 'Zur Entstehungsgeschichte des islamischen Gebets und Kultus', *Abhandlungen der preussischen Akademie der Wissenschaften*, 2 (Berlin, 1913).

Arabs and those of the Jews of Medina, with whom Muḥammad came into contact after the *hijra*. In the period following the Prophet's death and the Arab-Muslim conquests in the Middle East, the still nascent Islam would then have been open to influences from many other religions, such as Christianity and Zoroastrianism.

An important theme in the writings of such scholars was the role of ritual in creating an early Islamic identity and in distinguishing nascent Islam from other religions of the time. It was Snouck Hurgronje who, in his study of the *ḥajj* referred to above, put forward an idea that has had a great influence on the academic study of early Islam. He argued that the adoption by Muḥammad of the Kaʿba as a cultic centre, together with the rituals performed in and around Mecca, represented an attempt to give the new religion a marked Arab identity that would clearly distinguish it from that of the Jews of Medina.

There is evidence in the Muslim tradition that prior to the development of specifically Muslim forms of rituals such as prayer and fasting, the emerging community had followed practices that might be understood in a broad sense as Jewish. Prayer was performed in the direction of Jerusalem, and fasting was kept on the Jewish Day of Atonement. The tradition reports that shortly after his move to Medina, the Prophet received revelations ordering him to abandon the Jerusalem *qibla* and to face towards Mecca in prayer instead, and to fast during the month of Ramaḍān. Fasting on the 10th day of the year, ʿĀshūrāʾ, the Jewish practice then became a matter of debate, some regarding it as entirely optional, others as disapproved of. Passages of the Qurʾan are understood as containing these revelations regarding the direction of prayer and the time of the fast.

Although Snouck Hurgronje's theory subsequently came in for some scholarly criticism, mainly on the grounds that his dating of verses of the Qurʾan was questionable, the idea that Islam at first defined itself in contrast to Judaism, and that Judaism had previously greatly influenced the emergence of the new form of monotheism, became widely accepted in academic scholarship on the emergence of Islam. Equally important with Snouck Hurgronje in this respect was A. J. Wensinck, whose work *Mohammed en de Joden te Medina* further elaborated the thesis of the earlier Dutch scholar.[3]

Many of the ideas, paradigms and methods that were common to the early academic scholars are now subjects of debate and questioning. The value of the Qurʾan and of other early Islamic literature for reconstructing the emergence of Islam; the idea that a complex religion like Islam can be ultimately traced to one individual who may be called its founder; the relative importance of Arabia and the wider lands of the Middle East for the formation of Islam; the legitimacy and significance of the idea of external influences on nascent Islam, and the mechanisms by which they operated; these are just some of the questions to which different scholars now give a variety of answers.

---

[3] A. J. Wensinck, *Mohammed en de Joden te Medina* (Leiden, 1908); English trans. as *Muhammmad and the Jews of Medina* (Freiburg im Breisgau, 1975).

As for the possible non-Islamic sources of, or influences on, Muslim ideas, rituals and institutions, since the time of the early scholars we have become much more aware of, and have evidence for, the diversity of religion in the Middle East at the time when Islam was forming. As a result, we can no longer talk broadly of Judaism, Christianity or Zoroastrianism as influences on the emergence of Islamic rituals; we have to ask what we mean when using such general terms. Samaritanism, Jewish Christianity, possible influences from the vanished Qumran community that had produced the Dead Sea Scrolls, Manichaeism, and other religious traditions are now commonly referred to by scholars seeking to relate Islamic ideas and practices to those of other religions. Indeed, one of the problems facing scholars who seek to analyse Islam as a reworking and revision of previous monotheist religion is the very diversity that a comparative analysis of Islamic doctrines, practices and institutions has brought to light.

While the study of the historical development of Islamic rituals has continued to occupy many, since about the 1960s the descriptions and analyses of anthropologists, and some other social scientists, have focused attention on the actual performances and understandings of rituals and festivals in specific Islamic societies. Although accounts based on – or claiming to be based on – observation of Islamic rituals 'on the ground' have been an ingredient of Western literatures since the Middle Ages,[4] the development of anthropological studies of the life of particular Islamic societies in the latter half of the 20th century introduced a new concern with a methodology that problematised the role of the observer and emphasised local agency. Clifford Geertz (d. 2006) and Ernest Gellner (d. 1995) were not the first to approach given Islamic societies from an anthropological perspective, but their works attracted attention from beyond as well as within the academic discipline of anthropology and became the focus of intense discussion about the possibility and nature of a field called 'the anthropology of Islam'.[5]

Anthropology has been the dominant discipline in the study of ritual, going back to founding figures such as Emile Durkheim and Arnold van Gennep, but as a self-conscious and methodologically aware field, ritual studies too really emerged in the second half of the 20th century, an important event being the creation of the *Journal of Ritual Studies* in 1987. Scholars such as Victor Turner (d. 1983), Mary Douglas (d. 2007), Clifford Geertz, Jonathan Z. Smith, Catherine Bell (d. 2008) and Ronald L. Grimes have had immense influence on the field, although the editors of the 2006

[4] This is not the place for a full bibliography but such works as Edward Lane's *Manners and Customs of the Modern Egyptians* (London, 1836) and Richard Burton's *Personal Narrative of a Pilgrimage to al-Madinah and Meccah* (London, 1855) come to mind as obvious examples.

[5] See, e.g., Gabriele Marranci, *The Anthropology of Islam* (Oxford and New York, 2008), pp. 35ff, and Jens Kreinath, ed., *The Anthropology of Islam Reader* (London and New York, 2012) for critical discussions of the idea with references to the contributions of scholars such as Hamid El-Zein, Talal Asad, Dale Eickelman, Akbar Ahmad, Richard Tapper, Daniel Varisco and others. Some of their reflections on the anthropology of Islam are included in Kreinath's volume.

publication, *Theorizing Rituals*, suggested that there is a gap between those concerned with theory and those working on specific instances of ritual: 'in practice ritual studies largely neglect matters of theory'.[6] How far that is true is debatable.

Not surprisingly, within the study of Shiʿi ritual life, it is those of Muḥarram, connected with ʿĀshūrā', that have received most attention, and not merely from anthropologists.[7] Comparisons have been made between the dramatic reconstructions of the events surrounding the Battle of Karbalā' and similar dramatic representations, such as the passion plays of pre-modern Europe, and the interaction of politics and religion in certain aspects of the mourning ceremonies has also proved a fertile area for investigation.[8]

Although it is understood primarily as a ritual of commemoration, it is clear that ʿĀshūrā' has its roots in ancient ideas of sin and atonement. That is reflected not merely in the prominence of practices of self-mortification, but also in the underlying association of ʿĀshūrā' with the Day of Atonement in Judaism. Both festivals occur on the tenth day of the first month of the year, and, if Muslim tradition accurately reflects historical development, it seems that before it became predominantly associated with the killing of al-Ḥusayn, ʿĀshūrā' in Islam was a day of fasting consciously modelled on the Day of Atonement. However, the understanding of atonement rituals can also evolve, and according to Islamic sources the Jews of Medina at the time of Muḥammad understood the Day of Atonement more as a commemoration of God's giving of the Torah to Moses.[9]

The chapter here by Sabrina Mervin displays a multifaceted methodology and focus of interest. Based on fieldwork in India and the Middle East, this comparative study of the Muḥarram rituals is especially concerned with different attitudes to pictorial representation of the sacred figures and heroes of the Shiʿa in the reenactments of the drama of Karbalā', and with conflicting views among the Shiʿi scholars regarding certain practices of self-mortification performed by those taking part in the ʿĀshūrā' ceremonies. Regarding the former issue, she notes that pictures of the Shiʿi heroes and martyrs are a prominent and normal component in the Middle

---

[6] Jens Kreinath, Jan Snoek and Michael Stausberg, ed., *Theorizing Rituals: Isssues, Topics, Approaches, Concepts* (Leiden and Boston, 2006).

[7] See the bibliography to the article 'ʿĀshūrā'' in *EI3* by Megan H. Reid. See further now the essays devoted to the festival in Alessandro Monsutti, Sylvia Naef and Farian Sabahi, ed., *The Other Shiites: From the Mediterranean to Central Asia* (Bern and Oxford, 2007).

[8] See, e.g., for discussion of the dramatic aspects of the ʿĀshūrā' rituals, E. Fulchignoni, 'Quelques considérations comparatives entre les rituels du ta'ziyeh Iranien et les "spectacles de la passion" du Moyen Age Chrétien en Occident', in P. J. Chelkowski, ed., *Taziyeh: Ritual and Drama in Iran* (New York, 1979); and, for a study relating socio-political and intellectual changes among the Shiʿi scholars, see Werner Ende, 'The Flagellations of Muḥarram and the Shīʿite ʿUlamā'', *Der Islam*, 55 (1978), pp. 19–36.

[9] For the association of ʿĀshūrā' with notions of atonement, see Mahmoud Ayoub, *Redemptive Suffering in Islam: A Study of the Devotional Aspects of ʿĀshūrā' in Twelver Shīʿism* (The Hague, 1978); G. R. Hawting, 'The Tawwābūn, Atonement and ʿĀshūrā'', *JSAI*, 17 (1994), pp. 166–181.

East whereas in Hyderabad they are completely absent, and she discusses why that may be the case. Differences regarding methods of self-mortification, on the other hand, do not occur consistently on a regional basis but over time: in the same place the drawing of blood by cutting or flagellating one's body may at different times be approved or forbidden by the scholars. On positions regarding that issue, she argues, complex and changing cultural and political pressures on the traditional scholars are decisive in altering their attitudes. Ultimately, Mervin is concerned with the function of the ʿĀshūrāʾ rituals within the communities she has studied, their relationship to wider society in which the Shiʿa live, and the ways in which they enable individuals to achieve emotional balance and to find a place in their societies.

If the commemorative festival of ʿĀshūrāʾ is quite well known, at least in general terms, and has been discussed from various aspects in scholarly literature, the ceremony known as *Chirāgh-i rawshan*, discussed by Hakim Elnazarov, and mainly associated with the mourning rites following a death, seems to be little-known and confined to Ismaili communities of Central Asia. Elnazarov's account of this ceremony is based mainly on oral sources, but he also refers to the *Chirāgh-nāma*, the text containing poems, prayers and verses of the Qur'an recited during its course.

Elnazarov raises the issue of the relationship between the texts recited and the various parts of the ritual. The history of the *Chirāgh-nāma* is obscure, so too whether it was consciously composed or developed as the result of accretions over time. It is possible or even likely that the ritual, or at least elements of it, is older than the texts, which have been incorporated into the ritual as it was adapted to serve the need of an Ismaili community. Without the texts, the ritual perhaps reflects ideas about spirits and ancestors that pre-date the introduction of Islam into the region.

As for the meanings of the *Chirāgh-i rawshan*, Elnazarov's chapter reflects some of the problems involved in assessing what any ritual means to those taking part and to the community at large. It seems that both the form and the understanding of the ritual have evolved over time, and that it has meant different things at different times to those taking part, to the community in which it is performed, and to the outside observer. While for those involved it may be a means of expressing and controlling emotion at a time of crisis, for the outsider it appears to be more concerned with issues of identity and solidarity within relatively small social groups. Gratitude is due to the author for drawing attention to this relatively little discussed aspect of the life of the Ismailis of Central Asia.

19

ʿĀshūrāʾ Rituals, Identity and Politics: A Comparative Approach (Lebanon and India)

Sabrina Mervin

The rituals that commemorate the month of Muḥarram in the Shiʿi world come with a stream of sounds, images and emotions, increasingly popularised through the media. A vibrant popular culture spread through the internet and satellite television channels stems from this 'invented tradition', which is reinvented every year, reproduced and readapted, with a tension between the local, and even micro-local level (at the level of a village or district), and the global level. For the last fifty years or so, massive population movements and urbanisation have led to the development of these rituals; politicisation has transformed them as the rise of Shiʿism in the Middle East has increased their visibility.

More than ever, these rituals enable the Shiʿa to reaffirm their presence and their identity, not always without a clash (in Pakistan or in Iraq, in particular, where acts of inter-community violence are often committed during the ceremonies). But they also enable them to convey a supposedly universal message: the message of the triumph of Good over Evil, the 'triumph of blood on the sword'. Yet the aim is to commemorate a defeat, the Battle of Karbalāʾ, and to mourn, for Ḥusayn the grandson of the Prophet Muḥammad and the third Shiʿi Imam, who died there as a martyr. What we call the Karbalāʾ paradigm[1] is based on a particular conception of history, peculiar especially to Twelver Shiʿism. A number of Shiʿi doctrines developed around this paradigm, while identities and social relations formed. After presenting and analysing this paradigm, we will detail what the rituals of Muḥarram consist of. Then, we will focus on two themes, each one of them opening onto a more general direction of thought. Our analysis is based on long-term fieldwork that took place in the Middle East (Lebanon, Syria and Oman) and in India (Hyderabad) between 1994 and 2009, to enable comparative approaches. The richness of the texts published on the occasion of ʿĀshūrāʾ, from the accounts of travellers to the extensive researches carried out over the last years, revealed both the unity and the extreme diversity of the discourses

[1] See Michael Fischer, *Iran from Religious Dispute to Revolution* (Cambridge and London, 1980), pp. 21–22.

and the practices at work in these ceremonies.[2] Such an approach seems to us fruitful for improving our knowledge of Shiʿism and Shiʿi societies as much as for religious studies in general, in particular studies of religious rituals in a comparative manner.

To do so, two themes seemed relevant to me, especially as they addressed questions that supposedly raise a number of issues that are controversial among religious

[2] For literature on the topic related to Iran, see K. Aghaie, *The Martyrs of Karbalāʾ: Shiʿi Symbols and Rituals in Modern Iran* (Seattle and London, 2004); K. Aghaie, ed., *The Women of Karbalāʾ: Ritual Performance and Symbolic Discourses in Modern Shiʿi Islam* (Austin, TX, 2005); P. Chelkowski, 'Shia Muslim Processional Performances', *The Drama Review*, 29 (1985), pp. 18–30; P. Chelkowski, 'Narrative Paintings and Painting Recitation in Qajar Iran', *Muqarnas*, 6 (1989), pp. 98–111, D. Thurfjell, *Living Shiʿism: Instances of Ritualisation Among Islamist Men in Contemporary Iran* (Leiden and Boston, 2006). For literature related to India, see D. Pinault, *The Shiites: Rituals and Popular Piety in a Muslim Community* (New York, 1992); D. Pinault, *Horse of Karbalāʾ: Muslim Devotional Life in India* (London, 2001); T. Howarth, *The Twelver Shīʿa as a Muslim Minority in India: Pulpit of Tears* (New York, 2005). For literature related to Afghanistan, see A. Monsutti, 'Entre effervescence religieuse et expression politique: l'Ashura parmi les Hazaras à Quetta (Pakistan)', online: http://www.ethnographiques.org/2005/Monsutti.html (accessed 13 August 2013). For literature related to Pakistan, see V. Schubel, *Religious Performance in Contemporary Islam: Shiʿi Devotional Rituals in South Asia* (Columbia, 1993); M. E. Hegland, 'The Majales Shiʿa Woman's Rituals of Mourning in Northwest Pakistan', in J. Brink and J. Mencher, ed., *A Mixed Blessing: Gender and Rituals Fundamentalism Cross Culturally* (New York, 1997), pp. 179–196; M. E. Hegland, 'Flagellation and Fundamentalism: (Trans)Forming Meaning, Identity, and Gender Through Pakistani Women's Rituals of Mourning', *American Ethnologist*, 25 (May, 1998), pp. 240–266; M. E. Hegland, 'The Power Paradox in Muslim Women's Majales: North-West Pakistani Mourning Rituals as Sites of Contestation over Religious Politics, Ethnicity and Gender', *Signs*, 23 (1998), pp. 391–428. For literature related to Lebanon, see L. Deeb, *An Enchanted Modern: Gender and Public Piety in Shiʿi Lebanon* (Princeton, 2006); L. Deeb, 'Living Ashura in Lebanon: Mourning Transformed to Sacrifice', *Comparative Studies of South Asia, Africa and the Middle East*, 25 (2005), pp. 122–137; L. Deeb, 'Emulating and/or Embodying the Ideal: The Gendering of Temporal Frameworks and Islamic Role Models in Shiʿi Lebanon', *American Ethnologist*, 36 (May 2009), pp. 242–257; S. Mervin, 'Fāṭima et Zaynab, deux Dames de l'Islam Chiite', in *L'éternel féminin au regard de la cathédrale de Chartres, Actes du colloque européen, 30/6 et 1/7/01*, AACMEC (Chartres, 2002), pp. 111–119; S. Mervin, 'Les larmes et le sang des chiites: corps et pratiques rituelles lors des célébrations de ʿashūrāʾ (Liban, Syrie)', *REMMM*, 113–114, *Le corps et le sacré dans l'Orient Musulman* (2006), pp. 153–166; S. Mervin, ''Āshūrāʾ: Some Remarks on Ritual Practices in Different Shiite Communities (Lebanon and Syria)', in A. Monsutti, S. Naef and F. Sabahi, ed., *The Other Shiites: From the Mediterranean to Central Asia* (New York, 2007), pp. 137–147; S. Mervin, 'Le théâtre Chiite au Liban, entre rituel et spectacle', in N. Puig and F. Mermier, ed., *Itinéraires esthétiques et scènes culturelles* (Beirut, 2007), pp. 57–75; M. Weiss, 'The Cultural Politics of Shiʿi Modernism: Morality and Gender in Early 20th-century Lebanon', *IJMES*, 39 (2007), pp. 249–270; M. Weiss, *In the Shadow of Sectarianism: Law, Shiʿism and the Making of Modern Lebanon* (Cambridge and London, 2010). For literature related to Azerbaidjan, see A. Volker, 'Why do They Cry? Criticisms of Muharram Celebrations in Tsarist and Socialist Azerbaijan', in R. Brunner, and W. Ende, ed., *The Twelver Shia in Modern Times: Religious Culture and Political History* (Leiden, Boston and Cologne, 2001), pp. 114–134. For literature related to Trinidad, see F. J. Korom, *Hosay Trinidad: Muharram Performances in an Indo-Caribbean Diaspora* (Philadelphia, 2003).

authorities. The first theme deals with the representation of the sacred figures of Shiʿism in different forms and, in particular, in the form of theatrical representation. This will bring us to comment on the conception of history that stems from it and on the politicisation – or the lack of politicisation – of the discourses.

The second theme deals with the practices of mortification and the debates that they lead to among *ʿulamāʾ*. These two themes will enable us to see how the concerned actors seize on 'modernity' in their discourses on ʿĀshūrāʾ ceremonies. Furthermore, they will lead us to broaden the scope of our discussion of two complementary dimensions of the rituals; the collective dimension with its social function and the individual dimension with the central role played by emotion.

The Karbalāʾ Paradigm

The epic

In 61/680, Yazīd, appointed as a successor by his father Muʿāwiya who had just died, became the new caliph in Damascus, which corresponds to the first instance of dynastic succession in Islam. Ḥusayn, grandson of the Prophet, had complied until then with the peace agreement concluded between his elder brother Ḥasan and Caliph Muʿāwiya, but the political situation had changed. When Yazīd asked Ḥusayn to pledge allegiance the latter fled from Medina, where he had been living, to Mecca. There, he received messages from Kūfa, the city of ʿAlī, whose inhabitants assured him that they would support him if he joined them. Ḥusayn sent his cousin Muslim b. al-ʿAqīl scouting and he then left, with a small group of travelling companions, accompanied by women and children of his family. On 2 Muḥarram 61 (2 October 680), they were intercepted by Yazīd's soldiers who had come from Kūfa. The latter forced them to set up camp in Karbalāʾ, in the desert, next to the Euphrates. Negotiations were initiated but did not come to any agreement; Ḥusayn refused to pledge allegiance to Yazīd. The Umayyad army prevented those who were besieged from having access to water and they suffered from thirst.

Then, the battle started on 10 Muḥarram 61 (10 October 680), the Day of ʿĀshūrāʾ. Single combats, skirmishes and attacks followed one another throughout the whole day. Ḥusayn's companions perished one after the other, and so did his relatives: his two sons ʿAlī and ʿAbd Allāh, his nephew Qāsim, son of Ḥasan, his half-brother ʿAbbās, who was his standard bearer, and so forth. Eventually, Ḥusayn himself was injured several times before dying. He was beheaded and his body was trampled by horses. The victorious soldiers raised his head on a spear, like the heads of the other martyrs, and brought it to the caliph, leaving his body to be buried by the inhabitants of a nearby village.

The survivors of the battle were captured and taken away to the governor of Kūfa, then to Damascus to the court of Yazīd who let them leave for Medina. Among them was Zaynab, sister of Ḥusayn, and his son ʿAlī (also known as Zayn al-ʿĀbidīn) who, because he had been ill, had not been able to take part in the battle; the latter would later become the fourth Imam.[3] As for the people of Kūfa, they repented of having forsaken Ḥusayn.

Traditionists and historians narrate the Battle of Karbalāʾ in detailed accounts. These versions differ somewhat on certain points, such as the number of fighters in each camp, although they all agree on the unbalance of the forces present.[4] Among these narratives, there is the *maqtal* on Ḥusayn, the most commonly used being the *maqtal* written by Abū Mikhnaf (d. 157/774).[5] Moreover, a whole Shiʿa historiography, written in prose and verse, recounts the epic of the Imams and, in general, of the *ahl al-bayt*, especially the epic of Ḥusayn and of his family, in which elements of legend are intertwined with the narration of the facts.

This historiography developed along with the mourning rituals that commemorate the martyrdom of the Imam and of his relatives. According to traditions, these rituals were introduced just after Ḥusayn's death on the battlefield; in other accounts, they were introduced when the survivors of the battle, released by Yazīd and headed for Medina, stopped in Karbalāʾ to pray on Ḥusayn's tomb. There, Zaynab spoke in praise of her brother, cursed his murderers and preached a sermon that moved the audience to tears.[6] Later on, in AD 684, the pilgrimage of the 'Penitents' (*tawwābūn*) to Ḥusayn's tomb was introduced and, in AD 685, the revenge of Mukhtār, with his watchword 'Revenge for al-Ḥusayn'. Both served as a prototype for other kinds of public rituals.[7] These rituals became more diverse, codified and organised. If some of them disappeared,[8] others evolved and still exist. Indeed, every time the Shiʿa were in a position of strength or had the power (notably under the Būyids, then under the Safawids and later the Qajars), the observed practices were reinforced and new ones were established.

---

[3] Wilferd Madelung, 'Ḥusayn b. ʿAlī b. Abī Ṭāleb', *EIR*, online: http://www.iranicaonline.org/articles/hosayn-b-ali (accessed 13 August 2013).

[4] See, for instance, A. J. Hussain, 'The Mourning of History and the History of Mourning: The Evolution of Ritual Commemoration of the Battle of Karbalāʾ', *Comparative Studies of South Asia, Africa and the Middle East*, 25 (2005), p. 79, which recounts that the Umayyad army had at least 10,000 men and, in some accounts, as many as 100,000 men.

[5] The *maqtal* is a literary genre very common in the first four centuries of Islam. It corresponds to accounts of violent deaths. See Sebastian Günther, 'Maqātil Literature in Medieval Islam', *Journal of Arabic Literature*, 25 (1994), pp. 192–212, and Khalid Sindawi, 'The Image of Husayn ibn 'Ali in Maqatil Literature', *Quaderni di Studi Arabi*, 20–21 (2002–2003), pp. 79–104.

[6] M. Ayoub, *A Redemptive Suffering in Islam: A Study of the Devotional Aspects of ʿĀshūrāʾ in Twelver Shīʿism* (The Hague and Paris, 1978), pp. 152–153; Hussain, 'The Mourning of History and the History of Mourning', pp. 80–81; Y. Nakash, 'An Attempt to Trace the Origin of the Rituals of ʿĀshūrāʾ', *Die Welt des Islams*, 33 (1993), p. 163.

[7] See F. M. Denny, 'Tawwābūn', and G. R. Hawting, 'al-Mukhtār b. Abī ʿUbayd al-Thaḳafī', *EI2*.

[8] Jean Calmard mentions some rituals, such as burying oneself up to the head, which are no longer observed nowadays. See Calmard, 'Ḥosayn b. ʿAlī. ii. in Popular Shiʿism', *EIR*, online: http://www.iranicaonline.org/articles/hosayn-b-ali-ii (accessed 13 August 2013).

Five rituals

There are five main kinds of rituals, which are performed from the beginning of the month of Muḥarram and reach their climax on the tenth day ('Āshūrā'), some of them going on during the month of Ṣafar, until Arbaʿīn, which commemorates the 40th day of Ḥusayn's martyrdom. This is why these occasions are called Muḥarram ceremonies or, by extension, 'Āshūrā'.

All the rituals aim to commemorate the epic and the death of Ḥusayn and of his family. They recount this epic down to its smallest detail so as to enhance its emotional impact on the believers, who cry and lament the misfortunes of the *ahl al-bayt* and the atrocities perpetrated by their enemies. The first ritual is the pious visitation (*ziyāra*) of Ḥusayn's shrine in Karbalā', which was established, with its own liturgy, as early as the 10th century;[9] those who cannot afford this visitation are allowed to go to another shrine, such as the shrine of Sayyida Zaynab near Damascus, or to the shrines of other members of *ahl al-bayt*. The second ritual is the mourning gathering (*majlis ḥusaynī*), during which a recitant recounts, day after day, how the drama unfolded. These sessions are nowadays codified and all of them conform to the same pattern: prose tales alternating with elegies to the rhythm of the participants' breast-beating (*latm*) and sometimes accompanied by sermons.

For a long time, the narrators' reference book has been *Rawḍat al-shuhadā'*, written by Ḥusayn Wāʿiz Kāshifī (d. 910/1505) in 1502, a year after the Safawids came to power; it had such an influence on the sessions that the narrators were called *rawḍa-khān* (*rawḍa-khānī*).[10] The sessions can take place either in a private home (whose owner sometimes makes a wish on this occasion), or in a public place such as a school, or in an ad hoc place of worship, the *ḥusayniyya*.

The third kind of ritual corresponds to the public processions (*mawkib ḥusaynī*). It was also established as early as the 10th century during the reign of the Būyid ruler Muʿizz al-Dawla (d. AD 963); however, it was often forbidden whenever Shiʿis were able to openly express their doctrinal differences, but was later 'rediscovered'. Practices of mortification, which correspond to the fourth kind of ritual, developed during these processions; in addition to the simple breast-beating, more or less pronounced, came flagellation with chains (*zanjīr*) or with blades, incisions in the skull (*taṭbīr*) and other means of shedding blood.

Finally, the fifth ritual is the theatrical representation of the drama of Karbalā' and of the *ahl al-bayt*'s epic (*taʿziya* or *shabīh*), which was established as a continuation of the sessions and the processions, under the patronage of the Qajar princes, in the

[9] See Howarth, *The Twelver Shīʿa as a Muslim Minority in India*, where these sessions (in Hyderabad, India) are described and analysed.

[10] A. Amanat, '*Meadows of the Martyrs*: Kāshifī's Persianization of the Shiʿi Martyrdom Narrative in Late Tīmūrid Herat', in F. Daftary and J. W. Meri, ed., *Culture and Memory in Medieval Islam: Essays in Honour of Wilferd Madelung* (London, 2003), pp. 250–278, repr. in A. Amanat, ed., *Apocalyptic Islam and Iranian Shiʿism* (London and New York, 2009), pp. 91–109.

middle of the 18th century.[11] The rituals then drew on Iranian mythology, and this theatre patronised by the elite became quite popular in Iran, giving rise to what was acknowledged as quite an art.[12]

However, Muḥarram remains a time of mourning; believers must refrain from any expression of joy and must wear black or dark clothes. It is a time for lamentations, tears, sorrow and compassion; according to the words attributed to the Imam ʿAlī al-Riḍā, those for whom ʿĀshūrāʾ is a day of blessing (*baraka*) are doomed to hell.[13] The believers express love and devotion to the sacred family, cry over its misfortunes and renew, through these rituals, the pact that binds them to Ḥusayn, their martyr Imam. They pledge allegiance to him and ask him in return for his intercession in their quest for spiritual redemption.[14] The times and places of these rituals are dedicated to religiosity; they are also moments and places of socialisation.

The *ʿulamāʾ* and narrators consistently present ʿĀshūrāʾ as a 'school of thought' (*madrasa*). Scholars see the Battle of Karbalāʾ as a 'root metaphor'[15] from which Shiʿi doctrines and religious practices developed. In Twelver Shiʿism, the event corresponds to a founding myth re-enacted every year and internalised by the believers through the rituals. The epic of the *ahl al-bayt* is, for the Shiʿa, a sacred history from which they learn lessons, moral values and an ethos, by exalting the qualities and the attitudes of infallible or innocent figures (*maʿṣūm*), who are supreme examples to be followed.

The liturgical collection highlights the dichotomy between the *ahl al-bayt*'s purity and the Umayyads' villainy, between the friend and the enemy, between Good and Evil. This sacred story, which makes sense of the community's past, present and future, is subjected to rereadings and reinterpretations that vary according to the conditions of the time and place. All this constitutes the Karbalāʾ paradigm, which forges the group's collective memory, enables the community to imagine itself, participates in the identification process and reinforces its members' sense of affiliation. It also determines the social relations within the community and its relation to power.

---

[11] See, on this specific point, Jean Calmard, 'Le mécénat des représentations de taʿziye: I. Les précurseurs de Nâseroddin Châh', in *Le monde Iranien et l'Islam* (Geneva and Paris, 1974), vol. 2, pp. 73–126; Jean Calmard, 'Le mécénat des représentations de taʿziyé: II. Les débuts de Nâseroddin Châh', in *Le monde Iranien et l'Islam* (Geneva and Paris, 1977), vol. 4, pp. 133–162; Jean Calmard, 'L'Iran sous Nâseroddin Châh et les derniers Qadjars. Esquisse pour une histoire politique culturelle et socio-religieuse', in *Le monde Iranien et l'Islam* (Paris, 1977), vol. 4, pp. 165–194.

[12] This ritual theatre, and particularly the Iranian *taʿzieh* has been studied in detail, notably by Peter Chelkowski.

[13] Quoted by Nakash, 'An Attempt to Trace the Origin of the Rituals of ʿĀshūrāʾ', p. 166.

[14] Ayoub, *A Redemptive Suffering in Islam*, p. 198f, and D. Pinault, 'Shia Lamentation Rituals and Reinterpretation of the Doctrine of Intercession: Two Cases from Modern India', *History of Religions*, 38 (1999), pp. 285–305.

[15] Aghaie, *The Martyrs of Karbalāʾ*, p. 163, n. 3, using Victor Turner's analysis.

Reform, politicisation and gender discourse

This paradigm is not fixed. 'Āshūrā' rituals can be presented as pertaining to an immutable tradition passed on from generation to generation without being altered.

However, at least in part, these are invented traditions, reinvented as needed according to the circumstances, and perhaps even reinvented every year. As we saw, between the 10th century and the Safawid period, certain rituals disappeared whereas others appeared. The texts forming the collection of available narratives were also reorganised and recomposed. From the beginning of the 20th century onwards, there have been other changes in both the texts and the rituals.

These changes were first initiated by religious elites who, in order to preserve their roles and their status within society, had to adapt to the contemporary ethic influenced by the burst of European ideas, as well as to the social and political upheavals due to the formation of modern states. It was not so much an organised movement as individual initiatives that aroused debates, sometimes very stormy ones, within the clerical circles, before involving practical consequences in the performance of the rituals.[16]

These initiatives aiming at a modernist religious reform had two aspects: a discourse referring to a return to a 'genuine' Islam by eliminating superstitions (*khurāfāt*) and blameworthy innovations (*bid'a*); a discourse referring to the rationalisation and modernisation of the doctrines and practices. Thus, for instance, books were published which were intended to be read during the sessions. They were carefully organised and censored for marvellous narratives.[17]

This reform step (*iṣlāḥ*) was followed by another phase, the renewal (*tajdīd*), which came with a politicisation process across a large part of the Shi'i world (Iran, Iraq and Lebanon, then Afghanistan in particular) from the 1970s on. Except for 'Alī Sharī'atī, the initiators (Muṭahharī and Khumaynī in Iran; Mūsa Ṣadr in Lebanon; and Muḥammad Bāqir al-Ṣadr in Iraq) were still part of a religious elite, but were also the ideologists of 'mass' organisations or partisan structures (the Pasdarān, al-Da'wa, Amal and so forth).

The Karbalā' paradigm had already been used to political ends[18] but they really turned it into a vehicle for protest and mass mobilisation. Whereas their predecessors describe Ḥusayn's epic as an awakening (*nahḍa*),[19] the authors of this

---

[16] See Werner Ende, 'The Flagellations of Muḥarram and the Shi'ite 'Ulamā'', *Der Islam*, 55 (1978), pp. 19–36; Sabrina Mervin, *Un réformisme Chiite: Ulémas et lettrés du Jabal 'Âmil (actuel Liban-Sud) de la fin de l'Empire Ottoman à l'indépendance du Liban*, Karthala-CERMOC-IFEAD (Paris, 2000), especially ch. 6; Max Weiss, *In the Shadow of Sectarianism: Law, Shi'ism and the Making of Modern Lebanon* (Cambridge and London, 2010), especially ch. 2.

[17] For example, see Muḥsin al-Amīn, *al-Majālis al-saniyya* (5th ed., Najaf, n.d.). The first of the five volumes was published in 1924.

[18] From the Umayyad and Abbasid periods on, the symbolism of Karbalā' has been used in several rebellions; see Aghaie, *The Martyrs of Karbalā'*, p. 10.

[19] See the book by Iraqi reformist Hibat al-Dīn al-Shahrastānī (d. 1967), *Nahḍat al-Ḥusayn*. It should be noted that the term '*nahḍa*' is still used nowadays by certain authors.

generation presented it as a *thawra* (revolt, revolution);[20] Ḥusayn had refused to submit to tyranny and had risen up in spite of the strength of the enemy army. He was, therefore, an example to be followed. Sharīʿatī resorted to three concepts to describe Ḥusayn's movement – revolution, *jihād* and martyrdom – thereby introducing these terms into a new political and religious discourse.[21] Motahharī presented him as an example of rebellion against the Shah and against the imperialism of foreign powers.[22]

In the 1960s and 1970s in Iran, protestors were able to associate 'Āshūrā' celebrations with political demonstrations, thereby adding a sacred dimension to their struggle. Once in power, the revolutionaries would continue to use the rituals to political ends.[23]

In Lebanon, Mūsā Ṣadr initiated his political campaigns during the 'Āshūrā' ceremonies, drawing on the Karbalā' paradigm and transforming it. In a famous speech that he gave in Baalbek in 1974, he said:

> Do not allow ceremonies or lamentation to serve as a substitute for action. We must transform the ceremonies into a spring from which will gush forth the revolutionary fury and the constructive protest … Now let me ask you: If Husayn were living with us and saw that the rights of the people and justice were being trampled upon by the foot of pride, what would he do?[24]

Mūsā Ṣadr made use of the Muḥarram rituals to express a revolutionary spirit and to launch a political and social protest inside Lebanon, and the struggle against Israel was described by him as 'our Karbalā'' (*Karbalā'unā*).

In Iraq in the same year, 'Āshūrā' processions turned into a political protest as they did three years later in 1977.[25] After the success of the Iranian revolution, the politicisation of religious slogans and celebrations spread to other parts of the Shiʿi

---

[20] See, for instance, the famous book by Muḥammad Mahdī Shams al-Dīn, *Thawrat al-Ḥusayn,* translated into English as Shams al-Dīn, Shaykh Muḥammad Mahdī, *The Rising of al-Husayn: Its Impact on the Consciousness of Muslim Society*, tr. I. K. Howard (London, 1985).

[21] Aghaie, *The Martyrs of Karbalā'*, p. 103.

[22] Ibid., p. 110.

[23] Ibid., p. 131f.

[24] Salim Nasr, 'Mobilisation communautaire et symbolique religieuse: l'Imam Sadr et les Chiʿites du Liban (1970–1975)', in Olivier Carré and Paul Dumont, ed., *Radicalismes Islamiques* (Paris, 1985), pp. 119–158.

[25] Chibli Mallat, 'Religious Militancy in Contemporary Iraq: Muhammad Baqer al-Sadr and the Sunni-Shia Paradigm', *Third World Quarterly*, 10 (1988), pp. 723–724; F. A. Jabar, *The Shiʿite Movement in Iraq* (London, 2003), p. 185.

world such as Afghanistan,[26] and even as far as Indonesia,[27] not to mention Lebanon, where it has continued to spread more than ever under the leadership of Hizbullah.[28]

In Iran, the Karbalā' paradigm was practically monopolised by the Islamic government until June 2009 when the Green Movement emerged. The latter adopted the paradigm to turn its discourse against the regime. The political discourse therefore made use of the religious one, while at the same time the religious rituals became politicised: after being reformed and modernised, *ḥusaynī* pulpits (*manābir ḥusayniyya*) were used to deliver political messages.[29] In the 20th century, yet another phenomenon emerged that was to have an impact on the Karbalā' paradigm: a gender discourse which continued to be developed until it became what is now called Islamic feminism (although this term includes very different kinds of discourses).

'Āshūrā' rituals reinforce the social order; in these rituals, everyone has a function that mirrors the one that he/she has within society, which also means that everyone has a role assigned to himself/herself in the ceremonies. The *'ulamā'* bring religious support, the rich bring financial support, the storekeepers provide food to be shared, and so on. Likewise, men and women also have distinct functions within these rituals. We will later see in detail, when we present the practices of mortification, that the processions reproduce the departure for the battle; men symbolically go to fight while women play the role of martyrs and cry. Men play an active role while women play a passive supporting role. Yet throughout the 20th century, Muslim societies underwent big changes as women started to gain access to education, public spaces, employment and so forth, even if this emancipation should be considered in the context of the societies in question. It had an impact on social and religious institutions, but also on the Karbalā' paradigm and on the ritual practices of 'Āshūrā'.

On the one hand, a new discourse formed around Zaynab, Ḥusayn's sister, who lost her children at Karbalā' and who was brought captive and unveiled to the caliph's court. She delivered a sermon in which she defended her family's honour and turned public opinion against Yazīd. An example of abnegation and devotion, she is also an example to follow in terms of activism and courage; she is the eloquent (*nāṭiqa*) woman who expresses herself, stands up to the usurper caliph and defends the *ahl al-bayt*'s right to succeed to the Prophet.[30]

---

26 Monsutti, 'Entre effervescence religieuse et expression politique', p. 113f.

27 Zulkifli, *The Struggle of the Shi'is in Indonesia* (Ph.D. thesis, University of Leiden, 2009), pp. 120–121.

28 See Sabrina Mervin, 'Tu n'effaceras pas notre mémoire', in S. Mervin, ed., *Le Hezbollah, état des lieux* (Paris, 2008), pp. 213–219.

29 The reform and the modernisation of the pulpits took place, in particular, in Iraq around *Kuliyyat al-fiqh* who formed the *khaṭīb*, some of whom became famous outside Iraq, such as Shaykh Ahmad al-Wā'ilī (d. 2003) known as 'Prince of the pulpits'. See Ṣādiq Ja'far al-Rawāziq, *Amīr al-manābir* (Beirut, 2004); see also online: http://www.al-waeli.com (in Arabic) (accessed 13 August 2013).

30 Sabrina Mervin, 'Fāṭima et Zaynab, deux Dames de l'Islam Chiite', *L'éternel féminin au regard de la cathédrale de Chartres, Actes du colloque européen, 30/6 et 1/7/01*, AACMEC (Chartres, 2002), pp. 111–119; see also Aghaie, *The Martyrs of Karbalā'*, ch. 7.

On the other hand, although women do not challenge the sexual segregation that takes place during the performance of the rituals, they benefit from the separation from men by gaining independence through creating their own associations, organising their rituals in their *ḥusayniyya*, and by 'us[ing] their service experiences to consider and transform their self-images and worldviews'.[31] This phenomenon has been well noticed, which has led to valuable works.[32]

Reform, politicisation and gender discourse have all had an impact on 'Āshūrā' rituals, an impact that varies depending on the concerned groups and, therefore, on the local political and religious cultures, but also within the same group, according to doctrinal and political stands of religious authorities and of the other actors in presence. The two themes under consideration will be discussed with concrete examples which will demonstrate this and raise new questions.

Representing the Sacred Figure

Images and ritual objects

The representations of the Battle of Karbalā' and of the sacred figures of Shi'ism are common and, for the most part, related to 'Āshūrā' celebrations. They emerged from the passion play in Iran from the early Qajar period onwards, and developed through different media (e.g., canvas, murals) in coffee shops, *tekyeh*, private homes and so forth.[33] Under the Islamic government, other paintings or posters focused on the symbolism of Karbalā' appearing for directly political purposes.[34] But the portraits of the Imams and the representations of the battle continued to develop all the more quickly as artists can nowadays change or alter the images with a computer, by varying their compositions, by adding or removing certain elements, by changing the colours, and so on.[35] Furthermore, movies and cartoons are made. The faces of the Imams are either veiled or unveiled; this leads to controversies that divide religious authorities.

Besides, the Internet makes it possible to spread the images in a new way. They often come with a soundtrack, chants in particular (elegies or *laṭmiyyāt*), which broadens even more the range of possible messages. The images and the posters made in Iran are circulated in the Shi'i world; posted online, they are spread immediately and even further afield than before. They mirror and reproduce the canons of beauty;

---

31 Hegland, 'The Power Paradox in Muslim Women's Majales', p. 392.

32 See, for instance, Deeb, *An Enchanted Modern*; Aghaie, ed., *The Women of Karbalā'*; Hegland, 'The Majales Shi'a Woman's Rituals of Mourning in Northwest Pakistan'; and his 'The Power Paradox in Muslim Women's Majales'.

33 Chelkowski, 'Narrative Paintings and Painting Recitation in Qajar Iran'.

34 Peter Chelkowski and Hamid Dabashi, *Staging a Revolution: The Art of Persuasion on the Islamic Republic of Iran* (London, 2005).

35 The famous painting by Mahmoud Farschchian, *The Evening of Ashura*, widely reproduced and circulated, is also reinterpreted by artists who work with a computer.

the figure of 'Abbās, for instance, is represented with very delicate, almost feminine features, as well as with a body that is quite muscular and masculine. Moreover, he has 'attributes' that tell his story of Karbalā';[36] he wears a feather helmet, has an eye wound, bears a standard and has a goatskin attached to his belt. Like other heroes of Karbalā', he is represented so as to be easily recognised by the believers.

Other elements take part in the representation of Karbalā' and refer to its meanings; Ḥusayn's horse, Zuljanā, the sand of Karbalā', the water of the Euphrates. Other more symbolic elements refer to the heroes of Karbalā' and to the sacred figures of Shi'ism, such as Ḥusayn's head (which is symbolised by his turban), his standard, Ḥusayn's tomb or other shrine, the cradle of his son, the 'infant' (*al-ṭifl al-raḍī'*),[37] Noah's Ark, the hand of 'Abbās (*kaff 'Abbās*), or the hand of the five People of the Cloak (*panje*).[38] These representations, images and symbols rooted in Iranian culture were disseminated in the Shi'i world, spreading this culture that later on became locally integrated, either accepted in its original form or reappropriated and transformed.

The questions dealing with the representation of the sacred figures in Islam are complex; they lead to contradictory opinions from religious authorities and diversified practices. By examining how the images spread within the Shi'i world, one realises that the concerned Shi'i groups or communities sometimes react in an unexpected way. Thus, although the Arab Sunni world has a reputation for being iconoclastic, the Shi'a from the Middle East accepted these images wherever they were disseminated, next to places of worship (in particular the shrines in Iraq and Syria) or in bookshops.

By contrast, in Hyderabad, in a society in which Hindus coexist with Muslims, and therefore in a society used to the lavish representations of Hindu gods, these images did not 'take off' on the market. Objects are common though, such as small-scale replicas of the tombs (*zarī*) or of the cradle, and above all the standards (*'alam*, pl. *a'lām*), which are central to the religious practices and an important part of 'Āshūrā' celebrations.[39] As a consequence, the use of symbols is very prominent in India, although the representation of the sacred figures is not very common; besides, theatre is not well established there. This contrasts with the Middle East, where ritual objects are less widespread and where theatre, imported from Iran, is well established, as it exists from Turkey to Oman.

---

36 'Alī put 'Abbās in charge of protecting Ḥusayn. 'Abbās was Ḥusayn's standard-bearer, and the archetypal warrior. Caught in an ambush as he went to get water for Ḥusayn's children, he was injured several times. Both his arms were cut off before he was killed by the onslaught of arrows.

37 The latter was killed by an arrow while Ḥusayn was holding him in his arms.

38 A Prophetic *ḥadīth* says: 'My family is like Noah's Ark: whoever embarks upon it reaches salvation.'

39 On ritual objects and symbols in other parts of India, see S. Athar Rizvi, *A Socio-Intellectual History of the Ithnā'Asharī Shī'īs in India* (Canberra, 1986), vol. 2, pp. 347–352.

The standards of Hyderabad

These standards symbolically represent the main heroes and the martyrs of Karbalāʾ, all of them members of the sacred family: Ḥusayn, his half-brother ʿAbbās, his two sons ʿAlī Akbar and ʿAlī Aṣghar, his nephew Qāsim, his daughter Sakīna (who died after the battle, in Damascus), his sister Zaynab, and her two sons. One should not forget to mention Fāṭima because, although she died before the battle, she remains a central figure; to invoke her name means to invoke the whole family. Some of these *ʿalam*s, among the oldest ones, hold relics. According to the historian Naqvi, these are 'conventional copies of standards carried by Imam Ḥusayn in the Battle of Karbalāʾ';[40] David Pinault considers them to be 'copies of battle-standards or banners borne by the martyrs of Karbalāʾ'.[41] The disagreement between these two authors highlights the uncertainty that surrounds the process, consisting in attributing the standards to the various figures. On certain *ʿalam*s, the name of the figure to whom it is dedicated is engraved, but others do not bear any inscription. When asked about this, the owners of the standards invariably answer that they know with whom each *ʿalam* can be associated because it was passed on to them.[42] The history of their importation too remains quite vague;[43] the owners of *ʿalam*s say that the standards were brought by their families from Iran, Iraq or Lucknow when they settled in the Deccan two or three centuries ago.[44]

A technical knowledge developed regarding these *ʿalam*s, which constitutes a complex system; they are in metal (bronze, silver and alloy with gold for the most precious ones), adorned with designs (*panja*, a dragon's head, a shark's head, ʿAlī's sword, etc.) or with calligraphy, and each part of the object has its own name.[45] Some of them are covered with sandalwood paste. *ʿAlam*s are kept in wooden boxes, put in *ʿāshūr-khāna*, a term used here to refer to *ḥusayniyya*; they exist in any size, some of them are lavishly decorated, others are more simple, some are public, others belong to a certain family. Many of them are actually houses that are occasionally turned into places of worship. Indeed, according to a survey, 92 per cent of the Shiʿa families in Hyderabad have one or more *ʿalam*s in their homes.[46] Each family, depending on its social status and its financial situation, maintains the memory of these objects and has its own way of opening its home to the outside, to decorate it and to organise the rituals.

---

[40] Sadiq Naqvi, *The ʿĀshūr khānas of Hyderabad City* (3rd ed., Hyderabad, 2006), p. 10.

[41] Pinault, *The Shiites: Rituals and Popular Piety in a Muslim Community*, p. 80.

[42] Surveys, Hyderabad, December 2009.

[43] Naqvi (2006 b.), p. 160. This remark concerns Hyderabad. As for North India, according to Rizvi, *ʿalam* and processions might have been introduced by a Sufi saint as early as the beginning of the 15th century; see Rizvi, *A Socio-Intellectual History*, vol. 2, pp. 293–294.

[44] Ibid., p. 81.

[45] Naqvi, *The ʿĀshūr khānas of Hyderabad City*, pp. 11–16 and a diagram of the object, p. 20.

[46] Nadeem Hasnain and Abrar Husain, *Shias and Shia Islam in India* (Delhi, 1988), pp. 146–148.

On the first day of Muḥarram, the ʿalams are taken out of their boxes, wrapped in a 'shroud' or a coloured cloth, and displayed publicly. As the tenth day approaches, more and more people come to see them and, in the public *ʿāshūr-khāna*, such as the one of Bibi Ka Alava, a packed crowd of people rush to reach the Holy of the Holies, that is the place where the *ʿalams* are, to perform their devotions and to touch the *ʿalam*.[47] The believers bring garlands of flowers that they will lay on the *ʿalam* as offerings. They will consecrate plastic bracelets by moving them around the *ʿalam*. They ensure that they are protected by the *ʿalam* – and therefore by the sacred figure attributed to it – by tying a red thread around their wrists. They make wishes and ask for the sacred figure's intercession.

The seventh day is dedicated to Qāsim, 'the bridegroom of Karbalā'': one celebrates here his wedding to Fāṭima, Ḥusayn's daughter, before his departure for the battle and his martyrdom.[48] A big *majlis* is organised and patronised by a family of notables from the old town. After a sermon, Qāsim's *ʿalam* is brought into the middle of the crowd; men get 'presents' from their homes for the groom (henna, fruit, candles), which they carry in their outstretched arms while laboriously forcing their ways through the crowd, since everyone wants to touch the *ʿalam* and the offerings.

Then comes the ritual of *mātam*, which we will describe later on. Men leave the courtyard, while women remain confined to the courtyard during the *majlis*. They receive a white shroud covered with red stains and then leave the courtyard, which in the meantime becomes crowded with women who come from the outside. They fetch the *ʿalam*, stand it up and wrap it in the shroud while weeping. Then they walk through the courtyard forming a procession, and lay the *ʿalam* down in its initial position before concluding the ceremony with chanting.[49] It should be noted that when Pinault describes this ceremony that he observed in 1991, this ritual is performed by men; it seems that, since then, women have appropriated it. Thus, this celebration reproduces Qāsim's wedding, his martyrdom and burial.[50] The *ʿalam* represents Qāsim; in other places, a person embodies him, 'plays his role' in processions or passion plays.

In the last few evenings before 'Āshūrā', people bear the *ʿalam* of the great *ʿashūr-khāna* in a procession through the town. Thus, on the ninth evening dedicated to

---

47 Non-Muslims are welcome, but cannot enter this sacred place because their impurity (*najāsa*) would tarnish the *ʿalam* when touched; a part of the courtyard is reserved for them, where they can burn incense sticks and offer flowers.

48 The liturgy and the rituals of 'Qāsim's wedding' were adapted to the local culture as Karen Ruffle discussed in her paper, 'Karbalā' in the Indo-Persian Imaginaire: The Indianizing of the Wedding of Qasem and Fatima Kubra', in Denis Hermann and Fabrizio Speciale, ed., *Muslim Cultures in the Indo-Iranian World during the Early-Modern and Modern Periods* (Berlin, 2010), pp. 181–200. See also Pinault, *The Shiites: Rituals and Popular Piety in a Muslim Community*, p. 133.

49 Hyderabad (25 December, 2009).

50 A similar *majlis* has been organised since the late 1990s in a popular *ʿāshūr-khāna*. For a description, see Syed Akbar Hyder, *Reliving Karbalā': Martyrdom in South Asian Memory* (Oxford, 2006), p. 55.

ʿAbbās, the courtyard of Bargah Hazrat ʿAbbās is filled with believers who perform their devotions. Three *ʿalams* are carried by people in the procession. Standard-bearers, with white cloths around their waists, take the two other *ʿalams*, and then the remaining and largest one which is the *ʿalam* attributed to ʿAbbās. It holds a relic – a piece of his armour[51] – and is covered with sandalwood paste. Wrapped in a shroud as well as in green and red cloths and adorned with flowers, it looks like an effigy. The believers jostle in order to be able to touch it, weeping as they do so. It circumambulates the courtyard several times while held above the crowd before reaching the street.

On the following day, the fervour is at its height when people get Fāṭima's *ʿalam* in Bibi Ka Alava; carried on an elephant's back, it leads the great procession that continues until the evening. When it leaves the *ʿāshūr-khāna*, the crowd screams and some men incise their skulls with knives as it passes by them. The departure of the *ʿalam* symbolises the departure for the battle and therefore the martyrdom; when it returns, it is 'dead' and put back in place, symbolising burial, until the following year. The *ʿalam* is used here as a substitute for the sacred figure. It represents it, embodies it and is used as Marc Augé would perhaps describe it, as 'a god object'.[52]

In Hyderabad, there is no passion play of the drama of Karbalāʾ. One of the people whom I interviewed about this considers it to be 'wrong'. The cult of the *ʿalam*, which came from Iran, is a ritual 'graft' that 'took' in Hyderabad and, more generally, in South-East Asia, whereas elsewhere, and in particular in Lebanon, the *taʿziya* was established as the most accomplished mode of representation. Besides, it should be noted that one challenges the mode of representation adopted by the other, by describing it as non-Islamic.

The drama of Karbalāʾ, the ritual 'graft'

In the Ottoman Empire, the Shiʿa were not allowed to observe the public rituals peculiar to Shiʿism, in particular those in relation to ʿĀshūrāʾ. In Jabal ʿĀmil (today South Lebanon), the rituals have been therefore limited to quite informal *majlis*, until 1880 when a cleric from Najaf started to organise them, modelling them on the Iraqi rituals. Towards 1895, Iranians living around there observed their own rituals, in particular in terms of the representation of the drama of Karbalāʾ. On a local cleric's instigation, they were forbidden to do so. They asked for permission from the Ottoman authorities who granted them. Thus, Iranians were able to organise processions during which they engaged in practices of self-mortification, as well as in representations of the Battle of Karbalāʾ. ʿĀmilites joined them and, despite reservations and prohibitions from individual *ʿulamāʾ* who taxed the rituals with blameworthy innovations (*bidʿa*), these rituals became gradually established.

In the beginning, the passion plays were carnival playlets, with cavalcades, tents set on fire, captive women taken away on camels; people mimed their roles rather

[51] On this *ʿāshūr-khāna*, see Naqvi, *The ʿĀshūr khānas of Hyderabad City*, p. 71.

[52] Marc Augé, *Le dieu objet* (Paris, 1988).

than actually performing. In Nabatiyya, a commercial centre of Jabal 'Āmil, Shaykh 'Abd al-Ḥusayn Ṣādiq supported these representations. These playlets, which had been performed until then in Persian, were translated into Arabic and, in the 1930s, the script of a real passion play was written. Since then, the theatrical representation of 'Āshūrā' is the highlight of the celebrations in Nabatiyya, and other villages of Jabal 'Āmil also staged their own plays.[53] The 'Persian theatre'[54] became 'Lebanonised'. It has its own characteristics in matters of scenography (no stage-in-the-round, but wooden stages built with backdrops, props and a curtain), in the manner in which imagery and symbolism are used, in the organisation of the play and so on.[55]

Moreover, women play women's roles (in Iran, women's roles are played by men). Sometimes the sacred figures, such as Ḥusayn or Zayn al-'Ābidīn, are veiled so that their faces are not identified with those of ordinary men, although sometimes they are not. This depends upon the religious authority who supervises the play.

In Damascus at the end of the 19th century, the same process of establishment of the rituals was initiated by Iranians.[56] Yet, in the 1920s, the *mujtahid* who was the reference religious authority of the small Shi'i community in Syria, Muḥsin al-Amīn (d. 1952), started a reform of 'Āshūrā' rituals. He reorganised the *majlis*, codified them and modernised them. Furthermore, he prohibited two kinds of rituals, the practices of mortification (as we will see later on) and the passion plays, due to the fact that some men dressed as women and because female descendants of the Prophet were played by unveiled women.[57] According to him, this dishonoured the sacred family.

Muḥsin al-Amīn was obeyed by the believers and backed up by the French Mandate authorities; during the 'Āshūrā' ceremonies in Sayyida Zaynab, the playlets disappeared instead of developing. This prohibition has had quite an impression on the Shi'i community in Damascus for a long time. Not before Sayyida Zaynab became a cosmopolitan Shi'i centre supported by the Syrian government[58] did the first playlet reappear. On the morning of 'Āshūrā', next to the shrine in a soccer field, you can

---

[53] Mervin, *Un réformisme chiite*, pp. 245–248.

[54] I am referring here to Charles Virolleaud, *Le théâtre Persan, ou le drame de Kerbela* (Paris, 1950).

[55] Sabrina Mervin, 'Shiite Theatre in South Lebanon: The Karbalā' Drama and the Sabaya', in Peter Chelkowski, ed., *Eternal Performance: Ta'ziehs and Other Shiite Rituals (Enactments)* (Chicago, 2010), p. 327.

[56] Mervin, *Un réformisme Chiite*, pp. 248–249.

[57] Muḥsin al-Amīn detailed the prohibitions in his *Risālat al-tanzīh*. See ibid., p. 257 and the following pages on the controversies stirred up by his opinions. For more details about the issue of women, see Max Weiss, 'The Cultural Politics of Shi'i Modernism: Morality and Gender in Early 20th-Century Lebanon', *IJMES*, 39 (2007), pp. 249–270.

[58] Sabrina Mervin, 'Sayyida Zaynab: banlieue de Damas ou nouvelle ville sainte chiite?', *CEMOTI*, 22, 'Arabes et Iraniens' (1996), pp. 149–162; Paulo Pinto, 'Pilgrimage, Commodities and Religious Objectivation: The Making of Transnational Shiism between Iran and Syria', *Comparative Studies of South Asia, Africa and the Middle East*, 27 (2007), pp. 109–125.

now watch mimes and cavalcades representing the mounted army of the Umayyads burning the camp of Ḥusayn and capturing the survivors of the Battle of Karbalāʾ.[59]

In Lebanon, ʿĀshūrāʾ ceremonies became politicised in the 1970s as we saw, but it was first and foremost the Israeli invasion in 1982 that triggered the creation of certain plays. In the village of Majdal Silm, two men decided to stage plays for ʿĀshūrāʾ and the Arbaʿīn, in order to confront the occupation. One of them died in an Israeli operation in 1993, while the other continued to take care of these plays, but limited their themes to the Battle of Karbalāʾ and to the play entitled *Mawkib al-sabāyā* (*The Procession of the Captives*), which recounts the epic of the survivors of Karbalāʾ. Other villages stage the Battle of Karbalāʾ, such as Jibshit; in Kafar Kila, *The Procession of the Captives* is staged all year long in the village itself, but the troupe also visits nearby villages in order to perform. The inhabitants of a village take care of these plays, often under the more or less active supervision of a cleric. The actors are not professionals and do not get paid for their performances but, on the contrary, sometimes have to pay for their costumes. They perform 'for Ḥusayn' and for a reward in the Hereafter: 'When this work is done, we cash a cheque of good deeds (*chek ḥasanāt*)', an actor explains. Playing their roles enables them not only to experience community life and intense conviviality, but also to enjoy a spiritual experience. An actress remembers what she felt at the end of a play in which she played Zaynab's role: 'When the actors arrived and Imam Ḥusayn was on the ground, Lady Zaynab approached him. I couldn't stand any longer. I was going to faint … I started trembling. I said, "Truly, I feel I'm living in the time of Karbalāʾ".'[60] The audience, which often knows the lines of the plays by heart, weeps as it does in the *majlis* when the dramatic tension builds up, rediscovering scenes as if for the first time. This kind of theatre remains a ritual.

In the course of recent years, the performance has become more and more often a matter for professionals and has acquired a modern form in Nabatiyya, where the organisers try to attract and satisfy an audience that extends beyond the circle of the believers, in particular by entrusting the production to well-known professional directors.[61] Moreover, it has become even more politicised by Hizbullah, who have turned it into a means of communication and of mobilisation. The party, which has staged plays in schools, produced panoramas as well as sound and light shows about Karbalāʾ, started to stage a new version of the play in 2006. After the war against Israel, this play was updated and adapted into a DVD movie. The principle was to combine the past and the present, to present theatre scenes alternating with film projections, leading the spectator from the Battle of Karbalāʾ, its heroes and its sacred figures to the Islamic resistance, to its heroes, ideologues and fighters. The title of the play referred to Zaynab's words to Yazīd: 'You won't erase our memory'. These words, which became the slogan of the party, are also a common expression in all

---

59 I saw this for the first time in 2002.

60 Both interviews come from the documentary *The Procession of the Captives: A Shiite Tragedy* (2006), directed by S. Mervin, produced by CNRS Images-Momento.

61 Mervin, 'Shiite Theatre in South Lebanon', pp. 331–333.

the Shi'i communities, where they summarise the role of the commemorative rites of Karbalā': to conserve the group's memory and, thereby, its survival as an imagined community.

Shedding Blood for Ḥusayn: Rituals of Self-Mortification

'Bloody festivals'

The first accounts of the Shi'i rituals of self-mortification date back to the first half of the 17th century. Attested in the Caucasus and in Azerbaijan, these rituals first spread to the northern part of Iran, before reaching the central and the southern part of the country, as well as Iraq, in the 19th century; eastwards, they reached India where they became established.[62] Travellers, diplomats and later on scholars did not fail to describe these rituals, struck by the blood of the penitents and the fervour of the crowd. Thus, in the 1830s in India, a British administrator saw the Muslims 'inflamed to madness by the recollection of the really affecting incidents of the massacre of the grandchildren of their prophet ...' Beating their breasts, they were, according to him, 'ready to kill themselves and too anxious for an excuse to kill somebody else'.[63] Count Gobineau (d. 1882), posted to Iran in the 1860s, wrote: 'The Berberys begin to self-flagellate with their chains ... blood is shed, the crowd is elated and cries, exaltation becomes more and more intense ...'[64] Eugène Aubin (d. 1931), forty years later, wrote: 'In the background, a hideous crowd of people is thronging: squeezed up, staggering like drunkards, barefoot and white-clad men slashed their shaved heads with swords; blood streams down their faces and reddens their white clothes ...'[65] In 1912–1913, in Karbalā', Kāẓim al-Dujaylī observed similar practices, which he described in detail in the review *Lughat al-'Arab*.[66] In the mid-1950s, an American woman named Elizabeth Fernea, following the women of the Iraqi village where she lived, went to the pilgrimage in Karbalā'. Later on, she related the processions that she had witnessed and the exaltation of the sometimes rival groups of penitents.[67] More recently, historians and ethnologists looked into these practices, in particular

[62] Practices of self-mortification are attested in Oudh in 1784, when none other than the *nawāb* Asaf al-Dawla performed a violent self-inflicted beating. See Juan Cole, *Roots of North Indian Shī'ism in Iran and Iraq: Religion and State, in Awadh, 1722–1859* (Berkeley and London, 1988), p. 102.

[63] Pinault, *The Shiites: Rituals and Popular Piety in a Muslim Community*, p. 64.

[64] Joseph Arthur de Gobineau, *Les religions et les philosophies dans l'Asie centrale* (2nd ed., Paris, 1866), pp. 377–378.

[65] Eugène Aubin, *La Perse d'aujourd'hui* (Paris, 1908), p. 167.

[66] See Mervin, *Un réformisme Chiite*, pp. 241–242.

[67] Elizabeth Fernea, *Guest of the Sheik: An Ethnography of an Iraqi Village* (New York, 1965), pp. 242–244. Elizabeth Fernea (1927–2009) was at that time following her husband, the anthropologist Robert Fernea; later on she became an ethnologist herself as well as a filmmaker.

David Pinault, who made subtle observations and analyses of the groups of flagellators, the *gurūh*, in Hyderabad.[68]

Not only did these practices of self-mortification travel from one Shi'i region to the other, they also borrowed from local cultures and traditions. Thus, different techniques were more or less established and developed, depending on the location: scarification of the scalp (*taṭbīr*), use of knife blades, swords, razor blades or chains (*zanjīr*) on the breast or on the back. The believers aim to express their sorrow, their pain and their empathy for Ḥusayn's martyrdom, as well as to show that they are ready to die for him. To do so, some of them limit themselves to beating their breasts in step (*laṭm*), in a more or less pronounced way, with more or less sweeping and sophisticated gestures, which developed locally and progressively make the skin turn red.[69] Others use instruments to wound or gash themselves, in order to shed blood – and blood is shed in the *ḥusayniyya*, around the shrines and in the streets where the penitents march.

These spectacular shows did not fail to stir up reactions from the religious circles or the Sunni political authorities. Thus, in Lucknow, in 1927, the Nizam issued a *farmān* forbidding the practices of 'beating the breast and back with chains and planks studded with pointed barbs' in his dominions.[70] In the Ottoman Empire, the Shi'a subjects of the Sublime Porte were not allowed to observe the public rituals of Muḥarram. From the 1870s on, nevertheless, the Persian community of Istanbul, which already held its annual celebrations in the Valide Han, was able to add processions like those taking place in Iran to the sessions of mourning gatherings.[71] During these 'bloody festivals' in 1886, flagellators marched while beating themselves with chains along with white-clad penitents whose clothes turned red as the blood streamed from their scalps as they slashed themselves with swords in time with their steps.[72] Muḥarram celebrations were forbidden in Istanbul by the Ankara authorities in 1928, appearing again only in the 1980s.[73]

Banning attempts

After the fall of the Ottoman Empire, the Shi'a were able to express their identity in public and ceremonies developed, particularly in Iraq, Lebanon and even in Syria, around Sayyida Zaynab's mausoleum. Along with this new visibility, with tourists

---

[68] Pinault, *The Shiites: Rituals and Popular Piety in a Muslim Community*, Part III.

[69] Mervin, 'Les larmes et le sang des chiites', pp. 160–161.

[70] John Norman Hollister, 'The Shiite Community in India Today', *Moslem World*, 36 (1946), p. 172.

[71] Erika Glassen, 'Muharram-Ceremonies ('Azādārī) in Istanbul at the End of the XIXth and the Beginning of the XXth Century', in Zarcone and Zarinebaf-Shahr, ed., *Les Iraniens d'Istanbul* (Istanbul and Tehran, 1993), pp. 114–115.

[72] Kesnin Bey, *The Evil of the East or Truths about Turkey* (London, 1888), ch. 8: 'The Bloody Festival of Hasan and Hussein', p. 149.

[73] Thierry Zarcone, 'La communauté Chiite de Turquie à l'époque contemporaine', in Sabrina Mervin, ed., *Les mondes Chiites et l'Iran* (Paris, 2007), p. 140.

and others not familiar with Shiʿism and its tradition of bloody rituals, and then with local populations adopting practices imported by pilgrims,[74] came the first criticisms from the *ʿulamāʾ* who aimed to forbid the practices of self-mortification. Asadullāh Māmaqānī in Istanbul, Mahdī al-Qazwīnī (d. 1939) in Baṣra, and especially Muḥsin al-Amīn (d. 1952) in Damascus condemned the rituals based on bloodshed, which they considered to be blameworthy innovations (*bidʿa*). As these rituals are not part of the acts of worship (*ʿibādāt*) codified by Islamic jurisprudence (*fiqh*), they do not directly fall under categories subjected to normative discourses. Thus, in order to discuss this, reformist *ʿulamāʾ* and particularly Muḥsin al-Amīn, who was the most prolific,[75] used three lines of argument: the reference to previous *fatwa*s issued by recognised *mujtahid*; the ban on harming oneself (*iḍrār bi'l-nafs*), which is a principle of Islamic law; rulings that are more a matter of personal opinion and even common sense than, strictly speaking, the practice of *ijtihād*. Thus, for instance, each of them shared his own appreciation of the question of whether these rituals of self-mortification were harmful or not to those who indulged in them; in the ensuing controversies, the rulings diverged radically from one another. Likewise, each of them brought forth *fatwā*s that supported their arguments: if some of these *fatwā*s clearly asserted the licit or illicit nature of these practices, other more ambiguous ones were likely to be interpreted otherwise and such alternative interpretations did in fact exist. A number of great scholars indeed hesitated to take a stand against these rituals since they were not considered part of religion, rather they belonged to folklore and popular culture and consequently, somehow, they did not concern them.

Triggered by the calls for reform, the debate led to many publications, treatises and articles. Quite intense, particularly in the scholarly circles in Najaf, it even entailed insults thrown at reformists and violent incidents against supporters of the reforms. In addition, there were repercussions as far as India. On the one hand, reformists appealed to common sense and reason to defend the Shiʿi community as viewed by believers but also, first and foremost, as it was viewed by outsiders; they feared that the Shiʿa would represent themselves as savages or simpletons through these rituals. On the other hand, opponents to the reforms defended the Shiʿi identity that was displayed during these rituals as it showed they were no longer being repressed, thanks to the formation of more liberal modern states. Two clashing views on the place of Shiʿism within Islam and within the modern world overlapped with rivalries between ethnic groups, between conflicting communities, and between *mujtahids*.[76]

---

[74] In Iraq, for instance, Kāẓim al-Dujaylī noted in 1913 that, before the beginning of the century, rituals of self-flagellation were observed by Turkmen, Dervishes, Persians, Kurds, but not by Arabs. In 1919, the British administration mentioned in a report that hundreds of people performed *taṭbīr* in Najaf, but those were mostly Turks and Persians. These practices developed among local populations especially after World War II.

[75] He expounded his stand in the introduction of *al-Majālis al-saniyya* in the 1920s, and later on in a treatise entitled *Risālat al-tanzīh*.

[76] On Asad Allāh Māmaqānī, see Glassen, 'Muharram-Ceremonies ('Azādārī) in Istanbul at the End of the XIXth and the Beginning of the XXth Century', pp. 124, 127–128. On the two

After this wave of controversy that divided scholarly circles in the 1920s, few scholars ventured to reopen the debates. Yet *Marjaʿ* Hossein Borujerdi (d. 1961) attempted to oppose the practices of self-mortification. An anecdote about this is often told in Shiʿi circles: 'We follow you every day of the year, except on ʿĀshūrā'', said the *marjaʿ* to the representatives of a group of men observing these rituals.[77] One can see here the limit of the authority of the *marjaʿiyya*.

The calls for the reform of these practices in the name of modernity would not re-emerge until contemporary Shiʿi history entered a new phase. They came from promoters of a militant and rationalising political Islam. The debate was reopened, especially as the Shīrāziyya circle of influence encouraged the rituals,[78] and the other *marjaʿ*s did not often take such a clear-cut stance because their position was always open to interpretation. At the beginning of the 1980s in Lebanon, Muḥammad Ḥusayn Faḍl Allāh (d. 2010) encouraged his supporters to shed their blood in the Islamic resistance movement against Israel rather than shedding it in vain. He would later convey an increasingly intellectualised image of the Karbalā' paradigm and clearly ban the practices of self-mortification.[79] In Iran, Khumaynī opposed these rituals and later Khamenei issued a *fatwā* in 1994 banning them. Inside the country, believers could no longer observe them; outside, the supporters of the Supreme Leader also conformed to his rulings.[80] Once again, the debate was reopened, more intensely than ever. Abu'l-Qāsim al-Khū'ī (d. 1992) did not consider these rituals advisable, but he did not forbid them either, except when they 'undermine the sacrality of the [Shiʿa] sect (*ḥurmat al-madhhab*)'.[81] It seems that ʿAlī Sīstānī, whose *fatwā*s permitting the rituals are often cited by those who support them, changed his mind. In 2010, his office (*maktab al-istiftā'*) published a statement denying that he had issued rulings supporting *taṭbīr*, further to the statement of a Bahraini scholar who, as it were, manipulated his words.[82]

---

others, see Ende, 'The Flagellations of Muḥarram and the Shiʿite 'Ulamā''; Mervin, *Un réformisme Chiite*, ch. 6; Ibrahim Haydari, 'The Rituals of ʿAshura: Genealogy, Functions, Actors and Structures', in Faleh Abdul-Jabar, ed., *Ayatollahs, Sufis and Ideologues: State, Religion and Social Movements in Iraq* (London, 2002), pp. 445–460; Weiss, 'The Cultural Politics of Shiʿi Modernism', ch. 2.

77 I heard this on various occasions; from a Persian scholar living in London and from members of a group of penitents in Hyderabad.

78 The Shīrāziyya is a transnational politico-religious movement led by the Shīrāzī family, particularly strong in the Persian Gulf States. See Laurence Louër, *Transnational Shia Politics: Religious and Political Networks in the Gulf* (New York, 2008).

79 Muḥammad Ḥusayn Faḍl Allāh, *Ḥadīth ʿāshūrā'* (Beirut, 1997), pp. 220–221. His website is: http//arabic.bayynat.org.lb/achoura (accessed 13 August 2013).

80 Mervin, 'Les larmes et le sang des chiites', pp. 163–164.

81 Quoted by Faḍl Allāh, *Ḥadīth ʿāshūrā'*, p. 221.

82 '*Maktab al-Sīstānī yaṣdur takdhīban bi-sha'n ārā' mu'ayyida li'l-taṭbīr manṣūba li'l-marjaʿ*', published online at http://rassd.com on 24 October 2010; now available at: http://www.alrage.net/vb/t250965.html (accessed 28 October 2013).

Rationalised versus 'savage sacred'[83]

The *fatwās* issued by the great *marja'*s, as well as opinions issued by middle-rank scholars who belong to the intellectual and religious Shi'i circles, are nowadays published online. Those who support *taṭbīr* and the flagellations are particularly active on the internet, using this media to legitimise their stance;[84] they even monopolised the 'Tatbir' entry in Wikipedia, the online encyclopaedia.[85] However, there are also detractors who express themselves through internet forums and social networks (Facebook and Twitter), which intensifies the polemics – not to mention the Sunni Muslims who get indignant about these bloody practices displayed online[86].

These two camps coexist – and not only on the internet. Blood drives are organised in the Middle East and within the Shi'a diaspora community as a rational substitute for the bloodshed that sullies the image of the community. Some believers, however, combine the two practices, since they cannot resolve how to choose between what they consider to be two ways of getting closer to God, thanks to Ḥusayn's intercession. When a coercive force can impose the modernist and rationalising point of view, the believers limit themselves to breast-beating while marching, without going too far. This is particularly the case in Iran (even if certain believers self-flagellate in secret) and in the Hizbullah ranks, since the Lebanese party follows the Guide's rulings. As the party became hegemonic in the suburbs of South Beirut, it organised most of the processions there in a very well-ordered way. They mirror the order and the world view promoted by the party. On the other hand, in some South Lebanon cities, particularly in Nabatiyya, blood is shed every year, as in the holy cities in Iraq, in the Persian Gulf States where the Shīrāziyya remains influential, and in other Shi'i areas as far as the Philippines and India.

In Hyderabad, a consensus has almost been reached on this question: the practices of self-mortification constitute a good way of commemorating Ḥusayn's martyrdom, of expressing one's compassion, of showing that one is ready to shed one's blood for him, of calling for his intercession and so forth. I only met there one *mujtahid*, who had been studying for about twenty years in Qumm, who was critical of these rituals. On 'Āshūrā', from dawn to dusk, men perform *mātam*, breast-beating while holding razor blades between their fingers, beating their scalps with knives, or their backs with blades swung on chains. As David Pinault showed, the penitents congregate in *gurūh*, which try to outdo one another in skills. Within these groups, the young boys are initiated by the elders, whose gestures they imitate. A strong solidarity develops between men who are about to self-flagellate together; social differences smooth out. Each of them watches over the other, and the entire group watches over its members; when an individual enters a trance state and no longer controls his

---

[83] The expression is borrowed from Roger Bastide, *Le sacré sauvage* (Paris, 1975).

[84] See the following websites: http://wn.com/tatbeer (accessed 13 August 2013); and http://www.jafariyanews.com (accessed 13 August 2013).

[85] See http://en.wikipedia.org/wiki/Tatbir (accessed 13 August 2013).

[86] See http://www.shiachat.com/forum (accessed 13 August 2013).

gestures and running the risk of sustaining dangerous injuries, his colleagues rush to prevent him from doing so. It is about men displaying their virility; women's participation consists in shedding tears while watching men shedding their blood.[87]

Thus, these rituals are both rites of passage,[88] which enable the young to join the group, and rites of institution, which assign to each individual his or her role within society, depending on gender, age, social class, etc.[89] They enable the individual to express emotions that they have to contain during the rest of the year, while enabling them to focus on themselves while connecting with the group. It enables the group, on the one hand, to connect with the transnational and globalised Shiʿa community, and on the other hand, to negotiate its place as a (most often minority) community within the state. In order to perform these rituals in the public sphere, the Shiʿa show that they can be organised, while at the same time managing violence and maintaining order; meanwhile, in the background, the history of the local Shiʿa community and the story of the sacred family, the sole holders of legitimate power, are both being reaffirmed.

---

87 Observations and interviews in Hyderabad (December, 2009).

88 Arnold van Gennep, *Rites of Passage* (London, 2004).

89 Pierre Bourdieu, 'Les rites comme actes d'institution', *Actes de la recherche en sciences sociales*, 43 (1982), 'Rites et fétiches', pp. 58–63.

20

The Luminous Lamp: The Practice of *Chirāgh-i rawshan* among the Ismailis of Central Asia

Hakim Elnazarov

چراغ اوّل بدست مصطفی بود   دلیلش با علی مرتضی بود
چراغ مصطفی گیری تو در دست   بیا بنگر در إینجا چَند پند است.

The first Light was in the hand of Muṣṭafā,
Its *dalīl*[1] was with ʿAlī-yi Murtaḍā.
When you take the Light of Muṣṭafā in your hand,
Come and witness the guidance that is in here!

The Nizārī Ismailis who represent one of the largest and most culturally diverse communities of the global Muslim population, reside in more than 25 countries around the world. They are united in their adherence to the core Ismaili doctrine centred on the presence of a living Imam. The expressions of devotion and spirituality of the Ismaili communities bear the marks of their historical and cultural trends and are vividly manifested in their various religious rites and practices. In the mountainous regions of Central Asia, primarily Badakhshān, where Ismailis constitute a dominant Muslim group, the spread of Islam seems to have been a peaceful process in which diverse religious traditions intermingled over centuries and new belief systems evolved in conjunction with practices of the pre-Islamic era. The region is considered to be a pathway of the Great Silk Road. It was a meeting point of various civilisations and major religions, including Zoroastrianism, Nestorian Christianity, Buddhism, Manichaeism and Islam. This encounter shaped the cultural landscape of the region and finds its expression in the beliefs and practices of diverse Muslim communities in Central Asia.

Islam penetrated the mountain terrain of Central Asia as early as the 8th century. It was Shiʿi Islam, however, which firmly established itself in Badakhshān and was a driving force behind the dissemination of Islamic teachings to the indigenous

[1] In this context, it refers to a wooden piece which keeps the wick of a lamp upright. It also has a double meaning of *dalīl* (proof), i.e., that the proof of it is with ʿAlī.

mountain people.[2] According to oral tradition, the spread of Ismaili Shiʿism to the region was initiated by Nāṣir-i Khusraw (d. after 462/1070), the celebrated Persian Ismaili philosopher, traveller and poet who spent the last fifteen years of his life in exile in Badakhshān. A senior *dāʿī* (missionary) delegated by the Fatimid Imam-caliph al-Mustanṣir bi'llāh as his *ḥujja* (proof) in Khurāsān, Nāṣir found refuge from persecution at the court of the local Ismaili ruler, ʿAlī b. al-Asad, and wrote his most important works under his patronage.[3] Over time Nāṣir-i Khusraw's image transcended the historical figure and turned into a legendary personality endowed with supernatural powers capable of performing miracles. The religious practices of the community and many sacred places in the region are to this day associated with the name of Nāṣir-i Khusraw.

The Ismailis of Central Asia, who all belong to the Nizārī branch of Ismailism, are linguistically and culturally a diverse number of groups[4] and reside in the border regions of four countries, namely, the south-eastern part of Tajikistan, northern and central Afghanistan, northern areas of Pakistan as well as western China. Historically, the community was able to maintain its hermetic existence in the deep and narrow passages of the Pamir and Hindukush mountain ranges. The small principalities, which existed in the region, were by and large semi-independent on the fringes of great empires and dynasties stemming from the Sāmānid Empire (9th–10th centuries) down to the Bukharan Emirate (19th and early 20th centuries). The turning point in the history of the Ismailis of Central Asia was their encounter with the British and Russian superpowers on the highlands of the Pamirs at the end of the 19th century, which led to the foundation of the present territorial boundaries of the states where the Ismailis reside today.

The end of the Soviet era marked a new beginning for the Central Asian Ismailis, particularly those residing in Tajikistan, and paved the way for their integration into the global Ismaili community. The freedom of religious expression and globalisation processes opened new avenues for reinvigoration and modernisation of the local community. Religious practices, which hitherto had largely remained in the private domain, have attained public prominence and continue to evolve in an open space.

Among the most important traditional practices of the Central Asian Ismailis is the ceremony of *Chirāgh-i rawshan* (Luminous Lamp). Commonly performed in Badakhshān, it survived centuries of religious and ideologically motivated persecution of Ismailis in the region. At the same time, the practice enabled the community

---

[2] The oral and literary traditions of the Ismailis in Badakhshān are generally of a Shiʿi-Ismaili and Sufi nature. See, for example, A. E. Bertels and M. Baqoev, ed., *Alphabetic Catalogue of Manuscripts found by 1959–1963 Expedition in Gorno-Badakhshan Autonomous Region* (Moscow, 1967).

[3] For more details, see F. Daftary, *The Ismāʿīlīs: Their History and Doctrines* (2nd ed., Cambridge, 2007), pp. 206–207.

[4] The Central Asian Ismailis speak over 15 languages and dialects which belong to the eastern Iranian and Indo-Aryan group of languages, including Pamiri and Dardic. In addition, the Brushaski language, a language isolate, is widely spoken by the Ismailis of northern Pakistan.

to preserve its religious identity and served as a medium for the Ismaili *pīrs* and *dāʿīs* to disseminate their teachings to various parts of Central Asia. In the following sections, an attempt has been made to illustrate the tradition as a ritual which embodies both the rich cultural heritage of Central Asia as well as the core principles of the Ismaili faith. The depiction of the tradition draws on various materials, including the existing literature on the practice and oral traditions of the community.[5]

Chirāgh-i rawshan: The Luminous Lamp

The ceremony of *Chirāgh (Charāgh)-i rawshan* is the most distinguished and salient feature of the religious life of Ismailis in Central Asia. The practice is also known as *tsirow/tsiraw-pithid/pathid* in the local Pamiri languages (*tsirow*: *chirāgh*, and *pithid*: kindling, lighting-up). The ceremony takes place on two important occasions, namely the *Daʿwat-i fanā* (sermon of demise) and the *Daʿwat-i baqā* (sermon of eternity).[6] The concept of *daʿwa* (Persian, *daʿwat*), meaning 'sermon', 'call' or 'invitation' to join a cause, in the context of Central Asia also implies an 'assembly' or a 'gathering'. These functions of the *daʿwa* invariably went together in the past when a call for allegiance to the Ismaili Imam was a political function of the *daʿwa* institution.[7] The practice is also known as *Daʿwat-i Nāṣir*, in honour of Nāṣir-i Khusraw who is believed to have initiated the Ismaili *daʿwa* in Badakhshān.

The *Daʿwat-i fanā* traditionally takes place on the third day after the death of an Ismaili individual[8] and marks the end of the funeral ceremony. The *Daʿwat-i baqā*, on the other hand, is an infrequent event and is usually performed when an elderly member of a family decides to abandon all wrongdoing and submit himself wholly to the spiritual life. Unlike the *Daʿwat-i fanā*, which is obligatory upon a death of an Ismaili, the *Daʿwat-i baqā* is a personal endeavour.[9]

The *Chirāgh-i rawshan* is a complex ritual with various layers of meaning and significance designed to offer hope and spiritual elevation to the individuals who attend the ceremony. It is part of a larger burial ceremony that completes the formal observance of the funeral service with prayers for the soul of the deceased and

[5] The oral traditions of the Central Asian Ismailis, as collected by The Institute of Ismaili Studies, provide the bulk of the narratives which this chapter draws upon. I would also like to acknowledge and thank Dr Faqir Muhammad Hunzai, Dr Azizullah Najib, Dr Elbon Hojibekov and Mr Shohzodamamad Mamadsherzodshoev for their input in developing this chapter.

[6] The *Daʿwat-i baqā* is also referred to as '*Daʿwat-i ṣafā*' (sermon of purity) in the Ishkashim district of Badakhshān.

[7] See A. Nanji, *The Nizārī Ismāʿīlī Tradition in the Indo-Pakistan Subcontinent* (Delmar, NY, 1978), p. 4.

[8] The ceremony is currently performed in the evening of the second day after the death of a person, for pragmatic and economic reasons.

[9] The tradition of *Daʿwat-i baqā* ceased to exist in Tajikistan during the Soviet period, but it is still performed sporadically in parts of Afghan Badakhshān and the northern areas of Pakistan.

condolences to the bereaved family. The ceremony entails a series of rites, recitations and chanting which culminate in the kindling of a lamp. The symbolism and sanctity of light expressed in the Qur'anic verse on Light (*Nūr*: 24–35) is fundamental to the entire ceremony. The notion of light is of great significance in Shiʿi Islam in which the *nūr al-walāya* is transmitted from Imam to Imam.[10] For the Ismailis it denotes the light of the imamate that illuminates the world in every age through the presence of a living Imam. According to oral tradition, the light (*chirāgh*) also enlightens the path of the soul of the deceased towards finding peace and salvation in the afterlife. The practice seems to bind together various dimensions of human experience, including beliefs, emotions and hopes and spirituality associated with the afterlife.

The origins of the *Chirāgh-i rawshan* ceremony are obscure.[11] The ritualistic dimensions of the ceremony bear certain characteristics of pre-Zoroastrian religions, which also find expression in various rituals of other Muslim communities in Central Asia. The Ismaili theologians and intellectuals appear to have skilfully intertwined the performance of the ancient ritual with Qur'anic verses, stories about the prophets and Imams, supplications and a poetic commentary. As a result, they created an elaborate ritual text called the *Chirāgh-nāma* (Book of Light) which presents the *Chirāgh-i rawshan* as a sophisticated expression of *imam-shināsī*, that is, recognising and loving the Imam. Within this new form of expression, however, the ceremony has retained its primordial elements for the community as reflected in their belief in spirits, animal sacrifice and intimate connection between humanity and the natural world. These notions permeate the observance of the ceremony and enrich its significance for the community. Before discussing the rituals associated with the ceremony of *Chirāgh-i rawshan*, I briefly describe the *Chirāgh-nāma* text itself.

Chirāgh-nāma: The Book of Light

The *Chirāgh-i rawshan* ceremony is performed according to the compendium of Qur'anic verses, poems, supplications and instructions known as the *Chirāgh-nāma*. Much of this content has been evidently selected to evoke the divine light (*nūr*) by means of ritual glorification of God, the prophets and the Imams, thereby highlighting the continuity of divine guidance through history. The *Chirāgh-nāma* alludes to the light of the Prophet Muḥammad in the following verses:

---

10 For more details, see M. A. Amir-Moezzi, *The Spirituality of Shiʿi Islam* (London, 2011), pp. 51–52.

11 For discussion surrounding the origin of the *Chirāgh-i rawshan* ceremony, see A. Bertels, 'Naẓar-i barkhī az ʿurafā va Shīʿayān-i Ithnā ʿasharī rājiʿ bi arzish-i mīrāth-i adabī-yi Nāṣir-i Khusraw,' in *Yādnāma-yi Nāṣir-i Khusraw* (Mashhad, 1976), pp. 107–108; Umed Shozodamuhammad, *Manābeʿi Sunnat-i ʿCharāgh rawshan* (Dushanbe, 2009); A. Shokhumorov, '*Charāgh rawshankunī* – Sunnat-i Āriyā-ī va Ismāʿīlī-i mardum-i Badakhshān,' in *Masʿalahāi Pāmīrshināsī*, 5 (2003), pp. 156–162.

Mā charāgh az nūr-i shamʿ-i Muṣṭafā āwardaim,
Ruyi dil dar Kaʿba-i ahl-i ṣafāʾ āwardaim.
Har kasī ārad matāʿ-i khīshtan dar kuy-i dūst,
Mā charāgh az bahr-i mardān-i khudā āwardaim.

We have brought the lamp from the light of the *chirāgh* of Muṣṭafā;
We have brought the countenance of the heart into the Kaʿba of the people of piety.
Everyone brings his own offering to the presence of the friend;
We have brought the *chirāgh* for the (noble) men of Allah.[12]

We do not know much about the authorship of the *Chirāgh-nāma*. The existing Ismaili sources do not provide any record of the text or the practice other than the oral narratives of the community. Although the oral tradition attributes it to Nāṣir-i Khusraw, there are no indications or references to the *Chirāgh-nāma* in his works. But the original text of the *Chirāgh-nāma* may have been composed by some disciples of Nāṣir-i Khusraw, as indicated in one of the poems in the text which has the refrain 'Join the *daʿwat* of Nāṣir!' at the end of each verse:

Ay ʿāshiq-i ṣāḥibnaẓar, dar daʿwat-i Nāṣir darā!
Ay muʾmin-i ṣāf-i guhar, dar daʿwat-i Nāṣir darā! ...
Yak shab budam dar daʿwatash, chashmam gushūd az raḥmatash
Bastam kamar dar khidmatash, dar daʿwat-i Nāṣir darā!

O devotee, master of the vision, join the *daʿwat* of Nāṣir!
O believer of the pure jewel, join the *daʿwat* of Nāṣir! ...
One day I was present in his *daʿwat*, my eyes were opened by his mercy,
I fully submitted myself to his service, join the *daʿwat* of Nāṣir!

It is apparent that the text of the *Chirāgh-nāma* has been modified in the course of centuries. Several names appear in the text, such as Saʿdī, Kwaja Hamdīn, Shams and Shāh Niʿmatullāh, who are likely to be the source of some of the verses contained in the text, but whose identity is hard to ascertain.[13] The composition of the text attests

---

[12] The English translation of the verses is from text of the *Chirāgh-nāma* prepared by the IIS.

[13] Shāh Niʿmatullāh, whose name appears in some manuscripts, is believed to be the same as the founder of the famous Niʿmatullāhī Sufi order. This is among several interesting observations of Azizullah Najib regarding the authors of the text in his 'The Content and Practice of the Chirāgh-i rawshan Ceremony among the Ismailis of Northern Areas and Chitral of Pakistan', pp. 30–31 (unpublished report for the IIS).

to its close affinity to Sufism and Twelver Shiʿism which is expressed in the content, shared terminology and adoption of Persian lyrics.[14]

In some copies of *Chirāgh-nāma*[15] one finds a number of invocations in the name of Khwaja Aḥmad Yasavī, the founder of a Sufi order in Turkistan (end of 6th/12th century), Shaykh Farīd al-Dīn Shakar-Ganj, the Chishti Shaykh of India (d. 664/1266), the Twelver Imam ʿAlī b. Mūsā al-Riḍā (d. 203/818), Shams-i Tabrīz, the spiritual mentor of Jalāl al-Dīn Rūmī (d. 672/1273), and the Persian poet Ḥāfiẓ (d. 792/1390). The adoption of Sufi and Twelver Shiʿi elements by the Ismailis of Iran and Central Asia is clearly a feature of the post-Alamūt period (after 654/1256) in Nizārī Ismaili history following the Mongol invasions, when they were often obliged to practise *taqiyya* (precautionary dissimulation) to avoid persecution by their opponents.

The introductory part of *Chirāgh-nāma* illuminates some aspects of the text. It provides explanation and justification for the performance of the *Chirāg-i rawshan* ceremony which is presented as 'obligatory, incumbent, and blessing upon Muslims'.[16] Emphasising the supernatural origin of the *chirāgh*, it relates the story of the angel Jibraʾīl (Gabriel) bestowing the lamp on the Prophet Muḥammad on the event of his son ʿAbd Allāh's death and commanding him to perform the *Chirāgh-i rawshan* for his successors. Accordingly, the practice was passed down in the Prophet's progeny. The tradition maintains that Nāṣir-i Khusraw received it from the Fatimid Imam-caliph al-Mustanṣir biʾllāh (d. 487/1094) during his visit to Cairo and brought it with him to Badakhshan.[17]

The first section of the text which is recited at the beginning of the ceremony is called the *duʿa* of *pīsh-i takbīr* (prayers in the beginning of glorification) and consists of prayers and invocations in the name of Allah, his angels, the prophets and the Imams. Each invocation is accompanied with related verses from the Qurʾan. The subsequent poems and Qurʾanic verses further elaborate the notion of prophethood, Muḥammad being the seal of the prophets, and the continuity of the chain of imamate throughout human history.

---

[14] For more details see W. Ivanow, 'Sufism and Ismailism: *Chirāgh-nama*', *Revue Iranienne d'Anthropologie*, 3 (1959) pp. 13–39.

[15] The Central Asian Studies Unit of the IIS collected several copies of the *Chirāgh-nāma* of various quality and length from Central Asia, including from northern Pakistan, Afghanistan and Tajikistan. Among these texts the most elaborate and lengthy are manuscripts labelled as MS (h), MS (i), from northern Pakistan dated 1304/1886 and 1334/1915 respectively, and a manuscript from Tajik Badakhshān, dated 1334/1915, which is preserved at the Institute of Oriental Manuscripts in St Petersburg, Russia, under file 121, list 1. The discussion of the content of the text draws on these manuscripts.

[16] For more on the introductory part of *Chirāgh-nāma,* see Umed Mamadsherzodshoev Manobeʿi sunnati Charoghrawshan (Sources of the Tradition of Charoghrawshan)', *Merosi Ajam* (Dushanbe, 2009), pp. 8–9.

[17] Ibid., p. 9.

Ritual Aspects of *Chirāgh-i rawshan*

Traditionally, the *Chirāgh-i rawshan* ceremony is performed before dawn, following the night vigil and singing of devotional poetry, known as *maddāḥ* or *qaṣīda*. The *khalīfa*, a member of the local religious hierarchy, orchestrates and presides over the ceremony. As he performs the ritual and recites the corresponding texts from *Chirāgh-nāma*, the congregation joins him while reciting the last verses of the poems and chanting the glorification of God (*takbīr*).

The ceremony can be roughly divided into three stages: a preparatory stage, involving the ritual of sacrifice; the kindling of light; and third, the final stage of supplication and prayers for the bereaved family and participants of the ceremony. The preparatory stage begins with the recitation of *du'a-i pīsh-i takbīr* and *du'a-i takbīr*. The ritual associated with this stage is the animal sacrifice carried out at the end of the recitation of the *du'as*. The second stage entails the making and kindling of light while reciting verses from the *Chirāgh-nāma*. The ritual begins with the preparation of a long wick while the first poem in the *Chirāgh-nāma*, known as *Qandīl-nāma*, is recited. Once the wick is ready, the *khalīfa* cuts, folds and dips the wick in the oil and lights it. While holding the *chirāgh-dān* (kindle holder) in his hand, the *khalīfa* recites more verses from the *Chirāgh-nāma*. Finally, the *chirāgh-dān* is taken to the individual members of the bereaved family to obtain their blessings. In the final stage of the ceremony, the meal made from the sacrificial sheep is served to the congregation. After sharing the meal, prayers are offered for the bereaved family and for the salvation of the soul of the deceased. This ends the formal observance of the *Chirāgh-i rawshan* ceremony.

The ritual text is an important vehicle to construe the meaning of the ritual. At the same time, the meaning of the ritual is not limited to the text or to sermonising.[18] This can be observed in the case of the *Chirāgh-i rawshan* ceremony. The various meanings arise from the interpretations which are rooted in the oral tradition, the occasion, space and timing of the ritual.

The ceremony provides an occasion for the community to experience a heightened sense of unity and solidarity. While the *khalīfa* orchestrates and leads the ceremony, every individual becomes an active participant not just in a metaphorical sense, but in actual reality. They chant their portion of the sacred text, joining the *khalīfa* in glorifying the Lord. Most explicitly this occurs during the recitation of the *Qandīl-nāma* where each portion of the poem is accompanied by congregation reciting in unison the *Ṣalawāt*, that is, 'O Allah! Bless Muḥammad and the family of Muḥammad':

Guyim ba du'a zi dawr-i Ādam, Az Ādamu khātamash ba in dam
Bar jumlai mu'minān-i 'ālam, Khūsh gū ṣalawāt Muṣṭafā-rā
Ṣalawāt

[18] For a theoretical discussion of ritual and ritual texts, see Catherine Bell, *Ritual: Perspectives and Dimensions* (New York, 1975).

Chūn waqt-i duʿa wa daʿwat āmad, bigrikht balā-wu raḥmat āmad
Dilrā bikushā Muḥammad āmad, Khūsh gū ṣalawāt Muṣṭafā-rā
Ṣalawāt

We pray from the cycle of Ādam
To the Prophets' Seal and from him to this time
To all the faithful of the world:
Wholeheartedly recite *Ṣalawāt* on Muṣṭafā.
Ṣalawāt

When the time of *duʿa* and *daʿwat* came,
Calamities disappeared and blessings descended.
Open the heart, Muḥammad has come:
Wholeheartedly recite Ṣalawāt on Muṣṭafā.
Ṣalawāt

In all the subsequent poems too, after the recitation of Qurʾanic verses and corresponding acts, the congregation joins the *khalīfa* to say the *ṣalawāt*. Members of the community who know the verses by heart also join the *khalīfa* and his assistant to recite the poems from the *Chirāgh-nāma*. The participatory engagement of the congregation in the recitation is well expressed in the poem 'Join the *daʿwat* of Nāṣir', which begins with these verses:

Ai ʿāshiqi ṣāḥibnaẓar dar daʿwat-i Nāṣir darā
Ai muʾmini ʿālī guhar dar daʿwat-i Nāṣir darā.

Tā kay parishān miravī, majhūlu nādān miravī,
Bi amru farmān miravī, dar daʿwat-i Nāṣir darā.

O devotee, master of the vision, join the *daʿwat* of Nāṣir.
O believer of the pure jewel, join the *daʿwat* of Nāṣir.

How long will you wander in distress, in ignorance and unlettered,
And roam without the command? Join the *daʿwat* of Nāṣir.

Another instance, where the communal participation is essential, is in the glorification of God during the recitation of the *takbīrs*. In the final stage of the ceremony after each recitation of a Qurʾanic verse by the *khalīfa*, the congregation is expected to chant loudly after declaring 'We utter Your praise and recite':

Allāhu akbar, Allāhu akbar, lā ilāha illa-llāhu.
Allāhu akbar, Allāhu akbar wa li-llāh al-ḥamd.

Allah is great, Allah is great, there is no God but Allah.
Allah is great, Allah is great and may praise be to Allah.

The meaning of the ritual, which is embedded in the whole experience of the participants, entails the expression of grief for the lost one, consolation for the bereaved family, contemplation and the forging of communal unity. There is a strong sense of duty to ensure that the tradition is upheld and continued for the salvation of departed souls. In a communal sense, the collective effort of the participants in organising the ceremony, their mutual support in providing sustenance, offering prayers and consolation, as well as sharing in the meat of the sacrificial sheep, all contribute to strengthening their sense of belonging and fellowship.

Over the centuries the *Chirāgh-i rawshan* ceremony has evolved into a sophisticated ritual where each rite of passage has attained a symbolic meaning. The various segments of the ceremony form a chain of symbols which achieve greater significance and inclusivity than their discrete components. We consider the salient rituals of the ceremony in more detail in the following sections.

Animal sacrifice

The sacrifice, which expresses itself in various ways in all Abrahamic and other world religions, highlights the sense of submission, devotion and repentance of believers before the deity. In Islam, the ritual of sacrifice stems from the story of the Prophet Abraham and his submission to the will of God by preparing to forfeit his beloved son Ismail. The sacrifice of an animal, known as *qurbānī*, became deeply entrenched in the Islamic tradition. The food prepared from a sacrificial animal is distributed among the people, especially the poor and the needy, and reaffirms the sense of fraternity and ethical responsibility of the Muslims.

The ritual of sacrifice in the *Chirāgh-i rawshan* ceremony incorporates various layers of meaning and forms of intention, including supplication and expiation. The ritual commences with the placing of a plate with half-pounded wheat, salt, knife, candle and cotton in front of the *khalīfa* in the preparatory stage of the ceremony. The *khalīfa* takes a bit of wheat and salt and recites Qur'anic verses over them. Meanwhile, a sacrificial sheep is brought inside the house and kept under two pillars in the entrance. Prior to bringing the sheep inside the house, it is anointed by rubbing its face with water and cleaning its legs. Once the *khalīfa* completes his recitation of a *duʿa*, he hands over the wheat and salt to his assistant who feeds them to the animal. Thus, the ritual of purification of the sheep is completed and it becomes ready for sacrifice.

The slaughtering of sacrificial sheep should follow certain observances. It is important that the blood of the animal should not be spilled around or dropped on the ground. It is taken in a container when the animal is beheaded and then poured out in a clean or isolated place. The tradition requires that all edible parts of the animal should be used in the preparation of the consecrated meal called *bāj*, *būj* or *harisa*, which is made out of meat and wheat. *Bāj* is believed to be a sacred meal prepared exclusively for special occasions such as *Chirāgh-i rawshan* and a thanksgiving ceremony known as *khūda-ī* (lit., 'for God's sake'). The *bāj* prepared for *Chirāgh-i rawshan*, also referred to as *nasība* or *tabarruk* ('blessed meal'), is an indispensable part of the ceremony that is served to the congregation upon completion of the recitation of *Chirāgh-nāma* and kindling of the lamp.

The meaning which people of the Pamir Mountains attach to the ritual transcends the conventional connotation of *qurbānī*. In their system of religious beliefs, the notion of ancestral spirit or soul (sing. *rūḥ*; pl. *arwāḥ*) figures prominently. Since the ancestors are believed to watch over the deeds of people on earth, one is expected to be conscious of their presence, to revere them and act according to their satisfaction. As the popular saying goes, '*Khudā zadā viyat, arwāḥ zadā mave*' (You may be damned by God, but avoid being damned or reproached by the souls of the ancestors). Thus, reverence to the *arwāḥ* is a moral precept which keeps the individual responsible for their actions, not just to God, but also to the souls of their ancestors. In times of joy and sadness, either to express gratitude or to seek guidance and support, it is customary for the people to invoke the souls of their ancestors along with the names of God, prophets and Imams. The ritualistic dimensions of the *Chirāgh-i rawshan* ceremony maintains all these elements which are also intensely expressed in the ritual of sacrifice.

The oral tradition of the community maintains that the sacrificed sheep becomes a vehicle to assist the departed soul, which is believed to be in a state of confusion and uncertainty, in its journey towards the abode of peace. The animal may appear in the form of a white horse, known as Burāq, that takes the newly departed soul through the pool of judgement, or it may join the soul of the deceased and intercede for its passage to heaven.[19] The oil prepared for the kindling of the lamp is conventionally made out of the fat of the sacrificed animal, which melts and transforms into light, thereby symbolically enlightening the path of the departed soul to eternity.

The sacred meal *(bāj)* prepared from the meat of the sacrificial sheep is shared by the community at the end of the ceremony before offering the final prayers for the departed soul. The partaking of the sacred meal and offering of the prayers represent the final stage of the ceremony. The accomplishment of these rites is perceived by the participants as a completion of their duty and a spiritual endowment of the community towards the departed soul. It is believed to make the departed soul happy, as expressed in the final verdict of the *khalīfa* at the end of the ceremony: '*Arwāgān khushnūd*' ('The souls of the ancestors are happy'), while it also brings some comfort and satisfaction to the family in grief.

---

[19] Some ethnographic studies suggest that the sacrificial animal is believed to take on the sins of the deceased person as a 'scapegoat'. See M. S. Andreev, *Tadzhiki Doliny Khuf (The Tajiks of the Khuf Valley)* (Stalinabad, 1953), p. 196.

Kindling of the lamp

The main portion of the *Chirāgh-i rawshan* ceremony is the process of making and kindling of the lamp. The *khalīfa* and his assistant start preparing the wick, known as *fatīla*, by twisting the cotton and reciting *Qandīl-nāma*, which is the longest poem in the *Chirāgh-nāma*:

Qandīl-i chirāgh-i Muṣṭafāra, Ān nūr-i khudā wa-'ḍ-ḍuḥā-rā'
Paiwasta bikhān tu īn dū'ārā, Khūsh gū ṣalawāt Muṣṭafā-rā
Ṣalawāt

Tawfīq dahad khudā gadārā, Gūyam durūd Muṣṭafā-rā,
Khushnudī rūḥ-i awliyārā, Khush gū ṣalawāt Muṣṭafā-rā
Ṣalawāt

The candle of the lamp which belongs to Muṣṭafā,
The Light of Allah [mentioned in] '*wa-'ḍ-ḍuḥā*', [20]
Recite constantly this prayer:
Wholeheartedly recite *Ṣalawāt* on Muṣṭafā.
Ṣalawāt

May Allah grant success to the seeker,
So that I may recite *durūd* (*Ṣalawāt*) for Muṣṭafā
To please the souls of the friends of Allah:
Wholeheartedly recite *Ṣalawāt* on Muṣṭafā.
Ṣalawāt

Thereafter the *fatīla* is folded, cut, dipped into the oil, placed on the kindle (*chirāgh-dān*) and burnt up, each of these steps and gestures being accompanied by recitations of verses. Finally, while the kindle is lit and the *fatīla* burns, the final poem, *Ṣalawāt-nāma,* is recited. The poetry and selected Qur'anic verses amplify the visual performance of the ceremony. The light denotes several interrelated meanings where the centrality and continuity of the imamate is a binding point. Each step in the procedure of kindling the lamp represents the chain of the imamate which illuminates the path of believers over the centuries. The light symbolises the living Imam whose guidance enables individuals of every historical era to find meaning and salvation in this life, as well as to enlighten the path of the deceased towards peace and salvation in the afterlife. This as summed up in the final verse of *Ṣalawāt-nāma*:

In rishta-i imāmat thabt ast tā qiyāmat
Bahr-i najāt-i ummat Ṣalawāt bar Muḥammad.

---

[20] Ref. Q.93:1.

This line of imamate is established till the Day of Judgement
For the salvation of the *umma*, *Ṣalawāt* be on Muḥammad.

Once the recitation of *Ṣalawāt-nāma* is completed, the consecrated kindle with the burning light is taken to the members of the bereaved family. They individually hold the kindle or place their hands around it and rub them over their faces to obtain blessings from the light before proceeding to the final rite of prayer and invocation. Thus the light not only enlightens the path for those who have passed away but it also offers spiritual benefit and purification for the living members of the bereaved family.[21]

Time and space

Some variances exist in the timing of the *Chirāgh-i rawshan* ceremony among the Ismailis in various parts of Central Asia. In the Badakhshān regions of Tajikistan and Afghanistan, the ritual of sacrifice follows the evening prayers or late in the evening. While the sacred meal is being prepared the community engages in religious discourse, singing devotional poems and reading aloud *farmān*s (edicts, guidance) of the Imam.

Historically, the night vigil or *daʿwat* served as an important means of educating the community in religious matters. It provided an important platform for the community to talk about their faith and contemplate life after death. It provided a powerful experience of humility in the face of the unknown and the power of the Almighty. The *khalīfa*, as a religious authority, was in charge of religious instruction. His knowledge of the faith shaped the religious understanding of the community.

The singing of devotional poetry, known as *maddāḥ* or *qaṣīda*, is an integral part of the *Chirāgh-i rawshan* ceremony. The singing, led by the *maddāḥkhān* (singer of *maddāḥ*), is usually followed by a commentary from the *khalīfa* who interprets the meaning of the poems to the lay people. The poetic tradition of *maddāḥ*, which includes verses from Nāṣir-i Khusraw and the great Sufi poets such as Ḥakīm Sanāʾī, Farīd al-Dīn ʿAṭṭār and Jalāl al-Dīn Rūmī, has played a significant role in the formation of Ismaili Islam in Central Asia.

Traditionally, the kindling of light was performed before dawn. According to oral tradition, the soul of the deceased is ready to abandon its earthly presence on the third night before daylight. Upon completion of the ceremony, the soul is believed to depart from the world and the congregation disperses at the break of dawn to glimpse the sun's emerging light as the embodiment of God's light in the physical world.[22]

The ceremony of *Chirāgh-i rawshan* has traditionally taken place inside the local Pamiri house known in the Pamirs as *chid* or *chud*. The house is a spacious room

[21] For more details see Nazarova, 'K probleme izucheniia leksiki pogrebal'nogo obriada v ishkashimskom yazyke' (The problem of exploring the lexicology of funeral ceremony in the Ishkashimi language), in *Voprosī filologii* (Philological Issues), 3/6 (2000), pp. 52–59.

[22] At present, the night vigil is not observed in most Ismaili-populated districts of the region and the congregation usually disperses at midnight.

which has communal, social and religious functions. The construction of the traditional house is associated with the pre-Islamic tradition of the mountain-dwellers which was syncretic and related to Zoroastrianism. The various ancient Iranian tribes, whose languages are still spoken by local Ismailis, settled in the mountainous Pamir region long before the advent of Islam. Islam in its Ismaili form seems to have penetrated into the region through adaptation and assimilation with the ancient religious beliefs and practices.[23]

Since, according to the Arian (ancient Iranian) cosmology, the entirety of creation is the house of God, the Arians created their houses to resemble the creation of God as they perceived it. The Pamiri house is believed to embody this perception of the universe in terms of its architecture and social functions.[24] With the advent of Ismaili Islam in the region, the components which make up the Pamiri house were interpreted in accordance with Ismaili principles and cosmology. The five pillars which hold the two main columns of the ceiling were said to symbolise the five holy figures of Shiʿi Islam, namely, Prophet Muḥammad, his cousin and son-in-law ʿAlī, his daughter Fāṭima, and grandsons Ḥasan and Ḥusayn. The various rites of the ceremony are performed on a stand closest to the entrance of the house which is called *barnikh* (upper or superior stand). This stand is reserved for the *khalīfa,* his assistant, notables and elders of the community during the ceremonies.

One aspect of the *Chirāgh-i rawshan* ceremony, which signifies the relation between the space and the performance of the ceremony, is the ritual of *Bojkhambent* (lit., 'bringing down the *bāj*'), the consecrated food made from wheat and meat. The assistant of the *khalīfa* stands at the elevated stand of the house, namely *kitsornekh*, and descends holding a plate containing ritual items representing the heavenly origin of the items, namely, wheat, salt and the lamp. The spatial relations between the structural and religious functions of the Pamiri house are also expressed in other funeral rites, such as a dedicated space for washing the body of the deceased. Thus, the traditional house plays an important componential function in performing the *Chirāgh-i rawshan* ceremony and ensures its consistency and stability as a holistic ritual.

The societies and communities of hitherto isolated and mountainous regions of Central Asia have not escaped the problems and challenges posed by the processes of modernisation and globalisation. In particular, these processes are having various effects on the traditional forms of beliefs and practices that have survived for many centuries. As a result, the Ismaili community in Central Asia is today revisiting some of these beliefs and practices, including the *Chirāgh-i rawshan* ceremony, with the view of adapting them to the needs of the time.

---

23 This idea is reinforced by oral tradition and observations. See also A. A. Bobrinskiy, *Sekta Ismailiya v Russkikh i Bukharskikh vladeniiakh Tsentralnoĭ Azii* (The Ismaili Sect in Russian and Bukharan Domains of Central Asia) (Moscow, 1902); A. Shokhumorov *Pamir: Strana Ariev* (Pamir: The Land of Arians) (Dushanbe, 1998).

24 For more details on the Arian components of the Pamiri house, see Shokhumorov, 'Khonai Pairavoni Rostī' (The House of the Followers of the True Path') in Shokhumorov, *Pamir: Strana Ariev*, pp. 116–152.

PART VIII
PHILOSOPHY AND INTELLECTUAL TRADITIONS

*Introduction**

Daniel De Smet

What is Shiʿi Philosophy?

Henry Corbin was certainly the first Westerner to use the term 'Shiʿi philosophy'. This expression appears, inter alia, in the title of the volume containing his edition of two texts by the Iranian thinker Sayyid Ḥaydar al-Āmulī (d. after 787/1385), *Kitāb jāmiʿ al-asrār wa-manbaʿ al-anwār* (*The Sum of the Secrets and the Source of Lights*) and *al-Risāla naqd al-nuqūd fī maʿrifat al-wujūd* (*Treatise of Critical Examination of the Knowledge of Being*).[1] Western philosophers and most specialists of 'Arabo-Islamic philosophy' *(falsafa)* would certainly find it difficult to recognise in the works of Ḥaydar al-Āmulī a line of thought related to philosophy. They will consider them rather as a form of theology, mixed with mystical and 'esoteric' speculations.

Indeed, since the beginning of Western research in the 19th century on 'Arabic' philosophy, with the fundamental studies of Ernest Renan and Samuel Munk,[2] philosophical thought in Islam has often been reduced to a single current: *falsafa*, 'Hellenistic' philosophy in Arabic and, to a very limited extent, in Persian. Its main representatives – al-Kindī (d. 256/870), al-Fārābī (d. 339/950), Ibn Sīnā (d. 428/1037), Ibn Rushd (d. 595/1198) and Ibn Bājja (d. 533/1139) – openly recognised the authority of Aristotle, though they often interpreted him in a Neoplatonic sense. Most of the *falāsifa* were Sunnis. Ibn Sīnā certainly came from an Ismaili family from Central Asia, but already in his youth abandoned Ismailism and followed Sunni Islam of the Ḥanafī tradition. It is quite possible that al-Fārābī had Twelver Shiʿi convictions, although nothing in his biography allows us to establish this with certainty.[3] In any case, his philosophy has nothing specifically Shiʿi about it. What Corbin referred to as

* Translated from the French by Orkhan Mir-Kasimov.

[1] Sayyid Haydar Amoli, *La philosophie Shiʿite. 1. Somme des doctrines ésotériques (Jāmiʿ al-asrār). 2. Traité de la connaissance de l'être (Fī maʿrifat al-wujūd)*, ed. Henry Corbin and Osman Yahia (Tehran and Paris, 1969).

[2] Ernest Renan, *Averroès et l'averroïsme* (Paris, 1866); Samuel Munk, *Mélanges de philosophie juive et arabe* (Paris, 1859).

[3] Dimitri Gutas, 'Avicenna's Maḏhab with an Appendix on the Question of his Date of Birth', *Quaderni di Studi Arabi*, 5/6 (1987–1988), pp. 323–336; Dimitri Gutas, 'Fārābī. 1. Biography', *EIR*, vol. 9, p. 212.

'Shiʿi philosophy' is clearly different from the *falsafa*. But did he refer to 'philosophy' at all? Many scholars continue to doubt it until now.

It is therefore hardly surprising that Raymond Quenau, editor of the prestigious *Encyclopédie de la Pléiade*, received with amazement the manuscript of the first volume of the *History of Islamic Philosophy* that Henry Corbin had written on his demand. Unusual for that time, the 'Hellenistic philosophers' are to be found in this book only after more than 200 pages, mostly devoted to Shiʿism: Ismailism, Twelver Shiʿism, the alchemical corpus attributed to Jābir b. Ḥayyān and the Ikhwān al-Ṣafā'.[4] To a Western reader, whose interest in 'Arabic' philosophy was traditionally linked to the influence that the latter has had on Latin scholasticism, such an approach could only be confusing.

Henry Corbin has the immense merit of having made known in the West, through his countless text editions and studies, a large part of medieval Muslim thought belonging to the Shiʿi tradition (both Ismaili and Twelver), which was almost totally unknown before he began his research. He can therefore rightly be considered the true founder of the study of 'Shiʿi philosophy'. However, Corbin was not only a scholar in the field of intellectual history but was a great thinker himself. This implies that he has often given very personal interpretations of the texts he studied, and introduced some ideas and concepts that are not necessarily those of the Shiʿi authors.

Corbin said that he used 'the term "Shiʿi philosophy" in the sense of the term *ḥikmat ilāhiyya,* as the equivalent of the Greek *theosophia*; still more specifically, in the sense attributed in the Shiʿi milieu to the expression *ḥikmat nabawiyya wa-walawiyya,* "prophetic and imamic philosophy", as the word *ḥikmat*, or philosophy, came to designate the implementation and the exercise of that *ta'wīl* of which *Jāmiʿ al-asrār* (of Ḥaydar al-Āmulī) offers us many examples. It is neither exactly philosophy nor theology in the sense that the current use attributes to these words in the West.'[5]

As we shall soon see, this characterisation of 'Shiʿi philosophy' is in itself absolutely pertinent. However, in the general context of Corbin's thought, it acquires a meaning that reveals itself more problematic. In fact, Corbin considered Shiʿi philosophy a 'theosophy', a 'Shiʿi gnosis' (*ʿirfān-i Shīʿī*), related to a *sophia perennis* shared by authors as different as Ibn Sīnā, Ibn ʿArabī, al-Suhrawardī, Swedenborg and Jacob Boehme. The first manifestations of this tradition would have been found in the apocryphal Gospels of the first centuries of our era. A phenomenological and deliberately ahistorical (if not anti-historical) approach enabled Corbin to interpret

[4] Henry Corbin, *Histoire de la philosophie Islamique des origines à la mort d'Averroès* (Paris, 1964). The second volume, *La philosophie Islamique depuis la mort d'Averroès jusqu'à nos jours* (Paris, 1974) is mostly devoted to the Iranian Shiʿi thinkers. English tr. in one vol. by Liadain and Philip Sherrard as *History of Islamic Philosophy* (London, 1993).

[5] Henry Corbin, in S. Haydar Amoli, *La philosophie shiʿite*, p. 58.

an author in the light of another, without having to focus on the actual 'sources' used by this author.[6]

Such an approach, often related to the use of a semantically charged and ambiguous terminology (such as 'theosophy' or 'hierognosis'), was adopted by some scholars such as Seyyed Hossein Nasr but categorically rejected by others, such as Hossein Ziai.[7] It resulted in all kinds of confusion that for a long time undermined the field of 'Shiʿi philosophy' and delayed its inclusion within the history of Islamic philosophy. It is, therefore, necessary to define the concept of 'Shiʿi philosophy'.[8] In order to grasp its specificity, it seems necessary to me to identify beforehand some general characteristics which distinguish philosophy from other fields of knowledge in the Muslim world. Of course, this is not an exhaustive list of absolute criteria which appear with equal prominence in the works of all authors, in all currents and all ages:

1. Philosophical thought always involves, in one way or another, a rational reflection based on reason (*ʿaql*); it is formulated in the form of a demonstration (*burhān*) and constructed in accordance with the rules of logic (*manṭiq*). With the growing influence of Muʿtazilism on Twelver Shiʿism, the use of *ʿaql* and *burhān* no longer remained confined to philosophy but also characterised other fields of knowledge, particularly *ḥadīth* criticism and the criticism of the traditions attributed to the Shiʿi Imams, law *(fiqh)* and theology *(kalām).*
2. Philosophy focuses on topics as diverse as the origin and functioning of language, the rules of reasoning (logic), God and the first immaterial principles (metaphysics), the origin of the world (creation and emanation), cosmology and nature, human soul and its salvation, theory of knowledge and many other subjects.

---

6 The entire work of Corbin is impregnated by this approach; see, for example, Henry Corbin, *En Islam Iranien: Aspects spirituels et philosophiques. Tome 1: le Shīʿsme duodécimain* (Paris, 1971), pp. 43–53; Henry Corbin, 'Imāmologie et philosophie', in *Le Shīʿisme Imāmite, Colloque de Strasbourg (6–9 mai 1968)* (Paris, 1970), pp. 143–174; Henry Corbin, *Philosophie iranienne et philosophie comparée* (Paris, 1985). Specifically for the Ismaili case, see Daniel De Smet, 'Henri Corbin et les études Ismaéliennes', in Mohammad Ali Amir-Moezzi, Christian Jambet and Pierre Lory, ed., *Henry Corbin: Philosophies et sagesses des religions du livre* (Turnhout, 2005), pp. 105–118.

7 See, for example, Seyyed Hossein Nasr, 'The Meaning and Concept of Philosophy in Islam', in Seyyed Hossein Nasr and Oliver Leaman, ed., *History of Islamic Philosophy* (London, 2003), p. 24; Seyyed Hossein Nasr, 'Mullā Ṣadrā: His Teachings', in Nasr and Leaman, ed., *History of Islamic Philosophy*, p. 659; Hossein Ziai, 'Mullā Ṣadrā: His Life and Works', in Nasr and Leaman, ed., *History of Islamic Philosophy*, pp. 635–642. It should be highlighted that the same volume contains articles supporting exactly the opposite conceptions of Shiʿi philosophy.

8 For a general overview, see Mohammad Ali Amir Moezzi and Christian Jambet, *Qu'est-ce que le Shīʿisme? (*Paris, 2004), pp. 287–353 ('Shīʿisme, sagesse et philosophie').

3. Philosophy has a theoretical aspect, the acquisition of knowledge, and a practical aspect, obtaining happiness through a virtuous life. These two aspects are inseparable in Islamic philosophy (Sunni and Shiʿi), just as in ancient philosophy.[9]
4. Although deeply inspired by the Qurʾan and Islamic tradition, philosophy in Islam depends directly or indirectly on Greek sources. Many philosophers openly recognise their affiliation to this Greek legacy and rely on the authority of the great philosophers of Antiquity, such as Pythagoras, Empedocles, Plato, Socrates and Aristotle.

What we call 'Shiʿi philosophy' is philosophy in the sense that it has these criteria in common with other forms of philosophical thought in Islam. But it differs from them in some essential features that can be defined as follows:

1. Shiʿi philosophy relates directly or indirectly to the teachings of the Imams, the only source of knowledge after the Qurʾan. Particularly in Ismailism, it represents the teaching of the Imam or his missionaries *(duʿāt)* operating under his direct authority. However, in the absence of the Imam, the Twelver philosophers build their philosophical doctrines on many traditions attributed to the historical Imams. Shiʿi thinkers who explicitly claim affiliation to the philosophers of Antiquity often consider the latter as the 'inspired wise', whose knowledge derives from the prophets and Imams of their time. Shiʿi philosophy is therefore a 'revealed philosophy', which stands out from the *falsafa* by emphasising the term '*ḥikma*' ('wisdom').
2. Taught by Imams or deriving from their teaching, this *ḥikma* is related to the *bāṭin* – the hidden meaning of the revelation of the prophets – to be released from the apparent meaning *(ẓāhir)* of the revealed Books by an exegesis *(taʾwīl)*. In this regard, Shiʿi philosophy is an 'esoteric philosophy'.
3. Shiʿi philosophy is a 'religious philosophy' because it is rooted in the Shiʿi conception of Islam. This is part of Ismaili doctrine, from which it is inseparable. Closer to the Sunni tradition, Twelver Shiʿism has produced some fierce opponents to any form of philosophical thought. But for those who accept it, philosophy is integrated into other fields of knowledge, such as the interpretation of the Qurʾan and *Ḥadīth*, theology and mysticism. This means that, under the pen of the same author and in the same work, philosophy, *kalām*, prophetology, imamology, mysticism, logic, and even alchemy and astrology are intertwined to the point where they form a more or less harmonious unity, which constitutes the specificity of Shiʿi thought.

[9] On this complementarity of knowledge and moral virtue, see Pierre Hadot, *Qu'est-ce que la philosophie antique?* (Folio – Essais 280) (Paris, 2007); Christian Jambet, *Qu'est-ce que la philosophie Islamique?* (Folio – Essais 547) (Paris, 2011).

This plurality of forms, linked to a rare ability to assimilate concepts and doctrines from various intellectual traditions, represents the wealth of Shiʿi Islam. But, at the same time, it explains its immense complexity. There exists no single unique 'Shiʿi philosophy', but there are as many different forms as there were different currents and authors. Within each movement, the thought has evolved over centuries and sometimes led to the emergence of significant differences. Moreover, both Ismailism and Twelver Shiʿism have had a distinct history and doctrinal evolution, which also contributed to this complexity.

No global synthesis of philosophical thought in Shiʿi Islam has been written to date and it is impossible to even consider here such an undertaking, which would be enormous. In this brief introduction, I will only present a *status quaestionis* – necessarily incomplete – involving three main areas: the first Shiʿi Imams and philosophy; Ismailism; and Twelver Shiʿism.

The First Shiʿi Imams and Philosophy

According to a belief widespread in the Shiʿi tradition, ʿAlī b. Abī Ṭālib (d. 40/661) was 'the first philosopher of Islam'.[10] This idea, surprising at first sight, is related to the *Nahj al-balāgha,* the famous collection of speeches and maxims attributed to ʿAlī, which was compiled long after his death by al-Sharīf al-Raḍī (d. 406/1015). The *Nahj al-balāgha* is certainly not a work of philosophy but it has nourished philosophical reflection within Twelver Shiʿism for many centuries. The discourses attributed to ʿAlī indeed contain a whole set of elements that lend themselves to a philosophical reading, in particular the use of demonstration (*burhān*), and the concept of *ʿaql* (intellect), which plays a central role in this work. It is possible, as suggested by Mohammad Ali Amir-Moezzi, that the term *ʿaql* has to be understood in early Imamism in a pre-philosophical sense.[11] Nevertheless, it would be worthwhile to study the *Nahj al-balāgha* in the light of its later philosophical interpretations which, to my knowledge, has never been done.

The same remark comes to mind concerning the corpus of traditions attributed to the first Shiʿi Imams. Thus, the *Kitāb al-kāfī* of al-Kulaynī (d. ca. 328/940) contains a long chapter which brings together the *ḥadīth*s related to *ʿaql.* Like the *Nahj al-balāgha,* it was widely used and interpreted by the Twelver Shiʿi philosophers. According to one of the *ḥadīth*s reported by al-Kulaynī, the sixth Imam Jaʿfar al-Ṣādiq (d. 148/765) said: 'The first thing God created was the intellect (*al-ʿaql*). God said: "Advance!" and it advanced. He then said: "Go back!" and it went back. God

---

[10] This argument is put forward, in particular, by Abbas Muhajirani, 'Twelve-Imām Shiʿite Theological and Philosophical Thought', in Nasr and Leaman, ed., *History of Islamic Philosophy*, pp. 122–141.

[11] Mohammad Ali Amir-Moezzi, *Le guide divin dans le Shīʿisme originel: Aux sources de l'ésotérisme en Islam* (Lagrasse, 1992), pp. 15–33.

said: "By My power and majesty, I have not created any creature more noble than you; by you, I take and I give; by you, I reward and I punish. "'[12]

Already in 1909, Ignaz Goldziher had recognised in this *ḥadīth*, of which there are several variants, a Neoplatonic influence.[13] And indeed, it is repeatedly cited by Ismaili philosophers who give to it an interpretation in accordance with their Neoplatonic conception of the intelligible world: the *ʿaql* – which corresponds to the second hypostasis of Plotinus (the *Nous)* – is the first being created by God. From this point on, it is important to know whether such philosophical readings of the traditions attributed to the Imams are merely the result of later interpretations, or whether they are already implicated in the traditions themselves. In the present state of research and in the absence of studies concerning the possible influence of philosophy on the Shiʿi *ḥadīth* literature, the debate continues.

This issue is immediately related to the very sensitive question concerning the presence of a philosophical activity in the immediate entourage of the Imams, especially of Jaʿfar al-Ṣādiq. Among the many disciples of the latter, Hishām b. al-Ḥakam (d. 179/795–796) developed a highly original theology, considered heterodox by most of the later Shiʿa. The extant accounts concerning his doctrine show that he had an advanced knowledge of antique philosophy, especially of Aristotelianism and even of Stoicism, and used a philosophical terminology similar to that of the later *falāsifa*. If the evidence and the citations related to the thought of Hishām b. al-Ḥakam are reliable, it would follow that philosophical works circulated among the followers of Jaʿfar al-Ṣādiq, at a time when the movement of Greek–Arabic translation, sponsored by the Abbasids in Baghdad, had just started.[14]

This brings us to another disciple of Jaʿfar al-Ṣādiq, much more famous than Hishām b. al-Ḥakam, namely Jābir b. Ḥayyān (fl. 2nd/8th century). Under his name a large corpus of alchemical writings of Shiʿi inspiration have been transmitted, which contain many literal quotations from Greek philosophical and scientific works. The attribution of these writings to Jābir is a very controversial matter which has been a matter of contention among the scholars since the early 20th century up to our days. The debate revolves around the so-called 'Jābir problem'.[15]

---

[12] For one version of this *ḥadīth*, see Amir-Moezzi, *Le guide divin*, pp. 18–21.

[13] Ignaz Goldziher, 'Neuplatonische und gnostische Elemente im Ḥadīṯ', *Zeitschrift für Assyriologie*, 22 (1909), pp. 317–324.

[14] On Hishām b. al-Ḥakam, his doctrine and the accounts concerning his works, see Josef van Ess, *Theologie und Gesellschaft im 2. und 3. Jahrhundert Hidschra: Eine Geschichte des religiösen Denkens im frühen Islam. Band I* (Berlin and New York, 1991), pp. 353–379, 398–399.

[15] On the 'Jābir problem' see, in particular, Paul Kraus, 'Dschābir ibn Ḥajjān und die Ismāʿīlijja', *Forschungs-Institut für Geschichte der Naturwissenschaften in Berlin: Dritter Jahresbericht* (Berlin, 1930), pp. 23–30; Henry Corbin, 'Le Livre du Glorieux de Jābir Ibn Ḥayyān', *Eranos Jahrbuch*, 18 (1950), pp. 52–54; Fuad Sezgin,'Das Problem des Ǧābir ibn Ḥayyān im Lichte neu gefundener Handschriften', *ZDMG*, 114 (1964), pp. 255–268; Martin Plessner, 'Ǧābir ibn Ḥayyān und die Zeit der Entstehung der arabischen Ǧābir-Schriften', *ZDMG*, 115 (1965), pp. 23–35.

For the supporters of the authenticity of the corpus, it would reflect the intense philosophical and scientific activity in the entourage of Ja'far al-Ṣādiq and his followers, during the second half of the 8th century. The writings of 'Jābir' contain literal quotations, sometimes rather long, from the works of Aristotle, Alexander of Aphrodisias and Galen,[16] whereas the first Arabic translations of these writings preserved or recognised by the bibliographical sources date only from the first half of the 9th century. For this reason, Paul Kraus, followed by many other scholars, considered the writings attributed to Jābir as apocryphal, written by several authors over a long period that extends from the second half of the 9th to the first half of the 10th century. Circulating in a Shi'i milieu, the corpus would have been put under the symbolic authority of Imam Ja'far al-Ṣādiq and attributed to his disciple Jābir b. Ḥayyān.

The truth probably lies somewhere in between these two opposed theories. Indeed, one of the writings from the Jābirian corpus, the *Kitāb al-taṣrīf,* contains a long quotation from Aristotle's *De Generatione et Corruptione*, provided with a comment attributed to Alexander. It is quite certain that both come from the commentary of the *De Generatione et Corruptione* by Alexander of Aphrodisias, lost in Greek. Its Arabic translation by Abū Bishr Mattā b. Yūnus (d. 329/940) has also been lost, with the exception of some fragments cited in particular by Ibn Rushd (d. 595/1198). By comparing the citation reported in the *Kitāb al-taṣrīf* with the fragments of Alexander's commentary quoted by Ibn Rushd and with the technical vocabulary used in other translations of Mattā b. Yūnus, Emma Gannagé was able to show that the author of the Jābirian treatise used this commentary of Alexander in the translation of Mattā. Therefore, the *Kitāb al-taṣrīf* cannot be earlier than the first half of the 10th century, a century and a half after the death of Ja'far al-Ṣādiq.[17]

However, the study of the citations from Aristotle contained in other writings of the Jābirian corpus would reveal a clear difference with the translations made in Baghdad on behalf of the Abbasids. These citations would be distinguishable, in particular, by their more archaic vocabulary sometimes closer to Syriac.[18] If this fact was proved, it would follow that some parts of the Jābirian corpus could be prior to the 9th century and indeed go back to the time of Ja'far al-Ṣādiq. In the present state of research, the 'Jābir problem' is far from being resolved. An important part of the Jābirian corpus remains unpublished. Since the seminal work of Paul Kraus, the knowledge of the Graeco-Arabic translations has substantially evolved and the whole

---

[16] See the inventory established by Paul Kraus, *Jābir ibn Ḥayyān. Contribution à l'histoire des idées scientifiques dans l'Islam: Jābir et la science grecque* (Cairo, 1942), pp. 319–339.

[17] Emma Gannagé, 'Alexandre d'Aphrodise *In De generatione et corruptione apud* Ǧābir b. Ḥayyān, *K. al-Taṣrīf*', *Documenti e studi sulla tradizione filosofica medievale*, 9 (1998), pp. 35–86.

[18] Such is the argument proposed by Nomanul Haq, *Names, Natures and Things: The Alchemist Jabir ibn Ḥayyān and his* Kitāb al-Aḥjār *(Book of Stones)* (Dordrecht, 1994), in particular, see pp. 24–29.

file of citations and references to the philosophers of Antiquity in the writings of 'Jābir b. Ḥayyān' should be reassessed anew.

The interest of such a research for the study of Shiʿi philosophy is indeed considerable. The possible presence of philosophical elements in the traditions attributed to the first Shiʿi Imams and in the *Nahj al-balāgha,* to which should be added the diffusion of Greek philosophical works in Imāmī circles in the 8th century (Hishām b. al-Ḥakam, Jābir b. Ḥayyān), seems to provide arguments in favour of a close relationship between Shiʿism and philosophy from the early centuries of Islam. Further study of the relationships between the first Shiʿi Imams and philosophy is absolutely necessary in order to understand the emergence of philosophical thought within Shiʿism.

'Ismaili Neoplatonism'

Ismaili thought, one of the major currents of Shiʿi Islam, developed a doctrine profoundly influenced by Neoplatonic philosophy so that today we can speak of 'Ismaili Neoplatonism'. The oldest extant Ismaili texts, dating from the late 9th century, already show the concern to harmonise the teachings of the prophets and Imams with a vision of the universe rooted in the Neoplatonic philosophy of Late Antiquity. From the 10th century onwards, the Ismailis adopted and assimilated the contributions of *falsafa*, in particular some elements from the thought of al-Kindī and al-Fārābī. However, in Ismailism, philosophy is not one discipline among others but is simply integrated into the teachings of the Imams, which expose the hidden meaning *(bāṭin)* of the revealed books, primarily of the Qur'an.

Despite the lack of doctrinal unity, the Ismailism of the Qarmaṭī and Fatimid traditions emphasises the use of reason (*ʿaql*) and of demonstration (*burhān*), which are indispensable tools for the understanding of the 'real' (*ḥaqīqa*) meaning of the revelation. The result is a system whose major components can be summarised as follows. The Ultimate – referred to as *al-mubdiʿ* ('the Originator') – is conceived of as an ineffable and unknowable principle, located beyond being and nonbeing. He produced by his Will or Command, depending on the mode of creation *ex nihilo (ibdāʿ),* the Intellect, the first originated being, which carries the 'forms' or models of which the genres and species of the sensible world are the material embodiments. From the Intellect emanate successively the inferior hypostases *(ḥudūd)* of the intelligible world, Soul and Nature, or – according to the system developed by Ḥamīd al-Dīn al-Kirmānī (d. ca. 411/1020) – the ten Intelligences of the spheres. Then are generated the heavenly bodies and the matter of the sublunary world, with which the demiurge (the Soul or the Tenth Intelligence) shapes our earthly world. The human soul, united in this world to a material body, must purify and perfect itself by receiving the teachings (*taʿlīm*) of the prophets and Imams. Knowledge of *bāṭin* of the revelation related to the practice of a virtuous life by observing the precepts of *sharīʿa,* allows the soul to attain the liberation from the body after the death of the latter, and join the intelligible world to which it originally belonged.[19]

Before 1950, Ismailism was poorly known in the West, the majority of the sources available at that time being of an anti-Ismaili polemical nature, generally from the Islamic currents openly hostile to Shiʿi Ismailism. In the second half of the 20th century, through the publication of a growing number of authentic works, Ismaili studies have developed remarkably. This development continues today at an accelerated pace. However, in the field of philosophy, thorny issues remain, and many grey areas have still to be clarified by future research. I will try to present briefly some points which I consider as a priority.

The introduction of Neoplatonic philosophy into Ismaili doctrine

Most scholars admit today that Neoplatonic doctrine was originally introduced into Ismailism by the Iranian *dāʿīs* of Qarmaṭī tendency, in what Wilferd Madelung called the 'Persian School'. According to this hypothesis, the first representative of this 'School' was Muḥammad al-Nasafī (executed for heresy in 332/943), whose *Kitāb al-maḥṣūl* – dated by Madelung to around the year 300/912 – would have been the first example of 'Ismaili Neoplatonism'. This penchant of al-Nasafī and of some Iranian colleagues (as Abū Tammām, Abū Yaʿqūb al-Sijistānī and Abū Ḥātim al-Rāzī) for philosophy would not have been appreciated by the Fatimid Imam-caliph al-Muʿizz (r. 341–365/953–975), especially since the 'western' *daʿwa,* that of the Fatimids in Ifriqiya and Egypt, propagated a 'non-philosophical' Ismailism, as shown by the abundant work of al-Qāḍī al-Nuʿmān (d. 363/974).[20]

I am not convinced by this hypothesis concerning the 'introduction' of philosophy into Ismaili doctrine. 'Introduction' implies indeed that there had been an earlier phase, pre-philosophical of some kind, and a later phase in which the 'original' Ismailism would have been thoroughly rethought and redesigned with the help of the philosophical concepts and doctrines ubiquitous in most of the extant Ismaili works. Since I have already presented elsewhere the reasons for my doubts, it does not seem useful to repeat them here.[21] It will be enough to recall the case of the *Risāla*

---

[19] For a general overview of Ismaili philosophy, see Paul Walker, 'The Ismāʿīlīs', in Peter Adamson and Richard Taylor, ed., *The Cambridge Companion to Arabic Philosophy* (Cambridge, 2005), pp. 72–91; Daniel de Smet, 'Ismāʿīlī Philosophical Tradition', in Henrik Lagerlund, ed., *Encyclopedia of Medieval Philosophy: Philosophy Between 500 and 1500* (Wiesbaden, 2011), pp. 575–577.

[20] For a detailed discussion of this issue, with bibliographical references, see Daniel De Smet, 'Les bibliothèques Ismaéliennes et la question du néoplatonisme Ismaélien', in Cristina D'Ancona, ed., *The Libraries of the Neoplatonists* (Leiden, 2007), pp. 483–486.

[21] See Daniel De Smet, 'The *Risāla al-Mudhhiba* Attributed to al-Qāḍī al-Nuʿmān: Important Evidence for the Adoption of Neoplatonism by Fatimid Ismailism at the Time of al-Muʿizz?', in Omar Alí-de-Unzaga, ed., *Fortresses of the Intellect: Ismaili and Other Islamic Studies in Honour of Farhad Daftary* (London, 2011), pp. 309–341, in particular pp. 309–310; Daniel De Smet, 'Les bibliothèques Ismaéliennes', pp. 486–488.

al-mudhhiba, a treaty strongly influenced by philosophical speculations of Neoplatonic inspiration. Even if its attribution to al-Qāḍī al-Nuʿmān cannot be established with certitude, I believe I was able to show with some degree of plausibility that this work was written at the time of al-Muʿizz and that its contents are related to the 'western' Fatimid *daʿwa*. Along the same lines, various works attributed to Jaʿfar b. Manṣūr al-Yaman (d. ca. 346/957), such as the *Kitāb al-fatarāt*,[22] the *Kitāb al-kashf* and the *Asrār al-nuṭaqā'*, contain some elements from philosophical sources, which should be further studied.

Therefore, given the incomplete state of currently available sources, it seems to me that the use of philosophical themes and concepts was not the sole privilege of the Iranian *dāʿīs*, but it also characterised some works from the western *daʿwa*. Therefore, an inventory, as complete as possible, of the philosophical elements in the Ismaili literature of the 9th and 10th centuries belonging to the Eastern tradition and to the Western *daʿwa* should be established.

The 'long recension' of the Pseudo-Theology *of Aristotle in its relationship with Ismailism*

One of the main philosophical sources that inspired the Ismaili *dāʿīs* of this period is the *Pseudo-Theology* of Aristotle, the Arabic paraphrase of the last three *Enneads* of Plotinus produced in the 'circle' of the philosopher al-Kindī. Already in 1954, Shlomo Pines had noticed that several elements of Ismaili doctrine – in particular, the presence of the Word or of the Divine Will as intermediary hypostasis between the Originator and His first creature, the Intellect – are found in the 'long recension' of the *Pseudo-Theology* of Aristotle. He concluded that the additions which distinguish this 'long recension' from the 'vulgate' (the version contained in the majority of the manuscripts) would have been interpolations made by an Ismaili author.[23]

At the time he formulated his thesis, Pines had access to only a few works of Nāṣir-i Khusraw (d. after 462/1070). Since then, thanks to the works of Paul E. Walker, we know that the Ismailis were reading, in all probability, the *Pseudo-Theology* of Aristotle in its 'long recension'.[24] But the question raised by Pines remains open: are the doctrines that characterise this 'long recension' of Ismaili origin or, conversely, were the Ismailis inspired by the 'long recension'? This question is of the utmost importance, both for the genesis of Ismaili doctrine and the history of the transmission and reception of Neoplatonism in the Muslim world. But it remains insoluble as long as the 'long recension' – of which only a few manuscripts, all of them Judaeo-

[22] See David Hollenberg, 'Neoplatonism in Pre-Kirmānian Fāṭimid Doctrine: A Critical Edition and Translation of the Prologue of the *Kitāb al-Fatarāt wa-l-Qirānāt*', *Le Muséon*, 122 (2009), pp. 159–163, who, independently from myself, came to the similar conclusion.

[23] Shlomo Pines, 'La longue récension de la *Théologie d'Aristote* dans ses rapports avec la doctrine Ismaélienne', *Revue des Études Islamiques*, 22 (1954), pp. 7–20.

[24] See, in particular, Paul E. Walker, *Early Philosophical Shiism: The Ismaili Neoplatonism of Abū Yaʿqūb al-Sijistānī* (Cambridge, 1993).

Arabic, are extant – remains unpublished. Paul Fenton, who has long ago prepared an edition with transliteration in Arabic, now seems ready to publish his work within the framework of the European Research Council (ERC) Project *Greek into Arabic: Philosophical Concepts and Linguistic Bridges* under the directorship of Cristina D'Ancona, University of Pisa. Once this edition is available, we will be able to get a better idea of the interpolations that constitute this 'long recension' and study its relation to Ismaili doctrine. At the same time, it will be necessary to measure the influence of this source on Ismailism of the 10th century. This opens up a vast field of research.

The Rasā'il Ikhwān al-Ṣafā' *and the* Risāla al-jāmiʿa

The 52 'Epistles of the Brethren of Purity' – this vast 'encyclopaedia' which covers all fields of knowledge from logic to magic, including arithmetic, astrology, cosmology, ethics, the doctrine of the soul and intellect, metaphysics, theology and many other fields – have generated an impressive secondary literature since the 19th century.[25] While it is clear that the 'Epistles' were written in a Shiʿi environment close to Ismailism, the identification of their authors and the exact date of their composition remain debatable. The same holds true concerning the relationships between the doctrine of the Ikhwān al-Ṣafā' and the Ismailism represented by the official *daʿwa*, that of the Qarmaṭīs and that of the Fatimids. The studies of Carmela Baffioni, for example, showed the existence of similarities but also of dissimilarities, which are sometimes significant.

Unlike the Ismaili *dāʿīs*, implicitly inspired by the Greek and Arab philosophers (especially by the Neoplatonic writings of Aristotle, al-Kindī and al-Fārābī) while rejecting the *falsafa* as an impious doctrine, the Brethren of Purity explicitly claimed the legacy of ancient philosophy and science. They cite and mention an impressive number of Greek sources and authors, including Pythagoras, Socrates, Plato, Aristotle, Plotinus, Archimedes, Euclid, Nicomachus of Gerasa, Ptolemy and Galen. Some citations seem to come from authentic works. Others, however, are clearly drawn from apocrypha. Carmela Baffioni has compiled many quotations and devoted a number of studies to several of them.[26]

If the research in the field of the Greek sources of the *Rasā'il* is now well under way, we are still far from being able to reconstitute the library which was available to the Ikhwān al-Ṣafā'. Admitting that the 'Epistles' were written in the early 10th century – dating accepted by most researchers – they have been able to take advantage of

---

[25] For an up-to-date summary on this issue, with a bibliography related to the philosophical sources and themes, see Daniel De Smet, 'Religiöse Anwendung philosophischer Ideen. 2. Die Enzyklopädie der Iḫwān aṣ-Ṣafā'', in Ulrich Rudolph, ed., *Philosophie in der islamischen Welt. Band I: 8–10 Jahrhundert* (Basel, 2012), pp. 531–539, 551–554. See also Nader El-Bizri, ed., *The Ikhwān al-Ṣafā' and their Rasā'il: An Introduction* (Oxford, 2008).

[26] Carmela Baffioni, *Frammenti e testimonianze di autori antichi nelle* Rasā'il *degli Iḫwān al-Ṣafā'* (Rome, 1994); see also the bibliography in my article mentioned in the previous footnote.

the Graeco-Arabic translations made in Baghdad under the patronage of the Abbasids. A comparison of all the citations given by the Ikhwān al-Ṣafā' with translations from official circles in Baghdad would be a major contribution to the question of whether or not a 'parallel' transmission has existed – for example, by the means of the 'Sabians' of Ḥarrān – upon which would depend mainly the authors belonging to the Shiʿi tradition: those who wrote the Jābirian corpus, the Ikhwān al-Ṣafā' and the Ismailis. This thesis, supported among others by Yves Marquet,[27] deserves a critical assessment because it concerns the sources of philosophy in Shiʿi Islam. From the same perspective, we should consider Yves Marquet's comparative study between the *Rasā'il Ikhwān al-Ṣafā'* and the other great 'encyclopaedia' of Shiʿi philosophy and science – the corpus of writings attributed to Jābir b. Ḥayyān.[28] We have already seen that the latter raises also many difficult and still unsolved problems.

The study of the sources and doctrines of the *Rasā'il Ikhwān al-Ṣafā'* has been much complicated by the lack of critical editions and index.[29] Thanks to the initiative of The Institute of Ismaili Studies, a critical edition with annotated English translation is currently being published, under the general editorship of Nader El-Bizri.[30] The realisation of this great project will make the 'Epistles' much more accessible and facilitate the study of its relationship to the Ismaili doctrine of the 10th century.

However, in my opinion, a serious problem remains, which is the nature and origins of the *Risāla al-jāmiʿa*. In the opinion repeatedly mentioned in the secondary literature, this epistle was written by the same author (or authors) as the *Rasā'il Ikhwān al-Ṣafā'*, of which it exposed the 'quintessence', that is, the esoteric meaning (*bāṭin*). However, there are at least two different versions of this work: the first is attributed to the Andalusian mathematician, astronomer and great enthusiast of the occult sciences, Maslama al-Majrīṭī (d. 398/1007); the second, transmitted by the Ṭayyibī Ismailis, circulated in the name of Aḥmad, the second 'hidden Imam'

---

[27] Yves Marquet, *Les 'Frères de la Pureté', pythagoriciens de l'Islam: La marque du pythagorisme dans la rédaction des Épîtres des Iḫwān aṣ-Ṣafā'* (Paris, 2006); see Daniel De Smet, 'L'héritage de Platon et de Pythagore: la "voie diffuse" de sa transmission en terre d'Islam', in Richard Goulet and Ulrich Rudolph, ed., *Entre Orient et Occident: la philosophie et la science Gréco-Romaines dans le monde Arabe* (Vandœuvres and Geneva, 2011), pp. 119–126.

[28] Yves Marquet, *La philosophie des alchimistes et l'alchimie des philosophes: Jābir ibn Ḥayyān et les 'Frères de la Pureté'* (Paris, 1988).

[29] The edition of reference, published in Beirut in 1957, includes four volumes which contain together about 2,000 pages. Neither an index nor a table of contents has been provided to help in the search for a name or a concept.

[30] Four volumes have been published up to 2011: Lenn E. Goodman and Richard McGregor, *The Case of the Animals versus Man before the King of the Jinn: An Arabic Critical Edition and English Translation of Epistle 22* (Oxford, 2009); Carmela Baffioni, *On Logic: An Arabic Critical Edition and English Translation of Epistles 10–14* (Oxford, 2010); Owen Wright, *On Music. An Arabic Critical Edition and English Translation of Epistle 5* (Oxford, 2010); Godefroid de Callataÿ and Bruno Halflants, *On Magic: An Arabic Critical Edition and English Translation of Epistle 52, Part 1* (Oxford, 2011).

after Muḥammad b. Ismāʿīl.[31] If some sections of the *Risāla al-jāmiʿa* are sometimes limited to a summary overview of the *Rasāʾil*, other sections have no equivalent in the *Rasāʾil* or introduce concepts foreign to the *Rasāʾil Ikhwān al-Ṣafāʾ*, as, for example, transmigration of souls or the fall of souls into matter.

Regarding the *Risāla al-jāmiʿa*, everything – or almost everything – needs to be done: a critical edition, an inventory of manuscripts with their dating, origin and diffusion; a comparison of the doctrines and terminology with the *Rasāʾil Ikhwān al-Ṣafāʾ*; and a comparison of the two versions of the *Risāla al-jāmiʿa*, and so on. From the point of view of its contents and its terminology, the *Risāla al-jāmiʿa* is, in my opinion, much more explicitly Ismaili than the *Rasāʾil*. But should we explain this by the fact that it exposes the *bāṭin* of the latter? Or would it have been written by another author, in order to integrate more easily the thought of the Ikhwān into the doctrine of the Ismaili *daʿwa*? Certainly this is the approach adopted by the Ṭayyibī authors who quote extensively from the *Risāla al-jāmiʿa*; they borrow some of their doctrines from it and refer to its authority in order to legitimise their own system of thought. In the present state of research, these questions remain open, especially because the use and interpretation of the *Rasāʾil Ikhwān al-Ṣafāʾ* and *Risāla al-jāmiʿa* in Ṭayyibī Ismailism have not yet been studied adequately.

The Ismaili philosophy of Qarmaṭī, Fatimid and Ṭayyibī traditions: continuity and ruptures

With the development of Ismaili studies in recent decades, some Ismaili thinkers of the 10th and 11th centuries began to be relatively well known, especially Abū Yaʿqūb al-Sijistānī (d. after 361/971) and Ḥamīd al-Dīn al-Kirmānī. Each of these two major figures has developed a philosophical system very distinct from the other. Just to limit myself to the field of cosmology, al-Kirmānī abandoned the Neoplatonist scheme of al-Sijistānī, according to which the intelligible world is composed of the hypostases of Plotinus (the One, the Intellect, the Soul and Nature), in favour of the system of ten Intelligences governing spheres and heavenly bodies, borrowed from al-Fārābī. Moreover, the philosophy of al-Kirmānī, while remaining deeply Ismaili, is on many other issues close to that of al-Fārābī, whose works he certainly used albeit without mentioning them.[32]

Even if we begin to better understand Ismaili thought, especially through the works of Wilferd Madelung and Paul E. Walker, and if a growing number of texts becomes available in reliable editions – the 'Ismaili Texts and Translations Series' of The Institute of Ismaili Studies plays a key role in this field – we are still far from

[31] *Al-Risāla al-jāmiʿa al-mansūba liʾl-ḥakīm al-Majrīṭī*, ed. Jamīl Ṣalībā (Damascus, 1949–1951), 2 vols; *al-Risāla al-jāmiʿa. Tāj Rasāʾil Ikhwān al-Ṣafāʾ wa-khullān al-wafāʾ. Taʾlīf Aḥmad b. ʿAbdallāh b. Muḥammad b. Ismāʿīl b. Jaʿfar al-Ṣādiq*, ed. Muṣṭafā Ghālib (Beirut, 1974).

[32] See Daniel De Smet, 'al-Fārābī's Influence on Ḥamīd al-Dīn al-Kirmānī's Theory of Intellect and Soul', in Peter Adamson, ed., *In the Age of al-Farabi: Arabic Philosophy in the 4th/10th Century* (London and Turin, 2008), pp. 131–150.

being able to write a 'history' of philosophy in Ismailism. Indeed, the research has not yet advanced enough to make possible the understanding of the evolution of this thought, and too many texts remain either unpublished or published in poor editions.[33]

The famous controversy dividing the Iranian 'Qarmaṭī' *dāʿī*s of the 10th century (Muḥammad al-Nasafī, Abū Ḥātim al-Rāzī and Abū Yaʿqūb al-Sijistānī) – a fact well known from the work of Wladimir Ivanow – has never been studied as a whole. It is unclear how the 'heterodox' Ismailism of such authors as al-Nasafī, Abū Tammām (the supposed author of the *Kitāb al-shajara*)[34] and al-Sijistānī has been revised in order to incorporate it into the Fatimid tradition of Ismailism. Al-Sijistānī, won over to the Fatimid cause at some point of his career, may have himself played an important role in this revision, as did al-Kirmānī after him. But the *Kitāb al-riyāḍ* of the latter – a crucial source in this area – is available only in a practically unusable edition and its contents deserve a separate study.

Why was the philosophical system developed by al-Kirmānī, particularly in his *Kitāb rāḥat al-ʿaql*, not adopted by the Fatimid *dāʿī*s after him? Why did al-Muʾayyad fi'l-Dīn al-Shīrāzī (d. 470/1078) and Nāṣir-i Khusraw return to an Ismaili doctrine similar to that developed by al-Sijistānī? At the moment, it is impossible to answer these questions. Before we can answer them, the impressive collection of 800 'lectures' (*majālis*) delivered by al-Muʾayyad in Cairo on the occasion of the 'Sessions of Wisdom' (*majālis al-ḥikma*), in the course of which Ismaili doctrine was taught to initiates, should be studied. The lack of a philosophical study of these *majālis*, only a small part of which have been published, is a shortcoming that severely hinders our understanding of the evolution of Ismaili thought in the Fatimid period.

The Ṭayyibīs of Yemen regard themselves as the direct inheritors of Fatimid Ismailism. In addition to the Ikhwān al-Ṣafāʾ, they frequently cite al-Kirmānī. They took over his system while apparently introducing foreign elements borrowed, in particular, from the *Rasāʾil Ikhwān al-Ṣafāʾ* and *al-Risāla al-jāmiʿa*, and from the literature of the *ghulāt* circles. Much of the Ṭayyibī literature of Yemen remains either unpublished or poorly edited, and very little studied. Why did the Ṭayyibīs come back to al-Kirmānī, while the Fatimids before them seem to have abandoned him? How do they read the *Kitāb rāḥat al-ʿaql*? How is their thought linked to the Fatimid tradition, and possibly even to that of the Qarmaṭīs? Too many issues remain open, before we can grasp the evolution of the Ismaili doctrine in its continuity and through the ruptures which separate different currents and periods of its evolution.

---

[33] For a first attempt, limited to the Qarmaṭī, Fatimid and Ṭayyibī traditions, see Daniel De Smet, *La philosophie Ismaélienne: un ésotérisme Chiite entre néoplatonisme et gnose* (Paris, 2012).

[34] See Paul E. Walker, 'Abū Tammām and his *Kitāb al-Shajara*: a New Ismaili Treatise from Tenth-century Khurasan', *JAOS*, 114 (1994), pp. 343–352.

Nizārī Ismaili philosophy

The same holds even more true for the Nizārī Ismaili tradition. In terms of the history of philosophy, it opens with the enigmatic figure of al-Shahrastānī (d. 548/1153), a contemporary of Ḥasan al-Ṣabbāḥ (d. 518/1124), the founder of the Nizārī *da'wa* in Iran. Al-Shahrastānī was a Sunni of the Shāfiʿī rite, adherent of the Ashʿarī *kalām*. But many of his works, including a Qur'anic commentary attributed to him, suggest a Shiʿi tendency which is without doubt Ismaili of the Nizārī tradition. How is it possible to be simultaneously Shāfiʿī, Ashʿarī and Nizārī? How can one and the same person belong simultaneously to currents as incompatible as Ashʿarism and Ismailism?

Toby Mayer's chapter in this part addresses exactly this issue of the relationship between al-Shahrastānī and Nizārī Ismailism. Starting with al-Shahrastānī's refutation of the philosophy of Ibn Sīnā (*Kitāb al-muṣāraʿa*), Mayer shows how al-Shahrastānī deconstructs Avicennism to rebuild, from some of its themes, a Shiʿi philosophical system of great originality and coherence. Despite al-Shahrastānī's polemics against Ibn Sīnā, it seems that Avicennism penetrated the Nizārī circles, as it penetrated almost everywhere at that time, including the Ashʿarī *kalām* (Fakhr al-Dīn al-Rāzī is a good example of this). Another significant figure of Nizārī philosophy, Naṣīr al-Dīn al-Ṭūsī (d. 672/1274), is somehow the opposite of al-Shahrastānī. A great admirer of Ibn Sīnā, he is the author of a famous commentary on his *Ishārāt*, and of a refutation of the *Kitāb al-muṣāraʿa*, in which he defends the philosopher from the attacks of al-Shahrastānī. Although al-Ṭūsī converted back to Twelver Shiʿism after the fall of Alamūt in 654/1256, his Nizārī works are deeply influenced by Avicennism, which holds true particularly for his *Rawḍat al-taslīm*.[35]

By the presence of Avicennism – either negative, as in the case of al-Shahrastānī, or positive, as in the case of al-Ṭūsī – the Nizārī tradition differs from the Fatimid and Ṭayyibī traditions, where the influence of Avicenna is much less apparent.[36] A better knowledge of the relationship between Nizārī philosophy and that of earlier Ismailism would, without doubt, make possible a better understanding of the Ismaili sources of al-Shahrastānī, who is situated at the beginning of the Nizārī tradition.

From 'philosophy' (*falsafa*) to 'divine wisdom' (*ḥikma ilāhiyya*): Twelver Shiʿism

Nizārī Ismailism is also distinguished from other Ismaili traditions on another point. Fatimid and Ṭayyibī literatures almost exclusively emanate from the *dāʿīs* writing

[35] Naṣīr al-Dīn al-Ṭūsī, *Paradise of Submission: A Medieval Treatise on Ismaili Thought*, ed. and tr. S. J. Badakhchani (London, 2005).

[36] Which does not mean that it is absent; see, for example, Daniel De Smet, 'Avicenne et l'Ismaélisme post-Fatimide, selon la *Risāla al-Mufīda fī īḍāḥ mulġaz al-Qaṣīda* de 'Alī b. Muḥammad b. al-Walīd (*ob.* 1215),' in Jules Janssens and Daniel De Smet, ed., *Avicenna and his Heritage* (Louvain, 2002), pp. 1–20.

under the authority of the Imam or his representative. The researcher can find there passages directly inspired by the Arabic translations of Plotinus, Proclus or Aristotle, as well as concepts and terms borrowed from the *falāsifa*. But these sources are almost never mentioned; philosophy is fully integrated into the religious doctrine taught by the Imams. By contrast, Nizārī philosophers like Naṣīr al-Dīn al-Ṭūsī and, without doubt, al-Shahrastānī, do not seem to have been religious dignitaries – at least not to my knowledge – but, rather, scholars and 'men of science'. Thus, al-Ṭūsī cites in his Nizārī works a multitude of sources, such as the works of Aristotle or Ibn Sīnā, to which he adheres explicitly. No Fatimid or Ṭayyibī author, with the exception of the Fatimid *daʿī* Nāṣir-i Khusraw, would have done this. The place of philosophy in Nizārī Ismailism seems thus to resemble the place it occupies in Twelver Shiʿism: the existence of philosophy is recognised as such and – if its legitimacy is accepted – it is integrated into all other fields of knowledge related to the Shiʿi interpretation of Islam. In this sense, the Ismaili Nizārī Naṣīr al-Dīn al-Ṭūsī, once he became Twelver, proved to be one of the first great philosophers of Twelver Shiʿism.

Under the influence of Naṣīr al-Dīn al-Ṭūsī, Twelver Shiʿism was to produce a whole line of thinkers interested both in *falsafa* (especially in the works of Avicenna) in the Muʿtazilī *kalām*, in the 'philosophy of enlightenment' (*ishrāq*) of al-Suhrawardī, in the mysticism of Ibn ʿArabī, in mathematical sciences, in astronomy, but also in Qurʾanic commentary, *ḥadīth* and jurisprudence. One of the first representatives of this 'universal' Shiʿi science was al-ʿAllāma al-Ḥillī (d. 726/1325), a disciple of Naṣīr al-Dīn al-Ṭūsī.[37]

During the three centuries between the time of al-Ṭūsī and the 'Safawid renaissance', the scholars in this line followed each other in succession. Their names and some of their writings were revealed in the West by Henry Corbin: Ḥaydar al-Āmulī, Ibn Turkah al-Iṣfahānī (d. ca. 830/1426), Ibn Abī Jumhūr al-Aḥsāʾī (d. ca. 906/1501), to name but a few. Some of them were, after Corbin, the subject of specialised studies[38] but, on the whole, this period remains little known. Yet it is these authors who, through commenting and meditating on the works of Avicenna in the light of al-Suhrawardī, Ibn ʿArabī and traditions attributed to the Imams, made possible the rise of philosophy under the Safawids. The same holds true of the Shiʿi philosophical school which existed in Bahrain in the 13th and 14th centuries. But its representatives (including Saʿāda al-Baḥrānī, ʿAlī b. Sulaymān, Mītham al-Baḥrānī) and their works have not yet received the academic attention they deserve.

This Shiʿi philosophy or 'divine wisdom' (*ḥikma ilāhiyya*), then in full development, was not unanimously accepted. On the contrary, the philosophers had to face the hostility of much of the Shiʿi clergy who saw in their thought only heresies and 'blameworthy innovations' (*bidʿa*). The 'divine wisdom' was thus not regarded as such by all the religious scholars and it certainly was not confounded with the

---

37 See Sabine Schmidtke, *The Theology of al-ʿAllāma al-Ḥillī* (Berlin, 1991).

38 Let us mention in this regard the outstanding study of Sabine Schmidtke, *Theologie, Philosophie und Mystik im zwölferschiʿitischen Islam des 9/14. Jahrhunderts: Die Gedankenwelt des Ibn Abī Jumhūr al-Aḥsāʾī* (Leiden, 2000).

teachings of the Imams, contrary to the doctrines expounded by the Ismaili *dāʿīs*. Herein lies a fundamental difference between Ismailism (at least Qarmaṭī, Fatimid and Ṭayyibī traditions) and Twelver Shiʿism.

The advent of the Safawid dynasty in Iran, who made Twelver Shiʿism their state religion, entailed a remarkable cultural flowering, which also brought benefits to philosophy. Mīr Dāmād (d. 1041/1631), Mullā Ṣadrā Shīrāzī (d. 1045/1636), Qāḍī Saʿīd Qummī (d. 1107/1696), and many others constitute the famous 'School of Iṣfahān', a designation that, however, did not appear in the contemporary sources, but was probably coined by Henry Corbin and Seyyed Ḥossein Naṣr.[39]

Heirs of the great mixing of ideas and systems made by previous generations, Safawid philosophers tried to harmonise Aristotelianism, Neoplatonism, Avicennism, *ishrāq* and the teachings of the Shiʿi Imams in a comprehensive system. They called the result of this process *ḥikma mutaʿāliyya* (transcendental wisdom), following the title of the monumental work of Mullā Ṣadrā: *al-Ḥikma al-mutaʿāliyya fi'l-asfār al-ʿaqliyya al-arbaʿa* (*Transcendental Wisdom Concerning the Four Journeys of the Intellect*). Many studies on Mullā Ṣadrā highlighted the originality of his thought and the prominent position he occupies in the history of philosophy. Concepts such as 'unity of existence', 'modulation of existence', 'priority of existence' (compared to essence), 'substantial movement' or the 'world of active Imagination' – 'le monde imaginal', a concept made famous by Henry Corbin – are relatively well known today beyond the limited circle of the specialists of Iranian Shiʿism.[40]

Despite the intense editorial activity in Iran, many works still remain unpublished and many have never been studied in the West. Serious gaps remain in what concerns the knowledge of the sources used by the Safawid thinkers. In addition to the rediscovery of the *Pseudo-Theology* of Aristotle, the manuscripts of which were widely copied and commented upon, the writings of this period contain innumerable references to the authors of Antiquity. It would be very useful to establish their inventory, in order to determine whether the authors of that time had access to translations of the texts of Antiquity that were unavailable before their own time. For example, one issue that arises is the numerous quotations from Plato: did they come from the apocryphal works or from translations included in the earlier Arabic sources? At first glance, the corpus of the Arabic Plato could be significantly expanded if we add the evidence from the Safawid period. To my knowledge, no study has been done in this area.

---

[39] On the beginnings of this 'School' and the significant figure of Mullā Ṣadrā, see Sajjad Rizvi, *Mullā Ṣadrā Shīrāzī: His Life and Works and the Sources for Safavid Philosophy* (Oxford, 2007).

[40] Thanks, in particular, to the studies of Cécile Bonmariage, *Le Réel et les réalités: Mullā Ṣadrā Shīrāzī et la structure de la réalité* (Paris, 2007); Christian Jambet, *L'acte d'être: La philosophie de la révélation chez Mollā Ṣadrā* (Paris, 2002).

A Shiʿi Philosophy in Modern Times and Contemporary Approaches

The 'transcendental wisdom' inaugurated by Mīr Dāmād and Mullā Ṣadrā had its representatives up to the 20th century. In the 19th century Shiʿi philosophy enjoyed a remarkable revival within the framework of the Shaykhī school, for the acquaintance with which we are in large part indebted to the pioneering work of Henry Corbin.[41] Even today, Ibn Sīnā and other major *falāsifa* of classical Islam are read and interpreted in some Shiʿi *madrasa*s, the fact which, after the Islamic Revolution, reanimated the old debate on the legitimacy of philosophy within Twelver Shiʿism. But can this traditional practice of philosophy interact with modern Western philosophy? Can we imagine a philosophy which, while preserving its Shiʿi inspiration, would integrate the inputs coming from the West? Whatever might be the answer to this question, the rich contribution here of Nader El-Bizri, whose intention is to reconsider some major theses of the ontology of Ibn Sīnā in the light of Hegel and Heidegger, shows that the Avicennism which, throughout the centuries, nourished the strand of philosophical thought within Shiʿism, remains a topical issue for a philosopher of the 21st century.

[41] Henry Corbin, *En Islam Iranien* (Paris, 1971–1972).

21

Shahrastānī's Ḥanīf Revelation: A Shiʿi Philosophico-Hermeneutical System

Toby Mayer

In the introduction to his polemical work *Struggling with the Philosopher* (*al-Muṣāraʿa*), Shahrastānī (d. 548/1153) presents his milieu as one in which Avicennism held sway to a remarkable degree over his learned contemporaries. It was widely accepted, he says, that 'no one will catch up with [Ibn Sīnā] in [philosophy], even though he urged on his racehorse', and he adds that the critical study of his writings 'is a door before which obstacles are thrown up, and which is kept shut by guards and look-outs'.[1] To this could be added the testimony of numerous other texts, such as Ibn Ghaylān al-Balkhī's 'Temporal Origination of the World' (*Ḥudūth al-ʿālam*), confirming the extraordinary impact of Ibn Sīnā on the intellectual life of eastern Islam around the time of the Saljūqs.[2]

Medieval Muslim polemics against Ibn Sīnā (d. 428/1037) have to an extent influenced the picture formed of him in modern scholarship. His philosophy is sometimes casually viewed as in some fundamental conflict with Islamic sensibilities and scriptural teachings. Yet a good case could be made for an opposite view: the extent of Ibn Sīnā's impact was *precisely* owed to his deep reconfiguration of the philosophical heritage in line with Islamic concerns. In this way, he strove to explain Muslim teachings on the reality and unity of God, on prophecy, the afterlife, causal determinism, angelology and many other subjects, using Aristotelian concepts and syllogistic. This is even the case with his most notorious teaching, the pre-eternity of the world. In stark contrast with Aristotle's (and later, Ibn Rushd's) concept of the world as an ontological 'given', whose need for God was only in its movement, Ibn Sīnā insisted that the world is radically in need of God from moment to moment in its

---

[1] Shahrastānī, *Kitāb al-muṣāraʿa*, ed. and tr. Wilferd Madelung and Toby Mayer as *Struggling with the Philosopher: A Refutation of Avicenna's Metaphysics* (London, 2001), p. 20.

[2] 'It has taken root in the hearts of a group of people in our age (*qawm min ahli zamāninā*) that the truth is [simply] what [Ibn Sīnā] says, no matter what, that error is totally impossible for him, and that whoever opposes him in anything he said is not to be counted amongst intelligent folk.' Ibn Ghaylān and Ibn Sīnā, *Ḥudūth al-ʿālam and al-ḥukūmāt*, ed. M. Mohaghegh (Tehran, 1998), p. 13.

very existence. It is therefore, according to Ibn Sīnā, very much incepted – albeit in its essence, not in time (he distinguishes *al-ḥudūth bi'l-zamān*, temporal inception, from *al-ḥudūth bi'l-dhāt*, essential inception). Thus the Avicennan God is indeed the creator of the world, except that He has been creating it through all eternity. We see that even here Ibn Sīnā's impulse is basically Islamic – Aristotle's eternal cosmos has been wholly reformulated in terms of an emphasis on the world's createdness.

The Avicennan paradigm, however, contained a paradox. It seemed to many religious intellectuals of Shahrastānī's day to compromise the faith in its very accommodation of it. A prophet, according to Ibn Sīnā, is fundamentally akin to a philosopher – and is indeed endowed with such acute powers of intuition (*ḥads*) that he may dispense with the laborious scientific and syllogistic procedures used by the philosopher-sage. Both discover and give teachings on exactly the same divine, universal order. The religious systems propagated by prophets, however, depict this order in metaphors and images derived from the compositive imagination (*al-mutakhayyila*), which is the only way of making it accessible to the unphilosophical masses. This, for instance, is how Ibn Sīnā understands the creation-story and also the religious narrative on the afterlife. Even the religious law (*al-sharīʿa*) is cast as a philosophically motivated expedient to dissociate human beings from physical distractions and foster a measure of contemplativity.[3] So, though there is a powerful accommodation of revealed religion in Ibn Sīnā's thought, it comes at a high price, seeming to demote it to the status of philosophy's poorer cousin.

The more searching religious intellectuals of Shahrastānī's time were responding to this problem, whether explicitly or implicitly, consciously or unconsciously. It struck them, simply, as too weak a basis for religious truth. Abū Ḥāmid Muḥammad al-Ghazālī (d. 505/1111), for instance, responded to the challenge by supplying the faith with an ongoing empirical verification in the form of the mystical cognitions which resulted from Sufi practice. For Ghazālī, a central function of the mystical cadre within wider Muslim society was to confirm, generation by generation, the data of prophecy. Shahrastānī was Ghazālī's younger contemporary and like him was known as a Shāfiʿī in law, an authority in Ashʿarī Kalām, and even held an appointment at the Baghdad Niẓāmiyya college of which Ghazālī had been head some twenty-five years earlier. Shahrastānī can, moreover, be shown to have been consumed by a somewhat similar quest for religious certainty. He hints at this in the introduction to his Qur'an commentary. For a philosophically sophisticated, but religious, personality like Shahrastānī, the split epistemology produced by the Avicennan approach was intolerable. While he, of course, takes over the customary differentiation of revelation and philosophy (*al-sharʿ wa'l-ḥikma*) throughout his works,[4] in his higher thought Shahrastānī can nevertheless be seen to promote a deeper system merging both ways

---

[3] See, for example, Ibn Sīnā, *al-Shifāʾ*, *Ilāhiyyāt*, 10th *maqāla*, *faṣl* 3: *Fi'l-ʿibādāt wa manfaʿatihā fi'l-dunyā wa'l-ākhira* (= Avicenna, *The Metaphysics of the Healing*, tr. M. Marmura (Provo, 2005), p. 367ff).

[4] E.g., *al-Milal wa'l-niḥal* is divided into two halves, the first on the teachings of communities with revealed scriptures, and the second 'on the people of opinions and sects (*niḥal*) who

of seeing – a radically philosophical form of religion. He was given it, he states, by an anonymous teacher, to whom he refers using highly charged Qur'anic expressions relating to the divine servant encountered by Moses during his quest for the waters of immortality – in other words, the 'Green Sage', al-Khiḍr.[5] In presenting the supposedly correct teaching on each successive issue dealt with in his critique of Ibn Sīnā, Shahrastānī mentions the enigmatic system in question, using such expressions as the 'Methodology of the Prophets' (*minhāj al-anbiyā'*), the 'Standard Measure of Prophecy' (*mi'yār al-nubuwwa*) and (perhaps most noteworthy) 'the explicit, pure, Ḥanīf Revelation' (*al-shar' al-ẓāhir al-ḥanīfī al-ṭāhir*). Exponents of Ismaili teaching in the period sometimes designated it in just such terms,[6] and there is gathering evidence to identify Shahrastānī's system of ideas with trends within contemporary Ismaili thought. There is no scope here to rehearse this evidence afresh.[7]

The Architecture of the Ḥanīf Revelation

In the passage in his introduction to his Qur'an commentary in which he speaks of this life-changing encounter with the anonymous sage, he refers to a set of key ideas which the teacher had entrusted to him, and it is these concepts which basically constitute the so-called Ḥanīf Revelation. Shahrastānī explains these keys more amply in chapters nine and ten of his twelve-chapter introduction and goes on to apply them strikingly methodically in the course of his commentary. His approach to the text of the Qur'an covers each verse from many angles, with sections on lexicology, semantics, tradition-based exegesis and so on. It is not these, but the final section on each verse, with the heading secrets or arcana (*al-asrār*) which sees our thinker apply the structure of concepts from his unknown teacher to unlock, systematically, the hidden levels of meaning within scripture. The hermeneutical keys can be arranged as a set of dyads. The four chief dyads are creation and the Command

are ranged against the adherents of religions in the manner of opposition'. Shahrastānī, *Kitāb al-milal wa'l-niḥal*, ed. M. Al-Fāḍilī, 2 vols in 1 (Beirut, 1420/2000), vol. 2, p. 6.

[5] Shahrastānī, *Mafātīḥ al-asrār wa-maṣabīḥ al-abrār*, trans. of the commentary on *Sūrat al-Fātiḥa* tr. by Toby Mayer as *Keys to the Arcana: Shahrastānī's Esoteric Commentary on the Qur'an* (Oxford, 2009), p. 65.

[6] Ismailism was sometimes described as the 'Ḥanīf faith' and the Ismaili Imam as 'Protector of the Ḥanīf faith' (*'iṣmat al-dīn al-Ḥanīf*). For example, Pieter Smoor, "Umāra's Odes Describing the Imām', *Annales Islamologiques*, 35 (2001), pp. 549–626, at 559.

[7] Primarily responsible for drawing attention to the Ismailism of Shahrastānī's later works are Wilferd Madelung in the case of the *Muṣāra'a*, Guy Monnot in the case of the *Mafātīḥ al-asrār* and Diane Steigerwald for the *Majlis-i maktūb*. See W. Madelung, 'Aspects of Ismā'īlī Theology: The Prophetic Chain and the God Beyond Being', in S. H. Nasr, ed., *Ismā'īlī Contributions to Islamic Culture* (Tehran, 1977), pp. 51–65; G. Monnot, 'Islam: exégèse coranique', in *Annuaire de l'École des Hautes Études*, 95 (1986–1987), pp. 253–259 (Monnot's presentation of the *Mafātīḥ* is spread in the Annuaire, from volume 92 to 101); Shahrastānī, *Majlis: Discours sur l'ordre et la création*, French tr. D. Steigerwald (Saint-Nicolas, Québec, 1998).

(*al-khalq wa'l-amr*), hierarchy and opposition (*al-tarattub wa'l-taḍādd*), the accomplished and the inchoate (*al-mafrūgh ʿanhu wa'l-musta'naf*), and generality and specificity (*al-ʿumūm wa'l-khuṣūṣ*). Other complementarities come in too, but this list covers the main ones. Each dyad may be sketched only very briefly here.

The world of creation and of the Command can be interpreted as broadly corresponding with sensibilia and intelligibilia, that is, things with an externally perceptible existence and with an intellectual reality, respectively. There is some reference here to the familiar Qur'anic notion (possibly in turn picking up on the model of God's production of the cosmos in the Hexaemeron in Genesis, chapter 1), whereby God projects things into existence through His Word 'Be!' or 'Let there be (such and such)!' This was the seed for a rich doctrinal growth in different schools of thought in Islam – and in Ismaili thought it bore fruit in cosmologies which presented the divine Command as a hypostasis intermediate between the existent cosmos and the godhead, presupposed by creation but outside it. Moving on, the dyad hierarchy and opposition expresses the idea that all realities under God are disposed in relationships of relative superiority or inferiority, and relationships of mutual contrariness. This dyad is particularly suggestive of the historical links with earlier religious manifestations of Neoplatonism, and rendering Arabic *tarattub* with the word 'hierarchy' is an attempt to highlight those links. *Hierarchia* is the Greek technical term coined by Pseudo-Dionysius the Areopagite to express the system of ranks arranged beneath the supreme figure of the *hierarch* or high priest. For Pseudo-Dionysius it is crucial that there is an archetypal celestial hierarchy *and* an ecclesiastical hierarchy on earth which reflects it.[8] In a similar way, the principle of *tarattub* has simultaneous cosmological and socio-political (rather, pedagogic) implications in Shahrastānī's Ismaili system, in which the metaphysical principle of vertically differentiated levels is directly mirrored in the various religious rankings of disciples and teachers beneath the Imam, in other words the *ḥudūd al-dīn* ('ranks of the faith', up to 11 in number) of the medieval Ismaili organisation.[9] Likewise, 'opposition' (*taḍādd*) for Shahrastānī is not only a principle informing metaphysics and cosmology, but also human society and religious history.[10] Shiʿi ideas, notably *al-tabarru'* (self-acquittal

[8] For Pseudo-Dionysius, the divine aim in duplicating the hierarchies is to bring God-realisation (*theosis*) within the scope of humanity, by providing it with a perceptible image of the spiritual hierarchy. This comes out, for example, in the following passage from the Celestial Hierarchy: 'The source of spiritual perfection [i.e., God] provided us with perceptible images of these heavenly minds. He did so out of concern for us and because He wanted us to be made godlike. He made the heavenly hierarchies known to us. He made our hierarchy a ministerial colleague of these divine hierarchies by an assimilation, to the extent that is humanly feasible, to their godlike priesthood.' Pseudo-Dionysius, *The Complete Works*, tr. C. Luibheid and P. Rorem (New York, 1987), p. 147.

[9] The Ismaili doubling of cosmological and 'ecclesiastical' hierarchies is probably most fully explored in the works of Ḥamīd al-Dīn al-Kirmānī (d. after 411/1021) where it is called the 'balance of religion' (*mīzān al-diyāna*). See S. Calderini, '*ʿĀlam al-dīn* in Ismāʿīlism: World of Obedience or World of Immobility?', *BSOAS*, 56 (1993), pp. 459–469.

[10] E.g., Shahrastānī, *Keys*, p. 116.

through dissociation), surely leave their trace here. An example of one of the very many places where Shahrastānī finds the dyad hidden within the Qur'anic plaintext, as a deep principle explaining its outward form, is verses 6 and 7 of the Opening Chapter (*al-Fātiḥa*). The prayer to 'Guide us on the straight path' in verse 6 is appropriate to those who seek guidance from God's designated authorities. They are thus the students subordinate to the 'rightly guided guides' (*al-hudāt al-mahdiyūn*) who are referred to in verse 7 as 'Those whom God has graciously favoured' – theirs is the 'straight path' referred to, a path involving a religious hierarchy.[11] These categories are then contrasted with the vessels of divine wrath (*al-maghḍūb ʿalayhim*) who are the negative equivalent of the good guides, and those who are led astray by them (*al-ḍāllūn*), the negative equivalent of the seekers in verse 6. This is also, then, a kind of unholy hierarchy (Shahrastānī uses the word *tafāwut*, 'disparity of levels'), and it relates to the aforementioned groups through the principle of opposition.[12]

The accomplished and inchoate are a dyad which Shahrastānī also employs extensively in commenting on scripture. Yet it shows with special clarity how his conceptual system works equally as a way of interpreting the Qur'an *and* as an approach to issues in philosophy. These terms refer to two perspectives on causality which, according to Shahrastānī, must be affirmed together, despite their apparent conflict with the principle of non-contradiction. From one angle, events unfold piecemeal on the basis of the action of secondary causes and their effects. We act, in this view, freely, and the course of events is inchoate. But from the other angle, God has absolute foreknowledge of all events, all of which are already accomplished. Shahrastānī traces the terminology back to a *ḥadīth* in which the Prophet speaks to Abū Bakr and ʿUmar of created reality as a mighty angel, whose nature is, however, highly paradoxical. It is made, as it were, half of ice and half of fire, and yet subsists perfectly through divine power. On the basis of this dyad Shahrastānī can resolve the apparent contradiction between Qur'anic verses urging quietism (e.g., 'It is all the same for them if you warn them or do not warn them. They will not believe', Q.2:6) and those urging activism (e.g., 'Speak to him a gentle word, perhaps he will pay heed or become god-fearing', Q.20:44). The first type of verse is rooted in the accomplished point of view, and the second type of verse is rooted in the inchoate point of view.[13] But clearly, as Shahrastānī explains, the dyad not only allows us to coordinate conflicting verses, but also conflicting positions in the philosophy of action, that is, the views of determinists (Jabariyya) and libertarians (Qadariyya).[14] In other words, it is simultaneously a hermeneutical *and* philosophical key.

The last dyad presented here, generality and specificity, similarly faces two directions, one hermeneutical and the other philosophical, namely, the duality deeply informs both the scriptural and the *cosmic* text. As unfolded by Shahrastānī we find that the terms are vectors, so to speak, not distinct categories: there are four,

11 Ibid., p. 178.
12 Ibid., pp. 184–185.
13 Ibid., p. 115.
14 Ibid., p. 114.

or even more degrees, extending to resolving the specific into an actual individual (*tashkhīṣ*), and even possible resolutions beyond this degree.[15] A good case of the duality of general and specific working in interpreting scripture is with the divine names al-Raḥmān and al-Raḥīm in the opening formula of the Qurʾan *Bi-ʾsmiʾ Llāhi ʾl-Raḥmāni ʾl-Raḥīm* ('In the Name of God, the Absolutely Compassionate, the Merciful'). On the basis of venerable traditions which distinguish levels of divine mercy (*raḥma*), Shahrastānī says that the most general level which is betokened by the first, more intensive, name al-Raḥmān, extends to all existents whatsoever, while a relatively specific kind of divine mercy is betokened by the second, less intensive name al-Raḥīm – extending to believers in general (though not, he says significantly, exclusive to Muslim believers).[16] The Prophet himself is also sometimes called an epiphany of divine mercy (*raḥma liʾl-ʿālamīn*) in the Qurʾan, and this is of course the yet more specific degree of individualisation (*tashkhīṣ*) within the reality in question.

Though, as mentioned, certain other dyads are invoked by Shahrastānī in his interpretation, the list above seems to be the real core of his system. Moreover, it is crucial that these dyadic structures which underlie both the outer world and human thought, directly imply a radical theology. For the divine cause of this world must be wholly above the dyads. That God cannot fall within thought-structures which involve counterparts (*qasīm*, pl. *aqsimāʾ*), is supported by proof-texts like Q.2:22: 'Do not knowingly set up rivals (*andād*) for God'. Yet this seems a stance on divine predication so radical as to be unworkable, and indeed, the Qurʾan itself very often identifies God using terms with counterparts. Shahrastānī's response is to propose that all such terms which ostensibly associate the divine with the created must be taken to be equivocal (*bi-ʾshtirāk al-lafẓ*). Though the idea, as ascribed to creatures, may be familiar, it exits the realm of human conception when ascribed to God. Or rather, it *virtually* exits it, because Shahrastānī says that at least *one* sense of such divine predicates stands as viable and defensible. When God is characterised with X, where X has a counterpart, this does not mean that God has X in any familiar sense of X, but is equivalent to saying that God is the *cause* of both X and its counterpart. So for instance, when God is called *al-Ḥayy*, the Living, in the Qurʾan this is no mere truism that God is not dead, but means that God is the creator of life and death in others, and is beyond either. Shahrastānī implements this teaching on divine attributes without faltering. Most striking of all, he takes over the philosophical term for the godhead popularised in this period by Ibn Sīnā, *wājib al-wujūd* (the Necessary

---

15 Ibid., pp. 109–110. For an example of four levels from pure generality down, see the analysis of divine guidance (*hidāya*), p. 179. A further resolution (*talkhīṣ*) of guidance is mentioned, p. 178.

16 Ibid., pp. 109–110. In the passage in question, which builds on Q.7:156–157, Shahrastānī points out that divine mercy (in itself unlimited and all-encompassing), is firstly specified by God for a 'certain people' (*khaṣṣa ʾl-raḥmata bi-qawmin*), those 'who are God-conscious and give the poor-due and those who believe in [God's] signs'. This is clearly a broader community than the believers who specifically follow Islam, i.e., 'those who follow the Messenger, the unlettered prophet'.

Being). According to Shahrastānī, this must be taken to mean that God necessitates the existence and the non-existence of others, but in Himself is above the opposition, and is beyond existence. Here, then, is the well-known Ismaili, and earlier Neoplatonic, teaching that God is a hyper-existent reality (*huperousion*), which Shahrastānī does on occasion acknowledge frankly, both in his critique of Ibn Sīnā and his Qur'an commentary.[17] However, he usually presents God's absolute transcendence a little differently, ascribing existence to God but adding the vital proviso that existence is *equivocal* – something inconceivably expanded in the case of divine reality.

In brief, this seems to be the basic structure of the system known inter alia as the Ḥanīf Revelation, which is used by Shahrastānī in *Struggling with the Philosopher* in setting right the claimed slips of Avicennism, and which is, at bottom, one and the same as his keys for unlocking the deep semantics of the Qur'an, as referred to in the very name of his commentary, *Keys of the Arcana* (*Mafātīḥ al-asrār*). The author's own real sense of his lattice of dyads (and the radical theology which they imply) is seen in this nomenclature. They are *mafātīḥ*, unlocking devices, that is, means of access, not some rational edifice accessed in its own right, another speculative 'system' answering to, say, Avicennism. The point could also be made thus: the Ḥanīf Revelation is not in itself a constituted discourse, but is, rather, *the way* to constitute a discourse,[18] be it hermeneutical or philosophical. The same point may be made through the mathematical analogy of algorithms: Shahrastānī uses the ideas of the Ḥanīf Revelation *algorithmically*, to resolve indefinite new problems in scriptural hermeneutics and philosophy.

Philosophical Applications of the Ḥanīf Revelation

In the remainder of this chapter, it is the philosophical, not the scriptural, application of the Ḥanīf Revelation which will be sampled, through details of Shahrastānī's

---

[17] For this teaching in the critique of Ibn Sīnā see, for example, Madelung and Mayer, *Struggling*, p. 32, as referred to below in this chapter. For the same teaching in the Qur'an commentary see, for example, his *Keys*, p. 145. Here, Shahrastānī credits the four letters of the name *Allāh* (*alif*, *lām*, *lām*, *hā'*) with an ultimate cosmogonic role. The cosmogonic sequence is clearly framed here such that existence is beneath the godhead and does not include it, as follows: the godhead, then the four transcendental letters (*al-ḥurūf al-ʿulwiyya*), then the four intelligible root-principles (*al-mabādī' al-ʿaqliyya*), finally, the existence of existents (*wujūd al-mawjūdāt*). Earlier in the same passage Shahrastānī states that the name *Allāh* alone amongst naming words 'comprehends' God, since all other names are those of things within existence (*asmā' al-mawjūdāt*): 'No letter of any of the names of existents points to any part or attribute of the thing [here] named, only this highest name' (idem, slightly amended translation). This again implies that God as such does not fall within existence.

[18] This distinction is adapted from a remote context. It was proposed by the British anthropologist Graham Townsley in relation to the language of Yaminahua shamans in the Peruvian Amazon. G. Townsley, 'Song Paths: The Ways and Means of Yaminahua Shamanic Knowledge', in *L'Homme*, 126–128, vol. 33, nos 2–4 (1993), pp. 449–468.

polemic against Ibn Sīnā. Elements of the author's Ismaili system can be found at work throughout the refutation which is divided into five chapters challenging Ibn Sīnā's formal division of being, his way of proving God's existence, his way of proving God's oneness, his teaching that God only knows sublunary particulars in a universal way, and his teaching that the world is eternal.

1. The division of being

Shahrastānī's discussion of the division (diaeresis) of being is certainly recondite, dismissing in turn the *kalām* division, then Ibn Sīnā's, then proposing his own. He gives two interpretations of Ibn Sīnā's division, one with existence split into substance and accident, and substance then split into necessary substance (i.e., God) and contingent substance; the other interpretation splits existence between necessary existence (i.e., God) and contingent existence, which is then further split. On either interpretation, says our critic, Ibn Sīnā has situated God within a structure of counterparts. Shahrastānī next takes up Ibn Sīnā's own Peripatetic principles which on the one hand treat anything within any genus as a conceptual composite of the genus and a differentia, and which on the other hand insist on divine simplicity. On the first interpretation of Ibn Sīnā's division, he has made God subordinate to the genus substantiality (*jawhariyya*), making Him a composite of this and the differentia necessity; and on the other interpretation, he has made God subordinate to the quasi-genus existence, making Him a composite of this and, again, the differentia necessity. The basic problem here, supposedly, is including God within any such diaeretic exercise – violating the demand of the Ḥanīf Revelation that God be raised above all counterparts. This unavoidably involves Ibn Sīnā in compromising his *own* theological axiom of divine simplicity.

Shahrastānī's own diaeresis is elaborate and need not detain us. The main point to note is that, notwithstanding its complexity and comprehensiveness, God is carefully, *nowhere* included. Our author moreover prefaces and ends his own exercise with statements which are, likewise, clearly reflexes of his hidden Ismaili system. He begins his great tree of divisions by saying that it is a purely mental exercise, involving no suggestion that its subject is *objectively* divisible in this way. Shahrastānī must say this because he believes that existence has incommensurable meanings, that it is equivocal, and 'that which does not consist in univocal terms is not susceptible to division in regard to the [actual] meaning'.[19] There is simply no homogeneous reality, 'existence', which can function as the basis of the diaeresis, which thus becomes a strictly hypothetical exercise. As already mentioned, this claim of the equivocity of being is a strong feature of our author's Ismaili system. Then, at the very close of Shahrastānī's hypothetical arrangement of being into a many-branched diaeresis, in turning specifically to souls and intellects he alludes to crucial features of his own assumed cosmology: 'it is necessary for every soul to have an intellect, just as every heavenly sphere has a soul, and it has active not passive intellections. It is also neces-

[19] Madelung and Mayer, *Struggling*, p. 30.

sary for the universal soul to have a universal intellect, and the intellect has a universal intellection from which emanates the absolute good upon everything by the medium of the soul, and existence ends up in it, just as existence originated *from* it, as an ordered series (*silsila mutarattiba*) connected to the Command of the Creator, who is exalted and sanctified above His glory falling within the hierarchy of existents or contrariety in beings.'[20] Much here is hinted on Shahrastānī's Ismaili cosmology. The passage envisages the cosmos as a hierarchy (*tarattub*), with the body of each celestial sphere governed by a soul which is in turn governed by an intellect. This is of course the famous Fārābian scheme, first infused into Ismaili thought by Ḥamīd al-Dīn al-Kirmānī (d. after 411/1021). The limit of the cosmological enquiry is then said by Shahrastānī to be the topmost soul and its relevant intellect, designated the *Universal* Soul and the *Universal* Intellect. This last is explicitly stated by our author to be the upper bound of existence: 'existence ends up in it, just as existence originated from it'. The Creator, and possibly, to judge from the ambiguous structure of Shahrastānī's syntax, *also* the Command of the Creator surpasses this level. This crucial detail of Shahrastānī's cosmology is more aligned with the ideas of Abū Ya'qūb al-Sijistānī (d. ca. 361/971) than those of Kirmānī. The differentiation of the Command from the first, or 'universal', intellect, is typical of Sijistānī's Ismaili thought, while Kirmānī strove to identify them.[21] Sijistānī's divine Command has profound ontic ambiguity, in a relation with the realm of being that emerges through it, but also in a relation with the God beyond being.

2. The proof of God

In the second issue, on Ibn Sīnā's proof of God, Shahrastānī starts with a series of quotations, many of which, confusingly, have more to do with God's oneness than His existence. This is because our critic is especially concerned, throughout the chapter, with the philosopher's violation of divine simplicity, and his continuous suspension of this, his *own* principle, by the way he reasons in practice in his theology. The pre-eminent instance of the said violation is, however, of course taken to be Ibn Sīnā's proof of God, known elsewhere as the 'Proof of the Sincere' (*Burhān al-ṣiddīqīn*). Shahrastānī begins by quoting the famous opening proposition of this argument (which as a whole is in fact given in rather different forms in Ibn Sīnā's works): 'We do not doubt that there is existence. And it is subdivided into the Necessary in Itself and the necessary by another, which is contingent in consideration of itself.'[22] In this, we are straight back with the problems broached in the diaeresis in the First Issue – for the *Burhān al-ṣiddīqīn*, clearly, also builds on a division of existence

---

20 Ibid., p. 32.

21 Paul E. Walker, *Ḥamīd al-Dīn al-Kirmānī: Ismaili Thought in the Age of al-Ḥākim* (London and New York, 1999), p. 85.

22 Madelung and Mayer, *Struggling*, p. 33. Compare Ibn Sīnā, *Najāt*, ed. M. Al-Kurdī (Tehran, 1346 Sh./1967), p. 235.

into necessary and contingent, and places God under the quasi-genus 'existence'. God therefore becomes a composite of the generic existence and a differential, 'necessity'.

I have elsewhere explored at some length the structure of Ibn Sīnā's argument and proposed that, in terms of the Kantian classification of proofs of God, Ibn Sīnā's is largely cosmological but contains an elusive and fascinating ontological element.[23] These separate aspects of the proof follow from the division of existence *in intellectu*, as just quoted. (1) From the necessary mode of existence follows God's existence *in re*, otherwise it would not in fact be *necessary* at all. This is patently, an ontological train of thought. Next (2), from the contingent mode of existence, God's existence *in re* also follows: contingent beings are not a sufficient explanation of themselves, so even if contingents formed an infinite series, they would collectively remain in need of some external cause – a truly *non*-contingent being. This is, then, a cosmological train of thought.

The concern here is strictly with Shahrastānī's objections, especially in view of their Ismaili content, and this is not the place to delve anew into the structure of Ibn Sīnā's proof. Shahrastānī makes clear in passing that he himself understands the proof – to frame matters, again, in terms of Kant's categorisation – to be simply cosmological, not ontological: '[Ibn Sīnā] set about proving [God] by saying that contingents depend on the Necessary of Existence in Itself.'[24] Shahrastānī seems well aware that Ibn Sīnā's preliminary to his proof is to set up God's nature and what would directly be implied by it, but he does not take this as part of the actual argument, which he says, simply uses the need of contingent beings for an external cause: 'It is as though [Ibn Sīnā] grasped It by Its species-status in the mind (*bi-nawʿiyyatihi fi'l-dhihn*) and established what follows from Its species-status consisting in the negation of these [deficient] features; then he grasped It by Its individuality (*akhadhahu bi-ʿayniyyatihi*) such that he proved It on the basis of the contingency in contingents and their dependence on something which is Necessary of Existence in Itself.'[25] Though such a formulation shows that for Shahrastānī the Avicennan proof is firmly cosmological, the ontological aspect hovers on the brink of his recognition, being implied by the mentioned preliminary negation of deficient features imposed by God's 'species-status'. For, surely, the foremost such deficiency ruled out by God's nature would be the very possibility of *not* existing?

It is, anyway, the portentous opening gambit of the *Burhān al-ṣiddīqīn*, with its clear, double basis for inferring God's reality (via the idea of necessary existence *and* of contingent existence), which chiefly concerns our critic through the chapter. As he spells out his specific problem with it: 'It is implied by that, that existence includes two divisions which are equal in respect of existence-status, so that it is suited to be a genus or a concomitant tantamount to a genus. And one of the divisions is distinguished by a meaning which is suited to be a differentia or tantamount to a

[23] Toby Mayer, 'Ibn Sīnā's Burhān al-Ṣiddīqīn', *Oxford Journal of Islamic Studies*, 12 (2001), pp. 18–39.

[24] Madelung and Mayer, *Struggling*, p. 36.

[25] Ibid.

differentia. Thus the essence of the Necessary of Existence is compounded … [and] that contradicts unity and it contradicts absolute independence.'[26] The interest in the following is that Shahrastānī explores how the only escape from Ibn Sīnā's plight is for him to admit the full equivocity of existence instead of its univocity – there is no middle option. The middle option, which would have allowed Ibn Sīnā to take existence as the basis of a division encompassing God without compounding God, would be to declare existence *mushakkak*, ambiguous (or 'amphibolous').[27] What is intriguing here is that Ibn Sīnā does, precisely, back this doctrine of existence's ambiguity (*tashkīk al-wujūd*) in some places, such as his *Mubāḥathāt*. This is a philosophical innovation on his part, as Shahrastānī sees it: 'When the man had become aware of the like of this absurd implication, he invented for himself a category beyond the univocal, designating it "the ambiguous". That is not in the logic of the sages, nor will it protect him from starvation, nor is the absurd implication fended off by it!'[28] The doctrine of the ambiguity of existence is championed by Naṣīr al-Dīn al-Ṭūsī (d. 672/1274) in his defence of Ibn Sīnā against Shahrastānī (titled 'Wrestlings with the Wrestler', *Maṣāriʿ al-muṣāriʿ*), as it had also earlier been used by him in his defence of Ibn Sīnā against Fakhr al-Dīn al-Rāzī (titled 'Solution to the Difficulties of the Allusions', *Ḥall mushkilāt al-ishārāt*). The ambiguity of existence would go on to have a long history in the philosophical schools of eastern Islam, much later becoming the keynote of the thought of Mullā Ṣadrā in the 11th/17th century. In fact (*pace* Shahrastānī) we can trace it back rather earlier than Ibn Sīnā, who did not simply innovate it. Fārābī makes reference to it, and it may be traced back yet earlier to Alexander of Aphrodisias, and even, in seed form, to Aristotle.[29]

In finally presenting the supposedly right approach to proving God, Shahrastānī proceeds to employ a simple but memorable metaphor: 'Contraries are litigants and variant things are legal appellants, and their Judge is not numbered amongst either of His two appellants, the two litigants before Him. Instead, "the Real" (*al-ḥaqq*) is applied to the [Divine] Judge in the sense that He manifests the real and establishes it, not in the sense that He disputes with one of the two litigants such that He would sometimes be equal to him and at others at variance with him.'[30] The metaphor exploits the twofold connotation of *ḥaqq*: 'legal right' and 'true' (or 'real'). At any rate, here we appear to have the groundwork for Shahrastānī's own proposed proof of God, an approach which effectively takes away with one hand what it gives with the other. God is, as it were, the judge who confers and sustains all others' rights; but

---

26 Ibid., pp. 37–39.

27 An ambiguous predicate supposedly retains sufficient unity for it to be a basis for mental division, but would not be a genus (which must be predicated univocally) that would inflict genus-differentia composition on what falls within it.

28 Madelung and Mayer, *Struggling*, p. 38.

29 H. A. Wolfson, 'The Amphibolous Terms in Aristotle, Arabic Philosophy and Maimonides', in I. Twersky and G. H. Williams, ed., *Studies in the History of Philosophy and Religion* (Cambridge, MA, 1973), vol. 1, p. 457.

30 Madelung and Mayer, *Struggling*, p. 43, with slightly amended translation.

to consider Him in terms of *His* right is to treat him as just another litigant within His court. This is to be interpreted: God can be known to be real only insofar as He makes others existent or non-existent. A cause must be acknowledged beyond the opposition of either existence or non-existence, through which both come about. Confirming that this is Shahrastānī's intended argument, he has stated a little earlier: '[God] is necessary in His existence in the sense that He necessitates the existence of other than Him, and annihilates'.[31] Yet this basis for inferring God's reality involves a bewildering paradox. For, if God is inferred as the cause of existence, as a whole, and non-existence, in that case the very act of trying to prove God is self-defeating, since it immediately drags Him down into the alternative, proper to His effects, of either having existence or non-existence.

There is thus a clear sense in which, for Shahrastānī, the very notion of proving God is wrong-headed. In the course of the chapter he says, quoting an Imāmī *ḥadīth*: 'Why did [Ibn Sīnā] not say: "When the discourse comes to God, let them abstain"?'[32] These brief formulations above are thus the closest we may come to a proof, in Shahrastānī's view, since God is quite above human ideation and it should not be pretended otherwise. In sum, we are confronted by Shahrastānī with a highly elusive kind of cosmological proof – one that is distinctively Ismaili in pointedly approaching God via the dyad of both being *and* non-being, and also in paradoxically admitting that, in truly transcending His effect, God is after all quite indemonstrable: God would not *be* God if we could prove God. The proof thus retreats from the very idea of proving God, in proving God. A striking philosophical honesty seems to impose the antinomic character of this stance.

3. The proof of God's oneness and the formula 'only one proceeds from the one'

Next, various features of Shahrastānī's critique of Ibn Sīnā's arguments for God's oneness also stand out for their link to the so-called Ḥanīf Revelation. As quoted by Shahrastānī, Ibn Sīnā's thinking on God's oneness generally begins with laying down the Necessary Being as a species, and then shows on various grounds that there may only be one individual instance of that species. For example, some cause or other is supposed in the proliferation of a species as a series of individuals, and also some matter or substrate, as (so to speak) the 'stuff' in which the species can become multifarious. But the status of 'Necessity of Existence' obviously rules out any proliferative cause, and its immateriality too rules out serial individuations of the species. As expected, Shahrastānī is unhappy with this whole framework, with its talk of a distinction of a divine species and individuum. We must not introduce a generic level to our thinking on God, which is only really needed in a case where there are

[31] Ibid.

[32] Muḥammad Bāqir al-Majlisī, *Biḥār al-anwār* (Tehran, 1376–1392/1956–1972), vol. 3, p. 259. Quoted, Madelung and Mayer, *Struggling*, p. 35.

multiple instances of the reality considered. In introducing that level, there is some split inevitably acknowledged in the subject's identity.[33]

This problem could be framed in terms of the now familiar claim that composition follows from Ibn Sīnā's ways of thinking about God, which the reader may, from this point in the text, begin to feel is better viewed as an *ad hominem* argument on Shahrastānī's part. While earlier in the polemic the stress on keeping divine simplicity is, doubtless, linked to the extreme transcendentalism of Shahrastānī's Ismaili theology, it is really axiomatic within Avicennan theology, and it is noticeable that our critic's own argument for God's oneness in *Struggling* shuns all reference to simplicity. That it could be seen, in Ismaili terms, as a crude, even deficient, way of articulating God's transcendence, may be confirmed by Shahrastānī's observation that even the separate intellects are distinguished by having 'simple non-compound realities (*bi-ḥaqā'iqihā al-basīṭati ghayr al-murakkaba*)'.[34] Ibn Sīnā, it is true, described the celestial intellects within his cosmos as relative simplexes, so simplicity, of a kind, characterises even certain non-divine realities. This is part of a wider trend in Shahrastānī's attack, blaming Ibn Sīnā's view of the divine for being too low – the characteristics that he gives God really belong to beings which, though exalted in their cosmological rank, are still non-divine. Is this not in keeping with the venerable Ismaili trend to view the 'gods' of other systems of thought as beneath the true God?[35] This trend enters Shahrastānī's critique here, part of which states that the grounds used by Ibn Sīnā to prove God's oneness fail, because they also apply to certain lesser beings. The lack of any material substrate, for instance, also characterises celestial intellects in Ibn Sīnā's system. Despite this, and despite their being simple, Ibn Sīnā assumes that there are many of them. Why in these terms then, might there not be many gods too?[36]

---

[33] As Shahrastānī says (*Struggling*, p. 46): 'the individual, like Zayd, is not sometimes grasped unqualifiedly, so you call attention to its concomitants and adjuncts, and at other times individually, so you call attention to *its* concomitants and adjuncts. For if it is grasped unqualifiedly it departs from being the individual Zayd.'

[34] Ibid., p. 49.

[35] Out of many possible examples of the said trend: Nāṣir-i Khusraw views the great entity attributed with the simplicity and oneness normally ascribed to God, as in fact the Universal Intellect, below God and the Command. Nāṣir-i Khusraw, *Knowledge and Liberation*, ed. and tr. F. M. Hunzai (London, 1998), p. 91. The Necessary Being (*hast-i wājib*) is similarly identified by him as the Universal Intellect, not God. He takes over Ibn Sīnā's division of existence into necessary and contingent, the aforementioned basis of the *Burhān al-ṣiddīqīn*, and applies it systematically to cosmological realities below God: existence as such is identified with the Command (*amr-i bārī*), necessary existence with the Universal Intellect, and contingent existence with the Universal Soul. Ibid., p. 41ff.

[36] 'Amongst substances is that which is distinguished by itself and its reality from the like of it and the opposite of it, without being associated in a genus and differentiated by a differentia, such as the separate intellects, for they do not have something they are associated in, like genus or like matter, nor something through which they are distinguished, like differentia or like form. Despite that they are variant in their realities and distinct in their forms by

An issue dealt with in passing in this chapter of Shahrastānī's polemic is the Avicennan cosmogonic formula that 'Only one proceeds from the One' (*lā yaṣduru ʿan al-wāḥidi illā wāḥid*). For our critic, this is imputing a kind of deficiency to God in trying to exalt Him. While it seems to keep God's absolute elevation above the realm of multiplicity despite His being the cause of that realm, in Shahrastānī's terms it is absurdly limitative. Amongst other arguments, he asks: if God can know more than one thing, why may He not *originate* more than one?[37] Moreover, a single source of multiple effects is well known in physics, for both whiteness and blackness can arise from the sun's single radiation into two material substrates, and both solidity and liquefaction in two different bodies.[38] In the section headed 'The Correct Choice' (i.e., of teaching), Shahrastānī significantly says that it is in a sense true that only one proceeds from the One. But this is sufficiently explained, he suggests, through the dyad of generality/specificity (part of the basic conceptual structure of his Ḥanīf Revelation). For through a graduated progress of thought, there can be a total ascent from the specific to the general, and in view of absolute generality, the world-effect is indeed, truly a single thing. In this sense, only one proceeds from the One. The passage well brings out the coalescence of philosophical and religious elements, since Shahrastānī roots his generality-specificity distinction in a series of Qurʾanic proof-texts, rather than (say) the Corpus Aristotelicum. This is, surely, through his wish to stress that his counter-Avicennan philosophical system is prophetic, not Peripatetic, in authority and origin. Certain of the proof-texts in question are also invoked in his discussion of generality and specificity in chapter nine of his introduction to the Qurʾan commentary – so there is a clear overlap.[39]

Thus, though it is in some sense true that only one proceeds from the One – namely, in view of the reality of the perspective of absolute generality – Shahrastānī is quite against the theory that God's direct effect is only the First Intellect, and that He

themselves and nothing else. So why do you not say likewise in regard to two necessaries of existence?' Madelung and Mayer, *Struggling*, p. 47.

37 Ibid., p. 54.

38 Ibid., p. 50.

39 The passage in question at this point of the *Struggling* (pp. 57–58): 'The generality and particularity of the relation is mentioned in the revelation and is accepted by people of intellect. God (Exalted is He!) says, 'There is not one thing in the heavens and the earth but it comes to God as a worshipper' (Q.19:93). This is due to the generality of the relation with Him. And He says (the mention of His name is glorious!), 'And the worshippers of the All-Merciful are those who walk gently on earth' (Q.25:63). This is due to the particularity of the relation with Him. The general can be particularised step by step till it reaches a limit in a single thing which is a 'worshipper', just as the particular can be generalised step by step till it reaches a limit in 'the universe'. The uppermost worshippers of God are His angels 'brought nigh'. The status of the Spirit which rises as a rank, and the angels as a rank (Q.78:38), is the status of the universe in company with its parts, or the First Active Intellect in company with the separate intellects which direct by the Command. And just as particularity and generality are two things both rational and revealed in regard to 'worship', likewise their status occurs in regard to origination and creation, and in the relation of Lordship to the worshippers as His statement (Exalted is He!): 'the Lord of the worlds, the Lord of Moses and Aaron' (Q.7:121–122).'

is not an immediate cause for anything else. For even on this view, as he points out, there will inevitably be more than one single effect implied. We can, after all, objectify or reify the relation (*nisba*) of the supposedly single effect with God, and this *nisba* is also a thing of some kind, so God's single concomitant has immediately turned out to be *two* concomitants.[40]

It is not that Shahrastānī's cosmology lacks its own clear concept of a hierarchy of beings. Hierarchy is, as noted above, a cardinal principle of his Ḥanīf Revelation. But the Avicennan principle that 'only one proceeds from the One' subjects God, effectively, to the cosmological hierarchy of which He is the cause, treating Him simply as the top member of the great pyramidal structure.[41] More than once it emerges from Shahrastānī's discussion that the comparative relations of superior and inferior, and the mediated causation by which a member of higher rank acts upon ranks at removes beneath it, all are features *internal* to the hierarchy, simply inapplicable to the cause of the hierarchy per se. That cause has the unique ability to project things absolutely into being. He is the existentialiser, and everything else, be it higher or lower in the cosmic hierarchy, is uniformly characterised by the contingency of its being. Though unthinkably superior, an angel or immaterial intellect in fact has the self-same ontological contingency which characterises a lower life form and even a dust-mote. While the relative causal sequence internal to the hierarchy is from the higher to the lower, yet all ranks are codependent on God in their undermost existential contingency.[42] The subtlety and ingenuity of this are striking: Shahrastānī has here adopted a fundamental insight of Ibn Sīnā's own ontology, to challenge the great philosopher's cosmogony. More importantly, the role here of key elements of Shahrastānī's Ḥanīf Revelation is prominent – notably, hierarchy and the generality/specificity dyad.

But to return to the main issue of his chapter: what is Shahrastānī's own preferred way of proving God's oneness? Here again, his Ismaili system is by no means out of the picture. He ventures firstly that paired realities need a cause of their pairing:

---

40 Ibid., p. 58.

41 This is a point stressed earlier by Ismaili philosophers like Kirmānī, who states that the top member of the cosmic series is the First Intellect, not God. See Walker, *Ḥamīd al-Dīn al-Kirmānī*, p. 86.

42 As Shahrastānī says (*Struggling*, p. 51): 'there is no existentialiser for beings other than God (Exalted is He!), the Necessary of Existence in Himself. Thus it is necessary for all contingents to be related to Him in the same way, without the mediation of an intellect, a soul and a nature.' Again, Shahrastānī makes the same point about the equal dependence of the entire hierarchy on the divine source of its existence, when he says (p. 58): 'The secret of it is that the aspect through which contingents are in need of the Originator is their contingent existence, and existents are equal in regard to this aspect. So there is no difference between what is abstracted from matter and what is associated with matter from the point of view of contingency, nor in respect of contingent existence, and the two divisions are only disparate in rank for *another reason*. So it is appropriate that the First Principle is a principle for everything in a single manner, and the "intermediaries" are different due to the disparity of levels (*tafāḍul al-darajāt*).'

'incongruent things when paired and paired things when combined need something absolutely independent to combine them'.[43] Next there is also a sense in which anything twofold depends on its partner, if only in its characterisation *as* twofold. On both scores, a *wholly* independent being that is one of a couple is a contradiction in terms.[44] The now familiar reflex of raising God above any scheme of counterparts surely stirs in this thinking. This reflex then joins with another familiar one: the claim of equivocity. Unity is equivocal and God's oneness is *unlike* any other conceivable sense of oneness. That 'God is one' only renders the truth that God is the transcendent cause both of all unity and all multiplicity. Shahrastānī traces relative unities in the cosmos back to this transcendental, primordial unity, and in an intensely Neoplatonic turn of expression, presents this divine superabundance of unity as overflowing in the kinds of oneness to be found in the world: 'Unity is applied to Him (Exalted is He!) and to existents purely equivocally. He is one *unlike* the "ones" mentioned – one such that the two opposites, unity and multiplicity, both emanate from Him, one in the sense that He brings things that are "one" into existence. He was unique in unicity, then He made it overflow on His creation (*tafarrada bi'l-waḥdāniyya thumma afāḍahā ʿalā khalqihi*).'[45] Beyond the powerfully Neoplatonic way that Shahrastānī here articulates the solution to the problem in terms of divine superabundance, lie the familiar algorithms of his higher theology.[46]

4. God's knowledge

Needless to say, the last two issues of Shahrastānī's *Struggling with the Philosopher* (respectively, on God's knowledge and the world's eternity) show these patterns too, directly traceable to his so-called Ḥanīf system. There is no scope here to explore these in all their detail. Hierarchy and opposition, and God's radical transcendence of either, are the key to his thinking on the question of God's knowledge. Ibn Sīnā's teaching that the objects of divine knowledge are universals and that God only knows particulars in a universal way (*ʿalā naḥwin kulliyyin*) is again, for Shahrastānī, an ill-conceived bid to exalt God. If it is intended to explain how God's knowledge transcends time and temporal processes of understanding, it fails, for 'knowledge might

---

[43] Ibid., p. 55.

[44] 'The [status of being] "absolutely independent" cannot be realised for two since each of the two would be in need as well as needed, in *being two*.' Ibid., p. 55. Let it be noted here, that the argument is not really to do with divine simplicity, which is used in one type of Avicennan proof of God's unity, i.e., an absolute simplex could not be twofold, because it could be analysed in terms of a factor in which they share, and a factor which distinguishes them as two separate individuals.

[45] Ibid., pp. 56–57. For an example of similar thinking in a Neoplatonic text, see Plotinus, *Ennead* V. 13. Plotinus here speaks of the inclusive unity of the Intellect deriving from the exclusive unity of the One, through being 'poured down' (*epibrisantos*) from it.

[46] I.e., When God is said to be X (here, 'one'), where X has a counterpart (i.e., 'multiple'), the reality in question (unity) is equivocal and the proposition amounts to saying that God is the *cause* of both X and its counterpart.

be universal and be within time!'[47] Likewise, universal knowledge may take the form of conditional propositions, that is, 'if it is so and so, then it is so and so'. But divine knowledge is no more conditional than it is temporal. The alternative, universal *or* particular, is in fact a classic case of an opposition (*taḍādd*) from which our thought must strive to release God. The truth of the matter may also be approached through the principle of hierarchy, a noetic hierarchy, described here in eloquent terms by Shahrastānī:

> The sages who are the authorities in philosophy have said: the First is not grasped by way of His essence but is only grasped by way of His traces. And each thing that grasps Him does so only in the measure of the trace which is consigned to it and it is endowed with. So each animal praises Him in the measure of what it bears of His workmanship, and of the trace of [His workmanship] which it finds in its nature. And since man's endowment with His works is more ample and his share of His graces more numerous, his cognition is more powerful and his praise more comprehensive. Since the rank of the archangels which are in the highest heaven is [yet] more elevated and exalted, and the graces of workmanship in respect of their substances are more radiant and magnificent, their cognitions are purer. And just as the animal cannot attain the modes of man's cognitions, likewise man cannot attain the modes of the archangels' cognitions. And none of them can attain the mode of the Creator's comprehension of all existents (Exalted is He!), summarily and in their details, their universals and their particulars. Moreover one universal does not distract Him from another, and both of them are equal in relation to Him.[48]

Shahrastānī closes the chapter by proposing that 'intellect' (*'aql*) is – as in so many other cases – an equivoque. It even applies to human beings and angels equivocally, for angelic intellection dispenses with the conceptualisation, assent, definitions and syllogisms on which human intellection depends. All the more, says Shahrastānī, we must raise divine intellection which is 'a knowledge higher than all the divisions'.[49] Deep reflexes of the Ḥanīf Revelation are at work in all this: the raising of God above oppositions, the insistence on equivocity in divine predication, the principle of hierarchy. Incidentally, Shahrastānī has an almost identical use of the principle of hierarchy in his Qur'an commentary when he defends the scripture's inimitability on the grounds of a hierarchy in *nuṭq* (i.e., speech or reason). Very simply put: just as humanity's speech is inimitable for lesser beings, prophetic speech is inimitable for human beings.[50]

---

47 Madelung and Mayer, *Struggling*, p. 73.
48 Ibid., pp. 72–73.
49 Ibid., p. 74.
50 Shahrastānī, *Keys*, pp. 120–121.

5. Against the world's pre-eternity

Shahrastānī's last major discussion, against the world's pre-eternity, prominently uses arguments of a type traceable to the late antique Christian philosopher John Philoponus (d. ca. 570) in his critiques of Aristotle and Proclus. In such arguments, Aristotle's own principle is turned against him, that though an actual or fully traversed infinite is contradictory and in fact absurd, a potential, or unfolding, infinite is no problem. It follows from this that space must be finite, because it is actual in character, while time may supposedly be infinite, because it is unfolding and potential in character. Shahrastānī skilfully develops the Philoponian kind of argument against this convenient Aristotelian differentiation, taking up mathematical and geometrical proofs that space may not be infinite, and showing that they can be readily transferred to time and to temporal causal sequences. There is no room to delve into these ingenious proofs here. The link-up with our discussion is, however, that the arguments in question basically bring out, through deductive reasoning, the deep parity of time and space. Such proofs therefore, simply bear out truths passed down on the authority of the Ḥanīf Revelation, for time and space are of course counterparts of precisely the kind typifying creation according to the Ḥanīf Revelation, and God must in turn be raised above either of them. So underlying the elaborate discussion is this wholly typical turn of Shahrastānī's higher thought.

To explore this in a little more detail: Shahrastānī holds that much of Ibn Sīnā's thinking in his claim that the world is pre-eternal, fails to grasp a fundamental kinship of time with space. He fails to limit time, like space, to creation, thus inflicts it on God. The notion, for instance, that if the world began, God would absurdly have had to change suddenly from inactivity to activity, and from un-creativity to creativity, subtly assumes that time is applicable beyond the beginning and outside the universe. For change in God, as in anything else, presupposes time. How could there be change in the absence of time?

A daring aspect of Shahrastānī's attack is that he compares Ibn Sīnā's position with that of the notorious contemporary anthropomorphist Muslim sect known as the Karrāmīyya, who held that God is orientated in space. Though this seems shockingly polemical on Shahrastānī's part, the comparison is objective in his terms. For Ibn Sīnā's thought-experiments to prove the world's pre-eternity discreetly transfer time-sequences to God, much as Karrāmī thought extended spatial notions like direction and location to Him; yet if time, like space, is confined to the created universe, and God is raised quite beyond both, then there would be no question of change in God when He incepts the world. He would simply be the unchanging creator of a time-bound world, isolated from any factor of change relating to this event. So here, in brief, is a highly specific case of the imperative to raise God above paired realities, a definitive pattern of thought in the Ḥanīf Revelation. Shahrastānī puts the point with rhetorical power, wielding the talisman of scriptural authority: 'The Lord (Exalted is He!) is the First without any first which was prior to Him, and the Last without any last which will be subsequent to Him. For He is "the First and the Last", i.e., His existence is not temporal, "and the Outward and the Inward", i.e., His existence is not spatial. Such antonyms coincide in meaning in His case (Exalted is He!), and time and place are twins competing in a single womb, sucking from a single breast and mollified in a single cradle.'[51]

Finally, this critique of the world's pre-eternity is additionally informed by Shahrastānī's principle of equivocity, in particular, the equivocity of existence. He unearths vital grounds for the co-eternity of God and the world in Ibn Sīnā's thought – namely, that the world's existence derives from that of God and is held in common with Him. The reasoning is that since God's being has no beginning, neither does the world's. In answer, Shahrastānī in effect removes the common denominator between God and the world, that is, existence, through his doctrine of equivocal predication. The existence of the world is wholly *other* than that of God, and it is wrong to say that 'the world exists through God's existence' (*mawjūd bi-wujūdihi*). The correct proposition is rather: 'the world exists through God's existentiation' (*mawjūd bi-ījādihi*). Equivocity also applies, according to Shahrastānī, to eternity (*dawām*), for God's eternity is such that nothing else may share in it. In God's case 'eternity' amounts to His intrinsic necessity and to the absurdity of supposing non-existence for Him – it has nothing per se to do with extension in time (*istimrār al-zamān*) because God is quite above time. Given that the term eternity is equivocal (*lafẓ al-dawāmi mushtarak*) in this manner, the world cannot share in God's eternity.[52]

Conclusion

In all the above, the numinous body of ideas which make up Shahrastānī's 'Ḥanīf Revelation', are seen to be deeply at work in every single issue of his critique of Ibn Sīnā. It is fascinating to follow in detail the many uses to which this Ismaili system is put by our author. Its function in setting right the supposed errors of Avicennan thought complements its profound function in interpreting the scripture of Islam and unlocking the secret meanings within its verses. These interacting principles and algorithms of thought thus amount overall to a compelling philosophico-hermeneutical system, simultaneously rational and religious in its force. Shahrastānī indeed stresses that despite their coherence on a rational level, the elements of the system are traceable to the highest religious authorities: the prophets and Imams. This can be seen as reacting, albeit perhaps at a subliminal level, to the Avicennan epistemological model, in which philosophy was the real source of insight, with revealed religion foreshadowing its great truths for the dimmer masses. The intuition (ultimately

---

51 Madelung and Mayer, *Struggling*, pp. 90–91, quoting Q.57:3.

52 Ibid., p. 79. For a fuller presentation than possible here, of Shahrastānī's critique of time's pre-eternity and Ṭūsī's reply, see my discussion in 'The Absurdities of Infinite Time: Shahrastānī's Critique of Ibn Sīnā and Ṭūsī's Defence', in Rotraud Hansberger, M. Afifi al-Akiti and Charles Burnett, ed., *Medieval Arabic Thought: Essays in Honour of Fritz Zimmermann* (London and Turin, 2012), pp. 105–134.

Ismaili) of Shahrastānī seems to invert this model. Instead of a rational cosmos foreshadowed in religious symbols, he puts forth a religious cosmos – a world at whose centre lies a religious mystery – foreshadowed in reason.

Lastly, though he himself would have resented the very question: what of Shahrastānī's originality? The direct precursors of his system are demonstrably the great Fatimid period Ismaili philosophers, and it is in relation to their thought that the exact extent of his own contribution would have to be gauged. The four chief dyads of his system and the radical, 'supra-ontological' theology which they imply, are heirlooms to which Shahrastānī lays no claim at all. While working out a more detailed lineage for his ideas remains a desideratum, the following brief comment must here suffice: generality and specificity are familiar from the wider Muslim hermeneutical tradition; the distinction of creation from the Command is a mainstay of earlier Ismaili thought, as are the principles of hierarchy and opposition; and lastly, the fascinating distinction of the dimensions of the accomplished and inchoate, based by Shahrastānī on the *ḥadīth* of the paradoxical angel, is hard to trace earlier than his own use of it.[53] The implied theology in which God is raised above any counterparts, and is strictly only approached as their ineffable cause, is well-attested in the thought of major Ismaili theologians such as Sijistānī, Kirmānī, and Nāṣir-i Khusraw. That said, it seems to be on his own initiative that Shahrastānī elaborates this as a doctrine of the sheer equivocity of divine predicates. This was doubtless his own extrapolation from earlier Ismaili thinking, prompted by his deep acquaintance with the discussion of types of predication in the Avicennan tradition, and also – let it be stressed – with Ashʿarism. In the latter school of Sunnī Kalām, to which Shahrastānī had deep and highly public links, a remarkably subtle stance on divine attributes had been formulated which conscientiously affirmed them, but elevated them above all comparability (*al-ithbāt bi-ghayri'l-tashbīh*). The relevance of this to Shahrastānī's doctrine of the equivocity of divine predicates should not be missed, despite the shift to an Ismaili intellectual context. Neither is this the only feature of our author's system in which Ismaili and Ashʿarī teachings arguably dovetail.[54]

---

53 Oddly, though the distinction of the accomplished and inchoate is used extensively in Shahrastānī's scripture commentary and is also presented in his Persian language sermon, the *Majlis*, it is absent from *Struggling with the Philosopher*. The distinction, nevertheless, nicely exemplifies the utility of the dyads to interpret scripture and solve problems of philosophy, resolving, as it does, the clash of determinism and free-will – as I mentioned in introducing it, above.

54 Another noteworthy example is Shahrastānī's critique of the principle that 'only one proceeds from the One', discussed above. Here, we may either interpret as Ismaili or Ashʿarī his central argument that despite provisional cause-effect relations within the cosmic hierarchy, everything of the latter, as uniformly contingent in its existence, is equally dependent on the unmediated existentialiser, God. Neo-Ashʿarism, heralded by Ghazālī, famously accommodated natural causes within a framework of occasionalism – God was viewed as the sole agent of existence, who consistently regenerates the cosmos according to the pattern of His choosing, i.e., with all its regular sequences and cause-effect relations.

In the end, a focus on how, or how not, this or that element of Shahrastānī's system can be traced may blind us to what is most significant and original of all about it: the very fact that it has been formulated by him *as* a system. Our thinker has drawn together and coordinated diverse principles into a highly defined organon, which he has then shown, in detail, can apply to the problems of both philosophy and sacred scripture – the achievement of a magnificent project.

22

Philosophising at the Margins of 'Shiʿi Studies': Reflections on Ibn Sīnā's Ontology

Nader El-Bizri

Philosophical thinking in the history of ideas in Islam was closely associated with the scholarly expressions of the Shiʿi theological traditions. This state of affairs is still evident in the pivotal role that is assigned to *falsafa* and *ḥikma* in the unfolding of Islamic thought (*al-fikr al-Islāmī*) within the Shiʿi intellectual milieu. The connections with *falsafa* and *ḥikma* are didactically nurtured and intimately woven within the fabric of theological contemporary commentaries, exegesis and hermeneutic interpretations, in response to current debates in philosophy, along with their epistemic directives in our age of modern techno-science. Taking this into account, it is doubtful whether philosophising about the fundamental concepts of *falsafa* and *ḥikma* should be excluded from the new and emerging broad field of 'Shiʿi Studies'. This is the case, given that the disciplinary boundaries of 'Shiʿi Studies' are still being negotiated in the processes of becoming relatively more defined as an 'area study', while at the same time being gradually inserted within the wider and comparatively more established domains of 'Islamic Studies' in mainstream Europeanised and Americanised academia. Situating philosophy at the margins of so-called 'Shiʿi Studies' neglects the integrative role that philosophising played and continues to perform within Islamic thought in Shiʿism. However, any attempt to grasp the nature of philosophical thinking in Shiʿi scholarship cannot be undertaken without a focus on the fundamental notions that historically preoccupied the exponents of *falsafa* and *ḥikma*. Having this in mind and, by way of initiating some reflections on the renewal and rekindling of philosophical thinking in connection with Islamic thought, and in relation to contemporary Shiʿi scholarship, it is vital to focus on the interpretation of the most representative traditions in *falsafa* and *ḥikma*. In view of this, the present chapter is therefore focused on investigating the ecumenical metaphysical legacy that is exemplified by the foundational ontology of the 'Chief Philosopher', '*al-Shaykh al-Raʾīs*', Abū ʿAlī ibn Sīnā (known in Latin as 'Avicenna'; d. 428/1037). This line of enquiry consists of exegeses and hermeneutic interpretations, which are guided by historiography and epistemic analysis, while being metaphysically situated against the background of contemplating 'the question of *being*' (*masʾalat al-wujūd*) in our epoch of techno-science.

Conceptual Intricacies

Before we engage directly in our investigation of Ibn Sīnā's ontology (*ʿilm al-wujūd*; metaphysical study of '*being qua being*') it is essential that we undertake some preparatory steps in terms of accounting for the fundamental question concerning the connection and distinction between philosophy and religion. This is the case, given that the epistemic frameworks of philosophy are not unequivocally determined by way of religious directives. This is particularly the case due to the cognitive structure of their intrinsic methods of enquiry, the logical sequence of their inferential propositions, and the critical-analytical elements that secure the internal coherence of their modes of reasoning, explication, justification and verification. These structural and cross-cultural dimensions of thought neutralise the potential direct impact of religiosity on investigations in epistemology, and even in ontology. Nonetheless, philosophical reflections respond dialectically to the broader intellectual milieu in which they are concretely situated. The ethical-political horizons of the societal reception and applied appropriations of philosophy are partly conditioned by the tangible and dynamic situational circumstances of material culture and its evolution.

Classical traditions in philosophy can be examined from the standpoint of historiography, and the sociology of knowledge, in relation to specific intellectual histories, within the intercultural sequence of civilisations. This applies to investigations that focus on the history of philosophy in classical Islamic cultures while taking into account the diversity of religious expressions and theological doctrines in Islam, with their tacit impress on the formulation of fundamental questions in metaphysics. In order to account for the principal conceptual aspects that modulate the relationships between philosophy and theology, we have to go beyond the archival spheres of historiography and philology in terms of enquiring about the sense by virtue of which one can talk about a 'philosophical theology' per se. This interrogation belongs to reflections on the question concerning the philosophical impetus within the intellectual history of 'Abrahamic monotheism' in general, and the handed down legacies of Islamic thought in particular. The pathways of such enquiries are labyrinthine in character due to the ambiguities surrounding the proximity of the philosophical propositions to the utterances of theologians. However, we wonder whether the bifurcating divide between philosophy and theology is indeed bridgeable, or if their division can be eliminated by a reductive unifying singularity.

In reflecting on the differential relationships between theology and philosophy, faith is not readily contrasted with knowledge, nor is revelation set as a binary opposite of reason. The use of the appellation 'theology' in the context of commenting on Islamic thought is not simply reducible to being a mere designator that represents the schools of *kalām*, but more essentially it refers to systemic religious thinking that expresses a creedal grasp of the world and of life based on revelation and faith. While theology uses certain philosophical propositions in support of its doctrines, philosophy proceeds by way of attempting to unfold its modes of reasoning in constructs that are independent from revelation or faith. We thus have two distinct world views: one theological and the other philosophical, and both potentially point to the foundational disclosure of a region of *being*, albeit each in its own way. And yet, every region of *being* requires its own modes of knowledge and of uncovering the processes by which physical and human events occur. The *science* that investigates beings is marked by a *positive* character, in the sense that it carries a presupposed axiomatic '*positum*' that can be nature, history, economy, space, number, a sense of the sacred, and so forth. This state of affairs points to the act of *positing*, namely, of letting something be laid down, set, emplaced, posted and stationed. The reliance on presupposed givens in theology can be contrasted with the way ontology, as the study of *being qua being*, shifts its vision from beings to *being*, without losing sight of beings in terms of modifying the manner by which it lets them appear, or brings them forth from concealment into un-concealment.[1]

A *positive* knowledge, as is the case with theology (in its normative mode of enquiring about the *positum* of religiosity), is different from philosophy as ontology. Theology *posits* a given being or phenomenon as a possible theme of objectification, whose disclosure is already illuminated by a certain understanding of *being* or existence. This theological qua religious *positum* is presupposed in such a way that it is already disclosed, in the sense that it came about historically through handed down oral, textual and ritualistic communicative traditions. The presuppositions of theology are witnessed through the unfolding of the history of religion, and they are also present in concrete institutions, in actual cults, communities and groups, and in modes of receiving and reading scriptures. Theology is a mode of systemic knowledge that uses philosophical utterances in view of rendering the conditions of the enactment of the directives of such credal traditions possible. What is a posited given for theology is 'faith', namely, as a way of life that arises from what lies at the roots of religious thinking in the form of belief and conviction in what is revealed. What gives rise to faith is an assumed relationship with the Divine, with God. One experiences faith by way of believing, and through an historical communal partaking in the creedal events of receiving revelation in faithfulness. And yet this carries a sense of circularity, since the occurrence of revelation in faithfulness self-discloses itself only to faith. Hence, faith belongs to the context of its own self-disclosure, in being seized by what one cannot see as evidence, only through deeply rooted convictions and beliefs. In this sense, theology gains its meaning and legitimacy when it functions as an ingredient of faith, and when faithfulness holds sway at the roots of theological thinking.

Theology confronts philosophy with the challenges of the conceptual objectification and experiential constitution of what cannot be objectified and constituted, namely, the *telos* of faith: divinity! What is objectively definable compromises the specificity of faithfulness, whereby religious phenomena encompass series of experiences, convictions and beliefs that underpin the pre-given articles of faith; hence, that are knowable in advance as the foundations of theological enquiry. However, faith is

---

[1] Martin Heidegger reflected on this question in relation to Christian theology and its relationship with philosophy in *Wegmarken*, *Gesamtausgabe Band 9* (Frankfurt am Main, 1976); Martin Heidegger, *Pathmarks*, ed. William McNeill (Cambridge, 1998).

not readily assumable as being a criterion of knowledge for a philosophical explication of the fundamental concepts of theology, which rests on exercising the functioning of reason autonomously from revelation, or from the historical and communal ethos and praxis as well. Religious and theological concepts are manifest through faith and its determination of the sense of *being*. Philosophy offers directives to theological constructs, and, moreover, in the form of ontology, philosophical thinking may assist in illuminating the content of some of the basic concepts of theology. It is from the standpoint of the difference between philosophy and theology that one hesitates to talk about 'monotheistic philosophy' ('Jewish', 'Christian', 'Islamic'), or to entertain dilettante idioms about 'Sunni' or 'Shiʿi' philosophy ('Catholic' or 'Protestant', etc.) despite the contemporary relativistic popularity of such appellations.

The consideration of the question concerning the difference between philosophy and theology involves also reflections on the 'non-objectifying modes of thinking and speaking' that do not situate beings over and against us, nor place us in this mode of receiving them. Language is manifest in this context as that which is not simply an instrument to manipulate objects, or a tool within the regions of our human powers of disposal, or that which is of our mere human doing, or of the order of what is amenable to human possession as such. Rather, humans belong to language and they pay heed to the way it opens up the world for them. 'Poetic thinking lets God's presence be said' without letting divinity stand over against us as objectified presence. In avoiding a direct focus on what may be ambivalently called in facile terms 'Shiʿi philosophy', and by way of bracketing and suspending its religious discourses on revelation, prophecy, imamate, intercession, infallibility, spiritual guidance, authority, martyrdom, eschatology, and so on, we turn our gaze towards the ontology of Ibn Sīnā.

Ontological Modalities

Ibn Sīnā laid down the foundations of his naturalised causal ontology by way of logical investigations of the question of *being* (*wujūd*). In the logic divisions of his *Kitāb al-shifāʾ* (*Book of Healing*) and the *Kitāb al-najāt* (*Book of Deliverance*), Ibn Sīnā posited three modalities: necessity (*wujūb*), contingency qua possibility (*imkān*), and impossibility (*imtināʿ*, *istiḥāla*).[2] His analytics entailed the following ontological-logical propositions: The *necessary* (*al-wājib*) cannot but be; it is impossible for it not to be; and affirming its non-being is a contradiction; the *impossible* (*al-muḥāl*, *al-mumtaniʿ*) cannot be; it necessarily does not exist; and affirming its being entails a contradiction;[3] the contingent qua possible (*al-mumkin*) can either be or not be; its

[2] Ibn Sīnā, *Kitāb al-shifāʾ*, *Metaphysics II*, ed. G. Anawati, I. Madkour and S. Zayed (Cairo, 1975), p. 35; Ibn Sīnā, *Kitāb al-najāt*, *Metaphysics I*, ed. M. Fakhry (Beirut, 1985), p. 255.

[3] A distinction can be made between different types of 'impossibility', or of distinct levels of hardness and softness of this modality. For instance, a 'unicorn' is an impossible existent; however, its impossibility is existential and synthetic a posteriori. We can imagine a unicorn,

being or non-being is neither necessary nor impossible; it is ontologically neutral as a pure potentiality to exist or not to exist; and affirming its existence or nonexistence does not result in a contradiction. The contingent is in need of something other than itself to bring it from non-being to *being*; since it is mere potentiality *due-to-itself* (*bi-dhātih*), and exists necessarily in actuality only *due to something other than itself* (*bi-ghayrih*).

A reflection on *being* in terms of necessity results in two differential ontological-logical modes of existing: that of the *Necessary Existent due-to-itself* (*wājib al-wujūd bi-dhātih*), and that of the *necessary existent due-to-something-other-than-itself* (*wājib al-wujūd bi-ghayrih*); the latter being an *actualised contingent* that has been brought into existence as an effect of an existential cause (*'illa wujūdiyya*) that is prior to it, and is external to its essence. Ultimately, the *necessary existent due-to-something-other-than-itself* is brought into actualised existence by way of a continuous, finite, hierarchical grand chain of causation that connects it with the *Necessary Existent due-to-itself*. In an onto-theological prima facie account, one may precipitately hold that the *Necessary Existent due-to-itself* is conceptually derivable from a contemplation of the question of Divinity. When *being* is accounted for in terms of necessity per se, that which 'necessarily *is*' gets posited *ontologically* (from a perspective on *being/existing*) as 'necessary *being*' qua 'necessary existing;' yet, *ontically* (from a perspective on *beings/existents*) it is grasped as 'A Necessary Existent'. However, this 'Necessity of *being*/existing', or this 'Necessary Existent', is ultimately self-sustained *cum* self-derived, in the sense that it *necessarily exists due-to-itself*. Consequently, the 'Necessary' per se (*al-wājib*) is necessitated in a radically different ontological mode than the manner the contingent becomes *necessary due to what is other than itself*; namely, by being brought into existence by what is *other*, and continues to exist, or ceases to be, because of *otherness* (and due also to its inherent corruptive nature [*fasād*] as a generated being [*muḥdath*]). The metaphysical structure of a contingent is that of borrowed-granted *being*, which does not sustain the reasons of existence in its quiddity qua essence;[4] it is *mumkin* in-itself, *wājib* through-another.

Causality and Actuality

Rethinking Ibn Sīnā's modalities of *being* leads us to account for the workings of the principles of causation (*'illiyya*; *sababiyya*) in his ontology. Unlike necessary *being* and impossible *being*, which are not united with a cause, contingents depend on causation in being brought forth into existence and in continuing to be sustained

---

represent it in plastic and visual arts, and comment on it with meaningful poetic and mythological terms. In contrast, a 'squared circle' designates an a priori logical and analytical impossibility by definition; it is an impossible existent that cannot be imagined or represented.

4 *Avicenna Latinus, Liber De Philosophia prima sive Scientia divina I-IV*, ed. S. Van Riet, introduction G. Verbeke (Leiden, 1977), p. 72*.

within it.[5] We may in this context establish a nuance between *generation* and *preservation*; namely between what causes something to exist, and what sustains it in existence.[6] What is generated and brought into existence, by virtue of something else other than itself, is also in need of *another* in order to subsist in its own being, which is essentially marked by becoming, and destined to corruption. In actualisation, the realising external cause is itself brought from a state of potentiality into a state of actuality by way of bringing forth its receptive effect. Any existing entity, for which existence is not intrinsically necessary, is contingent in itself,[7] and a contingent would not exist in actuality unless it gets realised as a necessary effect of an existential cause that is other than itself. This is the case, given that the cause of an existent entity is that which is other than it; and a cause qua cause is *what it is* by virtue of letting an effect emerge out of it by necessity. However, a stress on the necessary connection between an effect and its cause invites the positing of 'Occasionalist' counterarguments with regard to creation, as well as enabling a sceptical penchant concerning the soundness of inductive reasoning,[8] along with the assertion of dependency conceptions in reference to an ever-sustaining emanation (*al-ṣudūr*; *al-fayḍ*). A conception of contingency in relation to causality relies on the continual intervention on the part of causes to support the actualisation of their effects. Ultimately, something is always dependent on what is other than itself in order for it *to be* or *not to be*. In this sense, Ibn Sīnā posited 'The Necessary Existent due-to-Itself' (*wājib al-wujūd bi-dhātih*) as the sustaining ontological-cosmological source, ground and *telos* for all existents.[9]

Based on Ibn Sīnā's causal explications, it can be claimed that the quiddities of existents are unworthy of *being*, *if and only if* abstracted from the Necessary Existent due-to-Itself. Accordingly, a quiddity (*māhiyya*) that is separated from its relation with the Necessary deserves 'non-being';[10] a contingent removed from the *existential causal chain* would not be; given that, in-itself, a contingent has an indeterminate relation to being or non-being. Existing is thus actualised against the horizon of production in terms of a causal metaphysics of presence qua actuality. Existence is thus external to the substantial structure of beings and their essence is not inclusive of their *being*. Existence is an *event* that happens to the essence of a thing, while

[5] Ibn Sīnā, *Danish nameh (Metaphysica of Ibn Sīnā)*, tr. Parviz Morewedge (New York, 1973), p. 50.

[6] Ibid., p. 52.

[7] Ibid., p. 48.

[8] This matter is best exemplified in the critique that al-Ghazālī advanced in his *Tahāfut al-falāsifa*, particularly in the 17th discussion of the physical sciences part, which centred on doubts raised in reference to the necessary connection between causes and effects that is reminiscent of what we attest centuries later with David Hume's interrogation of the justification of induction. See al-Ghazālī, *Tahāfut al-falāsifa (The Incoherence of the Philosophers)*, tr. Michael Marmura (2nd ed., Provo, UT, 2000), pp. 166–177.

[9] Ibn Sīnā, *Danish nameh*, p. 76; A.-M. Goichon, *La philosophie d'Avicenne et son influence en Europe médiévale* (2nd ed., Paris, 1984), pp. 24–27.

[10] *Avicenna Latinus, Liber De Philosophia prima*, pp. 73*–74*; Goichon, *Philosophie d'Avicenne*, p. 50.

this happening cum eventuality gets elucidated in cognitive and intellective terms by way of causal naturalised explanations. Yet there cannot be a cause of a cause ad infinitum,[11] given that the causal nexus is not circular and self-referential due to its inherent complexity. The self-subsisting (*qā'im bi-dhātih*) One is thus *posited* in cosmological terms as the Primary Principle of the All.[12]

Eternity and Necessity

Thinking about the subtle existential entailments of necessity, the Arabic expression '*wājib al-wujūd*' is usually rendered (*ontically*) as 'A Necessary Existent', and occasionally it is ambivalently interpreted (*ontologically*) as 'Necessary *Being* [Existing]', whilst literally meaning 'that whose existence [or *being*] is necessary'. However, rather than merely entailing the existence of an Absolute Deity, the appellation '*wājib al-wujūd*' points also to a *neuter* uncanny sense of '*being*' (*wujūd*) that is ontologically different from that of 'a being' (*mawjūd*).

In cognitive terms, Ibn Sīnā's 'Necessary Existent due-to-Itself' (*wājib al-wujūd bi-dhātih*) is not prior to *being* nor is it beyond it. The Necessary rather figures in an epistemic anteriority with respect to *being* and to *necessity*, as a modal derivative. This view preserves to *being* its logical, ontological and epistemic priority cum principality as what is encountered in the mind with immediacy, given that the notion of a 'Necessary Existent' is not self-evident, but is rather derived from the *necessity* of *being*.[13] Metaphysics does not thus begin with the *modality* of a 'Necessary Existent due-to-Itself' as its primitive term, rather this appellation, and what it entails, both get unveiled and disclosed in the course of an ontological enquiry.[14] Yet, this does not simply imply that we exclusively undertake demonstrative proofs with respect to the '*Necessary Existent due-to-Itself*'; nor does this entail that a refutation of *the ontological idea* of a 'Necessary Existent' results in a rejection of the notion of 'Divinity'.[15]

Ibn Sīnā argued that there cannot be more than one 'Necessary-Existent-due-to-Itself' without having *differentia* (*faṣl*) that allows one *Existent* to be distinguished from another. In case there is more than one Necessary Existent that is Necessary due-to-Itself, then these proclaimed *Necessary Existents* would need to be separated by what is external to them as *differentia*. And yet, this entails that they would not be necessary due to themselves, given that they depend on *differentia* to separate them

[11] Ibn Sīnā, *Kitāb al-shifā', Metaphysics II*, pp. 327–328, 340.

[12] Ibn Sīnā, *Danish nameh*, p. 59.

[13] Refer to Michael Marmura's contribution to the *Metaphysics* section under 'Ibn Sīnā' in *Encyclopaedia Iranica*, vol. 3, p. 75.

[14] Parviz Morewedge, *Islamic Philosophical Theology* (Albany, NY, 1979), pp. 191–192.

[15] Ibn Sīnā, *Kitāb al-shifā', Metaphysics II*, p. 354. Regarding Ibn Sīnā's version of the ontological argument, and the scholarly debates around it, along with his cosmological proofs, see Lenn E. Goodman, *Avicenna* (London, 1992), p. 64; Morewedge, *Islamic Philosophical Theology*, pp. 188–222.

from each other. Each will then be necessary-due-to-itself and necessary-due-to-another, which does not hold following the logic of non-contradiction. We perhaps could then argue that this problem may be resolved through dialectical methods that account for what is *determined in itself* as contrasted with what is *determined by what is other than itself*. Yet, even a dialectical account does not allow for the simultaneous occurrence of the determination of something due to itself with a concurrent determination of that thing due to what is other than itself. After all, it is logically problematic to assert something while at the same time refuting it, unless we adopt the quasi-logic of ambiguity, which does not obey the logic of non-contradiction, and yet, its utterances would not be within the provenance of *logos* but are rather inscribable within the narratives of *mythos*.[16]

Essence and Existence

Being that which has no quiddity/essence (*lā māhiyya lahu*), Ibn Sīnā's '*wājib al-wujūd bi-dhātih*' overcomes Aristotle's *ousia* (*substantia/essentia*; *jawhar*). His metaphysics thus moves away from an *ousia*-based ontology (namely, '*ousiology*'): what has no essence other than existence is not a substance (*jawhar*). *Being qua being* (*al-wujūd bi-mā huwa wujūd*) reflects the most general encounter in the mind, without definition (*ḥadd*) or description (*rasm*), which cannot be readily accounted for in terms of quiddity qua essence (*māhiyya*), given that it is neither genus (*jins*) nor *differentia* (*faṣl*).

Ibn Sīnā's thought about *being* overcomes the unfolding of Aristotle's *ousiology* (*ousia*-based ontology) within the course of development of the history of medieval metaphysics. This matter becomes clearer by addressing Aristotle's *Metaphysics* and the way it advanced ontology as an enquiry into *being qua being*: *on hē on*. And yet, despite investigating *being qua being*, an *onto-theological* turn is already attested with Aristotle's conception of *metaphysics* as *theology*. Nonetheless, a new foundational phase in metaphysical thinking arises with Ibn Sīnā's systemic conferral of autonomy to ontology from the determinants of theology-theosophy in investigating the question of *being*.

Aristotle enunciated that the dealing with 'beings in the primary sense' leads any enquiry to what 'all other beings are referred back to;' namely *ousia* (substance).[17] Based on this reading, everything that *is* (namely, all that is assumed under the

[16] Ibn Sīnā, *Danish nameh*, pp. 43-47; Ibn Sīnā, *Kitāb al-ishārāt wa'l-tanbīhāt*, ed. S. Dunia (Cairo, 1960), vol. 3, p. 65; Ibn Sīnā, *Livre des directives et remarques*, ed. and tr. A.-M. Goichon (Paris, 1951), p. 353; Louis Gardet, *La connaissance mystique chez Ibn Sīnā et ses présupposés philosophiques* (Cairo, 1952), pp. 37, 67; Ibn Sīnā's *Risāla fī al-ʿishq*, in *Traités mystiques d'Avicenne*, ed. M. Mehren (Leiden, 1894), pp. 2–3.

[17] Martin Heidegger, *Aristotle's Metaphysics, IX 1–3: On the Essence and Actuality of Force*, tr. Walter Brogan and Peter Warneck (Bloomington, IN, 1995), p. 2; Aristotle, *Metaphysics*, ed. W. D. Ross (Oxford, 1997).

categories) shows that 'first being' is *ousia*; and what '*is*' in the primary sense is *ousia* (*Metaphysics*, 1028a13ff). For, substance is herein said to be primary in definition, knowledge and time. The long-standing metaphysical question: 'what *is* that which *is*?' namely 'what is *being*?' is thusly reducible to the question: 'what is *substance*?'[18] The core of the question is: 'what is this *is*?' Namely, the '*is*' (qua verbal '*to be*') that continually figures in concealment within interrogations about essence and existence. This is the case even though the distinction between essence and existence is hinted at with ambivalence in the Aristotelian tradition in terms of thinking about what is intended from the saying *tode ti* (the 'thisness' of a present extant thing, as 'singularity in identity'),[19] in contrast with the vague concept that is hard to apprehend, *to ti ēn einai* ('what it was for something to be the thing it is!'). Aristotle's doctrine of *being* (developed in its historical unfolding as a 'doctrine of substance'), carries two determinations: it answers the question about the essence of something, while also positing that thing as an individual (*Metaphysics*, 1028a 10). In addition, given the manifoldness of beings and, consequently, that *being* has many meanings, these do nonetheless refer in unity to *ousia* (*Metaphysics*, 1003a 33), which acts as some sort of *hupokeimenon*, namely as what always already lies present at the basis of all the meanings of *being*. In this, there is some sort of a 'sustaining and guiding basic meaning' upon which the other meanings 'can be said'. In speaking about beings something alongside is murmured, namely *being* itself, wherein the sustaining and leading fundamental meaning of *being* (*einai*; *on*), to which all the other categories are carried back, is: *ousia*.

'Avicenna Latinus'

Ibn Sīnā's ontological reflections underpinned the medieval debates of European scholasticism over the *distinctio* and *compositio* between the quiddity qua *essentia* of a being and its way of being qua *existentia*. The distinction between essence and existence was expressed into a *distinctio realis* (in reality) within the tradition of Thomism (Thomas Aquinas), and it was rendered as a *distinctio formalis* or *modalis* (formal or modal) within the legacy of Scotism (Duns Scotus), and articulated as *distinctio rationis* (rational, in the mind) within the teachings of Francesco Suárez.[20] The scholastic ontology was structured in terms of disjunctive binaries, dyads such as: *ens infinitum* vs *ens finitum* (infinite vs finite); *ens increatum* vs *ens creatum* (uncreated vs created); *ens necessarium* vs *ens contingens* (necessary vs contingent); *ens per essentiam* vs *ens per participationem* (essential being vs participatory being);

---

18 Aristotle, *Metaphysics*, 1028b 2–4.

19 John Duns Scotus coins the term '*haecceitas*' (*Ordinatio* II, d.3, p.1, q.2, n.48) as a Latin rendition of the Greek '*tode ti*,' and in contrast with the expression *quidditas*, namely, *thisness* versus *whatness*.

20 Respectively in Aquinas' *Quaestiones Quodlibetales*, *Summa theologiae*, and *De veritate*; in Duns Scotus' *Reportata Parisiensia*; and Suárez's *Disputationes metaphysicae*.

actus purus vs *ens potentiale* (actuality vs potentiality); *ens a se* vs *ens ab alio* (being due to self vs being due to another), etc. Consequently, the Divine, conceived as *ens perfectissimum*, is also *ens a se, ens infinitum, ens increatum, ens necessarium, ens per essentiam, actus purus.* (The Perfect essentially exists due-to-itself, as an infinite, uncreated, and purely actual Existent). These Latinate notions rested on *adaptations* of Ibn Sīnā's reflection on the ontological difference between: *wājib al-wujūd bi-dhātih (Necessary-Being-due-to-Its-Self)* and *wājib al-wujūd bi-ghayrih* (*necessary-being-due-to-something-other-than-itself/contingent-being-in-itself*).[21]

The scholastic meditations on the *distinctio* and *compositio* between the *quiddity qua essentia* of a being and its way of *being qua existentia*, which were inspired by adaptive interpretations and assimilative re-conceptualisations of Ibn Sīnā's ontology, eventually underpinned 'the Kantian thesis about *being*', which speculated about 'the impossibility of having an ontological proof', in terms of also reflecting on the transcendental dialectical inferences of pure reason. *Being* was not grasped as 'real predicate' and it only figured as a 'copulative function' (what may be termed: *wujūd rābiṭ*). Kant's thesis read as follows:

> Being is obviously not a real predicate; that is, it is not a concept of something which could be added to the concept of a thing. It is merely the positing of a thing or of certain determinations as existing in themselves — Logically, it is the copula of a judgement. (Immanuel Kant, *Kritik der reinen Vernunft*: *Critique of Pure Reason*, A598–B626)

Consequently, the distinction between *essentia* and *existentia* does not readily correspond with the ontological difference between beings and *being*, rather it belongs to one or the other side of this binary bifurcation; hence, positing *primordial essence* as an opposite counterpart of *primordial existence*; and each instating a whole new tradition in metaphysics – the principality of essence or that of existence, *aṣālat al-māhiyya* vs. *aṣālat al-wujūd.*

Dialectics

Despite Ibn Sīnā's groundbreaking and foundational novel directions in ontology (overcoming Aristotle's *ousiology*, the reflection on the connection and distinction between essence and existence, the unveiling of the ontological difference between *being* and beings), his ontological thinking still self-announces some profound internal tensions and unresolved incongruities in relation to the doctrine of *being*. In view of attending to this matter to be thought, we will critically reconsider the question of

21 Ibn Sīnā, *Kitāb al-shifāʾ*, pp. 36–39, 43–47, 350–355; Ibn Sīnā, *Kitāb al-najāt*, pp. 255, 261–265, 272–275, 283–285; Ibn Sīnā, *al-Ishārāt waʾl-tanbīhāt*, p. 65; Ibn Sīnā, *Kitāb al-hidāya*, ed. M. ʿAbdū (Cairo, 1874), pp. 262–263.

being under the modality of '*wājib al-wujūd bi-dhātih*', while also attempting to offer modern ontological prolongations in its interpretation.

As noted above, the expression '*wājib al-wujūd bi-dhātih*' literally means: 'that whose existence or *being* is necessary due to itself.' In a neutralised conception, this modality points to an ambiguous and uncanny necessity in existing. The first sense of '*wājib al-wujūd bi-dhātih*' would be '*necessary being due to itself*' or '*necessary existing due to itself*', while the second significance of this appellation would be '*The Necessary Existent due to Itself*'. Given that with both renditions, '*wājib al-wujūd bi-dhātih*' is without quiddity, all we could confidently utter about this modality is that it designates *necessary-existing-due-to-itself*.

By rendering '*wājib al-wujūd bi-dhātih*' as 'necessary *being* due to itself', namely as the ground from which the *hypostasis* emanates, all we might be able to say about this uncanny *presencing* is that 'there is!' ('*il y a*!' '*es gibt Sein*!' '*huwa*!' or '*hunālika*!').[22] Accordingly, the Necessary (*al-wājib*) is not addressed as a determinate onto-theological Being qua Existent, but is rather posited as an immediate pure *being* that is equal to itself, namely *being-itself* as what does not need the mediation of anything other than itself for it to be. Consequently, it is indifferent to any determinateness of *being*.[23] As a simple self-relation that is posited a priori, it is *necessary*. However, when we render '*wājib al-wujūd bi-dhātih*' as 'The Necessary Existent due to Itself' we move from pure *being* to a determinateness in *being*. The Necessary Existent due to Itself is not merely *being-itself* but is rather a self-posited *being-for-itself*, which surges by way of excluding otherness, namely *the All* as contingents. It thus maintains Itself as the One by the exclusion of the many through an act of repulsion that posits *the All* as what issues forth from Its own *coming-out-of-Itself* into otherness. In this, the One, namely *The Necessary Existent due to Itself*, remains related to what It excludes by way of attraction; wherein everything is quasi-detached and ultimately returns to the One from which it came forth. For, attraction is an integrative gathering of everything in the One.

In the double movement of repulsion and attraction, of emanation and return, the 'Necessary Existent due to Itself' is revealed as being the initiating ground and the final destiny (*al-mabda' wa'l-ma'ād*).[24] As ground, *It* is assumed as an ever-present origin for all that issues forth from *It*. *It* thus acts as what always already lies present at the basis of what follows from *It*. Polemically, *It* bears the character of a *hupokeimenon*, as attested with Aristotle's *ousia*. In this, 'The Necessary Existent due to Itself' is: (i) *being-for-self*, as what excludes *the All*, namely, repulses (emanates) the many from the One, and is also (ii) *being-for-other*, as a self-repulsion of Itself into otherness that re-gathers *the All* in attraction qua return.[25] We could say that pure *being*, as

[22] Given that 'there is' ('*il y a*'), *absence* turns into some sort of *presence* of an impersonal 'existing' (*exister*); see Emmanuel Levinas, *Le temps et l'autre* (4th ed., Paris, 1991), pp. 25–26.

[23] This is what Hegel attributes to Greek ontology in his *Science of Logic*, tr. A. V. Miller, ed. H. D. Lewis (Atlantic Highlands, NJ, 1996), pp. 95–101.

[24] Hegel, *Science of Logic*, pp. 170–177.

[25] Ibid., pp. 164–165.

entailed by the *neuter* expression 'necessary *being* due to itself', becomes a derivative determinate being qua existent as *The Necessary Existent due to Itself.* Even by saying 'necessary *being*', we already let *being* show itself as determinateness, and even when uttering '*there is*', Ibn Sīnā's consideration of *being* under the modality of necessity bears some form of determinateness; for it is not implying that the '*there is*' ('*il y a*') is that of a paradoxical mode of 'existing without existent' ('*exister sans existant*'; '*wujūd bi-lā mawjūd*').[26]

This determinateness occurs by way of what may be described as '*sublation*' (*Aufheben*), namely the transcending eventuality of being *preserved and kept*, as well as being at the same time *surpassed and ended.* Something is thus *sublated* when it enters into a seemingly self-effacing unity with its opposite by being also elevated through the leverage that takes place in dialectics. However, what acts as the starting ground for a process of becoming is subsumed also within the folds of what issues forth and follows from it.[27] Pure *being* is thus self-*sublated* by becoming determinate *being*, even if such determinateness is not associated with quiddity. For, as what is indeterminate, it is *sublated* into what is determinate as '*The [Godhead] Necessary Existent due to Itself*' (with what this entails in terms of contemplating the divine essence and attributes). We could even say that pure *being*, as what is utterly indeterminate, is even self-*sublated* when considered as necessary '*being*', while being moreover subjected to further determinateness by becoming 'a determinate being', namely the One qua *The Necessary Existent due to Itself*; in this, *pure being* lets *determinate being* appear. The determinateness of *being* in the modality of *The Necessary Existent due to Itself* is ultimately a movement from *being-itself* to *being-for-self.* It thus appears as being a self-mediated and determinate *subject* that turns Itself into *being-for-other.* With *The Necessary Existent due to Itself*, something else is posited, namely what is *other.* Through Its own Nature, through Its-Self, *The Necessary Existent due to Itself* relates to what is other than Itself. *Being-within-self* includes negation within itself as an indeterminate *being-for-other*, which ultimately becomes a determinate otherness in *the All*; namely every contingent that has turned in actuality into *a necessary existent due to something other than itself* via a hierarchical existential chain of actualising causes.

Based on this interpretive reading, pure *being*, as what is utterly indeterminate, is in its immediacy necessary *being* that is as such as *being-itself.* It then passes into determinateness as *a determinate being*, namely *The Necessary Existent due to Itself* that is as such as *being-for-self.* As the One, *The Necessary Existent due to Itself* turns into *being-for-other* by way of Its own self-repulsion into the manifold many qua otherness. Pure *being*, which is without quiddity, definition or description, and is said to be beyond the categories while being non-mediated, utterly indeterminate and only equal to itself, seems perplexingly to be also construed as *a determinate being.* Pure *being* thus becomes *The Necessary Existent due to Itself*, which is not simply

---

26 This paradoxical notion was suggested by Levinas in *Le temps et l'autre.*

27 Hegel, *Science of Logic*, pp. 70–74, 107–108.

'what It is due to Itself', but, ultimately, and by way of all existing beings, is also *being-for-other*.

Pure *being* cannot be simply understood as '*a Being*', nor can *being* be readily defined by attributing beings to it.[28] Pure *being qua being-itself* and *The Necessary Existent due to Itself qua being-within-Itself* (as *being-for-self/being-for-other*), both describe divergent moments in Ibn Sīnā's ontology. 'Pure *being qua being-itself*' unveils the ontological difference between *being* and beings, while '*The Necessary Existent due to Itself qua being-within-Itself*' (as *being-for-self* and *being-for-other*) re-veils it. Although this state of affairs may be seen by some as being indicative of a classical tendency to cede the question of the meaning of *being* into forgetfulness, Ibn Sīnā did nonetheless raise the question of *being* anew, even if the moment of unveiling and un-concealment was unpredictably coupled with another that veiled and concealed. Ibn Sīnā's foundational ontology did creditably reveal the perennial paradox that confronts those who attentively address the subtleties of the question of *being* in contemplating the thought-provoking mysteries of the uncanny 'self-sending' and 'self-withdrawal' of *being*. What concerns us in this context, and must be thought about with mindfulness, mysteriously turns away from us, while drawing us along nearer in the draft of its own pulling withdrawal.[29] This is not poetising, rather questioning that calls for thinking.

---

[28] This reflects the attempt to avoid the use of the verbal '*to be*' that entails a tautological self-predication of *being* (as in saying: '*being is* …'). See Jeff Owen Prudhomme, *God and Being: Heidegger's Relation to Theology* (Atlantic Highlands, NJ, 1997), p. 152.

[29] Martin Heidegger, *Was Heisst Denken?* (Tübingen, 1954), Lecture I, Part 1; in reflection on the ontological bearings of Friedrich Hölderlin's *Mnemosyne* verse.

Epilogue

Azim Nanji

Arguably, a critical moment in modern, Western studies of the Shiʿi tradition was marked by a seminal article, published in 1955 in the *Journal of the American Oriental Society*, by the late Marshall Hodgson. This article and Hodgson's later magisterial book, *The Venture of Islam*, challenged scholars to revise assumptions as well as to rethink the language and vocabulary they employed for the study of Muslim history and society.

With regard to the Shiʿa in particular, Hodgson showed that the formation of their identity ought to be located in the context of early Muslim history as an expression of a shared but contested vision of how order should prevail in the *umma* and under whose custody its beginnings could be best sustained. His approach overturned the assumption of a normative Islam, homogenous in forms and concepts, from which departures and deviations led to sectarianism. Rather, the diversity of groups and the pluralism of interpretation among early Muslims showed how identity came to be constructed in relation to each others' differences, as the mode of discourse among emerging traditions became modified and modified each other, a process that was indeed continuous. The studies in this volume reflect the process that has taken place since the 1950s, in further developing some of these ideas and new insights and perspectives that have emerged since.

Perhaps the most important trend is the necessary cosmopolitanism of the scholarship itself. One no longer speaks of Western scholarship, though many still like to point to the continuing influence of 'orientalism'. A great deal of modern scholarship is taking place among scholars living in the Muslim world; many more sources have come to light, and there is much greater information among all scholars, who consistently share and critique each others' research. One can speak, tentatively, of an ethic of global relatedness, which is grounded in the values of pluralistic scholarship. The abundance of current scholarship embodies the intellectual, spiritual and institutional pluralism of Shiʿi Islam, as indeed of Islam.

As contemporary geopolitical events lead to a focus and present-mindedness on current developments, the trajectory of this volume and its perspectives remind us that the task of good and enduring scholarship is to help us to develop and retain mediating intellectual categories that allow us to resist the simplicity of relying on homogeneous and historical assumptions about differences in exploring an academically grounded space where mutual understanding can and should take place.

Index